MAMMALS OF NEVADA

MAMMALS OF NEVADA

By E. RAYMOND HALL

Foreword by TIMOTHY E. LAWLOR

UNIVERSITY OF NEVADA PRESS

Reno   Las Vegas   London

9 8 7 6 5 4 3 2 1

Library of Congress Cataloging-in-Publication Data

Hall, E. Raymond (Eugene Raymond), 1902–1986
    Mammals of Nevada / by E. Raymond Hall ; foreword by Timothy E. Lawlor.
      p. cm.
    Originally published: Berkeley : University of California Press, 1946.
    Includes bibliographical references (p.   ) and index.
    ISBN 0-87417-261-6 (acid-free paper)
    1. Mammals—Nevada.   I. Title
  QL719.N3H3   1995
  599.09793—dc20   95-6601
                                          CIP

CONTENTS

[v]

ILLUSTRATIONS

FIGURES IN TEXT

DISTRIBUTION MAPS

Among E. Raymond Hall's many accomplishments (he published more than 350 articles and books in his prolific career as a mammalogist), the *Mammals of Nevada* ranks as one of the very best. It has long consitituted the standard against which other state surveys of mammals have been measured. There are many reasons for this. The book was, and remains, a thoroughly documented treatise on the species occurring in the state. Hall personally conducted or directed a huge field effort to ensure an exhaustive accounting of mammals in all parts of Nevada. Together with materials obtained by earlier workers, notably those involved with the U.S. Biological Survey in the late 1800s, he carefully examined thousands of specimens to attain taxonomic thoroughness and accuracy. The book is a treasure trove of natural history information as well. Sections of the book dealing with such topics as speciation, life zones, and factors influencing geographic distributions integrate natural history information, ecological interpretations, and mammalian evolution. The result is a book of much larger dimensions than usual treatments of its kind, and it was used as a model by Hall's students for other faunal surveys, such as the mammals of Washington (Dalquest, 1948), Nebraska (Jones, 1964), Wyoming (Long, 1965), and Utah (Durrant, 1952).

The *Mammals of Nevada* was published originally by the University of California in Berkeley, where Hall did his doctoral work. He later served as curator of mammals and eventually acting director of the university's Museum of Vertebrate Zoology before continuing his distinguished career at the University of Kansas Museum of Natural History. Hall's extensive notes of fieldwork in Nevada remain on file at the Museum of Vertebrate Zoology in Berkeley. During my own studies of mammals in the state, I read many of them, for they enabled me to locate places that Hall and his field crews had visited. It is a testament to the detail with which he conducted his fieldwork that, on one occasion, I was able to locate and use as an observation post a limber pine Hall had used more than fifty years earlier in Greenmonster Canyon of the Monitor Range.

A great deal has been learned about Nevada mammals since the publication of *Mammals of Nevada* in 1946. To the best of my knowledge, no species has disappeared from the state; indeed, seven, and possibly eight, species have been added to the Nevada fauna. These include three bats (Allen's long-eared bat, *Idionycteris phyllotis;* the cave myotis, *Myotis velifer;* and the western mastiff bat, *Eumops perotis*); two carnivores (the wolverine, *Gulo gulo;* and the lynx, *Lynx lynx*); two rodents (the western gray squirrel, *Sciurus griseus;* and the spiny pocket mouse, *Chaetodipus spinatus*); and one artiodactyl (the white-tailed deer, *Odocoileus virginianus*), although the existence of the last species is disputed (Adams, 1963). A recent general treatment of mammals occupying the intermountain region, including Nevada, is provided by Zeveloff and Collett (1988).

At least one species of Nevada mammal has become celebrated for what it leaves behind. Middens of the packrat (*Neotoma cinerea*) have proven particularly useful in reconstructing paleobotanical and other changes that resulted from post-Pleistocene climate change (Betancourt *et al.*, 1990). Middens are ancient latrines, only briefly mentioned by Hall (1946). They consist of accummulated urine and feces, often several feet thick, that have hardened and been preserved in protected rock crevices or caves near packrat nests. Because packrats are consummate collectors, they also inadvertently deposit plant parts, pollen, skeletal remains, and other materials with their excrement, so middens can be used to document biotic changes in a community over thousands of years on a relatively fine scale.

Such studies, together with other paleontological and archaeological investigations, have clarified much of the late Pleistocene and Holocene history of Great Basin mammalian fauna (for reviews, see Grayson, 1993, 1994). As in other places in North America, Nevada saw widespread extinctions in the late Pleistocene of species that no longer occur on the continent, including camels, mammoths, mastodons, horses (modern horses were introduced), ground sloths, and saber-toothed cats.

Nevada and other parts of the Great Basin also witnessed the disappearance of several montane species that survive elsewhere in North America. These include martens (*Martes americana*), least weasels (*Mustela nivalis*), bog lemmings (*Synaptomys borealis*), and heather voles (*Phenacomys intermedius*). Of course, the fact that montane species were disproportionately affected by the gradual warming that has taken place since the Pleistocene is no accident. The isolation of many mountain ranges in Nevada and other parts of the Great Basin subjects montane species to population fragmentation and local extinctions; both would have been particularly acute as montane habitats moved upslope in response to warming. With these factors in mind, Brown (1971, 1978), in a now classic study, examined species occurrences on mountaintops in the Great Basin. Using data gathered mostly from Hall's *Mammals of Nevada,* he found a very strong relationship between number of species and mountaintop area. His explanation was straightforward. Because post-Pleistocene warming progressively caused montane mammals to become isolated in patches of coniferous forest on mountaintops, Brown reasoned that any extinctions should occur without replacement, and because small mountain ranges should lose species at rates faster than large ones (mammals in small areas have fewer habitats available to them and have smaller population sizes), they should end up with far fewer species than large ones over time. Recently, McDonald and Brown (1993) and Murphy and Weiss (1992) extrapolated from Brown's (1971, 1978) analyses to predict that substantial numbers of species should disappear from Nevada mountain ranges in the next century if expected global warming promotes further shrinkage in montane habitats.

However, recent information suggests that the foregoing scenario is incomplete. My own work (Lawlor, in preparation), as well as that of Grayson (1993) and Grayson and Livingston (1993), indicates that many of the mammals purported to be missing in small mountain ranges were not really absent but simply unreported. The newly emerging picture is as follows. Most mountain ranges in Nevada, irrespective of size, have about the same number of species. Although there have been some local extinctions without subsequent immigration, as evidenced by montane species no longer occurring in the state (see above) and by the patchy distribution in Nevada of once widespread montane species—for example, pikas, *Ochotona princeps,* and yellow-bellied marmots, *Marmota flaviventris* (Grayson, 1987, 1993; Lawlor, in preparation)—these have involved mostly montane obligates. By contrast, most species frequenting Nevada mountains are woodland forms with good dispersal abilities. Evidently these species are capable of relatively free movement from one mountain range to another. Indeed, Hall (1946) predicted as much when he suggested that montane species might cross desert valleys in winter.

As Hall (1946) recognized, habitat modifications stemming from human activities have greatly affected the Nevada landscape in ways that have changed the distributional occurrences and abundances of mammals. Piñon-juniper forests are invading desert valleys in many parts of the state, encouraging range expansions of woodland mammals and contractions of valley species. Although rangelands are in better condition now than in settlement times, native grasses have largely disappeared and are being replaced increasingly by alien species, the dominant ones of which are unpalatable to both native and domestic large herbivores (Young, 1994). Because water is a limiting factor in arid environments for both human and wildlife needs, impacts from the capture of water for irrigation are greatest on species dependent on riparian habitats. These habitats are absent in many places where creeks now run dry, especially in desert valleys. Many watercourses have also been highly degraded by livestock, although efforts are underway to limit the impact of cattle and sheep by reducing their numbers and by protecting springs and other vital sources of water.

Although not treated in detail by Hall (1946), feral horses and burros constitute important modern components of the Nevada landscape (for example, see Berger, 1986). High densities of horses have prompted extensive recent gathers on lands administered by the Bureau of Land Management.

Using archaeological and other historical information, Berger and Wehausen (1991) suggested that the modern abundance of mule deer resulted largely from an increase in browse plants brought about by intensive livestock grazing during the last century. In Berger and Wehausen's view, this in turn has led to increases in populations of predators such as mountain lions, which like mule deer were evidently rare in Nevada during the early settlement period.

Despite these concerns, some species seem to be thriving. Mule deer (*Odocoileus hemionus*) are very common in many parts of the state, having perhaps reached modern highs in abundance in the last decade. There has been a successful program of reintroductions of bighorn sheep (*Ovis canadensis*) to many parts of northern Nevada from which the species had disappeared prior to fifty years ago when Hall wrote about them, and they continue to prosper in southern mountain ranges.

The basis and inspiration for many studies that succeeded publication of *Mammals of Nevada* stem directly from that early work. Indeed, the contexts in which modern distributions and abundances of Nevada mammals are placed, and the management of current populations of mammals depend to varying degrees on comparisons to and information from that baseline study. Perhaps most important is the fact that the information and synthesis about mammals provided by Hall produced a framework for ecological and other insights that have had relevance far beyond the state of Nevada.

TIMOTHY E. LAWLOR
ARCATA, CALIFORNIA, 1995

SPECIES ADDITIONS AND TAXONOMIC CHANGES

The following list of additions or revisions to names of Nevada mammals is arranged according to the checklist provided by Hall in *Mammals of Nevada* (pp. 70–77). Species designations follow those of Jones *et al.* (1992) and Wilson and Reeder (1993); unless otherwise noted, subspecies names conform to Hall (1981). The foregoing publications also provide references for tracing the basis for the taxonomic changes. Listed species and subspecies include only those for which there has been an addition or change in nomenclature since publication of the original edition of *Mammals of Nevada.*

Common Name	Scientific Name in Hall (1946)	Taxonomic Revision or New to List (1995)

Order INSECTIVORA

SORICIDAE: SHREWS

Vagrant shrew	*Sorex vagrans amoenus*	*Sorex vagrans vagrans*
Dusky shrew	*Sorex vagrans monticola*	*Sorex monticolus obscurus*
Dusky shrew	*Sorex obscurus obscurus*	*Sorex monticolus obscurus*

Order CHIROPTERA

PHYLLOSTOMIDAE: LEAF-NOSED BATS

California leaf-nosed bat	*Macrotus californicus*	*Macrotus waterhousii*

VESPERTILIONIDAE: EVENING OR COMMON BATS

Long-eared myotis	*Myotis evotis chrysonotus*	*Myotis evotis evotis*
California myotis	*Myotis californicus pallidus*	*Myotis californicus stephensi*
Small-footed myotis	*Myotis subulatus melanorhinus*	*Myotis ciliolabrum melanorhinus*
Cave myotis[1]		*Myotis velifer brevis*
Allen's big-eared bat[1]		*Idionycteris phyllotis*
Townsend's big-eared bat	*Corynorhinus rafinesquii intermedius*	*Plecotus townsendii pallescens*

(continued on next page)

Common Name	Scientific Name in Hall (1946)	Taxonomic Revision or New to List (1995)
Townsend's big-eared bat	*Corynorhinus rafinesquii pallescens*	*Plecotus townsendii pallescens*

MOLOSSIDAE: FREE-TAILED BATS

Brazilian free-tailed bat	*Tadarida mexicana*	*Tadarida brasiliensis mexicana*
Greater mastiff bat[1]		*Eumops perotis californicus*

Order CARNIVORA

MUSTELIDAE: WEASELS AND ALLIES

Marten	*Martes caurina sierrae*	*Martes americana sierrae*
Ermine	*Mustela cicognanii lepta*	*Mustela erminea muricus*
Wolverine[1]		*Gulo gulo luteus*
River otter	*Lutra canadensis nexa*	*Lutra canadensis pacifica*
River otter	*Lutra canadensis brevipilosus*	*Lutra canadensis pacifica*
Western spotted skunk	*Spilogale putorius saxatilis*	*Spilogale gracilis gracilis*
Western spotted skunk	*Spilogale putorius gracilis*	*Spilogale gracilis gracilis*
Badger	*Taxidea taxus jeffersoni*	*Taxidea taxus taxus*

CANIDAE: FOXES AND COYOTES

Red fox	*Vulpes fulva necator*	*Vulpes vulpes necator*
Coyote	*Canis latrans estor*	*Canis latrans mearnsi*

FELIDAE: CATS

Lynx[1]		*Lynx lynx canadensis*

(continued on next page)

Common Name	Scientific Name in Hall (1946)	Taxonomic Revision or New to List (1995)

Order RODENTIA

SCIURIDAE: SQUIRRELS

Common Name	Scientific Name in Hall (1946)	Taxonomic Revision or New to List (1995)
Yellow-bellied marmot	*Marmota flaviventer flaviventer*	*Marmota flaviventris flaviventris*
Yellow-bellied marmot	*Marmota flaviventer avara*	*Marmota flaviventris avara*
Yellow-bellied marmot	*Marmota flaviventer nosophora*	*Marmota flaviventris nosophora*
Yellow-bellied marmot	*Marmota flaviventer parvula*	*Marmota flaviventris parvula*
Townsend's ground squirrel	*Citellus townsendii canus*	*Spermophilus townsendii canus*
Townsend's ground squirrel	*Citellus townsendii mollis*	*Spermophilus townsendii mollis*
Richardson's ground squirrel	*Citellus richardsoni nevadensis*	*Spermophilus richardsoni nevadensis*
Belding's ground squirrel	*Citellus beldingi oregonus*	*Spermophilus beldingi oregonus*
Belding's ground squirrel	*Citellus beldingi beldingi*	*Spermophilus beldingi beldingi*
Belding's ground squirrel	*Citellus beldingi crebrus*	*Spermophilus beldingi creber*
Rock squirrel	*Citellus variegatus grammurus*	*Spermophilus variegatus robustus*
Rock squirrel	*Citellus variegatus grammurus*	*Spermophilus variegatus utah*
California ground squirrel	*Citellus beecheyi fisheri*	*Spermophilus beecheyi fisheri*
Antelope ground squirrel	*Citellus leucurus leucurus*	*Ammospermophilus leucurus leucurus*
Round-tailed ground squirrel	*Citellus tereticaudus tereticaudus*	*Spermophilus tereticaudus tereticaudus*
Golden-mantled squirrel	*Citellus lateralis chrysodeirus*	*Spermophilus lateralis chrysodeirus*

(continued on next page)

Common Name	Scientific Name in Hall (1946)	Taxonomic Revision or New to List (1995)
Golden-mantled squirrel	*Citellus lateralis trepidus*	*Spermophilus lateralis trepidus*
Golden-mantled squirrel	*Citellus lateralis certus*	*Spermophilus lateralis certus*
Least chipmunk	*Eutamias minimus scrutator*	*Tamias minimus scrutator*
Yellow-pine chipmunk	*Eutamias amoenus celerus*	*Tamias amoenus celerus*
Yellow-pine chipmunk	*Eutamias amoenus monoensis*	*Tamias amoenus monoensis*
Panamint chipmunk	*Eutamias panamintinus*	*Tamias panimintinus panamintinus*
Uinta chipmunk	*Eutamias quadrivitattus inyoensis*	*Tamias umbrinus inyoensis*
Uinta chipmunk	*Eutamias quadrivitattus nevadensis*	*Tamias umbrinus nevadensis*
Palmer's chipmunk	*Eutamias palmeri*	*Tamias palmeri*
Lodgepole chipmunk	*Eutamias speciosus frater*	*Tamias speciosus frater*
Allen's chipmunk	*Eutamias townsendii senex*	*Tamias senex*
Long-eared chipmunk	*Eutamias quadrimaculatus*	*Tamias quadrimaculatus*
Cliff chipmunk	*Eutamias dorsalis grinnelli*	*Tamias dorsalis grinnelli*
Cliff chipmunk	*Eutamias dorsalis utahensis*	*Tamias dorsalis utahensis*
Gray squirrel[1]		*Sciurus griseus griseus*

HETEROMYIDAE: POCKET MICE, KANGAROO RATS, AND ALLIES

Long-tailed pocket mouse	*Perognathus formosus melanurus*	*Chaetodipus formosus melanurus*
Long-tailed pocket mouse	*Perognathus formosus mohavensis*	*Chaetodipus formosus mohavensis*
Long-tailed pocket mouse	*Perognathus formosus incolatus*	*Chaetodipus formosus incolatus*
Desert pocket mouse	*Perognathus penicillatus sobrinus*	*Chaetodipus penicillatus sobrinus*

(continued on next page)

Common Name	Scientific Name in Hall (1946)	Taxonomic Revision or New to List (1995)
Desert pocket mouse	*Perognathus penicillatus penicillatus*	*Chaetodipus penicillatus penicillatus*
Spiny pocket mouse[1]		*Chaetodipus spinatus spinatus*
Desert kangaroo rat[2]		*Dipodomys deserti aquilus*

MURIDAE: RATS AND MICE

Northern grasshopper mouse	*Onychomys leucogaster fuscogriseus*	*Onychomys leucogaster brevicaudus*
Arizona cotton rat	*Sigmodon hispidus plenus*	*Sigmodon arizonae plenus*
Montane vole	*Microtus montanus yosemite*	*Microtus montanus montanus*
Long-tailed vole	*Microtus longicaudus mordax*	*Microtus longicaudus longicaudus*
Sagebrush vole	*Lagurus curtatus curtatus*	*Lemmiscus curtatus curtatus*

DIPODIDAE (=ZAPODIDAE): JUMPING MICE AND ALLIES

Western jumping mouse	*Zapus princeps alleni*	*Zapus princeps pacificus*
Western jumping mouse	*Zapus princeps nevadensis*	*Zapus princeps oregonus*
Western jumping mouse	*Zapus princeps palatinus*	*Zapus princeps oregonus*

Order LAGOMORPHA

LEPORIDAE: HARES AND RABBITS

Pygmy rabbit	*Sylvilagus idahoensis*	*Brachylagus idahoensis*

Order ARTIODACTYLA

CERVIDAE: DEER AND ALLIES

Wapiti or elk	*Cervus canadensis nelsoni*	*Cervus elaphus nelsoni*
White-tailed deer[3]		*Odocoileus virginiana ochroura*

(continued on next page)

[1] New to original list of Nevada species provided by Hall (1946).

[2] Recently described subspecies. Another race, *Dipodomys deserti deserti*, is found elsewhere in the southern part of the state and was reported by Hall (1946).

[3] New to original list of Nevada species provided by Hall (1946), but its possible occurrence is mentioned in the account of mule deer (*Odocoileus hemionus*). Records of this species in Nevada are disputed by Adams (1963).

ERRATA

The following corrections to *Mammals of Nevada* are modifications of the substance of the text. They are based on notations inscribed by Hall in personal copies of the book and were provided through the kindness of Hubert Hall, one of E. R. Hall's sons. Minor typographical or other changes, of which there are few, are not included.

Page	Line	Erratum
81	32	"small" should read "big."
89	36	"thirty-two" should read "thirty."
89	39	"thirty" should read "twenty-eight."
127	40	"coracoid" should read "clavicle."
203	3	"*Spilogale gracilis saxatilis*" should read "*Spilogale saxatilis*."
203	5	Add as next line of synonymy: "*Spilogale gracilis saxatilis* Howell, N. Amer. Fauna, 26:23, November 24, 1906."
447	1–3	Reference to Johnson (ms) pertains to *Thomomys bottae centralis*, not to *Thomomys talpoides*.
482	21	"1/0" should read "1/1."
489	Table 13	"*C. castor*" should read "*C. canadensis*."
564	25	"*baileyi*" should read "*bernardi*."
679	Fig. 482	"interorbital" should read "postorbital."
680	6	"three" should read "two"; insert "three" before "in lower."
680	7	"twelve" should read "ten."

REFERENCES

Adams, L. 1963. Do white-tailed deer occur in northeastern California? Journal of Mammalogy. 44:518–522.

Berger, J. 1986. Wild horses of the Great Basin: social competition and population size. Chicago: University of Chicago Press.

Berger, J., and J. D. Wehausen. 1991. Consequences of a mammalian predator-prey disequilibrium in the Great Basin desert. Conservation Biology. 5:244–248.

Betancourt, J. L., T. R. Van Devender, and P. S. Martin. 1990. Packrat middens: the last 40,000 years of biotic change. Tucson: University of Arizona Press.

Brown, J. H. 1971. Mammals on mountaintops: nonequilibrium insular biogeography. American Naturalist. 105:467–478.

———. 1978. The theory of insular biogeography and the distribution of boreal birds and mammals. Great Basin Naturalist Memoirs. 2:209–227.

Dalquest W. W. 1948. Mammals of Washington. University of Kansas, Museum of Natural History Publication no. 2:1–444. Lawrence.

Durrant, S. D. 1952. Mammals of Utah: taxonomy and distribution. University of Kansas, Museum of Natural History Publication no. 6:1–549. Lawrence.

Grayson, D. K. 1987. The biogeographic history of Great Basin small mammals: observations on the last 20,000 years. Journal of Mammalogy. 68:359–375.

———. 1993. The desert's past: a natural prehistory of the Great Basin. Washington, D. C.: Smithsonian Institution Press.

———. 1994. The extinct Late Pleistocene mammals of the Great Basin. In Natural history of the Colorado Plateau and Great Basin, ed. K. T. Harper, L. L. St. Clair, K. H. Thorne, and W. M. Hess, 55–85. Niwot: University Press of Colorado.

Grayson, D. K., and S. D. Livingston. 1993. Missing mammals on Great Basin mountains: Holocene extinctions and inadequate knowledge. Conservation Biology. 7:527–532.

Hall, E. R. 1946. Mammals of Nevada. Berkeley: University of California Press.

———. 1981. The mammals of North America. 2 vols. New York: John Wiley and Sons.

Jones, J. K., Jr. 1964. Distribution and taxonomy of mammals of Nebraska. University of Kansas, Museum of Natural History Publication no. 16:1–356. Lawrence.

Jones, J. K., Jr., R. S. Hoffmann, D. W. Rice, C. Jones, R. J. Baker, and M. D. Engstrom. 1992. Revised checklist of North American mammals north of Mexico, 1991. Texas Tech University Museum Occasional Papers no. 146:1–23. Lubbock.

Long, C. A. 1965. The mammals of Wyoming. University of Kansas, Museum of

Natural History Publication no. 14:493–758. Lawrence.

McDonald, K. A., and J. H. Brown. 1993. Using montane mammals to model extinctions due to global change. Conservation Biology. 6:409–415.

Murphy, D. D., and S. B. Weiss. 1992. The effects of climate change on biological diversity in western North America: species losses and mechanisms. In Global warming and biological diversity, ed. R. L. Peters and T. E. Lovejoy, 355–368. New Haven: Yale University Press.

Wilson, D. E., and D. M. Reeder, eds. 1993. Mammal species of the world. A taxonomic and geographic reference. 2nd ed. Washington, D.C.: Smithsonian Institution Press.

Young, J. A. 1994. Changes in plant communities in the Great Basin induced by domestic livestock grazing. In Natural history of the Colorado Plateau and Great Basin, ed. K. T. Harper, L. L. St. Clair, K. H. Thorne, and W. M. Hess, 113–123. Niwot: University Press of Colorado.

Zeveloff, S. I., and F. R. Collett. 1988. Mammals of the intermountain west. Salt Lake City: University of Utah Press.

INTRODUCTION

Mammals are abundant in Nevada, even in the most sandy areas which, because they appear so barren, have but slight if any appeal to the casual visitor. One of these uninviting areas is the big sand dune at Sand Springs (see frontispiece). The dune, and the lesser ridges and mounds of wind-blown sand round about, which the scattered shrubs are ever ineffectually attempting to hold in place, is an unalluring prospect on almost any day. In every one of a hundred Nevadan valleys, on the leeward side of a playa, it is much the same. The sand's smooth surface is relieved only by sharp-edged, cut-out hollows where the wind races round a bush and fires out a sandblast that stings the cheeks, tortures the eyes, and coats one's teeth with grit. The sun's reflected heat, which burns through the soles of stout boots, drives even the lizards and antelope squirrels to the shade of bushes. Repellent though the dune is in the daytime's glare and wind's full grip, it becomes a quiet and friendly place the instant the sun has set. In the long twilight no glare blinds the eye and the wind has entirely gone. It is the rare person who then can resist the temptation to linger, even if he has a hundred traps to place for specimens of the small mammals there. In the cool of early morning it is not uncommon to find in his traps eighty or more individuals of a dozen kinds. More informative than the animals themselves, in many ways, is the maze of their footprints and tail marks on the sand. The tracks of a *Dipodomys* reveal where it paused to dig for a morsel of food, and at another place show where the animal leaped out of the way of a larger cousin the tracks of which continue on in a straight line; a little way farther on, the smaller "Dipo's" feet sank deeply in the sand and thereafter the tracks are farther apart and the tail no longer drags as the speed was increased. There, ahead, one sees the tracks of a kit fox. Marks farther along in the sand clearly tell of a fatality.

The tracks of pocket mice, kangaroo mice, and kangaroo rats reveal that these animals follow along the bottom of any tire-mark or similar depression which they encounter in their nocturnal foraging. Their accumulated experience conditions these small mammals to search in depressions more than elsewhere for seeds. Once the seeds are on the ground the wind drives them rapidly over the sand until they find lodgment in a depression. Knowledge of this habit of desert rodents explains why the collector drags the toe of his boot through the loose sand to make a furrow in which the mousetraps are set.

Scores of burrow openings around sandy dunes attest the density of population of small mammals—a density equaled in few other habitats—and inspection discloses that in nearly every burrow, a short distance back from the entrance, the occupant has snugly packed a plug of moist sand to shut him away from the dangers of day. Before a person's curiosity is half satisfied about the burrows and the dozens of stories told by the tracks, the sun is up— and with it the wind, the wind that obliterates every telltale mark and burrow opening, leaving only smooth sand in their places. Little by little the heat returns. But the mice are safely buried in the sand's cool depths and care not a whit about events above, unless it be repairs that they must make to the burrows which now and then cave in under the weight of the mammal collector as he walks across the sand.

Whence comes the food to support this host of creatures? It lies there buried in the sand for all those who have keen noses to find it and the will to dig it out—seeds of grasses and other desert plants. In an occasional spring, moisture enough falls to sprout the seeds and to make of this sandy waste a flower garden which people drive as many as eight hundred miles to see. They find a profusion of blossoms so great as almost to conceal the ground. Greater still was the number of seeds that grew, matured, and fell into the sand in response to a provision of nature for plants in places where moisture may not come again for 3 years.

This provision by plants is of course typical of Temperate Zone deserts everywhere, and explains why the sandy wastes which by day appear almost barren of life, instead, are most populous, and therefore of absorbing interest to the student of small mammals. Much of Nevada is like this. To me it is readily understandable that anyone who spends much time in the desert becomes deeply attached to it, for the unobscured work of the elements, the clear sky and nearness of celestial bodies at night, and the quiet of evening and dawn truly give to the desert a charm all its own.

With Miss Annie M. Alexander, a real affection for the desert was combined with a recognition of the large opportunity in Nevada for advancing our knowledge of the natural history of the vertebrates. This dual interest led her to plan and support an expedition to Nevada from the Museum of Vertebrate Zoölogy in its second season of field work; subsequently, she herself, with Miss Louise Kellogg, visited many parts of the state, in all seasons, intelligently sampling the mammalian fauna as against the time when a general report on it would be made. My own eagerness, in 1927, to carry on additional studies there she furthered in generous fashion. Her continued interest and my encouragement by the late Professor Joseph Grinnell, Director of the Museum of Vertebrate Zoölogy, make it possible to add the following account of the mammals of Nevada to the Museum's previously published accounts of the vertebrates of the Pine Forest Mountains (Taylor, 1911, 1912) and the Toyabe Mountains (Linsdale, 1938) and the summation of knowledge about the distribution of birds, reptiles, and amphibians (Linsdale, 1936, 1940). This book, then, is a part of Miss Alexander's program of making better known the vertebrate fauna of North America, especially the mammals, as begun by her in 1907 or earlier. She participated in the field work in Nevada from the very beginning to the end, additionally provided financial support, and repeatedly gave personal encouragement. It is strictly true, therefore, to say that without Miss Alexander there would have been no book on the mammals of Nevada.

ACKNOWLEDGMENTS

As a result of Miss Alexander's interest, a number of staff members of the Museum of Vertebrate Zoölogy enthusiastically participated in the field work which forms the basis for this report. According to field notes, these members of the staff, a larger number of graduate students, and a few others who joined in the work are:

Joseph Raymond Alcorn
Annie M. Alexander
Howard T. Anderson
John Ronald Anderson
Lee W. Arnold
Dale Arvey
Carrie N. Baldwin
Paul H. Baldwin
George A. Bartholomew
Seth Bertram Benson
Lloyd Morgan Boyers
J. Stanley Brode
Monroe D. Bryant
Lawrence Verlyn Compton
Walter W. Dalquest
William B. Davis
J. Kenneth Doutt
Stephen David Durrant
Elton R. Edge
Carl H. Engler
Dawson A. Feathers
Harvey Irvin Fisher
Henry Sheldon Fitch
Francis Clair Gale, Jr.
Frank W. Gorham
Thomas Conrad Groody
E. Raymond Hall
Hubert Handel Hall
Mary Frances Hall
William Joel Hall
Ronald Patrick Harville

Donald Marshall Hatfield
Milton T. Hildebrand
Emmet T. Hooper
David Horn Johnson
Louise Kellogg
Chester Converse Lamb
Ole Lilleland
Jean Myron Linsdale
William M. Longhurst
Anatole Stepanovitch Loukashkin
William C. Matthews
Alden Holmes Miller
Virginia Dove Miller
Robert Dunham Moore
Robert Thomas Orr
Fletcher Greenleaf Palmer
Albert Edwin Peterson
Frank Alois Pitelka
H. Robert Poultney
Charles Howard Richardson
William Bebb Richardson
Thomas Lathan Rodgers
Ward Cairns Russell
Dwight C. Smiley
Ruben Arthur Stirton
Ned W. Stone
Walter Penn Taylor
Alfred W. Ward
Halstead Guilford White
Paul Thomas Wilson

For help with the preparation of the manuscript in one way and another, I am grateful indeed to several persons, especially to J. R. Alcorn, Jean T. Boulware, Mary F. Hall, and Donald F. Hoffmeister. Of these, Mr. Hoffmeister expended the most time, and his recording of information and efficient attention to detail contributed much and greatly lightened the total labor. The assistance of F. O. Kelsey of the University of California Press is deeply appreciated. Source of the illustrations is acknowledged on page 11.

I am indebted also to persons who obtained specimens of mammals in Nevada before and while the Museum of Vertebrate Zoölogy carried on its work there; the published accounts and sometimes examination of the specimens resulting from this early work provided most useful information.

Specimens probably from within the present boundaries of Nevada were gathered in

1859 by C. S. McCarthy, taxidermist, and other members of the party led by Captain J. H. Simpson when exploring for a direct wagon route from Camp Floyd, Utah, to Genoa, Nevada. Some of these specimens were deposited in the Smithsonian Institution.

The field work of the Death Valley Survey of 1891, led by Clinton Hart Merriam, was productive of many specimens of mammals from the southern part of Nevada. These were obtained by Vernon Bailey, A. K. Fisher, Theodore S. Palmer, Clinton Hart Merriam, Edward W. Nelson, and Frank Stephens. Under Dr. Merriam's direction, and that of succeeding administrative officers who directed the work of the United States Bureau of Biological Survey, Vernon Bailey, Harry C. Oberholser, Clark P. Streator, Edward A. Goldman, Luther J. Goldman, Stanley E. Piper, Ernest G. Holt, and E. Raymond Hall, among others, did field work which involved the saving of mammals from Nevada, which are housed in the United States National Museum.

W. W. Price, from Stanford University, with associates, collected mammals in Douglas County between 1894 and 1900. The specimens were distributed to various collections. I recall the names of A. W. Greely, who collected *Eutamias panamintinus* at Anderson's Ranch in 1895, and W. W. Price and P. O. Simons, who obtained in 1898, at Gardnerville, the type specimen of *Peromyscus crinitus scitulus*.

Donald R. Dickey supported the work of Laurence M. Huey and May Canfield in southern Esmeralda County in 1922 and that of William H. Burt, who had the assistance of Thomas E. Dawson and Harry H. Sheldon in 1928, 1929, and 1930. Burt's (1934) report on the mammals of a cross section of southern Nevada was an important paper and followed by only 3 months the valuable contribution by Adrey E. Borell and Ralph Ellis (1934a), entitled "Mammals of the Ruby Mountains Region of Northeastern Nevada." The field work on which the last-mentioned paper was based was done in 1927, 1928, and 1929, by Adrey E. Borell, assisted in the field at one time or another by Bernard Bailey, Raleigh A. Borell, Lawrence Verlyn Compton, Raymond M. Gilmore, Harry H. Sheldon, and Ralph Ellis. The last-named, who financed the work, at this writing (December, 1944), retains in his private collection, housed in the Museum of Natural History at the University of Kansas, most of the mammals obtained in the Ruby Mountains and adjoining areas.

The field work done in Nevada by the Museum of Vertebrate Zoölogy, which accounts for most of the specimens of mammals accumulated and for most of the other materials used in drawing up the present report, was in the following chronological order: Work was begun in the summer of 1909 when Walter P. Taylor, Charles H. Richardson, and, for part of the summer, Miss Annie M. Alexander and Miss Louise Kellogg carried on studies of Recent vertebrates. The report, "Mammals of the Alexander Nevada Expedition of 1909," by Taylor (1911) was one result of this work. In 1922 Miss Alexander arranged for Halstead G. White to make additional collections in the same general area. This was followed by collecting in many parts of the state by Miss Alexander and Miss Kellogg from 1925 until 1940. Jean M. Linsdale worked in several parts of Nevada, beginning in 1927, but particularly in the Toyabe Mountains area from 1930 to 1933. In 1924 and 1925, in the interests of the United States Bureau of Biological Survey, and each year from 1926 to 1941, for the Museum of Vertebrate Zoölogy, I made studies in several parts of Nevada. The routes traveled in the total of 573 days that I spent in field study are shown in figure 1.

The many residents of Nevada constitute still another important source of information. By their helpfulness in numerous ways, they contributed greatly to the final result. I would single out for special mention J. R. Alcorn, Mrs. Anna Bailey Mills, her two sons, Claude and Vernon, and her daughter, Laura, all of Fallon. W. C. Kirkland, Louis Mattice, Mr. and Mrs. Doyle C. Robison, and E. B. Vandall, of White Pine County, and Mr. and Mrs. Fred Glazier, of Elburz, are others. There are many more who have helped me greatly. Although the names of several of these appear on the pages that follow, most are recorded only in my grateful remembrance of their assistance.

E. R. H.

University of Kansas, Lawrence, August 30, 1945.

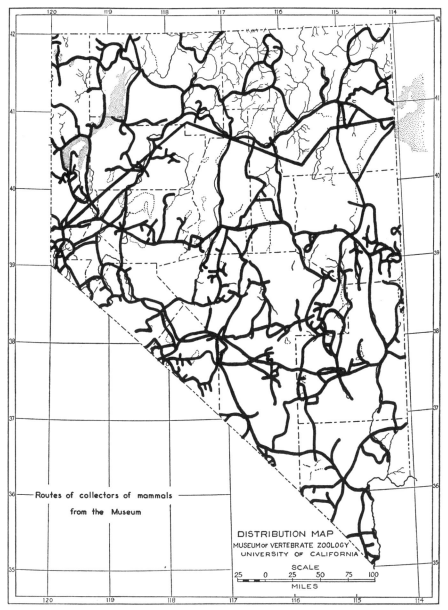

Fig. 1. Routes traveled by collectors of mammals for the Museum of Vertebrate Zoölogy. Red indicates routes of the author; blue, the routes of other collecters.

AIMS

Aims in preparing this account of the Recent mammals of Nevada were:

1. To find out what species of mammals occur in the state.
2. To ascertain the geographic range of each and the kinds of places in which it lives.
3. To ascertain and then catalogue the geographic variation in each species.
4. To provide such information on habits as would be incidentally obtained in pursuit of aims 1, 2, and 3.
5. To appraise the economic relation to man of the badger, coyote, pocket gopher, and beaver.
6. To provide a key, with descriptions and illustrations, by means of which a person without special zoölogical knowledge can identify kinds of mammals.

These aims add up to a presentation of natural history information which stresses geographic distribution and systematics as these bear on speciation, with additional selected information about Nevadan mammals set down either because it is regarded as new or because it is thought to have special significance otherwise.

METHODS

In the field studies there was another aim which, although not directly pertinent to the present account, nevertheless greatly influenced the results obtained and methods employed. This aim was to give instruction in vertebrate natural history, including practice in the techniques of field study, to several advanced students each year from 1930 to 1936. The three to five students chosen each spring were those who seemed most likely to continue with some phase of vertebrate natural history as a life occupation. With Ward C. Russell and myself included, the party ordinarily numbered six or seven (three to nine). We traveled in a light automobile and a truck. Often camp was made on the flank of a mountain range. When concentrating on mammals two members of the party in late afternoon would set out traps and explore in different directions on a contour with or above camp. Four others with traps and sleeping bags would leave in the light car. The driver might go as far from camp as 40 miles, leaving his companions, one at a place, 10, 20, and 30 miles from camp. Each person set out 90 to 130 mouse traps and sometimes traps of other kinds, and slept near by. Next morning, before the sun was up, he collected the traps and catch, and in the automobile returned to camp. Thus, with six hundred or more small traps, it was possible to test each night a considerable area and many habitats. The routine included the giving of attention to specimens from right after breakfast until well after lunchtime, followed by the preparation of field notes and setting of traps again. This routine sometimes allowed us to satisfy ourselves about the mammals of a given area in 2 or 3 days, and, following lunchtime of, say, the third day at a camp site, we moved on 90 or 100 miles to a new location and repeated the procedure. In this way we ordinarily obtained between one and two thousand specimens on a 5- or 6-week trip.

Work of this general nature was of course supplemented by trips that only two or three persons in a party made in search of special desiderata. Miss Alexander, with Miss Kellogg, spent much time in search of these special items.

In general, the desert is an easy place for the collector of mammals to work. Mammals are abundant, easily caught, and their skins and skulls dry readily. A technique that we found helpful when the weather was hot was to eviscerate the mammals selected for preparation right after they were weighed and measured. The mammals were wrapped in waxed paper, and then in a wet burlap sack. In the dry desert climate the rapid evaporation of water from the burlap

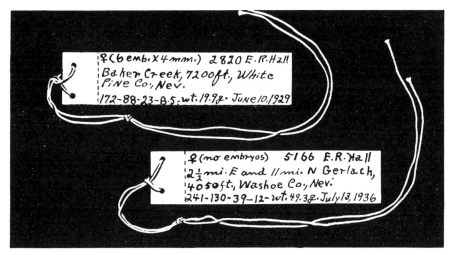

Fig. 2. Samples of labels used for attachment to stuffed study skins of mammals. X 1. These show kinds of data which, at the time of preparation of a stuffed study skin in the field, the collector records on the label that he attaches to the specimen.

kept the mammals cool, which in turn delayed bacterial action for a couple of days. Thus, it was a simple matter to keep all specimens in a condition good for the preparator. Possibly because we stressed preparation of relatively full field notes and often prepared specimens in special ways for other than systematic study, we came to regard ten to fourteen skins per day per person as a fair average for a trip of, say, 30 days, 3 or 4 days of which were spent in traveling to and from the field. Thus, in a month, we found that an experienced person averaged between three and four hundred "regular specimens," that is, skins with skulls.

Standard data obtained from the freshly caught, dead animal is of the kind shown on specimen labels in figure 2.

At each locality, we sought to obtain several individuals of each of the more geographically variable species, and within any major center of suspected differentiation made effort to obtain from some one place a series of thirty individuals. This latter number included young of different ages and ten adults of each sex.

In the laboratory, study of geographic variation was made by selecting for comparison from different localities skulls, skins, and external measurements of animals of equal age, of the same sex, taken in the same season. This was done after study of a large series from one place had yielded knowledge of the range of individual variation in a population thus uniform for age, sex, and season.

PLAN OF TREATMENT

For a subspecies, the intent is to give information under seven headings, as follows:

1. The accepted scientific name, selected in accordance with the international rules of zoölogical nomenclature, is the first of these headings, and is followed, on the same line, by the name of the authority. Some of the kinds of mammals here treated as subspecies have by some earlier writers been regarded as full species. In the present work, if a change in systematic status is made for the first time, reasons are given. These reasons have to do with the presence or absence of intergradation between the kind of animal in question and one or more related kinds. Intergradation, or lack of it, is accepted as the criterion of a subspecies and species, respectively. That is to say, if at a place where the ranges of the two kinds meet, the populations freely interbreed in a state of nature, the two are said to intergrade and accordingly are treated as subspecies of one species. If, on the other hand, the two kinds do not crossbreed at any place where their ranges meet or overlap, this constitutes lack of intergradation, and the two kinds, therefore, are treated as distinct species. This criterion can be applied satisfactorily to variants of a species if the species has a continuous geographic range. Where populations are separated from others by areas of terrain inhospitable to them, it is sometimes difficult to decide whether the different kinds are two or more full species or merely different subspecies of one species. This is true of Nevadan pikas (*Ochotona*), of which there are no less than three separate populations. Each population is entirely isolated from the others. All of these populations, one in the Sierra Nevada, one in the Ruby Mountains, and one in the Toyabe Mountain Range and near-by ranges in the central part of the state, inhabit country of high elevation that is isolated by low-lying territory uninhabited by pikas. The situation is comparable to one in which each of three kinds of mammals is confined to a separate island in the sea. A seemingly useful criterion in instances of this kind is set up by the following procedure: Study the continuously distributed mainland stock where there are different kinds with a view to determining if intergradation does occur. Where intergradation occurs estimate the maximum degree of difference between any two kinds that intergrade with each other. If between the insular or otherwise isolated kinds, the degree of difference is no greater than it is between the two mainland kinds, treat the two insular kinds as subspecies of one species. If the maximum degree of difference on the mainland is less than that between the two insular kinds, treat the latter as two species. According to this procedure the pikas (*Ochotona*) are only subspecies of a single species.

In order that other zoölogists may better gauge my systematic treatment of taxonomic categories lower than the genus, I add to the above remarks on the nature of a subspecies this definition of a Recent (as opposed to an extinct) mammalian species: A species is an evolved (and often evolving), reproductively isolated natural population in which individuals of similar age and sex (in at least one age group of one sex) possess in common certain heritable, morphological characters that are distinctive.

2. Next, there is the vernacular name. The same vernacular name is used for each one of

the several subspecies of a given species. There seems to be nothing gained, and something seems to be lost, by providing distinctive common (vernacular) names for different subspecies of a single species of mammal. For example, the name northern grasshopper mouse suffices whether the subspecies be *Onychomys leucogaster fuscogriseus* or, instead, *Onychomys leucogaster brevicaudus*. The scientific (Latin) subspecific names are based on features which are significant usually only to the specialist who is making studies of evolution. For most other purposes scientific subspecific names do not apply and were not intended to apply. Therefore, there is hardly any use in coining a vernacular subspecific name. Let us suppose that for the use of visitors the custodian of Lehman Cave National Monument makes a list intended to be scientifically accurate. In this list of mammals "northern grasshopper mouse (*Onychomys leucogaster brevicaudus*)" would be entirely adequate, less confusing, and more often used than "short-tailed northern grasshopper mouse (*Onychomys leucogaster brevicaudus* Merriam)." Laymen and amateur naturalists wrongly feel that there must be some reason, albeit unknown to them, why they should use a common name distinctive of subspecies in anything that they *write* about a mammal. Actually, for nonmigratory kinds of mammals (in which no more than one subspecies occurs in a place) common names of species almost everywhere suffice if the locality concerned is stated. If a subspecific name is needed, the scientific (Latin) one should be used. Even the scientific subspecific name is rarely required, and even the terminal part of it (*"brevicaudus,"* in the instance cited above) can be dropped without loss of significant meaning, providing the locality of capture of the animal is stated. Certainly, attempts to invent vernacular names complicated enough to distinguish subspecies usually lead to more confusion than clarification of the data which the person attempts to present. For these reasons, then, the common name at the heading of each subspecific account is the same for each one of the several subspecies of a single species.

3. Following the accepted scientific and common names, there is a synonymy which gives, first, the citation to the account in which the accepted scientific subspecific name was proposed (original description of zoölogical terminology), followed by indication of the type locality. The second citation is to the account in which the combination of names (generic, specific, and subspecific) used in the present account was first employed, unless the combination in the original description was the same as now employed. Nomenclaturally, so far as the first usage of a combination of names is concerned, the binomial combination *Antrozous pallidus* is considered to be the same as the trinomial *Antrozous pallidus pallidus*. The reason for this is that as soon as more than one subspecies of the species *Antrozous pallidus* is named, the binomial name automatically becomes trinomial. Where both combinations appear in a synonymy, the purpose of such duality is merely to list information pertaining strictly to Nevada under the form of the name used by the author who there is cited. The trinomial in such an instance is not used to provide a citation to the first usage of the name-combination that I have employed for the animal. Third, any other combinations of scientific names known to have been applied to Nevada-taken specimens are given along with some other published references. The latter are selected for inclusion because they contain information pertaining to the mammal in Nevada, which information it is now judged will be useful to the future student. A pure synonym is recognizable as such because in the citation the type locality immediately follows the name. For example, in the synonymy on page 506 *Peromyscus crinitus scitulus* Bangs is regarded as a pure synonym of *Peromyscus crinitus crinitus* (Merriam). In the synonymy a comma is interposed between a scientific name and the name of the author who used it, unless the author proposed the name (terminal word in the name-combination), in which event no punctuation appears between the scientific name and name of the author. Parentheses around the name of an authority following a scientific subspecific or specific name signify that the name was first proposed in combination with a generic name different from the generic name used in the present account. Absence of parentheses

signifies that the generic name used is the same one used when the name concerned first was proposed.

4. In the next category, *Distribution*, the statement of distribution is supported by a reference to the distribution map; the information thus provided is essentially geographical. Distribution according to life-zones, habitats, kinds of soils, or other features when known is given mainly in the account of the species.

5. Under *Remarks* the external measurements of total length (excluding hair on the tip of the tail), length of tail (measured from point on top where it bends at right angles with the back to tip, excluding hair on distal end), and length of hind foot (from back of heel to tip of the longest claw when foot is laid out flat) are given in the order mentioned. A fourth measurement, length of ear (measured from notch), is sometimes given. Any other measurements given are named or explained at the place where' they are recorded. All linear measurements are in millimeters unless otherwise indicated (25.37 millimeters equal 1 inch). Weight is given whenever available. Ordinarily the weight is expressed in grams (2.2 pounds equals 1,000 grams), but for some of the kinds of larger mammals it is recorded in pounds or ounces. Unless indication is made to the contrary, measurements and weights are of fully adult individuals, the females of which are nonpregnant. These data are followed by a statement, usually comparative in nature, of the characters by which the subspecies can be distinguished from other subspecies the geographic ranges of which border on that of the first. In describing and comparing color, capitalized color terms are those of Ridgway (1912), and uncapitalized color terms are unreferred to any precise standard of color. Finally, information on geographic variation, and sometimes on other kinds of variation, is given, together with remarks on intergradation and other data thought to pertain restrictedly to the subspecies.

6. *Records of occurrence* are divided into two parts: first, Specimens examined and, second, Additional records. Records of the first part are based upon specimens which I myself have examined. Effort is made to be exactly as precise as was the locality data on the labels of the specimens. Unless otherwise indicated, specimens are in the Museum of Vertebrate Zoölogy. At the time the first lists of specimens examined were prepared, the specimens listed as being in the D. R. Dickey Collection were at the California Institute of Technology, Pasadena, California, but at this writing (December, 1941) are housed by the University of California, Los Angeles. The specimens of mammals in the collection of Ralph Ellis, while this manuscript was being prepared, were housed at the University of California, Berkeley, and, finally, at the University of Kansas, Lawrence. At a late stage in the preparation of this account, 17,861 specimens from Nevada had been examined. More than fifteen thousand of these are in the Museum of Vertebrate Zoölogy; the exact numbers examined from any one collection are ascertainable by summing up those, of each category, recorded in the lists of specimens examined for each subspecies.

The additional records, given in the second paragraph of this section, are not based on specimens examined by me, but are records which have occurred in literature and field notes. Such records are included only if they are of undoubted accuracy and if they provide significant additions to a knowledge of the extent of range of a subspecies. Places from which specimens have been examined by me and also recorded in the literature are listed only under specimens examined.

The order of listing is first by counties, beginning in the northwest corner of the state and running in north-to-south tiers, in the following order (see map, fig. 475, p. 651):

Washoe	Humboldt	Esmeralda	Elko
Ormsby	Pershing	Lander	White Pine
Douglas	Churchill	Eureka	Lincoln
Storey	Mineral	Nye	Clark
Lyon			

Within a county, localities are listed from north to south, although where two localities are on the same parallel the western one precedes the eastern.

One change in county boundaries in recent years introduces some slight, apparent discrepancy in the above order of listing. This results from the incorporation into Lyon County of a considerable area along the East Walker River that formerly was in Mineral County. In the present account specimens from this area, for example those from Wichman, are listed under Mineral County, although at present this area is in Lyon County.

7. In tables of cranial measurements the ages of specimens that are juveniles, young, or subadults are designated as such by the abbreviations "juv.," "yg.," and "sad.," respectively. In the absence of such designation the specimen is understood to be adult. When the name of the state does not follow a locality, the locality is in Nevada.

The plan of treatment just outlined for a subspecies is deviated from when only one subspecies of a species is recorded from the state. In that event, the section on *Remarks* under the account of the subspecies includes also any information offered on habitat preferences, reproduction, food, secondary sexual difference, and any other natural history information. It is thereby possible to dispense with a separate account for the full species. When there are two or more subspecies of a species, the information just mentioned, beginning with habitat preferences, is presented in the account of the full species, together with a characterization of the species sufficient to differentiate it from other full species of the genus. The natural history information on habits pertains almost always to findings *in* Nevada. In every instance where such information was not the result of studies in Nevada, the source of the information is clearly stated to be extralimital.

Because the main emphasis in the present account is placed on species and subspecies, accounts of the characteristics of orders, families, and genera are omitted, unless it is felt that the inclusion of an account of one of these higher systematic categories contributes importantly to understanding the mammals of Nevada. Even the names of families and genera are omitted from the systematic section, but are incorporated in the check list of mammals on page 70. Characterizations of these higher groups are to be found in such general works as "Mammals Living and Extinct," by Flower and Lydekker (1891); "Die Säugetiere," by Max Weber (1927); "Field Book of North American Mammals," by H. E. Anthony (1928); or textbooks on vertebrate zoölogy.

Most of the drawings accompanying the key for identification of the species were made by Mary M. McAllister. And these are, for the most part, copies of previously published illustrations; only a few are original. Figures 169–171 were drawn by Frank B. Richardson. The rest of the drawings throughout the book are the work of Harry Adamson and Viola Memmler. Initials on the drawings identify the individual's work. For funds to defray the cost of many illustrations, I am grateful to the Committee on Research Grants of the University of California. Most of the distribution maps were prepared by Jean T. Boulware. On the small-scale maps showing ranges of species in North America, boundaries of some states are purposely omitted to avoid obscuring the boundaries of ranges of the mammals. Drawings of skulls as large as those of deer were made by means of a Bausch and Lomb reducing prism (camera lucida) with the skull about 3 feet from the prism. All drawings of skulls of smaller size were made by use of a Bausch and Lomb home balopticon, no. 41141. By the use of these instruments a view is obtained that is essentially photographic in the sense that perspective is about the same as registered upon a negative by the lens of a camera. In making these drawings and in computing the degree of reduction, the greatest length of the skull when viewed from below was used as the control—that is to say, if the drawing was made three times natural size, the image of a skull 20 millimeters long would, in ventral view, be focused upon the drawing board so that the greatest length was exactly 60 millimeters. In lateral view the same over-all length was used. In dorsal view the occipitonasal length was made to match the length of the same part shown in lateral view.

PLATES

a. East face of Wheeler Peak, White Pine County. Note the large area above timber line which is at about 11,000 feet. This peak is nearly 13,000 feet high. Photo by R. D. Moore, July 29, 1930.

b. Meadow on south flank of Mount Rose, Washoe County. This meadow of 8600-feet elevation is overgrazed by domestic sheep and supports large populations of mountain pocket gophers and Belding ground squirrels. Photo by J. M. Linsdale, July 10, 1932.

a. Cleve Creek, White Pine County, looking down from an elevation of 8100 feet toward the cliffs which have Douglas firs at their base. This was the habitat of the bushy-tailed wood rat. Photo by R. D. Moore, August 4, 1930.

b. Limber pines on Pine Forest Mountains, Humboldt County. Photo by W. P. Taylor, July 1, 1909.

PLATE 3

a. Trail through aspens at 8000 feet along North Twin River, Nye County. Photo by L. V. Compton, June 20, 1933.

b. Toyabe Mountains, Nye County, looking southeast from the divide along North Twin River at 9000 feet. This territory forms a part of the South Twin River watershed. Photo by J. M. Linsdale, June 20, 1933.

a

b

a. Meadow of *Balsamorrhiza* and grass on Duffer Peak, Humboldt County. Photo by W. P. Taylor, July 11, 1909.

b. Canyon of Wisconsin Creek, 7800 feet, Nye County. In this downstream view, piñons dot the slopes; willows and birches line the stream. Photo by J. M. Linsdale, May 31, 1930.

a. Sagebrush along South Twin River, 6500 feet, Nye County. The foreground shows typical habitat of sagebrush vole (*Lagurus curtatus*) which was trapped at this place. Photo by J. M. Linsdale, May 12, 1930.

b. Pond in Reese River, 8 miles west and 4 miles south of Austin. Ponds in rivers comprise one of the habitats of the muskrat. Photo by L. V. Compton, June 23, 1933.

a. Snake Valley, 5800 feet, White Pine County, looking north from Baker. This view is typical of Nevada in that it shows a single farmstead in a wide expanse of mountain range and valley. This same sparsity of settlement holds for most of the areas of the state. Photo by R. D. Moore, July 28, 1930.

b. Carson River Valley, Lyon County, 1½ miles upriver from Dayton. This shows the meadowland along the river, where *Microtus* and *Thomomys* live; the cottonwood trees lining the stream, where *Neotoma cinerea* has its home far below the rat's normal Boreal range; the area of northern desert shrub and sagebrush, where *Dipodomys* and *Perognathus* abound; and, on the mountain in the distance there are junipers and piñons, in which *Peromyscus truei* and other mammals find suitable habitat. Photo by W. C. Matthews, October 31, 1941.

a

b

PLATE 7

a. Foreground is habitat of *Perognathus formosus melanurus.*
View looking north from a point ¼ mile north of the Truckee
River, Washoe County, opposite the diversion dam of the
Truckee Canal, on north side of highway. Photo by W. C.
Matthews, November 2, 1941.

b. Habitat of *Microdipodops pallidus pallidus.* A westerly view
from a point 8 miles west of Fallon, at the intersection of the
highways from Carson City and from Reno. The wind-drifted
sand, with bushes of *Sarcobatus,* supports a dense population
of rodents. Note mouth of burrow, probably of kangaroo rat, at
side of bush in right foreground. Photo by W. C. Matthews,
November 2, 1941.

a

b

PLATE 8

a. Creosote bush association in the Lower Sonoran Life-zone, 14 miles east of Searchlight, Clark County. View west from Colorado River just above high-water line. Habitat of *Dipodomys merriami* and *Perognathus penicillatus*. Photo by Seth B. Benson, January 24, 1934.

b. Cottonwood trees and grass on bottom land along Colorado River, ½ mile north of California-Nevada Monument, Clark County. In the right foreground, on partly inundated land, is habitat of cotton rat; grass growing up through the twigs of fallen limb provided ideal cover. Photo by S. B. Benson, February 2, 1934.

a

b

a. Northern desert shrub at Quinn River Crossing, 4100 feet, Humboldt County. This flora is typical of large areas in the bottoms of valleys and in the low trough along the eastern base of the Sierra Nevada. Photo by W. P. Taylor, May 18, 1909.

b. Big Smoky Valley, 6800 feet, Nye County, looking north from South Twin River toward the playa (dry lake). A typical view in Nevada. Photo by L. V. Compton, June 17, 1933.

a. Kit fox and two young at den on the shore of Lake Mead, Hemenway Wash, Clark County. Photo by R. K. Grater, May 16, 1938.

b. Townsend ground squirrel, caught and photographed February 27, 1941, ¼ mile southwest of Soda Lake, Churchill County, by T. J. Trelease.

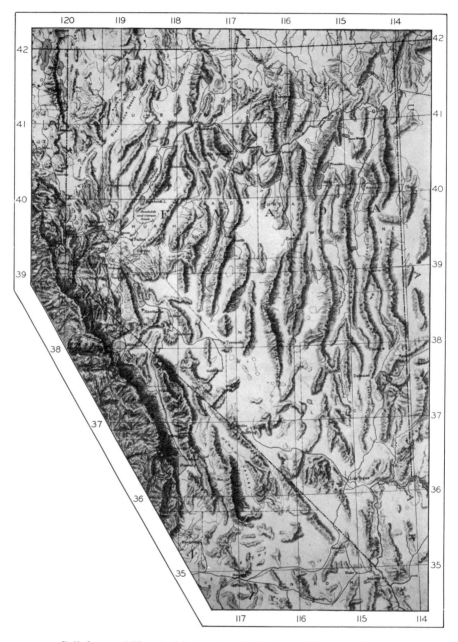

Relief map of Nevada. Map no. 1, after Lawson, Gilbert, *et al.* (1908).

TOPOGRAPHY

Nevada is made up of parallel, north-to-south mountain ranges and narrow and flat-floored valleys. Reference to plate 11 shows that many of these ranges are more than 150 miles long. Only two peaks rise above 13,000 feet, but many peaks and a number of ridges are more than 11,000 feet high. The floors of the valleys are about 4000 feet above sea level in the western part of the state, and about 5800 feet in the eastern part. The succession of parallel ranges and intervening valleys with their long axes in a north-to-south direction are relieved by two features: first, the narrow valley of the Humboldt River which in an east-to-west course cuts through seven mountain ranges in the north-central part of the state, and, second, the low-lying trough along the eastern base of the Sierra Nevada. From the Oregon boundary this trough extends southward to Walker Lake, thence angles southeast, erasing the southern ends of the mountain ranges as it continues on through successively lower levels, finally to fall away rapidly into Death Valley, just over the state boundary in California. Another wide arm that divides and reunites around Charleston Peak drops off into the valley of the Colorado. The trough along the eastern base of the Sierra Nevada has had much greater effect on the distribution and speciation of mammals than has the Humboldt River Valley.

The valley of the Colorado River, where it leaves the extreme southern tip of the state, is only about 500 feet above sea level, and the southern part of the state below 37 degrees latitude drops off rather abruptly to the river.

Of the north-to-south mountain ranges, those parts which lie north of the Humboldt River end at the river valley as low hills, and, together with high intervening valleys, comprise a divide between tributaries of the Humboldt River on the one hand and streams that flow northward out of the state into the Snake River of Idaho on the other hand. In addition to the Humboldt River and its tributaries and the tributaries of the Snake River, the principal streams in Nevada are the Truckee, Carson, and Walker rivers. These three rivers flow eastward from out of the Sierra Nevada; one, the Carson River, like the Humboldt, empties into a sink. The other two flow into lakes, Pyramid and Walker, which have no outlets. These lakes, and the aforementioned sinks, all lie within the trough along the eastern base of the Sierra Nevada. From Walker Lake northward this trough is part of the basin of the Quaternary Lake Lahontan of which Pyramid and Walker lakes are remnants.

In the southern, the drier, part of the state, the Muddy River and the Virgin River, which enter Nevada from Utah via northwestern Arizona, unite and flow into the Colorado River, which forms the southeastern boundary of the state. Of these streams, the Colorado has the most obvious effect on the distribution and speciation of the mammalian fauna. The river is a barrier so effective to the movements of land mammals that many species have developed distinct subspecies on the two sides and a few species have not crossed it.

The streams which course down the sides of the steep mountains flow into lake basins that are dry during all seasons of most years. The water is either lost by absorption or, if a lake is temporarily formed, by evaporation. The resulting playa or dry alkali flat is a characteristic feature in Nevada, almost every valley having one. This reflects the fact that stream action has not cut the low points in the rims of the valleys to provide drainage. If moisture were abundant, almost every valley would be the basin of a sizable lake. As already noted, these dry flats offer opportunity for the wind to move sediments that in more moist regions are transported by streams. On the leeward, usually eastern, side of nearly every playa, the wind has piled up sand or other fine particles of soil in dune formations. These wind-drifted deposits are the preferred habitat of many species of heteromyid rodents, the densest populations of which occur in these places.

CLIMATE

Notable features of the climate are wide range of temperature within a 24-hour period, bright sunshine, dryness of the air, slight amount of rainfall in the valleys and deserts, and heavy snowfall in the mountains. The lowest winter temperatures in all of the United States in some years are recorded in northeastern Nevada. In the extreme southern part of the state no temperature as low as 0° F. is recorded, but the winter temperature there does drop below freezing. In summer, temperatures well above 100° F. are recorded at many places, although, except in the southern part of the state, the nights are cool. In the northern part, killing frosts may occur in any month of the year, but ordinarily the months of June, July, August, and September are without frost. The length of the growing season depends mainly on altitude; at higher altitudes it is short.

The low trough at the eastern base of the Sierra Nevada receives the least rain of any part of the state, particularly in the southern part along the eastern edge of Death Valley. The adjoining eastern slope of the Sierra Nevada receives the most. Linsdale (1936) has recorded that "January has the greatest precipitation, and August the least. . . . The number of days per year with 0.01 inch or more of precipitation varies from 14 at Clay City, southern Nye County, to 67 at Tahoe. At Marlette Lake the annual snowfall is 255 inches while at Logandale, Clark County, it is less than one inch. Evaporation at Clay City, on the eastern edge of Death Valley, averages more than 11 feet per year."

The prevailing winds are from the south, southwest, and west. Wind velocities are generally low, and severe windstorms over large areas are uncommon. The nights are calm, and at many places the wind begins to blow at almost the same time every day and from the same direction. In summer, rains that do fall come mostly in the daytime.

Adaptations in the mammalian fauna that are responses to this climate include: winter whitening of weasels, white-tailed jack rabbits, and snowshoe

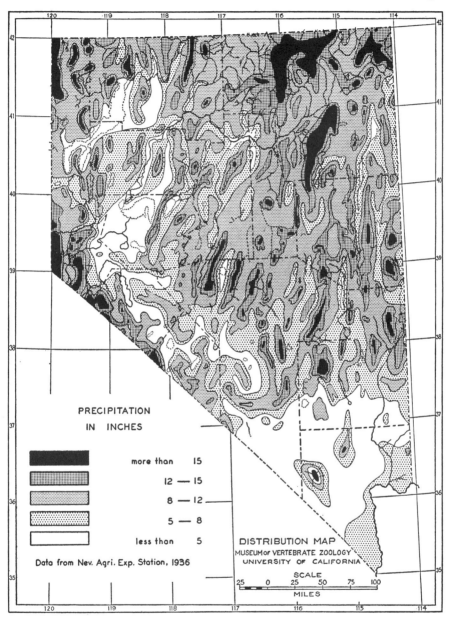

PRECIPITATION
IN INCHES

more than   15
12 — 15
8 — 12
5 — 8
less than   5

Data from Nev. Agri. Exp. Station, 1936

DISTRIBUTION MAP
MUSEUM of VERTEBRATE ZOOLOGY
UNIVERSITY OF CALIFORNIA

SCALE
25   0   25   50   75   100
MILES

Fig. 3. Average annual precipitation in different parts of the state. The data from which this map is compiled are of two sorts: (1) actual measurements of rainfall and other forms of precipitation made by governmental agencies and private citizens, and (2) inferences from the native flora of areas from which actual measurements of precipitation are lacking.

rabbits; estivation of some kinds of ground squirrels and adult marmots; hibernation of many kinds of mammals; watersaving mechanisms which permit many kinds to survive without water to drink; large number of seed-eating species, as opposed to species which feed primarily on green herbage; small number of individuals of aquatic species.

FLORAL BELTS

The distribution of mammals is greatly influenced directly by plants, as well as by climate. The presence or absence of individuals of a kind of plant, or more often of a group of species of plants, determines the presence or absence of food, shelter, and safe breeding places for kinds of mammals; therefore the presence or absence in a given area of certain kinds of mammals depends on whether or not certain kinds of plants are present. The sagebrush vole (*Lagurus curtatus*) seems to be a good illustration; this animal relies for food in large measure upon the leaves and inner bark of one or a few species of *Artemisia*, and nowhere in Nevada have adult voles of this species been found except in close association with *Artemisia*, usually, and perhaps always, the species *Artemisia tridentata*. The porcupine (*Erethizon epixanthum*) in Nevada finds an area suitable for permanent habitation only in places having some trees.

Beginning at the highest elevations, eight plant belts of Nevada may be listed as follows:

Alpine belt.—This is the area above timber line, and the number of kinds of plants found there is small. Nearly all are low-growing species which extend down into the next lower belt. *Polemonium confertum* is an example of this group of plants.

Subalpine belt.—Bristlecone pine (*Pinus aristata*), with associated plants, forms a second belt. In Nevada neither this nor the alpine belt supports mammals that are restricted to these belts; the mammals which occur there live also in lower belts of plants.

Spruce-fir belt.—The extensive stands of spruce (in my field notes *Picea pungens*, as well as *Picea engelmanni*, is listed as being on Wheeler Peak) along the Utah boundary, the red fir (*Abies magnifica*) in the Sierra Nevada along the California boundary, and the white fir (*Abies concolor*) at lower elevations cover a considerable area in and above which several species of mammals occur, particularly in the Sierra Nevada. Marten and northern flying squirrel are two. Elsewhere in Nevada the area of any one representation of the spruce-fir belt is so small that not many mammals are restricted to it; those which occur there are found also in lower belts of plants.

Aspen belt.—The aspens (*Populus tremuloides*) form a definite belt on the eastern slopes of Wheeler Peak and in some other places. In a large number of the higher mountain ranges in the interior of the state, for example the Toyabe Mountain Range and considerable areas of the high rolling country in the northeastern part of the state, aspens, sometimes of stunted growth-form, cover areas of several acres. Across areas many miles in extent these aspens of more or less stunted growth-form are the most conspicuous of all the larger plants. I know of no mammals which are limited in their distribution to the aspen belt. Indeed, pure stands of aspen are relatively barren of mammals. A number of species, for example *Mustela cicognanii* and *Microtus longicaudus*, find the lower limit of their vertical range in or near the lower margin of this belt.

Yellow pine belt.—The flora of this belt in Nevada occurs in patches rather than in belts. Moreover, yellow pines (*Pinus ponderosa*) themselves do not occupy any considerable part of the total area assigned to this belt. Relatively good stands of yellow pine occur on Charleston Peak and in the Sheep Range, but at few other places. In the Sierra Nevada of the western part of the state, the related Jeffrey pine (*Pinus Jeffreyi*) replaces the yellow pine almost everywhere. The total area occupied by Jeffrey pine and yellow pine is much less than that occupied by mountain mahogany (*Cercocarpus ledifolius*). The mahogany covers areas that in many other parts of western North America would support yellow pines. Where both occur in the same area, the yellow pines are on the deeper soils with more moisture and the mountain mahogany is on the slopes with less moisture. In the southeastern part of the state, for example, in parts of the Quinn Canyon Mountains, the yellow pines and mountain mahogany in some measure both give way to oak brush (*Quercus* sp.), which, along with squaw apple (*Peraphyllum ramosissimum*) and some other plants, indicates an intrusion into this area of conspicuous elements of the flora typical of this plant belt in northern Arizona and southern Utah. In the yellow pine belt the replacement of the yellow pine itself by other species of plants is reflected also in the mammalian fauna, because many of the species of mammals characteristic of the yellow pine belt elsewhere in the western United States are absent or sparsely represented.

Piñon-juniper belt.—The piñons (*Pinus edulis* and *Pinus monophylla*) and junipers (*Juniperus utahensis* and *Juniperus scopulorum*) form a broad belt in the foothills and on the lower mountain ranges. The junipers occur lower down than the piñons and the two together extend up to the lower edge of the yellow pine belt. In northwestern Nevada, juniper occurs to the exclusion of piñon. The Merriam shrew, Panamint chipmunk, cliff chipmunk, and piñon mouse are characteristic mammals of this belt.

Sagebrush belt.—*Artemisia tridentata* is the dominant shrub of this belt, which in northern and central Nevada covers more territory than any other belt here recognized. This plant (*Artemisia tridentata*) or some variety of it extends on up through the piñons and junipers, and on south-facing slopes passes upward even beyond the yellow pines and aspens; on exposed slopes it occurs well above 10,000 feet. Sagebrush, species *A. tridentata*, often occurs in pure stands from 2 to 7 feet high. Mammals the areas of distribution of which seemingly are determined by that of the sagebrush are the least chipmunk and sagebrush vole. In the lower parts of the valleys and on other soils that have a high content of alkali, *Artemisia tridentata* gives way to *Chrysothamnus, Sarcobatus, Atriplex,* and other plants able to live under adverse conditions. These plants, with the exception of *Artemisia tridentata,* usually occur in the bottoms of the valleys. Therefore, in general, these plants occur at lower elevations than *Artemisia tridentata.* In the salt-desert shrub there are several species of mammals which occur sparsely, if at all, in pure stands of *Artemisia tridentata.* If the area which supports *Artemisia tridentata* and the area of salt-desert which supports *Sarcobatus vermiculatus, Atriplex confertifolia, Chrysothamnus, Tetradymia,* and *Gutierrezia* be considered as one belt, several species of mammals can be pointed to as largely confined to this belt. In addition to the sagebrush chipmunk and sagebrush vole, in this category there are the following: Townsend ground squirrel, long-tailed pocket mouse, two species of *Microdipodops,* Ord kangaroo rat, northern grasshopper mouse, and pigmy rabbit.

Creosote bush belt.—The creosote bush (*Larrea tridentata*) is more extensive than any other type of vegetation in this belt. The plants are notable for their dark green color and even spacing. Areas of salt-desert within this belt often support desert saltbush (*Atriplex polycarpa*). The upper part of the creosote bush belt has a plant association which might almost be given the status of a belt because it separates the sagebrush and creosote bush. The association referred to includes the Joshua tree (*Clistoyucca brevifolia*), blackbrush (*Coleogyne*), hop-sage (*Grayia spinosa*), and several cacti. No full species of mammal is restricted to this association, but one subspecies, *Dipodomys panamintinus caudatus,* in Nevada, so far as known, occurs here only. Five species of mammals, the California leaf-nosed bat, round-tailed ground squirrel, desert pocket mouse, cactus mouse, and hispid cotton rat are restricted to the creosote bush belt.

LIFE-ZONES

Life-zones, as recognized by C. Hart Merriam, are clearly discernible in Nevada and are nearly as useful in studying the distribution of organisms as they are in the rest of the western United States. The word "nearly" is injected as a qualifier because the Upper Sonoran Life-zone is enlarged at the expense of the Transition Life-zone, and in many places the Transition Zone is absent as ascent is made from the Upper Sonoran to the Canadian Life-zone. As its name implies, the Transition Zone was a zone of change from one well-defined zone to another (Upper Sonoran to Canadian), and the fauna, of vertebrates at least, was a mixture of those of the two adjoining life-zones. Because the Transition Life-zone in Nevada is absent or faintly expressed in so many places where it might be expected to occur, the distinctness of the Sonoran and Boreal faunas and floras, and hence the life-zone concept, is emphasized. The change from one to the other, because of its abruptness, is more striking than in places where a broad Transition Life-zone effects a gradual change. Viewed in this way—and this viewpoint is eminently justified, I think—life-zones in Nevada

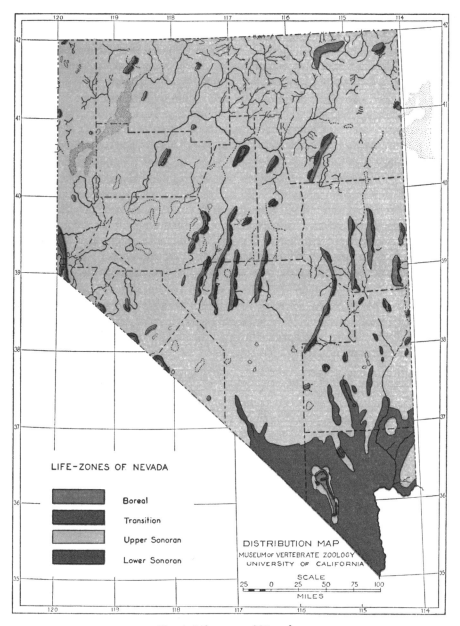

Fig. 4. Life-zones of Nevada.

are more useful to the biologist than in most other parts of the western United States. Nevertheless, it should be pointed out that the combination of factors which are responsible for the ascendancy of the Sonoran Zone over the Transition Zone has permitted the Sonoran to usurp also a part of the Boreal Zone. The Canadian Life-zone, and in a few places even the Hudsonian Life-zone, is clearly cut through by upward extensions of flora and fauna of the Upper Sonoran Life-zone. Sagebrush extends to timber line on some high mountains. This circumstance—at least for the student who classifies the biota of the high country—makes the life-zone concept less useful than it is in some other areas. Everything considered, then, life-zones in Nevada are about as useful to the biologist who chooses to use them as they are in the other parts of the western United States.

Although the approximate boundaries of a life-zone were set (Merriam, 1890:32) by two isotherms which marked a limited range of variation in mean temperature for the reproductive season, the biologist in the field ordinarily classifies a given area as to life-zone on the basis of the presence or absence of certain species of organisms which study in other areas has shown occur only, or mostly, in one life-zone. Organisms useful in this way are referred to as indicators. Among plants, some of these are mentioned in the account of plant belts on page 32.

A concordance between those belts of plants and life-zones of Merriam would be about as follows:

LIFE-ZONES	PLANT BELTS
Alpine-arctic	alpine
Hudsonian	subalpine
Canadian	spruce-fir and aspen
Transition	yellow pine
Upper Sonoran	piñon-juniper and sagebrush
Lower Sonoran	creosote bush

Indicators, in Nevada, among mammals would be as follows:

ALPINE-ARCTIC LIFE-ZONE

None found

HUDSONIAN LIFE-ZONE

None found

CANADIAN LIFE-ZONE

Sorex palustris, water shrew   *Eutamias speciosus*, lodgepole-pine chipmunk
Martes caurina, marten   *Glaucomys sabrinus*, northern flying squirrel
Mustela cicognanii, short-tailed weasel   *Aplodontia rufa*, mountain beaver
Vulpes fulva, red fox   *Lepus americanus*, snowshoe rabbit

TRANSITION LIFE-ZONE

Sorex trowbridgii, Trowbridge shrew   *Myotis evotis*, long-eared myotis

UPPER SONORAN LIFE-ZONE

Sorex merriami, Merriam shrew
Myotis subulatus, small-footed myotis
Citellus townsendii, Townsend ground squirrel
Eutamias minimus, least chipmunk
Eutamias panamintinus, Panamint chipmunk
Eutamias dorsalis, cliff chipmunk
Perognathus parvus, long-tailed pocket mouse

Microdipodops megacephalus, dark kangaroo mouse
Microdipodops pallidus, pallid kangaroo mouse
Dipodomys ordii, Ord kangaroo rat
Onychomys leucogaster, northern grasshopper mouse
Sylvilagus idahoensis, pigmy rabbit

LOWER SONORAN LIFE-ZONE

Macrotus californicus, California leaf-nosed bat
Bassariscus astutus, ring-tailed cat
Citellus tereticaudus, round-tailed ground squirrel

Perognathus penicillatus, desert pocket mouse
Peromyscus eremicus, cactus mouse
Sigmodon hispidus, hispid cotton rat

Reference to the chart on pages 39–41 will show that there are sixty-nine Sonoran and thirty-eight Boreal species. Four, the hairy-winged bat, river otter, bobcat, and coyote, seem to me to belong about as much to the Boreal region as to the Sonoran region.

In Nevada the Upper Sonoran Life-zone is not only the most extensive in area but has the largest number of species. The number of species of mammals which occur in each life-zone are:

Lower Sonoran, 53	Transition, 68	Hudsonian, 37
Upper Sonoran, 83	Canadian, 54	Alpine-arctic, 4

In any one of the three divisions (see chart, pp. 39–41) of the Upper Sonoran Life-zone, there are more species than in all of the Lower Sonoran Life-zone.

OCCURRENCE OF MAMMALS IN NEVADA
ACCORDING TO LIFE-ZONE

Width of horizontal bar in the table of occurrence indicates relative abundance of the species; the widest place in the bar indicates the place, zonally, where the population is thought to be densest. If there is reason to think that a species ranges beyond what is shown by actual facts available, the extension is indicated by a broken line. The zonal distribution in the table is based on findings for Nevada only; therefore the table does not show the distributional situation for each species over all of western North America. For most species, nevertheless, the distribution shown for Nevada is essentially correct for the species in parts of its range outside Nevada. The widths of the colored areas representing life-zones indicate in rough measure the relative areas of the state included within each zone. For example, the Upper Sonoran Life-zone includes more of the total area of the state than any other zone. The relative areas shown here are only approximately correct; the errors of area are in favor of the life-zones of smaller extent.

CHART 1

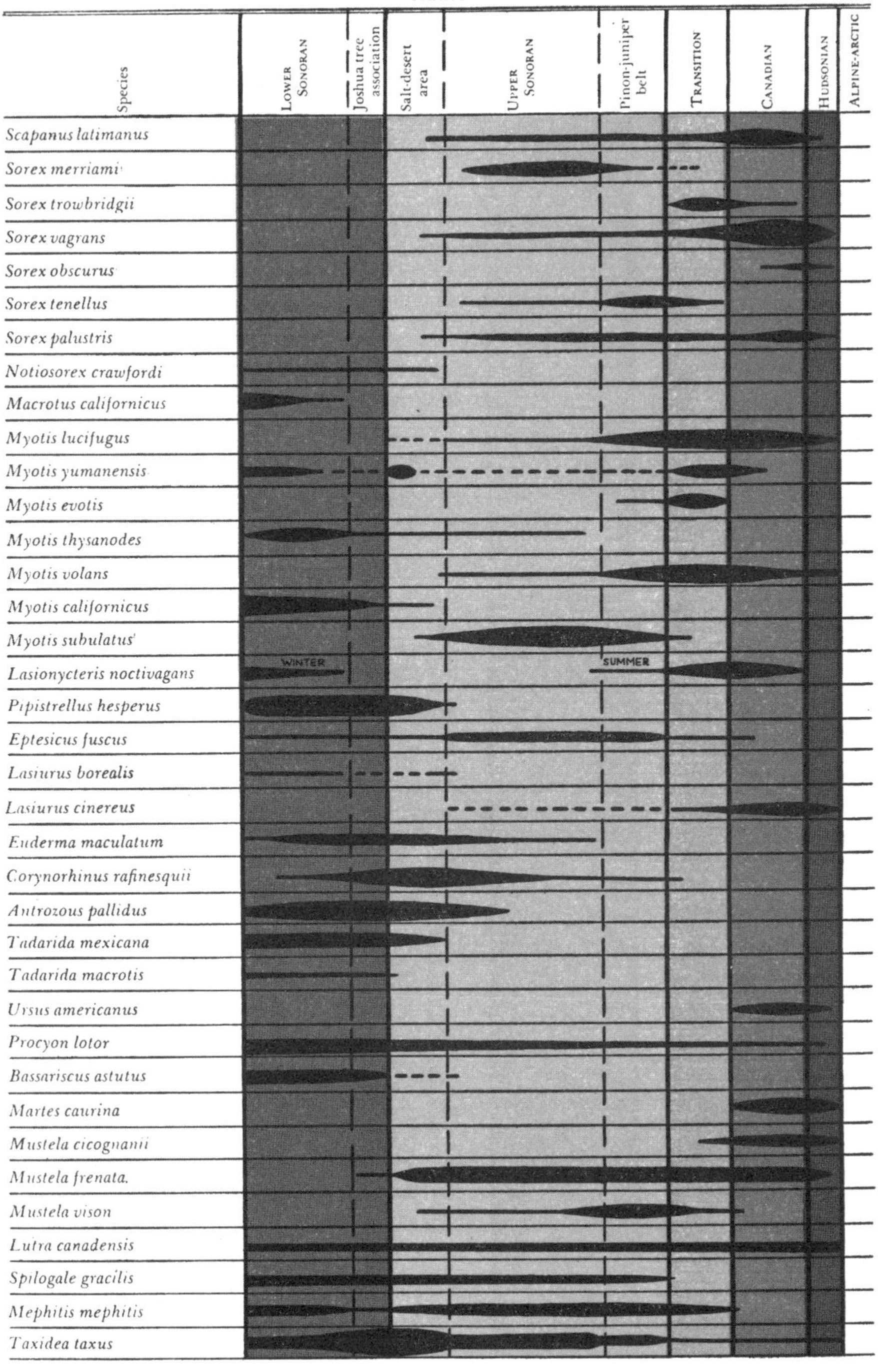

Species	LOWER SONORAN	Joshua tree association	Salt-desert area	UPPER SONORAN	Piñon-juniper belt	TRANSITION	CANADIAN	HUDSONIAN	ALPINE-ARCTIC
Scapanus latimanus									
Sorex merriami									
Sorex trowbridgii									
Sorex vagrans									
Sorex obscurus									
Sorex tenellus									
Sorex palustris									
Notiosorex crawfordi									
Macrotus californicus									
Myotis lucifugus									
Myotis yumanensis									
Myotis evotis									
Myotis thysanodes									
Myotis volans									
Myotis californicus									
Myotis subulatus									
Lasionycteris noctivagans	WINTER				SUMMER				
Pipistrellus hesperus									
Eptesicus fuscus									
Lasiurus borealis									
Lasiurus cinereus									
Euderma maculatum									
Corynorhinus rafinesquii									
Antrozous pallidus									
Tadarida mexicana									
Tadarida macrotis									
Ursus americanus									
Procyon lotor									
Bassariscus astutus									
Martes caurina									
Mustela cicognanii									
Mustela frenata									
Mustela vison									
Lutra canadensis									
Spilogale gracilis									
Mephitis mephitis									
Taxidea taxus									

CHART 1—(Continued)

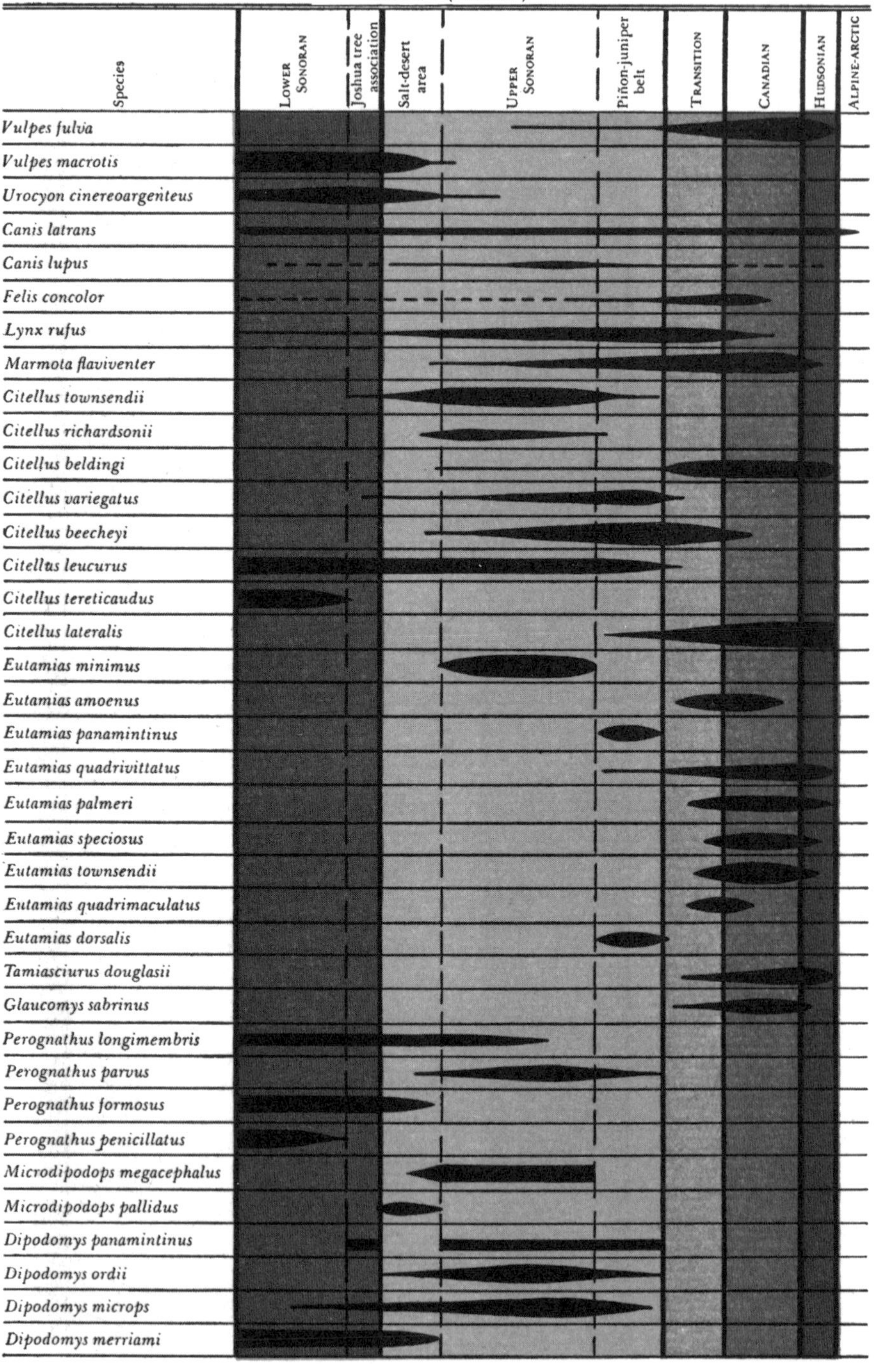

Species	LOWER SONORAN	Joshua tree association	Salt-desert area	UPPER SONORAN	Piñon-juniper belt	TRANSITION	CANADIAN	HUDSONIAN	ALPINE-ARCTIC
Vulpes fulva									
Vulpes macrotis									
Urocyon cinereoargenteus									
Canis latrans									
Canis lupus									
Felis concolor									
Lynx rufus									
Marmota flaviventer									
Citellus townsendii									
Citellus richardsonii									
Citellus beldingi									
Citellus variegatus									
Citellus beecheyi									
Citellus leucurus									
Citellus tereticaudus									
Citellus lateralis									
Eutamias minimus									
Eutamias amoenus									
Eutamias panamintinus									
Eutamias quadrivittatus									
Eutamias palmeri									
Eutamias speciosus									
Eutamias townsendii									
Eutamias quadrimaculatus									
Eutamias dorsalis									
Tamiasciurus douglasii									
Glaucomys sabrinus									
Perognathus longimembris									
Perognathus parvus									
Perognathus formosus									
Perognathus penicillatus									
Microdipodops megacephalus									
Microdipodops pallidus									
Dipodomys panamintinus									
Dipodomys ordii									
Dipodomys microps									
Dipodomys merriami									

CHART 1–(Concluded)

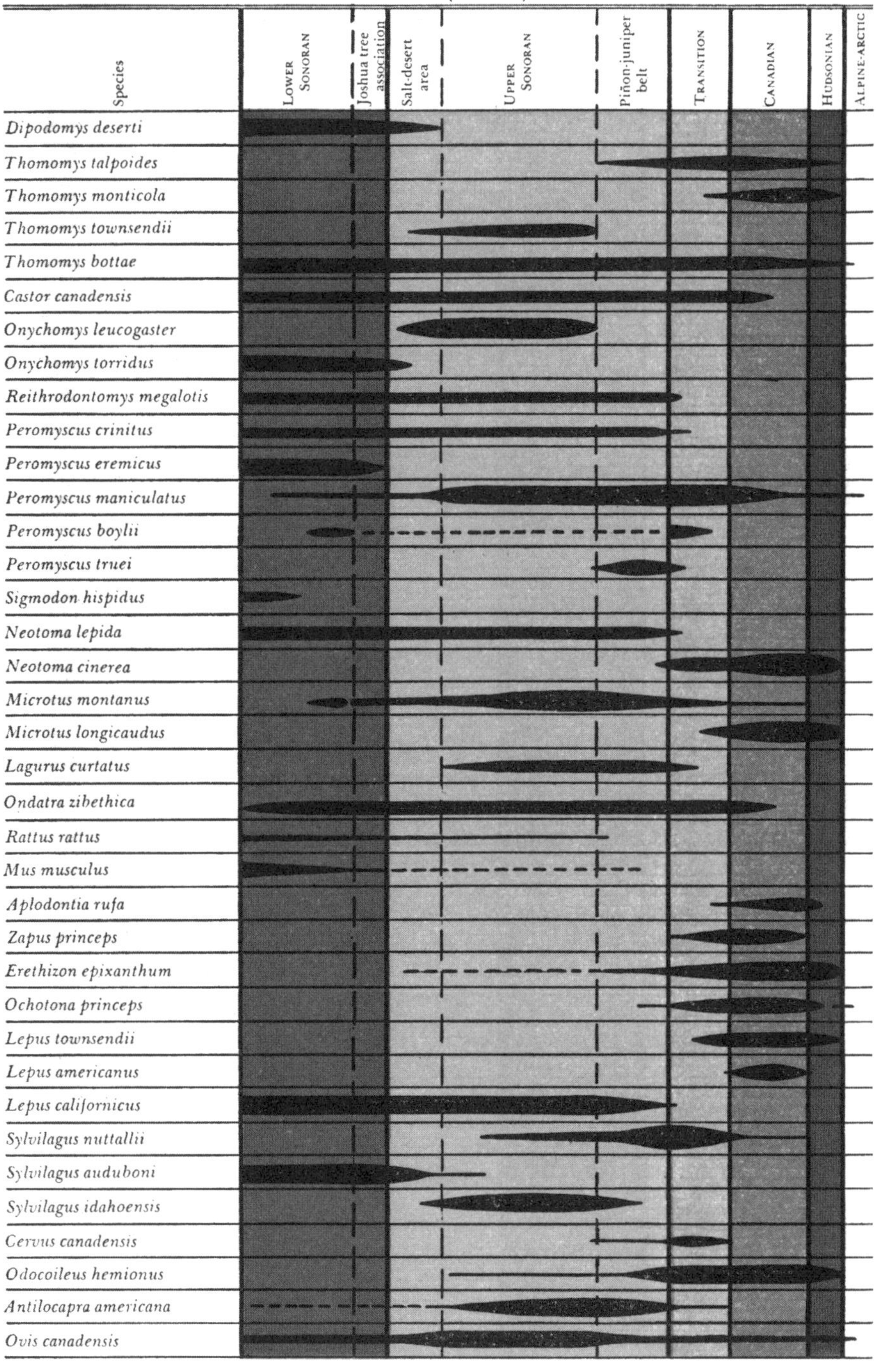

Species	Lower Sonoran	Joshua tree association	Salt-desert area	Upper Sonoran	Piñon-juniper belt	Transition	Canadian	Hudsonian	Alpine-Arctic
Dipodomys deserti									
Thomomys talpoides									
Thomomys monticola									
Thomomys townsendii									
Thomomys bottae									
Castor canadensis									
Onychomys leucogaster									
Onychomys torridus									
Reithrodontomys megalotis									
Peromyscus crinitus									
Peromyscus eremicus									
Peromyscus maniculatus									
Peromyscus boylii									
Peromyscus truei									
Sigmodon hispidus									
Neotoma lepida									
Neotoma cinerea									
Microtus montanus									
Microtus longicaudus									
Lagurus curtatus									
Ondatra zibethica									
Rattus rattus									
Mus musculus									
Aplodontia rufa									
Zapus princeps									
Erethizon epixanthum									
Ochotona princeps									
Lepus townsendii									
Lepus americanus									
Lepus californicus									
Sylvilagus nuttallii									
Sylvilagus auduboni									
Sylvilagus idahoensis									
Cervus canadensis									
Odocoileus hemionus									
Antilocapra americana									
Ovis canadensis									

CHART 2

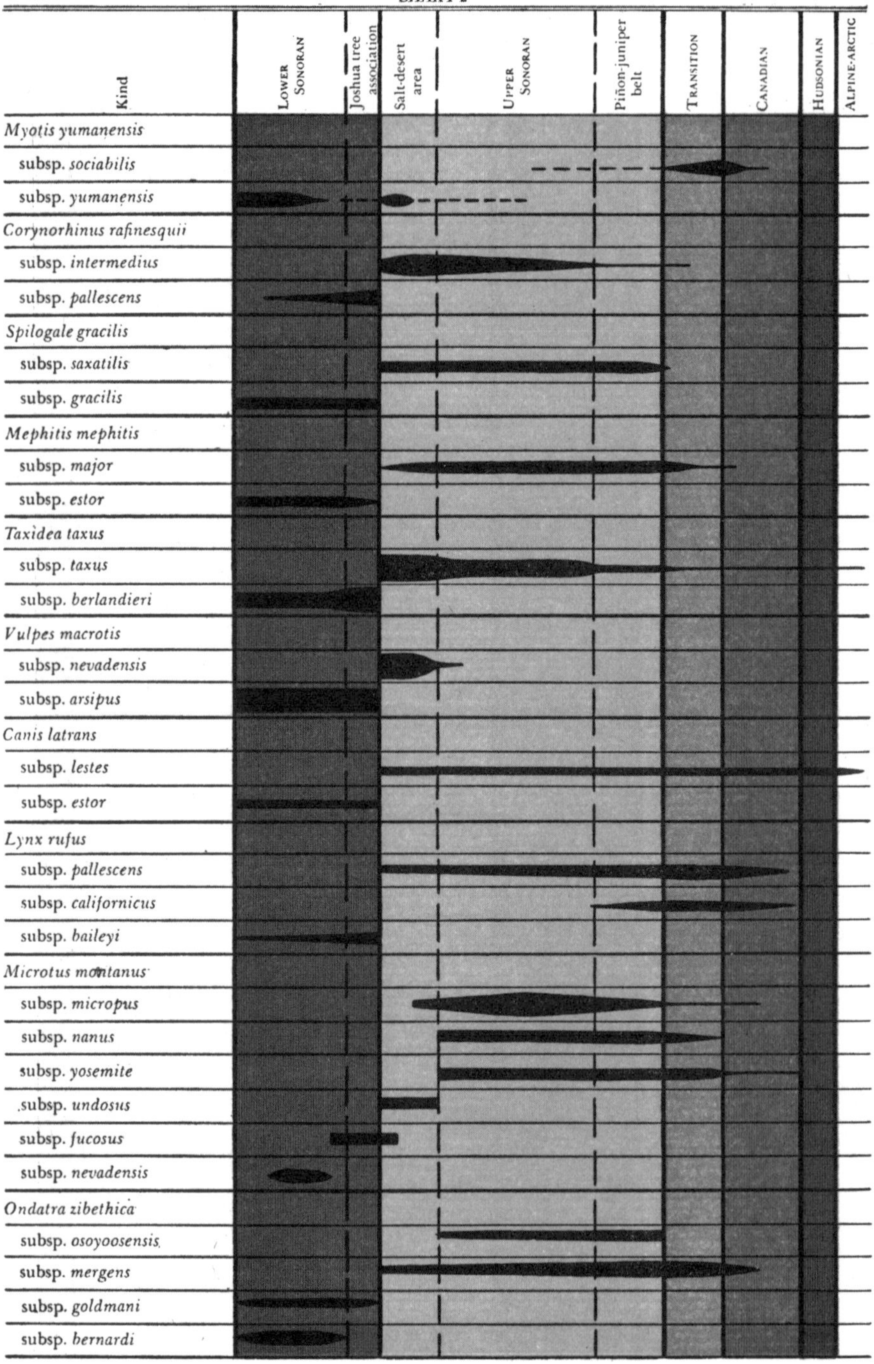

Kind	Lower Sonoran	Joshua tree association	Salt-desert area	Upper Sonoran	Piñon-juniper belt	Transition	Canadian	Hudsonian	Alpine-arctic
Myotis yumanensis									
subsp. *sociabilis*									
subsp. *yumanensis*									
Corynorhinus rafinesquii									
subsp. *intermedius*									
subsp. *pallescens*									
Spilogale gracilis									
subsp. *saxatilis*									
subsp. *gracilis*									
Mephitis mephitis									
subsp. *major*									
subsp. *estor*									
Taxidea taxus									
subsp. *taxus*									
subsp. *berlandieri*									
Vulpes macrotis									
subsp. *nevadensis*									
subsp. *arsipus*									
Canis latrans									
subsp. *lestes*									
subsp. *estor*									
Lynx rufus									
subsp. *pallescens*									
subsp. *californicus*									
subsp. *baileyi*									
Microtus montanus									
subsp. *micropus*									
subsp. *nanus*									
subsp. *yosemite*									
subsp. *undosus*									
subsp. *fucosus*									
subsp. *nevadensis*									
Ondatra zibethica									
subsp. *osoyoosensis*									
subsp. *mergens*									
subsp. *goldmani*									
subsp. *bernardi*									

Whereas the margins of the geographic ranges of several full species coincide with the boundaries between life-zones, the margins of the geographic ranges of only a few subspecies do so. The zonal boundary most significant for full species is that between the Sonoran zones and the Boreal zones. The Upper Sonoran Life-zone and the Canadian Life-zone, as indicated above, meet because the Transition Life-zone is absent in many places in Nevada. Thinking more especially of the sequence of life-zones from north to south than about their sequence altitudinally, the boundary between the Upper Sonoran Life-zone and the Lower Sonoran Life-zone is most significant for subspecies; it is this boundary which marks the northern limit of occurrence of several subspecies and the southern boundary of their geographically complementary subspecies of more northern occurrence. A much smaller percentage of subspecies than of full species has a margin of range coinciding with the boundary between two life-zones. This difference is partly to be accounted for, I think, as follows: The termination of the geographic range of a full species at the junction of the Boreal and Sonoran zones automatically rules out this place as a boundary *between* subspecies of this species. Several factors, for example kind of soil and amount of moisture, are more potent in fostering or in preserving heritable modifications in structure, the basis for subspecies, than are variations in temperature which are made the basis for separating life-zones.

In each of ten species there appears to be some significance attached to the fact that the demarcation line between subspecies coincides with that between life-zones. The zonal range of each of the subspecies is shown in the table of occurrence.

Analyzed on the basis of their geographical range, regardless of range by life-zone, the 111 full species recorded from Nevada comprise 33 northern, 33 southern, 10 western, 11 Great Basin, 22 ranging on all sides of Nevada, and 2 introduced from the Old World. Most of the 10 western forms barely enter Nevada along the Nevada-California boundary and the number of individuals of these in the state probably is less than that of any other category except the Old World kinds. Leaving these two categories out of account, it is seen that 33 kinds are northern species, 33 are southern species, and 33 are confined to the Great Basin or occur in it and widely on each side of it. It is noteworthy that no species having its main range in eastern and central North America sends an extension into Nevada. The north-to-south direction of the main mountain chains in North America limits the spread of mammals east and west and in part accounts for the absence in Nevada of kinds which could be said to be species of eastern North America.

FAUNAL AREAS AND CENTERS OF DIFFERENTIATION

Another useful way to generalize about the distribution of mammals is to set up faunal areas. If these areas are indicative of different groups of full species, centers of differentiation of subspecies theoretically should be found within a faunal area. Practically, this is what occurs in some of the faunal areas shown in figure 5; but partly because some of the faunal areas here recognized are small (for convenience of treatment), the distinction between faunal area and center of differentiation does not everywhere hold. With full recognition of this imperfection, the following arrangement expresses some of the effects on mammals of varying topography, climate, and their plant and animal associates. Faunal areas, five in all (see fig. 5), are:

1. Sierra Nevadan
2. Northern Great Basin
   A. Lava beds center of differentiation (other centers within this faunal area lie outside Nevada)
3. Central Rocky Mountain
   A. Elko center of differentiation
      a. Goose Creek subcenter
   B. Toyabe center of differentiation
4. Lower Sonoran–Lahontan Lake Basin
   A. Lahontan Lake Basin center of differentiation
   B. Amargosa-Pahranagat center of differentiation
   C. Charleston Peak center of differentiation
   D. Colorado River center of differentiation
      a. Virgin River Valley subcenter
      b. Colorado River Valley subcenter
5. Bonneville Basin

The Sierra Nevadan faunal area is characterized by twelve species which do not occur in any other part of the state. Trowbridge shrew, marten, Douglas squirrel, mountain beaver, and snowshoe rabbit are examples. With respect to the number of species peculiar to it and the absence of species which are found widely in the rest of the state, this is the most strongly marked of the faunal areas. It is also a center of differentiation; twelve species (one bat, three carnivores, and eight rodents) ranging also over other parts of the state have subspecies restricted, or nearly restricted, to this area. In general, the subspecies are dark-colored and individuals are of large size.

The Northern Great Basin faunal area extends into Nevada from Oregon and northeastern California. In Nevada no full species is restricted to it; species that are most nearly restricted to it occupy also parts of faunal areas 3 and 4. Thirteen subspecies are restricted to this Northern Great Basin faunal area. The part of this area which is in Nevada is more truly a center of differentiation which includes also northeastern California and the adjoining part of Oregon than it is a faunal area. Some of these subspecies are: *Antrozous pallidus cant-*

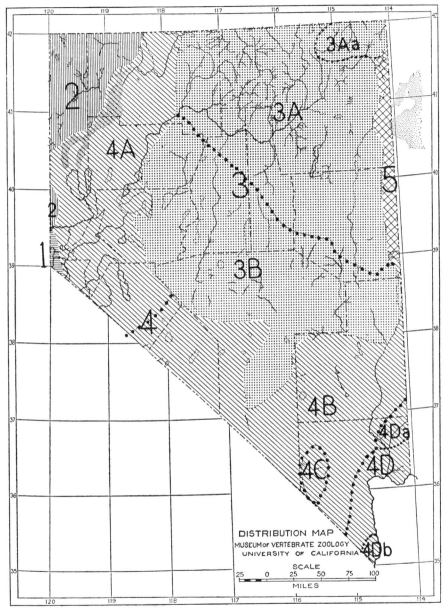

Fig. 5. Faunal areas and centers of differentiation as defined on page 44.

welli, Citellus townsendii canus, Microdipodops megacephalus oregonus, Dipodomys microps aquilonius, Onychomys leucogaster fuscogriseus, and *Ochotona princeps schisticeps.* These subspecies tend to be of large size and dark color. Lava beds of dark color are extensive in this area. Several species that range throughout it tend to be darker colored but insufficiently so to warrant subspecific differentiation. The harvest mouse and canyon mouse are examples. As a center of differentiation this area stands out strongly, but it is the most poorly defined faunal area in the state.

The Central Rocky Mountain faunal area is part of a much larger area in the Rocky Mountains northeast from Nevada. Most species of this area have ranges which extend also into the northern part of faunal area 4, or more often into faunal area 2. The Richardson ground squirrel is one species restricted to this area. Several subspecies, among which are *Sorex vagrans amoenus* and *Zapus princeps nevadensis,* characterize the Elko differentiation center of this area. Animals in this center tend to be large-skulled and of medium shade of color. The Goose Creek subcenter of differentiation is faintly marked. *Microtus montanus nanus* and *Marmota flaviventer nosophora* are subspecies that, in Nevada, occur only here. The Toyabe center of differentiation perhaps should be regarded only as another subcenter. *Zapus princeps palatinus* and *Ochotona princeps tutelata* are two subspecies restricted to this differentiation center of the Central Rocky Mountain faunal area.

The Lower Sonoran–Lahontan Lake Basin faunal area is second only to the Sierra Nevadan faunal area in being strongly distinct on the basis of the number of full species that are restricted to the area. The California myotis, Mexican free-tailed bat, kit fox, long-tailed pocket mouse, Merriam and desert kangaroo rats, and southern grasshopper mouse range throughout most of the area and are lacking in the faunal areas already mentioned. The Lahontan Lake Basin center of differentiation is one in which a large number of species have developed separate subspecies, especially the species characteristic of the Lower Sonoran Life-zone. In some of the species the geographic variation is so slight as not yet to warrant subspecific recognition. It is judged that subspecific change is proceeding at a rapid rate at the present time in the Lahontan Lake Basin.

The Amargosa-Pahranagat center of differentiation is the main area of true Lower Sonoran Life-zone; faunally, it is really a part of the Mohave Desert which covers a wide area in California. Many of the subspecies, for example *Perognathus longimembris panamintinus, Perognathus formosus mohavensis,* and *Dipodomys deserti deserti,* range over large areas of the Mohave Desert and adjoining areas.

The Charleston Peak center of differentiation truly is a strongly marked center, but the subspeciation in mammals there, which sets it apart as a center, is mostly concerned with the Boreal species from faunal areas 1, 2, and 3, which here are isolated in the high mountains. In a way, then, it might be regarded as a faunal area or as an isolated center of differentiation of the Central Rocky Mountain faunal area. *Citellus lateralis certus, Eutamias palmeri* (a full species), and *Neotoma cinerea lucida* are kinds restricted to the Spring Mountains, of which Charleston Peak is the highest part. Each of the three is a Boreal species. Small size and light color are characters of these subspecies.

The Colorado River center of differentiation has some but slightly less claim to being a faunal area than the Charleston Peak center. The round-tailed ground squirrel, desert pocket mouse, and cotton rat are full species which in Nevada occur only in this low terrain. The subspecies *Perognathus penicillatus sobrinus* has been differentiated here. Two subcenters of differentiation are the valley of the Virgin River and the wide valley of the Colorado River in the extreme southern tip of the state. A few miles above the state boundary the valley plays out and the river is lined with low mountains. In the wide valley of the Colorado River, the presence of the subspecies *Perognathus penicillatus penicillatus, Onychomys leucogaster pulcher,* and *Neotoma lepida grinnelli* comprise northeastern, marginal occurrences of a center of differentiation in and along the lower Colorado River Valley, and cause this area (including the part of it outside Nevada) to be regarded as a distinct center of differentiation. This is also the only place in the state where the cotton rat occurs. The Virgin River subcenter of differentiation is an intrusion of that subcenter which lies mainly in southwestern Utah, although the very northwestern part of Arizona is included. Subspecies peculiar to this subcenter are *Perognathus longimembris virginis, Thomomys bottae virgineus,* and *Ondatra zibethica goldmani.* Small size and red color are characteristic of mammals in this subcenter. This is true even of the populations of some species which have not become differentiated here to a degree that warrants their recognition as separate subspecies.

The Bonneville Basin faunal area owes its physical features to the same cause as does the Lake Lahontan Basin center of differentiation, namely, the drying up of a Quaternary lake that left sediments which, with the contained salts, produced extensive areas of sand and light-colored soils. The part of the area in Nevada is merely the western edge of the area that extends eastward-to the base of the Wasatch Mountain Range in Utah. *Perognathus longimembris gulosus, Perognathus formosus incolatus, Dipodomys ordii celeripes, Dipodomys microps bonnevillei, Peromyscus crinitus pergracilis,* and *Peromyscus truei nevadensis* are subspecies characteristic of the area. The differentiation of these and the absence of any full species peculiar to the area are reasons for its designation as a differentiation center rather than as a faunal area. The full species there are part of those of the Central Rocky Mountain faunal area and part of those of the Lower Sonoran–Lahontan Lake Basin faunal area. So far as full species are concerned, and, therefore, according to the definition here set up, the strongest claim that can be made for status as a faunal area is in its lack of certain species. If asked to select one of the areas here discussed as typical of the Great Basin, I think I should choose the Lake Bonneville Basin.

FACTORS RESPONSIBLE FOR GEOGRAPHIC DISTRIBUTION

(which factors are responsible also for speciation through natural selection of adaptive variations)

EDAPHIC FACTORS

In Nevada, as in many other desert areas, rock-covered areas are large, both in horizontal and vertical extent. These rocks are a positive distributional factor for several mammals. The particular kind of shelter which crevices and interstices in rocks afford is used by several terrestrial species that elude enemies, neither by running nor by flying, but by finding safety in retreats, even though the animals themselves are mostly ill-equipped by structure for digging burrows of their own. The bobcat is without talent for digging, but gains security, when resting, almost always by choosing a small cave in the side of a cliff, or a place among boulders. The yellow-bellied marmot, so much preyed upon by all of the large carnivores, finds the security afforded by rocks or huge boulders of survival value in addition to that gained by burrowing in the earth; every one of its dens found by us was under a boulder, between boulders, or was reached through a crevice in some pile of huge boulders. Green food is essential to this animal, but in Nevada such food must be near rocks.

The piñon mouse, *Peromyscus truei*, in Nevada has a strong predilection for rocks, but, like the marmot, must have suitable plant life in or near the rocks. For this mouse, the plant is the piñon tree. The canyon mouse (*P. crinitus*) of the same genus is even more intimately associated with rocks and boulders. Of the several hundred that I have seen caught, only one, a young individual, was as far as 50 feet from rocks. It is reasonable to suppose that, in response to population pressure, this young mouse was in quest of a new home when trapped between places suitable for adults of its kind.

The long-tailed pocket mouse (*Perognathus formosus*) almost everywhere lives on stony ground, and the subspecies *P. f. melanurus*, the northernmost representation of the species, lives only on ground where stones lie so thickly that if as many again of the same size were there laid down, the ground would be entirely covered. The diameter of the stones is from 1½ to 12 centimeters; the smaller or the larger of these stones by themselves do not meet the requirements of the mice. Plate 7, *a* shows a typical habitat.

When, in the marginal part of its geographic range, a species is sharply restricted to a particular fraction of the environment, as is *P. f. melanurus*, the chances are that several features of the environment are intolerable for the species. By noting, in the marginal part of the range, which feature of the environment is common to the places in which the species does live, the most important positive distributional factor for the species throughout its range often can be ascertained more quickly than through study of areas near the center of the geographic range. Near the centers of the ranges of many species of land mammals conditions favorable for existence are present over larger parts of the land's surface. The species is therefore usually more abundant here and often the population is more dense. The population pressure resulting from this density often causes the species, near the center of its range, to occur in environments that are not optimum for it. For these reasons, study in the marginal rather than in the central part of the range of a species often is profitable.

The pika, *Ochotona princeps*, lives only in talus (rock slides)—nowhere else. The animal, so far as I have seen, ventures away from the talus no more than 30 feet, and rarely that far, to gather plants that it dries for food. The "hay" is piled on the flat top of a boulder which is beneath other boulders that effectively protect the hay from the large herbivores, bighorn, and deer that would eat it, were it in a position accessible to them. The combination of cover and good drainage, in fact, dryness, which is thus afforded the pile of hay may be one reason why the animal lives in talus, but a more important factor in this restriction to rock slides probably is the almost complete protection afforded the pika itself from flesh-eating animals of large size.

The desert wood rat, *Neotoma lepida*, everywhere is partial to rocks, and at and near the northern margin of its range, for example, along Goose Creek in Elko County, was found only in talus.

Rock squirrels, *Citellus variegatus*, in Nevada live in burrows along cliffs or in boulder-strewn areas, the entrances to which burrows may be several yards from any boulder. It seems to me that the special value of the rocks and boulders to this animal is the provision of elevated lookout posts from which the squirrel detects approaching danger when the danger is yet a considerable distance away.

Stones, boulders, and rocks, then, are positive distributional factors for at least the eight species enumerated above. Many other species of Nevadan mammals occur in the same kinds of places, but their presence in a given area is not dependent upon the presence of stones, boulders, or rocks.

Type of soil greatly influences the distribution of many species in Nevada; indeed, I know of no kind of mammal that occurs on all types of soil. The deer mouse, *Peromyscus maniculatus*, and the coyote, *Canis latrans*, are two species with tolerances seemingly wider than most species for different kinds of soils. If the Nevadan species were arranged in order of decreasing tolerance for variety of soil, the pallid kangaroo mouse, *Microdipodops pallidus*, and the desert kangaroo rat, *Dipodomys deserti*, would stand at the bottom of the list. No kind of mammal lives on the water-laid silt of the surface of dry lakes, and only occasionally do individuals of a few species attempt to cross one of these areas if its expanse is more than a few hundred yards.

The pallid kangaroo mouse lives only in fine sand. It is true that the sand must support some plant growth, but regardless of the plants, which vary in kind from place to place where the mice occur, the sand must be of a fine texture. Furthermore, the top sand must be fine, wind-blown particles; if the sand is overlain by or mixed with pebbles, the mice will not inhabit it.

The desert kangaroo rat also requires fine sand which must be at least 20 inches deep. Drying of the surface layer of the sand may cause the tunnels to cave in unless they can be dug to a depth of 20 or more inches. Also, at any depth of less than 20 inches, insulation against high daytime temperatures probably would be insufficient.

PLANTS

TREES

As a category of plants, trees determine the distribution of the porcupine. Although the porcupine frequently retreats to dens among boulders in the day, feeds on low-growing herbaceous plants on some nights, and perhaps never climbs a tree for several consecutive days, still much of its time is spent in trees; never have we found one more than a few yards from trees of some kind. This restricted occurrence is significant of the effect of trees on the distribution of the porcupine, I think, because north of 37 degrees latitude the porcupine occurs where there are trees, not elsewhere.

Evergreen trees—conifers, to be still more precise—it seems, are essential to the existence of the Douglas squirrel, *Tamiasciurus douglasii*, and the northern flying squirrel, *Glaucomys sabrinus*. In any event, in Nevada, the two species have been found only in conifers. Perhaps the flying squirrel is not directly dependent upon the conifers, but instead responds to meteorological conditions favorable also to conifers of Boreal species. However that be, the Douglas squirrel relies for a large part of its food on the nuts provided by the pine cones. Food source for the Douglas squirrel seems to be one important factor, although there may be others; conceivably the same meteorological factors which were suggested as limiting the range of the flying squirrel hold for the Douglas squirrel.

Conifers of a particular kind, namely, piñons, alone furnish suitable habitat for two species of chipmunks. In my personal experience the Panamint chipmunk, *Eutamias panamintinus*, occurs only in piñons. I have had reports of its occurrence in junipers, but even there I suppose that piñon trees were mixed with the junipers. The geographically complementary cliff chipmunk, *Eutamias dorsalis*, in Nevada occurs in piñons and less often in junipers. Where both of these kinds of trees are absent in Nevada, there are no cliff chipmunks. Piñons—and in a few places, junipers—in combination with rocks or boulders form a positive distributional factor for the aptly named piñon mouse, *Peromyscus truei*.

BUSHES

For at least four species of mammals in Nevada, bushes are judged to be a positive distributional factor. The brush mouse, *Peromyscus boylii*, has been taken only in stands of shrubs. I have formed no opinion concerning the precise manner in which the brush mouse is dependent on shrubs, but I have learned that each of three other exclusively brush-inhabiting species utilizes for food the inner bark and leaves of the shrubs among which it lives. The shrub is sagebrush (*Artemisia tridentata*) and the mammals are the least chipmunk (*Eutamias minimus*), sagebrush vole (*Lagurus curtatus*), and pigmy rabbit (*Sylvilagus idahoensis*). The pigmy rabbit makes use of the bushes as cover in eluding enemies, as does also the least chipmunk. The sagebrush vole, in some places at least, constructs its nest from shredded bark of sagebrush. Actual dependence of the animals upon sagebrush has yet to be proved, because there remains the possibility that some factor, now unknown, is responsible for the distribution of both the animals and the plant. Although the animals probably depend upon the sagebrush, the known facts are merely that the animals occur only where there is sagebrush and that the animals use the brush for food and shelter.

HERBS

Herbs provide the major share of the food of many mammals. It might be supposed that the distribution of some kinds of rodents is determined by the herbaceous plants that they use for food and in other ways. Seedeaters, including the antelope ground squirrel (*Citellus leucurus*), the little pocket mouse (*Perognathus longimembris*), and the Ord kangaroo rat (*Dipodomys ordii*), probably are dependent upon certain plants. Nevertheless, the number of kinds of these plants is large, and one or more kinds can be found in almost any area. I am therefore unable to say that the geographic range of one of these rodents is determined by the presence or absence of a particular herb or group of herbs.

GRASS

Grass is essential to the presence of the montane meadow mouse (*Microtus montanus*). In the growing season for plants, the mouse relies principally on grass for food. At all seasons its nest is made of dried blades and shredded parts of stems of grass. In winter, as well as in summer, grass is relied upon for cover beneath which the mouse extends its sharply defined runways. The harvest mouse (*Reithrodontomys megalotis*) does not confine itself so closely to grass-lands as does the montane meadow mouse, but ordinarily is most abundant in grassy areas. If an abundant crop of grass grows in spring and early summer on a given area, that area may support a large population of harvest mice throughout the year only if the mice can find some other kind of cover to screen them from enemies after the grass is gone. Probably the principal positive factor for the mice in an instance of this kind is the supply of grass seeds which the mice eat throughout the year.

MOISTURE

Reference to figure 3, on page 31, shows the slight precipitation characteristic of the larger part of Nevada; as might be expected, moisture in nearly all of its forms is scarce. Although many of the lakes are of high salt content, each is to be classified as fresh-water, not marine. The fresh-water streams and lakes in Nevada are essential to the existence of five species, as follows:

water shrew, *Sorex palustris*   beaver, *Castor canadensis*
mink, *Mustela vison*   muskrat, *Ondatra zibethica*
river otter, *Lutra canadensis*

The Humboldt River, its tributaries, especially those from the north, and the streams of the extreme northern part of Nevada which flow northward into the Snake River nearly all originally contained beavers in large numbers. Within historic time this never has been true of any other considerable area of the state. None of the other four species mentioned above now has a large population in Nevada. Streams and lakes are so few that there is but little habitat suitable for aquatic mammals. The dependence on fresh water is absolute in each of the five species mentioned. Food such as occurs only in or at the margin of fresh water and security from enemies which individuals of the five species gain by their ability to swim beneath the surface are factors involved in this matter.

Among lakes, the water or moisture of which may have influenced the distribution and speciation of Nevadan mammals, the Quaternary Lake Lahontan and its remnants, including Pyramid and Walker lakes, warrant special consideration. The effects of these lakes have been of a somewhat indirect nature, as explained on pages 59-62.

The Colorado River, which forms the southeastern boundary of Nevada, is a stream large enough to prevent the dispersal southeastward of several kinds of land mammals found in Nevada. Conversely, it prevents the dispersal northwestward of several kinds that occur in Arizona. Goldman (1937b:427–435) has written of the varying degrees of potency of different parts of the river in restricting the movements of mammals, and Grinnell (1914) gave a detailed account of this same effect of that part of the Colorado River which forms the southeastern boundary of California. Estimate of the river's effectiveness as a barrier to dispersal can be made in two principal ways. One is to note which full species, or genera, range as far as the river without crossing over to the other side. The second way is to note, within a species which has populations on the two sides, how much if any morphological dissimilarity there is between animals on opposite sides. From studies of this kind made by various students it is clear that the small streams comprising the headwaters of the river are no barrier, or only partial barriers, to dispersal of mammals. Lower down, along its middle course, the Colorado River is wider and deeper and flows in a permanent channel, a steep-walled canyon. For mammals adapted to live in the desert this part of the river is an effective barrier to interchange of individuals between populations of the two sides.

In its lower reaches, the river, although wider than anywhere else, pursues a meandering course in a semipermanent channel through a wide, shallow valley. At times, in spring freshets, the river rises and in places cuts across the neck of a piece of land which projects out into the river, and thus transfers this piece of land and its mammalian fauna from one side to the other. Frequent shifting of the channel of the river has caused the faunas of the two sides of the lower course of the river to be more nearly alike than are the faunas along the two sides of the middle course of the river.

The part of the river touching Nevada is nearly all like the already-described middle course. There is a permanent channel, for the most part in a high-walled canyon, through which the broad, deep river flows swiftly.

Full species restricted to the side in Nevada and other full species restricted to the part in Arizona directly opposite are:

NEVADA	ARIZONA
Citellus leucurus	Citellus harrisii
Perognathus formosus	Perognathus intermedius
Perognathus parvus	Perognathus amplus
	Neotoma albigula*

* Downriver from Nevada this species occurs on both sides.

Several species which occur on both sides of the part of the river common to the two states have the population on one side of the river so trenchantly different in morphological features from the population on the other side that subspecific status has been accorded each of the geographic variants. Along this part of the river there is no direct intergradation between the variants on the two sides. Here, a pair of subspecies of one species, in that they are reproductively isolated in nature, bear, each to the other, the same relation as would full species. Subspecific rather than specific status is accorded these forms because intergradation occurs around the headwaters of the river, or along its lower course, or at both places. Kinds of mammals which fall within this category are:

SPECIES	NEVADAN SUBSPECIES	ARIZONAN SUBSPECIES
Vulpes macrotis.....................	macrotis	arizonensis*
Eutamias dorsalis.....................	utahensis	dorsalis
Thomomys bottae.....................	centralis	suboles
Perognathus penicillatus...............	sobrinus	penicillatus†
Onychomys torridus...................	longicaudus	perpallidus

* The degree of difference may not warrant subspecific separation.

† P. p. penicillatus occurs on both sides of the river below the area of occurrence of P. p. sobrinus, as well as directly across the river from sobrinus.

The Colorado River, it will be seen, has had important effect on the Sonoran fauna of Nevada: (1) by preventing potential occupants from reaching Nevada from Arizona on the southern side of the river and (2) by aiding in the formation of subspecies through geographically isolating populations on the north (Nevadan) side of the river. The effects of natural selection operating on mutations probably are hastened by the aid of isolation. As a matter of general interest, it may be pointed out that the species which are subspecifically distinct on the two sides of the river mostly live on ground higher than the bottom land. The considerable number of species without subspecific differentiation which occur on the two sides of the river include all of the aquatic species (the beaver and muskrat) and most of the kinds which live in the riparian growth, for example, the raccoon (*Procyon lotor*) and harvest mouse (*Reithrodontomys megalotis*), and most of those in the low bottom land, for example, the cotton rat (*Sigmodon hispidus*) and Audubon cottontail (*Sylvilagus audubonii*).

Flooding is a factor in distribution which, probably in every year, depopulates a few restricted areas. Members of the family Heteromyidae suffer most in this respect. Pocket mice and kangaroo rats, in particular, are quick to invade sandy areas laid bare by the drying up of shallow lakes in the bottoms of closed valleys. Perhaps in one season of exposure to the air, and certainly in two, areas of this kind produce plants requisite for food for the pocket mice and kangaroo rats, which after that time quickly and densely populate the place. Following rapid melting of deep snow, or heavy and long-continued rains in adjacent mountains, such areas again may be inundated with resultant drowning of all the mammals there. Pocket gophers invade some of these low areas and suffer the same fate as the kangaroo rats when the area is flooded. On page 440 an account is given of the drowning of pocket gophers.

Cloudbursts wipe out populations of mammals. I saw and doubt that I shall ever forget an instance of this. It was about 5:30 of an evening on August 13, 1930, that a companion and I were driving north along the west side of Steptoe Valley some 15 miles south of Ely, when over the mountains on our left, a black cloud blotted out the sun. Presently the rain was falling in torrents in the high mountains on our side of the range, although it did not even sprinkle, until later in the afternoon, where we were, at the base of the lowest foothills. Crossing one after another of the dry washes that led down to the floor of the valley, we soon came to one that had yellow water on its floor. Stopping the car on the side of the draw, I explored the nature of the bottom of the wash and the depth of the water, which was less than a foot. As I did so, the water was rising, and with the rise there came to us a grinding, roaring sound—an ominous sound—which came through the ground as well as through the air. An increasing volume of water rushed down toward us. Backing our car to higher ground, which we hoped was safe from inundation—as it proved to be—we watched the water rise. There was no wall of it, exactly, but it rose rapidly, we estimated to 10 feet, in a few minutes, certainly in less than 20 minutes. The spectacle was awe-inspiring, as boulders rolled down the wash, grinding against one another and now and then showing themselves above the flood. The water level fell more slowly than it rose, but in less than 2 hours the water was practically gone. The subsidence of the torrent revealed a ditch with steep-cut banks 7 feet high, instead of about a foot as before, and we realized then that the water had been nearer 20 than 10 feet deep. Large boulders, some with a diameter greater than an average man's height, lay along the torrent's course. As we drove down parallel to this course, seeking a way northward across it, we passed areas of several acres that had been under water. Bushes had been flattened, some uprooted and washed away. Boulders and stones were piled where only fine soil lay 2 hours before. In low places water still stood in pools. It was almost inconceivable that any of the population of desert rodents in their burrows there could have survived. Contemplation of these huge boulders now far below where any had been when we went down the valley that morning brought realization that this sort of thing might not have happened there in several centuries. Perhaps it would not happen again for several centuries more. It seemed, therefore, that as great and locally complete as the mortality to small mammals might have been in the canyon, along the wash on the alluvial fan, and around the margin of the lake in the bottom of the valley, the flood, when viewed in proper perspective with regard to interval of occurrence, area involved, and rate of repopulation of limited areas by small mammals, was of but little importance. Flooding of any and all kinds in Nevada, spectacular as it may be, in general is unimportant in limiting the distribution of mammals.

Rainfall has no direct effect, to which I can point, on the geographic distribution of mammals in Nevada. If wider annual fluctuations between the maximum and minimum fall occurred, it is expectable that there would be appreciable effects. Through regulation of the number and size of streams and lakes, regulation of amount of soil-moisture, and regulation of the kind of flora, rainfall indirectly has great importance.

Snowfall is an important factor in determining the limits of geographic distribution of several kinds of mammals. By burrowing through or under the snow, meadow mice (see under the account of *Microtus montanus*) and shrews in winter can cross areas devoid of other cover while eluding the watchful eyes of carnivorous mammals and raptorial birds. In this way snow in valleys permits kinds of animals that are adapted to live in mountains to cross from one mountain range to another—a thing they cannot do in summer because of the, for them, fatally high temperatures on the floors of the valleys. Probably they would not cross in autumn or spring either, for want of adequate ground cover. In the mountains the abundant earth-plugs left by pocket gophers attest to their habit of burrowing through the snow. Through this medium gophers sometimes cross over areas of naked granite from their burrows in one area to begin burrows in a new area which they probably never would have reached except for the snow. White-tailed jack rabbits (*Lepus townsendii*) descend to lower levels in winter when snow blankets the ground. Possibly the individuals that we found near the southern margin of the range of the species got there in winter by crossing snow-covered valleys from mountains to the northward. Residents of the areas concerned reported rabbits in the valleys only in winter. Snow in a valley, it is seen, aids in the interchange between populations of mammals which live in the mountains on either side, in somewhat the same way that ice on a river allows interchange between the populations of nonhibernating land mammals that inhabit the two sides. In Nevada, ice on streams has no appreciable effect on the geographic distribution of the mammals; the only stream large enough to constitute an effective barrier to dispersal is the Colorado River, and it does not freeze over in winter.

Humidity does not directly limit, so far as I know, the distribution of mammals in Nevada. I judge that humidity, in combination with low temperature, is responsible for the permanent occupancy by the bushy-tailed wood rat (*Neotoma cinerea*) of certain areas in the Upper Sonoran Life-zone. The areas that I have in mind are the shaded banks of Smoke Creek, near its mouth, and the similarly shaded banks of the lower course of the Carson River. Here, in the lower part of the Upper Sonoran Life-zone, *N. cinerea*, otherwise an inhabitant of the Boreal zones, occurs where the evaporation of moisture from the shaded places near the stream makes a situation temperature-wise, and possibly humidity-wise, attractive to the animal. Probably for the same reasons the deer mouse (*Peromyscus maniculatus*) occurs abundantly in the Lower Sonoran Life-zone only in and beneath the riparian plant growth along the Colorado River.

Soil-moisture, as explained elsewhere, is a positive factor in the distribution of the broad-footed mole (*Scapanus latimanus*). On the eastern edge of its geographic range, the broad-footed mole inhabits some soils when they are moist (ordinarily in spring) and withdraws from them when they are dry (ordinarily in summer and autumn). Soil-moisture, when present in an amount and under conditions that will produce sod, attracts the montane meadow mouse (*Microtus montanus*). This species permanently lives only where there is grass, which, when green, provides food, and when dry, is used to make nests; the grass provides also concealment from enemies, when green or dry.

NUMBERS OF MAMMALS

The number of mammals caught by us in certain areas where traps were set for several successive nights in the same place gives some basis for estimating the total number of mammals in the state. Over the whole of Nevada, I guess that the average population is about 20 mammals per acre. A square mile would therefore have 12,800 individuals; and the whole of Nevada, with its 109,740 square miles, would have 1,403,672,000, or approximately a billion and a half mammals.

The suitability of the environment—especially the presence of food, safe breeding places, and shelter from enemies—is the primary factor in determining the number of mammals. The manner in which some parts of the environment, such as soil and moisture, operate to permit or prevent occupancy by mammals has been described in the preceding pages.

Natural enemies and diseases, in the sense that these terms are used by many writers, it seems to me, are secondary factors so far as numbers of prey-species are concerned. When considering populations of herbivorous and gramnivorous mammals, especially rodents, the term "natural enemies" is used to include carnivorous mammals, raptorial birds, and certain kinds of snakes. For all of these creatures the Merriam kangaroo rat, of occurrence primarily in the Lower Sonoran Life-zone, is a prey-species. The natural enemies mentioned do take heavy toll of the rats and exert a checking effect upon the species. The numbers of rats thus eliminated in the reproductive season, and in the ensuing summer, autumn, and winter, combined with mortality from other causes, leaves only two rats in early spring where there were seven (two parents and their five young) 11 months before. So it goes, year after year, if we can rely on the records of catches in our traps in different seasons. Although natural enemies in the Lower Sonoran Life-zone may have more effect on the numbers of small mammals than in the higher life-zones, even in this low zone the reduction in numbers effected by the natural enemies is apparent only within the period of 1 year and not over longer periods.

In the higher life-zones, for instance, the Canadian, there is, in addition to the seasonal fluctuation just described for the Lower Sonoran Life-zone, yet another type of fluctuation which may be designated as multiannual. This is superimposed on the seasonal fluctuation in the higher life-zones. In this multiannual fluctuation, peaks in numbers of a prey-species are reached at intervals of more than a year, say, every 3 or 5 years. Of snowshoe rabbits, for example, there may be more each successive spring than the year before until there are scores where only two or three lived 5 years before. Given favorable meteorological conditions, safe breeding places, food, and cover which provides protection from enemies, the increase goes on, checked but not stopped by the natural enemies. Indeed, the direction of the regulation of numbers of individuals is here, in a manner, reversed from that in the Lower Sonoran Life-zone, because in the Canadian Life-zone the natural enemies of the snowshoe rabbit increase in response to the more abundant food provided by the rabbits! The decrease in numbers of the snowshoes is rapid; a population built up to large numbers over several years usually decreases in but a few months to a tenth or less of the numbers present at the peak. The numbers of the flesh-eaters, such as the red fox and bobcat, that are dependent mostly on rabbits for food also decrease. An inadequacy of food causes some females of the flesh-eaters to bear no young; those that do have young produce fewer per litter than in other years, and some adults die directly or indirectly of starvation. The decrease in numbers of flesh-eaters is more gradual, the low point in their numbers being reached about a year later than that of the rabbits. When the peaks and low points of multiannual fluctuations are spaced regularly, the fluctuation is properly spoken of as cyclic. In the Transition and Upper Sonoran life-zones the patterns of fluctuation in numbers of small mammals are intermediate between that characteristic of the higher Canadian Life-zone and

that characteristic of the Lower Sonoran Life-zone. For one thing, in the intermediate zones a trend toward a multiannual peak is frequently abortive, and
multiannual fluctuations which do occur seldom are truly cyclic. For these
reasons peaks in numbers cannot be so accurately predicted 1 to 3 years in
advance, as in the life-zones that are higher and, of course, those that are
lower. Even so, in any life-zone and under natural conditions, the influence of
the prey-carnivore relationship, as it affects the numbers of individuals of the
prey-species, is felt over a period of, at most, a few years. Therefore, contrary to
the statements of some naturalists that natural enemies are responsible for the
continual rarity of a species, the cause is to be sought in some part of the environment other than that of natural enemies. Finally, in comparing numbers
of mammals in different areas, the conclusion is reached that: Fluctuation in
numbers of small mammals is mainly seasonal below the Upper Sonoran Life-
zone and is both multiannual and seasonal above the Transition Life-zone.

Disease, as caused by the multiplication of viruses, bacteria, nematodes, and
other parasites, ordinarily is the agent which effects sudden decrease in a population of mammals like that described above in the snowshoe rabbit. Some
observers have thought that the onset of an epidemic followed only when the
hosts were weakened by unfavorable climatic conditions, whereas others have
contended that an epidemic appeared when the environmental conditions were
no less favorable for the hosts than they were for a long time before. A view
commonly expressed is that after immunities are built up, when only the
disease-resistant individuals are left, in short, when the disease has run its
course in the population, then the increase in numbers of the originally diseased
species begins again. Although evidence from Nevada is insufficient to con-
clusively prove or disprove these views, in the broad view the effect of disease
on a species is essentially the same as the effect of carnivorous predators; both
tend to check any excessive increase in numbers of a species of small mammal.

But there is this additional difference: When a population of, say, chipmunks, in the Transition Life-zone, the numbers of which ordinarily are held
within bounds, does increase considerably beyond normal, the checking effect
of the macroscopic enemies becomes insignificant; then the microscopic enemies find an environment suitable to them, and disease accomplishes, in a
relatively short time, the reduction ordinarily effected slowly by the appetites
and stalking abilities of carnivores among mammals, raptors among birds, and
kinds of snakes that prey on chipmunks and other small mammals.

Among all the enemies of wild mammals, it appears that man is the most
effective. In Nevada he has brought about the extinction of at least one species,
the wolf, and his activity has profoundly affected the numbers of individuals
of other species, notably, mountain sheep. Sometimes the toll that he takes has
no lasting effect on the numbers of a species. The apparent increase in numbers
of mule deer in Nevada in recent years, despite man's hunting them year after
year, is a case in point. Deer hunters hunt down also the natural enemies of the

deer which, like some other large mammals, but unlike most small mammals, under modern conditions frequently respond to removal of their natural enemies by thereafter maintaining larger populations. In some other instances where man has directly reduced the numbers of a given species and also those of one or more of its natural enemies, the results have been the reverse of that in the deer. Therefore, the results of such activities on the part of man are hardly predictable. For example, no one predicted that poisoned baits distributed for coyotes, and traps set for that species, instead of eliminating the coyote, which fairly well held his own, would in some valleys exterminate the kit fox. But, in general, man has reduced the total number of mammals. This he has done in three principal ways: (1) by grazing domestic livestock, (2) by hunting for sport with modern weapons (high-powered rifles), and (3) by the distribution of poisoned (suet) baits. The kit fox, already mentioned, fell a victim to poisons. Grazing of domestic sheep and hunting with rifles combined to exterminate mountain sheep in the northern part of the state, and everywhere in Nevada greatly reduced the number of prong-horned antelope. The latter species has regained something of its former numbers in parts of the northern half of the state since man there reversed his earlier tendency and sought by discontinuing hunting and by excluding domestic sheep from some areas to improve conditions for the antelopes. Efforts directed to the same end for the mountain sheep have resulted in an upturn in numbers of the subspecies inhabiting southern Nevada, but the action was taken too late to benefit the other two subspecies, now extinct in Nevada, which ranged in the western and northeastern parts of the state. The white-tailed deer, once probably a resident of parts of Nevada, may have been exterminated by man. The native wapiti once reported from White Pine County did not persist in later years; possibly its disappearance should be charged to man. The one full species which is everywhere extinct in the state, certainly as a result of man's persecution, is the wolf (*Canis lupus*). The record of man's effect on native wild species of mammals in the state is definitely not commendable. Still, only three, at most—and possibly only one—full species have been entirely exterminated by man in Nevada, which number is less than can be pointed to by almost any one of the other forty-seven states.

Only a small fraction of the area of Nevada has ever been cultivated, a few areas have been only lightly grazed by domestic stock, and the state has always been sparsely populated by man. These circumstances, combined, explain why, compared with other states, man's influence on the numbers of individuals of wild mammals has been slight in Nevada.

FLUCTUATIONS IN LAKE LAHONTAN

Shifts of environment, such as have occurred certainly within the late Quaternary Period, and probably even within the Recent Epoch, have had much to do with fluctuations in total numbers of mammals of some kinds and appar-

ently have had some effect in subspeciation. The shifts that I have in mind are
those concerned with the Quaternary Lake Lahontan in the low area of western
Nevada. Pyramid and Walker lakes are remnants of this lake, and cover only

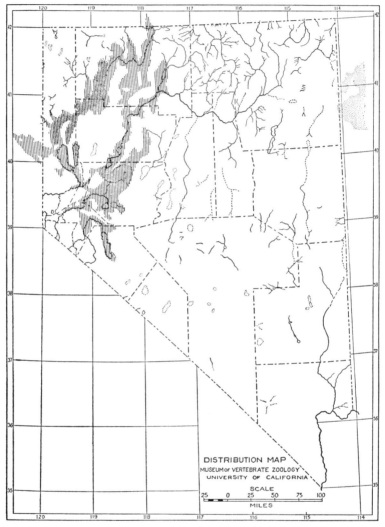

Fig. 6. The shaded area shows that part of Nevada covered by the Quaternary Lake Lahontan when at its highest level. After Russell (1885).

about 250 square miles of the total of 8,422 square miles occupied by Lake
Lahontan when it was at its highest level. In the Quaternary Period, Lake
Lahontan extended from a short distance north of the present Nevada-Oregon
boundary south about 250 miles to a short way south of the present Walker

Lake, and surrounded an island with an area about half that of the lake itself. If there were 20 mammals to the acre, the lake at its highest level reduced the population of land mammals by about 8,860,160. In long range of time, however, the effect of the lake may have been to increase the number of mammals. From the sediments exposed by the drying up of the lake, extensive areas of wind-drifted soil were formed. These fine soils and sands provide habitats in which maximum densities of populations of small mammals are attained. Much of the area of the former bed of Lake Lahontan now is as densely populated by mammals as any other terrain in Nevada.

Lake Lahontan was a factor important in causing geographic variation among small mammals. The student of subspeciation would immediately suppose that a water barrier 250 miles long would hasten subspeciation, through isolation of land mammals on the two sides. Isolation might be expected to have left its mark also on the mammals of the principal island that was formed, as well as upon those of some of the smaller islands. In *Microdipodops* and in some other mammals, the lake did seem to further subspeciation by isolating one population from another, but subspeciation seems to have been furthered still more by the formation of fine soils. These soils, especially fine sands that were derived from the sedimentary deposits in this trough after extensive areas of the lake had dried up, provided a habitat that was suitable for many species otherwise of more southern distribution. Some of these now are otherwise of exclusively Lower Sonoran occurrence. Here, in the old bed of Lake Lahontan, soil, meteorological conditions, flora, and possibly the nonmammalian fauna were significantly different from corresponding parts of the immigrants' homeland. In response to the new environment in the lake basin, a considerable number of geographic variants developed among the mammals which invaded the area. In some variants the degree of morphological distinctness now is so great as to warrant subspecific status. Examples of species which invaded the area and developed subspecies peculiar to it are:

Vulpes macrotis nevadensis	*Dipodomys ordii inaquosus*
Perognathus formosus melanurus	*Thomomys bottae canus*
Microdipodops megacephalus ambiguus	*Microtus montanus undosus*

The two first-mentioned species are otherwise of more southern occurrence. Two other species of the Lower Sonoran Life-zone which have developed somewhat less strongly differentiated geographic variants in the dry bed of Lake Lahontan are:

Dipodomys merriami   *Dipodomys deserti*

Five additional species of, in general, more southern distribution which have extended into this area, but without producing recognizable geographic variants, are:

Myotis californicus	*Pipistrellus hesperus*	*Onychomys torridus*
Myotis yumanensis	*Antrozous pallidus*	

The effectiveness of Lake Lahontan in causing subspeciation is judged to have resulted mainly from the extinction of one fauna when the lake was formed, and then the repopulation of the area, after the waters subsided, by animals that were, or became, adapted to the finer type of soils. That the lake was not more effective in causing speciation through isolation of the various populations that lived on the two sides and on the islands was because of the short time in which the lake functioned as a barrier. Antevs (1925:101) says: "The Pleistocene deposits of the Lahontan Basin, so far as they are exposed, seem to record three or perhaps four distinct moist stages, during which the valleys were flooded by deep waters, with preceding and intervening arid periods during which the water-level receded to about the present stand or even farther. Besides, they record oscillations of lesser amplitude." The rapidity with which small mammals reinvade areas exposed by receding waters of this lake was impressed upon me once with especial acuity. I was driving across the dry floor of Winnemucca Lake on July 21, 1941, incidentally noting abundant signs of small mammals, including burrows of *Dipodomys*, when I suddenly realized that at this same place in July, 1924, each of two fishermen in a boat about a half mile off shore caught his limit of Sacramento perch. A detailed record of the levels of Pyramid and Winnemucca lakes in the 96 years preceding 1940 is recorded by Hardman and Venstrom (1941). From their account it appears that Winnemucca Lake was dry at the beginning of this 96-year period, as it is now, but in an intervening time it attained a depth of 87 feet. Meanwhile, the level of Pyramid Lake fluctuated 64 feet. As indicated in the account of the genus *Dipodomys*, some species of kangaroo rats reoccupy land made available by receding lakes after the land has been exposed for only a year or two. Taking into account this rapid rate of movement into newly available territory and the ephemeral nature of large expanses of Lake Lahontan, it is readily understandable why the lake, unlike the Colorado River, did not serve more effectively to hasten speciation by isolating populations one from the other.

CLINES

Long geographical character-gradients, or clines, as Huxley (1939) has termed them, which are referred to in the accounts of some full species on later pages and upon which further information may be obtained by comparing corresponding parts of the accounts of subspecies within a species, would not be expected in Nevada; the longest straight line that can be drawn within the boundaries is 560 miles. Size, as expressed in weight of the freshly killed animal and to a lesser extent in linear measurements, provides clines in certain species. The broad-footed mole, at least seven of the species of carnivores, the canyon mouse, the muskrat, and the porcupine are much heavier and larger in the north. Individuals of only two species, the montane meadow mouse and the sagebrush vole, are heavier and larger in the south.

Variation in length of tail, however, in four species (gray fox, Merriam kangaroo rat, canyon mouse, and desert wood rat) shows an increasing length to the south; in one species, the golden-mantled ground squirrel, it increases to the north. The gradients in weight of the entire animal and length of the tail which are evident in Nevada continue southward outside Nevada, and extend from the northern to the southern limits of the range of the individual species concerned. For example, badgers of Canada are even heavier than those in northern Nevada, and badgers of Mexico are even lighter in weight than those in southern Nevada. Each of the clines mentioned has a north-to-south direction. None is evident in an east-to-west direction. This, I take it, is significant of response to climate, probably temperature, which, within any given distance, ordinarily varies more from north to south than from east to west.

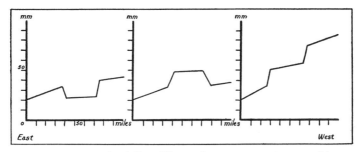

Fig. 7. Three kinds of clines illustrating east-to-west geographic "behavior" of increasing size of a mammal.

Some of the character-gradients mentioned may have an even increase, but some certainly do not. The length of tail relative to length of head and body in the Merriam kangaroo rat is an example of one that does not. (See fig. 306, p. 426.) Here the cline has a nearly uniform slope except near the middle, where a slope is lacking. The horizontal bar between Schurz and Arlemont marks a place where the population is small (not sparse). It is small because the topography between the two places is such that terrain suitable for occupancy by *D. merriami* along much of the distance is only a few miles wide—2 miles or less over a considerable part. Perhaps the small population here has something to do with the uniformity of length of tail to length of head and body, but exactly how I do not know.

One or another of these character-gradients has been used, in combination with other features, to distinguish subspecies, but the majority of the characters used for distinguishing subspecies of mammals in Nevada are not of this nature. Instead, most of the characters of a given subspecies are comparatively stable throughout most of the geographic range of that subspecies; where three subspecies occur in lineal sequence geographically, the character is about as likely to behave in one way as in either of the other two ways shown in figure 7.

In this connection, however, it should be remembered that in Nevada three or more subspecies in lineal geographic sequence occur more often from east to west than from north to south. Characters that vary in an east-to-west direction probably are less dependent on climate than are those which vary from north to south. The barriers of parallel valleys and mountain ranges that run from north to south in Nevada, then, may help to remove from the category of characters used for distinguishing subspecies those character-gradients with sustained, even slope. In one sense the characters without an even gradient may be more significant, in that they probably reflect, of environmental effects, several features exclusive of temperature which cause subspeciation. The effects of temperature in causing variations in a species that ranges through many degrees of latitude are fairly well known anyhow. Allen's and Bergmann's rules are based on these well-known variations with latitude.

SPECIATION

When one thinks about the problem of how species form in mammals and contemplates the facts of geographic distribution, it seems to me necessary to remember that there is a geometric ratio of reproduction and that the tendency of a growing population is always to push outward forcefully. Barriers retard and ultimately check such spreading. As these barriers arise, they break up populations into stocks and subsequently tend to keep neighboring stocks from mixing. But there is a shifting of barriers, spatially, through time; and this movement, at least in some instances, is continual. One result of this is that species are forced to move about. The process is a drastic one, for, if it is not conformed to, the result is extinction of the species affected.

Phases of this "geographic behavior" include invasion of new territory by a part of a population, isolation of stocks, differentiation, and in some places reinvasion of the original territory. For some species there might be an almost continual migration to correspond with a change in physiography. This change would modify and probably multiply the environments (I have in mind habitats and within habitats, ecological niches) which therefore probably have an evolution of their own and are potential areas of speciation. I use the phrase "areas of speciation" here to imply ecological niches, habitats (associational areas), subfaunal areas, faunal areas, life-zones, regions, and realms. When modifications occur in these environments, especially in the smaller divisions, or when a shifting of a barrier occurs, kinds of mammals may enter into competition. Some kinds survive and others do not.

In considering further this survival, or disappearance, of kinds of mammals, it is profitable to compare species with subspecies. Although species and subspecies seem to have the same kinds of distinguishing characters, which appear to be inherited by means of essentially the same kinds of mechanisms in the germ plasm, two noteworthy differences between species and subspecies are detected. A species which is continually distributed over a given area has, at the boundary of its range, characters which are sharp, definite, and precise.

Some of its characters—size, shape, and color—at any one place, are either those of one species or, instead, unequivocally those of some other. The characters of a subspecies, however, particularly at or near the place where two subspecies meet, more often than not, are various combinations of the characters of the two subspecies, and in many individual characters there is blending. The second difference is that in a given epoch of geological time one or more subspecies of a given species may disappear and one or several new subspecies of it may be formed. Subspecies, therefore, are shorter-lived than species.

Now the disappearance of subspecies is to be expected on *a priori* grounds if we suppose that new subspecies are formed in every geological epoch. We have reason to believe that in the Pleistocene, the epoch of time immediately preceding the Recent, there were even more species of mammals than there are now. In each of several successively corresponding periods of Tertiary time before the Pleistocene, there were probably as many species as now. Probably, too, these species then were about as productive of subspecies as species are now. Had even half of these subspecies persisted, either as subspecies unchanged, or in considerable part by becoming full species, there would now be an array of species and subspecies many times as numerous as actually does exist. It is obvious therefore that many disappeared.

In accounting for this adjustment of numbers of kinds of mammals, I have spoken of the disappearance of subspecies rather than of their extinction. This is because I can imagine how a species, say, the pocket gopher, *Thomomys townsendii*, in the middle Pleistocene with three subspecies (geographic races) could have come down to the present by means of each one of the three subspecies having gradually changed its characters into those of one of the three subspecies existing today in the area of northern Nevada that I have in mind. In this way disappearance of subspecies living in the Pleistocene has come about without their having become extinct in the sense that the subspecies left no living descendants. Of course this has to be true for some of the subspecies of each successively preceding epoch if any animals at all persist, but what I wish to emphasize is the strong probability that many, perhaps more than 50 per cent, disappeared thus, without actually becoming extinct. In this regard it is pertinent to consider each of three Pleistocene kinds of pocket gophers which are known from places that are short distances outside Nevada to the northward. These three gophers are *Thomomys gidleyi* (ancestor of some subspecies of *T. talpoides*), *Thomomys vetus* (ancestor of some subspecies of *T. townsendii*), and *Thomomys scudderi* (ancestor of some subspecies of *T. bottae*). Each of the fossil gophers differs from its living representatives in greater width labially of the individual cheek teeth of the lower jaw. Significant for the thesis being defended is the point that each and all of these *Thomomys* in the early Pleistocene differed, at least in regard to the shape of the teeth, in the same way from the three living species which I feel confident are their descendants. I suggest, without dogmatism, that these externally narrower teeth of living *Thomomys* were developed by natural selection as better adapted for the probably different kind of food now used by the pocket gophers that live under climatic conditions somewhat altered from those of early Pleistocene time. In other words, the change in shape of teeth is supposed to have been a response to change in environment.

The hypothesis just advanced has a good chance of being more exhaustively tested before long. With the increasing amount of remains of small mammals of the Pleistocene available for study, it may be possible to ascertain the relation, or lack of it, between several subspecies of a single species at one general level of time then and subspecies of the corresponding species living now.

In accounting for the formation of species and subspecies, there is the matter of varying adaptability or plasticity of mammals. Members of some groups are readily modifiable by changing environments. This is evidenced by the numerous subspecies of certain groups, for example, *Thomomys bottae* and *Microtus montanus*. Other groups are resistant, that is, they do not produce subspecies, and this probably makes for their earlier extinction. Nevertheless, even within the relatively plastic groups, the mechanism of inheritance, in general, insures stability within narrow margins of modifiability in a subspecies. Although the fact of this stability is clear enough, a wholly satisfactory explanation for it in every instance, I think, yet has to be found. In illustration, where the ranges of two subspecies meet and intergradation occurs, why does not the swamping effect of crossbreeding cause one subspecies to disappear? Although swamping may occur in some instances, in most it does not. The response of almost every subspecies to some of the distinctive features of its environment apparently suffices to overcome the swamping effect. The hypothesis of harmoniously stabilized complexes of genes (Timofeeff-Ressovsky, 1940:124) may hold as an explanation, but in connection with this concept it is well to remember that any one of some characters which occur throughout a subspecies may be caused by several genes. Some characters of this kind may be favored by natural selection more than others. In the belt of intergradation between two subspecies, where two of these favored characters meet, a "biological tension," as Huxley (1939a:415) terms it, "will result, which will produce *partial discontinuity* between the two groups. Each group will evolve a gene-complex which is not only broadly adapted to the external environment of the central area of its range, but is also harmoniously stabilized, in adaptation to the internal genetic environment, by the selection of modifiers." Crosses, that is to say, intergrades, between the two subspecies will lack this stabilization, and will therefore be at a selective disadvantage. The zone of intergradation will as a result remain narrow; intermediates are constantly being brought into existence there by intercrossing, but are as constantly being extinguished by selection. Among mammals this hypothesis concerning the nature of inheritance of several characters which serve to differentiate pairs of contiguous subspecies needs testing by correlating ecological information with that obtained from breeding before we can accept it as the true explanation of constancy of subspecific characters over areas of vast extent in which there oftentimes is much greater change in environmental conditions than there is in subspecific characters. Nevertheless, the facts that are known about inter-gradation between several (but by no means all) pairs of subspecies of Nevadan mammals are adequately accounted for by this hypothesis.

In this organic change, or evolution of an initial sort, that is revealed by study of subspecies of Nevadan mammals, there is considerable divergent evo-lution. Obviously there is some monotypic evolution, for example, that indi-cated by the above-described change in pocket gophers since the Pleistocene, but there is much or more indication of divergent evolution. There is fair evidence that variations—often of a preadaptable kind, under the influence of natural selection, sometimes with the aid of isolation—are enhanced in a way that induces in aggregates of individuals development of strains and varieties into subspecies and sometimes on into species. Even so, the divergence that does take place, with what might take place, is small, indeed. The things which limit the divergences seem to be the limitations in the very same things which up to a certain point foster the divergence. These things are the parts and com-binations of the environment. The environments are varied, but for mammals they are far short of infinite, and in these higher vertebrates the courses of evolution, both divergent and monotypic, I judge, are maintained, controlled, and guided by the careers of changing and shifting environments.

DESERT CHARACTER OF THE MAMMALIAN FAUNA

As a whole, the mammalian fauna of Nevada shows adaptation to desert condi-tions. For one thing many species are able to live without water to drink. The mechanism which allows this has been studied in the kangaroo rats (*Dipodomys* [*panamintinus*] *mohavensis* and *Dipodomys agilis*) by Howell and Gersh (1935) who learned that individuals on a diet of air-dried food conserved water by resorbing it in the ducts of the renal papillae and walls of the urinary bladder. In addition, the habits of *Dipodomys* tend to conserve water. The animal is strictly nocturnal and hence is abroad when the rate of evaporation is at a minimum; during the day it sleeps curled up in an underground chamber which is closed off from the outside, sometimes from the main part of the burrow, by an earthen plug; under such conditions moisture which is exhaled is in part regained at the following inhalation. This ability to live without water to drink allows a relatively even distribution over the desert of individuals of kinds of mammals thus endowed; they are not concentrated in the vicinities of the widely spaced springs and watercourses. Several observations have been made on pocket mice and kangaroo rats (see Grinnell, 1922:28) which show that they are ineffectual swimmers compared with similar-sized land mammals which in-habit less arid regions. On nights when a light rain fell on the desert I noted that kangaroo rats remained in their burrows. It is clear that the long-time occupancy of the desert has brought to many of the kinds of heteromyids, and several species of other families, the ability to live for months, and probably throughout their normal life span, without water to drink; it has caused some species to avoid moisture, and has robbed some of even the ability to swim effectively when they by accident find themselves in water.

The large number of mammals which eat mainly seeds and enlarged roots of plants appears to be an adaptation to desert conditions. The antelope ground squirrel and round-tailed ground squirrel seem to rely primarily on seeds, as do also many of the heteromyids (pocket mice, kangaroo mice, and kangaroo rats). The pocket gophers are adapted to feeding on the underground parts of plants. The roots of desert plants, relative to the part of the plant above-ground, are large and therefore an important source of food.

Estivation, or summer dormancy, is an adaptation which permits the Town-send and Richardson ground squirrels to live in the desert. These two species retain the food habits of most of the other species of their genus; they eat green vegetation. By July 1, in many places, the vegetation mostly is dried up. Pre-paratory to this period of food shortage, the squirrels have laid up large quantities of fat which sustain them during annual periods of sleep and inactivity until the following spring brings another growth of green vegetation.

Another evidence of adaptation to desert conditions is the large number of kinds of small mammals, principally rodents, which have the ability to con-struct deep burrows. Nearly all the heteromyid rodents dig burrows of this kind, and thereby escape the intense heat of midday. Most of these animals, after entering a burrow, close it by means of a plug of sand. At any depth of more than a couple of feet below ground the high temperatures of daytime and low temperatures at night are hardly felt. These deep burrows in the Lower Sonoran Life-zone are a contrast to the subsurface burrows so common in the Lower Austral Life-zone of the eastern part of the continent.

In the Sonoran zones the high temperatures of the daytime are fatal if the animal is long exposed, and the low temperatures at night have chilling effects on small mammals. On sandy areas in summer there is no small mammal which can long remain in the sun and live. One mammal which can most nearly do so is the antelope ground squirrel. It has a black epithelium lining the visceral cavity, the color of which, I have thought, may screen out some harm-ful rays of the sun. This squirrel, although more active in the sunshine and heat of the day than any other small mammal of the desert, exposes itself only briefly to the direct sun in midday; most of the day it remains in the shade of shrubs and sometimes retires to the cool depths of its burrow.

As would be expected from the sparse growth of trees in the desert, few if any truly arboreal mammals live there. The cliff chipmunk is the nearest approach to an arboreal form among mammals of the desert in Nevada. The arboreal Douglas squirrel and volant flying squirrel within Nevada occur only in the Boreal zones of the Sierra Nevada along the western boundary of the state.

Neither species, so far as known, occurs in any of the isolated stands of timber in other mountains of the state. Truly arboreal mammals occur only where trees grow near enough together to permit mammals to pass from one tree to another without descending to the ground. If there is an exception to this rule, I do not know of it. The supply of moisture in deserts is so scanty that trees grow relatively far apart—so far apart that an arboreal mammal would have to descend to the ground to get from one tree to another. The wide spacing of Joshua trees and of the trees in most forests of piñons in Nevada, along with the absence of arboreal mammals, establishes evidence in support of the rule formulated here.

Saltatorial mammals, of which Nevada has many, are characteristic of all deserts. The five species of kangaroo rats and two species of kangaroo mice are examples. Lengthening of the distal segments of the hind leg in each of these species and reduction in number of toes in one are changes associated with saltatorial progression. Saltatorial rodents that travel on sand usually have a large surface area on the hind foot, and in most species the area is covered with stiff hair. This is true of each of the Nevadan kangaroo rats and kangaroo mice. Long hind legs (indicative of speed) and large ears (indicative of keen hearing) commonly are associated one with the other in nocturnal mammals that are preyed upon by carnivores. In saltatorial mammals that live on the surface of the ground, for example, the jack rabbit, the enlargement of the ears often is in the external part, the pinnae, but in saltatorial mammals that live in burrows, the enlargement in most species is in some inner part of the ear. The kangaroo rats and kangaroo mice, all burrowing forms, conform to this pattern in that the bones associated with the ear are inflated tremendously and form hollow resonating chambers. Indeed, the pallid kangaroo mouse surpasses any other mammal known, living or fossil, in this respect (see fig. 283, p. 378).

The generally light color of the pelage of Nevadan mammals is another indication of the desert environment in which they live. Light grays and light buffs are the predominating colors on the upper parts of the body, and the fur of the underparts commonly is pure white all the way to the base. This coloration is characteristic of mammals in deserts in any part of the world. The pallid coloration is especially characteristic of the Sonoran mammals in Nevada, but subspecies of most of the Boreal species which occur in Nevada also are paler than subspecies of the same species elsewhere.

Species and genera of Nevadan mammals typical of deserts, or plains and deserts, include the following:

Merriam shrew	pocket mice	grasshopper mice
kit fox	kangaroo rats	jack rabbits
Townsend ground squirrel	kangaroo mice	pigmy rabbit
antelope ground squirrel	pocket gophers	prong-horned antelope
round-tailed ground squirrel	cactus mouse	

CHECK LIST OF NEVADAN MAMMALS

The 232 kinds (species and subspecies) of 111 full species which belong to 57 genera of 23 families of 6 orders of Nevadan mammals are:

Class MAMMALIA—mammals

Order INSECTIVORA—insectivores

Family TALPIDAE—moles

Genus **Scapanus** Pomel—western American moles

Scapanus latimanus dilatus True
Scapanus latimanus monoensis Grinnell } broad-footed mole

Family SORICIDAE—shrews

Genus **Sorex** Linnaeus—long-tailed shrews

Sorex merriami merriami Dobson
Sorex merriami leucogenys Osgood } Merriam shrew

Sorex trowbridgii mariposae Grinnell — Trowbridge shrew

Sorex vagrans amoenus Merriam
Sorex vagrans monticola Merriam } vagrant shrew

Sorex obscurus obscurus Merriam — dusky shrew

Sorex tenellus Merriam — dwarf shrew

Sorex palustris navigator (Baird) — water shrew

Genus **Notiosorex** Coues—gray shrews

Notiosorex crawfordi crawfordi (Coues) — Crawford shrew

Order CHIROPTERA—bats

Family PHYLLOSTOMIDAE—phyllostomid bats

Genus **Macrotus** Gray—leaf-nosed bats

Macrotus californicus Baird — California leaf-nosed bat

FAMILY VESPERTILIONIDAE—vespertilionid bats

Genus **Myotis** Kaup—mouse-eared bats

Myotis lucifugus carissima Thomas — big myotis

Myotis yumanensis sociabilis H. W. Grinnell
Myotis yumanensis yumanensis (H. Allen) } Yuma myotis

Myotis evotis chrysonotus (J. A. Allen) — long-eared myotis

Myotis thysanodes thysanodes Miller — fringe-tailed myotis

Myotis volans interior Miller — hairy-winged myotis

Myotis californicus pallidus Stephens — California myotis

Myotis subulatus melanorhinus (Merriam) — small-footed myotis

Genus **Lasionycteris** Peters—silvery-haired bats

Lasionycteris noctivagans (LeConte) — silvery-haired bat

Genus **Pipistrellus** Kaup—pipistrelles

Pipistrellus hesperus hesperus (H. Allen) — western pipistrelle

Genus **Eptesicus** Rafinesque—serotine bats

Eptesicus fuscus bernardinus Rhoads
Eptesicus fuscus pallidus Young } big brown bat

Genus **Lasiurus** Gray—hairy-tailed bats

Lasiurus borealis teliotis (H. Allen)   red bat
Lasiurus cinereus (Beauvois)   hoary bat

Genus **Euderma** H. Allen—spotted bat

Euderma maculatum (J. A. Allen)   spotted bat

Genus **Corynorhinus** H. Allen—long-eared bats

Corynorhinus rafinesquii intermedius H. W. Grinnell
Corynorhinus rafinesquii pallescens Miller } long-eared bat

Genus **Antrozous** H. Allen—nyctophyline bats

Antrozous pallidus cantwelli Bailey
Antrozous pallidus pallidus (LeConte) } pallid bat

Family MOLLOSIDAE—mollosid bats

Genus **Tadarida** Rafinesque—free-tailed bats

Tadarida mexicana (Saussure)   Mexican free-tailed bat
Tadarida macrotis (Gray)   big free-tailed bat

Order CARNIVORA—carnivores

Family URSIDAE—bears

Genus **Ursus** Linnaeus—bears

Ursus americanus californiensis J. Miller   black bear

Family PROCYONIDAE—raccoons and allies

Genus **Procyon** Storr—raccoons

Procyon lotor excelsus Nelson and Goldman
Procyon lotor psora Gray
Procyon lotor pallidus Merriam } raccoon

Genus **Bassariscus** Coues—ring-tailed cats

Bassariscus astutus nevadensis Miller   ring-tailed cat

Family MUSTELIDAE—weasels and allies

Genus **Martes** Pinel—martens and fisher

Martes caurina sierrae Grinnell and Storer   western marten

Genus **Mustela** Linnaeus—weasels, ferrets, and minks

Mustela cicognanii lepta (Merriam)   short-tailed weasel
Mustela frenata nevadensis Hall   long-tailed weasel
Mustela vison aestuarina Grinnell
Mustela vison energumenos (Bangs) } mink

Genus **Lutra** Brisson—river otters

Lutra canadensis nexa Goldman
Lutra canadensis brevipilosus Grinnell
Lutra canadensis sonora Rhoads } river otter

Genus **Spilogale** Gray—spotted skunks

Spilogale gracilis saxatilis Merriam
Spilogale gracilis gracilis Merriam } spotted skunk

Genus **Mephitis** Geoffroy and Cuvier—striped skunk

Mephitis mephitis major (Howell)
Mephitis mephitis estor Merriam } striped skunk

Genus **Taxidea** Waterhouse—American badger

Taxidea taxus taxus (Schreber)
Taxidea taxus berlandieri Baird } badger

Family CANIDAE—foxes, coyotes, and wolves

Genus **Vulpes** Oken—red foxes, kit foxes, and swifts

Vulpes fulva necator Merriam — red fox

Vulpes macrotis nevadensis Goldman
Vulpes macrotis arsipus Elliot } kit fox

Genus **Urocyon** Baird—gray foxes

Urocyon cinereoargenteus scottii Mearns — gray fox

Genus **Canis** Linnaeus—coyotes and wolves

Canis latrans lestes Merriam
Canis latrans estor Merriam } coyote

Canis lupus fuscus Richardson
Canis lupus youngi Goldman } wolf

Family FELIDAE—cats

Genus **Felis** Linnaeus—true cats

Felis concolor californica May
Felis concolor kaibabensis Nelson and Goldman } mountain lion

Genus **Lynx** Kerr—lynxes and bobcats

Lynx rufus pallescens Merriam
Lynx rufus californicus Mearns
Lynx rufus baileyi Merriam } bobcat

Order RODENTIA—rodents

Family SCIURIDAE—squirrels

Genus **Marmota** Blumenbach—marmots

Marmota flaviventer flaviventer (Audubon and Bachman)
Marmota flaviventer avara (Bangs)
Marmota flaviventer nosophora Howell
Marmota flaviventer parvula Howell } yellow-bellied marmot

Genus **Citellus** Oken—ground squirrels and spermophiles

Citellus townsendii canus (Merriam)
Citellus townsendii mollis (Kennicott) } Townsend ground squirrel

Citellus richardsonii nevadensis Howell — Richardson ground squirrel

Citellus beldingi oregonus (Merriam)
Citellus beldingi beldingi (Merriam)
Citellus beldingi crebrus Hall } Belding ground squirrel

Citellus variegatus grammurus (Say) — rock squirrel

Citellus beecheyi fisheri (Merriam) — Beechey ground squirrel

Citellus leucurus leucurus (Merriam)	antelope ground squirrel
Citellus tereticaudus tereticaudus (Baird)	round-tailed ground squirrel
Citellus lateralis chrysodeirus (Merriam)	
Citellus lateralis trepidus (Taylor)	golden-mantled ground squirrel
Citellus lateralis certus (Goldman)	

Genus **Eutamias** Trouessart—west American and Asiatic chipmunks

Eutamias minimus scrutator Hall and Hatfield	least chipmunk
Eutamias amoenus amoenus (Allen)	
Eutamias amoenus celeris Hall and Johnson	yellow-pine chipmunk
Eutamias amoenus monoensis Grinnell and Storer	
Eutamias panamintinus (Merriam)	Panamint chipmunk
Eutamias quadrivittatus inyoensis Merriam	Say chipmunk
Eutamias quadrivittatus nevadensis Burt	
Eutamias palmeri Merriam	Palmer chipmunk
Eutamias speciosus frater (Allen)	lodgepole-pine chipmunk
Eutamias townsendii senex (Allen)	Townsend chipmunk
Eutamias quadrimaculatus (Gray)	long-eared chipmunk
Eutamias dorsalis grinnelli Burt	cliff chipmunk
Eutamias dorsalis utahensis Merriam	

Genus **Tamiasciurus** Trouessart—red squirrels and allies

Tamiasciurus douglasii albolimbatus (Allen)	Douglas squirrel

Genus **Glaucomys** Thomas—American flying squirrels

Glaucomys sabrinus lascivus (Bangs)	northern flying squirrel

Family HETEROMYIDAE—pocket mice, kangaroo mice, and kangaroo rats

Genus **Perognathus** Wied—pocket mice

Perognathus longimembris nevadensis Merriam	
Perognathus longimembris panamintinus Merriam	little pocket mouse
Perognathus longimembris virginis Huey	
Perognathus longimembris gulosus Hall	
Perognathus parvus parvus (Peale)	Great Basin pocket mouse
Perognathus parvus olivaceus Merriam	
Perognathus formosus melanurus Hall	
Perognathus formosus mohavensis Huey	long-tailed pocket mouse
Perognathus formosus incolatus Hall	
Perognathus penicillatus sobrinus Goldman	desert pocket mouse
Perognathus penicillatus penicillatus Woodhouse	

Genus **Microdipodops** Merriam—kangaroo mice

Microdipodops megacephalus oregonus Merriam	
Microdipodops megacephalus californicus Merriam	
Microdipodops megacephalus nasutus Hall	
Microdipodops megacephalus ambiguus Hall	
Microdipodops megacephalus medius Hall	dark kangaroo mouse
Microdipodops megacephalus nexus Hall	
Microdipodops megacephalus megacephalus Merriam	
Microdipodops megacephalus sabulonis Hall	
Microdipodops megacephalus albiventer Hall and Durrant	

Microdipodops pallidus pallidus Merriam
Microdipodops pallidus ruficollaris Hall
Microdipodops pallidus ammophilus Hall
Microdipodops pallidus purus Hall

} pallid kangaroo mouse

Genus **Dipodomys** Gray—kangaroo rats

Dipodomys panamintinus leucogenys (Grinnell)
Dipodomys panamintinus caudatus new subspecies

} Panamint kangaroo rat

Dipodomys ordii columbianus (Merriam)
Dipodomys ordii inaquosus Hall
Dipodomys ordii celeripes Durrant and Hall
Dipodomys ordii monoensis (Grinnell)
Dipodomys ordii fetosus Durrant and Hall

} Ord kangaroo rat

Dipodomys microps preblei (Goldman)
Dipodomys microps aquilonius Willett
Dipodomys microps centralis Hall and Dale
Dipodomys microps occidentalis Hall and Dale
Dipodomys microps bonnevillei Goldman

} chisel-toothed kangaroo rat

Dipodomys merriami merriami Mearns   Merriam kangaroo rat

Dipodomys deserti deserti Stephens   desert kangaroo rat

Family GEOMYIDAE—pocket gophers

Genus **Thomomys** Wied—smooth-toothed pocket gophers

Thomomys talpoides quadratus Merriam
Thomomys talpoides gracilis Durrant
Thomomys talpoides fisheri Merriam
Thomomys talpoides falcifer Grinnell
Thomomys talpoides monoensis Huey

} northern pocket gopher

Thomomys monticola monticola Allen   mountain pocket gopher

Thomomys townsendii bachmani Davis
Thomomys townsendii elkoensis Davis
Thomomys townsendii nevadensis Merriam

} Townsend pocket gopher

Thomomys bottae canus Bailey
Thomomys bottae depressus Hall
Thomomys bottae lucrificus Hall and Durham
Thomomys bottae cinereus Hall
Thomomys bottae lacrymalis Hall
Thomomys bottae solitarius Grinnell
Thomomys bottae fumosus Hall
Thomomys bottae curtatus Hall
Thomomys bottae vescus Hall and Davis
Thomomys bottae concisor Hall and Davis
Thomomys bottae abstrusus Hall and Davis
Thomomys bottae brevidens Hall
Thomomys bottae latus Hall and Davis
Thomomys bottae centralis Hall
Thomomys bottae virgineus Goldman
Thomomys bottae nanus Hall
Thomomys bottae phelleoecus Burt
Thomomys bottae melanotis Grinnell
Thomomys bottae oreoecus Burt
Thomomys bottae providentialis Grinnell

} Botta pocket gopher

Family CASTORIDAE—beavers

Genus **Castor** Linnaeus—beavers

Castor canadensis taylori Davis ⎫
Castor canadensis baileyi Nelson ⎬ beaver
Castor canadensis repentinus Goldman ⎭

FAMILY MURIDAE—mice and rats

Genus **Onychomys** Baird—grasshopper mice

Onychomys leucogaster fuscogriseus Anthony ⎫
Onychomys leucogaster brevicaudus Merriam ⎬ northern grasshopper mouse

Onychomys torridus longicaudus Merriam ⎫
Onychomys torridus pulcher Elliot ⎬ southern grasshopper mouse

Genus **Reithrodontomys** Giglioli—American harvest mice

Reithrodontomys megalotis megalotis (Baird)   western harvest mouse

Genus **Peromyscus** Gloger—white-footed mice

Peromyscus crinitus crinitus (Merriam) ⎫
Peromyscus crinitus pergracilis Goldman ⎬ canyon mouse
Peromyscus crinitus stephensi Mearns ⎭

Peromyscus eremicus eremicus (Baird)   cactus mouse

Peromyscus maniculatus gambelii (Baird) ⎫
Peromyscus maniculatus sonoriensis (LeConte) ⎬ deer mouse

Peromyscus boylii boylii (Baird) ⎫
Peromyscus boylii rowleyi (Allen) ⎬ brush mouse

Peromyscus truei truei (Shufeldt) ⎫
Peromyscus truei nevadensis Hall and Hoffmeister ⎬ piñon mouse

Genus **Sigmodon** Say and Ord—cotton rats

Sigmodon hispidus plenus Goldman   hispid cotton rat

Genus **Neotoma** Say and Ord—wood rats

Neotoma lepida nevadensis Taylor ⎫
Neotoma lepida lepida Thomas ⎬ desert wood rat
Neotoma lepida grinnelli Hall ⎭

Neotoma cinerea alticola Hooper ⎫
Neotoma cinerea acraia (Elliot) ⎬ bushy-tailed wood rat
Neotoma cinerea lucida Goldman ⎭

Genus **Microtus** Schrank—meadow mice

Microtus montanus micropus Hall ⎫
Microtus montanus nanus (Merriam) ⎪
Microtus montanus yosemite Grinnell ⎬ montane meadow mouse
Microtus montanus undosus Hall ⎪
Microtus montanus fucosus Hall ⎪
Microtus montanus nevadensis Bailey ⎭

Microtus longicaudus mordax (Merriam) ⎫
Microtus longicaudus latus Hall ⎬ long-tailed meadow mouse
Microtus longicaudus sierrae Kellogg ⎭

Genus **Lagurus** Gloger—short-tailed voles

Lagurus curtatus intermedius (Taylor) ⎫
Lagurus curtatus curtatus (Cope) ⎬ sagebrush vole

Genus **Ondatra** Link—muskrats

Ondatra zibethica osoyoosensis (Lord)
Ondatra zibethica mergens (Hollister)
Ondatra zibethica goldmani Huey
Ondatra zibethica bernardi Goldman
} muskrat

Genus **Rattus** G. Fischer—Old World house rats

Rattus rattus alexandrinus (Geoffroy)   black rat

Genus **Mus** Linnaeus—house mice

Mus musculus subsp.? Linnaeus   house mouse

Family APLODONTIDAE—mountain beaver

Genus **Aplodontia** Richardson—mountain beaver

Aplodontia rufa californica (Peters)   mountain beaver

Family ZAPODIDAE—jumping mice and allies

Genus **Zapus** Coues—jumping mice

Zapus princeps curtatus Hall
Zapus princeps alleni Elliot
Zapus princeps nevadensis Preble
Zapus princeps palatinus Hall
} big jumping mouse

Family ERETHIZONTIDAE—American porcupines

Genus **Erethizon** F. Cuvier—North American porcupines

Erethizon epixanthum epixanthum Brandt
Erethizon epixanthum couesi Mearns
} porcupine

Order LAGOMORPHA—hares, rabbits, and pikas

Family OCHOTONIDAE—pikas

Genus **Ochotona** Link—pikas

Ochotona princeps schisticeps (Merriam)
Ochotona princeps nevadensis Howell
Ochotona princeps tutelata Hall
Ochotona princeps muiri Grinnell and Storer
Ochotona princeps sheltoni Grinnell
} pika

Family LEPORIDAE—hares and rabbits

Genus **Lepus** Linnaeus—hares

Lepus townsendii townsendii Bachman   white-tailed jack rabbit

Lepus americanus tahoensis Orr   snowshoe rabbit

Lepus californicus wallawalla Merriam
Lepus californicus deserticola Mearns
} black-tailed jack rabbit

Genus **Sylvilagus** Gray—cottontails and allies

Sylvilagus nuttallii nuttallii (Bachman)
Sylvilagus nuttallii grangeri (Allen)
} Nuttall cottontail

Sylvilagus audubonii arizonae (Allen)   Audubon cottontail

Sylvilagus idahoensis (Merriam)   pigmy rabbit

Order ARTIODACTYLA—even-toed ungulates

Family CERVIDAE—deer and allies

  Genus **Cervus** Linnaeus—wapiti

    Cervus canadensis nelsoni Bailey   wapiti

  Genus **Odocoileus** Rafinesque—black-tailed and white-tailed deer

    Odocoileus hemionus hemionus Rafinesque   black-tailed or mule deer

Family ANTILOCAPRIDAE—pronghorn or American antelope

  Genus **Antilocapra** Ord—prong-horned antelope

    Antilocapra americana americana (Ord)   prong-horned antelope

Family BOVIDAE—cattle, sheep, goats, and allies

  Genus **Ovis** Linnaeus—sheep

    Ovis canadensis californiana Douglas
    Ovis canadensis canadensis Shaw   } mountain sheep
    Ovis canadensis nelsoni Merriam

Scapanus latimanus. × ½.

Sorex vagrans. × 1.

KEY TO SPECIES OF NEVADAN MAMMALS

1 Tooth rows continuous, that is to say, without true diastemae (no spaces, so long as first lower molar devoid of teeth); canine teeth present above and below; six incisor teeth in upper jaw. Moles, shrews, bats, and carnivores.

    2 Canine teeth but little if any larger than teeth on either side of same; snout long and pointed (see figs. 9–31, pp. 111, 115). Order INSECTIVORA.

        3 No visible external ear; forefeet flattened for digging, being about as broad as long; total length, exclusive of tail, more than 108;[1] skull with complete zygomatic arches................**Scapanus latimanus**, broad-footed mole, p. 109.

        3' External ear visible; forefeet not flattened and no larger than hind feet; total length, exclusive of tail, less than 108; skull lacking zygomatic arches. Family SORICIDAE.

            4 Tail more than 30; five unicuspid teeth on each side of upper jaw.

                5 Hind foot less than 17, nonfimbriated, or only slightly so; total length less than 130; tail less than 55.

                    6 Third unicuspid not smaller than fourth.....................
......................**Sorex merriami**, Merriam shrew, p. 114.

                    6' Third unicuspid smaller than fourth.

                        7 Tail sharply bicolor; underparts of body scarcely, if any, paler than upper parts; ridge extending from apex of unicuspid toward interior edge of cingulum only slightly pigmented and rarely pigmented to cingulum, separated from cingulum by longitudinal groove, and never ending in a distinct cusplet...
..............**Sorex trowbridgii**, Trowbridge shrew, p. 117.

                        7' Tail not sharply bicolor; underparts of body distinctly paler than upper parts; ridge extending from apex of unicuspid toward interior edge of cingulum well-pigmented usually to cingulum, not separated from cingulum by longitudinal groove, and usually ending in a distinct cusplet more or less pigmented.

                            8 Foramen magnum placed relatively ventrad, encroaching less into supraoccipital and more into basioccipital (see fig. 21, p. 115); cranial breadth more than 7.4.

                              9 Total length usually less than 110; tail usually less than 44; least interorbital breadth usually less than 3.3; brain case flattened posteriorly..............
...........**Sorex vagrans**, vagrant shrew, p. 118.

                              9' Total length usually more than 110; tail usually more than 44; least interorbital breadth usually more than 3.3; brain case raised posteriorly...............
.............**Sorex obscurus**, dusky shrew, p. 121.

                          8' Foramen magnum placed relatively dorsad, encroaching more into supraoccipital and less into basioccipital (see fig. 23, p. 115); cranial breadth less than 7.4.........
.................**Sorex tenellus**, dwarf shrew, p. 122.

                5' Hind foot more than 17, fimbriated; total length more than 130; tail more than 55.................**Sorex palustris**, water shrew, p. 123.

            4' Tail less than 30; three unicuspid teeth on each side of upper jaw.........
...........................**Notiosorex crawfordi**, gray shrew, p. 126.

    2' Canine teeth larger than teeth on either side of same.

[1] All measurements are in millimeters unless otherwise specified.

Myotis lucifugus. × 1.

10 Fingers lacking claws (thumb has claw) and are longer than forearm; fingers supporting a membrane for flight; teeth with high styles, adapted to crushing hard-shelled insects. Order CHIROPTERA.

    11 Snout with pointed nose leaf; three completely bony phalanges in third finger; premaxillae united, with two incisors above on each side.........................

    ....**Macrotus californicus**, California leaf-nosed bat, p. 129.

    11' Snout without nose leaf; fewer than three completely bony phalanges in third finger; premaxillae separated, or when united (*Eumops*), with only one incisor above on each side.

        12 Tail not extending more than 3, if any, behind uropatagium; anterior border of ear lacking horny excrescences (and forearm always less than 67); anterior border of palate truncate or rounded, lacking a distinct emargination. Family VESPERTILIONIDAE.

            13 Total length usually less than 105; color always brownish; three premolars on each side above. Genus *Myotis*.

                14 Underside of wing furred to level of elbow; skull with occiput unusually elevated (see fig. 37, p. 131).......................

                ....**Myotis volans**, hairy-winged myotis, p. 138.

                14' Underside of wing not furred to elbow; skull with occiput normal (see fig. 36, p. 131).

                    15 Foot large, its length usually ranging from 48 to 60 per cent of that of tibia; occipital depth of skull more than 4.8.

                        16 Ear when laid forward not extending noticeably beyond tip of muzzle; free border of uropatagium without fringe of hair, or at most with faintly developed fringe; maxillary tooth row less than 5.9.

                          17 Forearm ranging from 36 to 40; hairs on back have conspicuously burnished tips; greatest length of skull ranging from 14.3 to 15.3. (Sometimes 14.0 or less in *M. l. phasma*, not yet recorded from Nevada)................

                          ......**Myotis lucifugus**, small myotis, p. 132.

                          17' Forearm ranging from 32 to 37; hairs on back without conspicuously burnished tips; greatest length of skull ranging from 13.2 to 14.2.......

                          ....**Myotis yumanensis**, Yuma myotis, p. 133.

                      16' Ear when laid forward extending noticeably beyond tip of muzzle; free border of uropatagium with a noticeable fringe of stiff hairs; maxillary tooth row more than 5.9.

                        18 Ear more than 18; forearm 40 or less; fringe on uropatagium present but not conspicuous; maxillary breadth at M3 less than 6.3......

                          .....**Myotis evotis**, long-eared myotis, p. 136.

                        18' Ear less than 18; forearm 41 or more; fringe on uropatagium conspicuous; maxillary breadth at M3 more than 6.3.......................

                      Myotis thysanodes, fringe-tailed myotis, p. 138.

                  15' Foot small, its length usually ranging from 40 to 46 per cent of that of tibia; occipital depth of skull less than 4.8.

Myotis californicus. × 1½.

Pipistrellus hesperus. × 1½.

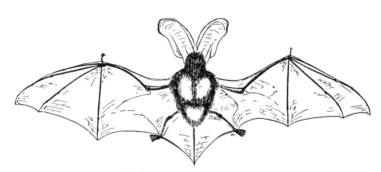

Euderma maculatum. × ⅓.

19 Ears blackish or brownish; skull with rounded occiput and abruptly rising forehead (see fig. 39, p. 131)..............**Myotis californicus**, California myotis, p. 140.

19' Ears black; skull with flattened occiput and gradual slope from rostrum to top of brain case (see fig. 42, p. 131)......**Myotis subulatus**, small-footed myotis, p. 143.

13' Total length more or less than 105, but usually more when color is brown; color various; less than three premolars on each side above.

20 Ear less than 25 from notch; incisors on one side above and below totaling four or five (when five, premolars may be $\frac{1}{2}$, $\frac{2}{2}$, or $\frac{2}{3}$; those with $\frac{2}{2}$ have condylobasal length less than 12.5, and those with $\frac{2}{3}$ have maxillary tooth row not less than 6.5).

21 Fur everywhere blackish to base, some hairs tipped with white; basal half of upper surface of uropatagium well-furred; three premolars on each side below..............**Lasionycteris noctivagans**, silvery-haired bat, p. 145.

21' Fur not black to base, even when tipped with white, and fur sometimes red or gray; uropatagium either naked or entirely furred on upper surface (not furred on basal half only); two premolars on each side below.

22 Color gray; total length less than 91; membranes naked; eight teeth in each upper jaw......**Pipistrellus hesperus**, western pipistrelle, p. 147.

22' Color brown, red, or blackish overcast with white; total length more than 91; membranes naked or furred; less than eight teeth in each upper jaw.

23 Color brown; membranes naked; one upper premolar.........
.....................**Eptesicus fuscus**, big brown bat, p. 151.

23' Color red or black, hairs often tipped with white; uropatagium densely furred over all of upper surface and on underside of wing along the bones of the forearm and slightly beyond the ends of these bones; two upper premolars. Genus *Lasiurus*.

24 Color red or reddish yellow; inside area of pinna of ear naked; total length about 104; forearm less than 50; breadth of brain case less than 8.6....................
.....................**Lasiurus borealis**, red bat, p. 155.

24' Color brownish-black overcast with white; inside area of pinna of ear densely furred; total length about 135; forearm more than 50; breadth of brain case more than 8.6.......
...................**Lasiurus cinereus**, hoary bat, p. 155.

20' Ear more than 25 from notch; incisors on one side above and below totaling three or five (when five, premolars never $\frac{1}{2}$, but $\frac{2}{2}$ or $\frac{2}{3}$; those with $\frac{2}{2}$ have condylobasal length more than 12.5 and those with $\frac{2}{3}$ have maxillary tooth row less than 6.5).

25 Color black with three white spots on upper parts; premolars $\frac{2}{2}$ ....
..............................**Euderma maculatum**, spotted bat, p. 156.

25' Color light-brownish; premolars $\frac{2}{3}$ and $\frac{1}{2}$.

26 Natal Brown to Army Brown above; forearm less than 48; well-developed glandular swelling on each side of muzzle; skull with interorbital region concave; incisors $\frac{2}{3}$; premolars $\frac{2}{3}$ ....
...................**Corynorhinus rafinesquii**, long-eared bat, p. 158.

26' Pallid tawny above; forearm more than 48; weakly developed, low, flattened swelling on each side of muzzle; skull with interorbital region convex; incisors $\frac{1}{2}$; premolars $\frac{1}{2}$ .. **Antrozous pallidus**, pallid bat, p. 162.

Tadarida mexicana. × ⅓.

Ursus americanus. × 1/35.

Procyon lotor. × 1/20.

Bassariscus astutus. × 1/15.

12' Tail extending conspicuously behind uropatagium; anterior border of ear with or without (when without, forearm more than 67) six to eight horny excrescences; anterior border of palate with a distinct emargination, or with premaxillae united (when premaxillae are united, condylobasal length more than 25.5). Family MOLOSSIDAE.

27 Forearm less than 67; anterior edge of ear with six to eight horny excrescences; anterior border of palate with a distinct emargination; condylobasal length less than 25.5.

28 Second phalanx of fourth finger less than 5; well-developed pocket in membrane at angle of tibia and femur; ears when laid forward extending well beyond nose; two incisors on each side below; condylobasal length of skull more than 17.

29 Forearm less than 52; condylobasal length of skull less than 19.5. **Tadarida femorosacca**, pocketed bat (not yet found in Nevada).

29' Forearm more than 52; condylobasal length of skull more than 19.5............**Tadarida macrotis**, big free-tailed bat, p. 169.

28' Second phalanx of fourth finger more than 5; no pocket in membrane at angle of tibia and femur; ears when laid forward not extending beyond nose; two and generally three incisors on each side below; condylobasal length of skull less than 17..................................
................**Tadarida mexicana**, Mexican free-tailed bat, p. 168.

27' Forearm more than 67; anterior edge of ear without horny excrescences; premaxillae united; condylobasal length more than 25.5. **Eumops perotis californicus**, mastiff bat (not recorded from Nevada).

10' Fingers have claws and are not so long as forearm; fingers not supporting a membrane or other adaptation for flight; teeth sectorial, adapted to cutting flesh. Order CARNIVORA.

30 Hind foot with five toes; thirty-four, thirty-six, thirty-eight, forty, or forty-two teeth; when forty-two, P4 not trenchant and width across upper tooth rows greater across second upper molars than across fourth premolars.

31 Total length more than 1,200 (47 inches) in adults; tail less than 14 per cent of total length; forty-two teeth; three molars in each lower jaw...........
................................**Ursus americanus**, black bear, p. 171.

31' Total length less than 1,200 (47 inches); tail more than 14 per cent of total length; less than forty-two teeth; two molars in each lower jaw.

32 Tail with conspicuous rings; forty teeth; two molars in each upper jaw.

33 Black rings on tail complete all around, numbering usually six, not counting black tip; tail, excluding hair at tip, near $\frac{1}{3}$ of total length; posterior margin of hard palate extending behind last upper molars for a distance of more than combined lengths of M1 and 2.....................**Procyon lotor**, raccoon, p. 175.

33' Black rings on tail incomplete, being absent on ventral side, numbering usually eight, not counting black tip; tail, excluding hair at tip, near $\frac{1}{2}$ of total length; posterior margin of hard palate on a line with last upper molars, or extending behind them for a distance of less than combined lengths of M1 and 2...........
..................**Bassariscus astutus**, ring-tailed cat, p. 179.

32' Tail without rings; less than forty teeth; one molar in each upper jaw.

Martes caurina. × $\frac{1}{11}$.

Mustela cicognanii. × $\frac{1}{8}$.

Mustela frenata. × $\frac{1}{8}$.

Mustela vison. × $\frac{1}{8}$.

Lutra canadensis. × $\frac{1}{20}$.

Spilogale gracilis. × $\frac{1}{10}$.

Taxidea taxus. × $\frac{1}{20}$.

Mephitis mephitis. × $\frac{1}{10}$.

34 General color of upper parts some shade of brown; thirty-eight, thirty-six, or thirty-four teeth, but when thirty-four, m1 lacks an internal cusp (metaconid).

35 Size small, total length of adults amounting to less than 786 (31 inches); hair on tail longer than on back; fleshy part of tail normal, that is, not thickened at base so as to merge gradually with body; thirty-four or thirty-eight teeth; P4 with simple deuterocone, not expanded into a basined structure; m1 lacking a metaconid.

36 Light-colored underparts Ochraceous Orange (in some places Cinnamon Buff) and restricted to throat, pectoral region, and a narrow line down belly to vent; ear more than 25 in height as measured from crown; premolars $\frac{4}{4}$; palatilar length more than 30 . . . . **Martes caurina**, marten, p. 183.

36' Light-colored underparts white or Buff Yellow to Straw Yellow, ochraceous yellow in some young, and in broad band amounting to more than $\frac{1}{4}$ of circumference of the body (weasels), or restricted to a few white spots or absent (minks); ear less than 25 in height as measured from crown; premolars $\frac{3}{3}$; palatilar length less than 30.

37 Light-colored area of underparts broad, amounting to more than $\frac{1}{4}$ of circumference of body; basilar length less than 50.

38 Total length less than 285; tail amounting to less than 31 per cent of total length; basilar length less than 33. . . . .
. . . . **Mustela cicognanii**, short-tailed weasel, p. 184.

38' Total length in adults more than 285; tail amounting to more than 31 per cent of total length; basilar length more than 33. . . . .
. . . . **Mustela frenata**, long-tailed weasel, p. 188.

37' Light-colored area of underparts absent or restricted to a few white spots; basilar length more than 50. . . . **Mustela vison**, mink, p. 193.

35' Size large, total length of adults amounting to more than 786 (31 inches); hair on tail about same length as on back; fleshy part of tail thickened at base, thus merging gradually with body; thirty-six teeth; P4 with deuterocone expanded into a basined structure; m1 with well-developed metaconid. . . . .
. . . . **Lutra canadensis**, river otter, p. 195.

34' General color of upper parts black and white, or black and white on head with silvery back and sides; thirty-four teeth, m1 always with well-developed internal cusp (metaconid).

39 Color black and white; tail amounting to more than 27 per cent of total length; basilar length less than 80; palate not projecting behind molars for a distance of more than the length of M1.

40 Back with four or more lines of broken white stripes, or white spots; total length of adults less than 500; length of upper tooth rows less than 23.5; length of m1 less than 8 . . . . **Spilogale gracilis**, spotted skunk, p. 199.

40' Back with two white stripes; total length of adults more than 500; length of upper tooth rows more than 23.5; length of m1 more than 8 . . . .
. . . . **Mephitis mephitis**, striped skunk, p. 204.

39' Color black and white on head with silvery back and sides and a single white stripe on middle of head extending a varying distance toward or to the tail; tail amounting to less than 27 per cent of total length; basilar length more than 80; palate projecting behind molars for a distance of more than length of M1. . . . .
. . . . **Taxidea taxus**, badger, p. 214.

Vulpes macrotis. × 1/15.

Urocyon cinereoargenteus. × 1/15.

Canis latrans. × 1/20.

Felis concolor. × 1/35.

Lynx rufus. × 1/20.

30′ Hind foot with four toes; thirty, thirty-two, or forty-two teeth; when forty-two, P4 trenchant and width across upper tooth rows less across second upper molars than across fourth premolars.

  41 Muzzle long and narrow; claws not retractile; forty-two teeth; two molars on each side above.

    42 Adults weigh less than 15 lbs.; postorbital processes thin and concave dorsally; basilar length of skull less than 147.

      43 Backs of ears black or grayish brown; tail without dark stripe all the way down upper side; skull of adults with sagittal crest or with temporal ridges low; inferior margin of lower mandible without prominent "step."

        44 Tip of tail white; ears black on outside; distance between orbit and anterior opening of infraorbital canal more than height of foramen magnum. . **Vulpes fulva,** red fox, p. 228.

        44′ Tip of tail black or dark brown; ears grayish brown on outside; distance between orbit and anterior opening of infraorbital canal less than height of foramen magnum . . . . **Vulpes macrotis,** kit fox, p. 233.

      43′ Backs of ears red; tail with dark strip all the way down upper side; skull of adults with high lyrate temporal ridges; inferior margin of lower mandible with distinct "step" midway between tip of angular process and a line dropped from the anterior border of coronoid process. . . . **Urocyon cinereoargenteus,** gray fox, p. 239.

    42′ Adults weigh more than 15 lbs.; postorbital processes thick and convex above and evenly continuous with inflated frontal area; basilar length of skull more than 147.

      45 Weight of adults usually less than 40 lbs.; width of rostrum measured across bases of upper canines less than $1\frac{3}{4}$ of the antero-posterior extent of auditory bulla. . **Canis latrans,** coyote, p. 242.

      45′ Weight of adults usually more than 40 lbs.; width of rostrum measured across bases of upper canines more than $1\frac{3}{4}$ of the anteroposterior extent of auditory bulla. **Canis lupus,** wolf, p. 266.

  41′ Muzzle short and broad; claws retractile; thirty or thirty-two teeth; one molar on each side above.

    46 Tail more than 30 per cent of total length (about 30 inches long in adults); thirty-two teeth, three upper premolars on each side; basilar length more than 132 . . . . **Felis concolor,** mountain lion, p. 269.

    46′ Tail less than 30 per cent of total length (about 6 inches long in adults); thirty teeth, two upper premolars on each side; basilar length less than 132 . . . . **Lynx rufus,** bobcat, p. 275.

1′ Tooth rows with diastemae (spaces as long as or longer than first lower molar, which spaces are devoid of teeth); canine teeth absent below and sometimes above; none to four incisor teeth in upper jaw.

  47 One or two incisor teeth on each side above; feet provided with claws.

    48 One incisor tooth on each side above. Order RODENTIA.

      49 Body and tail without quills; facial opening of infraorbital canal smaller than foramen magnum.

        50 Hair on middle of tail longer than diameter of fleshy part of tail (tail always longer than hind foot; and always more than three cheek teeth); skull with well-developed postorbital processes on frontal bone. Family SCIURIDAE.

Marmota flaviventer. × 1/12.

Citellus beldingi. × 1/5.

Citellus leucurus. × 1/5.

51 Length of hind foot and basilar length of skull each more than 66; postorbital processes broad, projecting at nearly right angles to skull (see fig. 188, p. 283); anterior lower premolar with a protoconule.........**Marmota flaviventer**, yellow-bellied marmot, p. 282.

51' Length of hind foot and basilar length of skull each less than 66; postorbital processes narrow, projecting downward and backward (see fig. 217, p. 317); anterior lower premolar without a protoconule.

  52 No loose fold of skin on side between fore- and hind leg, and no line of black color there which separates light-colored underparts from dark-colored upper parts; anterior part of zygomatic arch twisted toward a horizontal plane.

    53 Side of head lacking stripes; infraorbital canal (not mere foramen) present; anterior border of zygomatic notch in maxillary opposite M1 (see fig. 196, p. 305).

      54 Upper parts brownish or grayish or mixture of both (not striped or dappled); when gray, hairs on tail longer than on back, and tail less than ½ length of head and body; parastylar ridge on M1 and M2 joining the protocone with an abrupt change of direction; anterior opening of infraorbital canal circular.

        55 Hind foot less than 40; greatest length of skull less than 41......
........**Citellus townsendii**, Townsend ground squirrel, p. 290.

        55' Hind foot more than 40; greatest length of skull more than 41.

          56 Tail usually more than 75, Ochraceous-Buff below; length of nasals usually more than 79 per cent of cranial breadth
..**Citellus richardsonii**, Richardson ground squirrel, p. 303.

          56' Tail usually less than 75, reddish, often Hazel below; where this species occurs with *C. richardsonii* length of nasals usually less than 79 per cent of cranial breadth..........
.........**Citellus beldingi**, Belding ground squirrel, p. 306.

      54' Upper parts striped, or dappled, or red, or gray and dappled; when gray (or red), hairs on tail no longer than on back, and tail more than ½ length of head and body; parastylar ridge on M1 and M2 join the protocone without an abrupt change of direction; anterior opening of infraorbital canal higher than wide.

        57 Tail more than 135; greatest length of skull more than 50 (usually more than 56).

          58 Nape and shoulders without dark median area..........
................**Citellus variegatus**, rock squirrel, p. 310.

          58' Nape and shoulders with dark median area..............
........**Citellus beecheyi**, Beechey ground squirrel, p. 313.

        57' Tail less than 135; greatest length of skull less than 50 (usually less than 44).

          59 Tail white beneath, and flattened, its width three times its depth; one stripe only, and that white, on each side of back; upper incisors stout and distinctly recurved (see fig. 219, p. 318)....**Citellus leucurus**, antelope ground squirrel, p. 314.

          59' Tail red, or white beneath; when red, flattened, as in 59, but when white, width less than twice the depth; one stripe of white and one or two of black on each side of back, or back plain (without stripes); upper incisors slender and not distinctly recurved (see figs. 221, 223, p. 318).

Citellus lateralis. × ⅕.

Eutamias minimus. × ⅓.

60 Upper parts plain-colored, red or gray; tail short-haired and round; length of nasals less than 12.7; postorbital processes short and stout. . . . .
. . . . **Citellus tereticaudus,** round-tailed ground squirrel, p. 318.

60′ Upper parts with one white stripe and one or two black stripes on each side of back; length of nasals more than 12.7; postorbital processes long and slender. . . . .
. . . . **Citellus lateralis,** golden-mantled ground squirrel, p. 319.

53′ Side of head striped; infraorbital foramen (not canal) present; anterior border of zygomatic notch in maxillary opposite P4 (see fig. 245, p. 328).

  61 Length of head and body usually less than 110; greatest length of skull less than 31.5. . . . . **Eutamias minimus,** least chipmunk, p. 329.

  61′ Length of head and body usually more than 110; greatest length of skull more than 31.5.

    62 Length of head and body less than 130; greatest length of skull less than 36.

      63 Submalar dark stripe obsolete anteriorly; dark dorsal stripes (excepting median one) either reddish, or grayish, and almost obsolete; dorsal face of skull flattened (see fig. 237, p. 328).

        64 Dark dorsal stripe next to median one reddish, and distinct; edging of tail buffy; incisive foramina parallel. . . . .
. . . . **Eutamias panamintinus,** Panamint chipmunk, p. 336.

        64′ Dark dorsal stripe next to median one grayish and indistinct; edging of tail whitish; incisive foramina converging anteriorly.
. . . . **Eutamias dorsalis,** cliff chipmunk, p. 347.

      63′ Submalar dark stripe complete anteriorly; dark dorsal stripes black, or more blackish than reddish, never gray; dorsal face of skull rounded (see fig. 236, p. 328).

        65 Length of head and body usually less than 120; greatest length of skull usually less than 33.5. . . . .
. . . . **Eutamias amoenus,** yellow-pine chipmunk, p. 333.

        65′ Length of head and body usually more than 120; greatest length of skull usually more than 33.5.

          66 Submedian dark dorsal stripe brownish without black center; tail beneath Ochraceous Tawny. . . . .
. . . . **Eutamias palmeri,** Palmer chipmunk, p. 342.

          66′ Submedian dark dorsal stripe with black center; tail below lighter than Ochraceous Tawny.

            67 Submalar stripe without black center below eye; upper incisors not much recurved, their tips anterior to posterior borders of their alveoli when cranium is resting, teeth down, on horizontal surface. . . . .
. . . . . . **Eutamias quadrivittatus,** Say chipmunk, p. 339.

            67′ Submalar stripe with black center below eye; upper incisors strongly recurved, their tips posterior to posterior borders of their alveoli when cranium is resting, teeth down, on horizontal surface. . . . .
Eutamias speciosus, lodgepole-pine chipmunk, p. 344.

    62′ Length of head and body more than 130; greatest length of skull more than 36.

      68 Ears short (17.5 [16.2–18.7] from notch, dry), not pointed; submalar dark stripe not black below ear; rostrum broad (see fig. 232, p. 327).
. . . . **Eutamias townsendii,** Townsend chipmunk, p. 345.

Tamiasciurus douglasii. × ⅕.

Glaucomys sabrinus. × ⅕.

Perognathus longimembris. × ½.

68′ Ears long (19.5 [18.1–20.4] from notch, dry), pointed; submalar dark stripe expanding into conspicuous black area below ear; rostrum narrow (see fig. 233, p. 327).....**Eutamias quadrimaculatus**, long-eared chipmunk, p. 346.

52′ Either a loose fold of skin on side between fore- and hind leg or a line of black color there which separates light-colored underparts from dark-colored upper parts; anterior part of zygomatic arch vertical.

  69 Black stripe on side separating color of upper parts from color of underparts; no loose fold of skin on side between fore- and hind leg; postorbital breadth more than length of nasals; P3 absent or vestigial......................
.... **Tamiasciurus douglasii**, Douglas squirrel, p. 352.

  69′ No black stripe on side, but a loose fold of skin on side between fore- and hind leg; postorbital breadth less than length of nasals; P3 present and in crown surface amounts to approximately ⅕ that of P4......................
.... **Glaucomys sabrinus**, northern flying squirrel, p. 353.

50′ Hair on middle of tail shorter than diameter of fleshy part of tail (except *Aplodontia*, where tail is shorter than hind foot, and except *Neotoma cinerea*, where there are only three cheek teeth); skull without postorbital processes on frontal bone.

  70 External, fur-lined cheek pouches; auditory bulla longer than crown surface of upper cheek teeth and longer than incisive foramina.

    71 Tail more than ¾ length of head and body; claws on forefeet less than 1¾ as long as those on corresponding toes on hind feet; nasals projecting anteriorly to incisors; auditory bulla exposed on parietal face of skull.

      72 Soles of hind feet naked (in *P. longimembris*, hair on region between heel and plantar surface); greatest width of head less than distance between tip of nose and posterior end of eye; interparietal more than ¼ of greatest width of skull. Genus *Perognathus*.

        73 Hind foot less than 20; occipitonasal length less than 24........
.... **Perognathus longimembris**, little pocket mouse, p. 358.

        73′ Hind foot more than 20; occipitonasal length more than 24.

          74 Side of body with olivaceous line; tail not crested; supraoccipital without lateral indentations by mastoid on each side. **Perognathus parvus**, Great Basin pocket mouse, p. 364.

          74′ Side of body without olivaceous line; tail crested; supraoccipital with lateral indentation by mastoid on each side;

            75 Ear large; height, measured from notch, more than 10. mastoid side of parietal longest............ **Perognathus formosus**, long-tailed pocket mouse, p. 369.

            75′ Ear small; height, measured from notch, less than 10; mastoid side of parietal shortest................. **Perognathus penicillatus**, desert pocket mouse, p. 375.

      72′ Soles of hind feet densely haired; greatest width of head more than distance between tip of nose and posterior end of eye; interparietal less than ¼ of greatest width of skull.

        76 Tail with terminal tuft; hind foot more than 32; dermal gland between shoulders; lacrimal throughout its entire length applied to maxillary root of zygomatic arch; crown surface of P4 elliptical. Genus *Dipodomys*.

          77 Five toes on hind foot; breadth across bullae less than 27, and interorbital breadth less than half of basal length.

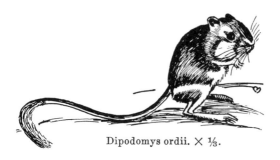

Dipodomys ordii. $\times$ ⅓.

Microdipodops pallidus. $\times$ ½.

Thomomys bottae. $\times$ ¼.

78 Lower incisors with anterior faces rounded, awllike; width of maxillary arm of zygoma, at lower angle, more than length of first three upper cheek teeth.

79 Ventral tail-stripe terminates short of end of vertebrae, or distally narrowed; hind foot less than 44; length of nasals less than 14.7; basal length less than 26.7; width of interparietal more than crown-length of P4 and M1..................................

...................**Dipodomys ordii,** Ord kangaroo rat, p. 410.

79' Ventral tail-stripe retains width to end of tail; hind foot more than 44; length of nasals more than 14.7; basal length more than 26.7; width of interparietal not more than crown-length of P4 and M1. **Dipodomys panamintinus,** Panamint kangaroo rat, p. 407.

78' Lower incisors with anterior faces flat, chisellike; width of maxillary arm of zygoma, at lower angle, less than length of first three upper cheek teeth. .**Dipodomys microps,** chisel-toothed kangaroo rat, p. 416.

77' Four toes on hind foot; breadth across bullae more than 27 (*deserti*), or when less than 27 (*merriami*) with interorbital breadth more than half of basal length.

80 Hind foot less than 46; tail with terminal inch of hairs black; ventral tail-stripe well-defined; basal length of skull less than 27.3 (23.0–25.3); greatest breadth of skull less than 26.2 (21.7–24.2)..................

...............**Dipodomys merriami,** Merriam kangaroo rat, p. 424.

80' Hind foot more than 46; tail with terminal inch of hairs white; ventral tail-stripe absent or poorly defined; basal length of skull more than 27.3 (29.3–32.5); greatest breadth of skull more than 26.2 (28.2–32.0)......

...................**Dipodomys deserti,** desert kangaroo rat, p. 428.

76' Tail without terminal tuft; hind foot less than 32; no dermal gland between shoulders; lacrimal forming a distinct process separated from maxillary root of zygomatic arch by deep notch; crown surface of P4 triangular. Genus *Microdipodops*.

81 Upper parts blackish; top of tail distally tipped with black; incisive foramina widest posteriorly or at middle; premaxillae extending but little posteriorly to nasals (see fig. 279, p. 378)...

..............**Microdipodops megacephalus,** dark kangaroo mouse, p. 383.

81' Upper parts near (*e*) light Pinkish Cinnamon; top of tail not black distally but same color as base; incisive foramina parallel-sided; premaxillae extending far behind nasals (see fig. 282, p. 378).............................

...................**Microdipodops pallidus,** pallid kangaroo mouse, p. 396.

71' Tail less than ¾ length of head and body; claws on forefeet more than 1¾ as long as those on corresponding toes on hind feet; nasals not projecting anteriorly to incisors; auditory bulla not exposed on parietal face of skull.

82 Color brownish; skull lacking sphenorbital fissure (see fig. 316, p. 436); anterior opening of infraorbital canal posterior to anterior palatine foramina; occlusal face of anterior prism of p4 not less than ¾ that of posterior prism.

83 Pinna of ear round; temporal ridges on skull usually parallel; os penis less than 18..............**Thomomys talpoides,** northern pocket gopher, p. 445.

83' Pinna of ear pointed; temporal ridges on skull diverging posteriorly; os penis more than 18........**Thomomys monticola,** mountain pocket gopher, p. 451.

82' Color grayish, blackish, or ochraceous; skull with sphenorbital fissure (see fig. 318, p. 436); anterior opening of infraorbital canal not posterior to anterior palatine foramina; occlusal face of anterior prism of p4 less than ¾ that of posterior prism.

Castor canadensis. × 1/20.

Onychomys leucogaster. × 1/2.

Onychomys torridus. × 1/2.

Reithrodontomys megalotis. × 1/2.

84 Size large; usually in males hind foot more than 35 and basilar length more than 39.2, in females corresponding measurements are 33 and 36.5..................
.......................**Thomomys townsendii,** Townsend pocket gopher, p. 451.

84' Size medium; usually in males hind foot less than 35 and basilar length less than 39.2, in females corresponding measurements are 33 and 36.5.................
.............................**Thomomys bottae,** Botta pocket gopher, p. 453.

70' No cheek pouches; auditory bulla shorter than crown surface of upper cheek teeth or shorter than incisive foramina and usually shorter than each.

85 Tail flattened dorsoventrally; incisive foramen shorter than first two upper cheek teeth...................................**Castor canadensis,** beaver, p. 481.

85' Tail not flattened; incisive foramina longer than first two upper cheek teeth.

86 Tail longer than hind foot; cheek teeth $\frac{3}{3}$.

87 Annulations on tail nearly or completely concealed by hair; cheek teeth with cusps (or prisms that remain when cusps are worn down) in two longitudinal rows (see fig. 345, p. 503). Family CRICETIDAE.

88 Cheek teeth with cusps, no flat occlusal area composed of lakes of dentine surrounded by enamel.

89 Cusps on cheek teeth not flattened and not divided into S-shaped lophs; tooth row less than 5.0; guard hairs not prominent and pelage smooth to the touch.

90 Tail less than 60 per cent of length of head and body; coronoid process of mandible high (see figs. 347, 349, p. 503).

91 Tail usually less than $\frac{1}{2}$ length of body; M3 as long as broad; M1 less than $\frac{1}{2}$ length of tooth row...........................**Onychomys leucogaster,** northern grasshopper mouse, p. 491.

91' Tail usually more than $\frac{1}{2}$ length of body; M3 broader than long; M1 more than $\frac{1}{2}$ length of tooth row......................**Onychomys torridus,** southern grasshopper mouse, p. 494.

90' Tail more than 60 per cent of length of head and body; coronoid process of mandible low (see figs. 351, 353, p. 503).

92 Head and body usually less than 80; upper incisors grooved on anterior face....**Reithrodontomys megalotis,** western harvest mouse, p. 496.

92' Head and body usually more than 80; upper incisors not grooved (smooth) on anterior face.

93 Total length less than 185; greatest length of skull less than 26.8 (and premaxillae not extending posteriorly to nasals).

94 Tail usually longer than head and body, or at least more than 90 per cent of length of head and body; dorsal tail-stripe broad, not sharply defined; fur long and lax; maxillary breadth 11.0 or less......**Peromyscus crinitus,** canyon mouse, p. 504.

Peromyscus maniculatus. × ½.

Sigmodon hispidus. × ⅕.

Neotoma lepida. × ¼.

Microtus montanus. × ½.

94' Tail shorter than (less than 90 per cent of) length of head and body; dorsal tail-stripe narrow, sharply defined; fur of average length; maxillary breadth more than 11.0....................................
......................**Peromyscus maniculatus**, deer mouse, p. 511.

93' Total length more than 185; greatest length of skull more than 26.8, or if less than 26.8 (only in *eremicus*) premaxillae extend posteriorly to nasals, and M1 and M2 without accessory cusps between the principal buccal cusps.

95 Ear, measured from the notch in fresh specimens, shorter than hind foot; dorsal tail-stripe broad; auditory bullae small and not greatly inflated (see fig. 344, p. 503).

96 Body small, weight averaging 24.1 grams; sole of hind foot naked to end of calcaneum; two pair mammae (inguinal); general color of upper parts light; greatest length of skull less than 26.8; M1 and M2 without accessory cusps between the principal buccal cusps; premaxillae projecting posteriorly to nasals...........
..................**Peromyscus eremicus**, cactus mouse, p. 509.

96' Body large, weight averaging 32.1 grams; proximal $\frac{2}{5}$ of underside of hind foot hairy; three pair mammae (one pair pectoral, two pair inguinal); general color of upper parts dark (mixed with brown and red); greatest length of skull more than 26.8; M1 and M2 with accessory cusps between the principal buccal cusps; premaxillae not projecting posteriorly to nasals.................
......................**Peromyscus boylii**, brush mouse, p. 517.

95' Ear, measured from notch in fresh specimens, longer than hind foot; dorsal tail-stripe narrow; auditory bullae large and inflated (see fig. 345, p. 503)......................**Peromyscus truei**, piñon mouse, p. 520.

89' Cusps on cheek teeth flattened and divided into S-shaped lophs; tooth row more than 5.0; guard hairs prominent and pelage rough to the touch................
................................**Sigmodon hispidus**, hispid cotton rat, p. 525.

88' Cheek teeth without cusps, flat occlusal area composed of lakes of dentine surrounded by enamel and separated by re-entrant angles.

97 Ears thinly haired and height from notch more than $\frac{2}{3}$ length of hind foot; teeth rooted, and posterior ends of M1 and M2 rounded.

98 Tail with hairs on side less than 20 long; ear, measured from notch, more than $\frac{3}{4}$ length of hind foot; sphenopalatine vacuities wide...................
..............................**Neotoma lepida**, desert wood rat, p. 528.

98' Tail with hairs on side more than 20 long; ear, measured from notch, less than $\frac{3}{4}$ length of hind foot; sphenopalatine vacuities closed.............
......................**Neotoma cinerea**, bushy-tailed wood rat, p. 533.

97' Ears thickly haired and height from notch less than $\frac{2}{3}$ length of hind foot; teeth not rooted, and posterior ends of M1 and M2 angled.

99 Tail round, not laterally compressed; length of hind foot less than 35; length of cheek teeth less than 10.

100 Color grayish-black to reddish-black; tail long, reaching beyond hind feet when these are extended posteriorly; m3 with three prisms (see fig. 374, p. 541).

101 Tail usually less than 30 per cent of total length; upper parts blackish and reddish, uniformly colored; skull heavily ridged, with incisive foramina abruptly constricted posteriorly (see figs. 372, 378, p. 541).......................................
........**Microtus montanus**, montane meadow mouse, p. 540.

Ondatra zibethica. × ⅙.

Mus musculus. × ¼.

Aplodontia rufa. × ⅕.

Erethizon epixanthum. × ¹⁄₁₅.

Zapus princeps. × ½.

Ochotona princeps. × ¼.

101' Tail usually more than 30 per cent of total length; upper parts grayish, with reddish middorsal longitudinal band; skull weakly ridged, with incisive foramina gradually tapered posteriorly or as wide as anteriorly (see figs. 372, 378, p. 541)..... **Microtus longicaudus,** long-tailed meadow mouse, p. 550.

100' Color light gray; tail short, not reaching beyond hind feet when these are extended posteriorly; m3 with four prisms (see fig. 384, p. 541).................................

..............**Lagurus curtatus,** sagebrush vole, p. 556.

99' Tail flattened, laterally compressed; length of hind foot more than 35; length of cheek teeth more than 10.....................

........................**Ondatra zibethica,** muskrat, p. 561.

87' Annulations on tail revealed by sparse hairiness; cheek teeth with cusps in three longitudinal rows (see fig. 398, p. 569). Family MURIDAE.

102 Hind foot more than 25; occlusal face of upper incisors viewed from side lacks a notch; M1 shorter than combined lengths of M2 and M3.

103 Tail not shorter than head and body; length of parietal, measured along a temporal ridge, less than greatest distance between temporal ridges.....................

.....................**Rattus rattus,** black rat, p. 569.

103' Tail shorter than head and body; length of parietal, measured along a temporal ridge, about equal to greatest distance between temporal ridges. **Rattus norvegicus,** Norway rat (not yet found in Nevada).

102' Hind foot less than 25; occlusal face of upper incisors viewed from side has a pronounced notch (see fig. 403, p. 572); M1 longer than combined lengths of M2 and M3...............

.......................**Mus musculus,** house mouse, p. 571.

86' Tail shorter than hind foot, or, instead, longer by $\frac{1}{5}$ than head and body; well-defined dark middorsal area set off by yellowish or ochraceous sides; cheek teeth $\frac{5}{4}$ or $\frac{4}{3}$.

104 Tail shorter (vestigial) than hind foot; length of head and body more than 130; cheek teeth $\frac{5}{4}$..... **Aplodontia rufa,** mountain beaver, p. 573.

104' Tail $\frac{1}{5}$ longer than head and body; well-defined, dark middorsal area set off by yellowish or ochraceous sides; cheek teeth $\frac{4}{3}$.............

.......................**Zapus princeps,** big jumping mouse, p. 576.

49' Body and tail with quills; facial opening of infraorbital canal larger than foramen magnum...........................**Erethizon epixanthum,** porcupine, p. 581.

48' Two incisor teeth on each side above (a minute tooth flat against the large anterior tooth). Order LAGOMORPHA.

105 Hind legs scarcely larger than forelegs; hind foot less than 40; nasals widest anteriorly; no supraorbital process on frontal; five cheek teeth on each side above...

....**Ochotona princeps,** pika, p. 587.

105' Hind legs larger than forelegs; hind foot more than 40; nasals widest posteriorly; supraorbital process on frontal; six cheek teeth on each side above.

Lepus californicus. × ¼.

Sylvilagus nuttallii. × ¼.

106 Hind foot more than 105; interparietal fused with parietals (see figs. 425–427, p. 594).

   107 Top of tail white (dark brownish in *L. americanus*, in summer); upper parts white in winter pelage; postorbital projection of supraorbital process not touching skull; anterior process absent or shorter than greatest width of posterior process.

      108 Hind foot more than 138; ear from notch more than 100; alveolar length of cheek teeth more than 14.5; supraorbital process with an anterior projection which is sometimes partly, but never entirely, fused along its medial border with frontal. . . . . **Lepus townsendii**, white-tailed jack rabbit, p. 598.

      108′ Hind foot less than 138; ear from notch less than 100; alveolar length of cheek teeth less than 14.5; supraorbital process without anterior projection. . . . . **Lepus americanus**, snowshoe rabbit, p. 601.

   107′ Top of tail black; upper parts not white in winter pelage; postorbital projection of supraorbital process touching skull, leaving an aperture; anterior process longer than greatest width of posterior process. . . . . **Lepus californicus**, black-tailed jack rabbit, p. 602.

106′ Hind foot less than 105; interparietal not fused with parietals (see fig. 439, p. 608).

   109 Tail white beneath; antorbital projection of supraorbital process less than ½ length of posterior projection; tip of posterior projection touches skull; alveolar length of cheek teeth more than 10.5; anterior face of first upper cheek tooth has three re-entrant angles (see fig. 442, p. 608).

      110 Ears of adults, measured from notch in flesh, less than 72 (less than 65 on dried skin); ears heavily haired on inner surface; antorbital projections of supraorbital processes pointed; posterior margin of palate usually without a spine; lateral diameters of posterior halves of second, third, and fourth lower molariform teeth amounting to ½ lateral diameters of anterior halves (for cranial features, see figs. 439–448, pp. 608, 609). . . . . **Sylvilagus nuttallii**, Nuttall cottontail, p. 607.

      110′ Ears of adults, measured from notch in flesh, more than 72 (more than 65 on dried skin); ears sparsely haired on inner surface; antorbital projections of supraorbital processes not pointed (blunted or serrated); posterior margin of palate usually with a spine; lateral diameters of posterior halves of second, third, and fourth lower molariform teeth amounting to about ⅘ lateral diameter of anterior halves (for cranial features, see figs. 439–448). . . . . **Sylvilagus audubonii**, Audubon cottontail, p. 612.

   109′ Tail not white (reddish buff) below; antorbital projection of supraorbital process more than ½ length of posterior process; tip of posterior projection not touching skull; alveolar length of cheek teeth less than 10.5; anterior face of first upper cheek tooth has one re-entrant angle (see fig. 444, p. 608). . . . . **Sylvilagus idahoensis**, pigmy rabbit, p. 614.

Cervus canadensis. × 1/40.

Odocoileus hemionus. × 1/40.

Antilocapra americana. × 1/40.

Ovis canadensis. × 1/40.

47′ No incisor teeth above; feet provided with hooves.

111 Males have antlers; females without antlers or horns.

112 Tail straw-colored; row of upper cheek teeth more than 110; knoblike canine tooth at union of maxillary and premaxillary bones.............

................................**Cervus canadensis,** wapiti, p. 618.

112′ Tail with black tip below white central part; row of upper cheek teeth less than 110; no canine tooth..

........................**Odocoileus hemionus,** black-tailed deer, p. 621.

111′ Males and females have horns (permanent bone core covered with horny sheath).

113 Underside of neck crossed by two white bars; horns with single fork in males, rarely 8 inches long in males and 2 inches in females; two hooves on each foot, there rarely being one additional false hoof; crown of M3 not more than 18 long...

.................**Antilocapra americana,** prong-horned antelope, p. 629.

113′ Underside of neck without white bars; horns not forked, but curving up, back, and down, and in males outward and upward at tip; horns more than 8 inches long; four hooves (including two false hooves) on each foot; crown of M3 more than 18 long.....................................

.............................**Ovis canadensis,** mountain sheep, p. 634.

ACCOUNTS OF SPECIES AND SUBSPECIES

Order INSECTIVORA
Insectivores

Scapanus latimanus
Broad-footed Mole

A true mole has velvety fur, broad flat forefeet, a long pointed snout, no external ear conchs, and at first glance appears to lack external eyes. By the two characters last mentioned, moles may be distinguished from their smaller relatives, the shrews, genus *Sorex*. Moles are larger than shrews and have a zygomatic arch that is lacking in their smaller relatives. The moles which occur in Nevada have more teeth (i. $\frac{3}{3}$, c. $\frac{1}{1}$, p. $\frac{4}{4}$, m. $\frac{3}{3}$) than any shrews found there, although this is not everywhere true outside of Nevada. Moles' teeth are adapted to a diet of insects and worms. Probably more than 99 per cent of a mole's life is spent underground where it makes runs of two sorts: one, commonly called mole-run, made by "swimming" along just beneath the surface of the ground so as to leave a raised ridge, and the other, made by digging at a greater depth and expelling the loose earth through a vertical shaft. The soil thus thrust up by the mole cascades down, leaving a concentrically ringed mound, as viewed from above, in contrast to the half-ringed mound of the pocket gopher which pushes its loads of excavated earth to the surface through an inclined tunnel, one load being thereby thrust out partly on top of the one before.

Moles have been found in Nevada only along the western edge of the state in the Hudsonian, Upper Sonoran, and intervening life-zones. This distribution may result from a varying degree of moisture in the soil. The greater rainfall in and near the Sierra Nevada and the soil moisture provided by seepage from the several streams which flow eastward from these mountains ensure soils moist enough to meet moles' needs throughout the year. As pointed out by Palmer (1937:281), moles cannot dig effectively in dry, baked soils, although certain soils which fail to attract moles in the dry season support them in a wet season. We noted evidence of this along the East Walker River in July, 1934. At that time the moles were confined to the moist soil along the river bank, but in the preceding spring they had worked several yards back from the river. This was shown by old workings in dry, baked soil, which at that earlier time had been moist enough to meet their needs. Evidence of this same extension and contraction of range, which is probably seasonal, in response to amount of moisture in the soil was noted 1 mile west of Hausen and at other places. Palmer (1937:283) points out also that "dry soils of a 'looser' type, in which moles can dig, probably are often uninhabited by moles because of the scarcity of invertebrate life suitable for food. The invertebrates that are present must be so adapted to high temperatures and aridity, by hard exoskeletons and other adaptations to prevent desiccation, that they are not of the type best suited for food. Also, the number of invertebrates in such dry situations is probably so low, as compared with their number in moister and

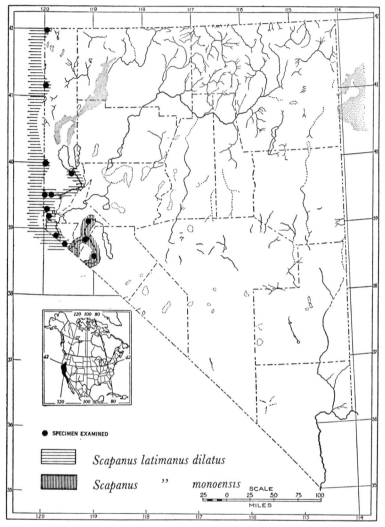

Fig. 8. Distribution of subspecies of the broad-footed mole, *Scapanus lati-manus*, with insert showing distribution of the species.

cooler soils, that their bulk in the forage radius of an individual mole is below its minimum food requirements."

It was Ward C. Russell's knowledge of moles' predilections for moist soils that enabled him to take most of our specimens. He caught moles even in relatively dry areas by saturating with water the ground around a mole sign before setting a mole trap of the stabbing variety.

Scapanus latimanus dilatus True
Broad-footed Mole

Scapanus dilatus True, Diagnoses of new North American mammals, p. 2, April 26, 1894 (reprint: Proc. U. S. Nat. Mus., 17:242, November 15, 1894). Type from Fort Klamath, Oregon.
Scapanus latimanus dilatus, Grinnell, Proc. California Acad. Sci., 3:270, August 28, 1913; Jackson, N. Amer. Fauna, 38:72, September 30, 1915; Palmer, Journ. Mamm., 18:291, August 14, 1937.

Distribution.—Moist soils along western border of state south to central Douglas County. See figure 8.

Remarks.—Measurements of five males from 12-mile Creek, N side State-line Peak, ½ mi. W Verdi, 3 mi. S and ½ mi. W Mt. Rose, and 3 mi. S Mt. Rose are, respectively, as follows: 190, 171, 176, 153, 151; 36, 31, 41, 32, 36; 21, 22, 22, 22, 22; weight, 85.0, 76.5, 65.5, ——, —— grams. No undoubted females are available. The secondary sexual difference in size is thought to be less than in the subspecies *monoensis* (see Palmer, 1937:287).

Compared with the one other subspecies, *monoensis*, found in Nevada, *dilatus* differs in: external measurements larger; skull longer and relatively narrower; upper tooth rows less sharply bent; bar lateral to infraorbital foramen thicker and more nearly vertical; interorbital constriction more marked; foramen magnum not encroaching so far dorsally into supraoccipital.

In the southern part of its range, near that of the smaller *monoensis*, specimens of *dilatus* average smaller. The measurements of a skull of a specimen from the East Fork of the Carson River, south and east of Minden, are instructive in this regard, because they are intermediate between those of *monoensis* and *dilatus*, although, all points considered, they show greater resemblance to the latter. The skull is long (35.5 mm.), as in *dilatus*, and a unique feature is the slight (4.1 mm.) rostral breadth. A specimen from the West Fork of the Walker River, 10½ miles south of Yerington, referred to *monoensis*, shows some resemblance to *dilatus*. These two specimens provide good evidence of intergradation between *dilatus* and *monoensis*. The specimen from Holbrook recorded by Jackson (1915: 74) has not been examined.

Records of occurrence.—Specimens examined, 10, as follows: *Washoe Co.:* 12-mile Cr., ½ mi. E Calif. boundary, 5300 ft., 1; N side State-line Peak, 4400 ft., 1; W side Truckee River, 4900 ft., ½ mi. W Verdi, 1; 3 mi. W Reno, 2; 3 mi. S and ½ mi. W Mt. Rose, 1; 3 mi. S Mt. Rose, 2; Marlette Lake, 8000 ft., 1. *Douglas Co.:* 5 mi. S and 3¾ mi. E Minden, 4900 ft., 1.
Additional records: *Washoe Co.:* (Hall, on July 15, 1934, noted "workings") 1 mi. W Hausen, 4650 ft.; (Alcorn, MS, noted "workings") S end Pyramid Lake, 4 mi. W Nixon; (Carl P. Russell, MS) 2 mi. S Reno. *Douglas Co.:* (Jackson, 1915:74) Holbrook.

Scapanus latimanus monoensis Grinnell
Broad-footed Mole

Scapanus latimanus monoensis Grinnell, Univ. California Publ. Zoöl., 17:423, April 25, 1918. Type from Taylor Ranch, 2 miles south of Benton Station, Mono County, California; Palmer, Journ. Mamm., 18:307, August 14, 1937.

Distribution.—Moist soils along Walker River and its forks from near Wabuska southwestward to California border. See figure 8.

Remarks.—Measurements of three males, nos. 63517, 63518, 63520, and one female, no. 63519 (all but 63517 from Lyon Co.), are as follows: 169, 162, 169, 163; 36,

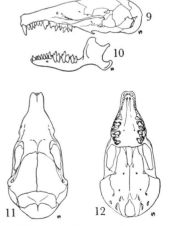

Figs. 9–12. *Scapanus latimanus monoensis*, East Walker River, 2 miles northwest Morgans Ranch, no. 63520, ♂. × 1.

36, 38, 34; 20, 21, 22, 21; weight, 69.5, 61.9, 58.7, 52.2 grams. The generally smaller size of the female is typical of this subspecies.

Comparison with *Scapanus latimanus dilatus* is made in the account of that form. Palmer (1937:308) has pointed out that the male from the West Walker River, 10½ miles south

TABLE 1
CRANIAL MEASUREMENTS* (IN MILLIMETERS) OF SCAPANUS

Sex	Catalogue no.	Greatest length of skull	Palatal length	Mastoidal breadth	Interorbital breadth	Maxillary breadth	Rostral breadth	Depth of skull	Length of orbit	Maxillary tooth row	Mandibular molar-premolar row
					Scapanus latimanus dilatus 12-mile Creek						
♂	73111	36.4	16.3	17.2	7.6	10.2	4.9	9.9	7.8	11.2	11.0
					½ mi. W Verdi						
♂	73112	35.9	15.9	16.7	7.6	9.8	4.5	10.1	8.4	10.9	10.7
					3 mi. S and ½ mi. W Mount Rose						
♂	88229	35.3	15.6	16.8	8.0	9.6	4.2	10.1	7.8	11.1	11.1
					3 mi. S Mount Rose						
♂	88230	34.8	15.7	16.8	7.9	9.7	4.3	9.9	8.0	11.2	11.1
					Scapanus latimanus monoensis 10½ mi. S Yerington						
♂	63517	34.1	15.2	17.2	7.9	10.3	4.7	10.1	7.8	10.0	10.1
					2 mi. NW Morgans Ranch						
♂	63518	32.8	14.8	16.4	7.5	9.7	4.4	9.5	7.5	9.7	10.2
♂	63520	33.2	14.5	16.6	7.8	9.7	4.3	10.2	7.1	10.1	10.0
♀	63519	32.6	14.4	16.0	7.2	9.4	4.0	9.8	7.1	10.1	10.1

* Measurements as taken by Palmer (1937:287).

of Yerington, is larger than any one of the males from the East Walker River. Possibly this is to be interpreted as intergradation with *dilatus*. The specimen from the East Fork Carson River, referred to *dilatus*, strengthens this possibility because it is still larger and is from a place farther north, toward the range of *dilatus*. Palmer (*loc. cit.*) has noted also that the Nevadan specimens from near Morgans Ranch have rostra broader than topotypes of *monoensis*.

Records of occurrence.—Specimens examined, 4, as follows: *Lyon Co.:* West Walker River, 10½ mi. S Yering-ton, 4500 ft., 1. *Mineral Co.:* East Walker River, 2 mi. NW Morgans Ranch, 5050 ft., 3.
Additional record (Alcorn, MS): in bend of Walker River, 4½ mi. E Wabuska.

Genus **Sorex** Linnaeus
Long-tailed Shrews

Long-tailed shrews average smaller in size than mice, have a long, sharp-pointed nose, velvetlike pelage, forefeet only about the size of the hind feet, minute but evident eyes, a well-developed ear conch, skull with all bones

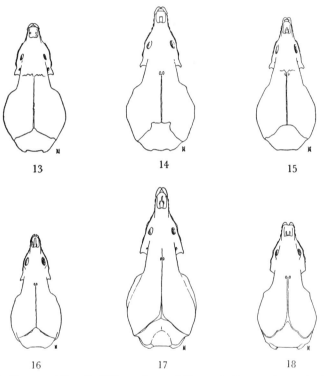

Figs. 13–18. Shrews. All, ×2. (Other views of these skulls are shown in figs. 19–31.)
Fig. 13. *Sorex merriami leucogenys,* Chiatovich Creek, no. 38398, ♀.
Fig. 14. *Sorex trowbridgii mariposae,* ½ mile northeast Dutch Flat, Placer County, California, no. 88148, ♀.
Fig. 15. *Sorex vagrans amoenus,* Baker Creek, 11,100 feet, no. 88042, ♀.
Fig. 16. *Sorex tenellus,* Rainbow Falls, no. 86842, ♂.
Fig. 17. *Sorex palustris navigator,* Cottonwood Creek, Mount Grant, 7400 feet, no. 63521, ♂.
Fig. 18. *Notiosorex crawfordi crawfordi,* 5 miles east and 1 mile north Grapevine Peak, no. 92391, ♂.

anastomosed in adults, no zygomatic arch, posterior border of palate truncate, and teeth characterized by an enlarged first incisor both above and below, followed by a series of teeth essentially unicuspidate back to P3 and m1 which, with succeeding teeth, have high cusps adapted to an insectivorous diet. The dental formula is i. $\frac{3}{1}$, c. $\frac{1}{1}$, p. $\frac{3}{1}$, m. $\frac{3}{3}$. The teeth are in a continuous row and are sharp-pointed. By either of these features shrews can be conveniently differentiated from other kinds of Nevadan mammals of about the same size except bats. The other small mammals are rodents and all have a space (diastema) between the first incisor tooth and the more posterior teeth. The smallest mammal in Nevada is a shrew, probably *Sorex tenellus.*

Judging from our experience, all kinds of Nevadan *Sorex*, except *S. merriami* and possibly *S. tenellus,* are restricted to the vicinity of water. Even so, traps set in moist places usually are much more productive of rodents than of shrews, and the total number of shrews in Nevada probably is small as compared with the number in a better watered area of similar extent at the same or a higher latitude.

No bait that we tried was especially effective in attracting shrews. We obtained most of them by so placing the trap that the shrew necessarily crossed the treadle in following along a runway. The scent left on a trap by a caught shrew may attract other shrews; at any rate the trap which catches a shrew on one night, more often than any other trap, catches another the following night.

Traps left set for 48 hours or more generally caught shrews only at night; this I take as evidence that shrews are nocturnal or that they are active aboveground mostly at night.

Shrews rely primarily upon insects for food but, at least in captivity, are carnivorous; I have found small, partly eaten mice in traps under circumstances which suggested that they had been fed upon by shrews.

Eight kinds of long-tailed shrews, belonging to six full species, have been found in the state.

Sorex merriami
Merriam Shrew

The Merriam shrew frequents places drier than those in which other kinds of shrews live. The area of its range as a whole is arid. The specimen from Mount Magruder was trapped (L. M. Huey, *in litt.*) on a dry hillside amid sagebrush. The specimen taken by Miss Louise Kellogg in the near-by White Mountains was trapped "among sage brush on the floor of the narrow canyon whose sides were clothed with juniper, pinyon and sage brush, although the edge of the creek was fringed with aspens, willows and cottonwoods" (Hall, 1933:153). The third Nevadan specimen is from Desert Ranch where, according to Jackson (1928:80), Edmund Heller recovered it from a house cat. The pale color of these shrews parallels that of other mammals which live in arid regions.

The shrew from Mount Magruder contained two embryos, a small number relative to that recorded for any other kind of *Sorex.*

The specimen from Chiatovich Creek is near (*j*) Hair Brown above and whitish below.The feet are whitish and the tail is distinctly bicolored. Measurements are given in table 1. The skull is relatively short and broad. The third unicuspid is larger than the fourth.

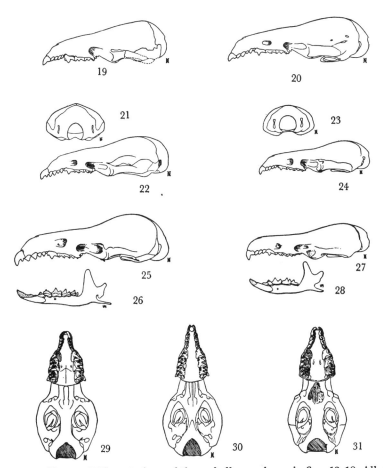

Figs. 19–31. Shrews. Different views of these skulls are shown in figs. 13–18. All, × 2.

Fig. 19. *Sorex merriami leucogenys*.
Fig. 20. *Sorex trowbridgii mariposae*.
Figs. 21, 22. *Sorex vagrans amoenus*.
Figs. 23, 24. *Sorex tenellus*.
Figs. 25, 26. *Sorex palustris navigator*.

Figs. 27, 28. *Notiosorex crawfordi crawfordi*.
Fig. 29. *Sorex merriami leucogenys*.
Fig. 30. *Sorex vagrans amoenus*.
Fig. 31. *Notiosorex crawfordi crawfordi*.

Sorex merriami merriami Dobson
Merriam Shrew

Sorex merriami Dobson, Monograph of the Insectivora, systematic and anatomical, part 3, fasc. 1, pl. 23, fig. 6, May, 1890. Type from Fort Custer, Bighorn County, Montana; Jackson, N. Amer. Fauna, 51:78, July, 1928.
Sorex merriami merriami, Benson and Bond, Journ. Mamm., 20:348, August 14, 1939.

Distribution.—Known from Desert Ranch, 100 miles northeast of Golconda, in Elko County. See figure 32.

Remarks.—Benson and Bond (1939:350), on the basis of the inadequate material available for study, point out that *merriami*, in comparison with *S. m. leucogenys*, differs as

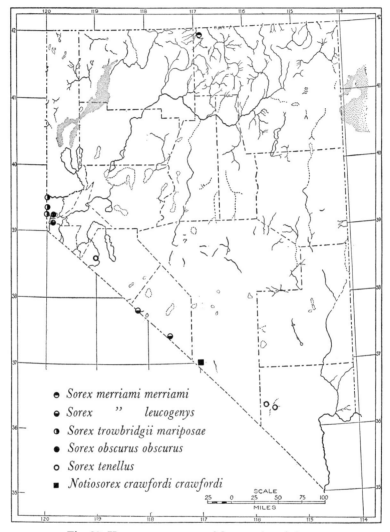

● *Sorex merriami merriami*
◔ *Sorex   ”   leucogenys*
◑ *Sorex trowbridgii mariposae*
● *Sorex obscurus obscurus*
○ *Sorex tenellus*
■ *Notiosorex crawfordi crawfordi*

SCALE
25   0   25   50   75   100
MILES

Fig. 32. Known occurrences of five species of shrews.

follows: actually smaller in total length, length of hind foot, condylobasal length, and cranial breadth; averages smaller in all measurements except least interorbital breadth. The exception, "least interorbital breadth," noted by Benson and Bond may not be an exception, because Jackson's measurements recorded by them were of "interorbital breadth," not "least interorbital breadth." Relative to the condylobasal length, the palate is longer and the maxillary breadth greater.

Record of occurrence.—(Jackson, 1928:81) *Elko Co.:* Desert Ranch, 100 mi. NE Golconda.

Sorex merriami leucogenys Osgood
Merriam Shrew

Sorex leucogenys Osgood, Proc. Biol. Soc. Washington, 22:52, April 17, 1909. Type from mouth of the canyon of Beaver River, about 3 miles east of Beaver, Beaver County, Utah; Jackson, N. Amer. Fauna, 51:81, July, 1928; Hall, Journ. Mamm., 13:260, August 9, 1932; Hall, Journ. Mamm., 14:154, May 15, 1933.

Sorex merriami leucogenys, Benson and Bond, Journ. Mamm., 20:348, August 14, 1939.

Distribution.—Known from two localities near the western border of Esmeralda County. See figure 32.

Remarks.—Measurements of two females from Chiatovich Creek and Mount Magruder are, respectively, as follows: 97, 105; 36, 40; 12, 12; weights not available. Comparison with *S. m. merriami* is made in the account of that form.

Records of occurrence.—Specimens examined, 2, as follows: *Esmeralda Co.:* Chiatovich Creek, 8200 ft., 1; Indian Spring [about ½ mi. SE of], 7700 ft., Mount Magruder, 1 (D. R. Dickey Coll.).

Sorex trowbridgii mariposae Grinnell
Trowbridge Shrew

Sorex montereyensis mariposae Grinnell, Univ. California Publ. Zoöl., 10:189, March 20, 1913. Type from Yosemite Valley, 4000 feet, Mariposa County, California.

Sorex trowbridgii mariposae Grinnell, Univ. California Publ. Zoöl., 21:314, January 27, 1923; Jackson, N. Amer. Fauna, 51:98, July, 1928.

Distribution.—Southwestern Washoe County. See figure 32.

Remarks.—Measurements of a male and female from Incline Creek are: 131, 114; 60, 44; 14, 14; weights unavailable.

Of our two specimens, both taken by J. R. Alcorn, one was trapped among dry pine needles under conifers about 15 feet from Incline Creek at a place approximately a half mile from Lake Tahoe, and the second, in a moist place near the head of Incline Creek.

External features useful in identifying this species are the dark-colored underparts which are scarcely, if at all, paler than the upper parts, and the sharply bicolored tail, the average length of which is greater than that in any other shrew except the water shrew.

In the skulls the third upper unicuspid is smaller than the fourth. In contrast to the condition in *vagrans*, the ridge which extends lingually from the apex of the unicuspid toward the cingulum is only slightly pigmented (rarely pigmented to the cingulum), is separated from the cingulum by an antero-posterior groove, and never ends in a distinct cusplet. The teeth are narrower than in *obscurus*, and the skull is larger than in *tenellus*.

The actual range in Nevada of this species probably is not much more extensive than our records of occurrence indicate; the species ranges in the more humid territory of the Pacific coastal region from southern British Columbia south into California.

Records of occurrence.—Specimens examined, 2, as follows: *Washoe Co.:* 3 mi. S Mt. Rose, 8500 ft., 1; Incline (½ mi. N, up Creek), 1.

Additional record: (Jackson, 1928:100) Verdi.

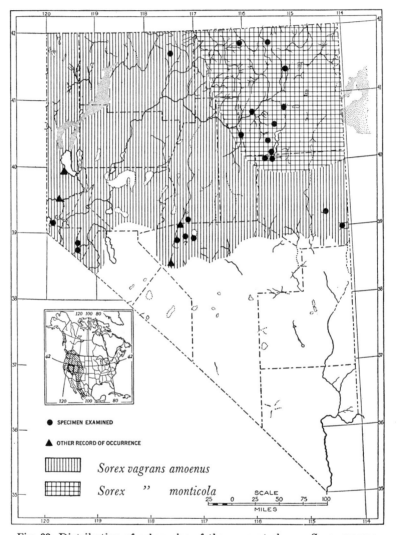

Fig. 33. Distribution of subspecies of the vagrant shrew, *Sorex vagrans*, with insert showing range of the species.

Sorex vagrans

Vagrant Shrew

This shrew and the water shrew are the two species most commonly taken in the state, and each has about the same area of geographic distribution.

The vagrant shrew has a total length of less than 120 mm.; above, in winter pelage, it is Fuscous-Black, with sides more drab-colored and underparts Smoke Gray, which gives it a tricolor pattern. The tail is indistinctly bicolor. In summer the upper parts and sides are slightly more brownish and differ from one another less than they do in winter. *S. vagrans* is easily confused with *S. obscurus*, but *vagrans* has a shorter tail, narrower rostral and inter-orbital regions, a shorter palate, smaller unicuspid teeth, and a brain case that is more nearly flat.

Specimens were taken mostly on the banks of streams or in marshy places. Only rarely was one taken on drier ground as far as 20 feet from water. In August, 1939, Alcorn (MS) took this species in mousetraps baited with rolled oats at 7000 feet in Kingston Canyon and at 11,100 feet on Baker Creek. At each place, a number of his traps, which were so large as easily to miss catching a shrew when sprung, had been set off supposedly by shrews. Shrew droppings on the traps were the basis for this supposition and suggested also that the animals were attracted to the bait of rolled oats which at other places, in my experience, shrews have generally disregarded.

The two specimens from Smiths Valley are young; the teeth are not fully erupted. Richard M. Bond took them from the stomach of a snake (*Coluber constrictor mormon*) on June 9, 1939.

Of the ten females judged, by wear on the teeth, to be old enough to have young, two were taken in June and eight in July. Four taken on July 24 and after contained embryos; three had five and the other had six.

Sorex vagrans amoenus Merriam
Vagrant Shrew

Sorex amoenus Merriam, N. Amer. Fauna, 10:69, December 31, 1895. Type from near Mammoth, 8000 feet, head of Owens River, Mono County, California.
Sorex vagrans amoenus Merriam, N. Amer. Fauna, 16:87, October 28, 1899.
Sorex nevadensis Merriam, N. Amer. Fauna, 10:71, December 31, 1895. Type from Reese River, 6000 feet, at line between Lander and Nye counties, Nevada.
Sorex vagrans nevadensis, Jackson, N. Amer. Fauna, 51:107, July, 1928.
Sorex vagrans, Linsdale, Amer. Midland Nat., 19:173, January, 1938.

Distribution.—Central Nevada from western to eastern border. See figure 33.

Remarks.—Measurements of five males showing wear on the teeth (two from Baker Creek and three from Toyabe Mts.) are: 97 (90–104), 35 (33–39), 13 (12–14). Each of two males weighed 6.7 grams.

From *S. v. monticola*, *amoenus* differs in more brownish (less grayish) color of the upper parts, smaller size, narrower rostrum, and, as apparent in dorsal contour of skull in longitudinal axis, more abrupt angle between brain case and preorbital part of skull.

The shrew named *Sorex nevadensis* by Merriam was known to him, and to Jackson (1928:107) when he revised the genus, by no more than four specimens, some of which were not adult. We have eleven specimens from the vicinity of the type locality, of which, un-fortunately, only two show much wear on the teeth. One of these has a skull that shows none of the features (more nearly flat skull, and weaker, more attenuated rostrum) alleged to be diagnostic of *nevadensis;* indeed, this skull has a heavier rostrum than even an average individual of *amoenus*, and its skull is not more flattened than in *amoenus*. The second adult skull has a narrower rostrum and a brain case more nearly flat, but I cannot distinguish it from many specimens of *amoenus* from California. Other differential characters by means of which *nevadensis* might be distinguished from *amoenus* have been sought, but with slight success. The topotypes of *nevadensis* are, by a barely appreciable degree, lighter colored than those of *amoenus* (summer pelages principally concerned). This lighter color is an approach toward the color of *monticola* and might well be regarded as evidence of intergradation between *amoenus* and *monticola*. Our specimens suggest also that *nevadensis* may average smaller than *amoenus*, but the difference, if there be any, is of only an average nature and slight in degree. It would seem, therefore, that Jackson (1928:108) was justified in regarding the status of *nevadensis* as "unsatisfactorily determined" and in saying that final decision will require additional topotypes that are fully adult. Study of the more abundant material, which in 1928 was unavailable to Jackson, increases the probability that *nevadensis* is indistinguishable from *amoenus*. Accordingly, the name *nevadensis* here is arranged as a synonym of *amoenus* which has priority.

The specimens from Baker Creek near the eastern border of Nevada agree with *amoenus*. The single specimen from north of Paradise Valley, which has only a slight amount of wear on the teeth, resembles *monticola* in total length and maxillary breadth, is intermediate in color between *monticola* and *amoenus*, and agrees with the latter in other features.

Records of occurrence.—Specimens examined, 29, as follows: *Ormsby Co.:* Marlette Lake, 8000 ft., 2; ½ mi. S Marlette Lake, 8150 ft., 2. *Lyon Co.:* West Walker River, ¼ mi. W Wellington, 5000 ft., 2 (coll. of J. R. Alcorn); 2 mi. S Hinds Hot Spring[s], 4700 ft., Smith[s] Valley, 2. *Humboldt Co.:* 13 mi. N Paradise Valley, 6700 ft., 1. *Lander Co.:* Kingston Ranger Station, 7500 ft., 3; Kingston Canyon, 7000 ft., 1. *Nye Co.:* Wisconsin Creek, 7800 ft., 3; 5 mi. SE Millett P. O., 5500 ft., 2; Bells Ranch, Reese River, 6890 ft., 2. *White Pine Co.:* Cleveland Ranch, 6000 ft., Spring Valley, 2; Baker Creek (11,100 ft., 4; 8000 ft., 2; 6600 ft., 1), 7.

Additional records: *Washoe Co.:* Hardscrabble Canyon, 5000 ft. [west side Pyramid Lake] (D. G. Nichols, MS, specimen in Amer. Mus. Nat. Hist.); Reno (Jackson, 1928:110). *Nye ? Co.:* Reese River, at line between Lander and Nye counties, Cloverdale (Jackson, *op. cit.:* 108).

Sorex vagrans monticola Merriam
Vagrant Shrew

Sorex monticolus Merriam, N. Amer. Fauna, 3:43, September 11, 1890. Type from San Francisco Mountain, 11,500 feet, Coconino County, Arizona.
Sorex vagrans monticola Merriam, N. Amer. Fauna, 10:69, December 31, 1895.
Sorex vagrans amoenus, Jackson (part), N. Amer. Fauna, 51:110, July, 1928; Borell and Ellis, Journ. Mamm., 15:18, 72, February 15, 1934.

Distribution.—Roughly northeastern fourth of state. See figure 33.

Remarks.—Measurements of sixteen males and females from the Ruby Mountains showing much wear on the teeth are: 108 (94–115), 39 (34–46), 12 (10–13). An adult from Evans hardly as large, I think, as the average for this race in Nevada weighed 6.8 grams.

Comparison with *S. v. amoenus* is made in the account of that form where comment is made also on the name *Sorex nevadensis* Merriam. Thirteen specimens from northeastern Nevada, which Jackson (1928:110), without comment, assigned to *amoenus* (in his revisionary paper), are here referred to *Sorex vagrans monticola*. This area of northeastern Nevada is separated, by nearly 230 miles, from the main range of *amoenus* (Sierra Nevada and southern Cascades), but adjoins the known range of *monticola*. Borell and Ellis (1934a:19), in identifying specimens from the Ruby Mountains, pointed out that their material was intermediate in character between *amoenus* on the west and *monticola* on the east, and said that the name *monticola* could apply as well as *amoenus*. In deference to Jackson's monographic treatment, they employed the name *amoenus*. From study of the specimens used by Borell and Ellis and also of additional material, it seems clear that this population in northeastern Nevada is referable to *monticola*. In detail, the specimens from the Ruby Mountains, although intermediate between *amoenus* and *monticola*, are nearer the latter in light (grayish) color, total length, cranial breadth and maxillary breadth, and geographic point of origin. Specimens from Cobb Creek and the Jarbidge Mountains agree with those from the Ruby Mountains. One from Marys River also agrees with *monticola* in most features, although it has a lesser maxillary breadth, as in *amoenus*. The single specimen (with much worn teeth) from Evans is intermediate between *amoenus* and *monticola* in some characters and in geographic point of origin; the total length is exactly intermediate. The skull is more nearly flat, and the maxillary breadth is less than in *monticola* but more than in *amoenus*. The heavy rostrum and broad brain case are as in *monticola*; indeed, the brain case is wider than in average specimens of *monticola*. A unique feature is the short tail (34 mm.), which is shorter than in any other specimen seen. The single specimen from 13 miles north of Paradise Valley, here referred to *amoenus*, in all its characters is almost exactly intermediate between *amoenus* and *monticola* and might with almost equal propriety be referred to either subspecies.

To make clear the basis of comparisons, it may be said that the same material of *amoenus* and *monticola* listed by Borell and Ellis (1934a:19) has here been employed. From the findings detailed above and in the account of *amoenus*, it is concluded that: *S. v. monticola* and *S. v. amoenus* are the two races of *S. vagrans* occurring in Nevada; these two races intergrade in Nevada; the name *S. v. nevadensis* is not recognized as a valid race and is placed as a synonym of *S. v. amoenus*.

Records of occurrence.—Specimens examined, 38 (unless otherwise noted, in the coll. of Ralph Ellis), as follows: *Eureka Co.:* Evans, 1 (Mus. Vert. Zoöl.). *Elko Co.:* Cobb Creek, 6 mi. SW Mountain City, 6500 ft., 2 (Mus. Vert. Zoöl.); summit between heads of Copper and Coon creeks, Jarbidge Mts., 3; Marys River, 22 mi. N Deeth, 5800 ft., 1 (Mus. Vert. Zoöl.); W side Humboldt River, 8 mi. WSW Elko, 5000 ft., 2 (coll. of J. R. Alcorn); summit of Secret Pass, 6200 ft., 2; Three Lakes, 9700 ft., 4; Long Creek, 7830 ft., 6; Harrison Pass Ranger Station, 6050 ft., 5; W side Ruby Lake, 3 mi. N White Pine Co. line, 6200 ft., 9 (1 in Mus. Vert. Zoöl.). *White Pine Co.:* Willow Creek, 2 mi. S Elko Co. line, 6500 ft., 2; W side Ruby Lake, 3 mi. S Elko Co. line, 6100 ft., 1.

Additional record: (Jackson, 1928:110) Mountain City.

Sorex obscurus obscurus Merriam
Dusky Shrew

Sorex obscurus Merriam, N. Amer. Fauna, 10:72, December 31, 1895 (renaming of *similis* Merriam).
Type from Timber Creek, 8200 feet, Lemhi Mountains, Lemhi County, Idaho.
Sorex vagrans similis Merriam, N. Amer. Fauna, 5:34, July 31, 1891 (name preoccupied).

Distribution.—Known only from the high Sierra Nevada east of Lake Tahoe. See figure 32, page 116.

Remarks.—Measurements of a male from Marlette Lake are: 110, 38, 12. Weight not available.

Search for this shrew of Boreal predilections was productive only at Marlette Lake and along the little stream running into its southern end. In this watershed, protected from grazing by domestic stock, the original flora and fauna are relatively undisturbed, and the dusky shrew here finds suitable habitat along the mossy-banked brooks which flow through channels cut in the deep accumulation of red fir  needles and other plant materials now constituting a thick covering over the granitic rocks. This covering is rich in insect life and is probably attractive to shrews; vagrant shrews and water shrews were taken along with the dusky shrew. *S. obscurus* previously had not been recorded from Nevada and it may occur in the state only in this high mountain area on the eastern side of Lake Tahoe where Wm. H. Dust saved the first specimens.

The brownish summer coat and more grayish winter coat, each with paler underparts and bicolored tail, hardly permit certain separation of *obscurus* from the slightly smaller *Sorex vagrans amoenus* on the basis of external characters alone. These external characters, the longer tail of *obscurus*, and the cranial characters, however, permit a person to distinguish specimens of the two species with fair ease. The cranial features in *obscurus* most apparent to me are: rostrum and interorbital region broader, palate longer, unicuspids larger, posterior part of top of brain case more raised (less flattened).

Records of occurrence.—Specimens examined, 5, as follows: *Washoe Co.:* Marlette Lake, 8000 ft., 2. *Ormsby Co.:* Marlette Lake, 8000 ft., 1; ½ mi. S Marlette Lake, 8150 ft., 2.

Sorex tenellus Merriam
Dwarf Shrew

Sorex tenellus Merriam, N. Amer. Fauna, 10:81, December 31, 1895. Type from Pipers Creek (Cottonwood Creek), near main peak of White Mountains, 9500 feet, Mono County, California.
Sorex myops, Burt, Trans. San Diego Soc. Nat. Hist., 7:391, May 31, 1934.

Distribution.—Along western border of state; known from Charleston Peak and East Walker River. See figure 32, page 116.

Remarks.—Measurements of seven of each sex, from Charleston Peak, are: ♂, 91 (86–95), ♀, 88 (85–91); 40 (37–41), 39 (36–41); 10.7 (10–11), 10.3 (9–11); weight of one male, 3.4 grams.

This small shrew of the *Sorex ornatus* group was found by Burt (1934:391) at three localities on Charleston Peak in shaded, damp situations near decaying logs and along the bases of cliffs in the bottoms of canyons not farther than 300 yards from running water. One shrew which Burt watched run across the treadle of a trap that caught the animal at early dusk led him to wonder if the species was habitually crepuscular as well as nocturnal. This observation also provided additional evidence for supposing that many of the shrews were caught because the treadle of the trap was placed in their path rather than because the shrews were attracted to the bait provided on traps. Burt (*loc. cit.*) mentions that 275 trap-nights, in late June and early July of 1928, on the bottom of one canyon yielded seven shrews and ninety-three *Peromyscus*. In June of 1939 Miss Annie M. Alexander and Miss Louise Kellogg trapped in places where Burt had obtained specimens, and caught fewer shrews per 100 trap-nights. The specimen from near Wichman was trapped on December 29, 1939, by Donald V. Hemphill near the base of a south-facing slope on the north side of the Walker River, about 100 yards from the stream, beneath a lava boulder, where *Artemisia tridentata*, *Ephedra*, and *Chrysothamnus* were the conspicuous plants.

The one specimen examined from Charleston Peak is drab grayish above and lighter, whitish, below, rivaling *S. m. leucogenys*, among Nevadan shrews, in pallor of coloration. From other Nevadan shrews of this general size, *tenellus* may be separated, when skulls are viewed posteriorly, by the fact that the foramen magnum encroaches dorsally, half way or more, into the total area of the occiput. In the other species the foramen magnum does not encroach so far into the supraoccipital. Other cranial features of *tenellus* are the lesser encroachment, than in *obscurus, vagrans, trowbridgii,* or *merriami,* of the foramen magnum into the basioccipital, and the smaller, more flattened skull.

Jackson (1928:173, 174) differentiated *tenellus,* known to him by one specimen, from *S. myops,* of which he had but two specimens, on the basis of narrower interorbital and rostral regions and weaker dentition. His measurements of interorbital breadth, maxillary breadth, and length of maxillary tooth row indicate these differences. Later, Burt (1934: 392) published measurements of thirteen specimens from Charleston Peak. The cranial measurements of the specimen of *tenellus* all fall within the extremes of the measurements of the series of specimens from Charleston Peak. Seemingly, therefore, *S. myops* falls as a synonym of *S. tenellus* which has more than 6 years' priority. The measurements of the specimen from ¼ mi. N Wichman fall within the range of variation shown by the series of specimens from Charleston Peak (Burt, *loc. cit.*), except in cranial breadth and maxillary breadth, which are, respectively, 0.1 millimeter and 0.2 millimeter larger. Nevertheless, these measurements are nearer to those of *tenellus* than to those of *S. o. ornatus,* but the maxillary breadth is as in *S. o. californicus,* known from the opposite, western, side of the Sierra Nevada. The cranial breadth, although, as indicated, a little larger than in any known *tenellus,* is still considerably less than in *californicus.* Although the specimen from near Wichman bridges the gap between *tenellus* (including *myops*) and *californicus* in some degree, and although it is geographically intermediate between these two races, here the conservative choice of treating *tenellus* as specifically distinct from *californicus* is made for the present. The one specimen at hand of *S. tenellus* from Charleston Peak and the specimen from Wichman almost agree in coloration and are considerably lighter colored than any specimen examined of thirty-four *californicus* or sixty of the subspecies *ornatus,* which is also a more western race of the species *ornatus.* The June-taken *tenellus* from Charleston Peak may be lighter colored by a slight degree than the December-taken specimen from Wichman.

Records of occurrence.—Specimens examined, 13 (unless otherwise noted, in D. R. Dickey Coll.), as follows: *Mineral Co.:* ¼ mi. N Wichman, 5500 ft., 1 (Mus. Vert. Zoöl.). *Clark Co.:* Clark Canyon, 8000 ft., 2; Kyle Canyon, 10,000 ft., 7; Rainbow Falls, 8200 ft., Kyle Canyon, 1 (Mus. Vert. Zoöl.); Kyle Canyon, 8000 ft., 2.

Sorex palustris navigator (Baird)
Water Shrew

Neosorex navigator Baird, Rept. Pacific R. R. Surv., 8; pt. 1, mammals, p. 11, 1857. Type from near head of Yakima River, Cascade Mountains, Washington.
Sorex palustris navigator, Stephens, California Mammals, p. 254, June, 1906; Taylor, Univ. California Publ. Zoöl., 7:301, June 24, 1911; Borell and Ellis, Journ. Mamm., 15:19, 72, February 15, 1934.
Sorex palustris, Linsdale, Amer. Midland Nat., 19:173, January, 1938.

Distribution.—Along rushing mountain streams from the White Mountains, Toyabe Mountains, and Snake Range northward in suitable habitat over the state. See figure 34.

Remarks.—Measurements of ten of each sex, showing marked wear on the teeth, from various localities in the state, are: ♂, 150 (140–159), ♀, 151 (142–162); 67 (57–71), 69 (58–78); 19.8 (18–21), 19.8 (19–21); weights of three males and seven females the teeth of which are much or moderately worn are, ♂, 14.2 (13.1–16.3), ♀, 13.2 (10.8–17.6) grams.

Size largest of Nevadan shrews; Fuscous-Black above, finely marked with white-tipped hairs; underparts lighter, often Light Grayish Olive but varying to Pale Smoke Gray; tail bicolored; winter pelage slightly less brownish; feet conspicuously fringed with hair which apparently provides added swimming ability; skull large, with condylobasal length more than 18.7 and cranial

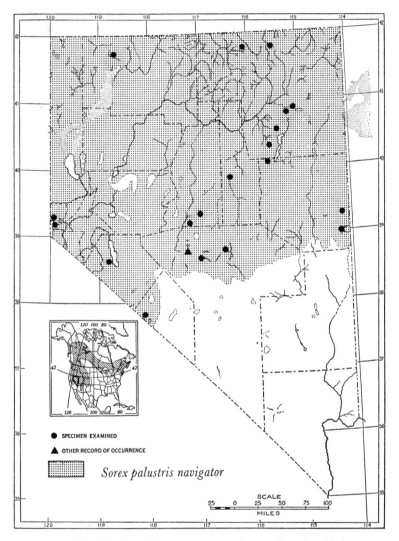

Fig. 34. Distribution of the water shrew, *Sorex palustris*, with insert showing range of the species.

breadth more than 9.2. The large size, fimbriated feet, long tail, and "silvery" coloration permit ready differentiation of this species from any other shrew in the state.

Although widely distributed over Nevada, the water shrew is narrowly restricted in habitat to cold mountain streams or their borders. About as many of our specimens were taken by traps set in the water as by those set at the water's edge. At Chiatovich Ranch we found it profitable to adopt R. A. Stirton's suggestion of extending out from each bank a board floating on edge on the surface of the water. Near midstream the ends of the boards were fastened by a wire so as to leave a 4-inch gap. A mousetrap secured in this gap caught several of the animals that presumably had been swimming downstream on the surface. In this way a fair series of specimens was obtained. This place, only 4900 feet in elevation, was the lowest point at which water shrews have been found in the state. Even at this low elevation, the cold water, from melting snow above, densely shaded by trees and shrubs, provided a cool habitat which permitted the animals to live in the narrow confines of the stream here, in the lower edge of the Upper Sonoran Life-zone, almost as well as in the Canadian Life-zone. I say almost as well, because I judge that a larger number of water shrews would have been obtained with the same effort at some places at higher elevations.

The fringe of stiff hairs on the sides of the feet which gives the animal greater propulsive power when swimming is one adaptation to a life in the water. Another aquatic adaptation is the imperviousness of the pelage to water. On Hendry Creek, David H. Johnson (MS) noted that only the tips of the hair were wet in a specimen which, caught in a trap, fell in the stream and remained immersed until he found it next morning. The bases of the hair and the skin were dry. The exceptional swimming ability was noted by Alcorn (MS) on May 13, 1939, at Kingston Creek, when he watched a shrew of this species swimming under water, with an almost unbelievable rapidity, back and forth over a 2-foot area near the center of a quiet pool. The reason for this extraordinary behavior was not learned, although the animal, finally obtained as a specimen, was observed for some time. It proved to be a female with mammary glands in a condition which suggested that she was nursing young.

Eleven females judged by amount of wear on the teeth to be old enough to bear young were taken, by months, as follows: May, 1; June, 4; July, 5; August, 2. One in June and one in July had six embryos each.

Records of occurrence.—Specimens examined, 88, as follows: Washoe Co.: 2 mi. W Mt. Rose summit, 1; 3 mi. S Mt. Rose, 8500 ft., 2. Ormsby Co.: ½ mi. S Marlette Lake, 8150 ft., 1. Humboldt Co.: head of Big Creek, 8000 ft., Pine Forest Mts., 2. Mineral Co.: Cottonwood Creek, 7400 ft., Mt. Grant, 4. Esmeralda Co.: Chiatovich Creek, 4900 ft., ½ mi. W Chiatovich Ranch, 4; Arlemont, 4900 ft., 3. Lander Co.: Birch Creek, 7000 ft., 5; Kingston Ranger Station, 7500 ft., 1; Kingston Canyon, 7000 ft., 5. Eureka Co.: 4 mi. S Tonkin, Denay Cr., Roberts Mts., 2. Nye Co.: Greenmonster Canyon, 7500 ft., Monitor Range, 5; 1 to 2 mi. E Jefferson, 7600–8000 ft., Toquima Range, 7. Elko Co. (unless otherwise noted, in coll. of Ralph Ellis): Cobb Creek, 6 mi. SW Mountain City, 6500–6550 ft., 6 (Mus. Vert. Zoöl.); summit between heads of Copper and Coon creeks, Jarbidge Mts., 1; Steels Creek, 7000 ft., 2; summit of Secret Pass, 6200 ft., 6; Three Lakes, 9700 ft., 2; Long Creek, 7830 ft., 1; Harrison Pass Ranger Station, 6050 ft., 11. White Pine Co.: Willow Creek, 2 mi. S Elko Co. line, 6500 ft., 6 (5 in coll. of Ralph Ellis); Hendry Creek, 9100 ft., 1½ mi. E Mt. Moriah, 7; Lehman Creek, 7500 ft., 1; Baker Creek, 11,100 ft., 3.

Additional records (Jackson, 1928:188): Nye Co.: South Twin River and Jet [= Jett] Canyon, both in Toyabe Mts.

TABLE 2

CRANIAL MEASUREMENTS (IN MILLIMETERS) OF SOREX AND NOTIOSOREX

Name and locality	Number of individuals averaged or catalogue no.	Sex	Condylobasal length*	Palatal length	Cranial breadth	Least interorbital breadth	Maxillary breadth	Maxillary tooth row	Wear of teeth
S. m. merriami									
Desert Ranch†....	210121‡	—	16.2	6.4	7.9		5.1	5.8	slight
S. m. leucogenys									
Chiatovich Creek.	38398	♀	16.5	6.9	8.4	3.7	5.3	6.1	moderate
Mount Magruder..	K572§	♀	16.9	6.7	8.4	3.8	5.5	6.0	slight
S. t. mariposae									
Incline...........	86087	—	18.5	7.6	9.3	4.0	5.6	7.0	much
S. v. amoenus.......									
Marlette Lake.....	67040	—	16.5	6.8	8.2	3.1	4.9	6.1	slight
Bells Ranch.......	35027	♂	16.6	6.5	8.4	3.3	4.9	5.8	much
Kingston Canyon..	88041	♂	16.4	6.6	8.2	3.1	4.8	6.0	slight
Baker Cr., 11,100 ft.	88042	♂	16.9	6.7	8.3	3.2	4.8	6.2	moderate
Baker Cr., 6600 ft..	41471	♂	16.8	6.7	8.4	3.2	4.8	6.1	much
S. v. monticola									
Ruby Mountains...	16 av.	♂, ♀	16.3	6.6	8.4	3.1	4.9	5.9	much
Ruby Mountains...	min.	♂, ♀	16.0	6.2	8.2	2.8	4.6	5.6	much
Ruby Mountains...	max.	♂, ♀	17.0	6.9	8.5	3.5	5.2	6.2	much
S. o. obscurus									
Washoe Co........	69639	♀	16.7	6.8	8.2	3.6	4.8	6.1	much
Ormsby Co., 8000 ft.	67039	♂	16.1	6.4	8.3	3.0	4.6	5.7	moderate
½ mi. S Marlette									
Lake...........	67041	—	17.1	7.0	8.6	3.4	5.1	6.4	moderate
S. tenellus									
Near Wichman....	64‖	—	15.1	6.1	7.3	3.2	4.5	5.5	much
Rainbow Falls.....	86842	♂	14.8	5.8	7.0	2.9	4.1	5.3	moderate
S. p. navigator									
Kingston Canyon..	86105	♀	18.8	7.6	9.7	4.1	6.1	7.0	much
Mount Grant......	63521	♂	20.4	8.6	9.7	4.0	6.0	7.7	moderate
Mount Grant......	63523	♂	20.7	8.8	9.8	3.2	6.0	7.8	moderate
N. c. crawfordi									
Nr. Grapevine Pk..	92391	♂	16.5	6.9	8.2	3.8	4.9	5.9	moderate

* Measurements taken in manner described by Jackson (1928:13), except that I have measured *least* interorbital constriction.
† Measurements from Jackson (1928:82). § D. R. Dickey Collection.
‡ United States National Museum. ‖ Collection of D. V. Hemphill.

Notiosorex crawfordi crawfordi (Coues)

Crawford Shrew

Sorex (Notiosorex) crawfordi Coues, Bull. U. S. Geol. and Geogr. Surv. Terr., vol. 3, p. 651, May 15, 1877. Type from near old Fort Bliss, about 2 miles above El Paso, El Paso County, Texas.
Notiosorex crawfordi, Merriam, N. Amer. Fauna, 10:32, December 31, 1895; Fisher, Journ. Mamm., 22:263, 1 pl., 2 figs., August 14, 1941.

Distribution.—Known only from near Grapevine Peak, Nye County. See figure 32, page 116.

Remarks.—Measurements of a male are: 89, 26, 10, ear from notch, 8; weight, 4.5 grams.

This, the only specimen known from the state, was caught on June 2, 1940, by Harvey I. Fisher in a mouse-trap baited with rolled oats. The trap was set beside a bush of *Chrysothamnus* on sandy soil thickly strewn with sharp-edged stones up to 5 inches in diameter, on a south-facing slope. The collector's notation that plants growing within 50 yards of the point of capture included *Artemisia*  *tridentata* and *Ephedra viridis* identifies the area as in the Upper Sonoran Life-zone.

The tail is both actually and relatively shorter than in other Nevadan shrews; ears large, projecting conspicuously beyond fur; fur plumbeous, on upper parts washed with brownish (near Sudan Brown and suggestive of chestnut); tail bicolored, lighter below; skull relatively broad, especially across rostrum, flattened; maxilla lacking the process present in *Sorex* at the labial margin of M3; dental formula is i. $\frac{3}{1}$, c. $\frac{1}{1}$, p. $\frac{1}{1}$, m. $\frac{3}{3}$, hence with three (rather than five, as in *Sorex*) unicuspids on each side above.

In comparison with six specimens from southern California and one from Brewster County, Texas, the Nevadan specimen is notable for more brownish color of upper parts. It is notable also for providing the northernmost record station of occurrence so far known.

Record of occurrence.—Specimen examined: *Nye Co.:* 5 mi. E and 1 mi. N Grapevine Peak, 5500 ft., 1.

Order CHIROPTERA
Bats

The modification of the forelimbs for flight is the most distinctive feature of bats. The distal part of the forelimb, the part corresponding to the hand of man, is particularly modified in that the bones are greatly lengthened. They support the wing which is made up of a double layer of skin. This is a live structure supplied with blood vessels and nerves, as opposed to the dead feathers (when fully grown) of a bird's wing. This skin, referred to as a membrane, extends back from the supporting finger bones to the leg, which forms another stay, or support, out about as far as the ankle, and it continues on posteriorly to envelop the tail. In two genera of Nevadan bats the distal part of the tail projects free behind the membrane. The power of flight necessitates adaptations in several parts of the body, but especially on the breast, where the breast bone, at least in most genera, is keeled to provide a larger area of attachment for the pectoral muscles the action of which is to pull the forearm downward. The coracoid, or collar bone, is large and other bones of the shoulder girdle are correspondingly strengthened. The elbow is formed by the humerus and radius, the ulna being small and of but slight or no functional value.

The degree of specialization for flight is the basis on which the order Chiroptera is divided into the two suborders, Megachiroptera and Microchiroptera. All Nevadan bats belong to the suborder Microchiroptera which is more highly adapted for flight. Members of this suborder differ from those of the Megachiroptera in having the second finger closely bound to the third, a humerus with the trochiter and trochin large, the former usually articulating with the scapula, a long, narrow (not a broad, low) angular process on the mandible, and an external ear the margin of which does not form a complete ring.

Of the many families in the suborder Microchiroptera, three, as mentioned beyond, occur in Nevada. The teeth of all these have sharp cusps and high styles which make them effective in masticating insects. Unlike insectivorous birds, most of which are diurnal and feed on insects that fly by day, bats are nocturnal or crepuscular and feed on kinds of insects which fly at night or at dusk or dawn when the light is poor. The total effect of bats as a natural check on these insects must be large. The mammalogist who spends some time looking for bats at dusk and listening for their shrill notes in an effort to estimate their numbers, generally concludes that they are, among mammals in most areas, numerically second only to rodents in abundance. Observation in an arid region like Nevada reveals also that the bats are most abundant where insects abound. This generally is where enough water exists to support luxuriant vegetation which in turn supports a large population of insects. Bats are attracted to the water itself; the dives which they make down to the surface of the water leave ripples which suggest that the bats drink by scooping up mouthfuls of water. In former centuries also, bats in Nevada concentrated near water. A cave, now uninhabited by bats, high up on the western side of the Snake Mountains, in White Pine County, in late years yielded many thousand sacks of decayed guano which was deposited by bats, probably when the waves of the Quaternary Lake Bonneville washed over the near-by beaches a few miles to the eastward.

Caves, crevices in rocks, and protected niches in rugged cliffs are occupied by the colonial species for daytime retreats. Only the deeper caves or mine tunnels are suitable as winter quarters for the kinds that hibernate, because they require a temperature above freezing. A relatively constant temperature but little modified by the temperature out of doors is maintained in these deeper caves. Our findings suggest, although they do not prove, that some species, for example *Corynorhinus rafinesquii*, choose for hibernation those places where the temperature is not so high as 65° F. Probably a high temperature makes it difficult for the bat to become semitorpid, a condition which is a means of conserving energy by a lowering of the metabolic rate.

Banding experiments of Griffin (1936:238) in New England indicate that bats usually return annually to the same caves to hibernate. Destruction of every individual in a wintering colony therefore might have more lasting effect on the number of bats than it would if they were less provincial. But colonies of bats may change from one winter roost to another; at any rate, many abandoned mine tunnels made only within the last hundred years now are used by bats as places of retreat. Not all of the tunnels and caves seemingly suitable for bats are occupied by them, which leads to the inference that the bats have some adaptability in selecting winter quarters. It is judged, therefore, that factors other than the number of suitable underground retreats limit the number of bats in Nevada. The number of suitable retreats near food, for instance, may be too few to support the maximum number of some species, but I think their numbers in Nevada are limited mainly by an over-all scarcity of food.

The population of most species of bats is maintained by the birth of only one or two young once a year, whereas most other kinds of mammals must necessarily produce far more young to maintain themselves. Therefore the mortality rate appears to be low in bats, and their existence is judged to be a relatively safe one. Although occasional individuals are taken by some carnivore or by some raptorial bird, I do not know of any Nevadan species of bat that is systematically preyed upon by any predator or group of predators, as, for example, the jack rabbit is preyed upon by coyotes and eagles, or as the ground squirrel is preyed upon by badgers.

The many popularly held superstitions about bats generally prove upon experiment to be groundless, but some of the actual facts learned by study of their behavior are no less curious than some of the fallacious stories that are told about them. Even with the knowledge that bats can detect sounds above the range audible to the human ear, and that they rely on the inner ear as a sense organ with which to locate stationary objects in their path of flight, one can explain only a part of their uncanny ability to travel widely and swiftly and to emerge evening after evening from intricate labyrinths so far underground that changing intensity of light would seem to be ruled out as a means of informing them of the correct time to emerge. So much remains to be learned about them and so little is known that they well repay study.

Macrotus californicus Baird
California Leaf-nosed Bat

Macrotus californicus Baird, Proc. Acad. Nat. Sci. Philadelphia, p. 116, 1858. Type from Old Fort Yuma, Imperial County, California, opposite present town of Yuma, Arizona; Burt, Trans. San Diego Soc. Nat. Hist., 7:393, May 31, 1934.

Distribution.—Known from three localities in the Lower Sonoran Life-zone of Clark County. See figure 93, page 157.

Remarks.—Measurements of two males and nine females taken January 15, 1934, 14 mi. E Searchlight, are: ♂, 96, 96; ♀, 96 (92–101); 35, 33; 35 (33–38); 15, 14; 13.5 (13–14); 35, 33; 34.8 (33–36); weight, 15.9, 13.3; 13.9 (11.0–15.1) grams. The collectors noted that the specimens were not especially fat.

According to Miller (1907:117), three completely bony phalanges in the third finger and the union of the premaxillae are family characters. The pointed nose leaf is a subfamily (Phyllostominae) character. A dental formula of i. $\frac{2}{2}$, c. $\frac{1}{1}$, p. $\frac{2}{3}$,

m. ⅔, and the extension of the tail for about 7 mm. behind the interfemoral membrane are generic characters. The large ear, which averages more than 30 millimeters, and slenderness of the skull, especially in the interorbital and rostral regions, are specific characters. The sooty Hair Brown tips of the fur on the back allow the white basal two-thirds of the hair to show through, particularly on the nape. The fold of skin across the head, which unites the bases of the ears and the pointed nose leaf, are two characters useful in distinguishing this bat from *Antrozous* and *Corynorhinus*.

The California leaf-nosed bat is colonial and lives in caves and in abandoned tunnels of mines. Burt's (1934:393) account of finding 120 that had been killed in late December in the far recesses of a mine at places reached through a tunnel 540 yards long, a shaft 160 ladder-steps deep, and short tunnels suggests that in winter the bats choose places that have a relatively constant temperature. On January 15, 1934, 14 miles east of Searchlight, when the temperature was about 54° F., after a period of colder weather, Hatfield (1937:96) records that bats of this species were first seen flying about. They were traced to a building where they hung up in the basement and in the rooms which gave greatest protection from the outside coolness. Hatfield (*loc. cit.*) and Benson (MS) found that the bats used the building only at night and concluded that they came there only after completing their feeding. The full stomachs of these bats, the presence of numerous droppings—but absence of hard parts of insects discarded by some kinds of bats which bring their prey to a perch to eat it—and the observation that the bats did not arrive until an hour or more after sunset support the conclusion of the observers.

The temperature was lower each succeeding night until January 19, when it was about 34° F. Each night fewer bats came to the building than on the night before until, on the 19th, none appeared. When alighting, the bats made a half-turn roll and hung straight down. In this position the ears were pendulous, but when disturbed the head was raised and the ears were horizontal. The eyes appeared unusually large and prominent. They reflected a straw-yellow light in the beam of an electric torch. The animals at no time squeaked, even when caught. Of the eleven captured, two were males and nine were females. Although embryos were looked for, none was found.

Records of occurrence.—Specimens examined, 17, as follows: *Clark Co.:* Frenchmans Mine, 7 mi. E Las Vegas, 2; Hemenway Wash, 1600 ft., 4 (U. S. Nat. Park Service, Boulder Dam Recreational Area Coll.); Jap Ranch, Colorado River, 500 ft., 14 mi. E Searchlight, 11.

Genus **Myotis** Kaup
Mouse-eared Bats

All of the American species of this genus, which occurs also in the Old World, are relatively generalized, small brownish-colored bats. The dental formula is i. ⅔, c. ⅟₁, p. ⅔, m. ⅔. So far as I know, none is truly migratory, although at the onset of winter they may choose, for hibernation, places which are considerably removed from their summer homes. In the temperate parts of North

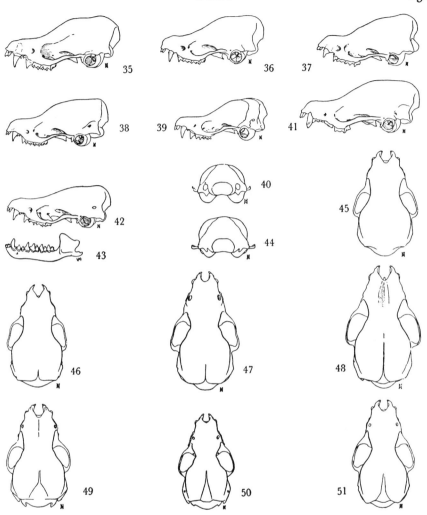

Figs. 35–51. *Myotis*. All, × 2.

Fig. 35. *Myotis evotis chrysonotus*, Burned Corral Canyon, no. 57366, ♂.
Fig. 36. *Myotis lucifugus carissima*, 3 miles south Mount Rose, no. 84076, ♂.
Fig. 37. *Myotis volans interior*, Smiths Creek, 5800 feet, Lander County, no. 63535, ♂.
Fig. 38. *Myotis yumanensis yumanensis*, ½ mile south Pyramid Lake, no. 88052, ♂.
Figs. 39, 40. *Myotis californicus pallidus*, Cave Spring, no. 40519, ♂.
Fig. 41. *Myotis thysanodes thysanodes*, Horse Spring, San Bernardino County, California,
    4750 feet, no. 86119, ♂.
Figs. 42, 43, 44. *Myotis subulatus melanorhinus*, 2 miles west Smith Creek Cave, Mount
    Moriah, no. 78379, ♂.
        (Figs. 45–51 are different views of the skulls shown in figs. 35–44.)

Fig. 45. *Myotis lucifugus carissima*.   Fig. 49. *Myotis volans interior*.
Fig. 46. *Myotis yumanensis yumanensis*.   Fig. 50. *Myotis californicus pallidus*.
Fig. 47. *Myotis evotis chrysonotus*.   Fig. 51. *Myotis subulatus melanorhinus*.
Fig. 48. *Myotis thysanodes thysanodes*.

America the animals are gregarious in winter and, at least the females of several species, colonial when the young are born. The systematic review of the American species by Miller and Allen (1928) is an indispensable work in the library of anyone who undertakes a serious study of bats of this genus.

Myotis lucifugus carissima Thomas
Big Myotis

Myotis (Leuconoe) carissima Thomas, Ann. and Mag. Nat. Hist., 13 (ser. 7):383, May, 1904. Type from Yellowstone Park, Wyoming.
Myotis lucifugus carissima, Miller and Allen, U. S. Nat. Mus., Bull. 144:50, May 25, 1928; Borell and Ellis, Journ. Mamm., 15:19, February 15, 1934.

Distribution.—Roughly, northern half of state. See figure 52.

Remarks.—Measurements of three males and six females taken in August at the north end of Lake Tahoe are: ♂, 87 (85–90), ♀, 86 (83–90); 37.3 (36–40), 33.8 (30–36); 10 (10–10); 9.8 (9–10); 14.3 (14–15), 14.3 (14–15); tragus from notch, 7.7 (7–8), 7.7 (7–8). A male and female taken July 1, 1936, ½ mi. W Verdi weighed 5.2 and 5.6 grams, respectively. Two females taken June 1, 1920, at the mouth of Little High Rock Canyon weighed 5.2 and 5.7 grams.

This is a medium-sized *Myotis*, Tawny-Olive above with a golden cast, and below near Light Grayish Olive. A glossy sheen is characteristic of the upper parts and helps to distinguish this species from the duller-toned *M. yumanensis*. The ear, when laid forward, reaches about to the end of the nose; the third metacarpal is the longest and when folded falls short of the elbow by about 2.5 mm.; the foot is large; the skull is characterized by a broad rostrum and flattened brain case the area of which, when viewed from above, exceeds that of the rostrum.

Specimens from Washoe County are relatively uniform in color and average darker than those from the Ruby Mountains of Elko County, which latter series, Borell and Ellis (1934a:20) have noted, contains one specimen as light-colored as *Myotis lucifugus phasma*, excepting that the ears are darker than in *phasma*. Typical *phasma*, the more southern, lighter-colored subspecies, has not been found in Nevada, although it probably occurs in the southern part of the state. *M. l. carissima* is distinguished from *M. l. alascensis* to the northwest, and *M. l. lucifugus* to the north and northeast of Nevada, by lighter color.

Borell and Ellis (1934a:20) record that this is the most numerous bat in the Ruby Mountains and that at Favre Lake they "sometimes came in numbers, especially on warm, cloudless evenings, to forage over the lake and to drink. Most of those shot . . . fell into the water. On five occasions large rainbow trout (which have been planted there) swallowed the dead or crippled bats before we could retrieve them." One trout was seen to seize an uninjured bat that swooped to drink.

The specimens that we took in western Nevada all were shot while flying near water at open places in the timber or at the edge of the timber. Ten were females taken between June 1 and August 23, but none contained embryos.

Records of occurrence.—Specimens examined, 48, as follows: *Washoe Co.*: mouth of Little High Rock Canyon, 5000 ft., 2; W side Truckee River, 4900 ft., ½ mi. W Verdi, 2; 3 mi. S Mt. Rose, 8500 ft., 1; Calneva, 6400 ft., 9. *Elko Co.* (coll. of Ralph Ellis): head of Ackler Creek, N end Ruby Mts., 6800 ft., 1; Three Lakes, 9700 ft., 18; Harrison Pass Ranger Station, 6050 ft., 1; W side Ruby Lake, 6 mi. N White Pine Co. line, 6200 ft., 1; W side Ruby Lake, 3 mi. N White Pine Co. line, 13 (1 in Mus. Vert. Zoöl.).

Additional record (Miller and Allen, 1928:52): Pyramid Lake.

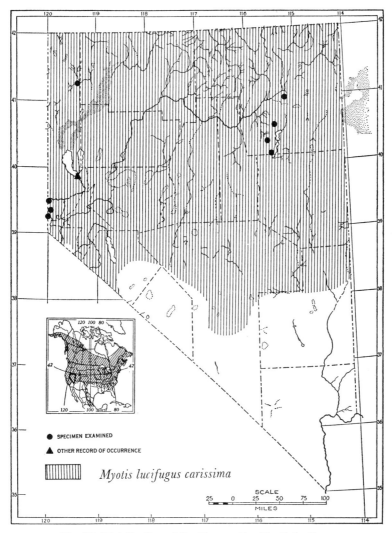

SPECIMEN EXAMINED

OTHER RECORD OF OCCURRENCE

Myotis lucifugus carissima

SCALE
25 0 25 50 75 100
MILES

Fig. 52. Distribution of the big myotis, *Myotis lucifugus.*

Myotis yumanensis
Yuma Myotis

This species is only slightly smaller than *Myotis lucifugus*, from which it usually may be told by the shorter forearm, shorter skull, and duller color. The ear, when laid forward, reaches about to the nose, the lower third of its external border, when erect, forming a shoulder (which is less pronounced than in *M. lucifugus*), and the upper two-thirds of the ear appearing narrower than in *lucifugus*; metacarpals are as described in *lucifugus*, except that the third falls only

1 to 2 mm. short of the elbow; the foot is large; the skull is characterized by a narrow rostral part and a more abruptly rising forehead than in *lucifugus*.
Of sixteen bats shot when flying through an opening in the coniferous trees

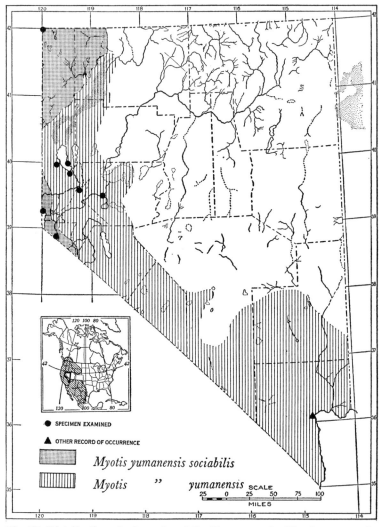

Fig. 53. Distribution of subspecies of the Yuma myotis, *Myotis yumanensis*, with insert showing range of the species.

at Calneva, at the north end of Lake Tahoe, in late August, seven were of this species and nine were *lucifugus*. The specimens from 12-mile Creek were shot while flying along the aspen- and willow-lined stream. They appeared at 1 to 3 minutes past 8 o'clock on each of the three evenings that we camped there,

July 16–18, 1936. The specimen from 7 miles south of Minden was seen by Alcorn as it alighted in the road at late dusk. He quickly picked it up and observed that it appeared to be in a healthy condition. Of the remaining specimens, all referred to the desert race *yumanensis*, those from 4 miles west of Fallon, from Wadsworth, and from a half mile south of Pyramid Lake were shot as they flew at late dusk about cottonwood trees adjacent to water. Those from 3 miles west of Sutcliffe were found on July 10, 1926, hanging in a cluster of about thirty individuals in the gable of a barn. The twenty-three adults saved were all females. Ten half-grown young also were saved and four females contained embryos. On July 11, 1924, in a cave on the eastern side of Pyramid Lake just opposite The Pyramid, I found several thousand bats of this species clinging to the rock roof of the cave. All those examined were females, either with embryos or newly born young. Young dropped to the dusty floor from time to time where tracks of a bobcat suggested that the cat had an interest in the bats. Droppings of a bobcat picked up near the entrance to the cave contained remains of bats. From all the evidence accumulated, it was concluded that a bobcat made regular visits to the cave where he found a supply of food easy to obtain. This same cave later (in late June, presumably 1927) was visited by Irving J. Perkins (1928:45) when he noted that the bats all were females and that of the twenty "collected, each possessed one embryo within a few days of birth, which would have taken place about July 1st."

Myotis yumanensis sociabilis H. W. Grinnell
Yuma Myotis

Myotis yumanensis sociabilis H. W. Grinnell, Univ. California Publ. Zoöl., 12:318, December 14, 1914. Type from Old Fort Tejon, Kern County, California.

Distribution.—Extreme western border of state from the Tahoe area northward. See figure 53.

Remarks.—Measurements of four specimens from Calneva are: 83 (82–85); 35 (32–38); 10 (9–10); 14 (14–15); tragus, 7.7 (7.2–7.8). Five females from 12-mile Creek weigh 6.9 (5.3–7.5) grams. The upper parts are darker (browner) than Tawny Olive above and the membranes are blackish. The color is intermediate between that of the pallid *Myotis y. yumanensis* to the southeast and *Myotis y. saturatus* to the west.

Of the seven specimens from Calneva, five appear typical of *sociabilis*, but two are almost as light colored as *yumanensis*, a circumstance that is not surprising when one considers that this is on the margin of the range of *sociabilis* where intergradation with the race *yumanensis* would be expected.

Records of occurrence.—Specimens examined, 14, as follows: *Washoe Co.:* 12-mile Creek, ½ mi. E Calif. boundary, 5300 ft., 6; Calneva, 6400 ft., 7. *Douglas Co.:* 7 mi. S Minden, 1.

Myotis yumanensis yumanensis (H. Allen)
Yuma Myotis

Vespertilio yumanensis H. Allen, Monogr. Bats N. Amer., Smithsonian Misc. Coll., 165:58, figs. 54–56, June, 1864. Type from Old Fort Yuma, Imperial County, California.
Myotis yumanensis, Miller, N. Amer. Fauna, 13:66, October 16, 1897.

Distribution.—Southern and low western part of state north at least to Pyramid Lake. See figure 53.

Remarks.—Measurements of five males from ½ mi. S Pyramid Lake are: 81 (73–86); 34 (31–38); 11 (10–11); 14 (13–15); weight, 4.7 (4.2–5.4) grams. The upper parts may be described as Pale Olive Buff or Pale Pinkish Buff with the qualification that they are grayer than either of these colors. The membranes and ears are whitish. The pale color of this bat permits ready separation of it from other Nevadan *Myotis*, although the pallid *Myotis lucifugus phasma*, not at this writing taken in the state, resembles *yumanensis* in color. I am at a loss to explain why specimens of *yumanensis* have not been taken at some of the collecting stations south of Fallon.

Records of occurrence.—Specimens examined, 52, as follows: *Washoe Co.:* 3 mi. W Sutcliffe, Pyramid Lake, 33; E shore Pyramid Lake, 15 mi. [by road ?] N Nixon, 8; ½ mi. S Pyramid Lake, 3950 ft., 5. *Churchill Co.:* 4 mi. W Fallon, 4000 ft., 4; Fallon, 1 (coll. of Mrs. Anna Bailey Mills).
Additional record (Miller and Allen, 1928:68): *Clark Co.:* Colorado River.

Myotis evotis chrysonotus (J. A. Allen)
Long-eared Myotis

Vespertilio chrysonotus J. A. Allen, Bull. Amer. Mus. Nat. Hist., 8:240, November 21, 1896. Type from Kinney Ranch, Sweetwater County, Wyoming.
Myotis evotis chrysonotus, Miller and Allen, Bull. U. S. Nat. Mus., 144:117, May 25, 1928; Borell and Ellis, Journ. Mamm., 15:21, February 15, 1934; Burt, Trans. San Diego Soc. Nat. Hist., 7:394, May 31, 1934.
Vespertilio albescens evotis, H. Allen, Bull. U. S. Nat. Mus., 43:89, March 14, 1894.
Myotis evotis, Miller, N. Amer. Fauna, 13:80, October 16, 1897; Linsdale, Amer. Midland Nat., 19:174, January, 1938.

Distribution.—Entire state in suitable habitat in Transition Life-zone. See figure 54.

Remarks.—Measurements of ten males and twelve females from various Nevadan localities are: ♂, 88 (81–95), ♀, 87 (82–97); 41 (36–47), 40 (35–49); 9.4 (8–10), 8.7 (7–10); 20.6 (20–22), 20.3 (18–22); tragus, 10.8 (10–12), 11.4 (9–13); weight, 5.2 (4.1–7.2), of nine nonpregnant females, 5.7 (4.5–7.5) grams.

This is a medium-sized *Myotis* near Cinnamon-Buff in color, easily distinguished from other Nevadan species of the genus by its long ears, which, when laid forward, extend about 6 mm. beyond the nose. The tragus is correspondingly long, nearly half as long as the ear. The third metacarpal is the longest, reaching to within 2 mm. of the elbow. The fourth and fifth fingers are of nearly equal length. The foot is large but slightly shorter than in *M. lucifugus*. The skull is slender throughout, especially in the rostrum.

All the localities of occurrence in Nevada fall within the Transition Life-zone except Pahranagat Valley, which is lower. Possibly the specimen taken there (Miller and Allen, 1928:117) was obtained in winter.

Nevadan specimens are relatively uniform in color and no geographic variation has been detected in other features.

Although a cluster of these bats once was found in a building in Colorado, the species otherwise, so far as I know, has not been found to be colonial. Two of our specimens were taken together in the attic of the Kingston Ranger Station. The individual from Goose Creek flew so closely about the head of A. E. Peterson (MS), while he was setting out traps for small rodents at late dusk, that he reached up and knocked the bat to the ground. All our other specimens were shot while flying at late dusk or later along mountain streams fringed with aspen, cottonwood, and mountain birch. Exception is to be made for the nine from Burned Corral Canyon, in that they were shot as they swooped down to one of two pools near together which provided the only water in the canyon. The pool was illuminated by the lights of two automobiles from about 8:30 until 11:00 P.M. Much of the shooting which yielded the nine *evotis* and thirteen bats of six other species was done at 10 o'clock and later. This was

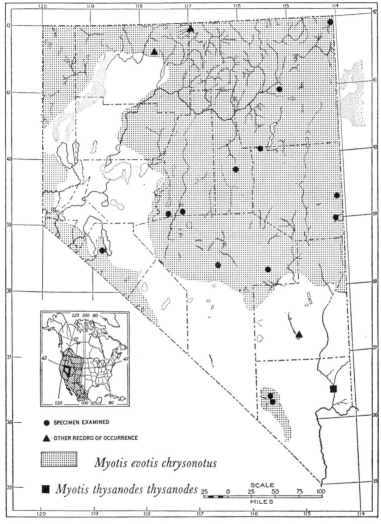

Fig. 54. Distribution of the large-eared myotis, *Myotis evotis*, and the fringe-tailed myotis, *Myotis thysanodes*, with insert showing range of *Myotis evotis*.

the largest number of this species obtained at any one place, and I judged that *evotis* emerges later in the evening than some other kinds of *Myotis* which have been shot in greater numbers earlier in the evening.

Of the fourteen females available, equal numbers were taken in June and July. The only embryos found were one each on June 14 and 24, 1937, at Mount Moriah.

Records of occurrence.—Specimens examined, 36, as follows: *Humboldt Co.:* Summit Lake road, 1. *Mineral Co.:* Cottonwood Creek, 7400 ft., Mt. Grant, 2. *Lander Co.:* Kingston Ranger Station, 7500 ft., 2; Peterson Creek, 7000 ft., Shoshone Mts., 1. *Eureka Co.:* 11½ mi. S Romano, Diamond Valley, 1. *Nye Co.:* Hot Creek Range, 7 mi. W Tybo, 7000 ft., 3; Burned Corral Canyon, 6700 ft., Quinn Canyon Mts., 9. *Elko Co.:* Goose Creek, 5000 ft., 2 mi. W Utah boundary, 1; head of Ackler Creek, 6800 ft., 1 (coll. of Ralph Ellis). *White Pine Co.:* Willow Creek, 6500 ft., 2 mi. S Elko Co. line, 1 (coll. of Ralph Ellis); 2 mi. W Smith Cr. Cave, 6300 ft., Mt. Moriah, 5; Baker Creek, 8000 ft., 1. *Clark Co.* (D. R. Dickey Coll.): Clark Canyon, 8000 ft., 3; Lee Canyon, 8200 ft., 4; Kyle Canyon, 9000 ft., 1.

Additional records (Miller and Allen, 1928:117): *Humboldt Co.:* Cottonwood Range. *Elko Co.:* Little Owyhee River. *Lincoln Co.:* Pahranagat Valley.

Myotis thysanodes thysanodes Miller
Fringe-tailed Myotis

Myotis thysanodes Miller, N. Amer. Fauna, 13:80, figs. 16, 17, October 16, 1897. Type from Old Fort Tejon, Kern County, California.
Myotis thysanodes thysanodes, Burt, Trans. San Diego Soc. Nat. Hist., 7:394, May 31, 1934.

Distribution.—To be expected in any part of the state, but known from only one locality, in Clark County. See figure 54.

Remarks.—Measurements of one male and two females from 6 mi. S St. Thomas are: 80, 83, 85; 34, 38, 36; 11, 11, 11; average and extreme measurements of nine females from the type locality, recorded by Miller and Allen (1928:128), are: 85.1 (81.0–88.4), 37.9 (35.4–39.6), 8.4 (7.6–9.0), 17.4 (16.4–18.0).

This, a medium-sized *Myotis* near Cinnamon-Buff in color above, is easily told among Nevadan species of the genus by the conspicuous fringe of hairs on the edge of the uropatagium. The ears, when laid forward, reach 3 to 5 mm. beyond the nose, but are shorter than in *evotis*. The tragus is a little more than half the length of the ear. Miller and Allen (1928:124) described the fur of the species as "not so full nor so golden in color" as in *evotis*. My own comparisons indicate the same difference as an average feature; individual specimens can be selected which are indistinguishable in color. The third metacarpal falls 1.5 to 2 mm. short of the elbow and is of about the same length as the fourth. The foot is large, especially in comparison with that of *californicus* and *subulatus*. The skull is slightly larger than that of *evotis* and broader in the rostral part.

This species is of lower zonal predilections than *evotis*. The single occurrence for Nevada is recorded by Burt (1934:394) who, on July 31, 1929, found three adults and thirteen young of the year in one bunch hanging from a rock in a large salt cave in Clark County.

Record of occurrence.—Specimens examined, 16, as follows: *Clark Co.:* 6 mi. S St. Thomas, 16 (D. R. Dickey Coll.).

Myotis volans interior Miller
Hairy-winged Myotis

Myotis longicrus interior Miller, Proc. Biol. Soc. Washington, 27:211, October 31, 1914. Type from Twining, Taos County, New Mexico.
Myotis volans interior, Miller and Allen, Bull. U. S. Nat. Mus., 144:142, May 25, 1928. Borell and Ellis, Journ. Mamm., 15:20, February 15, 1934; Burt, Trans. San Diego Soc. Nat. Hist., 7:394, May 31, 1934.
Vespertilio nitidus H. Allen, Bull. U. S. Nat. Mus., 43:96, March 14, 1894 (part). Pahranagat Valley, U. S. N. M. no. 28950.

Myotis lucifugus longicrus, Miller, N. Amer. Fauna, 13:65, October 16, 1897; Taylor, Univ. California Publ. Zoöl., 7:302, June 24, 1911.
Myotis volans, Linsdale, Amer. Midland Nat., 19:174, January, 1938.

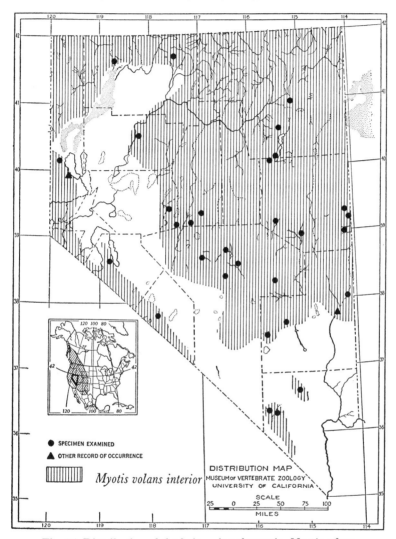

Fig. 55. Distribution of the hairy-winged myotis, *Myotis volans*.

Distribution.—Zonally from the upper margin of the Upper Sonoran Life-zone at least to upper margin of tree growth over entire state. See figure 55.

Remarks.—Measurements of ten males and twenty females from White Pine County are: ♂, 89 (80–95), ♀, 98 (85–105); 41 (34–45), 45 (38–49); 8.6 (8–10), 8.1 (6.5–9.6); 12.6 (11–14), 12.3 (10–14); tragus, 7.9 (7–9), 6.8 (4.5–8.0); weight, 7.5 (6.5–9.0), 6.2 (5.3–6.6) grams.

M. v. interior is of a size medium for the genus; it is Sayal Brown to Snuff Brown above and has a short rounded ear which, when laid forward, barely reaches the end of the nose. The third metacarpal is the longest and, when folded, falls short of the elbow by 1 to 1.5 mm. The foot is small, the calcar has a well-developed keel, and the under side of the membrane is furred to a line joining the elbow and knee. The skull is distinctive because of the high brain case; it is highest posteriorly. The rostrum is shortened relative to that of the species already mentioned. The extension of the fur on the ventral side of the membrane out to the elbow is a distinctive feature among Nevadan *Myotis* as also is the great height posteriorly of the brain case.

Despite the fact that a relatively large number of specimens of this bat were obtained at thirty localities, but little was learned concerning its habits. All the specimens were shot at dusk as they flew along the edge of a stream, lake, or pond. They were taken at elevations of from 5600 to 10,500 feet in White Pine County. They are relatively uniform in color and proportions. In these features we can detect no difference judged to be of systematic worth between those taken at high and low altitudes, nor between animals taken in different parts of the state. Of sixty-six females, thirty-three (eleven pregnant) were taken in June, twenty-three (three pregnant) in July, and three (none pregnant) in August. The inclusive dates for the pregnant animals were June 10 to July 14. The fourteen pregnant females had but one embryo each.

Records of occurrence.—Specimens examined, 132, as follows: *Washoe Co.*: Cottonwood Creek, 4400 ft., Virginia Mts., 1. *Humboldt Co.*: 14 mi. N Paradise Valley, 6700 ft., 1; Duffer Peak, 8400 ft., Pine Forest Mts., 1. *Pershing Co.*: El Dorado Canyon, 6000 ft., Humboldt Range, 1. *Mineral Co.*: Cottonwood Creek, 7400 ft., Mt. Grant, 4. *Esmeralda Co.*: Cave Spring, 6200 and 6248 ft., 2. *Lander Co.*: Smiths Creek, 5800–6800 ft., 3; Birch Creek, 7000 ft., 2; Kingston Ranger Station, 7500 ft., 2; Kingston Creek, 7000 ft., 3; Peterson Creek, 7000–7500 ft., Shoshone Mts., 4. *Nye Co.*: Greenmonster Canyon, 7500 ft., Monitor Range, 1; 1 to 1½ mi. E Jefferson, 7600 and 7700 ft., Toquima Range, 2; 5 mi. N Hot Creek, 6700 ft., Hot Creek Range, 1; 7 mi. W Tybo, 7000 ft., Hot Creek Range, 20; Burned Corral Canyon, 6700 ft., Quinn Canyon Mts., 8. *Elko Co.* (coll. of Ralph Ellis): head of Ackler Creek, 6800 ft., 3; Three Lakes, 9700 ft., 2; W side Ruby Lake, 6200 ft., 3 mi. N White Pine Co. line, 3 (1 in Mus. Vert. Zoöl.). *White Pine Co.*: Willow Creek, 6500 ft., 2 mi. S Elko Co. line, 4 (coll. of Ralph Ellis); 2 to 3 mi. W Smith Cr. Cave, 6300 ft., Mt. Moriah, 22; 2 mi. E Smith Cr. Cave, 5600 ft., Mt. Moriah, 2; Hendry Creek, 6800 ft., 7½ mi. SE Mt. Moriah, 2; 2½ mi. SW Hamilton, 7300–8600 ft., 7; Stella Lake, 10,500 ft., Snake Mts., 1; Lehman Cave, 7200 ft., 2; Lehman Creek, 7800 ft., 1; Baker Creek, 7800–8500 ft., 6; Water Canyon, 8 mi. N Lund, 1. *Lincoln Co.*: Eagle Valley, 3½ mi. N. Ursine, 5700 ft., 2; E Slope Irish Mt., 6900 ft., 8; SW base Groom Baldy, 7200 ft., 1. *Clark Co.* (D. R. Dickey Coll.): Hidden Forest, 8500 ft., 1; Clark Canyon, 8000 ft., 3; Kyle Canyon, 10,000 ft., 1; Kyle Canyon, 8000 ft., 4.

Additional records: *Washoe Co.*: Sutcliffe, 4000 ft., 1 (D. G. Nichols, MS). *Lincoln Co.*: Panaca (Miller and Allen, 1928:144).

Myotis californicus pallidus Stephens
California Myotis

Myotis californicus pallidus Stephens, Proc. Biol. Soc. Washington, 13:153, June 13, 1900. Type from Vallecito, San Diego County, California; Burt, Trans. San Diego Soc. Nat. Hist., 7:395, May 31, 1934.
Myotis californicus, Miller, N. Amer. Fauna, 13:71, October 16, 1897 (part).
Vespertilio nitidus ciliolabrum, H. Allen, Bull. U. S. Nat. Mus., 43:101, March 14, 1894.

Distribution.—Sonoran life-zones of southern and western parts of state. See figure 56.

Remarks.—External measurements of two males and three females from Esmeralda County, with the averages for females in parentheses, are: ♂, 81, 78; ♀, 82, 78, 85 (82); 37, 40; 41, 35, 42 (39); 6.5, 6.0; 6.5, 7.0, 5.5 (6.3); 12.3, 13.0; 11.9, 13.0, 14.0 (13.0); weight, 3.9 and 2.6; 2.9 and 3.9 grams.

This is a small bat, near Light Ochraceous-Buff above. The ear, when laid forward, exceeds the nose by 1 to 3 mm. The third metacarpal is longest and when folded back is about the same length as the forearm. The foot is small. The ears and membranes are dark brownish. The skull is delicate, has a long, tapering rostrum, and in lateral profile the forehead rises higher and more sharply than in *Myotis subulatus melanorhinus*, which has also darker membranes and ears than *M. c. pallidus*.

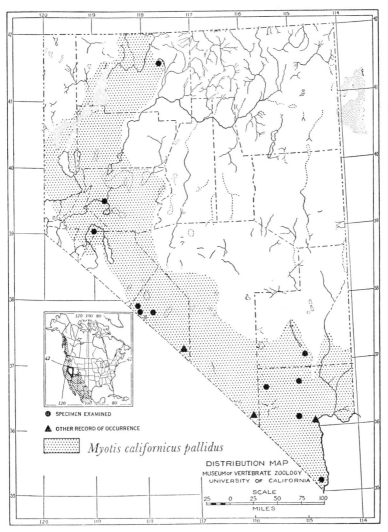

SPECIMEN EXAMINED

OTHER RECORD OF OCCURRENCE

Myotis californicus pallidus

DISTRIBUTION MAP
MUSEUM of VERTEBRATE ZOOLOGY
UNIVERSITY OF CALIFORNIA

SCALE
25   0   25   50   75   100
MILES

Fig. 56. Distribution of the California myotis, *Myotis californicus*.

From the records of occurrence available it is clear that in Nevada this bat inhabits the Sonoran life-zones. None was taken as high as the Transition Life-zone. The restriction of this species to the western part of the northern half of the state is explained by the lower zonal conditions that obtain there as compared to the same latitude farther east. Miller and Allen (1928:158) record two specimens, in the California Museum of Vertebrate Zoölogy, from Little High Rock Canyon, Humboldt County. The specimens seem to me to be referable, instead, to *Myotis subulatus melanorhinus*. Miller and Allen (*loc. cit.*) record one also from the Rabbit Hole Mountains, but it and the one other (U. S. Nat. Mus. cat. nos. 94381 and 94382) from that place seem to me to be *M. s. melanorhinus*.

The five specimens from Esmeralda County were shot while flying near water at early dusk, and the three from Hiko Spring were knocked down with a bundle of twigs as they swooped low over a trough of water. In Esmeralda County, Seth Benson and I noted that the course of flight, presumably in quest of insects, was varied by sharp changes in direction, up, down, or to either side. We judged that the path of flight was largely determined by sounds of insects which the bats followed to obtain for food. The sound-receptor formed by the conch of the ear in this species is so directed as to receive sounds from a wide arc. The ear of the pipistrelle taken at the same place looks to be adapted to catching sounds from a smaller arc, an arc more to the side of the animal. Its course of flight was correspondingly different; its sharp changes of direction were mostly to one side or the other and it was much easier to shoot on the wing than the California myotis. The third species of bat which appeared there in numbers at about the same time in the evening was the Mexican free-tailed bat, the easiest one of the three to shoot. Nearly all of its deviations from a straight, horizontal line of flight were downward swoops. Its ear conchs are directed to detect sound coming from below. We thought that there was a positive correlation between the direction of the opening of the external ear and the direction taken by the bat in pursuing the insects which it caught for food.

The three females obtained here in Esmeralda County were taken on June 3, June 23, and July 4. Only that one taken on the last date was pregnant; it had one embryo.

Bats of this species hibernate in mine tunnels, and I suppose that they hibernate also in caves. One specimen in a semitorpid condition was obtained on December 27, 1939, by J. R. Alcorn from a small crevice in the roof of a mine tunnel 9 miles east and 2 miles north of the town of Yerington. The temperature inside the mine where the bat was found was 55° to 60° F. and the outside temperature between 40° and 50°. Another bat of the same species, on the same day, was found clinging to the rock wall of the Royal Blue Mine in Esmeralda County by Emery F. Johnson.

Records of occurrence.—Specimens examined, 21, as follows: *Lyon Co.:* 9 mi. E and 2 mi. N Yerington, 1. *Humboldt Co.:* Cottonwood Range, 2 (U. S. N. M. cat. nos. 80907, 80911). *Churchill Co.:* Fallon, 1 (coll. of Mrs. Anna Bailey Mills). *Esmeralda Co.:* Royal Blue Mine, Royston, 5500 ft., 1; 7 mi. N Arlemont, 5500 ft., 1; Arlemont, 4850 ft., 2; Cave Spring, 6200–6248 ft., 3. *Lincoln Co.:* Coyote Spring, 1 (coll. of S. G. Jewett). *Clark Co.:* Mormon Well, 6500 ft., 1 (D. R. Dickey Coll.); Indian Springs, 3120–3280 ft., 2 (D. R. Dickey Coll.); 4 mi. NW Las Vegas, 2100 ft., 2 (D. R. Dickey Coll.); Hiko Spring, 1900 ft., Dead Mts., 3.

Additional records (Miller and Allen, 1928:158): *Esmeralda Co.:* Gold Mountain. *Nye Co.:* Pahrump Valley. *Clark Co.:* Colorado River.

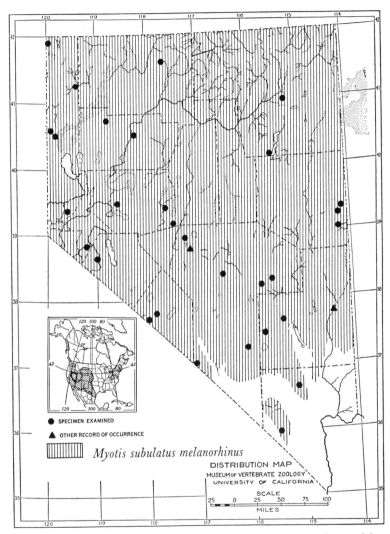

Fig. 57. Distribution of the small-footed myotis, *Myotis subulatus*, with insert showing range of the species.

Myotis subulatus melanorhinus (Merriam)
Small-footed Myotis

Vespertilio melanorhinus Merriam, N. Amer. Fauna, 3:46, September 11, 1890. Type from Little Spring, north base of San Francisco Mountain, 8250 feet, Coconino County, Arizona.

Myotis subulatus melanorhinus, Miller and Allen, Bull. U. S. Nat. Mus., 144:168, May 25, 1928; Borell and Ellis, Journ. Màmm., 15:20, February 15, 1934; Burt, Trans. San Diego Soc. Nat. Hist., 7:395, May 31, 1934.

Distribution.—Upper Sonoran Life-zone and more rarely in Transition Life-zone over entire state. See figure 57.

Remarks.—Measurements of ten of each sex from Nye County are: ♂, 81 (75–84), ♀, 82 (60–90); 38 (32–44), 39 (36–45); 7.5 (7–9), 7.6 (7–9); 13.4 (12.0–15.5), 13.8 (12–16); tragus, 7.8 (6–9), 8.6 (6–10); weight, 4.0 (3.5–4.7), of five nonpregnant, 4.7 (3.3–5.9) grams.

This small species, near Light Ochraceous Buff above, is proportioned about as is *Myotis californicus pallidus*. Often the color is a trifle brighter, the wing membranes and ears are darker (black rather than dark brownish), and the thumb averages longer. In my experience the blacker ears are the most distinctive external feature, but this is not always sufficient to permit distinguishing the two species for certain. The skull can be distinguished from that of *californicus* by slightly larger size, broader, flatter brain case, and, in lateral profile, lack of abrupt step between the rostrum and the brain case (see figs. 39 and 42, p. 131).

Of the seventy-three specimens taken in spring and summer, three were found flying about in houses, and the others were shot while flying along streams or at the edges of ponds. All were taken at dusk. None was taken at a high elevation or in a place which suggested that the species is tolerant of Boreal habitats. Nevadan occurrences are in the Transition and Upper Sonoran life-zones. No evidence was obtained which indicates that this species is colonial at any season. One was found on December 24, 1939, 12 miles east and 1 mile south of Fallon, ensconced in a crevice in the roof of the entrance to a cave. The temperature inside the cave was 55° F. and 40° outside. The bat may have been "awakened" when the observer (Alcorn) entered the cave. When he came out and found the bat, it had its eyes open, ears erect, mouth closed, and its respiratory rate was 252 per minute. From somewhere close by, a second bat flew on out of the cave and alighted near the entrance. One of these was a male and the other a female. On December 28, 1940, in the Muriel Bee Mine, 4 miles west of Wichman, D. V. Hemphill found one male hanging from the rock roof of the tunnel, about 75 feet from the entrance. The roof of the tunnel was about 5 feet high. The temperature on the side of the tunnel was 46° F. and the outside temperature was 38°. Of the twenty-five other females, one was taken in May, seven (one pregnant) in June, and seventeen (three pregnant, July 7 and 9) in July. Each of the pregnant females carried but a single embryo.

Records of occurrence.—Specimens examined, 85, as follows: *Washoe Co.:* Barrel Sprs., 5700 ft., 9½ mi. E and 3½ mi. N Ft. Bidwell, 1; mouth of Little High Rock Canyon, 5000 ft., 8; Smoke Creek, 4½ mi. E Calif. boundary, 3900–3950 ft., 6; Smoke Creek, 9 mi. E Calif. boundary, 3900 ft., 2. *Storey Co.:* 6 mi. NE Virginia City, 6000 ft., 1. *Lyon Co.:* West Walker River, 12 mi. S Yerington, 4600 ft., 2. *Humboldt Co.:* Cottonwood Range, 2 (U. S. N. M. cat. nos. 80908 and 80909 [= M.C.Z. 33204]). *Churchill Co.:* 12 mi. E and 1 mi. S Fallon, 3950 ft., 2. *Mineral Co.:* East Walker River, 2 mi. NW Morgans Ranch, 5050 ft., 3; Muriel Bee Mine, 4 mi. W Wichman, 5300 ft., 1. *Esmeralda Co.:* Cave Spring, 6200–6248 ft., 6; Fish Lake, 4850 ft., 1. *Pershing Co.:* Rabbit Hole Mts., 2 (U. S. N. M. cat. nos. 94381 and 94382); El Dorado Canyon, 6000 ft., Humboldt Range, 1. *Lander Co.:* Smiths Creek, 5800 ft., 1; Peterson Creek, 7000 ft., Shoshone Mts., 3. *Nye Co.:* Wisconsin Creek, 7000 ft., 1; Hot Creek Range, 7 mi. W Tybo, 7000 ft., 12; Quinn Canyon Mts. (Burned Corral Canyon, 6700 ft., 7; Big Creek, 5800 ft., 1) 8; ½ and 2 mi. S Oak Spring, 5700 ft., 2; 2½ mi. E and 1 mi. S Grapevine Peak, 6700 ft., 1. *Elko Co.* (coll. of Ralph Ellis): head of Ackler Creek, 1; W side Ruby Lake, 6200 ft., 3 mi. N White Pine Co. line, 6 (2 in Mus. Vert. Zoöl.). *White Pine Co.:* 2 mi. W Smith Creek Cave, 6300 ft., Mt. Moriah, 1; 2 mi. E Smith Creek Cave, 5600 ft., Mt. Moriah, 2; S side Mt. Moriah, 7000 ft., 1; Lehman Cave (not in Cave), 7200 ft., 3. *Lincoln Co.:* E slope Irish Mtn., 6900 ft., 2; SW base Groom Baldy, 7200 ft., 1. *Clark Co.:* Hidden Forest, 8500 ft., Sheep Mts., 1 (D. R. Dickey Coll.); N side Potosi Mtn., 7000 ft., 1.

Additional records: Miller and Allen (1928:171): *Nye Co.:* Pablo. *Lincoln Co.:* Panaca.

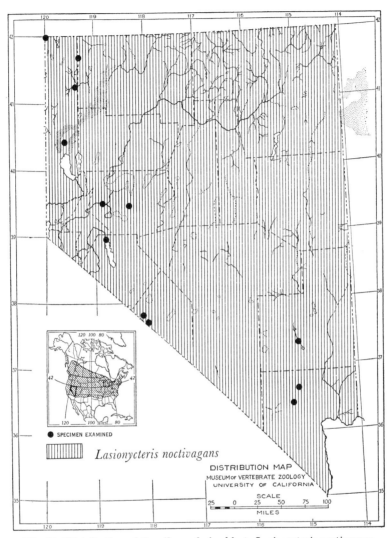

Fig. 58. Distribution of the silvery-haired bat, *Lasionycteris noctivagans*.

Lasionycteris noctivagans (LeConte)
Silvery-haired Bat

V[espertilio] noctivagans LeConte, McMurtie's Cuvier, Animal Kingdom, 1:431, 1831. Type from eastern United States.

Lasionycteris noctivagans, Peters, Monatsber. K. Preuss. Akad. Wissensch. Berlin, 1865:648; Miller, N. Amer. Fauna, 13:87, October 16, 1897; Burt, Trans. San Diego Soc. Nat. Hist., 7:395, May 31, 1934.

Distribution.—Known certainly only from the western and southern parts of the state, but probably occurs over all of Nevada. See figure 58.

Remarks.—Measurements of three males and four females are: ♂, 98, 95, 91, ♀, 100 (95–108); 40, 40, 31, 40 (37–46); 9, 8, 8, 9 (8–10); 12, 11, 13, 14 (12–14); tragus, —, —, —, 7 (6.3–7.0); weight, 7.3, 5.8, 8.0, 9.1 (6.8–11.4) grams.

This is a medium-sized bat, black in color, with some of the hairs on the upper and under surface tipped with whitish. The ears and membranes are black. These parts are naked, except for the basal half of the interfemoral membrane. The third metacarpal, when folded back, falls about even with the elbow. The skull is flattened, particularly in the rostral region, where there is a distinct concavity on each side between the lacrimal bone and anterior nares. The dental formula is i. $\frac{2}{3}$, c. $\frac{1}{1}$, p. $\frac{2}{3}$, m. $\frac{3}{3}$. The silvery cast to the pelage is reminiscent of *Lasiurus cinereus*, but *Lasionycteris* can be distinguished readily by the naked distal half of the upper surface of the interfemoral membrane, by the naked inner surface of the pinna of the ear (these parts are densely haired in *Lasiurus cinereus*), by the black rather than the brownish ground color of the fur, and, finally, by the smaller size.

This bat is known to be solitary and generally is a tree-living species. In the eastern part of North America at least, it is migratory and frequents the higher life-zones in summer, retiring to more southern places in winter. Less is known of the animal in western North America regarding its change of range with season. The specimen from Fallon and one from 4 miles west of that place were taken on September 12 and October 12. Because none has been taken near Fallon in summer, it might be inferred that these two were migrants. Nevertheless, our other specimen from Churchill County, and those from Washoe, Mineral, and Esmeralda counties came from places as low zonally as Fallon and were taken in May, June, and July. All were shot while flying, two at least when flying from the direction of piñon-covered hills toward marshy areas at lower elevations where abundant insect life was available. In view of the direction of flight of the two individuals and because of what is known of the habits of the species in the eastern United States, I suppose that in Nevada the taking of specimens in the zonally low western and southern parts of the state is not indicative of the true summer range of the species. They may have flown to these places, for purposes of feeding, from daytime retreats in a higher life-zone. The taking of the two specimens in Clark County conforms to what was postulated about winter and summer range; one taken on July 8, 1929, was at an elevation of 8500 feet amid yellow pines and white firs, whereas the other, found dead in January, 1940, at Corn Creek Ranch, at an elevation of about 3000 feet, was in the Lower Sonoran Life-zone.

Of the eight specimens the sexes of which are recorded, four were males and four were females. None was pregnant. The skull and part skeleton from 4 miles south of Alamo was recovered by Richard M. Bond (1940:165) from an owl pellet.

Records of occurrence.—Specimens examined, 17, as follows: *Washoe Co.:* 12-mile Creek, 5300 ft., ½ mi. E Calif. boundary, 1; mouth of Little High Rock Canyon, 5000 ft., 4; Horse Canyon, Pahrum Peak, 5800 ft., 1. *Humboldt Co.:* Badger, 2 (U. S. Nat. Mus.). *Churchill Co.:* 4 mi. W Fallon, 4000 ft., 1; Fallon, 1 (coll. of Mrs. Anna Bailey Mills); Mountain Well, 5600 ft., 1. *Mineral Co.:* 3 mi. S Schurz, 4100 ft., 1. *Esmeralda Co.:* Arlemont, 4850 ft., 1; Fish Lake, 4800 ft., 1. *Lincoln Co.:* 4 mi. S Alamo, 1. *Clark Co.:* Hidden Forest, 8500 ft., 1 (D. R. Dickey Coll.); Corn Creek Ranch, 1.

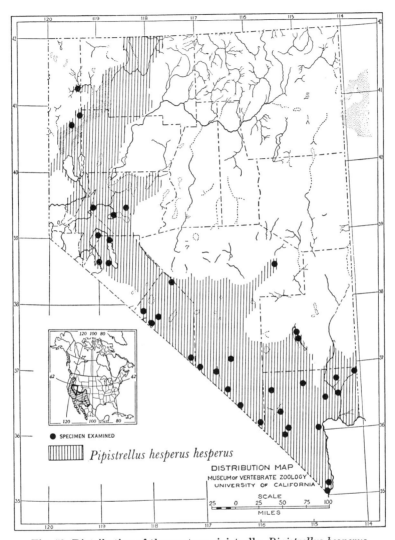

Fig. 59. Distribution of the western pipistrelle, *Pipistrellus hesperus*.

Pipistrellus hesperus hesperus (H. Allen)
Western Pipistrelle

Scotophilus hesperus H. Allen, Monogr. Bats N. Amer., p. 43, June, 1864. Type from Old Fort Yuma, Imperial County, California, on right bank of Colorado River, opposite present town of Yuma, Arizona.

Pipistrellus hesperus, Miller, N. Amer. Fauna, 13:88, October 16, 1897.

Pipistrellus hesperus hesperus, Burt, Trans. San Diego Soc. Nat. Hist., 7:395, May 31, 1934; Hatfield, Journ. Mamm., 17:257, August 14, 1936.

Distribution.—Sonoran life-zones in western and southern parts of the state. See figure 59.

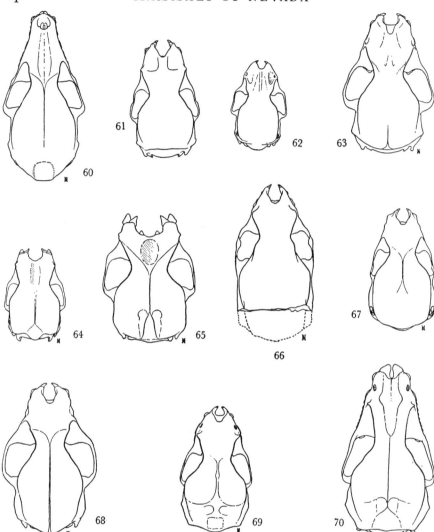

Figs. 60–70. Bats, exclusive of *Myotis*. All, ×2. (Other views of these skulls are shown in figs. 71–91.)

Fig. 60. *Macrotus californicus*, 14 miles east Searchlight, no. 61421, ♂.
Fig. 61. *Lasionycteris noctivagans*, 4 miles west Fallon, no. 88058, ♂.
Fig. 62. *Pipistrellus hesperus hesperus*, Crystal Spring, no. 52203, ♂.
Fig. 63. *Eptesicus fuscus pallidus*, Irish Mountain, no. 47851, ♂.
Fig. 64. *Lasiurus borealis teliotus*, 4 mi. N Dixon, Solano Co., California, no. 71601, ♂.
Fig. 65. *Lasiurus cinereus*, Camp Verde, Yavapai County, Arizona, no. 71588, ♀.
Fig. 66. *Euderma maculatum*, Reno, no. 65171, sex ?.
Fig. 67. *Corynorhinus rafinesquii pallescens*, 7 miles south Cleveland Ranch, no. 45899, ♂.
Fig. 68. *Antrozous pallidus pallidus*, Fish Lake, Esmeralda County, no. 40556, ♂.
Fig. 69. *Tadarida mexicana*, Greenmonster Canyon, no. 57472, ♂. (Another view of this skull is shown in fig. 485.)
Fig. 70. *Tadarida macrotis*, Pine Canyon, Chisos Mountains, Brewster County, Texas, 6000 feet, no. 81683, ♀.

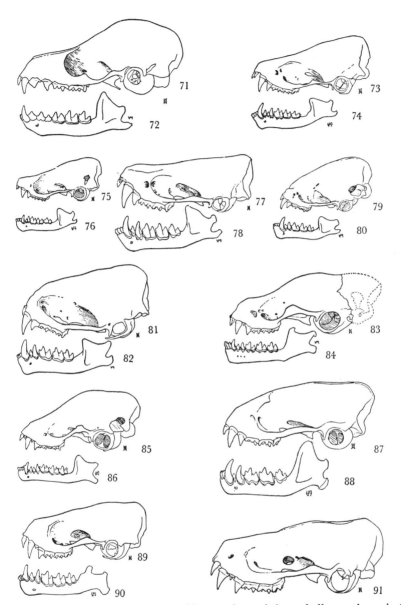

Figs. 71–91. Bats, exclusive of *Myotis*. Different views of these skulls are shown in figs. 60–70. All, × 2.

Figs. 71, 72. *Macrotis californicus.*
Figs. 73, 74. *Lasionycteris noctivagans.*
Figs. 75, 76. *Pipistrellus hesperus hesperus.*
Figs. 77, 78. *Eptesicus fuscus pallidus.*
Figs. 79, 80. *Lasiurus borealis teliotus.*
Figs. 81, 82. *Lasiurus cinereus.*

Figs. 83, 84. *Euderma maculatum.*
Figs. 85, 86. *Corynorhinus rafinesquii pallescens.*
Figs. 87, 88. *Antrozous pallidus pallidus.*
Figs. 89, 90. *Tadarida mexicana.*
Fig. 91. *Tadarida macrotis.*

Remarks.—Measurements of ten males from various localities and ten females from 3 to 4 mi. NE Beatty are: ♂, 73 (69–81), ♀, 75 (69–78); 29 (25–31), 29 (26–31); 6.2 (5–8), 6.1 (6–7); 11.2 (10–12), 11.2 (11–12); tragus, 4.7 (4–5), 5.1 (5.0–5.5); weight, 3.7 (2.7–4.1), of eight nonpregnant females, 3.6 (3.1–5.0) grams.

The pipistrelle is the smallest Nevadan bat. Above, it is between Drab Gray and Smoke Gray; ventrally, it is slightly lighter, Smoke Gray to Pale Smoke Gray. The ears are short and, when laid forward, do not reach to the end of the nose; the tragus is less than half as high as the ear; the ears and membranes are blackish; the skull is flattened and there is no abrupt "step" between the brain case and the rostrum. The dental formula is i. $\frac{2}{3}$, c. $\frac{1}{1}$, p. $\frac{2}{2}$, m. $\frac{3}{3}$.

From *Pipistrellus hesperus merriami*, the race to the westward, *hesperus* differs in lighter (grayer, as opposed to browner) color and slightly smaller average size. *P. h. hesperus* differs similarly from *australis*, the race to the southward, in color, but is larger than *australis*. From *P. h. santarosae*, the race to the eastward, *hesperus* differs in lighter color and smaller size. From *P. h. maximus*, the race to the southeast, *hesperus* differs mainly in smaller size. Hatfield (1936) has revised the races of this species.

The pipistrelle emerges earlier in the evening than any other kind of Nevadan bat. This time of appearance, the small size, and jerky, erratic flight usually permit a person to distinguish it on the wing from other species. Whether or not it is colonial I do not know, but it appears not to migrate. Alcorn, on December 27, 1939, 9 miles east and 2 miles north of Yerington, found two, a male and a female, in two separate crevices, clinging singly, in the roof of a mine tunnel where the temperature was 55° to 60° F. The temperature outside was between 40° and 50°. The pipistrelles had their eyes open but were semitorpid.

In early February they were flying along the Colorado River from the California boundary north for 5 miles. The five then taken all were males. They seem to segregate by sex in the summer, too; of thirty shot on May 19 to 23, 1931, along the Amargosa River, twenty-seven were females and only three were males. There was a similar disproportion in numbers of the two sexes taken at some other places.

All of our specimens, except the two mentioned above, were shot while flying. Because these bats on several evenings were first seen flying near rocky ledges, and twice near stone houses, it is thought that they spend the day in crevices between the rocks. It may be that they find concealment also in trees. Near the mouth of the Walker River, a place far from any rocks that would afford shelter for bats, pipistrelles were seen early in the evening flying about the fairly thick stand of cottonwood trees.

On July 29, 1939, at Stormy Spring, a pipistrelle was shot as it flew about in apparently normal fashion in the bright sunshine at 8 A.M. What had caused it to forsake its daytime retreat we did not learn.

On several evenings between May 16 and 26, 1932, at Crystal Spring, when the prevailing wind was from the north, pipistrelles were concentrated at the southern end of the lake, in pursuit of insects. Apparently the insects which arose from the marsh vegetation had drifted southward with the wind. Much the same thing was observed on May 20, 1928, at Fish Lake, where pipistrelles and nighthawks both were heading northwest into the wind below the lake; they seemed to have found good feeding conditions there, for they remained on this side of the lake; on quiet evenings they would be found more evenly distributed all about it.

Of seventy-three females, forty-seven (five pregnant) were taken in May, seventeen (ten pregnant) in June, and nine (none pregnant) in July. Fourteen of these pregnant females had two embryos each and the other but one.

Records of occurrence.—Specimens examined, 153, as follows: *Washoe Co.:* mouth Little High Rock Canyon, 5000 ft., 8; 12 mi. N and 2 mi. E Gerlach, 4000 ft., 1; Deep Hole, 4000 ft., 1. *Lyon Co.:* 9 mi. E and 2 mi. N Yerington, 2. *Churchill Co.:* Lahontan Dam, 1 (coll. of Mrs. Anna Bailey Mills); 4 mi. W Mountain Well, 5000 ft., 1; 12 mi. SE Fallon, 2. *Mineral Co.:* 3 mi. S Schurz, 4100 ft., 6; East Walker River, 2 mi. NW Morgans Ranch, 5050 ft., 1; Cottonwood Creek, Mount Grant, 7400 ft., 2. *Esmeralda Co.:* 7 mi. N. Arlemont, 5500 ft., 4; Cave Spring, 6200–6248 ft., 9; Fish Lake, 4800 ft., 12; Gold Mountain, 1 (U. S. Nat. Mus.). *Nye Co.:* Middle Stormy Spring, 11 mi. S Lock's Ranch, 5000 ft., 1; NW base Timber Mtn., 4200 ft., 1; 2½ mi. E and 1 mi. S Grapevine Peak, 6700 ft., 1; Amargosa River, 3400–3500 ft., 3 to 4 mi. NE Beatty, 30; Amargosa Desert, 20 mi. SE Beatty, 2500 ft., 1; Ash Meadow, 2½ mi. W Devils Hole, 2173 ft., 2; Pahrump Valley, 1 (U. S. Nat. Mus.); Pahrump Ranch, 1 (D. R. Dickey Coll.). *Lincoln Co.:* Crystal Spring, 4000 ft., Pahranagat Valley, 12; 5 mi. S Crystal Spring, Pahranagat Valley, 1; Ash Spring, 3800–4000 ft., Pahranagat Valley, 5. *Clark Co.:* "Beaverdam," in Nevada, 1 (U. S. Nat. Mus.); 10 mi. N. Overton, 1300 ft., 1; Mormon Well, 6500 ft., 1 (D. R. Dickey Coll.); Hidden Forest, 8500 ft., 1 (D. R. Dickey Coll.); Indian Springs, 3120 and 3280 ft., 13 (D. R. Dickey Coll.); Kaolin and ¼ mi. SW, 1220 ft., 2; Valley of Fire, 12 mi. SW Overton, 3; Kyle Canyon, 4500 ft., 2 (D. R. Dickey Coll.); Charleston Mts., 1 (D. R. Dickey Coll.); Charleston Mts., 6000 ft., 1 (D. R. Dickey Coll.); Cottonwood Springs [= Spring], 1 (U. S. Nat. Mus.); Boulder City, 2400 ft., 1 (U. S. Nat. Park Service, Boulder Dam Recreational Area); N side Potosi Mtn., 7000 ft., 1; Hiko Spring, 8 mi. SSE Dead Mtn., 1900 ft., 5; 3 mi. SW Hiko Spring, 2400 ft., 3; Colorado River, 6 mi. N Calif. boundary, 500 ft., 5; same as preceding except 5 mi. N, 1; Colorado River, 2 mi. N Calif.-Nev. Monument, 500 ft., 2; Colorado River, ½ mi. N Calif.-Nev. Monument, 500 ft., 1.

Eptesicus fuscus
Big Brown Bat

The medium size, total length of about 115 mm., brown color which resembles that of several species of *Myotis*, naked ears that are black, and the nearly naked membranes combine to make this bat easily distinguishable from any other Nevadan species. Superficially it looks like a *Myotis*, but the larger size is distinctive. The number of teeth is less, the dental formula being i. $\frac{2}{3}$, c. $\frac{1}{1}$, p. $\frac{1}{2}$, m. $\frac{3}{3}$. The skull is markedly flattened, with a nearly straight superior outline in lateral view, and the rostrum is about as broad as long.

The two subspecies in Nevada differ mainly, and perhaps only, in color. These bats leave their roosts relatively early in the evening, only a little while after pipistrelles appear, to fly about in search of food. The flight is steady and slow. The big brown bat is colonial, at least in the breeding season when the colonies that we located appeared to be made up of females only. Burt (1934: 396) thought that in summer there may be a segregation of the sexes by life-zones in southern Nevada. He points out that: "No females were taken at any time above the low creosote bush-mesquite belt whereas all of the males except one were taken in either piñon pine-juniper or yellow pine associations."

Often a colony of this species contains a smaller number of Mexican free-tailed bats. By placing an insect net over an opening between two stones in the wall of a rock house, which was 3½ miles north of Ursine, on August 2, 1933, eighteen big brown bats and two free-tails were caught as they emerged at dusk. All but two of the brown bats were females. Two years before, at the same place, between June 24 and 28, seven other specimens were shot while flying. All were females and six of them contained an embryo each. In Green-monster Canyon, from July 11 to 17, 1933, on consecutive evenings, we took by shooting, as the bats left a small cave or crevice near the top of a big rock about 80 feet high, a total of twenty-five adults. Each of several of these fe-males had one small young clinging to her. The two young saved measured 54 and 58 millimeters in total length and weighed 1.9 and 3.3 grams. Small young were found clinging to five of six females taken July 20, 1933, 5 miles north of Hot Creek P. O. Here also there was but one young to each female.

These six individuals were found at night clinging to the top of the insides of brick, beehive-shaped charcoal kilns. Beneath the bats was a pile of feces, mostly old. On this were relatively fresh remains of insects—hard parts of camel crickets and elytra of scarabaeid beetles. Evidently the big brown bats and, at times, possibly other species hung up here to devour at their leisure insects caught elsewhere. We knew that the bats were not in the same place in the daytime because no bats were there the day before when Ward C. Russell first found the pile of feces of bats and discarded hard parts of insects. It was because of this evidence that we went back to the place after dark, on the same day, with results as described. The daytime retreat of one colony which Borell and Ellis (1934a:20) discovered on May 30, 1928, near the summit of Overland Pass, was a small cave near the top of a cliff 40 feet high. The hundred or so bats that they flushed from the place all appeared to be of this one species. All eight specimens which were procured the next day from a crevice about 50 yards distant from the cave were females; four contained one small embryo each. Burt (1934:396) found an immature individual on July 31, 1931, in a salt cave 6 miles south of St. Thomas. This information is all that is available concerning the places of concealment used by these bats in Nevada. It is not known for certain that they are resident throughout the year in the state, but, judging from what is known of them in other states, I suppose that they hibernate there, within 10 miles or less of their summer quarters.

Sometimes the big brown bat engages insects too large for it successfully to manage for food. At late dusk on August 17, 1935, for example, the fire guard at Incline brought me an adult female big brown bat and a 60-milli-meters-long pinewood sawyer beetle (*Ergates spiculatus* Lec.), the mandibles of which were firmly fixed in the side of the bat. While driving his car the fire guard saw moving objects in the track ahead of him too late to avoid crushing them with the wheels of his automobile. Upon examination he found the two crushed, freshly killed animals, bat and beetle. He quickly brought them to me to ask if it were possible that bats were preyed upon by these huge insects. Considering the general feeding habits of the bat, it seemed more probable that the bat had seized the insect in flight, and was borne to the ground by the weight of its intended prey, when an end was put to both by the automobile tire.

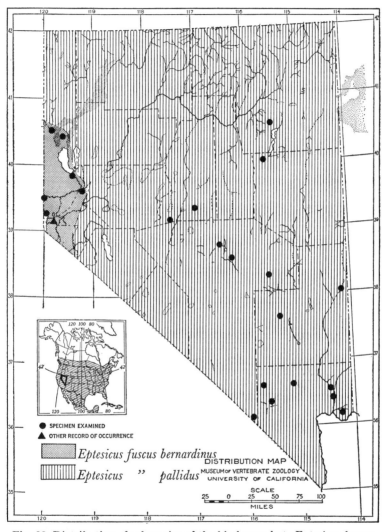

Fig. 92. Distribution of subspecies of the big brown bat, *Eptesicus fuscus*.

Of eight females taken in May, four were pregnant; of seven in June, six were pregnant; of thirty-three in July, nine were pregnant; and of fourteen taken in August, none was pregnant. The extreme dates for pregnant females are June 24 and July 14. The fifteen pregnant females had only one embryo each.

Eptesicus fuscus bernardinus Rhoads
Big Brown Bat

Eptesicus fuscus bernardinus Rhoads, Proc. Acad. Nat. Sci. Philadelphia, 1901:619, February 6, 1902.
Type from near San Bernardino, San Bernardino County, California; Engels, Amer. Midland Nat., 17:653, May, 1936.
Adelonycteris fuscus, H. Allen, Bull. U. S. Nat. Mus., 43:112, March 14, 1894.
Vespertilio fuscus, Miller, N. Amer. Fauna, 13:96, October 16, 1897.

Distribution.—Western part of state from the general region of Lake Tahoe north at least to Smoke Creek. See figure 92.

Remarks.—Measurements of four males from Smoke Creek, and two females from west of Verdi are: 119, 114, 111, 112, 124, 116; 45, 44, 46, 44, 48, 43; 11, —, 13, 10, 12, 12; 18, 14.5, 17, 18, 16, 19; tragus, 7, 5, 9, 11, 8.5, 9.0; weight, 15.7, 19.4, 14.4, 14.8, 16.8, — grams.

The color above ranges from near (*l* 16′) Dresden Brown to Prout's Brown and is lighter below than above. From *E. f. pallidus, bernardinus* differs in darker color, and averages slightly smaller at a given latitude. The specimens here referred to *bernardinus* are all typically dark colored. The single specimen from 8 miles southwest of Ravendale, Lassen County, California, referred by Engels (1936:657), on the basis of color, to *E. f. pallidus,* might with equal propriety be referred to either *pallidus* or *bernardinus.* Therefore, and because the specimens from near-by localities in Nevada all clearly are referable to *bernardinus,* the one from Lassen County also now is referred to that race.

Records of occurrence.—Specimens examined, 15, as follows: *Washoe Co.:* Smoke Creek, 9 mi. E Calif. boundary, 3900 ft., 4; Horse Canyon, Pahrum Peak, 5800 ft., 1; Pyramid Lake, 4 (U. S. Nat. Mus.); W side Truckee River, ½ mi. W Verdi, 4900 ft., 2; Incline, 6250 ft., 1. *Lyon Co.:* Wadsworth, 4100 ft., 3.
Additional record: *Ormsby?* Co.: Carson Valley (Miller, 1897:98).

Eptesicus fuscus pallidus Young
Big Brown Bat

Eptesicus pallidus Young, Proc. Acad. Nat. Sci. Philadelphia, 1908:408, October 2, 1908. Type from Boulder, Boulder County, Colorado.
Eptesicus fuscus pallidus, Miller, Bull. U. S. Nat. Mus., 79:62, December 31, 1912; Burt, Trans. San Diego Soc. Nat. Hist., 7:396, May 31, 1934; Engels, Amer. Midland Nat., 17:656, May, 1936.
Eptesicus fuscus, Linsdale, Amer. Midland Nat., 19:174, January, 1938.
Eptesicus fuscus fuscus, Borell and Ellis, Journ. Mamm., 15:20, February 15, 1934.

Distribution.—All but western part of state. See figure 92.

Remarks.—Measurements of five males from Nye and Lincoln counties are: 110 (105–119); 44 (39–51); 11 (9–12); 16 (13–17); tragus, 8.7 (7–9); weight, 15.4 (13.6–19.0) grams. Corresponding measurements of ten adult females from Greenmonster Canyon and ten from Eagle Valley, all measured by the same collector, are, respectively: 121 (116–125), 118 (106–130); 51.5 (45–58), 48.4 (40–55); 11.4 (10–13), 10.8 (10–11); 16.3 (16–17), 16.5 (15–17.5); tragus, 8.5 (8–10), 8.6 (7.5–9.0); weight of nonpregnant animals, 20.0 (15.3–23.0), 17.8 (15.8–20.4) grams.

The color above varies from near (*h* 18′) Buckthorn Brown to Dresden Brown and is slightly ligher below. The palest animals come from 3½ miles north of Ursine, but all others here referred to *pallidus,* with one exception, are distinct on basis of color from the race *bernardinus.* The exception is the one animal from Birch Creek, Lander County, which is as dark as some specimens of *bernardinus.* The pale color of *pallidus* is the feature distinguishing it from *bernardinus* to the west, *peninsulae* to the south, and *fuscus* to the east. Also, *pallidus* is larger than *peninsulae.*

Records of occurrence.—Specimens examined, 84, as follows: *Lander Co.:* Birch Creek, 7000 ft., 1; Peterson Creek, 7000 ft., Shoshone Mts., 1. *Nye Co.:* Greenmonster Canyon, 7500 ft., Monitor Range, 27; 5 mi. N Hot Creek, 6700 ft., Hot Creek Range, 5; Burned Corral Canyon, 6700 ft., Quinn Canyon Mts., 2; Pahrump Ranch, 2667 ft., 1. *Elko Co.:* Three Lakes, 9700 ft., 1 (coll. of Ralph Ellis). *White Pine Co.:* Overland Pass,

8 mi. S Elko Co. line, 7 (coll. of Ralph Ellis). *Lincoln Co.:* Eagle Valley, 3½ mi. N Ursine, 5900 ft., 22; E slope Irish Mtn., 6900 ft., 1. *Clark Co.* (unless otherwise noted, in D. R. Dickey Coll.): Hidden Forest, 8500 ft., 11; Indian Springs, 3120 ft., 1; ¼ mi. SW Kaolin, 1220 ft., 1 (Mus. Vert. Zoöl.); 6 mi. S St. Thomas, 1250 ft., 1; Lee Canyon, 8200 ft., 1; Cedar Basin, 3500 ft., 1.

Genus **Lasiurus** Gray
Hairy-tailed Bats

Two species of this genus occur in Nevada. They may be distinguished from other species by the densely haired dorsal surface of the interfemoral membrane and the densely haired underside of the wing along the bones of the forearm, upon which the hairs extend all the way to the ends and slightly beyond. The ears are short and round. The metacarpals of the hand are graduated from the third to the fifth, the fifth being much the shortest. The skull is short and deep. The dental formula is i. $\frac{1}{3}$, c. $\frac{1}{1}$, p. $\frac{2}{2}$, m. $\frac{3}{3}$.

The two Nevadan species occur widely over North America, are migratory, solitary, and tree-inhabiting, and have more than one young. The red bat has two, three, or even four young at a time; in this respect it differs from other bats, which have but one or two young.

Lasiurus borealis teliotis (H. Allen)
Red Bat

Atalapha teliotis H. Allen, Proc. Amer. Philos. Soc., 29:5, April 10, 1891. Type from unknown locality, probably some part of California.
Lasiurus borealis teliotis, Miller, N. Amer. Fauna, 13:110, October 16, 1897.

Distribution.—In Nevada known only from Churchill and Clark counties. See figure 93.

Remarks.—The female in alcohol yields external measurements of 104, 42, 6. The ears are short and round, being about 11 mm. long, as measured from the notch; the tragus is about half that height. The forearm in our specimen, a female, measures 40.5 mm. Over most of the body the base of the hairs is black, but this is concealed by the much wider yellowish band and a tip of reddish color, which in some lights is near Kaiser Brown. The ear is naked on the inside of the pinna.

No. 72439, a female from Clark County, was obtained for Dwight C. Smiley by a friend, Garner Anderson, who discovered it about sundown on June 25, 1936, in a mesquite bush in Overton. The male from Churchill County was obtained on July 19, 1942, for J. R. Alcorn by Paul L. Condee.

Records of occurrence.—Specimens examined, 2, as follows: *Churchill Co.:* 5 mi. SW Fallon, 1. *Clark Co.:* Overton, 1.

Lasiurus cinereus (Beauvois)
Hoary Bat

Vespertilio cinereus (misspelled *linereus*) Beauvois, Catal. Raisonné Mus. Peale, Philadelphia, p. 18 (p. 15 of English edition by Peale and Beauvois), 1796. Type locality, Philadelphia, Philadelphia Co., Pennsylvania.
Lasiurus cinereus, H. Allen, Monogr. N. Amer. Bats, p. 21, 1864; Miller, N. Amer. Fauna, 13:114, October 16, 1897.

Distribution.—Known certainly only from the western and southern parts of the state, but probably occurs over all of Nevada. See figure 93.

Remarks.—External measurements of two males from 12-mile Creek and Burned Corral Canyon, and a female from Crystal Spring, are, respectively: 134, 126, 141; 53, 48, 63; 11, 9, 14; 17, 18, —; tragus, 8, 7, —; weight, 26.9, 23.2, 25.2 grams.

This large bat, which has in general a brownish-black coloration that is overcast with white, appears at first glance as though the fur were coated with hoarfrost. The white tips of the hairs are succeeded by a dark brownish band, a light yellowish band, and a basal band of blackish or dark plumbeous color. This dark coloration with frosted appearance and large size—for example, forearm more, rather than less, than 50 millimeters—readily distinguishes the hoary bat from the red bat.

Three of our specimens were shot while in flight at late dusk. Two of these, from 12-mile Creek and Burned Corral Canyon, taken in July, were males, and possibly had flown down from near-by places of higher zonal position to feed. The remains of one of unknown sex, killed 2 weeks before by Mr. Cornell when he found the bat on a willow sprout, were picked up on July 10, 1936, along Smoke Creek. Probably it was not a migrant as perhaps was the one shot in flight on October 24, 1938, at Fallon, or the dead female found floating in the lake at Crystal Spring on May 19, 1932, or the one taken by C. Hart Merriam on April 30, 1891, in Vegas Valley. Bailey (1936:386) suggests that one found on June 27, 1928, by Anna Bailey Mills hanging in the green foliage of a plum tree 3 miles west of Fallon was a migrant.

B. P. Bole, Jr. (MS), on August 28, 1932, at the Patterson Ranch, 3 miles south of Dyer, Esmeralda County, noted two or three hundred bats which, so far as he could determine, were all of this species. This was in daylight, when the sun was just setting. The bats were flying about some cottonwood trees in "great numbers, and the two males [saved] fell to the ground in front of me, fighting and squealing." This locality is in the lower part of the Upper Sonoran Life-zone, although only about 6 miles in an air line from Boreal habitats in the White Mountains to the westward.

Records of occurrence.—Specimens examined, 6, as follows: *Washoe Co.:* 12-mile Creek, 5300 ft., ½ mi. E Calif. boundary, 1 (♂, July 17, 1936); Smoke Creek, 3950 ft., 4½ mi. E Calif. boundary, 1 (sex ?, about June 27, 1936). *Churchill Co.:* 4 mi. W Fallon, 1 (sex ?, October 24, 1938). *Nye Co.:* Burned Corral Canyon, 6700 ft., Quinn Canyon Mts., 1 (July 30, 1933). *Lincoln Co.:* Crystal Spring, 4000 ft., Pahranagat Valley, 1 (May 19, 1932). *Clark Co.:* Vegas Valley, 1 (April 30, 1891).

Euderma maculatum (J. A. Allen)
Spotted Bat

Histiotus maculatus J. A. Allen, Bull. Amer. Mus. Nat. Hist., 3:195, February 20, 1891. Near Piru, Ventura County, California.
Euderma maculata, H. Allen, Bull. U. S. Nat. Mus., 43:61, March 14, 1894.
Euderma maculatum, Hall, Journ. Mamm., 16:148, May 15, 1935.

Distribution.—In Nevada taken only at Reno, but may occur in any part of the state. See figure 93.

Remarks.—Measurements from the dried skin (no. 65171) are 107, 49, 10, 37; tragus, 7. The fur of the upper parts is black with three white spots, one at the base of the tail and one on each shoulder. The basal halves of the hairs making up these white spots are black.

The same is true of the whitish underparts. The ears and membranes are light yellowish when dry. The ears, wider than in *Corynorhinus*, are united at their bases. The forearm measures 50 mm.; the metacarpal of the fifth digit is longer than that of the fourth and about equal to that of the third. The skull has the lacrimal region raised to form a ridge,

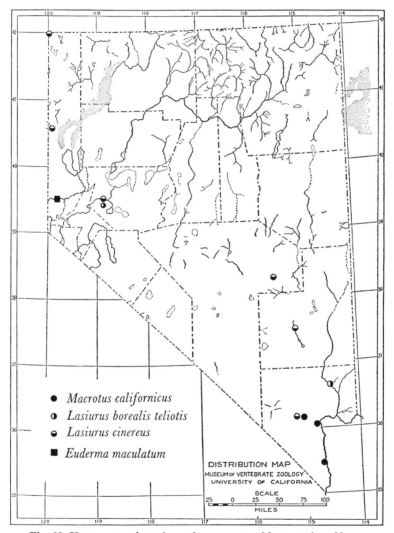

Fig. 93. Known record stations of occurrence of four species of bats.

the dorsal profile in lateral view is more nearly straight than in *Corynorhinus*, and the brain case is broader. The dental formula is i. $\frac{2}{3}$, c. $\frac{1}{1}$, p. $\frac{2}{2}$, m. $\frac{3}{3}$.

This rare bat at the present writing has been recorded only eight times. The area of known occurrence is bounded by a line the marginal reference

points of which are: Reno; Salt Lake City, Utah; Mesilla Park, New Mexico; Yuma, Arizona; and Piru, California. Donald D. McLean tells me (see Hall, 1935:148) that the specimen from Reno was taken about September 10, 1922, when it was found alive in the zoölogical laboratory at the University of Nevada. The animal was saved as a stuffed study skin by Professor C. L. Brown and ultimately was placed by him and Professor Peter Fransden in the California Museum of Vertebrate Zoölogy.

Miller (1897:49) quotes Merriam as saying, "While in Vegas Valley, Nevada, I was told by the Stuarts, the owners of the Vegas Ranch, that a very large bat 'with ears like a jackass and a white stripe on each shoulder' is abundant at that place in summer, but does not occur in spring or fall. They stated that it had not yet arrived at the date of our visit, May 1, 1891."

In July, 1928, John Chiatovich, then about 45 years of age, told me that when he was a boy he once saw a bat, with big ears and white shoulder patches, in the root cellar of his parents' ranch in Fish Lake Valley, Esmeralda County.

These indications of the bat's occurrence suggest that it will be found in southern Nevada.

Record of occurrence.—Specimen examined: *Washoe Co.*: Reno, 1.

Corynorhinus rafinesquii
Long-eared Bat

The long-eared bat averages about a hundred millimeters in total length, has ears about one-third the length of the body, is Natal Brown to Army Brown above, slightly lighter below, and has a large glandular swelling on each side of the muzzle between the eye and the nose. The ears and membranes are brownish colored and naked. The skull is relatively smooth, with zygomatic arches appressed, brain case rounded, interorbital region depressed, and rostrum small; its greatest breadth amounts to less than a third of the length of the skull. The dental formula is i. $\frac{2}{3}$, c. $\frac{1}{1}$, p. $\frac{2}{3}$, m. $\frac{3}{3}$.

From *Antrozous*, this bat may be told by: darker color; narrower ear; shorter forearm, which is less than 48 mm. (about 43 as opposed to 53); a lump on each side of muzzle; concave, rather than convex, interorbital region of skull; and larger number of teeth.

Long-eared bats inhabit caves. The females are colonial when carrying embryos and when with young; at these times the females remain apart from the males. The number of adult females found together in Nevada always has been less than fifty—usually about twenty-five. At the time of year when the females are in colonies the males were found singly. The species appears not to range higher than the Transition Life-zone, and is most abundant in the Sonoran life-zones. Long-eared bats are thought to be nonmigratory. In hibernation the females as well as the males hang singly, not in clusters, head downward, in caves or from the naked rock roofs of mine tunnels. The ears are folded up in circular fashion and the wings envelop the sides and underparts of the body and head (Alcorn, MS). A female hanging thus was found on December 27, 1939, by Alcorn 18 feet back from the mouth of a short (26-foot) mine tunnel 9 miles east and 2 miles north of Yerington; the temperature inside the tunnel was 50° F. On the same date, a male was found 650 feet from the entrance of a tunnel more than a thousand feet long, 3½ miles southwest of Yerington; the temperature both inside and outside this tunnel was about 40°. A day earlier, D. V. Hemphill took a hibernating male from a tunnel 4 miles west of Wichman, and on January 1, 1940, he obtained a male and a female from the Stanmoore Mine in Lapon Canyon; in both tunnels the temperature was above freezing. Alcorn examined a cave, but found no bats present, on December 24, 1939, 10 miles southeast of Fallon—where *Corynorhinus* was found on August 15, 1938; the temperature was 70°. He thought that bats might never choose places to hibernate as warm as this because the high temperature would hinder long continued torpidity. Probably this torpidity is a means of conserving energy in the winter when insect food is not obtainable. The bats taken by Alcorn and Hemphill were much fatter than specimens taken in summer. These findings accord in all particulars with Whitlow's more detailed observations of this species in southeastern Idaho (Whitlow and Hall, 1933:243), where it was found that the bats hibernated in mine tunnels in which the temperature remained above freezing. In preparation for this period of hibernation the bats put on fat; in the spring, when the store of energy thus provided was used up, they weighed a fifth less than in autumn. It was noted that these bats clung singly, not in clusters, to the faces of inclined rocks when hibernating. This is in contrast to the behavior of females in summer which collect in clusters.

Observations in spring and summer, which support generalizations made above about their habits in those seasons, include the following: Of six adult males, each was alone, four were in tunnels of as many different mines and two were in cellars of houses. The dates of capture of these males were May 28, June 16 and 27, July 13 and 30, and August 8. The bat taken by Burt (1934: 397) on May 31, in a mine tunnel, was also a male.

Females were taken ten times in spring and summer. Only three times were they taken singly: June 6, under circumstances unknown; July 6, when a bat flew into a house after dark; and July 30, when one was found hanging on a wooden beam in a rock house. Long after dark, on May 22, 1931, 3½ miles northeast of Beatty, two females were obtained in an old stone house. Judging from the discarded hard parts of insects found on the floor of the house, these bats came here only at night to devour prey caught on the wing. One contained an embryo. The six other occurrences of females were instances in which clusters of females, sometimes with young, hung from the rock roofs of caves or mine tunnels. On May 19, 4½ miles east of Stillwater, nine females (six with small embryos from 1 to 7 mm. in crown-rump length) were selected at random from a lot of about thirty-five bats. On May 27, at Springdale, ten females (from a lot of thirty-three or more) included four with embryos. On June 28, 1924, at the north end of Pyramid Lake, nineteen females (see Bailey, 1936: 388) included fourteen with a newly born young attached to the fur of each, another with a young one attached by the umbilical cord, another with a young one only half extruded from the vagina, and three, each containing one large fetus ready for birth. In this same cave a little more than 7 years later (July 5, 1931) a cluster of about twenty-five bats, mostly young, was examined. The six adults saved all were females. One was flying about with a young one attached to her, but, mostly, the females flew without the young. The one young saved was as large as any of the other young and larger than most. Its permanent teeth had not yet attained full height. On July 3, 1928, 1 mile southeast of Dyer Ranch, a cluster hanging from the top of a mine tunnel was made up of about thirty-five adults and an equal number of young. Eighteen adults the sex of which was ascertained were females. The young, although mostly of one size, varied from those only a few days old to some almost large enough to fly. On August 15, 10 miles southeast of Fallon, Alcorn (MS) found about fifty of these bats, two of which he saved, an adult female and an immature male. Of the ten females with embryos, nine had but one each and one had two embryos. All these data point to the last week of June as the time when young are born.

The clusters of females all were far enough back in tunnels or caves to be in dim light, but no bats that I found were in darkness so intense as to require artificial light to see them if a person allowed as much as a minute for his eyes to become accustomed to the semidarkness. When at rest these bats fold the ears in a circular fashion, but as they become alarmed the ears are extended. When this is done in a strong draft, such as blew out of the cave in The Pinnacles at the north end of Pyramid Lake, the effect holds one's attention, for the long, vibrating, semitransparent ears appear to be casting about to detect sounds, as indeed may be true. Here at The Pinnacles, where the daytime temperature in summer is well above 100° F., it seems that the bats may have chosen their roost because of the strong downdraft of cooling air which swept over them and then outward through a lower entrance of the cave.

Corynorhinus rafinesquii intermedius H. W. Grinnell
Long-eared Bat

Corynorhinus macrotis intermedius H. W. Grinnell, Univ. California Publ. Zoöl., 12:320, December 4, 1914. Type from Auburn, Placer County, California.
Corynorhinus rafinesquii intermedius H. W. Grinnell, Univ. California Publ. Zoöl., 17:344, January 31, 1918; Whitlow and Hall, Univ. California Publ. Zoöl., 40:245, September 30, 1933.
Corynorhinus rafinesquii pallescens, Bailey, N. Amer. Fauna, 55:388, August 29, 1936.

Distribution.—Western part of state north of Pine Grove, and probably northern part of state. See figure 94.

Remarks.—Three males from Horse Canyon, Deep Hole, and Pine Grove have measurements, respectively, as follows: 104, 103, 96; 48, 45, 46; 11, 10, —; 36, 32, 35; tragus, 16, 15, —; weight, 7.7, ——, 8.5 grams. Corresponding, average and extreme, measurements of ten females from The Needles, at the north end of Pyramid Lake, and of seven females

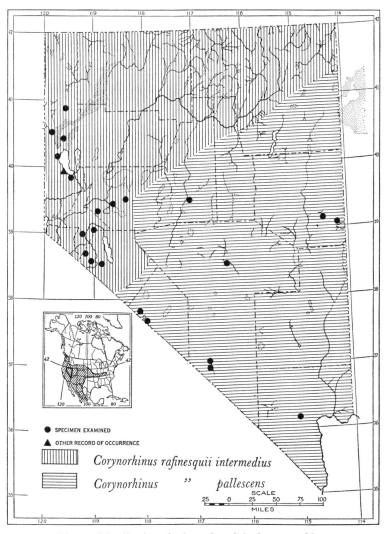

Fig. 94. Distribution of subspecies of the long-eared bat,
Corynorhinus rafinesquii.

from 4½ mi. E Stillwater are: 96 (89–108), 101 (98–106); 45.5 (43–47), 48.4 (46–51); 11.6 (10.0–12.5), 11 (11–11); 30.5 (30–32), 36.7 (34–41); tragus, 12.6 (10–15), 16.0 (15–17); weight, 11.7 grams for one nonpregnant female.

The animals here referred to the race *intermedius* are near Natal Brown above, in contrast to the Bone Brown upper parts of the darker-colored race *tonwsendii* to the northwest. Allen (1916:346), the last reviser of the genus, had no specimens from Nevada, but regarded those from eastern California, which are colored about like our animals from western Nevada, as intergrades between *pallescens* and *townsendii*. Whitlow and Hall (1933:246) chose to employ the name *intermedius* on the ground that animals of this medium-dark coloration have a wide geographic range, a large part of which is not geographically intermediate between that of *townsendii* and that of *pallescens*. It is on this ground that the specimens from western Nevada are referred to *intermedius*; otherwise I would refer them to the race *pallescens*, even though they are darker than the specimens from the southern part of Nevada. The two taken in hibernation from Stanmoore Mine are lighter than others to the northward and suggest intergradation with *pallescens*.

Records of occurrence.—Specimens examined, 28, as follows: *Washoe Co.:* 10 mi. NNW Deep Hole, 5150 ft., 1; Smoke Creek, 3900 ft., 9 mi. E Calif. boundary, 1; Horse Canyon, 5800 ft., Pahrum Peak, 1; The Needles, 4000 ft., N end Pyramid Lake, 7; 1 mi. SW Pyramid Lake, 1. *Lyon Co.:* 9 mi. E and 2 mi. N Yerington, 4700 ft., 1; Bluestone Mine, 3½ mi. SW Yerington, 5200 ft., 1. *Churchill Co.:* 4½ mi. E Stillwater, 4000 ft., 7; 10 mi. SE Fallon, 2; 10 mi. S and 5 mi. W Fallon, 4300 ft., 1 (coll. of J. R. Alcorn). *Mineral Co.:* 2 mi. SW Pine Grove, 7250 ft., 1; Muriel Bee Mine, 4 mi. W Wichman, 5800 ft., 1 (coll. of D. V. Hemphill); Stanmoore Mine, about 7000 ft., Lapon Canyon, Mt. Grant, 2 (coll. of D. V. Hemphill). *Lander Co.:* ¼ mi. WNW Austin, 1.
Additional record: *Washoe Co.:* Sutcliffe, 3700 ft. (D. G. Nichols, MS).

Corynorhinus rafinesquii pallescens Miller
Long-eared Bat

Corynorhinus macrotis pallescens Miller, N. Amer. Fauna, 13:52, October 16, 1897. Type from Keam Canyon, Navajo County, Arizona.
Corynorhinus rafinesquii pallescens, Grinnell, H. W., Univ. California Publ. Zoöl., 17:344, January 31, 1918; Whitlow and Hall, Univ. California Publ. Zoöl., 40:245, September 30, 1933; Burt, Trans. San Diego Soc. Nat. Hist., 7:397, May 31, 1934.

Distribution.—From Esmeralda County and southern White Pine County southward over the state. See figure 94.

Remarks.—Measurements of three males from Cleveland Ranch, Lehman Cave, and Arlemont, respectively, are: 96, 103, 103; 49, 52, 55; —, 11, 10.4; 32, 37, 35; tragus, —, 13, 15; weight, 7.6, 8.8, — grams. Corresponding, average and extreme, measurements of ten females from 1 mi. SE Dyer Ranch are: 104 (100–109); 51.2 (48–58); 10.1 (9.5–10.6); 34.4 (33.0–36.0); tragus, 14.4 (14.0–15.0); weight of six nonpregnant females, 9.3 (8.4–9.8) grams.

The animals here referred to the race *pallescens* average a little darker than specimens from Arizona and are near Army Brown above. The two from White Pine County are the darkest and suggest intergradation with the race *intermedius* from which, so far as we can see, *pallescens* differs only in lighter color.

Records of occurrence.—Specimens examined, 83, as follows: *Esmeralda Co.:* Chiatovich Ranch [= Arlemont in 1928], 4850–4900 ft., 3; 1 mi. SE Dyer Ranch, 5300 ft., 59. *Nye Co.:* 1 mi. W Hot Creek, Hot Creek Range, 6; Springdale, N end Oasis Valley, 10; Amargosa River, 3½ mi. NE Beatty, 3400–3500 ft., 2. *White Pine Co.:* 7 mi. S Cleveland Ranch, 6000 ft., Spring Valley, 1; Lehman Cave, 7200 ft., 1. *Clark Co.:* 7 mi. E Las Vegas, 1 (D. R. Dickey Coll.).

Antrozous pallidus
Pallid Bat

Compared with other members of the Vespertilionidae, this is a large bat, measuring from 100 to 135 mm. in total length, with large ears, a pallid tawny coloration above, and whitish underparts. The muzzle is squarely truncate, with low, flattened swellings on each side. The ears and membranes are brownish colored and naked. The metacarpals of the third, fourth, and fifth fingers are roughly of equal length and fall short of the elbow when folded back along the forearm. The skull has a distinct sagittal crest which is highest posteriorly. The dental formula is i. $\frac{1}{2}$, c. $\frac{1}{1}$, p. $\frac{1}{2}$, m. $\frac{3}{3}$.

From *Corynorhinus*, this bat may be told by its lighter color, wider ear, longer forearm, which is more than 48 mm. (about 53 as opposed to 43), much less pronounced lump on each side of muzzle, convex rather than concave interorbital region of skull, and fewer teeth.

Pallid bats separate by sex in spring before the young are born. The females then are in colonies. About fifty females is the largest number observed in one colony. The males obtained by us all were taken singly. These colonies of females inhabit caves, as at places 12 to 14 miles southwest of Fallon; or in some other places they are found in hollow trees. In winter we have found them hibernating in mine tunnels.

In the Carson Basin of Churchill County, Alcorn (MS) regards the pallid bat as the most common species of the order, noting, nevertheless, that it frequents the edges of the basin, foraging there as well as roosting in the caves along the outcrops of rock at the foot of the hills. He has noted that the pipistrelles, which in the evening emerge from these same rock outcrops, fly toward the center of the basin where irrigated land may provide food to their liking, but that the pallid bats, which emerge some time later, fly instead along the edge of the hills, apparently taking insects on the wing as they go. On May 30, 1927, in the highly eroded area known as the "fossil beds," 7 miles north of Arlemont, I noticed that two of these bats flew out from a cliff in the evening and went directly across the area devoid of plant growth to the areas of sagebrush, where their flight changed to an erratic course as they presumably pursued one insect after another. Both animals were females.

On May 22, 1931, on the Amargosa River, a cluster of these bats, all females, was found about 11 P.M. hanging in the apex of the roof of an empty building. Observations made at the same place before and after this time showed that this was a nighttime retreat only. Another man-made wooden structure that they utilized, in this instance for a daytime retreat, was a railroad bridge 3 miles west-southwest of Lahontan Dam (Alcorn, MS, August 7, 1939), where the bats ensconced themselves in the crevices, $\frac{1}{2}$ to 1 inch in width, between the 18-inch timbers on the under side of the bridge. At Ash Meadows on May 17, 1933, William B. Davis (MS) found five pallid bats roosting in a hole in a cottonwood tree. The three obtained were females. Three others, also females, were taken there at late dusk by means of an insect net as the bats flew low to the ground past Davis. Of the seven others obtained at this locality on May 17, Davis (MS) says: "Last night about 10:30 . . . *Antrozous* . . . [was] numerous, flying low under the cottonwood trees. The wind was blowing quite a breeze, and often the bats would light and hang in small bunches on the bole of the trees. Ward [Russell] killed 7 with two shots. . . . I caught one with the net after it had come to rest on a tree." In all, thirteen *Antrozous*, all females, were taken at this locality. At about 10:30 P.M., on May 27, 1928, at Fish Lake,

Esmeralda County, Seth B. Benson shot two that came to rest, singly, in poplar trees. He thought they alighted to obtain insects on the foliage.

At both Ash Meadows and at Fish Lake the bats flew lower to the ground

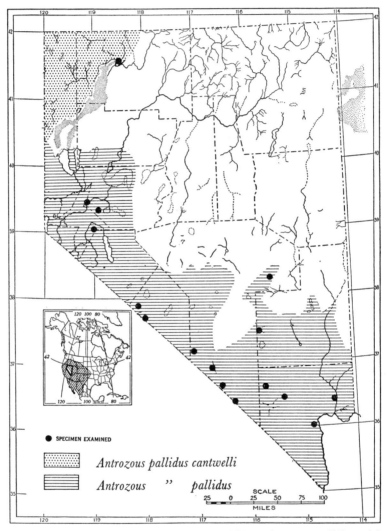

Fig. 95. Distribution of subspecies of the pallid bat, *Antrozous pallidus*, with insert showing range of the species.

and closer around the foliage of the trees than did the other kinds of bats which were active there at the time. At Fish Lake these were *Pipistrellus*, *Tadarida*, and two species of *Myotis*. Burt (1934:397) noted this same tendency to fly near the ground, and he details also how at Indian Springs they alighted on the ground to obtain June beetles of the genus *Polyphylla.*

It may well be that these traits of behavior, flying close to the ground and alighting on the ground and on trees and at other places to obtain food and to devour food already captured, expose them to many dangers that are escaped by kinds of bats which fly higher and capture and eat all their food in the air. This suggestion that their existence is more hazardous than that of, say, *Myotis yumanensis*, which has but one young, is supported by the fact that the pallid bat has from one to three young, an average of two.

Of our twenty-one females taken in May, six may not have been examined for embryos. Thirteen had embryos, two each in eleven females, and one and three in two others. It was noted that the embryos taken on May 17 measured only 3 mm. from crown to rump. The female taken on June 4, 6 miles south of St. Thomas, had two embryos nearly ready for birth, and the embryos found on June 7 at Indian Springs (Burt, 1934:397) also were nearly full term. On June 15, 1939, in crevices in the roof of a cave 10 miles west and 5 miles south of Fallon, Alcorn (MS) found about fifty females nearly every one of which had one or two young securely fastened to her mammae. Bailey (1936:392) found a colony of females with young in the same cave on June 27, 1927. The young of one female, he thought, were but one day old. Burt (1934:397) mentions young bats nearly full grown taken at Indian Springs on August 2 and 3; our specimen taken August 7, west of Lahontan Dam, is of similar age. It appears that young ordinarily are born in the first half of June.

The colony found by Bailey was a mixed one made up of pallid bats and Mexican free-tailed bats; otherwise the Nevada-taken *Antrozous* of which I have record were not found with *Tadarida.*

The hibernating individuals consisted of two males found December 27, 1939, in a mine tunnel 9 miles east and 2 miles north of Yerington, 120 and 138 feet from the mouth of the tunnel. Each bat was in a crevice in the roof of the tunnel and had its ears erect and eyes open. The bats were unable to fly and their movements were slow. The temperature inside the mine where the bats were was 60° F.; outside the mine it was between 40° and 50° F. (Alcorn, MS). In this same mine tunnel, but nearer the entrance, two *Pipistrellus hesperus* and one *Myotis californicus* were taken on this same date.

Antrozous pallidus cantwelli Bailey
Pallid Bat

Antrozous pallidus cantwelli Bailey, N. Amer. Fauna, 55:391, August 29, 1936. Type from Rogersburg, Asotin County, Washington.
Antrozous pallidus pallidus, Taylor, Univ. California Publ. Zoöl., 7:303, June 24, 1911.

Distribution.—Northwestern part of state. See figure 95.

Remarks.—The one bat referred to this race has lighter-colored fur than specimens of *cantwelli* from northeastern California and eastern Oregon, but the ears are typically dark colored. Its forearm measures 42 millimeters. External measurements were not recorded by the collector. Available specimens of *cantwelli* show its distinctness from *pallidus*, but are insufficient clearly to show differences from *pacifica*. I suppose that the race *cantwelli* bears much the same relation to *pallidus* and *pacifica* as *Corynorhinus rafinesquii intermedius* does to *C. r. pallescens* and *C. r. townsendii.*

Record of occurrence.—Specimen examined: *Humboldt Co.:* Quinn River Crossing, 1.

Antrozous pallidus pallidus (LeConte)
Pallid Bat

V[*espertilio*]. *pallidus* LeConte, Proc. Acad. Nat. Sci. Philadelphia, 7 (1854–5):437, 1856. Type from El Paso, El Paso County, Texas; Miller, N. Amer. Fauna, 13:45, October 16, 1897.
Antrozous pallidus, H. Allen, Smithsonian Misc. Coll., 7, article 1:68, June, 1864; Burt, Trans. San Diego Soc. Nat. Hist., 7:397, May 31, 1934.
Antrozous pallidus cantwelli Bailey, N. Amer. Fauna, 55:392, August 29, 1936 (part).

Distribution.—Southern and western part of the state north at least to Fallon. See figure 95.

Remarks.—Measurements of two males from Fish Lake and Burned Corral Canyon are: 112, 113; 48, 50; 13.5, 12.0; 31, 30; tragus, 15, 15; weight, 16.0, 18.4 grams. Corresponding, average and extreme, measurements of females, four from Fish Lake Valley, five from Amargosa River, and ten from Ash Meadows, are, respectively, as follows: 116 (111–121), 107 (101–112), 113 (110–120); 48 (46–51), 43 (40–46), 43 (39–51); 13 (11–14), 11.8 (11–12), 10.4 (10–12); 31.3 (31–33), 30.5 (30–31), 32.6 (30–34); tragus, 15.5 (15–16), 15.8 (15–16), 15.6 (14–17); weight, 19.4 (one specimen), 20.0 (16.9–22), 13.6 (12.7–15.5) grams.

There is a gradual increase in size northward among Nevadan specimens, and on basis of size the two from 7 miles north of Arlemont and those from Fallon might almost as well be referred to *cantwelli* as to *pallidus.* In color they agree with the latter. The specimen from the Quinn Canyon Mountains is darker than average for *pallidus;* it may be an extreme individual or an intergrade with *cantwelli,* but I have no evidence of the occurrence of the species directly to the north of the Quinn Canyon Mountains. The skull of this male is intermediate in size between those of *pallidus* and *cantwelli.* From the races *pacificus* to the westward and *cantwelli* to the northward, *pallidus* is distinguished by smaller size and lighter color, and allegedly from *pacificus* in narrower upper premolar. Each of the Nevadan specimens, including the one referred to *cantwelli,* has P1 narrow, as Miller (1897:45, fig. 6a) has represented it in *pallidus.*

The increase in size toward the north in Nevadan specimens is clearly evident in measurements of the skull, especially its length. Possibly Bailey's (1936:392) reference of specimens from the vicinity of Fallon to *cantwelli* is correct. Specimens from the same place are here referred to *pallidus* because of their lighter color, although it is recognized that they are larger than typical *pallidus.*

Records of occurrence.—Specimens examined, 47, as follows: *Lyon Co.:* 9 mi. E and 2 mi. N Yerington, 2, *Churchill Co.:* 3 mi. WSW Lahontan Dam, 1; 10 mi. W and 5 mi. S Fallon, 4 (1, coll. of J. R. Alcorn). *Esmeralda Co.:* 7 mi. N Arlemont, 5500 ft., 2; Fish Lake, 4800 ft., 3. *Nye Co.:* Burned Corral Canyon, 6700 ft., Quinn Canyon Mts., 1; near Thorp Mill, 1 (U. S. Nat. Mus.); Amargosa River, 3½ mi. NE Beatty, 3400 ft., 5; Amargosa Desert, 22 mi. SE Beatty, 2500 ft., 1; Ash Meadows, 2½ mi. W Devils Hole, 2173 ft., 13. *Lincoln Co.:* Timpahute Mts., 2 (U. S. Nat. Mus.). *Clark Co.:* Indian Springs, 3120–3280 ft., 9 (D. R. Dickey Coll.); Salt Cave, 6 mi. S St. Thomas, 1200 ft., 1; Corn Creek, 1 (D. R. Dickey Coll.); Boulder City, 2400 ft., 1 (U. S. Nat. Park Service, Boulder Dam Recreational Area).

Genus **Tadarida** Rafinesque
Free-tailed Bats

Two species of this genus are recorded from Nevada. Selected family characters are: fifth finger scarcely longer than metacarpal of first; tail projecting conspicuously behind uropatagium; wings narrow; fibula complete, bowed

outward from tibia, its diameter about half that of latter, entering conspicuously into the functional mechanical scheme of the leg. Other characters, of
generic rank, include: bony palate with conspicuous median emargination

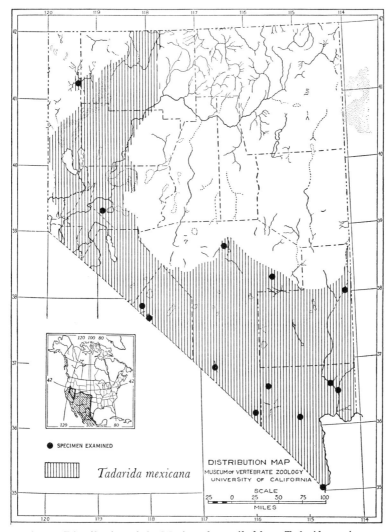

Fig. 96. Distribution of the Mexican free-tailed bat, *Tadarida mexicana*.

extending back of roots of incisors; anterior border of ear with six to eight
horny excrescences; forearm without warty excrescences. The dental formula is
i. $\frac{1}{2}$ or $\frac{1}{3}$, c. $\frac{1}{1}$, p. $\frac{2}{2}$, m. $\frac{3}{3}$. Of the two Nevadan species, *macrotis* has only two
incisors below on each side and *mexicana* ordinarily has three.

Tadarida mexicana (Saussure)
Mexican Free-tailed Bat

Mollosus mexicanus Saussure, Rev. et Mag. d. Zoöl., 12 (ser. 2): 283, July, 1860. Type from Cofre de Perotae, 13,000 feet, Vera Cruz, Mexico.

Tadarida mexicana, Miller, Bull. U. S. Nat. Mus., 128:86, April 29, 1924; Burt, Trans. San Diego Soc. Nat. Hist., 7:398, May 31, 1934.

Distribution.—Lower Sonoran Life-zone and lower part of Upper Sonoran Life-zone of southern and western parts of state. See figure 96.

Remarks.—Measurements of ten of each sex from various localities in Nevada are: ♂, 96 (88–103), ♀, 97 (89–112); 35 (31–40), 35 (31–41); 9.6 (8.0–11.5), 9.6 (8–12); 17 (15–19), 16.6 (14–20); tragus, 4.8 (4–6), — (— – —); weight, 11.1 (8.3–13.0), 11.4 (8.4–14.4) grams.

Characters of *mexicana* which distinguish it from *macrotis* are given in the account of that form. *T. mexicana* is a duller-colored animal than *T. macrotis*, and *T. femorosacca* is intermediate in this respect.

T. mexicana is colonial, frequents caves, crevices in cliffs, spaces in the walls of buildings, and the sexes apparently separate in spring before the young are born. This species is thought to be nonmigratory in Nevada. Specimens were taken, shot while flying, in extreme southern Clark County the first week in February.

The line of flight of these bats when foraging is relatively straight. The deviations in search of insects are mostly downward rather than upward or to the side. The Mexican free-tails are not only colonial but often associate themselves, when roosting, with other kinds of bats. Bailey (1936:392), on June 27, 1927, found them and *Antrozous* roosting together in a cave 10 miles south and 5 miles west of Fallon. At Greenmonster Canyon, on July 12 and 13, a few free-tails flew out from a small cave at dusk along with greater numbers of big brown bats. At Eagle Valley, Ward C. Russell and Davis (MS) obtained two free-tails and twelve big brown bats (*Eptesicus*) from a crevice between the stones of a rock house. Our thirteen females were taken by months, as follows: June, 5 (3 pregnant on June 8, 13, and 22); July, 2 (1 pregnant, July 13); August, 1; January, 1; February, 4. In addition, on June 15, 1939, in a cave 10 miles south and 5 miles west of Fallon, Alcorn (MS) examined four adults from a large colony and found them all to be pregnant females. On August 13 of the preceding year, eight individuals selected from several hundred in this same cave proved to be a mixture of adult females and nearly full-grown young of both sexes. The young appear to be born mostly in late June and early July, but Burt (1934:398) took a female carrying a 30-mm. embryo as late as July 28, 1939, at St. Thomas. The pregnant females recorded above had but one embryo each.

Records of occurrence.—Specimens examined, 45, as follows: *Washoe Co.*: mouth of Little High Rock Canyon, 5000 ft., 1. *Churchill Co.*: 10 mi. S and 5 mi. W Fallon, 4300 ft., 8. *Esmeralda Co.*: 7½ mi. N Arlemont, 5500 ft., 2; Fish Lake, 4800 ft., 5. *Nye Co.*: Greenmonster Canyon, 7500 ft., Monitor Range, 4; Burned Corral Canyon, 6700 ft., Quinn Canyon Mts., 1; Amargosa River, 3½ mi. N Beatty, 3400 ft., 1; Pahrump Ranch, 2667 ft., 4 (D. R. Dickey Coll.). *Lincoln Co.*: Eagle Valley, 3½ mi. N Ursine, 5900 ft., 2. *Clark Co.*: Overton, 2; Colorado River, 5 mi. N Calif. boundary, 500 ft., 1; Colorado River, ½ mi. N Calif.-Nev. Monument, 500 ft., 10.

Additional records (Burt, 1934:398): *Clark Co.*: Indian Springs, 3280 ft., 1 (D. R. Dickey Coll.); ½ mi. E St. Thomas, 1250 ft., 1 (D. R. Dickey Coll.); Las Vegas, 2100 ft., 2 (D. R. Dickey Coll.).

Tadarida macrotis (Gray)
Big Free-tailed Bat

Nyctinomus macrotis Gray, Ann. Nat. Hist., 4:5, September, 1839. Type from interior of Cuba.
Tadarida macrotis, Miller, Bull. U. S. Nat. Mus., 128:86, April 29, 1924; Shamel, Proc. U. S. Nat. Mus., 78:15, May 6, 1931.
Nyctinomus macrotis nevadensis, H. Allen, Bull. U. S. Nat. Mus., 43:171, March, 1894. Type from Nevada.
Nyctinomus nevadensis, J. A. Allen, Bull. Amer. Mus. Nat. Hist., 6:326, November 7, 1894.
Nyctinomops depressus, Miller, Proc. Biol. Soc. Washington, 15:250, December 16, 1902.
Tadarida nevadensis, Miller, Bull. U. S. Nat. Mus., 128:87, April 29, 1924.

Distribution.—Recorded once from Nevada without precise locality.

Remarks.—Extremes of external measurements (after Shamel, 1931:23) are about as follows: 108–129; 48–57; 8.9–13. In addition to its greater size, macrotis may be told from mexicana by the following features: second phalanx of fourth finger shorter (2.0–4.4 mm., rather than 6.6–9.2 mm.); ears extending well beyond end of rostrum when laid forward, rather than only to its end or short of it; inner edges of ears united at base for about 2 mm., rather than not united at base; pocket well developed in membrane at angle of femur and tibia, rather than slightly developed or absent; in skull, width of rostrum anteriorly scarcely more, rather than much more, than interorbital constriction; sagittal crest weaker; upper incisors parallel rather than converging at tips.

The describer of the subspecies nevadensis based his original account on "Two specimens from Nevada in the National Museum...." J. A. Allen (1894:326) showed that each was a young specimen retaining the milk teeth, and that one was labeled "California. John Mullan." I have examined, in the United States National Museum, the other specimen said to have come from Nevada. Its skull is numbered 60660 and the skin is in alcohol. I can add nothing further about its origin. Judging from the localities of capture for the

TABLE 3

CRANIAL MEASUREMENTS (IN MILLIMETERS) OF BATS (CHIROPTERA)

Name and locality	Catalogue no.	Sex	Greatest length	Condylobasal length	Zygomatic breadth	Interorbital constriction	Breadth of brain case	Occipital depth	Mandible	Maxillary tooth row	Maxillary breadth at M3	Mandibular tooth row	Wear of teeth*
Macrotis californicus													
14 mi. E Searchlight.....	61421	♂	22.5	20.3	11.5	3.4	9.0	7.9	15.3	9.9	7.5	10.0	1
	61417	♀	23.6	21.0	11.5	3.6	9.2	7.6	15.3	10.0	7.6	9.9	2
Myotis l. carissima													
3 mi. S Mount Rose......	84076	♂	14.4	13.0	9.0	3.8	7.2	5.3	10.1	6.4	5.9	6.4	2
Calneva.................	65196	♀	14.6	13.6	8.8	3.9	7.4	5.5	10.0	6.5	5.8	6.5	0
Myotis y. sociabilis													
Calneva.................	65188	♂	13.5	12.6	8.2	3.8	6.9	5.3	9.8	6.0	5.6	6.2	0
12-mile Creek...........	73113	♀	14.4	13.3	8.7	3.8	7.1	5.2	10.4	6.3	5.6	6.7	0
Myotis y. yumanensis													
½ mi. S Pyramid Lake..	88052	♂	13.6	12.9	8.1	3.8	7.0	5.3	9.6	6.0	5.3	6.1	1
4 mi. W Fallon..........	88057	♀	13.4	12.7	8.6	3.8	7.2	5.5	9.8	5.8	5.4	6.0	2

* 0, unworn; 1, worn; 2, considerably worn.

TABLE 3—(*Continued*)

Name and locality	Catalogue no.	Sex	Greatest length	Condylobasal length	Zygomatic breadth	Interorbital constriction	Breadth of brain case	Occipital depth	Mandible	Maxillary tooth row	Maxillary breadth at M3	Mandibular tooth row	Wear of teeth*
Myotis e. chrysonotus													
Burned Corral Canyon..	57366	♂	15.1	14.5	9.2	3.7	7.4	5.3	11.2	7.2	5.9	7.5	0
Burned Corral Canyon..	57369	♀	16.0	14.9	9.5	3.6	7.5	5.4	11.8	7.2	6.2	7.5	2
Myotis t. thysanodes													
Horse Spring, San Bernardino Co., Calif......	86119	♂	16.1	15.1	10.3	4.1	7.9	5.7	12.4	7.4	6.7	7.9	2
6 mi. S St. Thomas......	16275	♂	16.5	15.3	10.0	4.0	7.9	6.0	12.0	7.5	6.1	7.9	2
6 mi. S St. Thomas......	16276	♀	16.3	15.3	10.0	3.8	7.7	5.8	12.0	7.4	6.5	7.9	1
Myotis volans interior													
Smiths Creek............	63535	♂	13.8	13.5	8.8	4.1	7.3	5.5	10.4	6.4	5.8	6.8	2
Cottonwood Creek.......	63532	♀	13.9	13.4	8.7	4.0	7.3	5.4	10.1	6.5	6.0	6.4	1
Myotis c. pallidus													
Cave Spring............	40519	♂	12.7	12.1	7.7	2.9	6.1	4.3	9.1	5.2	4.8	5.8	0
7 mi. N Arlemont........	38506	♀	12.8	12.0	7.7	2.8	6.2	4.5	8.9	5.8	5.0	6.0	1
Myotis s. melanorhinus													
2 mi. W Smith Cr. Cave.	78379	♂	14.3	13.5	8.6	3.2	6.7	4.7	10.1	6.5	5.4	6.8	1
Burned Corral Canyon..	57427	♀	13.8	13.3	8.5	2.9	6.7	4.7	10.0	6.2	5.3	6.5	2
Lasionycteris noctivagans													
4 mi. W Fallon..........	88058	♂	15.6	15.2	9.5	4.2	8.1	5.5	11.6	6.7	6.2	6.9	0
12-mile Creek...........	73131	♀	16.4	15.8	9.8	4.4	8.2	5.6	12.1	7.1	6.5	7.2	2
Pipistrellus h. hesperus													
Crystal Spring...........	52203	♂	11.7	11.2	7.6	3.0	6.3	4.1	8.2	4.8	5.1	5.0	1
12 mi. SE Fallon.........	86884	♀	12.7	11.9	7.9	3.3	6.8	4.3	8.9	5.2	5.4	5.3	0
Eptesicus f. bernardinus													
Smoke Creek............	73133	♂	19.4	18.2	13.0	4.4	9.7	6.2	14.3	8.3	8.0	8.6	1
½ mi. W Verdi..........	73136	♀	19.5	18.7	12.9	4.5	9.7	6.2	14.2	8.1	8.3	8.7	2
Eptesicus f. pallidus													
E slope Irish Mountain..	47851	♂	18.0	17.3	12.5	4.1	9.1	6.1	14.7	8.3	8.1	8.9	0
Greenmonster Canyon...	57447	♀	18.2	17.1	12.8	4.6	9.3	6.4	14.2	7.9	8.2	8.3	1
Lasiurus b. teliotus													
4 mi. N Dixon, Calif.	71601	♂	12.0	11.7	8.7	4.3	7.3	5.6	9.1	4.5	5.5	5.6	0
Lasiurus cinereus													
Burned Corral Canyon..	57467	♂	16.0	16.0	12.4	5.2	9.9	6.8	12.7	6.7	8.6	7.7	0
Euderma maculatum													
Reno...................	65171	?	....	....	10.3	4.3	10.3	...	12.4	7.0	7.0	7.2	0
Corynorhinus r. intermedius													
Horse Canyon..........	78390	♂	15.9	14.4	8.8	3.7	8.3	6.0	10.3	6.1	5.9	6.6	0
Smoke Creek............	73141	♀	16.4	15.2	9.2	3.6	8.7	5.7	10.5	6.1	6.1	6.8	0
Corynorhinus r. pallescens													
7 mi. S Cleveland Ranch	45899	♂	16.1	15.1	8.9	3.7	8.5	6.0	10.5	6.2	6.0	6.5	1
Springdale..............	59121	♀	16.3	15.1	8.7	3.6	8.4	5.9	10.8	6.0	5.9	6.8	1
Antrozous p. cantwelli													
Quinn River Crossing....	7895	♀	....	18.9	12.2	4.0	9.5	...	14.6	8.2	...	8.8	0
Antrozous p. pallidus													
Fish Lake..............	40556	♂	20.0	18.6	13.0	4.0	9.5	6.9	14.6	8.0	7.8	8.8	1
7 mi. N Arlemont........	38512	♀	21.2	19.9	12.8	4.2	9.6	7.5	15.4	7.6	8.1	8.5	2
Tadarida mexicana													
Greenmonster Canyon...	57472	♂	16.6	15.8	9.9	3.9	8.6	6.0	11.5	7.2	7.1	7.0	0
10 mi. SW Fallon........	86092	♀	16.7	15.6	10.0	4.1	8.6	6.3	11.4	6.9	7.0	6.8	1
Tadarida macrotis													
Pine Canyon, Brewster Co., Texas............	81683	♀	23.1	21.9	12.8	4.3	11.1	8.0	16.6	10.2	9.2	10.4	0

* 0, unworn; 1, worn; 2, considerably worn.

species outside Nevada, it would be expected to occur in the southern part of the state. Shamel (1931:17), the last reviser of the genus, points out that when more specimens are available, some of the names now regarded as synonyms of *Tadarida macrotis* may prove to pertain to recognizable subspecies or distinct species. In the present instance, with less material available than Shamel had, it has seemed best to follow him in arranging Harrison Allen's name, *nevadensis*, as a synonym of Gray's earlier name, *macrotis*.

Record of occurrence.—Specimen examined: Nevada, 1 (U. S. Nat. Mus.).

Order CARNIVORA
Carnivores (Flesh-eating Mammals)

Ursus americanus californiensis J. Miller
Black Bear

Ursus Californiensis J. Miller, True bear stories, Rand McNally & Co., Chicago and New York, p. 250. 1900. Type locality, California. 1900.
Ursus americanus californiensis, Grinnell, Univ. California Publ. Zoöl., 32:396, July 19, 1929.

Distribution.—In Nevada known only from the Sierra Nevada in the vicinity of Lake Tahoe. See figure 253, page 354.

Remarks.—Black bears of this subspecies attain a total length of 1,750, hind foot of 250, and a weight slightly in excess of 500 pounds. This weight and the measurements given are near the maximum for males. Females average smaller than males, but just how much I cannot say. My guess is that, by weight, they are a third to a half smaller than males. Cinnamon-colored and black-colored individuals occur in the same litter of young. In the race *californiensis*, the cinnamon color phase is the more common.

Selected features of bears, which are animals that almost everyone can recognize at sight, are the short tail, which serves merely as an anal operculum, loose protrusible lips, and short, broad feet. Both the fore and hind feet have five toes. Most of the foot sole is naked. The claws are much longer on the forefeet than on the hind feet. Bears are referred to as plantigrade because, in walking, the entire length of a hind foot may be applied to the ground. But, according to persons who have carefully watched how the animals walk, the heel does not always touch the ground. The dental formula is i. $\frac{3}{3}$, c. $\frac{1}{1}$, p. $\frac{4}{4}$, m. $\frac{2}{3}$. Actually, few adult bears have as many as sixteen premolars; the anterior teeth of this series are small and frequently are lost with advancing age.

Two convenient means for distinguishing black bears from grizzly bears are the lesser length in black bears of the claws on the front feet (about 40 mm., as opposed to 75 mm. in the grizzly bear) and the lesser length and breadth of the last upper molar.

Relying on skulls of the subspecies *californiensis* from the Sierra Nevada of California, that race is found to differ from *Ursus americanus altifrontalis* Elliot, the subspecies next to the west, in less abruptly sloping forehead, the highest part of skull being situated farther posteriorly. From *Ursus americanus cinnamomum* Audubon and Bachman, the subspecies next adjacent to the east, *californiensis* differs in longer skull, relatively longer rostrum, higher brain case, more abruptly sloping forehead, and larger last upper molar tooth.

The molariform teeth are obviously adapted to an omnivorous diet, and their crown surfaces are reminiscent of those of men and pigs, which animals also have omnivorous food habits.

At localities where the winters are cold, black bears retire to sheltered places in late autumn and sleep for a long period, often until spring. But this, in a

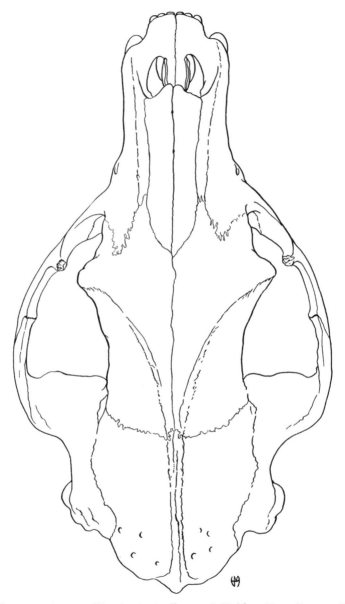

Fig. 97. *Ursus americanus californiensis*, 6 miles north Weldon, Kern County, California, no. 16269, ♂. × ½. (Other views of this skull are shown in figs. 98, 99, 100).

strict sense, is not hibernation. The temperature of the bear's body is not low-ered to near that of its immediate environment, and its rate of heartbeat and respiration are thought not to be lowered much below normal, whereas in

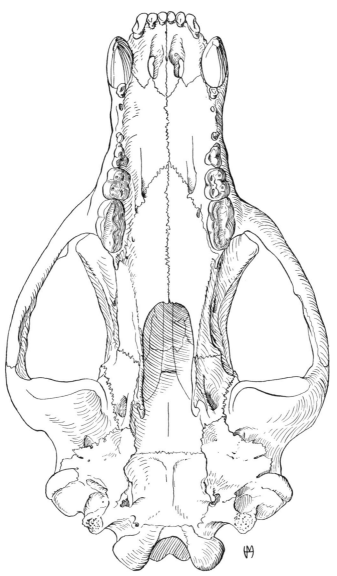

Fig. 98. *Ursus americanus californiensis*. A different view of this
skull is shown in fig. 97. × ½.

animals which truly hibernate, the pulse and breathing are slowed down to but
a small fraction of what they are when the animals are active in spring, and
the temperature of the body, as, for example, in a ground squirrel, may drop
almost to that of freezing. One pertinent bit of evidence in this connection is

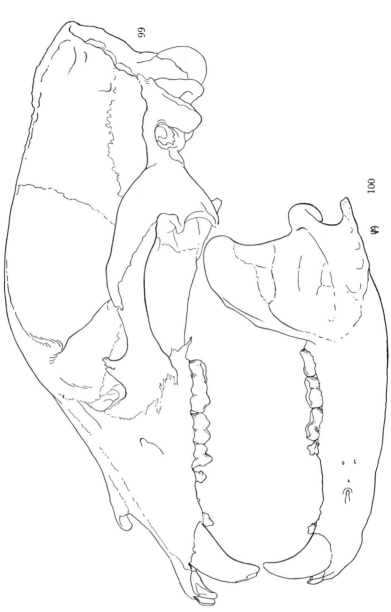

Figs. 99, 100. *Ursus americanus californiensis*. A different view of this skull is shown in fig. 97. × ½.

that bears always are found awake when their winter dens are broken into; they are not torpid, as are hibernating ground squirrels.

On August 21, 1934, at 7100 feet elevation, ¼ mile south of Incline Creek, Washoe County, I found sign of bear, including feces which contained remains of insects. Reports were common, at this time, of bears invading camps along Incline Creek, presumably in search of stored food. In the summer of 1935, William H. Dust, caretaker at Marlette Lake, reported tracks of bears being frequently seen about the lake and said that in early August of that same year guests coming to the lake saw a large bear which was of the cinnamon color phase.

No reports regarded as trustworthy have been had of bears in other parts of the state. All the bears, at least now, in the vicinity of Lake Tahoe are thought to be black bears, and no information about grizzly bears, if they ever occurred in Nevada, has come to my attention.

Specimens examined.—None. Records of occurrence additional to those given above and as obtained by Alcorn (MS) on basis of tracks and other sign: *Washoe Co.:* head of Hunters Creek, 1½ mi. SW Hunters Lake, 8000 ft., 2½ mi. S Mt. Rose. *Douglas Co.:* 1 mi. E Zephyr Cove.

Procyon lotor
Raccoon

Externally, the raccoon may be known by his black mask, dark grayish color, and ringed tail. The tail is round, shorter than the body, and is marked by six white rings, six black rings, and a black tip. The rings go all the way around the tail. The upstanding ears measure about 45 millimeters from the notch on the dried skin. All the feet are provided with five clawed digits. The entire sole of the hind foot is naked, and the track left by it is not unlike that made by the foot of a child. The forefeet and forearms are relatively long. These forefeet are used by the raccoon deftly to manipulate its food, to wash its food, and to do many other things. The skull has a short rostrum, rounded dorsal profile, relatively large brain case, and a hard palate which extends behind the molars. The dental formula is i. $\frac{3}{3}$, c. $\frac{1}{1}$, p. $\frac{4}{4}$, m. $\frac{2}{2}$.

The population of raccoons in Nevada is small. This is because the animals require water in their habitat, and Nevada has relatively little territory which meets this requirement. The places where the animals do occur are close to water. They are said to utilize, for daytime retreats, crevices in rocky cliffs. At the lower end of Wilson Canyon on the East Walker River, I noted, from the tracks, that a large raccoon visited one section of the river only about every 5 days. Presumably each adult animal, excepting females with small young, has a beat which requires several days for it to cover. The two specimens obtained from Marlette Lake provide an unusually high record station of occurrence, zonally as well as altitudinally. I know of no other specimens caught in the Sierra Nevada at an elevation of as high as 8000 feet nor of any others taken in the Hudsonian Life-zone.

The value of raccoons' furs has fluctuated from year to year. On February 16, 1942, when the price on this species was low, W. B. Gallagher received $2.50 each for two pelts trapped in the Carson Valley. In some years the price has been as much as three times higher.

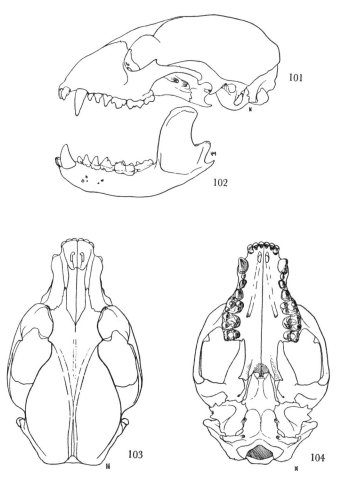

Figs. 101–104. *Procyon lotor psora*, south end Marlette Lake, no. 70003, ♀, subadult. ✕½.

Drawing on information gathered about raccoons outside of Nevada, it is known that they frequent the hardwoods and are expert climbers. Water is important to them because they obtain a part of their food from the animal life in it. The specific name *"lotor"* refers to the habit which raccoons, at least captive ones, have of washing their food in water. Nevertheless, a considerable part of their food is obtained away from streams or lakes; the animals are truly omnivorous. Over much of the United States they are hunted at night by dogs taught to trail the animals. Usually the chase ends when the raccoon climbs a tree from which it is dislodged by one means or another. Raccoons are

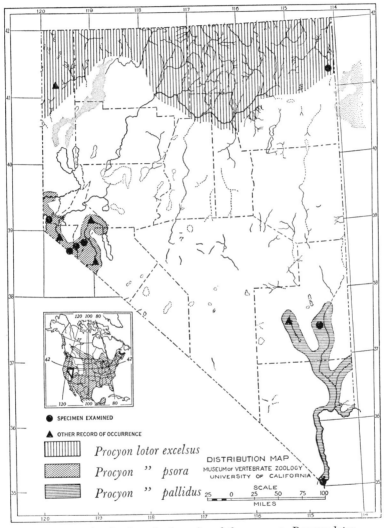

Fig. 105. Distribution of subspecies of the raccoon, *Procyon lotor*.

nocturnal, but occasionally venture forth in the daytime. In autumn they store up much fat which sustains them in their periods of winter sleep. In cold weather they hole up until the temperature rises or the storm passes. A single litter of three to six is born each year.

Procyon lotor excelsus Nelson and Goldman

Raccoon

Procyon lotor excelsus Nelson and Goldman, Journ. Mamm., 11:458, November 11, 1930. Type from Owyhee River, near mouth of North Fork, Malheur County, Oregon.

Distribution.—Northern part of state in suitable habitat. See figure 105.

Remarks.—External measurements of adults of this subspecies are not available. But judging from the size of the skull, these external measurements would equal or exceed those given for the subspecies *psora*. According to the original description of this subspecies, individuals of it attain larger size than those of any other race; the color resembles that of *Procyon lotor psora*, but is paler; the color is paler than that of *Procyon lotor pacifica*, especially on the top of the head, which is grayer; skull similar to that of *psora*, but larger and more angular, with frontal region broader and generally flattened; skull with frontal region broad as in *pacificus*, but brain case more elongated and entire skull larger; cranially differs from forms east of the Rocky Mountains in larger size and has "broad, flat frontal region, with prominent postorbital processes (frontal region generally high and narrow, and postorbital processes weak, or obsolescent, in forms east of Rocky Mountains)." (See original description.)

A fur trapper in northern Washoe County, living 8½ miles east of Hausen, pointed out to me, in 1936, a place 6 miles farther east where he had caught a raccoon. I gathered that this was the only raccoon caught by him in several years' trapping in this area. The place was in a canyon where water and some cottonwood trees were to be found. In 1935, reports were had of the occurrence of raccoons on a small creek northeast of San Jacinto, Elko County. A fur buyer in Reno reported receiving skins from the vicinity of Elko and Winnemucca and understood that along the Humboldt River between these two towns the animals found refuge in crevices in the rock walls of canyons.

Records of occurrence.—Specimens examined, 2 (in U. S. Nat. Mus., Biol. Surv. Coll.), as follows: *Humboldt Co.:* near Golconda, 1 (skull only). *Elko Co.:* Montello, 1.

Additional record: *Washoe Co.:* 14½ mi. E Hausen (report of trapper).

Procyon lotor psora Gray

Raccoon

Procyon psora Gray, Ann. and Mag. Nat. Hist., 10:261, December, 1842. Type locality, Sacramento County, California.

Procyon lotor psora, Grinnell, Univ. California Publ. Zoöl., 40:98, September 26, 1933.

Distribution.—Sierra Nevada, in vicinity of Lake Tahoe and along streams which course eastward from these mountains, from the Truckee River south at least to East Walker River. See figure 105.

Remarks.—External measurements of an adult male from Topaz Lake and a subadult female from ½ mi. S Wichman are: 911, 879; 370, 314; 128, 125; ear from notch, 51, 57; weight, 7,756, —— grams. Recorded weights of males in California are from 4,082 to 8,392 grams and of females, 5,443 to 7,600 grams.

Comparison with *P. l. excelsus* has been made in the account of that race. As described in the account of *pallidus*, *psora* differs from it in darker color. The material from along the eastern base of the Sierra Nevada reveals differences between the raccoons there and topotypical *psora*. The Nevadan skins average darker in color, but in this are indistinguishable from selected extreme specimens of *psora* taken in the Central Valley and coast ranges of California. The scanty material of *excelsus* makes it difficult to say whether it also averages lighter than the Nevadan specimens of *psora*. The specimens of *excelsus* (from Montello, Nevada, and Modoc County, California) and Nevadan animals from the Walker River system agree among themselves but differ from California-taken *psora* in that the black rings on the tail are wider and in that the intervening light-colored rings are either buffy rather than white or yellowish rather than grayish. The animals from Marlette Lake are intermediate in this particular and more nearly resemble California-taken animals. The skulls of the Nevadan animals are broad interorbitally, as in *excelsus*, but in other features agree better with skulls of *psora* from the Central Valley and coast ranges of California.

Raccoons occur regularly all along the Walker River system in Nevada. The two from Marlette Lake mark a zonal occurrence (Hudsonian) that is high for the species, and I think that they are uncommon there. Their tracks are seen more frequently lower down along the streams which course eastward from the Sierra Nevada.

Records of occurrence.—Specimens examined, 10, as follows: *Ormsby Co.:* S end Marlette Lake, 1; SE side Marlette Lake, 1. *Douglas Co.:* Topaz Lake, West Walker River, 1. *Lyon Co.:* Wilson Canyon, 2 (1 in U. S. Nat. Mus., Biol. Surv. Coll.); West Walker River, sec. 26, T. 11 N, R. 23 E, Mt. Diablo Base and Meridian, 1. *Mineral Co.:* East Walker River (5 mi. N Wichman, 1; ½ mi. S Wichman, 5050 ft., 2 [1 in coll. of D. V. Hemphill]; 1½ mi. SW Wichman, 1), 4.

Additional records: *Washoe Co.:* E side Lake Tahoe (Hall, MS). *Douglas Co.:* East Fork Carson River, 4900 ft., 5 mi. SE Minden (Alcorn, MS). *Lyon Co.:* Walker River, 14 mi. N Yerington (Alcorn, MS).

Procyon lotor pallidus Merriam
Raccoon

Procyon pallidus Merriam, Proc. Biol. Soc. Washington, 13:151, June 13, 1900. Type from New River, Colorado Desert, Imperial County, California.
Procyon lotor pallidus, Grinnell, Univ. California Publ. Zoöl., 40:99, September 26, 1933.

Distribution.—Along Colorado River, Virgin River, Meadow Valley Wash, north at least to Caliente, and in Pahranagat Valley. See figure 105.

Remarks.—In external measurements and cranial features not known to differ from *psora*. Relying on California-taken specimens, *pallidus*, in comparison with *psora*, differs in lighter color. The black areas are smaller, individual hairs have less black, the black color is less intense, and the underfur is paler.

The skull without skin that we have from the Colorado River is identified on geographic grounds. The two skins with skulls from Meadow Valley Wash are of young animals which are practically as dark colored on the foreparts of the body and head as are young *psora*. No skins of *pallidus* of comparable age are available. Specimens of raccoons are lacking from Pahranagat Valley, but reliable reports attest their occurrence there.

Records of occurrence.—Specimens examined, 3, as follows: *Lincoln Co.:* 3 mi. S Tennille Ranch, 10 mi. S Caliente, 2. *Clark Co.:* Colorado River, ½ mi. N Calif.-Nev. Monument, 500 ft., 1 skull.

Additional record: *Lincoln Co.:* Pahranagat Valley, 2 mi. N Crystal Spring (report of one killed).

Bassariscus astutus nevadensis Miller
Ring-tailed Cat

Bassariscus astutus nevadensis Miller, Proc. Biol. Soc. Washington, 26:159, June 30, 1913. Type from El Dorado Canyon, Clark County, Nevada. Hall, Univ. California Publ. Zoöl., 30:46, September 8, 1926; Hall, Univ. California Publ., Bull. Dept. Geol. Sci., 16:444, March 17, 1927; Goldman, Proc. Biol. Soc. Washington, 45:87, June 21, 1932; Burt, Trans. San Diego Soc. Nat. Hist., 7:398, May 31, 1934.

Distribution.—Southern part of state; definitely known from El Dorado Canyon and Meadow Valley Wash. See figure 110.

Remarks.—Miller (1913:159) gives approximate external measurements of the type specimen, a female, as 640, 310, 57. Grinnell, Dixon, and Linsdale (1937:171) record external measurements of a female and male from Union Mine, west slope of Inyo Mountains, Inyo County, California, as: 715, 715; 375, 373; 64, 63. These two Californian specimens, which, for several weeks at least, had been in captivity, weighed 955 grams and 1,000 grams, the female being the heavier.

The long erect ears (35 mm. from notch in dried skins from Lincoln County) help to give this animal a foxlike appearance. The tail is longer than the body, and the feet have five

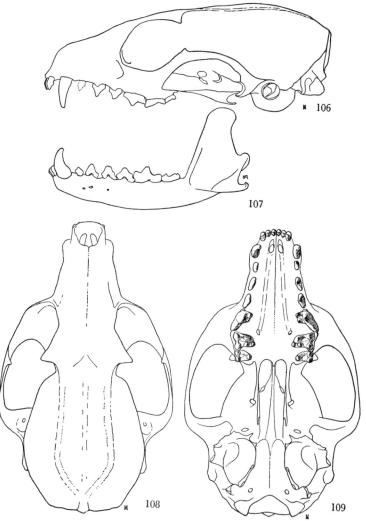

Figs. 106–109. *Bassariscus astutus nevadensis*, 10 miles south Caliente, no. 51665, ♂. × 1.

toes, each of which is provided with a claw. The general color above is Light Buff overcast with blackish and dark brownish pigment in the tips of the overhairs. The eye is ringed with black except that in some animals the back part of the superior border is white. The supraorbital, suborbital, subauricular patches, and upper lips are white, as also are the underparts, except that the belly may be tinged with Light Buff. The tail is ringed, usually with eight white rings and eight black rings plus a black tip. The black rings are incomplete, being absent on the underside of the tail, which is flattened. In the race *nevadensis* the white bands are wider than the black bands in every specimen but one; in it they are of equal width. The dental formula is i. $\frac{3}{3}$, c. $\frac{1}{1}$, p. $\frac{4}{4}$, m. $\frac{2}{2}$.

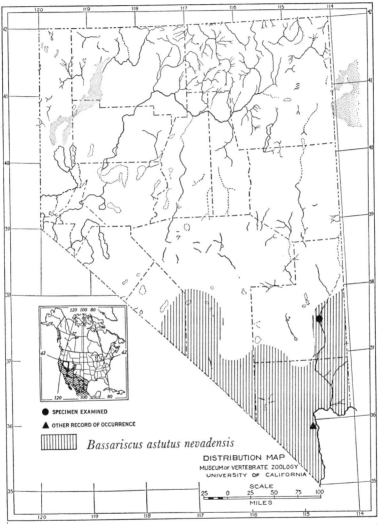

Fig. 110. The two known record stations of occurrence of the ring-tailed cat, *Bassariscus astutus*, which probably ranges over the southern third of the state.

In comparison with *Bassariscus astutus raptor* (Baird) to the northwest, *nevadensis* is lighter colored throughout, especially on the feet, and is smaller. From *Bassariscus astutus octavus* Hall, *nevadensis* differs in lighter color and greater breadth across the molars. *Bassariscus astutus arizonensis* Goldman is known to me by six specimens from localities in

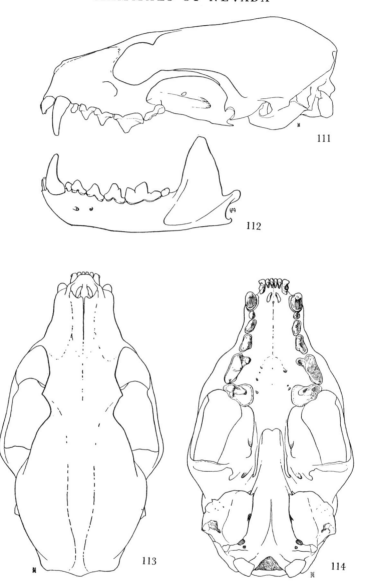

Figs. 111–114. *Martes caurina sierrae*, Marlette Lake, no. 69634, ♂, subadult. ×1.

Arizona, as follows: Blue River, Greenlee County, 1; Roosevelt, Gila County, 2; 3 mi. N Phoenix, Maricopa County, 1; 1 mi. W Paradise, Cochise County, 2. Some of these specimens are as described by Goldman in the original description. They are more blackish than *nevadensis*. Others are lighter, but two of these lighter-colored animals are more ochraceous than *nevadensis*, and are reminiscent of *Bassariscus astutus flavus*. One of these light-colored animals is indistinguishable from *nevadensis*. Comparison of the skulls shows no distinctive difference between *nevadensis* and *arizonensis* in width of rostrum or expansion of the zygomatic arches, as alleged in the original description, but the smaller size of the foramen ovale in *nevadensis* and, on the average, the lesser inflation of its tympanic bullae anteriorly, features also mentioned in the original description, seem to hold. Thus, from *arizonensis*, *nevadensis* may be thought of as differing in lighter color, smaller foramen ovale, and generally less inflation anteriorly of the auditory bullae.

In 1929 trappers received up to $4.50 each for pelts of ring-tailed cats, but in 1930–1931 the price had dropped to about $1 and has not risen much if any above that until now, spring of 1942.

Drawing on what is known about this animal in states other than Nevada, it can be said to be nocturnal, to be a good climber, to make its den in a dry crevice of a cliff or in a hole in a tree not farther than ¼ mile from water, to feed mainly upon mice and round-tailed wood rats, although taking berries in season, and to have two to four young. It is said that the animals are easily tamed and that the name miner's cat, which in the early days was given to them in parts of the western United States, resulted from the frequency with which ring-tails were tamed enough to take up residence about the cabins of miners.

Records of occurrence.—Specimens examined, 4, as follows: *Lincoln Co.:* Meadow Valley Wash, 7 mi. S Caliente, 3; Meadow Valley Wash, 10 mi. S Caliente, 1.
Additional record: *Clark Co.* (Miller, 1913:159): El Dorado Canyon.

Martes caurina sierrae Grinnell and Storer
Western Marten

Martes caurina sierrae Grinnell and Storer, Univ. California Publ. Zoöl., 17:2, August 23, 1916. Type from head of Lyell Canyon, 9800 feet, Yosemite National Park, Tuolumne County, California.

Distribution.—Sierra Nevada in vicinity of Lake Tahoe. See figure 253, page 354.

Remarks.—Average and extreme measurements of nine males from the Sierra Nevada of California (Grinnell, Dixon, and Linsdale, 1937:185) are as follows: 631 (576–730); 199 (170–240); 85 (79–90). Measurements of two females from the same source are: 551, 557; 177, 180; 76, 70. Adult males weigh 1,038 (874–1,123) grams, and the two females weigh 809 and 639 grams.

The color of the one specimen available from Nevada, a subadult male taken in February, 1935, agrees with selected specimens from California (for detailed description see Grinnell, Dixon, and Linsdale, 1937:184). The general coloration of the body is Snuff Brown, which results from a blending of the color of the underfur of lighter tint with that of the overhair of darker shade; color of tail at base is like that of body but gradually darkens to blackish at tip; head, paler than body, light drab; throat, pectoral region, and a narrow (15 mm.) line down belly to vent is Ochraceous Orange and in some places Cinnamon Buff. The facial and carpal vibrissae are black. The soles of the feet are densely haired, excepting the tips of the digital pads, which are bare. Generic characters of the skull are a basilar length, depending on the sex, of between 60 and 75 mm., facial angle slight, tympanic bullae moderately inflated but not in close contact with the paroccipital processes, and palate projecting behind the last upper molars. The dental formula is i. $\frac{3}{3}$, c. $\frac{1}{1}$, p. $\frac{4}{4}$, m. $\frac{1}{2}$. The inner moiety of M1 is larger than the outer. P4 has a simple deuterocone. In m1 the trigonid is larger than the talonid, the metaconid is small and appressed to the protoconid, the hypoconid is large, and the talonid is semibasined.

The specific name *caurina* is used in accordance with current nomenclature. I do not know whether *caurina* is a species distinct from *americana*, and the species name should be regarded as tentative pending a revision of the genus. The insert showing the range in North America of martens gives the range for the subgenus *Martes*, not alone that of *Martes caurina*.

From *Martes caurina humboldtensis*, the race to the northwest, *sierrae* differs in larger average size, darker coloration generally, and larger skull with a broader rostrum. From *Martes caurina caurina*, the race to the northward, *sierrae* differs in having a narrower rostrum, and from Idaho-taken specimens of *caurina*, in a more reddish (less yellowish) pelage.

The single specimen of marten from Nevada was trapped in February, 1935, by W. H. Dust, on the western shore of Marlette Lake. Here a dense stand of large red fir trees come near to the shore of the granite-bound lake. There are reports of martens from several other parts of the high mountain country in Nevada from Mount Rose south to Monument Peak.

From what is known of the species in areas outside Nevada, particularly in California, it appears that martens feed principally on rodents, are active all winter, although they may hole up for a day or two, travel as much as 10 miles in a night, bear one litter of three to four young per year after a long gestation period of 259 to 275 days, and produce a valuable fur. According to Grinnell, Dixon, and Linsdale (1937:205), "The average value to the trapper of marten pelts in California for the 5-year period, 1920–1924, was $15.71. The highest average price for any one year was $25.08, and the lowest $6.51." Prices received for the few caught in Nevada would be expected to run about the same as for those in California.

Record of occurrence.—Specimen examined: *Ormsby Co.:* Marlette Lake, 8000 ft., 1.

Genus **Mustela** Linnaeus
Weasels, Ferrets, and Minks

Members of this genus are slender-bodied and small, with the diameter of the head only slightly exceeding that of the neck. In the skull the rostrum is relatively short; facial angle slight; tympanic bullae greatly inflated (moderately in *Mustela vison*), cancellous and with paroccipital processes closely appressed; palate behind upper molars; dental formula, i. $\frac{3}{3}$, c. $\frac{1}{1}$, p. $\frac{3}{3}$ or $\frac{3}{2}$, m. $\frac{1}{2}$; inner moiety of M1 larger than outer; P4 with simple deuterocone; in m1 trigonid longer than talonid, metaconid absent, talonid trenchant. Three species, the short-tailed weasel, the long-tailed weasel, and the mink occur in Nevada.

Mustela cicognanii lepta (Merriam)
Short-tailed Weasel

Putorius streatori leptus Merriam, Proc. Biol. Soc. Washington, 16:76, May 29, 1903. Type from Silverton, San Juan County, Colorado.
Putorius cicognanii, Taylor, Univ. California Publ. Zoöl., 7:298, June 24, 1911.
Mustela cicognanii, Linsdale, Amer. Midland Nat., 19:174, January, 1938.

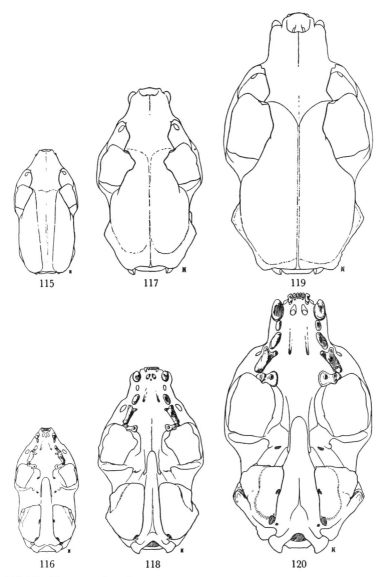

Figs. 115–120. Three species of the genus *Mustela*. All ×1. (Other views of these skulls are shown in figs. 121–126.)

Figs. 115, 116. *Mustela cicognanii lepta*, Baker Creek, 8500 feet, no. 41501, ♂.
Figs. 117, 118. *Mustela frenata nevadensis*, Baker Creek, 8400 feet, no. 41508, ♂.
Figs. 119, 120. *Mustela vison energumenos*, Goose Creek, 5000 feet. no. 74391. ♂.

Distribution.—Boreal zones in higher mountains of at least northern half of state. See figure 127.

Remarks.—External measurements of a male and female from Baker Creek are: 220, 190; 56, 42; 26, 23; weight, 57.7 and 33.8 grams. In summer pelage the color is brown above. The underparts, including the lips and medial sides of the legs, but no part of the tail, are white. The distal fourth of the tail is black or blackish brown. The winter pelage is

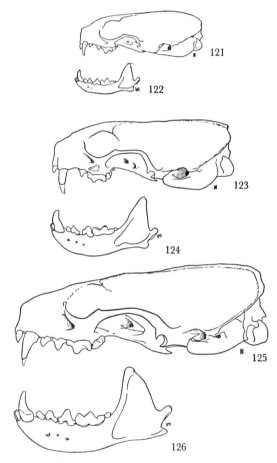

Figs. 121–126. Three species of the genus *Mustela*. Different views of these skulls are shown in figs. 115–120. All ×1.

Figs. 121, 122. *Mustela cicognanii lepta,* ♂.
Figs. 123, 124. *Mustela frenata nevadensis,* ♂.
Figs. 125, 126. *Mustela vison energumenos,* ♂.

all white except the tip of tail, which is black. Ventrally the tympanic bullae are flush with the squamosal bone anterior to the bullae, the length of the two lower mandibles in normal position is less than the postglenoid length (glenoid fossa to exoccipital condyle), and the skull lacks a sagittal crest.

Of the six specimens available, two were taken in mousetraps baited with rolled oats, and two were taken in rattraps baited with rolled oats. Notes are lacking concerning the means by which the young female from South Twin

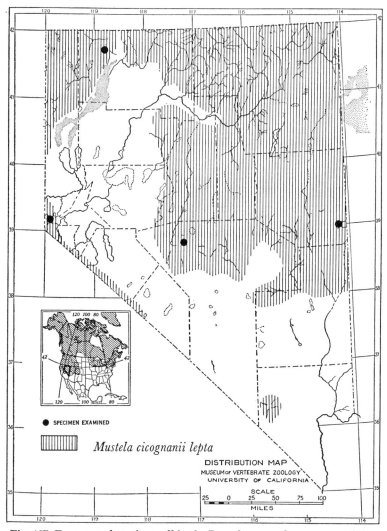

Fig. 127. Four record stations, all in the Boreal zones, of occurrence of the short-tailed weasel, *Mustela cicognanii*.

River was procured, or the exact habitat in which it was found. The sixth specimen, an adult female, was taken in one of three no. 1 steel traps the pans of which had been smeared with the scent from the anal glands of an adult male of the same species caught in a rattrap the night before. Concerning the pair of specimens last mentioned, the collector, R. D. Moore, in his field notes, says: "Baker Creek, . . . White Pine Co., Nevada, June 18, 1929. The male . . . was secured on the upper edge of the *Artemesia* and just below the Mountain Mahogany at 8675 ft., in a small talus. . . . One [steel] trap set about thirty feet from the trap which caught the male . . . caught a female. . . . She was caught by the shoulders with both feet and her head pressed down against the pan of the trap." The animal from Ormsby County was taken beside a dead stump on the bank of a stream 12 inches wide, beneath larkspur, monkshood, and associated plants in the red fir-aspen belt. The elevation was 8150 feet, in the saddle ½ mile south of Marlette Lake.

This species is clearly restricted to the Boreal life-zones and in summer, at least, appears not to occur lower down than the upper part of the Transition Life-zone. Burt (1934:399) thought it probable that this animal occurred on Charleston Peak.

The name *Putorius* (*Arctogale*) *muricus* Bangs, with type specimen from Echo, Eldorado County, California, might be expected to apply to the specimen from Marlette Lake, but I can find no difference judged to be of systematic worth between *P. muricus* and the earlier-named *P. leptus*.

Records of occurrence.—Specimens examined, 6, as follows: *Ormsby Co.:* ½ mi. S Marlette Lake, 8150 ft., 1. *Humboldt Co.:* Alder Creek, 6000 ft., Pine Forest Mts., 1. *Nye Co.:* South Twin River, Toyabe Mts., 1 (U. S. Nat. Mus.). *White Pine Co.:* Baker Creek, 8675 ft., 2, and 11,100 ft., 1.

Mustela frenata nevadensis Hall
Long-tailed Weasel

Mustela frenata nevadensis Hall, Carnegie Institution of Washington Publ. no. 473:91, November 20, 1936. Type from 3 miles east of Baker, White Pine County, Nevada.
Mustela (sp. ?), part, Burt, Trans. San Diego Soc. Nat. Hist., 7:398, May 31, 1934.
Putorius arizonensis, Taylor, Univ. California Publ. Zoöl., 7:299, June 24, 1911.
Mustela arizonensis, Borell and Ellis, Journ. Mamm., 15:20, February 15, 1934; Linsdale, Amer. Midland Nat., 19:174, January, 1938.

Distribution.—Over the entire state, except in areas of extreme desert; not reported from along the Colorado River. See figure 128.

Remarks.—Measurements of three males and six females are: ♂, 421 (410–437), ♀, 328 (311–354); 157 (154–160), 137 (113–135); 46 (45–47), 37 (35–40). Two males average 279 (250, 308) grams in weight and three nonpregnant females, 127 (122–134) grams.

In summer pelage the color is brown above. The underparts, including the medial sides of the legs, parts of the feet, and proximal fourth of underside of tail, are Buff Yellow to Straw Yellow and sometimes Ochraceous Yellow in young. The chin, lower lips, and sometimes upper lips are white. In winter, all white, except tip of tail, which is at all times black or, on upper parts, rarely near Snuff Brown or lighter than Brussels Brown with a smoked effect. The tympanic bullae are well inflated and project below the squamosal bone anterior to the bullae; the length of the two lower mandibles in normal position is more than the postglenoid length (glenoid fossa to exoccipital condyle); and the skull of an adult male has a well-developed sagittal crest.

From the subspecies *latirostra*, *pulchra*, *xanthogenys*, *oregonus*, and *altifrontalis* on the west, *nevadensis* differs in absence, or great reduction, of light-colored facial markings. From *saturata* and *washingtoni*, other races to the westward, it differs in lighter color and extension of the light color of the underparts onto the ankles and underside of the tail.

From *effera* of northeastern Oregon and southeastern Washington, *nevadensis* differs in larger size, and from *oribasa* of the northern Rocky Mountains in smaller size. *M. f. alleni* of the Black Hills is lighter colored and smaller than *nevadensis*, whereas *longicauda* of

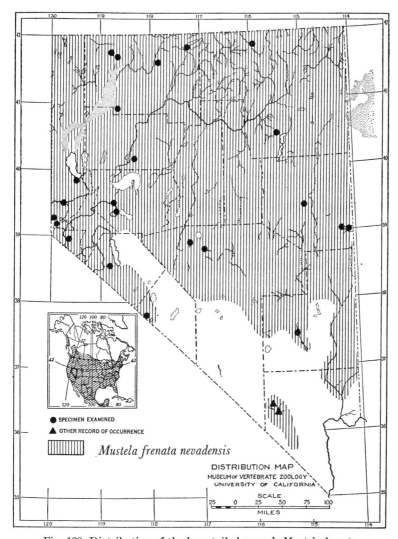

Fig. 128. Distribution of the long-tailed weasel, *Mustela frenata.*

the Great Plains also is lighter colored, but larger. *M. f. neomexicana* of the southwestern United States also is larger and lighter colored than *nevadensis* and has well-developed, light-colored facial markings that are lacking in *nevadensis*. From *arizonensis* of the high plateau country of Arizona, *nevadensis* differs in larger size and less inflated tympanic bullae.

The places where weasels have been taken or seen are scattered pretty much over the entire state. All the records are from the mountains, along streams, or from irrigated lands in the desert. None has been found far out in the waterless, sandy desert, and there are no records of weasel, so far as known, from along the Colorado River in Nevada. Seemingly, the subspecies *nevadensis* is ill-adapted to live amid Lower Sonoran zonal conditions such as obtain along the Colorado River. The animal has been found just inside the upper margin of this zone in Pahranagat Valley at an elevation of less than 4000 feet, but this occurrence probably is exceptional. In the other direction it shows no lack of tolerance of climatically cooler life-zones; it appears to be as abundant in the Hudsonian Life-zone around Marlette Lake as it is in the Canadian, Transsition, or Upper Sonoran life-zones. Probably it lives regularly at and even above timber line; I saw one in a rock-slide on Wheeler Peak at near 11,000 feet elevation, and Frank Gorham took a specimen at 10,700 feet altitude on Mount Jefferson.

Weasels deserve the reputation which they have gained for quickness. Although a man can outrun one, the weasel is so alert and agile that by quickly dodging, it is next to impossible for a person to catch an uninjured animal, except by driving it into a hole. Even then the chances are in favor of the weasel, for almost invariably a weasel caught in a person's bare, or thinly gloved, hands manages to manipulate its snakelike neck and head so as to sink its strong canine teeth deeply into one's finger or hand. That they climb with facility is known from our attempting to capture one in a cottonwood tree at Fallon (Alcorn, MS). A female, unaware of my presence, I think, in running across a field near Baker, at every bound bent the back up so far as to remind me of a measuring worm. For part of the time when running, the tail was held off the ground straight out behind, and then, for a while, inclined upward at an angle of about 45°.

The males are larger than the females, and about twice as heavy. Because of their larger size they may range more widely than the females. If this is true, it helps to explain why about three out of four specimens taken in steel traps at meat baits are males. Judging from the sexes of young animals captured in White Pine County, a litter contains about equal numbers of each sex.

Long-tailed weasels may be mostly nocturnal, but they are certainly to some extent diurnal. They do not hibernate. Two burrows in White Pine County from which young animals about 8 weeks old were trapped yielded, of adults, only one female each. This suggested that the males remain apart. Furthermore, at this time, and some 200 yards from one of these nurseries, an adult male was captured in a burrow which when excavated proved to have no other occupant, although it obviously had been used for some days as a weasel lair. I infer that the long-tailed weasel is solitary, except when the female remains with her young and when the two sexes come together to mate.

Just when mating takes place I do not know, but I have learned by keeping captive a female taken on the California shore of Lake Tahoe that the gestation period is long for so small an animal—at least 104 days (Hall, 1938a). Possibly the gestation period is much longer even than 104 days and it may equal or exceed that of the marten. It is fairly certain that there is but one litter per year. With one adult female we took two young about 8 weeks old, and with another, three young in the same stage of development. Probably these were the survivors of a litter of a greater number at the time of birth. Hamilton (1933:327) found that two captives of the eastern subspecies of this same species gave birth to litters of six and seven young.

The young taken by us in White Pine County on June 4 and June 25, 1929, are estimated to be about 8 weeks old. If this estimate is correct, the young were born in April. By December, when 8 to 9 months old, the animals have attained adult size.

All the three dens that were excavated in White Pine County were originally burrows of pocket gophers (*Thomomys bottae*). From each of two of these burrows we had trapped an adult female and young weasels, and from the third an adult male weasel. In no burrow was there a nest. Some enlargements of the burrows were trampled and much-used, suggesting that the weasels used these as places of shelter and rest. No remains of vertebrates were found in or near these burrows.

Although we have found weasels in many situations in Nevada, four times in rock-slides and once in an unused marmot burrow, for example, they most often were obtained from the burrows of pocket gophers. Excluding the weasels taken by Alcorn, more specimens of the remaining lot were caught in traps set in the burrows of pocket gophers than by all other means combined. All of the 22 weasels taken by Alcorn were obtained in gopher traps. These were obtained within 10 miles of Fallon as a result of setting 43,572 traps on 41,272 acres. Yields of all other animals included 14,695 pocket gophers and about 22 Townsend ground squirrels. This trapping was carried on in areas where an attempt to poison all the pocket gophers had been made about 45 days before the traps were set. Alcorn (MS) estimates that 80 per cent of the total population of gophers was killed by the poisoning. Taking these poisoned gophers into account, and assuming that no weasels were killed or driven out of the area by the poisoning, and that all the weasels in the areas concerned were trapped, and that all the gophers were killed, a ratio of 1 weasel to 6,675 pocket gophers on each 1,876 acres of land planted to alfalfa is obtained. By years, the data are as follows: In 1936, from August to December, inclusive, 9,011 traps on 6,527 acres yielded 2,568 gophers and 10 weasels. In 1937, from January to November, inclusive, 19,556 traps on 10,595 acres yielded 7,241 gophers and 10 weasels. In 1938, from July to November, inclusive, 15,005 traps on 24,150 acres yielded 4,886 gophers and only 2 weasels. Because each year about 95 per cent of the traps were set on areas where poisoned baits (strychnine-coated rolled oats, or sections of sweet potato, carrot, and Irish potato) and traps were used the year before, the figures suggest to Alcorn (MS) that the population of weasels in the 3-year period was reduced proportionately more than was the population of pocket gophers. Because of the variables involved, the figures do not permit positive conclusions on the questions raised.

That weasels use pocket gophers as food is suggested by the catching of so many of the former in gopher traps. The use by weasels of abandoned gopher burrows as dens for themselves leads one to wonder if the gophers that made the burrows did not fall victim to the weasels. Several of the twenty-two weasels taken near Fallon were caught by Alcorn (MS) in one trap of a two-way set when the other trap held a pocket gopher. At one time, in July, 1939, near Stillwater, Alcorn pursued, on foot, a not full-grown weasel and caused it to drop from its mouth a pocket gopher which was about two-thirds grown. On August 16, 1939, at an elevation of 7000 feet in Kingston Canyon, Alcorn watched a weasel chase a golden-mantled ground squirrel (*Citellus lateralis*). The two animals ran in different directions when frightened by him and his companion. At an earlier date, the same observer saw a weasel 5 miles west of Fallon that was carrying a Townsend ground squirrel (*Citellus townsendii*). On May 13, 1936, 3 miles east of Reno, Richardson (MS) watched a long-tailed weasel carry a half-grown round-tailed wood rat (*Neotoma lepida*) across a rock-slide. These are all the actual data that we have on the food of weasels in Nevada. Probably they take individuals of all kinds of smaller rodents.

Because the approximate proportion of animals caught is in the relationship of three males to one female, some persons have thought that there were only about a third as many females in nature as males. Since females weigh only about half as much as males, females more often pass over traps without springing them; this, I suspect, is the reason why more males are caught.

In Nevada the long-tailed weasel has two molts per year, one in autumn and the other in spring. The winter coat was white (ermine to the fur trade) in all but two individuals seen. These were from western Nevada and had the smoked effect which readily distinguishes the brown winter coat from the brown summer coat. Two skins with white fur, on March 17, 1942, brought $1 each at Reno; this was the average price for males that year. Females, at this time, were bringing about 75 cents each.

Records of occurrence.—Specimens examined, 42, as follows: *Washoe Co.*: Pyramid Lake, 1 (U. S. Nat. Mus.) ; 3 mi. E Reno, 1; Incline Creek, 7100 ft., 1; 2½ mi. S Incline, 6250 ft., 1; Marlette Lake, 8000 ft., 1; E side Marlette Lake, 8000 ft., 1. *Ormsby Co.*: ½ mi. S Marlette Lake, 8150 ft., 1. *Douglas Co.*: Mt. Siegel, 1 (Field Mus. Nat. Hist.). *Humboldt Co.*: Alder Creek, 7000 ft., Pine Forest Mts., 1; head of Big Creek, 8000 ft., Pine Forest Mts., 1; Cottonwood Range, 1 (U. S. Nat. Mus.); Calico Mtn., Little Owyhee River, 1 (U. S. Nat. Mus.); Mahogany, Little Owyhee River, 2 (U. S. Nat. Mus.); Sulphur, 1 (U. S. Nat. Mus.). *Pershing Co.*: Lovelocks, 1 (U. S. Nat. Mus.). *Churchill Co.*: Fallon, 3970 ft., 1; 2, 3, 4, and 5 mi. W Fallon, 4; 5 mi. S Fallon, 1; 8 mi. E and 3 mi. S Fallon, 1. *Mineral Co.*: Lapon Canyon, 8900 ft., Mt. Grant, 1. *Esmeralda Co.*: Arlemont, 4850 ft., 1. *Nye Co.*: Arc Dome, 1 (U. S. Nat. Mus.); ½ mi. SW Jefferson Peak, Toquima Range, 1. *Elko Co.*: Mountain City, 3 (U. S. Nat. Mus.); Three Lakes, 9700 ft., Ruby Mts., 1 (coll. of Ralph Ellis). *White Pine Co.*: Gleason Creek, 7500 ft., 1; Baker Creek, 6600–8450 ft., 8; 3 mi. E Baker, 5700 ft., 1. *Lincoln Co.*: 3 mi. S Crystal Spring, 3900 ft., Pahranagat Valley, 1 (coll. of Joe and Dean Thiriot).

Additional records: *Clark Co.*: Charleston Peak, Willow Creek, and Little Falls (Burt, 1934:399).

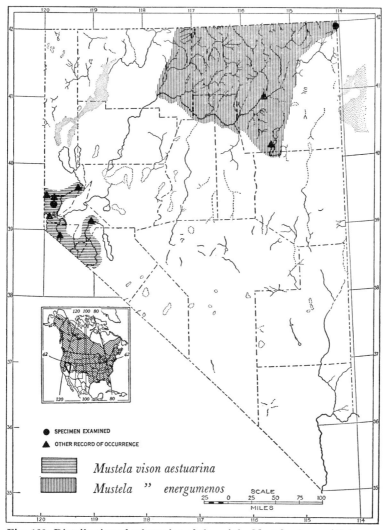

Fig. 129. Distribution of subspecies of the mink, *Mustela vison*, with insert
showing range of the species.

Mustela vison
Mink

The mink is dark brown; some, but not all, individuals have white spots on
the throat, chest, or belly. The brown color is of darkest shade near the tip of
the tail and along the middle of the back. A mink is weasellike, but larger than
a weasel, heavier bodied, and has a shorter and bushier tail. The ears are short
(13 mm. from notch in dried skin of female from Washoe County) and scarcely

project above the fur. The skull can be differentiated from that of the long-tailed weasel by larger size and more nearly flat tympanic bullae. See measurements in table 4 on pages 280–281, and figures 118 and 120.

Because minks live only in areas provided with lakes or streams, the animals have a restricted range in Nevada, which has large areas devoid of surface water. From what is known of minks in areas other than Nevada, it may be said that they make their dens in holes in the ground, under logs, or in crevices in rocks. The mink is an excellent swimmer, even under water, and is equally at home on land. It is not so proficient a climber as the long-tailed weasel. The mink is largely nocturnal. Litters of young numbering as many as seven and as few as four have been recorded. Food includes small vertebrates up to the size of a rabbit and aquatic animals, crayfish, for example. Birds are rarely eaten, but fish are commonly taken. In many temperate and boreal parts of the United States, mink are successfully raised in captivity for fur, but relatively few attempts at "farming" mink have been made in Nevada.

The fur of mink is durable and in nearly all years commands a good price. Skins taken in the Truckee River were being sold in 1942 by trappers at an average price of $8 each.

Mustela vison aestuarina Grinnell
Mink

Mustela vison aestuarina Grinnell, Proc. Biol. Soc. Washington, 29:213, September 22, 1916. Type from Grizzly Island, Solano County, California.

Distribution.—Western Nevada, in lakes and along streams which course eastward from the Sierra Nevada, from Truckee River south to Walker River. See figure 129.

Remarks.—Average external measurements of ten males and ten females, including in each sex adults and subadults, are: 573, 512; 194, 165; 69, 59 (Grinnell, Dixon, and Linsdale, 1937:236). An adult female from 7 mi. S Reno measures 560, 190, 65.

The race *aestuarina*, to which Grinnell, Dixon, and Linsdale (1937:237) ascribe a much more extensive geographic range than was indicated in the original description, is separable from *energumenos* on the basis of smaller skull, with the auditory bullae being shorter, shallower, and their sides steeper. Our specimen from Nevada is large, but the bullae are short and shallow. They are not particularly steep-sided. If the race *aestuarina* be recognized as distinct from *energumenos*, our one Nevadan specimen would be referable to *aestuarina*. On the average, *aestuarina* is lighter-colored than *energumenos*.

Although mink occur along the Truckee, Carson, and Walker rivers, it is known (Alcorn, MS) that they do not occur along the lower part of the Carson River, as, for example, at Fallon and Carson Lake. Some mink which were kept in captivity 4 miles west of Fallon by W. H. Alcorn and which were imported from the northeastern United States escaped in 1930. We have had no opportunity to obtain information, one way or the other, about the occurrence of mink farther down the Truckee River than Wadsworth and farther down the Walker River than the big bend 14 miles north of Yerington.

Record of occurrence.—Specimen examined: *Washoe Co.:* 7 mi. S Reno, 1 (coll. of Ralph Ellis).

Additional records: *Washoe Co.:* Truckee River at Verdi, and on outskirts of Wadsworth (Alcorn, MS, personal observation of sign); Truckee River, near Asylum, in vicinity of Reno, 1 specimen saved (coll. of Carl P. Russell, MS); E shore Lake Tahoe near Sandy Point (reported as taken by trapper). *Douglas Co.:* E Fork Carson River, 5 mi. SE Minden (Alcorn, MS, testimony of fur trapper). *Lyon Co.:* Walker River, 14 mi. N Yerington (Alcorn, MS, reported by local trapper).

Mustela vison energumenos (Bangs)
Mink

Putorius vison energumenos Bangs, Proc. Boston Soc. Nat. Hist., 27:5, March, 1896. Type from Sumas,
  in British Columbia.
Mustela vison energumenos, Miller, Bull. U. S. Nat. Mus., 79:101, December 13, 1912; Borell and Ellis,
  Journ. Mamm., 15:21, February 15, 1934.

Distribution.—Northeastern part of state along Humboldt River, Ruby Lake, and streams north thereof. See figure 129.

Remarks.—No external measurements of Nevadan specimens are available. Judging from those taken in Idaho, *energumenos* in northeastern Nevada would be expected to average not more than 5 per cent larger in linear measurements than *aestuarina*. Almost all individuals of *M. v. energumenos* are darker-colored than those of *aestuarina*. From the geographically adjoining races east of the Rocky Mountains it differs in smaller size and smaller teeth.

Borell and Ellis (1934*a*:21) mention that in the Ruby Mountains area minks occur "along the streams and about Ruby Lake." They are reported to occur also at Deeth and probably occur all along the Humboldt River and in permanent streams to the northward, although no specimens from these streams have been examined.

Record of occurrence.—Specimen examined: *Elko Co.*: Goose Creek, 5000 ft., 100 yds. W Utah boundary, 1.
Additional records: *Elko Co.*: Ruby Lake (Borell and Ellis, 1934:21); Deeth (Hall, MS, testimony of local trappers).

Lutra canadensis
River Otter

The deep brown color of river otters is only a little lighter than that of the mink. The animals are highly modified for aquatic life. The ears are short, the neck is of a diameter nearly as great as the head, the legs are short and powerful with large feet on which the toes are fully webbed, and the tail is so thick at the base as to make it difficult for one to decide where the pointed tail begins and the body stops. All these features combine to give the body a streamlined form that aids the animals in their life in the water. The skull is flattened in longitudinal dorsal outline, the tympanic bullae are flattened and not in contact with the paroccipital processes, the palate projects behind the upper molars, and the diameter of the infraorbital canal is greater than that of the alveolus of the canine; the dental formula is i. $\frac{3}{3}$, c. $\frac{1}{1}$, p. $\frac{4}{3}$, m. $\frac{1}{2}$. M1 is rhombic and large. P4 has a basined deuterocone. In m1 the talonid and trigonid are of roughly equal length, the metaconid is large, and the talonid is basined.

On land, river otters travel long distances, humping the back at each bound of their heavy gallop. They seem much less at home on land than in the water, where their speed and grace are truly marvelous. They are fond of sliding on their underparts, often in play, from the muddy banks of streams into the water. These slides are one kind of sign indicating their presence in a given locality. So far as I know, otters have few enemies other than man. The high value of their fur has led to great reduction in their numbers. They eat crayfish and fish. There are one to three young per litter.

For two pelts taken in 1941 on the Humboldt River, a fur dealer in Reno paid the trapper $35 each—more than these particular skins were worth. In 1942, on the same river, at Golconda, M. C. Bauder received $12 for a pelt, which for that year was probably near the average price.

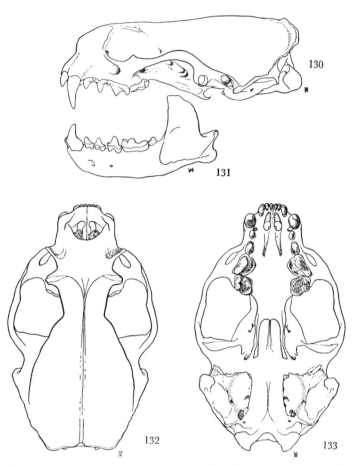

Figs. 130–133. *Lutra canadensis sonora*, Colorado River, 8 miles upriver from Needles, San Bernardino County, California, no. 61451, ♂. × ½.

Lutra canadensis nexa Goldman

River Otter

Lutra canadensis nexa Goldman. Proc. Biol. Soc. Washington, 48:182, November 15, 1935. Type from near Deeth, Humboldt River, Elko County, Nevada.

Distribution.—Northeastern part of state along Humboldt River and on streams to the north. See figure 134.

Remarks.—External measurements of one subadult female from Bull Head Ranch, 45 mi. N Golconda, are: 1,066, 393, 121.

In the original description (Goldman, 1935:183) this race is characterized as: "A medium-sized, comparatively light-colored subspecies, with cranium broad, low, smoothly rounded and weakly developed. Color of type (winter pelage): Upper parts near mikado brown (Ridgway, 1912) in general tone, the tips of longer hairs somewhat lighter and producing an indistinctly grizzled effect; under parts overlaid with much

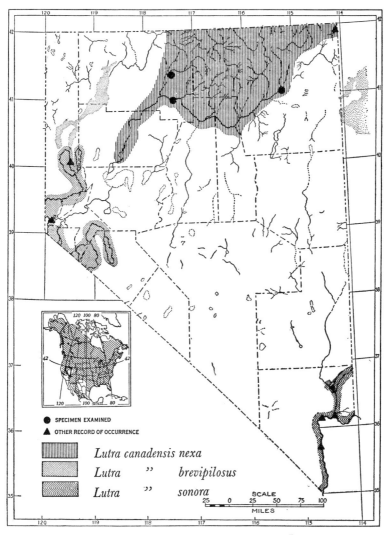

SPECIMEN EXAMINED

OTHER RECORD OF OCCURRENCE

Lutra canadensis nexa

Lutra " brevipilosus

Lutra " sonora

SCALE
25 0 25 50 75 100
MILES

Fig. 134. Distribution of subspecies of the river otter, *Lutra canadensis*.

lighter brown, paling gradually anteriorly to silvery grayish on throat, cheeks, and lips; feet light brownish; tail above about like back, somewhat paler below. Similar in general to *L. c. brevipilosus* from the lower Sacramento–San Joaquin River drainage, California, but apparently paler; skull more weakly developed, less angular; braincase usually lower and broader; postorbital processes of both frontals and jugals shorter and less prominent;

mastoid processes less deflected downward, less hook-like; bullae and dentition about the same. Color paler and skull decidedly smaller, less angular, than in *L. c. pacifica* of the Cascade Mountains region of Washington; braincase similar in height, but skull differing otherwise in about the same details as from *brevipilosus*. Similar in size to *L. c. interior*, of Nebraska, but color paler and skull less angular; zygomata more slender; postorbital processes of frontals and jugals shorter, more weakly developed; audital bullae less inflated; dentition about the same. Resembling *L. c. sonora* of the Verde River drainage, Arizona, but skull less angular; postorbital processes shorter; lambdoid crest less developed (projecting and trenchant in *sonora*); audital bullae less inflated, less projecting below plane of basioccipital; maxillary tooth row longer; dentition, especially the upper molars, somewhat heavier."

In the spring of 1925 at Halleck I was shown the skin of an otter taken in the Humboldt River near that place. On June 12 and 13, 1935, I saw tracks of an otter along Goose Creek in the northeasternmost township of Nevada. Otters now are rare in Nevada, probably because so many have been taken by fur trappers.

Records of occurrence.—Specimens examined, 7, as follows: *Humboldt Co.:* "Bull Head Ranch," near Paradise Valley, 3 (U. S. Nat. Mus., Biol. Surv. Coll.); 1 mi. E Golconda, 2. *Elko Co.:* "near Deeth," 2 (U. S. Nat. Mus., Biol. Surv. Coll.).

Additional record: *Elko Co.:* Goose Creek, 5000 ft., 2 mi. W Utah boundary (tracks noted by Hall).

Lutra canadensis brevipilosus Grinnell
River Otter

Lutra canadensis brevipilosus Grinnell, Univ. California Publ. Zoöl., 12:306, October 31, 1914. Type from Grizzly Island, Solano County, California.

Distribution.—Western Nevada in lakes and along streams which course eastward from the Sierra Nevada. See figure 134.

Remarks.—Average and extreme external measurements of eight males and six females, subadults and adults from California (Grinnell, Dixon, and Linsdale, 1937:273), are as follows: 1126 (1020–1164), 1094 (1000–1158); 423 (335–507), 414 (385–447); 127 (110–138), 122 (120–125). Weight, 17⅛ (11–23⅛), 15⅝ (11½–17) pounds.

L. c. brevipilosus, in comparison with *pacifica*, the race to the northward, is smaller, paler-colored, has shorter pelage and a narrower, relatively higher cranium. From *sonora*, *brevipilosus* differs in darker color and smaller skull. Comparison with *nexa* is made in the account of that form.

In 1924, at the Reno office of the federal predatory animal leader, I examined two otter skins that were said to have been taken in Pyramid Lake a few years before. In the course of my own stay at this lake, for about three months in the summer of 1924, I heard other reports of their former occurrence about Anaho Island, and myself found and entered a small cave, on the eastern shore of the lake a short distance north of Anaho Island, that appeared to have once been an otter den. Entrance to this small cave was gained by a passage about 8 feet long leading upward at an angle of about 40°. The entrance to the passage was partly above water line in 1924, but in previous years had been below water. The cave itself, relying on my memory, not written notes, was 4½ feet high, 5 feet wide, and 7 feet long. The floor was thickly carpeted with the bones of fish, including many of lake trout.

In the autumn of 1935 an otter was in the habit of including Marlette Lake in its beat. W. H. Dust, caretaker there, set some no. 4 traps for it and on the night of October 14–15 caught it. The otter carried the trap and attached drag some distance into a clump of willows and pulled free. Fresh otter tracks at that place next were seen on October 24.

Otters probably occurred along the Carson River and Walker River, but I have no records of their presence there.

In the absence of actual specimens, the identification of the otters in western Nevada as being of the subspecies *brevipilosus* is open to doubt. *L. c. brevipilosus* is thought to be the race in the Sierra Nevada of California. The chances of continuity between the populations of otters of the Truckee drainage system and the Sierra Nevada is of course far greater than between the populations of the Truckee system and the race *nexa* of the Humboldt drainage system.

Records of occurrence.—Washoe Co.: Pyramid Lake (as described above). *Ormsby Co.:* S end Marlette Lake (W. H. Dust, MS).

Lutra canadensis sonora Rhoads
River Otter

Lutra hudsonica sonora Rhoads, Trans. Amer. Philos. Soc., n. s., 19:431, September, 1898. Type from Montezuma Well, Beaver Creek, Yavapai County, Arizona.
Lutra canadensis sonora, Allen, Bull. Amer. Mus. Nat. Hist., 10:460, November 10, 1898.

Distribution.—Along Colorado River, and perhaps originally along Virgin River. See figure 134.

Remarks.—No external measurements are available of otters taken in the Colorado River. The skulls of two specimens taken in this river in California, 8 miles upriver from Needles and a tanned skin from the same place are available. These specimens of *sonora* indicate for it, in comparison with *brevipilosus*, lighter color both above and below and larger, more angular skull with more inflated tympanic bullae. Comparison with *nexa* is made in the account of that race.

Under date of March 7, 1936, Dwight C. Smiley wrote me that Harry Armitage of Las Vegas, in the winter of 1915–1916, caught an otter "at the mid-point of Boulder Canyon which is 14 miles long. Armitage caught no others when he trapped from 1912–1918, but found where one had eaten a fish at junction of Virgin and Colorado. Tracks seen at times elsewhere on Colorado River by Armitage." On February 1, 1934, John Leam, locally known as "California Jack," reported to me that on or about November 15, 1933, he saw an otter playing on a sand bar at the mouth of El Dorado Wash.

Records of occurrence.—Clark Co.: Colorado River, at its junction with Virgin River, and at a point midway of Boulder Canyon (D. C. Smiley, MS, report of a trapper); mouth of El Dorado Wash (report by John Leam, Hall, MS).

Spilogale gracilis
Spotted Skunk

The spotted skunk is so named because the four to six white stripes on its back and sides are broken into segments. Except for the white patch on the forehead, the irregular broken white stripes, and the white tip of the bushy tail, the animal is black, with an occasional brownish tint to the blackish parts. These animals are easily distinguished from the larger striped skunks by their color pattern and by their smaller size and weasellike actions. The upstanding ears measure about 20 mm. from the notch. Each foot has four pads and five clawed digits. The male is about twice as heavy as the female.

The skull, ranging in basilar length from 35 to 56 mm., is flattened in longitudinal dorsal outline and is of nearly equal height in parietal and frontal regions. The mastoidal bullae are highly inflated, the palate is nearly on a line with the posterior borders of the upper molars, and the anteroposterior and transverse diameters of M1 are each less than the outside length of P4. The dental formula is i. $\frac{3}{3}$, c. $\frac{1}{1}$, p. $\frac{3}{3}$, m. $\frac{1}{2}$. The infraorbital canal opens above the anterior half of P4. The metaconule of M1 is not distinct, and the inferior margin of the mandible is relatively straight and without the "step" seen in *Mephitis*, except that this "step" is weakly developed in *Spilogale lucasana;* in m1 the trigonid is longer than the talonid, the metaconid is high and distinct from the protoconid, the hypoconid is low, and the entoconid is low but separated from the protoconid by a wide notch.

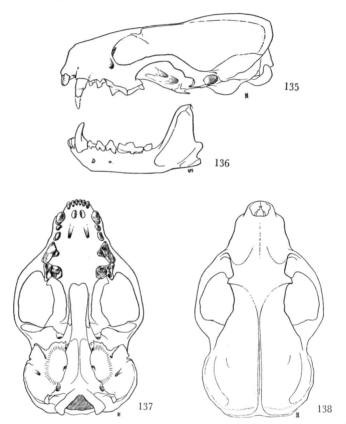

Figs. 135–138. *Spilogale gracilis saxatilis*, west side Ruby Lake, 6 miles north Elko Co. line, no. 4641, coll. of Ralph Ellis, ♂. × 1.

Because they are nocturnal and live mostly in inaccessible rocky situations, spotted skunks are but little known to most persons. Two of our specimens were taken in a stone building which was used daily by persons living near by; two were taken near rock-slides in willow thickets along rivers; and one was in a cellar. Several others were trapped along ledges of rock. Vernon L. Mills found one in a hollow log. Tracks of another were noted in a mine tunnel. It is always in or near places which afford shelter and protection that these animals may be found. No record of the species is available for the desert or sandy hills, although small mammals probably suitable as food for the skunks are plentiful in these areas. When not molested, the spotted skunks sometimes make their homes in cellars, under barns, or under other buildings, and persons may not even suspect the presence of the animals in the locality until one of these "civets" or "civet cats," as they are known to the fur trade, takes up residence in the buildings occupied by persons.

Litters of related subspecies in areas outside Nevada number two to six. Two specimens taken in eastern Nevada on June 20 were more than half-grown; they were probably born in March or April.

The food of spotted skunks probably varies with the season; I suppose that many insects are eaten in summer and that in winter small mammals constitute the major part of the diet. One, in Nevada, was known to have eaten chickens' eggs; one was caught in a trap baited with rolled oats; another in a trap baited with a rabbit; another had eaten part of a ham stored in a building; and a miner related that one lived under his cabin and ate scraps of food which were placed near the door.

Spotted skunks are often found far from water, but those living near water do not hesitate to wet their feet. On the Walker River one was taken in a steel trap set in shallow water. Where these small skunks inhabit barns and other buildings, the rats and mice are said soon to disappear; for destroying such rodents some persons value spotted skunks almost as highly as they do cats.

The scent is thought by many to be stronger and more disagreeable than that of the larger striped skunk. The musk is pale yellow in color and, as in the larger skunks, is used for defense against enemies. When faced with danger, these animals attempt to escape, but if prevented from doing so, they often attempt to frighten the enemy or warn him to keep his distance. If stamping the front feet on the ground fails to stop the enemy, the tail is lifted and the body bent in a U-shape, so that both the front and rear of the animal point toward the intruder. In this position the skunk waits for an attack, or what it thinks is one, before discharging its musk.

A miner near Austin related that food placed in the doorway of his cabin attracted a spotted skunk which lived under the building. Any attempt to frighten or remove the skunk from the building before it finished its meal resulted in the animal stamping its front feet on the floor. A large male spotted skunk while being captured on the Wilson Ranch, Lyon County, only once raised its tail as though he might discharge musk. This was when a can was dropped on a cement floor. After a moment's quietness on the part of his pursuers the tail was lowered. The skunk was induced to run into a 4-inch pipe from which it was transferred to a sack. The animal's pursuers were surprised at his weasellike quickness.

Whether the "hand stand" is done to frighten or to warn enemies, or is only part of the playfulness of the spotted skunk, is not known. The hand stand consists of throwing the body up and standing on the front feet alone. Although this behavior has not been observed in Nevada, it has been reported from several other parts of the range of the species. Spotted skunks are said to climb trees well, but again there is no record of their doing so in Nevada. Because

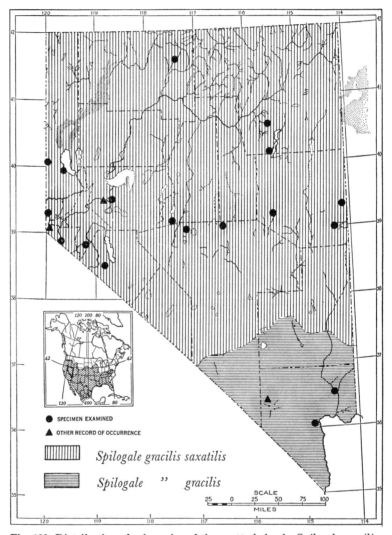

Fig. 139. Distribution of subspecies of the spotted skunk, *Spilogale gracilis*.

of their odor and the relatively low price of their fur (average price 50 cents each in the Reno fur market in the winter of 1942), the animals are usually killed and discarded when accidentally caught in traps set for other fur bearers in Nevada.

Spilogale gracilis saxatilis Merriam
Spotted Skunk

Spilogale gracilis saxatilis Merriam, N. Amer. Fauna, 4:13, October 8, 1890. Type from Provo, Utah County, Utah; Borell and Ellis, Journ. Mamm., 15:21, February 15, 1934.
Spilogale gracilis, Linsdale, Amer. Midland Nat., 19:174, January, 1938.

Distribution.—Over most of state in suitable habitat above the Lower Sonoran Life-zone. See figure 139.

Remarks.—External measurements of two adult males, one from Stanmoore Mine and the other from 5 mi. SE Minden, and of two subadults, one from Wilson Ranch and the other from ¼ mi. W Hamilton, are, respectively, as follows: 431, 420, 401, 383; 149, 145, 118, 120; 45, 46, 47, 44.5; ear from notch, 26, 26, 28, 24. Weight of the adult from 5 mi. SE Minden, 536 grams, of subadult from near Hamilton, 349 grams. Corresponding measurements of three adult females from Wilson Canyon, Wilson Ranch, and Peterson Creek are, respectively: 355, 348, 351; 130, 100, 120; 38, 39, 38; ear from notch, —, 22, 24; weight, 224, —, 269 grams.

Nevadan specimens differ from six adult topotypes of *saxatilis* in that the zygomatic arches are less bowed upward and that the tooth rows are longer and, as measured across the fourth upper premolars, are narrower. In eight males and seven females from Nevada the average and extreme measurements are as follows: length of tooth rows, ♂, 21.2 (20.1–21.9), ♀, 19.2 (18.6–19.5); breadth across upper fourth premolars, 19.4 (18.9–19.5), 17.9 (17.3–18.3). Corresponding measurements for four male topotypes and two Utah-taken females of *saxatilis* are: ♂, 20.9 (20.5–21.4), ♀, 18.9 (18.8–19.0); 19.9 (19.5–20.3), 18.5 (18.4–18.5).

From *S. phenax phenax*, the subspecies to the west, *S. g. saxatilis* differs in smaller size (approximately 1/9 less in external measurements), absence or poorer development of lateralmost white stripe, and more nearly straight, as opposed to dorsally convex, superior outline of skull when viewed from the side. From *S. g. gracilis*, *saxatilis* is said by Howell (1906:23, 24) to differ in larger size, absence or poorer development of the lateralmost white stripe, slightly larger skull with broader brain case, better developed postorbital processes, and a more pronounced ridge on each mastoid. From *S. g. tenuis*, the race to the eastward—as known by four specimens, one from South Park, one from Furnace Canyon in southwestern Baca County, one from 18½ miles south of Lake George, Fremont County, all in Colorado, and another from 20 miles south of Lake George—*saxatilis* differs, so far as I can see, only in slightly greater average size and in the greater extent of the individual white markings. Cranial differences judged to be of systematic worth are not apparent between *tenuis* and *saxatilis*.

Records of occurrence.—Specimens examined, 25, as follows: *Washoe Co.:* N side State-line Peak, 4400 ft., 1; Sutcliffe Station, 3950 ft., Pyramid Lake, 1 (U. S. Nat. Mus., Biol. Surv. Coll.); near Calneva, 1 (U. S. Nat. Mus., Biol. Surv. Coll.). *Douglas Co.:* 5 mi. SE Minden, 4900 ft., Carson River, 1. *Lyon Co.:* Wilson Canyon, 1; Wilson Ranch, mouth of Wilson Canyon, 4600 ft., 2. *Humboldt Co.:* Cottonwood Range, 1 (U. S. Nat. Mus., Biol. Surv. Coll.). *Churchill Co.:* 2. mi. ESE Fallon, 4000 ft., 1. *Mineral Co.:* Stanmoore Mine, 7750 ft., Mt. Grant, 1 (coll. of D. V. Hemphill). *Lander Co.:* Peterson Creek, Shoshone Mts., 7300 ft., 1. *Nye Co.:* Potts, 2; Millett P. O., 1. *Elko Co.:* Kleckner Creek, 4 mi. E Lee, 2 (coll. of Ralph Ellis); west side Ruby Lake, 3 mi. N White Pine Co. line, 6200 ft., 4 (coll. of Ralph Ellis). *White Pine Co.:* ¼ and 3 mi. W Hamilton, 8200 and 8600 ft., 2; Pole Canyon, W slope Snake Mts., 1; ½ and 1 mi. W Smith Creek Cave, Mt. Moriah, 6000 ft., 2.

Additional records: *Washoe Co.:* near Sandy Point, Lake Tahoe (Frank Peters, trapper, report to Hall, MS). *Douglas Co.:* Glenbrook (Tony Petroff, trapper, report to Hall, MS). *Churchill Co.:* 4 mi. W Fallon (coll. of Mrs. Anna Bailey Mills, Alcorn, MS).

Spilogale gracilis gracilis Merriam
Spotted Skunk

Spilogale gracilis Merriam, N. Amer. Fauna, 3:83, September 11, 1890. Type from Grand Canyon of the Colorado (north of San Francisco Mountain), Coconino County, Arizona.
Spilogale gracilis gracilis, Burt, Trans. San Diego Soc. Nat. Hist., 7:399, May 31, 1934.

Distribution.—Southern part of state; definitely recorded only from Clark County. See figure 139.

Remarks.—Extremes of external measurements for "five adult males from Grand Canyon, Arizona, and Panamint Mountains, California," according to Howell (1906:22), are: 334–400, 130–160, 41–46. The measurements given by him (*loc. cit.*) for an "Adult female from Inyo Mountains, California," are: 330, 120, 37.

Comparison with *S. g. saxatilis* has been made in the account of that form. From *S. phenax microrhina*, the race to the westward, *gracilis* differs in shorter tail (54 as opposed to 65 per cent of length of head and body), more extensive white tip of tail, less inflated mastoidal bullae, and tooth rows relatively wider across carnassials. Compared with *S. leucoparia* to the southward, *gracilis* differs in having slightly less white on the tail and less inflated mastoidal bullae. From *S. arizonae, gracilis* is said to differ in having a smaller, less angular skull. From *S. tenuis, gracilis* differs in being smaller.

Record of occurrence.—Specimen examined: *Clark Co.:* 1½ mi. NW Boulder City, 2500 ft., 1.
Additional record (Burt, 1934:399): *Clark Co.:* St. Thomas; ¼ mi. W Willow Creek.

Mephitis mephitis
Striped Skunk

The striped skunks are notorious for the ill-smelling, volatile musk which they release as a defense against enemies. The anal glands providing this musk are larger than in any other member of the family. The tail is shorter, by a little, than the head and body, the general size being about the same as that of a large domestic cat. The black coat is contrastingly marked with white on the upper parts, and part of the long-haired tail often is white. There are five clawed digits on each foot. Characters of generic worth in the skull are as follows: skull, ranging from 56 to 76 mm. in length, highly arched and deepest in frontal region; mastoidal bullae not inflated; posterior margin of palate nearly on a line with posterior borders of upper molars; anteroposterior and transverse diameters of M1 each about equal to (usually more than) outside length of P4; dental formula: i. $\frac{3}{3}$, c. $\frac{1}{1}$, p. $\frac{3}{3}$, m. $\frac{1}{2}$; infraorbital canal opening above posterior half of P4; metaconule of M1 not distinct; inferior margin of mandible curved; angle of mandible developed as a flattened face in a vertical plane producing a "step" or concavity in the inferior margin; coronoid process high and vertically inclined; in m1 trigonid longer than talonid, metaconid high and distinct from protoconid, hypoconid high, entoconid high and separated from protoconid by deep, wide notch. Characters of specific rank are white markings without admixture of black hairs, tympanic bullae relatively little inflated, and posterior margin of bony palate without a distinct notch.

The northern races of skunks have shorter tails than the southern races. This is reflected in specimens from Nevada where there is a gradient in relative length of the tail. In Elko County it is 40 per cent of the total length, in west-central Nevada 42 per cent, and in Clark County 46 per cent.

Since skunks live only where they can obtain water, their distribution is interrupted in the dry state of Nevada. They are common along streams, in the irrigated areas of western Nevada, and along the Colorado River.

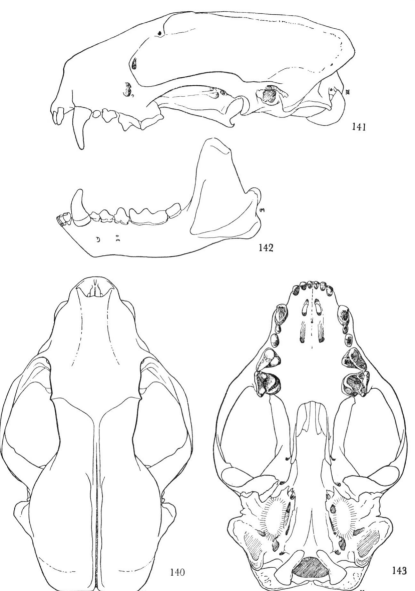

Figs. 140–143. *Mephitis mephitis major*, 1 mile southeast Lovelock, no. 90562, ♂. ×1.

In the species *Mephitis mephitis*, which ranges over southern Canada, the United States, and into Mexico, the color pattern is subject to much geographic variation. In the subspecies *M. m. nigra*, at least in central Ohio, for example, the animals generally are black with white present only in a patch on the top of the head and perhaps a white line on the forehead and a few hairs on the tip of the tail. At the other extreme, in *M. m. estor* of the lower part of the Colorado River Valley, most individuals have white also over nearly all the back and top of the tail. Between these extremes—animals with nearly white backs, and those with white only on the head—there are intermediate patterns, designated in the fur trade as short stripe, narrow stripe, and broad stripe. In the short stripe, the white is continued from the head down the back in two white stripes which end short of the base of the tail. In the narrow stripe, these white markings, less than an inch in width, continue to the base of the tail and sometimes onto it. In the broad stripe, the pattern is the same, but the stripes are wider. In several regions, for example in eastern Kansas, southwestern Missouri, and northern Arkansas, the four color patterns, black, short, narrow, and broad, occur in one place. At one time, 2½ miles south of Le Loup, Kansas, I found three patterns in one litter.

In Nevada the skunks show no such variation at one place. Over most of the state the stripes are narrow. In the southern part they are broad—so broad that the animals barely escape being white-backed. At any one place the population is relatively uniform. If hundreds of specimens were available from a given place, I do not doubt that an occasional pattern different from the normal one would be found. Nevertheless, these instances are so few as to constitute rare exceptions.

This black coloration extending over all the underparts and broken by white markings only on the upper parts may be concealing and therefore of survival value to the race by protecting the skunks from other kinds of animals which would do them harm. Possibly the black-and-white coloration is obliterative and of value to the skunks in enabling them more successfully to stalk small animals used for food. Most naturalists incline to the view that the color has warning significance, and that it is of survival value because it protects the skunks from would-be enemies, the enemies having learned that the black and white color is associated with the pungent musk. I incline to the latter view, but would not deny that the color serves two or even all three of the purposes mentioned.

The white hairs of skunks, of course, grow from follicles lacking pigment. The black hairs grow from pigmented follicles. As a result, even on newly born young and on large embryos in which the hair has not yet grown out of the skin, the areas destined to be white are clearly marked.

The most important defensive armament of the skunk is the musk glands, the attached muscles of which provide for expelling the musk or scent at will from either one or both of the anal musk glands. These glands are situated at the base of the tail, one on each side of the anus. A short duct leads from the muscular-walled gland to the edge of the anus and ends in a small papilla. The musk is a golden yellow, slightly phosphorescent, highly volatile fluid, one important ingredient of which is the sulphide known as mercaptan. The fluid can be directed with great accuracy for a distance of 10 feet or more. It can be discharged directly to the rear, but usually is shot sideways or even forward toward where the skunk is looking, the skunk having the ability to shoot the musk forward by contorting the body in an arc so that the papillae of the musk glands point to the place where the animal's eyes are directed.

The musk is used strictly for defense and in no sense for offense. Before releasing the musk, the skunk warns his tormenter to keep his distance. He does this by raising the tail, by hissing in a wheezy fashion, and by stamping or patting the forefeet on the ground. If given the chance, the skunk will go on about his business without releasing the musk. None discharged it at me when I stood still or retreated, but only when I made a quick movement near the animal or when I had injured one, did I become the recipient of his discharge. If a person moves cautiously, and, above all, deliberately, he may, short of striking or squeezing the skunk, do almost anything with a wild one caught in a place from which it cannot escape.

In order to illustrate some of the difficulties apt to be encountered by a person who changes from a deliberate to a hasty method of approach when dealing with skunks, but more particularly to illustrate the effectiveness of the musk in disabling an enemy, it is worth recording an experience of my own when I was about 12 years old.

Early one morning in the autumn of 1914 or 1915, two miles south of Le Loup, Kansas, I found a skunk in a steel trap which had been placed the day before just underwater at the edge of a branch (our word for a brook). The trap was set in the hope of catching a muskrat for a neighbor. He wanted to apply the fresh skin flesh-side-in between his shoulder blades. He thought this might cure him of his asthma. Because the pelt of a skunk was unprime so early in the autumn, I decided to take the animal alive and keep it until midwinter. Slowly picking up the pole to which the trap was secured, I lifted trap, skunk, and all safely up over the 4-foot bank onto level ground. Taking several minutes to the task, by slow stages I gained a position directly over the animal, with my left hand near his head and my right hand near his tail. Standing thus for a time, waiting for him to lower his tail that was raised aloft as a warning, my growing impatience caused me to decide on a quick movement. This consisted of my grasping the back of the skunk's neck in my left hand while my right hand grasped his tail and brought it down between his hind legs. When securely grasped in this manner, he could easily be freed from the trap without throwing musk on me. With this plan of action well in mind, I made my first quick move; but the skunk was quicker. All in an instant he turned on his back, sank his teeth into my left hand between the thumb and forefinger, and discharged his musk full in my face, completely blinding me. He also maintained his grip on my hand. Using my right hand to choke the little animal and to work blindly at his jaws, it required the better part of a minute to break his hold. Once free, I reeled backward and toppled over the bank into the water of the creek. In a way this was fortunate, for instinctively I washed my eyes and face. The pain in my eyes was intense, but in a few minutes, certainly in less than 10, I regained my sight, and the severe pain gradually disappeared, to be gone after 4 hours. Noticeable congestion of the mucous membranes in my nose cleared up even sooner, as I now remember it. Curiously, the burning on my cheeks and a resultant rash lasted all day. At one other time, a winter or two later, the liquid musk of a skunk struck me in one eye. The temporary blindness and ensuing irritation behaved about as in the first instance, when both eyes received the musk.

After recovering my sight (I am now referring to the first experience) I searched about and found a section of decayed willow limb with which I stunned the skunk by a blow on the head. After resetting the trap, I carried the skunk home and established him in one of several barrels that originally had been used for the storage of rock salt for livestock. These empty barrels made good cages when turned on their sides, faced with ½-inch wire mesh on the open end, and partly filled with hay. A ½-pint cup filled with warm milk night and morning and the hind quarter or similar-sized part of a cottontail rabbit once a day was the diet for each of my half dozen or so *Mephitis*. This fare seemed adequate, for they thrived, and when pelted in early January had glossy, thick-furred pelts. Because of individual traits and temperaments which made me fond of these animals, I found it difficult, in completing this commercial undertaking, to bring myself to kill them. The particular individual which had temporarily blinded me and whose bite resulted in an infection that required a month or more to heal was a broad stripe, commercially the least valuable of any one of my animals. After 3 months in captivity he escaped a night or two before I pelted the others!

One might suppose that the trouble and anxiety this skunk caused me was at an end once he escaped, but this was not true. Some 6 years later, when I was a freshman at the State University, I came across a book entitled "Fur-bearing animals: a monograph of the North American Mustelidae" which indicated that the bite of a skunk was invariably fatal, although, the book pointed out, the unfortunate person sometimes lived for as long as 12 years before the fatal seizure of rabies came on. My concern was the greater when I ascertained that the author of the book, Elliott Coues, was a medical doctor who, therefore, must surely know about the subject. Although a later rereading, in fact several rereadings, of the passages "On hydrophobia from skunk-bite, or the so-called 'Rabies mephitica,' " and a reading of related literature, gave me hope of survival, it is true that when the 12-year period elapsed I had a sense of relief somewhat akin, I suppose, to that which comes to outwardly more primitive men when some taboo is lifted or when a favorable omen is noted. I had this sense of relief notwithstanding the fact that two other skunks bit me about 8 years after the first. For some reason these later bites, compared to the first, caused me almost no concern.

To return to the subject of the skunk's use of musk in defense: Only one of my captives ever expelled musk, and that was when a dog sought to tear the wire from a cage. In captivity skunks quickly become tame and they make good pets. Individual temperaments vary and some are more vivacious than others, but every one of the animals that I kept became so tame within a few days as never to offer to expel the musk when I approached its cage. Skunks can, of course, be rendered incapable of emitting scent by a relatively simple surgical operation. As described by Seton (1929, 2:333), "There are four different ways of disarming: (a) by snipping off the nipples inside the rectum so that adhesive healing follows, permanently sealing the fluid in; (b) by cutting the ducts deep in near the sacs; (c) by pulling the sac out through the orifice that the nipple covers; (d) by totally cutting out both glands from the outside. There are grave objections to the first three. The last is the only one now followed by experts on the fur ranches."

The operation is most successfully and easily performed when the skunks are kittens but can be performed on adults. A general anesthetic is not necessary and may even be fatal to the skunk; a *Spilogale* on which this was tried died without regaining consciousness, and it is said that pneumonia frequently results from administering an anesthetic that is inhaled.

The odor of the skunk's musk is generally regarded as highly unpleasant. In concentrated form it is unpleasant, but in dilute form, to me, is rather the opposite. I have suspected that some persons who complained of it did so because of a prejudice gained, early in life, by noting the reactions of their elders, when, in truth, the odor in dilute form might just as well have been regarded as delightfully fragrant. The scent of the striped skunk (*Mephitis*) is recognizably different from that of the spotted skunk (*Spilogale*). The latter's musk is keener and has more of a "bite" to it. Also it has a certain character remindful of the scent excreted by the mink, which is lacking in the more mellow scent of the striped skunk.

Striped skunks are essentially nocturnal, but sometimes wander about in daylight. Ordinarily they come out at late dusk, and it is a common sight, where skunks abound, to see a female followed by her young in single file on their way from the den to a foraging place. The male does not stay with the female in the season when she is caring for the young, although he frequently occupies a den near by. Striped skunks are terrestrial, and, although they can climb the inclined trunk of a tree, they rarely do so; they probably are unable to climb a vertically straight tree. When walking, their gait is deliberate and graceful enough, but when hurried they resort to a clumsy gallop and hold the tail straight aloft or at some angle between this position and one where the tail projects straight out behind. One characteristic posture is that of half-sitting and half-standing on the hind legs with the forefeet entirely off the ground.

In the eastern United States striped skunks ordinarily occupy burrows dug by woodchucks. In California the digger ground squirrels do most of the excavating and skunks have only to enlarge these burrows to the required size. In Nevada the skunks mostly live in areas where woodchucks and digger ground squirrels do not occur. Therefore, the skunks must find burrows or places of concealment which are formed by other means. According to Alcorn (MS), these places are in the banks of rivers and irrigation ditches. He points out that near Fallon holes are formed by irrigation water which flows through and enlarges gophers' burrows or ground squirrels' burrows that extend from well out in an alfalfa field to the vertical bank of a creek or ditch. These holes are effectively plugged in the field by the rancher, but the lower end remains open and it is in these that the skunks make suitable homes. Of course, striped skunks seek out also crevices in rocky ledges and places in piles of stones where they can be relatively secure. The nest proper is made of dry grass and leaves which the skunk itself carries into the burrow. These nests are made not only by females, but solitary males also construct nests for themselves.

In these nests skunks commonly sleep below ground for several days, or even weeks, in winter when the weather is excessively cold. It is thought that skunks do not hibernate in the true sense, but, like bears, merely sleep for long periods of time. When the weather becomes warm and a thaw sets in, one may expect to see the tracks of the skunks, for they then emerge in response to the warmer weather out-of-doors. In winter there may be only one skunk to a burrow, but ordinarily an entire family will occupy a single burrow. In some instances large numbers of skunks—obviously more than a single family—occupy one burrow. I know of one in eastern Kansas that had fourteen animals in it. Possibly these were two or more families that had gone together. No food is stored within the burrow or elsewhere. In autumn striped skunks put on fat which doubtless gives the necessary reserve energy to sustain them in their long periods of sleep.

From general observations of the food habits of skunks and from the many careful studies of their food made in areas outside Nevada, it is known that, in the seasons when obtainable, almost 100 per cent of their food consists of insects. In winter, when insects are scarce, mice are the main food item. The characteristic cone-shaped pits dug by skunks in quest of insects or larvae of insects are one of the signs which permit the observant person to detect the presence of skunks. It is true that individual striped skunks learn to eat eggs and occasionally to kill young chickens. Others have been known to develop the habit of coming to feed with young chicks without ever harming the birds in the slightest. Spotted skunks may be responsible for molesting poultry more often than is *Mephitis*, although I can cite only a few instances in support of this opinion. It is certain, however, that the predilection displayed for eggs or for young chickens is found only occasionally, and then only in an individual skunk. It is definitely not characteristic of them as a race. A beekeeper near Fallon, Nevada, described to Alcorn (MS) the actions of a striped skunk he watched one night at one of his beehives, the essential parts of which were:

The skunk, with its forefeet, dug out a shallow basin in the sandy soil at the entrance of the hive. The bees, being disturbed, crawled out onto the fur of the skunk which lay down and rolled in the depression it had dug. Then it greedily ate from the sandy depression the bees that were dislodged from its long fur. Alcorn (MS) who himself has kept bees near Fallon found that skunks molested the hives mostly in late autumn and not at all in spring and summer. His suggestion is that the shortage of wild insects after freezing weather sets in causes the skunks to turn to the bees in hives. Behavior of skunks similar to the one described by this beekeeper has been reported in other states, but I have no personal knowledge of the methods which the animals employ to obtain bees. I have, however, often noted in eastern Kansas where striped skunks had dug out the ground nests of bumble bees. I supposed then that the skunks were seeking the honey to be found in these nests, but it may have been that they were seeking the bees themselves, or conceivably both the bees and the honey.

The gestation period of skunks has been given by Seton (1929, 2:353) as 63 days, and the number of embryos as ranging from two to sixteen. Vernon L. Mills, near Fallon, Nevada, on March 28, 1938, found seven embryos in one skunk. The young, according to Shaw (1928:66), average 31 grams at birth, which, in comparison with weights that he gives of adult individuals in the spring (op. cit., 68), amounts to 1/58 of the weight of an adult male and 1/52 of the weight of an adult female. Shaw (op. cit., 49) found that the eyes opened in the fourth week, and Seton (1929, 2:354) gives the time as 17 to 20 days after birth. The young are helpless at birth, and it is not until sometime between the fifth and seventh weeks that they are able to follow the mother on extended excursions in quest of food.

Rearing skunks for fur has been attempted in many places, but so far as I can learn, it has proved profitable only to those who have sold the animals at high prices to other fur farmers for breeding stock. It is understandable that raising these animals for their fur is rarely profitable when one considers that it requires almost as much food for a striped skunk as it does for a silver fox, that the skunk's pelt is worth on an average only about one-tenth as much as that of the fox, and that even the farming of silver foxes for fur more often results in financial loss than in gain. Nevertheless, because large numbers are taken, the skunk has considerable importance in the economy of the fur market. Skunk is not so valuable in Nevada as it is in California, where, in point of total sales, the skunk tops the list. Even so, in some limited areas of Nevada, for example in the vicinity of Minden and along the Colorado River, skunks are important because of the large numbers taken. For skunks caught in the Carson Valley and along the Walker River in the winter of 1941–1942 N. B. Gallagher received $1.50 each for a lot of 8 skins, and E. van Sickle received $1.35 each for a lot of 10. Skins from the northeastern part of the state, it is judged, would sell for considerably more. Those from the low, warmer, southern part of the state sell for much less: in 1940–1941, 387 skins from Moapa Valley sold for an average price of 55 cents each, and in the following winter the 15 to 18 caught in the same area sold at an average price of 65 cents each (G. H. Hansen, *in litt.*, June 3, 1942).

Mephitis mephitis major (Howell)
Striped Skunk

Chincha occidentalis major Howell, N. Amer. Fauna, 20:37, August 31, 1901. Type from Fort Klamath, Klamath County, Oregon.
Mephitis mephitis major, Hall, Univ. California Publ. Zoöl., 37:2, April 10, 1931; Borell and Ellis, Journ. Mamm., 15:21, February 15, 1934.

Distribution.—Over most of state in suitable habitat above the Lower Sonoran Life-zone. See figure 144.

Remarks.—External measurements of four males, from 1 mi. SE Lovelock, from 5 mi. SE Minden, from 12 mi. S Yerington, and from N end Walker Lake, are: 780, 710, 685, 695; 317, 340, 263, 267; 83, 78, 79, 75; 33, 35, —, 36. Corresponding measurements of three males, one adult, and two subadults from Kleckner Creek, Elko Co., are: 675, 710, 730; 270, 280, 300; 82, 80, 80. The animal from Kleckner Creek with the smallest linear measurements, taken on February 17, weighed 2,730 grams; one taken on March 5 from 12 mi. S Yerington weighed 1,388 grams; one taken February 27, 1940, at Lovelock weighed 3,409 grams. All were adults. An adult female taken in July from 12 mi. S Yerington measured 645, 310, 70, 30, and weighed about 1,400 grams.

The color is black with white markings, as follows: line, 2 to 5 mm. wide up center of face from nose pad to level of ears; white on nape narrowing posteriorly until at point about 140 mm. behind ears it divides into two white stripes, each 15 to 30 mm. wide, which continue to base of tail and often onto sides of tail; in some specimens these stripes unite across top of tail about one-third of its length from tip. Terminal hairs of tail black. In winter pelage, black hairs on the center of back attain a length of 60 mm.; white hairs in stripes of back reach a length of 80 mm. The longest hairs, 185 mm., on the tail are white. The longest claws on the forefeet may attain a length of 20 mm., which is about three times the length of the longest claws on the hind feet.

The specimens from Elko County have tails averaging 40 per cent of the total length and in this respect are about as near *M. m. hudsonica*, the race to the northward, as to *major*. Resemblance to *hudsonica* is shown also by the widely spreading zygomata of one specimen. Even the skin from 1 mile north of Crystal Spring at the lower margin of the Upper Sonoran Life-zone, in color pattern, short tail, and in some cranial dimensions, agrees with *major*. In general, however, the skull is smaller, more like that in *estor*. Despite these evidences of intergradation with *hudsonica*, all the Nevadan specimens taken above the Lower Sonoran Life-zone seem to be referable to *major*. From *M. m. notata*, *major* is judged to differ in longer tail and larger size, from *M. m. occidentalis* in larger size, from *M. m. estor* in larger size, relatively shorter tail, and lesser extent of white markings, and from *M. m. varians* in shorter tail and larger skull. Reliable reports are available of the occurrence of these skunks at Glenbrook and Hamilton.

Records of occurrence.—Specimens examined, 26, as follows: *Ormsby Co.:* Marlette Lake, 2. *Douglas Co.:* East Fork Carson River, 4900 ft., 5 mi. SE Minden, 4. *Lyon Co.:* West Walker River, 12 mi. S Yerington, 4600 ft., 2. *Humboldt Co.:* 35 mi. W and 6 mi. S Denio, Oregon, 2 (skulls only); Virgin Valley, 1 (skull only). *Pershing Co.:* 1 mi. SE Lovelock, 4000 ft., 1. *Churchill Co.:* 4 mi. W Fallon, 4000 ft., 1 (skull only); 2 mi. W Fallon, 3 (skulls only); 5 mi. SW Fallon, 1. *Mineral Co.:* N end Walker Lake, 4100 ft., 1 (skull only); 1 mi. NW Wichman, 1 (skull only, coll. of D. V. Hemphill). *Elko Co.:* Marys River, 22 mi. N Deeth, 5800 ft., 1 (skull only); Kleckner Creek, 4 mi. E Lee, 3 (coll. of Ralph Ellis). *Lincoln Co.:* 1 mi. N Crystal Springs, Pahranagat Valley, 1; Pahranagat Valley, 2 (skulls only).

Additional records: *Washoe Co.:* Vicinity of Spanish Spring, near Boynton Pond, E side Truckee Meadows (Carl P. Russell, MS); Reno (Howell, 1901:38). *Ormsby Co.:* Carson (Howell, 1901:38). *Douglas Co.:* Glenbrook. *Humboldt Co.:* Quinn River Crossing (Howell, 1901:38). *White Pine Co.:* Hamilton.

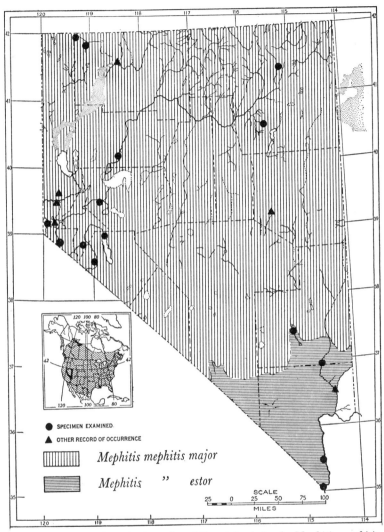

Fig. 144. Distribution of subspecies of the striped skunk, *Mephitis mephitis*, with insert showing range of the species.

Mephitis mephitis estor Merriam
Striped Skunk

Mephitis estor Merriam, N. Amer. Fauna, 3:81, September 11, 1890. Type from San Francisco Mountain, Coconino County, Arizona.

Mephitis mephitis estor, Hall, Univ. California Publ. Zoöl., 37:1, April 10, 1931.

Mephitis mephitis major, Burt, Trans. San Diego Soc. Nat. Hist., 7:399, May 31, 1934.

Distribution.—Southern part of state in suitable habitat below the Upper Sonoran Life-zone. See figure 144.

Remarks.—Average and extreme external measurements of eight males from along the

Colorado River are: 632 (568–683); 287 (255–315); 70 (66–75); 27 (26–28). A female from the same place, taken on January 19, measures 610, 320, —, 24, and weighs 903 grams.

Color is as described for *major*, except that: bifurcation of white occurs 10 mm. farther posteriorly; white stripes are wider, 20 to 50 mm. wide, and generally coalesce on rump; entire upper surface of tail white; terminal hairs of tail white; white markings on pectoral region in nine of ten specimens examined. The black area separating the stripes on the back is reduced to an elongated patch narrower than either white stripe. In winter pelage, black hairs on the center of the back attain a length of 45 mm.; white hairs in the stripes of the back reach a length of 80 mm. The longest hairs, 185 mm., on the tail are white. The claws and feet are essentially like those in *major*. The skull averages about 10 per cent smaller in linear measurements than that of *major*, and the posterior margin of the hard palate is usually anterior to a line drawn between the posterior borders of the last upper molars rather than on this line or posterior to it.

From each of the races the geographic ranges of which meet that of *estor*, it differs in the greater extent of the white markings, and from *occidentalis* and *major* it differs further in relatively longer tail.

The three specimens from "near St. Thomas" recorded by Burt (1934:399) under the name *Mephitis mephitis major* have not been examined by me, but the average of the population there would be expected to be nearer that of *estor* than to that of any other named race.

Records of occurrence.—Specimens examined, 12, as follows: *Lincoln Co.:* 1 mi. N Rox, 1. *Clark Co.:* Colorado River, Jap Ranch, 500 ft., 14 mi. E Searchlight, 2; same data, except Durban Ranch, rather than Jap Ranch, 2 (skulls only); 6 mi. N Calif.-Nev. Monument and 2 mi. W Colorado River, 1; Colorado River, ½ to 2 mi. N Calif.-Nev. Monument, 500 ft., 6.
Additional record: *Clark Co.:* near St. Thomas (Burt, 1934:399).

Taxidea taxus
Badger

The genus *Taxidea* includes only the one full species *Taxidea taxus* which does not occur outside North America. Many technical names have been proposed for supposed species and several names have been proposed for subspecies. All these names now are regarded as applying to a single full species, although of it there are no less than four, and perhaps as many as six, recognizable subspecies (geographic races), two of which occur in Nevada.

The American badger, compared to other mustelids, is a large animal, with short stout legs and a tail about a fourth the length of the head and body. The black and white markings on the face give way to a silvery gray color over most of the upper parts, except that a white stripe, which begins at the nose, extends down the mid-line of the back for a varying distance and reaches all the way to the tail in some specimens of the race *berlandieri*. The underparts are lighter-colored than the back and often are white along the mid-line. The overhairs are longer on the sides of the animal than on its back. The great enlargement of the claws on the forefeet, by which it is able to dig rapidly, is a conspicuous feature of the animal. Noteworthy features of the skull are: basilar length 100–130 mm.; occiput depressed; facial angle steep; tympanic bullae highly inflated but not in contact with paroccipital processes; palate behind upper molars; dental formula: i. $\frac{3}{3}$, c. $\frac{1}{1}$, p. $\frac{3}{3}$, m. $\frac{1}{2}$; M1 triangular, often with cusps arranged in rows transverse to long axis of skull; P4 with accessory cusp behind deuterocone; in m1, trigonid longer than talonid; metaconid, hypoconid, and entoconid large; talonid often with one, two, or three cusps additional to hypoconid and entoconid.

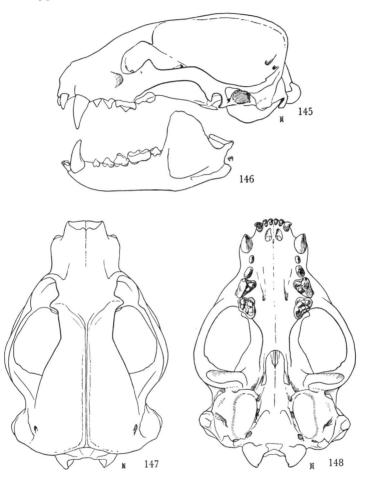

Figs. 145–148. *Taxidea taxus taxus*, Spring Valley, no. 41467, ♂. × ½.

A north-to-south size gradient in the species is evident, even within Nevada. Specimens from southern Nevada are smaller and have more extensive white markings than those from the northern part of the state. As evidence of this size gradient, fully adult males yield measurements as follows: Elko County, 778 mm.; Esmeralda County, 749; Clark County, 673.

Contrary to the statement sometimes made, females, among our specimens at least, average smaller than males, although the difference is not as much as in several other species of carnivores. Compared to males in Elko County, females are about 10 per cent smaller in external measurements, 8 per cent smaller in linear measurements of the skull, and 3 per cent smaller in linear measurements of the teeth.

The flattened appearance of the badger is reflected in the shape of its burrow, which is wider than high. A notable feature of this animal is that it lives nowhere else than in holes in the ground.

J. R. Alcorn, who has had extensive experience with badgers in western Nevada, has provided the following account: "Badgers occupy many kinds of soil in western Nevada. Their burrows are numerous in sandy valleys but are common also in gravelly or even stony areas. Apparently they avoid the clay and adobe soils; on these soils, especially on the playas which have no vegetation, badger diggings are seldom found—probably because the rodents which badgers catch for food are absent or rare at those places and because the stickiness of the soil when wet is a deterrent to any badger which might dig or even walk there. Marshy areas and those with dense vegetation are likewise avoided. Badgers are found in mountains at comparatively high elevations, but are most numerous on dry open hills and in valleys. The size of an area in which a badger lives is increased or decreased according to the distance he has to go for food. By following the fresh tracks of many badgers in the winters from 1930 to 1939, it was learned that a badger travels as far as a mile in one night, but at the end of that time, because the course taken while in search of food is very erratic, he may be only a few hundred feet from his starting point. As one follows the tracks and counts the number of shallow and deep diggings, some notion can be gained regarding the time when the badger will stop. If he has dug only a few shallow holes, the chances are that he has obtained insufficient food and will therefore continue farther in his search. If the holes are deep, the probabilities are that he has obtained sufficient food and will soon hole-up for 1 or 2 days, or possibly a week. But apparently a badger will sometimes hole-up before obtaining his fill. I followed the tracks of one in January, 1934, and noted that it had found but little to eat. All diggings were shallow (1 to 6 inches) and each probably rewarded the badger with, at most, a lizard or beetle, and from some excavations possibly nothing was obtained. After about a mile's travel the animal dug a burrow and holed-up.

"In 1937 I followed the tracks of several badgers into an area where poisoned baits had been placed for jack rabbits. When a badger found a dead rabbit, he dug a deep hole into which he took the rabbit. Some badgers remained there 1 or 2 days, and in several instances it was a week before the badger emerged. If, after emerging, the badger found another rabbit within 100 yards of the first, another hole was dug and with the rabbit for food the badger again remained holed-up for a few days. On several other occasions I have set traps baited with rabbits at the entrance to the burrow of a badger; on returning next day, I have found the trap sprung and the bait gone, the badger, as indicated by the absence of tracks, having returned to its subterranean retreat with the rabbit for food without so much as having gone farther than the entrance of the burrow."

Vernon L. Mills, of Fallon, Nevada, whose extensive experience with badgers qualifies him to speak of their habits, has written at length in answer to a query concerning how long a badger remains below ground in winter. From his reply the following somewhat condensed statements are offered:

"In the winter of 1937–1938, after a 2- or 3-inch snowfall, I trailed two badgers to their holes; in the afternoon of the same day I returned to their holes and set traps for them. One badger remained below ground for four days, and the other ventured out on the fifth night. On the morning following the third night, one of these badgers pushed about a quart of new dirt out of its burrow, leaving the opening slightly larger than before but still not nearly large enough for the animal to get through. Otherwise nothing about the holes was disturbed. I think the average stay of the badgers trailed to their burrows that winter was between 3 and 5 days. I cannot be sure of this, however, because the nights on which there was sufficient snow for the badgers to leave tracks were the cold nights, when I would not expect the fat badgers to venture out. I suspect that some badgers [near Fallon] go into hibernation in the fall and remain until spring."

With respect to burrows, Alcorn has this to say: "In digging holes, badgers loosen the soil with their front feet, then push it backward, under the belly. As the loose earth approaches the rear of the animal, the hind feet take up the pushing movement and push the soil on farther back—the dirt from the first 2 or 3 feet of the hole being that which is thrown out onto the surface. A burrow constructed in this manner is round only at the entrance. Within the burrow itself, loose earth lies deeply on the floor, beginning at a point several feet back in from the entrance.

"The rapidity with which badgers can dig has been clearly demonstrated to me on several occasions. In January, 1930, while driving through the desert, my father and I saw a badger run into a hole which was about 3 feet deep. We attempted to dig him out, but, although we could hear him digging in the stony soil and could get an occasional glimpse of him, he soon was out of sight and hearing. His progress was so fast and so much dirt did he push out behind, thus filling up his tunnel, that we found it difficult to follow his route. After an hour or two of digging we were at a depth of 4 feet and had covered about 15 feet laterally.

"In December, 1938, with the assistance of ten men, all with shovels, an attempt was made to dig out a badger in sandy soil. We worked as fast as possible for about 4 hours. At the end of that time we were at a depth of 6 feet and had traveled about 30 feet laterally when exhaustion prevented us from digging farther.

"Vernon Mills and I have attempted to dig, dynamite, and 'snake' badgers

from their subterranean retreats. After many futile attempts we concluded
that once a badger has entered the ground, his ability to dig rapidly makes it
almost impossible for man to reach him.

"Except during the time when the young are too small to leave the burrow,
badgers are thought not to regularly inhabit one burrow for long, and often
the animal may dig and occupy a new burrow following each time it appears
aboveground.

"Before the young are able to leave the burrow it is occasionally cleaned to
prevent sand, dirt, rocks, or other material from filling it up."

On May 26, 1929, at an 8100-foot elevation in a meadow alongside Lehman
Creek, White Pine County, Ward C. Russell and I trapped a half-grown
(weight 6½ lbs.) young badger in a burrow to which we were attracted by
scattered jay feathers. As we were pulling the trapped badger out of the hole,
another young one of about the same size followed the trapped animal to the
mouth of the burrow, but retreated back down the burrow when we attempted
to lay hands on it. With our shovel we took turns at digging, but, like Alcorn,
gave up after we had covered 18½ feet horizontally and were down to a depth
of 40 inches. This young badger filled the dirt in behind it so tightly that we
had difficulty in ascertaining the route it had chosen for burrowing.

Whether badgers have many enemies other than man, I do not know. It
surprised me to find in the well-filled stomach of a half-grown coyote shot on
June 20, 1928, 1 mile northeast of Cave Spring, remains of a badger only. I do
not for an instant believe that a coyote of this size could kill a grown badger,
and I doubt that an adult coyote would be a match for one.

Badgers obtain their food mostly by digging out small rodents, if we have
correctly interpreted the signs of their fossorial activity. Unlike other kinds of
Nevadan carnivores, which, when a favored food becomes scarce, direct their
foraging efforts to another area or to another food source, badgers as often as
not, especially in spring and early summer, thoroughly clean out the rodents of
a given area before moving on to another. One instance of this kind was noted
8 miles north of Sulphur, where a sand dune, surrounded by harder soil unpro-
ductive of rodents, had been so thoroughly worked that rodents had been
eliminated. Observations of similar work at other places in Nevada suggests
that badgers locally "control" rodents, whereas other kinds of carnivores act
more as "checks." Although I suppose that most of the areas from which rodents are eliminated by badgers in spring are repopulated within a few weeks,
or at most before autumn, and that the effect of the badgers foraging over a
6-month period therefore is, in the long run, mainly a checking effect after
all, it is conceivable that the depopulation of an area like the isolated sand
dune north of Sulphur, which is 200 feet long and a third as wide, would
produce a more lasting reduction of the rodent population.

A male trapped on June 21, 1928, at Cave Spring had only the remains of a
freshly eaten *Citellus townsendii* in its stomach. On the same date and at this

place, the viscera of two other *C. townsendii* were found in the freshly excavated earth at the mouth of a burrow made by a badger which was probably
in search of the luckless squirrels. In the Ruby Mountains area Borell and
Ellis (1934a:22) observed that: "On several occasions . . . badgers had dug out
and eaten ground squirrels (*Citellus elegans*) [= *Citellus beldingi oregonus*]."
An adult male badger taken 3 miles southeast of Kawich P. O., on September
24, 1931, about 5 P.M., was found to contain in its stomach three horned
toads (*Phrynosoma platyrhinos*), 80 per cent; one lizard (*Uta stansburiana*), 1
per cent; and insect remains. The latter, as identified by Clarence Cottam,
were: *Stenopelmatus* sp., with eggs, 10 per cent; fragment of one *Oedopodinae*
and one unidentified Acrididae, 4 per cent; fragment of one *Lasius* sp. and
undetermined Hymenoptera, trace; fragment of one *Vaejovis* sp., 4 per cent;
spider fragment, trace; fragment of one flower *Eriogonum* sp., trace. Because
the lizard and horned toads were partly digested, I thought that the insects,
in part, had come from the stomachs of the reptiles.

Relative to the food, Alcorn (MS) says:

"The food of badgers consists mostly of small mammals, insects, and lizards.
Eggs, snakes, birds, fish, and carrion also are eaten. In December, 1938, while
attempting to dig out a badger, I found the remains of three Piute ground
squirrels (*Citellus townsendii mollis*). Apparently these squirrels form a large
part of badgers' food; this is perhaps because the squirrels have short burrows
and are easily dug out. Especially in the 7 or 8 months during which time
these squirrels hibernate do badgers, to judge from sign, dig into the nests and
eat many squirrels.

"I have caught badgers in traps that were baited with many different things,
including fish, rabbits, dead sheep, chickens, ravens, carcasses of coyotes, and
the flesh of other animals, and many badgers were caught when the only lure
was coyote scent.

"I have seen two badgers killed by strychnine in eggs that were placed in
apiaries for skunks.

"In tracking badgers I have noted many holes dug in search of food, but
not once have I seen where food was buried. Judging from tracks, the food,
except when it is a very large item, is eaten immediately after it is obtained.
An animal of large size, such as a rabbit, which is already on top of the ground
is taken into the burrow to be eaten. A badger may even dig a burrow, if no
others be near, especially for this purpose.

"In the fall of 1937 Vernon Mills showed me tracks on a sandy part of the
desert near Fallon which indicated that a badger had come upon a snake—perhaps a rattlesnake—with which he did a considerable amount of fighting or
playing. It looked as if the snake had struck at the badger, but this could
not be definitely ascertained.

"The two female badgers which Vernon Mills keeps four miles west of Fallon
have their home in a large wooden box buried so that its top is flush with the

surface of the ground. When the lid is raised and small mammals or other foods are placed just outside the box, the badgers come out, eagerly grasp the food with their teeth, and crawl backward into the box to eat. On one occasion, after the badgers came out to get the seven or eight dead pocket gophers I had placed just outside the box, the lid of the box was closed, and they were prevented from reëntering it. Each carried away a gopher, buried it about 30 feet from the other's gopher, returned for another gopher, and so on, until all the gophers were disposed of—each having been buried by itself. At another time, when the badgers were between 6 and 9 months old, I offered them a large live pocket gopher (*Thomomys bottae canus*)—something that had never before been given them. Even though the pocket gopher "put up a mean front," one of the badgers quickly took the gopher in her mouth and dispatched it in one bite.

"As indicated by the fact that burrows often are many miles from the nearest water supply, badgers seem not to require water to drink. Captive animals, however, drink regularly."

Because no excrement identifiable as that of a badger was found in the course of our field work, I made inquiry on this point of Vernon Mills. He said that each of the two badgers kept by him digs a hole, deposits the feces, and covers it over with earth.

Concerning the behavior of badgers toward other animals, Alcorn writes as follows: "When approached closely by a person, dog, or other large mammal, a badger faces the intruder and crouches flat on the ground with the legs doubled up so as to enable it to jump at the enemy if occasion arises. The long hairs on the sides of the animal are extended outward, giving the badger the appearance of being flatter and much wider than it actually is. The nose is wrinkled, the lips are curled so as to show the teeth, and a low hissing sound is often made. If at this time a quick move is made in its direction, the badger feigns an attack by quickly advancing several feet and at the same time makes a loud hissing noise which lasts for a second or two. This is usually only a warning which the badger uses to discourage the intruder's further approach. But if the intruder persists, the badger will continue to feign attack.

"If the intruder is quiet and motionless for a few minutes, the badger rises on its feet and turns and runs. If pursued closely, it stops and, facing the pursuer, crouches flat on the ground, again ready to fight. If attacked, it uses its powerful jaws to inflict deep wounds in the enemy.

"When not alarmed, or when running, the badger stands erect and the long hairs on its sides hang down. Its legs hold its body surprisingly high off the ground. When a badger is hunting, its ears are erect and it has an alert expression on its face, reminding one more of a weasel than of the flat, wide badger known to most people."

Relative to the noise made by a badger that is cornered, I noted that a belligerent male trapped on June 20, 1928, at Cave Spring, snarled by drawing air in through the mouth; when this air was expelled through the nose, the snarl turned into a hissing sound. A further note on behavior is furnished by Ward C. Russell who, at 11:30 A.M., on May 2, 1931, 9½ miles east of Gold-field, saw an adult male running down a wash. When pursued and overtaken, the badger took refuge in a hole not more than a foot and a half deep. With head outward he defied the collector who was loath to damage the specimen by shooting it in the head, the only part exposed. When Russell, as though leaving the place, turned his back and walked away about 20 feet, the badger dashed out and away, probably in search of a deeper burrow; it was quick to take advantage of the chance to escape. Russell found the instinct to find safety by getting into the ground well illustrated in the autumn of 1940 near Fallon. When he came upon several badgers caught in traps set for coyotes, he saw that the badgers had almost completely buried themselves. After being released from the traps, they remained in the holes they had dug, and even when forcibly thrown out, they would dart back in. Their instinctive reaction to an injury or to danger is to seek safety *in* the ground.

Borell and Ellis (1934a:22) write of a badger observed in the Ruby Moun-tains area as follows: "At four o'clock one afternoon a large badger, apparently unaware of the observer, was watched for fifteen minutes as it foraged in a newly-mown alfalfa field. It would trot quickly ten or fifteen feet in one direc-tion and then stop abruptly and, standing or squatting on its haunches, sniff the air in various directions. Each time it repeated the maneuver, it traveled at an angle to the direction just taken and so made a zigzag trail across the fields. When trotting it held its nose close to the ground, but when standing or squatting it sometimes raised its nose upward to the full extent of its short neck. When disturbed it ran a short distance and took refuge in a burrow which had recently been excavated."

Alcorn (MS) has this to say about a badger's ability to swim to avoid being held captive: "Although many Nevadan badgers live in almost waterless deserts, they are able to swim and do not hesitate to do so when attempting to escape. I placed one on a ½-half-acre island one afternoon, but found it gone the following morning. Examination of tracks indicated that the animal had swum the 20 feet of water and then traveled for ¼ mile, as far as I followed, without digging a hole."

The reproductive tracts, preserved in alcohol, of seven females taken from November 7, 1940, to February 3, 1941, within 11 miles of Fallon by J. R. Alcorn are accompanied by skulls, weights, and external measurements. The diameter of the Fallopian tubes is smallest (2.6 mm.) in the animal taken first and largest in the animal taken last. The sizes of reproductive tracts of animals taken on intervening dates form a graded series, each reproductive tract being successively larger than the one taken on the last preceding date. Gross inspec-tion shows embryos in the last three: the one taken on January 13 had three embryos 9 mm. in diameter; that on January 25, two embryos, 12.5 mm.; and the one on February 3, four embryos, 21 mm. The diameter of the "embryos" was measured across the outside of the uterine horn. Study of the cleaned skulls reveals that the animal which contained two embryos was less than 1 year old. The female taken on November 17 was more than 1 year old. The ages of the other five females were not certainly ascertained. On March 16, 1929, in the Ruby Mountains area, Borell and Ellis (1934a:22) took a female containing three embryos. In normal position, freed from the embryonic membranes, one of these embryos measured 88 mm. long from crown to rump.

From these data it appears that swellings denoting the presence of embryos can be detected in the uterine horns about January 1 and that young are born approximately 80 days later. Females bear young when only 1 year old. The smallest number of embryos, two, was found in the only one judged certainly to be less than 1 year old. Records of embryos in the four pregnant females from Nevada are 2, 3, 3, and 4.

Concerning the weight of badgers, Alcorn (MS) says: "The weight of these animals at birth, which is thought to occur in March and April, is less than a pound. Two nonpregnant females, in captivity since a few days old, weighed 13½ and 14 pounds in February, 1940, when 24 months old (V. Mills, MS). Many fat adults in winter weigh more than 20 pounds. The largest badger of which we have record (Alcorn, MS) was caught south of Fallon in December, 1938; it weighed 30 pounds."

Of the economic status of the badger, Alcorn has this to say: "A population of badgers keeps down the numbers of rodents, the fur is valuable, and the burrowing activities are a factor in soil formation. Where badgers are left alone and not killed, ground squirrels seldom increase to the point where it is necessary to resort to artificial means of reducing their numbers.

"Most badgers are caught in early fall in traps set for coyotes. At this time of year the fur is of little or no value—seldom bringing more than 50 cents—and because the animal is difficult to release from a trap alive it is usually killed and thrown away unskinned. In the many warm days of September, badgers which are caught in the more than a few coyote traps put out in that month often die after a few hours of exposure to the sun. The fur of these 'slips' and is almost worthless. If these badgers could be turned loose, uninjured, the fur, like that of other badgers, would be worth ten times more in February. It is often found that where coyote trappers are inactive, badgers are more numerous than in areas where coyotes are extensively trapped or poisoned. Badgers are easily caught in traps, and, unlike coyotes, they will eat poisoned baits without hesitation."

To Alcorn's account I may add that the activities of the government hunters operating for the assumed benefit of the sheep growers appear to have an especially adverse effect on the populations of badgers. There are two principal reasons for this. One is that the government hunters use poisoned baits which private fur trappers rarely use. Badgers are less wary than coyotes and more readily fall victims to poisoned baits than do coyotes. Another reason why the work of the government hunters seeking coyotes is especially destructive of badgers is that they trap in summer and early autumn, which is the time when badgers are especially active. In late autumn and winter, when the private trappers operate (coyotes are the principal catch), many of the badgers are inactive, holed-up for so-called hibernation. Given two trap lines for coyotes, one set out in August and the other in December, other things being equal, more badgers, relative to coyotes, are taken in August.

Several government hunters operating in Nevada have complained of badgers being a nuisance in their efforts to trap coyotes in areas that had not been thoroughly poisoned in previous years. One trapper killed all badgers that he caught, his only excuse being that they were a nuisance. Other trappers liberated some of the badgers in accordance with instructions from their superior officers, but they expressed doubt that many of the so-liberated animals survived. My own experience in trapping a few badgers made me doubt this until I visited the trap line of one of the government trappers who got around to his traps only every 5 to 8 days. In these instances it was clear that a large proportion of the trapped badgers, still alive, were so injured as to be unable to survive for long after they were liberated.

A heavy toll of badgers, from 16 to 20 for every 100 coyotes, was reported in the trapping and poisoning work in the inclusive years 1916 to 1920 (see Records, 1919, 1921). After that time, badgers were not reported separately from the other smaller fur-bearing animals killed in efforts directed mainly at coyotes. Even in this 1916–1920 period the number of badgers killed, relative to coyotes, is thought to have been more than the figures indicate. Badgers are burrowing mammals and when poisoned it is believed that many retreat below ground to die out of sight, whereas coyotes, being essentially cursorial mammals, usually come to their death aboveground. This is probably the reason why a larger proportion of poisoned coyotes than of badgers was found. According to Biological Survey poisoners, many of the badgers found dead from poison had only their hindquarters aboveground; apparently before death overtook them the doomed, sick animals' natural burrowing instincts operated to a degree which permitted them to partly bury themselves.

It is sometimes denied by those supervising the work of government trappers that more badgers than coyotes are caught in some trap lines set in summer in areas not previously poisoned or intensively trapped. This is because the trappers who have taken large numbers of badgers in late years do not make a full report on them. Most trap lines of certain given areas, even in late summer, do not, as a matter of fact, catch anywhere near as many badgers as coyotes simply because so many badgers have been previously trapped or poisoned in that area that few remain. Furthermore, the lower birth rate of the badger, as compared with that of the coyote, prevents the badger from "coming back" in numbers as soon as does the coyote. The experience of members of our Museum field parties further bears out the contention that control measures directed at coyotes by government hunters is an appreciable factor in reducing the badger population. In areas where the government hunters have attempted control the year round—by trapping in some or all seasons and by using poison in some seasons—we found it always difficult and sometimes impossible to obtain badgers. In other areas where only private fur trappers had operated in late autumn and winter our collectors in summer found it relatively easy to procure badgers.

Turning now from the depletion in numbers, which, because of activities of government hunters, is so marked in some areas as to approach closely, or even reach, extermination, we come to the obvious fact that the activities of the private trappers seeking fur has been important, the most important factor, in reducing the numbers of badgers in many parts of the state. In 1929 and 1930, when dictates of fashion raised badger fur to a high price commercially, many trappers sought badgers, with the result that the population of badgers in certain areas was heavily levied upon.

Taking all of these factors into account, it is surprising to me that there are many badgers left in Nevada at all. Whether this reduction in numbers is a benefit or a loss, depends, of course, on the viewpoint of the person passing judgment. In general I have heard but few people in Nevada condemn the badger, among whom were: (1) some of the government trappers who, being desirous of taking as many coyotes as possible, found badgers to be a nuisance; (2) some riders who vaguely implied that badgers were in the nuisance category because their burrows constituted a menace to running horses and to the horses' riders; and (3) one rancher, like some others, no doubt, who objected to the burrows that badgers made in digging rodents out of a hay meadow. Taking the opposite view were: (1) many private fur trappers who are interested in taking and marketing the furs; and (2) two ranchers, doubtless like some others, who wished the animals to increase in numbers because of the control on rodent populations that the badgers exercised on their ranches.

The price of badger pelts has fluctuated greatly in the past 20 years. There was only slight demand for them before about 1927 when fashion in furs created a real demand for them and caused prices to rise to a peak in the late 1920's. In White Pine County I heard of one exceptionally fine pelt for which the trapper received $75. The precise prices received by trappers are not easy to verify, but invoice lists from the Funsten Fur Company reveal that Frank Garret, for badgers trapped in March and the first week of April, 1930, in Snake Valley, White Pine County, received $318.50 or an average of $9.37 per skin. The range in price per skin was from $2 to $20. Mr. Garret said that had his receipts for February, the month when he began trapping badgers, been included, the average price would have been higher. Change in fashion has resulted in a lesser demand for badger pelts, at least those of average and poor quality, since 1930 and, in Nevada, I think that the average price since then has been less than it was in 1930, but certainly less than it was in the late 1920's. In February, 1942, in Reno, badgers of average quality from around Fallon were bringing trappers only $3.50 each.

My own view is that the badger is a desirable member of the fauna, and that on public land as well as on much of the private land it should be preserved because it is one important part of the balance of nature and because it yields an important supplementary income to those who take and market its fur. From the information that we have, it appears to be second only to the coyote in total fur sales for the state, although in some years the badger may rank third, or fourth, depending on fur price for the year concerned. Wise use of the badger as a fur bearer would involve taking only a part of the annual increase so as to ensure a yearly income indefinitely. Three existing obstacles to doing this, in seeming order of decreasing importance, are: (1) lack of a state law prohibiting the distribution of poisoned meat (suet) baits for carnivores, either by governmental employees or by private individuals; (2) extensive trapping in summer and early autumn; and (3) overutilization by private fur trappers in the fur season.

Points 1 and 2 are discussed in more detail in the account of the coyote. In connection with point 3, which might most profitably be considered after difficulties in points 1 and 2 are resolved, I can suggest that some plan similar to that outlined on page 260 be put in practice. This involves the registration of private trap lines, the aim of which is the harvesting of prime fur only, simplifying law enforcement, and avoiding overtrapping.

Taxidea taxus taxus (Schreber)
Badger

Ursus taxus Schreber, Säugethiere, vol. 3, p. 520, 1778. Type said to be from Labrador and Hudson Bay but probably southwest of Hudson Bay.

Taxidea taxus, Rhoads, Amer. Nat., 28:524, June, 1894; Taylor, Univ. California Publ. Zoöl., 7:296, June 24, 1911; Linsdale, Amer. Midland Nat., 19:174, January, 1938.

Taxidea taxus taxus, Borell and Ellis, Journ. Mamm., 15:22, 72, February 15, 1934.

Distribution.—Over most of state above Lower Sonoran Life-zone. See figure 149.

Remarks.—External measurements are as follows: Male from near Big Creek Ranch, Humboldt Co., 725, 157, 110. Four males from Elko Co.: 778 (755–800), 149 (125–155), 116 (110–118), 55 (55– —). Four males (intergrades toward *berlandieri*) from Cave Spring, Esmeralda Co.: 749 (720–780), 131 (110–150), 120 (110–136), 53 (50–55); weight, in spring, 12 lbs. (= 5,443 gm.). Two females from Kleckner Creek, Elko Co.: 745, 690; 130, 131; 100, 96; weight, 13 lbs. (= 5,930 gm.), 13½ lbs. (= 6,154 gm., this one pregnant). The weight of seven females taken from November 7, 1940, to February 3, 1941, within 11 miles of Fallon, was 16 lbs. (= 7,278 gm.), with extremes of 14 lbs. (= 6,350 gm.) and 19 lbs. (= 8,614 gm.).

The white stripe, beginning on the nose, rarely extends back of the shoulders and in none of the specimens examined extends posteriorly to the root of the tail as it does in many individuals of *berlandieri*. Only two skins are available from northeastern Nevada, both from the Pine Forest Mountains. One has the tips of the overhairs markedly reddish, and in this feature shows approach to specimens of *Taxidea taxus neglecta* as known to me by specimens from Sonoma and Mendocino counties, California. The second specimen from the Pine Forest Mountains has the tips of the overhairs white as in other skins referred to *taxus* from farther east in Nevada. Five skins from the Warner Mountains, of California, a little farther west toward Fort Crook, the type locality of *neglecta*, have some red in the tips of the overhairs and in other parts of the pelage, which usually is

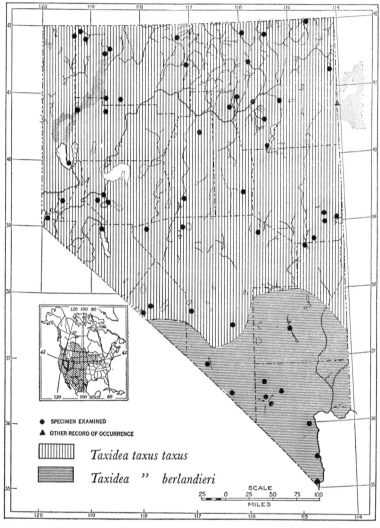

Fig. 149. Distribution of subspecies of the badger, *Taxidea taxus*, with insert showing range of the species.

white in *taxus*, but show greater resemblance to *taxus* than to *neglecta* from Sonoma and Mendocino counties. In summary, it can be said that the reddish color is thought to be the one distinguishing feature of *neglecta*, and that specimens from northwestern Nevada show evidence of intergradation with *neglecta*, but appear best referred to *taxus*.

T. t. taxus differs from *berlandieri* in larger size, shorter white line down the back, and relatively broader skull across the mastoidal processes and across the zygomatic arches. Intergradation with *berlandieri* is well-shown in size and in cranial proportions by several specimens, notably that from Kawich Valley and the four adult males from Cave Spring. The latter are almost exactly intermediate between badgers from Elko and Clark counties in cranial measurements, are intermediate but nearer *taxus* in external measurements, and are colored like *taxus*. These specimens all are referred to *taxus*.

Records of occurrence.—Specimens examined, 68, as follows: *Washoe Co.:* E shore Pyramid Lake, 4000 ft., 9 mi. NW Nixon, 1. *Ormsby Co.:* Marlette Lake, 1. *Storey Co.:* 6 mi. NE Virginia City, 6000 ft., 1. *Humboldt Co.:* 38 mi. W and 6 mi. S Denio, Oregon, 4; NW part Humboldt Co., 3; Virgin Valley, 4; Calico, 1; near Big Creek Ranch, Pine Forest Mts., 1; Leonard Creek, 6500 ft., Pine Forest Mts., 1; N of Bliss Ranch, Golconda, 1; Red Butte, Sulphur, 1; Clover Creek, Jungo, 1. *Pershing Co.;* 7 mi. NE Gerlach, 3925 ft., 1; 8 mi. S Sulphur, 4350 ft., 1. *Churchill Co.:* 5 mi. N Fallon, 1; 5 to 8 mi. SW Fallon, 4000 ft., 3; Carson Lake, 10 mi. SSE Fallon, 3900 ft., 1. *Mineral Co.:* 3 mi. S Schurz, 4100 ft., 1; Stewart Valley, 1. *Esmeralda Co.:* Cave Spring, 6200–6248 ft., 4. *Lander Co.:* Hilltop, 2; Gondolpho Ranch, 10 mi. W Austin, Reese River, 2. *Eureka Co.:* Palisade, 1; Reglis Ranch, Eureka, 1. *Nye Co.:* Millett P. O., 2; Marble, 1; Duckwater, 2; 9½ mi. E Goldfield, 5500 ft., 1; Kawich Valley, 3 mi. SE Kawich, 6000 ft., 1. *Elko Co.:* Cedar Creek, 10 mi. NE San Jacinto, 6000 ft., 1; Mountain City, 1; summit between heads of Copper and Coon creeks, Jarbidge Mts., 1 (coll. of Ralph Ellis); North Fork, 1; 2L-mile Ranch, Montello, 2; 15 mi. W Elko, 1 (coll. of Ralph Ellis); Elko, 1 (U. S. Nat. Mus.); summit of Secret Pass, 6200 ft., 1 (coll. of Ralph Ellis); near Wendover, 1 (Univ. Utah Dept. Zoöl.); Kleckner Creek, 4 mi. E Lee, 2 (coll. of Ralph Ellis); W side Ruby Lake, 3 mi. N White Pine Co. line, 6200 ft., 1 (coll. of Ralph Ellis). *White Pine Co.:* Cooper Canyon, Spring Valley, 1; Lehman Creek, 8100 ft., 1; Spring Valley, 3 mi. W Osceola, 6500 ft., 1; South [end of] Spring Valley, 4. *Lincoln Co.:* Cave Valley, 3 mi. W Cave, 6500 ft., 1.

Taxidea taxus berlandieri Baird
Badger

Taxidea berlandieri Baird, Mamm. N. Amer., p. 205, 1857. Type from Llano Estacado, Texas, near border of New Mexico.

Taxidea taxus berlandieri, Allen, Bull. Amer. Mus. Nat. Hist., 7:256, June 29, 1895; Burt, Trans. San Diego Soc. Nat. Hist., 7:399, May 31, 1934.

Distribution.—Southern part of state below the Upper Sonoran Life-zone, but also in higher zones in the isolated mountains of Clark County. See figure 149.

Remarks.—External measurements of a male from 2½ mi. N Calif.-Nev. Monument, Clark Co., are 673, 115, 105, 49. Corresponding measurements of two females, one from the same locality as the male and the second from the Jap Ranch, are 591, 615; 115, 115; 95, 102; 42, 43.

T. t. berlandieri differs from *taxus* in smaller size, in longer white stripe on back, and, on the average, in relative narrowness of skull as measured across the mastoidal processes and across the zygomatic arches. Four adult females from 14 miles east of Searchlight have, for example, average cranial measurements as follows: basilar length, 102.6; mastoidal breadth, 67.7; zygomatic breadth, 68.8. Corresponding average measurements of two adult females of *T. t. taxus* from Kleckner Creek, Elko County, for comparison, are 109.6, 75.9, 77.0. *T. t. berlandieri* differs from *T. t. neglecta* in the same way as it does from *taxus*. *T. t. neglecta* and *infusca* are more reddish than *berlandieri*. An additional difference from *infusca* is that the white stripe is not markedly wider on the nape than elsewhere. From *T. t. sonoriensis*, according to the describer, *berlandieri* differs in lighter color and more evenly V-shaped nasals.

Of the six specimens recorded from the D. R. Dickey Collection, only the skulls were seen.

Records of occurrence.—Specimens examined, 18, as follows: *Nye Co.:* Rhyolite, 1; Ash Meadows, 1 (U. S. Nat. Mus.). *Lincoln Co.:* Pahranagat Valley, 2. *Clark Co.:* Indian Springs, 1 (D. R. Dickey Coll.); Corn Creek, 1 (D. R. Dickey Coll.); above Willow Creek, 7200 ft., 2 (D. R. Dickey Coll.); Kyle Canyon, 8000 ft., 1 (D. R. Dickey Coll.); Boulder City, 1 (Boulder Dam Recreational Area Coll.); Colorado River, 14 mi. E Searchlight, 6; Colorado River, 2 to 2½ mi. N Calif.-Nev. Monument, 500 ft., 2.

Family CANIDAE
Foxes, Coyotes, and Wolves

Three genera, comprising five full species and a total of eight subspecies have been found in Nevada. These terrestrial, doglike carnivores, mostly of medium size, all have four clawed digits on the hind feet and in American kinds five digits on the forefeet, claws not retractile, sebaceous scent glands on the upper surface of the tail, tail long and usually bushy, muzzle elongated, alisphenoid canal present, and cheek teeth of combined trenchant and cutting type; the dental formula in American members is i. $\frac{3}{3}$, c. p.$\frac{1}{1}$, $\frac{4}{4}$, m. $\frac{2}{3}$.

Genus **Vulpes** Oken
Red Foxes and Kit Foxes or Swifts

Two species, the red fox and kit fox, occur in Nevada. Selected generic characters are the large ears, large cylindrical and bushy tail, small size (less than 15 lbs.), gland on top of tail less than 1/5 length of tail from its base, postorbital processes thin and concave on dorsal surface, temporal ridges closely paralleling one another or uniting to form a sagittal crest, and inferior margin of lower mandible without the step seen in *Urocyon*.

Vulpes fulva necator Merriam
Red Fox

Vulpes necator Merriam, Proc. Washington Acad. Sci., 2:664, December 28, 1900. Type from Whitney Meadows, 9500 feet, near Mount Whitney, Tulare County, California.
Vulpes fulva necator, Grinnell, Univ. California Publ. Zoöl., 40:108, September 26, 1933.

Distribution.—In the Sierra Nevada and in some other mountain ranges east as far as White Pine County and south to the Sheep Range. See figure 162.

Remarks.—External measurements of three males from the Sierra Nevada of California are 993 (937–1,022); 361 (349–365); 166 (162–171). Corresponding measurements of five females are 947 (881–1,003); 348 (311–373); 154 (145–168). The above measurements are from Grinnell, Dixon, and Linsdale (1937:385) who (p. 380) indicate that the weight of adult males averages about 4,205 grams (9¼ lbs.) and that of females about 3,295 grams (7¼ lbs.).

The coloration of red foxes in many localities, even among offspring of a single pair of adults, is variable. Four color phases are recognized: red, cross, silver, and black. In the cross and silver phases the color varies toward black, being more nearly black in the silver phase than in the cross phase. Intermediate amounts of the reddish, silver, and black color in many specimens make difficult the assignment of certain individuals to a particular color phase. All have the tip of the tail white. The tail is circular in cross section. The pads of the feet are concealed in winter by long fur.

In the Sierra Nevada of California more than half of the foxes reported (see Grinnell, Dixon, and Linsdale, 1937:378) are of the silver and cross phases,

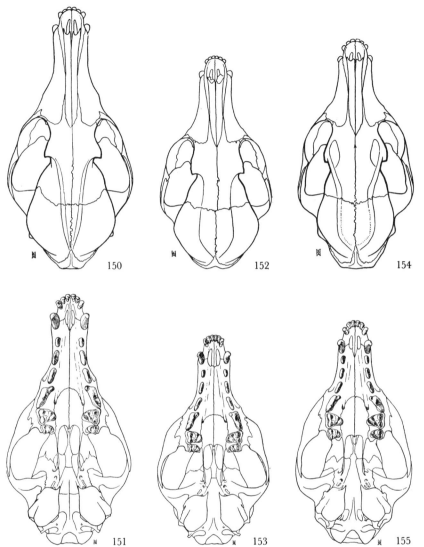

Figs. 150–155. Foxes. All, ×½. (Other views of these skulls are shown in figs. 156–161.)

Figs. 150, 151. *Vulpes fulva necator*, Marlette Lake, 8000 feet, no. 69636, ♂, subadult.
Figs. 152, 153. *Vulpes macrotis nevadensis*, 5 miles northeast Hazen, 4000 feet, no. 90014, ♂.
Figs. 154, 155. *Urocyon cinereoargenteus scottii*, Colorado River, 2 miles north Calif.-Nev.
Monument, no. 61465, ♂.

mostly the latter. The one skin from Nevada, no. 69635, taken in December, 1934, at 8000 feet elevation, at Marlette Lake, Ormsby County, is of this cross phase. Another taken in the same month at this place was described by the collector, W. H. Dust, as of the same color.

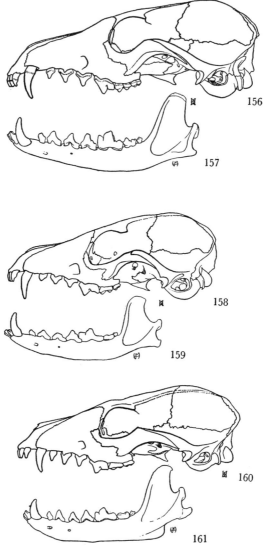

Figs. 156–161. Foxes. Different views of these skulls
are shown in figs. 150–155. All, × ½.

Figs. 156, 157. *Vulpes fulva necator*.
Figs. 158, 159. *Vulpes macrotis nevadensis*.
Figs. 160, 161. *Urocyon cinereoargenteus scottii*.

Available information about the occurrence of red foxes, from west to east, in the state
is as follows: On August 22, 1935, Tony Petroff reported having seen a red fox (not of the
cross, silver, or black phase) dash across the road about 2 miles south of Glenbrook,
Douglas County. In the winter of 1933–1934 Frank Peters trapped a silver fox at Sandy

Point, on the east side of Lake Tahoe. In December, 1934, W. H. Dust, at Marlette Lake, 8000 feet, in Ormsby County, trapped two cross foxes. These places are typical habitat for the red fox of the Sierra Nevada.

In April or May, 1911, Andy Fedor, a miner, at Fairview, Churchill County, dug "out of a hole in the ground" a fox about "the size of a large house rat" (F. Kendall, MS) which was shipped to a friend in San Francisco, California, and from him purchased by Mr. F. Kendall of the same city. In November, 1911, the fox died, and its skull, no. 16381, was given to the Museum of Vertebrate Zoölogy.

On July 9, 1933, an operator of a filling station at Little Rye Patch, about 10 miles south of Stone Cabin, Nye County, told of taking an occasional red fox as well as gray foxes and kit foxes in the fur trapping season in that vicinity. On July 19, 1933, one of the two Williams brothers at Hot Creek, also in Nye County, but 31 miles farther northeast, reported that in trapping fur bearers in winter he had taken one red fox in that vicinity. He knew also gray foxes and kit foxes of which only the former, in addition to the one red fox, had been taken at that place.

In June and July, 1928, Huey Stewart, Carl Reich, and Mr. McNett reported red foxes sometimes taken in the Silver Peak Mountain Range of Esmeralda County. There is the possibility that red individuals of *Urocyon* were confused with *Vulpes fulva*.

On August 20, 1930, at Hamilton, White Pine County, I examined two skins in the red phase, made into a muff and neckpiece, belonging to Mrs. Carl F. Muir of that place. These supposedly were the two red foxes trapped at Illipah (Mormon Ranch), about nine miles northeast of Hamilton, by a Mr. Kelley, but Mr. Kelley expressed to me his doubts that these were the skins of the animals trapped by him. In these the foot soles were not concealed by hair, whereas the hair did conceal the foot soles in the specimens which he trapped. It was his opinion that these were "southern foxes" substituted by the furrier who had made up the furs for Mrs. Muir. Mr. Ed Brrch, of Hamilton, who had trapped several red foxes in the White Pine Mountains near Hamilton also thought that the furs which I saw were not those trapped by Mr. Kelley. The fact emerged, however, that all the red foxes which Messrs. Brrch, Kelley, Muir, and E. B. Vandall knew of as having been trapped in the vicinity of Hamilton were of the red, not of the cross, silver, or black phase. On August 2, 1930, Lewis Mattice, a United States Biological Survey hunter, told me of a red fox that he poisoned in the Shell Creek Range of White Pine County in the course of coyote control work. Because the skin was spoiled when found he did not save it.

In the Museum of Vertebrate Zoölogy is the skull, together with the lower jaws, of a red fox (no. 90621) found, along with bones of a mountain sheep, on January 16 or 17, 1940, by J. C. Allen on the ground beneath the nest of a golden eagle, on the middle ridge, 9000 feet elevation, between Heyford Peak and Sheep Peak, 1 mile west of Hidden Forest, Sheep Range, Clark County.

At many other places seemingly as well suited for red foxes as those just mentioned, fur trappers have operated intensively in Nevada without ever taking red foxes. The present discontinuous distribution and especially the seeming absence of the foxes from several areas cannot be satisfactorily explained with the information now available.

No information is available that gives reason for doubting that the red fox is native to each of the four areas from which it is reported in the state. Nevertheless, the farming of foxes for fur commonly results in the escape of individuals and allowance for this should be made. In July, 1935, on the eastern outskirts of the town of Paradise Valley, an attempt at raising silver foxes was observed. Alcorn (MS) reports that in 1929 some foxes were kept 3 miles northeast of Fallon by U. S. Bentley. Probably similar attempts to "farm" foxes from imported stock have been made at other places in Nevada.

The three skulls available, all of subadult animals, one of which is represented also by the skin, agree with specimens from California assigned to the race *necator*. In the original description of this race, Merriam pointed out its close resemblance to *Vulpes macrourus*

Baird. Merriam (1900:665) thought that the geographic ranges of the two kinds were
"separated by the full breadth of the Great Basin" and that *necator* differed from *macrourus* in smaller size and especially in smaller tail, but only slightly, if at all, in cranial features. *V. macrourus* was based on material from the mountains along the eastern side

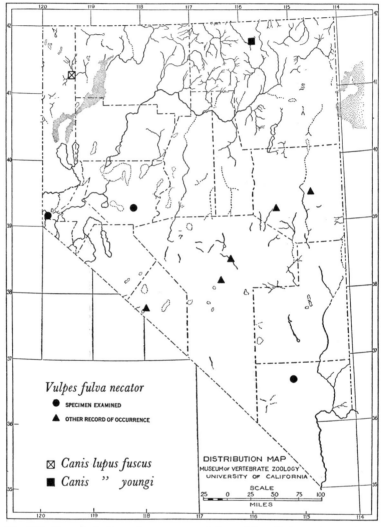

Fig. 162. Record stations of occurrence of the red fox, *Vulpes fulva*, and the
wolf, *Canis lupus*.

of Great Salt Lake, Utah. Probably *necator* and *macrourus* are at most subspecifically
distinct, but specimens from Utah are lacking, and no comparison can be made with the
fairly adequate material of *necator* from the Sierra Nevada. Conceivably, the two are not
recognizably different, in which event the earlier proposed name *macrourus* would apply.

If the two are recognizably different, it is possible that foxes from White Pine County differ from those from the Sierra Nevada, as at Marlette Lake, in the direction of *macrourus* and that more than one subspecies of *Vulpes fulva* occurs in Nevada. The reference of all to the one subspecies *Vulpes fulva necator* is merely the best that can be done with the information now available.

The secondary sexual difference in linear measurements of the skull amounts to about 5 per cent, if one may judge by specimens from the Sierra Nevada of California. The females are the smaller.

Information about the species which probably applies to the animals in Nevada is that they make their dens in natural cavities in the rocks, as well as in holes in the ground, have a gestation period of 51 days, and bear one litter per year of three to nine, of which the average number is six. The eyes of the young are said to open on the ninth day. The animals are mainly carnivorous, relying principally on rabbits and rodents for food.

The prices actually received by trappers in California for pelts of this species from the Sierra Nevada, before 1922, according to Grinnell, Dixon, and Linsdale (1937:397), were as follows:

black fox	$350 to $1,000
silver fox	80 to 350
cross fox	35 to 80
red fox	12 to 30

Because of the success attained in dying fox pelts and because fur farmers have raised increasing numbers of the black and especially silver color-phases, the values of these phases have declined and pelts often sell for a price no greater than that commanded by the cross and red phases. In the last 3 years, 1939 to 1942, I doubt that the average prices received for pelts of this species taken in Nevada is more than $20 for the cross phase and $7.50 for the red phase.

Records of occurrence.—Specimens examined, 4, as follows: *Ormsby Co.:* Marlette Lake, 8000 ft., 2. *Churchill Co.:* Fairview, 1. *Clark Co.:* 1 mi. W Hidden Forest, 9000 ft., Sheep Range, 1.

Additional records, on basis of information provided in the account above: *Nye Co.:* Hot Creek; vicinity of Little Rye Patch. *Esmeralda Co.:* Silver Peak Range. *White Pine Co.:* Shell Creek Range; Illipah; vicinity of Hamilton.

Vulpes macrotis
Kit Fox

This small fox is variously known in Nevada as kit fox, swift fox, swift, and desert fox. It is, at least in America, the smallest species of the genus. The weight of Nevadan adults is between 3 and 5 pounds, and the total length averages about 30 inches. The ears are unusually large, even for a fox. The tail is bushy, round in cross section, tapers slightly toward the tip, comprises about 40 per cent of the total length, and is black-tipped. The foot soles, at least in winter, are all concealed by long fur, except for a small exposed surface on each of the toe pads. Above, the color is grayish. The longest overhairs are tipped with black or with brown. The shorter overhairs are tipped with white or broadly banded near the tip with white. The underfur is tipped with brownish, then broadly banded with buffy, and the basal half is plumbeous. On the sides buffy color predominates and is present across the chest, on the backs of the ears, on the legs, and on all but the distal 2 inches of the underside of the tail. The underparts of the body are white. The sides of the muzzle, all vibrissae on the head, lower lip, and posterior third of the upper lip are blackish or brownish.

Selected differences of the skull of the kit fox in comparison with that of the red fox are: most linear measurements averaging about a fourth less; length of auditory bullae (measured from ventralmost union with paroccipital process to carotid foramen) more, rather than less, than greatest breadth of rostrum over canines, and more, rather than less, than distance between posterior border of P4 and anterior border of P3; distance between orbit and anterior opening of infraorbital canal less, rather than more, than height of foramen magnum; anterior palatine foramina extending posteriorly past, rather than only to middle of, alveoli of upper canines.

Among thirty-nine kit foxes (*V. macrotis* of subspecies *arsipus* and *nevadensis*) and twenty-one red foxes (*V. fulva necator*) at hand, the largest adult or subadult kit fox is smaller than the smallest adult or subadult red fox. Median figures for several measurements, which are more than in any kit fox and less than in any red fox, of the ages and races specified above are: total length, 815; length of tail, 303; length of hind foot, 135; basilar length of skull, 113; zygomatic breadth, 63; mastoidal breadth, 42.

Whether the kit foxes of the western United States and northern Mexico, all arranged under the specific name *macrotis*, are specifically or only subspecifically distinct from the shorter-eared animal of the Great Plains east of the Rocky Mountains in Canada and the United States I do not know, and specimens are not available from the area around the southern end of the Rocky Mountains where the ranges of the two kinds probably meet.

Measurements of skulls from Nevada suggest but do not prove that in linear dimensions females are about 2 per cent smaller than males. The same measurements likewise suggest that adult animals of comparable age and sex are about 2 per cent larger in Humboldt County than in Clark County, in the southern part of the state. This seeming increase in size to the northward and a slightly average darker color there provide the only evidence of a gradient, geographically, in the Nevadan populations.

The range in Nevada corresponds to areas of low zonal position. The records all are from places in or below the Upper Sonoran Life-zone. In western Nevada, if we may rely on reports of fur trappers and records of occurrence furnished by specimens in hand, the kit fox occurs only in the country of lower Upper Sonoran Life-zone complexion and does not occur in the higher areas which are the upper part of the Upper Sonoran Life-zone. Although the foxes occur in the lower, sandy parts of valleys, fur trappers report taking more of them at the edges of valleys a little above where the level valley floor breaks into the fanglomerates at the mouths of the canyons.

J. R. Alcorn (MS), in trap lines set for coyotes in Churchill and Pershing counties, has taken about twenty-five kit foxes among about eight hundred coyotes. There are reports of relatively larger numbers of foxes having been trapped near Tonopah, Coaldale, and in other areas where poisoned baits have not been distributed for coyotes. In areas where poisoned baits have been distributed, the population of kit foxes is reported to be quickly reduced, and some persons, including some of the United States Bureau of Biological Survey hunters who themselves distribute the poison, are of the opinion that the kit foxes have been exterminated in some areas, as, for example, in Spring Valley, White Pine County. It is certain that in several areas their numbers have been more greatly reduced than have those of the coyote for which the poisoned baits and traps, out of fur season, were placed.

The fur of the kit fox is attractive but inexpensive. Trappers were receiving only 75 cents to $1 per pelt in Reno in March, 1942. Frank Garret, in March, 1930, received $1.50 for a pelt taken in Snake Valley, when furs were higher in price than in 1942.

Kit foxes have been described as mainly nocturnal and are said to live in burrows in the ground which are described as having more than one entrance. A burrow 2 miles north of the Colorado River and about the same distance east of the California boundary, pointed out to us by an Indian who said he had trapped several kit foxes from it, had three entrances. The young are said to number four to seven in a litter. Food probably consists mainly of small rodents and, possibly in part, insects. In sandy areas I often have observed kit fox tracks from the course and arrangement of which I judged that kangaroo rats, and in some instances smaller rodents, had been pursued and caught. In Clark County, Burt (1934:400) found the remains of one cottontail rabbit and two kangaroo rats in the stomach of a kit fox.

Grater (1939:77–81) gives excellent flashlight photographs of a family of these foxes that he observed at their den about 4 miles north and 3 miles east of Boulder City on a north-facing slope of Hemenway Wash. In his words "a pair of kit foxes selected a large gravel bank in a dry wash above the shores of Lake Mead as a site for their den. . . . When the den was discovered, the pups had grown enough to be allowed out each night for a short play while waiting for their father to bring back their evening meal.

"Throughout the time that the little family was under observation a very similar procedure was followed each evening. About dusk the male fox would cautiously stick his head out of the den, and, after giving my motionless form a long scrutiny, would emerge and sit in front of his home for a few moments. . . . Finally, feeling that all was well he would climb the bank and without a sound disappear over the ridge like a small gray shadow. For almost half an hour everything would be quiet, as darkness finally blotted out the outline of the den. Then the slight sound of a rolling pebble would warn me that the mother fox had come out of the hole. . . . A low call from her and pandemonium would break loose as six eager pups scrambled over each other to get outside to play."

The female and the six pups quickly became accustomed to Grater's flashlight, the means by which he was able to observe the play of the young. In mimic combat resembling that of collie pups they growled and snarled. Campers with a dog on leash one night established themselves near the den, and the mother apparently was disturbed when the dog barked.

"When the dog barked again the [female] fox ran swiftly up on top of the low ridge . . . and stood there watching the camp below. Again the dog barked and she suddenly stamped her front feet several times, making a low but distinct thud each time. For some time she stayed on top of the ridge, nervously trotting back and forth, stopping every few moments to again stamp her feet. It was not until the dog became quiet that she returned to the den."

Grater was fortunate in witnessing the abandonment of the den—a result of rising water level in the artificial lake. The old foxes took turns in leading away the young, one at a time, a round trip requiring about 20 minutes (see plate 10, a)."The remaining pups sent up a series of protesting yelps and growls each time an old fox left with one of their number. . . . I watched the last pup finally scramble clumsily up to the top of the gravel bank and follow its mother out of sight into the night. . . ."

Vulpes macrotis nevadensis Goldman
Kit Fox

Vulpes macrotis nevadensis Goldman, Journ. Washington Acad. Sci., 21:250, June 4, 1931. Type from Willow Creek Ranch, near [20 miles north of] Jungo, Humboldt County, Nevada.

Distribution.—Western part of the state from the Oregon boundary south at least to Sodaville, and in interior valleys of central and eastern parts of state, mainly in Upper Sonoran Life-zone. See figure 163.

Remarks.—Measurements of a male and female from 5 mi. NE Hazen are, respectively: 699, 768; 230, 284; 132, 122; ear from notch, 93, 86. Each weighed 4⅛ lbs. (1,875 grams). These animals were trapped in late December.

The subspecies *nevadensis* is so slightly different from *Vulpes macrotis arsipus* as to make questionable the recognition of two races instead of one. The differences in *nevadensis* are black instead of brown or grayish upper lips, dark instead of light-colored forehead, and usually black instead of always brown tip on tail.

In the original description Goldman (1931:250) indicated that *nevadensis* differed from *arsipus* as follows: pelage "less silvery white, the black tips of hairs more in evidence over dorsum"; skull "broader, more robust; braincase larger, more fully inflated; nasals usually broader, more abruptly tapering." The specimens listed below include those examined by Goldman, and detailed comparisons have been made with those of *arsipus*. Of the latter, we have had the practical topotypes and other Californian specimens listed by Grinnell, Dixon, and Linsdale (1937:404) in addition to some material from Nevada.

With regard to color, the foxes from northwestern Nevada average darker than those from southern Nevada and California. The one constant difference detected is the black sides of the muzzle in *nevadensis* as contrasted with the brownish or dark grayish color of these areas in *arsipus*. Other differences include darker ears in some but not in all *nevadensis*, tip of tail black in most, but not in all, as opposed to brown in all *arsipus*; forehead darker in all *nevadensis*. The skins used by Goldman from the vicinity of Jungo and from Adelaide were all tanned and were trapped in 1915 and 1916. In comparison with untanned

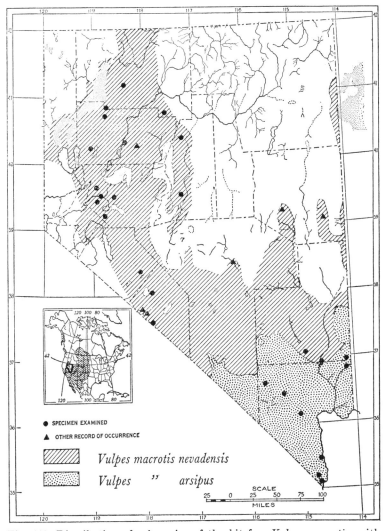

Fig. 163. Distribution of subspecies of the kit fox, *Vulpes macrotis*, with insert showing range of kit foxes in North America.

skins in the Museum of Vertebrate Zoölogy, which were trapped near by, at Rabbithole Springs, in 1939, the reddish color is everywhere enhanced in the older tanned skins. It turns out that the areas that are black in fresh skins are brownish in the tanned skins, this more buffy color in the tanned skins extending even to the bases of the fur on the back.

Although this discoloration may have resulted merely from "aging" of the skins, I suspect that chemicals used in the tanning process caused the discoloration. The tanned and untanned skins are comparable with respect to season, and season is an important consideration when comparing skins of kit foxes. Although Goldman (1931:250) pointed out that his tanned skins showed a reduced amount of silvery white when compared with skins of *arsipus*, our fresh untanned skins are not especially different in this respect from *arsipus*.

With regard to the skull, measurements show that the animals from northwestern Nevada average about 2 per cent larger than *arsipus*. Exception is to be made, however, for the orbitonasal length, which averages actually about the same in specimens from northern and southern Nevada. Therefore, the orbitonasal length is relatively (to the length of the skull) greater in *arsipus* from Nevada than in *nevadensis*, but the difference is only 1 per cent. Between *arsipus* from California and *nevadensis* the difference is only six-tenths of 1 per cent. Measurements show that the skull of *nevadensis* is not relatively broader, not even across the brain case. Its breadth, compared to the basilar length, is relatively less in males and relatively more in females of *nevadensis*. In each instance the average difference between the two series is less than one-half of 1 per cent. The nasals, allegedly broader in *nevadensis*, average actually narrower than in *arsipus* when measured both at the widest place anteriorly and at the waistlike constriction about halfway back along the nasals. Individual variation is great and the average differences between *nevadensis* and *arsipus* are so slight that I would expect them to disappear or to be reversed if a greater number of specimens were averaged. The alleged difference in shape of the nasals posteriorly is an average difference. In *nevadensis* more specimens have the nasals abruptly tapered than gradually tapered, but in *arsipus* the reverse is true. In both races each type of nasal occurs, the average condition of which might be reversed if additional specimens were taken into account. These data can be summarized as follows: The skull of *nevadensis* averages about 2 per cent larger in linear measurements. No other cranial variation regarded as geographic in nature has been detected. The cranial variations which Goldman relied upon as differentiating *arsipus* and *nevadensis* apparently were individual variations and those that he observed in the skin were adventitious variations resulting from the tanning process.

Too few external measurements of *nevadensis* and *arsipus* have been taken to permit of judging the two in these respects, if there are differences at all.

Relying on the darker color of the forehead and sides of the muzzle in *nevadensis* as diagnostic of that race, the tanned skin from Sodaville appears to have been intermediate between *nevadensis* and *arsipus*. The specimens from the vicinity of Rox are intermediate in the mentioned features and are nearer the average for *nevadensis*, although specimens from the vicinity of Mesquite, only 33 miles south of Rox, are typical of *arsipus*.

The records of occurrence for White Pine County are based upon the testimony of trappers. W. C. Kirkland, a United States predatory animal hunter, reported having taken "two swifts" on the fanglomerate below Osceola when he first began distributing poisoned baits for coyotes, but in several years of subsequent work he never found any others poisoned, nor did he take any in his traps (oral interview, June 20, 1929). Ed Brrch, of Hamilton, Nevada, reported (oral interview, August 20, 1930) having "caught swifts along the edge of the [White Sage] Valley. The most I ever got for one was $1.50." A fur trapper living 8½ miles southeast of Hausen reported that kit foxes did not occur in that area, but he knew of their occurrence "down by Smoke Creek in the desert."

Records of occurrence.—Specimens examined, 47, as follows: *Humboldt Co.:* "Trout Creek Ranch, Jungo," 1 (skull only, U. S. Nat. Mus.); "Sulphur Cow Creek," 1 (skin with skull, U. S. Nat. Mus.); Willow Creek Ranch, 4 (1 skull only and 3 skins with skulls, U. S. Nat. Mus.); "Jungo, water hole," 5 (4 skulls only and 1 skin only, U. S. Nat. Mus.); Sulphur, 1 (skin only, Hall, MS); Adelaide, 1 (skin with skull, U. S. Nat. Mus.); near Adelaide, 2 (skins with skulls, U. S. Nat. Mus.). *Pershing Co.:* Rabbithole Springs, 9 (skins only); Oreana, 3 (skulls only, U. S. Nat. Mus.); 30 mi. W and 4 mi. N Lovelock, 4300 ft., 1 (skull only). *Churchill Co.:* 5 mi. NE

Hazen, 4000 ft., 2 (skins, skulls, and skeletons); between Old River and Soda Lake, W of Fallon, 1 (skin with skull, U. S. Nat. Mus.); Carson Sink, 10 mi. E Fallon, 1 (skull with scalp, U. S. Nat. Mus.); 8 mi. SW Fallon, 1 (skeleton); 17 mi. S Fallon, 4100 ft., 1 (skin with skull). *Mineral Co.:* 5 mi. SE Sodaville, 1 (skin with skull, U. S. Nat. Mus.). *Esmeralda Co.:* Coaldale, 1 (skull only); 2½ mi. N Oasis, 5300 ft., 1 (part skeleton). *Lander Co.:* 35 mi. SW Argenta, 1 (skull only, U. S. Nat. Mus.); 2½ mi. W Railroad Pass, 1 (skin only). *Lincoln Co.:* Coyote Spring, 1 (skull only); 1 mi. N Rox, 5 (skins with skulls); 1 mi. NE Rox, 2 (skins with skulls).

Additional records: *Churchill Co.:* 17 mi. E Lovelock (Alcorn, MS). *Esmeralda Co.:* Chiatovich Ranch and Smith Ranch (Hall, MS). *Nye Co.:* Hot Creek (Hall, MS). *White Pine Co.:* White Sage Valley and Spring Valley near Osceola (Hall, MS).

Vulpes macrotis arsipus Elliot
Kit Fox

Vulpes arsipus Elliot, Field Columbian Mus., publ. 87, zoöl. ser., vol. 3:256, December, 1903. Type from Daggett, San Bernardino County, California.

Vulpes macrotis arsipus, Grinnell, Proc. California Acad. Sci., 4th ser., 3:287, August 28, 1913; Burt, Trans. San Diego Soc. Nat. Hist., 7:400, May 31, 1934; Benson, Proc. Biol. Soc. Washington, 51:23, February 18, 1938.

Distribution.—Southern part of state in suitable habitat below Upper Sonoran Life-zone. See figure 163.

Remarks.—Average measurements for six males and three females from California (Grinnell, Dixon, and Linsdale, 1937:405) are 741, 715; 286, 284; 120, 111. Weights of animals trapped in April and May were, for two males, 3¼ and 3⅜ lbs., and for three females, 3, 3, and 3⅓ lbs.

The lighter average color, the consistently lighter-colored forehead, and brownish or dark grayish, as opposed to blackish, sides of the muzzle are the characters differentiating this race from *nevadensis*. *V. m. arsipus* is smaller than individuals of surrounding races, namely, *nevadensis* on the north, *mutica* and *macrotis* on the west, *neomexicanus* and *zinseri* to the southeast. Possibly it is smaller than *tenuirostris* to the south. *V. m. arsipus* is also lighter-colored than *nevadensis*, *mutica*, *macrotis*, or *zinseri*. *V. m. tenuirostris* may be a valid race, but additional material is needed the better to judge of its relationship to *arsipus*. Comparisons are not made with *V. a. arizonensis* Goldman, because Benson (1938:20) showed that it is a synonym of *arsipus*.

Records of occurrence.—Specimens examined, 11, as follows: *Lincoln Co.:* 4 mi. N Mesquite, 2 (skins with skulls). *Clark Co.:* 3½ mi. NW Mesquite, 1 (skin with skull); 1½ mi. W Mesquite, 2 (skins with skulls); Indian Springs, 1 (D. R. Dickey Coll.); Corn Creek Station, 1 (D. R. Dickey Coll.); "vic. Las Vegas," 1 (D. R. Dickey Coll.); Durban Ranch, Colorado River, 14 mi. E Searchlight, 1 (skin only); 18 mi. S and 5 mi. E Searchlight, 1; 6 mi. N and 2 mi. W Calif.-Nev. Monument, 1 (skull only).

Urocyon cinereoargenteus scottii Mearns
Gray Fox

Urocyon virginianus scottii Mearns, Bull. Amer. Mus. Nat. Hist., 3:236, June 5, 1891. Type from Pinal County, Arizona.

Urocyon cinereo-argenteus scottii, Allen, Bull. Amer. Mus. Nat. Hist., 7:253, June 29, 1895.

Urocyon cinereoargenteus scottii, Burt, Trans. San Diego Soc. Nat. Hist., 7:401, May 31, 1934.

Urocyon cinereoargenteus, Linsdale, Amer. Midland Nat., 19:175, January, 1938.

Distribution.—Southern half of state in Transition and Sonoran life-zones. See figure 164.

Remarks.—Average and extreme external measurements of four males from along the Colorado River in the southern fourth of Clark County are 978 (935–1,030); 419 (405–435); 135 (133–145). A female from 2 mi. N Calif.-Nev. Monument measures 930, 405, 132. Weights of 7¼ (6½–8) lbs. for six males and 5¼ and 6 lbs. for two females from the Colorado River in California have been recorded by Grinnell, Dixon, and Linsdale (1937:434).

Nevadan specimens give basis for the recognition of only this one subspecies, *scottii*. Characters of a generic nature are: ears large; tail large, bushy, tipped with black, and triangular in cross section; size small (less than 14 lbs.); glandular area on top of tail in its middle third; line of long, stiff, black hairs along middle of upper side of tail for its entire length; coloration blackish gray above, underparts reddish brown becoming whitish on throat and middle of belly; postorbital processes thin and concave on dorsal surface; temporal ridges far apart, forming lyrate pattern on top of skull; inferior margin of

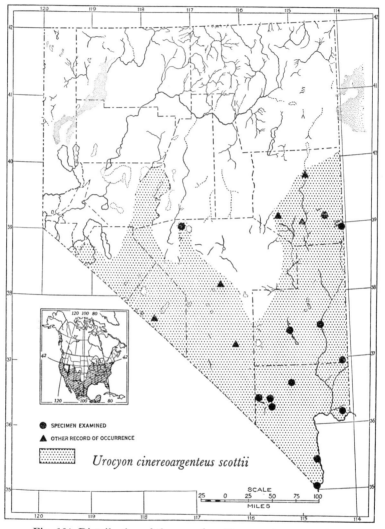

Fig. 164. Distribution of the gray fox, *Urocyon cinereoargenteus*.

lower mandible with distinct "step" midway between tip of angular process and anterior border of coronoid. The genus currently is divided into two species, *cinereoargenteus*, with about twelve races, and *littoralis*, of the coastal islands of southern California, with six races. From *littoralis*, *cinereoargenteus* differs in larger size and relatively as well as actually much longer tail. *U. c. scottii* differs in lighter coloration from the races *townsendi* to the west, *californicus* to the southwest, *colimensis* to the south, and *ocythous* to the east. The tail averages longer, actually as well as relatively, than in any of these races except possibly *colimensis*. The skull of *colimensis* in the original description is said to be smaller than that of *scottii* and to have a relatively broader rostrum and relatively deeper mandibular ramus. The smaller skull, paler color, and longer tail of *scottii*, compared to *townsendi* and *ocythous*, offer characters satisfactory for identification. From the race *californicus*, *scotti* is less easily distinguished; *californicus* averages darker and the tail averages shorter, but these are average differences.

Within Nevada there is a suggestion of geographic variation in size of skull among our specimens. Those from the northernmost localities, Millett P. O., Conners Canyon, and mouth of Snake Creek, average larger than skulls of the same sex from the southern part of the state. External measurements which would indicate the length of the tail are lacking for these specimens. The color of the coat is not appreciably different between animals from different parts of the state.

Information gathered from outside Nevada, but which probably applies to gray foxes in Nevada also, reveals that they are better climbers and more frugivorous than other foxes. Even so, their diet is made up largely of animal matter; wood rats and *Peromyscus* are two rodents commonly eaten by gray foxes in California. Burt (1934:401) found a snake (*Coluber*) in the stomach of a male trapped in August in Clark County, Nevada. Dens are made in crevices in cliffs, in rock piles, in holes in the ground, in hollow logs, and even in hollows in trees. It is thought that there is only one litter per year. The young number two to five, four being the usual number.

The fur value of this fox has never been as great as that of the red fox. In March, 1942, fur buyers in Reno were paying trappers from $1.25 to $1.50 per pelt. In 1928 to 1930 exceptional specimens were sold by trappers for as much as $5. As noted below, one trapper who sold direct to the consumer received $5 for each of his furs of this species.

Information about the occurrence of gray foxes, supplementary to that provided by actual specimens, was obtained from trappers. Donald V. Hemphill (MS in 1940) records that in about 1925 Warren Lewis caught several gray foxes near his ranch on the East Walker River, 3 miles south of Wichman. Hemphill also was told by John H. Wichman that about 1910 as he was driving up Aldridge Grade, about 8 miles south of Wichman, he had a good view of a gray fox. Huey Stewart reported them as common in the Silver Peak Range. In Nye County a trapper reported taking gray foxes in the vicinity of Little Rye Patch, and in the winter of 1930–1931 Ray Morris, at his cabin in the thick piñon timber 5½ miles northwest of Whiterock Spring, 7200 feet elevation, "caught numbers of gray foxes, all of which were sold for $5 each, to women in the southern part of the state who wanted them for furs." In White Pine County, Ed Brrch trapped these foxes in the foothills of the White Pine Mountains, and Lewis Mattice trapped two along Willow Creek, at an elevation of between 7500 and 8000 feet, under a mountain mahogany tree. On September 12, 1930, Chester C. Lamb recorded in his field notes that "there is a man at Cherry Creek Post Office that has a gray fox caught in this canyon."

Genus **Canis** Linnaeus
Coyotes, Wolves

Of this genus, there are known from Nevada two species, the coyote and the wolf. For the family Canidae, the size of these animals is large (20 to 100 lbs. or more). The tail is bushy, cylindrical, and of greatest diameter at the middle; glandular area on top of tail in its proximal third; postorbital processes thick, convex above, and evenly continuous with the inflated frontal area (sinuses); temporal ridges uniting to form a sagittal crest; inferior margin of lower jaw without the step seen in *Urocyon*.

Canis latrans
Coyote

Coyotes, on the average, weigh less than half as much as wolves, have a more slender muzzle, and relatively longer ears. From both dogs and wolves, as described in the account of the wolf, they differ in the better-developed talonid of the lower molar. Also, in the coyote, the width of the rostrum, measured across the bases of the upper canines, is less than one and three-fourths the anteroposterior extent of an auditory bulla, whereas in the wolf the width of the rostrum is more than one and three-fourths the anteroposterior extent of the bulla. The coyotes designated as adults in the systematic accounts below and in the table of measurements are judged to be more than 1½ years old. Females average about 5 per cent smaller than males in linear measurements of the skull and about 4 per cent smaller in measurements of the teeth.

In size the coyote resembles a collie dog, but is at once recognizable as a wild animal by reason of its erect ears, lower position of the tail, furtive air, and "lightness of foot." The coyote is probably the best known of Nevadan mammals in the sense that if everyone in the state were asked to list the native animals known to him, the coyote would have a score as high as, or higher than, any other. The animal occurs in all parts of the state and is of interest to nearly everyone; it is favorably known to fur trappers, unfavorably known to many sheep owners; it is a favorite target at all seasons for persons out "prospecting," and even those who lack special interest in the coyote itself, take a genuine interest in its weird and characteristic voice which is most likely to be heard shortly after nightfall.

Some general information, not all gathered from studies in Nevada, includes the following: The food is about a third rabbits, a fourth carrion, a fifth rodents, with the rest being divided among domestic stock and animals of various other kinds; 2 per cent is vegetable matter. The male shares with the female the task of bringing food to the young, of which there is one litter a year, born in the spring, after a gestation period of 60 to 63 days. The young average about seven to a litter, although as many as seventeen have been reported. These are born in a den which generally is dug in the ground. There is no nest. Eyes of the young open after 9 to 14 days. When about 3 weeks old the young are able to come out of the den, but they do not abandon it to live aboveground until they are 8 to 10 weeks of age. The young have distinctly thinner-toned voices of higher pitch than do adults. Mature coyotes yelp at any time of year, but are more prone to do so when their breeding season is at its peak. At that time, up to eight or more coyotes have been seen together.

Certainly the coyote is the most valuable fur bearer in Nevada; some fur buyers are of the opinion that in total annual sales the coyote is more valuable than all other fur bearers combined. Skins from the northern part of the state command highest prices, those from the southern part, the lowest prices, and those from the low west-central part of the state, an intermediate price. In west-central Nevada, J. R. Alcorn, from 1931–1932 to 1938–1939, has trapped and sold for fur more than eight hundred coyotes. In the preceding 4 years he and his father trapped in Owens Valley, California, where he thinks the quality of the fur is about the same as that in west-central Nevada. Average prices received by years are about as follows: 1927–1928, $15; 1928–1929, $15+; 1929–1930, $7; 1930–1931, no record; 1931–1932, $4; 1932–1933, offered $4, but held and eventually sold for $1.96; 1933–1934, $2.78; 1934–1935, no record; 1935–1936, $3–$3.50; 1936–1937, $4.50; 1937–1938, $5; 1938–1939, $4. In the spring of 1942, in Reno, fur buyers were paying $7 each for good average skins from west-central Nevada.

TRAPPING COYOTES

With respect to trapping this animal, Alçorn (MS) says: "The coyote is one of the most difficult animals in Nevada to catch in a trap. Most successful coyote trappers have had several years of experience. Many, using old desert roads, run their lines that may be 50 miles or more in length by automobile. Others use horses, trap in places inaccessible by automobile, and run short lines of less than 25 miles. The methods employed and baits used vary with the individual trapper, but certain rules are observed by all coyote trappers who are financially successful. Coyotes are to be trapped only when furs are prime, in October, November, December, and January. Furs taken in late September seldom are prime, and those taken in early February are often rubbed. These inferior furs are not worth half so much as prime furs.

"A good bait or scent is essential, failure or success often depending upon the kind used. Scent is preferred by many trappers because it is compact and easy to carry. It is easily made and does not attract magpies and flesh-eating birds,

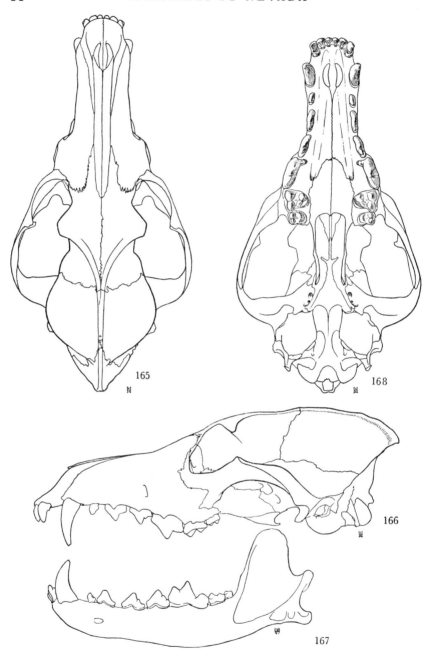

Figs. 165–168. *Canis latrans lestes*, 5 miles southeast Fallon, no. 89940, ♂. × ½.

as do meat baits. Most every trapper believes that the scent which he uses is better than any other and is loath to reveal the formula. From trappers who did tell me how the scents used by them were made and from experiments of my own with many different formulae, I conclude that some of the best ingredients come from the coyote itself. Of twenty different mixtures of fish oil, oil of anise, oil of rodium, brains, urine of coyote, clabbered milk from a fresh cow, and some other ingredients, certain of them were attractive to coyotes and others seemed to act as repellents. As shown by tracks, coyotes did not approach nearer than 30 feet to some scents.

"One of the best scents in my experience is made as follows: Remove from each of three or four coyotes the brains, the pads of the feet, the anus, and the bladder. Place in a glass jar and add enough coyote urine to cover the tissues. The jar should be buried or otherwise placed so that it will not freeze. Although this mixture, which eventually turns into a paste, may be used after only 2 or 3 weeks, it is better if kept for a year. Enough will adhere to a small stick dipped in the jar to make a satisfactory scent bait at a set. A small amount of ground beaver castor may be added to vary the formula. In many instances, I have observed from tracks where a coyote, passing near a set which was scented with this mixture, made a right-angle turn 20 yards or more from the trap and traveled upwind to it where it was caught.

"Another scent extensively used by trappers in Nevada is made by placing the anal tissues, including the anal scent glands, of several coyotes in the urine from a female coyote. To four parts of this mixture there is added one part of glycerine and a pinch of corrosive sublimate. This mixture may be used after it has set for only a week. The scent supposedly attracts coyotes other than those which are seeking food. The urine from the female coyote can be obtained by placing her in a small cage with a sloping metal floor provided with a trough at the lower end where the urine empties into a jar.

"Although scent has many advantages over baits, one of its disadvantages is that it attracts rabbits to the sets. If a rabbit springs a trap, the chances of catching a coyote in that trap is reduced by just that much. Some trappers who use scents exclusively, recommend an occasional variation of the formula.

"Excellent results are to be had in many localities by the use of meat baits, but where raptorial birds and magpies are plentiful it is almost impossible to place a meat bait that is acceptable to coyotes without having the birds find it before the coyotes do.

"I have caught many coyotes by using, as meat baits, carcasses of badgers, striped skunks, and coyotes, and the entire bodies of house cats, horned owls, fish (carp), rabbits, small rodents, cows, horses, and sheep. Small baits should be partly buried to prevent them from drying out quickly.

"In most parts of the year, especially in the fall months, the bodies of cows, horses, sheep, and other domestic stock are readily eaten by coyotes. It is generally a good practice to let the coyotes eat part of the animal before setting traps near it. In late winter, coyotes less often venture near freshly killed live-stock that is placed on the desert. This is especially true of a cow or horse. When large kinds of domestic livestock are to be used as bait, therefore, they should be put out in the early fall. On these animals, coyotes start eating at the anus, and a large hole is eaten there before the coyotes make much more than a start on other parts of the carcass.

"The preferred trap is a size no. 3, double outside-spring steel trap of a make the springs of which are not too strong. Many coyotes escape from traps with strong springs because the jaws of these traps pinch with such force as to deaden the nerve of the part of the leg or foot held in the trap. When the nerve is deadened or when the circulation of blood is cut off, allowing the foot to freeze, the coyote is apt to chew off his foot and thus escape. The Victor Special steel trap with offset jaws in size no. 3 is a good trap and is in wide use in Nevada.

"The trap is secured to a drag or to a stationary object. The drag may be a rock, piece of metal, or any compact object that has a rough surface and weighs about 10 pounds. In brushy country an iron bar bent on one end so as to form a hook is used by some trappers. Usually the hook catches on bushes and prevents the coyote from going far.

"Coyotes caught in traps tied to drags are customarily designated as 'travelers' or 'chewers,' according to their behavior. A traveler avoids bushes and travels a long distance, sometimes as much as 5 miles in 2 nights. Several travelers in my traps have drowned when they went to drink from, or cross, a canal from which, because of the weight of the drag and trap, they were unable to extricate themselves.

"The chewer, even with a light drag, usually goes only a short distance from where caught and may be more easily followed by the destroyed bushes left behind than by other sign. He becomes entangled in many bushes near his line of flight; by chewing and clawing them and by jerking the drag and trap chain through the bushes, he almost levels them to the ground.

"Coyotes caught in traps fastened to drags have a better chance to survive the hot days of, let us say, October, than those caught in traps secured to a stationary object. I have found in traps tied to a stake dead coyotes which had been caught within the day; some of them were worthless because the fur slipped. When the trap is fastened to a drag the coyote usually is able to get in some shade where, depending on the temperature, he may live for several days.

"Stationary objects suitable for use in anchoring traps are fences, large bushes of sage (*Artemisia tridentata*), or iron stakes 14 to 20 inches long—in other words, anything solid enough to hold a coyote. By continually pulling on the trap chain, the animals, especially when exposed to the hot sun, become exhausted and die after several hours.

"The selection of the location for setting a trap is of great importance. Regardless of the bait or the care used in setting the trap, the effort is wasted unless an animal comes to the location. Coyotes travel and hunt along small washes, old roads, cow trails, rivers, and the edges of farms and meadows. Their tracks often are numerous along the shores of Lahontan Reservoir, Pyramid, Winnemucca, Walker, and Soda lakes. I think that coyotes visit these places not only to drink, but to obtain dead or crippled water birds and an occasional fish. All these places are suitable for setting traps.

"Some successful trappers refuse to set a trap unless they find coyote tracks in the vicinity. Where both old and fresh tracks occur, the probabilities are that coyotes are regularly using the locality. One of the best places to set a trap is at a 'scent post.' One of these, along some route of travel or where

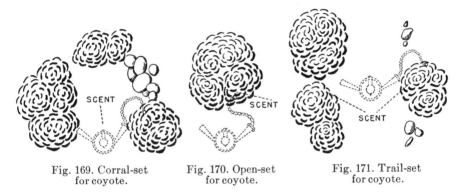

Fig. 169. Corral-set for coyote. Fig. 170. Open-set for coyote. Fig. 171. Trail-set for coyote.

routes cross, may be 10 to 20 feet across and is the place where coyotes stop to urinate or defecate. As indicated by tracks, most of the coyotes that come near the location stop and sniff of the different odors in the area, void body excrements, and then scratch the dirt with both fore and hind feet before going on their way.

"Sets of traps may be divided into three types: the corral-set (fig. 169), the open-set (fig. 170), and the trail-set (fig. 171).

"The corral, which is formed by nature or is constructed from brush, stones, or cow chips, prevents the coyote from reaching the bait or scent except by entering the opening where the trap is set. This type of set is especially effective in early autumn before many of the animals become 'trapwise.' Later, the other two types of sets are more effective. The open-set is probably so called because it is in the open, and the trail-set is so named because the trap is set where the animal runs (travels). The chances of the coyote stepping in the open-set are of course increased by placing the scent or bait so that in investigating it, the animal will step into the trap.

"The trapper should remember that it is more difficult to catch coyotes in thickets or near the trunk of a tree than in an open place where the animals have unobstructed vision. Coyotes more readily step on bare or soft soil than on sticks or rough plant material. When two or more coyotes are together they are bolder and easier to catch than is a lone individual.

"The behavior of coyotes in traps is a subject unpleasant to the average person, and the detailed description of it would contribute but little to a better understanding of the natural history of the animal. Coyotes caught in traps that are securely fastened desperately chew on the trap chain, snap at the trap, fiercely bite at sticks, claw at the earth in a way that often forms a sizable mound, and, except for periods in the hottest part of the day when they may lie down, continually struggle to pull free from the trap. When approached by a person, the coyote often empties its bladder. The behavior of adults is different than that of young; adults are bolder, often attempt to bite, and almost always are silent. The young have less control of the bladder, sometimes bark at a person, and more often howl in a pitiful fashion quite unlike the howl of a free animal. Coyotes that howl when trapped elevate the nose in doing so. Usually, however, they cease howling when closely approached. Even when grasped by the fur on the back of the neck and held they are silent.

"When hunting coyotes, certain of their actions can be predicted. At first sight of man, adults ordinarily run to a safe distance before stopping to look at the hunter. Usually this is to the top of a hill or edge of a thicket from which place their next move takes them out of sight.

"In a number of instances I have seen a coyote sitting motionless among the bushes of sagebrush near the top of some sandy hill. Such an animal will allow a fairly near approach when the person is on horseback, in an automobile, or even afoot, so long as motion is continued in a direction that will take the person *past* the coyote. If a stop is made, or if the direction of travel is switched to one directly toward the coyote, it is instantly away, over the hill.

"Coyotes often run across roads in front of automobiles, and when about 100 yards from the road, stop and watch the car pass. If the car stops near by, the coyote makes off with all speed. When a coyote thus once crossed in front of us, I stepped out of the moving car, as my father drove on down the road, and inexpertly shot at the coyote when it stopped. Of course it made off at great speed across the snow, and each time that I shot it twitched its tail and put on an extra burst of speed. Even though my first shot, I think, had not hit the coyote, it nevertheless then made a urinary discharge.

"Although coyotes have the ability to jump over fences, they seldom or never do so. Instead, they crawl under the fence or, if it is of woven wire, go through a hole in it.

"Coyotes visit dried hides and other desiccated remains of animals, especially immediately following rains. Then, they gnaw on bones and chew pieces of hide, a thing which they less often do when the animal-remains are thoroughly dry. I suppose that when these old remains are moist they give off more odor than at other times. In Washington Creek Canyon, Toyabe Mountains, Lander County, I once found that coyotes had eaten much of the posterior part of the remains of a deer that had become caught in a wire fence. I have frequently found apple peel in feces, and from other sign I know that apple trees near Fallon often are visited by coyotes. They visit also melon patches near Fallon and choose a ripe watermelon already cut open in prefer- ence to a whole one. Melon-eating coyotes have been caught in traps set about a cut-open, ripe melon in the field.

"On the sandy desert about a mile northwest of Soda Lake, Churchill County, on March 30, 1938, I tracked a coyote for about a half mile—the smooth sand, which shortly before had been blown by the wind, making the tracks easy to follow. The coyote, apparently looking for food, went here and there between the scattered bushes before finally going into an area where C. C. C. enrollees had been distributing strychnine-coated rolled oats for desert rodents. Sign indicated that the coyote had picked up and eaten several of the dead kangaroo rats and had continued on into the desert, out of the area where poison had been placed, still looking for food. As I picked up a dead kangaroo rat from the area, which had fifty-three kernels of rolled oats in the two cheek pouches, I wondered if coyotes might be killed by eating these poisoned rodents. To test the possibilities in this direction, I obtained ap- proximately fifty-three kernels of strychnine-coated rolled oats from the same batch the C. C. C. enrollees had been distributing. The next day these were forcibly fed to an unwanted pointer dog. In 20 minutes the dog was obviously distressed, and in 29 minutes it was dead. Because the dog's stomach was otherwise empty, and for other reasons, I do not regard the experiment as conclusive one way or the other. Although there was a canal of water about 30 feet away, the dog made no move to go to the water, as some persons who were experienced in poisoning coyotes report that coyotes do when they are suffering from strychnine poison."

"COYOTE CONTROL"
HISTORY OF CONTROL EFFORTS IN NEVADA

The coyote is the mammal at which the governmental efforts at predatory animal control at public expense are principally directed. Hardly any other phase of man's attempt to regulate the numbers of animals, which at times compete with him in agricultural or pastoral pursuits, has engendered more discussion than attempts at control (reduction) of the numbers of coyotes. Furthermore, Nevada, among all the western states, has given a relatively large measure of attention to the question, even though opinion in the state still is divided on the merits of this effort.

Some of the more obvious relationships of the coyote are suggested in figure 172 on page 250.

The beginning of predatory animal control by governmental employees at public expense in the United States may be said to have been in 1915 when

Congress appropriated $125,000 for the Bureau of Biological Survey, which was then a part of the United States Department of Agriculture. This coyote control work changed the Biological Survey's participation from the earlier basis of experiment, instruction, demonstration, and recommendation to one of service. The initial effort was directed mainly at wolves (*Canis lupus*) which made inroads on cattle. The work flourished as a wartime measure to conserve food; in fact, by late 1917, the view was held that this killing of wolves was a patriotic duty. It was contended that the beef cattle thus saved would be available to, and be needed by, our soldiers and allies in France. Soon after the wolf control measures were begun, and before the wolves were all but exterminated, the sheepmen, noting the assistance received by cattle-

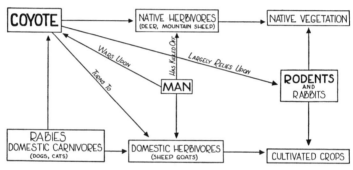

Fig. 172. Diagrammatic representation of food-chain relationships of coyote.

men at public expense, asked for and obtained the services of governmental employees to kill coyotes, the animals which especially at lambing time took toll of their flocks. The work was increased in scope, and what was in a way a wartime measure directed against the big wolves came to apply to coyotes and to be the biggest peacetime business of the Bureau of Biological Survey, which in 1930 was asking for a $1,000,000 annual appropriation for its share of the work. In that year biologists who were not in the employ of the Bureau of Biological Survey publicly objected to the extensiveness of the work and to some of the methods of control used. Nevertheless, by coöperative arrangement with states, counties, and wool growers' associations, and by drawing on federal resources appropriated for relief and unemployment, the work has been extended in most of the western states with but slight change in methods.

Speaking restrictedly of Nevada, it had as much or more to do with transfer of attention to coyotes and with expansion of the work as had any other state. This came about from the fact that in 1915, 1916, and 1917 coyotes in northern Nevada, as well as in adjoining parts of California and Oregon, contracted rabies. The infection spread widely among coyotes, and by transmitting the fatal disease to domestic animals, the coyotes caused considerable loss to many owners of livestock. In addition, some persons were bitten by rabid animals. In response to this emergency, aid was requested and obtained from the federal government. Employees of the United States Bureau of Biological Survey began killing coyotes in Nevada in the autumn of 1915. In January, 1916, a fund of about $85,000 was made available for the work by pooling funds advanced by the federal government ($55,914.78), the state of Nevada ($9,511.05), the state sheep commissioners ($10,000), and the state stock commissioners ($10,000). Early in 1917 the State Rabies Commission was formed, and a coöperative agreement entered into between it and the Federal Bureau of Biological Survey for the purpose of accomplishing the "practical extinction of predatory animals" (Records, 1919). From 1921 to early in 1923 some counties coöperated to the extent of spending $9,783.43 for the work, and in the fiscal year 1933–1934, when the appropriation by the state was reduced to $50 ($100 for the biennium), livestock owners were credited with providing the equivalent of $3,294.12.

A publication, "State of Nevada Biennial Report of the State Rabies Commission," was issued nine times, covering the 18¾ years from October 1, 1915, to June 30, 1934. The work directed against predatory animals was all carried out under the direction of E. R. Sans, representative for Nevada of the Federal Bureau of Biological Survey, and the reports of the State Rabies Commission appear for the most part to have been written by him, although all are signed by Edward Records, Secretary of the State Rabies Commission.

The original stated purpose of accomplishing the "practical extinction of predatory animals" (loc. cit.) was somewhat modified by 1923, when we read (Records, 1923:3) that the "absolute suppression [of rabies] . . . is . . . not to be expected in a state like Nevada so that keeping losses of livestock and injuries to human beings at a minimum is the actual object in view at this time." Four years later we read (Records, 1927:3): "There will always be some loss from predatory animals for we will never be able to exterminate the coyote or bobcat"; and in 1932 (Records, 1932:8): "Discussion has continued as to the propriety of the activities and expenditures of this commission. . . . Any final decision along this line of course rests with the people. . . ."

The discussion referred to had culminated in a referendum by the general electorate on November 4, 1930, when 11,586 voted for repeal of the "rabies law" and 11,567 voted for continuance of the law. The Attorney General ruled that a majority did not vote for repeal. This ruling was based on the fact that whereas 34,634 persons voted for choice of governor, less than half of those voted to repeal the "rabies law." On November 6, 1934, a second referendum resulted in repeal of the rabies law; at the same time a bounty law was enacted by a vote of 19,159 for and 8,840 against.

This bounty law specified that bounties were to be paid by the county clerks who were to perforate (mark) the skins of animals presented to them in a manner which would be evidence that bounty thereon had been paid in Nevada. Payments of bounty were held up pending receipt by the county clerks of the devices for perforating the skins. One interpretation of the law was that funds for purchasing these devices had not been specifically provided for in the original "bounty law"; hence, the devices were not forthcoming. In 1935 the 37th session of the Assembly and Senate approved an act (Assembly Bill 164) directing the state Controller to purchase the required devices and appropriate the funds. The Governor, however, did not sign the bill and it did not become law. Thus, the state ceased to participate in the predatory animal control, and the bounty law was never (up to 1941) put in operation.

Federal allotments for this work in Nevada were reduced year by year, so that by 1938–1939 an average of no more than 5 men were working (poisoning and trapping). Two changes of Bureau of Biological Survey leaders of predatory animal control for Nevada were made between 1934 and 1940. In 1940–1941, by use of funds obtained from various sources, a force equivalent to 37 men full-time (11,634 man-days) is said to have been again working to destroy coyotes under the direction of the Bureau of Biological Survey.

In the State Rabies Reports (Records, 1919 to 1934) it is recorded that in the 18½-year period, January 1, 1916, to June 30, 1934, a sum of about $984,103.07 was expended to account for 88,601 coyotes, 14,352 bobcats, 56 mountain lions, 4,959 badgers in the first 5 years, and 4,509 other animals, mostly or all fur bearers, including some badgers. All this was with an average of 43 full-time men in the field. Deducting $104,321.82, the sum returned to the state and counties from the sale of marketable furs, there remains $879,-781.25. Per man, per year, the take of coyotes was 111; of all predatory mammals (coyotes, bobcats, and mountain lions), 129; of other fur bearers, 12. For coyotes the cost averages $9.93 each, and for "predators" of all kinds $8.54. In the period reported upon, 3,703,157 poisoned-meat or suet baits were calculated to have been distributed.

METHODS OF CONTROL

The methods used by the Bureau of Biological Survey in taking coyotes were: (1) catching in steel traps, (2) poisoning, and (3) den-hunting before the young were old enough to leave the burrows. Most of the animals accounted for were taken by trapping, and fewest by den-hunting. A number were shot, and a few were taken in other ways. It is stressed in several of the published accounts of the work that of the animals reported, all are represented by scalps or by complete furs turned in to the office of the Bureau of Biological Survey, and that many of the animals killed by poison are never found. Other methods of control, some of which have been used only to a limited extent in Nevada, are: (1) use of dogs, (2) trapping by private individuals when the fur is prime, (3) organized drives by armed persons converging on a central point (may never have been used in Nevada), and (4) by offering bounties. Dogs—wolf hounds—were used, satisfactorily it is said, at Illipah, but their use extensively, so far as is known, has not been attempted elsewhere in Nevada. Private trappers working when the fur is prime take most of the coyotes killed in Nevada. This method of control meets with general approval, and some persons think that it alone is adequate for controlling the numbers of coyotes. Organized drives are generally regarded as impractical in most parts of Nevada because the country is so sparsely settled that it is difficult to form lines of beaters solid enough to keep the coyotes from escaping. Although the Legislature passed a bounty law, it never went into effect, and no bounties have been paid by the state. Some advantages claimed for the bounty system are reduced cost, less than $9.93 per coyote, and more equitable distribution of the tax money expended in control. Some objections are the likelihood of fraud through acceptance, for bounty payment, of animals taken outside Nevada and through substitutes being accepted in place of coyotes.

WHY CONTROL IS ADVOCATED

The question of whether some attempt at control is at all justified is answered in the affirmative by everyone with whom I have talked on the subject. When the owner of a flock of sheep detects a coyote killing his lambs, few if any would deny him the right to destroy the individual coyote. It seems that the owner is not only justified in doing so, but sometimes may be compelled to do so if he is to remain in business. He is, of course, justified only so far as the means adopted to solve his problem profits him more than it costs or damages his fellowmen. By way of illustration, let us say: Probably I would be justified in shooting three coyotes to eliminate one which had developed the habit of feeding on sheep to the point where it would kill ten of my sheep having a marketable value of $9 each, or $90 in all, but probably I would be unjustified in distributing poisoned meat baits (or employing any other method) to save the ten sheep if in so doing I killed, and wasted the fur of, eight coyotes, six badgers, five kit foxes, six gray foxes, two skunks, two bobcats, and a red fox, having a total potential fur value of $110.

Of the many debatable questions relating to coyote control, one is: Should it be done at federal expense? Arguments in favor include the following: The federal government collects grazing fees for use of some of its lands, and therefore should protect owners of livestock thereon from losses caused by coyotes; annual losses from coyotes, or predatory mammals collectively, of as much as 10 per cent of the value of a flock of sheep can be avoided by governmental predatory animal control, and some sheepowners can dispense with the services of some of their herders; the control can be done more economically by the government than in any other way, because the government agents, by employing traps and poisoned baits, can kill the coyotes *before* losses to livestock occur, rather than after a considerable loss has been sustained. Arguments in opposition include the following: The low grazing fees reflect and allow for the loss expectable from predatory animals; losses of 10 per cent are mostly from causes other than inroads of predatory mammals the depredations of which are much exaggerated by many sheepowners; sheepowners have no right to have animal life destroyed when the value to other persons of this animal life exceeds the sum actually lost in sheep killed by predatory mammals; sheepowners do not deserve favorite treatment to the extent of having their flocks protected at public expense in order that the cost of employing some herders can be avoided; citizens of the state are robbed of an important income because most of the coyotes killed by governmental hunters are taken in spring, summer, and early autumn when the furs are worthless; this out-of-season trapping so reduces the population of coyotes that, at the beginning of the regular trapping season when furs are prime, private trappers find it unprofitable to trap for furs in these areas, whereas if most of the coyotes were left until fall, about as many would be caught by private trappers in the fur season as are caught by government workers in the entire year; also the cost of control is more when done by governmental employees than if the control is done by an individual owner of sheep only when required. If some of these arguments, through assumptive reasoning or otherwise, are faulty, it may be said that they are presented as nearly as possible in the form used by adherents of one view or the other.

Another way to consider the federal government's relation to the work is to inquire if it should (1) devote no attention to the matter, (2) do all the work at federal expense, or (3) participate in some intermediate fashion. Many of those who favor the last-mentioned course think that instruction and demonstration would suffice, leaving the actual work to private individuals or to local political subdivisions in accordance with local or individual estimate of need. I do not certainly know the majority opinion in this matter.

Those who favor control at public expense, which now involves participation of the federal government on a service basis, are (1) the governmental employees engaged in the work, (2) owners of flocks of sheep, (3) roughly half of the sportsmen (hunters), and (4) an unknown percentage of the general public whose interests are not directly affected. Those opposed are (1) biologists not engaged in the work, (2) fur trappers, (3) roughly half of the sportsmen (hunters), and (4) an unknown precentage of the general public whose interests are not directly affected. Unanimity of opinion is lacking in every group mentioned. The nearest approach to agreement is among the sheepowners and governmental employees engaged in the work, who obviously favor governmental control, and the biologists not engaged in the work and the fur trappers, who are opposed. A few sheepowners in Nevada disapprove of the present system, one even disapproving of the killing of any coyotes not actually caught in the act of doing damage. Some governmental employees engaged in the work have said, in private, that they felt that the system is wrong. A few biologists, outside the government service, have at least failed to voice objection to the system, and therefore may favor it.

The claim made on occasion by both proponents and opponents of the system in question that public opinion favors their point of view seems to have been answered in one way through the elected representatives of the people when the State Rabies Commission was formed and in the opposite way when the "Rabies Law" was repealed by referendum vote. Some pertinent observations here are that persons whose personal interests are not involved and who are not trained biologists mostly inquire what value the animal has, and if they perceive no immediate usefulness of it to man, conclude that it should be eliminated. A considerable number of people, however, are much influenced by considerations of mercy and prevention of suffering. This takes expression in the many chapters of the humane society and related organizations. In general, persons of this type lean toward disapproval of killing of wild animals whenever clear justification is not shown, but a certain number react favorably to killing a carnivore—an animal which eats other animals. The general populace is relatively inarticulate in the matter. By propaganda the opponents and proponents of the present system have sought to influence the public toward their respective points of view.

The sportsmen's organizations are divided between those which advocate the elimination of animals which compete with the sportsmen in taking certain kinds of game and those which regard predation as a natural function relatively harmless or even beneficial to game species. Then, too, animals which some sportsmen regard as game, other sportsmen regard as nongame or even as inimical to game. In general, however, sportsmen lean toward disapproval of the coyote and also toward disapproval of the system of control which involves the use of poison—both the coyote and poison, a majority of the sportsmen feel, compete with them in killing game.

The "livestock owners" commonly are referred to as favoring the present system. Almost all owners of sheep favor it, but owners of cattle are individually unconcerned or opposed to it. Those who are opposed feel that coyotes help to hold in check rodents and rabbits which compete with their cattle for forage.

The above explains, in part, why opinion is divided on whether or not coyote control should be carried on at public expense.

Supposing, for the sake of presenting arguments *pro* and *con*, that control of coyotes at public expense is justified, then the question arises concerning the means of control that should be used.

ALLEGED GAINS AND LOSSES RESULTING FROM DIFFERENT METHODS OF CONTROL

Den-hunting of coyotes before the young are old enough to leave the burrow has been said to eliminate them before they are large enough to do harm. It is pointed out that in den-hunting the adults also can often be easily taken by traps set near the ruined den and beside the burial place of one of the dead whelps, one foot of which is left exposed. Objections made to den-hunting are that it destroys more coyotes which would be harmless or even beneficial than it does coyotes which would harm man's possessions. Some object also to the cruelty involved and the suffering. A sheepowner whose flock is levied upon by a parent coyote feeding young is apt to be especially favorable to den-hunting; and a fur trapper accustomed to trapping a given area in winter is apt to be equally opposed to den-hunting in his trapping area.

Trapping by paid government hunters the year through, it is maintained, provides a permanent force of men, so that a hunter always is available for sending where and when he is needed. Constant trapping prevents the population of coyotes from getting out of hand. No premium is placed on the number of coyotes taken, and it is possible for the trappers to concentrate on the individual coyotes that are causing damage. Young coyotes, because they are not trap-shy, are eliminated before they are old enough to learn to do damage. This method of control (use of traps) is selective, in that by setting the traps "stiff," animals lighter in weight than coyotes will not be caught; when an animal lighter in weight than a coyote steps on the pan of a trap the weight is insufficient to spring it. Opponents maintain the following: that trappers are assigned to areas where the most influential sheepowners have their flocks and not to places where coyotes are causing most damage; that the population is kept down, but think that the "wise" coyotes which do damage often escape the traps; that the success of trappers is rated by them and by their immediate superiors on basis of numbers of coyotes caught, and point to scalps purchased by, and given to, the government trappers as a means of swelling their total; that most of the coyotes caught when young would never do any damage if allowed to live; and that fur bearers are caught in large numbers but are not reported as caught. Furthermore, it has been maintained: that the fur taken out of season is wasted; that rodents increase in number because of removal of their natural enemies; that the average cost of trapping a coyote under this system is much too large; and that since the work is paid for out of the tax money, other persons in the state should be entitled to some of this tax money—the fruitgrower, for instance, who may argue with some justice that if the sheepman is to have this "free work," certainly, he, too, as a taxpayer, should have some "free work," say, governmental extermination of codling moths in his orchard.

Poisoning ordinarily is accomplished at poison stations, one of which may be prepared as follows: An unwanted horse, or, as second choice, a burro, is killed, eviscerated, and, at the place decided on, left to serve as a lure for coyotes. Next, caul fat (fat from around the kidneys) from some domestic animal is ground up, and in a quantity of this fat (often referred to as suet) a tablet of strychnine is inserted. The whole makes a pellet about ½ inch in diameter. When twenty to one hundred of these pellets have been prepared, the carcass of the horse is studded. Studding consists of inserting a long-bladed knife in the horse's flesh and placing one pellet, or bait, deeply in the incision. When each of the baits is thus placed, the carcass is rolled over, the upper surface on which the coyotes first feed being not studded. The theory of this is that the carcass will come to serve as food for many coyotes by the time the zone of poisoned baits is reached; thus, many, instead of a few coyotes will be killed at one time. Fifty to one hundred additional poisoned baits are prepared by (1) using the ground caul fat as described, (2) by slicing thin layers or chunks of caul fat from the freshly killed horse to encase strychnine tablets, or (3) by cutting the fresh liver in small chunks and inserting a tablet of strychnine in each. These baits, any one of which is spoken of as a "drop bait," are dropped on the ground around the carcass of the horse, where it is hoped that coyotes will find and eat them. A carcass, studded or not, with drop baits around it is termed a poison station, and is prepared ordinarily in autumn or early winter. One part of the procedure of poisoning coyotes by this method is to visit the poison stations in spring and at that time burn the studded carcasses. All the uneaten drop baits, in theory, are picked up at that time also.

Reasons advanced for using poison are that more coyotes can be killed at less expense and that poison is effective in wintry weather when steel traps, because of thawing and subsequent freezing of the soil, are prevented from springing. It is better for the "government" to put out poisoned baits than for the "people" to do it because the latter are more careless in placing them. The people have put out poison and will doubtless continue to do so if the government does not. The objections that have been made to the use of poison are these: The poisoned baits kill fewer coyotes than animals of other kinds— kinds of animals that are harmless or beneficial. When used in an area for the first time, poison often destroys most of the meat-eating, beneficial animals; its subsequent use in the same area does not destroy so many of the beneficial animals, the reason being that they were so thoroughly killed off when poison first was used. Because of their canny nature, many coyotes survive. Since the coyote's birth rate is higher than that of other carnivores of equal size, the population of large carnivores after a few years is made up principally of coyotes. The "killer coyote" is no more apt to be taken than any other; in fact, because of his knowledge of the ways of man, the killer coyote will be less apt to take the poison than will others of his kind. Many of the poisoned baits are buried by mice, carried afar by birds, or otherwise distributed where they are picked up by animals of various kinds. Attempts by man to pick up the undisturbed baits are ineffective because many are overlooked. The coyotes and other fur-bearing mammals killed by poison in winter mostly are found after the skins are spoiled. Many so killed are never found. Many dogs are killed by the poison. The suffering of poisoned animals is deplorable. The claim that it is best for the government workers to use poison as a means of reducing its use by private individuals is an admission of its being an unjustified means of control. The example set by federal and other governmental employees brings uncritical approval of the use of the poison and otherwise makes difficult or impossible the enactment of state laws against its use. In the nature of rebuttal to these objections, proponents of poison cite its effectiveness when an outbreak of rabies occurs. The implication may be that any method of killing animals is justified when, because of the animals, the lives of persons are in danger. The opponents concede its use in special instances in phraseology about as follows: ". . . the use of poison for the control of predatory mammals should be abandoned, except in cases of absolute necessity, such as might arise during an outbreak of rabies in coyotes."

Supposing, for the sake of presenting arguments *pro* and *con*, that control of coyotes is to be done privately; then the same questions arise about means proper and feasible to employ. Year-round trapping, den-hunting, organized drives, payment of bounty, and use of poisoned baits have about the same points in their favor and are open to about the same objections as noted above.

Trapping for fur is one method of private control. Some objections that have been made to it are: Control is exercised for only part of the year—only in the late fall and winter, when furs are prime. Private trappers work where coyotes are most abundant or where most easily caught and not where a coyote or coyotes are causing damage to man's property. Some private trappers release females from their traps in order to ensure an abundant fur crop the following trapping season. In years when coyote furs are low in price less trapping and hence less control is accomplished than in years when the fur is high in price. In support of this means of control it is maintained that where it alone has been used, the population of coyotes has been kept down to the same low level as obtains in other places where the other methods of control also, or alone, are used. Value of the fur places an attractive bounty on the animals. The coyotes are *used*. Taxpayers' money is not spent in getting them when private individuals trap the coyotes for their fur value. Instead, a means of livelihood is afforded to many persons. Most of the coyotes taken in Nevada are obtained by private trappers anyhow.

Dogs trained to hunt coyotes have been used mostly, if not entirely, by private parties. One common method is to take the pack of dogs to a coyote's fresh kill. From there the hound that runs by scent (trailing hound) leads the way until the coyote is sighted, when the hounds that run by sight overtake and. kill it. The aim is, in this way, to single out of the population of coyotes the individual which does the damage. Some objections made to the use of dogs for hunting coyotes are: It is too expensive. If an outbreak of rabies or other disease among coyotes occurred, then the dogs also would contract the disease. The dogs would kill other game. The dogs would be killed by poisoned baits. Advocates of the system say that it is cheaper than any other, that instances can be cited to show its effectiveness, that dogs trained for the work do not kill other game, that the dogs can be inoculated against rabies, that the killer coyote—the individual coyote causing damage—can be singled out and quickly eliminated, and that poisoned baits should not be distributed in areas where dogs are used, or, for that matter, anywhere.

FACTS BEARING ON THE CONTROL QUESTION

Some observations pertinent to the entire question of coyote control are these: The coyote has a higher reproductive ratio than any other Nevadan carnivore which approaches it in size. Therefore, the coyote is able to come back in numbers more quickly than are the other carnivorous mammals. In areas where the numbers of coyotes have been reduced to a low point, they will in two years, if unmolested by man, regain their normal abundance. This partly explains why they are a pest under certain conditions. Also they have certain instincts or cunning, or both, in a measure seemingly so much greater than any other kind of carnivorous mammal in Nevada that they can better survive man's efforts to exterminate them. They are omnivorous to a considerable degree and therefore can, and do, turn to a new food source when an old one is no longer available. To avoid actual or practical extinction of other kinds of flesh-eating mammals in areas where efforts are made to destroy coyotes, special care has to be taken to choose a method highly selective for coyotes.

The outbreak of rabies in Nevadan coyotes in the period 1915–1916 is thought to have resulted from transmission from the domestic dog. Some persons contend that coyotes are a constant reservoir of rabies; others say that rabies is periodically introduced into the coyote population from dogs, which if all properly muzzled for an appropriate length of time would result in the disappearance of the disease. Be that as it may, rabies among coyotes in Nevada has been on the decline since 1916 when examination of 217 suspected animals revealed that 151 were affected. By 1928 the number of suspected animals sent in to be examined by the state veterinary service had dropped to a point where no more than 25 were submitted for examination and less than 10 were found to be positive for rabies. For each of the 5 years following, similar declines in numbers submitted and found to be positive for rabies were shown. No reports for 1934 or later are available at this writing.

PERSONAL VIEWS ON COYOTE CONTROL

The writer's own personal views relating to control of coyotes, as might be expected, are based in considerable measure upon his personal experience and field studies in Nevada. Upon some points in controversy a satisfactory lot of firsthand evidence has been accumulated. On others it is regretfully meager or entirely lacking. The views, which are formulated on the basis of this evidence and information otherwise obtained, have undergone some changes from time to time in the past, and in expressing certain of them here I reserve the right of change in the future. In the suggested plan for dealing with the coyote problem in Nevada, I have taken into account, as nearly as I can, all the factors involved, and it is judged that the plan will best serve the long-time interests of Nevada's citizenry at large.

SUGGESTED PLAN FOR DEALING WITH THE COYOTE PROBLEM IN NEVADA

1. Private trapping for fur when the pelt is prime. This could well involve registration with the State Fish and Game Commission of trap lines on publicly owned lands (public lands reserved for game refuges or for some other purposes might be closed to trapping) and on privately owned lands on which trapping rights have been leased or otherwise assigned by owners.
2. Use of dogs against individual coyotes causing damage.
3. Enactment of legislation against the distribution of poisoned meat (suet) baits, or poisons on other baits when these poisons, like thallium, are cumulative in effect.
4. Acceptance of assistance from the federal government only in the form of advice and recommendation, except in an absolute emergency such as might arise in a serious outbreak of rabies in coyotes.

We may now take up these four points in reverse order.

If the federal government would abandon its participation on a service basis and operate instead in an advisory capacity, it would free itself of the danger of engaging in harmful practice—in response to the demands of special interests. In event of an emergency, as may have obtained in 1916 in northern Nevada, federal aid in appropriate form should be given if needed, but should be withdrawn when the emergency is past.

The enactment and enforcement of a state law against the use of poisoned meat or suet baits would permit the populations of valuable kinds of fur bearers to reëstablish themselves in areas where, because lethal poisoned meat baits are distributed at intervals, they cannot now do so. So far as I know, cumulative poisons, compounds of thallium for example, have not been used in Nevada on any kinds of baits. Thallium is referred to as cumulative because a lethal dose of it is almost as effective if taken in parts over a period of days as if taken in a single dose. Because thallium is not destroyed when taken into the tissues of an animal, as strychnine is, thallium is passed on from one animal which has eaten thallium to another which eats the first. By this means it has had far-reaching and costly effects upon various kinds of animal life. It is used in place of strychnine because of a slightly higher percentage of kills is claimed, particularly in some kinds of ground squirrels. In any legislation designed to prevent the use of poison, a clause to preclude the use of thallium against any vertebrate animal outside the limits of incorporated areas would seem to be a wise precautionary measure.

Whether strychnine-treated meat baits are truly essential to reduce the number of coyotes even where rabies became widespread is uncertain. Therefore, a law forbidding the use of poisoned meat baits would seem best drawn without provision for this emergency. If poisoned meat baits *were* shown to be an essential means of control, executive declaration in an emergency could meet the situation.

The use of dogs against coyotes is a valuable supplementary method—supplementary to trapping for fur—because the "killer" coyote through association with man has developed an exceptional ability to keep out of traps and otherwise avoid the death planned for him. By using one good trailing dog to start the wolf hounds that run by sight—and a pair of wolf hounds is sufficient—the killer can be singled out (see p. 252) at the scene of one of his misdeeds, followed, jumped, and quickly dispatched. Also, this method is economical of the harmless and beneficial kinds of mammals. It is dangerous, and impossible for long, to use such dogs in an area where poisoned meat baits are present.

Private trapping for fur accounts for more coyotes than any other method. Control (maintenance of the numbers below normal) of the population of coyotes by government hunters is accomplished principally by the large take of young coyotes between July 1 (about the time the pups leave the dens) and October 30. Indeed, more than half of all the coyotes obtained in the entire year by the government hunters are taken in this third of the year (Records, 1929). The control exercised by private trapping is between September 15 and March 1. This private trapping takes the surplus at a time when the fur is marketable. The coyote pup less than 1 year old seldom, if ever, damages livestock. Thus, by postponing for a few months the taking of the young coyotes, no appreciable increase in damage to sheep results.

The plan of registering trap lines on publicly owned land might be carried out under supervision of a state game commission as follows:

1. Allot to one trapper the fur rights of one and only one described area for his exclusive use upon payment of a small registration fee.

2. This registration can be renewed year after year upon receipt of a request accompanied by (a) list of furs taken, (b) record of average or total price received for each species, (c) names of firms or persons to whom furs were sold, and (d) payment of the annual registration fee.

3. If no trapping is done for two successive years, the right to renew the license is taken away from the trapper.

Some advantages of this plan are that fur is taken only when prime, and that the incentive to trap before or after the fur is prime in order to get ahead of someone else is removed—each licensee being restricted to a given area which is exclusively his own.

Game law enforcement is simplified, for there is strong incentive to trap only in the season prescribed by state law. Furthermore, one man, the licensee, is responsible for a given area, and it is to his best interests to see that all game laws are enforced in that area.

Overtrapping (depletion) is avoided because a sustained yield is the objective. The opportunity in any one year to trap the area lightly, to trap on only part of it, to trap only for certain species, or not to trap it at all, provides effective means for increasing a depleted stock and makes possible a sustained yield for following years. This is of particular importance if depletion or extinction is to be avoided, for no other species of Nevadan carnivore of a size comparable to the coyote has a reproductive rate as high as that of the coyote.

The transient trapper who exhausts an area and moves on to another is eliminated, with benefit to wildlife in general, to responsible trappers, and to the citizenry at large. The transient trapper is not only eliminated by law but by the insistence of a "warden"—the licensee—who naturally guards not only the license, but all of the rights guaranteed him by the license.

Where the system of registered trap lines has been most thoroughly tried out, in British Columbia, still other advantages are pointed out. Such a system brings ready enforcement of regulations prohibiting the placing of poisoned meat baits.

Under the proposed plan, on public lands, unnecessarily extensive poisoning of native rodents, the basic food of carnivores, probably would be lessened, and the use of a cumulative poison like thallium, which in turn kills the fur bearers which eat these poisoned rodents and birds, would be prevented. Possessors of registered trapping rights would be articulate in these matters. The registration system might fairly be expected to provide evidence (actual value of fur crop) to counterbalance the unwise demands of other special groups. For example, it would be easier to disallow the demands of hunters interested primarily in quail (many quail hunters advocate destruction of predatory mammals) because the owners of trapping rights would demand their "rights." Wildlife and the public domain itself would be expected to benefit, in this way: If, when a permit was granted to graze sheep, a permit was granted to someone else to trap fur bearers on the same area, drastic measures to meet the full demands of one grantee would not be carried out. For example, the fur trapper would not be allowed to exclude all sheep because sheep in some measure interfered with his harvesting of furs, and the sheepman would not be allowed to kill, or by other means exclude, all flesh-eating mammals because flesh-eating mammals in some measure interfered with his raising sheep. In this manner several natural resources, instead of only one, would be conserved and put to wise use.

The substance of the four-point program outlined above probably could best be given legal status by incorporating it in the state game code.

In review, let us set down the following points: The coyote, by reason of its high rate of reproduction, adaptability, and cunning, will persist in spite of efforts to exterminate it. Unless care be taken to select means of control, valuable species other than the coyote will be exterminated before the number of coyotes is greatly reduced. This already appears to have happened in some parts of Nevada. The coyote has virtues which make it worth encouraging in certain areas. Some of these are its value as a fur bearer, as a check (not necessarily a control) on the abundance of rodents, and its services as an eliminator of diseased and decrepit individuals among game species. The coyote has faults, noteworthy of which are that it contracts and sometimes spreads rabies, and that renegade individuals destroy sheep and sometimes poultry. When any of these faults become dangerous or overly burdensome, control should be resorted to. The most effective control is a method which permits singling out the individual that does the damage. The poorest methods of control, everything considered, are, first, poisoning, and, second, trapping out of season. The best method of general control is trapping when the fur is prime. Hounds can be used against individual culprits.

Canis latrans lestes Merriam
Coyote

Canis lestes Merriam, Proc. Biol. Soc. Washington, 11:25, March 15, 1897. Type from Toyabe Mountains, near Cloverdale, Nye County, Nevada; Taylor, Univ. California Publ. Zoöl., 7:293, June 24 1911; Linsdale, Amer. Midland Nat., 19:175, January, 1938.
Canis latrans lestes, Nelson and Goldman, Proc. Biol. Soc. Washington, 45:223, November 26, 1932; Borell and Ellis, Journ. Mamm., 15:22, 72, February 15, 1934.
Canis estor Merriam, part, Proc. Biol. Soc. Washington, 11:32, March 15, 1897.

Distribution.—Over most of the state above the Lower Sonoran Life-zone. See figure 173.

Remarks.—External measurements of males are as follows: From Kleckner Creek, Elko Co., 1,140, 1,220; 320, 387; 201, 205; from 15 mi. E Austin and 10 mi. W Austin (with hairs on tip of tail possibly included in measurements of total length and length of tail), 1,245, 1,230; 326, 355; 197, 216; from 5 mi. N Yerington, 1,019, 340, 205; from 8 mi. E Wabuska, 1,140, 323, 190. Corresponding measurements of two females from Elko Co. are 1,110, 1,148; 335, 350; 176, 185; of one from Millett P. O., 1,122, 300, 194. The second-mentioned female from Elko County weighed 8,846 grams (= 19½ lbs.). The four males (excluding those from near Austin) weighed 12,262 grams (approx. 27 lbs.), 9,923 grams (approx. 22 lbs.), approximately 13,636 grams (30 lbs.), and approximately 11,818 grams (26 lbs.).

The ears are erect, and the animal, compared with many domestic dogs of the same height, appears to stand disproportionately high at the shoulders; the tail is carried out behind, and usually points slightly downward. The general color is grayish above with blackish and some buffy. A subadult male taken January 17, 1927, at Millett P. O., Nye County, and hence a near topotype of the race *lestes*, answers well to a description earlier drawn up of this race (Grinnell, Dixon, and Linsdale, 1937:472) and which is essentially as follows: Gray of back extending well down on sides and merging gradually with whitish underparts. Black-tipped hairs form almost continuous, obscurely defined area down middle of back; hairs longest between shoulders, there forming a sort of mane. Pure white shows on the cheeks and throat, chest between forelegs, and on posterior half of belly. The whitish area extends down the inside of each hind leg. The color is Ochraceous-Buff on top of head and snout, on shoulders (where color results from distal parts of underfur), on front and outer parts of forelegs, and on flanks and outer parts of hind legs. Ochraceous-Buff darkest on snout and clearest and brightest on backs and bases of ears. Some black present on lower anterior part of foreleg. Forehead above and between eyes more grizzled than rest of head. A whitish band ½ inch wide borders upper lip and merges backward into white of throat. Vibrissae black, varying in length up to 65 mm. Overhairs on the back,

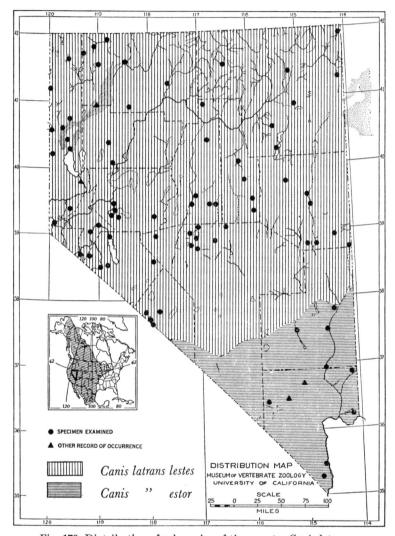

Fig. 173. Distribution of subspecies of the coyote, *Canis latrans.*

from base to tip, are banded black, white, black, white. On underparts overhairs are all white and grayish, or rarely an ochraceous appearance results from pigment in distal part of underfur. Underfur basally plumbeous. Tail cylindrical, about 3 inches in diameter at base and nearly 5 inches at middle, above colored like back. Underside of tail whitish toward base but distal half or two-thirds tawny; tip ordinarily all black, but sometimes a few of distalmost hairs white and rarely entire tip conspicuously white.

The black area down the middle of the back in many specimens is extended over the side of each shoulder. This and the less ochraceous color (of the underfur) showing on the back are the only two color features that I have been able to make out which differentiate *lestes* and *estor*. Also, *estor* of comparable age and sex, in Nevada, seems to average about 5 per cent smaller than *lestes* from Nevada. The specimens from southern Nevada agree well with topotypes at hand of *estor*, which name was based on specimens from southeastern Utah. The name *lestes* was based on animals from central Nevada, and our abundant material from there and from more northern localities in Nevada and elsewhere in western North America suggests that the type locality is near the southern margin of the geographic range properly assignable to *lestes*.

Some geographic variation in morphological features is shown within that part of the range of *lestes* which lies in Nevada. Coyotes from western Nevada in the vicinity of Fallon are smaller and lighter-colored than coyotes from northern and central Nevada. In this respect the animals from Fallon are intermediate between *estor* and *lestes*, but nearer the latter. The teeth in the animals from Fallon, nevertheless, are larger than in coyotes from any other part of the state.

Individual variation among coyotes seems to be of about the same degree as in other species of the family. This individual variation and the slight degree of geographic variation between coyotes in northern and southern Nevada make the allocation of individual specimens from the central part of the state to one or the other subspecies a difficult task. Therefore, an average of several individuals from one locality of one sex and one age has been relied upon. Also, the morphological distinctions between some named kinds is not so precisely known as would be desirable. From the information that is available, however, it appears that *lestes* differs from adjoining races in the following selected features: From *incolatus* to the northwest in less cinnamon, more black and white; skull larger, superior outline of anterior part of skull more nearly straight; width across tooth rows less, relative to length of tooth rows; zygomatic breadth less, relative to length of skull; least distance between orbit and anterior opening of infraorbital canal more, as opposed to less, than 41 per cent of distance across fourth upper premolars. From *nebracensis*, *lestes* is said to differ in darker, richer color. From *mearnsi*, *lestes* has been said to differ in about the same way as from *estor* (see above under discussion of differences between *estor* and *lestes*). From *ochropus* of the interior valleys of California, *lestes* is said to differ in larger size, less highly colored pelage, and larger skull and teeth.

Records of occurrence.—Specimens examined, 147, as follows: *Washoe Co.:* 4½ mi. NE Painted Point, 5800 ft., 1; 2 mi. N Hausen, 4700 ft., 1; 4 mi. W Deep Hole, 4200 ft., 1; 13 mi. W and 9 mi. S Deep Hole, 3850 ft., 1; Roop, 1; Horse Canyon, 4 mi. NW Pahrum Peak, 4200 ft., 1; same, except 3 mi. NW, 5000 ft., 1; Fox Canyon, 6 mi. S Pahrum Peak, 4800 ft., 1; 4 mi. NW Flanigan, 4200 ft., 1; Sand Harbor, E side Lake Tahoe, 1. *Ormsby Co.:* Marlette Lake, 1. *Storey Co.:* 6 mi. NE Virginia City, 6000 ft., 1. *Lyon Co.:* 8 mi. E Wabuska, 4400 ft., 1; 5 mi. N Yerington, 1; Desert Creek, 1; Desert Creek Ranch, 2. *Humboldt Co.:* Hot Springs, Thousand Creek Valley, 1; Virgin Valley, 30; Dry Lake, 1 mi. E Washoe Co. line and 19 mi. S Oregon boundary, 1; Quinn River Crossing, 2; Summit Lake, 1; Willow Point, 1; Jungo, 1. *Pershing Co.:* 3 mi. S Vernon, 4250 ft., 1; 2 mi. W Toulon, 4300 ft., 1. *Churchill Co.:* 5 mi. SE Fallon, 1; Carson Lake, 3900 ft., 10 mi. SSE Fallon, 1; 12 and 14 mi. S Fallon, 4; Eastgate, 4400 ft., 1; E side Carson Sink, 1 (coll. of Ralph Ellis). *Mineral Co.:* 3 mi. S Schurz, 4100 ft., 1; 5 mi. SW Pine Grove, 7250 ft., 1; Simon, 1; Lapon Canyon, Mt. Grant, 8900 ft., 1; 5 mi. S Wichman, 1. *Esmeralda Co.:* 1 mi. NE Cave Spring, 6400 ft., 1; Arlemont [=Chiatovich Ranch], 4850 and 4900 ft., 2; Fish Lake, 4800 ft., 2; Dyer Ranch, 4800 ft., 4. *Lander Co.:* 3 mi. S Izenhood, 1; Hilltop, 2; Reese River Valley, 7 mi. N Austin, 1; 20 mi. E Austin, 1; Gondolpho Ranch, Reese River, 10 mi. W Austin, 6; 10 mi. E Austin, 2; 15 mi. E Austin, 1. *Eureka Co.:* Winzell, 1; 4 mi. S Romano, Diamond Valley, 1; Reglis Ranch, Eureka, 1; 12 mi. S Eureka, 1. *Nye Co.:* Daniels Ranch, 12 mi. NE Millett P. O., 1; Potts, 2; Millett P. O., 5600 ft., 4; Marble, 1; 5 mi. SE Millett P. O., 5500 ft., 1; Monitor Valley, 6 mi. N Pine Creek Ranch, 6700 ft., 4; Darroughs Hot Springs, 5609 ft., 4; Millman Ranch, 19 mi. SE Millett P. O., 6400 ft., 2. *Elko Co.:* Goose Creek, 4 mi. W Utah boundary, 5200 ft., 2; Askov, 16 mi. W Deep Creek, 6; Marys River, 22 mi. N Deeth, 5800 ft., 5; Gamble Ranch, Montello, 1; Steels Creek, 7000 ft., 3 (coll. of Ralph Ellis); Kleckner Creek, 4 mi. E Lee, 3 (coll. of Ralph Ellis); W side Ruby Lake, 10 mi. N White Pine Co. line, 1 (coll. of Ralph Ellis). *White Pine Co.:* NW of 30-mile Spring, 1; Steptoe Creek, 10 mi. SE Ely, 7000 ft., 2; Pole Canyon, W slope Snake Mts., 1; Chimney

Rock Spring, 28 mi. S Ely, 7400 ft., 3; NE end Patterson Mtn., 27 mi. S Ely, 7100 ft., 1; Silver Creek, head of Cave Valley, 7200 ft., 1; Bullwhack Spring, S end Steptoe Valley, 7100 ft., 1; N end Lake Valley, 1.

Additional records: *Washoe Co.* (Carl P. Russell, MS): 6 mi S Pyramid Lake. *Humboldt Co.* (Merriam, 1897:32): Flowing Springs.

Canis latrans estor Merriam
Coyote

Canis estor Merriam, Proc. Biol. Soc. Washington, 11:31, March 15, 1897. Type from Nolands Ranch, San Juan River, San Juan County, Utah.

Canis latrans estor, Nelson and Goldman, Proc. Biol. Soc. Washington, 45:224, November 26, 1932; Burt, Trans. San Diego Soc. Nat. Hist., 7:402, May 31, 1934.

Distribution.—Southern part of state below the Upper Sonoran Life-zone and higher in isolated mountains. See figure 173.

Remarks.—A male from 14 mi. E Searchlight measured 1,195, 335, 200. A female from 1 mi. N Rox measured approximately 1,194 (47 inches), approximately 356 (14 inches). No weights are available.

Individuals of this race differ from *lestes*, so far as specimens examined show, in averaging about 5 per cent smaller, in less often having the black area along the middle of the back extending down over the shoulders, and in showing more ochraceous color on the back as a result of a brighter color on the distal parts of the underfur and also because the underfur is less completely covered by overhairs. In other words, *estor* tends to be smaller and more reddish than *lestes*. From *nebracensis*, *estor* is said to differ in smaller size and brighter color. In the original description, *estor* is said to be paler than *mearnsi*. Other accounts indicate that *estor* is smaller and paler, less reddish, than *ochropus*.

Records of occurrence.—Specimens examined, 16, as follows: *Lincoln Co.:* Panaca, 2; Meadow Valley Wash, 7 mi. S Caliente, 1; Crystal Spring, Pahranagat Valley, 1; Pahranagat Valley, 5; 1 mi. NE Rox, 1; 1 mi. N Rox Station, 1. *Clark Co.:* 1 mi. N and 1 mi. E Mesquite, 1; Wheeler Well, 1 (D. R. Dickey Coll.); Cedar Basin, 1 (D. R. Dickey Coll.); Colorado River, 14 mi. E Searchlight, 1; 7 mi. S and 1½ mi. E Dead Mountain, 2800 ft., 1.

Additional records (Burt, 1934:402): *Clark Co.:* Mormon Well, Corn Creek Station.

Canis lupus
Wolf

Wolves of this species weigh approximately twice as much as coyotes from which they are further distinguished by relatively shorter ears and broader head. The coloration above is grayish variously mixed with blackish and buff; the underparts are whitish often tinged with buff. Wolves in some localities, and possibly in Nevada, varied greatly in color at one locality; animals almost or quite black, some buffy in color, others whitish, and still others intermediate in colors were found. In Nevada most of the wolves are thought to have been more grayish than the coyotes there. The skull is more heavily proportioned than that of the coyote; the frontal sinuses appear more inflated and the rostrum is broader relative to its length. In the first lower molar, additional differences, as pointed out by Gidley (1913:102), are: talonid narrower, rather than about as wide as trigonid; length of talonid contained in length of entire tooth about four, rather than three and one-half or less times; protoconid and paraconid subconic, rather than bladelike; main cusps of talonid unequal in size, rather than of about same size.

The wolf is thought to be extinct in Nevada; the last one of which I have record is that taken on October 23, 1923, in the northeastern part of the state. This is mentioned in more detail under the account of *C. l. youngi*. From infor-

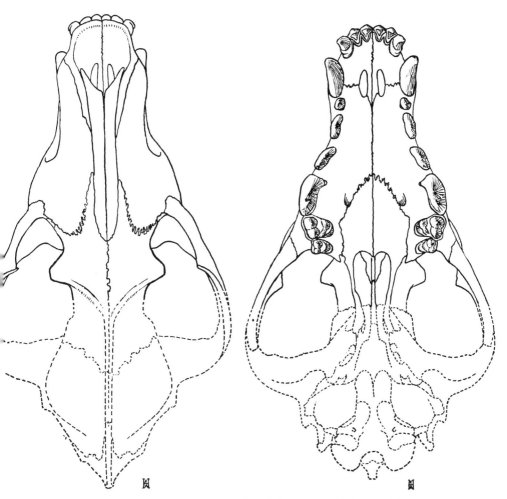

Figs. 174, 175. *Canis lupus youngi,* Gold Creek, no. 33428, ♂. × ½.

mation that has been placed on published record about wolves in other western states, it appears that: The dens for rearing young are in natural caves or burrows in the ground; the gestation period is 62 to 66 days; young are born ordinarily between March 9 and April 15; a litter comprises three to thirteen pups, six, seven, or eight being common numbers; and any kind of flesh is acceptable as food.

Canis lupus fuscus Richardson
Wolf

Canis lupus var. *fusca* Richardson, The Zoölogy of Captain Beechey's Voyage . . . in His Majesty's Ship Blossom . . . , p. 5, 1839. Type locality "California and banks of the Columbia [River]."

Distribution.—Northwestern part of state. Now probably extinct in Nevada. See figure 162, page 232.

Remarks.—External measurements are not available. A male taken near Litchfield, California, weighed 56 lbs.

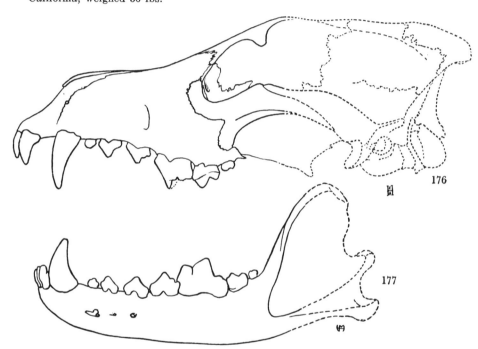

Figs. 176, 177. *Canis lupus youngi*, Gold Creek, no. 33428, ♂. ×½.

According to Goldman (1937a:40; 1941:111), *fuscus* differs from *C. l. columbianus*, the race to the northward, in lesser size, relatively shorter nasals which do not extend so far behind the maxillae, and relatively smaller second lower molar. From *C. l. youngi*, the race to the eastward, *fuscus* is said to differ in lighter color, rostrum more depressed near middle, and palate and nasals usually shorter. From *C. l. irremotus*, the race to the northeast, *fuscus* is said to differ in being smaller, in having a relatively as well as actually broader frontal region which slopes more abruptly to rostrum, and in having the rostrum and nasals shorter.

One reported occurrence is the sole basis for here ascribing the subspecies *fuscus* to Nevada. This is an animal which Stanley P. Young (MS) reported as having been taken near Leadville. Probably the individual to which Mr. Young refers is the same as reported to me on July 17, 1941, by Mr. Fred Vogel, who then lived about 10 miles north of Gerlach. For many years Mr. Vogel was employed, he said, by the United States Bureau of Biological Survey, first in killing wolves on the Great Plains and later in killing coyotes in

Nevada. Presumably, therefore, Mr. Vogel was competent to distinguish the northern wolf (*C. lupus*) from the coyote (*C. latrans*). Mr. Vogel said that in his work in Nevada he knew of only one wolf having been taken. In 1916 or 1917 he saw the skin of one trapped shortly before in Grass Valley [the same place, he thought, as Little High Rock Canyon] by William Denio, the son of the founder of the town of that name in Oregon.

Record of occurrence.—Specimen examined, none. The one reported occurrence, as mentioned above, from *Washoe Co.*: Little High Rock Canyon.

Canis lupus youngi Goldman
Wolf

Canis lupus youngi Goldman, Journ. Mamm., 18:40, February 14, 1937. Type from Harts Draw, north slope of Blue Mountains, 20 miles northwest of Monticello, San Juan County, Utah.

Distribution.—Northeastern quarter or more of state; now probably extinct in Nevada. See figure 162, page 232.

Remarks.—Approximate external measurements of the type specimen, after Goldman (1937a:40), who lists the animal as an adult male, are: 1,800, 470, 225.

According to Goldman (1937a:40–43), *youngi* differs from *C. l. irremotus*, the race to the northward, in color darker, cranium more convex in upper outline, and frontal area wider and less flattened. From *C. l. fuscus*, the race to the northwest, *youngi* differs in color darker, rostrum less depressed near middle, and palate and nasals usually longer. From *C. l. mogollonensis*, the race to the southward, *youngi* differs in color lighter, skull larger, zygoma less widely spreading, and inner margins of nasals tending to decurve less, thus forming a shallower V-shaped median groove; dentition relatively heavier. From *C. l. monstrabilis*, the race to the southeast, *youngi* differs in color lighter, pelage finer, skull more nearly flat, rostrum broader and less depressed near middle, nasals with inner margins turned less strongly downward forming a shallower V-shaped median trough, and auditory bullae less inflated. From *C. l. nubilus*, the race to the east, *youngi* differs in size larger, color darker, skull more flattened, and rostrum more elongated.

The only Nevada-taken specimen of wolf examined is the anterior half of a skull (Mus. Vert. Zoöl., no. 33424) labeled as taken July 29, 1922, at Gold Greek, Elko County, by a Mr. Charles Keas and sent to the Museum of Vertebrate Zoölogy by E. R. Sans, then supervising, in that state, predatory animal control work by the United States Bureau of Biological Survey. Under date of March 2, 1923, Mr. Sans wrote: "We have taken only one wolf in Nevada in the last two years." A second wolf was recorded (Records, 1925:5) as taken in Nevada in 1923, and on the monthly record of animals sent in to the state supervisor of predatory animal control, it is recorded that on October 23, 1923, George A. Nelson, a state trapper, post office address Mountain City, Elko County, trapped this wolf, a male, and sent its skin to the state supervisor. On June 4, 1941, Stanley P. Young, in indicating (MS) that he had record of only six wolves taken in Nevada in more than 2 decades of predatory animal work, said: "Three were taken in Elko County near Mountain City; one near Eureka in the same county; 1 in White Pine County and 1 near Leadville in Washoe County."

Record of occurrence.—Specimen examined: *Elko Co.*: Gold Creek, 1 (anterior half of skull).

Felis concolor
Mountain Lion, Cougar, or Puma

Of this species, two races, possibly three, occur in Nevada. The animals are 6 to 8 feet long, the tail comprising 2 to 2¾ feet of this length. The color in adults is tawny or grayish above and whitish below. Young are prominently spotted with blackish-brown on a pale fawn ground-color. The young, one to four per litter, are born after a gestation period of 91 to 97 days, often in a cave. More young appear to be born in April, in California at least, than in any other month. The young are about 12 inches long at birth. The male, so far as known, takes no part in rearing the young. Mountain lions kill and eat

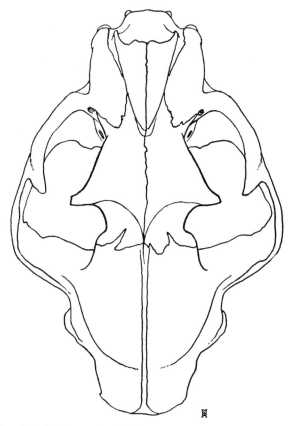

Fig. 178. *Felis concolor kaibabensis*, Potts, no. 37295, ♂. ×½.

various animals, but about three-fourths of their food is thought to be deer. They rely upon stealthy approach and a sudden dash to capture prey. It is a well-marked habit of mountain lions to cover up with loose earth and plant material the remains of an animal upon which they have fed to satisfaction. Often they return to this cache for one or more other meals. It is said that they only rarely eat animals not killed by themselves. Despite their large size, mountain lions are not often seen by persons, except when the lions are pursued and treed by dogs. This is because the lions are by nature given to concealing themselves; their success in capturing animals for food depends on stealth, and even in relatively scant cover a lion can remain out of sight of a person. D. H. Johnson was the only member of our field parties to see one in Nevada. His notes record that: "On June 26, 1937, at about 4 P.M., I saw a young lion about 4 miles north of Smith Creek Cave on the north fork of Smith Creek. I came down through a cleft in the rimrock on the south side

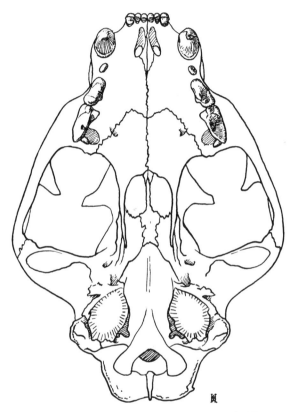

Fig. 179. *Felis concolor kaibabensis*, Potts, no. 37295, ♂. ×½.

of the canyon and saw the animal bound away along the base of a cliff. It stopped behind a pinyon and watched me for a second or two. When I fired at the lion, it disappeared around a corner of the cliff."

In the years 1916 to 1933 a total of fifty-six mountain lions, or an average of about three per year, were recorded as taken in Nevada by predatory animal hunters working under the direction of the Bureau of Biological Survey. How many were killed in this period by private individuals is not known, but I doubt that it was much in excess of fifty-six additional lions.

There is a marked secondary sexual difference in size; by weight, females are 27 per cent lighter than males. The difference is well enough marked so that with an adult skull of each sex in hand, it is possible to identify other skulls according to sex of animal even though this information is not recorded by the collector. The dental formula is i. $\frac{3}{3}$, c. $\frac{1}{1}$, p. $\frac{3}{2}$, m. $\frac{1}{1}$. The skull is readily distinguishable from that of the bobcat by three instead of two premolars in each upper jaw, larger size, and in that the anteroposterior diameter of the upper canine at the alveolus amounts to more rather than less than two-thirds

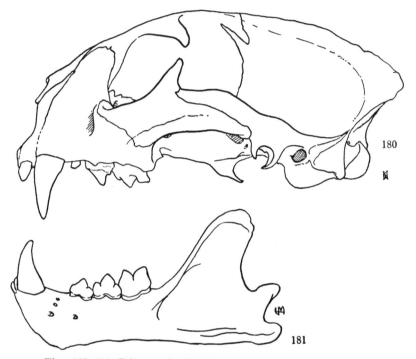

Figs. 180, 181. *Felis concolor kaibabensis*, Potts, no. 37295, ♂. ×½.

of the vertical diameter of the foramen magnum. Externally, the larger size, shorter fur, uniformly tawny, as opposed to mottled, color, and long rather than short tail are selected features which serve to distinguish mountain lions from bobcats.

Felis concolor californica May
Mountain Lion

Felis Californica May, California Game "marked down," 1896:22. Type probably from Kern County, California (see Grinnell and Dixon, Univ. California Publ. Zoöl., 21:327, April 7, 1923, but see also below, at end of *Remarks*, for additional comment).

Felis concolor californica, Nelson and Goldman, Journ. Mamm., 10:347, November 11, 1929.

Distribution.—Western Nevada in Sierra Nevada; eastward limits of range unknown. See figure 182.

Remarks.—Average and extreme external measurements of total length of fourteen males from California (see Grinnell, Dixon, and Linsdale, 1937:536) are 6 ft. 9¼ in. (6′2″–

7′3½″); of nineteen females, 6 ft. 2 in. (5′11″–6′9¾″); tail of three males, 28½″–30½″; of three females, 27″–30″; hind foot of three males, 11″, of three females, 9½″–11″. Average and extreme weights in pounds of fourteen males, 140 (100–165); of twenty females, 88 (65–105).

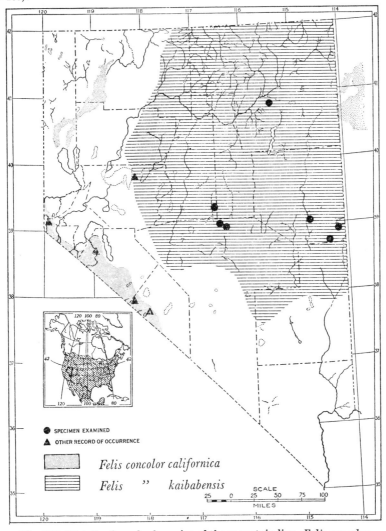

Fig. 182. Distribution of subspecies of the mountain lion, *Felis concolor*.

No specimen of this subspecies taken in Nevada has been examined. Mountain lions which live, or at least occasionally occur, in the Sierra Nevada in the vicinity of Lake Tahoe are probably of the race *californica*. Tony Petroff told me of a mountain lion seen by a tourist, in the winter of 1934, at Spooner. The lion was chasing a rabbit, and when a crew of men working near by on the road were notified, they went to the place and killed the lion. In December, 1939, Alcorn (MS) learned from W. E. Lewis and others. who lived near Wichman, that tracks of mountain lions had been seen there in the snow along the East Walker River. It was the belief of those who saw the tracks that mountain lions are resident on near-by Mount Grant. On June 18, 1928, Mr. D. H. McNett, resident for more than 50 years in Fish Lake Valley, told me that he had seen tracks of mountain lions in the Silver Peak Mountains, although they were not nearly so common there as in the White Mountains. In these mountains Ward C. Russell (MS) found fresh tracks on June 3, 1933, at an elevation of 8200 feet, along Pinchot Creek.

On geographic grounds it seems more reasonable to refer these records of occurrence to the race *californica* than to any other.

Some doubt attaches to the type locality of *Felis Californica* May. When Grinnell and Dixon (1923:327) revived the name they gave reason to suppose that Kern County, California, was the type locality. Nelson and Goldman (1929:347) say that the type locality is the "Upper Kern River, California." Grinnell (1933:114), ten years after he and Dixon first published concerning this name, writes of it as follows: "*Type locality*— Kern County, California; by subsequent action, restricted to Upper Kern River (Nelson and Goldman, Journ. Mammalogy, 10, 1929:347)." From the map facing page 49 of "The Genesis of California Counties" by Owen C. Coy (Publ. California Hist. Surv. Comm., 1923) it is learned that in 1895, before May proposed the name *Felis Californica* and before any of the other authors cited above wrote concerning it, Kern and Tulare counties had, essentially at least, the same boundaries as now (1942). Upper Kern River is mostly in Tulare County, not Kern. Perhaps Nelson and Goldman (1929:347) were the first really to designate a type locality. If so, they must be followed, but further restriction will be required if the type locality is to be fixed within one of the two counties above named. Perhaps, instead, Kern County is to be accepted as the type locality on the basis of information given in the original description or because of the association of the names "Kern County, California" and "*Felis Californica*" by Grinnell and Dixon when they revived the name *Felis Californica*.

Records of occurrence.—Source, as given above in text: *Ormsby Co.*: Spooner. *Mineral Co.*: vicinity of Wichman. *Esmeralda Co.*: Pinchot Creek, 8200 ft., White Mountains; Silver Peak Range.

Felis concolor kaibabensis Nelson and Goldman
Mountain Lion

Felis concolor kaibabensis Nelson and Goldman, Journ. Washington Acad. Sci., 21:209, May 19, 1931. Type from Powell Plateau, 8700 feet, Grand Canyon National Park, Arizona.
Felis concolor hippolestes, Borell and Ellis, Journ. Mamm., 15:23, February 15, 1934.
Felis concolor, Burt, Trans. San Diego Soc. Nat. Hist., 7:402, May 31, 1934.
Felis oregonensis, Linsdale, Amer. Midland Nat., 19:175, January, 1938.

Distribution.—Central and eastern part of state. See figure 182.

Remarks.—No external measurements or weights are available for this race which is thought to be slightly larger than *F. c. californica*, measurements of which have been given in the preceding account. Specimens available answer well to the original description, wherein Nelson and Goldman (1931:210) point out that *kaibabensis* differs from *hippolestes*, the race to the north and east, in paler color and narrower skull. From *F. c. azteca* to the southward it differs in larger size and narrower skull. From *F. c. browni* to the southwest it differs in larger size of skull and heavier dentition. From *F. c. californica* to the westward it differs in larger size, paler color, more elongated skull with a more flattened frontal region, and relatively less widely spreading zygomata.

The westernmost record of occurrence ascribed to this race in Nevada is the head of the left fork of Shady Run, Silver [= Stillwater] Range. Here, D. D. Kolstrup (MS) reports taking a male on November 6, 1927. The country here is such as would not be expected to support a population of mountain lions, and I suppose that the animal taken was a straggler from a more favorable habitat farther to the east.

Records of occurrence.—Specimens examined, 8, unless otherwise indicated each is a skull only, as follows: Lander Co.: 12 mi. SE Austin, 1. Nye Co.: Potts, 1 (skin with skeleton); Monitor Mts., near Potts, 1. Elko Co.: Cold Creek, Ruby Mts., 1. White Pine Co.: Steptoe Creek, 10 mi. SE Ely, 1 (humerus); John Henry Wash, Spring Valley, 1; 1 mi. SW of head of Choke Cherry Creek, Snake Range, 1; S end Snake Range, 1.

Additional record: Churchill Co.: head of left fork of Shady Run, Silver [= Stillwater] Range (D. D. Kolstrup, MS).

Lynx rufus
Bobcat

To the person whose concept of a cat is based on the house cat or other species of the same genus, the bobcat, seen in the wild, is notable for its long legs and apparent lack of tail. The animal appears to be brownish in general color. Viewed closely, the unworn coat is a mixture of tawny hairs tipped with black and white to produce a dappled effect. The chin and the underparts from the forelegs posteriorly to the inguinal region are white or distinctly whitish, as are also the medial sides of the legs and the ventral side of the tail. The tip of the tail is black. On the dorsal surface of the tail there are, depending on the individual, up to four additional blackish bars of decreasing intensity of color toward the base of the tail. The ears are whitish inside, blackish and grayish outside, and have a black apical patch and tuft. The "burnsides" of hair, longer than on immediately surrounding parts of the animal, have distinct black markings. Wear and fading combine to reveal more of the ground color. In individuals much worn, the general color is more tawny and the dappled markings are correspondingly less conspicuous. The dental formula is i. $\frac{3}{3}$, c. $\frac{1}{1}$, p. $\frac{2}{2}$, m. $\frac{1}{1}$. The skull is readily distinguishable from that of the mountain lion by two instead of three premolars in each upper jaw, smaller size, and in that the anteroposterior diameter of the upper canine at the alveolus amounts to less, rather than more, than two-thirds of the vertical diameter of the foramen magnum. Externally, as described in the account of the mountain lion, there are a number of characters which serve readily to differentiate the two species.

Among the names that have been used in Nevada for this animal are lynx cat, wildcat, and even lynx. Lynx cat is a name used by fur buyers for heavily furred animals, as opposed to bobcat for those less heavily furred. On this basis, of the animals taken in midwinter, nearly all from northern and central Nevada are lynx cats, and most of those from southern Nevada are bobcats. Wildcat is a name properly applied to an Old World species of the genus Felis. This wildcat has a longer tail than members of the genus Lynx, and bobcat seems to be a more correct name, as well as the one most commonly used for Lynx rufus. Some animals regarded as true lynxes, a species distinct from the bobcat, have been recorded (Bailey, 1936:271) from northern Nevada, but so far as I have been able to learn none of these records is supported by a preserved specimen. Probably the animals were unusually large bobcats. Aside from characters of a relative nature which distinguish bobcats from lynxes, there is the shape of the caudal half of the presphenoid bone. In the bobcat this is much narrower than long, and in the lynx nearly or quite as broad as long. Bangs (1897:48) has this to say of the two animals: In the bobcat, the "palatal exposure of presphenoid [is] strap shaped or slightly triangular," but in the lynx, the "presphenoid [is] broadly flask shaped."

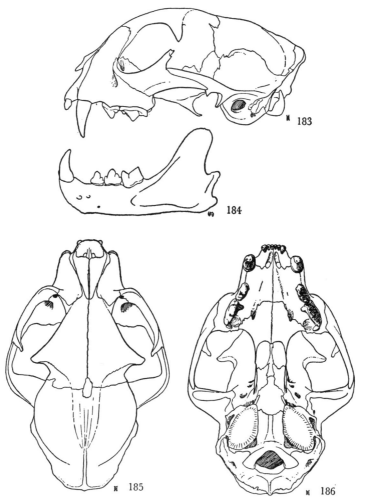

Figs. 183–186. *Lynx rufus pallescens*, Marble, no. 24584, ♂. ×½.

In the specimens examined, in addition to the variation resulting from wear, there also is, I judge, considerable individual variation otherwise in color, and certainly in size of skull. The variation resulting from age is appreciable in the skulls available, but is less than in most other kinds of Nevadan carnivores. The amount of secondary sexual variation is not enough in size of skull to permit certain recognition of sex by the shape or size of the skull alone. In adults, the skulls of males average about 3 per cent larger in linear measurements than females. Also in external measurements, the males average larger than females, but our data do not show to what degree. Likewise our data are too sparse for animals from the southern part of the state to show how much smaller are these animals than those in the northern part. The suggestion is that in size the secondary sexual difference at any one locality is less than the geographic difference between animals of the same sex from the northern and southern parts of the state.

The habitat favored by these cats is the rocky areas at the mouths of canyons. Here and in the other rocky parts of the mountains they are notably more abundant than in the valleys. Bobcats are more nocturnal than diurnal, I think, but many are active for at least part of the day. They frequent caves and fissures in the rocks, as is shown by their tracks, droppings, and places where they had lain. One bobcat, in the summer of 1924, on the eastern side of Pyramid Lake, had the habit of making regular visits to a cave harboring several thousand female bats (*Myotis yumanensis*) and their young. Many of the young bats dropped to the floor, and examination of the feces of the bobcat revealed remains of young bats. Here, evidently, was an easily obtained food of which the bobcat took advantage.

More indicative, I take it, of the normal food of bobcats is the finding by Alcorn of three kangaroo rats in the stomach of an adult female trapped on March 5, 1939, in Wilson Canyon. A female shot about 5 P.M. on June 10, 1932, 9 miles east of Eastgate, had in her stomach one *Eutamias minimus* and one *Lagurus curtatus*.

In the course of their predatory mammal control work, hunters working in Nevada under the direction of the United States Bureau of Biological Survey reported taking 14,352 bobcats in the 18½-year period, 1916 to June 30, 1934. For this period as a whole, which was a time when many of the hunters were in particular seeking coyotes, about one bobcat to every six coyotes was taken. Records (1929:4) says: "Reports received from county clerks show something over 5,000 bobcats were bountied during 1928 by private trappers. This gave them $10,000 over and above what they received for their furs, as a $2 bounty is paid on bobcats. Our [U. S. Biol. Surv.] hunters take about 4 coyotes to each bobcat."

In the winter of 1941–1942, at Reno, fur buyers were paying trappers $6 each for good, average skins. In 1929 and 1930, when furs were high-priced, good skins brought twice this amount.

Lynx rufus pallescens Merriam
Bobcat

Lynx fasciatus pallescens Merriam, N. Amer. Fauna, 16:104, October 28, 1899. Type from south side Mount Adams, near Trout Lake, Skamania County, Washington.

Lynx rufus pallescens, Borell and Ellis, Journ. Mamm., 15:23, February 15, 1934.

Lynx baileyi, Taylor, Univ. California Publ. Zoöl., 7:293, June 24, 1911.

Lynx rufus, Linsdale, Amer. Midland Nat., 19:176, January, 1938.

Distribution.—Northern and central Nevada. See figure 187.

Remarks.—Two males, adult and subadult, from Kleckner Creek, measure 878, 930; 187, 180; 162, 185; weight, 8,805 grams, 11,141 grams. Corresponding measurements of a subadult female from the west side of Ruby Lake are 880, 155, 175; weight, 20 lbs. (= 9,072

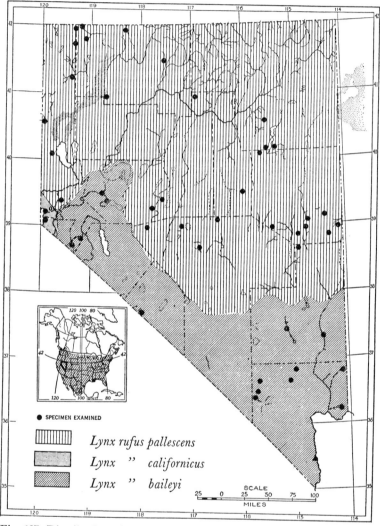

Fig. 187. Distribution of subspecies of the bobcat, *Lynx rufus*, with insert showing range of the species.

grams); an adult female from 9 mi. E Eastgate and another from Millett P. O. measure, respectively, 857, 753; 161, 150; 180, 170; weight, of the female from near Eastgate, 17 lbs. (= 7,711 grams).

This race is characterized by large size of all parts of the animal studied, ashy coloration, and relatively large, narrow brain case with well-developed sagittal crest and markedly protruding (posteriorly) lambdoidal crest. In these features it differs from both *baileyi* and *californicus*. From the latter it differs further in having a paler pinkish color below the tips of the fur. *L. r. pallescens* averages more ashy and less rusty than *baileyi*. In using the name *pallescens* for bobcats from all of northern Nevada I admit lack of personal knowledge concerning the morphological features of *Lynx uinta* Merriam, named from Bridger Pass, Carbon County, Wyoming. Adequate topotypical material of *uinta* is not available. It may be noted that Grinnell and Dixon (1924:350) regarded *uinta* as synonymous with the earlier proposed name *pallescens*, because some skulls "from the Modoc region are . . . identical in every critical respect with near-topotypes of *Lynx uinta*."

Records of occurrence.—Specimens examined, 77, as follows: *Washoe Co.:* "NE part of Washoe Co., and NW part of Humboldt Co.," 6; Little High Rock Canyon, 5000 ft., 1; Roop, 1; 2 mi. W Fish Springs, near Flanigan, 1. *Storey Co.:* 6 mi. NE Virginia City, 6000 ft., 1. *Humboldt Co.:* 38 mi. W and 6 mi. S Denio, Oregon, 5; Virgin Valley, 6; Paradise Valley, 1; Little Humboldt Ranch, Paradise, 2; Jackson Creek, Sulphur, 2. *Lander Co.:* 3 mi. S Izenhood, 1; 2½ mi. NE Smiths Creek Ranch, 5800 ft., 1; Roberts Creek Ranch, Eureka, 1. *Nye Co.:* Potts, 3; Millett P. O., 18; Marble, 2; Monitor Valley, 8 mi. E Toquima Peak, 1. *Elko Co.:* Kleckner Creek, 4 mi. E Lee, 5 (coll. of Ralph Ellis); W side Ruby Lake, 3 mi. N White Pine Co. line, 6200 ft., 1 (coll. of Ralph Ellis); Cooper Canyon, Connor Range, 2; Steptoe Creek, 10 mi. SE Ely, 7000 ft., 1; near head of White River, 10 mi. W Williams Ranch, 1; 5 mi. W Garrison, Utah, 1; mouth of Snake Creek, 1; E side Steptoe Valley, 20 mi. S Ely, 7100 ft., 1; Pole Canyon, Spring Valley, 1; NE end Patterson Mtn., 27 mi. S Ely, 3; Chimney Rock Spring, 28 mi. S Ely, 7400 ft., 1. *Lincoln Co.:* Shingle Pass, 4.

Lynx rufus californicus Mearns
Bobcat

Lynx rufus californicus Mearns, Preliminary diagnoses of new mammals of the genera Lynx, Urocyon, Spilogale, and Mephitis, from the Mexican boundary line, p. 2, January 12, 1897 (reprinted in Proc. U. S. Nat. Mus., 20:458, December 24, 1897). Type from San Diego, San Diego County, California.

Distribution.—The Sierra Nevada and eastern foothills in the vicinity of Lake Tahoe. See figure 187.

Remarks.—Average and extreme external measurements of twelve males and nine females from California (Grinnell, Dixon, and Linsdale, 1937:593) are: ♂, 827 (800–876), ♀, 768 (710–786); 157 (147–170), 143 (127–165); 170 (158–179), 156 (146–170). Weights likewise are lacking for Nevadan specimens of this subspecies, but, judging from the size of the skulls, animals of this subspecies are smaller than *pallescens* and a little larger than *baileyi*.

In comparison with *pallescens* and *baileyi*, *californicus* is distinctly darker-colored and has the dark bars better developed on the top of the tail. The size is less than in *pallescens* and greater than, or about the same as, in *baileyi*. The skulls of Nevada-taken specimens are smaller than in *pallescens* and have more rounded brain cases and slightly less-well-developed sagittal and lambdoidal crests. The skulls are larger than in *baileyi*, and in shape of brain case and degree of development of the sagittal crest are intermediate between *pallescens* and *baileyi*. In color, at least, there is no evidence of intergradation between our specimens of *californicus* and those of *pallescens* or *baileyi* in Nevada. A larger number of specimens from the eastern base of the Sierra Nevada might show that intergradation does occur there; general comparisons of specimens from outside of Nevada indicate that intergradation does occur between the two subspecies *baileyi* and *californicus*. Probably intergradation occurs also between the two subspecies *californicus* and *pallescens*.

Records of occurrence.—Specimens examined, 4, as follows: *Washoe Co.:* 2½ mi. NW Lakeview, 1; 2 mi. N Lakeview, 1; Sand Harbor, E shore of Lake Tahoe, 1. *Ormsby Co.:* Glenbrook, 1.

TABLE 4
CRANIAL MEASUREMENTS (IN MILLIMETERS) OF CARNIVORES (CARNIVORA)

Name and locality	Number of individuals averaged or catalogue no.	Sex and age	Basilar length (of Hensel)	Length of tooth rows	Least interorbital breadth	Orbitonasal length*	Mastoidal breadth	Zygomatic breadth	Length of tympanic bulla	Length of m1	P4 Lateral	P4 Medial
Ursus americanus californiensis												
6 mi. N Weldon, Cal.....	16269	♂	268.0	126.1	76.5	100.1	145.0	187.0	33.4	20.5	11.4	—
Yosemite region, Cal.....	21399	♀	231.1	112.2	57.9	86.0	117.5	159.0	31.0	17.9	10.4	—
Procyon lotor excelsus												
Parker Creek, Cal.......	11330	♂	99.5	55.4	26.6	45.0	73.5	89.7	21.0	10.7	8.9	—
Montello................	221728†	♀	104.5	50.4	28.8	43.1	68.5	85.9	20.0	9.7	7.7	—
Procyon lotor psora												
Topaz Lake.............	95041	♂	101.8	52.9	28.5	44.4	70.1	84.3	20.0	10.5	8.5	—
Sec. 26, T. 11 N, R. 23 E, Lyon Co...............	94805	♀	103.6	51.9	24.3	46.3	63.5	77.7	18.6	10.0	7.7	—
Bassariscus astutus nevadensis												
7 mi. S Caliente.........	51648	♂	68.0	34.2	14.1	30.6	33.4	46.3	12.1	7.1	6.6	7.9
10 mi. S Caliente........	51665	♂	69.2	35.2	15.3	31.8	33.6	47.6	13.4	7.5	7.0	7.8
Martes caurina sierrae												
Marlette Lake...........	69634	♂	71.1	33.3	17.9	26.2	36.2	45.2	16.5‡	9.5	8.6	9.4
Head Bear Cr., Trinity Co., Cal...............	13778	♀	64.8	30.2	16.0	24.2	33.1	42.9	15.8‡	8.6	7.9	8.6
Mustela cicognanii lepta												
Baker Creek, 8675 ft......	41501	♂	29.8	10.4	7.2	10.6	15.1	17.1	10.7‡	4.0	3.5	3.5
Baker Creek, 8675 ft......	41502	♀	27.3	9.3	6.3	9.5	13.9	15.8	10.0‡	3.4	2.9	3.1
Mustela frenata nevadensis												
Baker Creek, 8400 ft......	41508	♂	45.0	17.1	10.4	15.1	25.1	29.0	15.8‡	6.0	5.5	5.7
3 mi. E Baker............	41503	♀	37.7	14.4	8.8	13.6	20.6	22.7	13.5‡	5.0	4.6	4.7
Mustela vison energumenos												
Goose Creek..............	74391	♂	62.3	24.8	15.3	19.2	35.8	40.2	17.1	8.1	7.5	8.0
Mustela vison aestuarina												
7 mi. S Reno.............	7674§	♂	57.0	22.7	14.7	18.3	31.7	37.4	16.0	7.6	6.9	7.4
Lutra canadensis nexa												
Near Deeth..............	210572†	♂	101.2	44.9	20.3	26.8	71.2	75.0	—	14.8	11.7	—
Paradise.................	213136†	♀	98.8	43.2	23.3	25.0	68.9	70.5	—	13.5	11.3	13.1
Lutra canadensis sonora												
Colorado River, 8 mi. upriver from Needles, Cal.	61451	♂	117.7	47.9	29.8	28.6	75.0	81.7	25.8	14.9	13.3	14.2
Colorado River, 8 mi. upriver from Needles, Cal.	3633§	♀	106.1	44.4	26.3	25.9	71.4	73.7	24.5	14.1	12.5	14.0
Spilogale gracilis saxatilis												
W side Ruby Lake.......	4641§	♂	49.9	21.9	15.0	19.5	31.3	35.7		7.1	6.4	5.9
W side Ruby Lake.......	4640§	♀	43.2	19.5	12.5	17.1	26.2	29.3		6.7	6.3	5.2
Stanmoore Mine..........	303‖	♂	46.7	20.7	14.2	18.4	30.7	34.5		7.0	6.3	6.0
Mephitis mephitis major												
1 mi. SE Lovelock.......	90562	♂	70.9	30.5	24.2	28.2	44.8	52.5		10.0	7.1	7.4
Marlette Lake...........	68785	♀	64.5	29.7	22.0	27.1	39.7	45.7		10.0	7.4	7.1
Mephitis mephitis estor												
14 mi. E Searchlight......	61443	♂	60.2	29.2	20.9	25.4	36.5	42.6		9.6	7.1	7.2
14 mi. E Searchlight......	61442	♀¶	55.0	26.3	19.8	25.8	33.8	40.0		8.9	6.9	6.8

* Anterior median point of nasal to posterior base of postorbital process of frontal.
† United States National Museum. § Collection of Ralph Ellis. ¶ Subadult.
‡ Including paroccipital process. ‖ Collection of D. V. Hemphill.

TABLE 4—(*Continued*)

Name and locality	Number of individuals averaged or catalogue no.	Sex and age	Basilar length (of Hensel)	Length of tooth rows	Least interorbital breadth	Orbitonasal length*	Mastoidal breadth	Zygomatic breadth	Length of tympanic bulla	Length of m1	P4 Lateral	P4 Medial
Taxidea taxus taxus												
Between heads of Copper and Coon creeks.......	6638§	♂	121.0	54.1	30.0	44.2	81.1	86.5	30.3	13.6	11.9	14.4
4 mi. E Lee.............	6063§	♀	111.3	50.3	26.9	39.0	78.6	78.7	31.6	13.0	11.0	13.1
Taxidea taxus berlandieri												
2½ mi. N Calif.-Nev. Monument.............	61458	♂	112.1	51.3	25.3	41.7	75.8	74.0	27.0	13.4	11.7	13.9
14 mi. E Searchlight......	61457	♀	102.0	48.0	25.3	38.3	65.4	64.7	26.1	12.2	10.7	12.4
Vulpes fulva necator												
Marlette Lake...........	69636	♂	122.3	72.6	23.2	63.4	45.3	67.0	21.9	14.0	12.6	14.8
Vulpes macrotis nevadensis												
5 mi. NE Hazen.........	90014	♂	102.2	60.6	23.0	50.6	38.4	60.4	20.1	13.0	11.2	12.1
Nevada..................	12 av.	♀	102.8	60.0	21.2	50.8	38.8	60.0	19.9	12.4	10.3	11.4
Willow Creek Ranch.....	213115†	♀	99.2	57.4	20.9	50.4	37.4	——	19.2	12.3	10.0	11.1
Nevada..................	9 av.	♀	98.8	57.8	21.2	49.9	38.0	58.7	19.6	12.0	9.8	11.0
Vulpes macrotis arsipus												
4 mi. N Mesquite.........	51644	♂	100.7	59.6	20.6	51.3	37.4	57.8	19.9	11.1	9.7	10.7
1½ mi. W Mesquite.......	57330	♀	96.0	56.6	20.8	49.2	36.3	56.3	20.1	11.7	9.7	11.2
Urocyon cinereoargenteus scottii												
2 mi. N Calif.-Nev. Monument........ ~	61465	♂	106.8	61.3	23.8	55.1	41.1	63.0	18.0	11.8	10.2	11.5
½ mi. N Calif.-Nev. Monument.............	61467	♀?	104.7	56.5	21.3	51.8	41.2	58.5	18.2	10.7	9.1	10.6
Canis latrans lestes												
4 mi. E Lee.............	6068§	♂	175.9	104.7	31.3	91.8	60.9	98.6	24.5	21.6	19.8	19.6
Millett P. O.............	37293	♀	168.7	100.8	32.0	80.8	60.7	97.7	25.0	21.5	19.3	19.2
Canis latrans estor												
14 mi. E Searchlight......	61468	♂	173.2	101.6	33.8	89.8	61.1	99.7	23.8	21.5	19.6	20.0
1 mi. N Rox Station......	79823	♀	169.2	100.0	31.4	84.5	60.4	92.7	22.7	20.4	19.3	19.6
Canis lupus fuscus												
"Near Litchfield, Cal."...	34228	♂	211.5	124.0	45.7	106.5	78.7	134.6	28.9	30.1	25.8	27.1
Canis lupus youngi												
Gold Creek, Elko Co.....	33424	♂	——	119.2	46.2	106.0	——	——	——	27.7	23.7	23.1
Type specimen..........	224001†	♂	218.9	129.4	44.3	126.5	84.3	137.7	27.5	30.1	26.4	26.2
Felis concolor kaibabensis												
Potts, Nye Co...........	37295	♂	173.5	70.9	43.5	82.8	87.9	148.2	35.3	17.3	22.3	23.6
Monitor Mts., near Potts.	46909	♀	163.7	69.2	41.0	76.0	——	141.0	31.4	17.5	23.9	24.3
Lynx rufus pallescens												
Marble..................	24584	♂	106.0	45.7	25.0	59.3	59.0	90.2	25.5	11.9	15.1	15.4
NE part Washoe Co. or NW part Humboldt Co.	47211	♀	105.4	43.7	25.7	57.3	58.1	——	26.3	12.0	14.1	14.5
Lynx rufus californicus												
Sand Harbor............	65529	♂	100.4	43.5	24.8	53.0	55.4	86.3	22.8	10.6	13.2	13.5
2 mi. W Lakeview........	70001	♀¶	93.7	38.9	23.8	51.0	52.5	——	22.8	10.3	13.4	13.4
Lynx rufus baileyi												
Cabin Springs...........	91048	♂	98.9	43.3	25.4	——	53.0	86.8	23.2	11.9	14.8	14.6
	91047	♀¶	92.5	40.8	——	51.0	46.5	78.2	22.0	11.3	14.2	14.2

* Anterior median point of nasal to posterior base of postorbital process of frontal.
† United States National Museum.
§ Collection of Ralph Ellis.
¶ Subadult.

Lynx rufus baileyi Merriam
Bobcat

Lynx baileyi Merriam, N. Amer. Fauna, 3:79, September 11, 1890. Type from Moccasin Spring, Coconino County, Arizona.

Lynx rufus baileyi, Burt, Trans. San Diego Soc. Nat. Hist., 7:402, May 31, 1934.

Distribution.—Southern and low western area of Nevada north to Carson Sink, Churchill County. See figure 187.

Remarks.—No measurements of adult males are available. A female from Wilson Canyon, Lyon County, measures 810, 155, 155; weight 15 lbs. (= 6,804 grams). Animals from farther south, as judged by the skulls, are smaller.

This form is smaller and averages more reddish in coloration than *pallescens*. Our specimens suggest that *baileyi* is smaller than *californicus* and certainly it is much lighter-colored, being reddish, as opposed to blackish. Comparison of the skulls has been made in the accounts of *pallescens* and *californicus*. The specimens from Churchill and Lyon counties are intermediate toward *pallescens*, but are nearer *baileyi*.

Records of occurrence.—Specimens examined, 23, as follows: *Churchill Co.:* Fallon, 4000 ft., 1; Carson Lake, 3900 ft., 10 mi. SSE Fallon, 1. *Lyon Co.:* Wilson Canyon, 1; Desert Creek Ranch, S end of county, 2. *Esmeralda Co.:* Fish Lake, 4800 ft., 1. *Lincoln Co.:* Rainbow Canyon, 1; Pahranagat Valley, 5. *Clark Co.:* Cabin Springs, 2; 4 mi. S Mesquite, 1; 8½ mi. SW Mesquite, 1; Hidden Forest, 2 (D. R. Dickey Coll.); Indian Springs, 2 (D. R. Dickey Coll.); Cold Creek, 1 (D. R. Dickey Coll.); Wheeler Well, 1 (D. R. Dickey Coll.); Cedar Basin, 1 (D. R. Dickey Coll.).

Additional record: *Clark Co.:* Feathers (MS) records one from Jap Ranch, Colorado River, 14 mi. E Searchlight.

Order RODENTIA
Rodents (gnawing mammals)

Marmota flaviventer
Yellow-bellied Marmot

There are four races of this species in Nevada. Generic characters include large size, thick-set body, short legs, broad blunt nose, short and well-haired ears, tail amounting to from a fifth to a third of total length, claws stout, thumb almost rudimentary, mammae in five pairs, skull nearly flat on top, postorbital processes of frontal triangular and projecting nearly at right angles to axis of skull, upper molars with heightened inner cones, and P3 about a third as large as P4. The dental formula is i. $\frac{1}{1}$, c. $\frac{0}{0}$, p. $\frac{2}{1}$, m. $\frac{3}{3}$. Characters of the species include buffy patches on sides of neck; feet varying from Light Buff to Hazel (never black); nasals narrow posteriorly and their width there not more, and usually less, than that of adjacent branches of premaxillae; and maxillary tooth rows slightly divergent posteriorly.

M. flaviventer occurs in the western United States and ranges north a short distance into British Columbia. In past centuries, probably later than Pleistocene time, this species, as indicated by remains in kitchen middens from northern Arizona and remains in a cave in the Providence Mountains of California, occurred farther south than it does today. Because the species formerly occurred due south of Nevada, the species at this earlier time probably occurred farther south in Nevada itself than it does now. The animal subsists on green vegetation which is now rarely available for long periods of the year at the places where

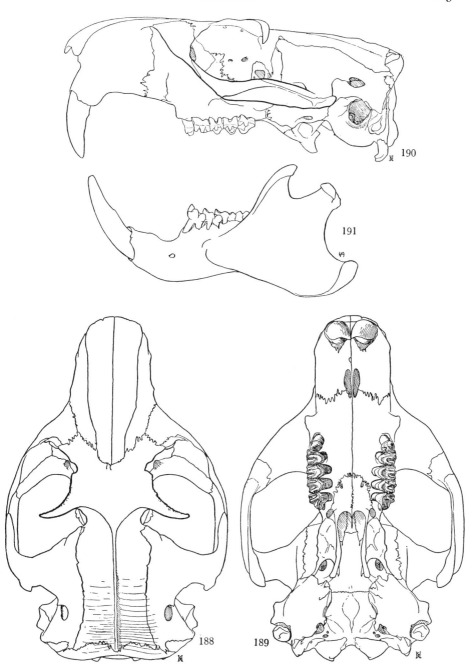

Figs. 188–191. *Marmota flaviventer parvula*, west slope Toquima Mountain, 10,000 feet, no. 57476, ♂. ×1.

the remains were found in Arizona and in the Providence Mountains. Possibly a decrease in annual rainfall or a slight retreat northward of plants characteristic of life-zones higher than the Lower Sonoran, or both, may account for the absence of marmots in these southern localities.

Farther north in Nevada, where marmots now occur, indications are that the animals, especially those more than 1 year old, commence estivation in early summer. This early retirement to dormancy, I suspect, is an adaptation to meet the shortage of green food which in many years is apparent by June. This response to an environmental factor seems to be now partly a "hereditary" matter, for in some years when rains occurred later than in most years and when green vegetation persisted correspondingly later, the adult marmots retired to estivate at about the same time as they did in dry years. These conditions seem to prevail where marmots occur in the Upper Sonoran, Transition, and lower part of the Canadian life-zones. In higher, more Boreal, surroundings, as, for example, the high country of the Ruby Mountains in the northeastern part of the state, some adult marmots, and perhaps all of them, are active all summer. The supposition is that the marmots have not, in this area, developed the hereditary trait of estivating early because green food is regularly available here in the summer. Another factor probably operating here, under Boreal conditions, is that breeding and the whole active (as opposed to the dormant) part of the life cycle of these animals is set at a later date than in the more southern localities in Nevada.

Safe refuges from enemies and dens for rearing young and for hibernation are provided mainly by piles of boulders. To be sure, the marmots dig burrows in the ground but, so far as we have observed, only beneath piles of stones or beneath some huge boulder. The name rock-chuck locally applied to this marmot is therefore appropriate. Favorite homesites are isolated groups of large boulders surrounded in spring by green vegetation. The adult animals spend much of their time basking in the sun atop boulders toward which it is difficult for a person to approach without being seen, for these boulders serve as lookout posts from which a marmot detects intruders when they are yet some distance away and scurries down from the top of the boulder into the den. In late spring an adult thus having left his place atop a boulder is apt to remain in the burrow all the rest of the day. By keeping vigil at one of these piles of boulders on August 21 and 22, 1930, at Hamilton, I learned that in the morning the animals emerged from the dens within 10 minutes after the sun first struck the tops of the boulders. Only two animals, each a young of the year, were observed (and obtained) here.

The feces of marmots are characteristic and commonly are deposited on the tops of the boulders which serve as resting places. This sign, or lack of it, atop boulders, is a useful means of learning whether marmots are present or not in an area, even after they have gone into estivation.

Along Hot Creek we learned that marmots lived in just one of the piles of boulders, a huge hill of broken rock at the base of which a crevice was emitting air so cold that on this day, June 20, 1933, icicles hung there. At this time the animals were not in sight and the live individuals were said by Mr. Marl A.

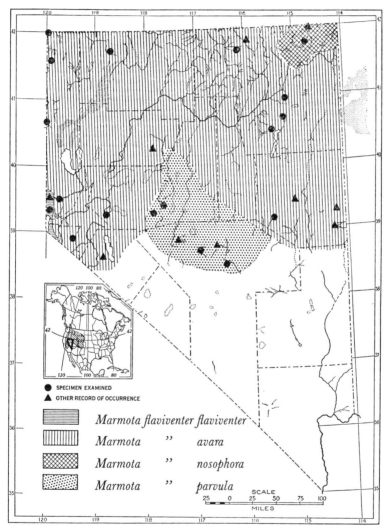

Fig. 192. Distribution of subspecies of the yellow-bellied marmot, *Marmota flaviventer*, with insert showing range of the species.

Page and Mr. Claude A. Page to be in estivation. In the preceding spring they said that they had shot and trapped twenty-three marmots. They found the desiccated carcasses of eight of these for us. Possibly the cold air emerging at the base of the rocks filtered through the pile and was an important factor in making this particular situation livable for the marmots.

On the basis of information recorded for this species in states other than Nevada, Howell (1915:12) gives the number of embryos as three to eight.

Marmota flaviventer flaviventer (Audubon and Bachman)
Yellow-bellied Marmot

Arctomys flaviventer Audubon and Bachman, Proc. Acad. Nat. Sci. Philadelphia, p. 99, 1841. Type from "Mountains between Texas and California." Fixed by Howell (N. Amer. Fauna, 37:39–40, April 7, 1915) as Mount Hood, Oregon.

[*Marmota*] *flaviventer*, Trouessart, Catal. Mamm., viv. foss., suppl., p. 344, 1904.

Marmota flaviventris flaviventris, Howell, N. Amer. Fauna, 37:39, April 7, 1915.

Distribution.—The Sierra Nevada in the vicinity of Lake Tahoe. See figure 192.

Remarks.—A male from 16 mi. W Bend, 6500 ft., Deschutes Co., Oregon, measures 600, 172, 80, 25, weight 1,942 grams. A female from Independence Lake, Nevada County, California, measured 575, 165, 85, and weighed 6¾ lbs. (3,062 grams).

Following the plan of description employed by Howell (1915:39), the coloration of a female from Independence Lake, California, may be described as follows: underfur of upper parts Deep Mouse Gray at base, succeeded by a broad band of buffy white, the latter shading on the hinder back to Pinkish Cinnamon or a darker shade, near Sayal Brown; long hairs Chestnut Brown or Clove Brown for basal three-fourths, then Light Buff on forepart of body and white on posterior part of body, except that the very tip of the hairs is black on all parts of the body; top of head and face Chestnut-Brown with buffy brown markings on face; sides of neck with large patches of Light Ochraceous-Buff; forelegs and feet Hazel; hind feet Light Ochraceous-Buff; tail Hazel; underparts mixed Ochraceous-Buff and Hazel; nose, chin, and lips whitish.

Individuals of this race average larger than those of any other. The skull is relatively narrow, although of large size, and the nasals project relatively far posteriorly to the premaxillae.

Intergradation with *avara*, the race to the eastward, is indicated by the specimens assigned to *avara* which, nevertheless, have the coloration of *flaviventer*. These are specimens from 3 miles east of Reno and one each from Mount Siegel and Winters Mine. The subspecific identity of marmots on Mount Grant is problematical. They might be *flaviventer*, but on the distribution map herewith are shown within the range of *avara*.

Records of occurrence.—Specimens examined, 4, from *Washoe Co.*: 3 mi. S Mt. Rose, 8500 ft., 3; 3 mi. SSW Mt. Rose, 9000 ft., 1.

Additional record: 1 mi. E Verdi (Hall, MS).

Marmota flaviventer avara (Bangs)
Yellow-bellied Marmot

Arctomys flaviventer avarus Bangs, Proc. New England Zoöl. Club, 1:68, July 31, 1899. Type from Okanagan, British Columbia.

[*Marmota flaviventer*] *avarus*, Trouessart, Catal. Mamm. viv. foss., suppl., p. 344, 1904.

Marmota flaviventris avara, Borell and Ellis, Journ. Mamm., 15:23, 73, February 15, 1934.

Marmota flaviventer, Taylor, Univ. California Publ. Zoöl., 7:211, June 24, 1911.

Distribution.—Over most of Nevada in suitable habitat north of latitude 38° 30', except in the Sierra Nevada, the central part of the state, and the northeastern corner. See figure 192.

Remarks.—Two males from the Ruby Mountains measure 640, 640; 180, 168; 78, 78. Two females from the same place measure 560, 515; 160, 130; 71, 70.

M. f. avara is of medium to small size and has relatively buffy-colored upper parts and light-colored underparts. Specimens from the Ruby Mountains differ from topotypes, as pointed out by Borell and Ellis (1934a:25), in slightly larger size, darker color above, especially over the shoulders, and more nearly flat skulls with slightly heavier rostra. The specimens from 3 miles east of Reno are not typical of *avara* in color but agree with *flaviventer*, although in size and in cranial features they agree with *avara*, to which race they here are referred. The two specimens from Douglas County have dark-colored underparts like those from 3 miles east of Reno, and in this particular agree with *flaviventer*. In size they seem to be more as in *flaviventer*, although each of the specimens from Douglas County is too young to show subspecific characters of the skull or those based on external measurements. The specimen from 16 miles south of Fallon, likewise, is a juvenile, and the specimens from northeastern Nevada also are young. The lack of fully adult (more than 2-year-old) specimens from several parts of the state prevents a satisfactory definition of ranges for the races concerned, although the material is more abundant than any lot previously assembled.

From *flaviventer*, *avara* differs in smaller size and lighter color, especially on underparts, and in the skull the nasals do not extend as far behind the premaxillae. Comparisons with *parvula* and *nosophora* have been made in the accounts of those forms.

Records of occurrence.—Specimens examined, 39, as follows: *Washoe Co.:* 12-mile Creek, 1 mi. E Calif. boundary, 5300 ft., 2; Barrel Spring, 5700 ft., 9½ mi. E and 3½ mi. N Ft. Bidwell, 1; 3 mi. W Vya, 6000 ft., 1; Smoke Creek, 4300 ft., Calif. boundary, 3; 4 2/5 mi. E Sparks, 1; 3 mi. E Reno, 4. *Douglas Co.:* Mt. Siegel, 1 (Field Mus. Nat. Hist.); Winters Mine, 1 (Field Mus. Nat. Hist.). *Humboldt Co.:* head of Big Creek, 8000 ft., Pine Forest Mts., 1 (piece of jaw). *Churchill Co.:* 16 mi. S Fallon, 4500 ft., 1. *Elko Co.:* 20 mi. S Owyhee, 3; head of Ackler Creek, 6800 ft., Ruby Mts., 12 (11 in coll. of Ralph Ellis); E base Ruby Mts., 10 mi. S Secret Pass, 2 (coll. of Ralph Ellis); Long Creek, 7830 ft., 4 (coll. of Ralph Ellis). *White Pine Co.:* ¼ mi. W Hamilton, 8200 ft., 2.

Additional records: *Pershing Co.:* Granite Mtn. (sign, Hall, MS). *Mineral Co.:* Mt. Grant (sign, Hall, MS). *Elko Co.:* Mountain City (Howell, 1915:45). *White Pine Co.:* Gleason Spring (sign, Hall, MS); Hendry Creek, 9100 ft., 1½ mi. E Mt. Moriah (seen, Lee R. Arnold, MS); ½ mi. N Treasury Lake, 12,200 ft. (sign, Alcorn, MS).

Marmota flaviventer nosophora Howell
Yellow-bellied Marmot

Marmota flaviventer nosophora Howell, Proc. Biol. Soc. Washington, 27:15, February 2, 1914. Type from Willow Creek, 4000 feet, 7 miles east of Corvallis, Ravalli County, Montana.

Distribution.—Northeastern corner of state. See figure 192.

Remarks.—Measurements (Howell, 1915:47) of three males, two from the Bitterroot Valley and one from the Pryor Mountains, in Montana, are 590, 600, 670; 159, 170, 165; 78, 79, 96. Howell (1915:47) gives corresponding measurements of seven females from the Bitterroot Valley of Montana as 565 (534–591); 165 (145–175); 78 (75–85).

The one specimen assigned to this race is a young male from 1 mile south of Contact. Reference to *nosophora* is made on the basis of the large auditory bullae and the conspicuous mantle of buff on the forepart of the back. In these features, characteristic of *nosophora*, the animal differs from other Nevadan specimens referred to *avara*. The specimen shows approach to *avara* in lighter color of the underparts and is notable for the extensively white face.

M. f. nosophora is said to differ from *engelhardti*, the race to the eastward, in longer tail and more ochraceous coloration above and below. These differences are not apparent in materials examined by me, and I wonder whether *nosophora* is distinct from *engelhardti*. From *avara*, *nosophora* differs in having darker-colored underparts, more often a buffy mantle over the anterior part of the back, and the auditory bullae averaging larger.

Record of occurrence.—Specimen examined: *Elko Co.:* 1 mi. S Contact, 4800 ft., 1.
Additional record: *Elko Co.:* Cedar Creek, 6000 ft., 10 mi. NE San Jacinto, where sign was noted (Hall, MS).

TABLE 5

CRANIAL MEASUREMENTS (IN MILLIMETERS) OF MARMOTA

Sex and age	Catalogue no.	Condylobasal length	Palatal length	Postpalatal length	Length of nasals	Zygomatic breadth	Breadth across mastoids	Least interorbital breadth	Breadth of rostrum	Maxillary tooth row
					Marmota f. flaviventer 16 mi. W Bend, Oregon					
♂	83590	88.6	52.3	32.2	39.4	60.7	41.3	20.9	23.5	19.2
					Independence Lake, California					
♀	11898	85.6	48.0	33.0	36.9	54.5	38.4	18.3	19.7	22.0
					Marmota f. avara† Head of Ackler Creek					
♂	6281	91.5	51.0	35.9	40.8	63.7	43.8	22.2	23.9	21.3
					Long Creek					
♀	5443	80.2	45.3	31.2	33.3	54.1	37.3	17.7	21.6	20.2
					Marmota f. nosophora Pocatello, Idaho					
♂	46529	90.3	51.5	35.1	40.0	59.2	44.5	20.5	21.8	22.0
					Craters of the Moon, Idaho					
♀ sad.	77895	79.7	44.7	30.8	32.5	53.0	37.7	17.8	19.4	19.0
					Marmota f. parvula W slope Toquima Peak					
♂	57476	89.6	51.0	35.5	40.0	61.0	42.0	19.0	23.3	20.1
					Jefferson					
♀	93690*	71.3	39.4	27.0	29.4	49.0	34.2	15.6	17.4	18.6

* After Howell (1915:56).   † Collection of Ralph Ellis.

Marmota flaviventer parvula Howell
Yellow-bellied Marmot

Marmota flaviventer parvula Howell, Proc. Biol. Soc. Washington, 27:14, February 2, 1914. Type from Jefferson, Nye County, Nevada.
Marmota flaviventris parvula Howell, N. Amer. Fauna, 37:44, April 7, 1915.
Marmota flaviventris, Linsdale, Amer. Midland Nat., 19:176, January, 1938.

Distribution.—In the Toyabe, Toquima, and Hot Creek ranges of central Nevada. See figure 192.

Remarks.—Measurements of a male from Toquima Mtn. (Peak) are 600, 165, 75, 30. Average and extreme measurements for three females from the Toyabe and Toquima ranges, as recorded by Howell (1915:45), are 480 (470–500); 141 (130–150); 70.

This race is characterized by the original describer as being of small size and darker color and having a narrower rostrum than in the race *avara*. The original series of specimens may be animals only 2 years old. The one specimen available at this writing, a practical topotype from Toquima Peak, is more than 2 years old; it is fully adult. In measurements it falls within the range of variation shown by males assigned to *avara* from the Ruby Mountains, but is not so large as the largest old male from there. Also, this topotype of *parvula* has darker-colored underparts, especially on the chest and under the chin, and in this respect is intermediate between the race *flaviventer* with dark-colored underparts and the race *avara* with lighter-colored underparts. Clearly, additional specimens more than 2 years old are needed to show if animals from the area of distribution assigned to *parvula* really are smaller than individuals of *avara*, and, if so, by how much. With the evidence available it seems best to treat *parvula* as a recognizable race. From *fortirostris* to the southwest, *parvula* is said to differ in having the nasals and posterior extensions of the premaxillae on the dorsal surface of the skull narrower, the entire rostrum and frontal region narrower, the incisors smaller, over-all size less, and coloration lighter. In size and color *parvula* differs in the same way, but more markedly from *sierrae* and *flaviventer* to the westward. Also, the skull is smaller than in *flaviventer*. From *avara* to the northward, *parvula* differs, on the average, in smaller size, darker color on the underparts, and smaller skull. From *nosophora* and *engelhardti* to the northeast and east, respectively, *parvula* differs in smaller size, lighter-colored underparts, and smaller auditory bullae.

Records of occurrence.—Specimens examined, 11, as follows: *Churchill Co.:* Eastgate, 1 (skin only) (coll. of J. R. Alcorn). *Lander Co.:* Smiths Creek, 7500 ft., 1 (broken skull only). *Nye Co.:* W slope Toquima Mtn. [= Peak], 10,000 ft., 1; Hot Creek Canyon, 6 mi. W Hot Creek P. O., Hot Creek Range, 8 (fractured skulls only).
Additional records (Howell, 1915:45): *Nye Co.:* Arc Dome, Toyabe Range; Jefferson. Reported to Hall from Monitor Range.

Genus **Citellus** Oken
Ground Squirrels and Spermophiles

The seven full species (thirteen subspecies) of this genus in Nevada include both plain-colored and striped kinds. Those with stripes are members of the subgenera *Ammospermophilus* and *Callospermophilus*. They differ in color pattern from the chipmunks (genera *Tamias* and *Eutamias*), with which they sometimes are confused, in that there are no stripes on the sides of the head. The dental formula is i. $\frac{1}{1}$, c. $\frac{0}{0}$, p. $\frac{2}{1}$, m. $\frac{3}{3}$. Skulls of *Citellus* are markedly less flattened than those of the much larger *Marmota*, have the postorbital process of the frontal projecting backward and downward to a greater degree, and the upper incisors are more compressed laterally and are more nearly flat on the anterior faces. From *Sciurus* and *Glaucomys*, *Citellus* differs in that the brain case is shallower, the zygomata are more contracted anteriorly, and the anterior portion of each zygoma is twisted toward a horizontal plane. From *Eutamias*, *Citellus* differs in having an infraorbital canal as opposed to an infraorbital foramen. Also, in *Citellus*, the anterior border of the zygomatic notch in the maxillary is opposite M1, rather than P4. Details of the skulls are shown in the illustrations below and are referred to in the key. To date, much the best exposition of the cranial differences and similarities between the genera of squirrels is that given by A. H. Howell (1938:34–52), to which the special student of sciurids will wish to refer for detailed characters of the teeth, skull, and baculum.

Citellus townsendii
Townsend Ground Squirrel

Two races of this species are known from Nevada. It is the smallest member of the subgenus *Citellus* which includes, of Nevadan species, *Citellus beldingi* and *Citellus richardsonii*. Distinctive features of *C. townsendii* include, in addition to small size (see measurements under subspecies), tail usually less than a third of the length of the head and body, hind foot less than 40 mm. (in Nevadan animals), gray-colored upper parts and whitish underparts, sometimes with a wash of cinnamon on the upper parts and underside of the tail, and a skull, in specimens measured, with greatest length less than 41 mm.

The species inhabits principally the Upper Sonoran Life-zone. The upper limit of altitudinal range noted in Nevada is 6890 feet at Bells Ranch on the Reese River. This is near the junction of the Upper Sonoran and Transition life-zones.

Where the two species *Citellus townsendii* and *Citellus richardsonii* occur in the same area, as, for example, 1 to 4 miles upriver from Winnemucca, *richardsonii* occupies the meadowland and first bottom, whereas *townsendii* lives on the sagebrush-covered benches next above the first bottom. This same difference in local distribution between *townsendii* and *beldingi* appears to obtain wherever they occur in the same area. Russell and Richardson (MS) noted on May 18, 1936, along the Reese River, 7 miles north of Austin, that *townsendii* occurred among the dry sagebrush and along the road, whereas the burrows of *beldingi* were in the meadows. Here the difference in voices of the immature animals was noted. *C. townsendii* made a "single tinny squeak" usually after the animal had disappeared down its burrow, whereas young *beldingi* gave three or four notes "starting high and going down the scale" often while at the mouth of the burrow.

The habits of Nevadan *townsendii* have been carefully studied by Alcorn, and in his account (1940a:160–170) it is recorded:

"The Piute ground squirrel (*Citellus townsendii mollis*) takes its common name from the Piute Indians who have used it for food since the time of earliest accounts left by white men of Nevada and according to Indian legends for countless years before. I first became aware of the importance of these animals to the Indians when I was carrying on poisoning operations in the desert near a ranch east of Fallon, Nevada. An elderly Indian drove up in a dilapidated wagon. He was a large, heavy-set man, and at first glance I knew that he was 'on the war path.' The conversation between us began as follows:

"Indian: 'What you doin'?'

"J. R. A[lcorn]: 'We are killing squirrels.'

"Indian: 'Who tell 'um you to kill squirrels?'

"J. R. A.: 'Many ranchers have asked the government to kill the squirrels because they are doing damage to crops. My boss has given me instructions to do the work.'

"Indian: 'Me boss too, me chief. I tell 'um you stop now.'

"J. R. A.: 'I couldn't do that.'

"Indian: 'I get sheriff after you. You better stop now; today. It's agin th' law to kill 'um squirrels. My people starve without squirrels. . . .'

"Everything considered, it seemed best to stop operations. I summoned my ten C. C. C. assistants and we moved to another location to finish the day's work. Many of the boys, who were fresh from New York City, were much impressed by this first meeting with an Indian.

"In June of any year it is a common sight to see an old buggy, drawn by a small pony, laden with numerous containers for carrying water, one buck Indian and several squaws. Often the Indians have traveled for several hours from the Reservation to find a place where the squirrels are numerous and close to water. At this place the squaws carry water from a few to several hundred feet and pour several buckets-full into a burrow. The buck Indian catches, by the neck, the squirrel that is forced out of the hole. If the squirrel is thin it is usually turned loose; if fat it is either killed or placed alive in a sack or box. Sometimes the squirrels are eaten within a few hours after they are killed; but Indians often take live squirrels many miles to trade or sell to other Indians.

"In June, 1937, I came upon two Indians who had several hundred live squirrels in the back of an old automobile. These two men, about twenty-four years of age, and obviously of some education, said that they themselves did not eat the squirrels, but had caught them to take to Pyramid Lake, fifty-five miles away. There they would sell the squirrels to other Indians for ten cents each or three for twenty-five cents. These two Indians said they had made from five to twenty dollars a day in this way. According to them the 'old timers' were better customers than younger Indians.

"The younger generation of Indians who eat these squirrels usually dress them and use modern methods to cook them but the 'old timers' do not. These old Indians bury the squirrels in hot coals. After the hair has burned off, the squirrel appears to be burned so much as to be unfit for food. However, when it is taken out of the fire one finds that only the skin is burned and that the meat and fat, the only parts eaten, are nicely roasted. I have eaten squirrels prepared in this way and in the modern way. Prepared by either method they are of good flavor and so fat as certainly to be highly nourishing.

"It is possible that Indians for generations have taken squirrels of this species from one valley to another and there liberated them in an effort to insure a stable food supply. In this manner the Piute ground squirrel may have come to occupy a range of larger size than it normally would have had.

"Close observation of these squirrels in the territory within ten miles of Fallon, Nevada, was undertaken in the spring of 1936 and continued into the summer of 1939. For part of this time I was supervising control measures directed at this squirrel by the United States Bureau of Reclamation in cooperation with the United States Bureau of Biological Survey, employing poisoned rolled oats distributed by C. C. C. enrollees. For the remainder of the time, I made observations in connection with work on my own ranch.

"HIBERNATION AND AESTIVATION"

"The squirrels emerge from hibernation in February while the weather is still severe. The earliest dates on which they were found active in four consecutive years are as follows:

Feb. 13, 1936. Four animals were seen when the weather was cloudy and when the extremes of temperature for the twenty-four hour period were 30 degrees and 53 degrees Fahrenheit.

Feb. 21, 1937. Eight animals were seen when the weather was clear and the extremes of temperature for the twenty-four hour period were 21 degrees and 50 degrees.

Feb. 14, 1938. Twelve animals were seen, when the weather was cloudy, a few hours after a trace of snow had fallen. Extremes of temperature for the day were 20 degrees and 43 degrees.

Feb. 15, 1939. Three animals were seen when the weather was partly cloudy and extremes of temperature for the day were 31 degrees and 48 degrees.

"Male squirrels emerge from hibernation before the females. Examination of individuals that had recently come out of hibernation, revealed fat in the abdominal cavity of the males whereas the females had little or no fat. Of eight shot on February 14, 1938, all were males; five poisoned on February 17, comprised three males and two females; nine shot on February 27 were males; twenty-three shot on March 3 comprised 17 males and six females; March 7, nine animals comprised five males and four females; March 9, 24 animals comprised 17 males and seven females. Additional information gathered in 1939 is in line with that just given for 1938.

"The time of year when these squirrels go into aestivation appears to be directly correlated with the amount of food available. In years when there is a normal supply of food, the males, for instance, become remarkably fat within a period of approximately 120 days after emergence, at the end of which time they go into aestivation.When food is scarce they... remain active [longer]. ...

"One male kept in captivity was not given food enough to become very fat. Instead of aestivating, when others kept in captivity did, he continued feeding for 40 days more, at the end of which time he escaped by gnawing a hole in the screen of the cage.

"Also, on several occasions, I have captured squirrels in the fall months after most of the animals were below ground and have found that these squirrels had no visible fat. My suggestion is that they are physiologically, as well as physically, not ready to hibernate because they lack sufficient fat.

"In contrast to the males, which ordinarily require about 120 days to become fat, the females and juveniles are usually active about 135 days before they become fat enough to aestivate.

"Once these squirrels go into aestivation, they normally stay underground for 7½ to 8 months before emerging in the following spring. If, however, the food supply is not sufficient to fatten the squirrel in 120 to 135 days, it may stay out longer, or may emerge for a time in the autumn after only a short period of aestivation.

"The young of both sexes also fatten later than do the adult males, and, although they may not be full grown, they usually go into aestivation about the same time as the females, namely, in the first week of July. Although females that do not bear young fatten early, I do not know whether or not they go into aestivation as soon as the males. A person with a little experience is usually able to distinguish a male from a female in the period from April 15 until the squirrels go into aestivation. The males then are much fatter and, in the latter part of June, if pursued by a person on foot, they appear to have difficulty in running, which probably results from the large accumulation of fat. The females do not appear to accumulate as much fat as the males. They are especially active if pursued by a person on foot.

"REPRODUCTION AND FLUCTUATION IN NUMBERS"

"Records of breeding habits for the year 1938 will now be described, because for that year they are the most complete that I have. Breeding apparently began between the fifth and twentieth of March. Evidence of this is shown by the enlargement of the uterine horns, observed at this time but not before.

"The horns of the uterus in the inactive period are approximately one millimeter in diameter, whitish in color, and flexible. About the time breeding begins, these tubes become inflated and have the consistency of sponge rubber. I do not know if the enlargement of these tubes indicates that implantation has occurred. After these tubes are inflated, enlargements, indicating developing embryos, appear in them. At one of these enlargements the uterine tube is approximately two millimeters in diameter. It is firm, almost hard, and white in color.

"On March 9, 1938, out of seven females shot, one had ten embryos and six had enlarged uterine horns. The presence of embryos in this one female was, for this year, the earliest evidence obtained that implantation had occurred. Of the many females whose reproductive tracts were studied in the breeding season of 1938, all of those examined on five selected dates are as follows:

Mar. 16, 1938. 9 embryos, 2 mm. diam.	Mar. 31, 1938. 8 embryos, 14 mm. diam.
"　　"　　"　　uterine horns enlarged	"　　"　　"　　13　　"　　14 mm. diam.
"　　"　　"　　10 embryos, 10 mm. diam.	"　　"　　"　　11　　"　　5 mm. diam.
"　　"　　"　　uterine horns enlarged	"　　"　　"　　10　　"　　5 mm. diam.
"　　"　　"　　"　　"　　"	"　　"　　"　　8　　"　　10 mm. diam.
"　　"　　"　　"　　"　　"	"　　"　　"　　9　　"　　21 mm. diam.
"　　"　　"　　10 embryos, 2 mm. diam.	"　　"　　"　　12　　"　　10 mm. diam.
"　　"　　"　　uterine horns enlarged	"　　"　　"　　11　　"　　7 mm. diam.
"　　"　　"　　"　　"　　"	"　　"　　"　　5　　"　　7 mm. diam.
"　　"　　"　　8 embryos, 2 mm. diam.	"　　"　　"　　14　　"　　17 mm. diam.
"　18,　"　　9 embryos, 2 mm. diam.	Apr.　8,　"　　16　　"　　19 mm. diam.
"　　"　　"　　uterine horns enlarged	"　　"　　"　　young already born
"　　"　　"　　12 embryos, 4 mm. diam.	"　　"　　"　　"　　"　　"
"　　"　　"　　10 embryos, 4 mm. diam.	"　　"　　"　　"　　"　　"
"　　"　　"　　uterine horns enlarged	"　　"　　"　　"　　"　　"
"　　"　　"　　"　　"　　"	"　　"　　"　　"　　"　　"
"　　"　　"　　11 embryos, 11 mm. diam.	"　　"　　"　　11 embryos, 13 mm. diam.
"　　"　　"　　9 embryos, 4 mm. diam.	"　9,　"　　young already born

"As indicating the length of the gestation period it may be pointed out that on March 16, 1938, implantation had occurred in 40 percent of the females and on March 18, in 60 percent. On April 8 and 9, 1938, 70 percent of the females already had given birth to young. This indicates that more than 20 days is required for gestation.

"By combining all of my figures (MS) from the sixteenth to the twentieth of March for the two years 1938 and 1939, I find that implantation, as indicated by the presence of small embryos, had previously occurred in 23 of the total of 45 females, or in 51 percent. Of eighteen females examined between April 8 and 12 inclusive, in 1938 and 1939, 13, or 72 percent, were suckling young. This suggests that the gestation period is about 24 days.

"Blind, pink, naked young squirrels, 15 in number, were found in a burrow excavated on April 8, 1937. About the same time (exact date not recorded) another nest, containing 17 young in the same stage of development, was found.

"Fewer young squirrels were produced in 1939 than in 1938, 1937, or 1936. On March 20, 1939, ten female squirrels were examined and only eight contained embryos. On April 12 and 18, 1939, ten female squirrels were examined and only two, or 20 percent, were suckling young; the other eight appeared to be barren. Further examination of 20 female squirrels in the later part of April, 1939, revealed that 60 percent were barren. It is not known why so few females bore young in 1939. In that year food conditions appeared to be normal and no extreme weather conditions were recorded.

"In 1937 and 1938, when the population of these squirrels was at its peak, the examination of 207 females showed that 90 percent produced young. Furthermore, the squirrel population was observed to be large in those years. For example, the distribution of strychnine-coated rolled oats on two measured acres, each judged to support an average-sized population, yielded 120 and 134 dead squirrels above ground. This was in April, when young of the year had become active above ground, but contrasted sharply with the smaller numbers found in similar work in 1939, on favorable areas not before treated with poisoned grain.

"During 1939, when the population of squirrels apparently was on the decrease, it is estimated that only about fifty percent of the females were producing young.

"The following summary, for 1938 and 1939, of pregnant females emphasizes the greater number of young per litter in 1938 than in 1939.

No. of embryos	5	6	7	8	9	10	11	12	13	14	15
1938, no. females examined	1	3	3	10	20	23	16	15	5	1	1
1939, no. females examined	2	5	10	16	10	3	1	1			

"The average number of embryos was ten (17 pregnant females) in 1937; ten (98 pregnant females) in 1938; and only eight (48 pregnant females) in 1939.

"In the examination of hundreds of these female squirrels, only a few embryos were found dead. Although no definite figures were kept in this regard, my estimate, from memory alone, is one-half of one percent. It was noted also that an embryo seldom died after it was half developed. Most dead embryos were approximately four millimeters in diameter.

"ACTIVITY OF YOUNG"

"The young, born naked and blind, live in the burrow with their mother until about two-thirds grown. The mother nurses them up to the time when, and sometime after, they are able to leave the burrow and forage for themselves. The young may be seen thrusting their heads out of the burrow about May 1. After several days of viewing the world from the entrance of the burrow, they venture out, gradually increasing the distance they wander in search of food, until they are able to travel as much as a hundred feet and still find their way back home. Many of the young squirrels on their first few trips from the burrow get lost and start squeaking. General observations lead me to believe that many of these lost young find their way back to their burrows unaided. Although I have watched for it, I never have seen any response from a female to the squeaking cries of the young.

"The young continue to suckle even after they have learned to eat green vegetation. This is shown by the following observation. On May 12, 1939, one mile north of Fallon, at 11:45 a.m., I saw, from a distance of fifty feet, a female squirrel standing erect supporting herself with her tail. This is the customary way for these squirrels to stand when watching or looking for an intruder. As she was standing thus, eight young squirrels were attempting to suckle her. Four of them appeared to be sucking on the four lowest teats while the other young attempted to nudge these four away. At 1 p.m. I placed carbon bisulphide in the main burrow and auxiliary burrow inhabited by this family. On excavating the burrows I found nine young, seven of which were females, dead in the main burrow. The stomach of each of them contained green vegetation.

"The nest was made of fibers from under the bark of a cottonwood tree, felled approximately thirty feet away. These young squirrels appeared to be about the same size as other young squirrels then appearing above ground. The total combined weight of these nine juveniles was 11 ounces. The adult female weighed 5½ ounces.

"By the middle of June, most of the young have either found an old burrow to occupy or have dug a new one. Only one young occupies a burrow. At this time they may be seen carrying dry grass and other loose material for a nest.

"The males appear to take no part in caring for the young. They obtain sufficient food to become fat enough to go into aestivation by the last week in June. The females with young expend much energy in producing and suckling their offspring. Possibly it is this expenditure of energy that delays accumulation of fat by the females until after the young have been weaned. Evidence in support of this possibility is furnished by my examination of 52 squirrels in this month. The males, on the average, were fatter than the females, and large accumulations of fat were to be noted in the abdominal cavity of each male examined.

"FAMILY AND INDIVIDUAL RELATIONS"

"Twenty-five inhabited burrows in all were excavated in the months of March and April. Each contained only one squirrel. In this period many squirrels were seen fighting. After the young had established themselves in individual burrows many of them, too, were seen fighting. On about a score of occasions, especially in 1938, I found small squirrels, only a few days old, partly eaten and often still squirming, lying at the entrance of a burrow. Once I saw an adult, at the entrance of a burrow, eating one of two young squirrels. Then within a minute's time or less another adult appeared from fifty feet to the north and immediately attacked the adult that was eating the young. A battle ensued. A shot from my gun killed both contestants. The adult that was eating the two young squirrels was a male, the other a female. Perhaps the male had gone into the female's burrow while she was away and had stolen the young. On several other occasions I saw adult squirrels eating young. In each instance evidence pointed to an adult of their own kind as responsible for the killing. The young squirrels eaten were only a few days old; their eyes were not yet opened.

"Although many of my field observations have shown these squirrels to be intolerant of others of their kind, the squirrels that I have kept in captivity appear to be sociable. Two males, three females, and one juvenile judged to be about twenty days old were all placed in a cage that was six feet long, four feet wide, and two feet deep, with one small box, one foot square, inside this cage for a nest. These squirrels, in captivity for six weeks, ate apples, rolled oats, meat, alfalfa, and four or five kinds of weeds. All slept in the same nest in the box and I saw no intolerance toward one another.

"BURROWS"

"The following table gives some information about a number of burrows that were excavated on wild land.

DIMENSIONS (IN CENTIMETERS) OF BURROWS OF *Citellus townsendii mollis* EXCAVATED 4 TO 8 MI. W OF FALLON, CHURCHILL CO., NEVADA

Date excavated	Length of burrow	Greatest depth of burrow	Greatest diameter of burrow	Number of openings	Depth below ground of nest	Diameter of nest chamber	Kind of soil	Number of auxiliary burrows
Home burrows of adults								
May 12, 1939	292	60.0	7.5	3	27.0	18.0	clay	1
May 1939	317	56.8	9.5	1	56.8	20.0	clay	1
May 1939	700	83.0	10.0	2	80.5	19.0	sand	?
May 18, 1939	1197	146.5	13.0	2	146.5	25.0	sand	3
May 19, 1939	1742	117.0	15.0	3	103.0	20.2	sand	?
May 19, 1939	642	117.0	10.0	2	92.6	19.4	sand	?
Auxiliary burrows at feeding places								
May 12, 1939	72.5	30.6	7.0	1	No nest		clay	—
June 1939	78.6	45.0	10.0	1	" "		clay	—
June 1938	78.6	38.1	10.0	1	" "		sand	—
April 1937	92.7	40.3	8.0	1	" "		sand	—
Home burrows of young								
June 1937	233.6	58.6	8.0	1	58.4	17.0	clay	none
June 1938	262.8	72.5	7.0	1	72.5	18.5	clay	none
June 1937	292.0	72.5	7.0	1	58.4	17.0	sand	none
June 1939	448.8	78.6	7.0	1	72.5	20.0	sand	none

"Three classes of burrows may be recognized: The main burrow of the adults, the main burrow of the young, and the auxiliary burrows used by both adults and young. As may be seen from the table, the burrow of one adult may extend for more than 50 feet. Many are 5 feet deep and have more than one opening.

"The auxiliary burrows are used only as places in which to hide and are usually dug close to good feeding grounds. Where the adult leaves the main burrow and goes more than 50 feet to forage, a well beaten path usually connects the opening of the main tunnel with that of the auxiliary tunnel. On leaving the main tunnel, the squirrel commonly goes directly to this auxiliary burrow, and there, after satisfying itself that all is well, begins to feed nearby. On being alarmed, the squirrel gives a shrill, short whistle as it runs to this burrow and sits up to see if danger has passed. Other squirrels in the vicinity on hearing the whistle of alarm run to their burrows. If a person approaches at this time, the squirrel may again give a short whistle denoting alarm and run into the auxiliary burrow. These burrows are seldom over 5 feet long. They have only one opening and no nest chamber.

"A main burrow of a juvenile squirrel seldom has more than one opening and its depth and extent are much less than in an adult's burrow. Home burrows of juveniles may be distinguished from the auxiliary burrows in that they usually contain a nest.

"In burrowing in sand near Fallon, the squirrels often encounter a hard stratum of clay from one-half to three or more inches in thickness at a depth of four or five feet. The major portion of the burrow often follows under this stratum of clay which prevents sand from caving into the burrow and nest chamber.

"Burrows dug into canal banks and in cultivated fields usually have one opening and are much shorter than those dug on the desert in sandy soil. A burrow dug in a good location and not molested may be cleaned out and used year after year, with the addition of a new nest chamber.

"During the time the female is suckling young, the tunnel within two or three feet of the nest chamber is often very dirty. Droppings and other waste materials collect in this vicinity, and many worms, insects, and larvae may be found in this unclean mixture. The insects included three kinds of histerid beetles and larvae of at least three kinds of flies (Diptera). On several occasions, in removing a new nest, decomposed young squirrels were found in the soil immediately underneath.

"The nests themselves also contained many insects. Those identified were numerous adult flies (family Miscidae), fleas (Siphonaptera), and what appeared to be mites. In many burrows, cave crickets (order Orthoptera, subfamily Rhaphidophorinae) and ants (family Formicidae) were found.

"The nests are made of whatever convenient material is closest to the burrow. On the desert where bunch grass (*Oryzopsis hymenoides*) is common, the nests were usually made of it. The bark of black sagebrush (*Artemisia tridentata*) was often used. Many bushes of this plant were completely cleaned of all loose bark from the ground up to as far as the squirrels could reach or climb. Juniper posts are used by ranchers in this district. When the loose bark has not previously been removed from the posts, the squirrels often take it as far from the ground as they are able to reach.

"SWIMMING AND CLIMBING"

"It is common knowledge among ranchers of the area about Fallon that these squirrels voluntarily swim across canals that are from ten to twenty feet wide. In the past four years, I have seen scores of squirrels, both old and young, swimming across the canals in this locality. On May 19, 1936, I was sitting on the bank of a canal watching a squirrel on the opposite side. The canal was full of water but there was little current. The squirrel entered the water and swam the twenty feet toward me. Apparently he did not know I was there until I captured him as he started up the bank on which I sat. He was fairly fat and apparently in good condition.

"To obtain food, nest material, or a better view, these squirrels often climb into the tops of bushes. I have seen many on fences made of wire netting, apparently attempting to see over the top of the grass. They are unable to climb a fence post that is set at right angles with the surface of the ground but they climb to the tops of posts that lean at an angle of forty-five degrees.

"FOOD"

"These squirrels subsist mainly on green vegetation, a predilection that explains their habit of concentrating around fields of alfalfa and growing grain. Here they burrow into the high ground near the supply of green food. They attack the crops at the edges of the fields. Around both alfalfa and grain fields, a marginal strip several hundred feet in width may be destroyed. Sprouting corn is also dug up and eaten. They are voracious eaters and their stomachs are kept full all day. The greatest amount of food is consumed in early morning when these animals are most active. These squirrels also eat members of their own species that are killed by automobiles, sometimes carrying the crushed body of one of these dead squirrels to a place of safety before feeding on it.

"ENEMIES"

"The ground squirrels are preyed on most heavily in the period from May 15 to July 1. During this period the juvenile squirrels apparently have not learned to recognize their enemies; at this time I have seen prairie falcons, Swainson hawks, red-tailed hawks, and rough-legged hawks catch them with seeming ease. Eleven Swainson hawks collected in June of 1937 and 1938 had Piute squirrels in their crops. Seven red-tailed hawks that were collected in June 1937 also had Piute squirrels in their crops. On several occasions, when gopher snakes were killed, examination revealed juvenile squirrels in their stomachs. Once I saw a weasel carrying a squirrel across a road. In November, 1937, while attempting to dig out a badger, I came upon fresh remains of three squirrels in the burrow. I do not know how badgers are able to find squirrels that are in hibernation; but I judge from signs that they dig out and eat many in winter.

"LOCAL MIGRATIONS"

"In an attempt to learn about local migrations, we exterminated all squirrels, as far as possible, on a cultivated field of 40 acres and on each side for one quarter of a mile back from the field. This field was surrounded by desert and there was no other ranch nearer than two miles. The animals were killed by placing strychnine-coated rolled oats in runways and at entrances to burrows. After several days, carbon bisulphide was placed in burrows that showed signs of having live occupants. No. 1½ Victor steel traps were set at some burrows.

"I estimated that there were thirty squirrels to the acre on the area before poisoning operations began and that at the end of the period of ten days, in which extermination was carried on, there was one animal per acre. Squirrels from the surrounding territory moved in on all the area and ten days after poisoning was discontinued I estimated eight squirrels to the acre. Fifteen days later (25 days after poisoning stopped), on July 15, 1939, I estimated 15 squirrels per acre. These observations show that at the season of greatest population-density, in a year when the species was only a little below the peak in numbers, some squirrels in a ten-day period travel a quarter of a mile or more."

Citellus townsendii canus (Merriam)
Townsend Ground Squirrel

Spermophilus mollis canus Merriam, Proc. Biol. Soc. Washington, 12:70, March 24, 1898. Type from Antelope, Wasco County, Oregon.
Citellus townsendii canus, Howell, N. Amer. Fauna, 56–67, May 18, 1938.
Citellus mollis, Taylor, Univ. California Publ. Zoöl., 7:216, June 24, 1911 (part).

Distribution.—In the northwestern corner of the state in the Upper Sonoran Life-zone. See figure 193.

Remarks.—Measurements of ten adults (Howell, 1938:67), presumably including both sexes, from Antelope, Gateway, and Prineville, Oregon, are 201 (190–217); 39 (37–42); 30.7 (29–33). No weights are available.

The size is small, the tail and hind foot being shorter than in the next described race, *mollis*, although the color is about the same as described for the gray phase of that subspecies. The skull, according to Howell (1938:67), in comparison with that of *mollis*, is shorter and relatively broader; zygomata more widely spreading; bullae averaging smaller; rostrum relatively short and broad. The seven available specimens from Nevada referred to this race by Howell comprise six immature individuals and one adult lacking external measurements and accompanied by only fragments of the skull. The assignment of these specimens to the race *canus* is in accordance with Howell's views; inadequate material prevents me from making an independent appraisal of the status of this race.

Records of occurrence.—Specimens examined, 7, as follows: *Washoe Co.:* Long Valley Ranch, 1 (coll. of U. S. Biol. Surv. Dist. Agent, Reno). *Humboldt Co.:* Hot Spring, Thousand Creek, 4300 ft., 3; Virgin Valley, 3.

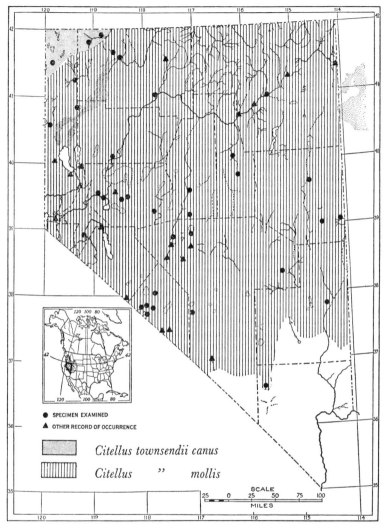

Fig. 193. Distribution of subspecies of the Townsend ground squirrel, *Citellus townsendii*, with insert showing range of the species.

Citellus townsendii mollis (Kennicott)
Townsend Ground Squirrel

Spermophilus mollis Kennicott, Acad. Nat. Sci. Philadelphia, 1863:157. Type from Camp Floyd, near Fairfield, Utah County, Utah.

Citellus townsendii mollis, Howell, N. Amer. Fauna, 56:63, May 18, 1938; Alcorn, Journ. Mamm., 21:160–170, 218, May 14, 1940.

Spermophilus mollis stephensi Merriam, Proc. Biol. Soc. Washington, 12:69, March 24, 1898. Type from Queen Station, near head of Owens Valley, Mineral County, Nevada.

[*Citellus*] *mollis*, Trouessart, Catal. Mamm. viv. foss., suppl., p. 339, 1904.

Citellus mollis, Taylor, Univ. California Publ. Zoöl., 7:216, June 24, 1911 (part); Linsdale, Amer. Midland Nat., 19:179, January, 1938.
Citellus mollis mollis, Bailey, N. Amer. Fauna, 55:154, August 29, 1936.
Citellus mollis stephensi, Burt, Trans. San Diego Soc. Nat. Hist., 7:405, May 31, 1934.
Citellus mollis washoensis Merriam, Proc. Biol. Soc.'Washington, 26:138, May 21, 1913. Type from Carson Valley [Douglas County ?], Nevada.

Distribution.—Typically Upper Sonoran Life-zone, but ranging into Lower Sonoran Life-zone from northwestern Clark County northward over all but the northwestern "corner" of the state. See figure 193.

Remarks.—Six males and six females, all in the gray phase, from within 6 miles of Fallon, measure: ♂, 236 (227–257), ♀, 228 (223–235); 51 (47–54), 51 (45–56); 36.0 (35–39), 34.5 (33–36). Two adult males in May weighed 313 and 215 grams, and an adult female in May, nursing young, weighed 190 grams. Eight males, on February 14, 1938, shortly after they had emerged from hibernation, averaged 185 grams (6½ ounces, with extremes of 5¼ and 8¾). When fat enough to begin estivation the weight is greater than that given above. Five males and six females, taken July 2, 1935, 1 to 4 miles northeast of Winnemucca, all were less than a year old. The males averaged 178 grams (229 mm. in total length) and the females 151 grams (211 mm. in total length).

Above, the coat is Smoke Gray, resulting from black-tipped overhairs having a wide subterminal band of light buff. A few of the overhairs above lack the buffy band. The nose and front of the face are Clay Color, the sides of head and body often washed with Pinkish Buff, the eyelids creamy white or Pinkish Buff, the front feet Pinkish Buff, the hind feet more whitish, thighs washed with Pinkish Cinnamon, and the tail strongly colored above and below with some shade of cinnamon, often with a white edge on the slightly flattened tail. As noted by Davis (1939:191), the terminal hairs of the tail have seven indistinct alternate light and dark bands of color. The underparts are whitish. The above description applies to what most writers term the "gray phase." The "buff phase" is described as having the upper parts strongly washed with Pinkish Buff. I have seen no specimens from Nevada referable to the buff phase, but in one area of about 16 square miles northwest of Soda Lake, Churchill County, Alcorn (1940b:218) notes that "ninety percent of the animals seen in the field appeared to be albinistic, though on close examination their eyes could be seen to be pigmented."

Concerning the albinistic color phase of squirrels, Alcorn goes on to say: "The pelage of squirrels in this limited area is of many varying shades of 'smoke gray' (Ridgway, Color Standards and Color Nomenclature, 1912). The guard hairs on all specimens handled were black for the full length of the hair. These black hairs help to give the light-colored squirrels a smoky gray color; if their guard hairs were removed, many individuals would be white. However, of about forty light-colored squirrels examined each had a brown supraorbital patch; the tail was wood brown, lighter on the dorsal surface. Possibly the pale color of the squirrels is protective; at any rate it closely matches the color of the soil in this restricted area."

Compared with topotypes of *mollis*, mostly animals less than a year old, the majority of the Nevadan specimens are slightly darker on the upper parts. When all of our specimens are assembled, it is found that the number of fully adult individuals, those more than 1 year old, are too few to allow of certain decision whether the names *washoensis* and *stephensi* are based on populations which differ from the earlier-named *mollis*. Except for the slightly darker color in many specimens which might be referred to *washoensis*, no constant differences have been detected. Therefore, in accordance with the arrangement proposed by Howell (1938:63), who examined nearly all of our material as well as additional specimens, the subspecific name *mollis* is applied to all of the squirrels of this species in Nevada, except those in the northwest corner of the state that are referred to the race *canus*.

Records of occurrence.—Specimens examined, 93, as follows: *Washoe Co.:* mouth of Little High Rock Canyon, 5000 ft., 1; 3 mi. E and 10 mi. N Gerlach, 4000 ft., 1; Smoke Creek, 3900 ft., 1. *Lyon Co.:* highway between Yerington and Wellington, 1. *Humboldt Co.:* Big Creek Ranch, Pine Forest Mts., 4350 ft., 4; Quinn River Crossing, 4100 ft., 17; 3 mi. NE Winnemucca, 4700 ft., 9; 1 mi. N Winnemucca, 4600 ft., 2. *Churchill Co.:* 3 mi. NW Soda Lake, 1; 7 mi. W and 1 mi. N Fallon, 4000 ft., 10; 1 mi. N Soda Lake, 4; 1 mi. NW Soda Lake, 1; 1 mi. N Fallon, 3; 5 mi. W Fallon, 2; 4 mi. W Fallon, 3; 1½ mi. SW Fallon, 1; 6 mi. E Stillwater, 3950 ft., 2; 5 mi. W Mountain Well, 4900 ft., 1; 2 mi. SE Eastgate, 1. *Esmeralda Co.:* 2½ mi. NW Blair Junction, 4950 ft., 1; 3 mi. N The Crossing, 5000 ft., 1; Chiatovich Ranch, 4900 ft., 1; Cave Spring, 6248 ft., 1; Fish Lake, 4800 ft., 2; Fish Lake Valley, 5300 ft., T. 6 S, R. 38 E, 1. *Lander Co.:* Reese River Valley, 7 mi. N Austin, 2; mouth of Kingston Canyon, 6000 ft., 1. *Eureka Co.:* Winzell, 1; 4 mi. S Romano, Diamond Valley, 2. *Nye Co.:* 5 mi. SE Millett P. O., 5500 ft., 1; Bells Ranch, Reese River, 6890 ft., 1; White River Valley, 15 mi. WSW Sunnyside, 1; 7½ mi. E Goldfield, 5700 ft., 1. *Elko Co.:* 3 mi. W Halleck, 4 (coll. of Ralph Ellis). *White Pine Co.:* Steptoe Valley, 9 mi. S Schellbourne, 6150 ft., 1; 1 mi. N Baker, 1; 2½ mi. E Baker, 5700 ft., 2; Spring Valley, 7 mi. SW Osceola, 6100 ft., 1. *Lincoln Co.:* 1 mi. W Panaca, 4700 ft., 1. *Clark Co.:* Indian Springs, 3280 ft., 1 (D. R. Dickey Coll.).

Additional records (unless otherwise noted, from Howell, 1938:64–65): *Washoe Co.:* Granite Creek; Virginia Mts.; Pyramid Lake; Nixon; Winnemucca Lake; Wadsworth. *Ormsby Co.:* Carson. *Humboldt Co.:* Paradise. *Churchill Co.:* Stillwater. *Mineral Co.:* 7 mi. NW Walker Lake (Hall, MS); Queen. *Esmeralda Co.:* Palmetto; Summit (= summit on road from Lida to Pigeon Spring, 4¾ mi. by air line SW of Lida, 7400 ft. elevation); Mount Magruder (Sugar Loaf Peak). *Nye Co.:* Indian Creek (near head); Round Mountain; Cloverdale; Peavine Creek; Springdale. *Elko Co.:* Tecoma, ¼ mi. W Utah boundary (Hall, MS); Metropolis; Elko; Carlin.

Citellus richardsonii nevadensis Howell
Richardson Ground Squirrel

Citellus elegans nevadensis Howell, Proc. Biol. Soc. Washington, 41:211, December 18, 1928. Type from Paradise, Humboldt County, Nevada. Borell and Ellis, Journ. Mamm., 15:26, February 15, 1934 (part); Bailey, N. Amer. Fauna, 55:159, August 29, 1936.

Citellus richardsonii nevadensis Howell, N. Amer. Fauna, 56-77, May 18, 1938.

Distribution.—Northeastern Nevada west to Winnemucca and south to Diamond Valley. See figure 194.

Remarks.—One adult and two subadult males, from within 3 miles of Winnemucca, measure 291, 293, 318; 80, 85, 100; 46, 46, 49; weight in grams, 286, 297, 411. Two females, a subadult from 13 mi. SSW Whiterock and an adult from Diamond Valley, measure 295, 315; 80, 85; 45, 45; weight in grams, 345.5, 393.

Upper parts Smoke Gray with Cinnamon Buff on some hairs, giving a dappled effect; underparts Cinnamon Buff or lighter; feet Pinkish Buff; eye ring buffy white; nose Mikado Brown to Pinkish Cinnamon; tail above blackish, mixed with Fuscous or some shade of cinnamon, but below Ochraceous-Buff in adults and at all ages with buffy-white border. Terminal hairs of tail with from five to seven alternately light and dark bands.

Of the four named races of this species, *nevadensis* is the "grayest," largest, and has the widest cheek teeth. It is noteworthy that its range appears not to meet that of the subspecies *elegans* to the east or *aureus* to the north. *C. r. elegans* also appears to have an area of distribution which does not meet that of any other race. A large area of central and southeastern Idaho, central Wyoming, and northern Utah separates the ranges of the three subspecies *nevadensis*, *aureus*, and *elegans*. This and related information led Davis (1939:51), as I see it, correctly to think that the species *richardsonii* at an earlier time occupied a nearly continuous range much of which now has been usurped by the ecologically similar species *beldingi* and *armatus*. The present distribution of *armatus* and *beldingi*, Davis thought, indicates that they are recent immigrants to the area now separating the ranges of the three races of *richardsonii*. Summed up, the evidence is that *nevadensis* is an isolated race of a species that in a sense is relict.

The Richardson ground squirrel in Nevada is apt to be confused only with the Townsend ground squirrel and the Belding ground squirrel. Compared with the latter, *C. richardsonii nevadensis* averages larger, has a relatively as well as actually longer tail, more cinnamon color on the nose and underparts, and an Ochraceous-Buff rather than reddish color on the under side of the tail. In the skull the interorbital breadth is less relative to the length of the skull, and the nasals are longer relative to the breadth of the cranium, if comparison is made with the subspecies *C. b. crebrus*. From the Townsend ground squirrel,

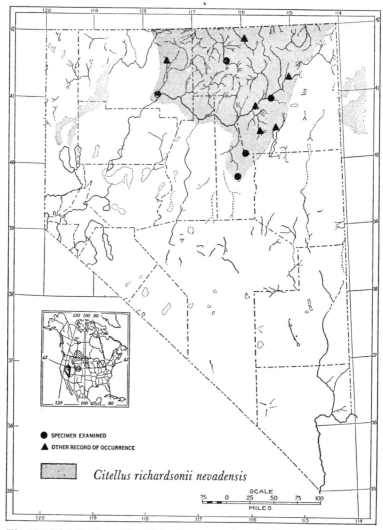

SPECIMEN EXAMINED

OTHER RECORD OF OCCURRENCE

Citellus richardsonii nevadensis

SCALE
25   0   25   50   75   100
MILES

Fig. 194. Distribution of the Richardson ground squirrel, *Citellus richardsonii*, with insert showing range of the species.

nevadensis differs in larger size, relatively and actually longer tail, cinnamon-colored rather than whitish underparts, and tail with, rather than without, the buffy-white border. In adult skulls the interorbital breadth is about the same as the length of the maxillary tooth row, but in *mollis* the length of the tooth row is more than the interorbital breadth.

Where found 13 miles south-southwest of Whiterock these squirrels lived in the sage-brush. Near Winnemucca they lived in the bottom land, and *Citellus townsendii* occupied the sagebrush-covered land. In general, Nevadan *richardsonii* lives in meadows or in meadowlike habitats, rather than amid shrubs on the desert, and it does not occur in timbered areas. Information is lacking about breeding habits. For another subspecies, *C. r. richardsonii*, Howell (1938:9) gives the gestation period as 28 to 32 days and says that only one litter per year is the rule, the number of young averaging 7.5, with extremes of 6

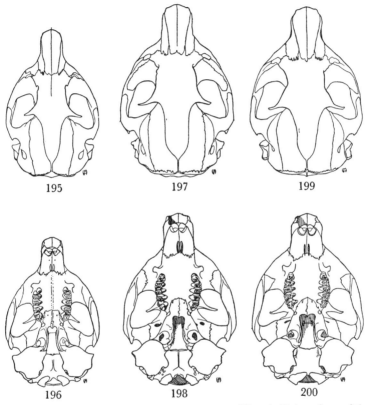

195   197   199

196   198   200

Figs. 195–200. Ground squirrels of the subgenus *Citellus*. All, × 1. (Other views of the skulls of these subspecies are shown in figs. 201–204.)

Figs. 195, 196. *Citellus townsendii mollis*, 6 miles east Stillwater, no. 41525, ♂.
Figs. 197, 198. *Citellus richardsonii nevadensis*, 4 miles south Romano, no. 70559, ♂.
Figs. 199, 200. *Citellus beldingi crebrus*, 7 miles north Austin, no. 70542, ♂.

and 11. For the race *C. r. elegans*, in Colorado, Howell (1938:10) records that fourteen females examined in 1916 had an average of 8.2 embryos, and in 1920, nineteen females had an average of only 4.6.

Records of occurrence.—Specimens examined, 11, as follows: *Humboldt Co.:* 3 mi. NE Winnemucca, 4700 ft., 2; 1 mi. N Winnemucca, 4600 ft., 1. *Eureka Co.:* 4 mi. S Romano, Diamond Valley, 2. *Elko Co.:* 13 mi. SSW Whiterock, 4; Elburz, 3 mi. S Halleck, 5200 ft., 1 (coll. of Ralph Ellis); 3 mi. SE Union, 1.

Additional records: Howell (1938:78): *Humboldt Co.:* Paradise. *Elko Co.:* Mountain City; Metropolis; Elko; Skelton; Ruby Valley.

Citellus beldingi
Belding Ground Squirrel

Three races of this species occur in the state in suitable habitat in the Transition and higher life-zones. The species occurs lower down than *Citellus lateralis*, and in a few places, as, for example, in the Carson Valley, 6 miles south of Minden, lives amid surroundings which have conspicuous elements of the Upper Sonoran Life-zone.

The size is a little less, and the tail considerably shorter, than in *C. richardsonii*. The upper parts are Smoke Gray mixed with reddish-brown or Pinkish Cinnamon, with the middorsal area darkened with Sayal Brown and the fore-

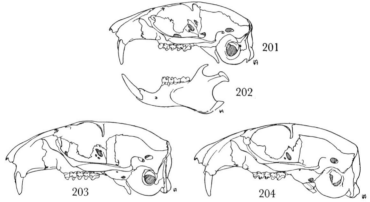

Figs. 201–204. Ground squirrels of the subgenus *Citellus*. Different views of the skulls of these subspecies are shown in figs. 195–200. All, ×1.

Fig. 201. *Citellus townsendii mollis*, 6 miles east Stillwater, no. 41525, ♂.
Fig. 202. *Citellus townsendii mollis*, 2½ miles east Baker, no. 41527, ♂.
Fig. 203. *Citellus richardsonii nevadensis*, 4 miles south Romano, no. 70559, ♂.
Fig. 204. *Citellus beldingi crebrus*, 7 miles north Austin, no. 70542, ♂.

head Pinkish Cinnamon. The underparts are grayish and have a wash of Pinkish Cinnamon which is most pronounced on the pectoral region, forelegs, and forefeet. The hind feet are similarly colored. The tail dorsally is the same color or, because of the greater amount of black, darker than the back. Beneath, the tail is distinctly reddish, often Hazel. The skull closely resembles that of *richardsonii*, but the interorbital breadth is greater relative to the ength of the skull, and in *C. b. crebrus* the nasals average shorter relative to the breadth of the cranium. Externally, from *richardsonii*, *beldingi* is readily distinguished by the shorter tail that is reddish rather than Ochraceous-Buff. Also, *beldingi* has more reddish in the pelage. From *C. townsendii*, *beldingi* may be distinguished by larger size, cinnamon-colored rather than whitish underparts, skull with maxillary tooth row more, rather than less, than 8.9 mm.

The habitat preferred by this species is the meadowland and its borders. The animals avoid marshy ground. At high elevations in the Sierra Nevada and Pine Forest Mountains it digs burrows in a wider variety of places, but steep hillsides, dense timber, dense brush, and, as already noted, marshy ground are avoided. These squirrels seldom climb. They are colonial in the sense that many burrows occur in a limited area. Linsdale (1938:178) estimated that five hundred of the squirrels lived in a belt 25 yards wide around the edge of a narrow meadow about ¼ mile long just above Kingston Ranger Station. The stomachs of those examined by him there contained green plant material, as did the stomachs of all those that I have examined from elsewhere in the state.

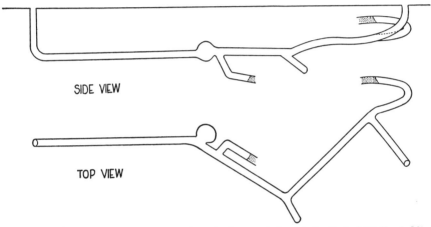

SIDE VIEW

TOP VIEW

Fig. 205. Diagrammatic representation of a burrow judged to be that of *Citellus beldingi* excavated on July 17, 1940, 3 miles south Mount Rose, 8300 feet, Washoe County. Drawing is one-fortieth natural size.

Adults go into estivation later than do those of *C. townsendii*, remaining until spring. Judging from the ages of specimens taken by us in the later part of the summer, young of the year remain aboveground later than do adults. Young are said to be born in April, and, so far as known, there is but one litter per year. The young, according to Howell (1938:12), number four to twelve per litter, with an average of eight.

The subspecies *C. b. beldingi* has a surprisingly large altitudinal range, in that it occurs from at least 9000 feet elevation in the Sierra Nevada on the eastern side of Lake Tahoe, down to 4850 feet elevation along the Carson River, 6 miles south of Minden.

The voice is high pitched, and the series of rapidly uttered notes almost blends into a trill.

A diagrammatic representation of a burrow judged to belong to one of these animals is shown in figure 205.

Citellus beldingi oregonus (Merriam)
Belding Ground Squirrel

Spermophilus oregonus Merriam, Proc. Biol. Soc. Washington, 12:69, March 24, 1898. Type from Swan
  Lake Valley, Klamath Basin, Klamath County, Oregon.
Citellus beldingi oregonus, Howell, N. Amer. Fauna, 56:83, May 18, 1938.

Distribution.—Northwestern Nevada south at least to Granite Mountain, Washoe
County. See figure 206.

Remarks.—Measurements of ten males and twenty females, taken in May at the type
locality, are: ♂, 270 (252–274), ♀, 269 (256–291); 61 (52–70), 59 (52–65); 42 (40–43), 41.2

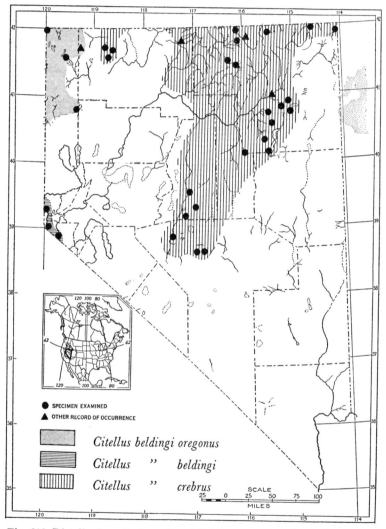

Fig. 206. Distribution of subspecies of Belding ground squirrel, *Citellus beldingi,* with insert showing range of the species.

(37–44); weight (mostly May-taken specimens) 246.5 (212.5–300.0) grams, 269.1 (233.6–330.1) grams.

The size is less than in *crebrus* and more than in *beldingi*. The color is intermediate between the two mentioned races. Over most of the range, in Oregon, the color is pale, as in *crebrus*, but in Nevada and in adjoining parts of California it is darker, although not so dark as in the race *beldingi*. In topotypes the underside of the tail is Chestnut Brown and therefore darker than in specimens from more eastern localities in which the color of this part is near (*j*) Hazel. The skull differs from that of *beldingi* in that the nasals extend farther posteriorly in relation to the premaxillae. From *crebrus*, *oregonus* differs in smaller size (weight, in comparable females, 269 as opposed to 355 grams) and smaller skull in which the interorbital region and rostrum are relatively as well as actually narrower, the nasals longer, and the postorbital region broader. The animals from 12-mile Creek are intermediate toward *crebrus;* the single specimen from Massacre Creek is so young as not to display characters diagnostic of the subspecies; and the occurrence at Badger is based on specimens not examined by me. The specimens from Rock Creek are intermediate toward *beldingi;* they show greatest resemblance to *beldingi* in color, but in cranial characters are referable to *oregonus*.

Records of occurrence.—Specimens examined, 9, as follows: *Washoe Co.:* 12-mile Creek, 1 mi. E Calif. boundary, 5300 ft., 2; Barrel Spring, 5700 ft., 9½ mi. E and 3½ mi. N Ft. Bidwell, 2; Massacre Creek, 5800 ft., 1; Rock Creek, 7000–7425 ft., 4.

Additional record: *Humboldt Co.:* Badger (Howell, 1938:84).

Citellus beldingi beldingi (Merriam)
Belding Ground Squirrel

Spermophilus beldingi Merriam, Ann. New York Acad. Sci., 4:317, December 28, 1888. Type from Donner, Placer County, California.

[*Citellus*] *beldingi*, Trouessart, Catal. Mamm., viv. foss., suppl., p. 339, 1904.

Distribution.—Sierra Nevada and adjoining Carson Valley in the vicinity of Lake Tahoe. See figure 206.

Remarks.—Measurements of ten males (Grinnell and Dixon, 1919:660) from the Yosemite section of the Sierra Nevada of California and ten females from the same mountain range in California (Independence Lake, Nevada County, south to the Yosemite section), are: ♂, 263 (230–280), ♀, 266 (241–280); 66 (60–74), 61.5 (51–68); 44 (41–44.5), 42.9 (41–45); weight, 222 (125.5–285.0), 246.6 (212.1–294.0) grams.

Individuals of *beldingi* average smaller than those of either of the other two races now recognized, and *beldingi* is distinguished by the well-defined dorsal band of dark reddish color which ranges from Kaiser Brown to Sayal Brown. The skull is small, and the nasals are shorter than in *oregonus*. In relation to the premaxillae, the nasals project posteriorly, about the same as in *crebrus*. Intergradation with *oregonus* is suggested by the specimens from Rock Creek, north of Pyramid Lake, referred to the race *oregonus*. The altitudinal range is from near 9000 feet or higher in the mountains on the eastern side of Lake Tahoe down to 4850 feet on the West Fork of the Carson River, 6 miles south of Minden.

Records of occurrence.—Specimens examined, 11, as follows: *Washoe Co.:* 3 mi. S Mt. Rose, 8500–8600 ft., 3. *Douglas Co.:* ¼ mi. E Zephyr Cove, 6300 ft., 1; 6 mi. S Minden, 4850 ft., 7.

Citellus beldingi crebrus Hall
Belding Ground Squirrel

Citellus beldingi crebrus Hall, The Murrelet, 21:59, December 20, 1940. Type from Reese River Valley, 7 miles north of Austin, Lander County, Nevada.

Citellus oregonus, Taylor, Univ. Calif. Publ. Zoöl., 7:213, June 24, 1911; Linsdale, Amer. Midland Nat., 19:178, January, 1938.

Citellus elegans nevadensis, Borell and Ellis (part), Journ. Mamm., 15:26, 72, February 15, 1934.

Distribution.—From the Pine Forest Mountains across northern Nevada and south in the central part of the state to north-central Nye County. See figure 206.

Remarks.—Measurements of ten males and fifteen females from southern Lander and northern Nye counties are: ♂, 282 (274–295), ♀, 282 (267–293); 65.2 (58–74), 68.7 (60–73); 43.9 (42–46), 43.3 (40–46); weight, 382.4 (322.1–550.0), 354.5 (290.0–448.6) grams.

Large size, light color, and a skull characterized by a broad rostrum, broad interorbital region, narrow postorbital region, and short nasals which in most specimens do not project so far posteriorly as do the premaxillae are the distinguishing subspecific characters. Comparisons with *beldingi* and *oregonus* are made in the accounts of those races.

Records of occurrence.—Specimens examined, 72, as follows: *Humboldt Co.:* Alder Creek, Pine Forest Mts., 5000 ft., 4; head of Big Creek, Pine Forest Mts., 8000 ft., 5; Big Creek, Pine Forest Mts.,6000–7000 ft.,2; head of Leonard Creek, Pine Forest Mts., 6500 ft., 1. *Lander Co.:* Reese River Valley, 7 mi. N Austin, 16; Birch Creek, 7000 ft., 2; Kingston Ranger Station, 7500 ft., 10. *Nye Co.:* Bells Ranch, Reese River, 6890 ft., 2; Toquima Range, Meadow Creek [= Valley] Ranger Station, 1; 2 mi. E Meadow Valley R. S., 2; Antone Creek, 1½ mi. SE Meadow Valley R. S., 2; Antone Creek, 2 mi. S Meadow Valley R. S., 1. *Elko Co.:* Owyhee, 1; Cedar Creek, 10 mi. NE San Jacinto, 6000 ft., 1; Goose Creek, 2 mi. W Utah boundary, 5000 ft., 1 (skull only); 3 mi. N Jarbidge, 1 (coll. of Ralph Ellis); 10 mi. S Owyhee, 1; Cobb Creek, 6 mi. SW Mountain City, 6500 ft., 1; 13 mi. SSW Whiterock, 5600 ft., 1; Jack Creek, 10 mi. S Deep Creek, 3; Steels Creek, N end Ruby Mts., 7000 ft., 1 (coll. of Ralph Ellis); summit of Secret Pass, 6200 ft., 3 (coll. of Ralph Ellis); Jerry Creek, 6700 ft., 1 (skull only) (coll. of Ralph Ellis); Lamoille, 2 (skulls only); Three Lakes, 9700 ft., 2 (coll. of Ralph Ellis); Harrison Pass R. S., Green Mountain Canyon, 6050 ft., 3 (coll. of Ralph Ellis); W side Ruby Lake, 3 mi. N White Pine Co. line, 6200 ft., 1 (coll. of Ralph Ellis); 2 mi. SE Union, 1.

Additional records (Howell, 1938:84): *Humboldt Co.:* Badger; Calico Mountain. *Elko Co.:* Mountain City; Halleck.

Citellus variegatus grammurus (Say)
Rock Squirrel

S[ciurus]. grammurus Say, Long's Expedit. to the Rocky Mountains, 2:72, 1823. Type from Purgatory River, near mouth of Chacuaco Creek, Las Animas County, Colorado.

[*Citellus variegatus] grammurus*, Elliot, Field Columb. Mus. Publ., zoöl. ser., 4:149, 1904; Howell, N. Amer. Fauna, 56:142, 1938.

Citellus grammurus grammurus, Burt, Trans. San Diego Soc. Nat. Hist., 7:404, May 31, 1934.

Otospermophilus grammurus, Linsdale, Amer. Midland Nat., 7:19, January, 1938.

Distribution.—Lower part of Transition Life-zone to upper part of Upper Sonoran Life-zone of the southeastern part of state from northern White Pine County south to Cedar Basin and from Toyabe Mountains east to Utah boundary. See figure 207.

Remarks.—Measurements of five males from Baker and Cleve creeks and three females from Willard Creek, Water Canyon, and 1 mi. W Smith Creek Cave, are: ♂, 468 (455–491), ♀, 451 (422–480); 197 (190–210), 187 (160–206); 59.2 (57–65), 56 (50–61); weight, 684.3 (580.3–742.5), 708.6 (643.5–795.5) grams.

Characters of the species are: size large (see measurements), variegated pattern on upper parts, anterior opening of infraorbital canal narrowly oval, and P3 about one-sixth size of P4.

There is but one molt, which occurs in summer. Specimens in hand, in fresh pelage, answer to Howell's (1938:143) description of color, which is essentially as follows: head and occiput Pinkish Buff; sides of nose Cartridge Buff; eye ring white; fore part of back, shoulders, and sides grayish white, slightly mixed with brownish; hinder part of back and rump Cinnamon Buff, varied with brownish; ears Hair Brown, shaded with Pinkish Buff; front legs buffy white; hind legs Cinnamon Buff; fore and hind feet Cartridge Buff; tail mixed Pinkish Buff and Bone Brown, edged with grayish white; underparts buffy white, shaded with Pinkish Buff.

Comparison of topotypes of *grammurus* and of *C. v. utah,* and of other specimens from various parts of the range of these two races, clearly shows that the Nevadan specimens are *grammurus,* and not *utah.* None of the Nevadan specimens is as tawny or otherwise as dark as are specimens of *utah.*

Most of the animals obtained and most of those seen were on, among, or in the vicinity of boulders. This was true in far more instances than for the Beechey ground squirrel of western Nevada. *C. v. grammurus* does not invariably live among rocks, for a few animals

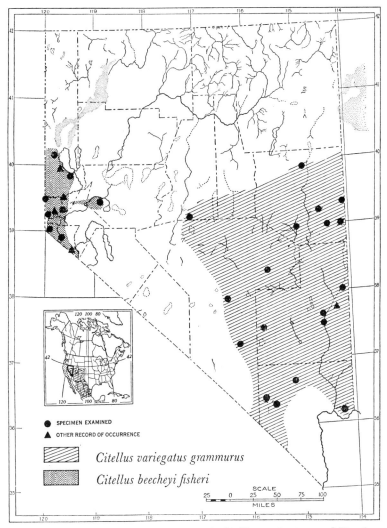

Fig. 207. Distribution of rock squirrel, *Citellus variegatus*, and Beechey ground squirrel, *Citellus beecheyi*, with insert showing combined ranges of the two species.

were found living in burrows more than a hundred feet from rocks. The squirrels found by us were shy, and successful hunting of them, in most places, required careful stalking. Trapping was more productive than hunting. Burt (1934:404) noted in southern Nevada that: "When danger was sensed by a squirrel he would utter his shrill whistle-like notes, whereupon all Rock Squirrels in the immediate vicinity would take to cover. We found them very shy and difficult to approach.''

The localities of occurrence here recorded greatly extend the known range within Nevada; previously this species was recorded only from the southern part of the state and to the westward only from the Providence Mountains of California. Although it occurs in the Sheep Mountains and on Charleston Peak, it is absent in the territory south thereof

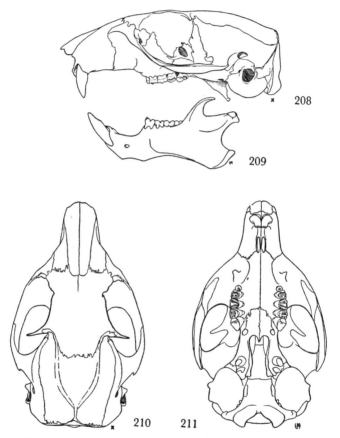

Figs. 208–211. *Citellus variegatus grammurus*, Baker Creek, 7300 feet, no. 41517, ♂. ×1.

and west of the Muddy River, as, for example, in the Dead Mountains and in the rocky canyon of the Colorado River. In Nevada the species inhabits the Upper Sonoran Life-zone and at no place that I know of does it live in typical Lower Sonoran surroundings. Its range does not, so far as known, meet that of *beecheyi*, the low territory of western Nevada separating the two. Because the difference between the two species is slight, it seems probable that in the not distant past both were part of a continuously distributed population.

None of the specimens in our collection contained embryos. One taken on July 19, 1937, in the juniper-piñon association 1 mile west of Smith Creek Cave was nursing young. Its cheek pouches contained about eighty fruits of *Ephedra,* and the stomach had finely chewed vegetable material much of which was fruits of *Ephedra.*

Records of occurrence.—Specimens examined, 55, as follows: *Lander Co.:* Kingston Canyon, 6350 ft., 1. *Nye Co.:* Quinn Canyon Mountains, 6 mi. NE Nyala, 7000 ft., 1; Haws Canyon, 7000 ft., 1; 2 mi. E Silverbow 6900 ft., 1; 2 mi. S Oak Spring, 5800 ft., 1; Belted Range, 5 mi. W White Rock Spring, 1. *White Pine Co.:* Cherry Creek, 6800 ft., 6; 1 mi. W Smith Creek Cave, Mt. Moriah, 6000 ft., 1; Cleve Creek, Shell Creek Range, 6900–7000 ft., 4; Willard Creek, Spring Valley, 7700 ft., 5; Baker Creek, Snake Mts., 7300–8450 ft., 5; Water Canyon, 8 and 10 mi. N Lund, 2. *Lincoln Co.:* Eagle Valley, 3½ mi. N Ursine, 5600–6000 ft., 5; 2 mi. N Caliente, 4250 ft., 1; Meadow Valley Wash, 7 mi. S Caliente, 4000 ft., 2; SW base Groom Baldy, 7200 ft., 3. *Clark Co.* (D. R. Dickey Coll.): Hidden Forest, 8500 ft., 1; Willow Creek, 6000 ft., 2; N slope "Charleston Mts.," 6000 ft., 1; "Charleston Mts.," 6000 ft., 4; Kyle Canyon, 8000 ft., 1; Kyle Canyon, 6500 ft., 2; Cedar Basin, 3500 ft., 4. Additional record: *Lincoln Co.:* 4 mi. NE Panaca (A. M. Alexander, MS).

Citellus beecheyi fisheri (Merriam)
Beechey Ground Squirrel

Spermophilus beecheyi fisheri Merriam, Proc. Biol. Soc. Washington, 8:133, December 28, 1893. Type from South Fork of Kern River, 3 miles above Onyx, Kern County, California.
Citellus beecheyi fisheri, Grinnell, Proc. California Acad. Sci. (4th series), 3:211, August 28, 1913.

Distribution.—Canadian to Upper Sonoran life-zones from southern Washoe County south into Douglas County, with one occurrence east as far as western Churchill County. See figure 207, page 311.

Remarks.—Measurements of a male and female from ½ mi. E Zephyr Cove are 431, 392; 152, 142; 63, 51. A male from ½ mi. W Verdi, in early July, weighed 651.7 grams.

Characters of the species are essentially the same as described for *Citellus variegatus,* except that: size less; white on anterior part of upper parts in two large patches, one on each shoulder and extending to about middle of back in two stripes separated by a triangular area of dark color; tail darker, more brownish and less whitish above and below; and skull averaging slightly smaller than in *variegatus.*

In the subspecies *fisheri,* the triangular area of dark color between the white shoulders is the same color as the hinder back, not black as in the more northwestern subspecies *douglasii.* From the subspecies *beecheyi* of western California south of San Francisco Bay, *fisheri* differs in: hind feet shorter; coloration both above and below paler, including light markings on shoulders which are clearer white; and skull averaging smaller. From *C. b. sierrae,* of the northern Sierra Nevada, *fisheri* differs in lighter-colored upper parts and head; feet more buffy (less whitish); and tail lighter and more buffy beneath.

The race *C. b. sierrae,* recorded from along the Californian side of Lake Tahoe. may occur in Nevada, but our specimens from the Nevada side of Lake Tahoe are not so dark-colored as are Californian specimens of *sierrae* at hand, from Crane Flat and the Merced Grove of Big Trees in Mariposa County. A complication entering into the identification of Nevadan specimens is that those from Incline Creek and near Zephyr Cove are in worn, faded pelage. Other available Nevadan specimens from lower elevations farther east, some in worn and some in fresh pelage, agree with these from along the eastern edge of Lake Tahoe in being lighter than *sierrae* and darker than *fisheri,* providing topotypes of *fisheri* and specimens from the southern part of its range are employed. A summary based upon the material available indicates no basis for ascribing more than one subspecies to Nevada, and the name seemingly best applied is *fisheri.*

This species occurs in the Virginia Mountains along the western side of Pyramid Lake and in the canyon of the Truckee River, where I have seen the animal, to at least 9½ miles east of Reno in Storey County, but not as far east as Wadsworth. The squirrel is present in the mountains about Virginia City as far down the Carson River as Dayton and on the headwaters of the Walker River in Smiths Valley, where Emmet Hooper (MS) observed it. Before 1943 the species had not established itself farther eastward in the low, hot desert, not even where it was irrigated and given over to agriculture, as, for example, about Fallon. On May 18, 1943, J. Rebol captured one individual, an adult, 5 miles west-southwest of Fallon, but did not report any others from this place, which is 35 miles west of previously known record stations and in an area where the species previously had been unknown to naturalists resident there for the past 30 years.

In open places in the forest about Lake Tahoe this species is common up to elevations of at least 7100 feet. The animals climb well for ground squirrels, and frequently I have seen them in bushes. At Dayton, Alcorn (MS) watched individuals search as high as 20 feet above the ground for catkins of cottonwood trees. Some Beechey ground squirrels are to be seen about piles of boulders, in which they take refuge, but a greater number live in holes in the ground. An adult male taken on July 2, 1936, a half mile west of Verdi, by Dwight Smiley, had 276 seeds of *Purshia* in the right cheek pouch and 261 seeds in the left. The combined weight of the seeds was 33.1 grams. A female taken March 24, 1938, 1 mile southwest of Pyramid Lake, by Alcorn, had seven embryos. In Nevada, young of the year as well as older animals are thought to hibernate.

Records of occurrence.—Specimens examined, 14, as follows: *Washoe Co.:* Cottonwood Creek, 4400 ft., Virginia Mts., 1; 1 mi. SW Pyramid Lake, 3950 ft., 1; W side Truckee River, ½ mi. W Verdi, 4900 ft., 1; Incline Creek, 7100 ft., 1; Incline Creek, 6300 ft., 1. *Douglas Co.:* ½ mi. E Zephyr Cove, Lake Tahoe, 2; Carson River, 5 mi. SE Minden, 5900 ft., 3; 6 mi. S Minden, 4850 ft., 1; 6½ mi. S Minden, 4900 ft., 1. *Storey Co.:* 1 mi. N Virginia City, 1. *Churchill Co.:* 5 mi. WSW Fallon, 1.

Additional records: *Washoe Co.:* Hardscrabble Canyon, 5000 and 5500 ft. (David Nichols, MS); Sutcliffe, 4000 ft. (David Nichols, MS); 500 yds. N Washoe City (Carl P. Russell, MS). *Ormsby Co.:* Carson City (Howell, 1938:156). *Douglas Co.:* Glenbrook (Howell, 1938:156); Smiths Valley (Emmet Hooper, MS).

Citellus leucurus leucurus (Merriam)
Antelope Ground Squirrel

Tamias leucurus Merriam, N. Amer. Fauna, 2:20, October 30, 1889. Type from San Gorgonio Pass (east of Banning), Riverside County, California.
Citellus leucurus, Elliot, Field Columb. Mus. Publ., zoöl. ser., 3:210, June, 1903.
Ammospermophilus leucurus, Linsdale, Amer. Midland Nat., 19:180, January, 1938.
Ammospermophilus leucurus leucurus, Taylor, Univ. California Publ. Zoöl., 7:219, June 24, 1911; Burt, Trans. San Diego Soc. Nat. Hist., 7:405, May 31, 1934; Howell, N. Amer. Fauna, 56:170, May 18, 1938.

Distribution.—Western and southern Nevada and along eastern border of state as far north as vicinity of Wendover. See figure 212.

Remarks.—Measurements of six of each sex, from Clark County, south of Searchlight, are: ♂, 212 (188–220), ♀, 210 (202–216); 56 (42–71), 61 (55–66); 36 (35–38), 37 (36–38); weight, 111.1 (103.7–116.8), 100.6 (96.2–104.5) grams.

This species clearly has two molts each year; the tail, however, appears to molt only when the animal is in its autumnal molt. In both the summer and winter coat, conspicuous features are the two white stripes (one on each side of the back extending from the shoulder onto the hip) and the white or creamy white undersurface of the tail (carried up over the back) edged with a narrow band of black. The summer coat is harsher to the touch and lacks most of the fine underfur of the softer winter coat. In summer the upper parts are Vinaceous Buff, underparts white or creamy white, front and hind legs Light Pinkish Cinnamon changing to buffy white on the feet, tail above mostly black but mixed with some whitish, although at the base it is colored like the back. In winter the hairs on the upper parts have longer black tips and the subterminal light band is more whitish (less buffy), giving a grayer tone to the pelage of the upper parts, the general effect being Pale Drab Gray. There are ten mammae.

In the abundant material available, I cannot detect any geographic variation, within the state, in coloration, in size of animal, or in proportions of the skull; nor were any secondary sexual differences found.

Zonally, the species occurs mainly below the Transition Life-zone; withal, so rarely does it occur in the Transition Life-zone that it can be said to be a species of the Sonoran zones. Exceptions are to be expected, as, for example,

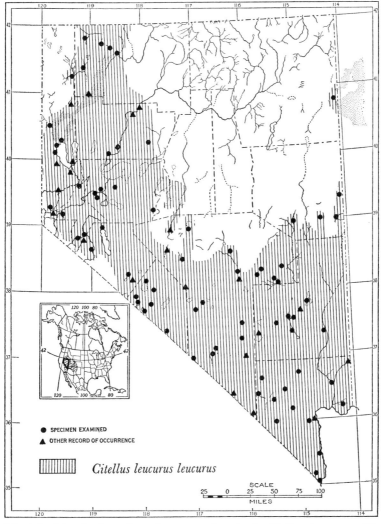

SPECIMEN EXAMINED

OTHER RECORD OF OCCURRENCE

Citellus leucurus leucurus

SCALE

25   0   25   50   75   100

MILES

Fig. 212. Distribution of antelope ground squirrel, *Citellus leucurus*, with insert showing range of the species.

occurrence of an individual at 8500 feet elevation on the western slope of the Sheep Mountains where yellow pines also occurred (Burt, 1934:405). In the Virginia Mountains on the western side of Pyramid Lake, David Nichols (MS) found the species to range no higher than the 5000-foot contour on the eastern side of the mountains.

This species, like *Citellus lateralis*, is mistakenly called chipmunk by many. Not only are the stripes fewer in number, but they do not extend onto the head as in true chipmunks. When a person walks through the desert these ground squirrels scurry under bushes or into burrows before the observer

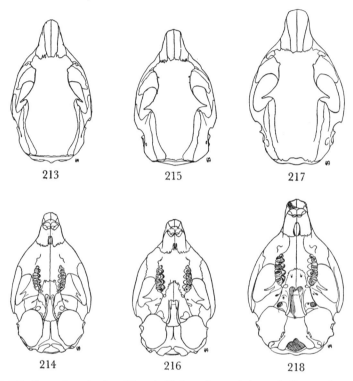

213   215   217

214   216   218

Figs. 213–218. Ground squirrels. All, ×1. (Other views of these skulls are shown in figs. 219–224.)

Figs. 213, 214. *Citellus leucurus leucurus*, 14 miles east Searchlight, no. 61472, ♂.
Figs. 215, 216. *Citellus tereticaudus tereticaudus*, Furnace Creek Ranch, Death Valley, Inyo County, California, 178 feet below sea level, no. 27381, ♀.
Figs. 217, 218. *Citellus lateralis trepidus*, Kingston Ranger Station, 7500 feet, no. 45473, ♀.

sees them. On horseback or in a car the observer sees many more of the squirrels. The brilliantly white undersurface of the animal's tail attracts the observer's attention, because it is turned up over the back, revealing the white underside, and because it is nervously twitched at short intervals.

The animals, at least in many areas, do not hibernate. At Indian Springs (Burt, 1934:406) they were active in February. D. V. Hemphill (MS), on December 31, 1940, at Wichman, trapped two, although on that day the temperature did not rise above 31° F. Throughout the winter, 4 miles west of Fallon, Alcorn reports them as active. The antelope ground squirrels are a minor nuisance to fur trappers in winter, Alcorn says, because they take the paper or cloth from the pans of steel traps set for coyotes and so render the set less effective for its intended purpose. When a jack rabbit is caught and killed in one of these coyote traps, the antelope ground squirrels clean all the fur off the exposed parts of the rabbit; this, Alcorn supposes, is used by them to construct warm underground nests.

On the firm soils of the fanglomerates at the bases of the mountains and on the sandy floors of the valleys, the squirrels are fairly evenly distributed—that

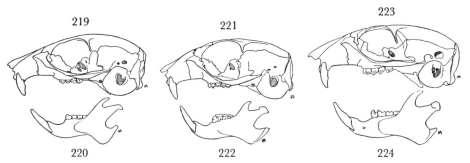

Figs. 219–224. Ground squirrels. Different views of these skulls are shown in figs. 213–218. All, ×1.

Figs. 219, 220. *Citellus leucurus leucurus.*   Figs. 221, 222. *Citellus tereticaudus tereticaudus.*
Figs. 223, 224. *Citellus lateralis trepidus.*

is to say, they do not live in colonies. Possibly this is because they do not rely on a kind of food which is concentrated in restricted areas. The stomach of one that I examined on May 28, 1932, 23 miles west of Panaca, contained some green plant material but mostly dry material which I thought had been seeds. Burt (1934:406) records finding 187 "seeds of cactus (*Opuntia*)" in the cheek pouches of an animal at Cedar Basin, and Alcorn (MS) mentions shooting animals in thickets of buck brush (buffalo berry, *Shepherdia*) near Fallon, the cheek pouches of which were filled with the berries of this plant. These data and other information indicate that seeds comprise a major share of the diet of these squirrels. Compared to other ground squirrels individuals of this species are good climbers and they use this ability to obtain their food.

On June 29, 1928, in Huntoon Valley, Louise Kellogg (MS) found one of these squirrels head first in the mouth of a rattlesnake.

There is record of ten pregnant females from Nevada. Of these, six were taken in March, one in April, two in May, and one in June. The embryos ranged in number from five to eleven, the mode being seven, and the mean 7.8. There are ten mammae.

Records of occurrence.—Specimens examined, 158, as follows: *Washoe Co.:* mouth Little High Rock Canyon, 5000 ft., 2; Smoke Creek, 9 mi. E Calif. boundary, 3900 ft., 2; mouth of Fox Canyon, 7½ mi. S Pahrum Peak, 4500 ft., 1; about 1 mi. NW The Needles, Pyramid Lake, 1; Pyramid Lake, 9 mi. S Sand Pass, 3800 ft., 1; Washoe Lake, 1 (coll. of Ralph Ellis). *Lyon Co.:* ½ mi. SE Wadsworth, 4200 ft., 1; 5 mi. S and E Dayton, 1 (coll. of U. S. Biol. Surv., Dist. Agent, Reno); Mason Valley, 11¾ mi. S and 2¾ mi. E Yerington, 4650 ft., 1;

West Walker River, 12 mi. S Yerington, 4600 ft., 1. *Humboldt Co.:* Virgin Valley, 5000 ft., 5; Alder Creek, Pine Forest Mts., 5000–5200 ft., 3; Big Creek Ranch, Pine Forest Mts., 4350 ft., 2; Quinn River Crossing, 4100 ft., 1; Soldier Meadows, 4600 and 4900 ft., 2. *Pershing Co.:* S base Granite Peak, East Range, 1; Lovelock, 4000 ft., 1; Toulon, 3900 ft., 1. *Churchill Co.:* 5 mi. N Stillwater, 4000 ft., 1; 4 mi. N Fallon, 1; 8 mi. W Fallon, 2; 8 mi. SW Fallon, 1; 8 mi. SE Eastgate, 1. *Mineral Co.:* 3 mi. S Schurz, 4100 ft., 6; East Walker River, 2 mi. NW Morgans Ranch, 5100 ft., 1; Marietta, 4900 ft., 2. *Esmeralda Co.:* Rockhill, 4600 ft., 3; 3½ to 4 mi. SE Coaldale, 4850 ft., 5; 7 mi. N Arlemont, 5500 ft., 1; 1½ mi. N Chiatovich Ranch, 4900 ft., 2; Cave Spring, 6200–6248 ft., 5; Fish Lake, 4800 ft., 2; Pigeon Spring, 6400 ft., 1. *Nye Co.:* 5 mi. SE Millett P. O., 5500 ft., 3; Hot Creek Range, 4 mi. N Hot Creek, 6400 ft., 1; 5¼ mi. NE San Antonio, 5700 ft., 1; White River Valley, 15 mi. WSW Sunnyside, 5500 ft., 1; Nyala, Railroad Valley, 5100 ft., 1; Twin Springs, S end Hot Creek Valley, 5250 ft., 1; Big Creek, Quinn Canyon Mts., 5700 ft., 1; Garden Valley, 8½ mi. NE Sharp, 3; White River Valley, 5 mi. E Sharp, 1; Cactus Spring, Cactus Range, 6500 ft., 1; Cactus Range, 2 3/10 mi. SW Cactus Spring, 6400 ft., 1; 14 mi. E Goldfield, 4900 ft., 1; Belted Range, 2 mi. N Indian Spring, 6700 ft., 1; 2 mi. NW Indian Spring, 6300 ft , 1; ½ to 1 mi. W Oak Spring, 6000–6100 ft., 2; ½ to 2 mi. S Oak Spring, 5600–5700 ft., 3; 1 mi. SW Oak Spring, 6000 ft., 1; 8 mi. NW Springdale, 4250 ft., 1; Amargosa River, 2 mi. E Springdale, 3850 ft., 1; 2½ mi. E and 1 mi. S Grapevine Peak, 7000 ft., 4. *Elko Co.:* 8 mi. S Wendover, 4700 ft., 2. *White Pine Co.:* 1 and 1½ mi. W Smith Creek Cave, Mt. Moriah, 6000 ft., 2; 1 mi. SE Smith Creek Cave, Mt. Moriah, 5800 ft., 2; 1 mi. E Lehman Cave, 7000 ft., 1; Baker Creek, 6900 and 7000 ft., 2; Spring Valley, 7 mi. SW Osceola, 6275 ft., 2; Water Canyon, 8 mi. N Lund, 1. *Lincoln Co.:* Desert Valley, 23 mi. W Panaca, 5300 ft., 1; Pahranagat Valley, 3 mi. N Crystal Spring, 4000 ft., 2; 4 mi. NE Crystal Spring, 4300 ft., 1; 1 mi. S Crystal Spring, 4000 ft., 1; 1 mi. SE Crystal Spring, 4000 ft., 1; 16 mi. E Groom Baldy, 4600 ft., 2; Ash Spring, Pahranagat Valley, 3800 and 4000 ft., 2; Alamo, 3570 ft., 1; Meadow Valley Wash, 24 mi. S Caliente, 3000 ft., 1. *Clark Co.:* Mormon Well, 5 (D. R. Dickey Coll.); Indian Springs, 1 (D. R. Dickey Coll.); ½ mi. E St. Thomas, 1250 ft., 1 (D. R. Dickey Coll.); Corn Creek, 2840 ft., 7 (D. R. Dickey Coll.); Wheeler Well, 6600 ft., 2 (D. R. Dickey Coll.); Kyle Canyon, 5000 ft., 4 (D. R. Dickey Coll.); 1 mi. NW Las Vegas, 2100 ft., 3 (D. R. Dickey Coll.); Cedar City, 3500 ft., 2 (D. R. Dickey Coll.); N side Potosi Mtn., 7000 ft., 1; Boulder City, on road to Dam, 1 (Boulder Dam Recreational Area Coll.); Colorado River, 14 mi. E Searchlight, Jap Ranch, 500 ft., 5; 7 and 8 mi. S Dead Mtn., 2700 ft., 6; Hiko Spring, 8 mi. SSE Dead Mtn., 1900 ft., 1; 12 mi. S and 5 mi. E Searchlight, 2600 ft., 1; 13 mi. S Dead Mtn., 1; ½ mi. N Calif.-Nev. Monument, 500 ft., 1.

, Additional records (unless otherwise indicated, after Howell, 1938:172–173): *Washoe Co.:* Granite Creek; Hardscrabble Canyon, 4900 to 5000 ft. (D. Nichols, MS); Sutcliffe, 3700–4500 ft. (D. Nichols, MS); Winnemucca Lake; 5 mi. S Pyramid Lake (Carl P. Russell, MS); 8 mi. E Reno (Carl P. Russell, MS). *Ormsby Co.:* Carson City. *Humboldt Co.:* Flowing Springs. *Pershing Co.:* Raspberry Creek, near Cosgrave; Imlay. *Mineral Co.:* 5 mi. N Pine Grove, 5500 ft. (Hall, MS); Candelaria. *Nye Co.:* Reese River; Cloverdale, 6 mi. S Golden; Arrowhead (Hall, MS); Tonopah (Hall, MS); Wahmonie (Hall, MS); Ash Meadows; Pahrump Valley. *Lincoln Co.:* Pahroc Spring; Emigrant Valley, N end of dry lake, south of Groom Baldy (Hall, MS). *Clark Co.:* Mesquite (Hall, MS); Black Canyon, Colorado River.

Citellus tereticaudus tereticaudus (Baird)
Round-tailed Ground Squirrel

Spermophilus tereticaudus Baird, Mamm. N. Amer., p. 315, 1857. Type from Old Fort Yuma, Imperial County, California.

Citellus tereticaudus, Elliot, Field Columb. Mus. Publ., zoöl. ser., 3:211, June, 1903.

Citellus tereticaudus tereticaudus, Burt, Trans. San Diego Soc. Nat. Hist., 7:405, May 31, 1934; Howell, N. Amer. Fauna, 56:185, May 18, 1938.

Distribution.—Lower Sonoran Life-zone in Clark and southern Nye counties. See figure 225.

Remarks.—Measurements of eleven specimens, probably of both sexes (Howell, 1938:186), from Fort Yuma and Pilot Knob, California, are 250 (235–266); 91.1 (81–102); 36.2 (33–38). A female from 4 miles northwest of Las Vegas measures 226; 79; 33. Weights of a male from 11 miles east of Mexicali, Mexico, taken in March, and of a nonpregnant female from Death Valley, California, taken in April, are, respectively, 148.1 grams and 145.0 grams.

This species appears to have two molts per year. The winter pelage has much more underfur than the summer pelage, which is coarser to the touch. In both winter and summer pelage there are two color phases, the "drab phase" and the "cinnamon phase." The latter, in unworn winter pelage, has the upper parts Light Vinaceous–Cinnamon, the hairs with a narrow whitish subterminal band, underparts, sides of face, eye ring, legs, and feet white (feet in some specimens Cartridge Buff), tail bicolor, Cartridge Buff below and colored like upper parts above, although terminally lighter and in some specimens edged with whitish. In the drab phase the color pattern is the same, but grayish above instead of Light Vinaceous–Cinnamon, and distal third of tail with more blackish above.

The small size, harsh pelage, and round, not flattened, long tail (more than half the length of head and body) are distinctive features of this ground squirrel, which has not been found north of 37° latitude. Specimens examined have ten mammae.

From the race *C. t. neglectus*, which occurs on the opposite side of the Colorado River, *tereticaudus* differs in longer tail and hind foot, lighter color, larger skull, with shorter nasals, broader rostrum, and broader interorbital region.

From information obtained mostly in areas other than Nevada, it is known that this squirrel is partial to sandy soil, digs burrows of its own and uses those of other rodents, climbs bushes and low trees, lives on seeds and also on green vegetation, and has litters of embryos ranging from six to twelve. Although the squirrels remain below ground most of the time in winter, they may not hibernate; some have been observed aboveground in nearly every month of the year.

Records of occurrence.—Specimens examined, 4, as follows: *Clark Co.:* ½ mi. E St. Thomas, 1250 ft., 2 (D. R. Dickey Coll.); 4 mi. NW Las Vegas, 2100 ft., 1 (D. R. Dickey Coll.); 12 mi. S and 5 mi. E Searchlight, 2600 ft., 1. Additional records (Howell, 1938:187): *Nye Co.:* Ash Meadows; Pahrump Valley. *Clark Co.:* Bunkerville.

Citellus lateralis
Golden-mantled Ground Squirrel

Three races of this species occur in Nevada. The animals typically live in the Transition and higher life-zones. At several places they occur about rocks among sagebrush, piñons, and junipers, but this is at the upper margin of the Upper Sonoran Life-zone where indicators of the Transition Life-zone can be found, if carefully sought.

On each side of the back, one white or buffy white stripe extends from the shoulder to the rump. This is bordered (in Nevadan races) on each side by a black stripe. The back between the black stripes is brownish, as also are the sides, although they are of a lighter tone. The underparts are buffy white, with the hair plumbeous basally. On the throat, on the insides of the legs, and over the feet the hair is buffy white to the base. A reddish "mantle" covers the head and sides and top of the neck. The tail is black above, mixed with a few hairs tipped with some shade of cinnamon, which color forms a border to the flattened tail that underneath is solidly reddish.

Unlike *C. leucurus*, the present species has but one molt each year. At any given locality in late spring and early summer the adult males acquire the new pelage, including the bright mantle, before the adult females acquire their new pelage. It is supposed that the physiological drain on the female resulting from her nursing of the young delays by a little the assumption of the new pelage. However that may be, the difference in pelage, particularly in color of mantle, is so great at the time of year mentioned that many collectors have been led to wonder if they had two species, until they obtained enough individuals to show that the difference in color resulted only from a difference in time of molt of the two sexes.

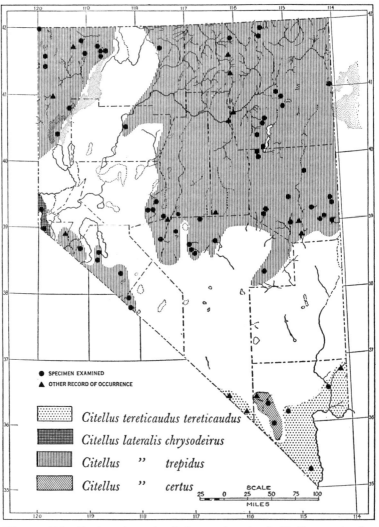

Fig. 225. Distribution of round-tailed ground squirrel, *Citellus tereticaudus*, and golden-mantled ground squirrel, *Citellus lateralis*.

Altitudinally, this squirrel occurs from as low as 4500 feet in the Pine Forest Range (Taylor, 1911:221) up to 11,200 feet in the Snake Mountains, and it probably ranges higher than this—up to timber line. The preferred habitat is open timber where rocks or fallen logs or both occur. The animals also frequent the edges of open meadows. Where sparse stands of old aspens remain in areas so heavily grazed by domestic sheep that reproduction of aspen has been stopped, these squirrels sometimes are numerous. Seemingly, the open forest habitat thus created by man's domestic animals is to the liking of the squirrels. Rock slides also are favored living quarters. In the small meadows, in open timberlands, and along the lower edges of the rock slides about Stella Lake at the head of Lehman Creek in the Snake Mountains, *C. lateralis*, in early July of 1929, was the most abundant mammal next to *Peromyscus maniculatus*.

Here, between the 10,000- and 11,000-foot elevation, burrows in the meadows mostly were beneath slabs of rock the tops of which protruded slightly aboveground. Whether at the mouth of a burrow or some distance away from it, *C. lateralis* rarely sits up picket-pin fashion, as does *C. beldingi*, but keeps its body more nearly on the horizontal plane. Fitch (MS), on Pahrum Peak, watched one "sprawled out on the top of a boulder basking in the sun." Engler (MS), on Mt. Rose, in August, watched one animal "stretch and yawn much like a cat. This was done in a sunny spot on loose dirt." Sometimes the animals climb trees and bushes. Durrant (MS), on July 1, 1933, at 8000 feet elevation on the south slope of Mount Jefferson, shot a specimen in "an old *Cercocarpus ledifolius* (mountain mahogany)." Another, Hall (1931b:54), on August 19, 1930, three miles west of Hamilton, was "shot as it sat on a limb fifteen feet above the ground hunched up against the trunk of a vertically growing white pine. Since there was no leaning snag or other inclined pathway which provided a means of reaching his position in the tree, the inference was that the ground squirrel had climbed" up the straight trunk.

Like other mammals which hibernate, these squirrels accumulate much fat in the autumn. Borell and Ellis (1934a:26) record that when in the Ruby Mountains from October 12 until November 6, 1929, none of this species was seen. Because the species was found abundantly in this same area in spring and summer, they inferred that the squirrels had gone into hibernation by October 12.

Probably all of the larger hawks and carnivores prey on golden-mantled ground squirrels. Alcorn (MS), on August 16, 1939, at 7000 feet in Kingston Canyon, watched a long-tailed weasel (*Mustela frenata*) pursue one, and Taylor (1911:221), on July 31, in the broad pass east of Duffer Peak in the Pine Forest Mountains, saw a "large western redtail (*Buteo borealis calurus*)" catch one of these squirrels. The writer, on July 31, 1935, fired a shot at a Cooper hawk flying rapidly through a grove of aspens, 13 miles north of Paradise Valley, and caused it to drop the near half-grown golden-mantled ground squirrel being carried in its talons.

These squirrels eat mainly seeds and berries. Brode (MS), on July 16, 1934, on Mount Grant, Mineral County, shot one of these squirrels that had a piñon nut in its cheek pouch. Engler (MS), on August 5, 1936, at 8500 feet on the south side of Mount Rose, shot a squirrel that had climbed into the lower branches of a bush where it was feeding on wild, ripe currants. Meat baits, at traps set for carnivores, are attractive to these squirrels, and some of the traps the pans of which were scented with musk from the glands of a short-tailed weasel (*Mustela cicognanii*) took several of these squirrels.

Most of our specimens from Nevada were taken in May or later in the spring and summer, and none of the females is recorded as pregnant. Howell (1938:32) says of the species, without reference to Nevada, that females have been recorded with four and six embryos, rarely with eight. Grinnell and Dixon (1919:680) record the embryos in six females taken in the Sierra Nevada of California as 5, 2, 5, 6, 6, and 5.

Citellus lateralis chrysodeirus (Merriam)
Golden-mantled Ground Squirrel

Tamias chrysodeirus Merriam, N. Amer. Fauna, 4:19, October 8, 1890. Type from Fort Klamath, Klamath County, Oregon.
Citellus lateralis chrysodeirus, Howell, N. Amer. Fauna, 56:203, May 18, 1938.
Citellus chrysodeirus chrysodeirus, Bailey, N. Amer. Fauna, 55:139, August 29, 1936.

Distribution.—Sierra Nevada in the vicinity of Lake Tahoe. See figure 225.

Remarks.—Measurements of ten "full-grown" males and ten "full-grown" females from the Sierra Nevada of California (Grinnell and Dixon, 1919:676) are 272 (253–290), 266 (243–285); 89 (75–104), 83 (67–100); 41 (38–43), 41 (39–44); weight, 181 (155–218), 199 (136–245) grams.

From *C. l. trepidus*, *chrysodeirus* differs in shorter tail, which averages less, not more, than half the length of the head and body, in darker color, and in having a skull the interpterygoid fossa and nasals of which average slightly wider. Between the stripes on the back, the color is browner, less grayish, and the underparts and hind feet are less whitish. Also the underside of the tail averages darker in color. Specimens from the Sierra Nevada in the vicinity of Lake Tahoe have tails which average between 45 and 48 per cent of the length of the head and body, as opposed to an average of 41 per cent in a series of topotypes from Oregon. Despite this geographic variation in length of tail, the specimens from the vicinity of Lake Tahoe are distinctly *chrysodeirus*, rather than *trepidus*. Intergradation with *trepidus* is discussed in the account of that race.

Records of occurrence.—Specimens examined, 6, as follows: *Washoe Co.:* 2 mi. W Mt. Rose Summit, 1; 3 mi. SSW Mt. Rose, 9000 ft., 1; Incline Creek, 7100 ft., 1. *Douglas Co.:* Zephyr Cove, 1; 1 mi. E Zephyr Cove, 1; ½ mi. N and 3 mi. E Edgewood, 1.

Citellus lateralis trepidus (Taylor)
Golden-mantled Ground Squirrel

Callospermophilus trepidus Taylor, Univ. California Publ. Zoöl., 5:283, February 12, 1910. Type from head of Big Creek, Pine Forest Mts., 8000 feet, Humboldt County, Nevada. Taylor, Univ. California Publ. Zoöl., 7:220, June 24, 1911.
Callospermophilus lateralis, Linsdale, Amer. Midland Nat., 19:177, January, 1938.
Callospermophilus chrysodeirus trepidus, Borell and Ellis, Journ. Mamm., 15:25, 72, February 15, 1934.
Citellus lateralis trepidus, Hall, The Murrelet, 12:2, May, 1931; Howell, N. Amer. Fauna, 56:206, May 18, 1938.

Distribution.—In suitable habitat from about latitude 38° northward over all the state, except in the vicinity of Lake Tahoe. See figure 225.

Remarks.—Measurements of three males and four females from the Pine Forest Mountains are: ♂, 280 (266–288), ♀, 270 (250–283); 104 (101–108), 101 (93–107); 40.7 (40–42),

40.2 (40–41). Corresponding measurements of ten males and seventeen females from southern Lander and northern Nye counties are 262 (250–279), 263 (250–295); 95 (90–105), 91 (85–103); 38.7 (36–42), 39.1 (36–42); weight, 146.9 (104.4–171.5), 169.3 (132.0–204.6) grams.

The long tail, whitish underparts, and grayish color of the back between the stripes are distinguishing features of this race. Comparison with *chrysodeirus* and *certus* are made in the accounts of those races. From several localities in western Nevada specimens here assigned to *trepidus* show intergradation with *chrysodeirus*. Animals from 12-mile Creek approach *chrysodeirus* in color, as does one specimen from Pine Grove and one from Mt. Grant. The two specimens last-mentioned have tails amounting to only 45 and 44 per cent of the length of the head and body; in this respect they also show approach to *chrysodeirus*. Another individual from Mount Grant, although light in color like *trepidus*, has a long tail amounting to 56 per cent of the length of the head and body. Even in the two specimens which show certain features of *chrysodeirus*, the light color of the underparts and resemblance in all features considered throw the animals with *trepidus*.

From north to south there is some geographic variation within the race *trepidus*. Size, as shown by each of the three external measurements, decreases toward the south. In the skull, the measurements of greatest length, palatilar length, and zygomatic breadth decrease toward the south, except that the populations in the White Mountains of Esmeralda County have skulls that are as large in most parts measured as those in the populations from along the northern border of the state. Nevertheless, the nasals in the animals from the White Mountains average short, as in animals from southern Lander County, northern Nye County, and White Pine County. All these have nasals which average shorter than those in animals from Humboldt and Elko counties farther north. The difference is slight, 13.7 mm. as against 14.4 mm., and insufficient to merit subspecific recognition. Whereas the tail amounts to about 60 per cent of the length of the head and body in the population from the Pine Forest Mountains, it is slightly less, 55 per cent, in animals from the Ruby Mountains of Elko County, as it is also in animals from the central part of the state, for example the Toyabe Mountains. The percentage is only 53 in the large series from the Snake Mountains of White Pine County, and still farther south in the race *certus*, on the Charleston Mountains, the percentage is only about 45. Here, then, from the Pine Forest Mountains, in northwestern-Nevada, there is a trend, to the eastward, but more pronouncedly to the southward, toward a tail both actually and relatively shorter.

Records of occurrence.—Specimens examined, 192, as follows: *Washoe Co.:* 12-mile Creek, ½ to 1 mi. E Calif. boundary, 5300 ft., 7; Barrel Spring, 5700 ft., 9½ mi. E and 3½ mi. N Ft. Bidwell, 2; ½ mi. N Vya, 6200 ft., 1; 10½ mi. S Vya, 5800 ft., 1; Rock Creek, Granite Range, 6400 and 7350 ft., 2; ½ mi. S Rock Creek, 6000 ft., 1; Horse Canyon, Pahrum Peak, 5800 ft., 2. *Humboldt Co.:* Virgin Valley, 5000 ft., 1; Alder Creek, 5000–7000 ft., 4; head of Big Creek, Pine Forest Mts., 8000 ft., 8; Big Creek, Pine Forest Mts., 6000 ft., 1; Big Creek Ranch, Pine Forest Mts., 4900–5000 ft., 17; 13 mi. N Paradise Valley, 6700 ft., 2; Pine Forest Mtn. [= Duffer Peak], 8400–9000 ft., 4; 5 mi. N Summit Lake, 5900 ft., 1; Leonard Creek, Pine Forest Mts., 6500 ft., 2. *Pershing Co.:* El Dorado Canyon, Humboldt Range, 6000, 7000, and 8000 ft., 3. *Churchill Co.:* 3 mi. W Carroll Summit (east of Eastgate), 1. *Mineral Co.:* 2 mi. SW Pine Grove, 7250 ft., 2; Cottonwood Creek, Mt. Grant, 7400 and 7700 ft., 2; Lapon Canyon, Mt. Grant, 8900 ft., 1; Endowment Mine, 6500 ft., Excelsior Mts., 1. *Esmeralda Co.:* Pinchot Creek, 8100–8200 ft., White Mts., 4; Chiatovich Creek, 8200 ft., 1. *Lander Co.:* Smiths Creek, 7100 ft., 2; ¼ mi. E Carroll Summit, 1; Peterson Creek, Shoshone Mts., 6500 ft., 3; Kingston Creek, 7100–9000 ft., 11; W of Kingston Ranger Station, 9300 ft., 1; Mahogany Canyon, 8000 ft., 1. *Nye Co.:* Wilson Creek, 7500 ft., Toquima Range, 1; Wisconsin Creek, 7000–7800 ft., 5; head of Wisconsin Creek, 11,000 ft., 1; Shoshone Mts., 2 mi. W Indian Valley, 9000 ft., 1; Greenmonster Canyon, Monitor Range, 7500–9000 ft., 4; S slope Mt. Jefferson, 8400–9300 ft., 3; SW slope Mt. Jefferson, 10,008 ft., 1; N slope Toquima Mtn., 9000 and 9400 ft., 2; Toquima Range, 1½ mi. E. Jefferson, 7750 ft., 1; 1½ mi. SE Jefferson, 9000 ft., 1; Toquima Range, 2 mi. W Meadow Creek Ranger Station, 1; Antone Creek, 2 mi. S Meadow Creek Ranger Station, 1; Quinn Canyon Mts., Burned Corral Canyon, 6700–6750 ft., 3. *Elko Co.:* (unless otherwise noted, in coll. of Ralph Ellis): Jarbridge Mts., 3 mi. N Jarbidge, 1; summit between heads of Copper and Coon creeks, Jarbidge Mts., 1; 6 mi. SW Mountain City, Cobb Creek, 6500–6550 ft., 5 (Mus. Vert. Zoöl.); Pilot Peak, ½ mi. W Debbs Creek, 6000–8200 ft., 4 (Mus. Vert. Zoöl.); head of Ackler Creek, 6800 ft., 2; Steels Creek, 7000 ft., 2; Jerry Creek,

TABLE 6
CRANIAL MEASUREMENTS (IN MILLIMETERS) OF CITELLUS

Name and locality	Number of individuals averaged or catalogue no.	Sex	Greatest length	Palatilar length	Zygomatic breadth	Cranial breadth	Interorbital breadth	Postorbital breadth	Length of nasals	Maxillary tooth row
Citellus townsendii canus										
Ontario and Vale, Ore. (after Howell,										
1938:66)	13 av.	♂, ♀	38.3	18.4	25.5	17.8	7.9	9.6	13.4	7.7
	min.		37.3	17.5	24.5	17.2	7.3	8.9	12.8	7.2
	max.		39.6	19.5	26.7	18.4	8.4	10.5	13.8	8.2
Citellus townsendii mollis										
Within 8 mi. Fallon	6 av.	♂	39.4	18.7	25.4	17.6	7.9	9.2	13.5	8.3
	min.		38.6	18.0	24.3	17.2	7.3	8.8	12.8	8.0
	max.		40.3	19.0	26.2	17.8	8.3	9.5	14.7	8.9
Within 8 mi. Fallon	6 av.	♀	37.3	17.8	24.0	17.0	7.7	9.2	12.6	8.1
	min.		36.5	17.4	22.9	16.5	7.4	8.7	11.9	7.5
	max.		38.7	18.8	25.0	17.7	8.3	9.8	13.0	8.6
Citellus richardsonii nevadensis										
3 mi. NE Winnemucca	67799	♂	45.5	22.5	30.2	19.9	—	—	16.7	10.1
4 mi. S Romano	70559	♂	45.9	22.1	31.0	20.3	9.8	10.9	15.6	10.0
4 mi. S Romano	70558	♀	47.2	22.8	31.4	20.4	9.5	10.8	16.5	10.3
13 mi. SSW Whiterock	78449	♀	44.8	21.6	29.1	19.6	9.3	11.0	15.3	10.1
Citellus beldingi oregonus										
Topotypes	10 av.	♂	44.5	21.2	29.2	19.5	9.3	10.9	15.7	9.5
	min.		43.3	20.0	28.0	19.0	8.8	10.4	15.1	8.9
	max.		45.8	22.1	31.2	20.8	10.1	11.6	16.8	9.7
Topotypes	20 av.	♀	44.2	21.0	29.3	19.3	9.2	10.9	15.6	9.5
	min.		42.3	20.0	28.4	18.5	8.8	10.1	14.5	9.2
	max.		46.0	22.3	30.5	20.6	9.6	11.7	16.7	9.8
Citellus beldingi beldingi										
Sierra Nevada, California	7 av.	♂	44.9	21.4	29.2	19.5	9.7	11.1	16.1	9.5
'	min.		43.6	20.8	27.7	19.0	8.9	10.4	15.2	9.2
	max.		46.0	21.8	30.2	20.2	10.4	11.7	16.8	9.8
Sierra Nevada, California	10 av.	♀	43.7	21.0	28.3	19.1	9.1	10.9	15.8	9.5
	min.		43.2	20.2	28.0	18.5	8.6	10.5	15.1	9.3
	max.		44.7	22.3	29.5	19.7	9.5	12.0	17.1	9.8
Citellus beldingi crebrus										
Lander and Nye counties	10 av.	♂	46.7	21.6	30.2	20.1	9.6	10.9	15.9	9.7
	min.		45.7	21.2	29.3	19.3	9.0	10.3	15.3	9.4
	max.		47.9	21.9	31.9	20.5	10.5	11.3	17.0	10.1
Lander and Nye counties	15 av.	♀	45.6	21.2	30.1	20.0	9.6	10.6	15.5	9.0
	min.		44.4	20.5	29.1	19.2	8.9	10.1	14.5	9.2
	max.		47.6	22.0	31.4	20.6	10.2	11.1	16.5	10.3
Citellus variegatus grammurus										
Baker and Cleve creeks	5 av.	♂	61.5	29.1	37.8	24.7	14.6	17.1	23.0	12.0
	min.		59.9	28.0	36.3	24.0	13.1	16.7	21.7	11.9
	max.		63.6	29.9	38.9	25.2	15.7	17.6	24.4	12.1
White Pine Co.	3 av.	♀	60.0	28.1	37.4	24.1	14.3	16.9	21.8	11.8
	min.		59.5	27.7	36.8	23.9	13.9	16.4	21.4	11.7
	max.		60.5	28.7	37.9	24.3	14.9	17.6	22.1	11.8

TABLE 6—(*Continued*)

Name and locality	Number of individuals averaged or catalogue no.	Sex	Greatest length	Palatilar length	Zygomatic breadth	Cranial breadth	Interorbital breadth	Postorbital breadth	Length of nasals	Maxillary tooth row
Citellus beecheyi fisheri										
½ mi. W Verdi........................	73160	♂	61.8	29.8	38.0	24.0	13.5	17.1	22.0	11.5
½ mi. E Zephyr Cove................	85184	♂	58.7	27.5	37.9	23.3	14.1	17.0	20.9	11.5
Incline Creek........................	65204	♂	56.5	26.3	34.5	22.8	11.7	16.1	19.2	11.1
		av.	59.0	27.9	36.8	23.4	13.1	16.7	20.7	11.4
½ mi. E Zephyr Cove................	85186	♀	55.0	25.1	—	22.3	12.2	15.8	18.7	11.5
Citellus leucurus leucurus										
Clark Co.............................	6 av.	♂	38.7	17.5	22.3	17.7	8.6	13.6	11.3	6.8
	min.		37.9	17.1	21.6	17.4	8.3	13.0	10.7	6.5
	max.		39.7	18.0	22.5	18.3	8.8	14.1	11.7	7.1
Clark Co.............................	6 av.	♀	38.1	17.3	22.0	17.6	8.4	13.5	11.0	7.0
	min.		37.5	16.7	21.5	17.0	8.1	12.9	10.1	6.8
	max.		38.7	18.0	22.7	18.0	8.7	14.2	11.7	7.5
Citellus tereticaudus tereticaudus										
Imperial Co., California...............	4 av.	♂	37.5	17.2	24.2	17.8	8.0	12.9	11.7	7.2
	min.		37.1	16.9	24.1	17.6	7.1	12.7	11.4	7.1
	max.		37.9	17.3	24.4	18.0	8.3	13.1	12.2	7.5
Imperial Co., California...............	4 av.	♀	35.7	16.3	21.8	17.2	7.6	12.4	10.5	7.5
	min.		34.4	15.7	21.2	17.0	7.0	11.7	9.9	7.4
	max.		36.4	16.6	22.2	17.3	7.9	13.6	11.1	7.5
4 mi. NW Las Vegas...................	15571*	♀	34.5	15.5	21.2	16.7	7.0	12.6	10.4	7.5
Citellus lateralis chrysodeirus										
Klamath Co., Ore. (after Howell,1938:204)	10 av.	♂	42.3	19.5	26.3	19.5	10.2	13.2	14.4	8.2
	min.		41.0	18.5	24.8	19.1	9.3	12.5	13.3	7.6
	max.		44.0	21.0	28.0	20.0	11.2	13.9	15.8	8.6
Klamath Co., Ore. (after Howell, 1938:204)	10 av.	♀	41.1	18.7	25.5	19.3	9.5	12.7	14.4	8.0
	min.		39.6	18.0	23.8	18.1	9.1	11.2	13.2	7.4
	max.		42.7	19.5	26.4	19.9	10.0	14.0	15.4	8.7
Citellus lateralis trepidus										
Lander and Nye counties...............	10 av.	♂	41.8	18.7	25.7	19.2	9.2	12.7	13.7	8.4
	min.		40.8	18.2	24.7	18.5	8.7	11.7	12.9	8.0
	max.		43.3	19.4	27.0	20.0	10.0	13.6	14.8	8.8
Lander and Nye counties...............	17 av.	♀	41.5	18.7	25.7	19.1	9.0	12.3	13.6	8.1
	min.		40.4	18.2	24.3	18.6	8.3	11.6	12.5	7.5
	max.		42.9	19.4	26.6	19.5	9.6	12.9	14.9	8.5
Citellus lateralis certus										
Topotypes (after Howell, 1938:208); includes subadults	6 av.	♂	42.5	19.9	26.0	19.9	9.8	13.2	13.8	8.1
	min.		41.0	19.0	25.0	19.3	9.2	12.8	13.3	7.8
	max.		43.4	20.5	27.2	20.3	10.4	13.8	14.2	8.6
Topotypes (after Howell, 1938:209)......	7 av.	♀	41.7	19.0	25.2	19.5	9.4	12.9	13.7	8.3
	min.		41.0	18.0	24.4	19.0	8.9	12.2	12.8	7.7
	max.		42.8	20.0	25.7	20.0	9.6	13.5	14.4	8.7

* D. R. Dickey Collection.

6700 ft., 1; Three Lakes, 6500 ft., 8; Long Creek, 7830 ft., 2; Harrison Pass R. S., 6050 ft., 1; W side Ruby Lake, 3 mi. N White Pine Co. line, 6200 ft., 4. *White Pine Co.*: Willow Creek, 2 mi. S Elko Co. line, 6500 ft., 3 (coll. of Ralph Ellis); Overland Pass, E slope Ruby Mts., 8 mi. S Elko Co. line, 1 (coll. of Ralph Ellis); 2 mi. SE Schellbourne, 7050 ft., 1; Gleason Creek, 7500 ft., 1; 3 mi. W Hamilton, 6800–8400 ft., 5; Rye Grass Canyon, 5 mi. N Mt. Moriah, 8400 ft., 1; 1 mi. E Mt. Moriah, 10,000–10,600 ft., 3; Hendry Creek, 9400 ft., 1½ mi. E Mt. Moriah, 2; Cleve Creek, Shell Creek Range, 8100 and 8300 ft., 2; 2½ mi. SW Hamilton, 7500 ft., 1; ¾ mi. N Stella Lake, Snake Mts., 11,200 ft., 1; Stella Lake, Snake Mts., 10,750 ft., 5; ½ mi. E Stella Lake, Snake Mts., 10,400 ft., 4; Lehman Creek, 8200 ft., 1; Willard Creek, Spring Valley, 7000–7700 ft., 5; Baker Creek, 8400–8675 ft., 9; Water Canyon, 10 mi. N Lund, 1.

Additional records:*Washoe Co.*: 20 mi. NNW Deep Hole (Hall, MS). *Douglas Co.* (Howell, 1938:208): Mount Siegel. *Humboldt Co.* (Howell, 1938:207): "Badger (20 miles northwest of Summit Lake, Humboldt County)." *Eureka Co.* (Howell, 1938:208): Palisade; Monitor Mts. "(25 miles southwest of Eureka)." *Nye Co.* (Howell, 1938:207): Arc Dome. *Elko Co.*: Deep Creek (Hall, MS); Taylors Canyon (Hall, MS); Carlin (Howell, 1938:207). *White Pine Co.* (Hall, MS): Willow Creek, 7100 ft., Egan Range; Chimney Rock Spring, 7400 ft., 28 mi. S Ely

Citellus lateralis certus (Goldman)
Golden-mantled Ground Squirrel

Callospermophilus lateralis certus Goldman, Journ. Mamm., 2:232, November 29, 1931. Type from north base of Charleston Peak, Clark County, Nevada; Burt, Trans. San Diego Soc. Nat. Hist., 7:403, May 31, 1934.

Citellus lateralis certus, Howell, N. Amer. Fauna, 56:208, May 18, 1938.

Distribution.—Limited to the Spring Mountains, Clark County. Does not occur outside of the state. See figure 225.

Remarks.—Two males measure 240, 257; 61, 74; 40, 37. The first weighs 189.2 grams. Three subadult females measure 249, 247, 249; 69, 70, 63; 40, 40, 38; weight, 200.0, 199.7, 192.0 grams. Howell (1938:208) records average measurements of eighteen adults, including both sexes, as 249, 77.4, 38.5.

Diagnostic features of *certus* are short tail (averages about 45 per cent of length of head and body), dark color of underside of tail, pale color of underparts and back, and short black stripes. In relation to the head and body, the tail is about the same length as in *chrysodeirus*, but shorter than in *trepidus*. The color of the underside of the tail is darker, and the black stripes are shorter than in either of these races; the feet and underparts lack the buffy color of *chrysodeirus*, and the back between the stripes is paler (less brownish); the zygomatic breadth averages slightly less (60 as opposed to 62 per cent), and the nasals are narrower posteriorly than in *trepidus*.

This race is isolated in the Spring Mountains and, according to our records, does not occur in the yellow pine and white fir associations of the near-by Sheep Mountains to the eastward.

Records of occurrence.—Specimens examined, 37, all from the Spring Mountains of Clark County, as follows: Lee Canyon, 8200 ft., 8 (D. R. Dickey Coll.); Charleston Peak, 10,000 ft., 6 (D. R. Dickey Coll.); Charleston Peak, 11,800 ft., 1 (D. R. Dickey Coll.); Charleston Park Resort, 8000 ft., Kyle Canyon, 21 (17 in D. R. Dickey Coll.); N side Potosi Mtn., 7000 ft., 1.

Additional record (Burt, 1934:403): *Clark Co.*: Wheeler Well.

Genus **Eutamias** Trouessart
West American and Asiatic Chipmunks

The thirteen kinds of chipmunks in Nevada belong to nine full species. These miniature squirrels, delicate in appearance and agile in marked degree, vary, depending on the species, from about 30 to 110 grams in weight, and range from about 185 to 265 mm. in total length. Of this length, the tail amounts to a little less than half. On the upper parts there are five or three blackish and four whitish stripes, all of approximately equal width. Alternating light and dark stripes on the sides of the head differentiate members of this genus from *Citellus* (ground squirrels), which lacks stripes on the head, although a few species of *Citellus* have stripes on the back. In the skull there

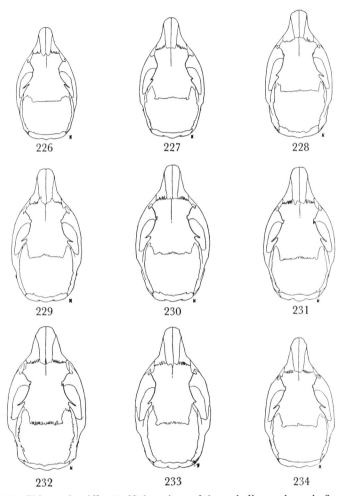

Figs. 226–234. Chipmunks. All, × 1. (Other views of these skulls are shown in figs. 235–245.)

Fig. 226. *Eutamias minimus scrutator*.
Fig. 227. *Eutamias amoenus celeris*.
Fig. 228. *Eutamias panamintinus*.
Fig. 229. *Eutamias quadrivittatus inyoensis*.
Fig. 230. *Eutamias palmeri*.

Fig. 231. *Eutamias speciosus frater*.
Fig. 232. *Eutamias townsendii senex*.
Fig. 233. *Eutamias quadrimaculatus*.
Fig. 234. *Eutamias dorsalis grinnelli*.

is no infraorbital canal, as in *Citellus*, but, instead, a foramen. Similarly, the anterior border of the zygomatic notch in the maxillary is opposite P4, instead of opposite M1, as in *Citellus*. From *Tamiasciurus* and *Sciurus*, the upper molars of *Eutamias* differ in that the transverse ridges diverge labially, whereas they are more nearly parallel in the tree squirrels. The dental formula is i. $\frac{1}{1}$, c. $\frac{0}{0}$, p. $\frac{2}{1}$, m. $\frac{3}{3}$. The first upper premolar (P3) is a mere spike, but is normally present. Its presence is a useful character in distinguishing *Eutamias* from *Tamias* of eastern North America in which this tooth is lacking.

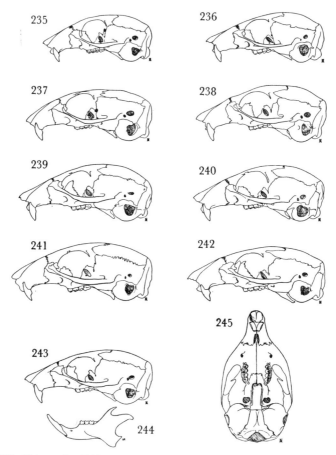

Figs. 235–245. Chipmunks. Different views of these skulls are shown in figs. 226–234. All, ×1.

Fig. 235. *Eutamias minimus scrutator*, Wisconsin Creek, 7800 feet, no. 45513, ♀.

Fig. 236. *Eutamias amoenus celeris*, Pine Forest Mountain, no. 7931, ♂.

Fig. 237. *Eutamias panamintinus*, ½ mile west Wheeler Well, no. 52149, ♂.

Fig. 238. *Eutamias quadrivittatus inyoensis*, mouth Pole Canyon, south side Baker Creek, east side Snake Mountains, no. 41574, ♂.

Fig. 239. *Eutamias palmeri*, 6 miles north Charleston Park Resort, 7800 feet, no. 86850, ♂.

Fig. 240. *Eutamias speciosus frater*, Galena Creek, 8950 feet, no. 88261, ♂.

Fig. 241. *Eutamias townsendii senex*, Blue Canyon, Placer County, California, 5000 feet, no. 18870, ♂.

Fig. 242. *Eutamias quadrimaculatus*, 3 miles south Mount Rose, 8500 feet, no. 88265. ♂.

Figs. 243–245. *Eutamias dorsalis grinnelli*, southwest base Groom Baldy, 7200 feet, no. 47949, ♂.

The species and subspecies of this genus are difficult to handle systematically because the kinds are so nearly alike, especially in the shape of the skull. Fortunately for the present account, the genus, including all the Nevadan species, has been carefully revised by A. H. Howell (1929), and, subsequently, D. H. Johnson, at the California Museum of Vertebrate Zoölogy, has intensively reworked the California chipmunks and at this writing (1940) has put his findings in manuscript form. This manuscript he has generously made available to me and I have freely drawn on it and on Howell's published accounts, citing the source for actual quotations; in many other places, even though I have drawn upon Howell and Johnson for information about systematic relationships, I have expressed the data partly or wholly in my own words, without citing the source.

Chipmunks of the genus *Eutamias* are essentially Boreal, rather than Sonoran in distribution. Excepting the species *E. minimus*, all of them in Nevada live in timbered areas, but their climbing is done more in bushes, among rocks, and over fallen tree trunks than it is in trees. To be sure, some species, for example, *E. speciosus* and to a lesser extent *E. dorsalis*, do climb in trees to a considerable degree. Between the species there are marked differences in climbing ability. Also, marked differences occur between species with respect to choice of habitats and ecologic niches in which each lives.

Chipmunks feed principally on seeds, nuts, and berries, and live in holes in fallen logs or in underground holes, generally beneath boulders or logs. In some areas, and possibly in all, they hibernate in winter, but in the southern part of the range of the genus, individuals of some species are active for at least part of the time in winter.

Males average about 3 per cent smaller than females in linear measurements. There are two molts per year, except that the tail undergoes but one molt.

Eutamias minimus scrutator Hall and Hatfield
Least Chipmunk

Eutamias minimus scrutator Hall and Hatfield, Univ. California Publ. Zoöl., 40:321, February 12, 1934. Type from 10,500 feet, near Blanco Mountain, White Mountains, Mono County, California.
Eutamias pictus, Taylor, part, Univ. California Publ. Zoöl., 7:222, June 24, 1911.
Eutamias minimus pictus, Howell, N. Amer. Fauna, 52:39, November 30, 1929; Borell and Ellis, Journ. Mamm., 15:26, February 15, 1934.
Eutamias amoenus monoensis, Howell, N. Amer. Fauna, 52:65, November 30, 1929, part.
Eutamias minimus, Linsdale, Amer. Midland Nat., 19:180, January, 1938.
Tamias minimus, Allen, Bull. Amer. Mus. Nat. Hist., 3:110, June, 1890.
Tamias minimus pictus Allen, Bull. Amer. Mus. Nat. Hist., 3:115, June, 1890.

Distribution.—In sagebrush, from Mount Magruder, Breen Creek, and Eagle Valley northward. The low valleys in the western part of the state are uninhabited as far north as the northern end of the Black Rock Desert, probably because their floors do not support sagebrush. See figure 246.

Remarks.—Measurements of ten of each sex from the Toyabe Mountains are: ♂, 184 (173–192), ♀, 194 (185–203); 77 (71–86), 84 (74–90); 29 (28–32), 29 (28–30); weight (April and May), 33.3 (30.0–36.6), 43.2 (37.9–54.0) grams.

This is the smallest of Nevadan chipmunks. In summer pelage the light and dark areas are well defined, not tending to blend as in the species *amoenus*. In dorsal view, the dark dorsal stripes appear wider than the light stripes. Howell (1929:39) describes the summer pelage essentially as follows: head Smoke Gray mixed with Light Pinkish Cinnamon; median dorsal stripe blackest; outer dark dorsal stripes with more brownish; lateralmost dark stripe Mikado Brown and continuous with cinnamon color of neck; outer pair of light dorsal stripes white; inner pair grayish white, mixed with Sayal Brown; sides Pinkish Cinnamon, fading in time to Light Pinkish Cinnamon; rump and thighs Smoke Gray; feet grayish-white, washed with Pale Pinkish Buff; tail above blackish-brown, the hairs tipped with a color between Pinkish Buff and Deep Olive-Buff; tail beneath, medially of this same olive color surrounded by black and fringed by the olive color; underparts whitish. Winter pelage more grayish (less reddish) over all of upper parts and sides, especially on anterior half of upper parts.

The small size and olive color of the ventral side of the tail are two distinguishing features of this chipmunk. The skull is smaller than in any other Nevadan species, is relatively high and narrow, and is strongly arched in lateral view, with appressed zygomatic arches and narrow interorbital region.

As compared with topotypes and other Utah-taken specimens of *Eutamias minimus consobrinus*, individuals of *E. m. scrutator* are lighter colored and less rufescent; their skulls are relatively shorter and the length of the tail relative to length of head and body is less.

From *Eutamias minimus pictus*, as known from twenty topotypes, *scrutator* differs as follows: tail relatively and actually shorter; coloration darker and more rufescent; top of head notably darker (less grayish); supraorbital dark stripe clearly defined rather than faint and anteriorly barely discernible; anterior half of median side of pinna of ear darker; postauricular patches more buffy and posteriorly more defined; inner pair of dark dorsal stripes wider; lateralmost dark stripe Mikado Brown rather than Snuff Brown, and continuous with cinnamon color of side of neck rather than continued anteriorly as a distinct stripe on side of neck, which in *pictus* is gray rather than cinnamon in color; tail above more blackish, overlain with Cinnamon Buff, brighter below than in *pictus;* feet darker; cinnamon generally present on anal region. Skull generally larger; relatively as well as actually broader, especially through rostrum and across lacrimals, but actually, as well as relatively, shallower through postorbital region; squamosal arm of zygoma projects more abruptly from cranium. The lesser depth of the skull (the vertical depth averaging less than 55 per cent of the zygomatic breadth) results from depression of the frontals and the anterior parts of the parietals. In *scrutator* the zygomata are nearly parallel, whereas in *pictus* each zygoma is bowed outward at the middle and the squamosal arm is shorter. This greater length of the squamosal arm in *scrutator*, coupled with the relatively wider skull and depressed frontoparietal region, gives the skull a markedly flattened appearance in comparison with that of the narrower, rounded skull of *pictus*. This condition is reflected in the circumstance that, when adult skulls are laid top down on a flat surface, those of *scrutator* are stable, whereas those of *pictus* are unsteady, and rock back and forth or twirl around at a slight touch. In this inverted position the occiput in *scrutator* is higher.

In making comparisons of color, only specimens in the summer coat have been used.

From *Eutamias amoenus*, the other species with which it is apt to be confused, *minimus* differs in smaller size, lighter color on sides of body, "olive" rather than reddish underside of tail, more whitish (less reddish) underparts, brownish rather than black lateral dark stripes, narrower and less-flattened tail (central reddish area on ventral side about 5 mm. wide and mixed with dark hairs, rather than 9 mm. wide and uniformly colored), less-flattened skull with more appressed zygomatic arches, shorter rostrum, and less-recurved incisors.

This is the only Nevadan chipmunk not restricted to the vicinity of coniferous trees. It lives amid the sagebrush (*Artemisia tridentata*) even at the highest elevations from which we have recorded it. The lowest elevations of occurrence are where sagebrush gives way to *Sarcobatus* and other shrubs of lower zonal distribution. Along Marys River, 22 miles north of Deeth, we found it amid *Chrysothamnus*, but near tall sagebrush, and at one and a half miles northeast of Tecoma some lived among *Sarcobatus* bushes. In a third instance, in Buena Vista Valley at 4600 feet elevation, I saw one amidst the *Sarcobatus*. These are the three exceptions, so far as my field notes go, and all the other observations recorded therein pertain to the animals' occurrence where sagebrush is the only or dominant shrub. Over the long stretches of the Black Rock Desert, in Railroad Valley, in the Carson Sink, and in similar places where *Sarcobatus*, *Atriplex*, and other shrubs predominate to the exclusion of *Artemisia tridentata*, this chipmunk does not occur.

It is a common sight to see these animals up in sagebrush and associated shrubs; scores of notebook entries emphasize the predilection for climbing. From such vantage points as often are thus attained, the animals "chirp" at the intruder in scolding fashion just about as fast as a person can count the notes, at every seventh or eighth of which the animal flips the tail two or three times. From having taken them from traps before sunrise—they were caught only a few minutes before—I know these animals to be early risers, in midsummer at least. Even so, it was light enough at the time to justify applying the term diurnal rather than nocturnal to their activities.

Their food, I think, is mostly seeds, but there is little positive information in our field notes on this point. On July 23, 1936, 5 miles north of Summit Lake, C. Engler (MS) watched one jump up and climb a stalk of tall grass until the stem bent over to the ground where the chipmunk cut off the head of seeds before repeating the maneuver on another stalk. The contents of the cheek pouches of a female taken on May 14, 1930, 5 miles southeast of Millett P. O., comprised 160 seeds of Russian thistle and 6 larger seeds, possibly Cruciferae. Howell (1929:10) writes that in June, 1893, at Halleck, Vernon Bailey found the least chipmunk "feeding extensively on the larvae and pupae of a web worm that was stripping the sagebushes. Several stomachs examined contained little else but these insects, and Mr. Bailey estimated that the caterpillars formed about 60 per cent of the chipmunk food at the time."

The considerable number of lactating females taken in May leads to the supposition that most of the young are born in April. A female taken on April 24, 1930, 4 miles southeast of Millett P. O. at an elevation of 5500 feet, contained six embryos.

Records of occurrence.—Specimens examined, 444, as follows: *Washoe Co.:* 12-mile Creek, ½ mi. E Calif. boundary, 5300 ft., 1; Barrel Spr., 5700 ft., 9½ mi. E and 3½ mi. N Ft. Bidwell, 1; 4 mi. S Diessner, 5800 ft., 2; 3 mi. N Vya, 5900 ft., 2; ½ mi. N Vya, 6000 and 6200 ft., 2; 2 mi. W Vya, 6500 ft., 2; 1 mi. W Vya, 6700 ft., 1;

3 mi. E Painted Point, 5850 ft., 2; 12 mi. S Vya, 5800 ft., 3; 13 mi. S Vya, 5800 ft., 1; 15 mi. S Vya, 5800 ft., 1; mouth Little High Rock Canyon, 5000 ft., 5; 10 mi. SE Hausen, 4675 ft., 6; 15 mi. NNW Deep Hole, 5500 ft., 3; 12 mi. N and 2 mi. E Gerlach, 4000 ft., 1; Rock Creek, Granite Mts., 6600 ft., 2; Horse Canyon, Pahrum Peak, 5800 ft., 2; 2¾ mi. SW Pyramid, 4300 ft., 1. *Douglas Co.:* 11 mi. E Gardnerville, 6000 ft., 1; Carson River, 5

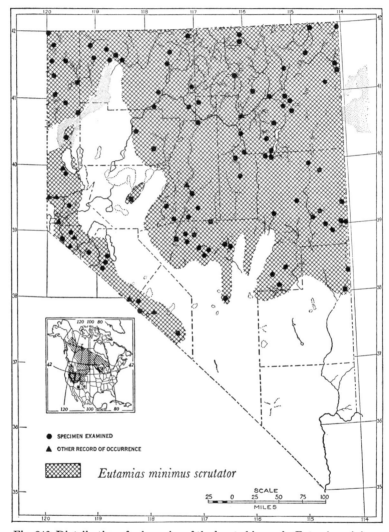

SPECIMEN EXAMINED

OTHER RECORD OF OCCURRENCE

Eutamias minimus scrutator

Fig. 246. Distribution of subspecies of the least chipmunk, *Eutamias minimus,* with insert showing range of the species.

Vi. SE Minden, 4900 ft., 1. *Storey Co.:* 6 mi. NE Virginia City, 6000 ft., 9. *Humboldt Co.:* 36 mi. NE Paradise malley, 5500 ft., 4; Virgin Valley, 3; Alder Creek, 6000–7000 ft., 4; head of Big Creek, 8000 ft., 7; meadow, near head of Big Creek, 7000 ft., 3; 12½ to 14 mi. N Paradise Valley, 6400–7000 ft., 12; Cottonwood Range, 1 (U. S. Nat. Mus., Biol. Surv. Coll.); Big Creek Ranch, 4350 ft., 4; 5 mi. N Summit Lake, 5900 ft., 4; Leonard Creek, 6500 ft., 7; ½ mi. W Quinn River Crossing, 4100 ft., 1; Quinn River Crossing, 4100 ft., 26; 5 mi. W Paradise Valley, Hansen Canyon, 8200 ft., 1; 18 mi. NE Iron Point, 4600 ft., 1; 16 mi. NE Iron Point, 4500 ft., 1;

7 mi. N Winnemucca, 4400 ft., 2; 1 mi. N Winnemucca, 4600 ft., 1; 1½ mi. NW Winnemucca, 4900 ft., 2; 3 to 5 mi. SW Winnemucca, 4500 ft., 8; 10 mi. SW Winnemucca, 4500 ft., 1; 23 mi. NW Battle Mountain, 1. *Pershing Co.:* El Dorado Canyon, Humboldt Range, 7800 and 8000 ft., 2; S slope Granite Peak, East Range, 2; S base Granite Peak, East Range, 1. *Churchill Co.:* 1½ mi. N Mountain Well, 6100 ft., 1. *Mineral Co.:* 2 mi SW Pine Grove, 7250 ft., 4; Cottonwood Creek, Mt. Grant, 7400 ft., 1; Lapon Canyon, Mt. Grant, 8900 ft., 2; Fletcher, 6098 ft., 1. *Esmeralda Co.:* Pinchot Creek, White Mts., 8200 ft., 1; Middle Creek, 9500 ft., 2; Chiatovich Creek, 8200 ft., 17; N side Mt. Magruder, 7400 ft., 1. *Lander Co.:* Izenhood, 1; 3 mi. S Izenhood, 1; 1 mi. E Battle Mountain, 1; Reese River Valley, 7 mi. N Austin, 2; Smiths Creek, 6800 ft., 1; Birch Creek, 7000 ft., 2; Kingston Ranger Station, 7500 ft., 6; Mahogany Canyon, 8000 ft., 1; Peterson Creek, Shoshone Mts., 7000 ft., 9. *Eureka Co.:* Evans, 1; Union, 2; Winzell, 5; 4 mi. S Romano, Diamond Valley, 3. *Nye Co.:* Toquima Range, Wilson Canyon, 7500 ft., 1; Wilson Creek, 7200 ft., 1; Wisconsin Creek, 7600–8200 ft., 17; 4 mi. S Millett, 5500 ft., 2; 4 to 5 mi. SE Millett P. O., 5500 ft., 16; 5 mi. S Millett P. O., 5500 ft., 1; Ophir Creek, 6500 ft., 2; ridge S of Wisconsin Creek, 8000 and 8400 ft., 2; Bells Ranch, Reese River, 6890 ft., 3; South Twin River, 6500 ft., 1; Greenmonster Canyon, Monitor Range, 7500–8600 ft., 7; Fish Spring Valley, ½ mi. N Fish Lake, 6500 ft., 1; S slope Mt. Jefferson, Toquima Range, 7600–8000 ft., 4; N slope Toquima Peak, 9400 ft., 1; Monitor Valley, 8 to 9 mi. E Toquima Peak, 7000 ft., 3; Toquima Range, 1 to 1¾ mi. E Jefferson, 7600–7800 ft., 5; Toquima Mts., 2 mi. W Meadow Valley Ranger Station, 1; White River Valley, 17 mi. W Sunnyside, 2; Burned Corral Canyon, Quinn Canyon Mts., 6700–6750 ft., 3; Quinn Canyon Mts., 7 mi. E Nyala, 6700 ft., 2; Garden Valley, 8½ mi. NE Sharp, 5; Breen Creek, Kawich Mts., 7000–7100 ft., 3; 2½ mi. NE Silverbow, 7000 ft., Kawich Mts., 1. *Elko Co.:* 7 mi. NE San Jacinto, 5300 ft., 2; Goose Creek, 2 mi. W Utah boundary, 5000–5800 ft., 13; Owyhee River, 7 mi. NW Mountain City, 5300 ft., 8; Cobb Creek, 6 mi. SW Mountain City, 6500 and 6550 ft., 3; 15 mi. S Contact, 5800 ft., 8; 13 mi. N Montello, 5000 ft., 3; 1½ mi. NE Tecoma, 4900 ft., 1; Tecoma, 4900 ft., 1; Marys River, 22 mi. N Deeth, 5800 ft., 2; 1 mi. SE Tuscarora, 5900 ft., 4; Cobre, 6100 ft., 2; 10 mi. N Elko, 1; Halleck, 1. The following specimens listed from Elko Co., unless otherwise noted, are in the coll. of Ralph Ellis: 2 mi. NW Halleck, 1; head of Ackler Creek, 6800 ft., 1; 3 to 5 mi. W Halleck, 5200–5300 ft., 15 (8 in Mus. Vert. Zoöl.); Steels Creek, 7000 ft., 2; summit of Secret Pass, 6200 ft., 1; Jerry Creek, 6700 ft., 4; Three Lakes, 9740 ft., 2; Harrison Pass R. S., 6050 ft., 3; W side Ruby Lake, 3 mi. N White Pine Co. line, 6200 ft., 2. *White Pine Co.:* Willow Creek, 2 mi. S Elko Co. line, 6500 ft., 1 (coll. of Ralph Ellis); W side Ruby Lake, 3 mi. S Elko Co. line, 6100 ft., 1 (coll. of Ralph Ellis); 5 mi. SE Greens Ranch, Steptoe Valley, 5900 ft., 1; E side Schellbourne Pass, 6800 ft., 2; Gleason Creek, 7500 ft., 3; Smith Creek, 3 mi. W Smith Creek Cave, 6700 ft., 1; Cleve Creek, Shell Creek Range, 8300–9200 ft., 6; 3 mi. W Hamilton, 8400 ft., 1; Steptoe Creek, 5½ mi. SE Ely, 6430–6500 ft., 3; Lehman Creek, 8200 ft., 1; Spring Valley, 7 mi. SW Osceola, 6100–6275 ft., 9; Willard Creek, Spring Valley, 7700 ft., 2; Baker Creek, 5800 ft., 2; 1 mi. N Baker, 4; 2½ mi. E Baker, 1; Baker Creek, 6600–8500 ft., 19; Spring Valley, 5 mi. NW Shoshone P. O., 6100 ft., 1. *Lincoln Co.:* lat. 38° 17′ N, ¼ to 1 mi. W Utah boundary, 7700 ft., 3; Eagle Valley, 3½ mi. N Ursine, 5900 ft., 6.

Additional records: Howell (1929:39) lists specimens from forty-one localities in Nevada. The following of his record stations importantly supplement the occurrences listed above for the purpose of outlining the geographic range of this race: *Washoe Co.:* Verdi; Reno. *Ormsby Co.:* Carson. *Douglas Co.:* Mt. Siegel; Holbrook. *Mineral Co.:* Queen Station, Owens Valley; Silver Peak Mountains (near summit). *Lander Co.:* Silver Creek, *Nye Co.:* Cloverdale Creek. *Elko Co.:* Carlin. D. G. Nichols (MS) records specimens from Hardscrabble Canyon, 6500 ft., on the west side of Pyramid Lake, Washoe Co.

Eutamias amoenus
Yellow-pine Chipmunk

Each of the three races occurring in Nevada average a little larger than *E. m. scrutator,* except that the tail is about the same length; therefore the tail is relatively shorter in *amoenus.* The animal is richly colored, especially in summer pelage, because much of the lighter colored area is suffused with ochraceous. Howell (1929:61) has described this pelage, for the subspecies *amoenus,* essentially as follows: top of head Smoke Gray mixed with Cinnamon; dark facial stripes Fuscous, the middle one and sometimes upper one Fuscous Black; dark dorsal stripes black, edged with, and sometimes mixed with, Ochraceous-Tawny; median pair of white stripes Pale Smoke Gray, sometimes with hairs of Cinnamon color; outer pair of light stripes white; sides Ochraceous-Tawny; rump and thighs Smoke Gray, washed with Cinnamon-Buff; tail above, Fuscous Black, overlain with Clay color; tail beneath, Cinnamon or Sayal Brown, margined with Fuscous-Black and edged with Clay color; feet Light Pinkish Cinnamon; underparts whitish, often washed with Light Buff. The skull is only a little larger than that of *E. minimus*, slightly shallower, with less appressed zygomatic arches, longer rostrum, and more recurved incisors.

Eutamias amoenus differs from *minimus, panamintinus,* and *quadrivittatus* as noted in the accounts of those species. *E. amoenus* differs from *speciosus* and *palmeri* in about the same features as noted in comparison with *quadrivittatus,* except that the differences in color are even more pronounced in comparison with the pale *palmeri.* From *townsendii* and *quadrimaculatus, amoenus* may easily be told on basis of lesser size alone, and the edging of the tail is distinctly buffy in *amoenus* (the race *celeris* excepted) rather than white or only faintly buffy as in the three larger sized species just named. The same difference in color of edging of the tail separates this species also from *dorsalis.* In comparison with it, *amoenus* has distinct (reddish-black) submedian dark dorsal stripes rather than grayish dark stripes that are indistinct or wanting, a skull less flattened dorsally, and incisive foramina that are parallel rather than convergent anteriorly.

The places where this species enters the state all have some yellow pines (or Jeffrey pines in vicinity of Lake Tahoe) as well as other plants characteristic of the Transition Life-zone. These places in Nevada are at the margins of the range of this species, which has a wide distribution outside Nevada to the west, north, and east. In parts of this wide range outside Nevada the species occurs in life-zones higher than the Transition, but rarely if anywhere in those lower. In Nevada our specimens mostly were taken on ledges of rocks or amid brush, but one was shot from the lower branches of a pine.

Eutamias amoenus amoenus (Allen)
Yellow-pine Chipmunk

Tamias amoenus Allen, Bull. Amer. Mus. Nat. Hist., 3:90, June, 1890. Type from Fort Klamath, Klamath County, Oregon.

E[utamias]. amoenus, Merriam, Proc. Biol. Soc. Washington, 11:191, July 1, 1897.

Eutamias amoenus amoenus, Howell, N. Amer. Fauna, 52:61, November 30, 1929; Borell and Ellis, Journ. Mamm., 115:72, February 15, 1934.

Distribution.—In Transition Life-zone where it enters state at two places: north-central Elko County and northwestern Washoe County. See figure 247.

Remarks.—Four males and six females from northern Elko County measure: ♂, 204 (197–213), ♀, 213 (201–224); 87 (82–94), 91 (80–98); 31.8 (31–32), 32.7 (32–34); weight of two males, 49.6 and 51.3 grams, of three females, 58.0, 66.0, and 71.7 grams.

The color and skull are as described for the species. From both *celeris* and *monoensis,* this race differs in longer hind foot, slightly longer tail, more brownish top of head, light facial and dorsal stripes more suffused with ochraceous, sides more intensely ochraceous, top and edges of tail and feet darker, and skull broader. The differences are greater between *amoenus* and *celeris* than between *amoenus* and *monoensis.*

Records of occurrence.—Specimens examined, 21, as follows: *Washoe Co.:* 12-mile Creek, ½ mi. E Calif. boundary, 3; 12 mi. E and 3 mi. N Ft. Bidwell, 5700 ft., 3. *Elko Co.:* Owyhee River, 7 mi. NW Mountain City, 1; 3 mi. N Jarbidge, 1 (coll. of Ralph Ellis); Cobb Creek, 6 mi. SW Mountain City, 6500–6550 ft., 7; summit between heads of Copper and Coon creeks, Jarbidge Mts., 6 (coll. of Ralph Ellis).

Eutamias amoenus celeris Hall and Johnson
Yellow-pine Chipmunk

Eutamias amoenus celeris Hall and Johnson, Proc. Biol. Soc. Washington, 53:155, December 19, 1940. Type from head of Big Creek, 8000 feet, Pine Forest Mountains, Humboldt County, Nevada.
Eutamias pictus, Taylor, Univ. California Publ. Zoöl., 7:222, June 24, 1911, part.
Eutamias amoenus monoensis, Howell, N. Amer. Fauna, 52-65, November 30, 1929, part.

Distribution.—Transition Life-zone and higher parts of the Pine Forest Mountains in Humboldt County. See figure 247.

Remarks.—Measurements of five male and three female topotypes are: ♂, 190 (187–194), ♀, 193 (189–195); 83 (78–86), 84 (82–85); 31.2 (30–32), 29 (29–30). No weights are available. The color and the skull are as described for the species. From *monoensis*, *celeris* differs in hind foot shorter, tail slightly shorter, top of head grayer, light facial and dorsal stripes clearer white, ochraceous color of sides more intense, top and edges of tail paler, feet paler, and skull narrower. Comparison with the subspecies *amoenus* is made in the account of that race.

A skin with skull, U. S. Nat. Mus., Biol. Surv. Coll., catalogue no. 80755, obtained on September 17, 1896, by Clark P. Streator, in the "Cottonwood Range," was sent on loan by Dr. H. H. T. Jackson in response to my query about the basis of Howell's (1929:66) record of *Eutamias amoenus monoensis* in the Santa Rosa Mountains [= Cottonwood Range], and proves upon examination to be *Eutamias minimus scrutator.* In advance of examining this specimen it was supposed that it would be referable to *E. a. celeris.* which now, however, so far as known, is limited to the Pine Forest Mountains.

Records of occurrence.—Specimens examined, 25, as follows: *Humboldt Co.:* Alder Creek, 7000–8000 ft., 4; head of Big Creek, 8000 ft., 13; Pine Forest Mountain [= Duffer Peak], 8400–9400 ft., 6; ridge near Pine Forest Mountains, 2.

Eutamias amoenus monoensis Grinnell and Storer
Yellow-pine Chipmunk

Eutamias amoenus monoensis Grinnell and Storer, Univ. California Publ. Zoöl., 17:3, August 23, 1916. Type from Warren Fork of Leevining Creek, 9200 feet, Mono County, California. Howell, N. Amer. Fauna, 52:65, November 30, 1929, part.
Eutamias amoenus amoenus, Howell, N. Amer. Fauna, 52:61, November 30, 1929, part.
Eutamias amoenus, Stone, Proc. Acad. Nat. Sci. Philadelphia, 1904:588, October 17, 1904.
Tamias amoenus Allen, Bull. Amer. Mus. Nat. Hist., 3:90, June, 1890, part.

Distribution.—Transition Life-zone and higher areas in Sierra Nevada in vicinity of Lake Tahoe. See figure 247.

Remarks.—Measurements of six males and five females from the Mono Lake area of California, including the type specimen, are: ♂, 190 (188–193), ♀, 199 (195–202); 81 (76–83), 81 (73–85); 30.2 (29.0–31.1), 30.4 (29.7–31.1); weight, 42.6 (37.9–49.3), 54.9 (45.9–66.0) grams.

Color and skull are as described for the species. Comparisons with *amoenus* and *celeris* are made in the accounts of those forms.

The specimens here assigned to *monoensis* from southern Washoe County are intergrades between *monoensis* and *amoenus*. By Howell (1929) they would be referred to *amoenus.* Indeed, the one from Washoe was so identified by him. Johnson (MS), in a later study, also recognized that these specimens were intergrades, but referred them, as I have done here, to *monoensis*.

Skin no. 11426 of the Academy of Natural Sciences of Philadelphia recorded by Stone (1904:588) and Howell (1929:52) is labeled as taken on July 17, 1898, at Mount Sugar, Nevada, by A. S. Bunnell (field no. 201). I have examined the skin and it seems to be species *amoenus*, not *minimus*. Other chipmunks taken on this same trip to Mount Sugar are, according to R. T. Orr, in the collection of the California Academy of Sciences. Orr says that they are correctly named *Eutamias minimus*. I note also that Howell (1929:40) records three *minimus* from Mount Sugar in the collection of the Museum of Comparative Zoölogy. Because no. 11426 is the only specimen of *amoenus* from east of the valley of the Carson River, I made special effort to work out the history of this individual. R. T. Orr, in the spring of 1942, interviewed the collector, A. S. Bunnell, and learned that Bunnell went to Mount Sugar (which turns out to be Sugar Loaf of modern maps, at 38° 51′ N, 119° 33′ W) directly from Mount Tallac, California, where he had been collecting alone. The opportunity to join W. W. Price and associates in getting to and collecting on Mount Sugar was taken advantage of by Bunnell. Because *Eutamias amoenus* is common at Mount Tallac, the possibility presents itself that a mixup in labels occurred. I would expect the chipmunks on Sugar Loaf to be *Eutamias panamintinus* and *E. minimus*. *E. panamintinus* has been taken in the same range of mountains at Andersons Ranch and Mount Siegel. Further collecting in the Pine Nut Mountains on and near Sugar Loaf will be required to learn if *amoenus* as well as *panamintinus* occurs here. At no other place in Nevada have the two species been taken this near together. Although the specimen in question is listed below under *amoenus* in specimens examined, the locality of capture of the specimen is not shown on the distribution map, figure 247. If Mount Sugar were there shown as being within the range of *Eutamias amoenus monoensis*, the small scale of the map would represent the ranges of *E. a. monoensis*, and *E. panamintinus* as meeting at the place shown as the northernmost occurrence of *panamintinus*.

Records of occurrence.—Specimens examined, 8, as follows: *Washoe Co.*: W side Truckee River, 1 mi. W Verdi, 4900 ft., 1; Incline Creek, 7100 ft., 1; Calneva, 6400 ft., 1; Washoe, 1 (U. S. Nat. Mus., Biol. Surv. Coll.). *Douglas Co.*: Zephyr Cove, 6200 ft., 3; Mount Sugar, 1 (Acad. Nat. Sci. Philadelphia). Additional records (Howell, 1929:52): *Douglas Co.*: Glenbrook; Edgewood.

Eutamias panamintinus (Merriam)
Panamint Chipmunk

Tamias panamintinus Merriam, Proc. Biol. Soc. Washington, 8:134, December 28, 1893. Type from Johnson Canyon, Panamint Mountains [near lower edge of piñon belt at about 5000 feet, vicinity of Hungry Bill's Ranch, *fide* Grinnell, Univ. California Publ. Zoöl., 40:128, September 26, 1933], Inyo County, California.

Eutamias panamintinus Merriam, Proc. Biol. Soc. Washington, 11:194, July 1, 1897; Howell, N. Amer. Fauna, 52:78, November 30, 1929.

Eutamias panamintinus juniperus Burt, Journ. Mamm., 12:298, August 24, 1931. Type from one-half mile west of Wheeler Well, west slope of Charleston "Mountains" [= Peak], Clark County, Nevada; Burt, Trans. San Diego Soc. Nat. Hist., 7:406, May 31, 1934.

Distribution.—Piñon-juniper areas along southwestern border of state from Douglas County south to Potosi Mountain at latitude 36°. See figure 247.

Remarks.—Measurements of four of each sex from Charleston Peak are: ♂, 201 (190–209), ♀, 210 (203–214); 84 (80–86), 82 (70–91); 31.5 (30–32), 31 (31–31). A male from Pine Grove which measures 211, 89, 30, ear 18.0 from notch, weighs 62.3 grams. Two other males from there weigh 45.0 and 62.0 grams, giving an average of 56.4 grams. Two females from Cottonwood Creek measure 208, 208; 90, 84; 27, 29; ear from notch 18, 18; and weigh 52.0 and 53.1 grams.

This small, brightly colored chipmunk, only a little larger than *minimus* and *amoenus*, may be described with respect to color, after the system of Howell (1929:92), as follows: in summer pelage: top of head Smoke Gray mixed with Light Pinkish Cinnamon and bordered on sides of crown with Fuscous; ocular streak blackish near eye, otherwise Mikado Brown, as is submalar stripe, although it is shaded with Fuscous; ears Mouse Gray or Smoke Gray shaded on posterior margin with buffy white; postauricular patches creamy

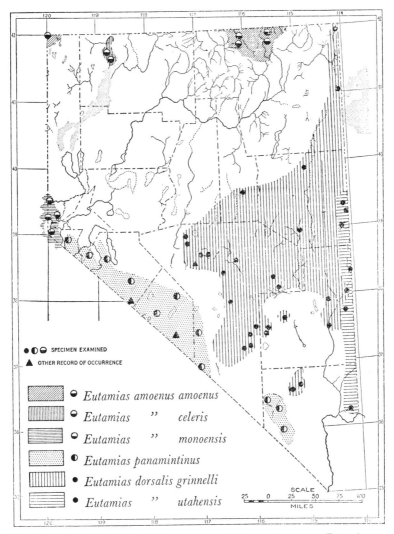

● ◐ ◖ SPECIMEN EXAMINED
▲ OTHER RECORD OF OCCURRENCE

◖ *Eutamias amoenus amoenus*
◖ *Eutamias " celeris*
◖ *Eutamias " monoensis*
◐ *Eutamias panamintinus*
● *Eutamias dorsalis grinnelli*
● *Eutamias " utahensis*

SCALE
25 0 25 50 75 100
MILES

Fig. 247. Distribution of three species of chipmunks, genus *Eutamias*.

white; median dorsal stripe black for short distance near middle of back, otherwise Mikado Brown, like other dark dorsal stripes; median pair of light dorsal stripes grayish-white, lateral pair white; sides Mikado Brown shading to Cinnamon below; rump and thighs Smoke Gray; feet Pinkish Buff, tinged with Smoke Gray; tail above Fuscous-Black overlain with Pinkish Buff; tail beneath Sayal Brown or Clay color bordered with

Fuscous-Black and tipped with Pinkish Buff; underparts buffy white. In winter pelage much grayer, dark dorsal stripes less blackish (more brownish), and stripes less contrasting in color.

Selected features in which *panamintinus* differs from *minimus* are: size larger; color more reddish, especially in the summer pelage; central area of underside of tail more reddish and broader; skull larger and top of brain case more flattened.

From *amoenus, panamintinus* differs in: slightly shorter feet and ears; lighter general coloration; gray rather than brown crown of head; narrower and lighter facial stripes; less conspicuous dark dorsal stripes of which only part of the median one is black and the lateral pair are almost obsolete; relatively narrower inner and broader outer light stripes; skull, in general, broader; roof of brain case flattened rather than rounded; nasals less prolonged anteriorly; incisive foramina longer; and upper incisors less recurved.

Comparison with *Eutamias quadrivittatus* has been made in the account of that form. From *E. palmeri, panamintinus* differs in about the same way as from *quadrivittatus*. From *speciosus, panamintinus* differs in color in about the same way as from *quadrivittatus* but more pronouncedly. The skull of *panamintinus* is of about the same length, but the brain case is much more flattened. From *senex* and *quadrimaculatus, panamintinus* can be distinguished by lesser size alone; also the tail has an edging of buff rather than white. From *dorsalis, panamintinus* differs in reddish rather than grayish tone of coloration of the upper parts, in reddish and distinct, as opposed to grayish and indistinct, submedian dark dorsal stripes, in more flattened brain case, and in incisive foramina that are parallel rather than convergent anteriorly.

D. H. Johnson, whose thorough study of Californian *Eutamias* has led him to examine related materials, writes (MS): "Examination of the series (except the type specimen) on which Burt . . . based the name *Eutamias panamintinus juniperus* and additional recently collected specimens from the vicinity of the Charleston Mountains reveals . . . differences from typical *panamintinus* . . . no greater than the differences between other series in the subspecies [and] I have considered *juniperus* a synonym of *E. a. panamintinus*." In deference to Johnson's special knowledge of *Eutamias*, his view is here made the basis for not recognizing *juniperus*. The population named *juniperus* averages smaller of skull than the few individuals from Pine Grove at the northern end of the geographic range of the species. More adequate material from the northern part of the range might reveal differences sufficiently great to warrant separation of these from the southern animals. The single specimen from Lone Mountain is notable for small size of skull. Additional specimens would be required to show if this is a feature common to all members of the population isolated on Lone Mountain and differentiating it from other populations of the species.

This species, like *dorsalis*, is an inhabitant of piñon areas, but *E. panamintinus* occurs only in the western part of the state, entirely west of the area occupied by *dorsalis*. On rock ledges, in bushes, or among the lower limbs of piñon trees, *panamintinus* is equally at home. One that I shot on April 5, 1936, in Springdale Canyon was abroad when the temperature in the shade was below freezing and even in the sunshine the temperature was so low as to make me suspect that most chipmunks of this species failed to hibernate. The specimen shot was in a low bush of *Salix* and when picked up had a willow catkin in its mouth.

Records of occurrence.—Specimens examined, 80, as follows: *Douglas Co.:* Andersons Ranch, 1 (Field Mus. Nat. Hist.); Mt. Siegel, 1 (Field Mus. Nat. Hist.). *Mineral Co.:* 2 mi. SW Pine Grove, 7250 ft., 4; Cottonwood Creek, Mt. Grant, 7400-7700 ft., 5; Endowment Mine, Excelsior Mts., 6500 ft., 1. *Esmeralda Co.:* Springdale Canyon, Lone Mountain, 6650 ft., 1; Cave Spring, 6248 ft., 2. *Nye Co.:* W side Stonewall Mtn., 6000 ft., 2; ½ mi.

E Grapevine Peak, 8500 ft., 1; 2½ mi. E and 1 mi. S Grapevine Peak, 6700 ft., 22; 2½ mi. E and ½ mi. S Grapevine Peak, 6700 ft., 1. *Clark Co.:* W slope Charleston Peak, Wheeler Well, 18 (9 in D. R. Dickey Coll.); Kyle Canyon, Charleston Peak, 7 (D. R. Dickey Coll.); 2 mi. SE Charleston Park Resort, 6900 ft., 1; N side Potosi Mtn., 5800–8000 ft., 13.

Additional records (Howell, 1929:79): *Mineral Co.:* Queen Station. *Esmeralda Co.:* Mount Magruder.

Eutamias quadrivittatus
Say Chipmunk

This species, with two subspecies, extends into Nevada from the east, where the species has an extensive range in the Rocky Mountain region. The size is medium for a *Eutamias,* and the color may be said to be the same. More in detail, and drawing on Howell's (1929:84) description, Nevadan specimens of *E. q. inyoensis* in hand in summer pelage may be described as: sides of nose Cinnamon-Buff; top of head Smoke Gray to Pale Smoke Gray, with wash of Pinkish Cinnamon on nose; stripes on side of head brownish rather than black, except that center of ocular stripe in some specimens is black; ears Fuscous or Chaetura Drab, shaded with Mouse Gray and bordered on posterior margin with buffy white; postauricular patches grayish-white; median dorsal stripe black margined with Sayal Brown; outer dark stripes blackish mixed with Sayal Brown or Mikado Brown; median pair of light stripes grayish-white; outer pair white; lateral dark stripes obsolete; sides Russet or Tawny, shading to Ochraceous-Tawny on sides of neck; thighs Cinnamon-Buff, shaded with Fuscous and Smoke Gray; feet Cinnamon-Buff or Light Pinkish Cinnamon; tail above Cinnamon mixed with Fuscous-Black, beneath Cinnamon, Cinnamon Buff, or Ochraceous-Tawny bordered with Fuscous Black and edged with Pinkish Buff; underparts creamy white. In winter pelage much paler; rump grayish and sides paler. Skull, in dorsal outline, strongly arched; rostrum narrow; upper incisors long and but slightly recurved.

This species is larger than *minimus* and smaller than *townsendii* and *quadrimaculatus;* and from these two larger species differs further in having a buffy, rather than white, edge on the tail.

From *amoenus,* it differs in larger size, grayer head and shoulders, narrower medial light dorsal stripes, less ochraceous suffusion over underparts, larger skull with relatively narrower brain case, more elevated rostrum, longer upper incisors, and more nearly parallel zygomatic arches.

From *panamintinus, quadrivittatus* differs in greater size, grayer shoulders, more solidly black and solidly white dorsal stripes; narrower and less-flattened brain case, longer upper incisors, larger cheek teeth, and more nearly parallel zygomatic arches.

Selected differences in comparison with *speciosus* are: ears shorter; tail averaging longer; colors paler, with light rather than dark elements in color pattern predominating; shoulders and crown of head gray rather than brown;

dark facial stripes paler, submalar stripe lacking black center below eye, and ocular stripe black only immediately adjacent to eye; medial pair of light dorsal stripes grayer and lateral pair purer white; neither pair heavily washed with ochraceous; subterminal black area on underside of tail more restricted, being about 10 mm. rather than 20 mm. anteroposteriorly; skull longer, and narrower except in interorbital region; upper incisors longer and less recurved, their outer borders forming an arc of a circle having a radius of about 5.7 mm. rather than 5.0 mm.; auditory bullae larger and zygomatic arches more nearly parallel.

Comparisons with *E. palmeri* and *E. dorsalis* are made in the accounts of those species.

The preferred habitat is among the conifers—yellow pines, white pines, and other conifers of high zonal position—which grow at an elevation higher than the piñons and junipers. The edges of meadows adjoining dense stands of timber and open places where logs and rocks occur were favorite sites about Stella Lake, on Wheeler Peak. There, on August 8, 9, and 10, 1938, at an elevation of approximately 10,500 feet, the females were suckling young and still were in winter pelage, but the males were in fresh summer pelage. Each adult male chipmunk and each adult female had a territory not shared with any other adult chipmunk, although many home territories were shared with *Citellus lateralis*. At this time, the young chipmunks big enough to be out of the burrow remained with the mothers. The home areas centered about fallen tree trunks in every instance. On this mountain the animals ranged up to at least 11,400 feet and, where adequate shelter was afforded, I suppose higher. A few, but not many, lived in thick stands of aspens, and at lower elevations they were common about ledges of rock and were found in mountain mahogany and in rock slides. They did not live in sagebrush where *Eutamias minimus* occurred, and only a few ventured into the piñons and junipers and then only for a short way. The belt of piñons and junipers was inhabited by *Eutamias dorsalis*. Likewise, in the Hot Creek Range and in the Quinn Canyon Range, a few *quadrivittatus* were taken in the upper part of the piñon timber, but *dorsalis* was the chipmunk far more abundant at each of these places.

In the Ruby Mountains, where *dorsalis* is lacking, *quadrivittatus* ranges right down to the lower edge of the junipers. In this mountain range, Borell and Ellis (1934a:27) note that most of these chipmunks "hibernate, or at least remain under cover, during the winter. However, a few were active during winter months. On December 23, 1927, two individuals were collected at 7000 feet altitude as they were running about the trunk of a juniper tree. A few days later another was seen sunning itself on top of a rock a short distance from where the first two were taken. At this time there was a foot of snow on the ground and the temperature at night was around 0° F., although the days were sunny and relatively warm. Where available, the pinyon nuts furnished a large part of the food for this species."

In 1929, on the eastern slope of Wheeler Peak, a female taken June 13, at 7500 feet, contained four embryos and another taken 5 days later, at 9000 feet, had five embryos.

Eutamias quadrivittatus inyoensis Merriam

Say Chipmunk

Eutamias speciosus inyoensis Merriam, Proc. Biol. Soc. Washington, 11:202, 208, July 1, 1897. Type from White Mountains (about 9000 feet, at southern end, near head of Black Canyon, *fide* Grinnell, Univ. California Publ. Zoöl., 40:129, September 26, 1933), Inyo County, California.

Eutamias quadrivittatus inyoensis, Howell, N. Amer. Fauna, 52:84, November 30, 1929, part; Borell and Ellis, Journ. Mamm., 15:27, February 15, 1934.

Eutamias quadrivittatus, Linsdale, Amer. Midland Nat., 19:182, January, 1938.

Distribution.—Transition and higher life-zones in White Mountains of Esmeralda County and in isolated mountain ranges of central part of state from the Desatoya Range eastward and from the Ruby Mountains southward to Kawich Mountains and Irish Mountain. See figure 248.

Remarks.—Measurements of ten of each sex from Baker Creek are: ♂, 213 (207–222), ♀, 217 (209–222); 86 (71–95), 87 (75–95); 32.1 (31–34), 32.5 (30–34); ear from notch, 17.2 (16.5–18.5), 17.6 (17–19); weight, 57.2 (51.4–63.6), 67.4 (52.6–80.5) grams.

Color and skull are as described in the account of the species. From *nevadensis*, this form differs in narrower light and dark dorsal stripes; greater extent of tawny areas; gray areas suffused with more dark color; more distinct facial markings; darker (more tawny) feet; tail much darker (more reddish) below, and bases of hair on top of tail more Cinnamon in color.

Intergradation in color between *inyoensis* and *nevadensis* was expected and looked for in the series of specimens from Irish Mountain. All are in winter pelage. They agree with *inyoensis* from the Snake Mountains and differ from *nevadensis* in every differential character noted above except one. That is the paler and less extensive dark facial stripes, in which feature the animals from Irish Mountain are intermediate. For comparisons with other forms, see the account of the full species, *quadrivittatus*.

Records of occurrence.—Specimens examined, 188, as follows: *Esmeralda Co.*: Chiatovich Creek, 8200 ft., 1. *Lander Co.*: Smiths Creek, 7100 ft., 2; Kingston R. S., 7500 ft., 4; Kingston Creek, 7100 ft., 2; Peterson Creek, Shoshone Mts., 6500–7600 ft., 3. *Eureka Co.*: 4 mi. S Tonkin, Denay Creek, Roberts Mts., 1. *Nye Co.*: Wilson Creek, 7500 ft., Toquima Range, 1; Wisconsin Creek, 7800 ft., 4; ridge S of Wisconsin Creek, 8000 ft., 4; Greenmonster Canyon, Monitor Range, 7500 ft., 3; S slope Mt. Jefferson, Toquima Range, 9300 ft., 1; Toquima Range, 1½ mi. SE Jefferson, 7800 and 8000 ft., 2; N slope Toquima Peak, Toquima Range, 9400 ft., 1; Monitor Valley, 8 to 9 mi. E Toquima Peak, 7000 ft., 3; 1 to 1½ mi. E Jefferson, 7600–7700 ft., 3; Hot Creek Range, 8 mi. W Tybo, 6700–6900 ft., 3; Burned Corral Canyon, Quinn Canyon Mts., 6700–7700 ft., 2; Quinn Canyon Mts., 6½ mi. E Nyala, 7000–8000 ft., 4; Kawich Mts., 2 4/5 mi. E Silverbow, 7300 ft., 3. *Elko Co.* (all in coll. of Ralph Ellis): head of Ackler Creek, 6800 ft., 1; Steels Creek, 7000 ft., 3; summit of Secret Pass, 6200 ft., 2; Three Lakes, 9740 ft., 12; Long Creek, 7830 ft., 5; Harrison Pass R. S., 6050 ft., 1; W side Ruby Lake, 6 mi. N White Pine Co. line, 6200 ft., 3; W side Ruby Lake, 3 mi. N White Pine Co. line, 6200 ft., 9. *White Pine Co.*: Willow Creek, 2 mi. S Elko Co. line, 6500 ft., 6 (coll. of Ralph Ellis); W side Ruby Lake, 3 mi. S Elko Co. line, 6100 ft., 5 (coll. of Ralph Ellis); Overland Pass, 8 mi. S Elko Co. line, 2 (coll. of Ralph Ellis); Cherry Creek, 6800 ft., 1; Halstead Creek, 1 mi. W Illipah, 6200 ft., 1; Deadman Creek, Mt. Moriah, 8100 and 9100 ft., 2; 1 mi. E Mt. Moriah, 10,400 ft., 1; Hendry Creek, 9800 ft., Mt. [Moriah, 2; Hendry Creek, 1½ mi. E Mt. Moriah, 9100–9400 ft., 6; Hendry Creek, 2½ mi. E Mt. Moriah, 8000 ft., 1; Cleve Creek, Shell Creek Range, 8200–8300 ft., 3; 3 mi. W Hamilton, 8100 and 8600 ft., 2; 2½ mi. SW Hamilton, 7600 ft., 1; Snake Mts., Teresa Lake, 10,500 ft., 1; Snake Mts., ½ mi. E Stella Lake, 10,400–10,500 ft., 9; Snake Mts., ¼ and ½ mi. W Stella Lake, 10,500 ft., 2; Lehman Creek, 8700 ft., 1; E side Wheeler Peak, Snake Mts., 9300 ft., 1; mouth Pole Canyon, S side Baker Creek, 7500 ft., 7; Pole Canyon, E slope Snake Mts., 8000 ft., 1; Baker Creek, 8000–8500 ft., 16; S side Baker Creek, 8600–9000 ft., 4; Water Canyon, 10 mi. N Lund, 1. *Lincoln Co.*: latitude 38° 17′ N, ¼ to 1 mi. W Utah boundary, 7300–7700 ft., 7; 10 mi. E Poney Springs, 6700 ft., 1 (found under hawk's nest); Wilson Peak, 7500 ft., Wilson Creek Mts., 7; Eagle Valley, 3½ mi. N Ursine, 5800 ft., 1; E and N slopes Irish Mountain, 7700–8300 ft., 13.

Additional records: Howell (1929:86) records specimens from seven localities in Nevada, all within the range outlined by specimens examined.

Eutamias quadrivittatus nevadensis Burt
Say Chipmunk

Eutamias quadrivittatus nevadensis Burt, Journ. Mamm., 12:299, August 24, 1931. Type from Hidden Forest, 8500 feet, Sheep Mountains, Clark County, Nevada. Burt, Trans. San Diego Soc. Nat. Hist., 7:407, May 31, 1934.

Distribution.—Transition and higher life-zones of Sheep Mountains. See figure 248.

Remarks.—Measurements of ten of each sex from the type locality are: ♂, 213 (210–222), ♀, 220 (215–224); 87 (74–91), 91 (81–96); 32.6 (31–34), 33.4 (32–35); weight of two females, 79.0 and 83.7 grams.

Size as in *inyoensis*. Color as described for *inyoensis* under account of the species except: thighs gray, feet Light Pinkish Cinnamon or gray, tail below Cinnamon-Buff. *E. q. nevadensis* is paler, especially less reddish and more grayish, than *inyoensis* in both summer and winter pelage. Comparison in more detail is made in the account of *inyoensis*. From *E. palmeri*, of the near-by Charleston Peak, *nevadensis* in summer pelage differs in much blacker as opposed to reddish dorsal stripes and anterior part of ears; underside of tail much lighter, and on its top grayish rather than showing Cinnamon color; skull with longer, more slender rostrum, and longer, more recurved upper incisors.

Records of occurrence.—Specimens examined, 36, as follows: *Clark Co.:* Hidden Forest, 7700 and 8500 ft., Sheep Mountains, 36 (27 in D. R. Dickey Coll.).

Eutamias palmeri Merriam
Palmer Chipmunk

Eutamias palmeri Merriam, Proc. Biol. Soc. Washington, 11:208, July 1, 1897. Type from Charleston Peak, 8000 feet, Clark County, Nevada. Howell, N. Amer. Fauna, 52:92, November 30, 1929; Burt, Trans. San Diego Soc. Nat. Hist., 7:409, May 31, 1934.

Distribution.—Transition and higher life-zones 7000 to near 12,000 feet on Charleston Peak. See figure 248.

Remarks.—Measurements of ten of each sex from Charlston Peak are: ♂, 214 (204–225), ♀, 218 (205–230); 86 (75–99), 87 (74–97); 32.8 (31–34), 33.7 (33–35); weight of three ♂, 65.1 (59.6–69.1), of two ♀, 75.4 and 75.6 grams.

The size is about as in *E. quadrivittatus inyoensis*. Specimens in hand answer to Howell's (1929:92) description of color, which is essentially: in summer pelage, sides of nose Light Pinkish Cinnamon; top of head Smoke Gray mixed with Light Pinkish Cinnamon and bordered on sides of crown with Fuscous; facial stripes Sayal Brown, shaded with Fuscous, median stripe with some Fuscous-Black in front of and behind eye; ears Sayal Brown on anterior part, buffy white on posterior part, clouded with Fuscous in middle; postauricular patches grayish white; median dorsal stripe narrow, Fuscous-Black, bordered with Mikado Brown; outer pair of dark stripes Mikado Brown, faintly shaded with Fuscous; median pair of light stripes Pale Smoke Gray; outer pair creamy white; no lateral stripes; sides Tawny or Cinnamon, shading to Pale Russet; rump and thighs Cinnamon Buff, shaded with Fuscous; feet Pinkish Buff to Pinkish Cinnamon; tail above Fuscous-Black with a more proximal, wide band of Cinnamon showing through; tail beneath Ochraceous-Tawny, bordered with Fuscous-Black and edged with Pinkish Buff; underparts creamy white. In winter pelage: upper parts more grayish, and dorsal stripes, both dark and light, less distinct; dark dorsal stripes Sayal Brown, median one Fuscous-Black in center; light dorsal stripes Pale Smoke Gray; nape and shoulders extensively washed with Pale Smoke Gray; rump and thighs Smoke Gray, washed with Cinnamon-Buff; sides Sayal Brown, shading to Cinnamon-Buff on sides of neck; feet and tail as in summer. The indistinctness of the dorsal stripes in winter is reminiscent of *Eutamias dorsalis*. The differences between coloration of winter and summer pelage is greater in *palmeri* than in its near relatives, *E. q. inyoensis*, *E. q. nevadensis*, or *E. s. frater*.

From *inyoensis*, *palmeri* differs, in summer pelage, in more brownish (reddish as opposed to blackish) dark dorsal stripes and grayer light dorsal stripes; more extensive gray

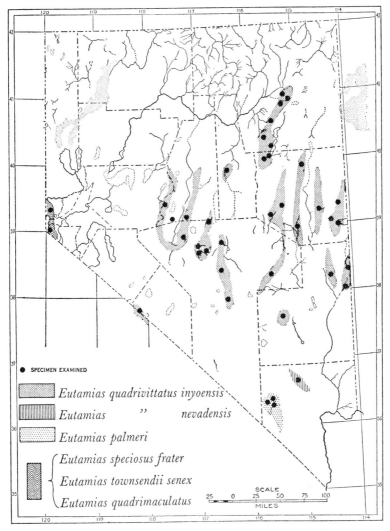

Fig. 248. Distribution of five species of chipmunks, genus *Eutamias*.

areas behind ears and over neck; tail above blacker and with more reddish (Cinnamon) showing through; more tawny color on underside of tail. Also in *palmeri*, the skull, rostrum, nasals, and upper incisors all shorter. Comparison with *E. q. nevadensis* is made in the account of that form.

Isolated on Charleston Peak, this chipmunk has developed characters which differentiate it so much from its near relatives of the species *E. quadrivittatus* as to justify full specific as opposed to subspecific separation for it. In habits, so far as is known, it closely resembles *E. quadrivittatus*. It ranges from 7000 feet altitude in the yellow pine belt up to timber line at about 12,000 feet. *E. panamintinus* occurs in the piñon and juniper belt which is below the range of *palmeri*. Burt (1934:408) judged from the numerous workings beneath conifers that seeds of these trees made up a considerable part of the food.

Records of occurrence.—Specimens examined, 85, unless otherwise noted in D. R. Dickey Coll., as follows: *Clark Co.:* Deer Creek, 8250 ft., 1 (Mus. Vert. Zoöl.); Charleston Peak, Kyle Canyon, 10,000 ft., 15; Kyle Canyon, 8000 ft., 30; Charleston Park, 8000 ft., 9; Charleston Park Resort, 7500 ft., 2 (Mus. Vert. Zoöl.); 2 mi. SE Charleston Park Resort, 6900 ft., 1 (Mus. Vert. Zoöl.); Clark Canyon, 2 mi. above sawmill, 8600 ft., 1; W slope Clark Canyon, 8000 ft., 1; head of Clark Canyon, 8500 ft., 1; W slope Clark Canyon, 8000 ft., 3 (1 in Mus. Vert. Zoöl.); N slope Lee Canyon, 8200 ft., 2; Lee Canyon, 8200 ft., 4; E slope Lee Canyon, 8200 ft., 6; Lee Canyon road, 6 mi. N Charleston Park Resort, 7800 ft., 2 (Mus. Vert. Zoöl.); N slope Charleston Peak, 7500 ft., 1 (Mus. Vert. Zoöl.); E slope, 11,800 ft., 4; E slope, 11,000 ft., 1; E slope, 8000 ft., 1.

Eutamias speciosus frater (Allen)
Lodgepole Chipmunk

Tamias frater Allen, Bull. Amer. Mus. Nat. Hist., 3:88, June, 1890. Type from Donner, Placer County, California.

Eutamias speciosus frater, Merriam, Proc. Biol. Soc. Washington, 11:194, 202, July 1, 1897.

Eutamias quadrivittatus frater, Howell, N. Amer. Fauna, 52:86, November, 1929.

Distribution.—Chiefly Canadian Life-zone, but invading, for a short distance, the Hudsonian and Transition life-zones in the vicinity of Lake Tahoe. See figure 248.

Remarks.—Measurements of ten of each sex from southern Tuolumne County, California, are: ♂, 211 (204–218), ♀, 210 (197–216); 88 (80–95), 87 (80–92); 33.0 (30–36), 33.7 (32–36); weight, 56.8 (50.6–60.8), 63.1 (55.2–69.5) grams.

In size, coloration, and cranial proportions *frater* resembles *Eutamias quadrivittatus*, but differs, as described in the account of that species, in several features. Although *quadrivittatus*, with its several races, was regarded by Howell as the same full species as *speciosus* (also with several races), D. H. Johnson (MS) has shown by study of Californian material from the area where the two kinds meet that they are two distinct species. In this critical area, Johnson (MS) points out that *speciosus* occurs only in or near the dense stands of lodgepole pine in the damper and more sheltered basins, whereas *quadrivittatus* was taken only in the vicinity of open forests of stunted limber pine and white bark pine on exposed and well-drained ridges and slopes near timber line. None of the specimens showed characters indicative of intergradation.

The zonal distribution of the species is from within the Transition Life-zone up into the Hudsonian Life-zone. The animals are notable for their climbing ability. When one is frightened it reportedly takes refuge in a tree. The number of embryos recorded from California by Grinnell and Storer (1924:183) in six pregnant females ranged from 3 to 6, with a mean of 4¼.

Records of occurrence.—Specimens examined, 17, as follows: *Washoe Co.:* 3 mi. SSW Mt. Rose, 9000 ft., 2; 3 mi. S Mt. Rose, 8500 ft., 6; Galena Creek, 8950 ft., 1; Incline Creek, 6300 ft., 1; 7100 ft., 2; 8400 ft., 2. *Douglas Co.:* Zephyr Cove, Lake Tahoe, 6250 ft., 1; 1 mi. E Zephyr Cove, 2.

Additional records (Howell, 1929:87): *Douglas Co.:* Glenbrook; Genoa (probably at higher elevation); Edgewood.

Eutamias townsendii senex (Allen)
Townsend Chipmunk

Tamias senex Allen, Bull. Amer. Mus. Nat. Hist., 3:83, June, 1890. Type from summit of Donner Pass, Placer County, California.

Eutamias townsendii senex, Howell, Journ. Mamm., 3:178, August 4, 1922; Howell, N. Amer. Fauna, 52:114, November 30, 1929.

Distribution.—Canadian and upper part of Transition life-zones of Sierra Nevada entering Nevada in Lake Tahoe area. See figure 248.

Remarks.—Measurements of seven males and ten females from the area extending from Cisco, Placer Co., to Donner Lake, Nevada Co., Calif., are: ♂, 241 (237–245), ♀, 249 (242–261); 100 (92–105), 101 (90–109); 35.4 (35–36), 35.7 (34–37); weight (ten adults of each sex from Yosemite National Park, California), 82.8 (66.8–96.3), 95.9 (73.0–108.5) grams.

This is the largest-bodied, heaviest, and darkest-colored species of the genus in Nevada. Following the plan of Howell (1929:115), the color of the winter pelage may be described as: top of head mixed Pinkish Cinnamon and Fuscous, sprinkled with grayish-white, bordered on each side with strip of Fuscous; sides of nose Cinnamon; dark facial stripes Sayal Brown, shaded with Fuscous, with blackish patch behind eye; light facial stripes grayish-white, tinged with buff; ears Fuscous or Fuscous-Black, bordered posteriorly with grayish-white; postauricular patches grayish-white; shoulders usually washed with Smoke Gray; dark dorsal stripes Fuscous-Black, more or less mixed with Mikado Brown, median stripe usually darkest; light dorsal stripes grayish-white, median pair grayest and sometimes clouded with Cinnamon; lateral dark stripes Mikado Brown; sides Clay Color; rump and thighs Dark Smoke Gray or Mouse Gray; hind feet Clay Color or pale Ochraceous-Tawny; toes Cinnamon-Buff; front feet Cinnamon-Buff; tail above, Fuscous-Black overlain with Pale Smoke Gray; tail beneath, Sayal Brown or paler than Ochraceous Tawny, bordered with Fuscous-Black and edged with Pale Smoke Gray; underparts creamy white. In summer pelage: sides darker, about Sayal Brown; and general tone of upper parts more ochraceous, lacking grayish wash on shoulders and rump; median pair of light dorsal stripes often strongly mixed with Pinkish Buff. Skull massive, broad, and flattened; brain case relatively small; zygomata widely expanded; rostrum broad anteriorly; nasals not separated anteriorly by notch; palate terminating posteriorly in slender spine.

Comparison with *quadrivittatus* is made in the account of that species. The large size (in both external and in most cranial measurements) and dark color distinguish it from all other Nevadan species.

Although this is the darkest-colored Nevadan kind of chipmunk, it is the lightest-colored subspecies of the species *townsendii*, which ranges northwestward from the Sierra Nevada into the humid Pacific coastal district.

E. t. senex is less of a climber than *speciosus*, and in the upper part of the Transition Life-zone and in the Canadian Life-zone the preferred habitats are in mature stands of coniferous trees or in areas where stumps and logs of large diameter abound. Of three pregnant females recorded (Grinnell and Storer, 1924:185) from the Sierra Nevada of California, one had two embryos, another four, and the third five.

Record of occurrence.—Specimens examined: *Douglas Co.:* Glenbrook, 2 (U. S. Nat. Mus., Biol. Surv. Coll.).

Eutamias quadrimaculatus (Gray)
Long-eared Chipmunk

Tamias quadrimaculatus Gray, Ann. and Mag. Nat. Hist., 20 (ser. 3):435, December, 1867. Type from Michigan Bluff, Placer County, California.
Eutamias quadrimaculatus, Merriam, Proc. Biol. Soc. Washington, 11:203, July 1, 1897; Howell, N. Amer. Fauna, 52:121, November 30, 1929.
Tamias macrorhabdotes, Allen, Bull. Amer. Mus. Nat. Hist., 3:78, June, 1890. Type from Blue Canyon, Placer County, California.

Distribution.—Lower part of Canadian Life-zone and upper part of Transition Life-zone of Sierra Nevada in vicinity of Lake Tahoe. See figure 248.

Remarks.—Measurements of nine males and six females from Merced Grove of Big Trees, California, are: ♂, 233 (230–239), ♀, 239 (230–245); 91 (85–100), 94 (90–101); 35.5 (34–37), 36.5 (35–37); weight, 78.6 (74.1–89.0), 91.9 (81.0–105.0) grams.

The size is only slightly less than in *E. t. senex*, and the color is as described in that form, except that: top of head lacking Pinkish Cinnamon; sides of nose Clay Color or Sayal Brown; dark facial stripes Fuscous-Black; submalar stripe shaded with Mikado Brown, broad, and reaching back beneath ear to postauricular patch; lateral dark stripes Fuscous mixed with Mikado Brown; median pair of light stripes grayish-white, frequently mixed with Sayal Brown; outer pair of light stripes creamy white; sides Sayal Brown to Snuff Brown; rump and thighs Neutral Gray mixed with Fuscous and sprinkled with grayish-white; hind feet deep Pinkish Cinnamon or Pinkish Buff; front feet similar, but paler; tail below Ochraceous-Tawny or Mikado Brown. In summer pelage, more ochraceous, the difference with season being about the same as described for *E. t. senex*. Skull small and lightly built for a member of the *townsendii* group of chipmunks; zygomatic arches flaring widely; rostrum narrow and shallow; nasals long; brain case short and broad; upper rows of teeth widely spaced, and individual teeth small.

Selected differences from *senex* are: lesser size; longer ears; more bushy tail; brighter coloration, with areas of white of purer quality; more extensive postauricular patches; lighter tail edging; blackish rather than brownish dark facial stripes; submalar dark stripe expanded into broad blackish spot below ear, rather than present as a narrow brownish stripe; longer nasals and greater interorbital breadth, but skull in most other parts smaller.

Next to *senex*, this is the largest Nevadan chipmunk. The large size, the dark color, the long, slender ear, with conspicuous, whitish postauricular patch and whitish edging on the tail, are features useful in distinguishing it from other kinds. It has a small range in the Sierra Nevada and, like *senex, frater,* and *monoensis,* occurs in Nevada only in the vicinity of Lake Tahoe, where some high parts of the Sierra are included in Nevada.

The zonal range is the upper part of the Transition and lower part of the Canadian life-zones. Open places in mature timber, where fallen trunks of large diameter afford shelter among manzanita bushes, comprise suitable habitat at the northern end of Lake Tahoe where I found the animal. Two pregnant females taken June 11, at the Merced Grove of Big Trees, California (Grinnell and Storer, 1924:189), had four and five embryos.

Records of occurrence.—Specimens examined, 3, as follows: *Washoe Co.:* 3 mi. S Mt. Rose, 8500 ft., 1; Calneva, 6400 ft., 1. *Douglas Co.:* 10 mi. NW Minden, 1.

Additional record (Howell, 1929:123): *Douglas Co.:* Glenbrook. Allen's (1890:79) mention of a specimen from Carson City probably refers to a specimen taken a mile or more west of Carson City.

Eutamias dorsalis
Cliff Chipmunk

Each of the two Nevadan subspecies is a chipmunk of medium size. The species is notable for the Smoke Gray or Neutral Gray tone of the upper parts and particularly for the indistinctness of the dorsal stripes which in some stages of pelage are obsolete. The median stripe is more pronounced than the lateral stripes but, at a little distance from the observer, the animals, particularly when in winter  pelage, appear to be grayish without stripes. The coloration in detail, following the plan of description adopted by Howell, and with specimens in hand of *Eutamias dorsalis grinnelli*, may be described, for the summer pelage, as: upper parts Smoke Gray in general tone, with top of head slightly darker than back; sides of nose Clay Color or Cinnamon Buff; facial stripes Sayal Brown shaded with Fuscous; postauricular patches grayish-white and poorly defined; median dorsal stripe Fuscous-Black mixed with Burnt Sienna; more lateral dark dorsal stripes Pale Fuscous, tinged with Cinnamon, but faintly indicated and often obsolete; light dorsal stripes likewise faintly indicated, creamy white; sides Pinkish Cinnamon or Light Pinkish Cinnamon; hind feet slightly paler than sides; tail above Fuscous-Black, overlain with Tilleul Buff; tail beneath Ochraceous-Tawny bordered with Fuscous-Black and edged with Tilleul Buff; underparts creamy white. Skull with brain case wide and dorsally flattened; rostrum relatively broad; incisive foramina diverging posteriorly rather than parallel. This feature of the incisive foramina and the indistinctness of the dorsal stripes are unique features among Nevadan species. Only *palmeri* and *panamintinus* in winter pelage have the stripes anywhere near as indistinct, and in those two species the general tone of coloration is reddish rather than gray. The flatness of the top of the skull is exceeded only in *panamintinus*, the skull of which is of smaller size and otherwise different, as described in the account of that form. The almost white edging of the tail is a feature held in common with the much larger and darker colored *senex* and *quadrimaculatus* and the much smaller *E. amoenus celeris*. In other Nevadan chipmunks the edging of the tail is distinctly buffy.

This species, like *panamintinus*, is an inhabitant of the piñon-juniper areas. In Garden Valley, 8½ miles northeast of Sharp, we found it well out in the valley, but restricted to a tongue of juniper trees that extended out from the main body of timber higher up. At many places *dorsalis* is abundant, but, except in a few localities, the animals were so shy that few were seen until caught in traps. For example, at Lehman Cave, we came to be able to recognize this chipmunk in the tops of piñon trees, but they usually saw us first and ran down to the ground and into hiding before we could approach within gunshot of them. Davis (1934:20-22) has remarked on the lack of shyness of *dorsalis* at three places in eastern Nevada, and Burt (1934:409) found the animals in the Sheep Mountains to be less shy than at other places where he saw them.

On Pilot Peak, where *quadrivittatus* was absent, *dorsalis* occurred on up through the white pines to 9900 feet. At this elevation Ward C. Russell shot one, and he saw another at a higher altitude. Near by, in the Ruby Mountains, where *quadrivittatus* but not *dorsalis* occurs, *quadrivittatus*, as already noted, occurs down through the piñon-juniper belt to its lower margin at 6000 feet elevation. It appears that each species exerts a limiting effect, with respect to range, on the other, for on mountains where but one species is present, it occupies not only its normal habitat, but also that normally occupied by the other species. Over the greater part of eastern Nevada, however, both species occur in most mountain ranges, *dorsalis* keeping to the piñons and junipers and *quadrivittatus* to the yellow pines, white pines, and other coniferous timber between the upper limit of the piñons and timber line. The only exception to this known to me is in the Sheep Mountains where Burt (1934:409) found *dorsalis* and *quadrivittatus* together in the yellow pine belt.

Probably a wide variety of seeds and fruits are taken as food. At South Twin River, on May 6, Linsdale found a piñon nut in the cheek pouch of an adult male. In the Hot Creek Range, 4 miles north of Hot Creek, J. Arnold found the animals climbing wild currant bushes in search of the berries. In the Quinn Canyon Mountains, at Burned Corral Canyon, in late July, the fruits of a species of *Prunus*, of *Rhus trilobata*, and of *Peraphyllum ramosissimum* were being eaten.

Relatively little is known of their breeding habits. Several lactating females have been taken in June.

Eutamias dorsalis grinnelli Burt
Cliff Chipmunk

Eutamias dorsalis grinnelli Burt, Journ. Mamm., 21:300, August 24, 1931. Type from Mormon Well, 6500 feet, Sheep Mountains, Clark County, Nevada. Burt, Trans. San Diego Soc. Nat. Hist., 7:409, May 31, 1934.
Eutamias dorsalis utahensis, Howell, N. Amer. Fauna, 52:133, November 30, 1929.

Distribution.—Among piñons and junipers in northeasternmost township of state southward to the Sheep Mountains; and in central part of state westward to Toyabe Mountains. See figure 247, page 337.

Remarks.—Measurements of five of each sex from Pilot Peak are: ♂, 217 (204–226), ♀, 222 (212–235); 92 (82–100), 95 (89–105); 33 (32–35), 33 (31–34); ear from notch, 20 (19–21), 20 (19–22); weight (July-taken), 59.5 (54.5–63.8), 62.9 (58.8–66.7) grams.

Corresponding measurements of fourteen males and twenty-one females from Groom Baldy, about 260 miles to the southward, are: ♂, 206 (193–222), ♀, 208 (186–218); 86 (78–95), 85 (72–94); 31 (30–34), 31 (29.5–33.0); ear from notch, 19 (15–22), 19 (18–21); weight (specimens taken in May and June), 51.3 (48.0–55.7), 53.3 (46.5–60.0) grams.

Comparison of the two sets of measurements indicates the smaller average size of the southern population. *E. d. grinnelli* differs from *utahensis* in more whitish dorsal coloration and less inflation of the brain case in the parietal region.

With specimens of *Eutamias dorsalis* in summer pelage arranged in geographic order, from Nevada, Utah, Idaho, Wyoming, Colorado, and northwestern Arizona, a major division on basis of color is apparent. Those from Nevada, excepting populations from along the eastern border, are lighter colored and more whitish above. A line separating the two types is shown on the distribution map (fig. 247) as the boundary between *E. d. utahensis* and *E. d. grinnelli*. The animals referred to *grinnelli* can be further divided into three groups: topotypes and those from the Hidden Forest in Clark County, which are of lightest color; specimens from Goose Creek and Pilot Peak in Elko County, which comprise a second group and average only a little darker; and the specimens from the several localities intervening between Elko and Clark counties, which are the darkest of this subspecies.

The more eastern populations, namely, those referred to *utahensis*, are divisible into a southern group with more distinct stripes and a northern group with less distinct stripes. The northern group is not uniform in that topotypes of *utahensis* have a dusky suffusion of the white parts of the cheeks that is most pronounced in specimens from northwestern Colorado. Nevadan populations also are less dusky cheeked than topotypes of *utahensis*. Those from Bridge, Idaho, are intermediate in this respect, but in general coloration of the dorsum are more whitish than *utahensis* and more nearly resemble the animals from Elko County; indeed, they are even lighter than this northern Nevadan group.

The brain case undergoes a decrease in degree of inflation from a maximum in topotypes of *utahensis* to a minimum in topotypes of *grinnelli*. The geographic variation in this character follows roughly that for coat color. Greatest length of skull also undergoes a decrease to the southward, reduction being evident in southern populations of both *utahensis* and *grinnelli;* the average difference between the two extremes is nevertheless only about 2½ per cent.

Topotypes of *grinnelli* are extreme for that race in whiteness of coloration, lack of inflation of brain case, and length of skull. Topotypes of *utahensis* stand near the opposite extreme in these characters.

Because of the lack of specimens in summer pelage from the vicinity of Mount Moriah and Wheeler Peak and the paucity of specimens from Cherry Creek and 8 miles west of Eureka, the specimens from Eureka and White Pine counties are less certainly identified with respect to subspecies than are the other populations.

Records of occurrence.—Specimens examined, 205, as follows: *Eureka Co.:* 8 mi. W Eureka, 1. *Nye Co.:* Wisconsin Creek, 7600 and 7800 ft., 2; ridge N of forks of Wisconsin Creek, 7500 ft., 4; South Twin River, 6500–7000 ft., 6; Toquima Range, 2 mi. E Jefferson, 7800 ft., 1; Monitor Valley, 8 mi. E Toquima Peak, 7000 ft., 1; Hot Creek Range, 4 mi. N Hot Creek, 6400 ft., 3; Hot Creek Range, 7 to 8 mi. W Tybo, 6700–7200 ft., 15; Burned Corral Canyon, Quinn Canyon Mts., 6700–7700 ft., 11; Quinn Canyon Mts., 7 mi. E Nyala, 6700 ft., 8; Garden Valley, 8½ mi. NE Sharp, 3; Kawich Mts., 2 1/10 mi. E Silverbow, 6950 ft., 2; 6 to 9 mi. E Cliff Spring, 6000 ft., 4; Belted Range, 3 mi. N Indian Spring, 6700 ft., 6; Indian Spring, Belted Range, 7450 ft., 1; S end Belted Range, 4½ to 5½ mi. NW White Rock Spring, 7200–7500 ft., 3; Oak Spring, 6400 ft., 2; Belted Range, 5 mi. W White Rock Spring, 6950–7050 ft., 7. *Elko Co.:* Goose Creek, 2 mi. W Utah line, 5000 ft., 1; Pilot Peak, ½ mi. W Debbs Creek, 6000–9900 ft., 13. *White Pine Co.:* Cherry Creek, 6800 ft., 2; Water Canyon, 8 to 10 mi. N Lund, 5. *Lincoln Co.:* Eagle Valley, 3½ mi. N Ursine, 5600 ft., 8; 2 mi. SE Pioche, 6000 ft., 1; E slope Irish Mtn., 6400–8250 ft., 20; W slope Groom Baldy, 8400 ft., 3; SW slope and base Groom Baldy, 7200–8400 ft., 33. *Clark Co.:* Mormon Wells, E slope Sheep Mts., 6500 ft., 13 (11 in D. R. Dickey Coll.); Hidden Forest, Sheep Mts., 8500 ft., 26 (D. R. Dickey Coll.).

Additional record (Howell, 1929:134): *Nye Co.:* Manhattan.

Eutamias dorsalis utahensis Merriam
Cliff Chipmunk

Eutamias dorsalis utahensis Merriam, Proc. Biol. Soc. Washington, 11:210, July 1, 1897. Type from Ogden, Weber County, Utah. Burt, Trans. San Diego Soc. Nat. Hist., 7:408, May 31, 1934.
Eutamias dorsalis, Linsdale, Amer. Midland Nat., 19:183, January, 1938.

Distribution.—Among piñons and junipers from Mount Moriah southward along eastern border of state to Cedar Basin almost to Colorado River. See figure 247, page 337.

TABLE 7
CRANIAL MEASUREMENTS (IN MILLIMETERS) OF EUTAMIAS

Name and locality	Number of individuals averaged or catalogue no.	Sex	Greatest length	Zygomatic breadth	Cranial breadth*	Interorbital breadth	Length of nasals
Eutamias minimus scrutator							
Toyabe Mountains	10 av.	♂	29.5	16.4	14.4	6.8	8.5
	min.		28.9	16.1	14.2	6.6	7.8
	max.		30.1	16.9	14.7	7.0	9.0
Toyabe Mountains	10 av.	♀	30.1	16.7	14.5	6.7	8.9
	min.		29.5	16.0	14.1	6.3	8.2
	max.		30.9	17.6	15.1	7.1	9.5
Eutamias amoenus amoenus							
Northern Elko Co	4 av.	♂	33.7	18.0	15.5	7.6	10.4
	min.		33.5	17.8	15.3	7.4	10.0
	max.		34.0	18.3	15.6	7.7	10.7
Northern Elko Co	6 av.	♀	33.8	18.2	15.4	7.5	10.6
	min.		33.5	18.0	15.2	7.3	10.3
	max.		34.1	18.6	15.6	7.8	10.7
Eutamias amoenus celeris							
Pine Forest Mountains	5 av.	♂	32.1	17.5	15.0	7.5	9.6
	min.		31.8	17.3	14.9	7.3	9.4
	max.		32.7	17.8	15.2	7.7	9.9
Near head Big Creek	7950	♀	32.5	17.7	15.2	7.3	9.8
Pine Forest Mountains, 9000 ft.	7958	♀	31.9	17.8	15.3	7.2	9.9
Pine Forest Mountains, 9000 ft.	7960	♀	—	17.6	15.0	7.4	—
Eutamias amoenus monoensis							
Southern Sierra Nevada, California	5 av.	♂	32.2	17.9	15.4	7.7	9.9
	min.		31.8	17.7	15.1	7.5	9.6
	max.		32.5	18.2	15.7	8.1	10.2
Robinson Creek, California	64774	♀	32.3	18.1	15.5	7.7	10.0
Pine City, California	32931	♀	31.8	18.4	15.3	8.0	9.0
Pine City, California	32993	♀	32.9	18.9	15.7	7.8	10.1
Eutamias panamintinus							
Charleston Peak	4 av.	♂	34.0	18.4	15.6	7.3	10.0
	min.		33.7	18.2	15.3	6.9	9.7
	max.		34.4	18.7	15.8	7.6	10.6
Charleston Peak	4 av.	♀	34.7	19.2	16.0	7.4	10.5
	min.		34.0	18.6	15.6	7.2	9.8
	max.		35.3	19.7	16.4	7.5	11.0
Eutamias quadrivittatus inyoensis							
Baker Creek	10 av.	♂	35.4	19.2	16.0	7.8	11.0
	min.		34.7	18.7	15.5	7.3	10.4
	max.		36.2	19.8	16.5	8.0	11.8
Baker Creek	10 av.	♀	35.8	19.6	16.0	8.0	11.3
	min.		35.0	19.1	15.8	7.5	10.8
	max		36.5	20.2	16.3	8.1	11.8

* Breadth of brain case taken with calipers set obliquely in constriction just posterior to zygomatic processes of squamosals and anterior to auditory bullae.

TABLE 7—(Continued)

Name and locality	Number of individuals averaged or catalogue no.	Sex	Greatest length	Zygomatic breadth	Cranial breadth*	Interorbital breadth	Length of nasals
Eutamias quadrivittatus nevadensis							
Hidden Forest	10 av.	♂	35.5	19.7	16.1	7.7	10.9
	min.		35.1	19.4	15.8	7.3	10.6
	max.		35.8	20.0	16.4	8.2	11.4
Hidden Forest	10 av.	♀	36.1	20.0	16.2	7.8	11.2
	min.		35.6	19.7	15.9	7.5	10.7
	max.		36.7	20.5	16.7	8.0	11.6
Eutamias palmeri							
Charleston Peak	10 av.	♂	36.4	19.9	16.3	8.0	10.9
	min.		35.8	19.1	15.8	7.7	10.5
	max.		37.0	20.2	16.7	8.4	11.6
Charleston Peak	10 av.	♀	36.5	20.0	16.1	8.0	11.0
	min.		36.0	19.8	16.1	7.6	10.3
	max.		37.1	20.3	16.8	8.3	11.6
Eutamias speciosus frater							
Southern Tuolumne Co., California	10 av.	♂	34.6	19.2	15.8	7.8	11.0
	min.		33.8	18.7	15.3	7.1	10.2
	max.		35.2	19.5	16.2	8.2	11.6
Southern Tuolumne Co., California	10 av.	♀	34.8	19.1	15.8	7.7	11.0
	min.		34.0	18.7	15.5	7.3	10.5
	max.		35.4	19.4	16.2	8.0	11.6
Eutamias townsendii senex							
Placer and Nevada counties, California	7 av.	♂	38.1	21.3	16.9	8.4	11.8
	min.		37.3	20.7	16.4	8.0	11.2
	max.		39.0	21.7	17.3	8.6	12.1
Placer and Nevada counties, California	10 av.	♀	38.6	21.5	17.0	8.4	12.2
	min.		37.8	21.3	16.6	8.2	11.7
	max.		39.2	22.1	17.3	8.8	12.6
Eutamias quadrimaculatus							
Merced Grove of Big Trees, California	4 av.	♂	36.7	20.8	16.9	8.9	12.6
	min.		36.1	20.5	16.5	8.6	12.4
	max.		37.2	21.0	17.0	9.4	12.9
Merced Grove of Big Trees, California	6 av.	♀	37.3	20.9	16.8	9.1	12.4
	min.		36.7	20.4	16.5	8.6	11.9
	max.		38.0	21.6	17.1	9.4	13.0
Eutamias dorsalis grinnelli							
Groom Baldy	21 av.	♂	34.7	18.9	16.2	7.7	10.3
	min.		33.5	18.4	15.9	7.0	9.8
	max.		36.2	19.4	16.5	8.2	11.0
Groom Baldy	14 av.	♀	34.7	18.8	16.2	7.6	10.2
	min.		33.9	18.5	15.9	7.3	9.5
	max.		35.3	19.5	16.7	8.0	10.7
Eutamias dorsalis utahensis							
38° 17′ N, ¼ mi. W Utah boundary	59455	♂	—	18.6	16.5	7.7	—
38° 17′ N, ¼ mi. W Utah boundary	59451	♂	34.3	18.8	16.2	7.6	10.4
38° 17′ N, ¼ mi. W Utah boundary	6 av.	♀	34.3	19.0	16.3	7.8	10.0
	min.		33.0	18.4	15.9	7.5	9.1
	max.		35.3	19.5	16.6	8.0	10.5

* Breadth of brain case taken with calipers set obliquely in constriction just posterior to zygomatic processes of squamosals and anterior to auditory bullae.

Remarks.—Six females, from latitude 38° 17′, ¼ mi. W Utah boundary, measure: 210 (192–225), 91 (84–102), 31 (29–32), ear from notch, 18 (17–19), weight, 53.7 (50.0–57.0) grams. The one male from this place has corresponding measurements of 213, 95, 32, 18, 56.4.

This race differs from *grinnelli* in darker (browner, less whitish) upper parts and broader brain case, which is more inflated in the parietal region. Variation within the subspecies is discussed in the preceding account of *grinnelli*.

Records of occurrence.—Specimens examined, 36, as follows: *White Pine Co.:* Smith Creek, Mt. Moriah, 6600 ft., 1; 1 to 2 mi. W Smith Creek Cave, Mt. Moriah, 6000–6300 ft., 5; Hendry Creek, 7½ mi. SE Mt. Moriah, 6800 ft., 1; Lehman Cave, 7400 ft., 2, and 7500 ft., 1; ½ mi. S Lehman Cave, 7200 ft., 1; Baker Creek, 7500 ft., 1. *Lincoln Co.:* ¼ mi. W Utah boundary, N. latitude 38° 17′, 7300 ft., 8; 11 mi. E Panaca, 6500 ft., 5, 6600 ft., 1, and 7100 ft., 1; Meadow Valley Wash, 7 mi. S Caliente, 4000 ft., 1, and 4500 ft., 2. *Clark Co.:* Cedar Basin, 30 mi. SE St. Thomas, 3500 ft., 6 (D. R. Dickey Coll.).

Tamiasciurus douglasii albolimbatus (Allen)
Douglas Squirrel

Sciurus douglasii albolimbatus Allen, Bull. Amer. Mus. Nat. Hist., 10:453, November 10, 1898 (renaming of *californicus* Allen). Type from Blue Canyon, Placer County, California.

Sciurus hudsonius californicus Allen, Bull. Amer. Mus. Nat. Hist., 3:165, November 14, 1890 (name preoccupied).

Distribution.—Coniferous timber of Transition and higher life-zones in the Sierra Nevada in the vicinity of Lake Tahoe. See figure 253.

Remarks.—Measurements of a male from 2 mi. E Incline are 325, 124, 51. Two females, one from Incline Creek and one from ½ mi. E Zephyr Cove, measure 330, 367; 130, 134; 55, 54; 25, —. Weights of five spring-taken adults of each sex from eastern Oregon are: ♂, 256, ♀, 255 grams.

Generic characters include: zygomata nearly parallel to long axis of skull; notch in zygomatic plate of maxilla opposite P4; penis without baculum; Cowpers glands minute, opening into urethra in the bulb; dental formula: i. $\frac{1}{1}$, c. $\frac{0}{0}$, p. $\frac{1}{1}$ or $\frac{2}{1}$, m. $\frac{3}{3}$ (P3 vestigial in some specimens but usually absent). Specific characters include blackish as opposed to reddish shade of coloration of upper parts and tail.

In summer pelage: upper parts dark brown, resulting from a mixture of black and Cinnamon-Buff bands on hairs; underparts white; tail, above and below, blackish, but lightly overlain with whitish and bordered with white, and in proximal part colored like back; side with distinct black band separating the brown upper parts and white underparts; feet, forearm, and front edge of thigh Cinnamon-Buff. In winter pelage color pattern the same, but middorsal area of back with more Cinnamon-Buff; rest of upper parts more gray, as result of more white bands on hairs; white border on tail wider; black stripe on side narrower; Ochraceous-Buff color lacking on foreleg and on front of thigh; underparts more plumbeous and laterally vermiculate rather than pure white.

From *T. d. mollipilosus* and *T. d. cascadensis*, the two races to the northwest the ranges of which meet that of *albolimbatus*, it differs in winter pelage in less cinnamon-colored middorsal band and lighter colored underparts. In summer pelage the underparts are white rather than heavily shaded with cinnamon, and the upper side of the tail has less of the cinnamon or reddish color.

In coniferous timber, from just above the piñons and junipers, this squirrel occurs up to timber line. In Nevada we have found it to be common among the white firs. The animal ranges through a wide variety of places. For example, it has tunnels underground where food is stored, it ranges over the surface of the ground, over trunks of trees and limbs, and out to the tips of twigs. Exploring as it goes, it finds food in one place and stores or eats it in another.

The squirrels of this genus are the smallest of North American tree squirrels and, like most of their relatives, are diurnal. They have a large "vocabulary" and often make their presence known by objecting loudly to some intruder in their "territory."

A large share of their food is made up of seeds of conifers. They cut up and eat the unripe cones as well as the nuts of the ripened cones. The base of a tree

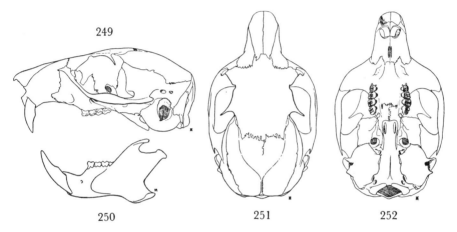

Figs. 249–252. *Tamiasciurus douglasii albolimbatus*, Incline Creek, 6500 feet, no. 65215, ♀. × 1.

or the top of a log or stump is a place favored by the squirrel for eating, and the refuse—discarded plant material—in such places may accumulate to a depth of more than a foot.

Nests, of which I have found none in Nevada, are made in hollows of trees and are constructed of leaves, shredded bark, and finer plant materials. Along Incline Creek, half-grown young were seen in August. Five embryos are recorded (Grinnell and Storer, 1924:211) in a female taken July 19, 1915, in Lyell Canyon, California.

Records of occurrence.—Specimens examined, 8, as follows: *Washoe Co.:* 3 mi. SSW Mt. Rose, 9000 ft., 2; 3 mi. S Mt. Rose, 8500 ft., 1; Incline Creek, 7100 ft., 1; Incline Creek, 6500 ft., 1; 2 mi. E Incline, 7700 ft., 1. *Douglas Co.:* ½ mi. E Zephyr Cove, 6500 ft., 1; 1½ mi. E Calif. boundary at S end Lake Tahoe, 1.

Glaucomys sabrinus lascivus (Bangs)
Northern Flying Squirrel

Sciuropterus alpinus lascivus Bangs, Proc. New England Zoöl. Club, 1:69, July 31, 1899. Type from Tallac, El Dorado County, California.
Glaucomys sabrinus lascivus, Howell, N. Amer. Fauna, 44:55, June 13, 1918.

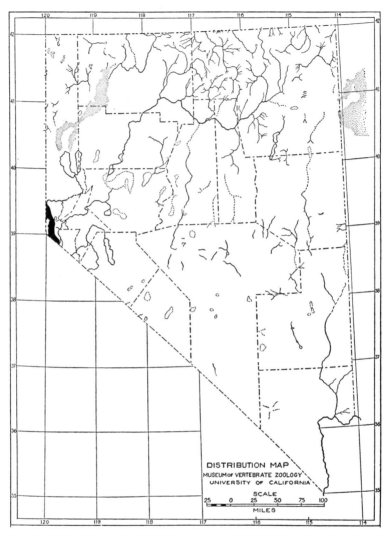

Fig. 253. The nine species listed below occur in the Sierra Nevadan faunal area shown in solid black. Several species occur in only a part of the area.

Black bear, *Ursus americanus*
Western marten, *Martes caurina*
Lodgepole-pine chipmunk, *Eutamias speciosus*
Townsend chipmunk, *Eutamias townsendii*
Long-eared chipmunk, *Eutamias quadrimaculatus*

Douglas squirrel, *Tamiasciurus douglasii*
Northern flying squirrel, *Glaucomys sabrinus*
Mountain beaver, *Aplodontia rufa*
Snowshoe rabbit, *Lepus americanus*

Distribution.—Coniferous timber of Transition and higher life-zones in the Sierra Nevada in the vicinity of Lake Tahoe. See fig. 253.

Remarks.—A male from Marlette Lake measures 290, 122, 40, 20. A male from California weighs 140 grams.

A subfamily character is the fold of skin on each side of the body between the fore and hind leg. Generic characters include: brain case deep; great constriction of the frontal bone interorbitally and postorbitally; incisors not recurved; notch in maxillary plate of zygoma opposite P4; dental formula: i. $\frac{1}{1}$, c. $\frac{0}{0}$, p. $\frac{2}{1}$, m. $\frac{3}{3}$. Specific characters, in contrast to *G. volans*, the other American species, which does not occur in Nevada, are: length of hind foot more than 33 mm.; greatest length of skull more than 35.9 mm.

The adult male from Marlette Lake, in winter pelage, agrees with Howell's (1918:55) description of color, which is essentially as follows: upper parts Wood Brown, shading to drab; sides of face Smoke Gray (shaded with Pale Fuscous in some specimens); upper surface of flying membrane blackish-brown; ears Fuscous-Black; hind feet Hair-Brown, toes shaded with whitish (or buff in some specimens); forefeet Mouse Gray; tail above Fuscous-Black mixed with Wood Brown (pale Snuff Brown in some specimens), below strongly washed with Avellaneous; underparts grayish-white faintly washed with Avellaneous. The summer pelage is more brownish, with more pinkish color in the underparts. The fur is dense, of silky texture, and of even length over the upper parts. It is shorter on the underparts. An immature specimen which retains the milk premolar above differs in sooty black coloration of the upper surface of the tail and only slightly more grayish color over the upper parts of the body. The underparts are more plumbeous than in adults.

G. s. lascivus is the subspecies found in, and limited to, the Sierra Nevada. From the race *flaviventris* to the north it differs in lesser average size and whiter, less yellowish underparts. From *californicus*, the race to the south, *lascivus* differs in darker, less grayish upper parts and face and larger skull.

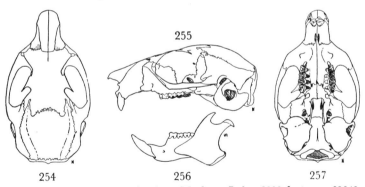

255

254   256   257

Figs. 254–257. *Glaucomys sabrinus lascivus*, Marlette Lake, 8000 feet, no. 69640, ♂. ×1.

The flying squirrel is the only nocturnal squirrel in Nevada. With the legs spread wide and by aid of the flattened tail, the animal can volplane down from well up in a tree to a lower level on another, and in so doing can change the direction of its glide at will. The species occurs only in coniferous timber. The specimen from Marlette Lake came from a forest of large red firs. The imma-ture male taken on August 22, 1934, on the west side of Incline Creek at 7100 feet elevation was caught in a snap rattrap nailed head-high, and baited with a partly dry prune, on the trunk of an incense cedar. The large cedar, some 5 feet in diameter, was dead, but bark still clung to the trunk, and high up in the tree there were woodpecker holes. At the place where the trap was set, the bark of the cedar was frayed as though much used by sharp-clawed animals of small size. These claw marks and the presence near by of some white firs suggested that the flying squirrel, or squirrels, used the frayed place on the bark of the incense cedar as a landing place after gliding to it from near-by firs.

TABLE 8

Cranial Measurements (in Millimeters) of Tamiasciurus and Glaucomys

Sex	Catalogue no.	Locality	Greatest length	Zygomatic breadth	Mastoidal breadth	Least interorbital breadth	Postorbital breadth	Length of nasals (over all)	Alveolar length of maxillary tooth row
			Tamiasciurus d. albolimbatus						
♂	88266	2 mi. E Incline........	49.1	28.5	21.8	15.0	15.2	15.0	8.0
			Glaucomys s. lascivus						
♂	69640	Marlette Lake.........	41.8	23.1	18.0	7.7	9.2	13.0	8.4

From information obtained outside Nevada, it is known that squirrels of this species make nests in hollows of trees and behind loose pieces of bark, and that they sometimes have "outside" nests of globular shape. The animals do not hibernate—at any rate many are taken in steel traps set for fur-bearing mammals in winter. Although attracted by meat baits, the principal food of flying squirrels is thought to be nuts. The young are said to number up to six in a litter. Of the subspecies *lascivus*, Grinnell and Storer (1924:214) record that of four pregnant females from Yosemite National Park, California, two had two embryos each and the others four each.

Records of occurrence.—Specimens examined, 2, as follows: *Washoe Co.*: Incline Creek, 7100 ft., 1; Marlette Lake, 8000 ft., 1.

Family HETEROMYIDAE
Pocket Mice, Kangaroo Rats, and Kangaroo Mice

Three genera, *Perognathus*, *Dipodomys*, and *Microdipodops*, representative of this family, occur in Nevada. All are characteristic of plains or desert regions. In Nevada several exhibit the extreme of specialization among North American mammals for successful existence under desert conditions. The reduction in number of toes on the hind feet of the big desert kangaroo rat and the tremendous enlargement of the auditory bullae of the skull in kangaroo mice are specializations of this sort, or at any rate are associated with adaptation to life in deserts. The dental formula is i. $\frac{1}{1}$, c. $\frac{0}{0}$, p. $\frac{1}{1}$, m. $\frac{3}{3}$.

Genus **Perognathus** Wied
Pocket Mice

The four Nevadan species live in arid situations, as do nearly all species of the genus. In Nevada none lives in timbered areas, except that *Perognathus parvus* does occur in scattered stands of juniper and piñon. *Perognathus longimembris* is the smallest rodent in the state. The size of each of the other species is about the same as in *Peromyscus*, from which *Perognathus* can readily be differentiated by its smaller ears and fur-lined cheek pouches. The pocket mice are all nocturnal. They forage over the surface of the ground in quest of plant food, taking seeds principally. Some species, and probably all, store seeds below ground. They live in burrows which they themselves excavate. The soil is left in a pile at the entrance to the burrow, but ordinarily this is soon leveled down by the wind, often in a few hours. In the daytime the burrow usually is closed from the inside by a plug of sand or other soil, and on most days, in sandy areas, the wind drifts sand into the opening and erases every trace of it. In many of the places where the mice live they have no opportunity to obtain water. Captive individuals live well on air-dry foods without water to drink. *P. penicillatus* probably does not hibernate. Each of the other three species, particularly *parvus* and *longimembris*, lives in parts of the state where temperatures fall far below zero and where snow lies deeply for long periods. Under such conditions the mice are not active aboveground and they probably hibernate, although actual proof of this for Nevadan animals is lacking.

As with other small rodents of the temperate regions, the numbers of *Perognathus* in a given region fluctuate markedly in different years. I have noticed this particularly in connection with *Perognathus longimembris*.

There seems to be only one annual molt, which occurs in late summer. In the following accounts, unless otherwise indicated, only fresh pelage is used in making comparisons of color.

Cranial measurements were taken as follows: occipitonasal length, from the tip of the nasals to the most posterior projection of the supraoccipital directly above the middle of the foramen magnum; frontonasal length, from the tip of the nasals along the mid-line to the frontoparietal suture, ignoring the median posterior projections of the frontals which exist in some species; mastoidal breadth is greatest breadth across mastoids; length of bulla, from posteriormost projection of mastoidal bulla to anteriormost point dorsolateral to squamosal arm of zygomatic arch; interorbital breadth is least interorbital breadth immediately behind lacrimals; alveolar length of upper molariform tooth row is self-explanatory.

Perognathus longimembris
Little Pocket Mouse

Of this, the smallest rodent in the state, four races are recognized in Nevada. It occurs in the Lower Sonoran Life-zone and in the Upper Sonoran Life-zone below the piñon-juniper growth. The highest elevation from which we have recorded it is 6500 feet at Cactus Spring. Sometimes the little pocket mouse is taken on the fine sandy soil in the center of valleys, but is found more often, and more abundantly, on the firmer soils of the slightly sloping margins of the

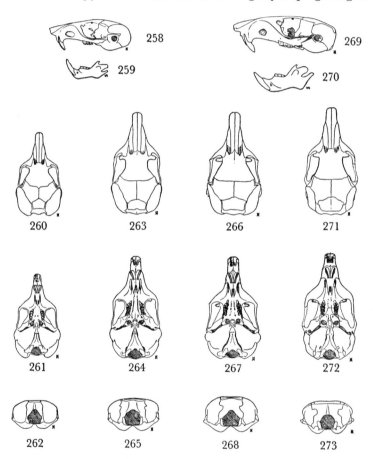

Figs. 258–273. Pocket mice. All, ×1.

Figs. 258–262. *Perognathus longimembris panamintinus*, R. 38 E, T. 6 S, Esmeralda County, no. 38586, ♀.

Figs. 263–265. *Perognathus parvus olivaceus*, Wisconsin Creek, 7800 feet, no. 45599, ♂.

Figs. 266–268. *Perognathus formosus melanurus*, latitude 40° 28′, 6 miles east California boundary, no. 73442, ♂.

Figs. 269–273. *Perognathus penicillatus penicillatus*, 14 miles east Searchlight, no. 61569, ♂.

valleys. Here, although it occurs along with many kinds of plants, it is associated in my mind with the low-growing, rose-pink *Sidalcea*. On these firm soils of sand overlain with pebbles and supporting widely spaced, low-growing shrubs, *P. longimembris* frequently is the most abundant mammalian species. In some places I have estimated the population to be as high as four hundred per acre. Our trapping records suggest that *longimembris* fluctuates markedly in numbers, seasonally, and from year to year; at some places where it was found to be the most abundant mammalian species, traps set out at later dates took none, and the absence of signs (tracks and excavations made in search of food) of the species further attested to its scarcity. In late May of 1931, in southern Nye County, this was the most abundant mammal. How far one of these mice normally travels I don't know, but Burt has recorded (1934:411) that one which lost its tail one night in a mousetrap was caught in another 350 yards away on the next night. How long the mice live in the wild state I do not know, but one taken at Cactus Flat by Orr (1939:505) in September, 1931, lived in captivity in San Francisco, California, for a few days more than 7 years.

Although I have no proof, I suppose that these mice hibernate. Trapping in cold weather in places where the species probably occurs has yielded no specimens and indicates that the mice are not then active aboveground. The seed-filled cheek pouches of trapped specimens suggest that food is stored. The contents of the pouches of one taken on June 17, 1928, at Cave Spring, consisted of the flowers of *Eriogonum gracillimum*. Another taken on May 23, 1931, three miles northeast of Beatty, had in its cheek pouches only seeds of *Chenopodium album*. Burt (1934:411) trapped three animals the cheek pouches of which contained seeds, "the following plants being represented: burro-weed (*Franseria dumosa*), plantain (*Plantago* sp.), and grass (*Festuca* sp.)."

The annual molt appears to take place in July and August. Among the numerous specimens taken from May to October, there are twenty-five in process of molt for which the inclusive dates of capture were July 3 to August 1. The pelage in April or early May is not much different than that in August or September, but by June the pelage is much faded. There is but slight secondary sexual variation—less than the individual variation between animals of similar age from a single locality. In nine series measured, males were in six instances no larger than females in total length, and in nine instances the tail was no longer than in females. The hind foot averaged longer in males in five series, the length of the skull was more in males in six series, and the mastoidal breadth was more in males in eight of the nine series.

Apparently there is only one litter born per year. Of 382 adult females, 30 were pregnant. For embryos per litter, the mode was 5, the mean 4.3, and the extremes 2 and 8. By months, the females were distributed as follows: April, 2; May, 149 (29 pregnant); June, 75 (1 pregnant); July, 130; August, 12; September, 13; November, 1.

Perognathus longimembris nevadensis Merriam
Little Pocket Mouse

Perognathus nevadensis Merriam, Proc. Acad. Nat. Sci. Philadelphia, 1894:264, September 27, 1894.
Type from Halleck, Elko County, Nevada; Osgood, N. Amer. Fauna, 18:31, September 20, 1900, part; Bailey, N. Amer. Fauna, 55:249, August 29, 1936.

Distribution.—Northern and central Nevada; northwestern Nevada west of the Black Rock Desert; east of the Black Rock Desert from the Oregon boundary south to Smiths Creek Valley and east to Halleck and near Eureka. See figure 274.

Remarks.—Measurements of ten male and five female topotypes are: ♂, 129 (124–138), ♀, 132 (128–137); 70 (62–75), 73 (68–77); 18.6 (18–19), 18.8 (18–19); weight of two males, 8.7 and 8.5 grams.

Size medium for the species; upper parts with the Pinkish Buff subterminal bands almost concealed by an overlay of blackish; underparts with hair white only in limited area on chest, otherwise plumbeous basally and Pinkish Buff or a darker shade of buff distally; tail bicolored, blackish above and buffy below; skull of medium size for the species; mastoidal breadth amounting to about 59 per cent of occipitonasal length; mastoidal bullae projecting behind supraoccipital; mastoidal side of parietal longest; ascending branches of supraoccipital, at sides of interparietal, threadlike; supraoccipital, viewed from posterior, straight-sided without lateral indentations by mastoids.

From *P. l. panamintinus, nevadensis* differs in dark-colored, as opposed to white, underparts. Possibly it averages slightly darker on the upper parts. In color of the underparts it differs in the same way from *gulosus* and *virginis*. From the latter, *nevadensis* is further distinguished by smaller mastoidal and tympanic bullae.

With respect to color of the underparts, specimens here assigned to *nevadensis* are typical of that race. Intergradation with *panamintinus* is shown by specimens from the Black Rock Desert and as far south as Toulon. These are commented on under the account of *panamintinus*, the race to which they are referred.

Records of occurrence.—Specimens examined, 76, as follows: *Washoe Co.:* 10 mi. SE Hausen, 4675 ft., 1. *Humboldt Co.:* 36 mi. NE Paradise Valley, 5500 ft., 1; Jackson Creek Ranch, 17½ mi. S and 5 mi. W Quinn River Crossing, 4000 ft., 2; 16 mi. NE Iron Point, 4500 ft., 1; 5 mi. NE Golconda, 2; 2 mi. E Golconda, 1; 10 mi. SW Winnemucca, 4500 ft., 3; 23 mi. NW Battle Mountain, 1. *Pershing Co.:* 15 mi. SW Winnemucca, 1. *Lander Co.:* 3 mi. S Izenhood, 1; 1 mi. E Battle Mountain, 5; 1½ mi. NW Cortez, Cortez Mts., 1; Reese River Valley, 7 mi. N Austin, 8; 2½ mi. NE Smiths Creek Ranch, 5800 ft., 2; Smiths Creek, 5800 ft., 5; Smiths Creek Valley, 3 mi. W Railroad Pass, 5500 ft., 2. *Eureka Co.:* 5 mi. N Beowawe, 4; ½ mi. S Beowawe, 6; Winzell, 6; 8 mi. E Eureka, 1. *Elko Co.:* 2 mi. NW Halleck, 5200 ft., 2 (coll. of Ralph Ellis); 3 to 5 mi. W Halleck, 5200–5300 ft., 19 (14 in coll. of Ralph Ellis); 3 mi. S Halleck, 1.
Additional record (Osgood, 1900:31): Devil Gate, 12 mi. W Eureka.

Perognathus longimembris panamintinus Merriam
Little Pocket Mouse

Perognathus longimembris panamintinus Merriam, Proc. Acad. Nat. Sci. Philadelphia, 1894:265, September 27, 1894. Type from Perognathus Flat, 5200 feet, Panamint Mountains, Inyo County, California. Burt, Trans. San Diego Soc. Nat. Hist., 7:411, May 31, 1934.
Perognathus nevadensis, Taylor, Univ. California Publ. Zoöl., 7:279, June 24, 1911; Hall and Linsdale, Journ. Mamm., 10:295, 302, November 11, 1910.
Perognathus longimembris, Linsdale, Amer. Midland Nat., 19:185, January, 1938.
Perognathus panamintinus, Osgood, N. Amer. Fauna, 18:29, September 20, 1900.

Distribution.—Western Nevada from Quinn River Crossing in Humboldt County south into Clark County. See figure 274.

Remarks.—Measurements of ten males and seven females from the vicinity of Arlemont, Esmeralda County, are: ♂, 130 (112–138), ♀, 136 (133–138); 67 (50–76), 73 (67–75); 18.8 (17.5–20), 19.1 (18–20); weight, 7.9 (7.7–8.3), 9.4 (7.3–10.3) grams.

Size, color, except underparts, as described below, and skull as described for *P. l. nevadensis*.

The selection of a subspecific name for the population of *P. longimembris* in western Nevada requires consideration of the names *P. longimembris* (Coues) 1875, *P. panamin-*

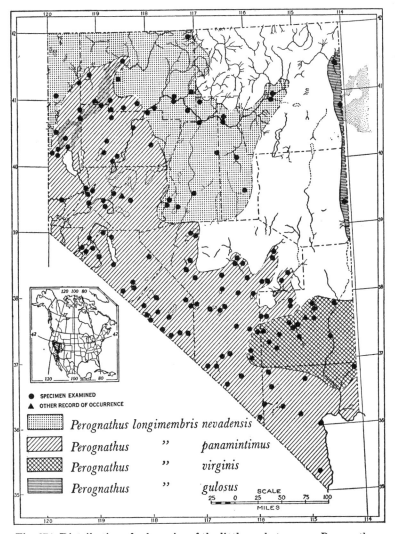

Fig. 274. Distribution of subspecies of the little pocket mouse, *Perognathus longimembris*, with insert showing range of the species.

tinus Merriam 1894, *P. bangsi* Mearns 1898, *P. pericalles* Elliot 1903, and *P. salinensis* Bole 1937. *P. bangsi*, if distinct from *longimembris*, may be of a color lighter than that of *longimembris* and of a size less than that of the Nevadan animals. *P. pericalles* and *P. salinensis*, so far as I can see, are based on populations which do not significantly differ from other populations of southeastern California to which the names *longimembris* and *panamintinus* have been applied. With abundant topotypes of *panamintinus* in hand and with a series of specimens from Pecks Butte, in northeastern Los Angeles County, which may be typical of *longimembris*, the Nevadan specimens are found to be longer of tail and longer over all than *longimembris*, but about the same as *panamintinus*. Osgood (1900:29) thought that the specimens from western Nevada comprised an incipient form, which he chose not to recognize by name. The one difference that I can find is the greater average length of the upper molariform tooth row in topotypes of *panamintinus* than in Nevadan specimens. It should be noted that both the topotypes of *panamintinus* and the animals from many of the Nevadan localities are in worn, faded pelage of late spring. If topotypes of *panamintinus* in fresh pelage were available for comparison with the specimens in that pelage from western Nevada, differences in color might be apparent, although I doubt it.

Intergradation with *nevadensis* is clearly shown by specimens from more than a score of localities in northwestern Nevada. Excepting the specimen from 10 miles southeast of Hausen, the others from northwestern Nevada are intergrades. These may be bounded by a line drawn from the mouth of Little High Rock Canyon to Flanigan to Toulon to a point 11 miles east of Jungo to the point of beginning. But, in addition, the animals from Quinn River Crossing are to be included. At some of these places, the hair of the underparts is everywhere white, but at most places it is plumbeous at the base, as in *nevadensis*, although the distal part of the hair lacks the buffy color. In some specimens the hair on only a small part of the underparts is plumbeous basally. Indeed, all variations occur between the condition in *nevadensis* and that in *panamintinus*. Those from 1 mile west of Humboldt and from 9 to 9½ miles east of Fanning are typical of *panamintinus*, that is to say, they are pure white below, whereas those from the vicinity of Toulon are intermediates.

Records of occurrence.—Specimens examined, 779, as follows: *Washoe Co.:* mouth of Little High Rock Canyon, and 1 mi. E thereof, 5000 ft., 2; 12 mi. N and 2 mi. E Gerlach, 4000 ft., 1; 5 mi. N Gerlach, 3950 ft., 2; 3½ mi. NE Gerlach, 4000 ft., 2; Smoke Creek, 9 mi. E Calif. boundary, 3900 ft., 6; 4 mi. NW Pahrum Peak, 4200 ft., 8; Fox Canyon, 6 mi. S Pahrum Peak, 4800 ft., 3; N side Sand Pass, 3900 and 3950 ft., 2; 3½ mi. NW Flanigan, 4200 ft., 11; 2 mi. NW Flanigan, 4250 ft., 6; ½ mi. NW Flanigan, 4200 ft., 8; 2½ mi. E Flanigan (4200 ft., 1, and 4250 ft., 4), 5; 3½ mi. E Flanigan, 4200 ft., 5; 1½ mi. N Wadsworth, 4100 ft., 8; 3 mi. E Reno, 1. *Lyon Co.:* 6 mi. N Fernley, 2; ½ to 1 mi. SE Wadsworth, 4200 ft., 4; 3½ mi. to 4 mi. W Hazen, 4250 ft., 9; West Walker River, 6 mi. S Yerington, 4500 ft., 3; Mason Valley, 11¾ mi. S and 2¾ mi. E Yerington, 4650 ft., 6; Smith[s] Valley, 7½ mi. NE Wellington, 4900 ft., 9; Mason Valley, 12 mi. E Wellington, 5000 ft., 8. *Humboldt Co.:* 1½ mi. N Quinn River Crossing, 4100 ft., 4; Quinn River Crossing, 4100 ft., 7; Soldier Meadows, 4600 ft., 6; 9½ mi. N Sulphur, 4050 ft., 4; 8 mi. E and 1 mi. N Jungo, 4200 ft., 3; 11 mi. E and 1 mi. N Jungo, 4200 ft., 1; 2 mi. E Antelope, 4400 ft., 1; 1¼ mi. N Sulphur, 4050 ft., 6; 1 mi. W Sulphur, 4040 ft., 4; ¾ mi. S Sulphur, 4050 ft., 1. *Pershing Co.:* 10½ mi. W and 6 mi. N Sulphur, 4000 ft., 1; 10 mi. W and 6 mi. N Sulphur, 4000 ft., 1; 8 mi. S Sulphur, 4350 ft., 3; 1 mi. W Humboldt, 4180 ft., 18; 3 mi. SW Vernon, 4300 ft., 1; 2½ mi. S Vernon, 4250 ft., 3; 3 mi. S Vernon, 4250 ft., 12; 9 mi. E Fanning, Buena Vista Valley, 4100 ft., 2; 9½ mi. E and 1 mi. S Fanning, Buena Vista Valley, 4100 ft., 7; 21 mi. W and 2 mi. N Lovelock, 4000 ft., 4; 3 mi. NNE Toulon, 3900 ft., 1; 1½ to 3½ mi. NE Toulon, 3900–3950 ft., 6; 1 mi. W Toulon, 4100 ft., 3; Toulon, 3900 ft., 1. *Churchill Co.:* 8 mi. NE Fallon, 3950 ft., 1; 1 mi. S Soda Lake, 4000 ft., 1; 4 mi. W Fallon, 4000 ft., 1; 5 mi. W Fallon, 4000 ft., 1; 100 yds. N Lahontan Dam, 4100 ft., 1; 1 mi. W Mountain Well, 5350 ft., 2; Mountain Well, 5600 ft., 6; 7 mi. SW Fallon, 1. *Mineral Co.:* 7 mi. NW Schurz, 4500 ft., 17; 3 mi. S Schurz, 4100 ft., 15; 8 mi. SE Schurz, 4100 ft., 3; Mason Valley, 5 mi. N Pine Grove, 5300 ft., 18; Fingerrock Wash, Stewart Valley, 5400 ft., 7; East Walker River, 2 to 3 mi. NW Morgans Ranch, 5050–5100 ft., 21; Cat Creek, 4 mi. W Hawthorne, 4500 ft., 2; 2 mi. E Hawthorne, 4300 ft., 1; Marietta, 4900 ft., 3; S side Teels Marsh, 4900 ft., 3; Huntoon Valley, 5700 ft., 8. *Esmeralda Co.:* 3½ to 4 mi. SE Coaldale, 4850 ft., 3; 13½ mi. NW Goldfield, 4850 ft., 12; 13 mi. N Goldfield, 5100 ft., 2; 7 mi. N Arlemont, 5500 ft., 26; Arlemont, 4900 ft., 4; Cave Spring, 6248 ft., 9; 2½ mi. N Dyer, 4850 ft., 1; Fish Lake Valley, 4945 ft., 3; 5 mi. SE Silver Peak, 4500 ft., 6; 8 mi. SE Blair, 4500 ft., 4; Dyer, 4900 ft., 5 (D. R. Dickey Coll.); 2½ mi. SE Dyer, 4950 ft., 1; R. 38 E, T. 6 S, 5300 ft., 6; 2 mi. NW Palmetto, 5900 ft., 2 (D. R. Dickey Coll.); Lida, vicinity of, 36 (D. R. Dickey Coll., as follows: ¾ mi. E, 5900 ft., 2; 2 mi. E, 5800 ft., 4; 3 mi. E, 5500 ft., 8; 4½ mi. E, 5350 ft., 8; 5½ mi. E, 5200 ft., 5; 6½ mi. E, 5100 ft., 4; 8 mi. E, 5000 ft., 2; 10 mi. E, 4875 ft., 3); Palmetto Wash, 5700 ft.,, 6 (D. R. Dickey Coll.); mouth of Palmetto Wash, 5350 ft., 6 (D. R. Dickey Coll.); 1 mi. SE Palmetto, 6200 ft., 6 (D. R. Dickey Coll.); Pigeon Stamp Mill, 6500 ft., 1 (D. R. Dickey Coll.). *Nye Co.:* 2 mi. S Millett P. O., 5500 ft., 1; 4 mi. S Millett P. O., 5500 ft., 1; 5 mi. S Millett P. O., 5700 ft., 5; 5 mi. SE Millett P. O., 5500 ft., 2; Railroad Valley, 2½ to 3¼ mi. S Lock's

Ranch, 5000 ft., 2; Railroad Valley, 9 mi. S Lock's Ranch, 5000 ft., 2; Hot Creek Valley, 6½ mi. N Hot Creek, 5900 ft., 12; 11½ mi. NE San Antonio, 5700 ft., 1; 4 to 6 mi. NE San Antonio, 5650–5700 ft., 8; Hot Creek Valley, ¼ mi. W Hot Creek, 5900 ft., 1; Hot Creek Valley, 3½ mi. E Hot Creek, 5650 ft., 12; San Antonio, 5407 ft., 1; White River Valley, 15 mi. WSW Sunnyside, 1; 14½ mi. NNE Sharp, 1; 9 mi. W and 3 mi. S Tybo, 6200 ft., 22; Ralston Valley, 15½ mi. NE Tonopah, 5800 ft., 9; S end Hot Creek Valley, 2½ mi. E and N Twin Springs, 5400 ft., 7; Railroad Valley, 3 mi. S Nyala, 5600 ft., 1; Big Creek, Quinn Canyon Mts., 5700 ft., 4; Ralston Valley, 34 mi. E and 1 mi. N Tonopah, 5650 ft., 13; Old Mill, N end Reveille Valley, 6200 ft., 1; Railroad Valley, 9½ mi. E New Reveille, 5100–5200 ft., 3; N shore Mud Lake, S end Ralston Valley, 5300 ft., 3; Kawich Mts., 5½ mi. SW Silverbow, 6000 ft., 9; Cactus Flat, 6½ mi. SW Silverbow, 5750 ft., 4; Cactus Spring, Cactus Range, 6500 ft., 2; Cactus Flat, 11½ mi. SW Silverbow, 5400 ft., 5; Gold Flat, 6 mi. W Kawich P. O., 5150 ft., 1; Belted Range, 2 to 4½ mi. NW Indian Spring, 5700–6300 ft., 18; NW base Timber Mtn., 4200 ft., 11; 8½ mi. NE Springdale, 4250 ft., 2; 8 mi. E Grapevine Peak, 5000 ft., 6; 7 mi. E and 2 mi. N Grapevine Peak, 5100 ft., 3; Amargosa River, 3½ mi. NE Beatty, 3400 ft., 4; 1 mi. N Beatty, 3400 ft., 13 (D. R. Dickey Coll.); NW base Skull Mtn., 3500 ft., 15; Amargosa Desert, 20 mi. SE Beatty, 2500 ft., 13; 3 mi. N Pahrump Ranch, 1 (D. R. Dickey Coll.); Pahrump Ranch, 2667 ft., 2 (D. R. Dickey Coll.). *Lincoln Co.:* E side Coal Valley, 14 mi. N Seeman Pass, 4850 ft., 35; E side Coal Valley, 10 mi. N Seeman Pass, 4600 ft., 2; 11 mi. NE Belted Peak, 1; Penoyer Valley, 14 mi. NNW Groom Baldy, 3. *Clark Co.* (unless otherwise noted, in D. R. Dickey Coll.): Indian Spring Valley, 14 mi. N Indian Springs, 3100 ft., 4 (Mus. Vert. Zoöl.); Mormon Well, 6500 ft., 6; Indian Springs, 3280 ft., 9; W slope Charleston Mts., 4000 ft., 9 mi. NE Pahrump, 5; Kyle Canyon, 4500 ft., 14; 3 mi. NW Las Vegas, 2100 ft., 2; Boulder City, 7 (Mus. Vert. Zoöl.); 12 mi. S and 5 mi. E Searchlight, 2600 ft., 7 (Mus. Vert. Zoöl.).

Additional records (Osgood, 1900:29, 31): *Humboldt Co.:* Flowing Springs. *Churchill Co.:* Stillwater. *Nye Co.:* 10 mi. W Oasis Valley.

Perognathus longimembris virginis Huey
Little Pocket Mouse

Perognathus longimembris virginis Huey, Trans. San Diego Soc. Nat. Hist., 9:55, August 31, 1939. Type from Saint George, 2950 feet, Washington County, Utah.

Perognathus panamintinus, Osgood, N. Amer. Fauna, 18:29, September 20, 1900, part.

Distribution.—Virgin River Valley and southern half of Lincoln County west into Nye County. See figure 274.

Remarks.—Measurements of ten of each sex from 5 miles north of Summit Spring measure: ♂, 144 (135–151), ♀, 142 (133–147); 79 (71–82), 75 (68–81); 19.5 (18–20), 19.0 (18–20); weight, 8.4 (6.8–9.6), 9.1 (7.1–10.6) grams.

Size large; color dark, upper parts near Ochraceous-Buff heavily overlain with blackish; underparts white; skull large, mastoidal and tympanic bullae particularly large.

Topotypes fully confirm the characters pointed out by the original describer. The color of Nevadan animals is not so dark as that of topotypes. Large size of animal, including its skull and particularly the large size of the mastoidal bullae, are features which set the series from southern Lincoln County apart from *nevadensis* and *panamintinus*. Proceeding westward, the large size of the bullae is, in *virginis*, the last subspecific character to disappear and the change in size is gradual. The greater size of bullae (length of mastoidal bullae) is evident as far to the northwest as Hot Creek, Nye County, although, on the basis of all features, specimens from there are referable to *panamintinus*.

Comparison of topotypes and other specimens of *P. l. arizonensis* with those of *virginis* shows the latter to be differentiated by more blackish coloration and greater frontonasal length. The large size of mastoidal bullae differentiates *virginis* from *gulosus*, *nevadensis*, and *panamintinus*.

Records of occurrence.—Specimens examined, 234, as follows: *Nye Co.:* 9 mi. E Wheelbarrow Peak, 1; ½ to 2 mi. S Oak Spring, 5700 ft., 4; 2 to 4½ mi. SE Oak Spring, 4700–5500 ft., 19; Emigrant Valley, 9 to 9½ mi. S Oak Spring, 4400 ft., 10. *Lincoln Co.:* Desert Valley, 20 mi. SW Pioche, 5400–5700 ft., 21; 2 mi. N Panaca, 4800 ft., 1; Desert Valley, 21 mi. W Panaca, 5300 ft., 14; 12 mi. E Hiko Spring, 4800 ft., 9; 16 mi. W Caliente, 5000 ft., 8; Pahranagat Valley, 31 (9 1/5 mi. NW Crystal Spring, 4800 ft., 9; 1½ to 4 mi. NE Crystal Spring, 4100–4300 ft., 12; 1 2/5 mi. W Crystal Spring, 4100 ft., 1; Crystal Spring, 4000 ft., 6; ¼ to 4 mi. E Crystal Spring, 4000 and 4300 ft., 3); 9 mi. W Groom Baldy, 5500 ft., 19; 16 mi. E Groom Baldy, 4600 ft., 17; Desert Valley, 8 mi. SW Hancock Summit, 5200–5300 ft., 22; Pahranagat Valley, 9 mi. SW Crystal Spring, 4800 ft., 4; 8 mi. N Summit Spring, 8; Alamo, 3570 ft., 6; Meadow Valley, 24 mi. S Caliente, 3000 ft., 1; 14½ mi. S Groom

Baldy, 4; 5 to 5½ mi. N Summit Spring, 4700 ft., 30; Summit Spring, 4800 ft., 4. *Clark Co.:* Virgin River [south side], ¾ mi. E Mesquite, 1750 ft., 1.

Additional records (Osgood, 1900:29): *Lincoln Co.:* Panaca; Pahroc Spring.

Perognathus longimembris gulosus Hall
Little Pocket Mouse

Perognathus longimembris gulosus Hall, Proc. Biol. Soc. Washington, 54:55, May 20, 1941. Type from near [¼ mi. S] Smith Creek Cave, 5800 feet, Mount Moriah, White Pine County, Nevada.

Distribution.—Eastern Nevada south from near Montello in Elko County to near Baker in White Pine County. See figure 274.

Remarks.—Measurements of one male and five females from the vicinity of the type locality are: ♂, 136, ♀, 132 (125–137); 73, 72 (70–74); 16, 17.8 (17–19); weight, 7.4, 7.5 (6.1–8.9) grams.

Size medium for the species; color pale, sides Pinkish Buff, underparts white; skull resembling that of *nevadensis* and *panamintinus*, but upper tooth row shorter than in *panamintinus*. From *nevadensis*, this race differs in pure white underparts rather than having the hairs of the underparts plumbeous basally and tipped with buffy. From *P. l. arizonensis* to the southeast, *gulosus* differs in paler color (more grayish and less reddish) of sides and upper parts. From *P. l. virginis*, *gulosus* differs in lighter (less blackish and less reddish) upper parts and sides and in smaller skull, especially the smaller mastoidal bullae. From *P. l. panamintinus*, *gulosus* differs in less ochraceous sides and shorter upper tooth rows.

Among named races, *gulosus* most closely resembles *P. l. panamintinus*. Specimens of *gulosus* in fresh pelage are indistinguishable on basis of color from *panamintinus* in much worn pelages in late June. In comparable pelage, for example worn pelage of June-taken specimens, the sides are Pinkish Buff rather than Light Ochraceous Buff. This same difference in color is shown also by the rest of the upper parts beneath the overlay of dark brownish or blackish. In *gulosus* the area of buffy color averages smaller than in *panamintinus*.

So far as known, the ranges of *gulosus* and *panamintinus* do not meet. Between the southern end of the known range of *nevadensis* and the northern end of the range of *virginis* there is an area from which no mice of this species have been recorded. If the mice do occur here it almost certainly is only in the valleys. These are separated by north-south mountain ranges where living conditions are unsuited to this species of *Perognathus*.

Records of occurrence.—Specimens examined, 21, as follows: *Elko Co.:* 13 mi. N Montello, 5000 ft., 2; 8 mi. S Wendover, 4700 ft., 12; near Smith Creek Cave, Mt. Moriah, 5800 ft., 2; 1 mi. SE Smith Creek Cave, Mt. Moriah, 5800 ft., 1; 2 mi. E Smith Creek Cave, Mt. Moriah, 5600 ft., 3; 4 mi. E Smith Creek Cave. 1.

Perognathus parvus
Great Basin Pocket Mouse

These mice in Nevada are inhabitants of the Upper Sonoran Life-zone. Altitudinally they range from 3900 feet at Smoke Creek up to 10,000 feet on the sagebrush-covered slopes of Mount Grant. The species occurs in a wide variety of habitats as regards kind of soil and associations of plants. In these respects it is the most catholic of the Nevadan pocket mice. Although taken along with *Perognathus longimembris* at many places, the upper and lower limits, zonally and altitudinally, are each lower for *longimembris*, and *longimembris* is less often taken on soils made up principally of humus. *P. formosus* also has been taken at some places with *P. parvus*, but *formosus* ranges upward only into the lower part of the Upper Sonoran Life-zone, and even there it is closely restricted to soils strewn with stones. In Nevada we never have found *P. penicillatus*, which is a species of the Lower Sonoran Life-zone, associated with *P. parvus*. Between the areas of occurrence of these two species, a belt of territory in the upper part of the Lower Sonoran Life-zone seems to be uninhabited by either, although this belt does have a big pocket mouse of comparable size, namely, *P. formosus*. It is found on all stony places and sometimes even on ground not particularly stony, which if zonally higher would be inhabited by *P. parvus* and if lower by *P. penicillatus*.

The great distance from water at which specimens have been trapped in abundance indicates that this species, like others of the genus, obtains from food all the water that it requires. Nevertheless, the frequency with which specimens of *P. parvus* have been taken in mousetraps set along small streams at the water's edge suggests that they come to such places more often than the other kinds of Nevadan *Perognathus*. On May 30, 1937, at 5600 feet on Pahrum Peak, David H. Johnson took several of these mice on a night when rain "seemed to discourage other mammals than these from getting into the traps."

Indication of the kind of food eaten is furnished by the contents, listed below, of the cheek pouches of several specimens. Unless otherwise indicated, there was only one mouse from each locality.

Wild gooseberry seeds................ Each of 3 mice, 2 mi. SW Pine Grove, June 29, 1934

Eriogonum sp. (20 achenes)...........
Cruciferae gen. et sp. (455 pods of seed) } Lapon Canyon, July 13, 1934

Polygonum (*buxiforme* ?) (seeds)....... Kingston R. S., June 5, 1930

Rosa (*Woodsii* ?) (seeds).............
Cuscuta sp. (1 seed)................. } Wisconsin Creek, May 27, 1930
Unidentified leaves..................

Gilia inconspicua (leaves, fruits).......
Descurainia sp. (pods and seeds)....... } South Twin River, May 5, 1930

Mustard seeds....................... 1 mi. E Jefferson, July 1, 1933

Amsinckia (nutlets)................... 10 mi. SW Midas, July 5, 1937

Leptotaenia multifida (seeds)..........
Dactylus glomerata (seeds)............ } East slope Irish Mountain, June 7, 1931

Burt (1934:412) recorded that, of specimens taken on Charleston Peak, "Seeds or twigs of the following species of plants were represented in the cheek pouch contents: *Gilia* sp., loco-weed (*Astragalus* sp.), goosefoot (*Chenopodium* sp.), mistletoe (*Phoradendron* sp.), and mustard (Cruciferae)."

Molt occurs in May, June, and July. So far as can be told by examination of Nevadan specimens, there is only one molt per year. Females average smaller than males of comparable age. The difference, as shown by measurements of the series from Wisconsin Creek, is about 19 per cent in weight, 6 per cent in total length and length of tail, and 4 per cent in linear dimensions of the skull.

Young are born in May, June, and July. The number of embryos in 33 pregnant females averaged 5.5 with extremes of 3 and 8. The mode is 5 or 6;

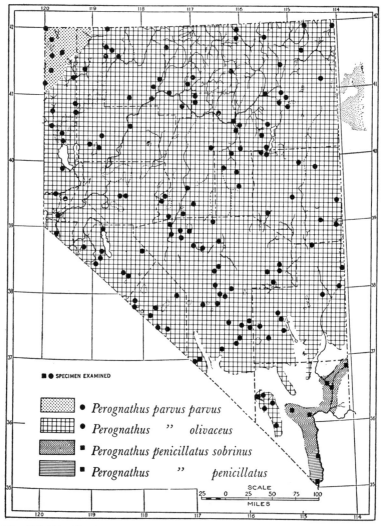

Fig. 275. Distribution of the Great Basin pocket mouse, *Perognathus parvus*, and the desert pocket mouse, *Perognathus penicillatus*.

equal numbers of females had 5 and 6 embryos. The 212 adult females are distributed by months as follows: April, 2; May, 59 (11 pregnant); June, 58 (16 pregnant); July, 65 (6 pregnant); August, 19; September, 9.

Perognathus parvus parvus (Peale)
Great Basin Pocket Mouse

Cricetodipus parvus Peale, U. S. Expl. Exp'd., 8 (Mamm. and Ornith.): 52–54, 1848. Type from Oregon; probably in neighborhood of The Dalles, Wasco County.

Perognathus parvus, Cassin, U. S. Expl., Exp'd. Mamm. and Ornith., pp. 48–49, 1858.

Distribution.—Northwestern Nevada. See figure 275.

Remarks.—Measurements of two males and one female from ½ mi. N Vya are: ♂, 197, 166, ♀, 174; 101, 81, 87; 25.0, 23.5, 24.0; weight, 26.2, 20.0, 20.2 grams.

Size and cranial proportions essentially as described below in *P. p. olivaceus;* color grayish above with ochraceous color absent or, if present, of slight extent.

Pending the completion of a revisionary study of *Perognathus* now under way by Seth B. Benson, the subspecific name *parvus* is applied to specimens from northwestern Nevada. These agree with topotypes in hand except that some have more ochraceous color than *parvus*. These more ochraceous individuals and the average of several other populations from farther south along the western border of Nevada approach the race *Perognathus parvus mollipilosus* of California to the west in color, but are of larger size than topotypes of *mollipilosus.*

Whatever name proves applicable to the gray-colored mice of this species in northwestern Nevada here referred to the race *parvus,* they are easily separable from the more ochraceous animals referred to *olivaceus.* Additional information on geographic variation is given under the account of *P. p. olivaceus.*

Records of occurrence.—Specimens examined, 15, as follows: *Washoe Co.:* 12-mile Creek, ½ mi. E Calif. boundary, 5300 ft., 1; Barrel Spr., 5700 ft., 9½ mi. E and 3 mi. N Ft. Bidwell, 1; 12 mi. E and 3 mi. N Ft. Bidwell, 5700 ft., 2; 4 mi. S Diessner, 5800 ft., 2; 3 mi. N Vya, 5900 ft., 1; ½ mi. N Vya, 6200 ft., 4; 4½ mi. NE Painted Point, 5800 ft., 1; 12 mi. S Vya, 5800 ft., 1; 15 mi. S Vya, 5800 ft., 1; 1 mi. W Hausen, 4650 ft., 1.

Perognathus parvus olivaceus Merriam
Great Basin Pocket Mouse

Perognathus olivaceus Merriam, N. Amer. Fauna, 1:15, October 25, 1889. Type from Kelton, Box Elder County, Utah.

Perognathus parvus olivaceus, Osgood, N. Amer. Fauna, 18:37, September 20, 1900; Taylor, Univ. California Publ. Zoöl., 7:274, June 24, 1911; Borell and Ellis, Journ. Mamm., 15:28, 73, February 15, 1934.

Perognathus parvus magruderensis Osgood, N. Amer. Fauna, 18:38, September 20, 1900. Type from Mount Magruder, 8000 feet, Esmeralda County, Nevada. Burt, Trans. San Diego Soc. Nat. Hist., 7:412, May 31, 1934.

Perognathus parvus, Hall and Linsdale, Journ. Mamm., 10:295, 297, November 11, 1929; Linsdale, Amer. Midland Nat., 19:186, January, 1938.

Distribution.—Upper Sonoran Life-zone throughout state. See figure 275.

Remarks.—Measurements of ten of each sex from Wisconsin Creek are: ♂, 187 (174–193), ♀, 176 (162–187); 97 (91–101), 91 (85–99); 25.0 (24–27), 24.2 (22–26); weight, 25.4 (21.5–31.0), 20.5 (16.5–28.5) grams.

Size large (in comparison with *P. longimembris*); above, near (c) Ochraceous-Buff overlain with blackish; ochraceous color revealed in nearly pure form above eyes and along side from vibrissae posteriorly to flank; underparts with hair white all the way to base; tail bicolored, its upper and lower colors corresponding to those on body. Some specimens have most of the underparts dark-colored, and in these animals the hairs are plumbeous basally and near (c) Ochraceous-Buff distally. Skull slightly rounded in dorsal longitudinal outline; auditory bullae barely or nearly meeting anteriorly; interparietal width less than interorbital breadth.

In the specimens here assigned to *P. p. olivaceus,* four geographic variants are recognizable. If the name *olivaceus* be assigned to one, there remain three incipient geographic races which appear insufficiently differentiated to warrant naming as subspecies.

One of these is the population in the Spring Mountains (specimens from Charleston Peak and Potosi Mountain) which is characterized by long skull, including relatively long frontonasal part of skull and enlarged mastoidal bullae. Pertinent average measurements of ten adult males from Charleston Peak, with corresponding measurements in parentheses for ten adult males from Wisconsin Creek, regarded as representative of *olivaceus*, are: occipitonasal length, 27.6 (27.2); frontonasal length, 18.8 (18.0); mastoidal breadth, 14.3 (14.0); length of mastoidal bulla, 9.0 (8.8). In these dimensions this southernmost Nevadan population averages larger than any other from within the state. Nevertheless, there is considerable overlap.

The second geographic variant comprises animals from the north end of Walker Lake (3 mi. S Schurz) which are nearly white. Animals from Mountain Well, about 45 miles to the north and east, also average lighter colored than other populations, those from near Schurz excepted. Furthermore, in these animals the total length, length of tail, and occipitonasal length each averages small, as they do in all the populations from the area of distribution shown in figure 304 for *Dipodomys microps occidentalis*. That the characters— small size and pale color—are the same as in *occidentalis*, probably is significant. Differences from *occidentalis* are that in this incipient race of *parvus* the reduction in size, in comparison with animals from surrounding areas, is not so much as in *occidentalis*, and the pallid coloration is not maintained over so wide an area, as in *occidentalis*. Nevertheless, at the locality 3 miles south of Schurz, the mice (species *parvus*) are more pallid in comparison with surrounding incipient races than are the rats (species *microps*) from that place when compared with those of surrounding subspecies.

The third incipient subspecies, that from Mount Magruder, is less strongly marked than the two already mentioned. In the animals from Mount Magruder, the tail averages longer, relative to the total length, by about 2 per cent than in any other Nevadan population. Otherwise, to me these mice are indistinguishable from those from central and eastern Nevada. The name *Perognathus parvus magruderensis* Osgood, once applied to them and to specimens from near-by parts of California, was given because of the supposed larger size. With the now more abundant material no such difference is apparent, excepting possibly the tendency to relatively longer tail.

The fourth geographic variant comprises the animals of roughly the northeastern half of Nevada. The most northern of these, particularly specimens from Cobb Creek, Elko County, average darker than others. Otherwise the specimens from this northeastern part of Nevada agree well with topotypes of *P. p. olivaceus*. Another name to be taken into account for animals of eastern Nevada is *Perognathus olivaceus amoenus* Merriam, from Nephi, Juab County, Utah, but study of topotypes leads to the conclusion, made by Osgood (1900:37), that *amoenus* is not distinguishable from *olivaceus*. The name *olivaceus* has priority.

Records of occurrence.—Specimens examined, 762, as follows: *Washoe Co.*: Little High Rock Canyon, 5000 ft., 1; 2¼ to 2½ mi. E and 11 mi. N Gerlach, 4050 ft., 2; Rock Creek, Granite Mts. (5000 ft., 7; 5200 ft., 3), 10; 12 mi. N and 2 mi. E Gerlach, 4000 ft., 1; 3½ mi. NE Gerlach, 4000 ft., 2; 17½ mi. W Deep Hole, 4750 ft., 2; 17 mi. W Deep Hole, 4800 ft., 4; Smoke Creek, 9 mi. E Calif. boundary, 3900 ft., 2; Horse Canyon, 3 mi. NW Pahrum Peak, 5000 ft., 3; Horse Canyon, 5600–6000 ft., Pahrum Peak, 8; Fox Canyon, 6 mi. S Pahrum Peak, 4800 ft., 1; 2¾ mi. SW Pyramid, 4300 ft., 1; 3 mi. E Reno, 4. *Ormsby Co.:* 3½ mi. E Carson City, 4700 ft., 1; 6 mi. E Virginia City, 6000 ft., 3. *Douglas Co.:* 6 mi. S Minden, 1 (coll. of J. R. Alcorn). *Humboldt Co.:* 1 mi. S Denio, Oregon, 4200 ft., 5; 13 to 14 mi. N Paradise Valley, 6400–6700 ft., 6; Martin Creek R. S., 1; meadow, Pine Forest Mts., 8000 ft., 1; head of Big Creek, Pine Forest Mts., 8000 ft., 1; Big Creek, Pine Forest Mts. (6000 ft., 2), 3; 7000 ft., 5; near Big Creek Ranch, 4800 and 4900 ft., 2; Big Creek Ranch, Pine Forest Mts., 4350 ft., 8; Leonard Creek, Pine Forest Mts., 6500 ft., 7; Quinn River Crossing, 4100 ft., 10; Hansen Canyon, 6200 ft., 5 mi. W Paradise Valley P. O., 1; Soldier Meadows, 4600 ft., 14; 18 mi. NE Iron Point, 4600 ft., 2; 7 mi. N Winnemucca, 4400 ft., 2; 1 mi. N Winnemucca, 4600 ft., 3; 5 mi. NE Golconda, 3; 3 to 5 mi. SW Winnemucca, 4500 ft., 3; 8 mi. E and 1 mi. N Jungo, 4200 ft., 2; 11 mi. E and 1 mi. N Jungo, 4200 ft., 3; 23 mi. NW Battle Mountain, 1. *Pershing Co.:* El Dorado Canyon, Humboldt Range (6000 ft., 7; 6100 ft., 2; 7800 ft., 1; 8000 ft., 1), 11; 2½ mi. S Vernon, 4250 ft., 1; 30 mi. W and 4 mi. N Lovelock, 4300 ft., 1; 21 mi.

W and 2 mi. N Lovelock, 4000 ft., 1; S side Granite Peak, East Range, 2. *Churchill Co.:* 1 mi. W Mountain Well, 5300 ft., 3; Mountain Well, 5600 ft., 1. *Mineral Co.:* 3 mi. S Schurz, 4100 ft., 3; 2 to 3½ mi. SW Pine Grove, 7250–7800 ft., 11; Fingerrock Wash, Stewart Valley, 5400 ft., 4; Omco, 6000 ft., 1; Cottonwood Creek, Mt. Grant, 7400 ft., 3; SW slope Mt. Grant, 10,000 ft., 4; Lapon Canyon, Mt. Grant, 8900 ft., 6; Cat Creek, Mt. Grant, 8900 ft., 1; Fletcher, 6098 ft., 1; Endowment Mine, Excelsior Mts., 6500 ft., 7; 4 mi. N Marietta, 6500 ft., 2. *Esmeralda Co.:* 13½ mi. NW Goldfield, 4850 ft., 1; 7 mi. N Arlemont, 5500 ft., 7; Chiatovich Creek, 7000–8200 ft., 29; 1 mi. N Valcalda Spring, 7000 ft., 2; Silver Peak Range, 2 mi. S Piper Peak, 7500 ft., 1; N side Mt. Magruder, 7400–8000 ft., 9; (following specimens from Esmeralda County, unless otherwise noted, in D. R. Dickey Coll.): Palmetto Wash, 5700 ft., 1; Lida, 6100 ft., 7; mouth of Palmetto Wash (5350 ft., 3; 5500 ft., 1), 4; Pigeon Spring, 6400 ft., 2 (Mus. Vert. Zoöl.); Pigeon Stamp Mill, 6500 ft., 1; 2 mi. E Pigeon Stamp Mill. 6600 ft., 1; Palmetto, 6100 ft., 1; 1 mi. SE Palmetto, 6200 ft., 1; Indian Spring, Mount Magruder, 7700 ft., 4; Little Log Spring (7000 ft., 4; 7100 ft., 5), 9; Stockade Springs, 7100 ft., 1. *Lander Co.:* Izenhood, 1; 3 mi. S Izenhood, 1; 1½ mi. NW Cortez, Cortez Mts., 22; Reese River Valley, 7 mi. N Austin, 3; 2½ mi. NE Smiths Creek Ranch, 5800 ft., 4; Smiths Creek, 5800–7700 ft., 17; Birch Creek, 7000 ft., 1; Kingston R. S. 7500 ft., 5; Peterson Creek, Shoshone Mts., 7000 ft., 5. *Eureka Co.:* 5 mi. N Beowawe, 1; Pine Creek, 2 mi. E Palisade, 12; Evans, 4; Union, 4; Winzell, 5; 4 mi. S Tonkin, Denay Creek, Roberts Mts., 1; 4 mi. S Romano. Diamond Valley, 1; 8 mi. W Eureka, 3. *Nye Co.:* Potts R. S., Monitor Valley, 6650 ft., 1; Dutch Flat School House, Reese River, 6715 ft., 2; Wisconsin Creek, 7800–8500 ft., 31; 5 mi. SE Millett P. O., 5500 ft., 1; Ophir Creek, 6500 ft., 2; Bells Ranch, Reese River, 6890 ft., 4; South Twin River, 6500 ft., 10; Greenmonster Canyon. Monitor Range, 7500 ft., 4; Toquima Range, 1 mi. NE Jefferson, 7600–7650 ft., 5; Toquima Range, 1 to 1½ mi. E Jefferson, 7600–8700 ft., 13; Monitor Valley, 7 to 9 mi. E Toquima Peak, 7000–7100 ft., 7; Meadow Creek R. S., Toquima Mts., 2; White River Valley, 17 mi. W Sunnyside, 4; Grant Mts., 19 3/5 mi. WSW Sunnyside, 1; Hot Creek Range, 8 mi. W Tybo, 6700 ft., 6; Hot Creek Range, 9 mi. W and 3 mi. S Tybo, 6200 ft., 4; Burned Corral Canyon, Quinn Canyon Mts., 6700 ft., 3; Garden Valley, 14½ mi. NNE Sharp, 1; Garden Valley, 8½ mi. NE Sharp, 3; Ralston Valley, 34 mi. E and 1 mi. N Tonopah, 5650 ft., 3; Old Mill, N end Reveille Valley, Monitor Range, 6200 ft., 1; Breen Creek, Kawich Mts., 7000 ft., 7; Kawich Mts., 2 4/5 mi. E Silverbow, 7300 ft., 1; Cactus Flat, 5 mi. SW Silverbow, 6000 ft., 1; Cactus Spring, Cactus Range, 6500 ft., 1; 7 to 7½ mi. E Cliff Spring, 5900 ft., 9; Gold Flat, 5½ mi. W Kawich P. O., 5150 ft., 1; 8 mi. NE Wheelbarrow Peak, 3; Belted Range, 2 mi. NW Indian Spring, 6300 ft., 11; 9 mi. E Wheelbarrow Peak, 1; S end Belted Range, 5½ mi. W White Rock Spring, 7250 ft., 1; Belted Range, 5 mi. W White Rock Spring, 6950 ft., 7; NW base Timber Mtn., 4200 ft., 2; 5 mi. E and 1 mi. N Grapevine Peak, 5500 ft., 2; 8 mi. E Grapevine Peak, 5000 ft., 2; 2½ mi. E and 1 mi. S Grapevine Peak, 6700 ft., 23. *Elko Co.:* Cedar Creek, 6 mi. NE San Jacinto, 5300 ft., 1; Goose Creek, 2 mi. W Utah boundary, 5000 ft., 3; Owyhee River, 7 mi. NW Mountain City, 5300 ft., 2; Cobb Creek, 6 mi. SW Mountain City, 6500–6550 ft., 7; summit between heads of Copper and Coon creeks, Jarbidge Mts., 2 (coll. of Ralph Ellis); 15 mi. S Contact, 8500 ft., 1; Marys River, 22 mi. N Deeth, 5800 ft., 7; 1 mi. SE Tuscarora, 5900 ft., 4; 11 mi. SW Midas, 1; Cobre, 6100 ft., 1; (following specimens from Elko Co., unless otherwise noted, in coll. of Ralph Ellis): head of Ackler Creek, Ruby Mts., 6800 ft., 1; 2 mi. NW Halleck, 5200 ft., 3; 2 mi. W Halleck, 5800 ft., 3 (2 in Mus. Vert. Zoöl.); Halleck, 5200 ft., 1; Steels Creek, Ruby Mts., 7000 ft., 3; summit of Secret Pass, Ruby Mts., 6200 ft., 1; Jerry Creek (Jerry Crab Springs), Ruby Mts., 6700 ft., 2; Long Creek, Ruby Mts., 7830 ft., 2; 5 mi. E Raines, Sulphur Spring Mts., 10 (Mus. Vert. Zoöl.); Harrison Pass R. S., Green Mtn. Canyon, 6050 ft., 10; W side Ruby Lake, 3 mi. N White Pine Co. line, 13 (1 in Mus. Vert. Zoöl.). *White Pine Co.:* Willow Creek, 2 mi. S Elko Co. line, 6500 ft., 25 (22 in coll. of Ralph Ellis); W side Ruby Lake, 3 mi. S Elko Co. line, 6100 ft., 4 (coll. of Ralph Ellis); Cherry Creek, 6800–6900 ft., 3; E side Schellbourne Pass, 6800 ft., 4; Gleason Creek, 7500 ft., 6; 2 mi. W Smith Creek Cave, Mt. Moriah, 6300 ft., 1; Smith Creek, 4 mi. W Smith Creek Cave, 6900 ft., 1; 2½ mi. SW Hamilton, 7300 ft., 4; Spring Valley, 7 mi. SW Osceola, 6100 and 6275 ft., 2; Willard Creek, 7150–8300 ft., 10; Baker Creek, 7200–8000 ft., 11; 2 mi. SE Lehman Cave, 6700 ft., 3; mouth Pole Canyon (E slope Snake Mts.), 7200 ft., 1. *Lincoln Co.:* Duck Valley, 3 mi. S Geyser, 6050 ft., 1; latitude 38° 17′ N, ¼ mi. W Utah boundary, 3700 ft., 5; Eagle Valley, 3½ mi. N Ursine, 5900 ft., 2; 2 mi. S Pioche, 6000 ft., 1; 2 mi. SE Pioche, 6000 ft., 1; E slope Irish Mtn., 6900–6950 ft., 4; Pahranagat Valley, 9 1/5 mi. NW Crystal Springs, 4800 ft., 1; 9 mi. W Groom Baldy, 5500 ft., 2; SW base Groom Baldy, 7200–7250 ft., 4; Pahranagat Valley, 9 mi. SW Crystal Springs, 4800 ft., 2; 5½ to 8 mi. N Summit Springs, 4700 ft., 4. *Clark Co.* (unless otherwise noted, in D. R. Dickey Coll.): Willow Creek, 6000 ft., 3; ½ mi. N Wheeler Well, 1; ¼ mi. N Wheeler Well, 6; Charleston Mts., Kyle Canyon (6500 ft., 16; 6300 ft., 9), 25; Trout Canyon, 6500 ft., 1; N side Potosi Mtn., 5800 ft., 4 (Mus. Vert. Zoöl.).

Perognathus formosus
Long-tailed Pocket Mouse

The geographic variants of this species are arranged as three subspecies. All differ from *P. longimembris* in greater size, grayer color, and crested tail. Compared with *P. parvus* and *P. penicillatus, formosus* is grayer, has a more heavily crested tail, and the fur on the body is longer and finer than in *peni-*

cillatus. The antitragus is narrow at the base and in this feature differs from *parvus* and more nearly agrees with *penicillatus.* The ear of *formosus* is longer than in any other Nevadan species. The skull has the cranium more arched

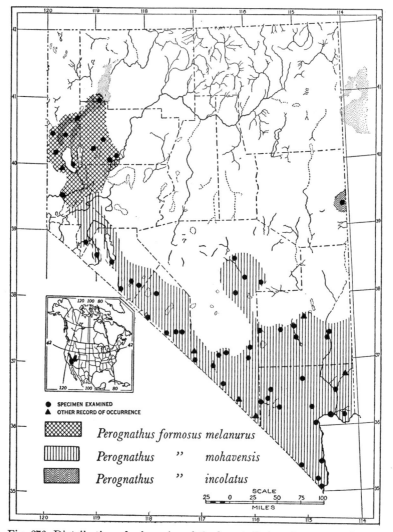

Fig. 276. Distribution of subspecies of the long-tailed pocket mouse, *Perognathus formosus,* with insert showing range of the species.

than in *penicillatus* and the mastoidal bullae are more inflated but less so than in *parvus.* The crested tail and indentation of the supraoccipital by the mastoids are features allying *formosus* with the subgenus *Chaetodipus,* to which

Perognathus penicillatus belongs, but the characters of *formosus* otherwise place it in the subgenus *Perognathus* along with *P. longimembris* and *P. parvus*.

I think of *formosus* as an inhabitant of the Lower Sonoran Life-zone, but it extends also into the lower part of the Upper Sonoran Life-zone, as, for example, in the low western part of the state and again in the extreme eastern part, on the southwestern edge of the basin of Lake Bonneville. The animals' preference for stony ground is well-marked. In western Nevada, especially, they are closely confined to slopes where stones from the size of walnuts up to those 8 inches or even more in diameter are scattered over and partly imbedded in the ground (see pl. 7, *a*). Therefore, places below talus or below cliffs often are suitable for the mice. This predilection for stony ground is evident everywhere throughout the animals' range in Nevada, but it is most pronounced in the northern part of the state. Here, again, is illustrated the principle that the preferred habitat of a species is most clearly revealed at and near the margin of its geographic range, in which area the population of a species faces hostile environment and therefore occupies only the least hostile parts.

In a fairly wide belt across southern Nevada, *formosus* occurs to the exclusion of any other pocket mouse of similar size. At the upper margin of this belt, however, *formosus* and *parvus* have been taken on the same ground, and at the lower margin of this *formosus*-belt *penicillatus* occurs along with *formosus*.

The contents of the cheek pouches of each of two animals taken on June 13, 1932, at a point 2½ miles north of Hoover (Boulder) Dam Ferry, by A. M. Alexander (field nos. 1395 and 1398) consisted of seeds of *Plantago* (*insularis*?) and nutlets and calyces of *Plectocarya linearis*. The pouches of 1395 contained also pods and seeds of Cruciferae. The pouches of a specimen taken on May 20, 1931, 3½ miles north of Beatty, by J. K. Doutt (field no. 574) contained fruits tentatively identified by Frank Richardson as *Oryctes nevadensis*.

Ninety-one females old enough to bear young were taken by months as follows: January, 1; February, 4; May, 33; June, 19; July, 34. Only two contained embryos. These were animals taken in July, and the number of embryos in each instance was six.

Individual variation is less in this species than in *P. penicillatus*. Even so, it is more than the secondary sexual variation. Males average larger than females by about 3 per cent in linear dimensions and by about 6 per cent in weight.

Perognathus formosus melanurus Hall
Long-tailed Pocket Mouse

Perognathus formosus melanurus Hall, Proc. Biol. Soc. Washington, 54:57, May 20, 1941. Type from 40° 28′ N, 6 miles east of California boundary, 4000 feet, Washoe County, Nevada.

Distribution.—Upper Sonoran Life-zone from southwestern Humboldt County southward through western Pershing County and Washoe County to Truckee River. See figure 276.

Remarks.—Measurements of ten males and eleven females from Washoe and Pershing counties are: ♂, 199 (187–211), ♀, 196 (185–211); 107 (100–115), 108 (97–118); 24.7 (23–26), 24.9 (23–26); weight, 21.9 (19.8–24.7), 20.2 (16.8–23.3) grams.

This race may be described as: size large; color blackish over upper parts with faint tinge of buffy; underparts white, or buffy and white; hind feet buffy; tail black above, and below buffy or rarely with a black stripe; skull with small tympanic bullae, long frontonasal region, and widespread maxillary arms of zygomata causing jugals to be nearly parallel.

From *P. f. mohavensis*, this race on the average differs in larger size, always in darker color of upper parts including dorsal tail-stripe, and in smaller tympanic bullae. From *P. f. formosus* and *P. f. incolatus*, *melanurus* differs in the same way as it does from *mohavensis*, although the color difference is less in comparison with *formosus* and more in comparison with *incolatus*. Furthermore, *formosus* and *incolatus* have the maxillary arm of each zygoma inclined more posteriorly, resulting in the zygomatic breadth being less anteriorly rather than about equal anteriorly and posteriorly as in *melanurus*.

Intergradation with the race *mohavensis* is suggested by specimens from several localities in Mineral County. Although these are darker than the average for *mohavensis*, they are referable to that subspecies.

The locality of occurrence north and west of Sulphur is the northernmost one known for the species. Places farther north, which to the collector's eyes appeared to be suitable for these mice, were tested by setting traps; but no long-tailed pocket mice were taken. Places tested were, for example, within 5 miles of Quinn River Crossing.

Records of occurrence.—Specimens examined, 42, as follows: *Washoe Co.:* 1 mi. NE Gerlach, 4000 ft., 2; latitude 40° 28′ N, 6 mi. E Calif. boundary, 4000 ft., 8; 4 mi. NE Pahrum Peak, 4200 ft., 1; 2½ mi. E Flanigan, 4250 ft., 4; Fremont Point [= E shore Pyramid Lake opposite The Pyramid], 1 (coll. of T. J. Trelease and Ira La Rivers); 8 mi. E Reno, 4500 ft., 1; N side Truckee River, 10 and 11¾ mi. E Reno, 4500 ft., 8. *Humboldt Co.:* 10½ mi. W and 6 mi. N Sulphur, 4000 ft., 1. *Pershing Co.:* 3 mi. SW Vernon, 4300 ft., 8; 30 mi. W and 4 mi. N Lovelock, 4300 ft., 1; 30 mi. W and 3 mi. N Lovelock, 4300 ft., 1; 3½ mi. NE Toulon, 3950 ft., 1; 1 to 3½ mi. W Toulon, 4100–4500 ft., 5.

Perognathus formosus mohavensis Huey
Long-tailed Pocket Mouse

Perognathus formosus mohavensis Huey, Trans. San Diego Soc. Nat. Hist., 9:35, November 21, 1938. Type from Bonanza King Mine, Providence Mountains, San Bernardino County, California.
Perognathus formosus, Osgood, N. Amer. Fauna, 18:40, September 20, 1900.
Perognathus formosus formosus, Burt, Trans. San Diego Soc. Nat. Hist., 7:412, May 31, 1934.

Distribution.—Lower Sonoran Life-zone into lowermost part of Upper Sonoran Life-zone in western Nevada north as far as Walker River and across southern Nevada northward into Hot Creek Valley of eastern Nye County. See figure 276.

Remarks.—Measurements of four males and seven females, from 5 mi. E and 1 mi N Grapevine Peak, are: ♂, 192 (188–199), ♀, 188 (182–196); 113 (108–116), 103 (98–105); 24.3 (24–25), 24.4 (24–25); weight, 21.1 (19.0–25.3), 20.7 (16.7–24.5) grams.

Size medium to large; color pale; skull with tympanic bullae large; maxillary arms of zygomata inclined posteriorly to a degree which causes breadth across zygomatic arches to be less anteriorly than posteriorly. Comparison with *melanurus* and *incolatus* is made in the accounts of those forms. From *formosus*, *mohavensis* differs in lighter color, and in most populations the tympanic bullae are less inflated. From *mesembrinus*, *mohavensis* differs in larger size of nearly all parts measured except the mastoidal bullae which are roughly the same size.

Some geographic variation is displayed by the Nevadan specimens. Northern populations are larger than the most southern. For example, the average measurements of four adult males from Big Creek, Quinn Canyon Mountains, followed by corresponding measurements of three adult males from ½ mi. N Calif.-Nev. Monument and vicinity, roughly two hundred miles south of Big Creek, are: external measurements, 197, 188; 109, 107; 24.7, 23.0; weight, 21.6, 16.1 grams; occipitonasal length, 27.5, 26.5; mastoidal breadth, 14.4, 13.7. These specimens from the southern tip of Nevada average smaller than those of any other Nevadan population. This small size suggests intergradation with the race *P. f. mesembrinus*. Even so, the average for these specimens is nearer that which I obtain for *mohavensis*, and if *mohavensis* be recognized as distinct from *mesembrinus*, all our specimens from southern Nevada seem to be referable to it.

Records of occurence.—Specimens examined, 296, as follows: *Lyon Co.:* West Walker River, 12 mi. S Yerington, 4600 ft. [= Wilson Canyon], 8. *Mineral Co.:* East Walker River, 2 mi. NW Morgan's Ranch, 5050–5100 ft., 12; Cat Creek, 4 mi. W Hawthorne, 4500 ft., 3; Marietta, 4900 ft., 5; 1 mi. W Candelaria Junction, 5500 ft., 1; Huntoon Valley, 5700 ft., 4. *Esmeralda Co.* (unless otherwise indicated, in D. R. Dickey Coll.): 2½ mi. NW Blair Junction, 4950 ft., 1 (Mus. Vert. Zoöl.); 2½ mi. SE Dyer, 4950 ft., 2 (Mus. Vert. Zoöl.); ¾ mi. E Lida, 5900 ft., 1; 2 mi. E Lida, 5800 ft., 1; 3 mi. E Lida, 5500 ft., 1; 4½ mi. E Lida, 5350 ft., 1; 6½ mi. E Lida, 5100 ft., 1; 8 mi. E Lida, 5000 ft., 1; Palmetto Wash, 5700 ft., 4. *Nye Co.:* Hot Creek Valley, 6½ mi. N Hot Creek, 5900 ft., 1; S end Hot Creek Valley, 2½ mi. E and N Twin Springs, 5400 ft., 3; Big Creek, Quinn Canyon Mts., 5700–5800 ft., 20; Old Mill, N end Reveille Valley, 6200 ft., 1; ½ mi. E Oak Spring, 6400 ft., 1; ½ mi. S Oak Spring, 5700 ft., 8; 1 to 4½ mi. SE Oak Spring, 3750–6200 ft., 4; 9 to 9½ mi. S Oak Spring, 4400 ft., 6; NW base Timber Mtn., 4200 ft., 8; 8½ mi. NE Springdale, 4200 ft., 1; 7 mi. E and 2 mi. N Grapevine Peak, 5100 ft., 2; 5 mi. E and 1 mi. N Grapevine Peak, 5500 ft., 5; 8 mi. E Grapevine Peak, 5000 ft., 8; Amargosa River, 3½ to 4 mi. NE Beatty, 3400–3500 ft., 47; 1 mi. N Beatty, 3400 ft., 15 (D. R. Dickey Coll.); Amargosa Desert, 20 mi. SE Beatty, 2500 ft., 1. *Lincoln Co.:* Pahranagat Valley, 1½ mi. NE Crystal Spring, 4100 ft., 2; 9 mi. W Groom Baldy, 5500 ft., 6; 16 mi. E Groom Baldy, 4600 ft., 1; Meadow Valley, 5½ mi. N Elgin, 4000 ft., 3; Meadow Valley Wash, 21 mi. S Caliente, 3200 ft., 8; Alamo, 3570 ft., 4. *Clark Co.:* Mormon Well, 6500 ft., 1 (D. R. Dickey Coll.); Indian Springs, 3280 ft., 16 (D. R. Dickey Coll.); ½ mi. SE St. Thomas, 1250 ft., 2 (D. R. Dickey Coll.); ½ mi. S St. Thomas, 1250 ft., 4 (D. R. Dickey Coll.); Lost City, 1 (D. R. Dickey Coll.); Willow Creek, 6000 ft., 1 (D. R. Dickey Coll.); W slope Charleston Peak, 9 mi. NE Pahrump, 4000 ft., 4 (D. R. Dickey Coll.); Kyle Canyon, 4500 ft., 6 (D. R. Dickey Coll.); island in Las Vegas Wash, 1150 and 1250 ft., 2 (Boulder Dam Recreational Area Coll.); 2½ mi. N Hoover (Boulder) Dam Ferry, 8; Cedar Basin, 3500 ft., 2 (D. R. Dickey Coll.); Hemenway Wash, 1150 ft., 4 (Boulder Dam Recreational Area Coll.); Colorado River, 14 mi. E Searchlight, Jap Ranch, 500 ft., 3; 9 mi. W and 5 to 5½ mi. S Searchlight, 4300 ft., 2; 7 mi. S Dead Mtn., 2700 ft., 5; Hiko Spring, 8 mi. SE Dead Mtn., 1000 ft., 2; 3 mi. SW Hiko Spring, 2400 ft., 10; W side Colorado River, 500 ft., 6 mi. N Calif. boundary, 10; Colorado River, ½ to 1 mi. N Calif.-Nev. Monument, 450–500 ft., 13.

Additional records (Osgood, 1900:41): *Nye Co.:* Thorp Mill; Ash Meadows; Pahrum Valley. *Lincoln Co.:* Pahroc Spring. *Clark Co.:* Bunkerville.

Perognathus formosus incolatus Hall
Long-tailed Pocket Mouse

Perognathus formosus incolatus Hall, Proc. Biol. Soc. Washington, 54:55, May 20, 1941. Type from 2 miles west of Smith Creek Cave, 6300 feet, Mount Moriah, White Pine County, Nevada.

Distribution.—Eastern slope of Mount Moriah on eastern border of state. See figure 276.

Remarks.—Measurements of four females are 185 (177–190), 102 (97–106); 22.8 (22–23); weight, 18.9 (16.8–21.5) grams.

Size medium; color grayish and pale, the upper parts a mixture of white, light buffy, and reduced amount of blackish; sides with buffy markings faintly indicated; hind feet and underparts white; tail bicolored, buffy below, and colored like upper parts above; skull with large tympanic bullae, and maxillary arms of zygomata inclined posteriorly so that width across zygomatic arches is less anteriorly than posteriorly.

From *P. f. formosus* this race differs in lighter color and in the shape of the interparietal, which has the anterior border more nearly straight; in *formosus* the suture between the interparietal and the parietals has the form of an open, inverted V. From *P. f. mohavensis*, *incolatus* differs in the same way as from *formosus*, but the difference in color is less. Judging from the material at hand, the hind foot is shorter in *incolatus* than in either of the other two races just mentioned. The taking of specimens near the eastern base of Mount Moriah by Lee W. Arnold, Henry S. Fitch, and David H. Johnson was the first intimation that we had of the occurrence of this species in the basin of the Pleistocene Lake Bonneville.

Records of occurrence.—Specimens examined, 5, as follows: *White Pine Co.:* 2 mi. W Smith Creek Cave, Mt. Moriah, 6300 ft., 2; near (within ¼ mi. of) Smith Creek Cave, 5800 ft., Mt. Moriah, 3.

TABLE 9

CRANIAL MEASUREMENTS (IN MILLIMETERS) OF PEROGNATHUS

Sex	Name and locality	Number of individuals averaged or catalogue no.	Occipitonasal length	Frontonasal length*	Mastoidal breadth	Length of bulla*	Interorbital breadth	Alveolar length of upper molariform teeth
	P. longimembris nevadensis							
♂	Topotypes..................	10 av.	21.1	14.4	12.4	8.2	5.3	3.0
		min.	20.1	14.0	12.0	7.9	5.1	2.8
		max.	21.8	14.8	12.9	8.5	5.5	3.3
♀	Topotypes..................	5 av.	21.0	14.3	12.3	8.1	5.3	3.0
		min.	20.6	14.1	12.2	8.0	5.2	2.9
		max.	21.4	14.5	12.4	8.2	5.5	3.2
	P. longimembris panamintinus							
♂	7 mi. N Arlemont............	10 av.	21.3	14.4	12.4	8.2	5.2	3.2
		min.	20.6	14.0	12.0	8.0	5.0	3.0
		max.	21.9	14.9	12.8	8.3	5.4	3.2
♀	7 mi. N Arlemont............	7 av.	21.4	14.4	12.3	8.1	5.3	3.1
		min.	20.5	13.9	12.1	7.8	5.2	3.0
		max.	22.2	14.9	12.6	8.4	5.4	3.2
	P. longimembris virginis							
♂	5 mi. N Summit Spring.......	10 av.	22.0	15.0	12.5	8.5	5.3	3.1
		min.	21.3	14.5	12.0	8.2	4.9	2.9
		max.	22.6	15.4	12.8	9.0	5.5	3.3
♀	5 mi. N Summit Spring.......	10 av.	21.7	14.8	12.3	8.5	5.2	3.2
		min.	21.1	14.5	11.8	8.0	5.0	2.9
		max.	22.3	15.3	12.8	9.0	5.4	3.5
	P. longimembris gulosus							
♂	8 mi. S Wendover..........	46088	21.7	14.6	12.7	8.4	5.4	3.0
♂	Near Smith Creek Cave.....	78767	21.1	14.2	12.5	8.2	5.3	3.0
♀	Near Smith Creek Cave.....	5 av.	21.1	14.4	12.5	8.2	5.2	3.0
		min.	21.0	14.0	12.3	8.1	5.1	2.9
		max.	21.2	14.6	12.6	8.3	5.3	3.1
	P. parvus parvus							
♂	4 mi. S Diessner............	73382	27.2	18.0	14.2	9.4	6.1	4.0
♂	½ mi. N Vya..............	73386	27.7	17.9	13.7	9.0	6.0	4.0
♂	½ mi. N Vya..............	73387	25.3	16.8	13.0	8.3	5.8	3.7
♀	½ mi. N Vya..............	73385	25.9	16.8	13.8	8.8	6.0	3.8
	P. parvus olivaceus							
♂	Wisconsin Creek............	10 av.	27.2	18.0	14.0	8.8	6.2	3.9
		min.	26.3	17.4	13.5	8.6	5.8	3.7
		max.	27.9	18.9	14.6	9.1	6.6	4.1
♀	Wisconsin Creek............	10 av.	26.2	17.4	13.7	8.7	6.0	3.8
		min.	25.2	16.4	13.2	8.0	5.7	3.6
		max.	27.4	18.4	14.4	9.1	6.2	3.9
	P. formosus melanurus							
♂	NW Nevada................	10 av.	27.2	18.8	14.3	9.0	6.9	4.0
		min.	26.5	18.0	13.9	8.7	6.7	3.6
		max.	28.2	19.6	14.7	9.3	7.3	4.3
♀	NW Nevada................	11 av.	26.8	18.5	14.0	8.8	7.0	3.8
		min.	25.5	17.6	13.4	8.6	6.6	3.7
		max.	27.3	19.4	14.7	9.0	7.5	4.0

* For explanation of measurements, see page 357.

TABLE 9—(*Continued*)

Sex	Name and locality	Number of individuals averaged or catalogue no.	Occipitonasal length	Frontonasal length*	Mastoidal breadth	Length of bulla*	Interorbital breadth	Alveolar length of upper molariform teeth
♂	*P. formosus mohavensis* Near Grapevine Peak.......	4 av. min. max.	27.3 26.8 27.3	18.6 18.2 19.4	14.2 13.8 14.9	9.0 8.7 9.5	6.8 6.5 7.1	3.9 3.7 4.2
♀	Near Grapevine Peak.......	7 av. min. max.	26.9 26.1 28.0	18.1 17.6 18.9	14.0 13.5 14.6	9.0 8.8 9.2	6.7 6.5 7.0	3.8 3.7 4.1
♀	*P. formosus incolatus* Near (within 2 mi. of) Smith Creek Cave..............	4 av. min. max.	26.8 26.0 27.3	18.1 17.7 18.3	13.9 13.7 14.4	8.9 8.8 9.1	6.7 6.4 6.9	3.7 3.7 3.7
♂	*P. penicillatus sobrinus* Near mouth Vegas Wash....	15 av. min. max.	27.0 25.7 28.8	18.5 17.7 19.2	13.1 12.6 13.6	8.0 7.5 8.5	6.5 6.1 6.8	4.0 3.9 4.3
♀	Near mouth Vegas Wash....	7 av. min. max.	25.1 25.6 28.8	18.1 17.6 19.6	13.0 12.7 13.4	7.9 7.7 8.4	6.4 6.1 7.2	4.0 3.9 4.2
♂	*P. penicillatus penicillatus* 14 mi. E Searchlight........	10 av. min. max.	27.9 26.1 29.5	19.0 17.9 20.5	13.8 12.9 14.4	8.3 7.9 8.7	6.7 6.2 7.2	4.1 3.9 4.4
♀	14 mi. E Searchlight........	10 av. min. max.	26.6 24.5 28.0	18.2 17.0 19.5	13.3 12.2 13.6	7.9 7.2 8.4	6.4 6.1 6.5	4.1 3.9 4.5

* For explanation of measurements, see page 357.

Perognathus penicillatus
Desert Pocket Mouse

Two races, both from Clark County, are known of this species which is confined to the Lower Sonoran Life-zone. Among Nevadan species of *Perognathus* it may be described as: size largest; pelage coarsest; brownish gray above and white below; tail averaging longer than head and body; soles of hind feet naked; ears measuring less than 10 mm. from notch (about 8 mm. on dried skins); tail heavily crested and penicillate; skull large; mastoidal side of parietal shorter than any other side (rarely about equal to squamosal side); ascending branches of supraoccipital wide on top of skull; auditory bullae separated anteriorly by a distance equal to more than half the width of the posterior end of the basisphenoid.

Indidivual variation in this species is great; the actual amount is indicated by the measurements given. These show that the males average about 4 per cent larger than females in linear measurements and 20 per cent greater in weight.

Fifteen miles east of Searchlight, twenty-one specimens were taken in January when the nights were cold. Apparently this species does not hibernate. None of the ten females taken here was pregnant. Most of the specimens were taken in thickets of arrowweed, although 4 were trapped at the edge of a mesquite thicket. All were on the fine, silty soil of the bottom land along the river. In the same locality, *P. formosus* was taken on more gravelly soil.

Perognathus penicillatus sobrinus Goldman
Desert Pocket Mouse

Perognathus penicillatus sobrinus Goldman, Journ. Mamm., 20:257, May 14, 1939, as a substitute for the preoccupied name *P. p. seorsus* Goldman. Type from "Virgin River, 7 miles above Bunkerville, Clark County, Nevada."

Perognathus penicillatus seorsus Goldman, Proc. Biol. Soc. Washington, 52:34, March 11, 1939, not *Perognathus spinatus seorsus* Burt, Trans. San Diego Soc. Nat. Hist., 7:167, October 31, 1932.

Perognathus penicillatus, Osgood, N. Amer. Fauna, 18:45, September 20, 1900.

Perognathus penicillatus penicillatus, Burt, Trans. San Diego Soc. Nat. Hist., 7:413, May 31, 1934.

Distribution.—Sandy and alluvial soils along the Muddy, Virgin, and Colorado rivers north from Boulder Dam. See figure 275, page 366.

Measurements.—Measurements of eleven males and three females from near the mouth of Vegas Wash along the Colorado River are: ♂, 200 (180–215), ♀, 188 (178–200); 110 (99–121), 103 (97–108); 24.9 (23.5–26.0); 25.1 (24.5–26.0); no weight available.

In addition to characters as described for the species, *sobrinus* is characterized by Pinkish Buff color on underparts, nasals posteriorly depressed below premaxillae, mastoidal breadth slight, and maxillary arm of zygoma broad.

These features differentiate *sobrinus*, as pointed out by the original describer, from *P. p. penicillatus* on the opposite side of the Colorado River in Arizona and from farther down the Colorado River on its western side. The pinkish (less grayish) color is only slightly different from that of other populations, and I cannot affirm that it is not the result of fading in animals which live in soils with a high content of alkali. The depression of the nasals permits separating about three-fourths of the specimens of *sobrinus* from those *penicillatus* east of Searchlight in Nevada. The narrower mastoidal breadth of *sobrinus* is diagnostic in roughly the same, or a slightly lesser, proportion of the specimens. As noted in the account of the subspecies *penicillatus*, the Nevadan animals from east of Searchlight mostly have the maxillary arm of the zygoma as broad as in *sobrinus* and in this feature are intermediate between *sobrinus* and populations of *penicillatus* farther to the west. The race *sobrinus* is weakly differentiated from the populations to which the subspecific name *penicillatus* is applied.

Records of occurrence.—Specimens examined, 40, as follows: *Clark Co.:* 7 mi. above Bunkerville, 2 (U. S. Nat. Mus., Biol. Surv. Coll.); 5 mi. SE Overton, 1200 ft., 1; ½ mi. SE St. Thomas, 2 (D. R. Dickey Coll.); island in "Boulder Lake" at mouth of Virgin River, 1; Vegas Valley, 13 (U. S. Nat. Mus., Biol. Surv. Coll.); near mouth of Vegas Wash, Colorado River, 21 (U. S. Nat. Mus., Biol. Surv. Coll.).

Perognathus penicillatus penicillatus Woodhouse
Desert Pocket Mouse

Perognathus penecillatus [sic] Woodhouse, Proc. Acad. Nat. Sci. Philadelphia, 6:200, 1852. Type locality uncertain; see below under *Remarks*.

Distribution.—Sandy and alluvial soils along the Colorado River south to California from a latitude at least as far north as Searchlight. See figure 275, page 366.

Remarks.—Measurements of ten of each sex, from 14 mi. E Searchlight, along the Colorado River, are: ♂, 200 (184–216), ♀, 191 (171–208); 107 (98–118), 103 (92–112); 25.7 (24–27), 25.3 (22–28); weight, 25.6 (19.5–32.8), 21.1 (13.9–29.9) grams.

The description given for the species applies here, and differences from *sobrinus* are noted in the account of that race. Comparison of Nevadan specimens with others from the opposite side of the Colorado River near Searchlight Ferry, from Mellen, and from Cibola reveals agreement in essential features, except that in most (not all) of the Nevadan animals the maxillary arm of the zygoma is broader. In this respect the animals from extreme southern Nevada and from along the Nevadan side of the River east of Searchlight are intermediate toward *sobrinus*.

These Nevadan specimens are distinguishable from topotypes of *P. p. angustirostris* by greater average size, by broader rostrum the sides of which, as pointed out by Goldman in the original description of the race *sobrinus* (1939a:34), are less evenly tapered anteriorly, owing to more swollen premaxillae over roots of incisors, by broader maxillary arm of zygoma, and by broader upper incisors. Compared to *P. p. stephensi* from Death Valley, Nevadan specimens differ in still greater degree; adults of comparable sex and age by actual weight are about twice as heavy (males 25.6 and 11.9 grams).

The name *penicillatus* (see Goldman, 1939a:33) is poorly established because in the original description the animal was said to be from San Francisco Mountain, a place probably unsuitable for this species. The assumption is that the specimen used by Woodhouse came from somewhere else. Indeed, because Woodhouse did not designate a type specimen by number, there is some doubt whether the specimen commonly regarded as the type specimen in the United States National Museum is actually the one on which Woodhouse based his description. For the present it seems best to follow current usage and apply the name *penicillatus* to the race of mouse, here under consideration, which ranges to the south, east, and west from and including our most southern localities of occurrence in Nevada.

Records of occurrence.—Specimens examined, 33, as follows: *Clark Co.*: Colorado River, 14 mi. E Searchlight, Jap Ranch, 500 ft., 21; Colorado River, 5 and 6 mi. N Calif. boundary, 500 ft., 2; opposite Fort Mohave, 10 (8 in U. S. Nat. Mus., Biol. Surv. Coll.).

Genus **Microdipodops** Merriam
Kangaroo Mice

There are two species in the genus *Microdipodops* Merriam, each of which occurs in Nevada.

Microdipodops has many unique structural features which mark it as a genus distinct from other heteromyids. Selected features of this nature are the great enlargement of the auditory bullae, which in many specimens extend anteriorly to the glenoid fossae, high degree of fusion of the cervical vertebrae, length and slenderness of the manus, and fusion of the tibia and fibula throughout almost three-fifths of their length. *Microdipodops* exceeds *Dipodomys* in degree of enlargement of the auditory bullae and agrees with that genus in thickly furred soles of the hind feet and general shape of the external ear. Agreement with *Perognathus* is shown in absence of a dermal gland between the shoulders, relative length and color pattern of the tail, and unexpanded zygomatic process of the maxilla. Among living genera of heteromyids, *Microdipodops* is in many features intermediate between *Dipodomys* and *Perognathus*, but shows greater resemblance to the latter. The most comprehensive account of the osteology and dentition is that of Wood (1935). Hatt (1932) has compared the vertebral column with that of other ricochetal rodents.

Merriam (1891:115), in his original description of the genus, called attention to many of its outstanding structural features. His mention of rootless molars was properly queried by Wood (1935), whose limited material prevented him from satisfying himself on this point. In the present study teeth extracted from specimens in the Museum of Vertebrate Zoölogy show that M1 is rooted in both old and young specimens of *M. pallidus* and that the roots are present

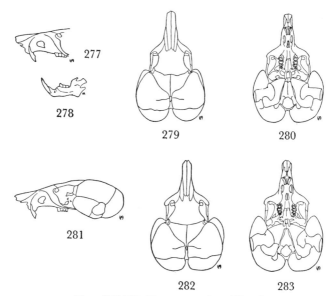

Figs. 277–283. Kangaroo mice. All, × 1.

Figs. 277–280. *Microdipodops megacephalus megacephalus*, Winzell, no. 70942, ♀ (except fig. 278, lower jaw, which is no. 58077, ♂, from 6½ miles north Fish Lake, 6700 feet, Fish Spring Valley, Nye County).
Figs. 281–283. *Microdipodops pallidus pallidus*, 8 miles southeast Blair, no. 59344, ♀.

in both adult and young topotypes of *M. megacephalus*, although the roots are small in the young. Indeed, in one of two young topotypes no indication of roots was found. Thus, Merriam's statement probably was correct for the specimen examined by him, but actually the anterior molar above is normally rooted, as also is the first molar below, the upper and lower premolar, and sometimes the second upper and lower molar. The third molar, above and below, is single rooted.

The short-haired tail of *Microdipodops* is notable for being larger in the middle and along most of the proximal third than at either the base or the tip. Probably this fleshiness near the middle permits it to function as a balancing organ in somewhat the same way as does the tail in *Dipodomys* and *Perog-*

nathus, but what *Dipodomys* accomplishes by a combined lengthening of the
tail and growth of long hairs on its tip, or what *Perognathus* accomplishes by
lengthening of the tail, *Microdipodops* accomplishes by an increase in diameter
of the middle part of the tail. The adaptation resembles that in the fat-tailed
mice of the desert of northern Africa, but the degree of "fattening" in *Microdipodops* is much less.

If any list of genera might be spoken of as characteristic of the Nevadan
fauna, the genus *Microdipodops* would have to be included. Outside of Nevada
it ranges only into the low country of eastern Oregon, into California only
along its eastern border and in Utah to a point about 65 miles east of the
Nevada boundary. Altitudinally, the mice have been taken from as low as
3900 feet at Smoke Creek up to 7600 feet in Monitor Valley, 9 miles east of
Toquima Peak. All of the known occurrences, without as well as within
Nevada, are in the Upper Sonoran Life-zone. Within this zone, edaphic
features control the distribution of the species and even some of the subspecies.

The subspecies *M. m. megacephalus* and *M. m. sabulonis* occur on gravelly
soil, more often where gravel is mixed with either fine or coarse sand, and at
some places, for example at Cobre, the animals seem to avoid fine sand. Where
mice of these two races have been found on sandy soil, it is as often as not
packed and firm. The species *M. pallidus*, including all its subspecies, is restricted to fine, loose, wind-blown sand. At eleven of the twelve places where
the two species were taken together, careful note was made of the character
of the soil on which each species was caught, and in every instance *M. pallidus*
was restricted to the fine sand and *M. megacephalus* to coarser soils. This was
true in Great Smoky Valley where, northeast of San Antonio, the ranges of the
two meet. Along the eastern bank of the wash in the center of the valley, *M.
pallidus* ranged continuously from San Antonio, on fine sand of uniform character, northward for 4¾ miles. Here a smaller side wash, 10 feet wide and 4
feet deep, with fine sand in the bottom and with gently sloping sandy sides,
comprised the boundary between the ranges of the two species. The sand itself
is indistinguishable north and south of this wash, but, beginning at its center
and extending for an undetermined distance northward, dark-colored gravel
up to the size of the ball of a man's thumb is mixed with the sand, giving the
sandy soil a much darker color. On this darker soil, only *M. megacephalus*
was taken. An individual of *M. pallidus* was caught in the bottom of the wash
on the fine sand only 4 feet from its edge, and an individual of *M. megacephalus*
was caught only 35 feet farther north on the darker colored, coarser soil. A
change in flora was as abrupt as that in the soil and in the mice. South of the
wash the shrubs were a third taller than those to the north. *Atriplex canescens*
was dominant on the south side and absent on the north. *Parosela* sp. (blue
flowers) was common on the south side and represented by a mere trace on the
north side. *Chrysothamnus viscidiflorus* var. *pumilis* occurred on the north side

only. *Tetradymia* sp. was equally common on the two sides. From observations at other places where the ranges of the two species of *Microdipodops* meet, it is concluded that the difference in flora, like the difference in the mice, depends on the change in type of soil; the change in type of flora was not the limiting factor for the mice or vice versa.

At this place, as at ten other places where the two species of mice were taken together, there was no evidence of crossbreeding. At the twelfth place, Penoyer Valley, north of Groom Baldy, the difference in color between the two species, by reason of addition of much buff color in each of the two kinds, is less than at any of the eleven other places. Also the difference in length of hind foot is less than at most other places where the two kinds meet or occur together. These resemblances, at first glance, suggest that crossbreeding to some degree has occurred. Shape of the incisive foramina, breadth of the interorbital region, width of skull across the auditory bullae, and color, when closely examined, nevertheless, permit ready identification as to species of all but three of the fifty-seven specimens.

Specimen no. 52672 has the color and incisive foramina like that in *megacephalus*, and the interorbital breadth and greatest breadth of the skull is similar to that in *pallidus*. No. 52728 is intermediate in color and interorbital breadth, and is like *pallidus* in shape of incisive foramina and like *megacephalus* in greatest breadth across auditory bullae. No. 52718 has the color and interorbital breadth like that in *pallidus*, the breadth across the auditory bullae and the breadth across the maxillary processes of the zygomata similar to that in *megacephalus*, and the incisive foramina of an intermediate shape. My impression is that these three specimens are the result of crossbreeding between the two species. Because only three of a total of fifty-seven specimens appear to be of this nature, they are regarded as hybrids rather than intergrades. Unfortunately, the field notes for this catch record only that the mice were taken on sandy areas alternating with areas of hard-packed soil, and it is not recorded whether the seeming hybrids were taken on the hard-packed soil or on a sandy area.

The geographic distribution of *M. pallidus* is confined to the lower part of the Upper Sonoran Life-zone. In this zone it occupies the same areas as does *Dipodomys deserti*, *D. merriami*, and some other mammalian species of predominantly Lower Sonoran distribution. Edaphic conditions appear suitable for *M. pallidus* at several places in the Lower Sonoran Life-zone of Nevada, but it does not occur at any of these places.

By referring to the three individuals described above from Penoyer Valley as hybrids, it is not intended to imply that they are infertile. Although no conclusive information is available on that point, it is supposed that the three hybrids are fertile, because individuals of the two kinds at this locality closely resemble one another in color and in the relation of nasals to premaxillae and are indistinguishable in length of hind foot, three of the several features by which the two kinds can be distinguished at all other places where they have been found in the same locality.

Two explanations which come to mind for the situation existing in Penoyer Valley are (1) that two full species, long separated without any crossbreeding between them, happen now to crossbreed at this one place among the several at which their ranges meet, or (2) that this is a species in the making—an instance where the two kinds have ceased to crossbreed except at this one place where separation never has been wholly accomplished.

No evidence has been found which supports the first explanation to the exclusion of the second. Some evidence which lends credence to the second explanation and not to the first is this: The northern, western, and eastern limits of the geographic range of *pallidus* coincide with those of several other mammalian species, for example, *Dipodomys merriami*, *D. deserti*, and *Perognathus formosus*. The southern limit of the range of each of the other species does not coincide with the southern limit for *pallidus*, but is much farther south, well down in the Lower Sonoran Life-zone. The other species differ from their nearest relatives to the northward more than *pallidus* does from *megacephalus*, its nearest relative to the northward. The differentiation from one another of *megacephalus* and *pallidus* probably, therefore, has occurred relatively recently. Considering all the evidence, the most logical explanation seems to be that two species are in the making.

If this hypothesis should prove to be correct, the question will remain concerning the manner in which this division of one species into two took place. Possibly it began by an ecological separation of the animals living on the fine sand from those on firmer soils. Like many plants and some kinds of animals which live in the bottom of the valley on the fine sands, the *Microdipodops* there may have begun their reproductive cycle earlier than mice of their kind on firmer soils, which in general are at a higher elevation, with the result that a measure of isolation occurred because of physiological differences. The possibility that some physiological separation now exists was first considered on May 31, 1932, when adults and a few young of both species were taken 14½ to 15 miles south of Groom Baldy. The young of *pallidus* were older than those of *megacephalus*.

To speculate further, but with less factual basis: If from Penoyer Valley the incipient species *pallidus*, adapted to existence in the fine sand, spread to the westward (appropriate soils occur in that direction), a plausible explanation of the limits of range of *pallidus* is provided. When the area of Lake Lahontan to the westward of the main range of *megacephalus* progressively receded, *megacephalus*, like *pallidus*, too, may have extended its range into the areas made available by this recession. Even though such westward extension of the range of *megacephalus*, to judge from its present distribution, would have put the extended area somewhat north of that first invaded by *pallidus*, *megacephalus* may have extended its geographic range around the northern end of

Lake Lahontan and then on southward along the western shore. When populations of the two species met west of Penoyer Valley, for example in Cactus Flat and at the southern end of Great Smoky Valley, it is conceivable that, by slight change in each kind, differentiation had progressed to the point where no crossbreeding at all could occur.

At still more western localities, for example in the area about Mono Lake, California, and in the eastern part of its range, as at Skull Valley, Utah—places reached and now inhabited by *megacephalus* but probably never reached by *pallidus*—*megacephalus* has several characters of *pallidus*, namely, long hind foot, large auditory bullae, and white underparts. In these places *megacephalus* lives in the fine sand. This parallelism between sand-inhabiting populations of *megacephalus* lends greater probability to the view that *pallidus* has developed some of its characters as a result of adaptation to living in the one kind of soil—fine sand. Also, the fact that *megacephalus* inhabits fine sand only on the margins of its range—places far removed from known occurrences of *pallidus*—lends greater probability to the above-postulated origin of *pallidus* in Penoyer Valley or in some near-by part of south-central Nevada.

The larger tympanic bullae of *pallidus* indicate that it is the more specialized of the two species, and I think of it as the offspring rather than the parent or even sibling of *megacephalus*. Because *M. pallidus* lives on the fine sands in the bottoms of valleys where plants and animals associated with *Microdipodops* prosper most—population-densities for most species are greater there than on any one type of the firmer soils—it appears to be the more advanced of the two species. *M. megacephalus* has a wider tolerance with respect to kind of soil, which fact, together with its more generalized structure (smaller auditory bullae), is an indication of its greater potentialities in speciation; if additional species of *Microdipodops* are formed, they probably will stem from *megacephalus* rather than from *pallidus*.

In review, a hypothesis sufficing for the meager factual information now available is that: The two species are at the stage, rarely observed, which can be designated as that between the last stage of a subspecies and the first stage of a species. The progress registered toward the formation of two full species has been accomplished by ecological separation, physiological separation, and extension of the geographic range, in the order mentioned.

The mice are regarded by some naturalists as rare, but they are abundant in some places. Ten years before and after 1900, when the earlier collections of mammals were made in Nevada, the collectors relied on horses for transportation and stops for overnight trapping were made where water and, if possible, green forage were to be had. *Microdipodops* prefers a habitat more arid than is ordinarily found at a place of this kind and, therefore, but few were taken. The collections here reported upon were made mostly between 1927 and 1937, when automobiles were used for transportation, making it easy to stop overnight in dry places far removed from water. This change in means of transportation, I think, was responsible more than anything else for the taking of large numbers of kangaroo mice in later years and the consequent modification of naturalists' estimates of their abundance. Of course, once it was learned where profitably to look for the *Microdipodops*, effort was made to get them; even so, it probably is fair to say that the automobile is responsible for the present abundance of study specimens of *Microdipodops*.

Kangaroo mice are nocturnal. In the daytime they live below ground in burrows which are closed to the outside, probably by earth that the mice push into the openings; in any event, the wind soon after sunrise ordinarily drifts sand over the mouths of the burrows. A caged mouse invariably kept the entrance to its small nest box closed with sand during the day. Like *Dipodomys* and several species of *Perognathus*, *Microdipodops* is able to live without water to drink. The one kept for 6 months in captivity was not given water.

Tracks of kangaroo mice are essentially miniatures of those of kangaroo rats. The relatively large impressions of the hind feet usually are not parallel but have the toes pointing outward. This position permits the hind feet, equipped as they are with stiff, projecting hairs on the sides of the soles, to function effectively in the sand when the animal leaps, which it does by using the two hind feet at the same time rather than alternately. Impressions of the forefeet usually are present, but, if not, the consecutive pairs of tracks left by the hind feet are farther apart than otherwise. This indicates that rapid progress is accomplished mainly or wholly by use of the hind feet. The mark ordinarily left by the dragging tail is absent when the consecutive tracks of the hind feet are far apart; it seems that the tail is carried higher off the ground when the animal makes haste. One young kangaroo mouse at Halleck repeatedly jumped out of a can 17 inches high and only 10 inches in diameter without touching the sides.

Attributes peculiar to the species, of which there appear to be but two, are discussed below.

Microdipodops megacephalus
Dark Kangaroo Mouse

Nine subspecies occur in Nevada. The upper parts are brownish, blackish, or grayish, depending upon the subspecies. The basal two-thirds of the hair is plumbeous, thence, distally, it is brownish or buffy and the tips of most of the longer hairs are darker brown or black. The underparts are lighter. Usually the hair is plumbeous basally and white in its distal half. In some subspecies it is white to the  base and in others is plumbeous basally, then white and tipped with buffy. The color of the light-colored underparts extends over the fore and hind legs, flanks, and sides of the head, but does not encroach as far upward as the base of the ear or the lower lid of the eye. On the back the hair attains an average length of 12 millimeters and on the underparts is as much as 8 millimeters long. The facial vibrissae extend behind the ear and are about 35 millimeters long. A supraorbital light spot is present in many populations and all but a few have a light postauricular patch shaded with buffy. The antipalmar and antiplantar faces of the feet are short-haired and grayish or brownish. The tail likewise is short-haired and, although not sharply bicolor, is the same shade below as the underparts and the same color above as the upper parts, except that the distal sixth to distal half ordinarily is darker than the back, sometimes black.

The races *M. m. megacephalus* and *M. m. sabulonis* in comparison with *M. pallidus* (all races included) differ in brownish or blackish rather than whitish or light buffy upper parts; buffy rather than white postauricular light patches; hair of underparts plumbeous basally rather than everywhere white entirely to base; tail above tipped with black rather than without darker color terminally; hind foot shorter (23 to 25 rather than 25 to 27); skull with less inflated auditory bullae and hence less in maximum width; upper incisors more recurved; anterior palatine foramina wider posteriorly and tapering to a sharper point anteriorly rather than narrow and parallel-sided with less obviously tapered anterior ends; nasals extending posteriorly quite or almost as far as do the premaxillae rather than extending posteriorly to a point considerably short of that reached by the premaxillae. At the eleven places where the race *M. m. sabulonis* and some race of *M. pallidus* meet or occur together, the two kinds are easily distinguished either by the skins or by the skulls. Exception is to be made only for Penoyer Valley, as described in detail under the account of the genus, where three seeming hybrids were found among a total of fifty-seven animals, including thirty-four of *M. pallidus ruficollaris* and twenty of *M. megacephalus sabulonis.*

In the other, more western, subspecies of *M. megacephalus*, only one of the characters, the darker colored upper parts, above mentioned as being diagnostic of *M.m.megacephalus* and *M.m.sabulonis* everywhere holds. The narrower skull, as measured across the mastoids and especially in relation to the basal length, is nearly always diagnostic of populations but less often of individuals. The terminal darkening of the tail and the basally plumbeous pelage of the underparts serve to distinguish most specimens of *M. megacephalus* from *M. pallidus*, but at a few localities most specimens resemble *M. pallidus* in these two features. The shape of the incisive foramina closely approaches that in *M. pallidus*, and the curvature of the upper incisors is in even more specimens like that in *M. pallidus*, as also is the relation to one another of the posterior ends of the nasals and premaxillae. The hind foot is longer in these western forms of *M. megacephalus*, often being as long as in *M. pallidus*. Furthermore, these western forms of *megacephalus* are partial to fine wind-drifted sand, as is *M. pallidus*. At only one place in this western region, in Granite Spring Valley, 21 miles west and 2 miles north of Lovelock, have we found the two species together. If there was a difference in type of soil occupied by the two, we did not note it at this place. The two specimens of *M. megacephalus* are easily told from the eleven *M. pallidus* by color and by lesser width across the auditory bullae. Otherwise, the forty-six places of capture of these western races of *M. megacephalus* and the nineteen places of capture of *M. pallidus* west of Nye County yielded mice of only a single kind at any one locality. Between the sandy soils supporting the two kinds of mice, some barrier of soil inhospitable to mice of this genus intervenes. For example, the sand about Wadsworth and southeastward for a mile and a half harbors *M. megacephalus.* Twenty-five miles southward, near Fallon, the fine sand proves hospitable to *M. pallidus.* To the east of Fernley, in the low pass connecting the two sandy areas, *Microdipodops* does not occur, according to our testing (365 traps) and observation of the area. Along the eastern base of the Sierra Nevada, *M. megacephalus* keeps to the sandy areas, and *M. pallidus* occupies similar soils in the generally slightly lower and hotter terrain in the bottom of the trough lying along the eastern base of these mountains. In this general area, then, not an edaphic difference, but some other difference or factor unknown at this writing, accounts for the different ranges of the two kinds.

In view of the foregoing it may reasonably be asked whether these western, dark-colored *Microdipodops* (races *oregonus, californicus, ambiguus, nexus, medius, nasutus,* and the Californian race *polionotus*) are conspecific with *M. megacephalus.* The test of actual intergradation, involving continuous geographic distribution, probably cannot be applied to these mice because they have an interrupted distribution conforming to the distribution of a few types of soils. Therefore, actual crossbreeding does not occur between some populations. The critical area respecting the relation (intergradation or lack of it) between the above-mentioned races of supposed *megacephalus* and the race *M. m. megacephalus* is the territory of northern Eureka County and a part of northern Lander County, or the country (see fig. 284) between the eastern border, as now known, of the race *M. m. nexus* and the westernmost known occurrence of *M. m. megacephalus.* The easternmost *nexus* were taken in sand and the westernmost *M. m. megacephalus* on firmer, less sandy soil. Between the two places there are areas judged by Ward C. Russell and Wm. B. Richardson, who tested the area for *Microdipodops,* to be unsuitable for either of the subspecies concerned. Apparently the two kinds do not actually meet. Nevertheless, the difference between the two, as set forth in the accounts of the subspecies, is relatively slight. Also, *M. m. nexus* is, in color, in length of the hind foot, and in some cranial proportions, intermediate between the *M. m. megacephalus* known from about 75 miles to the eastward and the *M. m. ambiguus* known from 5 miles or less to the westward. This is the basis for regarding the western, dark-colored races (*oregonus, californicus, nasutus, polionotus, medius, ambiguus,* and *nexus*) as conspecific with *M. megacephalus* rather than as a third species in the genus distinct from *M. megacephalus* and, of course, from *M. pallidus.*

Although *megacephalus* is distinct from *pallidus* where the ranges of the two actually meet, *megacephalus* ranges farther west (into California, as at Mono Lake) and farther east (into Utah). In these peripheral populations of *megacephalus*, no one of the differential characters (cranial, color, or body proportions) everywhere holds. For example, *M. m. leucotis* has upper parts as pale as *pallidus*; *M. m. polionotus* has pure white underparts; *M. m. ambiguus* has hind feet as long as *pallidus*; and cranial characters, which in south-central Nevada differentiate *pallidus* from *megacephalus*, appear in these marginal races of *megacephalus*.

Ordinarily the wanderings of one of these mice over the sand cannot be traced far because the tracks tend to be blotted out by the tracks of others. Once, however, 5 miles west of Halleck, I followed the tracks of one individual between two points 70 yards apart. I do not know whether the mice come out in the snow, but I have trapped them on nights when it was so cold that their bodies were solidly frozen in the traps in the morning. On nights when rain falls they seem not to come out of their burrows; traps then caught but few and sometimes none in places where kangaroo mice were known to be numerous.

Although commonly thought of as rare, these mice, like other desert rodents, at times become truly abundant in their preferred habitat. For example, on July 10, 1933, 9 miles west and 3 miles south of Tybo, 313 traps yielded 121 kangaroo mice and thirty-five other rodents. Several of these show the molt well. In all, seventy-four specimens of *M. megacephalus* were in process of molt. Fourteen of these were taken in May, one in June, and the other fifty-nine in July. These all are adult animals, and each shows wear on the permanent fourth upper premolar. With the present information I cannot satisfactorily account for the molt in May, since all other evidence that I have indicates that there is only one molt per year, which occurs in July.

Secondary sexual variation is of slight degree, if there is any at all. Comparison of the average measurements of seventy adults of each sex from northwestern Nevada reveals that males average 0.4 per cent smaller than females in external measurements and 0.9 per cent more in weight. In cranial measurements the males average 0.4 per cent larger in greatest breadth and maxillary breadth, but from 0.15 to 1 per cent less in the other cranial measurements. This lack of, or slight, difference in size between the two sexes is a feature in which *Microdipodops* differs from *Dipodomys*.

Probably most of the food consists of seeds. Several times, seeds were found in the cheek pouches. Nevertheless, six specimens had animal matter in the pouches: one had the freshly killed larva of an insect 13 mm. long and 5 mm. in diameter; a second mouse had the larva of an insect in each pouch; a third had several plant seeds and one larva of an insect in each pouch; a fourth had the remains of one larva of an insect and a whole roach (*Arenivaga erratica*); a fifth had one fecal pellet, five seeds of a grass, remains of two larvae of insects, and a whole tenebrionid beetle (*Eusattus*, probably species *dubius*); and a sixth had in the two pouches a few fragments of a leopard lizard (*Crotaphytus wislizenii*) in addition to fifty-seven plant seeds.

Of the 478 adult females, 54 were pregnant. The embryos ranged from 2 to 7

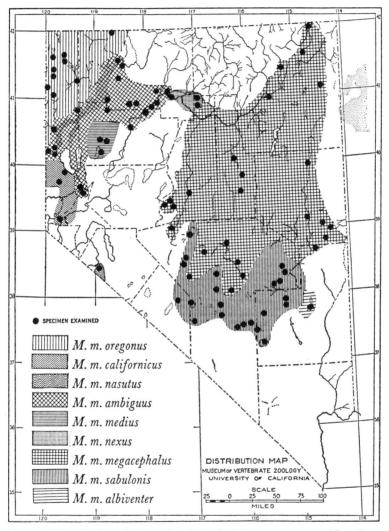

● SPECIMEN EXAMINED

M. m. oregonus

M. m. californicus

M. m. nasutus

M. m. ambiguus

M. m. medius

M. m. nexus

M. m. megacephalus

M. m. sabulonis

M. m. albiventer

DISTRIBUTION MAP
MUSEUM OF VERTEBRATE ZOOLOGY
UNIVERSITY OF CALIFORNIA

SCALE
25 0 25 50 75 100
MILES

Fig. 284. Distribution of subspecies of the dark kangaroo mouse, *Microdipodops megacephalus*.

per litter, with an average of 3.9 and a mode of 4. Inclusive dates for pregnant females range from April 28 to September 22. No specimens at all are availabl-
for the months of November to March. By months the females are distributed

as follows: April, 14 (5 pregnant); May, 91 (8 pregnant); June, 102 (34 pregnant); July, 198 (5 pregnant); August, 26 (0 pregnant); September, 45 (2 pregnant); October, 2 (0 pregnant).

Microdipodops megacephalus oregonus Merriam
Dark Kangaroo Mouse

Microdipodops megacephalus oregonus Merriam, Proc. Biol. Soc. Washington, 14:127, July 19, 1901. Type from Lake Alvord, Alvord Desert, Harney County, Oregon. According to Bailey, N. Amer. Fauna, 55:241, 1936, the type locality, more restrictedly, is "Wild Horse Creek, 4 miles northwest of Alvord Lake." Hall, Zoöl. Series, Field Mus. Nat. Hist., 27:248, December 8, 1941.

Distribution.—Northwestern Nevada northwest of the Black Rock and Smoke Creek deserts. See figure 284.

Remarks.—Ten of each sex from the vicinity of Vya measure: ♂, 169 (158–177), ♀, 170 (159–175); 93 (88–96), 92 (86–100); 25.2 (24–26), 25.3 (24–26); weight, 14.6 (13.5–16.0), 14.7 (12.5–16.9) grams.

Tail and hind foot long; upper parts, including upper side of tail, blackish with a reddish hue; tail black above distally; feet dusky; postauricular and supraorbital light patches small or wanting; underparts often with faint plumbeous shade basally, but otherwise whitish except for light terminal wash of buffy in some populations; skull with greatest breadth averaging less than basal length in Nevadan populations; incisive foramina averaging widest posteriorly, but sometimes widest near middle; nasals extending posteriorly almost as far as premaxillae.

From *M. m. californicus*, this race differs in: upper parts darker, more reddish, and less grayish; hair of underparts more often plumbeous basally and sometimes tipped with buffy rather than white entirely to base; skull narrower interorbitally and across maxillary arms of zygomata. From *M. m. ambiguus*, *oregonus* from Nevada differs in: body longer; upper parts darker, more reddish, and less grayish; feet darker colored; skull averaging broader across auditory bullae and across maxillary arms of zygomatic arches.

Intergradation with *ambiguus* is indicated by specimens of that race from Smoke Creek, 9 miles east of the California boundary, and by specimens assigned to *oregonus* from south of Denio.

Records of occurrence.—Specimens examined, 85, as follows: *Washoe Co.*: 3 mi. N Vya, 5900 ft., 4; 4½ mi. NE Painted Point, 5800 ft., 10; 8½ mi. E Vya, 5900 ft., 7; 3 mi. E Painted Point, 5850 ft., 3; S of Vya, 5800 ft. (10½ mi., 2; 11 mi., 1; 12 mi., 4; 13 mi., 1; 15 mi., 1), 9; Little High Rock Canyon, 5000 ft., 1; mouth of Little High Rock Canyon, 5000 ft., 11; 1 mi. E mouth Little High Rock Canyon, 5000 ft., 1; 1 mi. W Hausen, 4650 ft., 4; Hausen, 4800 ft., 3; 10 mi. SE Hausen, 4675 ft., 13. *Humboldt Co.*: 1 mi. S Denio, Oregon, 4200 ft., 19.

Microdipodops megacephalus californicus Merriam
Dark Kangaroo Mouse

Microdipodops californicus Merriam, Proc. Biol. Soc. Washington, 14:128, July 19, 1901. Type from Sierra Valley, near Vinton, Plumas County, California.
Microdipodops megacephalus californicus, Hall, Zoöl. Series, Field Mus. Nat. Hist., 27:250, December 8, 1941.

Distribution.—Western Nevada from Pyramid in Washoe County southward at least to 3½ miles east of Carson City in Carson River Valley. See figure 284.

Remarks.—Average and extreme measurements of four males from 2¾ mi. SW Pyramid, and measurements of one female from the same place and two female topotypes, are: ♂, 162 (160–163), ♀, 158, 157, 169; 88 (84–91), 81, 88, 100; 25.2 (24–25.5), 25, 25, 25; weights not recorded.

Tail and hind foot medium to long; upper parts grayish brown, with reddish hue; tail distally blackish or dark brownish; postauricular and supraorbital light patches usually present, but sometimes absent; feet grayish; hair of underparts white all the way to base; skull with width across auditory bullae not much if any greater than basal length; broad across zygomatic arms of maxillae and interorbitally; incisive foramina generally widest near middle; relation between posterior ends of nasals and premaxillae variable, but nasals usually extend almost as far posteriorly as premaxillae.

Comparisons with *oregonus*, *ambiguus*, and *nasutus* are made in the accounts of those forms.

The specimens from Washoe County agree closely with topotypes. The one specimen from near Carson City is notable for the large, nearly white postauricular patches and for the narrowness of the skull, as measured across the auditory bullae (17.1 mm.) and across the maxillary processes of the zygomata (11.2). The basal length is 18.4.

Records of occurrence.—Specimens examined, 10, as follows: *Washoe Co.:* 2¾ mi. SW Pyramid, 4300 ft., 6; Junction House, 4500 ft., 3. *Ormsby Co.:* 3½ mi. E Carson City, 4700 ft., 1.

Microdipodops megacephalus nasutus Hall
Dark Kangaroo Mouse

Microdipodops megacephalus nasutus Hall, Zoöl. Series, Field Mus. Nat. Hist. 27:251, December 8, 1941. Type from Fletcher, 6098 feet, Mineral County, Nevada.

Distribution.—Known only from the type locality. See figure 284.

Remarks.—Measurements of two of each sex are: ♂, 159, 150; ♀, 151, 158; 86, 79; 78, 88; 26, 24; 26, 25; weights not recorded.

Tail of short-to-medium length; hind foot long; upper parts grayish, marked with blackish; tail with distal half to fourth blackish; supraorbital patches faint or absent; postauricular patches light gray rather than white or buffy; feet light gray; underparts white, but light plumbeous basally; skull with greatest breadth slightly exceeding basal length; broad across zygomatic arms of maxillae and interorbitally; incisive foramina broad, either parallel-sided or widest posteriorly; relation of posterior ends of nasals and premaxillae variable, but premaxillae extending well behind nasals in three of four adults.

From *californicus*, this race differs in slightly shorter tail and body, grayer (distinctly less reddish) upper parts, and greater breadth of skull across auditory bullae. From *polionotus*, *nasutus* differs in longer body, relatively shorter tail, longer hind foot, relatively greater breadth across auditory bullae, and longer nasals.

More material of this race is desirable both to learn the limits geographically of its range and to learn about the range of variation in some of its apparently diagnostic features. The color of the underparts in one specimen has the hair white entirely to the base and in two others there is a faint wash of buffy on the terminal part of the hair.

Record of occurrence.—Specimens examined, 6, as follows: *Mineral Co.:* Fletcher, 6098 ft., 6.

Microdipodops megacephalus ambiguus Hall
Dark Kangaroo Mouse

Microdipodops megacephalus ambiguus Hall, Zoöl. Series, Field Mus. Nat. Hist., 27:252, December 8, 1941. Type from 1¼ miles north of Sulphur, 4050 feet, Humboldt County, Nevada.

Distribution.—Smoke Creek and Black Rock deserts and lower part of Humboldt River Valley from Quinn River Crossing southwest to Flanigan, south to Humboldt, and east to Golconda. See figure 284.

Remarks.—Measurements of ten males and seven females from the vicinity of Sulphur are: ♂, 165 (162–176), ♀, 164 (157–172); 91 (85–98), 92 (88–95); 24.9 (24–26), 25.0 (24–26); weight, 12.4 (10.2–14.0), 12.4 (11.2–13.6) grams.

Tail and hind foot long; upper parts grayish, with olive hue; tail black above distally; feet whitish; postauricular and supraorbital light patches of moderate size; hair of underparts white, plumbeous at base in topotypes, but white all the way to base in many populations; skull with tympanic bullae much inflated, resulting in greatest breadth of skull amounting to more than basal length; narrow across zygomatic arms of maxillae; interorbital breadth medium; incisive foramina generally widest posteriorly, but sometimes widest at middle; nasals projecting nearly as far posteriorly as premaxillae in northern populations, but falling much short of premaxillae in southern populations, although variable there.

From *californicus*, this race differs in shorter body and longer tail, lighter (more grayish-olive and less reddish) color; skull broader across auditory bullae, but narrower across maxillary arms of zygomata and interorbitally. Comparisons with *oregonus* and *medius* are made in the accounts of those forms. From *nexus*, *ambiguus* differs in shorter tail, lighter color of upper parts (more yellowish and less blackish and less reddish); upper side of tail like back; hair of underparts often white entirely to base rather than plumbeous basally. From the race *megacephalus*, *ambiguus* differs in longer tail and hind foot, markedly lighter upper parts including upper side of tail, postauricular patches white or nearly so rather than buffy, underparts white rather than buffy, black on upper side of tail far more extensive and intense, skull broader across tympanic bullae and interorbitally. The geographic range of *ambiguus* is relatively large, and in it there are exposures of many different geological formations. On these are varied products of relatively recent volcanic activity, and, in addition, there are the even more recent deposits left by the Quaternary Lake Lahonton. These diverse formations have contributed to the production of many different kinds of sandy soils suitable for occupancy by *Microdipodops*. The populations of mice themselves show a wide variation. This is true to some extent of the skulls, is even more evident in the external porportions, and is most pronounced in the coloration. The palest of the animals are those from one mile west of Humboldt. In increasing order of darkness the others are those from the vicinities of Jungo, Sulphur, Flanigan, Winnemucca, and Wadsworth. The difference in color is not, however, entirely a matter of lightness and darkness. Those from Smoke Creek are intermediate in color, as they are also geographically, between *oregonus* and *ambiguus* and therefore resemble *californicus* in color, although the resemblance in this particular instance is judged not to be the result of continuity in geographic range with *californicus* nor the result of close genetic relationship with it. Those from Jackson Creek Ranch approach in color the population from Denio assigned to *oregonus;* those from Wadsworth show approach in color to *californicus*, those from Winnemucca tend toward *nexus*. Thus, intergradation is evidenced with each of the subspecies of *megacephalus* the range of which meets or closely approaches that of *ambiguus*.

In external measurements, evidence of intergradation with near-by races is provided by the greater length of tail in animals from 9 to 10 miles north of Golconda, as well as by the shorter body. These strongly resemble *nexus*. The reduced length of tail in animals from Quinn River Crossing is a feature better developed farther north in the populations of *oregonus*.

Cranially, animals from Quinn River Crossing and from Flanigan tend to be broad interorbitally, much as in *oregonus* and *californicus*. This suggests intergradation in this feature. The incisive foramina are widest posteriorly in animals from the vicinities of Quinn River Crossing and Golconda, as they generally are in animals from Sulphur. At Flanigan the incisive foramina are widest near the middle in most specimens.

Of populations assigned to *ambiguus*, that from the vicinity of Flanigan, including the animals from the vicinity of Warm Spring, just across the boundary in California, is the most aberrant. At the same time, the variation between individuals here is greater than at any other locality. In the population as a whole, the body is long, the tail is short, the hind foot is long, the weight is great, the color is light, and the skull is narrow across the auditory bullae and wide across the maxillary arms of the zygomata and in the interorbital region. The cranial proportions mentioned suggest intergradation of *ambiguus* with *californicus*, as does the longer body, but the other features enumerated tend to set the population from Flanigan apart from any of the surrounding races. The incisive foramina tend to be widest at the middle rather than posteriorly, as in most of the dark races. The situation is complicated because the variation in color between individuals is greater here than at any other locality. In one animal the color is as dark as in *oregonus* and in some others as light as in *pallidus*. Nearly all of the specimens agree in color with topotypes of *ambiguus*. The skulls are more uniform, and those of the dark and light animals agree with the skulls of the specimens colored as in typical *ambiguus*.

With the information now available it appears that the population of *Microdipodops* from the vicinity of Flanigan and Warm Spring (1) agree in essential characters with *ambiguus*, (2) in several features are intermediate toward the race *californicus* to the southwestward, (3) in a few characters differ from any of the surrounding subspecies, and (4) embrace a few individuals which in color and color pattern have preserved the characters of near-by races.

This interpretation is the best that I can offer for the facts in hand, but additional field work, particular attention being given to type of soil on which the animals of different colors occur, may bring different conclusions.

Peromyscus maniculatus and some other mammals in this low area about Flanigan show a high percentage of light-colored individuals, such as predominate in populations farther to the southeast. *Microdipodops*, then, is not unique in showing much color variation here.

Records of occurrence.—Specimens examined, 252, as follows: *Washoe Co.:* 2½ mi. E and 13 mi. N Gerlach, 4050 ft., 1; 2½ mi. E and 11 mi. N Gerlach, 4050 ft., 4; 3 mi. E and 10 mi. N Gerlach, 4000 ft., 1; Smoke Creek, 9 mi. E Calif. boundary, 3900 ft., 9; N side Sand Pass, 3900 ft., 5; 4 mi. NW Flanigan, 4200 ft., 7; 3½ mi. NW Flanigan, 4200 ft., 17; ½ mi. NW Flanigan, 4200 ft., 3; 2½ mi. E Flanigan, 4200 ft., 8; 3½ mi. E Flanigan, 4200 ft., 4; 1½ mi. N Wadsworth, 4100 ft., 2. *Lyon Co.:* ½ mi. SE Wadsworth, 4200 ft., 4; 1 mi. SE Wadsworth, 4200 ft., 12. *Humboldt Co.:* ½ mi. W Quinn River Crossing, 4100 ft., 2; 2 mi. SW Quinn River Crossing, 4000 ft., 7; 2½ mi. SW Quinn River Crossing, 4100 ft., 1; 4½ mi. S Quinn River Crossing (4000 ft., 5; 4100 ft., 3), 8; Jackson Creek Ranch, 17½ and 5 mi. W Quinn River Crossing, 4000 ft., 7; 7 mi. N Winnemucca, 4400 ft., 20; 9 mi. NW Golconda, 21; 10 mi. NNW Golconda, 12; 6 mi. N Golconda, 19; Flowing Spring, 2 (U. S. Nat. Mus., Biol. Surv. Coll.); 9½ mi. N Sulphur, 4050 ft., 6; 8 mi. E and 1 mi. N Jungo, 4200 ft., 22; 11 mi. E and 1 mi. N Jungo, 4200 ft., 1; 3 mi. SW Winnemucca, 4500 ft., 2; 5 mi SW Winnemucca, 4; 10 mi. SW Winnemucca, 4500 ft., 7; 1¼ mi. N Sulphur, 4050 ft., 14; 1 mi. W Sulphur, 4040 ft., 3; ¾ mi. S Sulphur, 4050 ft., 3. *Pershing Co.:* 15 mi. SW Winnemucca, 1; 1 mi. W Humboldt, 4180 ft., 13.

Microdipodops megacephalus medius Hall
Dark Kangaroo Mouse

Microdipodops megacephalus medius Hall, Zoöl. Series, Field Mus. Nat. Hist., 27:256, December 8, 1941.
Type from 3 miles south of Vernon, 4250 feet, Pershing County, Nevada.

Distribution.—Southwestern Pershing County. See figure 284.

Remarks.—Average and extreme measurements of nine of each sex from the type locality are: ♂, 164 (155–177), ♀, 167 (160–173); 90 (84–95), 90 (83–95); 24.6 (23–26), 24.9 (24–26); weights not recorded.

Tail of short to medium length; hind foot short; upper parts including upper side of tail blackish with a reddish hue; tail blackish above distally; feet light dusky; postauricular light patches well developed and whitish; supraorbital light patches present but less conspicuous than postauricular patches; underparts white, although hair often plumbeous at base; skull with auditory bullae moderately inflated; interorbital breadth "average" for the species; incisive foramina widest posteriorly; premaxillae extending relatively far, for this species, behind the nasals, but variable.

From *ambiguus*, this race differs in: color of upper parts darker, more blackish, and more reddish (less gray); skull narrower as result of lesser inflation of auditory bullae. From *M. m. oregonus, medius* differs in: color of upper parts lighter, less blackish, and slightly less reddish; feet lighter; postauricular patches more prominent; underparts white rather than frequently tipped with buffy; hind foot shorter; skull broader as a result of greater inflation of auditory bullae; premaxillae extending farther behind nasals.

Surrounded on three sides by the geographic range of the subspecies *M. m. ambiguus*, *medius* seems to have its main range in dark-colored, sandy soils, as, for instance, those on which it was taken near Vernon. That *medius* ranges onto lighter colored soils is shown by the taking of two animals 21 miles west and 2 miles north of Lovelock along with eleven individuals of the different species, *M. pallidus*. Here the soil was of lighter color. In addition to a difference in color, each of the two individuals of *medius* has less inflated auditory bullae than any one of the eleven *pallidus*. The measurement of greatest breadth of skull in the two specimens is 18.3 and 19.2, whereas the minimum measurement for *pallidus* at this place was 19.3 (average 19.7).

Records of occurrence.—Specimens examined, 21, as follows: *Pershing Co.:* 3 mi. SW Vernon, 4300 ft., 1; 3 mi. S Vernon, 4250 ft., 18; 21 mi. W and 2 mi. N Lovelock, 4000 ft., 2.

Microdipodops megacephalus nexus Hall
Dark Kangaroo Mouse

Microdipodops megacephalus nexus Hall, Zoöl. Series, Field Mus. Nat. Hist., 27:257, December 8, 1941. Type from 3 miles south of Izenhood, Lander County, Nevada.

Distribution.—From 5½ miles northeast of Golconda in Humboldt County eastward to Izenhood in Lander County. See figure 284.

Remarks.—Measurements of ten of each sex from the type locality and from 3 miles north thereof are: ♂, 165 (160–170), ♀, 167 (162–176); 93 (88–99), 95 (86–103); 24.7 (24–26), 25.3 (24–27); weights not recorded.

Tail and hind foot long; upper parts grayish-brown; tail distally black; supraorbital spots indistinct; postauricular patches buffy; underparts white, but plumbeous basally; skull with auditory bullae much inflated, resulting in greatest breadth amounting to more than basal length; narrow across zygomatic arms of maxillae; interorbital breadth medium; incisive foramina generally parallel-sided, but rounded posteriorly and sharply pointed anteriorly; premaxillae extending a relatively short way behind nasals.

Comparisons with *ambiguus* and *megacephalus* are made in the accounts of those forms. The range of this race is separated from that of *ambiguus* by a low range of mountains which extend in a northeast direction from Golconda. In isolated populations from 5½ miles northeast of Golconda to Izenhood, the characters are maintained in uniform fashion. In color these animals are almost exactly intermediate between *ambiguus* and *megacephalus* and thus bridge the gap between the western gray mice and the black mice from farther east. Geographically there is a gap of about 75 miles between *nexus* and *megacephalus* to the eastward. In 1936 vain search was made for *Microdipodops* in this area, about Battle Mountain, Cortez, and Beowawe, by Ward C. Russell and William B. Richardson, who concluded that the mice did not occur there.

Records of occurrence.—Specimens examined, 36, as follows: *Humboldt Co.:* 5 mi. NE Golconda, 16. *Lander Co.:* Izenhood, 6; 3 mi. S Izenhood, 14.

Microdipodops megacephalus megacephalus Merriam
Dark Kangaroo Mouse

Microdipodops megacephalus Merriam, N. Amer. Fauna, 5:116, July 30, 1891. Type from Halleck, East Humboldt Valley, Elko County, Nevada. Hall, Zoöl. Series, Field Mus. Nat. Hist., 27:257, December 8, 1941.

Distribution.—Northeastern Nevada from northern Elko County south to northern Nye and Lincoln counties and from western Lander County east almost to Utah boundary. See figure 284.

Remarks.—Measurements of four males and six females from Marys River, 15 miles south of Contact, and from Cobre and vicinity are: ♂, 157 (155–158), ♀, 153 (145–163); 78 (68–86), 73 (67–80); 24.3 (24–25), 23.7 (23–24.5); weight, 12.7 (12.3–13.2), 14.4 (14.3–14.5) grams.

Body large, tail and hind foot short; upper parts dark brown mixed with black; distal fourth to half of tail black; supraorbital spots faintly developed or absent; postauricular patches buffy; feet dusky; underparts with hair whitish to base only on throat; otherwise deep plumbeous basally, with terminal wash of buffy; skull with auditory bullae moderately inflated, resulting in greatest width slightly exceeding basal length; maxillary and interorbital breadth moderate to slight; incisive foramina widest posteriorly and sharply pointed anteriorly; nasals projecting posteriorly nearly as far as premaxillae.

From *nexus*, this race differs in shorter tail and hind foot, more blackish and less reddish color of upper parts, including upper side of tail; hair of underparts distally buffy rather than white; skull narrower across tympanic bullae. From *sabulonis*, *megacephalus* differs in tendency to slightly longer hind foot, in color in almost the same way as from *nexus*, and in tendency to slightly narrower incisive foramina. From *M. m. paululus*, the subspecies to the eastward in Utah, *megacephalus* differs in longer body and tail, color above slightly darker, hair of underparts plumbeous basally and buffy distally rather than everywhere white to base, postauricular light patches buffy rather than white, and skull longer. Comparison with *albiventer* is made in the account of that form.

So far as is known to me, there are no fully adult topotypes of this race in any collection. Ten adult specimens from northeast of Halleck, Elko County, differ from other populations here assigned to the race in longer body and shorter tail. These are the only specimens of the genus in which the tail is shorter than the combined length of the head and body. In some of the specimens from Elko County the incisive foramina are widest near the middle. Except in these particulars the animals do not differ from others farther south. For this reason, and because adult topotypes of *megacephalus* are unknown, it seems best to refer these short-tailed specimens to *megacephalus*. Geographic variation is shown by other populations. The darkest specimens are from central Nevada, those from Reese River Valley and from Eureka County being darker even than specimens from Elko County. Specimens from Eureka County are notable for long tail, which possibly reflects intergradation with *nexus*. Specimens from Dutch Flat Schoolhouse in Reese River Valley have short tails like the population of *sabulonis* which occurs near Millett in the next valley (Great Smoky Valley) to the east. Specimens from Steptoe Valley, 5½ miles south of Ely, are notable for generally large size but narrow interorbital regions. Specimens from Greens Ranch, 50-odd miles to the north in the same valley, are not exceptionally large, but of a size about average for the subspecies.

Intergradation with *sabulonis* is complete. Specimens referred to *megacephalus*, which have lighter (less blackish and more reddish) upper parts and the hairs of the underparts white or only lightly tipped with buffy, are those from Hot Creek Valley south to Old Mill at the north end of Reveille Valley and those from Ralston Valley, 15½ miles northeast of Tonopah. Specimens from Spring Valley, near Osceola and Shoshone, are lighter (grayer) above, lack the buffy terminal tipping of the hair of the underparts, which in many specimens is white entirely to the base, and thus are intermediate toward *paululus* known from Utah.

Records of occurrence.—Specimens examined, 296, as follows: *Lander Co.*: Reese River Valley, 7 mi. N Austin, 4; 6 mi. ENE Smiths Creek Ranch, 5550 ft., 11; 2½ mi. NE Smiths Creek Ranch, 5800 ft., 5; Smiths Creek Valley, 2 mi. W Railroad Pass, 5550 ft., 4. *Eureka Co.*: Winzell, 18; 4 mi. SE Romano, Diamond Valley, 18; 8 mi. W Eureka, 15. *Nye Co.*: Dutch Flat Schoolhouse, Reese River, 6715 ft., 10; 30 mi. N Belmont, Monitor Valley, 1 (U. S. Nat. Mus., Biol. Surv. Coll.); 6½ mi. N Fish Lake, Fish Spring Valley, 6700 ft., 14; 9 mi. E Toquima Peak, Monitor Valley, 7600 ft., 2; 10½ mi. E Toquima Peak, 6900 ft., Monitor Valley, 24; 5 mi. N Belmont, Monitor Valley, 1 (U. S. Nat. Mus., Biol. Surv. Coll.); 3½ mi. E Hot Creek, Hot Creek Valley, 5650 ft., 17; 15½ mi. NE Tonopah, Ralston Valley, 5800 ft., 13; 2½ mi. E and N Twin Spring, S end Hot Creek Valley, 5400 ft., 3; Old Mill, N end Reveille Valley, 6200 ft., 36. *Elko Co.:* 9 mi. NE San Jacinto, 5300 ft., 1; 15 mi. S Contact, 5800 ft., 6; Marys River, 22 mi. N Deeth, 5800 ft., 9; Cobre, 6100 ft., 5; 2 mi. SW Cobre, 2; 3 to 5 mi. W Halleck, 5200–5300 ft., 6 (1 in coll. of Ralph Ellis). *White Pine Co.:* 5 mi. SE Greens Ranch, Steptoe Valley, 5900 ft., 11; 5½ mi. SE Ely, Steptoe Creek, 6400–6500 ft., 7; 7 mi. SW Osceola, Spring Valley, 6275 ft., 24; 5½ mi. NW Shoshone P. O., 6100 ft., 3; 4 mi. S Shoshone, Spring Valley, 5900 ft., 16. *Lincoln Co.:* 3 mi. S Geyser, Duck Valley, 6050 ft., 10.

Microdipodops megacephalus sabulonis Hall
Dark Kangaroo Mouse

Microdipodops megacephalus sabulonis Hall, Proc. Biol. Soc. Washington, 54:59, May 20, 1941. Type from 5 miles southeast of Kawich Post Office, 5400 feet, Kawich Valley, Nye County, Nevada. Hall, Zoöl. Series, Field Mus. Nat. Hist., 27:260, December 8, 1941.

Microdipodops megacephalus, Linsdale, Amer. Midland Nat., 19:188, January, 1938.

Distribution.—Eastern Esmeralda County eastward across Nye County to western Lincoln County. See figure 284.

Remarks.—Measurements of ten of each sex from 4 to 5 miles southward from Millett are: ♂, 150 (142–155), ♀, 151 (140–158); 78 (72–82), 79 (72–86); 24.3 (23–26), 24.5 (23.8–26.0); weight, 11.6 (10.2–13.0), 11.2 (10.0–14.9) grams.

Tail and hind foot short; upper parts brownish, with much reddish; distal fourth to sixth of tail dark brown or black; supraorbital and postauricular patches light buffy; feet light gray; underparts white (basally plumbeous); skull with auditory bullae much inflated for this species, which results in greatest width exceeding basal length; maxillary and interorbital breadth moderate to slight; incisive foramina widest posteriorly; nasals extending posteriorly almost as far as premaxillae.

From *albiventer*, this race differs in longer body and tail, relatively longer tail, longer skull including nasals, darker (more reddish) upper parts including upper side of tail, and in hair of underparts sometimes plumbeous basally rather than always white. From *paululus*, a race which occurs to the eastward in Utah, *sabulonis* differs in longer body and much longer tail, in color in the same way as described for *albiventer*, and in shorter, narrower skull.

Specimens assigned to *sabulonis* from Coal Valley closely approach *albiventer* in pallor of coloration and indicate intergradation of the two. Specimens from Garden Valley also are lighter colored than most populations of *sabulonis* and differ also in larger size of all parts measured, although relative proportions of the parts are about as in other populations. The animals from Great Smoky Valley (near Millett and San Antonio) have as much red in the upper parts as any other population and more than most. Topotypes have longer tails than most specimens. At some localities, occasional specimens have a light wash of buffy on the tips of the hairs of the underparts.

This subspecies of *megacephalus* occurs in the same general area as *ruficollaris*, a race of the different species *pallidus*. The firmer soils were favored by *sabulonis* at each of the eleven places where the two species were taken in the same trap line. *M. pallidus* occupied the fine sands. It follows from the distribution of these two types of soils that *sabulonis* occurs on the sides of the valleys and has a more nearly continuous distribution than does *pallidus*, which occurs generally in the lowest part of the valley. The two kinds are easily distinguished by the color, and to me the difference is more easily perceivable in the live or freshly killed animals than in prepared study skins. The occurrence of three seeming hybrids among the fifty-seven animals (thirty-four *pallidus*, twenty *megacephalus*, and three "crosses") saved from Penoyer (Sand Spring) Valley makes desirable further study at this place to learn for certain if two free-living species of wild mammals do here hybridize. If they do so, opportunity to study an unusual stage in the formation (or extinction by dilution) of a species would be afforded. The characters of the seeming hybrids are discussed in detail under the account of the genus.

Records of occurrence.—Specimens examined, 413, as follows: *Esmeralda Co.:* 13½ mi. NW Goldfield, 4850 ft., 22. *Nye Co.:* 4 mi. SE Millett, 5500 ft., 17; 5 mi. SE Millett, 4; 4 mi. S Millett, 5500 ft., 5; 11½ to 13 mi. NE San Antonio, 5700–6700 ft., 26; 4¾ to 6 mi. NE San Antonio, 5650–5700 ft., 29; 17 mi. W Sunnyside, White River Valley, 12; 9 mi. W and 3 mi. S Tybo, 6200 ft., 43; 15 to 16½ mi. WSW Sunnyside, White River Valley, 5500 ft., 11; 14 to 15 mi. NE Sharp, Garden Valley, 23; 8½ mi. NE Garden Valley, 28; 34 mi. E and 1 mi. N Tonopah, 5650 ft., 6; N shore Mud Lake, S end Ralston Valley, 5300 ft., 2; 1½ to 3 2/5 mi. S Silverbow, Kawich Mts., 6200–6400 ft., 19; 5 to 6½ mi. SW Silverbow, Cactus Flat, 5700–6000 ft., 18; 11½ mi. SW Silverbow, Cactus Flat, 5400 ft., 9; 14 mi. SE Goldfield, Stonewall Flat, 4700 ft., 2; 7½ mi. E Cliff Spring, 5900 ft., 37; 4½ mi. NW Indian Spring, Kawich Valley, 5700 ft., 6; 5 to 5 7/10 mi. SE Kawich P. O., Kawich Valley, 5400 ft., 12. *Lincoln Co.:* 14 mi. N Seeman Pass, 4850 ft., E side Coal Valley, 26; 10 mi. N Seeman Pass, 4650 ft., Coal Valley, 14; 17 mi. N Groom Baldy, Penoyer Valley, 14; 14 to 15 mi. NNW Groom Baldy, Penoyer Valley, 8; 9 mi. W Groom Baldy, 5500 ft., 13; 11½ mi. E Johnnies Water, 1; 14½ to 15 mi. S Groom Baldy, 6.

Microdipodops megacephalus albiventer Hall and Durrant

Dark Kangaroo Mouse

Microdipodops pallidus albiventer Hall and Durrant, Journ. Mamm., 18:357, August 14, 1937. Type from Desert Valley, 5300 feet, 21 miles west of Panaca, Lincoln County, Nevada.
Microdipodops megacephalus albiventer, Hall, Zoöl. Series, Field Mus. Nat. Hist., 27:263, December 8, 1941.

Distribution.—Desert Valley in central Lincoln County. See figure 284.

Remarks.—Average and extreme measurements of nine males and five females from the type locality are: ♂, 150 (141–158), ♀, 149 (138–155); 79 (74–87), 80 (72–89); 24.3 (23.2–25.3), 23.8 (23.0–25.0); weight, 12.6 (11.6–13.6), 14.2 (13.5–15.3) grams.

Tail, body, and hind foot short; upper parts grayish and faintly lined with brownish, top of tail at tip with blackish markings faint or absent; postauricular patches white; supraorbital patches white, sometimes with trace of buffy; hair of underparts white to base; skull with auditory bullae much inflated and greatest width of skull greatly exceeding basal length; maxillary breadth slight; interorbital breadth moderate for the species; incisive foramina widest posteriorly; nasals short and not extending nearly so far posteriorly as premaxillae.

From *megacephalus*, this race differs in lesser average size of external measurements, lighter colored upper parts, white rather than buffy postauricular patches and underparts, and almost white rather than distinctly blackish distal part of upper side of tail; skull with shorter nasals. From *M. m. paululus*, the race to the eastward in Utah, *albiventer* differs in longer tail, lighter colored upper parts, more blackish on tip of tail; larger skull in all parts measured except length of nasals, which is less. From *M. m. sabulonis*, the subspecies next to the west with an extensive instead of a restricted geographic range, *albiventer* differs in shorter body and tail, relatively shorter tail, shorter skull including nasals, lighter (less reddish) upper parts including upper side of tail, and in hair of the underparts white entirely to the base instead of sometimes plumbeous basally.

This is the palest race of the species *M. megacephalus* in Nevada. When *albiventer* was named, the describers knew that there were two full species of *Microdipodops* in western Lincoln County and because of the pale color of *albiventer* assigned it to the paler of the two full species. Subsequent study, which revealed cranial differences between the two species, indicates that *albiventer* is, instead, a race of the species *M. megacephalus*. In the original description, animals from Pine Valley, Utah, were assigned to the race *albiventer*, but these later (Hall and Durrant, 1941:5) were separated from *albiventer* and made the basis of *Microdipodops megacephalus paululus*. Thus, *albiventer* as here understood is restricted to Desert Valley in central Lincoln County. Animals from Coal Valley, about 25 miles to the west and north, although assigned to the race *sabulonis*, are much paler than typical specimens and approach *albiventer* in color.

Record of occurrence.—Specimens examined, as follows: *Lincoln Co.:* Desert Valley, 21 mi. W Panaca, 5300 ft., 23.

Microdipodops pallidus
Pallid Kangaroo Mouse

Four subspecies occur in Nevada. The upper parts are near (e) Light Pinkish Cinnamon, lightly marked with buffy or blackish. The basal two-thirds or more of the hair is plumbeous and the distal third buffy, some races having a short terminal tip of blackish. The hair of the underparts is everywhere white to the base, as is that on the legs, feet, and underside of the tail. Above, the tail is about the same color as the upper parts of the body, but lacks the black tip of *megacephalus*. The length of the hair and facial vibrissae are about as described in the last-mentioned species. The postauricular patch is prominent and pure white in all races. The supraorbital spots, one above each· eye, are white or faintly tinged with buffy. In some forms they are faintly developed or wanting. The hind foot is large, averaging more than 25 mm. in length, the auditory bullae show the maximum of inflation for the genus, the upper incisors are relatively straight, the incisive foramina are parallel-sided and the premaxillae extend well behind the nasals. Several of these features are of a comparative nature and are mentioned in greater detail in the preceding account of *M. megacephalus*.

Fine sand supporting some plant growth meets the requirements of this species; as previously pointed out (Hall and Linsdale, 1929:299), fine sand without plants does not meet the requirements of the mice. Because the finest sand ordinarily occurs in the bottoms of valleys, as on the windward side of a playa, the mice are most abundant in the low parts of valleys. The distribution of the species is less continuous than that of *M. megacephalus*, which lives in coarser soils.

Elevations of occurrence range from as low as about 3900 feet at Soda Lake up to 5700 feet in Huntoon Valley. At every place where taken, the vegetation is of a kind which favors a zonal position lower than places supporting *Artemisia tridentata*. *Atriplex* and *Sarcobatus* are shrubs characteristic of the areas in which the mice occur. Nowhere have they been found at a place low enough zonally to support the creosote bush, *Larrea*. If the upper, northern, limit of occurrence of this shrub be taken as the upper margin of the Lower Sonoran Life-zone, the mice have not been found in this life-zone. The nearest approach to occurrence in this zone was in the valley next west of Pahranagat Valley. In this valley Joshua trees, cholla, and *Artemisia tridentata* grew together.

The burrows found by us lacked nests and probably were only resting places for the animals during the day. Several that I excavated ranged from 8 inches to nearly 3 feet long and had maximum depths of 4 to 24 inches. The burrows are plugged with sand during the day.

Like the preceding species, this one is active on nights when the temperature is so low as to freeze to a state of stiffness the bodies of mice caught in traps. In some places they are so abundant that almost every second trap takes a

specimen. Once, ninety-two were taken in 150 traps. Satisfactory evidence of
secondary sexual variation in size is lacking. Comparison of average measurements of forty adults of each sex reveals that males average 0.8 per cent larger

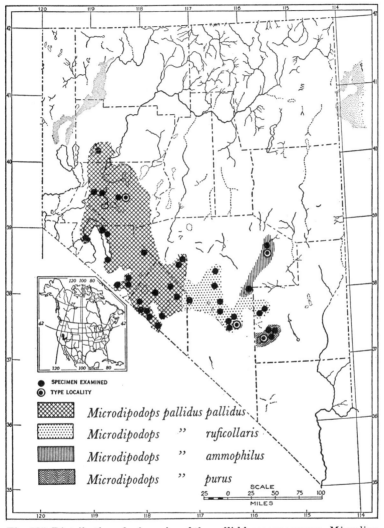

Fig. 285. Distribution of subspecies of the pallid kangaroo mouse, *Microdipodops pallidus*, with insert showing range of the species.

than females in external measurements and in weight. In breadth across the
tympanic bullae, males are 1.5 per cent larger, but in other cranial measurements only about one-half of 1 per cent larger. Because the difference is so
slight and also because for several parts it is just the reverse of the difference

shown by the corresponding measurements for *M. megacephalus*, it may be that the two sexes are of the same size.

The food of this animal probably consists mostly of seeds. The cheek pouches of a specimen taken on June 7, 1931, 5½ miles north of Summit Spring, contained twenty-three seeds of *Oryzopsis hymenoides*. In Fish Lake Valley, seeds of *Gilia* sp. and *Oryzopsis hymenoides* were found in cheek pouches, as was also a three-fourths-inch-long larva of an insect. In the next valley to the east, 8 miles southeast of Blair, W. B. Davis (MS) records that the contents of the cheek pouches of several of these mice comprised "2 scarabaeid beetles, 1 small centipede, the pupa of a moth, and several kinds of seeds. . . ." Insects apparently make up a considerable share of the food.

Twenty-five adult specimens were in process of molt. Two of these were taken in June and the others in July.

Of 286 adult females, 56 were pregnant. The embryos ranged from 2 to 6 per litter. The average number was 3.9 and the mode was 4. Inclusive dates for pregnant females are March 29 (the earliest date on which any specimens were taken) to September 22. No specimens are available for August, October, November, December, January, February, or the first twenty-eight days of March. By months the females are distributed as follows: March, 25 (14 of which are pregnant); April, 19 (0); May, 47 (13); June, 94 (23); July, 64 (4); September, 37 (2).

Microdipodops pallidus pallidus Merriam
Pallid Kangaroo Mouse

Microdipodops pallidus Merriam, Proc. Biol. Soc. Washington, 14:127, July 19, 1901. Type from 10 miles east of Stillwater, near sink of the Humboldt and Carson, Churchill County, Nevada. More restrictedly, according to Vernon Bailey (in *litt.*), the type locality is Mountain Well, Churchill County.

Microdipodops pallidus pallidus, Hall, Zoöl. Series, Field Mus. Nat. Hist., 27:269, December 8, 1941.

Microdipodops megacephalus lucidus Goldman, Proc. Biol. Soc. Washington, 39:127, December 27, 1926. Type from 8 miles southeast of Blair, 4500 feet, Esmeralda County, Nevada; Hall and Linsdale, Journ. Mamm., 10:299, November 11, 1929.

Microdipodops megacephalus dickeyi Goldman, Proc. Biol. Soc. Washington, 40:115, September 26, 1927. Type from 3 miles southeast of Oasis, 5150 feet, Mono County, California; Hall and Linsdale, Journ. Mamm., 10:299, pl. 22, November 11, 1929.

Distribution.—Low western part of Nevada from southern Pershing County southward to lower end of Fish Lake Valley in Esmeralda County. See figure 285.

Remarks.—Measurements of ten of each sex from within 1 mile of the type locality are: ♂, 164 (150–169), ♀, 160 (153–169); 87 (76–93), 85 (74–94); 25.5 (25–26), 25.6 (25–27); weight, 15.2 (14.7–16.8), 14.0 (12.2–16.4) grams.

Upper parts near (e) Light Pinkish Cinnamon; otherwise, as described for the species.

Compared with *ruficollaris*, this race differs in more reddish color of upper parts and absence of the collar. The nasals average slightly longer, as does the tail, but the differences in these measurements are slight. The difference in color is great and permits ready identification as to subspecies, except for a few populations which, from their geographic point of origin, would be expected to be intergrades. For example, animals from Millers Wells are intermediate in amount of red in the upper parts.

Within the range here assigned to the race *pallidus* there is some variation judged to be of a geographic nature. The population farthest north, that from west of Lovelock, is one of the two palest. The other population sample is from 8 miles southeast of Blair, in what may be the southernmost population of the subspecies. The northern population has a yellowish tinge in contrast to a reddish tinge present in the animals from Blair. Topotypes from Mountain Well are more reddish than any other specimens. Animals from Mountain Well and from the vicinity of Schurz have actually and relatively shorter tails than others. In most of the measurements taken, animals from Fingerrock Wash average larger than those from any other place. Specimens from 8 miles southeast of Blair average two-tenths of a millimeter less in basal length, one-tenth less in interorbital breadth, and one-tenth more in length of molariform tooth row. These inconstant features, and a lighter (less reddish) coloration, are all that has been found to differentiate this population from the one on which the name *Microdipodops megacephalus lucidus* Goldman was based. The color, however, is closely approached by specimens named *Microdipodops megacephalus dickeyi* by Goldman and based on specimens from 3 miles southeast of Oasis, California, in the valley next to the west. Topotypes and abundant material from other places in the same valley present no differences from other populations. Accordingly, both these names are placed as synonyms of *pallidus*.

Much to our surprise, intensive search for these mice in Humboldt Sink, in the vicinity of Toulon, yielded no trace of them. Because they do occur as far north as 21 miles west and 2 miles north of Lovelock, we suppose that they occur in places in the region of Humboldt Sink. Search for them in Buena Vista Valley, farther to the northeast, likewise was in vain, although seemingly suitable soils were found. In the sands of Carson Sink they have been found only near Soda Lake and at a point 9 miles west of Fallon, although in many other apparently suitable areas of sand they were sought in vain. Differences in soils of a minor but, by me, undetected nature may explain the presence of these mice in some places and absence in others of apparently equal suitability.

Records of occurrence.—Specimens examined, 386, as follows: *Lyon Co.:* 11¾ mi. S and 2¾ mi. E Yerington, 4650 ft., 23. *Pershing Co.:* 21 mi. W and 2 mi. N Lovelock, 4000 ft., 11. *Churchill Co.:* 9 mi. W Fallon, 4000 ft., 4 (Univ. Mich. Mus. Zoöl.); 1 mi. N Soda Lake, 4000 ft., 1; W end Soda Lake, 3900 ft., 2; 1 mi. W Mountain Well, 5350 ft., 16; Mountain Well, 5600 ft., 20. *Mineral Co.:* 3 mi. S Schurz, 4100 ft., 26; 8 mi. SE Schurz, 4100 ft., 2; Fingerrock Wash, Stewart Valley, 5400 ft., 34; Cat Creek, 4 mi. W Hawthorne, 4500 ft., 1; 2 mi. E Hawthorne, 4300 ft., 6; Marietta, 4900 ft., 3; Huntoon Valley, 5700 ft., 8; S side Teels Marsh, 4900 ft., 7. *Esmeralda Co.:* 1½ mi. W Millers Wells, 4800 ft., 16; 3½ to 4 mi. SE Coaldale, 4850 ft., 12; 13½ mi. NW Goldfield, 4850 ft., 2; 7 mi. N Arlemont, 5500 ft., 78; 1½ to 2½ mi. N Dyer, 4800–4850 ft., 17; Fish Lake Valley, 4945 ft., 1; 2 mi. SE Dyer, 4900–4950 ft., 10; 8 mi. SE Blair, 4500 ft., 46; mouth of Palmetto Wash (5350 ft., 3, 5500 ft., 1), 4 (D. R. Dickey Coll.). *Nye Co.:* NE of San Antonio (5½ mi., 5700 ft., 1; 4¾ mi., 5650 ft., 3; 4 2/3 mi., 5650 ft., 3; 4½ mi., 5640–5650 ft., 7; 4¼ mi., 5650 ft., 3), 19; San Antonio, 5407 ft., 17.

Microdipodops pallidus ruficollaris Hall
Pallid Kangaroo Mouse

Microdipodos [misspelling for *Microdipodops*] *pallidus ruficollaris* Hall, Proc. Biol. Soc. Washington, 54:60, May 20, 1941. Type from 5 miles southeast of Kawich Post Office, 5400 feet, Kawich Valley, Nye County, Nevada. Hall, Zoöl. Series, Field Mus. Nat. Hist., 27:272, December 8, 1941.

Distribution.—Western Nye County eastward to western Lincoln County. See figure 285.

Remarks.—Measurements of three males and seven females from the type locality are: ♂, 157 (156–158), ♀, 161 (154–164); 85 (83–88), 89 (85–91); 25.0 (25–25), 25.2 (25–26); weight, 12.1 (11.5–12.5), 12.3 (10.8–13.3) grams.

Upper parts near (e) Light Pinkish Cinnamon mixed with blackish, with a broad collar of more nearly cinnamon color; otherwise as described for the species.

From *purus*, this race differs in more reddish upper parts, presence of the cinnamon-colored collar, lesser maxillary breadth, and slightly less-inflated auditory bullae. Comparisons with *pallidus* and *ammophilus* are made in the accounts of those races.

There is surprisingly little variation between populations of this race, considering the fact that because it occurs mainly or entirely on fine sand its distribution is noncon-

TABLE 10

CRANIAL MEASUREMENTS (IN MILLIMETERS) OF MICRODIPODOPS

Locality	Number of individuals averaged	Basal length*	Nasal length	Greatest breadth	Maxillary breadth	Least interorbital breadth
		M. megacephalus oregonus				
Vicinity of Vya..............	20 (10♂, 10♀) av.	18.6	10.0	18.6	11.8	6.6
	min.	17.7	9.6	18.2	11.2	6.2
	max.	19.1	10.3	19.2	12.3	7.1
		M. megacephalus californicus				
2¾ mi. SW Pyramid..........	5 (4♂, 1♀) av.	18.7	10.1	18.3	12.0	6.8
	min.	18.6	9.9	17.9	11.9	6.7
	max.	18.9	10.6	18.6	12.2	7.1
		M. megacephalus nasutus				
Fletcher.....................	4 (2♂, 2♀) av.	18.5	10.1	18.9	12.0	6.8
	min.	18.0	10.0	18.2	11.2	6.5
	max.	19.2	10.4	19.4	12.4	7.2
		M. megacephalus ambiguus				
Vicinity of Sulphur............	17 (10♂, 7♀) av.	18.4	10.1	19.3	11.6	6.7
	min.	17.7	9.5	18.6	11.1	6.4
	max.	19.0	10.4	19.8	12.5	7.0
		M. megacephalus medius				
3 mi. S Vernon................	18 (9♂, 9♀) av.	18.6	10.1	19.1	11.7	6.5
	min.	18.0	9.4	18.8	11.2	6.2
	max.	19.1	10.6	19.6	12.2	6.9
		M. megacephalus nexus				
Izenhood and 3 mi. S..........	20 (10♂, 10♀) av.	18.5	9.9	19.3	11.5	6.6
	min.	17.8	9.4	18.8	11.0	6.3
	max.	19.0	10.2	20.0	12.2	6.8

* Basal length taken from anterior face of incisors.

TABLE 10—(*Continued*)

Locality	Number of individuals averaged	Basal length*	Nasal length	Greatest breadth	Maxillary breadth	Least interorbital breadth
		M. megacephalus megacephalus				
Elko County.................	10 (4♂, 6♀) av.	18.4	10.0	18.6	11.8	6.5
	min.	17.9	9.9	18.2	11.5	6.3
	max.	18.7	10.1	19.1	12.4	6.7
		M. megacephalus sabulonis				
5 mi. SE Kawich..............	9 (4♂, 5♀) av.	18.2	9.9	19.0	11.7	6.5
	min.	17.3	9.5	18.1	11.2	6.1
	max.	19.1	10.3	20.0	12.4	6.8
		M. megacephalus albiventer				
21 mi. W Panaca..............	14 (9♂, 5♀) av.	18.2	9.6	19.1	11.9	6.5
	min.	17.7	9.1	18.7	11.4	6.2
	max.	18.6	10.2	19.6	12.3	6.9
		M. pallidus pallidus				
Mountain Well................	20 (10♂, 10♀) av.	18.6	10.0	19.7	12.3	6.8
	min.	17.9	9.6	18.4	11.7	6.5
	max.	19.1	10.6	20.8	12.7	7.1
		M. pallidus ruficollaris				
5 mi. SE Kawich P. O..........	10 (3♂, 7♀) av.	18.3	9.9	19.6	12.2	6.9
	min.	18.0	9.5	19.2	11.8	6.7
	max.	18.7	10.3	20.1	12.7	7.3
		M. pallidus ammophilus				
3¼ to 12½ mi. S Lock's Ranch..	12 (8♂, 4♀) av.	18.3	9.7	19.5	12.2	6.9
	min.	17.9	9.3	18.8	11.6	6.7
	max.	18.9	9.9	20.4	12.6	7.1
		M. pallidus purus				
14½ to 15 mi. S Groom Baldy....	20 (10♂, 10♀) av.	18.7	9.8	19.6	12.4	6.7
	min.	18.1	9.4	19.1	11.9	6.4
	max.	19.2	10.3	20.2	12.9	6.9

* Basal length taken from anterior face of incisors.

tinuous. The population which shows the greatest departure from the mean is that in Penoyer Valley. These animals are more reddish than typical specimens, are by weight the heaviest of any, and have relatively short tails and greatly inflated auditory bullae. This inflation of the bullae is reflected in the great average breadth of the skull, which, actually (20.1 mm.) and also relatively to the basal length (18.5), is more than in any other population of Nevadan *Microdipodops* studied. Additional comment on this population from Penoyer Valley is made in the account of *M. p. purus*, in the account of *M. m. sabulonis*, and in the account of the genus *Microdipodops*.

Records of occurrence.—Specimens examined, 165, as follows: *Nye Co.*: 9 mi. W and 3 mi. S Tybo, 6200 ft., 2; 34 mi. E and 1 mi. N Tonopah, 5650 ft., 39; N shore Mud Lake, S end Ralston Valley, 5300 ft., 10; 1½ to 3 2/5 mi. S Silverbow, Kawich Mts., 6200–6400 ft., 3; 11½ mi. SW Silverbow, Cactus Flat, 5400 ft., 5; 6 mi. W Kawich P. O., Gold Flat, 5150 ft., 5; 5 to 5½ mi. W Kawich P. O., Gold Flat, 5100–5200 ft., 8; 5 to 5 7/10 mi. SE Kawich P. O., Kawich Valley, 5400 ft., 46; 6 mi. SW Kawich P. O., Gold Flat, 5100 ft., 12. *Lincoln Co.*: 17 mi. N Groom Baldy, Penoyer Valley, 25; 14 to 15 mi. NNW Groom Baldy, Penoyer Valley, 10.

Microdipodops pallidus ammophilus Hall
Pallid Kangaroo Mouse

Microdipodops pallidus ammophilus Hall, Zoöl. Series, Field Mus. Nat. Hist., 27:273, December 8, 1941. Type from Railroad Valley, Able Spring, 12½ miles south of Lock's Ranch, 5000 feet, Nye County, Nevada.

Distribution.—Railroad Valley in eastern Nye County. See figure 285.

Remarks.—Measurements of eight males and four females from 3¼, 9, and 12½ mi. S Lock's Ranch are: ♂, 164 (161–173), ♀, 157 (154–162); 90 (85–99), 86 (81–90); 25.5 (25.0–26.5), 25.6 (25.0–26.2); weights not recorded.

Upper parts near (*e*) Light Pinkish Cinnamon heavily mixed with blackish; a broad collar of cinnamon color lightly mixed with blackish; otherwise as described for the species.

In some ways this is the most handsome of all the kangaroo mice. Its ground color is that of the light-colored species *pallidus* overlain with a frosting of black. The collar is barely evident, much less so than in *ruficollaris*, from which *ammophilus* is further distinguished by the frosting of black. Specimens from 9½ miles east of New Reveille, which is at the southern end of Railroad Valley, show only slight approach to *ruficollaris* and indicate for *ammophilus* a range in Railroad Valley of 50 miles in extent in a southwest to northeast direction.

Records of occurrence.—Specimens examined, 30, as follows: *Nye Co.*: Railroad Valley, 5000 ft. (2½ to 3¼ mi. S Lock's Ranch, 10; 9 mi. S Lock's Ranch, 10; 12½ mi. S Lock's Ranch, Able Spring, 2), 22; 9½ mi. E New Reveille, Railroad Valley, 5100 ft., 8.

Microdipodops pallidus purus Hall
Pallid Kangaroo Mouse

Microdipodops pallidus purus Hall, Zoöl. Series, Field Mus. Nat. Hist., 27:273, December 8, 1941. Type from 14½ miles south of Groom Baldy, Lincoln County, Nevada.
Microdipodops pallidus albiventer Hall and Durrant (part), Journ. Mamm., 18:358, August 14, 1937.

Distribution.—Emigrant and Desert valleys in western Lincoln County. See figure 285, page 397.

Remarks.—Measurements of ten of each sex from the type locality are: ♂, 160 (152–168), ♀, 160 (153–167); 88 (83–94), 87 (83–90); 25.7 (25–26), 25.5 (25–26); weight, 13.3 (10.3–14.5), 13.9 (12.5–15.6) grams.

Upper parts near (*e*) Light Pinkish Cinnamon; distinctly whitish; otherwise as described for the species.

This race, at the type locality, is the palest and most nearly white of any. It is rivaled in this respect only by the population from 8 miles southeast of Blair here referred to the race *pallidus*. Cranially, the topotypes are notable for the greater average width across the maxillary processes of the zygomata and the reduced interorbital breadth. In the population from the next valley to the east, the interorbital breadth is larger, as in most other populations of the full species *pallidus*, but the narrowness across the zygomatic arches anteriorly is as in the topotypes.

Reference to the distribution map reveals that from the main geographic range of *ruficollaris* there are three projections to the eastward. These are (1) *ammophilus* to the northeast, (2) the populations in Penoyer Valley to the east, and (3) *purus* to the southeast. Each of these differs appreciably from *ruficollaris: ammophilus* is "blacker," animals from Penoyer Valley are "redder," and *purus* is "whiter." From one another, they differ far more than any one of them differs from *ruficollaris*. Perhaps this is, in a measure, the result of isolation from one another by hills and mountains, whereas closer connection is maintained with *ruficollaris*. A low pass through which mice of this species may occur connects the range of *ammophilus* with that of *ruficollaris*, and a similar pass connects Penoyer Valley with the range of *ruficollaris*, but there is no such low pass between Penoyer Valley and the range of *ammophilus*. The range of *purus* may not be continuous with that of *ruficollaris*, but the two are less isolated from each other than *purus* is from the population in Penoyer Valley.

The habitat of *purus* is the fine, exceptionally white sand which in large part probably results from the disintegration of Sieberts Tuff, a white deposit abundantly exposed in the area where *purus* occurs.

Records of occurrence.—Specimens examined, 38, as follows: *Lincoln Co.:* Desert Valley, 8 mi. SW Hancock Summit, 5300 ft., 3; 8 mi. N Summit Spring, 3; 5½ mi. N Summit Spring, 4700 ft., 3; 14½ to 15 mi. S Groom Baldy, 29.

Genus **Dipodomys** Gray
Kangaroo Rats

The five species of Nevadan kangaroo rats are concentrated in the Sonoran zones and do not range higher than the Transition Life-zone. *D. panamintinus* is the only one that I have caught among trees. The trees were scattered piñons and probably the rats (*D. p. leucogenys*) lived in the wider open places among them. The loose, sandy soils supporting widely spaced xerophitic shrubs are the places favored by kangaroo rats.

In size they range from the small *Dipodomys merriami*, with a total length of about 245 millimeters and a weight of 43 grams, up to the large *Dipodomys deserti*, with a total length of 340 millimeters and a weight of 119 grams. The coloration, and particularly the color pattern, is relatively uniform throughout the genus. The underparts, upper lips, spot above each eye, spot behind each ear, forelegs (except in some specimens which have pigmented hairs on the outer sides of the forelegs), forefeet, and antiplantar faces of hind feet are white. Also, there is a white stripe extending from the flank to the base of the tail which separates a patch of darker color on each hind leg. This patch, like the upper parts, is some shade of buff or brownish. The tail, although white all around at the base, is four-striped, having a white stripe on each side and a dark stripe on the top and bottom. Exception is to be made for *Dipodomys deserti*, in which the ventral dark stripe generally is lacking. The tail is tufted

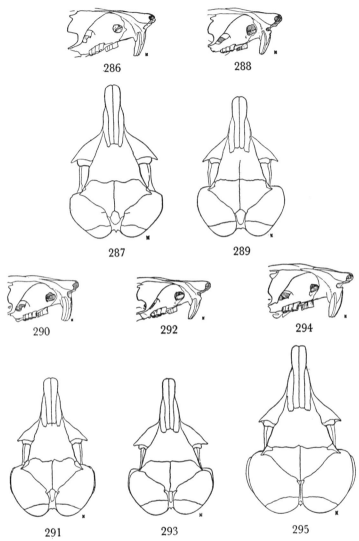

Figs. 286–295. Kangaroo rats. All, × 1. (Figs. 286, 288, 290, 292, and 294 are from antero-lateral aspect, perpendicular to dorsolateral face of maxillary arm of zygomatic arch.)

Figs. 286, 287. *Dipodomys panamintinus leucogenys*, Junction House, no. 49012, ♂.
Figs. 288, 289. *Dipodomys ordii columbianus*, 4½ miles northeast Painted Point, no. 73541, ♂.
Figs. 290, 291. *Dipodomys microps aquilonius*, 3½ miles east Flanigan, no. 73616, ♂.
Figs. 292, 293. *Dipodomys merriami merriami*, 14 miles east Searchlight, no. 61580, ♂.
Figs. 294, 295. *Dipodomys deserti deserti*, 21 miles west and 2 miles north Lovelock, 4000 feet, no. 73694, ♂.

at the end. The fur is of silky texture; it is plumbeous basally on the upper parts, but white all the way to the base on the underparts. The sleekness, in part, may result from the secretion of the dermal gland on the back between the shoulders. The tail, excepting its terminal fourth, and the ears, forefeet, and upper sides of the hind feet are short-haired. There is only one molt per year. Ordinarily it occurs in July, but in the southern part of the state it may begin in June. The forelegs and forefeet are small, but nevertheless they are used in digging and in bringing food to the face. The hind legs and hind feet are large. The fifth toe is vestigial or wanting. Like other members of the family, the cheek pouches are fur-lined. The eyes are relatively large and the external

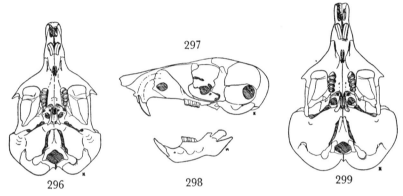

Figs. 296–299. Kangaroo rats. All ×1.

Figs. 296–298. *Dipodomys panamintinus leucogenys*, Junction House, no. 49012, ♂.
Fig. 299. *Dipodomys deserti deserti*, 21 miles west and 2 miles north Lovelock, 4000 feet, no. 73694, ♂.

ears relatively small. The head is broad posteriorly and the cervical vertebrae and associated structures are anteroposteriorly compressed, producing a short neck. In the skull the outstanding feature is the greatly enlarged mastoidal bones and other bones associated with the ear. The huge bullae are exceeded in relative (to the skull as a whole) size among American mammals only by those in the related genus *Microdipodops*.

Rapid locomotion is accomplished by leaping with the hind feet, both feet being used in the action at the same time. When speed is required, the tail does not touch the ground. In large size of auditory bulla, in silkiness of pelage, and in absence of the fifth toe, *Dipodomys merriami* and *Dipodomys deserti* appear to be more specialized than other Nevadan species of the genus. Even these most specialized species are less highly adapted to the saltatorial method of progression than are some Old World rodents of other families that are adapted for life in deserts. For example, some of the Asiatic and north African jerboas have the toes on the hind feet reduced to three in number, and the hind legs are relatively longer than in *Dipodomys*, especially in the distal segments. These characteristics are obvious adaptations to rapid progression by means of the hind limbs. Probably evolution toward perfecting rapid locomotion by use of the hind limbs in *Dipodomys* has been at work for a shorter time because our west American deserts are younger than those in the Old World. Given sufficient time, *Dipodomys deserti* may develop into an animal with longer hind legs, each terminating in only three instead of four toes. Structural modifications which adapt kangaroo rats to this saltatorial mode of progression have been studied and written about by Howell (1932) and Hatt (1932) among others. The paper by Grinnell (1922) also contains some information on this subject.

Kangaroo rats are nocturnal and do not show themselves aboveground in daylight except when accidentally forced out of their burrows, which they themselves dig. Nests of dried plant materials have been found in some burrows, but all that I have excavated lacked nests. It is not known whether the animals hibernate, but they are not active aboveground in the northern part of Nevada when the weather is coldest and snow lies deeply on the ground. In the southern part of the state the animals are active all winter. Evidence that they do not hibernate anywhere is comprised in the lack of large accumulations of fat in autumn, such as are found in rodents that are known to hibernate. Also, kangaroo rats, some species at least, store food below ground. This suggests that the animals are active in winter, even if confined to their burrows.

Plant material makes up nearly all the animals' food and seeds are an important, perhaps the most important, part of the total. Nevertheless, cuttings from green plants have frequently been found in the cheek pouches, and I have noted a half dozen or so rats the pouches of which were well filled with pupae of insects.

Like several rodents which live in deserts, *Dipodomys* does not need water to drink. Howell and Gersh (1935) mention that individuals of more than one species of the genus suffered no discernible ill effects from having lived on diets of dried cereals without water for several months in captivity. Under similar conditions, white rats (*Rattus*) lived no longer than a week. These investigators learned that when individuals of *Dipodomys* were kept on a dehydrated diet, they conserved metabolic water chiefly by resorbing it in the ducts of the renal papillae and in the walls of the urinary bladder. In addition, the habits of the animals help to conserve water. Being nocturnal, the animals are abroad only when the rate of evaporation is at a minimum; during the day they sleep curled up in an underground chamber which is closed off from the outside air by an earthen plug, and hence the moisture which is exhaled is, in part, regained at the following inhalation.

One thing that has impressed me about *Dipodomys* is the rapidity with which it invades new territory—territory previously unavailable because it was under water. At the northern end of Walker Lake, *Dipodomys microps* was trapped on sandy soil which was judged to have been exposed for less than two years. Apparently the kangaroo rats move into an area of this kind just as soon as plants sufficient to give a food source for the rats have established themselves. It is inferred that the kangaroo rats retreated and advanced in unison with the changing shorelines of Lake Lahontan of which Walker Lake and other lakes in the low, western part of Nevada are remnants. Whatever effect isolation of populations of these rats by a water barrier may have had in bringing about speciation, this effect conceivably was minimized by the rapid reinvasion of land areas exposed by a lowering of the lake. For example, when receding waters of the lake, which had its longest axis in a north to south direction, exposed a ridge of land cutting across the lake, as in the territory a few miles south of Fernley, genetic distinctness of populations of *Dipodomys microps* on the east and west sides of the lake would be expected to become less through crossbreeding between the two populations.

Dipodomys panamintinus
Panamint Kangaroo Rat

Two subspecies of Panamint kangaroo rat occur in Nevada, one in the Upper Sonoran Life-zone from the head of Owens Valley northward along the western boundary of the state to the Virginia Mountains, and the other in the Lower Sonoran Life-zone in the southern part of the state. At the latter place the animals, race *caudatus*, were taken at an elevation of 4300 feet on coarse sand among *Yucca brevifolia*, *Y. mohavensis*, *Y. baccata*, cholla and prickly pear, with cat claw along the washes. The more northern populations, race *leucogenys*, have been taken at elevations of 3950 to 8900 feet. *D. p. leucogenys* commonly lives at an elevation higher than that of *D. ordii* and *D. microps*, often where sagebrush areas are dotted with occasional piñons.

This species, in Nevada, is second in size to *deserti* and has relatively darkcolored upper parts, the general effect being only slightly lighter than Sayal Brown. The tail amounts to about 140 per cent of the length of the head and body or about 58 per cent of the total length. The hind foot has five toes. The auditory bullae are small, the interparietal is wide, and the dorsolateral face of the maxillary arm of the zygoma is wide.

Of six adults taken on July 31, in Clark County, one was in process of molt. No embryos were recorded in any of the females. Males average slightly more than 2 per cent larger than females in linear measurements, and in weight about 14 per cent heavier.

Dipodomys panamintinus leucogenys (Grinnell)
Panamint Kangaroo Rat

Perodipus leucogenys Grinnell, Univ. California Publ. Zoöl., 21:46, March 29, 1919. Type from Pellisier Ranch, 5600 feet, 5 miles north of Benton Station, Mono County, California.
Dipodomys leucogenys, Grinnell, Journ. Mamm., 2:95, May 2, 1921; Hall and Dale, Occas. Papers, Mus. Zoöl., Louisiana State Univ., (no.) 4:48, November 10, 1939.

Distribution.—Upper Sonoran Life-zone along western border of state from Pyramid Lake south to head of Owens Valley. See figure 300.

Remarks.—Measurements of nine males and ten females (three adult and seven subadult) are: ♂, 297 (280–308), ♀, 296 (286–307); 173 (165–182), 174 (165–189); 45.8 (45–47), 45.4 (43–47); weight, 85.8 (76.5–94.3), 74.3 (64.0–80.5) grams.

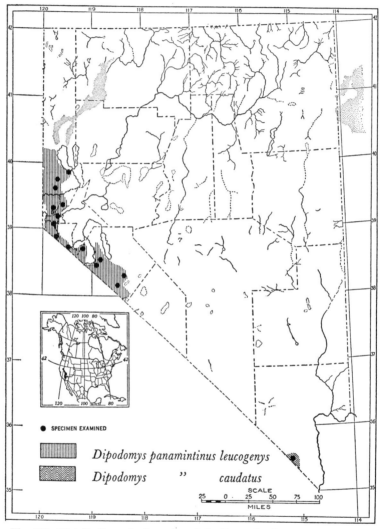

Fig. 300. Distribution of subspecies of the Panamint kangaroo rat, *Dipodomys panamintinus*, with insert showing range of the species.

For the species as a whole, individuals of this race can be characterized as of large size, medium color (general effect reddish-brown), tail heavily crested, skull relatively broad across auditory bullae.

From *D. panamintinus caudatus*, this race differs in slightly smaller average size, darker color, and lesser width across auditory bullae. From *D. panamintinus mohavensis*, found to the southward in California, *leucogenys* differs in slightly darker color of upper parts, more whitish cheeks, longer-haired tail, heavier rostrum, and wider interparietal. From *D. p. panamintinus*, also of California, *leucogenys* differs in longer hind foot, lighter color of upper parts, more whitish cheeks, longer-haired tail, heavier and longer rostrum, and longer skull of about equal breadth. Comparison with *D. p. caudatus* is made in the account of that form. From *D. heermanni californicus*, known from as far east as Petes Valley, Lassen County, California, only 50-odd miles northwest of known localities of occurrence of *leucogenys* near Vinton, California, the latter differs in smaller ear, five instead of four toes, much lighter color of upper parts, narrower interparietal, and other cranial features.

Examination of California-taken specimens in the Museum of Vertebrate Zoölogy from Owens Valley shows intergradation between *Dipodomys mohavensis* (Grinnell) and *D. leucogenys*. Comparison of topotypes and other specimens of *Dipodomys panamintinus* (Merriam) reveals differences of a nature which indicate no more than subspecific rank between it and *mohavensis;* the same applies to differences between *D. p. caudatus* and *D. panamintinus*. *D. panamintinus* is the oldest of these names, hence the name combination *Dipodomys panamintinus leucogenys* is here employed.

Records of occurrence.—Specimens examined, 45, as follows: *Washoe Co.:* ½ mi. S Pyramid Lake, 3950 ft., 1; Junction House, 4500 ft., 2; 8 mi. NE Reno, 2; 10 mi. S Reno, 3. *Ormsby Co.:* 3½ mi. E Carson City, 4700 ft., 2. *Douglas Co.:* 5½ mi. S Carson City, 4700 ft., 1; 6½ mi. S Minden, 4900 ft., 1; N end Topaz Lake, 1; 6 mi. NE Virginia City, 6000 ft., 10. *Mineral Co.:* 2 to 3½ mi. SW Pine Grove, 7250 ft., 17; Lapon Canyon, Mt. Grant, 8900 ft., 1; Fletcher, 6098 ft., 2; Endowment Mine, Excelsior Mts., 6930 ft., 1; Huntoon Valley, 5700 ft., 1.

Dipodomys panamintinus caudatus new subspecies
Panamint Kangaroo Rat

Type.—Female, adult, skin and skull; no. 80028, Mus. Vert. Zoöl.; 6 mi. S Granite Well, 3800 feet, Providence Mountains, San Bernardino County, California; December 18, 1937; obtained by F. Wallace Taber; original no. 121.

Range.—Providence Mountains region of northeastern San Bernardino County, California, and western Clark County, Nevada; principal center of abundance in the yucca belt. See figure 300.

Diagnosis.—Size large (see measurements, table 11, pp. 430–431); color slightly lighter than Sayal Brown, heavily washed with ochraceous; tail lightly crested; skull large and broad, averaging 25.0 mm. or more across auditory bullae.

Comparisons.—From *D. p. panamintinus*, *caudatus* differs in lighter color and larger size of skull in all parts measured. From *D. p. leucogenys*, *caudatus* differs in lighter color by a slight degree, less heavily crested tail, shorter hind foot, and greater breadth, actually and relatively, across tympanic bullae. From *D. p. mohavensis*, *caudatus* differs in shorter body and tail and smaller size of skull in all parts measured. From *D. stephensi*, *caudatus* differs in larger size in all parts measured, is lighter colored, and relative to the basilar length is narrower across the auditory bullae.

Remarks.—Measurements of three of each sex from Nevada are: ♂, 302 (294–312), ♀, 300 (285–310); 178 (168–185), 178 (174–186); 44 (42–46), 45 (43–46); weight, 85.2 (78.9–89.6), 77.0 (74.0–81.0) grams.

Average and extreme measurements of ten adults of each sex from the type locality and near-by localities in the Providence Mountains are: total length, ♂, 310 (289–334), ♀, 304 (294–318); length of tail, 180 (165–198), 181 (165–202); length of hind foot, 44.1 (42–47), 43.9 (42–46); basal length (from anterior border of incisor), 29.0 (27.9–30.0), 28.5 (27.7–29.0); length of nasal, 15.6 (14.7–16.2), 15.2 (14.8–15.0); greatest breadth of skull, 25.4 (24.2–26.2), 25.0 (24.0–25.7); maxillary breadth, 23.6 (23.0–24.0), 22.9 (21.9–23.9); interorbital breadth, 13.3 (12.2–14.4), 12.9 (12.4–13.7); weight, 77.9 (67.5–89.5), 69.7 (63.0–78.4) grams.

In the last few years parties from the California Museum of Vertebrate Zoölogy have obtained abundant materials of the kangaroo rat from the Providence Mountains of southeastern California which Grinnell (1922:61) tentatively referred to *Dipodomys mohavensis*—the kind of kangaroo rat known from along the western side of the Mohave Desert. Study of the now more abundant material from the general region of the Providence Mountains shows that it differs from any one of its relatives so much as to require separate designation by name.

The named relatives of this rat which show greatest morphological resemblance to it occur in adjacent regions, and are: *Dipodomys panamintinus* Merriam, 1894; *Dipodomys stephensi* Merriam, 1907; *Dipodomys mohavensis* Grinnell, 1918; and *Dipodomys leucogenys* Grinnell, 1919. In his paper, "A geographical study of the kangaroo rats of California," Grinnell (*op. cit.*) treated these four named kinds of kangaroo rats as distinct species. Specimens recently obtained from Owens Valley show that *D. leucogenys* and *D. mohavensis* intergrade there. *D. stephensi* may also intergrade with *D. mohavensis*, but material showing complete intergradation is lacking. *D. panamintinus* appears to be restricted to the Panamint Mountains in and above the upper part of the Lower Sonoran Life-zone, and therefore is judged to have no connection, geographically, at the present time, with the other named forms, because extensive areas of low Lower Sonoran Life-zone surround the Panamint Mountains. Nevertheless, the degree of difference between *panamintinus*, on the one hand, and *D. leucogenys*, *D. mohavensis*, and especially the animal in the Providence Mountains, on the other, is so slight that it seems best to give the new form only subspecific status. The oldest name among the mentioned forms is *Perodipus panamintinus* Merriam.

D. p. caudatus is indistinguishable in color from *D. p. mohavensis*. These two animals are the lightest colored of the forms here considered. *D. stephensi* is the darkest. *D. p. panamintinus* is slightly darker than *D. p. leucogenys*. The newly named race has the largest external measurements of any of the five forms, but this is only an average difference which alone does not permit separating the individual specimens of it from those of *panamintinus* and *leucogenys*.

It is principally David H. Johnson to whom I am indebted for the opportunity to include *D. p. caudatus* in the list of the fauna of Nevada. He obtained the first adequate series of specimens from the area of the Providence Mountains in California, recognized the distinctive characters of the subspecies, predicted that it would be found within Nevada, and in the summer of 1941 when in southern Nevada went to the appropriate habitat and with his field companions obtained the seventeen specimens here recorded. Furthermore, he intended to include an account of the new form in a paper of his own, partly written, on the biota of the Providence Mountains region, but generously allowed insertion of the first notice of the new race here.

Records of occurrence.—Specimens examined, 76, as follows: CALIFORNIA: *San Bernardino Co.:* 3 mi. N Cima, 4500 ft., 2; 2 mi. NNE Cima, 4100 ft., 2; Purdy, 4500 ft., 6 mi. SE New York Mts., 7; Cedar Canyon, 5000 ft., Providence Mts., 4; 2 mi. ESE Rock Spring, 4700 ft., Lanfair Valley, 5; 5 mi. NE Granite Well, 5400–5800 ft., Providence Mts., 16; 6 mi. S Granite Well, 3800 ft., Providence Mts., 23. NEVADA: *Clark Co.:* 9 mi. W and 3½ to 5½ mi. S Searchlight, 4300 ft., 17.

Dipodomys ordii
Ord Kangaroo Rat

Five subspecies of the Ord kangaroo rat occur in Nevada. One specimen in the D. R. Dickey Collection, labeled as being from a mile north of Beatty, comes from a place within the Lower Sonoran Life-zone. Otherwise, all the known stations of occurrence are within the Upper Sonoran Life-zone at elevations of between 3900 feet (Smoke Creek) and 7000 feet (9 miles east of

Toquima Peak). Although *D. microps* and this species occur together over most of the state, *D. ordii* does not extend so far southward nor range down zonally so low as *microps*, but does occur in the northwestern part of Nevada in the zonally high central part of Elko County where *microps* has not been found.

D. ordii is a medium-sized, relatively short-tailed, five-toed species of a color about average for the genus. The hind foot varies from 37 to 42 millimeters in total length, and the tail amounts to about 125 per cent of the length of the head and body or 56 per cent of the total length. The color (described in the accounts of the subspecies) is lighter than that of *D. panamintinus* and *D. microps*, darker than that of *D. deserti*, and darker, usually, than that of *D. merriami*. The dark stripe on the ventral side of the tail almost always tapers to a point and ends short of the terminal pencil. The skull has a relatively short rostrum, moderate-sized bullae, wide interparietal, and wide maxillary arm of the zygomatic arch.

There are thirty-one specimens clearly showing molt, and nearly all (twenty-three) were taken in July. The extreme dates are June 11 and August 27. Males average only slightly more than 1 per cent larger than females in linear measurements of the skull and external parts, and a little less than 4 per cent more in weight.

On July 9, 1935, 22 miles north of Deeth, W. B. Richardson trapped a female containing five nearly full-term embryos. Her cheek pouches contained dried blades of grass which he supposed she would have used in constructing a nest.

Including the animals reported by Alcorn (1941:88), there is record of 291 mature females examined for embryos. Of these, 80 were pregnant. The number of embryos averaged 3.5, with extremes of 1 and 6. The mode was 4 (1 ♀ with 1 embryo; 8 ♀ with 2; 28 ♀ with 3; 36 ♀ with 4; 5 ♀ with 5; 2 ♀ with 6). By months the females were distributed as follows: February, 34 (23 of which were pregnant); March, 26 (11); April, 33 (15); May, 23 (5); June, 62 (8); July, 93 (18); August, 11 (0); September, 9 (0). No females were taken in October, November, December, or January. The specimens recorded for February were taken on the 23d, 24th, and 25th of that month, and of the eleven not pregnant, 2 were suckling young and 7 others had the uterine horns much enlarged. Obviously, young are born from February to July, inclusive, most of them in the first three of these months. Alcorn (*loc. cit.*) suggests that there are two litters per year.

Dipodomys ordii columbianus (Merriam)
Ord Kangaroo Rat

Perodipus ordii columbianus Merriam, Proc. Biol. Soc. Washington, 9:115, June 21, 1894. Type from Umatilla, at mouth of Umatilla River, Plains of Columbia, Umatilla County, Oregon.
Dipodomys ordii columbianus, Grinnell, Journ. Mamm., 2:96, May 2, 1921; Borell and Ellis, Journ. Mamm., 15:29, February 15, 1934.
Perodipus microps levipes, Taylor, Univ. California Publ. Zoöl., 7:267, June 24, 1911, part.

Distribution.—Northwestern, northern, and most of northeastern quarter of state. See figure 301.

Remarks.—Measurements of six of each sex from northwestern Washoe County are: ♂, 255 (245–263), ♀, 247 (238–254); 143 (135–150), 138 (132–142); 41.3 (41–42), 41.0 (40–42); weight, 57.3 (52.6–59.5), 53.8 (50.1–61.0) grams.

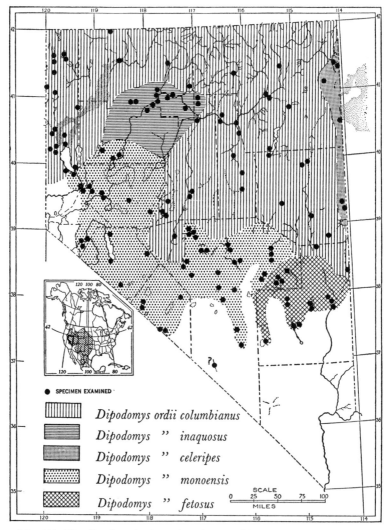

Fig. 301. Distribution of subspecies of the Ord kangaroo rat, *Dipodomys ordii*, with insert showing range of the species.

Size large; color dark, near (16″c) Cinnamon-Buff on upper parts, strongly mixed with blackish; white supraorbital spots small; black arietiform facial markings well developed; skull large; nasals long.

From *inaquosus*, *columbianus* differs in relatively longer tail, markedly darker color, smaller supraorbital spots, and prominently black rather than almost obsolete dark arietiform facial markings. From *celeripes, columbianus* differs in larger size, in color in about the same way as from *inaquosus*, smaller bullae, and broader interorbital region. From *monoensis, columbianus* differs in larger size of all parts measured, darker color, relatively longer tail, relatively longer nasals, and less arched brain case as its superior border is viewed from the side. From *fetosus, columbianus* differs in larger external measurements, except length of hind foot, which is about the same, darker color, more divergent frontomaxillary sutures, and more acute angle at junction of rostrum and maxillary arm of zygomatic arch.

Some geographic variation is shown by Nevadan specimens assigned to *columbianus*. Animals from Washoe County have shorter nasals than those to the eastward. Specimens from northern Eureka County are distinctly darker colored than any others. Some geographic variations appear to be the result of intergradation with surrounding races. For example, specimens from Sulphur and vicinity in west-central Washoe County approach *monoensis* in reduced size and in lighter color. In Elko County, the lighter color of specimens from along the eastern base of the Ruby Mountains reflects the influence of the pallid race *celeripes* to the eastward.

The series of specimens from northwestern Washoe County, of which cranial measurements are given below as typical of the race *columbianus*, have shorter nasals, lesser interorbital breadth, and in females a lesser width of skull as measured across the auditory bullae (greatest breadth) than populations from most parts of Nevada included within the range of *columbianus*.

Records of occurrence.—Specimens examined, 182, as follows: *Washoe Co.:* 3 mi. N Vya, 5900 ft., 3; 4½ mi. NE Painted Point, 5800 ft., 4; 8½ mi. E Vya, 5900 ft., 1; 3 mi. E Painted Point, 5850 ft., 1; Long Valley Ranch, 3 mi. S Vya, 5800 ft., 1; 10½ mi. S Vya, 5800 ft., 1; 11 mi. S Vya, 5800 ft., 2; 13 mi. S Vya, 5800 ft., 4; 1 mi. W Hausen, 4650 ft., 1; Hausen, 4800 ft., 3; 10 mi. SE Hausen, 4675 ft., 6; 2½ mi. E and 11 mi. N Gerlach, 4050 ft., 4; Smoke Creek, 9 mi. E Calif. boundary, 3900 ft., 5; latitude 40° 28′ N, 6 mi. E Calif. boundary, 4000 ft., 3; Horse Canyon, 3 mi. NW Pahrum Peak, 5000 ft., 1; 4 mi. S Pahrum Peak 4800 ft., 4; N side Sand Pass, 3950 ft., 2; 4 mi. NW Flanigan, 4200 ft., 1; 3½ mi. NW Flanigan, 4200 ft., 1; 3½ mi. E Flanigan, 4200 ft., 2; 4½ mi. N and 2½ mi. W Nixon, 1 (coll. of Ira La Rivers and T. J. Trelease); 2¾ mi. SW Pyramid, 4300 ft., 2. *Humboldt Co.:* 1 mi. S Denio, Oregon, 4200 ft., 6; Quinn River Crossing, 1; 2 mi. SW Quinn River Crossing, 4000 ft., 1; Cherry Creek Ranch, N end Paradise Valley, 1 (coll. of U. S. Biol. Surv. Dist. Office, Reno); 18 mi. NE Iron Point, 4600 ft., 3. *Lander Co.:* 1 mi. E Battle Mountain, 1; Reese River Valley, 7 mi. N Austin, 2; Malloy Ranch, 5 mi. W Austin, Reese River, 5500 ft., 3; 2½ mi. NE Smiths Creek Ranch, 5800 ft., 1; Campbell Creek, 6900 ft., 3; Campbell Creek Ranch, 5500 ft., 8. *Eureka Co.:* 5 mi. N Beowawe, 7; ½ mi. S Beowawe, 1; Pine Creek, 2 mi. E Palisade, 7; Evans, 4; Winzell, 3; 4 mi. SE Romano, Diamond Valley, 1; 8 mi. W Eureka, 12. *Nye Co.:* Bells Ranch, Reese River, 6890 ft., 1. *Elko Co.:* Marys River, 22 mi. N Deeth, 5800 ft., 3; 1 mi. SE Tuscarora, 5900 ft., 2; 2 mi. NW Halleck, 5200 ft., 2 (coll. of Ralph Ellis); 3 to 5 mi. W Halleck, 5200–5300 ft., 18 (9 in coll. of Ralph Ellis); Elburz, 3 mi. S Halleck, 3 (coll. of Ralph Ellis); Jerry Creek, N end Ruby Mts., 6 (coll. of Ralph Ellis); W side Ruby Lake, 3 mi. N White Pine Co. line, 6200 ft., 1 (coll. of Ralph Ellis). *White Pine Co.:* W side Ruby Lake, 3 mi. S Elko Co. line, 6100 ft., 4 (coll. of Ralph Ellis); 5 mi. SE Greens Ranch, Steptoe Valley, 5900 ft., 1; Cherry Creek, 6600 ft., 2; 1 mi. E Illipah, 6100 ft., 3; 5½ mi. SE Ely, 6500 ft., 6; 4 mi. S Shoshone, Spring Valley, 5900 ft., 6. *Lincoln Co.:* 3 mi. S Geyser, Duck Valley, 6050 ft., 1; latitude 38° 17′ N, ¼ mi. W Utah boundary, 7300 ft., 2.

Additional records (D. G. Nichols, MS): *Washoe Co.:* Hardscrabble Canyon, 4500–4900 ft., 3; Sutcliffe, 3700–4200 ft., 34.

Dipodomys ordii inaquosus Hall
Ord Kangaroo Rat

Dipodomys ordii inaquosus Hall, Proc. Biol. Soc. Washington, 54:58, May 20, 1941. Type from 11 miles east and 1 mile north of Jungo, 4200 feet, Humboldt County, Nevada.

Distribution.—Southeastern Humboldt County and northern Lander County. See figure 301.

Remarks.—Measurements of five males and two females from within 11 miles to the eastward of Jungo are: ♂, 246 (233–261), ♀, 252, 254; 136 (125–142), 140, 138; 39.7 (38–41), 41, 41; weight, 44.3 (33.8–49.0), 64.6, 51.7 grams.

Size large; tail relatively short; color pale, Pinkish Buff on upper parts, lightly marked with dusky; white supraorbital spots large; dark arietiform facial markings almost obsolete. Skull large; nasals long.

From *monoensis, inaquosus* differs in larger size of all parts measured and in lighter color. Comparison with *columbianus*, the one other race the range of which meets that of *inaquosus*, is made in the account of that form.

The pallor of coloration in this race almost equals that of *D. o. celeripes* of the Bonneville Basin to the eastward. The ranges of the two are separated by a wide area populated by darker colored animals referable to *columbianus*. The relatively short tail of *inaquosus* is found also in the race *monoensis* to the southward. An additional resemblance between the two is the dorsally convex superior outline of the skull. The convexity is less pronounced in most specimens of *inaquosus* than in *monoensis*.

Records of occurrence.—Specimens examined, 50, as follows: *Humboldt Co.:* 7 mi. N Winnemucca, 4400 ft., 4; 1 mi. N Winnemucca, 4600 ft., 8; 5 mi. NE Golconda, 7; 1 mi. W Golconda, 3; 3 to 5 mi. SW Winnemucca, 4500–4600 ft., 4; 8 mi. E and 1 mi. N Jungo, 4200 ft., 6; 11 mi. E and 1 mi. N Jungo, 4200 ft., 8; 10 mi. SW Winnemucca, 4500 ft., 1; 23 mi. NW Battle Mountain, 4. *Pershing Co.:* 15 mi. SW Winnemucca, 1. *Lander Co.:* Izenhood, 2; 3 mi. S Izenhood, 2.

Dipodomys ordii celeripes Durrant and Hall
Ord Kangaroo Rat

Dipodomys ordii celeripes Durrant and Hall, Mammalia, 3:10, March, 1939. Type from Trout Creek, 4600 feet, Juab County, Utah.

Distribution.—Eastern Nevada south from near Montello in Elko County to Mount Moriah in White Pine County. See figure 301.

Remarks.—Measurements of six males and nine females from near Tecoma are: ♂, 249 (244–250), ♀, 241 (232–249); 138 (131–140), 133 (127–138); 39.9 (39–41), 39.6 (38.5–40.0); weight, 53.7 (52.5–55.6), 55.5 (52.0–62.3) grams.

Size small; tail relatively short and hind foot relatively long; color pale, Pinkish Buff on upper parts, lightly marked with dusky; white supraorbital spots large; dark arietiform facial markings obsolete; skull large; nasals long.

Nevadan specimens referred to this race are larger and slightly darker colored than topotypes and are regarded as intergrades with *columbianus*. The external measurements given above and the cranial measurements of the series from near Tecoma (see measurements in table 11, pp. 430–431 are more like those in *columbianus* than those of the topotypes of *celeripes*. The color, although darker than in topotypes of *celeripes*, is distinctly more like the color in that race than that in *columbianus*.

Records of occurrence.—Specimens examined, 27, as follows: *Elko Co.:* 13 mi. N Montello, 5000 ft., 2; 1½ mi. N Tecoma, 4900 ft., 8; Tecoma, 4900 ft., 8; Cobre, 6100 ft., 3; Salt Springs, 4200 ft., 3. *White Pine Co.:* 2 mi. W Smith Creek Cave, Mt. Moriah, 6300 ft., 1; near Smith Creek Cave, Mt. Moriah, 5800 ft., 1; Hendry Creek, 8 mi. SE Mt. Moriah, 6200 ft., 1.

Dipodomys ordii monoensis (Grinnell)
Ord Kangaroo Rat

Perodipus monoensis Grinnell, Univ. California Publ. Zoöl., 21:46, March 29, 1919. Type from Pellisier Ranch, 5 miles north of Benton Station, 5600 feet, Mono County, California.
Dipodomys ordii monoensis Grinnell, Journ. Mamm., 2:96, May 2, 1921.
Dipodomys ordii, Linsdale, Amer. Midland Nat., 19:187, January, 1938.

Distribution.—Western Nevada from Pyramid Lake and Humboldt Sink southward to Beatty and, excepting the Reese River Valley, eastward over Nye County to the Quinn Canyon Mountains. See figure 301.

Remarks.—Measurements of ten males and three females from the vicinity of Fallon are: ♂, 237 (230–245), ♀, 239 (231–245); 131 (122–136), 129 (124–137); 39.2 (38–40), 38.7 (38–39); weight, 50.6 (47.1–55.3) grams, weight for females unavailable.

Size small, tail relatively short (less than 120 per cent of length of head and body in most series, although not in animals from Fallon); color pale, Pinkish Buff to near (16″) Pinkish Buff moderately marked with dusky; white supraorbital spots large; dark arietiform facial markings faintly indicated; skull small, nasals short, cranium highly arched. Comparisons with adjoining races are made in the accounts of those forms.

Intergradation with *columbianus* is shown by specimens from near the southern end of Pyramid Lake, by those from Great Smoky Valley (vicinity of Millett), and by those from the next valley to the eastward labeled as being from Toquima Peak. Populations from all these places, although referred to *monoensis* on basis of lighter color and some other features, at the same time closely resemble, or even agree with, *columbianus* in other features. Much the same is true of populations farther southeast in Nye County except that here intergradation is shown also with *fetosus*. Decision to refer these specimens to *monoensis* finally was made largely on the basis of their small size in most, although not in all, parts measured. Their lighter color distinguishes them from *columbianus*, but is not distinctive as between *monoensis* and *fetosus*. Intergradation with *inaquosus* is shown by specimens from the vicinity of Toulon.

Intergradation otherwise is shown by the populations here referred to *monoensis*. Topotypes from the head of Owens Valley in California are lighter colored and shorter tailed than animals from the opposite, eastern, side of the White Mountains as known by material from Arlemont in Fish Lake Valley. Also, the population in Owens Valley is one of the palest referred to this race. Nevertheless, excepting the populations from east-central Nye County, which are in truth intergrades with both *columbianus* and *fetosus*, *monoensis* is a relatively uniform race. The light color, small size, relatively as well as actually short tail, and short nasals are features maintained over a considerable area.

The correlation of light color and small size on the one hand with the low, hot territory of southern and western Nevada on the other is about the same in the two species, *Dipodomys ordii* and *Dipodomys microps*. The geographic area occupied by *D. m. occidentalis* is about the same as that occupied by the three races, *inaquosus*, *monoensis*, and *fetosus*, of *D. ordii*. Light color characterizes all of these, as it does *D. m. occidentalis*. The difference is that in *D. ordii* the range of variation in color is a little greater over the same geographic area than it is in *D. microps*. Much the same is true of range of size. The differences in geographic distribution of characters, then, is less than a comparison of the distribution maps would at first glance lead one to suppose.

Records of occurrence.—Specimens examined, 221, as follows: *Washoe Co.:* ½ mi. S Pyramid Lake, 3950 ft., 1; 1½ mi. N Wadsworth, 4100 ft., 2. *Lyon Co.:* 6 mi. NE Fernley, 1; 1 mi. SE Wadsworth, 4200 ft., 7; Wilson Canyon, 8 mi. NE Wellington, 1; West Walker River, Smiths Valley, 4700 ft., 4; Mason Valley, 10 mi. S Yerington, 4500 ft., 6. *Pershing Co.:* 21 mi. W and 2 mi. N Lovelock, 4000 ft., 2; 3 to 3¼ mi. NNE Toulon, 3900 ft., 7; ½ mi. NE Toulon, 3900 ft., 1; Toulon, 3930 ft., 5. *Churchill Co.:* 2 mi. W Hazen, 1; Truckee Canal, 2 mi. SW Hazen, 4000 ft., 1; 1 mi. NW Soda Lake, 4000 ft., 9; 1 mi. S Soda Lake, 4000 ft., 1; 5 mi. W Fallon, 4000 ft., 2; 4 mi. W Fallon, 4000 ft., 2; 1 mi. W Mountain Well, 5350 ft., 3; Eastgate, 4400 ft., 13. *Mineral Co.:* 8 mi. SE Schurz, 4100 ft., 18; Fingerrock Wash, 5400 ft., Stewart Valley, 4; Cat Creek, 4500 ft., 4 mi. W Hawthorne, 1; Huntoon Valley, 5700 ft., 1. *Esmeralda Co.:* 13½ mi. NW Goldfield, 4850 ft., 3; 7 mi. N Arlemont, 5500 ft., 6; Arlemont, 4900 ft., 16; mouth of Palmetto Wash, 5500 ft., 2 (D. R. Dickey Coll.); 2 mi. NW Palmetto, 5900 ft., 2 (D. R. Dickey Coll.); 1 mi. NW Palmetto, 6000 ft., 5 (D. R. Dickey Coll.); Palmetto, 6100 ft., 1 (D. R. Dickey Coll.); 1 mi. SE Palmetto, 6200 ft., 1 (D. R. Dickey Coll.); Pigeon Spring, 6400 ft., 1; Palmetto Wash, 7000 ft., 3 (D. R. Dickey Coll.); Indian Spring, Mt. Magruder, 7700 ft., 1 (D. R. Dickey Coll.). *Nye Co.:* 2 mi. S Millett P. O., 5500 ft., 1; 4 mi. SE Millett P. O., 5500 ft., 11; 5 mi. SE Millett P. O., 5500 ft., 5; 4 mi. S Millett, 5500 ft., 2; Millman Ranch, Moore Creek, 19 mi. SE Millett P. O., 6400 ft., 9; Meadow Creek Ranger Station, Toquima Mts., 2; 9 to 10½ mi. E Toquima Mtn., Monitor Valley, 6900–7000 ft., 19; ½ mi. N Fish Lake, Fish Spring Valley, 6500 ft., 3; Fish Lake, Fish Spring Valley, 6800 ft., 1; 2½ mi. S Lock's Ranch, Railroad Valley, 5000 ft., 1; 9 mi. S Lock's Ranch, Railroad Valley, 5000 ft., 1; 12½ mi. S Lock's Ranch, Railroad Valley, 5000 ft., Able Spring, 3; Hot Creek Valley, 3½ mi. E Hot Creek, 5650 ft., 1; Hot Creek Valley, 4/5 mi. S Hot Creek, 5900 ft., 1; 5½ mi. NE San Antonio, 5700 ft., 1; San Antonio, 5400–5406 ft., 2; 9 mi. W and 3 mi. S Tybo, 6200 ft., 2; 15½ mi. NE Tonopah, Ralston Valley, 5800 ft., 2; Nyala, 5100 ft., 5; Big Creek, Quinn Canyon Mts., 5800 ft., 1; 34 mi. E and 1 mi. N Tonopah, Ralston Valley, 5650 ft., 2; Old Mill, N end Reveille Valley, 6200 ft., 6; 1½ mi. S Silverbow, 6400 ft., Kawich Mts., 1; 5 7/10 mi. SE Kawich, 5400 ft., Kawich Valley, 2; 5 mi. W White Rock Spring, 6950 ft., Belted Range, 2; 1 mi. N Beatty, 3400 ft., 1 (D. R. Dickey Coll.).

Dipodomys ordii fetosus Durrant and Hall
Ord Kangaroo Rat

Dipodomys ordii fetosus Durrant and Hall, Mammalia, 3:14, March, 1939. Type from 2 miles north of Panaca, 4800 feet, Lincoln County, Nevada.

Dipodomys ordii, Hall and Dale, Occas. Papers, Mus. Zoöl., Louisiana State Univ., (no.) 4:48, November 10, 1939.

Distribution.—Southeastern Nevada in Lincoln County and east of the Quinn Canyon Mountains in Nye County. See figure 301.

Remarks.—Measurements of six males and seven females from the vicinity of Panaca are: ♂, 240 (232–249), ♀, 232 (226–237); 133 (126–140), 127 (123–134); 41.8 (40–43), 40.6 (40.0–41.5); weight of three males and one female from 21 mi. W Panaca, ♂, 59.7 (56.0–65.0), ♀, 49.1 grams.

Size small in external measurements, excepting hind foot, which is large; color pale, near (16″) Pinkish Buff on upper parts, marked with fine lines of dusky; white supra-orbital patches small; black arietiform facial markings poorly developed anteriorly; skull large; nasals of moderate length.

From *monoensis, fetosus* differs in longer tail and hind foot, in slightly more reddish coloration, and in larger skull. Comparison with *columbianus* is made in the account of that race.

The greater total length of animals from Coal Valley and Garden Valley and the slightly darker color of animals from the latter valley indicate intergradation with *columbianus*. The circumstance that few of the animals referred to *fetosus* are in fresh pelage makes difficult an accurate appraisal of the difference in color obtaining between it and *monoensis*. Although the upper parts are slightly more reddish than in *monoensis*, there is nowhere near so much reddish in the pelage of *fetosus* as there is in that of *D. o. cupidineus*, the race to the eastward.

The interorbital breadth in topotypes is less than in other populations from Lincoln County assigned to this race. Thus, the figure given in the table of cranial measurements (table 11, pp. 430–431) is less than it normally is in this race.

Records of occurrence.—Specimens examined, 99, as follows: *Nye Co.:* White River Valley, 15 mi. WSW Sunnyside, 5500 ft., 27; same, except 16½ mi., 6; Garden Valley, 14 mi. NNE Sharp, 1; Garden Valley, 14½ to 15 mi. NE Sharp, 4; Garden Valley, 8½ mi. NE Sharp, 17. *Lincoln Co.:* E side Coal Valley, 14 mi. N Seeman Pass, 4850 ft., 4; 2 mi. SE Pioche, 6000 ft., 1; Coal Valley, 10 mi. N Seeman Pass, 4650 ft., 1; Desert Valley, 5400 ft., 20 mi. SW Pioche, 1; 2 mi. N Panaca, 4800 ft., 16; Desert Valley, 5300 ft., 21 mi. W Panaca, 10; Panaca, 4700 ft., 7; Crystal Spring, 4000 ft., Pahranagat Valley, 2; 10 mi. E Crystal Spring, 1; 15 mi. S Groom Baldy, 1.

Dipodomys microps
Chisel-toothed Kangaroo Rat

Five races of the chisel-toothed kangaroo rat are known from Nevada; this is the "metropolis" of the species, for it ranges only a short way into each of the adjoining states. *D. microps* is a medium-sized, five-toed kangaroo rat of a color slightly darker than average for the genus. The hind foot varies from 39 to 44 millimeters in length, and the tail amounts to about 135 per cent of the length of the head and body or 57 per cent of the total length. The color, employing specimens of the race *centralis*, may be described as follows: upper parts nearest (16"c) Cinnamon-Buff mixed with blackish; underparts, inside of hind legs and hind feet (soles excepted), forelegs and feet, upper lips, hip stripes, and lateral stripes of tail and its superior base white; supraorbital spots and postauricular patches white, with a few black hairs; vibrissae, arietiform facial markings, soles of hind feet, dorsal and ventral stripes of tail, and sometimes inside of cheek pouches blackish. Notable features of the skull are: interparietal narrow; dorsolateral face of maxillary arm of zygomatic arch narrow; lower incisors with anterior faces flattened. The flat face is a unique feature among Nevadan species.

302   303

Figs. 302, 303. Anterior view of lower jaws showing awl-shaped lower incisors in *Dipodomys ordii* and chisel-shaped lower incisors in *Dipodomys microps*. Both, × 2.

Fig. 302. *Dipodomys ordii columbianus*, 4½ miles northeast Painted Point, no. 73541, ♂.
Fig. 303. *Dipodomys microps aquilonius*, 3½ miles east Flanigan, no. 73616, ♂.

The Upper Sonoran Life-zone is the home of *microps*. In this zone it is to be looked for from the sagebrush belt down through the shadscale into the greasewood belt, rather than in the more elevated, timbered belt where piñons and junipers grow. In these shrub-supporting areas, *microps*, although widely distributed, does not live so far out on alkaline lands toward, for example, a true salt flat devoid of vegetation, as does *Dipodomys merriami*. Despite the zonal preference just noted, *microps* does occur in the Lower Sonoran Life-zone, for example near Las Vegas. At the other extreme, we have found it just entering the piñon-juniper belt. This was at Breen Creek in the Kawich Mountains of Nye County. The elevation there is 7000 feet. Ninety per cent or more of the available specimens come from elevations of between 3500 and 6500 feet.

Part of the range of *microps* is shared with *Dipodomys deserti*, a much larger, lighter colored animal with only four toes on the hind foot, and with *Dipodomys merriami*, an animal smaller than *microps*, and, like *deserti*, with only four toes on the hind foot. Along the western margin of its range, *microps* is sometimes taken in the same place as *Dipodomys panamintinus*, also a five-toed species which resembles it in color. Most of the populations of *panamintinus* occur at elevations higher than those of *microps*. *D. panamintinus* is larger, and in my experience can always be distinguished from *microps* by the larger hind foot, which is more than 44 millimeters long in areas where the two species occur together. *D. microps*, *D. merriami*, *D. deserti*, and *D. ordii* have repeatedly been taken together on the same ground. The last-mentioned species occurs over all but the southwestern part of the range.of *microps*. There, *microps* is able to tolerate slightly lower zonal territory and pushes farther south than does *ordii*.

Compared with *ordii*, *microps* generally has the color darker, the dark ventral stripe on the tail extended all the way to the tip rather than terminated short of the tip, black stripes on tail wider than white stripes, lining of cheek pouches dusky rather than white, hind foot longer, interparietal and zygomatic arm of maxilla narrower, and upper incisors subequally, rather than equally, grooved. Nevertheless, no one of these characters can be relied upon to distinguish the two species at all localities. The similarity of the two animals probably explains why *microps* was unrecognized until as late as 1904. The two species can readily be distinguished by the shape of the incisors in the lower jaw. In *microps* these teeth are flat on the anterior face and chisellike, whereas in *ordii* they are rounded and awllike (see figs. 302, 303).

The contents of the cheek pouches of five rats of this species, as identified by Frank B. Richardson, are recorded below. To the right of the items identified there is given the locality, date, name of the collector, and his field number.

Atriplex confertifolia (leaves)............ ⎫ Marietta, 4900 feet, Mineral Co., June 2,
Grayia spinosa (leaves).................⎭ 1928 (L. Kellogg, 242).

Lepidium Fremontii (leaves)............. 5½ mi. SE Oasis, 5300 ft., Esmeralda Co., June 16, 1927 (E. R. Hall, 1872).

Atriplex (argentea?) (leaves)............. 2 mi. S Millett P. O., 5500 ft., Nye Co., June 3, 1930 (J. M. Linsdale, 3264).

Trifolium (variegatum?) (leaves)........ ⎫ 5 mi. SE Millett P. O., 5500 ft., Nye Co.,
Atriplex (confertifolia?) (2 leaves)....... ⎭ April 22, 1930 (J. M. Linsdale, 2908).

Cryptantha circumcissa (seeds and carpels) ⎫ 9 mi. W Groom Baldy, 5500 ft., Lincoln Co.,
Grass (a few blades)................. ⎬ May 29, 1931 (J. K. Doutt, 676).
Compositae (one seed)............... ⎭

The pouches of another animal trapped near Vernon held green leaves of *Sarcobatus*.

Burt (1934:414) found both dry seeds and green vegetation in the cheek pouches of these rats in southern Nevada and mentions "plantain (*Plantago* sp.), peppergrass (*Lepidium* sp.), sage brush (*Artemisia* sp. leaves), and quail brush (*Atriplex* sp. leaves)."

C. N. Baldwin (MS) credits kangaroo rats, thought to be of this species, with vocal calls. At late dusk, on June 2, 1932, in Penoyer Valley, 17 miles north of Groom Baldy, he frightened from beneath a bush, two rats that ran ahead and stopped, each in an open space, approximately 35 feet away. The rats were about 35 feet apart. "Immediately after I had disturbed them one . . . started a . . . call. One could probably have heard it clearly five rods away."

The call was continued "for 5 minutes with only occasional interrupted periods of silence sufficient to allow respiration."

Of 315 mature females examined for embryos, 39 were pregnant. The num-

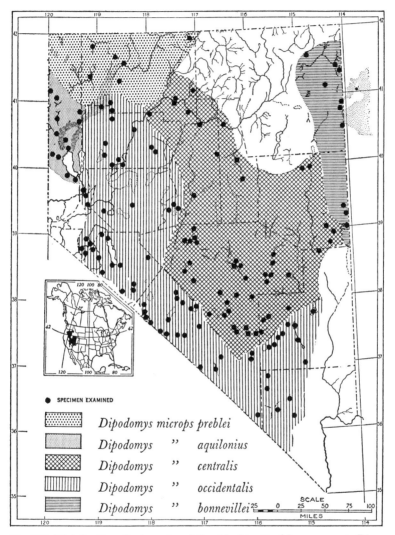

Fig. 304. Distribution of subspecies of the chisel-toothed kangaroo rat, *Dipodomys microps*, with insert showing range of the species.

ber of embryos averaged 2.3, with extremes of 1 and 4. The mode was 2 (2 ♀ with 1 embryo; 27 ♀ with 2; 7 ♀ with 3; 3 ♀ with 4). By months the females were distributed as follows: April, 11 (5 of which were pregnant); May, 82 (16);

June, 72 (11); July, 138 (7); August, 20 (0); September, 29 (0). No females were taken from October to March, inclusive. From what is known of other species in the genus, I suppose that most of the young are born before April.

Dipodomys microps preblei (Goldman)
Chisel-toothed Kangaroo Rat

Perodipus microps preblei Goldman, Journ. Mamm., 2:233, November 29, 1921. Type from Narrows, Malheur Lake, Harney County, Oregon.
Dipodomys microps preblei, Miller, Bull. U. S. Nat. Mus., 128:297, April 29, 1924; Hall and Dale, Occas. Papers, Mus. Zoöl., Louisiana State Univ., (no.) 4:54, November 10, 1939.
Dipodomys microps levipes, Taylor, Univ. California Publ. Zoöl., 7:267, June 24, 1911, part.

Distribution.—Northeastern Washoe County and northern Humboldt County south to 17 miles south of Quinn River Crossing. See figure 304.

Remarks.—Measurements of three males from Narrows, Buena Vista, and Summer Lake, Oregon, and a young female from Narrows, Oregon, are: ♂, 275 (269–281), ♀, 264; 162 (158–167), 155; 41.6 (41–42), 40.0. No weights are available.

Size medium, except that body is short; color about as in *centralis*, but less blackish and more cinnamon on sides, with dark tail-stripes brownish rather than blackish; skull small, but relatively broad interorbitally.

From *centralis*, *preblei* differs in: body shorter; color darker; skull smaller in all measurements taken except interorbital breadth and breadth of nasals. From *aquilonius*, *preblei* differs in: color lighter; body and hind foot shorter; nasals relatively longer; maxillary breadth actually greater and especially greater relative to greatest breadth of skull and to basal length. From *occidentalis*, *preblei* differs in: color darker; skull relatively narrower across bullae, but relatively as well as actually broader interorbitally; maxillary breadth greater relative to greatest breadth.

There are still too few adult specimens of *preblei* from Oregon in the vicinity of the type locality to give an accurate measure of its characters. Evidences of intergradation with more southern races are furnished by specimens from Lake Alvord, Oregon. In these, the breadth across the maxillary processes of the zygomatic arches amounts to only 80.6 per cent of the greatest breadth across the auditory bullae. In this character the specimens are more nearly like *aquilonius* and *occidentalis*. Specimens from Quinn River Crossing, although referable to *preblei*, resemble *aquilonius* and *centralis* in longer hind foot, greater basal length of skull, and greater breadth across tympanic bullae.

The single specimen from 36 miles northeast of Paradise Valley is too young to display fully the characters relied upon in differentiating *preblei*. Adult specimens from there might prove to be referable to some other subspecies.

Records of occurrence.—Specimens examined, 30, as follows: *Humboldt Co.:* 36 mi. NE Paradise Valley, 5500 ft., 1; Virgin Valley, 1; Big Creek Ranch, base of Pine Forest Mts., 1; 1½ mi. N Quinn River Crossing, 4100 ft., 6; Quinn River Crossing, 7; 2 mi. SW Quinn River Crossing, 4000 ft., 1; 2½ mi. SW Quinn River Crossing, 4100 ft., 1; Soldier Meadows, 4600 ft., 8; Jackson Creek Ranch, 4000 ft., 17½ mi. S and 5 mi. W Quinn River Crossing, 4.

Dipodomys microps aquilonius Willett
Chisel-toothed Kangaroo Rat

Dipodomys microps aquilonius Willett, Journ. Mamm., 16:63, February 14, 1935. Type from 3 miles east of Eagleville, Modoc County, California. Hall and Dale, Occas. Papers, Mus. Zoöl., Louisiana State Univ., (no.) 4:55, November 10, 1939.
Perodipus microps preblei, Bailey, N. Amer. Fauna, 55:239, August 29, 1936.

Distribution.—Washoe County from Surprise Valley south to near southern end of Pyramid Lake. See figure 304.

Remarks.—Measurements of four males and two females from within 10 miles of Hausen are: ♂, 276 (260–289), ♀, 274 (274, 273); 156 (142–170), 156 (152, 159); 42.8 (41–44), 41.8 (41.0, 42.5); weight, 65.0 (60.9–75.6), 57.1 (56.4, 57.7) grams.

Size medium; color dark; upper parts heavily mixed with blackish, which is present in maximum degree for the species throughout the dark-colored areas; skull medium-sized, relatively narrow across the maxillary processes, and broad interorbitally.

From *centralis*, *aquilonius* differs in darker color and narrower skull. For comparison with *preblei*, see account of that form. From *occidentalis*, *aquilonius* differs in: color darker; body averages longer; weight greater; skull broader interorbitally.

D. m. aquilonius is a long-bodied form, but its range is separated from those of the other long-bodied forms by the ranges of the shorter-bodied *occidentalis* and *preblei*. The dark color of *aquilonius* is especially distinctive in comparison with the adjoining light-colored race, *occidentalis*. *D. m. aquilonius* is darker also than *preblei*. Cotypes of *aquilonius* are paler than other specimens, possibly as a result of preservation for a time in a salt-alum-pickle solution.

Records of occurrence.—Specimens examined, 45, as follows: *Washoe Co.*: 1 mi. W Hausen, 5650 ft., 2; Hausen, 4800 ft., 1; 2½ mi. SE Hausen, 5200 ft., 3; 10 mi. SE Hausen, 4675 ft., 2; 12 mi. N and 2 mi. E Gerlach, 4000 ft., 3; 3 mi. E and 10 mi. N Gerlach, 4000 ft., 2; Granite Creek, 1 (U. S. Nat. Mus., Biol. Surv. Coll.); 17½ mi. W Deep Hole, 4750 ft., 1; 5 mi. N Gerlach, 3900 ft., 3; 1 mi. NE Gerlach, 4000 ft., 2; Smoke Creek, 9 mi. E Calif. boundary, 3900 ft., 7; 4 mi. NW Pahrum Peak, 4200 ft., 2; Fox Canyon, 6 mi. S Pahrum Peak, 4800 ft., 5; Flanigan, 4200 ft. (3½ mi. NW, 1; 3½ mi. NE, 1; ½ mi. NW, 1; 2½ mi. E, 2; 3½ mi. E, 2), 7; 2¾ mi. SW Pyramid, 4300 ft., 2; ½ mi. S Pyramid Lake, 3950 ft., 2.

Dipodomys microps centralis Hall and Dale
Chisel-toothed Kangaroo Rat

Dipodomys microps centralis Hall and Dale, Occas. Papers, Mus. Zoöl., Louisiana State Univ., (no.) 4:52, November 10, 1939. Type from 4 miles southeast of Romano, Diamond Valley, Eureka County, Nevada.
Dipodomys microps, Linsdale, Amer. Midland Nat., 19:187, January, 1938.

Distribution.—Central Nevada from the Humboldt River Valley south to Pahute Mesa and from northeastern Pershing County, Reese River Valley, Great Smoky, and Ralston valleys east to Steptoe and Spring valleys. See figure 304.

Remarks.—Measurements of three males from near Romano and three females from near Battle Mountain and Cortez are: ♂, 286 (282–288), ♀, 272 (266–277); 167 (164–169), 156 (151–161); 43.3 (43–44), 41.3 (41–42); weight, 73.2 (70.8–76.1), 63.1 (61.2–66.3) grams.

Size medium; color dark, as described for the species; skull of medium size.

Comparisons with adjoining races are made in the accounts of those forms.

In the southern part of its range, *centralis* approaches *occidentalis* in color, but otherwise agrees with topotypes. *D. m. centralis* occupies a central position geographically in the species. Its position with respect to structure is similar; it is neither the darkest nor the lightest, and in size is larger than some races and smaller than others.

Records of occurrence.—Specimens examined, 302, as follows: *Humboldt Co.*: 18 mi. NE Iron Point, 4600 ft., 5; 16 mi. NE Iron Point, 4500 ft., 4; 5 mi. NE Golconda, 4; 2 mi. E Golconda, 2; 23 mi. NW Battle Mountain, 2. *Pershing Co.*: 15 mi. SW Winnemucca, 1. *Lander Co.*: 1 mi. E Battle Mountain, 2; 1½ mi. NW Cortez, Cortez Mts., 4; Reese River Valley, 7 mi. N Austin, 2. *Eureka Co.*: ½ mi. S Beowawe, 3; Winzell, 1; 4 mi. S Romano, Diamond Valley, 3; 4 mi. SE Romano, Diamond Valley, 6. *Nye Co.*: 4 mi. N Millett, 5500 ft., 1; 2 mi. S Millett P. O., 5500 ft., 6; 4 mi. SE Millett, 5500 ft., 3; 4 mi. S Millett, 5500 ft., 2; Ophir Creek, 6500 ft., 1; 5 mi. SE Millett P. O., 5500 ft., 6; 5 mi. S Millett (5500 ft., 1; 5700 ft., 2), 3; South Twin River, 6500 ft., 28; Railroad Valley, 2½ to 3¼ mi. S Lock's Ranch, 5000 ft., 10; Railroad Valley, 9 mi. S Lock's Ranch, 5000 ft., 4; Hot Creek Valley, 6½ mi. N Hot Creek, 5100 ft., 2; 11½ mi. NE San Antonio, 5700 ft., 3; Railroad Valley, 12½ mi. S Lock's Ranch, Able Spring, 5000 ft., 1; Hot Creek Valley, ¼ mi. W Hot Creek, 5900 ft., 3; Hot Creek Valley, 4/5 mi. E Hot Creek, 6000 ft., 3; Hot Creek Valley, 3½ mi. E Hot Creek, 5650 ft., 9; 4 to 5¾ mi. NE San Antonio, 5650–5700 ft., 4; San Antonio, 5400 ft., 1; Railroad Valley, 2 mi. N Nyala, 5100 ft., 3; Railroad Valley, 2 mi. NE Nyala, 5100 ft., 9; White River Valley, 15 mi. WSW Sunnyside, 5500 ft., 2; S end

Hot Creek Valley, 2½ mi. E and N Twin Spring, 5400 ft., 5; Ralston Valley, 15½ mi. NE Tonopah, 5800 ft., 18; Railroad Valley, Nyala, 5100 ft., 6; Railroad Valley, 3 mi. S Nyala, 5600 ft., 1; Ralston Valley, 34 mi. E and 1 mi. N Tonopah, 5650 ft., 15; N end Reveille Valley, Old Mill, 6200 ft., 14; Railroad Valley, 9½ mi. E New Reveille, 5100 ft., 3; Breen Creek, Kawich Range, 7000 ft., 8; 1½ mi. S Silverbow, Kawich Mts., 6450 ft., 2; 2 mi. S Silverbow, 6400 ft., 3; 3 2/5 mi. S Silverbow, 6200 ft., 1; Cactus Flat, 6000 ft., 5 mi. SW Silverbow, 1; 5½ mi. SW Silverbow, 6000 ft., 7; Cactus Flat, 5750 ft., 6½ mi. SW Silverbow, 2; 1 mi. SW Cactus Spring, Cactus Range, 1; Gold Flat, 5200 ft., 5 mi. W Kawich P. O., 1; 4½ mi. NW Indian Spring, Kawich Valley, 5700 ft., 3; 8 mi. NE Wheelbarrow Peak, 1; Kawich Valley, 5400 ft., 5 mi. SE Kawich P. O., 4; Gold Flat, 6100 ft., 6 mi. SW Kawich P. O., 3; 2½ mi. NW Indian Spring, Belted Range, 6200 ft., 1; 9 mi. E Wheelbarrow Peak, 2. *White Pine Co.:* Cherry Creek, 6600 ft., 2; 5 mi. SE Greens Ranch, Steptoe Valley, 5900 ft., 2; 7 mi. SW Osceola, Spring Valley, 6100 ft., 9; R. 67 E, T. 12 N, 5½ mi. NW Shoshone P. O., 6100 ft., 2; Spring Valley, 4 mi. S Shoshone, 5900 ft., 2. *Lincoln Co.:* Duck Valley, 3 mi. S Geyser, 6050 ft., 1; Coal Valley, 10 mi. N Seeman Pass, 4650 ft., 5; Penoyer Valley, 17 mi. N Groom Baldy, 10; Penoyer Valley, 14 mi. NNW Groom Baldy, 2; 9 mi. W Groom Baldy, 5500 ft., 22.

Dipodomys microps occidentalis Hall and Dale
Chisel-toothed Kangaroo Rat

Dipodomys microps occidentalis Hall and Dale, Occas. Papers, Mus. Zoöl., Louisiana State Univ., (no.) 4:56, November 10, 1939. Type from 3 miles south of Schurz, 4100 feet, Mineral County, Nevada. *Dipodomys microps levipes*, Burt, Trans. San Diego Soc. Nat. Hist., 7:414, May 31, 1934.

Distribution.—Western and southern Nevada: south from southern Humboldt County to Las Vegas; east from Black Rock Desert and southwestern boundary of state to Smiths Creek Valley in Lander County; east from Mud Lake in Nye County (south of Pahute Mesa) to a point 21 miles west of Panaca in Desert Valley. See figure 304.

Remarks.—Measurements of four males and seven females from the vicinity of Schurz are: ♂, 260 (254–266), ♀, 271 (256–274); 148 (140–156), 160 (146–168); 42.0 (40–42), 41.5 (40–43); weight, 60.4 (57.0–63.2), 56.4 (48.4–62.9) grams.

Size small; body short; color pale, less blackish in upper parts and arietiform facial markings more restricted than in *centralis;* darkest areas brownish as opposed to blackish; skull small.

From *centralis*, *occidentalis* differs in: color lighter, as noted above; skull smaller and relatively narrower across bullae and maxillary processes. From *levipes*, a race to the westward, in California, *occidentalis* differs in: external measurements less, especially length of body; weight a fourth less in males and a fifth less in females; skull smaller in all measurements taken, except breadth of nasals and interorbital breadth, which are about the same in the two races, but skull relatively broader. From *microps,* another race to the westward, in California, *occidentalis* differs in: size slightly greater; color slightly darker; skull larger, relatively as well as actually broader; nasals relatively shorter; maxillary breadth 81 per cent, as opposed to 86 per cent of breadth across bullae. From *celsus*, a race to the southeastward, in Arizona, *occidentalis* differs in: external measurements smaller; weight a fourth (24 per cent) less in males and a fifth (18 per cent) less in females; color lighter; skull smaller in all measurements taken, with uniformly shorter nasals; nasals relatively as well as actually shorter. From *bonnevillei, occidentalis* differs in: body shorter; all cranial measurements less except breadth of nasals in females and interorbital breadth in both sexes, the latter breadth averaging relatively larger. For comparisons with *preblei* and *aquilonius*, see accounts of those forms.

In the northern part of its range, specimens of *occidentalis* average larger and darker than in the vicinity of the type locality. Intergradation with *centralis* is shown by the animals from Smiths Creek Valley, which in the sum of their characters are only a little nearer *occidentalis* than *centralis*. This was surprising, because on geographic grounds it was expected that they would agree with *centralis*. Most of the specimens referred to *occidentalis* from southern Nevada south of the range of *centralis*, although light in color, have long bodies suggestive of *celsus, bonnevillei,* and *centralis*.

Records of occurrence.—Specimens examined, 350, as follows: *Washoe Co.:* 1½ mi. N Wadsworth, 4100 ft., 2. *Lyon Co.:* ½ mi. SE Wadsworth, 4200 ft., 1; 3½ mi. W Hazen, 4200–4250 ft., 9; 4 mi. W Hazen, 4250 ft., 6; West Walker River, 6 mi. S Yerington, 4500 ft., 1; 11¾ mi. S and 2¾ mi. E Yerington, 4650 ft., Mason Valley, 2; West Walker River, Smiths Valley, 4700 ft., 1; 12 mi. S Yerington, 4600 ft., West Walker River, 2; Smiths Valley, 7½ mi. NE Wellington, 4900 ft., 1; Mason Valley, 12 mi. E Wellington, 5000 ft., 2. *Humboldt Co.:* 9½ mi. N Sulphur, 4050 ft., 2; 1¼ mi. N Sulphur, 4050 ft., 2; 1 mi. W Sulphur, 4040 ft., 3; ¾ mi. S Sulphur, 4050 ft., 1. *Pershing Co.:* 10 mi. W and 6 mi. N Sulphur, 4000 ft., 1; 8 mi. S Sulphur, 4350 ft., 8; 1 mi. W Humboldt, 4180 ft., 7; 3 mi. SW Vernon, 4300 ft., 3; 2½ mi. S Vernon, 4250 ft., 1; 3 mi. S Vernon, 4250 ft., 12; 9 mi. E Fanning, 4100 ft., 7; 9½ mi. E and 1 mi. S Fanning, 4100 ft., 7; 10 mi. E and 3 mi. S Fanning, 4100 ft., 2; S slope Granite Peak, East Range, 1; 21 mi. W and 2 mi. N Lovelock, 4000 ft., 9; 3 mi. NNE Toulon, 3900 ft., 3; 1½ mi. NE Toulon, 3900 ft., 2; 3½ mi. NE Toulon, 3950 ft., 6; 3½ mi. W Toulon, 4500 ft., 3; 2 mi. W Toulon, 4300 ft., 12; 1 mi. W Toulon, 4000 ft., 1; Toulon, 3930 ft., 1; 3 mi. E Toulon, 3900 ft., 1. *Churchill Co.:* 1 mi. W Mountain Well, 5350 ft., 1; Mountain Well, 5600 ft., 1; 7, 8, and 12 mi. SW Fallon, 3 (coll. of J. R. Alcorn). *Mineral Co.:* 7 mi. NW Schurz, 4500 ft., 3; 3 mi. S Schurz, 4100 ft., 11; Mason Valley, 5 mi. N Pine Grove, 5300 ft., 3; East Walker River, 5100 ft., 2 mi. NW Morgans Ranch, 1; Fingerrock Wash, 5400 ft., Stewart Valley, 1; Cat Creek, 4500 ft., 4 mi. W Hawthorne, 3; Fletcher, 6098 ft., 1; Marietta, 4900 ft., 2; S side Teels Marsh, 4900 ft., 2; Huntoon Valley, 5700 ft., 7. *Esmeralda Co.:* ½ mi. W Millers Wells, 4800 ft., 1; 2½ mi. NW Blair Junction, 1; Lone Mtn., 12½ mi. W and 2½ mi. S Tonopah, 6600 ft., 1; 4 mi. SE Coaldale, 4850 ft., 1; 13 mi. N Goldfield, 5100 ft., 1; 13½ mi. NW Goldfield, 4850 ft., 3; 7 mi. N Arlemont, 5500 ft., 5; 1½ mi. N Chiatovich Ranch, 4900 ft., 2; 2½ mi. N Dyer, 4850 ft., 6; Fish Lake, 4900 ft., 1; 5 mi. SE Silver Peak, 4500 ft., 1; 2 mi. SE Dyer, 4800 ft., 3; 2½ mi. SE Dyer, 4950 ft., 3; R. 38 E, T. 6 S, 5300 ft., 3; 1 mi. NW Palmetto, 5 (D. R. Dickey Coll.); 2 mi. E Lida, 1 (D. R. Dickey Coll.); 4½ mi. E Lida, 2 (D. R. Dickey Coll.); 8 mi. E Lida, 2 (D. R. Dickey Coll.); 10 mi. E Lida, 5 (D. R. Dickey Coll.). *Lander Co.:* 6 mi. ENE Smiths Creek Ranch, 5500 ft., 2; 2½ mi. NE Smiths Creek Ranch, 5800 ft., 2; Smiths Creek Valley, 5550 ft., 2 mi. W Railroad Pass, 10; Smiths Creek Valley, 5550 ft., 3 mi. W Railroad Pass, 1; Smiths Creek, 5800 ft., 1. *Nye Co.:* N shore Mud Lake, 5300 ft., S end Ralston Valley, 4; Stonewall Flat, 4700 ft., 14 mi. SE Goldfield, 2; 8½ mi. NE Springdale, 4250 ft., 1; 4½ mi. SE Oak Spring, 4500–4750 ft., 3; Emigrant Valley, 9½ mi. S Oak Spring, 4400 ft., 5; 7 mi. E and 2 mi. N Grapevine Peak, 5100 ft., 4; 5 mi. E and 1 mi. N Grapevine Peak, 5500 ft., 1; 8 mi. E Grapevine Peak, 1; Amargosa River, 3½ mi. NE Beatty, 3400 ft., 2; 1 mi. N Beatty, 23 (D. R. Dickey Coll.); 1½ mi. N Pahrump, 3 (D. R. Dickey Coll.). *Lincoln Co.:* Desert Valley, 5300 ft., 21 mi. W Panaca, 3; 9 1/5 mi. NW Crystal Spring, 4800 ft., Pahranagat Valley, 1; 3 mi. N Crystal Spring, 4000 ft., Pahranagat Valley, 1; 1 2/5 mi. W Crystal Spring, Pahranagat Valley, 6; Crystal Spring, 4000 ft., Pahranagat Valley, 6; ¼ mi. E Crystal Spring, 4000 ft., Pahranagat Valley, 5; ½ mi. E Crystal Spring, 4000 ft., Pahranagat Valley, 1; 16 mi. E Groom Baldy, 4600 ft., 5; Desert Valley, 8 mi. SW Hancock Summit, 5200–5300 ft., 10; Alamo, 3570 ft., 3; 5½ mi. N Summit Spring, 4700 ft., 1; 5 mi. N Summit Spring, 4700 ft., 1; 14½ mi. S Groom Baldy, 3; 15 mi. S Groom Baldy, 3; Coyote Spring, 2800 ft., 1. *Clark Co.:* Indian Spring Valley, 14 mi. N Indian Springs, 3100 ft., 1; Indian Springs, 9 (D. R. Dickey Coll.); Corn Creek Station, 23 mi. NW Las Vegas, 6 (D. R. Dickey Coll.); Kyle Canyon, 4500 ft., 8 (D. R. Dickey Coll.); 4 mi. NW Las Vegas, 3 (D. R. Dickey Coll.).

Dipodomys microps bonnevillei Goldman
Chisel-toothed Kangaroo Rat

Dipodomys microps bonnevillei Goldman, Proc. Biol. Soc. Washington, 50:222, December 28, 1937. Type from Kelton, about 4300 feet, Box Elder County, Utah. Hall and Dale, Occas. Papers, Mus. Zoöl., Louisiana State Univ., (no.) 4:58, November 10, 1939.

Distribution.—Eastern Nevada south from near Contact in Elko County to northern Lincoln County. See figure 304.

Remarks.—Measurements of eight males and ten females from 13 miles north of Montello are: ♂, 278 (263–297), ♀, 273 (265–293); 156 (142–174), 154 (145–173); 41.6 (40–43), 40.6 (40–43); weight, 67.3 (60.8–73.7), 65.0 (58.8–72.5) grams.

Size medium, but hind foot short; color pale, less blackish in upper parts, and arietiform facial markings less extensive in *centralis;* darkest areas brownish, as opposed to blackish; skull large and of a shape average for the species.

From *centralis*, *bonnevillei* differs in: hind foot shorter; color lighter; interorbital region narrower. From *celsus*, the race to the southeast, in Utah and Arizona, *bonnevillei* differs in: external measurements less; color lighter; skull smaller in all parts measured; nasals relatively as well as actually shorter; upper incisors wider at tips. For comparison with *occidentalis*, see account of that form. *D. m. bonnevillei* is a light-colored race, and its range corresponds closely to the outline of the Quaternary Lake Bonneville when it was at its maximum height.

Records of occurrence.—Specimens examined, 98, as follows: *Elko Co.:* 15 mi. S Contact, 5800 ft., 7; 13 mi. N Montello, 5000 ft., 16; 1½ mi. NE Tecoma, 4900 ft., 2; Tecoma, 4900 ft., 7; Cobre, 6100 ft., 4; 3 mi. S Wendover, 4250 ft., 4; 8 mi. S Wendover, 4700 ft., 16; Salt Springs, 4200 ft., 1. *White Pine Co.:* 2 mi. W Smith Creek Cave, Mt. Moriah, 6300 ft., 1; near Smith Creek Cave, Mt. Moriah, 5600–5800 ft., 22; 3 mi. E Smith Creek Cave, Mt. Moriah, 5500 ft., 1; Hendry Creek, 8 mi. SE Mt. Moriah, 6200 ft., 1; 1 mi. N Baker, 15; 2½ mi. E Baker, 5700 ft., 1.

Dipodomys merriami merriami Mearns
Merriam Kangaroo Rat

Dipodomys merriami Mearns, Bull. Amer. Mus. Nat. Hist., 2:290, February 21, 1890. Type from New River, between Prescott and Maricopa, Maricopa County, Arizona. Hall and Dale, Occas. Papers, Mus. Zoöl., Louisiana State Univ., (no.) 4:48, November 10, 1939.

Dipodomys merriami nevadensis Merriam, Proc. Biol. Soc. Washington, 9:111, June 21, 1894. Type from Pyramid Lake, Washoe County, Nevada. Taylor, Univ. California Publ. Zoöl., 7:272, June 24, 1911.

Dipodomys merriami merriami, Burt, Trans. San Diego Soc. Nat. Hist., 7:413, May 31, 1934.

Distribution.—Lower Sonoran Life-zone of southern Nevada and low western part of state in the salt-desert area north to Quinn River Crossing, Humboldt County. See figure 305.

Remarks.—Average and extreme measurements of ten of each sex from 14 miles east of Searchlight are: ♂, 249 (243–259), ♀, 248 (240–254); 150 (142–161), 146 (140–156); 38.6 (37.9–39.2), 38.1 (36.0–41.0); weight, 42.5 (38.4–46.9), 39.2 (34.9–44.7) grams.

By weight, *D. merriami* is the smallest Nevadan species of the genus; tail amounts to 147 per cent (shorter to northward) of length of head and body and 60 per cent of total length; hind foot slender and four-toed; upper parts often lighter than Ochraceous-Buff; auditory bullae large; interparietal small, narrow; unique among Nevadan species in that interorbital breadth is more than half of basal length.

Typically, *D. merriami* is an inhabitant of the Lower Sonoran Life-zone, and, like some other species of that zone, ranges far northward in the Upper Sonoran Life-zone along the eastern base of the Sierra Nevada. There, the low-lying territory, which consists of sinks and alkali flats alternating with sandy areas and which supports *Atriplex*, *Sarcobatus*, and related shrubs of a zonal position lower than *Artemisia tridentata*, provides habitats favorable to the species *merriami*. It was in this kind of territory that we found *merriami* on Gold Flat, which is isolated by higher terrain of different floral aspect from the rest of the known range of the species.

D. merriami has been caught in the same places as each of the other four Nevadan species, but it ranges farther out on alkali flats than any of the others. Sometimes, *Dipodomys merriami* is the only species of its genus to be found on crusted areas where only an occasional bush grows and catches fine sand, but farther back, away from the alkali flat, other species, often along with *merriami*, abound.

Several names proposed for subspecies of *merriami* might apply to Nevadan populations. *Dipodomys merriami nevadensis* Merriam, with type locality at Pyramid Lake, is one. The features mentioned in the original description which differentiate it from *D. m. merriami* are shorter tail, longer hind foot, and lighter color. Certainly, the first and last features hold. Benson (1934:182) has pointed out that topotypes of *D. m. merriami*, although darker than near-by populations, scarcely differ from these near-by populations in other features. He shows also that the variation, darker color, of topotypes is reproduced at widely separated points within the range of the animal currently designated as the subspecies *merriami*. On this account the slight difference in color between topotypes of *merriami* and topotypes of *nevadensis* is regarded as of but slight importance systematically. Geographically, length of hind foot behaves in much the same way as color. Length of tail, on the contrary, is in a different category. It is definitely shorter to the northward.

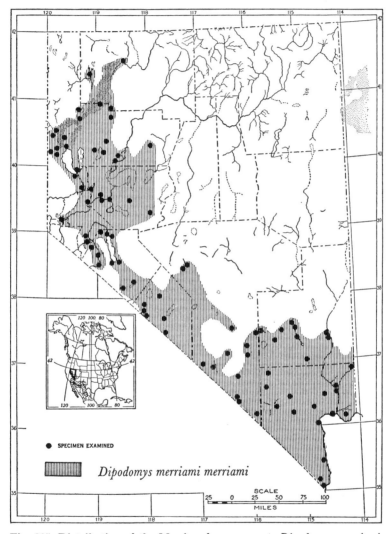

Fig. 305. Distribution of the Merriam kangaroo rat, *Dipodomys merriami*, with insert showing range of the species.

Between Soldier Meadows, Humboldt County, and the extreme southern tip of Nevada, near Searchlight, a distance of 467 miles from northwest to southeast (404 miles north to south), the change in length of tail is actually 14 millimeters.

In figure 306, which shows variation in length of tail at seven places in this distance, it may be seen that the length increases to the southward and that the trend is gradual. Pertinent facts not ascertainable from this figure are that over the Lower Sonoran Life-zone, within Nevada, the tail is of relatively constant length. For example, the length, expressed as a percentage of the length of the head and body, in animals from Meadow Valley Wash, 21 to 25 miles south of Caliente, is 143 per cent, about the same as at Beatty, 125 miles westward. Also, in the southern tip of the state, about 160 miles south of the two places just mentioned, the length is only slightly more.

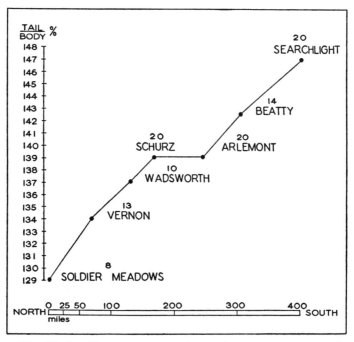

Fig. 306. Graphic representation showing increase in length of tail of Merriam kangaroo rat, *Dipodomys merriami*, from Soldier Meadows in the north to Searchlight in the south.

In addition to shorter tail to the northward, animals there have slightly smaller mas-toidal bullae, and the dorsal longitudinal outline of the skull, as viewed from the side, is more rounded. This, then, is the geographic variation found.

As to use of the name *nevadensis* for the northern animals, it may be said that Merriam was correct in his selection of features differentiating topotypes of *merriami* and *nevadensis*. Because two of these features, length of hind foot and color of upper parts, vary first one way and then the other from place to place, only length of tail remains as distinctive of animals over a considerable geographic area. This variation appears to be as well shown by description as by employing the subspecific name *nevadensis*. The name is arranged as a synonym of *D. m. merriami*.

None of the Nevadan specimens shows characters of *Dipodomys merriami vulcani* from northwestern Arizona, nor of *Dipodomys merriami frenatus* from southwestern Utah, which appears to be a synonym of *vulcani*.

Dipodomys merriami nitratus Merriam, described from Keeler, on the east side of Owens

Lake, Inyo County, California, now is known to owe its supposedly distinctive color to fading of the pelage caused by alkali in the soil where the animal lives. Several specimens from widely separated places in Nevada (Quinn River Crossing, Dyer, and Toulon) in old pelage have this same tawny coloration which extends even to the normally dusky terminal tuft on the tail. The names *Dipodomys merriami mortivallis* Elliot, based on specimens from Death Valley, California, and *Dipodomys merriami kernensis* Merriam, based on specimens from Onyx, California, are regarded as synonyms of *D. m. merriami*.

The amount of secondary sexual variation is slight and less than the range of individual variation in animals of one sex at any given locality. Males average larger than females. The difference is about 2 per cent in linear measurements, including those of the skull, and about 6 per cent in weight.

Individuals in process of molt were taken from July 18 to August 3.

At many places in the Lower Sonoran Life-zone, *merriami* appears to outnumber all other species of rodents combined. Along the Colorado River, 14 miles east of Searchlight, in January and February, 1934, Fitch trapped Merriam kangaroo rats in the arrowweed on sandy soil. They were taken abundantly in sparse, low arrowweed and were uncommon in the tall arrowweed.

Of their food, in Clark County, Burt (1934:413) writes that it "consists of green leaves and seeds as well as the dry seeds of plants. Many of the specimens had dry seeds in their cheek pouches, others green seeds and seed pods or green leaves. Seeds of the following plants were represented in cheek pouch contents: grass (*Festuca octoflora*), pepper-grass (*Lepidum* sp.), goosefoot (*Chenopodium* sp.), mustard (*Cruciferae*), loco-weed (*Astragalus* sp.), *Pentstemon* (?), and mesquite (*Prosopis* sp.)." The contents of the cheek pouches of one of these rats taken on May 10, 1933, at Boulder City (A. M. Alexander, field no. 2107) consisted entirely of seeds and leaves of *Cryptantha circumcissa*. In 1928, at 7 miles north of Arlemont in Fish Lake Valley, seeds of *Malacothrix torreyi* were found in the cheek pouches of one of these rats taken June 1, and the pouches of another taken the following day 1½ miles east of Dyer contained seeds of *Cleomella brevipes*.

Including the animals reported by Alcorn (1941: 88), I have record of 324 mature females examined for embryos. Of these, 72 were pregnant. The number of embryos per litter averaged 3, with extremes of 1 and 5. The mode was 3 (3 ♀ with 1 embryo; 17 ♀ with 2; 30 ♀ with 3; 19 ♀ with 4; 3 ♀ with 5). By months, the females were distributed as follows: January, 19 (0 pregnant); February, 10 (2 of which were pregnant); March, 68 (22); April, 20 (6); May, 54 (15); June, 34 (10); July, 64 (15); August, 42 (1); September, 8, (0); October, 2 (0); November, 0; December, 3 (0). From these data it appears that most of the young are born in spring, from March on through July, although in July relatively fewer females are pregnant than in any one of the four preceding months. On the basis of part of the data given here, Alcorn (*loc. cit.*) suggested that there are two litters per year.

Records of occurrence.—Specimens examined, 601, as follows: *Washoe Co.:* 12 mi. N and 2 mi. E Gerlach, 4000 ft., 2; 11 mi. N and 2½ mi. E Gerlach, 4050 ft., 1; 3 mi. E and 10 mi. N Gerlach, 4000 ft., 1; 5 mi. N Gerlach, 3950 ft., 1; Smoke Creek, 9 mi. E Calif. boundary, 3900 ft., 5; latitude 40° 28' N, 6 mi. E Calif. boundary, 4000 ft., 2; 4 mi. NW Pahrum Peak, 4200 ft., 2; Fox Canyon, 6 mi. S Pahrum Peak, 4800 ft., 3; N side Sand Pass, 3950 ft., 2; 4 mi. NW Flanigan, 4200 ft., 3; 3½ mi. NW Flanigan, 4200 ft., 1; 2 mi. NW Flanigan, 4250 ft., 1; ½ mi. NW Flanigan, 4200 ft., 2; 2½ mi. E Flanigan, 4200–4250 ft., 6; 3½ mi. E Flanigan, 4200 ft., 3; 4½ mi. N and 2½ mi. W Nixon, 1 (coll. of T. J. Trelease); ½ mi. S Pyramid Lake, 3950 ft., 2; 2¼ mi. S Pyramid Lake, 1; ½ mi. N Wadsworth, 4100 ft., 2; 1 mi. W Wadsworth, 12 (9 in coll. of Ralph Ellis, some of which are labeled 34 mi. E Reno). *Ormsby Co.:* 3½ mi. E Carson City, 4700 ft., 1. *Lyon Co.:* 6 mi. NE Fernley, 5; ½ to 1 mi. SE Wadsworth, 4200 ft., 28; 3½ to 4 mi. W Hazen, 4250 ft., 10; West Walker River, 6 mi. S Yerington, 4500 ft., 1; Mason Valley, 10 mi. S Yerington, 4500 ft., 1; Mason Valley, 11¾ mi. S and 2¾ mi. E Yerington, 4650 ft., 2. *Humboldt Co.:* Quinn River Crossing, 1; Soldier Meadows, 4600 ft., 8; 1¼ mi. S Sulphur, 4050 ft., 2. *Pershing Co.:* 10½ mi. W and 6 mi. N Sulphur, 4000 ft., 1; 10 mi. W and 6 mi. N Sulphur, 4000 ft., 2; 8 mi. S Sulphur, 4350 ft., 8; 3 mi. SW Vernon, 4300 ft., 5; 2½ mi. S Vernon, 4250 ft., 1; 3 mi. S Vernon, 4250 ft., 3; 9½ mi. E and 1 mi. S Fanning, Buena Vista Valley, 4100 ft., 3; 30 mi. W and 4 mi. N Lovelock, 4300 ft., 7; 30 mi. W and 3 mi. N Lovelock, 4300 ft., 1; 21 mi. W and 2 mi. N Lovelock, 4000 ft., 6; 3 to 3¼ mi. NNE Toulon, 3900 ft., 6; 3½ mi. NE Toulon, 4500 ft., 2; Toulon, 3930 ft., 12. *Churchill Co.:* 1 mi. NW Soda Lake, 4000 ft., 2; 1 mi. S Soda Lake, 4000 ft., 2; 5 mi. W Fallon, 1; 4 mi. W Fallon, 4000 ft., 2; Fallon, 3970 ft., 1; 1 mi. W Mountain Well, 5350 ft., 1; Mountain Well, 5600 ft., 1; Eastgate, 4400 ft., 3. *Mineral Co.:* 7 mi. NW Schurz, 4500 ft., 6; 3 mi. S Schurz, 4100 ft., 20; 8 mi. SE Schurz, 4100 ft., 2; Mason Valley, 5 mi. N Pine Grove, 5300 ft., 5; East Walker River, 2 to 3 mi. NW Morgans Ranch, 5050–5100 ft., 8; Cat Creek, 4 mi. W Hawthorne, 4500 ft., 3; 2 mi. E Hawthorne, 4300 ft., 2; Wichman, 5500 ft., 2 (coll. of D. V. Hemphill); Marietta, 4900 ft., 1; Huntoon Valley, 5700–6000 ft., 10. *Esmeralda Co.:* 3½ to 4 mi. SE Coaldale, 4850 ft., 2; 7 mi. N Arlemont, 5500 ft., 4; Arlemont, 4900 ft., 20; 1½ mi. N Dyer, 4800 ft., 2; Dyer, 5 (D. R. Dickey Coll.); 1½ mi. E Dyer, 4800 ft., 6; 2 mi. SE Dyer, 4800 ft., 1; 8 mi. SE Blair, 4500 ft., 2; mouth of Palmetto Wash, 5500 ft., 5 (D. R. Dickey Coll.); Palmetto Wash, 5700 ft., 1 (D. R. Dickey Coll.). *Nye Co.:* 4½ to 5¾ mi. NE San Antonio, 5640–5700 ft., 5; San Antonio, 5400 to 5407 ft., 8; Gold Flat, 6 mi. W Kawich P. O., 5150 ft., 1; 9 mi. E Wheelbarrow Peak, 1; ½ mi. N Oak Spring, 6500 ft., 1; NW base Timber Mtn., 4200 ft., 4; Emigrant Valley, 9 to 9½ mi. S Oak Spring, 4400 ft., 5; 8 mi. E Grapevine Peak, 5000 ft., 7; Amargosa River, 3 to 3½ mi. NE Beatty, 3400 ft., 16; 1 mi. N Beatty, 12 (D. R. Dickey Coll.); NW base Skull Mtn., 3500 ft., 12; Ash Meadows, 4 4/5 mi. NW Devils Hole, 2200 ft., 1; Ash Meadows, 2½ mi. W Devils Hole, 2173 ft., 2; 3 mi. N Pahrump, 2667 ft., 2 (D. R. Dickey Coll.); 1½ mi. N Pahrump, 2667 ft., 2 (D. R. Dickey Coll.). *Lincoln Co.:* 3 mi. N Crystal Spring, 4000 ft., 3; Crystal Spring (¼ mi. NE, ¼ mi. E, ½ mi. S, ¾ mi. S), 4000 ft., 12; 9 mi. W Groom Baldy, 5500 ft., 6; 16 mi. E Groom Baldy, 4600 ft., 1; Alamo, 3570 ft., 5; Meadow Valley, 21 mi. S Caliente, 3200 ft., 11; Meadow Valley, 24 to 25 mi. S Caliente, 3000 ft., 22; 8 mi. N Summit Spring, 3; Coyote Spring, 2800 ft., 1. *Clark Co.:* Virgin River, ¾ mi. E Mesquite, 1750 ft., 4; Indian Spring Valley, 14 mi. N Indian Springs, 3100 ft., 3; Indian Springs, 3280 ft., 9 (D. R. Dickey Coll.); 5 mi. SE Overton, 1200 ft., 1; Lost City, 1250 ft., 3 (D. R. Dickey Coll.); ½ mi. E St. Thomas, 1250 ft., 7 (D. R. Dickey Coll.); 2 mi. S St. Thomas, 1250 ft., 1 (D. R. Dickey Coll.); Valley of Fire, 12 mi. SW Overton, 1; Corn Creek, 2840 ft., 5 (D. R. Dickey Coll.); Kyle Canyon (6500 ft., 4; 6300 ft., 3), 7 (D. R. Dickey Coll.); Charleston Mts., 4500 ft., 10 (D. R. Dickey Coll.); 3½ to 4 mi. NW Las Vegas, 2100 ft., 13 (D. R. Dickey Coll.); 2½ mi. N Hoover (Boulder) Dam Ferry, 1; Cedar Basin, 3500 ft., 12 (D. R. Dickey Coll.); Boulder City, 2500 ft., 10; ¼ mi. S Boulder City, 2500 ft., 5; Hemenway Wash, 1 (Boulder Dam Recreational Area Coll.); 14 mi. E Searchlight, Jap Ranch, Colorado River, 500 ft., 29; 9 mi. W and 3½ to 5½ mi. S Searchlight, 4300 ft., 5; 7 mi. S Dead Mtn., 2700 ft., 1; 8 mi. SSE Dead Mtn., Hiko Spring, 1900 ft., 2; 3 mi. SW Hiko Spring, 2400 ft., 1; W side Colorado River, 500 ft., 6 mi. N Calif. boundary, 7; ½ mi. N Calif.-Nev. Monument, 500 ft., 26; opposite Fort Mojave, 4.

Dipodomys deserti deserti Stephens
Desert Kangaroo Rat

Dipodomys deserti Stephens, Amer. Nat., 21:42, January, 1887. Type from Mohave River [bottom at "upper crossing" on old road from Cajon Pass to Rabbit Springs, "3 or 4 miles" from, and opposite Hesperia, according to Grinnell, Univ. California Publ. Zoöl., 40:165, September 26, 1933], San Bernardino County, California. Hall and Linsdale, Journ. Mamm., 10:295, November 11, 1929; Hall and Dale, Occas. Papers, Mus. Zoöl., Louisiana State Univ., (no.) 4:48, November 10, 1939.

Dipodomys deserti deserti, Burt, Trans. San Diego Soc. Nat. Hist., 7:415, May 31, 1934.

Distribution.—Lower Sonoran Life-zone of southern Nevada and low western part of state in salt-desert area north to southern Humboldt County. See figure 307.

Remarks.—Measurements of ten males and six females from Pershing and Churchill counties are: ♂, 340 (325–365), ♀, 328 (316–340); 197 (189–212), 191 (180–198); 54.7 (51–58), 51.5 (50–54); weight, 119.1 (105.1–138.0), 111.5 (95.3–118.8) grams.

This is the largest, lightest-colored species of the genus in Nevada. The tail amounts to about 143 per cent of the length of the head and body or about 58 per cent of the total length. Distinctive features are Pale Ochraceous Buff color of upper parts, white-tipped

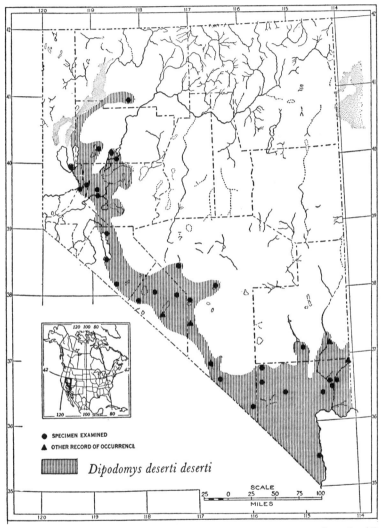

Fig. 307. Distribution of the desert kangaroo rat, *Dipodomys deserti*, with insert showing range of the species.

tail, absence in most specimens of a ventral, dark tail-stripe, four-toed hind foot, and relatively, as well as actually, maximum-sized auditory bullae. The enlargement of the mastoidal bullae has so restricted the space for the interparietal and the supraoccipital that these bones on the dorsal face of the skull are barely discernible. The distal third of the tail is crested, and the long hairs comprising the crest are dusky, except that the distal 25 millimeters of the tail is white.

Geographic variation detectable in Nevadan specimens is comprised in the presence of a well-defined, dark, ventral tail-stripe, darker dorsal tail-stripe, and more dusky fur at the base of the long facial vibrissae in the young specimen from near Jungo, in the three adults from 21 miles west and 2 miles north of Lovelock, and in the two from 4½ miles north and 2½ miles west of Nixon. These are the northwesternmost localities of known occurrence. Specimens from near Toulon are variously intermediate between the northwestern specimens and those from the vicinity of Fallon and farther south. This darkening of facial and caudal coloration parallels that in *Perognathus formosus*, another species of the Lower Sonoran Life-zone which occurs about equally far north. Another parallel is furnished by *Vulpes macrotis*.

The differentiation of northern populations of the mentioned species of *Perognathus* and *Vulpes* is sufficient to warrant distinction by subspecific name, but in *Dipodomys deserti* the difference is of less magnitude. Even in extreme southern Nevada and in Arizona an occasional adult *deserti* has a dark, ventral tail-stripe which prevents designation of this feature as distinctive of the northern populations. In these northern animals no difference of size of external parts or of cranial proportions has been found to be correlated with the darker coloration. The opinion at this writing is that although differentiation has begun, it is not yet of a degree which warrants recognition of the northwestern animals by separate subspecific name.

D. deserti is generally thought of as restricted to the Lower Sonoran Life-zone and previously has not been recorded north of the 37th parallel. Nevertheless, in the low, hot, area of the Upper Sonoran Life-zone along the eastern base of the Sierra Nevada, the species extends 275 miles farther north to about the 41st parallel. Wherever found, it was in wind-drifted sand not less than 20 inches deep. The large size of the burrow-openings and frequently the trails which are traceable between burrows permit a person to recognize the presence of the animals in advance of obtaining specimens. Having found the species so much farther north than we at one time supposed that it occurred, special lookout was kept for sign of it in southern Nye County. There, in Cactus Flat, Gold Flat, and Kawich Valley, edaphic conditions looked to be suitable, but no animals or traces of them were found.

In an area of deep sand 7 miles north of Arlemont, 5500 feet elevation, on the morning of June 8, 1927, Jean M. Linsdale trapped numbers of this species and (MS) noted that the burrows were in firm sand where the bushes were widely spaced and about 2 feet high. On the preceding day, wind had eliminated all tracks and trails; thus, on this morning, the marks left in the sand by the animals all were made the night before. At a set of burrows there were from six to twelve openings, only two of which appeared to be used. Several at each place had been filled by wind-borne sand. In the neighborhood of each set of openings there usually were several miniature sinks 10 inches to 2 feet in diameter which appeared to have been made by the caving in of the burrows. Fresh, well-beaten trails, ordinarily two, leading in opposite directions and averaging 5 inches wide, extended out from each set of burrows. At one burrow a trail by actual measurement was 75 yards long, and the one in the opposite direction was even longer. The paths turned aside for bushes and other obstructions, but as a rule they ran in nearly straight lines and were conspicuous features of the environment.

From one burrow being excavated by Linsdale, 10 linear yards having been already excavated, a young *deserti* rat broke out at the opposite end of the burrow about 10 yards ahead. It ran rapidly to and entered another hole 20 feet away, and immediately ran out of this hole and under a dead bush where the rat was obtained. At the opening, where digging was started, the hole was plugged with sand for about 2 inches. The burrow averaged 4 inches in diameter, and at the deepest part, which was near the middle, it was a little more than 2 feet below the surface of the ground.

Males average 2½ per cent larger than females in linear measurements of both the skull and external features and about 7 per cent more in weight. Three adults, taken on July 26, July 29, and August 12, clearly were in process of molt.

The cheek pouches of a specimen taken June 2, 1927, 7 miles north of Arlemont, by J. M. Linsdale (field no. 2224) contained seeds and heads of *Glyptopleura marginata* and two seeds of *Lupinus* (*concinnus* ?). The pouches of another taken May 29, 1933, 13½ miles northwest of Goldfield, by W. B. Davis (field no. 154) contained leaves and flower heads of *Gilia leptomeria* and two leaves of *Atriplex* sp. In Clark County, Burt (1934:415) found in cheek pouches of rats "seeds of creosote bush (*Larrea*), leaves of sage bush (*Artemisia* sp.), and fragments of stem and fruiting capsule of Scrophulariaceae (probably *Pentstemon*)."

Six females contained embryos: 2 had 3 embryos, 2 had 4, and 2 had 5. Alcorn (MS) noted that 3 females taken on March 24, 1939, near Fallon, were suckling young. The 35 adult females of which we have record respecting time of capture were taken by months as follows: January, 6 (1 pregnant); February, 1; March, 5; April, 0; May, 12 (3 pregnant); June, 8 (2 pregnant); July, 2; August, 0; September, 1.

Records of occurrence.—Specimens examined, 135, as follows: *Washoe Co.*: 4½ mi. N and 2½ mi. W Nixon, 2 (coll. of Ira W. La Rivers and T. J. Trelease). *Lyon Co.*: 6 mi. NE Fernley, 2; ½ and 1 mi. SE Wadsworth, 4200 ft., 2. *Humboldt Co.*: 8 mi. E and 1 mi. N Jungo, 4200 ft., 1. *Pershing Co.*: 21 mi. W and 2 mi. N Lovelock, 4000 ft., 3; 3¼ mi. NNE Toulon, 3900 ft., 1; 3 mi. E Toulon, 3900 ft., 4. *Churchill Co.*: 1 mi. NW Soda Lake, 4000 ft., 1; 1 mi. S Soda Lake, 4000 ft., 2; 5 mi. W Fallon, 4000 ft., 1; 4 mi. W Fallon, 4000 ft., 2. *Mineral Co.*: 8 mi. SE Schurz, 4100 ft., 1; Cat Creek, 4 mi. W Hawthorne, 4500 ft., 1; Huntoon Valley, 5700 ft., 4. *Esmeralda Co.*: 3½ to 4 mi. SE Coaldale, 4850 ft., 4; 13 mi. N Goldfield, 5100 ft., 1; 13½ mi. NW Goldfield, 4850 ft., 13; 7 mi. N Arlemont, 5500 ft., 20. *Nye Co.*: San Antonio, 5400 ft., 1; 34 mi. E and 1 mi. N Tonopah, Ralston Valley, 5650 ft., 1; N shore Mud Lake, 5300 ft., S end Ralston Valley, 2; 1 mi. N Beatty, 3400 ft., 7 (D. R. Dickey Coll.); Amargosa Desert, 20 mi. SE Beatty, 2500 ft., 4; 3½ mi. N Pahrump, 2667 ft., 1 (D. R. Dickey Coll.); 1½ mi. N Pahrump, 2667 ft., 1 (D. R. Dickey Coll.). *Lincoln Co.*: Coyote Spring, 2800 ft., 4. *Clark Co.*: Indian Spring Valley, 14 mi. N Indian Springs, 3100 ft., 11; 7 mi. N (on Virgin arm of) Lake Mead (east side), 920 ft., 1; 5 mi. SE Overton, 1; Indian Springs, 3280 ft., 14 (D. R. Dickey Coll.); island, mouth Virgin River, 1; St. Thomas, 2 (Boulder Dam Recreational Area Coll.); ½ mi. E St. Thomas, 2 (D. R. Dickey Coll.); Corn Creek, 2840 ft., 4 (D. R. Dickey Coll.); Valley of Fire, 12 mi. SW Overton, 1; 14 mi. E Searchlight, Colorado River, Jap Ranch, 500 ft., 12.

Additional records (animals or unmistakable sign noted, Hall, MS): *Esmeralda Co.*: 8 mi. SE Blair. *Nye Co.*: Stonewall Flat, 14 mi. SE Goldfield. *Lincoln Co.*: Carp (R. T. Orr, MS). *Clark Co.*: Mesquite (Hall, MS).

TABLE 11

CRANIAL MEASUREMENTS (IN MILLIMETERS) OF DIPODOMYS

Name and locality	Number of individuals averaged or catalogue no.	Sex	Basal length*	Length of nasal	Greatest breadth	Maxillary breadth	Interorbital breadth
Dipodomys panamintinus leucogenys							
Western Nevada	9 av.	♂	28.6	15.8	24.9	23.3	13.2
	min.		27.6	15.0	24.4	21.8	12.6
	max.		29.4	16.1	25.3	24.3	13.9
Western Nevada	10 av.	♀	28.0	15.4	24.1	22.7	12.9
	min.		26.7	14.5	23.6	21.5	12.3
	max.		28.9	16.2	24.6	24.0	13.8
Dipodomys panamintinus caudatus							
Western Clark Co	3 av.	♂	29.1	15.6	25.6	24.1	13.4
	min.		28.5	15.1	25.0	24.0	13.1
	max.		29.5	16.1	26.0	24.3	13.7
Western Clark Co	3 av.	♀	28.9	15.3	25.0	23.2	13.0
	min.		28.5	14.9	24.8	22.6	12.6
	max.		29.1	15.5	25.1	23.6	13.3
Dipodomys ordii columbianus							
Northwestern Washoe Co	6 av.	♂	25.9	13.6	23.9	20.5	11.7
	min.		25.4	13.1	23.1	20.4	11.2
	max.		26.1	13.9	24.4	20.8	12.1
Northwestern Washoe Co	6 av.	♀	25.6	13.3	23.4	20.0	11.7
	min.		25.1	12.8	22.9	19.5	11.4
	max.		26.2	14.0	23.6	20.1	11.9
Dipodomys ordii inaquosus							
8 and 11 mi. eastward from Jungo	6 av.	♂	25.6	13.7	24.0	20.2	11.8
	min.		25.2	13.2	23.1	19.8	11.6
	max.		26.0	14.1	24.8	20.6	12.0
8 mi. E and 1 mi. N Jungo	73574	♀	26.0	13.6	23.9	20.1	11.7
11 mi. E and 1 mi. N Jungo	73582	♀	25.0	14.3	23.9	20.2	12.0
D. o. celeripes (intergrades with *columbianus*)							
1½ mi. N and 1½ mi. NE Tecoma	6 av.	♂	25.7	13.9	23.9	20.5	11.9
	min.		24.8	13.3	23.3	19.9	11.7
	max.		26.2	14.8	24.5	20.7	12.3
1½ mi. N and 1½ mi. NE Tecoma	9 av.	♀	25.5	13.8	23.8	20.5	11.8
	min.		24.9	13.3	23.5	19.9	11.3
	max.		26.2	14.6	24.1	20.8	12.3
Dipodomys ordii monoensis							
Vicinity of Fallon	10 av.	♂	25.4	13.5	23.5	20.0	11.7
	min.		25.0	13.1	22.5	19.2	11.2
	max.		26.1	14.3	24.1	20.5	12.1
Vicinity of Fallon	3 av.	♀	25.3	13.3	23.0	19.9	11.4
	min.		24.6	13.3	22.7	19.6	11.0
	max.		26.0	13.3	23.3	20.4	11.7
Dipodomys ordii fetosus							
2 mi. N Panaca	6 av.	♂	26.0	13.6	23.9	20.2	11.7
	min.		25.6	12.8	23.3	19.5	11.4
	max.		26.3	14.0	24.2	20.5	12.1
2 mi. N Panaca	7 av.	♀	25.4	13.4	23.3	20.0	11.6
	min.		24.7	12.8	22.4	19.1	10.8
	max.		26.6	14.0	24.1	21.4	12.7

* Basal length taken from anterior face of incisors.

TABLE 11—(*Continued*)

Name and locality	Number of individuals averaged or catalogue no.	Sex	Basal length*	Length of nasal	Greatest breadth	Maxillary breadth	Interorbital breadth
Dipodomys microps preblei							
Malheur Co., Oregon	3 av.	♂	27.3	13.0	23.9	19.3	12.1
	min.		27.1	12.7	23.4	19.0	12.0
	max.		27.5	13.1	24.2	19.5	12.2
Narrows, Oregon	1 yg.	♀	25.2	11.7	——	18.6	11.6
Dipodomys microps aquilonius							
Near Hausen	4 av.	♂	26.7	12.2	23.3	18.6	12.2
	min.		26.0	11.9	22.8	18.1	12.0
	max.		27.4	12.7	24.1	19.3	12.4
Near Hausen	2 av.	♀	26.3	12.1	23.0	18.6	11.9
	min.		26.2	12.1	22.6	18.6	11.7
	max.		26.3	12.1	23.3	18.6	12.1
Dipodomys microps centralis							
Near Romano	3 av.	♂	27.3	13.0	23.9	19.3	12.1
	min.		27.1	12.7	23.4	19.0	12.0
	max.		27.5	13.1	24.2	19.5	12.2
Near Battle Mountain (town) and Cortez	3 av.	♀	26.5	12.9	23.9	19.6	12.4
	min.		26.3	12.6	23.4	19.3	12.3
	max.		26.8	13.3	24.5	19.8	12.5
Dipodomys microps occidentalis							
Near Schurz	4 av.	♂	25.9	12.1	22.6	18.5	11.7
	min.		25.5	11.8	21.7	17.9	11.1
	max.		26.3	12.4	23.1	19.1	12.0
Near Schurz	7 av.	♀	25.8	12.4	23.0	18.4	11.7
	min.		25.1	11.9	22.7	18.0	11.2
	max.		26.6	13.1	23.4	18.8	12.0
Dipodomys microps bonnevillei							
Near Montello	8 av.	♂	26.8	12.7	23.8	19.5	11.9
	min.		26.1	12.1	23.3	19.0	11.4
	max.		27.1	13.3	24.6	20.1	12.6
Near Montello	10 av.	♀	27.1	12.8	23.5	19.2	11.6
	min.		26.4	12.2	22.9	18.4	10.9
	max.		27.9	13.1	24.5	20.0	12.1
Dipodomys merriami merriami							
14 mi. E Searchlight	10 av.	♂	24.6	13.4	22.8	19.5	13.0
	min.		23.7	12.6	22.0	19.0	12.0
	max.		25.1	14.4	23.3	19.8	13.4
14 mi. E Searchlight	10 av.	♀	24.3	13.2	23.0	19.4	13.1
	min.		23.8	12.3	23.7	19.0	12.5
	max.		24.9	13.9	22.4	20.2	13.5
Dipodomys deserti deserti							
Fallon, N to Lovelock	10 av.	♂	31.2	16.3	30.5	23.8	14.8
	min.		30.0	15.7	29.5	22.1	13.5
	max.		32.5	17.3	31.9	25.0	16.1
Fallon, N to Lovelock	6 av.	♀	30.3	15.9	29.5	23.2	14.9
	min.		29.3	15.1	28.4	22.6	14.1
	max.		31.4	16.9	30.2	24.6	16.2

* Basal length taken from anterior face of incisors.

Genus **Thomomys** Wied
Smooth-toothed Pocket Gophers

The four species of Nevadan pocket gophers belong to the one genus, *Thomomys*. There are several other genera of pocket gophers in North and Central America. Most zoölogists have accorded these genera of pocket gophers the rank of a full family (Geomyidae) distinct from the Heteromyidae comprising the Recent genera *Heteromys, Liomys, Perognathus, Dipodomys*, and *Microdipodops*. In 1937 Hill (see Literature Cited) pointed out that the two groups had the following in common: external, fur-lined cheek pouches, with almost identical musculature; infraorbital canal sunken in the side of the rostrum and opening anteriorly near the premaxillo-maxillary suture; premolar present; dental formula i. $\frac{1}{1}$, c. $\frac{0}{0}$, p. $\frac{1}{1}$, m. $\frac{3}{3}$; similarities in both the permanent and deciduous dentition; fused and reduced anterior horns of hyoid; vestigial stapedial canal; similar arrangement of fissures and foramina around the tympanic bulla; pseudostyloid process on radius; tibia and fibula solidly fused; and common features in the muscular system, digestive system, and external genitalia. Hill (1937) regarded these similarities as outweighing the dissimilarities, and pointed out that the latter are correlated with the different manners of life of these rodents. Some of these dissimilarities which serve to set the geomyids apart from the heteromyids are: infraorbital foramina not connected by an opening through the nasal septum; no entepicondylar foramen; posterior angular process of mandible elevated and strong; internal pterygoid muscle invades sphenopterygoid canal; caudal angle of scapula not greatly produced; and the pubic symphysis short or lacking. To Hill the resemblances so far outweighed the differences as to indicate subfamily rather than family rank for the pocket gophers. Also, the most generalized members of this group of mammals appear to be the spiny pocket mice. Because of the relationships indicated above, the pocket gophers in the present work, in the order of listing, are made to follow rather than precede the pocket mice. The close relationship of the pocket gophers and heteromyids can be indicated by according family rank to each group under the superfamily Geomyoidea, or the closeness can be emphasized by placing both groups in the one family Heteromyidae.

In addition to the characters indicated above for the family, the genus *Thomomys* is characterized by having: each upper and lower molar with both anterior and posterior enamel plate; upper incisors plain with only a minute groove near inner edge of each; forefeet more slender and claws smaller than in other genera.

The four full species in Nevada are naturally arranged in two groups. *T. monticola* and *T. talpoides* agree in general shape of the lower premolar, in absence of a sphenoidal fissure, and in having a narrow rostrum, and they closely resemble each other in coloration. *T. townsendii* and *T. bottae* agree in shape of the lower premolar, presence of a sphenoidal fissure, broad rostrum, and in some other features. The differences between the individual species are mentioned in the following accounts.

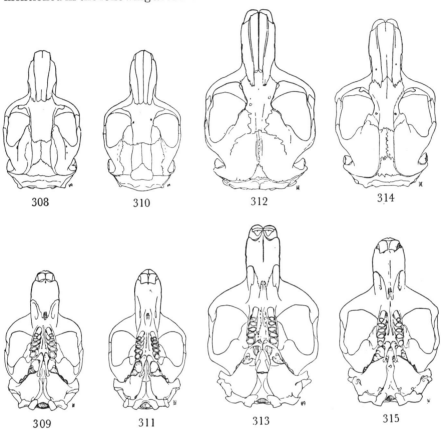

Figs. 308–315. Pocket gophers. All, × 1. (Other views of these skulls are shown in figs. 316–321.)

Figs. 308, 309. *Thomomys talpoides monoensis*, Lapon Canyon, Mount Grant, no. 63697, ♂.
Figs. 310, 311. *Thomomys monticola monticola*, 3 miles south Mount Rose, 8600 feet, no. 65219, ♂.
Figs. 312, 313. *Thomomys townsendii nevadensis*, Malloy Ranch, 5 miles west Austin, no. 37073, ♂.
Figs. 314, 315. *Thomomys bottae canus*, Deep Hole, no. 41652, ♂.

There is no overlapping in the ranges of the four species. This is true of the species of the genus elsewhere and even of the genera within the family. To be sure, specimens of both *Thomomys talpoides* and *Thomomys townsendii* were taken at the same time, in a field 5 miles west of Austin, but this was a place where the ranges of the two species met.

Variations in nature of soil and conditions associated with altitude seem to be responsible for different species occupying different areas. For example, *Thomomys monticola* occurs at high altitudes in the Sierra Nevada where temperatures are lower than in the habitat of the species *bottae* on the lower terrain to the eastward. Between the geographic ranges of these two species, in a belt which is narrow and relatively cool and where soils are often thin, *T. talpoides* occurs, as it does also widely in northern Nevada where, over the area as a whole, climatic conditions are similar. In some of the higher, north-south ranges of mountains in the central part of the state *talpoides*, as would be expected, occurs much farther south, as, for example, in the Toyabe and

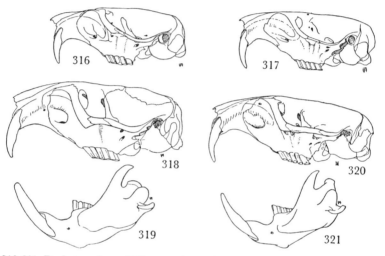

Figs. 316–321. Pocket gophers. Different views of these skulls are shown in figs. 308–315. All, × 1.

Fig. 316. *Thomomys talpoides monoensis*.   Figs. 318, 319. *Thomomys townsendii nevadensis*.
Fig. 317. *Thomomys monticola monticola*.   Figs. 320, 321. *Thomomys bottae canus*.

Monitor mountain ranges. The greater altitude there provides temperatures to which *talpoides* is adapted, whereas in the different climate at lower elevations at the same latitude, the species *T. bottae* occurs to the exclusion of *talpoides*. *Thomomys townsendii* is restricted to deep soils of a lacustrine origin in the Humboldt River Valley, in similar soils northwest of this valley, and in the Reese River Valley. To this species, type of soil is the important factor; climate seems to have little or no effect. The winter temperature at Elko is in some years as low as recorded anywhere in the United States, whereas at Toulon, the other, western, end of the range of the populations of *townsendii* inhabiting the Humboldt River Valley, the winter temperature is relatively high. There enters into this matter of present geographic ranges also the antiquity of the species. For example, in the higher parts of the mountains of eastern White Pine County, *bottae* occurs from low to high elevations. *T.*

bottae, I suppose, was the only kind of pocket gopher around the bases of Wheeler Peak and Mount Moriah when the higher elevations of these peaks became available for gopher-occupancy. Probably *bottae* worked slowly upward, developing populations with individuals adapted to living at these higher elevations as it went. Even yet they are not abundant, as is *T. talpoides* in the higher parts of the Cleve Creek Range to the westward. If *talpoides* had had access to these high elevations on Wheeler Peak and Mount Moriah when they became habitable for pocket gophers, probably the rate of occupancy would have been faster and the present gopher population would be more abundant

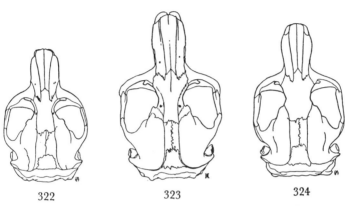

322   323   324

Figs. 322–324. Pocket gophers. All, × 1. Note geographic difference between adult male skulls of two subspecies, figs. 322, 323, and sexual dimorphism between adults, figs. 323, 324.

Fig. 322. *Thomomys bottae phelleoecus,* Hidden Forest, 7700 feet, no. 93119, ♂.
Fig. 323. *Thomomys bottae canus,* Deep Hole, no. 41652, ♂.
Fig. 324. *Thomomys bottae canus,* Deep Hole, no. 41660, ♀.

there. In this instance, then, antiquity of a species, or presence of one species and absence of another, seems to have been one factor responsible for present occurrence.

Although pocket gophers occur in all parts of Nevada and although the full species have wide geographic ranges, the range of an individual animal is small. Many a gopher probably lives its entire life in an area of less than an acre. This sedentary existence may operate in some measure, as does geographic isolation, to assist in preserving morphological variations of a heritable nature. At any rate, no other genus of mammal has as many races in Nevada as does *Thomomys.* The twenty-nine recognized kinds differ in size of animal, color of pelage, and in proportions of the skull and extent of individual cranial bones in such a fashion as to suggest that the variations are responses to environment— responses which better fit the animals to live where they do. These responses apply to subspecies rather than to individual animals. For example, there is good evidence that secondary sexual variation in size is greatest in deep soils at low elevations and least in thin soils at high elevations. A case in point is *T. bottae nanus*. Throughout most of its geographic range the soil is thin, and the absence, or slight degree, of secondary sexual variation is maintained throughout the geographic range of the subspecies, even at places where the soil is deep. *T. bottae centralis* has a range in soil that in general is deeper, and the secondary sexual difference in size is greater—greater even where the animals range into thin soil. In other words, heritable characters of a subspecific nature prevail over variations which are responses in but a small fraction of the population to environmental influences—responses peculiar to the particular area in which this small fraction of the population lives. Even so, differences of subspecific rank appear in pocket gophers in areas of smaller extent than in other rodents of less sedentary habits.

Although not directly bearing on the points just discussed, it is worth noting that thin soil and high altitude appear to be productive of small gophers, and low altitude and deep soils productive of large gophers. The suggestion that greater abundance of plant food at lower elevations in the deep soils may in one generation make the difference between small and large size is unsatisfactory because of the relative uniformity of size in a given subspecies, even where some individuals occur in an unusual (for the subspecies) kind of soil. Also, what we know of the heritable nature of similar differences in subspecies of *Peromyscus* and *Microtus* indicates that such differences as distinguish, say, typical *T. b. brevidens* from typical *T. b. nanus* are hereditary and not of a kind that can be produced by a change in food or environment in one or even in a few generations.

Superimposed on these variations in size, which are correlated with altitude and nature of soil, is a size gradient from north to south in the species *Thomomys bottae*. The largest animals of it occur in the north and the smallest in the south. It is true that large and small kinds (subspecies) occur in the central part of the state and have contiguous ranges. An example of this is furnished by the large *T. b. canus* and small *T. b. depressus*. Nevertheless, *T. b. depressus* is larger than subspecies in the southern part of the state which occupy equally arid and thin soils. Also, no forms as large as *canus* occur in the southern part of the state, even where soils are deep.

In viewing the twenty-nine kinds of Nevadan pocket gophers in relation to their environment, it is pertinent to recall that the genus *Thomomys*, to which all of them belong, is restricted to that part of North America west of the Mississippi River between the 55th and 20th degrees of north latitude. Over the larger part of this area the climate is characterized by sharp alternation of dry and wet seasons. Linked with this character of climate is a larger relative number of plants with nutritious and thickened underground roots than in the flora of the region east of the Mississippi where the climate is more evenly moist throughout the year. These nutritious and thickened underground roots comprise the major share of the pocket gopher's food.

As these enlarged underground structures of the plants developed in response to increasingly arid seasons, probably so did the ancestral pocket gophers become more fossorial. Now a point has been reached at which, at certain seasons, all their food is obtained below ground. The pocket gopher is the most efficiently adapted of any living North American rodent for utilizing this underground food source. Many parts of the pocket gopher's body are highly developed for a life underground. As Grinnell (1923:139) says: "a pocket gopher spends at least ninety-nine one-hundredths of its existence below ground. Its world is limited by the earthen walls of a cylinder. In one direction this cylinder brings safety from enemies; at the other end it brings accessibility to food. . . . the gopher is deficient relatively to other rodents with respect to eyesight. Its hearing likewise is below the average and seems to be keenest for sounds of very low rate of vibration, such as jarrings of the ground. Its sense of touch is localized not only in the nose and surrounding vibrissae, but also at the tip of the tail. The animal moves quite as well backward in its burrow as forward; it needs to be appraised of conditions in both directions." The forelimbs, used for moving soil, are larger than the hind limbs and have strong forefeet provided with long claws used in digging. The incisor teeth are large, have the lips meeting behind them so as to exclude dirt from the mouth, and are used by the animal in prying and otherwise loosening soil. Just as with the forefeet, a strong base is required for teeth strong enough to be used in the way that the pocket gopher uses his. This base, the skull, is large in proportion to the body of the animal. Indeed, the neck, shoulders, and entire forepart of the animal, in comparison with these parts in other rodents, are disproportionately large, giving the pocket gopher the muscular force and strength of bone to burrow through the soil. In these modifications the pocket gopher, among rodents, is second only to *Spalax*, a burrowing rodent of the arid parts of the Eurasiatic and African continents. Rodents of the genus *Spalax* inhabit deserts and semideserts much older than those of the western United States and have reached a point in specialization for fossorial activity which our pocket gophers may not attain until several millions of years hence.

This specialization for a life below ground has lessened the ability to get along aboveground. The structure of the limbs makes it impossible for the animal to run or leap rapidly on the surface of the ground. Its sight is poor. Sounds made by potential enemies probably are not readily heard from any considerable distance. The animals seem instinctively to avoid fully exposing themselves aboveground, for when one does come out of its burrow to eat the stems and leaves of plants, it ventures only as far from the mouth of the burrow as it can go while still keeping its hindquarters in the burrow. Even so, many are snatched up by owls. This inability to travel overland makes areas of lava and rock real barriers and, in part, explains why the extent of territory occupied by a pocket gopher is so small.

Pocket gophers do, in rare instances, travel over the exposed surface of the ground at night. Evidence of this travel was furnished by several pocket gophers accidentally caught in rat- and mousetraps. All so caught by us were young animals which probably had just left the burrows of their parents and were seeking new homes. Young animals make burrows of smaller diameter than those of adults, and many of the tunnels made by young are shallow. Many, when excavated, proved to be short, and their manner of construction was such as to show that the animal went a little way overland between the mouths of the short burrows. Exposure aboveground is dangerous for a gopher, and young gophers with the least fossorial inclinations probably are most quickly eliminated by enemies.

Important enemies of Nevadan pocket gophers are weasels, owls of larger size, and snakes of several kinds. Other carnivorous mammals and raptorial birds eat pocket gophers when opportunity presents itself. On a meadow along Baker Creek we took a female weasel and her four young from a gopher burrow. This burrow was dug out and found to contain no gopher, nor did other burrows in this same meadow. We made the latter conclusion because no fresh dirt was thrown out, because holes leading into burrows remained open day after day, and because traps set in the burrows took no gophers. It was assumed that the weasel had used all the gophers in the meadow as food for herself and her young. The pellets regurgitated by barn owls and some pellets probably regurgitated by horned owls contained remains of *Thomomys*. At Cleveland Ranch, in Spring Valley, conditions in late July, 1930, were ideal for *Thomomys*, except that the hundreds of acres of land there, pretty much surrounded by water, supported an unusually large population of snakes. We saw many gopher snakes (*Pituophis catenifer deserticola*) and blue racers (*Coluber constrictor mormon*). One of the men at the ranch said that whenever he was traveling about the country he made it a practice to pick up all the nonpoisonous snakes that he saw and take them back to the ranch and release them there in the fields. His belief that the snakes eliminated the pocket gophers seemed reasonable to me because thorough search for "gopher-workings," by three of us, on two days, revealed workings in only one limited area where five gophers in all were trapped.

Another hazard for these rodents is the flooding of areas in the valleys that occurs at rare intervals following cloudbursts, heavy rains, or rapid melting of deep snows in the mountains. Linsdale (1938:184) witnessed an instance of this kind in a meadow 5 miles southeast of Millett in Great Smoky Valley. He says, "During the 3 days before May 19, 1932, while flood waters from South Twin River were running across this meadow, many gopher burrows were filled with water and the occupants forced from them. At noon on May 19, 2 live gophers and 3 dead ones were noted on small islands. One of the live ones remained quiet, and when disturbed, it finally withdrew into a small part of the tunnel that was still above the water level. The other one was pugnacious and it bit at the end of a gun barrel that was placed near it. When pushed off its mound into the water, it immediately swam back to it. Apparently it was characteristic for these gophers to stick to their homes even after being forced to the surface rather than to start out in search of more suitable home sites. And they remained despite an almost certain fate of being chilled to death or of being picked up by some one of the numerous predators which soon discovered this easily accessible food source and congregated there to take advantage of it."

Gophers do not need water to drink. Many live in places where they could not get water to drink, and I have no evidence indicating that they do drink in the wild, even in places where they could do so.

Pocket gophers do not hibernate, being active the year round. Where the ground freezes and there is little or no snow, the animals work below the level of frost. Soil which the gophers move when constructing new tunnels is not brought to the surface, but is shoved into previously made burrows. This is the normal situation over much of the range of *T. bottae*, as, for example, about Fallon. In the range of *T. monticola*, and over much of the range of *T. talpoides*, there is deep snow for many months. In this snow the gophers burrow freely, often several inches above the surface of the ground, and pack into the tunnels in the snow the soil that they excavate. As the snow melts, the soil in these tunnels becomes moist, consolidates, and is lowered to the ground. There the cores lie atop of sticks and stones, as though expelled like toothpaste from a giant tube.

Snow probably is an important means of allowing the animals to reach new territory. In the Sierra Nevada for example, areas of soil deep enough for pocket gophers to live in, in some places, are of small extent and are surrounded by granite rocks; when snow lies deeply here, the rocks are passed over by the gophers which, in the absence of the snow, would be unable to move from one of these limited areas of soil to another without exposing themselves to enemies.

Like most mammals which do not hibernate, pocket gophers do not accumulate large stores of fat in autumn. Once, however, in January, 1934, at two places on the Colorado River, the Durban Ranch, and ½ mile upriver from the Nevada-California Monument, the gophers were exceptionally fat. Each had a thick layer which adhered closely to the skin. The animals were feeding on the roots of saltgrass which grew in a narrow strip just above flood-water level at the lower margin of the dry upland.

Spring is the season when greatest evidence of the burrowing activities of pocket gophers is to be seen. The more numerous mounds then thrown out are probably caused by the fact that the soil then is usually moist all the way to the surface—a condition which does not hold in summer or in autumn when the upper part of the soil is dry and hard. It is in the spring that the mounds guide the observer to the animals, which are widely distributed and which may occur almost anywhere except in rock or in the bare alkali flats. Where the surface of the ground freezes in winter and is not covered by snow, little or no earth then is brought to the surface. In the summer, when most of our collecting in Nevada has been done, the animals appear to be restricted to the vicinity of springs and moist places, where in truth they are present in great numbers, but in these places the earth may be brought to the surface over a longer period of time than in drier areas.

The workings of moles, which occur in western Nevada, and those of pocket gophers are apt to be confused. The ridges of raised earth which moles make by pushing along an inch or two below the surface of the ground are of course recognizable as the work of moles, but the mounds of earth which they bring to the surface from deeper burrows do resemble mounds made by pocket gophers. Knowledge of how the mounds of each are constructed makes it easier to distinguish one from the other. The lateral burrow of the pocket gopher is ordinarily inclined at a considerable angle to the surface of the ground. Through this burrow successive loads of earth are pushed out in one direction, each partly on top of the one before, making a mound on which half circles are visible. The "lateral" through which the mole expels earth ordinarily comes straight up to the surface of the ground. The soil brought to the surface though this "lateral" cascades down, like water from a fountain, so that the successive loads form a nearly circular mound.

Pocket gophers use their forefeet and face in pushing loads of loose earth. The cheek pouches, contrary to popular opinion, are not used in transporting earth. These pouches are used for carrying food.

Pocket gophers are of great economic importance. This is because of the damage that they do in cultivated areas and because of the benefits which they confer in uncultivated areas. In orchards they are a definite menace. They eat the roots of fig trees and apricot trees, so many of which roots may be severed near the base of the trunk that, before the orchardist is aware anything is amiss, the tree may be killed. In flower gardens a pocket gopher is capable of cutting the stems of many plants just beneath the surface of the ground, and oftentimes an entire plant is dragged below ground. Vegetable gardens, too, have suffered from the work of pocket gophers. Alfalfa fields are favorite places for pocket gophers because the roots of alfalfa provide abundant food. Although many plants, the main roots of which are severed, will eventually reestablish themselves through the other roots, some of them are killed. Where a spring-toothed cultivator is run over the field in spring to kill newly sprouted weeds, these insecurely rooted alfalfa plants, in some soils, are dragged out, and the full effect of the pocket gopher's destructive potentialities is realized. Although the mounds of dirt thrown up by a pocket gopher are a nuisance when the rancher is mowing, or using a buckrake, the burrows themselves are the cause of most trouble in any irrigated field. After water has run down and enlarged a burrow, the entire flow of a small lateral ditch may run down the burrow indefinitely and so defeat the efforts of the rancher to spread the irrigation water evenly over the field. The burrows made by these animals in the banks of raised ditches sometimes allow water to seep through; with eventual enlargement of the burrow, a break occurs. In larger ditches or canals the loss from such a break, and the cost of repairs, mount to important figures. Almost anyone in the West who has had experience in farming or in gardening where pocket gophers abound will recall instances of the sort mentioned and probably will take the view, with which I agree, that pocket gophers wherever possible should be eliminated from cultivated lands. I know of one rancher, however, who encouraged the pocket gophers in the soil of his silty, not sandy, alfalfa field. He pointed to the more luxuriant growth of alfalfa where the gophers had cultivated the soil and judged that the animals were an asset. Nevertheless, on most farmland the benefits which the animals confer by loosening the soil, by serving as a food source for carnivorous fur-bearing mammals, and by acting in other ways to advance man's interests are generally more than offset by the damage they do. Therefore, they should be eliminated or their numbers should be kept at low ebb in cultivated areas.

Of the several means of doing this, one is substitution of flooding in place of irrigating in furrows or within narrow checks. When large areas are covered with water by flooding, the pocket gophers drown.

Plowing to a depth of 6 inches and subsequent cultivation of the soil, as is done in a cornfield, suffices to remove all or nearly all of the pocket gophers of the kinds found in Nevada. In heavily infested, large fields, where neither of these means could conveniently be employed, poisoning has been tried, with fair results being recorded. Probably the best method of all, especially where the problem is to keep gophers out of a given area, is to use traps of the Macabee pattern, by means of which the animals are easily and inexpensively eliminated. If traps are set in burrows as soon as gophers begin to invade the area and if a sort of patrol is maintained about the borders, a large area can be kept free of gophers. This method of control takes account of the fact that prevention of damage by these rodents is accomplished best by continued effort. Desirable as it might be to eliminate all the animals by one operation, and thus make further efforts at control unnecessary, this is seldom possible, for no matter what means be employed, animals always work in later from the edges of the treated area. Therefore, trapping about the margins is the cheapest method, in the long run, for one desiring to keep an area free of pocket gophers.

The general statement, frequently made, that rodents increase on newly cultivated, previously wild, land is open to question, because some kinds of rodents certainly decrease in an area that is planted to growing crops. Pocket gophers, however, do appear to increase on previously arid wild land brought under irrigation (lands irrigated by flooding are excepted) and applied to growing alfalfa or other crops which have an abundant root supply on which the pocket gophers can feed.

Turning now to the credit side of the ledger, it can be pointed out that the pocket gopher is one of the burrowing rodents the activity of which has an important place in naturally tilling the wild lands. Some of the ways in which the pocket gophers are thought to promote the growth of plants are mentioned below.

The humus content of the soil is increased by the vegetation being buried beneath the mounds of earth thrown up by pocket gophers, as it is also by the bits of vegetation that are carried below ground and never eaten, and by the vegetation carried below ground and used in constructing nests. Similarly, excreta deposited below ground by the animals contributes to the humus content of the soil and its fertility. The loosening of soil by pocket gophers counteracts the packing effect on grazing lands where hoofed animals abound. Loosening of soil makes it possible for rootlets to penetrate the soil more easily. The vivid green spots that one sees on hillsides in spring prove, upon investigation, to be superior growths of grass often upon mounds of earth thrown out by pocket gophers—growths of grass more luxuriant and more vividly green than grown on the surrounding soil not so recently worked over by the pocket gophers.

Many of the mounds thrown out by pocket gophers are of earth from the layer of subsoil. By being thus brought to the surface, the material undergoes an increased rate of weathering and deepens the top soil. The gopher burrows are one means by which air, water, and contained solvents are carried underground. The water thus conserved lessens the immediate runoff and distributes the supply to streams and springs over a longer period of time. Water is conserved indirectly by the greater plant growth on the soils loosened by the burrowing activities of the pocket gophers.

These rodents serve as food for carnivorous fur-bearing mammals and for raptorial birds. The value to man in this regard is difficult to estimate and may be much or little, depending upon local conditions.

On the mountain meadows subjected to varying degrees of use by livestock, particularly sheep, along the Nevadan side of Lake Tahoe, pocket gophers are abundant in the overgrazed meadows and scarce in the other meadows. In the long-overgrazed meadows, the native grasses are partly replaced by dog fennel and other hardy plants well known as indicators of overgrazing, the large roots of which are one of the special adaptations which permits them to live under adverse conditions. It is mainly the abundance of this food supply of roots that is responsible for the large number of pocket gophers. These animals, in such a meadow, in one season may cover up with soil brought from below ground half the surface of the "meadow." Their action in cultivating the soil and in actually destroying the plants which have replaced the grasses and other native vegetation hastens the return of meadow conditions. It is true that by eradicating the pocket gophers in one year a greater amount of forage would be available for domestic stock the following year, but over a longer period, say, 5 or 6 years, it is thought that the pocket gophers would increase the amount of food for livestock by hastening the return of meadow conditions, providing the area was closed to grazing, as, it seems to me, it should be if already overgrazed to the point where these thick-rooted plants which attract pocket gophers and indicate overgrazing are numerous.

Some persons have thought that in situations of this kind the activity of pocket gophers is responsible for gully-erosion. The presence of burrows of the pocket gophers within a foot or two of the brink of a gully that has already formed in a meadow of the overgrazed type conceivably would hasten further erosion. Over most of the meadow, however, the earth plugs left from the hibernal activities of the gophers and the copious burrow system, permitting entrance of water into the ground, would retard erosion. It is a matter of common observation that the real cause of scarcity of vegetative cover and unnaturally rapid erosion in these mountain meadows is overgrazing by domestic stock. Since the activities of pocket gophers are thought to retard erosion and to hasten the return of favorable grazing conditions, control activities directed against the gophers in such places appear to be more harmful than beneficial.

What we have learned of the pocket gopher in Nevada leads to the opinion that on most cultivated land it should be eradicated because of the damage that it does, but that on uncultivated lands, especially on wild lands, it should be unmolested by man because it is distinctly beneficial there.

Thomomys talpoides
Northern Pocket Gopher

Five races of this species occur in Nevada. In general, the species occupies the northern half of the state and a narrow strip of territory along the eastern flank of the Sierra Nevada between the ranges of *T. monticola* and *T. bottae*.

Color of this species in summer is brownish above; whitish, or whitish and buffy, on the underparts; blackish on the nose; black postauricular patches; white on the lower lips and chin; in winter lighter, grayer, usually with a more smoky effect; ears short (5 to 6 mm.) and round; mammae usually ten, three pairs pectoral and two pairs inguinal; skull lacking sphenoidal fissure; anterior opening of infraorbital canal posterior to anterior palatine foramina; occlusal face of anterior prism of p4 with a distinct anteromedial notch, and area of its occlusal face three-fourths or more that of posterior prism.

The above characters serve easily to distinguish *talpoides* from *T. townsendii* and *T. bottae*. Differential features distinguishing *talpoides* from *monticola* are mentioned in the account of the latter.

As with other species of *Thomomys*, only one adult is ordinarily taken from

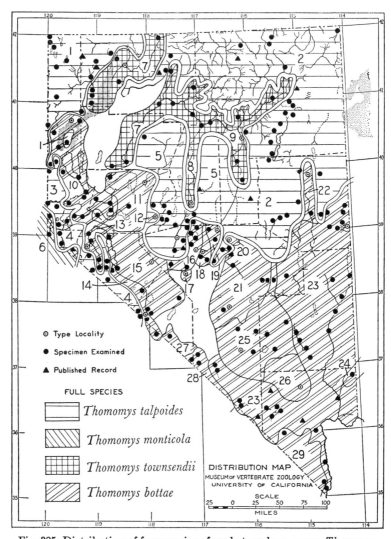

Fig. 325. Distribution of four species of pocket gophers, genus *Thomomys*.

Genus *Thomomys*	6. *T. m. monticola*	14. *T. b. lacrymalis*	22. *T. b. latus*
subspecies	7. *T. t. bachmani*	15. *T. b. solitarius*	23. *T. b. centralis*
guide:	8. *T. t. nevadensis*	16. *T. b. fumosus*	24. *T. b. virgineus*
1. *T. t. quadratus*	9. *T. t. elkoensis*	17. *T. b. curtatus*	25. *T. b. nanus*
2. *T. t. gracilis*	10. *T. b. canus*	18. *T. b. vescus*	26. *T. b. phelleoecus*
3. *T. t. fisheri*	11. *T. b. depressus*	19. *T. b. concisor*	27. *T. b. melanotis*
4. *T. t. monoensis*	12. *T. b. lucrificus*	20. *T. b. abstusus*	28. *T. b. oreoecus*
5. *T. t. falcifer*	13. *T. b. cinereus*	21. *T. b. brevidens*	29. *T. b. providentialis*

a burrow, but Johnson (MS) on June 22, 1937, caught a male and female in the same burrow high on Mount Moriah in a place that had been free of snow for only two weeks. Our field notes record six instances in which gophers of this species were caught in oatmeal-baited mousetraps set on top of the ground. All six of the gophers were immature animals. Of the 112 adult females examined for embryos, 1 was taken in April, 5 in May, 7 (3 pregnant) in June, 31 (1 pregnant) in July, 50 in August, 12 in September, and 6 in October. One of the pregnant females had 4 embryos, another 5 embryos, and 2 had 6 embryos each, giving an average of 5.3.

Thomomys talpoides quadratus Merriam
Northern Pocket Gopher

Thomomys quadratus Merriam, Proc. Biol. Soc. Washington, 11:214, July 15, 1897. Type from The Dalles, Wasco County, Oregon.

Thomomys talpoides quadratus, Goldman, Journ. Mamm., 20:234, May 14, 1939.

Thomomys quadratus quadratus, Bailey, N. Amer. Fauna, 39:115, November 15, 1915, part; Hall and Davis, Univ. California Publ. Zoöl., 40:388, 400, March 13, 1935.

Thomomys fuscus fisheri, Taylor, Univ. California Publ. Zoöl., 7:258, June 24, 1911.

Thomomys quadratus fisheri, Hall and Davis, Univ. California Publ. Zoöl., 40:388, 401, March 13, 1935, part.

Distribution.—Northwestern Nevada: east to Pine Forest Mountains; south to head of Smoke Creek and Granite Peak; and in an isolated colony on Pahrum Peak. See figure 325.

Remarks.—Measurements of three males from 4½ mi. NE Painted Point, from 4 mi. S Diessner, and from 12-mile Creek, and measurements of two females from 4½ mi. NE Painted Point and from 3 mi. S Vya, are: ♂, 194 (192, 195, 196), ♀, 196 (195, 197); 58 (50, 60, 64), 57 (53, 61); 26.3 (27, 24, 28), 24 (24, 24); weight, 97.6 (107.0, 89.6, 96.3), 83.3 (81.6, 85.0) grams.

Size medium; color dark, Mars Brown above; skull broad; premaxillae extended well behind nasals; tympanic bullae relatively uninflated dorsoventrally.

From *T. t. gracilis*, *quadratus* differs in: skull broader; nasals shorter; interpterygoid space averaging broader; basioccipital narrower, more often constricted at middle. From *T. t. fisheri*, *quadratus* differs in: size larger throughout, color darker, premaxillae extending farther behind nasals, tympanic bullae less inflated dorsoventrally.

T. t. quadratus in northwestern Nevada differs from topotypes in slightly more blackish color and slightly smaller skull. *T. t. quadratus* is less sharply distinct from *gracilis* than from *fisheri*. Specimens from the Pine Forest Mountains and from the Santa Rosa Mountains are intermediate between *quadratus* and *gracilis*. Specimens from along the eastern base of Granite Peak (5 mi. E and 3½ mi. N thereof, and from 10 mi. N and 2 mi. E Gerlach) are intermediate in that a few specimens have more inflated tympanic bullae and short premaxillary tongues, as in *fisheri*. The majority show greater resemblance to *quadratus*. The population isolated on Pahrum Peak at the northern end of Pyramid Lake agrees with *quadratus* in all but one character, greater inflation of the tympanic bullae, which is more nearly like that in *fisheri*.

Records of occurrence.—Specimens examined, 42, as follows: *Washoe Co.:* 12-mile Creek, 5300 ft., ½ mi. E Calif. boundary, 1; Barrel Spr., 5700 ft., 9½ mi. E and 3½ mi. N Ft. Bidwell, 1; 4 mi. SW Diessner, 5800 ft., 1; 4½ mi. NE Painted Point, 5800 ft., 2; ½ mi. N Vya, 6200 ft., 1; Long Valley Ranch, 5800 ft., 3 mi. S Vya, 2; 8½ mi. SE Hausen, 4800 ft., 1; 10 mi. N and 2 mi. E Gerlach, 4000 ft., 5; Smoke Creek, on Calif.-Nev. boundary, 4300 ft., 1; Horse Canyon, 5600–5800 ft., Pahrum Peak, 4. *Humboldt Co.:* meadow, Big Creek, 7000 ft., Pine Forest Mts., 5; head of Big Creek, 8000 ft., Pine Forest Mts., 1; 5 mi. N Summit Lake, 5900 ft., 1; Soldier Meadows, 4600 ft., 12. *Pershing Co.:* 5 mi. E and 3½ mi. N Granite Peak, 3900 ft., 4.

Additional records (Bailey, 1915:115, 116): *Humboldt Co.:* Badger; Summit Lake.

Thomomys talpoides gracilis Durrant
Northern Pocket Gopher

Thomomys quadratus gracilis Durrant, Bull. Univ. Utah, 29:3, February 28, 1939. Type from Pine Canyon, 6600 feet, 17 miles northwest of Kelton, Box Elder County, Utah.

Thomomys talpoides gracilis Durrant, Bull. Univ. Utah, 30:6, October 24, 1939.

Thomomys quadratus fisheri, Bailey, N. Amer. Fauna, 39:116, November 15, 1915, part; Borell and Ellis, Journ. Mamm., 15:27, 72, February 15, 1934; Hall and Davis, Univ. California Publ. Zoöl., 40:388, 400, 401, March 13, 1935, part.

Distribution.—Northeastern Nevada west to Santa Rosa Mountains north of Humboldt River and west into Eureka County and Monitor Mountain Range south of Humboldt River. See figure 325.

Remarks.—Measurements of ten males and six females from the Ruby Mountains are: ♂, 196 (182–207), ♀, 185 (178–190); 55 (50–62), 55 (45–63); 26.2 (24–28), 25.5 (24–26); weight of four males and ten females from the east side of Schellbourne Pass are 101.7 (95.3–107.0), 83.2 (75.1–93.7) grams.

Size medium; color light, in summer pelage Prouts Brown (6 mi. SW Mountain City) to Brussells Brown (Goose Creek) above; skull of medium length, relatively narrow; tympanic bullae moderately inflated dorsoventrally, and truncate anteriorly; basioccipital wide and straight-sided.

From *T. t. falcifer*, *gracilis* differs in: skull shorter and relatively narrower across zygomata; nasals straight-sided, rather than constricted near middle; rostrum relatively as well as actually shorter; basioccipital wider; tympanic bullae more globular; upper incisors shorter. Comparison with *T. t. quadratus* is made in the account of that form.

As might be expected, the difference between specimens of *gracilis* from northeastern Nevada and specimens referred to *quadratus* from northwestern Nevada is not so great as between topotypes of *gracilis* from Utah and topotypes of *quadratus* from Oregon. Specimens from the Santa Rosa Mountains north of Paradise Valley in structural features are intermediate and might be referred to *quadratus* almost as well as to *gracilis*. Furthermore, there is considerable geographic variation shown by the different populations here referred to *gracilis*. Animals from Cobb Creek are the darkest colored of any and a few specimens from there have the basioccipital constricted, as in *falcifer*. This hourglass-shape is seen in about half of the specimens from the east side of Schellbourne Pass and in nearly all of those from Gleason Creek and in those from the vicinity of Hamilton. In specimens from the Monitor Range and from Fish Spring Valley, the basioccipital is wide, the nasals are straight-sided, and, except in the one series from the Nay Ranch, the rostrum is short. These features place the animals with *gracilis* rather than with *falcifer* to which, on geographic grounds, one might expect them to be referable.

Records of occurrence.—Specimens examined, 190, as follows: *Humboldt Co.:* 13 mi. N Paradise Valley, 6700 ft., 4; Hansen Canyon, 6200 ft., 5 mi. W Paradise Valley P. O., 3. *Nye Co.:* Monitor Range, Greenmonster Canyon, 7500–8200 ft., 5; Fish Spring Valley, 6½ mi. N Fish Lake, 6600 ft., 3; Monitor Valley, Nay Ranch, 7200 ft., 8. *Elko Co.* (unless otherwise indicated in coll. of Ralph Ellis): Goose Creek, 5000 ft., 2 mi. W Utah boundary, 11 (Mus. Vert. Zoöl.); ½ mi. W Jarbidge, 1; summit between heads of Copper and Coon creeks, Jarbidge Mts., 9; 6 mi. SW Mountain City, 6500 ft., Cobb Creek, 11 (Mus. Vert. Zoöl.); Marys River, 5800 ft., 25 mi. N Deeth, 2 (Mus. Vert. Zoöl.); head of Ackler Creek [6800 ft.], 1; Steels Creek [7000 ft.], 1; summit Secret Pass, 6200 ft., 7; Jerry Creek [6700 ft.] (Jerry Crab Spring), 1; Three Lakes [9740 ft.], 10; Long Creek [7830 ft.], 4; 5 mi. E Raines, Sulphur Spring Mts., 1 (Mus. Vert. Zoöl.); Harrison Pass R. S., Green Mountain Canyon, 10; W side Ruby Lake, 6200 ft., 3 mi. N White Pine Co. line, 5. *White Pine Co.:* Willow Creek [6500 ft.], 2 mi. S Elko Co. line, 10 (9 in coll. of Ralph Ellis); W side Ruby Lake, 6100 ft., 3 mi. S Elko Co. line, 9 (coll. of Ralph Ellis); E side Schellbourne Pass, 6800 ft., 17; Gleason Creek, 7500 ft., 25; Cleve Creek, 8100–8600 ft., Shell Creek Range, 22; 1 mi. E Illipah, 6100 ft., 3; Cottonwood Creek, 6400 ft., 7 mi. SW Illipah, 1; 3 mi. W Hamilton, 8400 and 8600 ft., White Pine Mts., 2; 2½ mi. SW Hamilton, 7600 ft., 2; 3 mi. SW Hamilton, 8400 ft., 2.

Additional records (Bailey, 1915:116): *Humboldt Co.:* Cottonwood Range. *Eureka Co.:* Eureka. *Elko Co.:* Bull Run; Wells.

Thomomys talpoides fisheri Merriam
Northern Pocket Gopher

Thomomys fuscus fisheri Merriam, Proc. Biol. Soc. Washington, 14:111, July 19, 1901. Type from Beck-
with, Sierra Valley, Plumas County, California. Taylor, Univ. California Publ. Zoöl., 7:288, June 24,
1911, part.
Thomomys talpoides fisheri, Goldman, Journ. Mamm., 20:234, May 14, 1939.
Thomomys quadratus fisheri, Bailey, N. Amer. Fauna, 39:116, November 15, 1915, part; Hall and Davis,
Univ. California Publ. Zoöl., 40:388, 401, part.

Distribution.—Southwestern Washoe County and Ormsby County east of the range of
T. m. monticola. See figure 325.

Remarks.—Measurements of a male topotype and a subadult female from 3½ mi. E
Carson City are 205, 173; 57, 48; 26, 24; weight, 114.5, —— grams.

Size small; color light, in summer pelage Argus Brown above; skull small; premaxillae
extending only slightly behind nasals; tympanic bullae small but much inflated dorsoventrally; molariform teeth small.

From *T. t. monoensis, fisheri* differs in: external measurements less; color slightly darker;
skull much smaller; molariform teeth smaller. Comparison with *T. t. quadratus* is made
in the account of that race.

Records of occurrence.—Specimens examined, 17, as follows: *Washoe Co.:* Cottonwood Creek, Virginia Mts.,
4400 ft., 7; N side State-line Peak, 4400 ft., 3; 8 mi. S Reno, 1 (coll. of Ralph Ellis). *Ormsby Co.:* 3½ mi. E
Carson City, 4700 ft., 2; ¼ mi. S Carson City, 4700 ft., 1. *Storey Co.:* 6 mi. NE Virginia City, 6000 ft., 3.
Additional records (Bailey, 1915:116): *Washoe Co.:* Verdi; Reno.

Thomomys talpoides falcifer Grinnell
Northern Pocket Gopher

Thomomys falcifer Grinnell, Univ. California Publ. Zoöl., 30:180, December 10, 1926. Type from Bells
Ranch, 6890 feet, Reese River Valley, Nye County, Nevada.
Thomomys talpoides falcifer, Goldman, Journ. Mamm., 20:234, May 14, 1939.
Thomomys quadratus falcifer, Hall and Davis, Univ. California Publ. Zoöl., 40:388, 400, 401, March 13,
1935; Durrant, Bull. Univ. Utah, 29(6):5, February 28, 1939.
Thomomys quadratus fisheri, Bailey, N. Amer. Fauna, 39:116, November 15, 1915, part.
Thomomys quadratus, Linsdale, Amer. Midland Nat., 19:185, January, 1938.

Distribution.—Central Nevada: north and west to Unionville; south to head of Reese
River; east at least to Toyabe Mountains. See figure 325.

Remarks.—Measurements of seven males and five females from the type locality are:
♂, 216 (209–223), ♀, 200 (186–218); 56 (52–59), 52 (44–58); 27.0 (26–28), 25.9 (25–27);
weights not available.

Size large to medium; color Verona Brown to Snuff Brown above; skull large; rostrum
long; upper incisors long; nasals constricted medially; basioccipital hourglass-shaped.

The range of this form meets that of *gracilis,* but apparently does not meet the range of
any other subspecies of *Thomomys talpoides* in Nevada. At the time the name *falcifer* was
proposed, only the series of specimens from the type locality were available to the describer. Subsequently, specimens have become available from several other localities.
Study of all of this material shows that the exceptionally long, sickle-shaped incisors are
present in a larger percentage of topotypes than in specimens from any other locality.
Furthermore, the bodies of topotypes average larger than those of other specimens, as
do also the skulls which are more heavily ridged. Selected specimens from Cottonwood
Creek and from Kingston Creek closely approach topotypes in long upper incisors and in
heavy ridging of the skull. The animals from Cherry Creek Spring have large skulls,
closely approaching, but not equaling, those of topotypes in size. From Smiths Creek and
Peterson Creek, which places lie between Cherry Creek and the type locality of *falcifer,*
the size of skull is less. Nevertheless, all these populations have a relatively long rostrum,

hourglass-shaped basioccipital, and in most instances medially constricted nasals, which features make the specimens referable to *falcifer*. The series from Birch Creek, as might be expected from its geographic position, shows some approach to *gracilis*, namely, in straight-sided nasals, shorter rostrum, and in some specimens wide basioccipital. The specimens from 2 mi. E Unionville are of relatively large size and the basioccipital is narrow, both of which features are common to *falcifer*. Because these specimens are from the floor of the valley east of the West Humboldt Range, it is assumed that the species *talpoides* in that general area occupies the low country as well as the higher, more mountainous areas where, in view of its occupancy of higher territory to the southward, the species would be expected to occur. Specimens from western Lander County and eastern Eureka County are needed to ascertain what kind of *Thomomys* occurs there.

Records of occurrence.—Specimens examined, 133, as follows: *Pershing Co.:* 2 mi. E Unionville, 4500 ft., 9. *Churchill Co.:* Alpine, 13; Cherry Creek (Spring), 5000 ft., 10; Cherry Valley (Meadows), 6450 ft., 12; Edwards Creek Ranch, 8; ½ mi. W divide on highway between Eastgate and Campbell Creek Ranch, 6100 ft., 7. *Lander Co.:* Malloy Ranch, 5 mi. W Austin, 5500 ft., Reese River, 1; Smiths Creek, 7100 ft., 3; Smiths Creek, 5900 ft., 3; Birch Creek Ranch, Big Smoky Valley, 5650 ft., 16; Campbell Creek Ranch, 5500 ft., 16; Peterson Creek, 7000 ft., Shoshone Mts., 5; Kingston R. S., 7500 ft., 3. *Nye Co.:* junction San Juan and Cottonwood creeks, 2; Bells Ranch, 6890 ft., Reese River Valley, 20; Wisconsin Creek, 8500 ft., 2; Slys Ranch, 7400 ft., Indian Valley, Shoshone Mts., 3.

Additional records (Bailey, 1915:116): *Lander Co.:* Silver Creek (north of Austin). *Nye Co.:* Arc Dome.

Thomomys talpoides monoensis Huey
Northern Pocket Gopher

Thomomys quadratus monoensis Huey, Trans. San Diego Soc. Nat. Hist., 7:373, May 31, 1934. Type from Dexter Creek Meadow, 6800 feet, at confluence of Dexter and Wet creeks, Mono County, California.
Thomomys talpoides monoensis, Goldman, Journ. Mamm., 20:234, May 14, 1939.
Thomomys quadratus fisheri, Bailey, N. Amer. Fauna, 39:116, November 15, 1915, part ?; Hall and Davis, Univ. California Publ. Zoöl., 40:388, 400, 401, March 13, 1935, part.

Distribution.—Higher areas along western boundary of state from northern Douglas County south to northern end of White Mountains, Esmeralda County. See figure 325.

Remarks.—Measurements of ten of each sex from Lapon Canyon are: ♂, 209 (191–221), ♀, 196 (181–207); 61 (58–63), 59 (44–66); 28.3 (26–30), 27.3 (25–30); weight, 109.5 (89.5–131.4), 90.3 (76.0–101.5) grams.

Size large to medium; color pale, in summer Sudan Brown above; skull of medium size; rostrum relatively long; nasals straight-sided; tympanic bullae small but relatively much inflated dorsoventrally; basioccipital wide.

Comparison with *T. t. fisheri* is made in the account of that race, the only Nevadan race the range of which meets that of *monoensis*. Intergradation is indicated by specimens from 4½ mi. NE Genoa, which are darker colored than *monoensis* and which have molar teeth intermediate in size between those of *fisheri* and *monoensis*. With topotypes of *monoensis* in hand, it is seen that they and specimens from Pinchot and Chiatovich creeks in the northern end of the White Mountains differ in more slender skull from other specimens here referred to *monoensis*. The only significant cranial difference noted between the animals from the White Mountains and topotypes is that the premaxillae in the latter extend only about 1, rather than 2, millimeters behind the nasals. All the Nevadan specimens, those from 4½ mi. NE Genoa excepted, have large molariform teeth like topotypes.

The tail in the series of topotypes is recorded as being longer than in Nevadan specimens, but this may be the result of different techniques in measuring.

Records of occurrence.—Specimens examined, 90, as follows: *Douglas Co.:* N side Carson River, 4700 ft., 4½ mi. NE Genoa, 7; 6 mi. S Minden, 1. *Mineral Co.:* 2 mi. SW Pine Grove, 7250 ft., 9; Cottonwood Creek, 7400 and 7700 ft., Mt. Grant, 2; Lapon Canyon, 8900 ft., Mt. Grant, 25; Cat Creek, 8900 ft., Mt. Grant, 6; Sonoma, East Walker River, 5800 ft., 11; Fletcher, 6098 ft., 7. *Esmeralda Co.:* Pinchot Creek, 8200 ft., White Mts., 2; Middle Creek, 9500 ft., 1; Chiatovich Creek, 8200 ft., 19.

Additional records (Bailey, 1915:116): *Douglas Co.:* Mt. Siegel; Sugar Loaf.

Thomomys monticola monticola Allen
Mountain Pocket Gopher

Thomomys monticolus Allen, Bull. Amer. Mus. Nat. Hist., 5:48, April 28, 1893. Type from Mount Tallac, 7500 feet, Eldorado County, California.

Thomomys monticola monticola, Bailey, N. Amer. Fauna, 39:121, November 15, 1915; Hall and Davis, Univ. California Publ. Zoöl., 40:388, 400, 401, March 13, 1935.

Distribution.—In Nevada: Sierra Nevada in southwestern Washoe, western Ormsby, and western Douglas counties. See figure 325.

Remarks.—Measurements of two males and a subadult female from 3 mi. S Mt. Rose are 215, 204, 210; 61, 56, 75; 26, 28, 29.5; weights unavailable.

Size small; color near Mummy Brown above; below, dark plumbeous tipped with buffy; lips, nose, and postauricular patches black; wrists white; ears long (8 to 9 mm.) and pointed; mammae usually eight, two pairs pectoral and two pairs inguinal; skull lacking sphenoidal fissure; anterior opening of infraorbital canal posterior to anterior palatine foramina; occlusal face of anterior prism of p4 with a distinct anteromedial notch, and area of occlusal face three-fourths or more that of posterior prism.

The above-mentioned characters serve easily to distinguish *monticola* from *T. townsendii* and *T. bottae*. *T. monticola*, where its range meets that of *talpoides* in Nevada, differs as follows: color darker; ears longer (8 to 9 rather than 5 to 6 mm.) and pointed rather than rounded; two, not three, pairs of pectoral mammae; rostrum longer relative to length or breadth of brain case; zygomatic breadth less relative to length of skull; temporal ridges diverging posteriorly, rather than nearly parallel; interparietal longer relative to its breadth; tympanic bullae larger.

Records of occurrence.—Specimens examined, 12, as follows: *Washoe Co.:* W side Truckee River, ½ mi. W Verdi, 4900 ft., 1; 3 mi. S Mt. Rose, 8500 and 8600 ft., 6. *Douglas Co.:* Zephyr Cove, 5.

Additional records (Bailey, 1915:123): *Ormsby Co.:* Carson [W of city ?]. *Douglas Co.:* Glenbrook, Sugar Loaf.

Thomomys townsendii
Townsend Pocket Gopher

Three races of this species occur in Nevada, occupying the deep soils of the Humboldt River Valley, valleys of tributaries of the Humboldt River, and deep soils northwest from Humboldt Sink to the Oregon boundary. Individuals of *Thomomys townsendii* attain larger size than any other Nevadan species of the genus. Additional characters are: color above grayish washed with buff, or, instead, black; ears short (5 to 8 mm.) and rounded; mammae usually eight, two pairs pectoral and two pairs inguinal; skull with sphenoidal fissure; anterior opening of infraorbital canal anterior to or on a plane with anterior palatine foramina; occlusal face of anterior prism of p4 rounded and less than three-fourths the area of the occlusal face of the posterior prism.

The above-mentioned characters serve to distinguish *townsendii* from *T. talpoides* and *T. monticola*. From *T. bottae*, *townsendii* differs in greater average size. The relation of the two species is discussed in detail in the account of

T. bottae. The revisionary paper by Davis (1937) outlines the known range of the species both within and without the state, except for a few localities from which specimens have been obtained in Nevada since his paper was written. The large size of this gopher is reflected in the size of the mounds. Taylor (1911:266) recorded one mound at Big Creek Ranch that "was three feet long and 2 feet wide, and contained a freshly dug out stone three inches long and 2 inches in diameter."

Thomomys townsendii bachmani Davis
Townsend Pocket Gopher

Thomomys townsendii bachmani Davis, Journ. Mamm., 18:150, May 14, 1937. Type from Quinn River Crossing, 4100 feet, Humboldt County, Nevada.
Thomomys nevadensis, Taylor, Univ. California Publ. Zoöl., 7:262, June 24, 1911.
Thomomys nevadensi nevadensis, Bailey, N. Amer. Fauna, 39:44, September 30, 1915.
Thomomys townsendii nevadensis, Hall and Davis, Univ. California Publ. Zoöl., 40:388, 400, 401, March 13, 1935, part.
Thomomys perpallidus canus Bailey, N. Amer. Fauna, 39:73, November 15, 1935, part.

Distribution.—In Nevada: Quinn River Valley, Little Humboldt River Valley, and Lower Humboldt River Valley from Toulon upriver to Battle Mountain. See figure 325.

Remarks.—Measurements of three male and seven female topotypes are: ♂, 267 (261–276), ♀, 251 (240–262); 86 (82–92), 83 (73–86); 37 (36–38), 35 (33–36). Three males from 1 mi. W Winnemucca weigh 242.2, 287.5, and 255.6 (average, 261.4) grams, and a female from the same place weighs 236.0 grams.

Upper parts grayer than Buffy Brown; under parts Light Grayish Olive; nose Mummy Brown; postauricular patches black; throat-patch, tail, and upper surfaces of feet white. Nasals extending to or beyond frontal tongues; sphenorbital fissure slightly expanded dorsally.

Compared with *nevadensis,* this form differs in: tail longer; nasals longer and extending to or beyond frontal tongues; zygomatic arch heavier; sphenorbital fissure less expanded dorsally; alveolar length of maxillary tooth row longer. Differences in comparison with *T. t. elkoensis* are: anterior edge of alisphenoid covering, rather than not covering, root capsule of M2; distal end of maxillary arm of zygomatic arch larger; rostrum less depressed. Also, a larger number of specimens of *bachmani* than of *elkoensis* are light-colored (gray, as opposed to blackish).

Records of occurrence.—Specimens examined, 75, as follows: *Humboldt Co.:* McDermitt, 2 (U. S. Nat. Mus., Biol. Surv. Coll.); Big Creek Ranch, 4; Quinn River Crossing, 14; Schwartz Ranch, 1 mi. W Paradise, 1 (coll. of U. S. Biol. Surv. Dist. Agent, Reno); Paradise, 9 (U. S. Nat. Mus., Biol. Surv. Coll.); 30 mi. N Golconda, 4100 ft., 3; Jackson Creek Ranch, 4000 ft., 17½ mi. S and 5 mi. W Quinn River Crossing, 1; 18 mi. NE Iron Point, 4600 ft., 7; Flowing Springs, 7 mi. E and 3½ mi. N Division Peak, 4200 ft., 4 (1 in U. S. Nat. Mus., Biol. Surv. Coll.); 6 mi. E Division Peak, 4200 ft., 4; 11½ mi. E and 22 mi. N Gerlach, 1; 1 mi. N Winnemucca, 5; 1 mi. E Golconda, 4000 ft., 2; 18 mi. W Battle Mountain, 1 (U. S. Nat. Mus., Biol. Surv. Coll.). *Pershing Co.:* Lovelock, 2; Toulon, 1. *Lander Co.:* Battle Mountain, 13 (U. S. Nat. Mus., Biol. Surv. Coll.); Argenta, 1 (U. S. Nat. Mus., Biol. Surv. Coll.).

Thomomys townsendii elkoensis Davis
Townsend Pocket Gopher

Thomomys townsendii elkoensis Davis, Journ. Mamm., 18:151, May 14, 1937. Type from Evans, Eureka County, Nevada.
Thomomys townsendi nevadensis, Bailey, N. Amer. Fauna, 39:44, September 30, 1915.
Thomomys townsendii nevadensis, Hall and Davis, Univ. California Publ. Zoöl., 40:388, 400, 401, March 13, 1935, part.

Distribution.—Upper part of Humboldt River drainage system downriver to Carlin. See figure 325.

Remarks.—Measurements of nine males and six females from within a radius of 4 miles of Halleck are: ♂, 279 (265–290), ♀, 255 (235–264); 87 (81–95), 74 (68–81); 38.3 (37–41), 36.2 (35–37). Two males from Evans and Winzell weigh 288.5 and 280.8 grams. Four females, three from 4 mi. S Romano and one from Winzell, weigh 211.8, 231.2, 227.5 and 244.3 (average 228.7) grams.

Upper parts darker than Sepia; underparts darker than Dark Mouse Gray; nose sooty black; postauricular patches black; throat-patch, tail, and upper surfaces of feet white. Nasals long, extending posteriorly to frontal tongues; anterior face of alisphenoid curved posteriorly, exposing root capsule of M2; sphenorbital fissure contracted dorsally.

Compared with *T. t. nevadensis*, this form differs in: size larger; color more often blackish; nasals extending posteriorly beyond frontal tongues, rather than terminating anteriorly thereto; anterior face of alisphenoid posterior, rather than anterior, to root capsule of second upper molar; sphenorbital fissure contracted, rather than expanded, dorsally. Most of the specimens examined are in the dark (blackish, as opposed to grayish) phase.

Records of occurrence.—Specimens examined, 25, as follows: *Eureka Co.:* Independence Valley, 1 (U. S. Nat. Mus.); Evans, 2; Winzell, 2; 4 mi. S Romano, 3. *Elko Co.:* 4 mi. W Halleck, 1; 2 to 3 mi. W Halleck, 5200 ft., 9 (8 in coll. of Ralph Ellis); 3 mi. S Halleck, 5200 ft., 7 (coll. of Ralph Ellis).

Thomomys townsendii nevadensis Merriam
Townsend Pocket Gopher

Thomomys nevadensis Merriam, Proc. Biol. Soc. Washington, 11:213, July 15, 1897. Type from Reese River, 5 miles west of Austin, Lander County, Nevada.

Thomomys townsendi nevadensis, Bailey, N. Amer. Fauna, 39:44, September 30, 1915, part.

Thomomys townsendii nevadensis, Hall and Davis, Univ. California Publ. Zoöl., 40:388, 400, 401, March 13, 1935, part.

Distribution.—Known only from the vicinity of the type locality in Reese River Valley. See figure 325.

Remarks.—Measurements of twelve male and eight female topotypes are: ♂, 257 (239–270), ♀, 237 (232–244); 67 (60–73), 58 (53–60); 36.4 (34–38), 34.2 (34–35); weights not available.

In winter pelage: light Cinnamon-Buff above, lighter below; chin, tail, and upper surfaces of feet white. Nasals short, seldom extending posteriorly to plane of frontal tongues; sphenorbital fissure enlarged dorsally and exposed to view; root-capsule of M2 covered by alisphenoid.

All of the specimens seen and those recorded by Bailey (1915:44) now assignable to this race are of the grayish, as opposed to the blackish, phase.

Comparisons with *bachmani* and *elkoensis* are made in the accounts of those races.

Records of occurrence.—Specimens examined, 22, as follows: *Lander Co.:* Malloy Ranch, 5 mi. W Austin, Reese River, 5500 ft., 21; E side Reese River, 8 mi. W and 5 mi. S Austin, 1.

Thomomys bottae
Botta Pocket Gopher

Of this species, twenty races, more than of any other species, are recognized in Nevada. In general, the range of *bottae* is over the southern and low western parts of the state. In the northern races the size exceeds that of *Thomomys monticola* and *T. talpoides*, but averages considerably less than that of *T. townsendii*.

Size medium; color above, buffy or grayish, with some

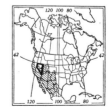

overlay of buff; underparts whitish; ears short (5 to 8 mm.) and rounded; mammae usually eight, two pairs pectoral and two pairs inguinal; skull with sphenorbital fissure; anterior opening of infraorbital canal anterior to or on a plane with anterior palatine foramina; occlusal face of anterior prism of p4 rounded and less than three-fourths the area of the occlusal face of the posterior prism.

The above-mentioned characters serve to distinguish *bottae* from *T. monticola* and *T. talpoides*. The differential features between *bottae* and *T. townsendii* mentioned in the account of the latter species apply to the two full species occurring in Nevada. Their ranges across most (the eastern two-thirds) of Nevada are separated by the range of *Thomomys talpoides*. It is only in the low, western part of the state that the ranges of *bottae* and *townsendii* are contiguous. There the races *T. bottae depressus* and *T. bottae canus* approach or meet the range of *T. townsendii bachmani* at three places. One place is the Humboldt Sink, where an adult female of *T. bottae depressus* from 1 2/5 miles northeast of Ocala differs from an adult female of *T. townsendii bachmani* from Toulon, 10 miles to the northward, in smaller size (total length, 205 versus 242; hind foot, 30 versus 33; basilar length of skull, 32.2 versus 37.5; weight of skull, including lower jaws, 3.3 grams versus 5.2 grams); postauricular black patches well developed rather than almost wanting. Weights of other individuals of *depressus* comparable to the specimen from near Ocala are less than 100 grams. The female from Toulon weighed 285.5 grams, or more than twice as much. The great difference in size makes it easy at this point to separate *townsendii* and *bottae*. No pocket gophers could be found in the territory between the two mentioned localities of occurrence.

Farther to the northwest, where the range of the large *Thomomys bottae canus* approaches that of *Thomomys townsendii relictus* (a Californian race), the structural difference between the two kinds is less. In California, specimens referred to *relictus* have been taken as far east as Amedee and 4 miles ESE thereof. In western Nevada, five female specimens referred to *canus* are available from 4½ miles south of Flanigan, which is 15 miles southwestward from the easternmost record station of *relictus*. Between these easternmost specimens of *Thomomys townsendii relictus* and westernmost specimens of *Thomomys bottae canus*, I can detect no differences of a qualitative kind; *T. townsendii relictus* is larger in size of body and skull. Intensive search in this 15-mile-wide gap between the known ranges of *T. t. relictus* and *T. b. canus* indicates that no pocket gophers live there. The third place where the ranges of the two species closely approach one another is in the general vicinity of Gerlach. The type locality of *T. b. canus* at Deep Hole is only about 26 air-line miles (11½ miles east and 22 miles north of Gerlach) southwest of the Jackson Ranch where *T. t. bachmani* occurs. By way of the meandering trough of low desert the distance is perhaps 10 miles farther; the edge of the desert, not the high country, nor the barren desert floor, affords habitat suitable for *canus* and *bachmani.* Indeed, *canus* was taken by Clark P. Streator in 1896 at Granite Creek, which place, as set forth in the account of *canus,* I judge is nearly 8 miles east of Deep Hole and only about 21 miles south and west of the *bachmani* locality, as distance is measured along the edge of the desert. Repeated search in this 21-mile strip, the third critical area, yielded no trace of gophers. Indeed, at some time since Streator's visit, *canus* seems to have disappeared from the mouth of Granite Creek and from the other moist places between there and Gerlach. The difference in size (and no other differences have been detected) between *T. bottae* at Deep Hole and *T. townsendii* at the Jackson Ranch is less even than at either of the two other places where the ranges of the two species closely approach.

Even so, the one specimen from the Jackson Ranch can be distinguished from any specimen of *canus.* The specimens of *T. t. bachmani* from 6 miles east of Division Peak are larger and near the upper limit of size for that race; therefore they are by size easily distinguished from any *T. b. canus.* The four specimens from Flowing Springs, 3 miles farther north, are smaller. Nevertheless, they are larger in most measurements than *T. b. canus* from Deep Hole. If one compares these specimens from Flowing Springs with *T. b. canus* from along the Truckee River, east of Reno, the difference in size is still less. In every measurement taken, there is some overlap between the two species, although if a combination of all measurements ordinarily employed in recording size of skull be taken into account, any specimen of *bachmani* can be distinguished from any one of *canus.* On the basis of degree of difference, *bachmani* and *canus* are only subspecifically distinct. Intergradation, where populations closely approach one another, does not occur, but it probably did relatively recently. Because intergradation does not now occur, I treat the two as distinct species.

Furthermore, it appears that the actual severance of one kind into two kinds occurred so recently that if stocks of *T. b. canus* from Deep Hole and *T. t. bachmani* from Flowing Springs were allowed to intermingle, they would crossbreed in nature. This instance provides, as I see it, another example of how two species are formed by the cutting in two of the geographic range of one species by a physical change in the habitat, namely, by an increase in the aridity of the soil to a point where it will not support the animals. At present the effect of isolation is coming into play. Within the past 40-odd years, populations have disappeared entirely, thereby widening the uninhabited area between the geographic ranges of the two kinds.

Thomomys bottae eats a variety of plants. Field notes record that on June 6, 1937, at a half mile west of Smith Creek Cave, an adult female was feeding on roots of "prickly pear cactus." On June 21, 1937, at 9100 feet elevation along Hendry Creek, one was feeding on grass. On January 17, 1934, at the Durban Ranch on the Colorado River, the animals were feeding on the roots of salt grass and roots of fig trees in an abandoned orchard. On February 13, 1934,

8 miles SSE of Dead Mountain, *Ephedra* (the part growing aboveground) was being eaten and some was being stored underground.

According to Alcorn (MS), "Pocket gophers often have storage chambers for food. Usually these chambers are situated a few inches to one side of the main tunnel and are 6 to 10 inches in diameter. On February 9, 1938 [at 4 miles east of Fallon], two or three poisoned (strychnine alkaloid) carrot baits 2 inches long by ½ inch in diameter were placed at several different places in a gopher tunnel. The system of which this tunnel was a part, when dug out the next day, was found to have 345 feet of tunnels, none of which was at a depth of more than 1½ feet. The nest, the top of which was 1½ feet below ground and in a cavity 10 inches in diameter, was made of dry, cut pieces of grass. Four or five pieces of alfalfa roots 1½ inches long were found in the nest along with one piece of poisoned carrot, the end of which had been eaten. Two feet from the nest was a cavity 5 inches in diameter filled with gopher droppings and seven pieces of alfalfa roots about ¼ inch wide by 1¼ inches long with all the bark eaten off.

"This rubbish or waste had been tightly packed into the cavity, as it also was in two other cavities near by. One of these, 4 feet from the nest, was of the same size, and had eighty-seven pieces of alfalfa roots packed into it. Another, 5 feet from the nest, had forty pieces of alfalfa roots with the bark peeled off. All three cavities were apparently garbage rooms for the gopher and all were tightly packed with droppings and the pieces of roots. Some distance from the nest three food-storage chambers were found. One, 30 feet away, contained 876 pieces of alfalfa roots. Another, 100 feet from the nest, had 1,561 pieces of alfalfa roots, and a third, 115 feet from the nest, contained 336 dry, hard pieces of alfalfa roots. Apparently this third chamber had been forgotten, or else the gopher had cut more food than he could eat, for, in the dry soil of the knoll upon which the chamber was situated, the alfalfa roots had dried out. I noticed that when these roots were dug out and left in the dry air they dried out in a day or so and got as hard as wood. A gopher usually stores these roots far enough under ground so that they keep moist. The roots in the first and second cavities were in moist ground which kept them soft and edible for some time. The gopher, a good-sized male, was found dead about 30 feet from the nest." Alcorn (MS) adds that although he recorded only the number of pieces of alfalfa roots stored, almost every cache contained also pieces of roots of sour dock (*Rumex*) which, as a food for the pocket gophers in the cultivated district about Fallon, is second only to alfalfa. On occasion, grain (wheat) is stored below ground.

Additional information recorded by Alcorn (MS) includes the following: "Presumably to escape from the heat, the old gophers in summer dig tunnels several feet deep and pack the laterals [burrows which lead from the main tunnel to the surface] all the way to the surface with soil. In early spring most of the tunnels are only 4 to 8 inches deep. The young, born in spring, and apparently more active in summer than the adults, now and then throw out a fresh mound of soil, whereas an old gopher may not push out a mound for 2 months.

"The nest chamber may be an empty food chamber or one excavated for a nest. It is usually filled with dry grass cut into pieces or with other loose material gathered from the surface. Both males and females have nests.

"A burrow system excavated in November, 1937, 4 miles west of Fallon, was 185 feet long. Along this were thirty-six mounds of earth which averaged 5.1 feet apart, with extremes of 2 and 12 feet. Three side tunnels had six additional mounds. The nest was 2 feet below the surface of the ground, and the food chamber, containing 736 pieces of alfalfa roots one-half to 5 inches long, was 20 inches below ground. The roots of 182 alfalfa plants had been cut by this gopher in the course of construction of the tunnel. Ninety-eight per cent of the tunnel was 6 to 8 inches deep; the rest, as at the nest, was deeper.

"On February 18, 1938, in an alfalfa field, 4 miles west and 2 miles north of Fallon, a burrow, in several parts of which poisoned carrot had been placed the day before, was dug out. A male gopher was found dead in the burrow. The crowns of forty-five alfalfa plants along the course of the burrow had been cut off. The tunnel system totaled 477 feet in length, and the fifty mounds of earth thrown out averaged 9.54 feet apart and varied from 2 to 24 feet apart. The depth of the tunnel below ground varied from 4 to 24 inches and averaged about 8 inches.

"The normal gopher tunnel system at this time (February, 1938) is 200 feet of tunnel, fifteen mounds, one nest 10 inches in diameter situated 1½ to 2 feet underground, and one or more storage chambers."

In supervising efforts of boys enrolled in the Civilian Conservation Corps to eradicate pocket gophers in the vicinity of Fallon, J. R. Alcorn had traps set in the "live" gopher burrows about 45 days after poison had been placed in them. "Live" gopher burrows designates those which showed evidences of use at the time traps were set, in contrast to "dead" burrows which showed no signs of use, presumably because the gophers therein had been killed by the poisoned baits that had been introduced into the burrows 45 days before. Record was kept of 43,572 traps set in the 3 years, 1936, 1937, and 1938, on 41,272 acres, in which a total of 14,695 gophers were caught. On the basis of an estimate that 80 per cent of the gophers had been killed by poison, the population of pocket gophers averaged 1.78 per acre.

Between July 20 and August 4, 1937, detailed record was kept of ninety-six sets (a set being one or more traps at a place). Only one set was made in what was judged to be the burrow system of one gopher. The following information was recorded for each set: (1) total number of mounds; (2) number of mounds less than 1 week old; (3) length of the "lateral," the tunnel leading from the mound of earth to the main tunnel where the set of traps, or of a trap, was made; (4) the length of the fill of the "lateral"; (5) depth below ground at which the "lateral" [tunnel] joined the main tunnel, measurement being made from the surface of the ground to the roof of the tunnel; (6) distance between the outside of the two mounds farthest apart in each burrow system; and (7) sex and size of the animal caught, and condition of the reproductive organs in each female. Data on the seven items mentioned, for eight males having a total length of 232 millimeters or more and for thirty females having a total length of 197 millimeters or more, are as follows:

DATA ON POCKET GOPHER WORKINGS

	8 males		30 females	
	Average	Extremes	Average	Extremes
Total number of mounds per burrow.......	6.8	1–14	9.3	3–36
Number of mounds less than one week old.	4.0	1–13	4.5	1–33
Length of lateral [tunnel]................	9.6 in.	4–20 in.	18.5 in.	2–61 in.
Length of the fill of the lateral [tunnel]....	6.4 in.	0–10 in.	10.1 in.	0–46 in.
Depth at lateral and main tunnel junction	4.6 in.	4–7 in.	6.5 in.	2–16 in.
Distance between mounds farthest apart..	38 ft., 5 in.	0–73 ft.	37 ft., 7 in.	6–105 ft.

From the above, it appears that the lengths of the tunnel systems of males and females are about the same, but that the females make more mounds of earth than males in excavating a tunnel of the same length. It should be emphasized that these observations were made in late July and early August, a time of year when adult gophers leave relatively few evidences of their activity on the surface of the ground. Certainly fewer mounds of earth are thrown out in summer than in March.

The taking of twenty-two weasels in the gopher traps which caught 14,695 gophers suggests that weasels are important enemies of gophers. The gopher snake (*Pituophis*) and the barn owl (*Tyto*) also are thought to kill many of the pocket gophers of this species.

In the vicinity of Fallon, Alcorn thinks that there is only one litter per year. In this area he kept record of the embryos in 37 females and found the mode to be 5, the mean to be 5.4, and the extremes 2 and 11. Adding to these, our records of other pregnant females of this species taken in Nevada, it is found that the 63 pregnant females contained an average of 4.8 embryos (mode of 4), with extremes of 2 and 11. It is obvious that the young are born in the first half of the year. By months, the adult females of which we have record are distributed as follows: January, 72 (6 pregnant, average size of litter, 3.8); February, 65 (13 pregnant, 5.1 per litter); March, 29 (12 pregnant, 5.8 per litter); April, 21 (8 pregnant, 6.4 per litter); May, 115 (15 pregnant, 3.5 per litter); June, 85 (6 pregnant, 5.2 per litter); July, 103 (3 pregnant, 2 per litter); August, 32; September, 21; October, 14; November, 0; December, 2. In the first 4 months, the animals recorded were nearly all of the race *canus* from the vicinity of Fallon. Most of those recorded in May are of the race *centralis* from White Pine County; the smaller number of embryos per litter in this month, compared to the months preceding and to June, possibly reflects a subspecific difference. The smaller number of embryos recorded at the end and at the beginning of the breeding season probably is correlated with the lesser age of the pregnant females. The litter size in January averages 3.8. Pregnant females in

January probably average 3 months younger than pregnant females in April, when the litters average 6.1 embryos. In July the 3 pregnant females, each of which contained but 2 embryos, may be young of the year. Whatever the reasons, the number of embryos per litter is smaller at the beginning and end of the reproductive period than near the middle of the period.

Thomomys bottae canus Bailey
Botta Pocket Gopher

Thomomys canus Bailey, Proc. Biol. Soc. Washington, 23:79, May 4, 1910. Type from Deep Hole, Washoe County, Nevada.

Thomomys bottae canus, Hall, Univ. California Publ. Zoöl., 26:333, February 27, 1932; Hall and Davis, Univ. California Publ. Zoöl., 40:394, March 13, 1935.

Thomomys perpallidus canus Bailey, N. Amer. Fauna, 39:73, November 15, 1915, part.

Distribution.—Margins of Black Rock Desert from Deep Hole southward to Carson River Valley; from near Dayton eastward to Fallon. See figure 325.

Remarks.—Measurements of seven male and fifteen female topotypes are: ♂, 247 (242–253); ♀, 224 (214–234); 80.7 (79–83); 70.7 (61–76); 32.6 (31–34), 31.0 (30–32); weight, 183.0 (154.0–201.5), 138.8 (119.0–164.3) grams.

Size large, with tail and hind foot long; color in both summer and winter pelage near Pale Mouse Gray with faint shade of buff; underparts white, but hairs basally plumbeous except on thoracic and often on inguinal regions where hairs white to base; skull large; rostrum and incisors long; rostrum constricted posteriorly; zygomata parallel; temporal ridges widest apart near middle of frontal bone; maxillofrontal suture on top of skull concave posteromedially; occiput relatively low and wide; tympanic bullae but little inflated.

Comparisons with *depressus, lucrificus,* and *cinereus* are made in the accounts of those races. There is considerable geographic variation in cranial characters. The animals from along the Carson River agree with *Thomomys bottae cinereus* in the shortness of the incisors and show approach to that form in smaller size, more arched dorsal outline of the skull in longitudinal axis, broader rostrum, and more inflated tympanic bullae. Agreement with *canus* is shown in depth of skull, flattened occiput, and in the more nearly parallel zygomata. Animals from the vicinity of Fallon have slightly more buff in the coloration than those to the northwest. Some geographic variation is shown also in the northern part of the range of *canus*. The three adults from Smoke Creek are smaller than topotypes.

On May 23, 1896, Clark P. Streator obtained two pocket gophers, *Thomomys bottae canus*, at a place designated by him as Granite Creek, Nevada. When I visited the area in question in July of 1936 and again in 1941, the name Granite Creek Ranch was applied to a ranch about 9½ miles by air line NNE of the railroad station of Gerlach. From the south base of Granite Peak this ranch is reached by going NNE along the edge of the alkali flat some 10 miles or more, crossing a low spur of Granite Peak, and then turning northeast to the ranch which is watered by the flow of two creeks, Rock Creek to the north and Granite Creek to the south, which unite into one stream I am told, before reaching the ranch. William Hart, resident at this ranch in July, 1936, told me that it had been known as Granite Creek Ranch for more than 60 years, and I supposed at that time that this was where Streator caught his two gophers, although through Mr. Hart I knew of Granite Station, 4 miles NNE of Gerlach. In July of 1941, Mr. Hart, who then was living at Granite Station, showed me the stone foundations of two old buildings there which served as a stage station, and said that the ranch 9½ mi. NNE of Gerlach in the early days was known as Granite Meadows, not Granite Creek Ranch! Water flows down to the latter place at least as late as July, but not this late to Granite Station. In July, 1941, we could find no *Thomomys* at Granite Station or vicinity, and at Granite Creek

Ranch [= Granite Meadows] trapped only *Thomomys talpoides*. Streator traveled from Smoke Creek, where he trapped three *T. b. canus* on May 8, 1896, to Deep Hole, to Granite Creek, and to Flowing Springs, and I suppose he stopped at Granite Station. My guess is that this is where he got his two gophers; Granite Meadows would have been somewhat off the most direct route of travel. Where on Smoke Creek he took his three *Thomomys* I do not know. In July of 1936 we found only *Thomomys talpoides* along this creek just east of the state boundary, and at and near the mouth of the creek could find no gophers of any kind, either in July, 1936, or in March, 1941. At some time in the elapsed 45 years, *Thomomys bottae canus* has apparently become extinct at Granite [Station ?] Creek and perhaps at the mouth of Smoke Creek also.

Records of occurrence.—Specimens examined, 108, as follows: *Washoe Co.:* Granite Creek, 2 (U. S. Nat. Mus., Biol. Surv. Coll.); Deep Hole, 30; Smoke Creek, 3 (U. S. Nat. Mus., Biol. Surv. Coll.); Round Hole, 3900 ft., 1; 4½ mi. S Flanigan, 4100 ft., 5; Pyramid Lake, 2 mi. W Sutcliffe, 1; 2 mi. N Nixon, 1; 1 mi. SW Pyramid Lake, 1; 1 mi. S Pyramid Lake, 1; 1 mi. N Wadsworth, 4100 ft., 2; western outskirts of Wadsworth [= 34 mi. E Reno on specimen label], 2 (coll. of Ralph Ellis); N side Truckee River, 9½ mi. E Reno, 4500 ft., 2. *Storey Co.:* S side Truckee River, 9½ mi. E Reno, 4500 ft., 3. *Lyon Co.:* 1 mi. S Fernley, 2; 2 mi. SE Fernley, 1; 5 mi. S Fernley, 1; S side Carson River, 4300 ft., 1 mi. E Old Ft. Churchill, 5; N side Carson River, 4300 ft., 2 mi. W Old Ft. Churchill, 1; same, except 6 mi. W, 2; same, except 10 mi. W, 2; N side Carson River, 4300 ft., 1 mi. E Dayton, 1. *Churchill Co.:* 2 mi. SW Hazen, 2; 4 mi. W Fallon, 7; 4 mi. W and 2 mi. S Fallon, 4000 ft., 1; Fallon, 3970 ft., 16; 1½ mi. SW Fallon, 12; 7 mi. S and 3½ mi. E Fallon, 1.

Thomomys bottae depressus Hall
Botta Pocket Gopher

Thomomys bottae depressus Hall, Univ. California Publ. Zoöl., 26:326, February 27, 1932. Type from Dixie Meadows [at south end of Humboldt Salt Marsh], 3500 feet, Churchill County, Nevada. Hall and Davis, Univ. California Publ. Zoöl., 40:394, March 13, 1935.

Thomomys quadratus fisheri, Hall and Davis, Univ. California Publ. Zoöl., 40:400, March 13, 1935, part.

Distribution.—Area around Carson Sink and Humboldt Salt Marsh. See figure 325.

Remarks.—Measurements of six male and seven female topotypes are: ♂, 224 (220–232), ♀, 207 (195–218); 62 (55–68), 59 (54–60); 29 (28–30), 28 (28–29); weight of two males and two females from vicinity of Mountain Well, ♂, 101.7, 110.4 (av. 105.7), ♀, 111.2, 90.6 (100.9) grams.

Size small; tail of medium length; hind foot short; color, in winter pelage, lighter than Mouse Gray above with slight tinge of buff; gray below with tinge of buff on pectoral region. Skull relatively broad, especially in female; rostrum broad, not constricted posteriorly, but depressed distally; tympanic bullae angular anterolaterally; foramen magnum evenly rounded above.

From *T. b. canus*, this race differs in smaller size; presence of a small amount of buff color; skull smaller; rostrum relatively shorter, as wide posteriorly as anteriorly, rather than constricted posteriorly, and more depressed distally; lacrimals larger; tympanic bullae more angular anterolaterally; interparietal wider than long, rather than longer than wide; ascending tongues of premaxillae extending farther behind nasals; foramen magnum evenly rounded above, rather than marked with median evagination; incisors shorter; maxillary tooth row relatively longer. From *fumosus*, *depressus* differs in: size smaller; color lighter (more gray); skull relatively broader; rostrum not constricted posteriorly; occiput relatively shallower; pterygoid space more broadly V-shaped; temporal ridges more widely separated; top of skull less depressed interorbitally; paroccipital processes less developed. Comparisons with *T. b. lucrificus* and *T. b. cinereus* are made in the accounts of those races.

The trace of buff in the pelage of *depressus* is to be expected on geographic grounds because *lucrificus* to the southeastward has an appreciable amount of buff. Also, specimens of *canus* from Fallon and vicinity display a trace of buff which is lacking in topotypes of *canus* and in other specimens from the northwestern part of the range of *canus*.

Topotypes have slightly more robust skulls than animals from other localities. In shape of the interpterygoid space they are intermediate between the narrowly V-shaped condition in the animals from near Mountain Well and the broadly U-shaped condition in the animals from Ocala. The latter have more extensive postauricular black patches than topotypes and specimens from the vicinity of Mountain Well. These specimens from near Ocala were erroneously referred (Hall and Davis, 1935:400) to *Thomomys quadratus fisheri*. They lived in alkaline soil and were feeding on the large (half the diameter of a lead pencil) roots of grass locally called Johnson grass. The animals at Mountain Well and 1 mile west of this place were living in sand dunes. The three young males from the hills 15 miles southwest of Fallon were taken in sandy soil. These specimens, although referable to *depressus*, show approach in some features to both *cinereus* and *canus*, especially to the latter. For example, the foramen magnum has the dorsal evagination of *canus* and the rostrum is constricted posteriorly.

Records of occurrence.—Specimens examined, 31, as follows: *Churchill Co.:* 1 2/5 mi. NE Ocala, 3900 ft., 3; Dixie Meadows, 3500 ft., 20; 1 mi. W Mountain Well, 3; Mountain Well, 5600 ft., 2; 15 mi. SW Fallon, 5000 ft., 3.

Thomomys bottae lucrificus Hall and Durham
Botta Pocket Gopher

Thomomys bottae lucrificus Hall and Durham, Proc. Biol. Soc. Washington, 51:15, February 18, 1938. Type from Eastgate, Churchill County, Nevada.

Distribution.—Known only from Eastgate and at an elevation 600 feet higher along the creek which flows westward from the Desatoya Mountains to Eastgate. See figure 325.

Remarks.—Measurements of six male and eleven female topotypes are: ♂, 255 (238–265), ♀, 229 (216–245); 81 (72–88), 72 (65–79); 32.2 (31–33), 30.2 (27–31); weight, 200.0 (two specimens, 198.5 and 201.5), 144.4 (130.6–156.0) grams.

Size large; tail of medium length; hind foot long; color, in winter pelage, near (18″ h to j) Tawny Olive above, or grayish, tinged with buff; plumbeous tipped with whitish below; summer pelage more reddish (less of smoked effect) above, and plumbeous lightly tipped with white below. In both pelages, pectoral region plumbeous sometimes with buffy tinge; inguinal region plumbeous or white; skull large; nasals expanded distally; hamular processes of lacrimals large; tympanic bullae angular anterolaterally and but little inflated; occiput anterodorsally inclined.

In size, *lucrificus* resembles *canus* and *fumosus* and is larger than *depressus* and *solitarius*. In color, *lucrificus* is intermediate between *canus* and *fumosus*, but shows greater resemblance to the latter in both winter and summer pelage. Adult male skulls differ from those of topotypes of *canus* and specimens of *canus* from the vicinity of Fallon, as follows: upper incisors shorter and narrower; nasopremaxillary sutures convex medially rather than straight; nasals expanded distally and bluntly extended medially rather than truncate anteriorly and straight-sided. Hamular processes of lacrimals larger; occiput more anterodorsally (less vertically) inclined; dorsal margin of foramen magnum rarely, as opposed to commonly, notched; interpterygoid space averaging more narrowly V-shaped; tympanic bullae anterolaterally angular rather than smoothly rounded, and less inflated ventrally and medially. Differences of the same nature but of lesser degree are shown by females. Selected differences of adult male and female skulls of *lucrificus* from those of *fumosus* are: larger size; relatively, as well as actually, greater zygomatic breadth; larger jugals; dorsal outline of skull, viewed laterally, without the marked dorsal convexity at junction of rostrum and interorbital region. Selected differences from *T. b. depressus* are: larger in external and most cranial measurements; rostrum less depressed distally and relatively longer; tympanic bullae less inflated. Differences from *T. b. solitarius* are: larger in all parts measured; weight about double; relatively broader across zygomatic arches; rostrum relatively longer and broader; tympanic bullae less inflated.

T. b. lucrificus appears to be as closely related to *T. b. fumosus* as to *T. b. canus*. The range of *canus* corresponds in general with the northwestern reaches of Lake Lahontan. The 50-odd miles of extremely arid desert between the type locality of *lucrificus* and the easternmost record station of *canus*, near Fallon, is not known to be inhabited by pocket gophers of any species. If any occur there, it is expected that they would be of, or closely related to, the race *T. b. depressus*. The 50-mile extent of country separating *T. b. lucrificus* from *T. b. fumosus* to the eastward is occupied by *Thomomys talpoides*, a distinct species. *T. b. lucrificus*, then, is thought to be geographically isolated from other races of its species, excepting possibly *T. b. solitarius* and *T. b. depressus*. An individual of either of these races is hardly half the mass of one of *lucrificus*, for adult males of *lucrificus* average 200 grams in weight and those of the other two mentioned races only 100 grams.

Records of occurrence.—Specimens examined, 37, as follows: *Churchill Co.:* Eastgate, 31; along creek flowing from the Desatoya Mountains to Eastgate, 5025 ft., 6.

Thomomys bottae cinereus Hall
Botta Pocket Gopher

Thomomys bottae cinereus Hall, Univ. California Publ. Zoöl., 26:327, February 27, 1932. Type from West Walker River, Smiths Valley, 4700 feet, Lyon County, Nevada. Hall and Davis, Univ. California Publ. Zoöl., 40:394, March 13, 1935.

Distribution.—Valleys of West Walker and East Walker rivers and downstream along Walker River as far as Walker Lake. See figure 325.

Remarks.—Measurements of three males and three females from the type locality are: ♂, 230, 240, 230 (average, 233), ♀, 203, 205, 228 (average, 212); 76, 71, 72 (73), 61, 60, 63 (61); 30, 31, 30 (30), 28, 28, 30 (29); weight of two males and six females from 9 mi. NE Wellington, 158.5 (154.3–162.6), 120.4 (97.3–142.5) grams.

Size, including length of tail and hind foot, medium for the species; color, in winter pelage, slightly lighter than Mouse Gray above; gray below except for white chin and anal region; some specimens faintly tinged with buff on forearms; in summer the same, but with tinge of buff in upper parts; skull relatively broad, especially in female; rostrum narrow, but not constricted posteriorly; tympanic bullae moderately inflated; zygomatic breadth greater posteriorly than anteriorly; pterygoid space with central spicule; pterygoid processes wide transversely.

Selected differences in *cinereus* as compared with *canus*, the race next adjacent on the north, are: smaller; dorsal outline of skull in longitudinal axis more arched; vertical depth of skull through maxillary teeth less; rostrum relatively broader; occiput less flattened; tympanic bullae more inflated; incisors shorter; and in females, zygomatic breadth less anteriorly than posteriorly, rather than about the same anteriorly and posteriorly; ascending tongues of premaxillae and whole rostrum relatively and actually wider.

Excepting the faint tinge of buff on the forearms of about half of the specimens of *cinereus*, the coloration is practically identical with that of *canus*. *T. b. canus, cinereus,* and *depressus* are the three palest of the known races of this species in Nevada.

In comparison with *lacrymalis*, the race next adjacent on the south, selected differences of *cinereus* are as follows: coloration more gray (less buffy); smaller; rostrum relatively more slender and constricted posteriorly; lacrimals smaller; posterior ends of ascending tongues of premaxillae more attenuated; tympanic bullae less inflated; zygomatic arm of maxilla at junction with jugal less thickened; pterygoid space more nearly U-shaped and with, rather than without, central spicule of vertical lamina of palate; each pterygoid process wider transversely; incisors shorter.

From *T. b. depressus, cinereus* differs in: external measurements larger; color slightly paler; interorbital breadth and length of maxillary tooth row actually as well as relatively less; rostrum less depressed distally; brain case more inflated anteriorly.

From *solitarius, cinereus* differs in larger size, grayer (less buffy) color, relatively longer rostrum, and more heavily ridged skull.

Topotypes of *cinereus* were employed in making the above comparisons. Specimens from the East Walker River average larger and are more cinnamon in color than topotypes. Specimens from 3 miles south of Schurz also are more cinnamon-colored than topotypes but have smaller skulls. These slight average differences are expectable when one recalls that the two races *solitarius* and *lacrymalis*, adjoining *cinereus* on the southward, are distinctly cinnamon-colored in comparison with *cinereus*. The specimens from 5½ to 12 miles south of Yerington agree closely with topotypes of *cinereus*.

Records of occurrence.—Specimens examined, 62, as follows: *Lyon Co.:* ½ mi. N Yerington, 1; 3 mi. S Yerington, 4500 ft., 1; 5½ mi. S Yerington, 4500 ft., 8; 11½ to 12 mi. S Yerington, 4600 ft., 3; Smiths Valley, 4700 ft., 6; 9 mi. NE Wellington, 4800 ft., 8. *Mineral Co.:* 3 mi. S Schurz, 4100 ft., 14; East Walker River, 5000 ft., 5 mi. NW Morgans Ranch, 7; East Walker River, 5050 ft., 2 mi. NW Morgans Ranch, 14; East Walker River, 5100 ft., Morgans Ranch, 4.

Thomomys bottae lacrymalis Hall
Botta Pocket Gopher

Thomomys bottae lacrymalis Hall, Univ. California Publ. Zoöl., 26:328, February 27, 1932. Type from Arlemont [= Chiatovich Ranch, Fish Lake Valley], 4900 feet, Esmeralda County, Nevada.

Distribution.—Fish Lake Valley north to south end of Walker Lake. See figure 325.

Remarks.—Measurements of five males and ten females from the type locality are: ♂, 241 (232–255), ♀, 216 (200–230); 63 (58–68), 59 (51–70); 31 (30–32), 28.6 (26.5–31.0); weight of male and female from McNett Ranch, 162.7 and 148.6 grams.

Size large; tail short; hind foot long; color, in summer pelage, slightly lighter than Cinnamon-Buff above; Neutral Gray below except for white inguinal region and presence of buff on pectoral region; skull broad, especially in male; rostrum relatively broad but constricted proximally; tympanic bullae large and smooth; lacrimals large and expanded at tips; zygomatic process of maxilla greatly thickened at junction with jugal; interpterygoid space narrowly V-shaped.

T. b. lacrymalis is similar in general size and coloration to *Thomomys bottae amargosae* Grinnell and *Thomomys bottae melanotis* Grinnell, but, on the average, the color is more cinnamon than in either of these forms. Also, available specimens of *melanotis* average slightly smaller than those of *lacrymalis* and *amargosae*. Selected cranial characters in which *lacrymalis* differs from *melanotis* are: skull larger; lacrimals relatively larger; maxillary tooth row longer; jugals bowed outward rather than straight; nasals and ascending tongues of premaxillae actually and relatively longer. Outstanding differences from *amargosae* are: jugal, in longitudinal axis, inclined forward and upward rather than horizontally; zygomatic process of maxilla, viewed dorsolaterally, slightly, rather than greatly, thickened at junction with jugal; zygomatic breadth actually and relatively less; nasals actually and relatively longer; anterior end of rostrum usually more depressed. For comparison with *T. b. cinereus, T. b. solitarius,* and *curtatus*, see accounts of those races.

Intergradation with *cinereus* is indicated by a series of specimens from Cat Creek, near the southern end of Walker Lake. With respect to size and shape of the tympanic bullae these specimens are almost exactly intermediate as between *cinereus* and *lacrymalis*. Agreement with *cinereus* is shown in smaller size of the animal and smaller lacrimals. In eight other differential characters as between *lacrymalis* and *cinereus*, the specimens from Cat Creek show precise agreement with *lacrymalis*. The only character noted as distinguishing the specimens from Cat Creek from both *lacrymalis* and *cinereus* is the more abrupt outward extension of the squamosal arm of the zygomatic arch. The specimens from Fish Lake Valley approach the specimens from Cat Creek in this respect more closely than do those of *cinereus*.

The two specimens from near Candelaria Junction are so young as not clearly to show diagnostic cranial characters. Their reference to the subspecies *lacrymalis* is therefore tentative. Indeed, certain features of these specimens suggest relationship with the subspecies *solitarius*.

Records of occurrence.—Specimens examined, 34, as follows: *Mineral Co.:* Cat Creek, 4 mi. W Hawthorne, 9; 1 mi. W Candelaria Junction, 5500 ft., 2. *Esmeralda Co.:* Arlemont [= Chiatovich Ranch, Fish Lake Valley], 4900 ft., 18; [upper] McNett Ranch, 5 mi. SW Arlemont, 5600 ft., 5.

Thomomys bottae solitarius Grinnell
Botta Pocket Gopher

Thomomys solitarius Grinnell, Univ. California Publ. Zoöl., 30:177, December 10, 1926. Type from Fingerrock Wash, Stewart Valley, 5400 feet, Mineral County, Nevada.
Thomomys bottae solitarius, Hall, Univ. California Publ. Zoöl., 26:333, February 27, 1932; Hall and Davis, Univ. California Publ. Zoöl., 40:395, March 13, 1935.
Thomomys bottae lacrymalis Hall, Univ. California Publ. Zoöl., 38:329, February 27, 1932, part.

Distribution.—Eastern Mineral County and northern Esmeralda County. See figure 325.

Remarks.—Measurements of five males and two females from the type locality are: ♂, 211 (205–216), ♀, 199 (194–203); 68 (64–73), 62 (58–66); 28.0 (28–28), 27.5 (27–28); weight of two males and five females from 7 mi. N and from 4 mi. NE Arlemont, ♂, 101.4 (95.3–103.5), ♀, 83.5 (73.6–93.3) grams.

Size small; tail of medium length; hind foot short; color, in winter and summer pelage, near Cinnamon-Buff; postauricular black patch large; underparts white or whitish with hair plumbeous basally except on inguinal region where white to base; skull small; rostrum constricted posteriorly; zygomatic breadth greater posteriorly than anteriorly; premaxillae extended well behind nasals; interpterygoid space widely V-shaped to narrowly U-shaped.

The two adult females from the south end of Walker Lake at one time (Hall, 1932:329) were tentatively referred to *lacrymalis*, but with more adequate material from surrounding areas were found to agree with *solitarius* and to differ from *lacrymalis* in small size, weaker ridging of skull, greater extension of premaxillae posteriorly to nasals, smaller lacrimals, more abruptly flaring zygomata posteriorly, and in the greater zygomatic breadth posteriorly than anteriorly. The relative width of the rostrum and degree of inflation of the tympanic bullae are intermediate between conditions obtaining in *lacrymalis* and *solitarius*. The type of soil in which these two animals were taken is unknown at the present writing. The animals from 4 miles northeast of Arlemont were taken in soil not more than 6 inches deep underlain with an impenetrable (for them) stratum of alkali. The specimens from 7 miles north of Arlemont were taken in dunes of drifted sand. The one adult male from Lone Mountain was taken in deep soil where *Sarcobatus* grew. This animal is larger than specimens of *solitarius* from Fish Lake Valley and in general appearance suggests *curtatus* which it resembles also in color. The longer incisors, the distally more depressed rostrum, and the sum total of its cranial characters indicate nearer relationship with *solitarius* than with any other named race. Since the place from which this specimen comes is in the center of an area otherwise unrepresented by specimens of *Thomomys*, study of additional materials from this area might make a different identification of this specimen necessary.

From *T. b. curtatus*, *solitarius* differs in shorter body and hind foot; skull averaging smaller in all parts measured; relatively narrower across zygomatic arches; temporal ridges less well developed and farther apart; rostrum less bent downward at end; tympanic bullae more angular anterolaterally. From *T. b. fumosus*, *solitarius* differs in shorter body and hind foot; longer tail, on the average; skull smaller in all parts measured; relatively narrower across zygomatic arches; relatively broader interorbitally; temporal ridges bowed outward or parallel rather than bowed inward; temporal ridges much farther apart; tympanic bullae more angular anterolaterally. For comparison with *T. b. cinereus* and *T. b. lucrificus*, see accounts of those forms.

Records of occurrence.—Specimens examined, 24, as follows: *Mineral Co.:* Fingerrock Wash,5400 ft.,7; S end Walker Lake, 4100 ft., 2. *Esmeralda Co.:* Lone Mtn., 6600 ft., 12½ mi. W and 2½ mi. S Tonopah, 1; 7 mi. N Arlemont, 5500 ft., 7; 4 mi. NE Arlemont, 4800 ft., 7.

Thomomys bottae fumosus Hall
Botta Pocket Gopher

Thomomys bottae fumosus Hall, Univ. California Publ. Zoöl., 26:329, February 27, 1932. Type from Milman Ranch, Moores Creek, 19 miles southeast of Millett Post Office, Nye County, Nevada. Hall and Davis, Univ. California Publ. Zoöl., 40:395, March 13, 1935.
Thomomys canus Bailey, part, N. Amer. Fauna, 39:73, November 15, 1915.
Thomomys perpallidus, Linsdale, Amer. Midland Nat., 19:184, January, 1938.

Distribution.—Great Smoky Valley and around southern end of Toyabe Mountain Range to Cloverdale Creek. See figure 325.

Remarks.—Measurements of seven males and eight females from the type locality are: ♂, 236 (223–247), ♀, 212 (192–233); 60 (53–70), 56 (50–66); 31.6 (30.5–32.0), 29.2 (27.0–31.5); weight of two males and two females from 5 mi. SE Millett, 171.0, 190.2 (average 180.6), 118.4, 138.2 (average 128.3) grams.

Size large; tail of medium length; hind foot long; color, in winter pelage, above near Deep Mouse Gray with smoky tinge, darkest on middorsal area; sides and pectoral regions tinged with buff; inguinal region and, at some localities, small areas on pectoral region with hair white to base; otherwise dark gray below, with occasional white markings on throat and chin; postauricular black patches large; in summer pelage similar except that most specimens have a slight tinge of Ochraceous-Buff on upper parts and sides; skull large and relatively long; rostrum large and greatly elongated; tympanic bullae moderately inflated and angular anteriorly; frontal region behind orbits depressed so as to form basin; incisors long; maxillary tooth row short.

In comparison with *T. b. centralis*, *fumosus* is of about the same size, but has a shorter tail and is Deep Mouse Gray rather than Cinnamon-Buff above. Other differences are: skull actually and relatively deeper throughout; incisors slightly larger and of much greater diameter; rostrum actually and relatively broader; zygomatic arm of maxilla carried farther anteriorly on rostrum; bullae more inflated; basioccipital tending to be Y-shaped rather than V-shaped. *T. b. fumosus* may be distinguished from *T. b. canus* by the following selected differences: coloration darker; cranium and body smaller; rostrum more depressed distally; interorbital region wider; occiput much less flattened; bullae less attenuated anteriorly; pterygoid space narrowly V-shaped and without central spicule, rather than U-shaped and with central spicule; interorbital region more depressed. For comparison with *T. b. curtatus*, *T. b. solitarius*, *T. b. vescus*, and *T. b. brevidens*, see accounts of those forms.

Seven specimens, taken on May 30, 1898, by Vernon Bailey, at Cloverdale, show intergradation with *T. b. lacrymalis* and in color are intermediate between *fumosus* and *T. b. solitarius*. These seven specimens have more Cinnamon-Buff color than has *T. b. lacrymalis*, although selected individuals in each series can be matched with selected individuals in the other series. Nevertheless, the specimens are smaller than those of *lacrymalis*, have less inflated tympanic bullae, and the hamulus of each lacrimal bone is smaller. Their relationships are more nearly with *T. b. fumosus* and *T. b. curtatus*. Agreement with *curtatus* is shown in general size of entire animal and in size of skull. Also, nearer approach is shown to *curtatus* in color and the relatively straight (not distally depressed) rostrum. In greater length of hind foot and in relative proportions of the skull, the specimens from Cloverdale show greater resemblance to *fumosus*, the race to which they are tentatively referred. Actually, they are intermediate in the aggregate of characters considered and are regarded as intergrades. Incidentally, search in 1933 by W. B. Davis and Ward C. Russell at Cloverdale failed to locate any *Thomomys*.

A series of twenty-three specimens from Peavine Ranch, 6000 feet, 7 miles north of San Antonio, was obtained in order to learn if individuals from that place were of the subspecies *T. b. curtatus* which is known only from San Antonio, the terminus of Peavine Creek. It was supposed that specimens from Peavine Ranch would be referable to *curtatus* and not, as our examination shows them to be, most nearly related among named races to *T. b. fumosus*, to which they are here referred. Selected differences from *curtatus* are: larger size of body and skull; relatively longer skull; longer incisors and slightly more inflated tympanic bullae. The majority of the structural features examined agree with features characterizing *fumosus*. This is true of five of six cranial measurements expressed in percentages of the basilar length and is true also of length of hind foot and coloration. Even so, some departures are noted from topotypes of *fumosus*. These are: rostrum less depressed distally; nasals relatively, but not actually, shorter; pterygoid wings longer and interpterygoid space more narrowly V-shaped. These departures, however, are of no greater degree than those shown by specimens referred to *fumosus* from 5 miles southeast of Millett P. O. and at some other places in the northern part of Great Smoky Valley.

If our reference of these specimens from Peavine Ranch and Cloverdale be correct, *T. b. fumosus* occupies not only Great Smoky Valley but also a strip of territory around the southern end of the Toyabe Mountains.

Records of occurrence.—Specimens examined, 96, as follows: *Lander Co.:* Kingston Ranch, 16 mi. N Millett P. O., 4. *Nye Co.:* Daniels Ranch, 12 mi. NE Millett P. O., 4; Millett P. O., 12; Mitchell Field, 5 mi. SE Millett P. O., 29; South Twin River, 7000 ft., 1; Milman Ranch, Moores Creek, 19 mi. SE Millett P. O., 16; Peavine Ranch, 7 mi. N San Antonio, 6000 ft., 23; Cloverdale [Ranch], 7 (U. S. Nat. Mus., Biol. Surv. Coll.).

Thomomys bottae curtatus Hall
Botta Pocket Gopher

Thomomys bottae curtatus Hall, Univ. California Publ. Zoöl., 26:329, February 27, 1932. Type from San Antonio, 5400 feet, Nye County, Nevada.

Distribution.—Known only from San Antonio. See figure 325.

Remarks.—Measurements of four males and four females from the type locality are: ♂, 223 (209–235), ♀, 211 (194–221); 66 (63–75), 63 (56–74); 29 (27–31), 29 (28–29); weight, 128.8 (117.2–155.5), 106.3 (91.0–119.3) grams.

Size, including tail and hind foot, medium for the species; color, in summer pelage, above slightly lighter than Cinnamon-Buff; below Neutral Gray except for white inguinal region and presence of buff on pectoral region; skull broad, especially in male; rostrum wide, constricted posteriorly, and but slightly depressed distally; tympanic bullae moderately inflated and angular anteriorly; dorsal outline of skull in longitudinal axis nearly straight; incisors short.

In comparison with *T. b. lacrymalis* to the southwest, *curtatus* is smaller in both external and cranial measurements and has a trifle more Cinnamon-Buff in the color of the upper parts with buff on the pectoral region. This buff is practically absent on the pectoral region of *lacrymalis*. The interorbital region is more basined and the upper face of the rostrum markedly less decurved than in *lacrymalis*. Also, in *curtatus* the incisors are much shorter and the tympanic bullae are less inflated posteromedially. Correlated with this degree of inflation of the bullae is the shape of the basioccipital, which is V-shaped in *curtatus* and Y-shaped in *lacrymalis*. From *T. b. fumosus*, the form next adjacent to the northward, *curtatus* differs, as follows: color reddish rather than grayish; although females are of similar size, males are smaller; skull relatively broader throughout and actually much shorter; incisors shorter; dorsal outline of skull in longitudinal axis nearly straight rather than much arched; rostrum notably less depressed distally and relatively and actually shorter; zygomatic arch thicker at junction of jugal and maxilla; tooth row relatively, and usually actually, longer. Comparison with *T. b. solitarius* is made in the account of that race.

Peavine Creek does not flow much farther than Peavine Ranch (7 miles north of and 600 feet higher than San Antonio) for most of the year and, probably as a result of the lack of moisture, the stream course between Peavine Ranch and San Antonio supports a type of vegetation not notably different from that elsewhere on the dry fanglomerate at the southern end of the Toyabe Range. This habitat is not favorable to *Thomomys*. At San Antonio proper, however, water rises to the surface in places and a more luxuriant vegetation in parts of this highly alkaline ground supports a population of *Thomomys* which appears to be isolated from adjacent races. Probably the combined effect of this isolation and long residence in the highly alkaline soil has contributed to developing the unique cranial features found in the subspecies *curtatus*.

Record of occurrence.—Specimens examined, 12, as follows: *Nye Co.:* San Antonio, 5400 ft., 12.

Thomomys bottae vescus Hall and Davis
Botta Pocket Gopher

Thomomys bottae vescus Hall and Davis, Univ. California Publ. Zoöl., 40:389, March 13, 1935. Type from Toquima Range, south slope of Mount Jefferson, 9000 feet, Nye County, Nevada.

Distribution.—Toquima Mountain Range in Nye County. See figure 325.

Remarks.—Measurements of five males and two females from the type locality are: ♂, 206 (187–221), ♀, 205, 207; 64 (56–69), 55, 66; 29 (27–32), 28, 30; weight of two males, 113.5, 122.0; of two females, 96.0, 112.0 grams.

Size in general small; tail and hind foot of medium length; color in summer pelage darker than Cinnamon-Buff above; whitish gray below; nose sooty black; black post-auricular patches small; dorsal surface of feet and distal one-third to one-half of tail white; skull relatively broad, especially across zygomata and mastoidal region; rostrum relatively short; interpterygoid space V-shaped; tympanic bullae sharply angular antero-laterally.

In comparison with *T. b. concisor* and *T. b. fumosus*, the two subspecies geographically adjacent, *vescus* is smaller and has a less massive skull; temporal ridges more widely separated in animals of advanced age; zygomatic arch relatively more slender at junction of jugal and maxilla, and relative to basilar length shallower; breadth across mastoids greater; tooth row relatively longer and incisors shorter and weaker. Additional differences from *concisor* are relatively longer nasals, relatively lesser zygomatic breadth, and absence of Cinnamon-Buff on the pectoral region. From *fumosus*, *vescus* differs also in relatively shorter nasals and in relatively broader rostrum, which is less depressed distally.

In comparison with *T. b. curtatus*, selected differences of *vescus* are: rostrum relatively narrower; jugals less nearly parallel; nasals relatively shorter; tooth row relatively shorter; and tympanic bullae more inflated.

T. b. vescus is of especial interest because of the distributional problem it presents. It is thought to be restricted to the Toquima Range, the central one of three parallel mountain ranges extending in a north and south direction through central Nevada. In the two adjacent mountain ranges, the Toyabe Range to the westward and the Monitor Range to the eastward, the species *T. bottae*, so far as is known, does not occur, these mountain ranges being inhabited by another species of the same genus, *T. talpoides*. These two southward projections of the species *talpoides* are thought to be connected with the larger distributional area, including both valleys and mountains, north of the Monitor and Toyabe ranges, occupied by *talpoides*.

For some reason that is not clear, *Thomomys talpoides* does not occur in the Toquima Range, and I think that its absence in this range has permitted *T. bottae* to invade the area from the two adjacent valleys and from territory to the southward. Here, in the more boreal environment, and in general stonier ground and thinner soil, structural differentiation has taken place which characterizes not only the animals from the higher parts of the mountains but those from the lower elevations of the mountains as well. For example, animals taken one mile east of Jefferson at 7600 feet elevation on the western side of the range as well as those from five miles east of Meadow Canyon Ranger Station, only a short distance above the mouth of Meadow Creek Canyon, exhibit the diagnostic features of *vescus*.

Although specimens were taken only as high as 9800 feet elevation, abundant workings were noted from that point up to 11,000 feet elevation at the base of the south summit of Mount Jefferson.

Certain similarities between *T. b. vescus* and *Thomomys bottae nanus* are as follows: both are mountain-inhabiting subspecies; each is small; and each has a more lightly constructed skull than have neighboring subspecies in the surrounding lowlands. In spite of these similarities, which indicate a correlation between certain structures and habitat, the two subspecies are readily distinguishable. The larger size of *vescus*, its cranial features, and its much longer and heavier incisors are distinctive and suggest that its response to inhospitable soil and boreal conditions has not reached the extreme seen in *nanus*.

Records of occurrence.—Specimens examined, 19, as follows: *Nye Co.:* 1 mi. E Jefferson, 7600 ft., 2; 1½ mi. E Jefferson, 8000 ft., 1; S slope Mt. Jefferson (8900 ft., 3; 9000 ft., 3; Jefferson, 9800 ft., 1), 7; Meadow Canyon R. S., 6; 5 mi. E Meadow Canyon R. S., 3.

Thomomys bottae concisor Hall and Davis
Botta Pocket Gopher

Thomomys bottae concisor Hall and Davis, Univ. California Publ. Zoöl., 40:390, March 13, 1935. Type from Potts Ranch, 6900 feet, Monitor Valley, Nye County, Nevada.
Thomomys canus Bailey, N. Amer. Fauna, 39:73, November 15, 1910, part.

Distribution.—Monitor Valley in Nye County. See figure 325.

Remarks.—Measurements of six males and ten females from the type locality are: ♂, 251 (232–260), ♀, 230 (210–243); 85 (73–94), 76 (66–84); 31.6 (29–33), 29.3 (27–32); weight, 189.0 (131.0–233.0), 141.3 (105.4–172.0) grams.

Size large; tail and hind foot long; color darker than Cinnamon-Buff above; grayish below; sides and pectoral and inguinal regions near (16″ *a*) Cinnamon-Buff; nose sooty black; black postauricular patches large; dorsal surface of feet and distal one-third to one-half of tail white; skull relatively broad and massive, especially across zygomata; rostrum short and broad (breadth, 50 per cent or more of length); interpterygoid space narrowly V-shaped; juncture of jugal and zygomatic arm of maxilla relatively heavy; tympanic bullae sharply angular anterolaterally.

Compared with *T. b. fumosus*, the subspecies which structurally most resembles *concisor*, adult females of the latter differ as follows: rostrum actually and relatively much broader (in females, ratio of breadth to length is 51 per cent in *concisor* and 40 per cent in *fumosus*) and distally less depressed; zygomatic breadth actually and relatively greater; nasals actually and relatively shorter. In size, skulls of adult males of *concisor* most closely resemble comparable skulls of *T. b. canus*. Selected differences of *concisor* are as follows: depth of rostrum immediately behind incisors greater; zygomatic breadth greater; tympanic bullae angular anterolaterally rather than rounded; pterygoid processes V-shaped rather than U-shaped; pelage brownish rather than grayish. Comparison with *T. b. vescus* is made in the account of that form.

T. b. concisor is closely related to *T. b. fumosus*, but is distinguished from it by greater size. Also, in *concisor*, the short, broad rostrum of the females and the large, heavy skulls of the males are distinctive.

Records of occurrence.—Specimens examined, 24, as follows: *Nye Co.:* Wilson Creek, 7200 ft., 2; Potts Ranch, 6900 ft., 20; 8 mi. N Pine Creek Ranch, 7050 ft., 2.

Thomomys bottae abstrusus Hall and Davis
Botta Pocket Gopher

Thomomys bottae abstrusus Hall and Davis, Univ. California Publ. Zoöl., 40:391, March 13, 1935. Type from Fish Spring Valley, 2 miles southeast of Tulle Peak, 7000 feet, Nye County, Nevada.

Distribution.—Known only from the northern part of Fish Spring Valley in Nye County. See figure 325.

Remarks.—Measurements of the type, a male, are: 245; 75; 31; weight, 207 grams. No adult females are available.

Size in general large; tail and hind foot of medium length; color darker than Cinnamon-Buff above; whitish gray below; nose dark brown to sooty black; black postauricular patches small; dorsal surface of feet and distal third or more of tail white; skull with rostrum actually and relatively long and narrow; zygomatic arches widest posteriorly; temporal ridges approaching one another closely (2 mm.) in the male of advanced age; brain case and occiput flattened, with interparietal but little above plane of external auditory meatus; incisors short; maxillary tooth row relatively short; interpterygoid space narrowly V-shaped; tympanic bullae sharply angular anterolaterally and relatively uninflated; paroccipital processes well developed and projecting well over and beyond the mastoidal bullae, which are relatively small and uninflated.

T. b. abstrusus is most nearly like *T. b. brevidens* with which it agrees in the yellowish color, small size of black postauricular patches, general size of body, and short incisors. It differs, however, in animals of comparable age, in much larger skull. Other differences in the skull are: rostral part much longer; brain case more nearly flat; temporal ridges approaching one another more closely; interpterygoid space more narrowly V-shaped; paroccipital processes better developed and tympanic bullae less inflated, especially in a dorsoventral direction.

The duller color, broad skull with markedly broader rostrum, and generally more massive build of *abstrusus* readily separate it from *brevidens*.

At the "Upper Crocker Ranch," the type locality of *T. b. abstrusus*, gophers were scarce at the time of our visit, which was on July 13, 1933. The ranch, though not on the very floor of Fish Spring Valley, is, nevertheless, well out of the Monitor Mountains and is properly to be spoken of as in the valley. The taking of specimens there naturally led us to believe that *T. bottae*, with in general a more southern distribution, occurred southward throughout the valley. We were surprised, therefore, when specimens taken at the "Lower Crocker Ranch," on the floor of the valley, eight miles south and one mile east of the type locality of *T. b. abstrusus*, proved to belong to another species, *T. talpoides*, which is more northern in distribution and known to occupy the adjacent Monitor Mountains. Finally, at a point five miles still farther south on the floor of the valley (one mile north of Fish Lake), *T. bottae* (subspecies *brevidens*) again was found to occur.

Fish Spring Valley, then, is an area in which occur two distinct species of pocket gophers, *Thomomys bottae* and *T. talpoides*. Taking into account the geographic distribution of these two species in adjacent territory, I conclude that the population of *bottae* at the "Upper Crocker Ranch"—here named *abstrusus*—has been cut off from the main range of that species by a flanking movement of *talpoides*. In this movement, *talpoides* is thought to have moved out, eastward, from the Monitor Mountain Range onto the floor of Fish Spring Valley and thus to have isolated *T. b. abstrusus* from the main area of distribution of the *bottae* stock to the southward.

Given the knowledge that *T. talpoides* occurred on the floor of Fish Spring Valley, one would not expect the species *T. bottae*, in general of more southern distribution, to occur in the northern end of the valley.

Record of occurrence.—Specimens examined, 5, all from the type locality.

Thomomys bottae brevidens Hall
Botta Pocket Gopher

Thomomys bottae brevidens Hall, Univ. California Publ. Zoöl., 26:330, February 27, 1932. Type from Breen Creek, 7000 feet, Kawich Range, Nye County, Nevada. Hall and Davis, Univ. California Publ. Zoöl., 40:396, March 13, 1935.

Distribution.—Central Nye County from Fish Lake south to Cactus Flat and east to western base of Quinn Canyon Mountains. See figure 325.

Remarks.—Measurements of five males and four females from the type locality are: ♂, 232 (217–241), ♀, 210 (200–220); 76 (73–80), 70 (64–75); 31 (30–32), 28.9 (27.5–30); weight of two males and four females from 3½ mi. E Nyala are 125.3 (120–130.5), 122.4 (106.5–134.0) grams.

Size medium for the species; tail relatively long; hind foot of medium length; color (May- and September-taken specimens) darker than Cinnamon-Buff above; whitish-gray below; skull relatively narrow; rostrum of average size, depressed distally and constricted posteriorly; tympanic bullae markedly inflated dorsoventrally; incisors short; parietal ridges widely separated even in animals of advanced age.

The skull of *brevidens*, compared with that of *T. b. fumosus*, is less depressed interorbitally, with heavier jugals and with the tympanic bullae more inflated dorsoventrally; and the skull, when laid top down on a horizontal surface, has the tips of the nasals lower and the occiput higher. Compared with topotypes of *T. b. centralis*, the tympanic bullae are more inflated and, on the average, the ascending tongues of the premaxillae extend farther posteriorly beyond the nasals.

T. b. brevidens differs from both *centralis* and *fumosus* as follows: entire animal about the same size externally but skull markedly smaller; incisors one-fourth to one-third shorter; rostral and mastoidal breadths relatively greater; tooth row relatively longer; temporal ridges not approaching one another so closely with advanced age; pterygoid space more broadly V-shaped; fossa, beneath overhanging edge of frontal and immediately posterior to foramen opticum, absent rather than present.

T. b. brevidens is less reddish and more yellowish than *centralis*. The Deep Mouse Gray of *fumosus* sets it sharply apart from *brevidens*, so far as color is concerned.

Compared with *nanus*, the color of *brevidens* averages a trifle lighter (less plumbeous). Its larger size and larger skull of different proportions, as mentioned in the account of *nanus*, are distinctive. The specimen from one mile north of Fish Lake, an adult male, agrees well with topotypes of *brevidens*, except in shape of the auditory bullae. The tympanic part of each is less inflated dorsoventrally. Also, the mastoidal part is less inflated and is more overshadowed by the paroccipital process. The lesser inflation of the bullae and the prominence of the paroccipital process are even better shown in *T. b. abstrusus*, which occurs farther north in Fish Spring Valley. Comparison with *abstrusus* is made in the account of that form.

The specimens from Nyala and those from points 3½ and 5 miles east of that place agree among themselves and differ only slightly from topotypes of *brevidens*. The observed differences are as follows: nasals, in males, but not in females, relatively and actually slightly shorter; zygomatic breadth averaging actually and relatively greater; tympanic bullae less inflated dorsoventrally.

Records of occurrence.—Specimens examined, 48, as follows: Nye Co.: 1 mi. N Fish Lake, 6500 ft., Fish Spring Valley, 1; ¼ mi. W Hot Creek [P. O.], 5900 ft., 1; Hot Creek P. O., 5800 ft., Hot Creek Valley, 5; Nyala, 5100 ft., 1; 3½ mi. E Nyala, 5750 ft., 16; 5 mi. E Nyala, 6000 ft., 10; Breen Creek, 7000 ft., Kawich Range, 13; Cactus Flat, 5700 ft., 7½ mi. SW Silverbow, 1.

Thomomys bottae latus Hall and Davis
Botta Pocket Gopher

Thomomys bottae latus Hall and Davis, Univ. California Publ. Zoöl., 40:393, March 13, 1940. Type from Cherry Creek, 6500 feet, White Pine County, Nevada.

Distribution.—Steptoe Valley in White Pine County. See figure 325.

Remarks.—Measurements of three males and six females from the type locality are: ♂, 233 (226–245), ♀, 219 (205–222); 73 (72–75), 67 (61–70); 31 (30–32), 29 (28–30); weight, 144.2 (117.8–169.0), 131.1 (107.4–161.3) grams.

Size, including length of tail and hind foot, medium for the species; color darker than Cinnamon-Buff above; lighter below, with more gray and a tinge of Pinkish Buff on inguinal and pectoral regions; nose dark gray or sooty black; distal half, or more than half, of tail white; skull relatively broad, especially across zygomata, rostrum, and upper tooth row (measured from the outside of one row to the outside of the other); tympanic bullae sharply angular anterolaterally.

Compared with topotypes of the structurally most similar and the geographically adjacent *T. b. centralis*, adult females of *latus* differ as follows: relatively broader through rostrum, through anterior part of brain case, and across zygomata; squamosal roots of zygomata projecting more abruptly; dorsal margin of foramen magnum more concave, rather than relatively straight; tympanic bullae more angular anterolaterally; distance across second upper molars (measured from outside to outside) more than, instead of less than, 7 mm.; palatal pits averaging shallower.

In external measurements and coloration, *T. b. latus* and *centralis* are to me indistinguishable. The greater breadth of the skull, especially across the zygomata, in *latus* is distinctive. Measured across the mastoidal region, the two forms are but little different, and this brings into contrast the greater zygomatic width of *latus*. The available male specimens of *latus* are young, but, like the adult females, they exhibit the greater spread of zygomata, greater inflation of brain case anteriorly, and more abruptly projecting squamosal root of the zygomata.

A series of sixteen specimens from 6½ miles southeast of Ely agree with *centralis* in three of the eight differential characters mentioned above. In three characters, namely, width across zygomata, broad brain case, and angular bullae, they agree with *latus*. In two respects, namely, depth of palatal pits and width across upper tooth rows, they are intermediate. Thus, so far as I can see, they may be referred with equal propriety to either *centralis* or *latus*. Because they come from the southern end of the same general valley into which Cherry Creek empties, they here are referred to *latus*.

Records of occurrence.—Specimens examined, 30, as follows: *White Pine Co.*: Cherry Creek, 6500 ft., 14; 6½ mi. SE Ely, 6400 ft., 16.

Thomomys bottae centralis Hall
Botta Pocket Gopher

Thomomys perpallidus centralis Hall, Univ. California Publ. Zoöl., 32:445, July 8, 1930. Type from 2½ miles east of Baker, 5700 feet, White Pine County, Nevada. Grinnell and Hill, Journ. Mamm., 17:5, February 14, 1936.
Thomomys bottae centralis Hall, Univ. California Publ. Zoöl., 26:333, February 27, 1932; Burt, Trans. San Diego Soc. Nat. Hist., 7:409, May 31, 1934; Hall and Davis, Univ. California Publ. Zoöl., 40:396, March 13, 1935.
Thomomys perpallidus aureus, Bailey, N. Amer. Fauna, 39:74, November 15, 1940, part.

Distribution.—From Mount Moriah southward over eastern Nevada, the Virgin River Valley excepted, across southern Nevada and northward to head of Amargosa River. See figure 325.

Remarks.—Measurements of nine males and seventeen females from the type locality and from low elevations in the Snake Mountains are: ♂, 237 (215–250), ♀, 214 (195–229);

75 (61–83), 65 (55–75); 30.3 (29.1–31.5), 28.8 (27–30); weight, 165.8 (147.0–197.5), 117.7 (102.3–133.0) grams.

Size in general large; length of tail and hind foot medium for the species; color in winter and in summer darker than Cinnamon-Buff above; underparts grayish with tinge of Pinkish-Buff on inguinal and pectoral regions; nose dark gray or sooty black; distal half, or more than half, of tail white; skull with tip of rostrum curved downward; parietal ridges usually parallel-sided; zygomatic arches about same width at anterior and posterior parts of arches; maxillofrontal suture on top of skull convex posteromedially.

Comparisons with Nevadan races, the ranges of which touch that of *centralis*, are made in the accounts of those races.

Specimens from the general region of the type locality have more slender rostra and generally narrower skulls than do referred specimens from many localities to the southward and southwestward. Compared with topotypes, specimens from Panaca have the brain case more inflated and the skull averages larger. Specimens from 7 miles south of Caliente also have more inflated brain cases and, on the average, the nasals are shorter and the tympanic bullae are slightly more inflated.

Of specimens taken in Pahranagat Valley, those from Alamo agree well with topotypes of *centralis*, except that the brain case is slightly more inflated and the rostrum averages broader. The specimens from Crystal Spring, in the same valley as Alamo, present a more extreme variation. Departures from topotypes are as follows: skull larger and heavier; zygomatic breadth and mastoidal breadth relatively less; nasals, on the average, broader and posteriorly less attenuated; interpterygoid space tending to be U-shaped, rather than strictly V-shaped; basisphenoid much wider and heavier; rostrum averaging relatively broader. These differences apply also in comparison with the specimens from Alamo, except that in breadth of the rostrum the specimens from Alamo are intermediate between those from Crystal Spring and the type locality. In external measurements and coloration, these specimens from Pahranagat Valley agree closely with topotypes of *centralis*.

Specimens from the Amargosa River Valley, namely, those in Ash Meadows from 2 miles west and 4½ to 5 miles northwest of Devils Hole, those from 3½ miles northeast of Beatty, and those from Springdale, were looked upon, in advance of study, as belonging to the race *Thomomys bottae amargosae* Grinnell. Actual comparison with topotypes of *amargosae*, however, reveals differences as follows: zygomatic breadth, mastoidal breadth, depth of skull, and length of hind foot are less. Also, expressed in percentage of the basilar length, in *amargosae* the zygomatic breadth is 73 per cent, the mastoidal breadth 62 per cent, and the length of the rostrum 65 per cent. In our specimens from the Amargosa Valley, corresponding percentages are 70, 60, and 69. These agree closely with the corresponding percentages in topotypes of *centralis*.

Even so, there are differences between topotypes of *centralis* and specimens from the Amargosa River Valley. These differences, in males from the Amargosa Valley, are: rostrum wider, actually and relatively to its breadth; premaxillae extending a lesser distance behind nasals; interpterygoid space V-shaped rather than Y-shaped; tympanic and mastoidal parts of auditory bullae more inflated; basioccipital Y-shaped rather than V-shaped; maxillary root of zygomata more nearly at a right angle with longitudinal axis of skull; zygomatic breadth greater. Except in the shape of the basioccipital and the angle of the maxillary root of the zygomata, the same differences exist between females. In spite of these differences, the specimens from the Amargosa Valley of Nevada, among described races of *Thomomys bottae*, most closely resemble *T. b. centralis*.

One adult male from 2½ miles west of Devils Hole is almost identical in size and relative proportions with *T. b. amargosae* and may be thought of as indicating intergradation between *amargosae* and *centralis*, even though the average of specimens from 2½ miles west of Devils Hole is nearer to that of *centralis*.

The southernmost populations to be mentioned in connection with the subspecies *centralis* are from the north side of the Colorado River in Clark County: Durban Ranch, 14 miles east of Searchlight, and the second from ½ mile north of the California boundary. Each of these, on the average, differs from a series of topotypes of *centralis* in having the rostrum actually broader and relatively shorter; mastoidal breadth and zygomatic expanse relatively and actually greater; tooth row longer; premaxillae not extended as far behind nasals. Each of the populations in question is constantly distinct from *Thomomys bottae suboles* Goldman, based on animals taken directly across the Colorado River from the Durban Ranch. Topotypes of *suboles* show much smaller size, indentations in lateral margins of nasals, greater convexity of dorsal outline of skull in both longitudinal and transverse axes, and other differences.

It should not be inferred from the remarks just made that these two populations from two separate valleys along the north side of the Colorado River agree with each other in all respects. They do not. In cursory comparison with the population-sample from ½ mile above the California boundary, that from the Durban Ranch (both males and females) differs on the average, and in some of its features differs constantly, in the following selected respects: rostrum broader (its breadth more, rather than less, than half its length); nasals and rostrum actually shorter and averaging shorter relative to the basilar length; interpterygoid space ordinarily V-shaped, rather than ordinarily U-shaped; tympanic bullae very slightly more inflated; premaxillae extended farther behind nasals; hind foot longer.

Records of occurrence.—Specimens examined, 305, as follows: *Nye Co.:* White River Valley, 16½ mi. WSW Sunnyside, 6; Grant Mts., 19½ mi. WSW Sunnyside, 6; Springdale, N end Oasis Valley, 11; Amargosa River, 3½ mi. NE Beatty, 3400 ft., 38; Ash Meadows, 4½ to 5 mi. NW Devils Hole, 2200 ft., 19; Ash Meadows, 2½ mi. W Devils Hole, 2173 ft., 10. *White Pine Co.:* Smith Creek, 6600–6700 ft., Mt. Moriah, 4; 1 to 2 mi. W Smith Creek Cave, 6000–6300 ft., Mt. Moriah, 4; near Smith Creek Cave, 5800 ft., 1; Mt. Moriah, 11,400 ft., 3; 2 mi. E. Mt. Moriah, 9800 ft., 1; Hendry Creek, 9800 ft., Mt. Moriah, 4; Hendry Creek, 9100 ft., 1½ mi. E Mt. Moriah, 9; Hendry Creek, 7900 ft., 4 mi. SE Mt. Moriah, 1; Cleveland Ranch, 6000 ft., Spring Valley, 5; Lehman Creek, 8400 ft., 1; head of Shingle Creek, 10,000 ft., Snake Mts., 2; Willard Creek, 7150–7400 ft., Spring Valley, 7; 2½ mi. E Baker, 5700 ft., 13; Baker Creek, 6600–6700 ft., 7; Baker Creek, 8400 and 8500 ft., 2; Stella Lake, 10,500 ft., 1; Pole Canyon, 7500 ft., Snake Mts., 3. *Lincoln Co.:* ¼ mi. W Utah boundary, 38° 17′ N latitude, 7300 ft., 1; Wilson Creek, 7500 ft., Wilson Creek Mts., 2; 3½ mi. N Eagle Valley [Ursine], 5600 ft., 7; Panaca, 4700 ft., 6; Meadow Valley Wash, 7 mi. S Caliente, 5; Crystal Spring to ¾ mi. S thereof, 4000 ft., Pahranagat Valley, 39; Alamo, 3570 ft., Pahranagat Valley, 10; 4 mi. S Alamo, 4; E side Lower Pahranagat Lake, 3800 ft., 2; Coyote Spring, 2800 ft., 1. *Clark Co.* (unless otherwise noted, in D. R. Dickey Coll.): ¼ mi. N Wheeler Well, 6600 ft., 1; Wheeler Well, 6600 ft., 1; ¼ mi. S Wheeler Well, 6600 ft., 1; Willow Creek, 6000 ft., 1; Cold Creek, 6000 ft., 5; Lee Canyon, 8200 ft., 1; Deer Creek, 8800 ft., Charleston Peak, 1; Kyle Canyon, 8000 ft., 6 (5 in Mus. Vert. Zoöl.); Kyle Canyon (6600 ft., 2; 6500 ft., 1; 5500 ft., 1), 4; Trout Canyon, 6500 ft., 6; Boulder City, 3 (2 in Boulder Dam Recreational Area Coll. and 1 in Mus. Vert. Zoöl.); Durban Ranch, Colorado River, 14 mi. E Searchlight, 15 (Mus. Vert. Zoöl.); ½ mi. N Calif.-Nev. Monument, Colorado River, 500 ft., 25 (Mus. Vert. Zoöl.).

Additional records: Specimens, probably referable to this subspecies, have been recorded by Bailey (1915:75) from Charleston Mts., Las Vegas, Black Canyon, and St. Thomas, all in Clark County, and by Burt (1934:410) from Indian Springs, Clark County, and Pahrump Valley, Nye County.

Thomomys bottae virgineus Goldman
Botta Pocket Gopher

Thomomys bottae virgineus Goldman, Proc. Biol. Soc. Washington, 50:133, September 10, 1937. Type from Beaverdam Creek, near confluence with Virgin River at Littlefield, 1500 feet, Mohave County, Arizona.
Thomomys bottae centralis, Hall and Davis, Univ. California Publ. Zoöl., 40:397, March 13, 1935, part.

Distribution.—Virgin River Valley. See figure 325.

Remarks.—Measurements of a male and four females from Mesquite are: ♂, 227, ♀, 219 (209–233); 69, 69 (66–73); 29.5, 29.2 (28–32); weight, ♂, 142.7, ♀, 111.2 (99.2–130.7) grams.

Size, in general, including length of tail and hind foot, medium for the species; color Cinnamon-Buff above; postauricular black patches small; tail Cinnamon-Buff all around and to tip in most specimens; underparts with hair plumbeous basally and tipped with white or buff; skull relatively broad; interparietal broad; zygomatic arches distinctly bowed in at middle of jugals; tympanic bullae angular anterolaterally; interpterygoid space narrowly U-shaped or broadly V-shaped.

In the original description Goldman noted that, in comparison with *T. b. centralis*, the skull was relatively narrower and that the premaxillae extended farther behind the nasals. Actually the reverse is true when topotypes of *centralis* and *virgineus* are compared. Goldman probably had, of *centralis*, specimens from some place southwest of the type locality. As noted under the account of *centralis*, specimens from south and west of the type locality have broader skulls. The skull of *virgineus* has a broader interparietal, broader brain case, and zygomata more bowed inward at the middle than topotypes or other specimens of *centralis*. The color is more reddish.

The specimens from Mesquite differ from the nine topotypes of *virgineus* used in drawing up the original description in slightly greater average size and in darker color (Cinnamon-Buff, rather than paler than Cinnamon-Buff). The animals from Mesquite are much more reddish. The shade is about as in *centralis*, but the color is purer. In topotypes of *virgineus* the distal third of the tail is white, but in animals from Mesquite it is Cinnamon-Buff.

Specimens from Mesquite originally were referred to *T. b. centralis* (Hall and Davis, 1935:397), and their strikingly reddish color was regarded as evidence of intergradation with the race *T. b. planirostris* Burt of Zion Canyon, Utah, farther up the Virgin River. With the recognition that the color of *virgineus* is paler than that of *planirostris* and that of the animals from Mesquite, and because *virgineus* comes from an area between Zion Canyon and Mesquite, it is evident that the reddish color at Mesquite is not the result of intergradation with *planirostris*, but is probably an independent intensification of reddish color. So far as color is concerned, these specimens from Mesquite possibly are more representative of the race *virgineus* than are topotypes. Burt's (1934:410) comment that specimens from St. Thomas, at the junction of the Virgin River and Meadow Valley Wash, approach *T. b. planirostris* in color suggests that at least this feature of reddish color may characterize pocket gophers all the way down to near the mouth of the Virgin River.

Record of occurrence.—Specimens examined, 5, as follows: *Clark Co.*: Mesquite, 1750 ft., 5.

Thomomys bottae nanus Hall
Botta Pocket Gopher

Thomomys bottae nanus Hall, Univ. California Publ. Zoöl., 26:331, February 27, 1932. Type from south end of Belted Range, 5½ mi. northwest of Whiterock Spring, 7200 feet, Nye County, Nevada. Hall and Davis, Univ. California Publ. Zoöl., 40:399, March 13, 1935.

Distribution.—Quinn Canyon Mountains south to near latitude 37°; from Pahute Mesa eastward to Irish Mountain. See figure 325.

Remarks.—Measurements of five males and ten females from the type locality are: ♂, 199 (185–210), ♀, 196 (188–204); 64 (57–70), 58 (48–69); 29 (28–30), 28 (25–29); weight, 99.1 (93.3–107.2), 86.8 (70.8–101.8) grams.

Size small; tail of medium length; hind foot short; color above, in summer pelage, darker than Cinnamon-Buff; black postauricular patch large; color of underparts highly variable, ranging from Cinnamon-Buff over all to light gray, with white pectoral and inguinal regions; skull small, lightly built, and relatively narrow; rostrum weak and narrow; tympanic bullae moderately inflated and truncate anteriorly; parietal ridges widely separated even in animals of advanced age; incisors strongly recurved.

Differences from *T. b. brevidens* are: size less; color grayer (less cinnamon); skull averaging smaller in all parts measured; rostrum relatively, to basilar length, shorter and narrower; skull relatively narrower across zygomata; tympanic bullae less inflated dorsoventrally. From *centralis*, *nanus* differs in: size less in all parts measured; color slightly more gray; incisors relatively shorter; skull relatively broader interorbitally and across mastoids; temporal ridges farther apart. Comparison with *T. b. phelleoecus* is made in the account of that form.

The six specimens from the head of Burned Corral Canyon at 8700 feet elevation agree well with topotypes of *nanus*. The specimen from 7700 feet, however, shows departures, in coloration and cranial features, toward *brevidens*. The specimen from 6700 feet shows still nearer approach to *brevidens* and especially to that sample of *brevidens* from 5 miles east of Nyala, at 6000 feet elevation, a place 2 to 3 miles farther down the main canyon of which Burned Corral Canyon is a tributary. Thus, here on the western side of the Quinn Canyon Mountains, intergradation seems to occur between the two subspecies *T. b. nanus* and *T. b. brevidens*.

The limits of range of *nanus* to the southward and the northward limit of range of *T. b. phelleoecus*, so far known only from the Sheep Mountains, remain to be determined.

Records of occurrence.—Specimens examined, 53, as follows: *Nye Co.*: Quinn Canyon Mts., Burned Corral Canyon (6700 ft., 1; 7700 ft., 1; 8700 ft., 6) 8; Kawich Range, 6000 ft., 1½ mi. E Kawich P. O., 1; S end Belted Range, 5½ mi. NW Whiterock Spring, 7200 ft., 37; 2 mi. SW Oak Spring, 5800 ft., 1; 4 mi. SE Oak Spring, 5800 ft., 1. *Lincoln Co.*: N slope Irish Mtn., 7000–8000 ft., 4; Summit Spring, 4800 ft., 1.

Thomomys bottae phelleoecus Burt
Botta Pocket Gopher

Thomomys phelleoecus Burt, Journ. Mamm., 14:56, February 14, 1933. Type from Hidden Forest, Sheep Mountains, Clark County, Nevada. Burt, Trans. San Diego Soc. Nat. Hist., 7:411, May 31, 1934.
Thomomys bottae phelleoecus, Hall and Davis, Univ. California Publ. Zoöl., 40:401, March 13, 1935.

Distribution.—Sheep Mountains. See figure 325.

Remarks.—Measurements of three males and six females from the type locality are: ♂, 198 (190–202), ♀, 181 (167–196); 56 (49–59), 54 (51–57); 27.3 (27–28), 26.8 (26–27); weight, 108.5 (96.0–123.3), 89.8 (71.3–106.4) grams.

Size small; tail and hind foot short; color above, in summer pelage, lighter than (near *h*) Sayal Brown; nose blackish; postauricular black patches small; underparts with hair plumbeous basally, tipped with whitish or cinnamon or both; cinnamon most prominent on pectoral region; skull small; nasals truncate posteriorly; temporal ridges parallel or slightly bowed outward; tympanic bullae globular but angled anterolaterally; interpterygoid space broadly V-shaped and rarely narrowly U-shaped.

Differences from *T. b. nanus* are: tail and hind foot shorter; color averaging slightly more reddish; upper incisors longer; skull narrower interorbitally; nasals broader posteriorly; basioccipital straighter sided, less hourglass-shaped; squamosal root of zygomatic arch less angled; brain case more flattened in males. From *T. b. centralis*, *phelleoecus* differs in: size less in all parts measured; relatively broader as measured across the zygomata, mastoids, and rostrum. The two specimens from low elevations in the canyon leading up to Hidden Forest from the west are larger than those from the type locality and indicate intergradation with *centralis*.

Records of occurrence.—Specimens examined, 14, as follows: *Clark Co.*: Hidden Forest, 7700 ft., 11; ridge N of Wiregrass [= Wire] Spring, 8250 ft., Sheep Mts., 1; Hidden Forest road, 5300 and 5450 ft., Sheep Mts., 2.

Thomomys bottae melanotis Grinnell
Botta Pocket Gopher

Thomomys melanotis Grinnell, Univ. California Publ. Zoöl., 17:425; April 25, 1918. Type from Big Prospector Meadow, 10,500 feet, White Mountains, Mono County, California.
Thomomys bottae melanotis, Hall, Univ. California Publ. Zoöl., 26:328, February 27, 1932.

Distribution.—Mount Magruder. See figure 325.

Remarks.—Measurements of four males and two females from Lida are: ♂, 235 (230–240), ♀, 215 (210–220); 72 (68–80), 64 (60–68); 31 (30–32), 30 (30–30). Weight not taken.

Size large; tail relatively long; hind foot of medium length for the species; color, in summer pelage, grayish washed with Cinnamon; nose blackish; postauricular black patches of medium size; below, hairs on underparts plumbeous basally, tipped with whitish or buff; skull large; interparietal small; nasals posteriorly emarginate; jugals relatively straight; bullae globular and rounded or weakly angled anterolaterally; interpterygoid space V-shaped.

In color and in size; *T. b. melanotis* closely resembles *lacrymalis*, the subspecies which, on the east, adjoins the geographic range of *melanotis;* actually the color averages slightly less Cinnamon in *melanotis*, and the size, on the average, is slightly less. Selected cranial differences in which *melanotis* differs from *lacrymalis* are: skull smaller; lacrimals relatively smaller; maxillary tooth row shorter; jugals straight rather than bowed outward; nasals and ascending branches of the premaxillae actually and relatively shorter. From *T. b. oreoecus, melanotis* differs in: size larger; skull larger; temporal ridges farther apart; mastoidal breadth less in relation to basilar length.

The six adult specimens from Lida are intermediate in size between topotypes of *lacrymalis* and *melanotis*. Of the ten linear measurements taken of each sex, nearer approach is shown to *melanotis* in eleven instances, to *lacrymalis* in eight instances, and in one instance the measurement is exactly intermediate. On the average, the rostrum of males is broad, as in *lacrymalis*, although the lacrimals are small and thus more like those of *melanotis*. Also, in males the upper incisors are short, stout, and incurved; all these are features found in *lacrymalis* and differentiate the animal at Lida from *melanotis*. Both males and females have, on the average, the zygomatic breadth greater anteriorly, relative to that posteriorly, than in *melanotis*, and in the females the same difference is noted also in comparison with *lacrymalis*. This greater width is a feature even better developed in *Thomomys bottae amargosae*. Color, likewise, is suggestive of *amargosae* in that there is more dark pigment than in most specimens of *melanotis* and *lacrymalis*. The only feature noted in which the population from Lida is in any measure unique is in the greater average distance of projection of the premaxillae behind the nasals. Judged by our study of some of the characters of the population at Lida, the animal at that place is slightly nearer *melanotis* than *lacrymalis*.

Record of occurrence.—Specimens examined, 22, as follows: *Esmeralda Co.:* Lida, 6100 ft., 22 (D. R. Dickey, Coll.).

Thomomys bottae oreoecus Burt
Botta Pocket Gopher

Thomomys oreoecus Burt, Trans. San Diego Soc. Nat. Hist., 7:154, July 28, 1932. Type from Greenwater 4300 feet [Black Mountains, 8 mi. SW Ryan], Inyo County, California.
Thomomys bottae oreoecus, Hall and Davis, Univ. California Publ. Zoöl., 40:399, March 13, 1935.
Thomomys perpallidus perpes, Bailey, N. Amer. Fauna, 39:72, November 15, 1915, part.

Distribution.—Grapevine Mountains. See figure 325.

Remarks.—Measurements of five males and two females from 2½ mi. E and 1 mi. S Grapevine Peak are: ♂, 195 (191–203), ♀, 186 (181–190); 54 (51–59), 55 (51–59); 27.4 (26–28), 27 (25–29); weight, 96.0 (85.6–103.2), —, 70.3 grams.

Size small; tail relatively short; hind foot short; color above, in summer pelage, grayish washed with Cinnamon, or over all near (*h*) Cinnamon; nose blackish; postauricular black patches of medium size; below, hairs plumbeous basally, tipped with whitish and buff; skull small; interparietal small; bullae relatively uninflated.

From *providentialis, oreoecus* differs in slightly more reddish coloration, narrower brain case, smaller interparietal, temporal ridges nearer together, and basioccipital more nearly hourglass-shaped, rather than straight-sided, and premaxillae extended farther behind nasals. These differences obtain between Nevadan specimens of each form. From *centralis* (populations from Ash Meadows), *oreoecus* differs in smaller size; more cinnamon on underparts; skull smaller; temporal ridges less prominent and farther apart; tympanic bullae more rounded anterolaterally. From *melanotis, oreoecus* differs in: size less, including skull; temporal ridges nearer together; mastoidal breadth significantly greater in relation to basilar length.

In the Nevadan specimens from the eastern slope of the northern end of the Grapevine Mountains, the skulls are relatively and actually broader than in topotypes and the rostrum is longer. In these respects some approach is shown to *melanotis* and *centralis*. The one, not fully adult, female from Grapevine Canyon, in nine differential features studied, agrees with, or most nearly approaches, *lacrymalis* in one, *melanotis* in four, and *oreoecus* in four. Its skull is more slender than typical skulls of any of the mentioned races. The one specimen from Thorps Mill also shows some approach in cranial characters to *centralis* and *melanotis*. Even these two specimens, and certainly the others here referred to *oreoecus*, are referable, among named races, to that form. The description of their intermediacy serves to illustrate, when considered in the light of the geographic origin of the specimens, how thoroughly intergradation occurs between the desert subspecies of *Thomomys bottae*, at least in certain areas.

Records of occurrence.—Specimens examined, 23, as follows: *Esmeralda Co.:* 4 3/10 mi. E Calif. boundary, 4200 ft., 1. *Nye Co.:* Thorps Mill, 1 (U. S. Nat. Mus., Biol. Surv. Coll.); Grapevine Mountains, 3 (U. S. Nat. Mus., Biol. Surv. Coll.); 2½ mi. E and 1 mi. S Grapevine Peak, 6700 ft., 15; 5 mi. E and 1 mi. S Grapevine Peak, 6000 ft., 3.

Thomomys bottae providentialis Grinnell
Botta Pocket Gopher

Thomomys providentialis Grinnell, Univ. California Publ. Zoöl., 38:1, October 17, 1931. Type from Purdy, 4500 feet, 6 miles southeast of New York Mountain, Providence Range, San Bernardino County, California.
Thomomys bottae providentialis, Hall and Davis, Univ. California Publ. Zoöl., 40:400, March 13, 1935.

Distribution.—Southern Clark County, except valley of the Colorado River proper. See figure 325.

Remarks.—Measurements of two males and eight females from 8 mi. S Dead Mtn. are: ♂, 222, 195, ♀, 195 (181–203); 80, 64, 63 (55–71); 29, 25, 28.0 (27–29); weight, 101.9, 84.1, 84.9 (74.7–88.2) grams.

Size small; tail relatively long; hind foot short; color above, in winter pelage, grayish lightly washed with Cinnamon; postauricular black patches small; nose dark gray; underparts with hair plumbeous but tipped with white; skull small; rostrum short; brain case broad; temporal ridges widely separated and parallel; tympanic bullae moderately inflated and anterolaterally rounded or weakly angled.

From *centralis, providentialis* differs in: size less; color, in most specimens, lighter; brain case wider and shallower relative to length of skull; temporal ridges farther apart. These are differences between specimens of *providentialis* from Dead Mountain and *centralis* from Ash Meadows and from along the Colorado River east of Searchlight. Greater differences obtain between topotypes of the two races.

In the specimen from Potosi Mountain, the rostrum and nasals are unusually short. Also, it is smaller than the other Nevadan specimens of *providentialis* and has the occiput more protruded posteriorly; 5 mm. of the supraoccipital is revealed on the dorsal face of the skull. The cinnamon color in the pelage of this specimen and the cinnamon color and small size of other specimens from the higher elevations of Charleston Peak suggest intergradation between *centralis* and *providentialis*.

Records of occurrence.—Specimens examined, 11, as follows: *Clark Co.:* N side Potosi Mtn., 5800 ft., 1; 7 mi. S Dead Mtn., 2700 ft., 7; 8 mi. SE Dead Mtn., 1900 ft., 3.

TABLE 12
CRANIAL MEASUREMENTS (IN MILLIMETERS) OF THOMOMYS

Name and locality	Number of individuals averaged or catalogue no.	Sex and age	Basilar length	Zygomatic breadth	Least interorbital constriction	Mastoidal breadth	Length of nasals	Breadth of rostrum*	Length of rostrum†	Alveolar length of maxillary tooth row	Palato-frontal depth‡	Extension of premaxillae posterior to nasals
T. talpoides quadratus												
4½ mi. NE Painted Point...	73243	♂	31.8	23.0	6.4	19.3	13.4	7.1	15.9	7.4	13.4	1.8
4 mi. SW Diessner..........	73238	♂	29.6	22.3	6.8	18.6	13.0	7.1	14.8	7.0	12.7	1.2
12-mile Creek..............	73237	♂	30.8	21.9	6.5	18.7	12.3	7.4	14.7	7.5	13.0	2.0
		av.	30.7	22.4	6.6	18.9	12.9	7.2	15.1	7.3	13.0	1.7
4½ mi. NE Painted Point...	73242	♀	28.6	21.2	5.8	18.1	12.3	6.6	14.4	6.6	12.6	1.9
Long Valley Ranch..........	73240	♀	29.7	21.6	7.1	17.6	11.7	6.6	15.0	7.0	13.0	2.0
T. talpoides gracilis												
Ruby Mountains§..........	10 av.	♂	30.0	21.2	6.3	18.0	12.6	7.1	15.3	7.1	12.9	1.7
		min.	28.6	18.7	6.1	17.1	11.6	6.7	14.0	6.8	12.1	1.3
		max.	31.9	23.2	6.7	19.0	13.6	7.5	16.4	7.4	13.8	2.1
Ruby Mountains§..........	6 av.	♀	28.2	19.9	6.3	16.9	11.7	6.6	14.1	7.0	12.5	1.5
		min.	27.5	19.6	6.0	16.1	11.6	6.4	13.6	6.6	12.1	1.0
		max.	28.8	20.4	6.7	17.5	11.8	6.7	14.5	7.3	12.9	1.7
T. talpoides fisheri												
½ mi. W Beckwith, Cal......	41306	♂	30.9	21.6	6.1	18.1	11.8	7.4	14.1	7.7	12.9	0.9
3½ mi. E Carson City.......	64856	♀ sad.	28.2	19.9	6.5	16.9	11.4	6.5	13.7	7.2	12.2	0.6
T. talpoides falcifer												
Type locality...............	7 av.	♂	33.7	24.3	6.4	19.4	14.3	7.6	17.3	7.8	14.5	1.5
		min.	31.6	22.9	6.0	18.4	13.7	7.4	16.5	7.1	13.9	1.0
		max.	34.5	24.8	6.8	20.4	15.2	7.9	18.1	8.5	15.1	2.1
Type locality...............	5 av.	♀	30.1	21.4	6.5	17.5	12.5	7.0	15.2	7.5	13.2	1.1
		min.	28.8	20.0	6.0	16.5	11.9	6.4	14.5	6.9	12.7	0.5
		max.	31.1	22.1	7.0	18.2	12.8	7.5	15.9	7.9	13.5	1.7
T. talpoides monoensis												
Chiatovich Creek...........	10 av.	♂	30.6	20.7	6.0	18.1	12.4	7.3	15.2	7.5	13.0	2.1
		min.	29.3	19.6	5.5	17.4	11.6	7.0	14.3	7.0	12.7	1.6
		max.	31.5	21.9	6.4	19.0	13.0	7.5	16.5	7.8	13.7	2.6
Chiatovich Creek...........	5 av.	♀	29.1	19.7	6.2	17.6	11.4	7.0	14.5	7.4	12.7	2.1
		min.	28.1	18.9	6.1	16.6	10.9	6.8	14.0	7.0	12.3	1.9
		max.	30.0	21.4	6.3	18.8	11.7	7.4	15.3	7.9	13.1	2.2
T. monticola monticola												
3 mi. S Mount Rose.........	65219	♂	31.7	21.2	6.3	17.6	14.5	7.5	16.6	7.4	13.6	0.3
3 mi. S Mount Rose.........	88275	♂	29.9	—	6.1	17.4	13.5	7.1	15.9	7.5	13.0	0.8
3 mi. S Mount Rose.........	65217	♀ sad.	28.7	18.9	6.4	16.7	12.7	7.6	15.1	7.2	12.4	0.3
T. townsendii bachmani												
Topotypes..................	3 av.	♂	41.2	31.2	7.1	25.7	16.9	10.1	19.1	9.8	18.5	2.7
		min.	39.3	29.7	7.0	24.8	15.8	9.6	17.9	9.1	17.8	2.3
		max.	42.7	32.0	7.3	26.2	17.4	10.7	20.4	10.4	19.0	2.9
Topotypes..................	7 av.	♀	38.6	29.2	7.0	23.9	15.4	9.1	17.5	9.5	17.4	2.6
		min.	37.6	28.2	6.7	22.1	14.5	8.8	17.0	9.1	16.8	2.0
		max.	39.4	30.5	7.4	25.0	16.3	9.4	18.4	9.8	17.7	2.8

* Taken where maxillary and premaxillary bones meet on sides of rostrum.
† Taken from the middle of the anterior border of the nasals to the maxilla at its lateralmost point of union with the hamular process of the lacrimal.
‡ Vertical distance between ventral face of palatine bones between second molars to mid-line of dorsal face of frontal bones at plane of least interorbital constriction.
§ Collection of Ralph Ellis.

TABLE 12—(Continued)

Name and locality	Number of individuals averaged or catalogue no.	Sex and age	Basilar length	Zygomatic breadth	Least interorbital constriction	Mastoidal breadth	Length of nasals	Breadth of rostrum*	Length of rostrum†	Alveolar length of maxillary tooth row	Palato-frontal depth‡	Extension of pre-maxillae posterior to nasals
T. townsendii elkoensis												
Within 4 mi. Elko	6 av.	♂	43.1	32.1	7.1	25.6	17.9	9.7	20.8	9.6	18.8	2.7
	min.		41.7	30.6	6.9	24.9	17.1	9.0	19.2	9.1	18.1	2.2
	max.		44.6	34.0	7.3	26.4	19.0	10.4	24.0	10.1	19.8	3.0
Within 4 mi. Elko	9 av.	♀	40.9	30.2	7.2	24.4	16.4	9.2	18.8	9.4	17.9	2.7
	min.		40.2	29.2	6.8	23.7	15.2	8.8	17.6	8.7	17.5	2.2
	max.		41.6	31.4	7.5	25.2	17.5	9.4	19.9	10.6	18.5	3.0
T. townsendii nevadensis												
Topotypes	12 av.	♂	40.4	29.7	6.9	25.1	15.4	9.4	19.2	9.4	18.1	3.6
	min.		38.8	28.5	6.3	23.9	14.6	9.0	18.2	9.2	17.4	3.3
	max.		42.9	31.4	7.3	26.3	16.7	10.0	20.2	9.9	19.0	4.0
Topotypes	8 av.	♀	37.8	28.3	6.8	23.7	13.9	8.9	17.5	9.4	16.9	3.4
	min.		37.0	27.1	6.4	22.9	13.3	8.8	16.5	9.0	16.4	2.7
	max.		38.4	29.5	7.1	24.7	14.4	9.1	18.4	9.7	17.6	3.9
T. bottae canus												
Topotypes	7 av.	♂	38.3	27.0	6.7	22.8	15.7	8.9	18.7	8.2	15.9	2.1
	min.		37.4	25.7	6.6	21.8	14.3	8.5	17.5	7.9	14.9	1.3
	max.		39.2	28.0	6.8	23.6	16.5	9.2	19.3	8.5	16.3	3.0
Topotypes	15 av.	♀	34.5	24.1	6.6	20.7	13.6	8.2	16.2	8.0	14.6	1.9
	min.		33.2	22.7	6.1	19.8	13.1	7.8	15.4	7.4	14.0	1.1
	max.		35.8	25.2	6.9	21.5	14.1	8.5	16.8	8.3	15.4	2.4
T. bottae depressus												
Topotypes	6 av.	♂	34.8	25.5	7.0	21.1	13.7	8.8	16.8	8.4	15.2	2.7
	min.		33.8	23.4	6.6	20.2	13.1	8.4	15.4	7.9	14.3	2.2
	max.		35.5	26.8	7.4	21.9	14.2	9.3	17.5	8.9	15.7	3.0
Topotypes	7 av.	♀	32.2	23.5	6.9	19.8	12.7	8.0	15.6	8.0	14.1	2.7
	min.		30.8	22.7	6.4	19.4	11.9	7.4	14.1	7.6	13.7	1.7
	max.		33.5	24.5	7.2	20.3	13.8	8.4	16.3	8.4	14.8	3.1
T. bottae lucrificus												
Topotypes	6 av.	♂	37.6	28.3	7.1	22.6	16.2	8.9	19.2	8.5	16.3	2.0
	min.		35.1	27.0	6.9	22.1	15.5	8.6	17.7	8.0	14.9	0.8
	max.		39.2	29.3	7.5	23.0	17.2	9.3	20.2	8.8	17.2	3.3
Topotypes	11 av.	♀	33.2	24.2	7.0	20.4	13.5	8.0	16.4	8.2	14.6	2.5
	min.		32.0	23.0	6.7	19.5	12.8	7.5	15.7	7.6	13.8	1.5
	max.		35.2	26.7	7.2	21.3	14.5	8.6	17.5	8.6	15.6	3.5
T. bottae cinereus												
Topotypes	3 av.	♂	34.5	24.6	6.7	20.9	14.2	8.4	17.4	8.6	15.2	2.8
	min.		33.1	24.1	6.5	20.2	13.5	8.3	16.8	8.4	15.0	1.7
	max.		36.0	25.2	7.0	21.5	14.9	8.5	17.9	8.8	15.3	3.9
Topotypes	3 av.	♀	32.4	23.6	6.5	19.9	14.2	8.4	15.8	8.3	14.5	2.0
	min.		31.7	22.7	6.2	19.5	12.1	7.9	15.1	8.0	13.9	1.5
	max.		33.7	24.3	6.9	20.3	13.4	8.2	15.5	8.6	14.9	2.2
T. bottae lacrymalis												
Topotypes	5 av.	♂	35.7	26.6	6.6	21.8	15.4	9.8	17.6	8.6	15.2	1.5
	min.		34.9	25.4	6.2	21.2	14.6	9.3	16.7	8.0	15.0	1.4
	max.		36.5	28.3	7.0	22.8	17.5	10.6	18.4	9.3	15.4	2.4
Topotypes	10 av.	♀	32.3	23.2	6.8	19.6	13.2	8.1	15.6	8.3	14.3	1.8
	min.		29.9	21.8	6.4	18.5	11.8	7.8	14.4	7.8	13.4	1.0
	max.		34.1	25.0	7.5	20.5	14.1	8.7	17.8	8.7	15.4	2.8

*, †, ‡. For explanation of these symbols, see first page of table.

TABLE 12—(*Continued*)

Name and locality	Number of individuals averaged or catalogue no.	Sex and age	Basilar length	Zygomatic breadth	Least interorbital constriction	Mastoidal breadth	Length of nasals	Breadth of rostrum*	Length of rostrum†	Alveolar length of maxillary tooth row	Palato-frontal depth‡	Extension of premaxillae posterior to nasals
T. bottae solitarius												
Topotypes	5 av.	♂	30.9	21.5	6.6	18.6	12.2	7.9	14.9	7.7	13.7	2.4
	min.		29.9	20.7	6.4	18.1	11.7	7.5	14.0	7.3	13.3	2.2
	max.		31.1	22.3	7.1	18.9	12.9	8.0	15.2	8.1	14.2	2.5
Topotype	36379	♀	29.6	20.4	6.6	18.4	12.1	6.9	14.1	7.3	13.3	2.5
Topotype	36383	♀	30.0	20.8	6.7	17.9	12.0	7.4	13.5	7.9	13.8	2.0
T. bottae fumosus												
Topotypes	7 av.	♂	36.1	25.5	6.9	21.0	14.8	8.7	17.3	8.1	15.6	2.3
	min.		33.5	24.1	6.6	20.3	13.3	8.1	16.4	7.5	14.7	1.3
	max.		37.5	26.7	7.3	21.6	16.6	9.3	18.1	8.7	16.1	3.3
Topotypes	8 av.	♀	32.8	23.0	6.9	20.0	12.8	8.1	15.3	7.7	14.3	2.3
	min.		31.4	22.1	6.4	19.0	11.8	7.6	14.1	7.2	13.6	1.1
	max.		34.8	23.9	7.2	20.9	14.6	8.5	17.0	8.0	15.4	3.1
T. bottae curtatus												
Topotypes	4 av.	♂	33.2	24.4	6.7	20.4	13.7	8.5	16.0	8.2	14.6	2.5
	min.		32.0	23.6	6.0	20.0	12.8	8.3	15.5	7.6	14.2	1.8
	max.		35.6	26.0	7.4	21.0	15.0	8.8	16.9	9.2	15.5	3.0
Topotypes	4 av.	♀	31.8	23.1	6.9	19.6	13.0	8.0	15.1	8.3	14.1	2.0
	min.		30.8	21.9	6.5	19.0	12.5	7.9	14.4	8.2	13.7	1.7
	max.		33.0	23.9	7.1	20.2	13.7	8.2	16.2	8.6	14.5	2.6
T. bottae vescus												
Topotypes	5 av.	♂	32.6	23.4	6.5	19.7	12.4	7.6	15.0	7.5	14.0	2.3
	min.		30.9	21.9	6.2	18.5	11.7	7.0	14.2	6.7	13.6	2.2
	max.		35.0	25.3	6.7	21.6	13.8	8.4	16.5	8.2	14.1	2.9
Topotype	57606	♀	31.2	22.0	6.4	18.3	11.8	7.2	15.1	7.4	13.8	2.9
Topotype (9800 ft.)	57603	♀	31.9	22.7	6.8	19.3	12.0	7.2	14.6	7.9	13.8	1.8
T. bottae concisor												
Topotypes	6 av.	♂	37.6	27.6	6.9	21.8	14.2	8.8	17.6	8.1	16.2	2.4
	min.		35.3	25.2	6.7	20.0	13.2	8.3	16.5	7.7	14.8	2.0
	max.		39.5	29.0	7.1	23.2	15.0	9.4	18.5	8.7	17.2	3.0
Topotype	10 av.	♀	33.3	24.1	6.8	20.2	12.5	8.0	15.7	7.7	14.9	2.5
	min.		32.2	22.4	6.5	19.6	11.5	7.5	14.8	7.1	14.0	2.2
	max.		34.6	25.7	7.1	20.9	13.1	8.5	16.3	8.2	16.3	3.0
T. bottae abstrusus												
Type	57613	♂	38.1	27.1	6.6	22.4	15.4	8.5	19.1	8.2	17.0	3.7
T. bottae brevidens												
Topotypes	5 av.	♂	33.5	23.5	6.6	19.7	13.3	8.6	15.5	8.0	14.7	2.3
	min.		32.5	23.2	6.2	19.3	12.5	8.3	14.9	7.8	14.3	1.5
	max.		34.5	24.1	6.8	20.1	14.0	8.9	16.5	8.4	14.9	2.9
Topotypes	4 av.	♀	30.4	21.4	6.4	18.6	11.6	7.5	14.1	7.4	13.7	2.6
	min.		29.7	20.8	6.2	18.0	11.4	7.1	13.9	7.2	13.6	2.5
	max.		30.8	22.4	6.5	19.2	11.8	7.9	14.5	7.6	14.0	2.8
T. bottae latus												
Topotypes	3 av.	♂	33.9	24.8	6.8	20.0	13.3	8.0	16.0	7.9	15.3	2.5
	min.		32.6	24.0	6.8	19.4	12.7	7.8	15.2	7.8	15.1	2.1
	max.		36.0	25.3	6.9	21.1	13.8	8.2	16.6	8.1	15.6	2.8
Topotypes	6 av.	♀	32.9	23.9	6.7	19.2	12.8	7.8	15.5	7.9	14.8	2.4
	min.		31.8	22.9	6.6	18.9	12.0	7.5	14.7	7.6	14.6	2.2
	max.		33.8	24.1	6.8	19.8	13.5	8.3	16.0	8.3	15.3	2.6

*, †, ‡. For explanation of these symbols, see first page of table.

TABLE 12—(*Concluded*)

Name and locality	Number of individuals averaged or catalogue no.	Sex and age	Basilar length	Zygomatic breadth	Least interorbital constriction	Mastoidal breadth	Length of nasals	Breadth of rostrum*	Length of rostrum†	Alveolar length of maxillary tooth row	Palato-frontal depth‡	Extension of premaxillae posterior to nasals
T. bottae centralis												
Near topotypes.............	9 av.	♂	36.3	25.2	6.6	20.7	14.6	8.5	17.7	8.0	15.5	3.2
	min.		34.5	24.6	5.8	19.7	13.9	8.1	17.1	7.5	14.7	2.2
	max.		38.0	26.1	7.2	21.9	15.9	8.9	18.6	8.7	15.9	4.5
Near topotypes.............	17 av.	♀	31.8	22.1	6.6	19.0	12.6	7.6	15.3	7.6	14.1	2.7
	min.		30.5	21.3	5.9	18.2	11.9	7.4	14.7	7.0	13.4	2.0
	max.		33.0	23.1	7.1	20.1	13.8	8.2	16.0	8.0	14.8	3.4
T. bottae virgineus												
Mesquite..................	49096	♂	34.8	24.8	6.5	21.1	14.6	8.5	17.5	7.9	15.1	3.2
Mesquite..................	4 av.	♀	31.2	22.4	6.3	19.3	11.9	7.6	14.7	7.7	13.9	2.7
	min.		30.1	21.4	6.0	18.6	11.4	7.5	14.2	7.2	13.3	2.4
	max.		33.3	24.0	6.5	20.2	12.5	8.0	15.6	8.2	14.8	3.3
T. bottae nanus												
Topotypes.................	5 av.	♂	29.7	20.6	6.4	17.9	11.0	7.1	13.7	7.5	12.9	2.7
	min.		28.2	19.8	6.2	16.9	10.7	6.5	12.7	6.8	12.5	1.3
	max.		31.9	21.8	6.6	19.0	11.6	7.4	14.7	8.0	13.4	3.3
Topotypes.................	10 av.	♀	28.8	20.2	6.4	17.7	10.6	7.0	13.3	7.6	12.9	2.6
	min.		26.9	19.1	6.2	17.4	9.9	6.6	12.0	7.0	12.4	2.3
	max.		30.4	20.8	6.7	18.3	11.2	7.4	14.0	8.0	13.2	3.0
T. bottae phelleoecus												
Topotypes.................	3 av.	♂	30.3	22.7	5.9	19.5	11.1	7.7	14.4	7.5	13.6	3.0
	min.		30.0	22.4	5.6	19.0	10.7	7.5	14.0	7.3	13.2	2.9
	max.		30.8	23.1	6.0	19.8	11.5	8.0	14.7	7.6	13.9	3.0
Topotypes.................	5 av.	♀	27.4	20.3	6.1	17.8	10.6	7.0	13.6	6.9	12.6	2.6
	min.		24.3	19.0	5.8	16.9	10.0	6.6	13.1	6.6	11.5	2.0
	max.		28.7	21.0	6.6	18.4	11.6	7.4	14.2	7.3	13.2	3.0
T. bottae melanotis												
Lida‖......................	4 av.	♂	35.3	25.5	6.4	20.9	13.5	8.8	16.8	8.3	15.5	3.2
	min.		34.4	23.4	6.0	19.4	12.7	8.1	16.4	8.0	14.9	2.6
	max.		36.9	27.0	6.8	22.3	14.4	9.1	18.0	8.5	16.4	3.6
Lida‖......................	K 864	♀	32.6	23.4	6.3	20.3	11.9	8.0	16.0	7.6	14.8	4.5
Lida‖......................	K 878	♀	31.9	22.8	6.3	19.0	12.7	7.7	15.3	8.0	14.3	1.9
T. bottae oreoecus												
Near Grapevine Peak.......	4 av.	♂	30.8	22.2	6.3	19.1	11.7	7.7	14.8	7.6	13.9	3.0
	min.		30.0	21.4	6.1	18.5	10.8	7.5	14.2	7.4	13.8	2.8
	max.		32.0	22.8	6.6	19.9	12.4	7.8	15.8	7.7	14.2	3.3
Near Grapevine Peak.......	92654	♀	27.8	19.7	6.0	17.5	11.6	6.8	13.6	7.3	12.8	2.1
Near Grapevine Peak........	92649	♀	28.8	20.1	6.0	17.5	10.8	6.6	13.3	6.9	13.0	2.8
T. bottae providentialis												
8 mi. S Dead Mountain.....	61501	♂	30.7	21.7	7.2	19.3	12.0	8.1	14.0	7.8	13.8	1.5
8 mi. S Dead Mountain.....	61502	♂	28.8	20.7	6.8	18.0	11.3	7.0	13.2	7.1	13.8	1.3
8 mi. S Dead Mountain.....	8 av.	♀	29.8	21.2	6.5	18.5	12.2	7.3	14.1	7.9	13.5	1.8
	min.		28.8	20.0	6.3	17.7	11.6	6.9	13.3	7.4	12.9	0.6
	max.		31.1	22.2	6.8	19.0	12.9	7.6	15.0	8.7	13.9	2.6
Potosi Mountain...........	92656	♀	28.4	20.1	6.5	17.8	10.5	7.0	12.8	6.8	13.0	2.2

*, †, ‡. For explanation of these symbols, see first page of table.
‖ D. R. Dickey collection.

Castor canadensis
Beaver

The beaver is the largest of North American living rodents and one of the most valuable fur-bearing mammals. Much of the early exploration of western North America by white men was incidental to their quest for beaver. Northern Nevada came in for its share of attention from these parties of beaver trappers. One such party of which there is written record (Elliott, 1910) is that led by Peter Skene Ogden in 1828 and 1829. Ogden, Thomas McKay, and their men reaped a rich harvest of beaver skins from the Humboldt River, its tributaries from the north, and probably also from some of the tributaries of the Snake River which head in Nevada. In one spring, that of 1829, 1,700 beavers were taken from a Nevadan stream, probably the Humboldt River.

Noteworthy features of the beaver are: underfur dense and sharply distinct from overhairs; neck and legs short; ears short, valvular, and nearly concealed by the pelage; hind feet much larger than the forefeet and webbed; tail scaly, paddle-shaped, and flattened in horizontal plane; rostrum of skull broad and deep; brain case narrow and angular; basioccipital hollowed out on ventral side; anterior opening of infraorbital canal much smaller than incisive foramen; cheek teeth hypsodont but not evergrowing; crown surfaces of cheek teeth exhibiting alternating layers of enamel and dentine. The dental formula is i. $\frac{1}{1}$, c. $\frac{0}{0}$, p. $\frac{1}{1}$, m. $\frac{3}{3}$. Many of the distinguishing features are of an adaptive kind which better fit the beaver for a life in the water. The dense fur, short and valvular ear, webbed hind foot, and flattened tail are modifications of this sort.

Although beavers can live for some time, perhaps for days, away from water, they never do so in the wild. If their place of habitation becomes depleted of water, they migrate to a place that meets their requirements for water. To beavers, water means, for one thing, safety. At hint of danger they dive into it and out of sight. Entrances to their homes, whether these be houses made of sticks and mud or burrows in banks of streams or lakes, are under water and thus closed to terrestrial enemies. To provide and maintain a depth of water sufficient for the needs just mentioned, the beavers in small streams, and sometimes in wide streams, work assiduously in cutting sticks and small poles and dragging them to the place where a dam is to be constructed. Faced with mud on the upstream side, these dams raise the water level to the height required by the beavers. In addition to providing refuge for themselves and covering for the entrances to their lodges and burrows, the pond serves as a waterway, up and down which the beavers travel and transport freshly cut willows used as food, and as a place in which they can store food and move about below the ice that in northern Nevada probably restricts their activity in winter.

Formation of a beaver pond in a small stream raises the water level in the stream and the water table in the near-by ground. As a result, trees within the area affected sometimes die, and limbs soon break off the dead trunks and

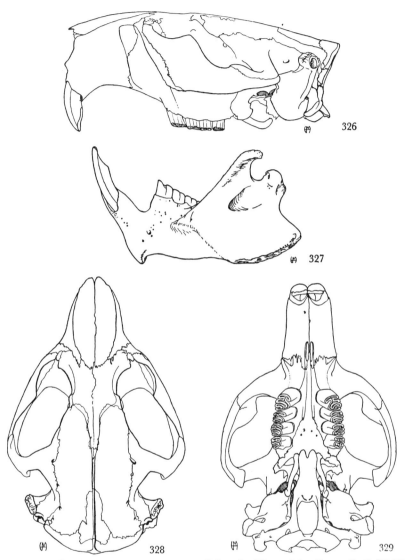

Figs. 326–329. *Castor canadensis repentinus*, Colorado River, ½ mile north Calif.-Nev. Monument, no. 61670, ♀. × ½.

allow the entrance of water, fungi, and other things which hasten the enlarge-ment of cavities so formed. Woodpeckers drill other holes into the dead trunks. These hollows provide nesting sites for tree swallows, some kinds of fly-catchers, bluebirds, wood ducks, and, depending on the locality, other kinds of birds which did not occur at the place before. Wood-boring insects multiply and provide food attractive to woodpeckers and other animals. Because of the higher water table and formation of swampy land, willows and other trees spring up in place of, and farther back than, those that died. A variety of other plants find a foothold and create a dense ground cover. About this area ducks nest, rear their broods, and hide while in the eclipse plumage, and a large number of other animals of different phyla find their preferred habitats created as a result of the beavers' work. Fish have rearing ponds, muskrats find conditions to their liking, and jack snipes live on the wet bottoms.

As the stream bed silts up behind the dams, the beavers build other dams higher up the stream, and in time a succession of ponds, later marshy places, and eventually meadows may be formed. In 1935, on Goose Creek, in the northeastern corner of the state, all stages of the results of beaver workings, from newly made pond to meadow, were to be seen.

The following summer, on 12-mile Creek, in the northwestern corner of Nevada, we saw only the terracelike remains of meadows, the beavers having been trapped out, to the last animal, long before. Where grass once grew, rabbit brush and sagebrush of the arid upland had taken over and was crowding down toward the stream which was now little more than a trickle, even in places disappearing entirely in midday. That the stream had been higher was proved by drift left on the sides of old trees by a spring freshet. But now, the beaver dams having been washed away, the water had cut deeply, and an ugly gully ran through the heart of the meadows. At a Fort Bidwell store, local residents told us that this was not as good cattle country as it was in the old days. "The meadows don't produce as much feed as formerly," they said. Among several buildings which once served an old ranch in this vicinity, a cabin, sometimes used overnight by a rider who came at intervals to look at the cattle, was the only one standing. The road to it was no longer passable, even for a wagon. Because of insufficient water, the area of alfalfa on this ranch that could be irrigated was much reduced! The water mostly ran off in early spring because there were no beavers keeping dams in repair to hold back the flood and equalize the flow, and thus prolong it into the dry months when most needed. Ducks no longer nested, muskrats were not to be found, trout were few, and many other creatures were scarce or entirely gone. Domestic animals found but scanty forage and even man himself had left!

On the streams of northern Nevada, beavers are valuable, several ranchers realizing this. Huge yields of native hay and abundant pasture along the creeks were credited by ranchers to the activities of the beavers. In summer, foremen cautioned the ranch hands not to destroy the beavers, even though they made nuisances of themselves by blocking up the intake gates of irrigation ditches. Vigilance in winter was necessary too, for unscrupulous individuals then appeared who were bent on taking the pelts of beavers.

In 1935, ranchers near Lovelock, at the lower end of the Humboldt River, had an attitude toward the beaver very much at odds with that of the ranchers on the upper reaches of the stream. By reason of early establishment, ranches at the lower end of the river had prior water rights. But, because the river is a meandering stream in which water requires a long time to flow all the way down, evaporation and losses from other causes, at the time of which we speak, prevented water from reaching Lovelock in quantities large enough to irrigate the fields. The rancher with whom I talked said he spoke for the majority of the ranchers in the vicinity of Lovelock in recommending extermination of the beavers because their dams retarded the flow of water. These ranchers wanted a rapid runoff which would produce a head of water big enough to flow as far as the intakes of their irrigation ditches.

At the time of our visit to Marys River, near the head of the Humboldt, a rancher, who, holding water rights which could be exercised only after the superior rights of those lower downstream were satisfied, was letting the flow pass his headgates, smilingly admitted that the flooding of a meadow as a result of beavers' raising the height of their dam was an act of nature over which he had no control! In his opinion the beavers were useful animals indeed; he was loath to allow us to take even one individual for a "scientific specimen," and would have been aghast at any suggestion about dynamiting the dams, as the rancher at the lower end of the river claimed had been done there.

In northeastern Nevada, on Goose Creek and Marys River, the beavers had two kinds of homes, both of which were in the ponds upstream from the dams. One kind was the house built of sticks and poles. Some of these houses were as much as 14 feet across at the base and 6 feet high, the entrances being under water. The other and more common kind of home was a burrow. The roofs of some had caved in, leaving holes in the meadow 10 feet or so back from the edge of the stream. These holes were covered over and partly filled in with sticks. A few abodes thus repaired were so nearly intermediate between a house and a burrow as to be easily classified in either category.

On Marys River, between July 5 and 9, 1935, I noticed several musk mounds. This was a time of year, so others had determined by study of localities elsewhere, when beavers are said to make few or no such deposits. The mounds were small, 4 to 8 inches in diameter, and each was more largely composed of soil than of vegetable matter. They were recognizable by the odor of the musk deposited there as well as by the heaped-up appearance of the places themselves. All feces that we found were in shallow water. No canals, such as beavers make in some places, were noted. The willows, the twigs and bark of which the beavers use for food, grew thickly right up to the water's edge and hung down into it. Thus, it was unnecessary for the animals to leave the water to obtain all the food they required. On Goose Creek, willows were less plentiful and some beavers went as far as 60 yards from the water in quest of food. The animals on this creek cut some sagebrush, but used it to build up the top of one of their dams and not, so far as we could learn, for food. Along the Colorado River, also, willows were the plants used as food.

In the steep-sided, rocky canyon of the Colorado River 10 miles below

Boulder Dam, the habitat requirements of beavers were clearly evident in the spring of 1940. These were: (1) a cut bank of soil in which burrows could be made and (2) willows near by for food. Along the nearly vertical rock walls

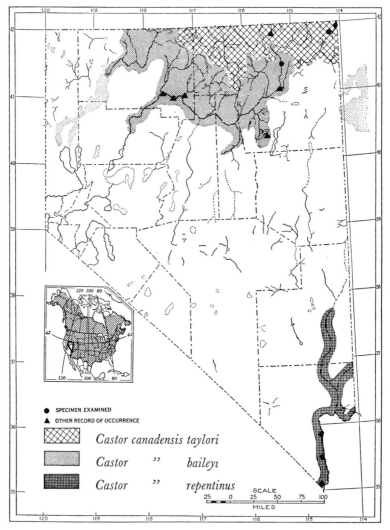

Fig. 330. Distribution of subspecies of the beaver, *Castor canadensis*, with insert showing range of the species.

there are incipient canyons at the bottoms of some of which soil has accumulated to a depth of several feet. More than half of these deposits have a cut bank. If willows grow on this soil or as near as a hundred yards to it, beavers occupy the place. A cut bank without willows near by was not occupied by beavers, and willow thickets were untouched if no cut bank was near. Only burrows in the banks, no houses, were seen on this river. The three parts of the Colorado personally examined by me were those 5 to 15 miles below Boulder Dam, a 2-mile stretch directly east of Searchlight, and the part from the California boundary upstream for 5 miles. Although it is thought that some beavers are trapped on this river each year, they nevertheless seem to maintain their numbers fairly well.

The construction of Boulder Dam and the consequent modification of the water levels in the Colorado River probably profoundly affected the beaver population there. R. K. Grater (*in litt.*, February 14, 1941) informs me that there are few beavers in Lake Mead. Fresh sign of beavers was found by him on the Muddy River arm of this lake several times in the preceding 2 years, and old cuttings, probably of one beaver, were noted at just one other place.

Below Boulder Dam the beavers appear to have been unfavorably affected by releases of large quantities of water that were allowed to go downriver to fill Havasu Lake behind Parker Dam at the time of its completion. For several hours on each of several days, says Grater, "water would pour down the river in quantity, flooding the narrow canyons and valleys downstream along the river. For example in the Willow Beach area the water would rise several feet. . . . These regular floodings had a marked effect upon the beaver population . . ., at least as far downstream as the Searchlight Ferry. . . . For several weeks beaver sign was rare in areas that heretofore were known to contain many of the animals. Whether they were forced to move and weeks later came back, I cannot say, but such seems to have been the case." Whether these fluctuations had more or less effect on beavers than the marked seasonal fluctuations in water level that occurred before Boulder Dam was built is unknown.

Of late years, beavers are reported to have been transported by man to places where they had become extinct or never occurred before. It is perhaps the result of one of these transplants that beaver occurred a few years before 1940 at Lahontan Reservoir on the Carson River. In this reservoir, 2 miles east of the dam, on February 25, 1940, J. R. Alcorn recovered the stump of a cottonwood tree, 4 inches in diameter, cut off by beaver more than a year before. No fresh beaver signs were seen. Otherwise, we have no records of beavers in the Carson, Truckee, or Walker rivers, and doubt that the animals ever occurred there naturally.

There is only one molt per year. The sexes are colored alike and there is but little if any secondary sexual variation in size. The two pair of mammae are pectoral. In beavers from areas outside Nevada, embryos have been found to range from one to eight in number, with an average of four.

Three subspecies of beavers are known from Nevada. Possibly a fourth subspecies, *Castor canadensis shastensis*, occurred in the extreme northwestern corner of the state in 12-mile Creek. Beavers are extinct there now, or were in 1936, and so far as known, no specimens were saved from that area.

Castor canadensis taylori Davis
Beaver

Castor canadensis taylori Davis, The Recent Mammals of Idaho, p. 273, April 5, 1939. Type from Big Wood River, Bellevue, Blaine County, Idaho.

Distribution.—Northern Nevada in streams tributary to the Snake River drainage. See figure 330.

Remarks.—External measurements of adult animals are unavailable, but judging from the tanned skins of topotypes the size is about the same as in *baileyi*.

Color between Cinnamon-Brown and Prouts Brown above; skull relatively narrow, nasals projecting behind premaxillae and elliptical in outline; anterolateral rim of orbit narrow (about 7 mm.). Comparison with *baileyi* is made in the account of that race.

C. c. taylori probably occurred on all the streams of any size in northern Nevada which flow into the Snake River. General reports indicate that they still are fairly common on many of these streams. Adrey E. Borell (MS) observed fresh working on the Jarbidge River in 1929. The animals were common along Goose Creek in July, 1935, from which place our only specimens were procured. These all are so young as not clearly to show the characters differentiating *baileyi* from *taylori*, and their reference to the latter race rests on geographic probability.

Records of occurrence.—Specimens examined, 4, as follows: *Elko Co.*: Goose Creek, 2 mi. W Utah boundary, 5000 ft., 3; Goose Creek, 10½ mi. W Utah boundary, 5150 ft., 1 (skull only).
Additional record: *Elko Co.*: Jarbidge River (Borell and Ellis, 1934b:73).

Castor canadensis baileyi Nelson
Beaver

Castor canadensis baileyi Nelson, Proc. Biol. Soc. Washington, 40:125, September 26, 1927. Type from Humboldt River, 4 miles above Winnemucca, Humboldt County Nevada; Borell and Ellis, Journ. Mamm., 15:29, February 15, 1934.

Distribution.—Humboldt River drainage. See figure 330.

Remarks.—Measurements of the type, said to be (Nelson, 1927:126) an adult male, and of another adult male from Marys River, are 1,064, 1,006; 254 (*sic*), 454; 183, 166; ear from notch, —, 34; weight, —, 46½ lbs.

Color near Cinnamon-Brown; skull relatively slender; nasals extending posteriorly to premaxillae; anterolateral rim of orbit broad (9 mm.) in specimen from Marys River.

From *taylori*, this race differs in: color lighter; incisors larger and more recurved; anterolateral rim of orbit and nasals wider. From *repentinus*, *baileyi* differs in: color darker and skull relatively broader.

The single adult specimen seen comes from the headwaters of the Humboldt River and probably differs in slightly darker color and somewhat wider skull from topotypes. I have not examined topotypes, and all that I know about them is that which is contained in the printed description.

Record of occurrence.—Specimens examined, 2, as follows: *Elko Co.*: Marys River, 25 mi. N Deeth, 5800 ft., 2.
Additional records: *Humboldt Co.* (Nelson, 1927:126): Humboldt River, 4 mi. above Winnemucca; Iron Point; Golconda. *Elko Co.*: Deeth (Nelson, *loc. cit.*); Toyn Creek, 7000 ft.; near summit of Harrison Pass (Borell and Ellis, 1934a:29).

Castor canadensis repentinus Goldman
Beaver

Castor canadensis repentinus Goldman, Journ. Mamm., 13:266, August 9, 1932. Type from Bright Angel Creek, Grand Canyon of the Colorado River, 4000 feet, Coconino County, Arizona.

Distribution.—Colorado River and probably formerly Virgin and Muddy rivers. See figure 330.

Remarks.—A female from ½ mile north of the Calif.-Nev. Monument measures 1,200, 530, 200, 35. Weights are unavailable.

Color near (*j*) Ochraceous-Tawny; nasals extending behind premaxillae; jugals narrow vertically at postorbital processes.

The Nevadan specimens referred to this race are the palest North American beavers examined. The one adult skull from Nevada is relatively narrower in the interorbital region than are topotypes.

From *baileyi, repentinus* differs in: color much lighter and skull relatively broader (comparing topotypes of the two races).

Dwight C. Smiley (*in litt.*, February 16, 1936) says that "Mr. Armitage of Las Vegas . . . trapped the region between Boulder Dam and Pierces Ferry . . . 85 mi. NE of the dam site . . . between the years 1912 and 1918. . . . beaver [were] sufficiently abundant to yield 2.5 animals out of six traps set night after night." I found them on the Nevada side of the Colorado River 10 miles below Boulder Dam on March 20, 1940.

Records of occurrence.—Specimens examined, 3, as follows: *Clark Co.*: Searchlight Ferry, 1 (skin only); ½ and 2 mi. above Calif.-Nev. Monument, 500 ft., 2.
Additional record (Hall, MS): 10 mi. below Boulder Dam.

TABLE 13

CRANIAL MEASUREMENTS (IN MILLIMETERS) OF CASTOR

Sex	Catalogue no.	Occipitonasal length	Condylobasal length	Basilar length	Zygomatic breadth	Mastoidal breadth	Interorbital constriction	Length of nasals	Greatest width of nasals
				C. castor taylori, Bellevue, Idaho					
♀	67588	132.2	131.5	115.9	95.4	67.6	25.2	49.8	22.5
				C. castor baileyi, 25 mi. N Deeth					
♂	68235	133.8	132.5	118.1	97.0	63.1	24.0	48.5	21.5
			C. castor repentinus, ½ mi. N Calif.-Nev. Monument						
♀	61670	141.3	139.3	121.2	98.5	70.1	22.9	52.0	23.0

Genus Onychomys Baird
Grasshopper Mice

There are only two living species of this genus, both of which occur in Nevada. *Onychomys leucogaster* is somewhat the larger of the two. Both resemble mice of the genus *Peromyscus* but are stouter-bodied and shorter-tailed. From *Peromyscus* they differ further in: sole of hind feet with only four tubercles (forefeet with five tubercles); nasals distinctly more wedge-shaped; coronoid process of mandible higher; molars more hypsodont, with anterior cusp of M1 more nearly in line with the outer row of cusps. The dental formula is i. $\frac{1}{1}$, c. $\frac{0}{0}$, p. $\frac{0}{0}$, m. $\frac{3}{3}$.

These mice have been treated systematically by Hollister (1914); Charles Sperry (1929) reported on their food habits, Vernon Bailey (1929) gave data on their general habits, and Ruth Dowell Svihla (1936) recorded valuable information about their food. Information extracted from these accounts, little or none of which relates to Nevada-taken specimens, indicates that the mice are nocturnal, probably do not hibernate, even in the northern part of their range, and subsist principally upon insects. Sperry (*op. cit.*) found insects to comprise 79 per cent of the food, and animal matter of all kinds made up 89 per cent of the food. La Rivers (1941: 67) implies that in Nevada the species *O. leucogaster* feeds on Mormon crickets (*Anabrus simplex*). Bailey (*op. cit.*) suggests from observation of captives that seeds may be stored up in winter when vegetable matter may comprise a larger share of the diet.

Some of the many kinds of insects eaten are injurious to cultivated crops. The grasshopper mice, or scorpion mice, as some naturalists term them, are therefore regarded by certain persons as beneficial to man. Vernon Bailey (*op. cit.*) found that if the cage of his captive mice were placed in a closed room at night with the door of the cage open, the mice would return to the nest in the cage after their nocturnal forays. He says that in the kitchen one of these mice "proved very useful in capturing and eating all the cockroaches that came out at night. At first they [cockroaches] were numerous and large, but after a few weeks they became scarce, and only the very small or young individuals were occasionally seen. Little groups of legs could be found all around the edges of the floor for a few nights, but the smaller young were eaten legs and all, and apparently most of the cockroaches in the house were destroyed within a month."

Like other insectivorous vertebrates, grasshopper mice decay quickly, and in our field work we early learned that specimens must be skinned soon after they were caught if "slipping" of the hair were to be avoided. The mice are rare. *O. torridus*, in our experience, was more common than *O. leucogaster*. Even so, by far the largest number, thirty-six, that we ever took at one time was of the species *leucogaster*. Ward Russell and I, on July 28, 1935, 16 mi. NE Iron Point, in 140 mouse traps, took sixteen, along with eight other mammals (one *Peromyscus maniculatus*, two *Perognathus longimembris*, and five *Dipodomys microps*). The traps were set on fine, chalky soil supporting *Atriplex* and thin lines of *Artemisia tridentata* along gullies 8 inches deep that cut across this flat at widely spaced intervals. At the same time, Albert E. Peterson and William B. Richardson, 2 miles farther northeast, in 150 traps set on gravelly, and in places stony, soil among *Artemisia tridentata*, took twenty *Onychomys* and fifty other mammals (thirty-four *Peromyscus maniculatus*, two *Peromyscus crinitus*, three *Perognathus parvus*, three *Dipodomys ordii*, seven *Dipodomys microps* and one *Eutamias minimus*). The relatively large number of *Onychomys* caught here was entirely unlike anything experienced in all our other collecting in Nevada. Ordinarily, when 125 mouse traps are placed out in a new place each night, yielding a catch of twenty-five to seventy-five rodents each time, the collector feels fortunate if he takes one *Onychomys leucogaster* in 2 or 3 weeks.

In writing of the voice of grasshopper mice, Svihla (*op. cit.*) says: "I have heard it clearly at a distance of at least 100 feet from the closed greenhouse in which the animals were kept. The mouse usually stands on its hind feet with its front feet resting upon a food dish or side of the cage, points its nose skyward and with the mouth wide open emits the shrill, clear, little 'wolf's howl.' The other sound, which Bailey terms similar to the 'barking of a tiny terrier,' is entirely different and is used in protest, anger or scolding. I also have heard a high-pitched note which may be called a modified 'wolf's howl' of lesser intensity, but of such ventriloquistic qualities that it is very difficult to locate."

Onychomys leucogaster
Northern Grasshopper Mouse

Two subspecies of *Onychomys leucogaster* occur in Nevada. In each, the tail is less than half the length of the head and body; upper parts in adults rich glossy avellaneous; the face, back, and rump darkened by brownish-tipped hairs; sides more reddish; ear tufts white or white and buffy, but not well differentiated in some adults; ears brownish, edged with white; tail grayish-brown above, with tip white; underparts, including lower cheeks, legs, feet,  and underside of tail, white, but fur plumbeous at base except on throat, where white entirely to base. The young are plumbeous or bluish-colored above, and, according to Svihla (1936:173), the brighter adult pelage is acquired when the mice are 5 or 6 months old. I have not been able to ascertain the time of molt or the number of molts per year.

In Nevada, *O. leucogaster*, compared with *O. torridus*, has an actually shorter tail (averaging less, rather than more, than half length of head and body), and the interorbital region is of the same breadth, but in all other measurements taken averages larger. To my eye, *leucogaster* is a stockier animal, and by actual weight it is a third heavier. In the skull, *leucogaster* is relatively narrower interorbitally, is larger in other parts, has higher crowned teeth of which the unworn cusps on M1 are higher than long, rather than vice versa, has M3 larger and as long as broad, rather than broader than long, and has M1 making up less, rather than more, than half of the length of the tooth row.

In my experience this species is less common than *O. torridus*. *O. leucogaster* keeps entirely to the Upper Sonoran Life-zone. The specimens available from Nevada well show the range, except in northern Lincoln County, where probably this species and not *O. torridus* occurs. Altitudinally, it has been

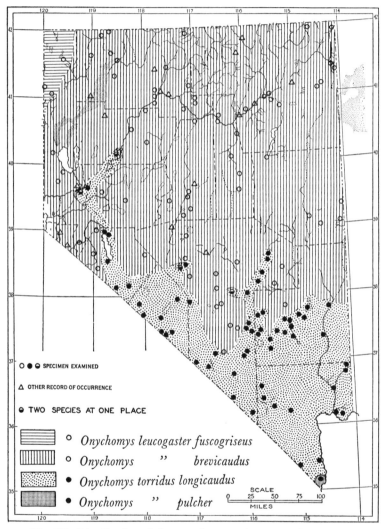

SPECIMEN EXAMINED

△ OTHER RECORD OF OCCURRENCE

TWO SPECIES AT ONE PLACE

○ *Onychomys leucogaster fuscogriseus*
○ *Onychomys   ,,   brevicaudus*
● *Onychomys torridus longicaudus*
● *Onychomys   ,,   pulcher*

SCALE
0   25   50   75   100
MILES

Fig. 331. Distribution of the grasshopper mice, genus *Onychomys*.

taken from as low as 3900 feet at Toulon up to 7500 feet on Kingston Creek.

Secondary sexual variation in size is of small amount; females average larger than males in external measurements by about 7 tenths of 1 per cent, by 6 per cent more in weight, and by about 5 tenths of 1 per cent in cranial measurements.

Mrs. Svihla (1936:173) obtained much information by breeding mice of this species, race *fuscogriseus*, in captivity at Pullman, Washington. The gestation period varied from 33 to 47 days in lactating females and was no longer than 32 days in a nonlactating female. At time of birth, young averaged 2.2 grams, or slightly less than 7 per cent of the weight here recorded for adult females of the race *brevicaudus*. The eyes opened on the 19th or 20th day. Of the ninety adult females from Nevada, only five had embryos: three females had five embryos, one female had four, and one female had three, which gives an average of 4.4 and mode of 5. By months the females were distributed as follows: February, 1 (0 pregnant); April, 1 (0); May, 17 (2); June, 9 (0); July, 47 (3); August, 5 (0); September, 5 (0); October, 4 (0); December, 1 (0).

Onychomys leucogaster fuscogriseus Anthony
Northern Grasshopper Mouse

Onychomys leucogaster fuscogriseus Anthony, Bull. Amer. Mus. Nat. Hist., 32:11, March 7, 1913. Type from Ironside, 4000 feet, Malheur County, Oregon.

Distribution.—Northern Washoe County. See figure 331.

Remarks.—A male from 1 mi. W Hausen measures 140, 35, 20; weight, 32.7 grams. In size, *O. l. fuscogriseus* is indistinguishable from *O. l. brevicaudus*, in the account of which average measurements are provided.

This is a weakly marked subspecies, in that it is distinguishable from *brevicaudus* only by color. The upper parts in adults are of a darker reddish-brown and the darker pelage of younger animals is more nearly black. Young specimens from Nevada show this darker color almost as well as do specimens from the Warner Mountains of California. In Oregon, young specimens of *fuscogriseus* seem not to be comparatively lighter than young specimens from California and Nevada. Intergradation with *brevicaudus* is shown by specimens referred to that race from places in western Humboldt County and by specimens from the vicinity of Flanigan. Adult specimens from these places, although intermediate in color between *fuscogriseus* and *brevicaudus*, show greater resemblance to the latter.

Records of occurrence.—Specimens examined, 7, as follows: *Washoe Co.:* 8½ mi. E Vya, 5900 ft., 1; 3 mi. E Painted Point, 5850 ft., 1; 1 mi. W Hausen, 4650 ft., 2; 2½ mi. SE Hausen, 5200 ft., 1; 10 mi. SE Hausen, 4675 ft., 2.

Onychomys leucogaster brevicaudus Merriam
Northern Grasshopper Mouse

Onychomys leucogaster brevicaudus Merriam, N. Amer. Fauna, 5:52, July 30, 1891. Type from Blackfoot, Bingham County, Idaho. Borell and Ellis, Journ. Mamm., 15:29, February 15, 1934.
Onychomys brevicaudus, Taylor, Univ. California Publ. Zoöl., 7:228, June 24, 1911.
Onychomys leucogaster, Linsdale, Amer. Midland Nat., 19:188, January, 1938.

Distribution.—Throughout the Upper Sonoran Life-zone of the state north of about latitude 37°, except northern Washoe County. See figure 331.

Remarks.—Average and extreme measurements of eight of each sex from an area in north-central Nevada embracing Winnemucca, Izenhood, and Battle Mountain, are: ♂, 144 (138–151), ♀, 142 (131–147); 40 (37–43), 40 (35–43); 20.4 (19–21.5), 19.8 (19–20); weight, 30 (24.8–33.3), 32.5 (26.3–37.5) grams.

The size is indicated by the measurements above and by the cranial measurements in table 14. The color is as described for the species, and comparison in this respect is made in the account of *fuscogriseus*. The skull averages less in size than in any other race of the species and is relatively broad and flat, with a stout rostrum. Seeming geographic variation in the subspecies is as follows: Animals from the area extending from Winnemucca to Eureka average slightly larger in most measurements taken than animals from other parts of the state. In width of brain case, this is particularly noticeable, and the wide brain case is found also in animals from Halleck and the Reese River Valley, in other words, in central Nevada. Four adults from the western edge of Lake Bonneville (vicinity of Montello and Tecoma) have small external measurements (136; 36; 19.0; weight, 28.0 grams). The minimum measurements of average size are shown by animals from central Nye County (9 mi. W and 3 mi. S of Tybo, south to the northwest base of Timber Mountain), the southernmost group of specimens. The eight adults, four of each sex, of this southernmost group yield average measurements of 139; 39; 18.9; weight, 25.5; condylobasal length, 24.3; greatest length of skull, 26.6; basilar length, 21.1; length of diastema, 6.8; postpalatal length, 9.3. In other cranial measurements, they differ by a smaller amount from more northern populations.

Records of occurrence.—Specimens examined, 211, as follows: *Washoe Co.:* 2½ mi. E Flanigan, 4200 ft., 8; 3½ mi. E Flanigan, 4200 ft., 3; 2¾ mi. SW Pyramid, 4300 ft., 1; Junction House, 4500 ft., 1. *Lyon Co.:* 1 mi. SE Wadsworth, 4200 ft., 1; West Walker River, Smiths Valley, 4700 ft., 1. *Humboldt Co.:* 1 mi. S Denio, Oregon, 4200 ft., 1; Hot Spring, Thousand Creek, 4300 ft., 5; 36 mi. NE Paradise Valley, 5500 ft., 1; Big Creek Ranch, base of Pine Forest Mts., 4350 ft., 1; 5 mi. N Summit Lake, 5900 ft., 1; 1½ mi. N Quinn River Crossing, 4100 ft., 2; 2½ mi. SW Quinn River Crossing, 4100 ft., 1; ½ mi. W Paradise, 1 (coll. of U. S. Biol. Surv. Dist. Office, Reno); Jackson Creek Ranch, 17½ mi. S and 5 mi. W Quinn River Crossing, 4000 ft., 2; 18 mi. NE Iron Point, 4600 ft., 16; 16 mi. NE Iron Point, 4500 ft., 16; 7 mi. N Winnemucca, 4400 ft., 1; 1½ mi. NW Winnemucca, 4900 ft., 1; 1 mi. N Winnemucca, 4600 ft., 6; 3 to 5 mi. SW Winnemucca, 4500 ft., 8; 10 mi. SW Winnemucca, 4500 ft., 11; 23 mi. NW Battle Mountain, 2. *Pershing Co.:* 15 mi. SW Winnemucca, 1; El Dorado Canyon, Humboldt Range, 6000 ft., 1; 9 mi. E Fanning, Buena Vista Valley, 4100 ft., 1; 3 mi. NNE Toulon, 3900 ft., 1; 1½ mi. NE Toulon, 3900 ft., 1. *Churchill Co.:* 1 mi. NW Soda Lake, 4000 ft., 2; 1 mi. W Mountain Well, 5350 ft., 1. *Mineral Co.:* 7 mi. NW Schurz, 4500 ft., 1; East Walker River, 2 mi. NW Morgans Ranch, 5100 ft., 1; Fingerrock Wash, Stewart Valley, 5400 ft., 2; Fletcher, 6098 ft., 1. *Lander Co.:* Izenhood, 2; 3 mi. S Izenhood, 2; 1 mi. E Battle Mountain, 7; Reese River Valley, 7 mi. N Austin, 5; Malloy Ranch, Reese River, 5 mi. W Austin, 5500 ft., 1; 6 mi. ENE Smiths Creek Ranch, 5550 ft., 1; Birch Creek, 7000 ft., 1; Kingston Ranger Station, 7500 ft., 1. *Eureka Co.:* 5 mi. N Beowawe, 1; ½ mi. S Beowawe, 3; Evans, 3; Winzell, 3; 4 mi. SE Romano, Diamond Valley, 1; 8 mi. W Eureka, 1. *Nye Co.:* 5 mi. S Millett, 5500 ft., 2; 11½ mi. NE San Antonio, 5700 ft., 1; 3½ mi. E Hot Creek, Hot Creek Valley, 5650 ft., 1; White River Valley, 17 mi. W Sunnyside, 2; San Antonio, 5400 ft., 1; 9 mi. W and 3 mi. S Tybo, 6200 ft., 1; 15 mi. NE Tonopah, Ralston Valley, 5800 ft., 2; Garden Valley, 8½ mi. NE Sharp, 1; 34 mi. E and 1 mi. N Tonopah, Ralston Valley, 5650 ft., 3; Old Mill, N end Reveille Valley, 6200 ft., 1; 3 2/5 mi. S Silverbow, Kawich Mts., 6200 ft., 1; 5½ mi. SW Silverbow, Kawich Mts., 6000 ft., 1; Gold Flat, 5½ mi. W Kawich P. O., 5150 ft., 2; 5 7/10 mi. SE Kawich P. O., Kawich Valley, 5400 ft., 2; NW base Timber Mtn., 4200 ft., 1. *Elko Co.:* 9 mi. NE San Jacinto, 5300 ft., 1; Goose Creek, 2 mi. W Utah boundary, 5000 ft., 1; 13 mi. N Montello, 5000 ft., 2; 1½ mi. NE Tecoma, 4900 ft., 4; Tecoma, 4900 ft., 3; Cobre, 6100 ft., 1; 2 mi. SW Cobre, 2; 2 mi. NW Halleck, 5200 ft., 7 (coll. of Ralph Ellis); 3 to 5 mi. W Halleck, 5200–5300 ft., 10 (5 in coll. of Ralph Ellis); Halleck, 5200 ft., 1 (coll. of Ralph Ellis); Elburz, 3 mi. S Halleck, 5200 ft., 4 (coll. of Ralph Ellis); summit of Secret Pass, 6200 ft., 1 (coll. of Ralph Ellis); 10 mi. SW Elko, 5600 ft., 1. *White Pine Co.:* W side Ruby Lake, 3 mi. S Elko Co. line, 6100 ft., 1 (coll of Ralph Ellis); 3 mi. E Smith Creek Cave, Mt. Moriah, 5500 ft., 1; Steptoe Creek, 5½ mi. SE Ely, 6400–6500 ft., 5; 1 mi. N Baker, 6; Spring Valley, 7 mi. SW Osceola, 6275 ft., 1. *Lincoln Co.:* Coal Valley, 10 mi. N Seeman Pass, 4650 ft., 1.

Additional records (Hollister, 1914:443): *Douglas Co.:* Gardnerville; Holbrook. *Humboldt Co.:* Golconda; Flowing Springs. *Pershing Co.:* Rabbit Hole Mountains. *Lander Co.:* Silver Creek. *Nye Co.:* Monitor Valley. *Elko Co.:* Mountain City; Bull Run Mountains; Wells; Elko; Carlin.

Onychomys torridus
Southern Grasshopper Mouse

Tail more than half the length of the head and body; upper parts in adults Light Pinkish Cinnamon marked with blackish on back and top of tail, but less marked with black on sides; cheeks, underparts, legs, feet, underside of tail and its tip white; hair of underparts basally plumbeous, but faintly so; young, bluish above; skull, in comparison with that of *O. l. brevicaudus*, small; teeth lower crowned; M3 small. Comparison with the species *Onychomys leucogaster* is made in the account of that species.

This species occupies the Lower Sonoran Life-zone and pushes far up north in Railroad Valley and in the low western part of Nevada as far as Toulon in south-central Pershing County. At four places, 3 miles NNE Toulon, 1 mile SE Wadsworth, San Antonio, and Old Mill at the north end of Reveille Valley, the two species have been taken together. Altitudinally, the species occurs from about 500 feet elevation at the lowest point in the state, along the Colorado River near the California-Nevada boundary, up to as high as 7200 feet at the southwestern base of Groom Baldy.

Females average a fraction of 1 per cent larger in external measurements and are 9 per cent heavier.

Of 62 adult females, 19 were pregnant. The number of embryos ranged from 2 to 6 with a mean of 3.9. There were 3 litters of 2, 5 litters of 3, 4 litters of 4, 5 litters of 5, and 2 litters of 6. By months the females were distributed as follows: January, 1 (0 pregnant); February, 1 (0); May, 18 (7); June, 25 (6); July, 11 (5); September, 5 (1); October, 1 (0).

Onychomys torridus longicaudus Merriam
Southern Grasshopper Mouse

Onychomys longicaudus Merriam, N. Amer. Fauna, 2:2, October 30, 1889. Type from Saint George, Washington County, Utah.

O[*nychomys*]. *torridus longicaudus* Merriam, Proc. Biol. Soc. Washington, 17:123, June 9, 1904.

Onychomys torridus longicaudus, Burt, Trans. San Diego Soc. Nat. Hist., 7:415, May 31, 1934.

Distribution.—Southern and low western part of the state, except extreme southern tip. See figure 331.

Remarks.—Average and extreme measurements of fifteen males and eight females from western Lincoln County are: ♂, 138 (126–145), ♀, 138 (131–143); 46 (39–52), 47 (44–51); 19.2 (18–20), 19.5 (19–20); weight, 22.8 (20.2–25.5), 22.4 (21.7–22.8) grams.

This race is as described in the account of the species, and differs from the race *pulcher* to the westward in darker color. From *O. t. perpallidus*, on the southeastern side of the Colorado River, *longicaudus* differs in lesser size, shorter ears, and lighter color.

Protracted study and mensuration of our fairly adequate adult material reveals what may be geographic variation in just two features. One feature is a lesser zygomatic breadth (12.7 to 12.9) in populations from Clark and Lincoln counties and southern Nye County, including Railroad Valley. The northern populations have this measurement averaging from 13.1 to 13.4. The other feature is a tendency to paler color in the southwest, which is indicative of intergradation with the race *pulcher*. *O. t. pulcher* is distinguished from *longicaudus* only by paler, more pinkish coloration. Occasional specimens, for example one from near Schurz, well to the north, are pale, and thus it is impossible to draw any hard and fast line regarding color.

Records of occurrence.—Specimens examined, 180, as follows: *Lyon Co.*: 1 mi. N and 8 mi. E Fernley, 1; 1 mi. NW Fernley, 4090 ft., 3; ½ and 1 mi. SE Wadsworth, 4200 ft., 2. *Pershing Co.*: 3 mi. NNE Toulon, 3900 ft., 1; 1 mi. W Toulon, 4100 ft., 1; Toulon, 3930 ft., 1. *Mineral Co.*: 3 mi. S Schurz, 4100 ft., 8; 8 mi. SE Schurz, 4100 ft., 1; Cat Creek, 4 mi. W Hawthorne, 4500 ft., 1; S side Teels Marsh, 4900 ft., 2; Huntoon Valley, 5700 ft., 1. *Esmeralda Co.*: 13½ mi. NW Goldfield, 4850 ft., 3; 7 mi. N Arlemont, 5500 ft., 1; 1½ mi. E Dyer, 1; 2 mi. SE Dyer, 4800 ft., 2; 8 mi. SE Blair, 4500 ft., 3; mouth of Palmetto Wash, 5350 ft., 1 (D. R. Dickey Coll.); 2 mi. E Lida, 5800 ft., 2 (D. R. Dickey Coll.); 3 mi. E Lida, 5500 ft., 2 (D. R. Dickey Coll.); 4½ mi. E Lida, 5350 ft., 2 (D. R. Dickey Coll.); 1 mi. SE Palmetto, 6200 ft., 1 (D. R. Dickey Coll.). *Nye Co.*: Railroad

Valley, 5000 ft. (2½ mi. S Lock's Ranch, 5; 9 mi. S Lock's Ranch, 4), 9; 4½ to 5½ mi. NE San Antonio, 5650–5700 ft., 3; San Antonio, 5400 ft., 2; 2 mi. NE Nyala, 5100 ft., Railroad Valley, 2; Nyala, 5100 ft., Railroad Valley, 2; Big Creek, Quinn Canyon Mts., 5700 ft., 1; Old Mill, N end Reveille Valley, 6200 ft., 1; 9½ mi. E New Reveille, Railroad Valley, 5100 ft., 1; N shore Mud Lake, S end Ralston Valley, 5300 ft., 1; 7½ mi. E

TABLE 14

CRANIAL MEASUREMENTS (IN MILLIMETERS) OF ONYCHOMYS

Sex	Number of individuals averaged or catalogue no.	Greatest length of skull	Basilar length	Greatest breadth of brain case	Interorbital constriction	Length of nasals	Shelf of bony palate	Palatine slits	Diastema	Postpalatal length	Alveolar length of maxillary tooth row
Onychomys leucogaster fuscogriseus, 1 mi. W Hausen											
♂	73922	26.9	21.5	12.0	4.6	10.3	5.0	5.0	6.8	9.5	4.1
Onychomys leucogaster brevicaudus, North-central Nevada											
♂	8 av.	27.4	21.7	12.6	4.8	10.4	5.1	5.2	7.1	9.7	4.1
	min.	26.9	21.2	12.3	4.5	10.2	5.0	4.9	6.7	9.4	4.0
	max.	28.0	22.3	13.1	5.0	10.6	5.3	5.5	7.2	10.1	4.1
♀	8 av.	27.3	21.6	12.7	4.8	10.4	5.1	5.0	7.0	9.6	4.0
	min.	26.8	21.1	12.5	4.6	10.2	4.9	4.6	6.8	9.4	3.9
	max.	27.8	22.1	13.0	5.0	10.5	5.5	5.2	7.5	9.8	4.2
Onychomys torridus longicaudus, Western Lincoln Co.											
♂	15 av.	24.9	19.1	11.3	4.8	9.4	4.4	4.4	6.1	8.8	3.8
	min.	24.3	18.5	11.1	4.6	8.8	4.2	4.1	5.9	8.5	3.5
	max.	25.7	19.6	11.6	5.0	9.7	4.8	4.8	6.4	9.2	4.0
♀	8 av.	24.9	19.0	11.3	4.8	9.2	4.5	4.3	6.0	8.9	3.8
	min.	24.1	18.3	11.1	4.7	8.5	4.3	4.1	5.6	8.5	3.7
	max.	25.2	19.3	11.6	5.0	9.6	4.7	4.7	6.3	9.0	3.9
Onychomys torridus pulcher, 8 mi. SSE Dead Mountain											
♂	61683	25.2	19.5	11.4	4.8	9.6	5.0	4.3	6.3	8.8	3.8
8 mi. S Dead Mountain											
♀	61682	25.8	19.9	11.7	5.2	9.6	4.4	4.6	6.6	9.3	3.7

Cliff Spring, 5900 ft., 1; 8 mi. NE Wheelbarrow Peak, 1; 9 mi. E Wheelbarrow Peak, 2; 8 mi. NE Springdale, 4250 ft., 1; 4½ mi. SE Oak Spring, 4700 ft., 1; 9 mi. S Oak Spring, 4000 ft., 5; 5 mi. E and 1 mi. N Grapevine Peak, 5500 ft., 3; 8 mi. E Grapevine Peak, 5000 ft., 7; Amargosa River, 3½ mi. NE Beatty, 3400 ft., 4; NW base Skull Mtn., 3500 ft., 1; Ash Meadows, 4 4/5 mi. NW Devils Hole, 2200 ft., 3. *Lincoln Co.:* Panaca, 4700 ft., 1; Desert Valley, 21 mi. W Panaca, 5300 ft., 1; Penoyer Valley, 17 mi. N Groom Baldy, 3; Penoyer Valley, 14 mi. NNW Groom Baldy, 1; 12 mi. E Hiko Spring, 4800 ft., 2; Pahranagat Valley (from Crystal Spring, 9 1/5 mi. NW, 1; 3 mi. N, 1; ½ to 4 mi. NE, 4000–4100 ft., 3; ¼ mi. W, 4000 ft., 1; Crystal Spring itself, 4000 ft., 2; ¼ mi. E, 4000 ft., 4; 2 mi. E, 5000 ft., 3; ½ mi. S, 4000 ft., 3), 18; 9 mi. W Groom Baldy, 5500 ft., 4; SW base Groom Baldy, 7200 ft., 1; 16 mi. E Groom Baldy, 4600 ft., 5; 11½ mi. E Johnnies Water, 1; Desert Valley, 8 mi. SW Hancock Summit, 5300 ft., 5; Pahranagat Valley, 9 mi. SW Crystal Spring, 4800 ft., 1; Alamo, 3570 ft., 1; Meadow Valley, 24 mi. S Caliente, 3000 ft., 4; 8 mi. N Summit Spring, 3; 5 to 5½ mi. N Summit Spring, 4700 ft., 9; Summit Spring, 4800 ft., 2. *Clark Co.:* Virgin River, 1 mi. N Mesquite, 1750 ft., 1; Virgin River, 1 mi. E Mesquite, 1750 ft., 1; Indian Springs, 3280 ft., 4 (D. R. Dickey Coll.); 1 mi. NE St. Thomas, 1250 ft., 1 (D. R. Dickey Coll.); Willow Creek, 6000 ft., 1 (D. R. Dickey Coll.); Kyle Canyon, 4500 ft., 7 (D. R. Dickey Coll.); 4 mi. NW Las Vegas, 1 (D. R. Dickey Coll.); Cedar Basin, 3500 ft., 4 (D. R. Dickey Coll.); Jap Ranch, Colorado River, 14 mi. E Searchlight, 500 ft., 4; 9 mi. W and 5 to 5½ mi. S Searchlight, 4300 ft., 3.

Additional records (Hollister, 1914:464): *Nye Co.:* Pahrump Valley. *Lincoln Co.:* Pahroc Spring. *Clark Co.:* Stones Ferry.

Onychomys torridus pulcher Elliot
Southern Grasshopper Mouse

Onychomys pulcher Elliot, Field Columbian Mus., pub. 87, zoöl. ser., 3:243, December, 1903. Type from Morongo Pass, east end of San Bernardino Mountains, San Bernardino County, California.
O[*nychomys*]. t[*orridus*]. *pulcher*, Hollister, Proc. Biol. Soc. Washington, 26:215, December 20, 1913.

Distribution.—Valley of the Colorado River south of Dead Mountains. See figure 331.

Remarks.—Measurements of a male and female from 8 mi. SSE Dead Mtn., and 8 mi. S Dead Mtn., respectively, are 140, 150; 50, 50; 20, 20; weight, 21.8 and 22.8 grams.

From *longicaudus*, this race differs in lighter color, and from *perpallidus*, it differs in lesser size, shorter ear, and brighter color. Specimens from only about 12 miles farther up the Colorado River (directly east of Searchlight) from the places in Nevada where the two individuals of this race were taken are appreciably darker colored and therefore referable to *longicaudus*.

Records of occurrence.—Specimens examined, 2, as follows: *Clark Co.:* 8 mi. SSE Dead Mtn., 1900 ft., 1; 8 mi. S Dead Mtn., 2700 ft., 1.

Reithrodontomys megalotis megalotis (Baird)
Western Harvest Mouse

Reithrodon megalotis Baird, Mamm. N. Amer., 1857, p. 451. Type from between Janos, Chihuahua, and San Luis Springs, Grant County, New Mexico.
Reithrodontomys megalotis megalotis, Borell and Ellis, Journ. Mamm., 15:29, January 15, 1934; Burt, Trans. San Diego Soc. Nat. Hist., 7:416, May 31, 1934.
Reithrodontomys megalotis, Allen, Bull. Amer. Mus. Nat. Hist., 5:79, April 28, 1893. Linsdale, Amer. Midland Nat., 19:189, January, 1938.
Reithrodontomys megalotis deserti Allen, Bull. Amer. Mus. Nat. Hist., 7:127, May 21, 1895. Type from Oasis Valley, Nye County, Nevada. Taylor, Univ. California Publ. Zoöl., 7:237, June 24, 1911.

Distribution.—Over all of state in the Sonoran life-zones. See figure 332.

Remarks.—Measurements of ten males and nine females from Pahranagat Valley, within 9 miles of Crystal Spring, are: ♂, 142 (136–150), ♀, 143 (135–148); 70 (67–76), 66 (61–70); 17.4 (16–19), 16.7 (15–18); weight, 12.0 (9.2–13.2), 13.9 (12.0–15.0) grams.

Generic characters, in addition to the murine appearance, are: tail long (about half the total length in Nevadan representatives), slender and sparsely haired; ear prominent; sole of hind foot with six tubercles; mammae in three pairs, one pectoral and two inguinal; anterior zygomatic plate not projecting anteriorly enough to be visible from directly above; posterior border of palate truncate; each upper incisor with a deep longitudinal groove near its middle. The dental formula is i. $\frac{1}{1}$, c. $\frac{0}{0}$, p. $\frac{0}{0}$, m. $\frac{3}{3}$.

Harvest mice, of the Nevada race, have the upper parts composed of mixed blackish-brown and light buff color, the back darkest, gradually changing to near pure buff on the sides; ears drab, usually with a tuft of ochraceous buff hairs at the anterior base; under-parts and feet white, but hair of underparts plumbeous basally; tail sharply bicolored, the white on the underside being more extensive than the dark brown upper side. The single character most useful for distinguishing these mice from *Peromyscus* is the grooved upper incisors; in *Peromyscus* the upper incisors are smooth on their anterior face. Young animals are less buffy and more plumbeous than adults, but the difference in color between young and old is less than in Nevadan species of *Peromyscus*.

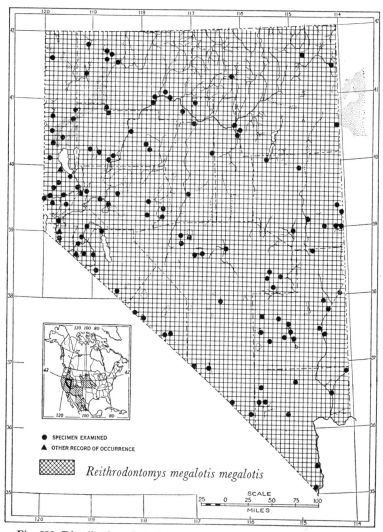

SPECIMEN EXAMINED

OTHER RECORD OF OCCURRENCE

Reithrodontomys megalotis megalotis

Fig. 332. Distribution of the harvest mouse, *Reithrodontomys megalotis*.

In seven adults from southern Clark County the tail averages longer than the head and body (the reverse being true of all other populations) and the weight is less than in any other population, being 8.9 grams in males and 9.8 in females, as opposed to 11.6 to 12.3 grams in males and 15.0 to 15.4 grams in females of other populations. Although all the specimens from southern Clark County were taken in winter (January and February), the others having been obtained in spring and summer, I would expect winter-taken specimens to be as fat as others. Also, in this population, as in all others the weights of which were averaged, pregnant females were excluded and only adults (animals with some wear upon each major cusp of each cheek tooth) were considered. This southern population is definitely small-bodied.

The name *Reithrodontomys megalotis deserti* Allen, with type locality from Oasis Valley, Nevada, Howell (1914:28) regards as presenting no differences of systematic worth in comparison with *megalotis*. The one difference detected by Howell (*loc. cit.*) was slightly larger skulls in mice "from the Death Valley region of southern California and Nevada." The Nevadan specimens examined by me, but not seen by Howell, bear out this tendency, for, in twelve adults from the west slope of Grapevine Peak, the skull averages larger than in any other population. The actual average measurements, corresponding to those given in table 15 for animals from Pahranagat Valley, for greatest length and breadth of skull and length of nasals are 21.7, 10.3, 8.3.

Goldman (1939b:355) named the subspecies *Reithrodontomys megalotis ravus* from specimens taken on Stansbury Island and the shore of the adjacent mainland of Great Salt Lake in Utah. He differentiates these from the subspecies *megalotis* on basis of duller, more grayish upper parts which lack "the ochraceous buffy suffusion," shorter tail, and shorter and relatively broader skull. Nevadan specimens from the eastern slope of Mount Moriah in White Pine County, which on geographic grounds might be expected to be referable to the race *ravus*, are here referred to the race *megalotis*, because they lack the short tail and broad skull of *ravus* and in color are indistinguishable from other specimens of *megalotis* to the south and west of Mount Moriah.

Howell (1914:32) named the subspecies *Reithrodontomys megalotis nigrescens* from Payette, Idaho, and ascribed to it a geographic range which suggests that specimens from northwestern Nevada might belong to the race *nigrescens*. In the original description, Howell indicated that it was distinct from the race *megalotis* on basis of longer nasals and darker color. Davis (1939:283) indicated that his study of material, not available to Howell, including topotypes of *nigrescens* as well as other specimens referable to it and to *megalotis*, showed the nasals to be of the same length in the two races. He felt that "color alone is not a trustworthy subspecific character in these mice." In reviewing Davis' work, Howell (1939:390) says that he joins in the inclination to doubt the validity of the race *nigrescens*. At this writing, about 100 skins from western Idaho and eastern Oregon are before me, and these do average darker than the Nevadan specimens assigned to *megalotis*, but so many specimens from the range ascribed to *nigrescens* are indistinguishable from many specimens within the range ascribed to *megalotis* that I see no adequate basis for recognizing *nigrescens* as distinct from *megalotis*.

In Nevada the harvest mouse is fairly sharply confined to the Sonoran life-zones and is further restricted, in the main, to grassy places near water. This characterization of occurrence requires some modification, in that specimens have been taken on the desert far from water, and one specimen was taken in the Pine Forest Mountains at an elevation of 8000 feet. Taylor (1911:242) regarded this exceptional occurrence as being in the lower part of the Transition Life-zone.

The mice are nocturnal and commonly use the runways, and even burrows, of meadow mice (*Microtus montanus*). In Clark County they were trapped also in the runways of cotton rats. In grassy places the mice make ball-like nests up to 5 inches in diameter on the surface on the ground, the opening of which is on the side. Alcorn (MS) records that on March 20, 1936, 4 miles west of

Fallon, in a 2-acre field thickly grown up to tumbleweeds of large size, the mice had built nests beneath the dead weeds. When these weeds were burned, his dog caught and ate more than fifty harvest mice within 30 minutes and many more were burned.

Enemies of harvest mice include horned owls, long-eared owls, and scorpions. Bond (1940:164) found harvest mice to comprise more than 11 per cent of the total of 394 food items identified in pellets of horned owl 4 miles south of Alamo in Pahranagat Valley. At Fish Lake in Esmeralda County, Seth Benson (MS) recovered a skull of a harvest mouse from a pellet of a long-eared owl.

TABLE 15

CRANIAL MEASUREMENTS (IN MILLIMETERS) OF REITHRODONTOMYS

Sex	Number of individuals averaged	Greatest length of skull	Basilar length	Greatest breadth of brain case	Interorbital constriction	Length of nasals	Shelf of bony palate	Palatine slits	Diastema	Postpalatal length	Alveolar length of maxillary tooth row
					R. m. megalotis, Pahranagat Valley						
♂	10 av.	21.3	15.7	10.0	3.1	8.3	3.4	4.5	5.1	7.2	3.2
	min.	20.9	15.4	9.8	2.9	7.7	3.1	4.2	5.0	6.9	3.0
	max.	21.7	15.9	10.2	3.4	8.8	3.6	4.7	5.2	7.4	3.3
♀	9 av.	21.3	15.9	10.0	3.1	8.1	3.4	4.5	5.0	7.3	3.3
	min.	20.5	15.3	9.6	3.0	7.7	3.1	4.4	4.7	6.9	3.1
	max.	21.8	16.3	10.5	3.3	8.4	3.6	4.9	5.4	7.6	3.4

On May 22, 1932, 1 mile northeast of Crystal Springs, Pahranagat Valley, Henry Fitch turned over a flat rock near the edge of the lake at that place and found a large scorpion devouring a still-warm, half-grown harvest mouse.

Measurements of sixty-four males and thirty-eight females reveal no secondary sexual variation in linear measurements, but females average 12 per cent heavier than males.

Of a total of 101 sexually mature females, 22 have embryos. The litters range in size from 1 to 6 embryos. Four is the average number and also the mode. By months, these females are distributed as follows: January, 9 (0 pregnant); February, 0; March, 0; April, 3 (0); May, 31 (9 pregnant); June, 16 (3); July, 27 (8); August, 4 (2); September, 3 (0); October, 2 (0); November, 6 (0); December, 0.

Records of occurrence.—Specimens examined, 446, as follows: *Washoe Co.:* 3 mi. N Vya, 5900 ft., 1; 3 mi. E and 10 mi. N Gerlach, 4000 ft., 1; Rock Creek, Granite Mts., 5000 ft., 1; 12 mi. N and 2 mi. E Gerlach, 4000 ft., 1; 17½ mi. W Deep Hole, 4750 ft., 1; 17 mi. W Deep Hole, 4800 ft., 3; 1 mi. NE Gerlach, 4000 ft., 1; Smoke Creek, 9 mi. E Calif. boundary, 3900 ft., 5; Horse Canyon, Pahrum Peak, 5800 ft., 1; Round Hole, 3900 ft., 2; N side Sand Pass, 3950 ft., 1; 4 mi. S Flanigan, 4100 ft., 1; 4½ mi. S Flanigan, 4100 ft., 1; ½ mi. S Pyramid Lake, 3950 ft., 1; Junction House, 4500 ft., 1; 10 mi. N Reno, 1 (coll. of Ralph Ellis); 34 mi. E Reno, 1; N side

Truckee River, 10 to 11¾ mi. E Reno, 4500 ft., 4; 4 mi. W Reno, 1 (coll. of Ralph Ellis); W side Truckee River, ½ mi. W Verdi, 4900 ft., 2; 7 to 8 mi. S Reno, 9 (7 in coll. of Ralph Ellis). *Ormsby Co.:* 3½ mi. E Carson City, 4700 ft., 1. *Douglas Co.:* Carson River, 4900 ft., 5 mi. SE Minden, 1; Desert Creek, Sweetwater Range, 6250 ft., 11. *Storey Co.:* Gilpin Spillway, Truckee Canal, 4000 ft., 3 mi. WSW Wadsworth, 1; 6 mi. NE Virginia City, 6000 ft., 5. *Lyon Co.:* 1 mi. NW Fernley, 4090 ft., 1; 2 mi. SSW Fernley, 2; 2 mi. N Yerington, 4350 ft., 1; West Walker River, 6 mi. S Yerington, 4500 ft., 6; Mason Valley, 10 mi. S Yerington, 4500 ft., 3; West Walker River, Smiths Valley, 4700 ft., 3; West Walker River, 12 mi. S Yerington, 4600 ft. (including 8 mi. NE Welling-

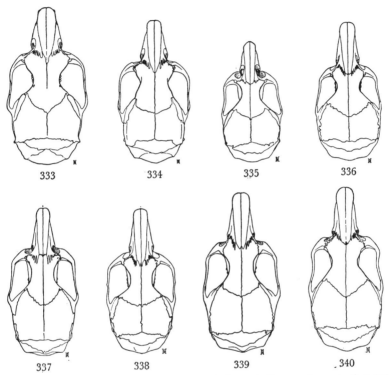

333   334   335   336

337   338   339   340

Figs. 333–340. Mice. All, × 1½. (Other views of these skulls are shown in figs. 341–345, 346–353.)

Fig. 333. *Onychomys leucogaster brevicaudus,* 16 miles northeast Iron Point, no. 68276, ♂.
Fig. 334. *Onychomys torridus longicaudus,* ¼ mile east Crystal Spring, no. 52957, ♂.
Fig. 335. *Reithrodontomys megalotis megalotis,* Crystal Spring, no. 52998, ♂.
Fig. 336. *Peromyscus crinitus pergracilis,* 2 miles west Smith Creek Cave, no. 79179, ♂.
Fig. 337. *Peromyscus eremicus eremicus,* Hiko Spring, Clark County, no. 61760, ♂.
Fig. 338. *Peromyscus maniculatus sonoriensis,* Stella Lake, 10,500 feet, no. 84093, ♂.
Fig. 339. *Peromyscus boylii rowleyi,* Ash Spring, no. 53145, ♂.
Fig. 340. *Peromyscus truei nevadensis,* ½ mile west Debbs Creek, no. 68476, ♂.

ton, 4700 ft.), 6; Desert Creek, Sweetwater Range, 6250 ft., 1. *Humboldt Co.:* Virgin Valley, 5000 ft., 1; head of Big Creek, Pine Forest Mts., 8000 ft., 1; Big Creek Ranch, Pine Forest Mts., 4350 ft., 4; Leonard Creek, Pine Forest Mts., 6500 ft., 2; Quinn River Crossing, 4100 ft., 20; 2½ mi. SW Quinn River Crossing, 4100 ft., 1; Soldier Meadows, 4600 ft., 4; 10 mi. NNW Golconda, 1; 6 mi. N Golconda, 1; 5 mi. NE Golconda, 1; 1 mi. N Winnemucca, 4600 ft., 1; 3 mi. SW Winnemucca, 4500 ft., 1; 1¼ mi. N Sulphur, 4050 ft., 4; 1 mi. W Sulphur, 4040 ft., 2; 23 mi. NW Battle Mountain, 1. *Pershing Co.:* 3½ mi. SE Sulphur, 4950 ft., 2; El Dorado Canyon, Humboldt Range, 6000 ft., 2; 9 mi. E Fanning, Buena Vista Valley, 4100 ft., 1; 9½ mi. E and 1 mi. S Fanning, Buena Vista Valley, 4100 ft., 1; S side Granite Peak, East Range, 3; 30 mi. W and 3 mi. N Lovelock, 4300 ft., 1; 21 mi. W and 2 mi. N Lovelock, 4000 ft., 2; 3 mi. NNE Toulon, 3900 ft., 1; 1½ mi. NE Toulon, 3900 ft., 1;

1 mi. W Toulon, 4100 ft., 1. *Churchill Co.:* Truckee Canal, 2½ mi. W Hazen, 5; 3 mi. N Stillwater, 3900 ft., 1; 5 mi. W Fallon, 4000 ft., 1; 4 mi. W Fallon, 4000 ft., 1; Cherry Creek (spring), 5000 ft., 3; 7 mi. SE Fallon, 3; 7 mi. S and 3½ mi. E Fallon, 1; Eastgate, 4400 ft., 3. *Mineral Co.:* Schurz Indian dam, Walker River, 4300 ft., 6; 3 mi. S Schurz, 4100 ft., 3; 2 mi. SW Pine Grove, 7250 ft., 1; East Walker River, 5 mi. NW Morgans Ranch, 5050 ft., 1; East Walker River, 2 mi. NW Morgans Ranch, 5050 ft., 1; 1 mi. NW Wichman, 5500 ft., 1 (coll. of D. V. Hemphill); ¼ mi. N Wichman, 5000 ft., 3 (coll. of D. V. Hemphill); Fletcher, 6098 ft., 1; Huntoon Valley, 5700 ft., 2. *Esmeralda Co.:* Chiatovich Creek, 7000 ft., 4; Arlemont, 4900 ft., 3; Fish Lake, 4800 ft., 19; Lida, 6100 ft., 4 (D. R. Dickey Coll.); Indian Spring, 7400 ft., Mt. Magruder, 1 (D. R. Dickey Coll.). *Lander Co.:* 3 mi. S Izenhood, 2; 1 mi. E Battle Mountain, 3; 1½ mi. NW Cortez, Cortez Mts., 1; Reese River Valley, 7 mi. N Austin, 1; Smiths Creek, 5800 ft., 3; Campbell Creek Ranch, 5500 ft., 1. *Eureka Co.:* Pine Creek, 2 mi. E Palisade, 1; Evans, 1. *Nye Co.:* Wisconsin Creek, 7800 ft., 3; Ophir Creek, 6500 ft., 2; 5 mi. SE Millett P. O., 5500 ft., 7; South Twin River, 6500 ft., 5, Fish Spring Valley, ½ mi. N Fish Lake, 6500 ft., 1; Toquima Range, 1 mi. E Jefferson, 7600 ft., 1; Toquima Range, 9 to 9¼ mi. E Toquima Peak, 7000 ft., 5; Troy Creek, 5400 ft., 2; White River Valley, 15 mi. WSW Sunnyside, 5500 ft., 2; Burned Corral Canyon, Quinn Canyon Mts., 6800 ft., 2; Garden Valley, 8½ mi. NE Sharp, 1; Breen Creek, Kawich Mts., 7000 ft., 3; 2½ mi. E and 1 mi. S Grapevine Peak, 6700–7000 ft., 13; Amargosa River, 4 mi. NE Beatty, 3500 ft., 12; Ash Meadows, 2½ mi. W Devils Hole, 2173 ft., 2; Pahrump Ranch, 2667 ft., 3 (D. R. Dickey Coll.). *Elko Co.:* 15 mi. S Contact, 1; 13 mi. N Montello, 5000 ft., 1; 1 mi. SE Tuscarora, 5900 ft., 1; Salt Springs, 4200 ft., 1; 5 mi. E Raines, Sulphur Spring Mts., 1. *White Pine Co.:* W side Ruby Lake, 3 mi. S Elko Co. line, 6100 ft., 10 (coll. of Ralph Ellis); Cherry Creek, 6800 ft., 1; Smith Creek, 4 mi. W Smith Creek Cave, 6900 ft., 1; Smith Creek, 3 mi. W Smith Creek Cave, 6700 ft., 2; 2 mi. W Smith Creek Cave, Mt. Moriah, 6300 ft., 2; Hendry Creek, 8 mi. SE Mt. Moriah, 6200 ft., 2; 5½ mi. SE Ely, 6450 ft., 1; 1 mi. N Baker, 5700 ft., 3; Lehman Cave, 7400 ft., 1; Baker Creek, 6600–7200 ft., 6; 2½ mi. E Baker, 5700 ft., 4; Water Canyon, 9 mi. N Lund, 1. *Lincoln Co.:* Duck Valley, 3 mi. S Geyser, 6050 ft., 1; Eagle Valley, 3½ mi. N Ursine, 5600 ft., 6; 2 mi. SE Pioche, 6000 ft., 1; Panaca, 4700 ft., 2; Penoyer Valley, 17 mi. N Groom Baldy, 1; E slope Irish Mtn., 6900 ft., 1; Pahranagat Valley (from Crystal Spring: ½ to 3 mi. N, 4000 ft., 8; ¼ to 1 mi. NE, 4000 ft., 7; Crystal Spring itself, 4000 ft., 15; ¼ mi. E, 4000 ft., 1), 31; Meadow Valley, 7 mi. S Caliente, 4000 ft., 4; SW base Groom Baldy, 7200 ft., 1; Ash Spring, 3800 ft., 8; Meadow Valley Wash, 5½ mi. N Elgin, 4000 ft., 1; Pahranagat Valley, 9 mi. SW Crystal Spring, 4800 ft., 1; Alamo, 3570 ft., 2; 8 mi. N Summit Spring, 1. *Clark Co.* (unless otherwise noted, in D. R. Dickey Coll.): Virgin River, ¾ mi. E Mesquite, 1750 ft., 6 (Mus. Vert. Zoöl.); Mormon Well, 6500 ft., 1; Indian Springs, 3280 ft., 3; ½ mi. E St. Thomas, 1250 ft., 1; Willow Creek, 6000 ft., 27; Cold Creek, 6000 ft., 1; ¼ mi. S Wheeler Well, 6600 ft., 2; 3½ mi. NW Las Vegas, 2100 ft., 2; Colorado River, 14 mi. E Searchlight, 500+ ft., 7 (Mus. Vert. Zoöl.); Colorado River, ½ mi. N Calif.-Nev. Monument, 500 ft., 11 (Mus. Vert. Zoöl.).

Additional records: *Washoe Co.:* Sutcliffe (D. G. Nichols, MS). *Douglas Co.:* Gardnerville (Howell, 1914:29). *Churchill Co.:* 15 mi. N Stillwater, near sloughs of Carson Sink, 1 (Carl P. Russell, MS).

Genus **Peromyscus** Gloger
White-footed Mice

Five species of *Peromyscus* occur in Nevada. Adults range from about 145 mm. to 210 mm. in total length, depending upon the kind. In these nocturnal mice, the tail is about as long as the head and body; they are usually bicolored, dark brown or blackish above and white below. The ears are membranous and project well beyond the fur. The upper parts are ochraceous, overlain with dark color, and the underfur is whitish at the tips. The eyes are relatively large and black. The sole of each hind foot has five or six tubercules (six in all Nevadan races) and medially is naked, at least for the distal half. There are two or three pairs of mammae. The skull is relatively smooth, the incisors are ungrooved, and there are three cheek teeth in each jaw. Of these, the anterior is largest and the posterior smallest. The dental formula is i. $\frac{1}{1}$, c. $\frac{0}{0}$, p. $\frac{0}{0}$, m. $\frac{3}{3}$.

The large number of distinct species, the considerable geographic variation shown by most species, and the wide distribution of the genus made it a difficult group for zoölogists to deal with. The publication of W. H. Osgood's "Revision of the mice of the American genus *Peromyscus*" in 1909 largely remedied this difficulty. Following this improved classification, F. B. Sumner and associates, and more recently L. R. Dice and associates, have published considerable data about the genus. Selected papers in this regard are Sumner (1932), dealing with genetics; Collins (1918, 1923), relative to molt; Dice (1935,

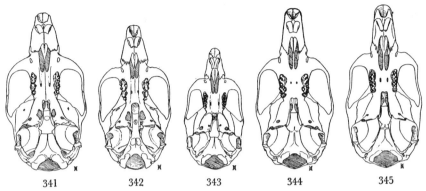

Figs. 341–345. Mice. Different views of these skulls are shown in figs. 333–340. All, × 1½.

Fig. 341. *Onychomys leucogaster brevicaudus.*
Fig. 342. *Onychomys torridus longicaudus.*
Fig. 343. *Reithrodontomys megalotis megalotis.*

Fig. 344. *Peromyscus boylii rowleyi.*
Fig. 345. *Peromyscus truei nevadensis.*

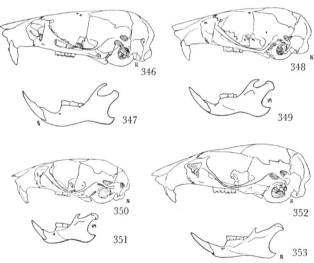

Figs. 346–353. Mice. Different views of these skulls are shown in figs. 333–340. All, × 1½.

Figs. 346, 347. *Onychomys leucogaster brevicaudus.*
Figs. 348, 349. *Onychomys torridus longicaudus.*
Figs. 350, 351. *Reithrodontomys megalotis megalotis.*
Figs. 352, 353. *Peromyscus truei nevadensis.*

and other papers), on variation and genetics; and Svihla (1932), on life histories. As a result of the many kinds of studies made by these and other persons, especially since Osgood's (1909) systematic revision, the mice of this genus, with respect to basis of understanding of biological processes in wild mammals, have come to be among the important, possibly are the most important.

The mice of this genus build nests of plant fibers. The young number one to nine per litter, and a female is thought to have more than one litter per year.

In the following accounts, individuals designated as adults are only those specimens in which each main cusp of each tooth shows considerable wear.

Peromyscus crinitus
Canyon Mouse

Three subspecies of *crinitus* occur in Nevada. The color above is Pale Ochraceous Buff, with many dusky-tipped hairs. The sides are more brightly colored (less dusky) than the back. The underparts are whitish, although, as in the other Nevadan species, the hairs are plumbeous basally. The plumbeous color shows especially prominently in the northern populations of *crinitus* because the white tips of the hairs are shorter. This gives a gray rather than white color to the underparts of some specimens. The coloration throughout is more dusky (less reddish) than that of *maniculatus*, and the pelage is long and lax. The tail is bicolored, and, in contrast to that of *eremicus*, is heavily haired and more nearly has a pencil. The tail is longer than the head and body except in some individuals of the northern populations where the tail occasionally is shorter. The ear, measured from the notch, on fresh specimens is about as long as the hind foot. The sole of the hind foot is naked to the distal end of the calcaneum. There are two pairs of mammae, both inguinal. The skull is the smallest among Nevadan species of the genus and has a short tooth row, slender and relatively long rostrum, and is narrow across the zygomatic arches anteriorly. The premaxillae do not extend behind the nasals. Minute accessory cusps between the three principal buccal cusps of M1 may or may not be present.

Mice of this species live in stony places among rocks. Just one of our specimens was caught as far as 50 feet away from rocks. This one, a young individual, probably was seeking new territory, and in so doing had wandered out of its habitat. The others were caught alongside or within a few steps of rocks. In Nevada one commonly finds these mice where the canyons from the mountains open out into the valleys. This is where rocks are exposed. Because of this close restriction to a special habitat, the geographic range of *P. crinitus* is markedly more discontinuous than that of *P. maniculatus*. Altitudinally, these mice range from the lowest elevations in the state, where suitable habitat exists, up to 10,000 feet. This exceptionally high occurrence—10,000 feet—was on Charleston Peak (Burt, 1934:416). The presence of yellow pines where the mice were caught identifies the place as being in the Transition Life-zone. This occurrence is not inconsistent with findings in other parts of the state, for, although I do not know that the mice elsewhere were found among yellow pines, in a few instances they were found in territory that could be classified as Transition Life-zone. Nevertheless, the mice were not found above the Transition Life-zone, although they were looked for repeatedly in rocky places in higher life-zones. *P. crinitus* has been taken along with *P. eremicus, P. maniculatus,* and *P. truei.* These other species invade and live in the habitat of *crinitus.* On February 6, 1934, at Hiko Spring, Clark County, Fitch (MS) noted that "many of the *eremicus* were parasitized with warbles, but none of these were found in *crinitus.*"

In this species there is an average secondary sexual difference, and females exceed males in size. The difference is indicated by average measurements for fifteen adults of each sex of *P. c. pergracilis* from White Pine County (all the adults that are available from that county) as follows: total length, ♂, 171 mm., ♀, 177; weight in grams, ♂, 16.6, ♀, 19.5; greatest length of skull, ♂, 24.8, ♀, 25.3. These females exceed the males by 3.5 per cent in total length, 17.5 per cent in weight, and 2.1 per cent in greatest length of skull. This average difference is less than the individual variation between animals of the same sex and age from one locality. Also, this degree of secondary sexual variation is less than the degree of geographic variation between animals from the northern and southern parts of the state.

Through Nevada there is a trend from north to south. The northern animals are heaviest, have longest bodies, shortest tails, and longest skulls. For example, among adult males, eleven specimens from just north of Elko County in southwestern Idaho have the tail averaging 104 per cent of the length of head and body; 200 miles south in White Pine County, the percentage for twenty-one animals is 107; 150 miles farther south in southern Nye and Lincoln counties, the percentage for eighteen specimens is 112; and 170 miles still farther south in the extreme southern tip of the state, the percentage for eleven animals is 113. This trend is not everywhere as gradual as these figures for eastern Nevada indicate. In the western part of the state the percentage remains relatively constant from about latitude 37° 30′ north to 39° 30′. Also, throughout the true Lower Sonoran Life-zone of the southern part of the state, the percentage is relatively constant. In west-central Nevada, north of latitude 39°, the percentage above referred to tends to be less than in any other part of the state. Therefore, many animals in this part of the state have tails shorter than the head and body. Also, in this area the skulls average shorter than at the same latitude in the eastern part of the state. This is discussed at greater length in the account of the race *P. c. crinitus,* to which reference should be made also for other details of geographic variation.

The 142 sexually mature females were taken by months as follows: February, 13 (0 pregnant); May, 30 (3); June, 51 (12); July, 35 (2); August, 4 (0); September, 7 (0); October, 2 (0). The mode and mean for the number of embryos for the litters in the 17 pregnant females were 4, and the extremes were 3 and 5.

Peromyscus crinitus crinitus (Merriam)
Canyon Mouse

Hesperomys crinitus Merriam, N. Amer. Fauna, 5:53, July 30, 1891. Type from Shoshone Falls, north side of Snake River, Jerome County, Idaho.

Peromyscus crinitus, Osgood, N. Amer. Fauna, 28:229, April 17, 1909; Taylor, Univ. California Publ. Zoöl., 7:235, June 24, 1911; Linsdale, Amer. Midland Nat., 19:190, January, 1938.

Peromyscus crinitus scitulus Bangs, Proc. New England Zoöl. Club, 1:67, July 31, 1899. Type from Gardnerville, Douglas County, Nevada.

Peromyscus crinitus crinitus, Borell and Ellis, Journ. Mamm., 15:30, February 15, 1934; Hall and Hoffmeister, Journ. Mamm., 23:56, February 14, 1942.

Peromyscus (truei) scitulus, Elliot, Field Columb. Mus., publ. 45, zoöl. ser., 2:429, 1901.

Distribution.—Western half of state south to latitude of Walker Lake. See figure 354.

Remarks.—Average and extreme measurements of four males and four females from northwestern Nevada north of latitude 41° are ♂, 172 (168–179), ♀, 175 (164–185); 89 (80–95), 90 (79–98); 20.8 (20–21), 20.1 (19–21); 18.0 (17–19), 19 (19–19); weight of three ♂, 15.0 (13.2–16.2), ♀, 18.1 (15.7–20.0) grams.

Among races of this species, the body is long and the tail is short, averaging only about 107 per cent of the length of the head and body. The upper parts are near (*j*) Hair Brown in general effect but mixed with some ochraceous, the underparts and feet are white, and the tail is dusky above. The skull is of medium size and the shelf of the bony palate is long.

This race differs from *P. c. pergracilis* to the eastward in slightly longer body and tail, notably darker color, and longer shelf of bony palate. In Nevadan specimens the external measurements are about the same in the two subspecies, but specimens of *crinitus* from Idaho average larger than Nevadan specimens of *pergracilis*. From *P. c. stephensi* to the southward, *P. c. crinitus* differs in greater average size, relatively shorter tail with longer hairs, notably darker color, larger skull, relatively longer shelf of bony palate, and a greater width across the zygomatic arches anteriorly relative to the width across these arches posteriorly.

Nearly all of the specimens of both *crinitus* and *stephensi* from western Nevada are intermediate in characters between topotypes of *crinitus* from Idaho to the north of Nevada and topotypes of *stephensi* from southern California. Specimens from the southern part of the range here assigned to the race *crinitus* are lighter colored and smaller than individuals of northern populations, in these respects showing approach to *stephensi*. Exception should be made for length of tail which, in general, increases from north to south. The animals named *Peromyscus crinitus scitulus* by Bangs and animals from near-by places have this intermediate character referred to and are different from either topotypes of *crinitus* or *stephensi*, although when all characters are taken into account they show greater resemblance to *crinitus*.

The color, except in specimens from the southern periphery (Mountain Well southward) of the range of *crinitus*, maintains its character of darkness. Indeed, the specimens from as far south as Reno are dark and the darkest individual of all the Nevadan specimens comes from only about 65 miles north of Reno at latitude 40° 28', 6 mi. E California boundary. This nearly black individual is darker than others taken at the same place and probably reflects the tendency to black coloration encountered among the mice as one goes westward into northeastern California.

Records of occurrence.—Specimens examined, 163, as follows: *Washoe Co.:* 12-mile Creek, ¾ mi. E Calif. boundary, 5300 ft., 2; 12 mi. E and 3 mi. N Ft. Bidwell, 5700 ft., 3; Painted Point, 9 mi. E Vya, 6000 ft., 1; mouth of Little High Rock Canyon, 5000 ft., 1; 17½ mi. W Deep Hole, 4750 ft., 1; 17 mi. W Deep Hole, 4800 ft., 3; 1 mi. NE Gerlach, 4000 ft., 7; 13 mi. W and 9 mi. S Deep Hole, 3850 ft., 1; latitude 40° 28', 6 mi. E Calif. boundary, 4000 ft., 8; Horse Canyon, 3 mi. NW Pahrum Peak, 5000 ft., 1; N side Sand Pass, 3900 ft., 1; Sand Pass, 3950 ft., 1; 3½ mi. NW Flanigan, 4200 ft., 1; ½ mi. NW Flanigan, 4200 ft., 3; 2½ mi. E Flanigan, 4250 ft., 1; ½ mi. S Pyramid Lake, 3950 ft., 1; 1 mi. SW Pyramid Lake, 3950 ft., 1; 1 mi. S Pyramid Lake, 1; N side Truckee River, 10 mi. E Reno, 1; 15 mi. E Reno, 1; 3 mi. E Reno, 14. *Douglas Co.:* Gardnerville, 7 (Mus.

Comp. Zoöl.); Carson River, 5 mi. SE Minden, 4900 ft., 4; Desert Creek, Sweetwater Range, 6250 ft., 8. *Lyon Co.:* West Walker River, 12 mi. S Yerington, 4600 ft., 3. *Humboldt Co.:* Virgin Valley, 5000 ft., 2; head of Big Creek, Pine Forest Mts., 8000 ft., 1; Big Creek Ranch, Pine Forest Mts., 4350 ft., 2; 14 mi. N Paradise Valley, 6400 ft., 2; 1½ mi. N Quinn River Crossing, 4100 ft., 3; Soldier Meadows, 4600 ft., 2; Jackson Cr. Ranch, 17½

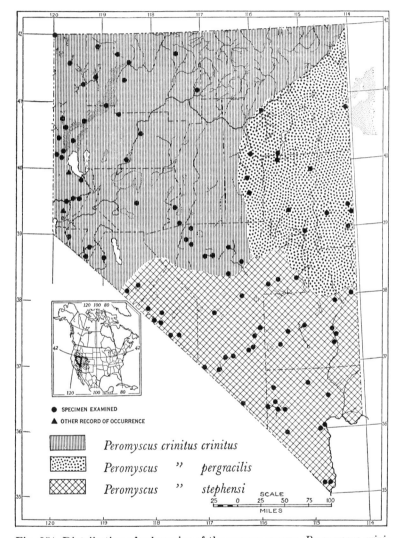

Fig. 354. Distribution of subspecies of the canyon mouse, *Peromyscus crinitus*, with insert showing range of the species.

mi. S and 5 mi. W Quinn River Crossing, 4000 ft., 1; 18 mi. NE Iron Point, 4600 ft., 2; 10 mi. W and 6 mi. N Sulphur, 4000 ft., 2. *Pershing Co.:* 3½ mi. SE Sulphur, 4950 ft., 4; El Dorado Canyon, Humboldt Range, 6000 ft., 4; 3½ mi. NE Toulon, 3950 ft., 1; 3½ mi. W Toulon, 4500 ft., 1. *Churchill Co.:* Mountain Well, 5600 ft., 5. *Mineral Co.:* East Walker River, 2 mi. NW Morgans Ranch, 5050–5100 ft., 4; ¼ mi. N Wichman, 5500 ft., 5 (coll. of D. V. Hemphill); Wichman, 5500 ft., 1 (coll. of D. V. Hemphill). *Lander Co.:* 2½ mi. NE Smiths Creek Ranch, 5800 ft., 2; Peterson Creek, Shoshone Mts., 6500 ft., 1; Kingston Canyon, 7000–7100 ft., 6.

Nye Co.: Ophir Creek, 6500 ft., 1; South Twin River, 6500 ft., 13; Greenmonster Canyon, Monitor Range, 7500 ft., 1; 1 mi. NE Jefferson, Toquima Range, 7600–7650 ft., 7; 1 mi. E Jefferson, Toquima Range, 7600 ft., 5; 7 to 8 mi. E Toquima Peak, Monitor Valley, 7100 ft., 2; 4 mi. N Hot Creek, Hot Creek Range, 6400 ft., 3; 7 to 8 mi. W Tybo, Hot Creek Range, 6700–7200 ft., 4.

Additional records: Osgood (1909:231) records specimens from several places which are not plotted on our distribution map because they fall within the area of occurrence shown by specimens examined.

Peromyscus crinitus pergracilis Goldman
Canyon Mouse

Peromyscus crinitus pergracilis Goldman, Journ. Mamm., 20:356, August 14, 1939. Type from south end of Stansbury Island, 4250 feet, Great Salt Lake, Toole County, Utah. Hall and Hoffmeister, Journ. Mamm., 23:58, February 14, 1942.

Distribution.—Eastern part of state in White Pine County and adjoining parts of Elko and Eureka counties. See figure 354.

Remarks.—Average and extreme measurements of nine males and eleven females from the vicinity of Mount Moriah are: ♂, 172 (165–186), ♀, 173 (164–186); 89 (82–97), 90 (86–96); 20.1 (19–21), 19.6 (18–21); 19.6 (18–21), 19.6 (18.0–21.5); weight, 16.6 (15.4–17.8), of six ♀, 17.5 (13.7–22.9) grams.

P. c. pergracilis differs from *stephensi* in shorter, more heavily haired tail, longer hind foot and ear, and larger skull. From *auripectus*, to the eastward, *pergracilis* differs in smaller hind foot, notably paler (grayer) color, and smaller skull except that bony palate is about the same or larger and hence relatively much longer. Comparison with *crinitus* has been made in the account of that race.

This race, named on the basis of a single aged individual in worn pelage, was judged by the describer to belong to a race restricted to Stansbury "Island," an area of land in Great Salt Lake, Utah, not entirely isolated from the mainland. When adequate topotypical material is available, the describer's judgment may be substantiated. Careful comparison of the type with specimens from Mount Moriah, Nevada, however, reveals that every one of the differential characters ascribed to *pergracilis* in the original description is duplicated among these Nevadan specimens. Search for additional characters to distinguish the specimen from Stansbury Island was in vain. It is true that no one of the Nevadan specimens shows exactly the same combination of characters as the type of *pergracilis*, but neither do any two Nevadan specimens show the same combination of characters. Therefore, the name *pergracilis* is here employed for all the pale mice which in general have a distribution corresponding to the former basin of Lake Bonneville, although specimens from as far west as eastern Eureka County are included. The slightly darker color of these suggests intergradation with *crinitus*. The specimen from Elko, likewise, is relatively dark. So far as can be judged from the broken skull of this specimen of subadult age, greater resemblance is shown to *pergracilis* than to *crinitus*.

Records of occurrence.—Specimens examined, 78, as follows: *Eureka Co.:* Union, 1; 4 mi. S Romano, Diamond Valley, 7; 8 mi. W Eureka, 2. *Elko Co.:* Elko, 1 (U. S. Nat. Mus., Biol. Surv. Coll.); 8 mi. S Wendover, 4700 ft., 6; W side Ruby Lake, 3 mi. N White Pine Co. line, 1 (coll. of Ralph Ellis). *White Pine Co.:* W side Ruby Lake, 3 mi. S White Pine Co. line, 6100 ft., 5 (coll. of Ralph Ellis); Cherry Creek, 6800 ft., 3; 2 mi. W Smith Creek Cave, Mt. Moriah, 6300 ft., 10; Deadman Creek, 6700 ft., Mt. Moriah, 3; near Smith Creek Cave, Mt. Moriah, 5800–7200 ft., 18; Halstead Creek, 1 mi. W Illipah, 6200 ft., 1; Cleve Creek, Shell Creek Range, 6900 ft., 7; Hendry Creek, 8 mi. SE Mt. Moriah, 6200 ft., 2; Baker Creek, 7300–7700 ft., 5; Water Canyon, 8 mi. N Lund, 5; Water Canyon, 10 mi. N Lund, 1.

Peromyscus crinitus stephensi Mearns
Canyon Mouse

Peromyscus stephensi Mearns, Proc. U. S. Nat. Mus., 19:721, July 30, 1897. Type from 3 miles east of Mountain Spring in Imperial County, California.
Peromyscus crinitus stephensi, Osgood, N. Amer. Fauna, 28:232, April 17, 1909; Burt, Trans. San Diego Soc. Nat. Hist., 7:416, May 31, 1934; Hall and Hoffmeister, Journ. Mamm., 23:59, February 14, 1942.

Distribution.—Southern third of state. See figure 354.

Remarks.—Average and extreme measurements of eleven males from Hiko Spring, 8 mi. SSE Dead Mountain, and ten females from Hiko Spring and 8 mi. S Dead Mountain, Clark Co., are: ♂, 176 (162–183), ♀, 175 (171–181); 93 (88–101), 93 (89–96); 18.9 (18–20), 19.0 (18–20); 19.1 (18–20), 18.9 (18–20); weight, 15.7 (12.8–17.2), 14.2 (12.6–15.2) grams.

Comparison of this small, long-tailed, light-colored race with *crinitus* and *pergracilis* has been made in the accounts of those forms. From *auripectus* to the eastward, *stephensi* differs in: smaller hind foot, gray as opposed to bright ochraceous coloration of upper parts, and a skull smaller in every part measured except the length of the bony palate, which averages larger in *stephensi*. Intergradation with *auripectus* is not indicated within Nevada, but takes place farther to the east. Specimens assigned to *stephensi* from northern Lincoln and eastern Nye counties show some approach to *pergracilis* and *crinitus* in coloration and larger size of skull. All the Nevadan specimens show approach to *crinitus* and *pergracilis* in that the tail relative to the length of the head and body is shorter than in topotypes of *stephensi* and in other populations from as far south as, and farther south than, the type locality.

Records of occurrence.—Specimens examined, 176, as follows: *Mineral Co.:* Marietta, 4900 ft., 2; Huntoon Valley, 5700 ft., 1. *Esmeralda Co.:* 7 mi. N Arlemont, 5500 ft., 1; Cave Spring, 6200–6245 ft., 2; Fish Lake, 4800 ft., 5; 2 mi. S Piper Peak, Silver Peak Range, 7500 ft.,6; Palmetto Wash.,5700 ft., 2 (D. R. Dickey Coll.); ¾ mi. E Lida, 5900 ft., 1 (D. R. Dickey Coll.); 2 mi. E Lida, 5800 ft., 2 (D. R. Dickey Coll.); 3 mi. E Lida, 5500 ft., 3 (D. R. Dickey Coll.). *Nye Co.:* 7 mi. E Nyala, Quinn Canyon Mts., 7000 ft., 2; 14 to 15 mi. SW Sunnyside, White River Valley, 5800 ft., 3; Big Creek, Quinn Canyon Mts., 5700–5800 ft., 13; Old Mill, N end Reveille Valley, 6200 ft., 1; 1 mi. SW Cactus Spring, Cactus Range, 1; 8½ mi. E Cliff Spring, 6200 ft., 2; 2 mi. NW Indian Spring, Belted Range, 6300–6500 ft., 5; Indian Spring, Belted Range, 7200–7400 ft., 3; ½ mi. S Oak Spring, 5700 ft., 6; 5 mi. W White Rock Spring, Belted Range, 7300 ft., 5; NW base Timber Mtn., 4200 ft., 2; 8½ mi. NE Springdale, 4250 ft., 1; 7 mi. E and 2 mi. N Grapevine Peak, 5100 ft., 3; 5 mi. E and 1 mi. N Grapevine Peak, 5500 ft., 5; 2½ mi. E and 1 mi. S Grapevine Peak, 7000 ft., 7; Amargosa River, 3 to 4 mi. NE Beatty, 3400–3500 ft., 2; Ash Meadows, 4 4/5 mi. NW Devils Hole, 2200 ft., 1. *Lincoln Co.:* Eagle Valley, 3½ mi. N Ursine, 5600–5900 ft., 3; 2 mi. S Pioche, 6000 ft., 1; 4 mi. NE Crystal Spring, 4300 ft., 4; 1½ mi. NE Crystal Spring, 4100 ft., 2; Meadow Valley Wash, 7 mi. S Caliente, 4500 ft., 6; 16 mi. E Groom Baldy, 4600 ft., 4; Meadow Valley Wash, 5½ mi. N Elgin, 4000 ft., 1; 5½ mi. N Summit Spring, 4700 ft., 1; Meadow Valley Wash, 21 mi. S Caliente, 3200 ft., 2. *Clark Co.:* Mormon Well, 6500 ft., 2 (D. R. Dickey Coll.); Hidden Forest, 8500 ft., 2 (D. R. Dickey Coll.); Indian Springs, 3300 ft., 1; Valley of Fire, 12 mi. SW Overton, 1; Willow Creek, 6000 ft., 1 (D. R. Dickey Coll.); Charleston Mts., 4000 ft., 9 mi. NE Pahrump, 4 (D. R. Dickey Coll.); Charleston Peak, 10,000 ft., 1 (D. R. Dickey Coll.); Charleston Mts., 6000 ft., 7 (D. R. Dickey Coll.); Kyle Canyon, 4500 ft., 10 (D. R. Dickey Coll.); 2½ mi. N Hoover (Boulder) Dam Ferry, 2; 4½ mi. W Boulder City, 2700 ft., 2; N side Potosi Mtn., 5800 ft., 2; 8 mi. S Dead Mtn., 2700 ft., 6; Hiko Spring, 8 mi. SSE Dead Mtn., 1900 ft., 22; 3 mi. SW Hiko Spring, 2400 ft.,2.

Additional records: Osgood (1909:234) records specimens from seven places not plotted on our distribution map which fall within the area of occurrence shown by specimens examined.

Peromyscus eremicus eremicus (Baird)
Cactus Mouse

Hesperomys eremicus Baird, Mamm. N. Amer., Pac. R. R. Repts., 8:479, 1857. Type from Old Fort Yuma, Imperial County, California, on Colorado River, opposite Yuma, Arizona.
Peromyscus eremicus, Allen, Bull. Amer. Mus. Nat. Hist., 7:226, June 29, 1895; Osgood, N. Amer. Fauna, 28:239, April 17, 1909.
Peromyscus eremicus eremicus, Burt, Trans. San Diego Soc. Nat. Hist., 7:416, May 31, 1934.

Distribution.—From base of Grapevine Peak and Meadow Valley Wash (21 miles south of Caliente) southward over state in Lower Sonoran Life-zone. See figure 355.

Remarks.—Average and extreme measurements of ten of each sex taken in January and February from along the Colorado River, from and below a point due east of Searchlight, are: ♂, 199 (192–205), ♀, 199 (187–214); 106 (100–109), 105 (92–113); 20.8 (20–22), 20.5 (19–22); 19.6 (18–20), 19.5 (18–20); weight, 24.1 (20.5–28.5), of eight ♀, 23.2 (20.0–27.3) grams.

The ochraceous buff upper parts are uniformly overlain, but not entirely concealed, by blackish; the ochraceous is more prominent on the sides. The underparts are whitish, as are the feet. The tail is bicolored, but not so sharply as that of *P. maniculatus.* The tail almost always amounts to more than half the total length, is finely annulated, short-haired, and lacks a marked pencil. The ears are large (see measurements above), rela-

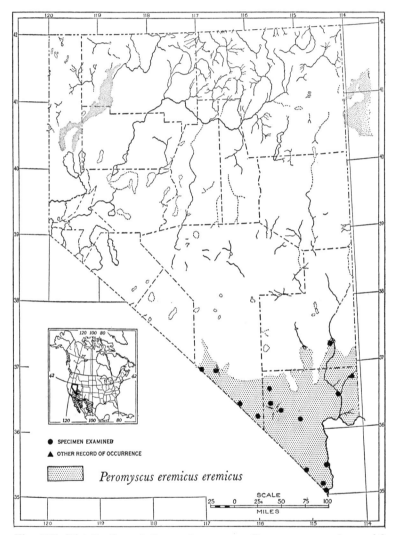

Fig. 355. Distribution of the cactus mouse, *Peromyscus eremicus*, with insert showing range of the species.

tively naked, and lack both the white border and also the preauricular white patch of *maniculatus.*The sole of the hind foot is naked to the end of the calcaneum.The mammae are inguinal, in two pairs. The premaxillae extend behind the nasals; the zygomatic breadth anteriorly is relatively (to maxillary breadth posteriorly) narrower than in *maniculatus*, slightly narrower than in *boylii* or *truei*, and wider than in *crinitus*. The skull is about the same size as that of *maniculatus*, smaller than that of *boylii* and *truei*, and larger than that of *crinitus*. M1 has only three buccal cusps.

No secondary sexual variation in this species in Nevada has been found, although it was looked for in external measurements and in cranial measurements.

Geographic variation is not certainly shown within Nevada in this species. The one adult from the northernmost locality, 21 mi. S Caliente, measures only 179, 92, 20, 17, and weighs 17 grams. The small size of this specimen may be only an individual variation. The Nevadan specimens, compared with specimens from the vicinity of the type locality, have tails about the same length, but longer bodies which average about 88 as opposed to 81 per cent of the length of tail. In a series from the Arizona side of the Colorado River (31 mi. N and 2½ mi. W Camp Mohave), the body averages 84 per cent of the length of tail, but in this series both the body and tail average actually shorter than in the Nevadan animals.

This is a species of the Lower Sonoran Life-zone, although in southern Nevada, as pointed out by Burt (1934:416), it does penetrate the "piñon pine–juniper belt." Over the arid parts of the Lower Sonoran Life-zone, *P. eremicus* replaces *P. maniculatus* as the common mouse of this genus, and the two occur together under cover of riparian growth along the Colorado River. Svihla (1932:19) gives the gestation period as 21 days for a female kept in captivity, remarks (*op. cit.*: 23) that the young are born in a more advanced stage of development than those of *P. maniculatus*, and says (*op. cit.*: 30) that the eyes open from 15 to 17 days after birth. Of six sexually mature females taken in January, two had three embryos each. In February, nine females had no embryos. In May, of four females, one had five embryos. Burt (1934:416) records a pregnant female with four embryos taken in June.

Records of occurrence.—Specimens examined, 88, as follows: *Nye Co.:* 2½ mi. E and 1 mi. S Grapevine Peak, 7000 ft., 1; Amargosa River, 3½ mi. NE Beatty, 3400 ft., 8; Ash Meadows, 4 4/5 mi. NW Devils Hole, 2200 ft., 2; Pahrump Ranch, 2667 ft., 4 (D. R. Dickey Coll.). *Lincoln Co.:* Meadow Valley Wash, 21 mi. S Caliente, 3200 ft., 2. *Clark Co.:* Indian Springs, 1 (D. R. Dickey Coll.); Kaolin Reservoir, 1400 ft., 1 (Boulder Dam Recreational Area Coll.); ½ mi. E St. Thomas, Muddy River, 1250 ft., 6 (D. R. Dickey Coll.); Willow Creek, 6000 ft., 1 (D. R. Dickey Coll.); Charleston Mts., 4 (D. R. Dickey Coll.); Kyle Canyon, 4500 ft., 8 (D. R. Dickey Coll.); 4 mi. W Las Vegas, 2100 ft., 1 (D. R. Dickey Coll.); Colorado River, 14 mi. E Searchlight, 17; 9 mi. W and 5 to 5½ mi. S Searchlight, 4300 ft., 8; 8 mi. S Dead Mtn., 2700 ft., 1; Hiko Spring, 8 mi. SSE Dead Mtn., 1900 ft., 11; 3 mi. SW Hiko Spring, 2400 ft., 4; Colorado River, 500 ft. (½ mi. N Calif.-Nev. Monument, 11; 6 mi. N Calif.-Nev. Monument, 1), 12.

Additional record: Bunkerville (Osgood, 1909:242).

Peromyscus maniculatus
Deer Mouse

Two subspecies of *maniculatus* occur in Nevada. The color depends in part upon the stage of molt, and in part upon the individual, as well as upon the place of geographic origin. Some students have recognized two "phases" of color, which I am not prepared to deny, in each of the two Nevadan subspecies. Some specimens, intermediate in color between the "phases," may be colored thus because the two phases are not sharply distinct, or it may be that stage of molt alone accounts for the specimens of an intermediate color. Collins (1918, 1923) has studied and reported upon this problem, and his work must be consulted by anyone who attempts to explain the color variation mentioned. The upper parts in some adults are a mixture of brown and black and vary from this to an ochraceous or reddish color of varying shade. The sides are usually, but not always, of a color less mixed than that on the back and generally are more reddish. The underparts are whitish, as are the feet. The tail is distinctly bicolored, the dark dorsal stripe being relatively narrow. The tail is about as hairy as that in *truei*, more than in *boylii*, and less than in *crinitus*. In each of the two Nevadan subspecies of *maniculatus* the tail is shorter than the head and body. The ears are of small size, and measured from the notch, in fresh specimens, are shorter than the hind foot. The ears have a fine edge of whitish and often a whitish or light reddish preauricular tuft of hairs. The mammae are in three pairs, one pectoral and two inguinal. This is a small mouse among Nevadan species, the total length being about the same as in *crinitus*, but the body is relatively longer and the tail shorter. The skull is relatively broad, especially anteriorly across the zygomatic arches. The premaxillae do not extend posteriorly to the nasals. M1 normally has accessory cusps between the major buccal cusps, but occasional specimens have these so much reduced that at first glance they appear to be absent.

In most areas of Nevada the deer mouse is the most abundant mammal. One exception to this is in the area of the Lower Sonoran Life-zone along the Colorado River where the deer mouse is fairly sharply restricted to the riparian association, being in part replaced, among the creosote bushes and cacti, by the cactus mouse, *Peromyscus eremicus*. Another exception is in most arid parts of the Upper Sonoran Life-zone where heteromyids of one kind or another may outnumber deer mice. In most trap lines set anywhere from in the Upper Sonoran Life-zone to above timber line, more deer mice than any other kind of nocturnal rodent are apt to be caught. This species occurs with each of the other four species of the genus in Nevada.

Among the 1,767 specimens at hand, there are two albinistic animals which, because of this unusual feature, were saved as specimens. One is a juvenal male taken June 20, 1937, by D. H. Johnson, 2 miles east of Mount Moriah, 10,250 feet elevation, White Pine County, and appears to be a complete albino, although no record of the color of its eyes is available. The other is a subadult female, taken September 13, 1931, 5 miles southeast of Millett, 5500 feet elevation, Nye County, by Chester C. Lamb. A large area on the back is white, although over part of this area the hair is plumbeous basally. The animal has crinkled ears which are shorter than normal. In the dry specimen the length of ear is 10 mm. from the notch, as opposed to 16 mm. in several normal specimens of corresponding age and sex. The skull of this animal is smaller and has a shorter rostrum than normal females. Of deer mice trapped, probably nine out of ten were not saved as specimens; hence, these two albinistic animals may have been selected from 17,670 specimens, rather than from only 1,767.

Nests have been found under logs and in walls of buildings. Several were made of plant fibers, and one found on June 17, 1937, along Hendry Creek, by H. S. Fitch, was composed largely of fur, probably of a wood rat. The nest was beneath some logs and was evidently used by a female and her several half-grown young which were seen when the logs were moved. Svihla (1932:15) gives the gestation period as 22 to 35 days and says (*op. cit.*:29) that the eyes open when the mice are from 12 to 17 days old. Of 592 sexually mature females available, 120 contained embryos, as recorded on the skin-labels by collectors. The mode for the number of embryos is 5, the mean is 5.3, and the extremes are 2 and 8. Pregnancy seems to be most common in May and June when about half of the sexually mature females are recorded as being pregnant. The 582 sexually mature females are distributed by months as follows: April, 17 (2 of these with embryos); May, 82 (24); June, 156 (53); July, 253 (34); August, 36 (4); September, 20 (2); October, 7 (1); November, 0 (0); December, 7 (0); January, 12 (0); February, 2 (0); March, 0 (0).

In field work around and on Mount Moriah, White Pine County, in June, 1937, record was made of the sex of all mice of this species caught by several collectors. Of the 218 individuals, 123 were males and 95 were females.

There is secondary sexual variation in size in this species, the females averaging 2 to 5 per cent larger than males in total length. In every large series, females (nonpregnant so far as known) averaged 4 to 19 per cent heavier than males. In greatest length of skull, females in six series were larger, in two series the males were larger, and in one series there was no average difference. From these crude data we conclude that females of this species in Nevada average larger than males.

Geographic variation is discussed in the accounts of the two subspecies.

Peromyscus maniculatus gambelii (Baird)
Deer Mouse

Hesperomys gambelii Baird, Mamm. N. Amer., Pac. R. R. Repts., 8:464, 1857. Type from Monterey, Monterey County, California.
Peromyscus maniculatus gambeli, Osgood, N. Amer. Fauna, 28:67, April 17, 1909.
Peromyscus maniculatus sonoriensis, Taylor, Univ. California Publ. Zoöl., 7:228, June 24, 1911, part.
[*Peromyscus*] [*texensis*] *gambeli*, Elliot, Field Columb. Mus., publ. 45, zoöl. ser., 2:130, 1901.

Distribution.—Northwestern Nevada from the Oregon boundary south to the Truckee River and from the California boundary east into the Black Rock Desert. See figure 356.

Remarks.—Average and extreme measurements of ten males and eight females from central Washoe County (15 mi. NNW Deep Hole south to Flanigan) are: ♂, 157 (145–165), ♀, 164 (152–178); 65 (60–70), 68 (62–80); 20.2 (18–21), 19.7 (19–21); 17.6 (15–20), 18.2 (17–20); weight, 19.8 (15.4–22.5), 20.4 (17.8–24.0) grams.

Size small. Color ochraceous above, heavily and nearly uniformly mixed with dusky; underparts creamy white, as also are the feet. A darker "phase" is characterized by Osgood (1909:67) as more vinaceous than ochraceous.

From *P. m. sonoriensis*, Nevadan specimens assigned to *gambelii* differ in lesser total length, relatively shorter tail, lesser weight, and smaller skull. For the most part these Nevada specimens may be regarded as intergrades between *sonoriensis* and *gambelii*.

Specimens which have been particularly difficult to assign to one race or the other are those from the Pine Forest Mountains (referred to *sonoriensis*) and those from along the Truckee River at points 3 and 11¾ miles east of Reno. Also, specimens from the eastern edge of the Black Rock Desert west of Sulphur are difficult to assign. The specimens from

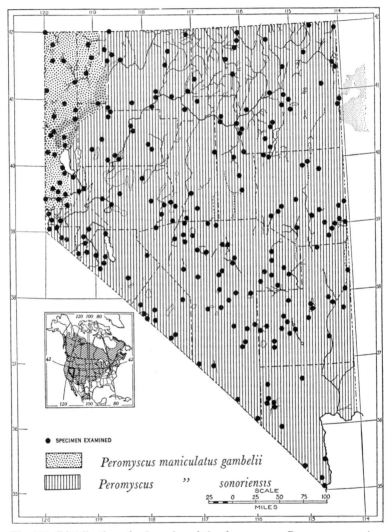

Fig. 356. Distribution of subspecies of the deer mouse, *Peromyscus maniculatus*, with insert showing range of the species.

10½ miles west and 6 miles north of Sulphur were taken on dark-colored rocks and average a little darker than those from lighter colored soils within a radius of 1 mile of Sulphur. In coloration, animals from Smoke Creek south to Flanigan more closely resemble *gambelii*, but in relative length of tail and in cranial size are more like *sonoriensis*. The low elevation, light-colored soil, and general extension westward of typical Great Basin conditions here probably explain this marked trend toward *sonoriensis*. Probably it was this same tendency which influenced Osgood (1909:93) to refer specimens from as far west as Honey Lake, California, to the race *sonoriensis*.

Records of occurrence.—Specimens examined, 157, as follows: *Washoe Co.:* 12-mile Creek, ½ mi. E Calif. boundary, 5300 ft., 5; 12-mile Creek, ¾ mi. E Calif. boundary, 5300 ft., 2; Barrel Spring, 5700 ft., 9½ mi. E and 3½ mi. N Ft. Bidwell, 4; 4 mi. SW Diessner, 5800 ft., 2; 4 mi. S Diessner, 5800 ft., 2; 3 mi. N Vya, 5900 ft., 7; ½ mi. N Vya, 6200 ft., 6; 2 mi. W Vya, 6500 ft., 4; 1 mi. W Vya, 6700 ft., 1; 4½ mi. NE Painted Point, 5800 ft., 5; 8½ mi. E Vya, 5900 ft., 2; Painted Point, 9 mi. E Vya, 6000 ft., 1; 3 mi. E Painted Point, 5850 ft., 2; mouth Little High Rock Canyon, 5000 ft., 3; 1 mi. W Hausen, 4650 ft., 4; Hausen, 4800 ft., 3; 2½ mi. SE Hausen, 5200 ft., 3; 15 mi. NNW Deep Hole, 5500 ft., 10; 12 mi. N and 2 mi. E Gerlach, 4000 ft., 1; 2½ mi. E and 11 mi. N Gerlach. 4050 ft., 1; 3 mi. E and 10 mi. N Gerlach, 4000 ft., 2; Rock Creek, Granite Mts., 5000 ft., 5, and 6000 ft., 1; 17½ mi. W Deep Hole, 4750 ft., 1; 17 mi. W Deep Hole, 4800 ft., 3; 1 mi. NE Gerlach, 4000 ft., 1; Smoke Creek, 9 mi. E Calif. boundary, 3900 ft., 13; latitude 40° 28′, 6 mi. E Calif. boundary, 4000 ft., 3; Horse Canyon, Pahrum Peak, 5800 ft., 4; Fox Canyon, 6 mi. S Pahrum Peak, 4800 ft., 2; 4 mi. NW Flanigan, 4200 ft., 1; 3½ mi. NW Flanigan, 4200 ft., 4; 3½ mi. E Flanigan, 4200 ft., 1; Sutcliffe, Pyramid Lake, 1; 2¾ mi. SW Pyramid, 4300 ft., 6; Junction House, 4500 ft., 2; 10 mi. N Reno, 1 (coll. of Ralph Ellis); 8 mi. NE Reno, 3 (2 in coll. of Ralph Ellis); 11¾ mi. E Reno, N side Truckee River, 4500 ft., 3; W side Truckee River, ½ mi. W Verdi, 4900 ft., 3; 4 mi. W Reno, 3 (1 in coll. of Ralph Ellis); 3 mi. E Reno, 2. *Humboldt Co.:* Virgin Valley, 5000 ft., 7; 5 mi. N Summit Lake, 5900 ft., 2; Soldier Meadows, 4600 ft., 9; 10½ mi. W and 6 mi. N Sulphur, 4000 ft., 1. *Pershing Co.:* 10 and 10½ mi. W and 6 mi. N Sulphur, 4000 ft., 5.

Additional records: Osgood (1909:71) lists specimens from Deep Hole, Flowing Springs, and Summit Lake, places which we have not attempted to plot on our distribution map because specimens have been examined from near-by localities.

Peromyscus maniculatus sonoriensis (LeConte)
Deer Mouse

Hesp[eromys]. sonoriensis LeConte, Proc. Acad. Nat. Sci. Philadelphia, 1853:413. Type from Santa Cruz, Sonora, Mexico.

Peromyscus maniculatus sonoriensis, Osgood, N. Amer. Fauna, 28:89, April 17, 1909; Taylor, Univ. California Publ. Zoöl., 7:228, June 24, 1911; Borell and Ellis, Journ. Mamm., 15:30, 73, February 15, 1934; Burt, Trans. San Diego Soc. Nat. Hist., 7:416, May 31, 1934.

Peromyscus maniculatus, Linsdale, Amer. Midland Nat., 19:189, January, 1938.

Distribution.—Over all of state, except northwestern part; distribution discontinuous only in the Lower Sonoran Life-zone where suitable habitat is rare. See figure 356.

Remarks.—Average and extreme external measurements of thirty-two males and twenty-eight females from the area of Mount Moriah and Wheeler Peak, White Pine Co., are: ♂, 161 (148–177), ♀, 165 (153–180); 68 (56–82), 68 (58–78); 20.2 (19–22), 19.7 (18.7–21.0); 18 (16.0–19.5), 18.2 (16–20); weight, 21.8 (19.5–25.4), 24.1 (19.8–30.0) grams. The length of tail in mice from this area is shorter than in most populations referred to *sonoriensis*.

Size small; color ochraceous above, mixed with fine dusky lines; underparts creamy white, as also are the feet. A darker "phase" has more dusky in the pelage of the upper parts.

Comparison with *gambelii* has been made in the account of that race. More in detail, for males, *sonoriensis* differs in total length, more than 160 mm.; in tail, more than 70 mm., averaging more than 72 per cent of length of head and body; in total length of skull, more than 25.4 mm.; and in nasals, 9.9 mm. or more. These are, of course, average differences. About the same differences obtain in females, which are somewhat larger than males. From *P. m. rufinus*, *sonoriensis*, so far as I have determined, differs chiefly in lighter coloration.

Considerable geographic variation is shown in Nevadan specimens here assigned to *sonoriensis*. The total length and weight is greater in the north, for example in Elko County, as compared with Clark County in the south. Relatively, the tail is shorter toward the north. Specimens from northern Elko County (northeastern Nevada) are darker than others and tend to have larger skulls. Those from close to the eastern boundary of the state, south of Wendover, and those from the western slope of Mount Moriah are a dark, but not bright, red and are suggestive of *rufinus*. This red coloration in mice from the western edge of Lake Bonneville suggests that the old lake basin has an appreciable effect on the coloration of the mice.

Records of occurrence.—Specimens examined, 1610, as follows: *Washoe Co.:* ½ mi. S Pyramid Lake, 1; 1 mi. S Pyramid Lake, 1; 34 mi. E Reno, 5 (3 in coll. of Ralph Ellis.); 3 mi. S Mt. Rose, 8500 ft., 2; Calneva, 6400 ft., 1; Incline Creek, 7100 and 8400 ft., 2. *Ormsby Co.:* Marlette Lake, 8000 ft., 1; ½ mi. S Marlette Lake, 8150 ft., 7; 3½ mi. E Carson City, 4700 ft., 1. *Douglas Co.:* Zephyr Cove, 6; 5½ mi. S Carson City, 4750 ft., 1; Carson River, 5 mi. SE Minden, 4900 ft., 2; 8 mi. SE Gardnerville, 5500 ft., 1; Desert Creek, Sweetwater Range, 6250 ft., 10. *Storey Co.:* 1 mi. S Wadsworth, Truckee Canal, 4100 ft., 2; 3 mi. SW Wadsworth, Gilpin Spillway, Truckee Canal, 1; 6 mi. NE Virginia City, 6000 ft., 6. *Lyon Co.:* 2 mi. N Yerington, 4350 ft., 1; West Walker River, 6 mi. S Yerington, 4500 ft., 6; West Walker River, 12 mi. S Yerington, 4600 ft., 8; Desert Creek, Sweetwater Range, 6250 ft., 7. *Humboldt Co.:* 1 mi. S Denio, Oregon, 4200 ft., 1; 36 mi. NE Paradise Valley, 5500 ft., 2; Alder Creek, Pine Forest Mts., 5000–7000 ft., 8; head of Big Creek, Pine Forest Mts., 60; Big Creek, Pine Forest Mts., 6000–7000 ft., 6; 12½ to 14 mi. N Paradise Valley, 6400–7000 ft., 16; Big Creek Ranch, Pine Forest Mts., 4350 ft., 3; Pine Forest Mtn. (= Duffer Peak), Pine Forest Mts.,8400–9400 ft., 12; Leonard Creek, Pine Forest Mts., 6500 ft., 7; Quinn River Crossing, 4100 ft., 20; Hansen Canyon, 5 mi. W Paradise Valley, 6200 ft., 4; 18 mi. NE Iron Point, 4600 ft., 6; 7 mi. N Winnemucca, 4400 ft., 1; 16 mi. NE Iron Point, 5000 ft., 1; 1 mi. N Winnemucca, 4600 ft., 4; 5 mi. NE Golconda, 2; 8 mi. E and 1 mi. N Jungo, 4200 ft., 2; 5 mi. SW Winnemucca, 4500 ft., 6; 10 mi. SW Winnemucca, 4500 ft., 1; 1¼ mi. N Sulphur, 4050 ft., 2; 1 mi. W Sulphur, 4040 ft., 3; 23 mi. NW Battle Mountain, 3. *Pershing Co.:* 3½ mi. SE Sulphur, 4950 ft., 2; 8 mi. S Sulphur, 4350 ft., 3; 1 mi. W Humboldt, 4180 ft., 1; El Dorado Canyon, Humboldt Range (6000 ft., 9; 7800 ft., 3), 12; 3 mi. SW Vernon, 4300 ft., 1; 9 mi. E Fanning, Buena Vista Valley, 4100 ft., 4; 9½ mi. E and 1 mi. S Fanning, Buena Vista Valley, 4100 ft., 4; S slope Granite Peak, East Range, 1; 30 mi. W and 4 mi. N Lovelock, 4300 ft., 3; 30 mi. W and 3 mi. N Lovelock, 4300 ft., 1; 3 to 3¼ mi. NNE Toulon, 3900 ft., 2; 1½ mi. NE Toulon, 3900 ft., 1; 2 mi. W Toulon, 4300 ft., 1; Toulon, 3930 ft., 5; 3 mi. E Toulon, 3900 ft., 3. *Churchill Co.:* Dixie Meadows, 3000 ft., 1; 3 mi. N Stillwater, 4000 ft., 1; 4 mi. W Fallon, 1; Fallon, 4000 ft., 1; Cherry Creek (Spring), 5000 ft., 2; 8 mi. SE Fallon, 3950 ft., 2. *Mineral Co.:* Schurz, Walker River, Indian dam, 4300 ft., 1; 3 mi. S Schurz, 4100 ft., 6; 2 to 3½ mi. SW Pine Grove, 7250–7800 ft., 16; 2 to 3 mi. NW Morgans Ranch, East Walker River, 5050–5100 ft., 11; Cottonwood Creek, Mt. Grant, 7400–7900 ft., 3; Fingerrock Wash, Stewart Valley, 5400 ft., 1; Wichman, 5500 ft., 2 (coll. of D. V. Hemphill); SW slope of Mt. Grant, 10,000 ft., 3; Lapon Canyon, Mt. Grant, 8900 ft., 7; Cat Creek, Mt. Grant, 8900 ft., 18; Fletcher, 6098 ft., 1; Endowment Mine, Excelsior Mts., 6500 ft., 1. *Esmeralda Co.:* 13½ mi. NW Goldfield, 4850 ft., 5; 7 mi. N Arlemont, 5500 ft., 4; Chiatovich Creek, ½ mi. W Chiatovich Ranch, 4900 ft., 1; Arlemont, 4900 ft., 2; Cave Spring, Silver Peak Range, 6200 ft., 1; Chiatovich Creek, 7000–8200 ft., 5; 2½ mi. N Dyer, 4850 ft., 1; 1½ mi. E Dyer, 4800 ft., 3; 2 mi. S Piper Peak, Silver Peak Range, 7500 ft., 1; N side of Mt. Magruder, 7400–7800 ft., 3; Pigeon Spring, Mt. Magruder, 6400 ft., 7. *Lander Co.:* 1½ mi. NW Cortez, Cortez Mts., 3; Reese River Valley, 7 mi. N Austin, 2; 6 mi. ENE Smiths Creek Ranch, 5550 ft., 2; Smiths Creek, 5800–7700 ft., 23; Smiths Creek Valley, 3 mi. W Railroad Pass, 5500 ft., 1; Birch Creek, 7000 ft., 1; Campbell Creek, 6900 ft., 8; Kingston R. S., 7500 ft., 5; Kingston Canyon, 7000 ft., 4; Peterson Creek, Shoshone Mts., 6500–7000 ft., 12. *Eureka Co.:* 5 mi. N Beowawe, 1; ½ mi. S Beowawe, 3; Pine Cr., 2 mi. E Palisade, 5; Evans, 2; Union, 9; Winzell, 1; 4 mi. S Romano, Diamond Valley, 4; 8 mi. W Eureka, 1. *Nye Co.:* Cottonwood Creek, at junction with San Juan Creek, Toyabe Range, 2; White Rock Mtn., Toquima Range, 10,177 ft., 2; 1 mi. N Penelas Mine, 1; Potts R. S., Monitor Valley, 6650 ft., 1; Wisconsin Creek, 7800–8500 ft., 3; 5 mi. SE Millett P. O., 5550 ft., 10; Bells Ranch, Reese River, 6890 ft., 2; ridge, south of Wisconsin Creek, 2; South Twin River, 6500–7000 ft., 14; Greenmonster Canyon, Monitor Range, 7500 ft., 14; 6½ mi. N Fish Lake, Fish Spring Valley, 6700 ft., 4; ½ mi. to 1,000 yds. SW Mt. Jefferson, 9800–9900 ft., 5; 1 to 1½ mi. E Jefferson, Toquima Range, 7600 ft., 9; 7 to 9¼ mi. E Toquima Peak, Monitor Valley, 7000–7100 ft., 13; 2½ mi. S Lock's Ranch, Railroad Valley, 5000 ft., 1; 4 mi. N Hot Creek, Hot Creek Range, 6400 ft., 12; 12½ mi. S Lock's Ranch, Railroad Valley, Able Spring, 5000 ft., 1; ¼ mi. W Hot Creek, Hot Creek Range, 5900 ft., 1; 4 mi. NE San Antonio, 5650 ft., 3; San Antonio, 5407 ft., 6; 7 to 8 mi. W Tybo, Hot Creek Range, 6700 ft., 4; 9 mi. W and 3 mi. S Tybo, Hot Creek Range, 6200 ft., 2; White River Valley, 17 mi. N Sunnyside, 5500 ft., 3; White River Valley, 15 mi. WSW Sunnyside, 5500 ft., 6; same as preceding, but 16½ mi. WSW, 3; White River Valley, 15 mi. SW Sunnyside, 5800 ft., 3; same as preceding, but 14 mi. SW, 4; Ralston Valley, 15½ mi. NE Tonopah, 5800 ft., 2; 2 mi. N Nyala, Railroad Valley, 5100 ft., 1; Nyala, Railroad Valley, 5100 ft., 1; Burned Corral Canyon, Quinn Canyon Mts., 6700–7000 ft., 31; Big Creek, Quinn Canyon Mts., 5700 ft., 2; 3 mi. S Nyala, Railroad Valley, 5600 ft., 1; Garden Valley, 8½ mi. NE Sharp, 34; 34 mi. E and 1 mi. N Tonopah, Ralston Valley, 5650 ft., 5; Old Mill, N end Reveille Valley, 6200 ft., 19; 9½ mi. E New Reveille, Railroad Valley, 5000 ft., 1; Breen Creek, Kawich Mts., 7000 ft., 19; 2 4/5 mi. E Silverbow, Kawich Mts., 7300 ft., 1; 2 mi. S Silverbow, Kawich Mts., 6400 ft., 2; 5½ mi. SW Silverbow, Kawich Mts., 6000 ft., 1; Cactus Spring, Cactus Range, 6500 ft., 1; Gold Flat, 5½ mi. W Kawich P. O., 5100 ft., 1; 7½ to 8½ mi. E Cliff Spring, 5900–6200 ft., 7; 2 mi. NW Indian Spring, Belted Range, 6300 ft., 2; Indian Spring, Belted Range, 7200 ft., 1; 5½ mi. NW White Rock Spring, S end Belted Range, 7200 ft.,

5; 5 mi. W White Rock Spring, Belted Range, 6905 ft., 2; Amargosa River, 3 to 4 mi. NE Beatty, 3400 and 3500 ft., 2; 7 mi. E and 2 mi. N Grapevine Peak, 5100 ft., 2; 5 mi. E and 1 mi. N Grapevine Peak, 5500 ft., 4; 8 mi. E Grapevine Peak, 5000 ft., 2; 2½ mi. E and 1 mi. S Grapevine Peak (7000 ft.), 31; 6700 ft., 51), 82; Ash Meadows, 4 4/5 mi. NW Devils Hole, 2200 ft., 1; Pahrump Ranch, 2667 ft., 1 (D. R. Dickey Coll.). *Elko Co.*: Cedar Creek, 10 mi. NE San Jacinto, 6000 ft., 2; Cedar Creek, 6 mi. NE San Jacinto, 5300 ft., 1; Cedar Creek, 2 mi. NE San Jacinto, 6000 ft., 2; Goose Creek, ½ to 2 mi. W Utah boundary, 5000 ft., 7; Owyhee River, 7 mi. NW Mountain City, 5300 ft., 7; Cobb Creek, 6 mi. SW Mountain City, 6550 ft., 13; summit between heads of Copper and Coon creeks, Jarbidge Mts., 4 (coll. of Ralph Ellis); 20 mi. S Owyhee, 2; 15 mi. S Contact, 5800 ft., 2; 13 mi. SSW Whiterock, 5600 ft., 2; 13 mi. N Montello, 5000 ft., 5; 1½ mi. NE Tecoma, 4900 ft., 13; Tecoma, 4900 ft., 1; Marys River, 22 mi. N Deeth, 5800 ft., 10; 1 mi. SE Tuscarora, 5900 ft., 10; 11 mi. SW Midas, 5000 ft., 1; Cobre, 6100 ft., 14; 2 mi. SW Cobre, 1; 2 mi. NW Halleck, 5200 ft., 1 (coll. of Ralph Ellis); 3 mi. W Halleck, 5300 ft., 3 (1 in coll. of Ralph Ellis); Elburz, 3 mi. S Halleck, 5200 ft., 2 (coll. of Ralph Ellis); head of Ackler Creek, Ruby Mts., 6800 ft., 7 (coll. of Ralph Ellis); Steels Creek, N end Ruby Mts., 7000 ft., 7 (4 in coll. of Ralph Ellis); summit of Secret Pass, 6200 ft., 8 (coll. of Ralph Ellis); 3 mi. S Wendover, 4300 ft., 4; 8 mi. S Wendover, 4700 ft., 2; Jerry Creek (Jerry Crab Springs), Ruby Mts., 6700 ft., 4; 10 mi. SW Elko, 5600 ft., 1; Three Lakes, Ruby Mts., 9700 ft., 8 (coll. of Ralph Ellis); 5 mi. E Raines, Sulphur Spring Mts., 2; Long Creek, Ruby Mts., 7830 ft., 5 (coll. of Ralph Ellis); Harrison Pass R. S., Green Mountain Canyon, 6050 ft., 10 (coll. of Ralph Ellis); W side Ruby Lake, 6 mi. N White Pine Co. line, 6200 ft. 1 (coll. of Ralph Ellis); W side Ruby Lake, 3 mi. N White Pine Co. line, 6200 ft., 22 (13 in coll. of Ralph Ellis). *White Pine Co.*: Willow Creek, 2 mi. S Elko Co. line, 6500 ft., 6 (coll. of Ralph Ellis); W side Ruby Lake, 3 to 3½ mi. S Elko Co. line, 6100 ft., 5 (coll. of Ralph Ellis); Overland Pass, E slope Ruby Mts., 8 mi. S Elko Co. line, 2 (coll. of Ralph Ellis); 5 mi. SE Greens Ranch, Steptoe Valley, 5900 ft., 2; Cherry Creek, 6800 ft., 7; E side Schellbourne Pass, 6800 ft., 5; Gleason Creek, 7300 ft., 4; Illipah, White Sage Valley, 6100 ft., 2; Cottonwood Creek, 6 mi. SW Illipah, 6400 ft., 2; Cleve Creek, Shell Creek Range, 6900–8300 ft., 10; 2 mi. W Smith Creek Cave, Mt. Moriah, 6300 ft., 9; near Smith Creek Cave, Mt. Moriah, 5600–5800 ft., 13; 2 mi. E Smith Creek Cave, Mt. Moriah, 1; 2 mi. E Mt. Moriah, 10,250 ft., 1; Hendry Creek, Mt. Moriah, 9800 ft., 3; Hendry Creek, 1½ mi. E Mt. Moriah, 9100 ft., 11; Hendry Creek, 8800 ft., Mt. Moriah, 1; 2½ to 3 mi. SW Hamilton, 7300–8400 ft., 14; 5½ mi. SE Ely, 6450–6500 ft., 6; Lehman Creek, 5700–8300 ft., 2; 7 mi. SW Osceola, Spring Valley, 6100–6275 ft., 5; Willard Creek, Spring Valley, 7150–8200 ft., 4; Pole Canyon, E slope Snake Mts., 7250–7500 ft., 3; Baker Creek, 6600–8850 ft., 44; Lehman Cave, 7200 ft., 2; 2 mi. SE Lehman Cave, 6700 ft., 4; 2½ to 3 mi. E Baker, 5700–5800 ft., 18; 1 mi. N Stella Lake, 11,500 ft., 1; Stella Lake, Snake Mts., 10,500–10,750 ft., 5; ½ mi. W Stella Lake, 10,500 ft., 2; ½ mi. E Stella Lake, 10,400 ft., 2; Baker Creek, 11,100 ft., 2; Spring Valley, 5½ mi. NW Shoshone P. O., 6100 ft., 3; Water Canyon, 8 mi. N Lund, 14; Spring Valley, 4 mi. S Shoshone, 5900 ft., 4. *Lincoln Co.*: 3 mi. S Geyser, Duck Valley, 6050 ft., 4; latitude 38° 17', ¼ mi. W Utah boundary, 7300 ft., 6; 3½ mi. N Ursine, Eagle Valley, 5800 ft., 2; 2 mi. SE Pioche, 6000 ft., 1; E side Coal Valley, 14 mi. N Seeman Pass, 4850 ft., 1; Desert Valley, 20 mi. SW Pioche, 5400–5700 ft., 3; 2 mi. N Panaca, 4800 ft., 3; Desert Valley, 21 mi. W Panaca, 5300 ft., 3; 11 mi. E Panaca, 6500 ft., 5; E slope and N slope Irish Mtn., 6900–8300 ft., 29; 12 mi. E Hiko Spring, 4800 ft., 5; Pahranagat Valley, 9 mi. NW Crystal Spring, 4800 ft., 5; Pahranagat Valley, 3 mi. N Crystal Spring, 4000 ft., 3; W slope Groom Baldy, 8000 ft., 1; Crystal Spring, Pahranagat Valley, 4000 ft., 9 (2 labeled 4900 ft.); within ½ mi. radius of Crystal Spring, 4000 ft., 9; 9 mi. W Groom Baldy, 5500 ft., 1; SW base Groom Baldy, 7200–7250 ft., 22; 16 mi. E Groom Baldy, 4600 ft., 3; Ash Spring, Pahranagat Valley, 3800 ft., 7; 5½ mi. N Summit Spring, 4700 ft., 1; Pahranagat Valley, 9 to 9 1/5 mi. SW Crystal Spring, 4800 ft., 6; Meadow Valley, 25 mi. S Caliente, 3000 ft., 2; ¼ mi. E Summit Spring, 4000 ft., 1. *Clark Co.* (unless otherwise noted, in D. R. Dickey Coll.): Mormon Well, 6500 ft., 15; Hidden Forest, 8500 ft., 6; Indian Springs, 3280 ft., 4; Willow Creek, 6000 ft., 3; ¼ mi. N Wheeler Well, 6600 ft., 4; Clark Canyon, 8000 ft., 2; Lee Canyon, 8200 ft., 11; N slope Charleston "Mts.," 7500 ft., 4; W side Charleston Peak, 2; summit Charleston Peak, 11,910 ft., 6; Charleston Peak (11,500 ft., 2; 11,000 ft., 1), 3; E slope Charleston Peak (11,800 ft., 9; 11,000 ft., 14), 23; Kyle Canyon (10,000 ft., 47; 8000 ft., 25; 6500 ft., 25; 6300 ft., 3; 4500 ft., 4), 104; N side Potosi Mtn., 7000 ft., 4 (Mus. Vert. Zoöl.); Colorado River, 14 mi. E Searchlight, 8 (Mus. Vert. Zoöl.); 9 mi. W and 3½ to 5½ mi. S Searchlight, 4300 ft., 4 (Mus. Vert. Zoöl.); 8 mi. S Dead Mtn., 2700 ft., 1 (Mus. Vert. Zoöl.); Colorado River, ½ mi. N. Calif.-Nev. Monument, 500 ft., 17 (Mus. Vert. Zoöl.); opposite Fort Mojave, 500 ft., 1 (Mus. Vert. Zoöl.).

Additional records: Osgood (1909:93) gives many additional localities of occurrence which are not entered on the distribution map (fig. 356) because they fall within the known range of this mouse as illustrated by the plotted occurrences of specimens examined.

Peromyscus boylii
Brush Mouse

Two subspecies of *boylii* occur in Nevada. The upper parts are brownish, consisting oftentimes of a pale buffy ground color overlain with dark brownish and blackish. The buffy color is pronounced on the sides, and in some specimens is the predominant color over all the upper parts.

The underparts are whitish, as are the feet. The tail is bicolored, whitish below, except where the flesh color of the skin shows through, and is longer than the head and body. Compared with *truei*, the tail is more sparsely and

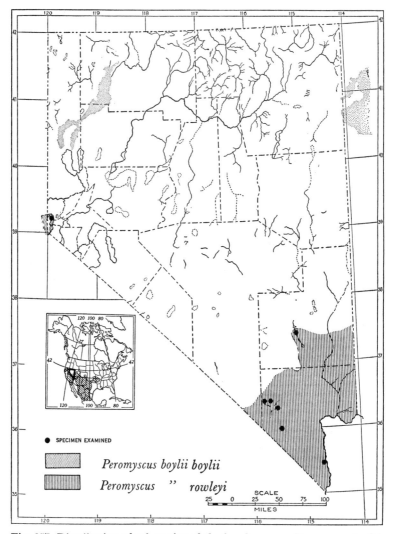

Fig. 357. Distribution of subspecies of the brush mouse, *Peromyscus boylii*, with insert showing range of the species.

shorter haired, and the annulations are coarser and less concealed. The ears are of medium size and, when measured from the notch in the flesh, are shorter than the hind foot. The mammae are in three pairs, one pectoral and two inguinal. The skull is large and may be distinguished from that of *truei* by the smaller size and lesser inflation of the auditory bullae. M1 has accessory cusps between the major buccal cusps.

This species is rare in Nevada, and where found, was in brush or, as along the Colorado River 14 miles east of Searchlight, in a dense growth of arrow-weed. Burt (1934:417), on Charleston Peak, likewise took his specimens on slopes densely covered with chaparral. A female taken May 29, 1932, at Ash Spring, 3800 feet, contained six embryos, each 16 mm. long. Burt (*loc. cit.*) took a female at 8000 feet altitude on Charleston Peak, June 10, 1928, which contained four embryos, and another on June 13, of the same year, that was suckling young.

Peromyscus boylii boylii (Baird)
Brush Mouse

Hesperomys boylii Baird, Proc. Acad. Nat. Sci. Philadelphia, 7:335, April, 1855. Type from Middle Fork of American River, near present town of Auburn, Eldorado County, California.
Peromyscus boylii, Mearns, Proc. U. S. Nat. Mus., 19:139, December 21, 1896.

Distribution.—In Nevada known only from the eastern shore of Lake Tahoe. See figure 357.

Remarks.—Measurements of three males from Eldorado County, California, a female from the same county, and a near adult female from Washoe County, Nevada, are: ♂, 200, 204, 201, ♀, 210, 197; 98, 112, 105, 107, 100; 22, 23, 22, 22, 22; weight, 27.6, 28.7, 25.5, 29.8, —— grams.

In addition to the characterization given for the species, it may be added that the race *boylii* is darker colored and has a smaller ear and smaller auditory bullae than the race *rowleyi*. The one skin and two skulls from Nevada, obtained by F. G. Palmer, agree well with topotypes.

Record of occurrence.—Specimens examined: *Washoe Co.:* 3 mi. E [SE] Incline, 6250 ft., east shore Lake Tahoe, 2.

Peromyscus boylii rowleyi (Allen)
Brush Mouse

Sitomys rowleyi Allen, Bull. Amer. Mus. Nat. Hist., 5:76, April 28, 1893. Type from Noland Ranch, San Juan River, San Juan County, Utah.
P[eromyscus]. b[oylii]. rowleyi, Mearns, Proc. U. S. Nat. Mus., 19:139, December 21, 1896.
Peromyscus boylei rowleyi, Osgood, N. Amer. Fauna, 28:145. April 17, 1909.
Peromyscus boylii rowleyi, Burt, Trans. San Diego Soc. Nat. Hist., 7:417, May 31, 1934.

Distribution.—Known only from Lincoln and Clark counties. See fig. 357.

Remarks.—Measurements of two males and three females from Ash Spring are: ♂, 201, 210, ♀, 211, 210, 198; 98, 113, 113, 107, 100; 21, 23, 24, 22, 22; 19, 20, 20, 21, 19; weight 30.2, 35.6, 35.2, ——, 27.3 grams.

Compared with *boylii*, *rowleyi* is paler (more reddish) and has a larger ear. Measurements of adult specimens from Nevada average larger than those recorded by Osgood (1909:145) for topotypes from southeastern Utah, but I am not certain but that this difference is ascribable to individual variation. At the same time, it may be pointed out, *rowleyi* has an extensive geographic range. Because of the large area of distribution, some geographic variation is expectable between populations from places far apart in this range.

Records of occurrence.—Specimens examined, 51, as follows: *Lincoln Co.:* Ash Spring, Pahranagat Valley, 3800 ft., 8. *Clark Co.* (unless otherwise noted, in D. R. Dickey Coll.): Cold Creek, 1; Cold Creek, 6000 ft., 1; Willow Creek, 1; Willow Creek, 6000 ft., 6; ½ mi. W Wheeler Well, 6700 ft., 3; N slope Charleston Peak, 6000 ft., 5; Charleston Peak, 10,000 ft., 1; Charleston "Mts.," 6000 ft., 2; Kyle Canyon, Charleston Park, 8000 ft., 16; Kyle Canyon, 6500 ft., 2; Potosi Mtn., 7000 ft., 1 (Mus. Vert. Zoöl.); Colorado River, 14 mi. E Searchlight, 4 (Mus. Vert. Zoöl.).

Peromyscus truei
Piñon Mouse

Two subspecies of *truei* occur in Nevada. The ochraceous buff upper parts are slightly overlain on the back with blackish; the ochraceous is most prominent on the sides of the body, on the face, and often on the nape. The underparts are whitish, as are the feet. The pelage is long and more lax than in any other Nevadan species except *crinitus*. The tail is sharply bicolored, white below, and usually shorter than the head and body. Compared with *boylii*, the tail is more closely and longer haired, and its annulations are finer and more nearly concealed. The ears are larger than in any other Nevadan species and, measured from the notch in the flesh, are longer than the hind foot. The hind foot has the calcaneum haired. The mammae are in three pairs, one pectoral and two inguinal. The skull is the largest among Nevadan species, slightly exceeding that of *boylii*, from which *truei* may be distinguished by the greater size and greater inflation of the auditory bullae. M1 has accessory cusps between the three major buccal cusps.

In Nevada we have generally found mice of the species *Peromyscus truei* on rocky areas which support a growth of piñon trees. Piñons without rocks and rocks without piñons seem not to provide habitats suitable to the mice. Exception to this generalization has to be made in that juniper trees may substitute for piñons in some places. Burt (1934:417) implies that on Charleston Peak these mice occur among the bristlecone pines in areas of rimrock. Svihla (1932) says that the gestation period is 25 to 40 days and that the eyes of the young open 15 to 20 days after birth. Of 16 pregnant females, 2 had 3 embryos, 7 had 4 embryos, and 7 had 5 embryos, yielding an average of 4.3. Of 6 sexually mature females in May, half were pregnant; of 26 in June, 10 were pregnant; and of 16 in July, 3 were pregnant. Of sexually mature females, 5 taken in August, 1 in September, 3 in October, 1 in March, and 2 in November, none had embryos. *P. truei* has been taken in Nevada along with each of the other species of the genus, and in only a few places was it found to outnumber any one of these other species.

Peromyscus truei truei (Shufeldt)
Piñon Mouse

Hesperomys truei Shufeldt, Proc. U. S. Nat. Mus., 8:407, September 14, 1885. Type from Fort Wingate, McKinley County, New Mexico.
P[eromyscus]. Truei, Thomas, Ann. and Mag. Nat. Hist. (ser. 6), 14:364, November, 1894.
[Peromyscus] truei, Elliot, Field Columb. Mus., publ. 45, zoöl. ser., 2:139, 1901.
Peromyscus truei, Osgood, N. Amer. Fauna, 28:165, April 17, 1909.
Peromyscus truei truei, Burt, Trans. San Diego Soc. Nat. Hist., 7:417, May 31, 1934; Hall and Hoffmeister, Univ. California Publ. Zoöl., 42:403, April 30, 1940.

Distribution.—Southern and western parts of state. See figure 358.

Remarks.—Average and extreme measurements of five males from northwestern Mineral County and a female from Pine Grove are: ♂, 186 (177–195), ♀, 183; 92 (87–98), 90; 23.4 (22.5–24.0), 22; 26 (24–27), 27; weight, 24.4 (20.0–29.1), 27.8 grams.

The size is small among races of *truei* and the body is relatively as well as actually short. The color is average for the species and is without marked suffusion of the upper parts by blackish or dark brown pigment. The skull is small, the zygomatic breadth anteriorly is great relative to that posteriorly, and the auditory bullae are greatly inflated.

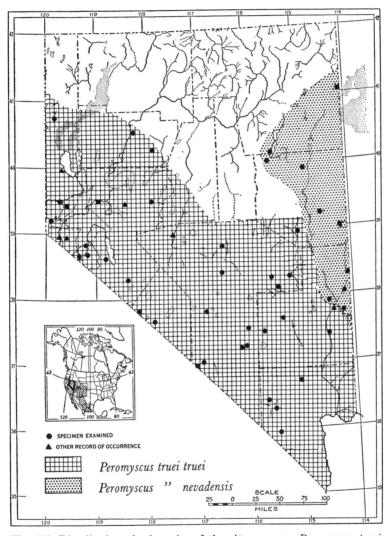

Fig. 358. Distribution of subspecies of the piñon mouse, *Peromyscus truei*, with insert showing range of the species.

From *P. t. preblei* of Oregon, *truei* differs in lighter color of upper parts, larger skull with relatively greater zygomatic breadth anteriorly, and larger upper incisors. From *P. t. gilberti* to the west, *truei* differs in smaller size, longer ear, lighter color above, smaller skull, and larger auditory bullae. From *P. t. montipinoris* to the southwest, *truei* differs

MAMMALS OF NEVADA

TABLE 16
CRANIAL MEASUREMENTS (IN MILLIMETERS) OF PEROMYSCUS

Sex	Number of individuals averaged or catalogue no.	Greatest length of skull	Basilar length	Greatest breadth of brain case	Interorbital constriction	Length of nasals	Shelf of bony palate	Palatine slits	Diastema	Postpalatal length	Alveolar length of maxillary tooth row
		Peromyscus crinitus crinitus, Northwestern Nevada, N of 41° latitude									
♂	4 av.	24.8	18.1	12.0	4.5	9.4	3.9	5.2	6.1	8.7	3.5
	min.	24.7	18.0	11.8	4.4	8.8	3.7	5.1	6.1	8.5	3.4
	max.	24.9	18.2	12.3	4.5	10.0	4.0	5.3	6.1	8.9	3.7
♀	4 av.	25.0	18.3	12.0	4.3	9.4	4.0	5.3	6.4	8.7	3.5
	min.	24.7	18.1	11.8	4.3	9.3	3.9	5.2	6.2	8.5	3.4
	max.	25.5	18.6	12.1	4.4	9.7	4.1	5.4	6.4	8.8	3.7
		Peromyscus crinitus pergracilis, Vicinity of Mount Moriah, White Pine Co.									
♂	9 av.	24.9	18.3	11.8	4.3	9.4	3.8	5.0	6.1	8.6	3.5
	min.	24.4	17.9	11.5	4.1	8.7	3.5	4.6	5.8	8.4	3.3
	max.	25.5	19.0	12.1	4.9	9.9	4.2	5.4	6.3	8.8	3.6
♀	11 av.	25.0	18.2	11.9	4.3	9.5	3.8	5.0	6.1	8.7	3.5
	min.	23.5	17.1	11.5	4.1	8.6	3.5	4.7	5.7	8.2	3.2
	max.	25.5	19.1	12.2	4.5	9.9	3.9	5.3	6.5	9.2	3.6
		Peromyscus crinitus stephensi, Hiko Spring, Clark Co.									
♂	11 av.	24.4	17.7	11.6	4.2	9.2	3.8	5.0	6.0	8.6	3.5
	min.	23.8	17.4	11.3	4.1	8.7	3.6	4.7	5.7	8.3	3.3
	max.	25.1	18.2	11.9	4.5	9.6	4.1	5.4	6.2	8.8	3.8
♀	10 av.	24.1	17.6	11.5	4.2	9.0	3.8	4.9	5.9	8.5	3.5
	min.	23.0	16.9	11.2	4.0	8.7	3.5	4.7	5.7	8.1	3.3
	max.	24.5	18.3	11.8	4.4	9.5	4.2	5.2	6.3	8.7	3.7
		Peromyscus eremicus eremicus, Southern Clark Co.									
♂	10 av.	25.6	19.7	11.9	3.9	9.1	4.2	5.0	6.3	9.4	3.9
	min.	24.4	19.0	11.5	3.8	8.5	3.8	4.7	6.1	9.0	3.8
	max.	26.2	20.2	12.3	4.1	9.7	4.6	5.3	6.5	9.9	4.1
♀	10 av.	25.6	19.8	11.9	3.9	9.2	4.2	5.1	6.4	9.3	4.0
	min.	24.6	19.2	11.7	3.7	8.7	3.7	4.8	5.9	8.7	3.8
	max.	26.3	20.1	12.3	4.0	9.4	4.4	5.4	6.6	9.7	4.1
		Peromyscus maniculatus gambelii, Central Washoe Co.									
♂	10 av.	25.2	19.0	11.6	3.9	10.0	3.8	5.5	6.7	8.7	3.8
	min.	24.1	18.2	11.2	3.7	9.4	3.4	5.1	6.2	8.4	3.5
	max.	26.3	19.6	12.0	4.1	10.9	4.2	6.2	6.9	9.0	4.0
♀	8 av.	25.5	19.4	11.6	3.9	10.1	3.8	5.6	6.7	9.1	3.7
	min.	24.5	18.4	11.2	3.8	9.4	3.3	5.4	6.4	8.7	3.5
	max.	26.5	20.3	11.9	4.1	11.0	4.2	5.7	7.2	9.4	4.0

TABLE 16—(*Continued*)

Sex	Number of individuals averaged or catalogue no.	Greatest length of skull	Basilar length	Greatest breadth of brain case	Interorbital constriction	Length of nasals	Shelf of bony palate	Palatine slits	Diastema	Postpalatal length	Alveolar length of maxillary tooth row
		Peromyscus maniculatus sonoriensis, Vicinity of Mt. Moriah and Wheeler Pk.									
♂	31 av.	25.4	19.1	11.7	4.0	10.1	3.9	5.5	6.7	9.0	3.8
	min.	23.9	18.2	11.0	3.7	9.5	3.5	5.2	6.1	8.2	3.5
	max.	26.5	20.1	12.3	4.2	10.9	4.2	6.0	7.4	9.7	4.1
♀	28 av.	25.5	19.2	11.7	4.1	10.2	3.7	5.5	6.8	9.1	3.7
	min.	24.3	18.3	11.2	3.7	9.4	3.2	5.1	6.3	8.2	3.5
	max.	26.5	20.0	12.2	4.4	10.9	4.3	5.9	7.2	9.7	4.1
		Peromyscus boylii boylii, Near topotype, Eldorado Co., California									
♂	84306	27.5	20.4	13.0	4.2	10.9	4.0	5.8	6.9	9.6	4.3
		3 mi. SE Incline, Washoe Co.									
♀	78318	27.8	20.4	12.5	4.3	10.3	4.5	6.0	6.6	9.3	4.5
		Peromyscus boylii rowleyi, Ash Spring, Lincoln Co.									
♂	2 av.	27.9	21.7	12.6	4.3	10.6	4.6	6.0	7.4	9.8	4.2
	min.	27.4	21.5	12.4	4.2	10.5	4.4	5.8	7.2	9.4	4.2
	max.	28.4	21.9	12.8	4.3	10.6	4.7	6.1	7.6	10.1	4.3
♀	3 av.	27.9	21.1	13.0	4.3	10.9	4.2	5.8	7.3	9.7	4.3
	min.	27.1	20.1	12.9	4.1	10.4	4.1	5.7	6.9	9.4	4.2
	max.	28.5	21.9	13.2	4.5	11.3	4.3	6.0	7.7	9.9	4.4
		Peromyscus truei truei, 2½ mi. E and 1 mi. S Grapevine Peak									
♂	5 av.	28.5	21.1	12.9	4.5	10.6	4.0	5.9	7.2	10.2	4.2
	min.	27.9	20.5	12.8	4.3	10.3	3.7	5.7	7.0	10.0	4.0
	max.	29.1	21.7	13.2	4.6	10.9	4.4	6.0	7.4	10.3	4.4
♀	5 av.	28.5	21.1	13.0	4.4	10.6	4.2	5.9	7.2	10.1	4.3
	min.	27.9	20.7	12.7	4.3	10.0	4.1	5.8	7.1	9.9	4.2
	max.	29.3	21.5	13.1	4.6	11.1	4.4	6.1	7.5	10.3	4.4
		Peromyscus truei nevadensis, Elko and Northern White Pine cos.									
♂	3 av.	28.8	21.2	13.3	4.6	10.8	4.3	5.9	7.1	10.3	4.2
	min.	28.7	21.0	13.1	4.5	10.6	4.1	5.8	7.0	9.9	4.2
	max.	28.9	21.3	13.4	4.6	11.0	4.5	6.0	7.1	10.7	4.3
		Elko Co.									
♀	3 av.	29.8	22.0	13.5	4.5	11.0	4.3	6.1	7.4	10.7	4.3
	min.	29.1	21.3	13.3	4.3	10.6	4.1	6.0	7.2	10.4	4.3
	max.	31.1	22.9	13.6	4.7	11.5	4.5	6.2	7.8	11.0	4.4

in about the same way as it does from *gilberti*, except that the tail is shorter, being longer than the head and body in *montipinoris* and averaging shorter than these parts in *truei*, and the auditory bullae are of about the same size. Comparison with *nevadensis* is made in the account of that form. The race *truei* has an extensive geographic range to the south and east of Nevada. The Nevadan specimens are remarkably uniform.

Records of occurrence.—Specimens examined, 184, as follows: *Washoe Co.:* 17 mi. W Deep Hole, 4800 ft., 1; 3 mi. E Reno, 1; 3 mi. SE Incline, 6250 ft., 1. *Douglas Co.:* Gardnerville, 1 (Calif. Acad. Sci.); Holbrook, 1 (Calif. Acad. Sci.); Desert Creek, 6250 ft., Sweetwater Range, 2. *Storey Co.:* 6 mi. NE Virginia City, 6000 ft., 2. *Lyon Co.:* West Walker River, 12 mi. S Yerington, 4600 ft., 4; ¼ mi. SW Ranger Station, 5000 ft., Wellington, 1 (coll. of J. R. Alcorn). *Pershing Co.:* El Dorado Canyon, 6000 ft., Humboldt Range, 1; S slope Granite Peak, East Range, 2. *Churchill Co.:* 3 mi. SW Lahontan Dam, 4100 ft., 1; Cherry Creek (Spring), 5000 ft., 3. *Mineral Co.:* 2 to 3½ mi. SW Pine Grove, 7250–7800 ft., 20; Cottonwood Creek, Mount Grant, 7400–7900 ft., 4; Endowment Mine, Excelsior Mts., 6500 ft., 2. *Esmeralda Co.:* Middle Creek, 8000 ft., 1; 2 mi. S Piper Peak, Silver Peak Range, 7600 ft., 1. *Nye Co.:* Greenmonster Canyon, Monitor Range, 7500 ft., 1; 8 mi. W Tybo, Hot Creek Range, 6700 ft., 2; Burned Corral Canyon, Quinn Canyon Mts., 6700 ft., 7; White River Valley, 14 to 15 mi. SW Sunnyside, 5500 ft., 2; Garden Valley, 8½ mi. NE Sharp, 8; 1 mi. SW Cactus Spring, Cactus Range, 1; 3 mi. N Indian Spring, Belted Range, 6700 ft., 1; Indian Spring, Belted Range, 7100 ft., 2; ½ mi. NE Oak Spring, 6600 ft., 3; 5 mi. W White Rock Spring, Belted Range, 7300 ft., 6; 5 mi. E and 1 mi. N Grapevine Peak, 5500 ft., 6; 8 mi. E Grapevine Peak, 5000 ft., 1; 2½ mi. E and 1 mi. S Grapevine Peak (7000 ft., 16; 6700 ft., 14), 30. *White Pine Co.:* Water Canyon, 8 mi. N Lund, 11. *Lincoln Co.:* E slope Irish Mtn., 6900 ft., 11; SW base Groom Baldy, 7200 ft., 2; Meadow Valley Wash, 4000 ft., 5½ mi. N Elgin, 1. *Clark Co.* (unless otherwise noted, in D. R. Dickey Coll.): Mormon Well, 6500 ft., 6; Hidden Forest, 8500 ft., 6; Willow Creek, 6000 ft., 3; Charleston "Mts." (7500 ft., 1; 6000 ft., 6), 7; E slope Charleston Peak, 11,000 ft., 1; Kyle Canyon, 6500 ft., 2; N side Potosi Mtn., 5800–7000 ft., 15 (Mus. Vert. Zoöl.).

D. G. Nichols (MS) records specimens from elevations of 5000 to 6500 feet in Hardscrabble Canyon in the Virginia Mountains on the western side of Pyramid Lake, Washoe County. Osgood (1909:169) records specimens not seen by me from the following places: *Douglas Co.:* Anderson Ranch. *Churchill Co.:* mountains, 16 mi. E Stillwater. Probably *Nye Co.:* Reese River. *Lincoln Co.:* Panaca. *Clark Co.:* Charleston Mountains.

Peromyscus truei nevadensis Hall and Hoffmeister
Piñon Mouse

Peromyscus truei nevadensis Hall and Hoffmeister, Univ. California Publ. Zoöl., 42:401, April 30, 1940. Type from ½ mile west of Debbs Creek, 6000 feet, Pilot Peak, Elko County, Nevada.
Peromyscus truei truei, Borell and Ellis, Journ. Mamm., 15:31, February 15, 1934.

Distribution.—Northeastern part of state from central Elko County south to northeastern Lincoln County and from the Utah boundary westward to the eastern slopes of the Ruby Mountains. See figure 358.

Remarks.—External measurements of three males (two topotypes and one from Cherry Creek) and three females (two topotypes and one from Ruby Lake) are: ♂, 200, 202, 191, ♀, 212, 201, 201; 94, 88, 89, 97, 93, 96; 23, 22, 23, 24, 24, 23; 25, 26, 24, 27, 25.5, 24; weight, 26.1, 23.4, 24.6, ——, 26.7, —— grams.

The size is medium among races of *truei*, and the body is relatively as well as actually long. The color is pale, the upper parts having only a small amount of blackish and a reddish or buff color of a markedly light tone. The skull is large, the rostrum is long, the zygomatic breadth is slight anteriorly relative to that posteriorly, and the auditory bullae are moderately inflated.

From specimens of *Peromyscus truei truei* from northern New Mexico, northern Arizona, and southern and western Nevada, *nevadensis* differs as follows: total length greater; body longer; length of tail averages 86 as opposed to 95 per cent of length of head and body; color paler, resulting from less blackish and a lighter tone of cinnamon in upper parts; skull averages larger in every measurement taken except in least interorbital constriction, in palatine slits, in diastema, and in maxillary tooth row, which are about the same as in *truei;* rostrum relatively as well as actually longer; auditory bullae slightly less inflated and with external auditory meatus slightly smaller. The range of *nevadensis* probably does not meet that of *preblei*, and is separated from that of *gilberti* by the range of the race *truei*, which extends northward at least to near latitude 41° in the low, western part of Nevada.

Intergradation with *truei* is indicated by three specimens from Pershing County which have the larger body and total length of *nevadensis* but cranial characters of *truei* to which they here are referred, although in the original description (Hall and Hoffmeister, 1940:403) they were referred to *nevadensis*. Similarly, the specimens originally referred to *nevadensis* from Water Canyon, 8 miles north of Lund, now are placed with *truei*, although in cranial characters they show some resemblance to *nevadensis*. A specimen from Green-monster Canyon, which has a relatively long body suggestive of *nevadensis*, a color intermediate between that of *truei* and *nevadensis*, though nearer the latter, and a skull as small as that of *truei*, is referred to *truei*. Some specimens from eastern Lincoln County also show approach to *truei*, although the average of all specimens from that general area is nearer that of *nevadensis*.

Records of occurrence.—Specimens examined, 49, as follows: *Elko Co.:* Pilot Peak, ½ mi. W Debbs Creek, 6000 ft., 18; W side Ruby Lake, 3 mi. N White Pine Co. line, 6700 ft., 1 (coll. of Ralph Ellis). *White Pine Co.:* W side Ruby Lake, 3 mi. S Elko Co. line, 7000 ft., 5 (coll. of Ralph Ellis); Overland Pass, E slope Ruby Mts., 8 mi. S Elko Co. line, 1 (coll. of Ralph Ellis); Cherry Creek, 6800–6900 ft., 6; Cleve Creek, 6900 ft., Shell Creek Range, 3; Lehman Cave, 7400 ft., 1; ½ mi. W Lehman Cave, 7500 ft., 2. *Lincoln Co.:* Latitude 38° 17′, ¼ mi. W Utah boundary, 7300 ft., 1; Eagle Valley, 5600 ft., 3½ mi. N Ursine, 2; 2 mi. S Pioche, 6000 ft., 3; 2 mi. SE Pioche, 6000 ft., 1; 11 mi. E Panaca, 6500–6600 ft., 5.

Sigmodon hispidus plenus Goldman
Hispid Cotton Rat

Sigmodon hispidus plenus Goldman, Proc. Biol. Soc. Washington, 41:205, December 18, 1938. Type from Parker, 350 feet, Yuma County, Arizona.

Distribution.—Extreme southern tip of state in bottom lands of Colorado River. See figure 370, *b*, page 537.

Remarks.—Measurements of the largest male and female available are: ♂, 338, ♀, 268; 143, 112; 37, 32; weight, 241.0 and 117.4 grams.

Tail less than half of total length; pelage coarse; upper parts mixed blackish and buffy, the total effect being blackish-brown; underparts with fur whitish distally but plumbeous base showing through; forefeet buffy; hind feet whitish or light buffy; tail with sparse, short, fine hair revealing scales, general color being dark brownish and scarcely lighter below than above; foot soles naked; mammae in five pairs; skull with short swollen rostrum; premaxillae projecting behind nasals; well-developed spinous process projecting anteriorly from outer wall of antorbital foramen; anterior margin of zygomatic plate concave, temporal ridges being continued as supraorbital ridge; palate ending behind plane of last upper molars and with median short spine; interpterygoid space spatulate; alveolar tubercle (marking basal end of lower incisor) on lateral face of mandible prominent; anterior faces of incisors smooth; cheek teeth semihypsodont. The dental formula is i. $\frac{1}{1}$, c. $\frac{0}{0}$, p. $\frac{0}{0}$, m. $\frac{3}{3}$.

From *Sigmodon hispidus eremicus* of the lower parts of the valleys of the Colorado and Gila rivers, this race differs in: skull larger; rostrum heavier; and interparietal longer anteroposteriorly.

All our specimens were taken from January 30 to February 2, 1934, ½ mile upriver from von Schmidt's meridian post, the post marking the boundary between Nevada and California. Here, Henry S. Fitch and Donald M. Hatfield found the animals confined to a tract of less than an acre. Water was flowing through this area, which supported cattails in places, Bermuda grass on the higher parts, and three mesquite bushes on the highest part. The cotton rats lived just above water level. The runways, some of which went through water an inch deep, averaged 8 centimeters wide, and were made either by the animals having cut off the grass near the ground or by the rats having run over and pressed down the grass. The food consisted of the bases of the stems of Bermuda grass. In several

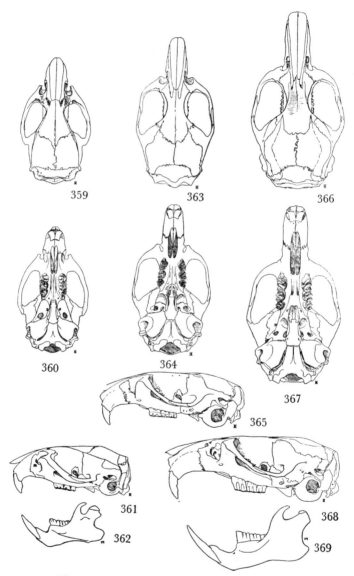

Figs. 359–369. Cotton rat and wood rats. All, ×1.

Figs. 359–362. *Sigmodon hispidus plenus*, Colorado River, ½ mile above Calif.-Nev. Monument, no. 61836, ♀.

Figs. 363–365. *Neotoma lepida lepida*, Baker Creek, 7300 feet, no. 42031, ♀.

Figs. 366–369. *Neotoma cinerea acraia*, Baker Creek, 8500 feet, no. 41994, ♀.

places every stem of grass had been cut by the rats over an area several feet square. No nests were found and there was no evidence of burrowing in the ground or of climbing in the mesquite bushes. Animals of several sizes were taken, the smallest of which is 132 mm. in total length and weighs only 17.5 grams, as against a length of 338 mm. and a weight of 241 grams for the largest, which was a male. About as many animals were caught in traps in the daytime as at night. *Peromyscus maniculatus* and *Reithrodontomys* were caught at night, but not by day, in the runways of the *Sigmodon*. One of the two females old enough to bear young had five embryos.

Record of occurrence.—Specimens examined: *Clark Co.:* Colorado River, ½ mi. N Calif.-Nev. Monument, 500 ft., 15.

TABLE 17

CRANIAL MEASUREMENTS (IN MILLIMETERS) OF SIGMODON

Sex	Catalogue no.	Greatest length of skull	Basilar length	Greatest breadth of brain case	Interorbital constriction	Length of nasals	Shelf of bony palate	Palatine slits	Diastema	Postpalatal length	Alveolar length of maxillary tooth row
					Sigmodon h. plenus, ½ mi. N Calif.-Nev. boundary						
♂	61833	41.3	34.6	16.5	—	16.5	8.5	9.5	11.8	14.6	6.6
♀	61836	33.9	27.7	14.9	5.0	12.8	7.0	7.6	8.9	11.4	6.5

Genus **Neotoma** Say and Ord
Wood Rats

Two species, the round-tailed desert wood rat of the subgenus *Neotoma* and the bushy-tailed wood rat of the subgenus *Teonoma*, have been found in Nevada.

Despite its superficial resemblance to the introduced *Rattus* (Old World rats), the round-tailed *Neotoma* belongs to a different family and can readily be distinguished by the occlusal faces of the cheek teeth which are made up of lakes of dentine surrounded by enamel, the lakes being more or less separated from one another by re-entrant angles. The cheek teeth of *Rattus* have definite cusps, and, except in aged individuals which have the cusps worn down, the occlusal faces of the cheek teeth have cusps opposing each other from above and below. In *Neotoma* the grinding faces of the cheek teeth are flat (see fig. 400, p. 560). The dental formula, which is the same as in *Rattus*, is i. $\frac{1}{1}$, c. $\frac{0}{0}$, p. $\frac{0}{0}$, m. $\frac{3}{3}$. The tail is slightly more hairy in *Neotoma*, and the outlines of the scales on the tail are less prominent than in *Rattus*. In each of the Nevadan species of *Neotoma* there are two pairs of mammae, both inguinal, as opposed to five or six pairs (two or three pairs pectoral and three pairs toward the inguinal region) in *Rattus*.

Neotoma lepida
Desert Wood Rat

The three subspecies of desert wood rat known from Nevada are distinguished from one another principally by color, relative length of tail and body, and size (not shape) of skull. The species as a whole, within Nevada, has a total length of about 300 millimeters; tail amounting to about three-fourths of length of head and body; foot soles and outer side of foot to tarso-metatarsal joint naked; ears thinly haired and projecting prominently beyond fur and only about 3 per cent shorter than hind foot; fur on feet, underside of tail, and chest white to base; fur elsewhere plumbeous at base; upper parts a mixture of blackish and buffy; underparts whitish or buffy; hair on back about 20 mm. long and about 10 mm. long on underparts; hairs on sides of tail attain a maximum length of about 6 mm.; first cheek tooth noticeably wider than last; medial side of first cheek tooth with one re-entrant angle; spheno-palatine vacuities wide.

Altitudinally, this species occurs from as high as 8700 feet in the Toquima Range down to the lowest parts of the state. Zonally, it occurs in the Lower Sonoran and Upper Sonoran life-zones and a short way into the Transition Life-zone. The high country comprising the greater part of Elko County, even in areas where sagebrush is the dominant shrub, seems to be too Boreal in character for *Neotoma lepida*, but is occupied by *Neotoma cinerea*.

Like other members of the genus, this species constructs houses of sticks, but in our experience the "houses" are invariably associated with burrows, the nest proper being in a burrow, or, sometimes, in a crevice in a rock. In some relatively open country known to be inhabited by these animals no sign of a rat house is to be found. The house-building instinct is evident, but poorly developed in comparison with that of some other species of wood rats.

The rats are most common where boulders or crevices in rocks afford shelter. For example, Fitch (MS), on May 20, 1932, noted that along the eastern side of Pahranagat Valley near Crystal Springs, a place which he describes as being on a certain level on a hillside where a continuous vein of rock formed ledges in many places, the wood rats were much more numerous than in surrounding territory.

Linsdale found the species to occur only sparingly along the eastern base of the Toyabe Mountains in 1930, and was told that a disease two years before had killed most of the rats. In 1930, along the Amargosa River and farther east at Oak Spring and about Groom Baldy, the rats were scarce and obviously at a low point respecting numbers. Only old burrows and houses with cobwebs in the passage ways were found.

Warbles, the larvae of botflies, often are found under the skin of this species and *Neotoma cinerea*. Probably many raptorial birds and carnivorous mammals prey on these rats. On May 13, 1936, 3 miles east of Reno, William B.

Richardson shot a long-tailed weasel that was carrying a half-grown wood rat across a rock slide.

Males average slightly larger than females. For fifty males and thirty-nine

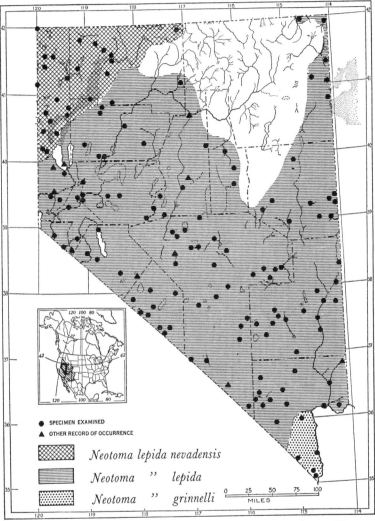

Fig. 370, *a*. Distribution of subspecies of the desert wood rat, *Neotoma lepida*, with insert showing range of the species.

females of comparable age the averages, for each sex, in total length, length of tail, and three of eight cranial measurements are identical. The hind foot and ear of males average 2 per cent longer; the weight is 10.5 per cent more, and five linear measurements of the skull range from 0.5 to 3.6 per cent more in males.

Of 148 sexually mature females, 25 were pregnant. The usual number of embryos (in 15 out of the 25) and also the average number was 3. The extremes were 1 and 5. By months these females were distributed as follows: January, 1 (0 pregnant); February, 3 (1 pregnant); March, 1 (0); April, 2 (0); May, 24 (10); June, 55 (14); July, 47 (0); August, 9 (0); September, 6 (0). Supplementary data are given by Burt (1934:418) who records 3 pregnant females taken by him on May 22, June 3, and June 7, in Clark County. Each contained 4 embryos. The female taken on June 3 was suckling 4 young about a fourth grown, which shows that more than one litter per year is produced.

Neotoma lepida nevadensis Taylor
Desert Wood Rat

Neotoma nevadensis Taylor, Univ. California Publ. Zoöl., 5:289, February 12, 1910. Type from Virgin Valley, 4800 feet, Humboldt County, Nevada. Taylor, Univ. California Publ. Zoöl., 7:243, June 24, 1911.

Neotoma desertorum, Goldman, N. Amer. Fauna, 31:76, October 19, 1910.

Neotoma lepida lepida, Goldman, Journ. Mamm., 13:61, February 9, 1932.

Distribution.—Northwestern Nevada. See figure 370, *a*.

Remarks.—Measurements of nine males and ten females from northern Washoe and Humboldt counties are: ♂, 279 (256–312), ♀, 285 (252–316); 116 (110–120), 122 (108–138); 31.1 (29–33), 30.4 (29–32); weight, 123.9 (119.5–132.2), 132.0 (96.0–157.7) grams.

Tail short; color blackish; upper parts blackish; upper side of tail black; underparts of many specimens overlain with buffy; tympanic bullae well inflated.

The dark color of this race is its principal distinguishing character, and is maintained in fairly uniform fashion over the northwestern part of the range of the species, which includes northeastern California, eastern Oregon, and parts of Idaho. Because of the uniformity of coloration and difference in coloration from *lepida*, it seems to me desirable to recognize the race *nevadensis* which Goldman (1910:76) regarded as inseparable from the race now called *lepida*. Animals from the type locality and from the Pine Forest Mountains near by to the eastward, are intergrades between *nevadensis* and *lepida*, and are not nearly so black as others farther to the northwest.

Records of occurrence.—Specimens examined, 84, as follows: *Washoe Co.:* 12-mile Creek, ½ mi. E Calif. boundary, 5300 ft., 2; Barrel Spring, 9½ mi. E and 3½ mi. N Ft. Bidwell, 5700 ft., 2; 12 mi. E and 3 mi. N Ft. Bidwell, 5700 ft., 2; ½ mi. N Vya, 6000 and 6200 ft., 2; Painted Point, 9 mi. E Vya, 6000 ft., 1; 10½ mi. S Vya, 5800 ft., 1; mouth Little High Rock Canyon, 5000 ft., 5; 1 mi. W Hausen, 4650 ft., 1; 15 mi. NNW Deep Hole, 5500 ft., 2; Rock Creek, Granite Mts., 6000 ft., 1; 17½ mi. W Deep Hole, 4750 ft., 2; 17 mi. W Deep Hole, 4800 ft., 2; 1 mi. NE Gerlach, 4000 ft., 2; 13 mi. W and 9 mi. S Deep Hole, 3850 ft., 3; Smoke Creek, 9 mi. E Calif. boundary, 3900 ft., 1; latitude 40° 28′, 6 mi. E Calif. boundary, 4000 ft., 4; Horse Canyon, 3 mi. NW Pahrum Peak, 5000 ft., 1; Sand Pass, 3950 ft., 1; 2 mi. NW Flanigan, 4250 ft., 3; ½ mi. NW Flanigan, 4200 ft., 3; 2½ mi. E Flanigan, 4250 ft., 3. *Humboldt Co.:* 36 mi. NE Paradise Valley, 5500 ft., 3; Virgin Valley, 5000 ft., 9; mouth Alder Creek, Pine Forest Mts., 5000 ft., 2; near Big Creek Ranch, Pine Forest Mts., 4350 ft., 3; 1½ mi. N Quinn River Crossing, 4100 ft., 1; Quinn River Crossing, 4100 ft., 1; 4½ mi. S Quinn River Crossing, 4000 ft., 1; 5 mi. S Quinn River Crossing, 4000 and 4100 ft., 2; Soldier Meadows, 4600 ft., 13; Jackson Creek Ranch, 17½ mi. S and 5 mi. W Quinn River Crossing, 4000 ft., 3; 10 mi. W and 6 mi. N Sulphur, 4000 ft., 2.

Neotoma lepida lepida Thomas
Desert Wood Rat

Neotoma lepida Thomas, Ann. and Mag. Nat. Hist. (ser. 6), 12:235, September, 1893. Type from along the 39th parallel somewhere between Camp Floyd, Utah, and Genoa, Nevada. Linsdale, Amer. Midland Nat., 19:190, January, 1938.

Neotoma desertorum, Goldman, N. Amer. Fauna, 31:76, October 19, 1910.

Neotoma lepida lepida, Goldman, Journ. Mamm., 13:61, February 9, 1932; Burt Trans. San Diego Soc. Nat. Hist., 7:417, May 31, 1934.

Distribution.—Most of state, except southern Clark, northern Washoe and Humboldt, and western and central Elko counties. See figure 370, *a*.

Remarks.—Measurements of ten males and five females from the sides of Great Smoky Valley are: ♂, 291 (282–305), ♀, 284 (276–295); 120 (113–128), 119 (108–131); 31.4 (30–34), 31.0 (29–32); weight, 158.3 (140.0–188.0), 139 (105.4–151.7) grams.

Tail short; color grayish; upper parts mixed blackish and buffy; underparts whitish; tympanic bullae well inflated.

From *nevadensis* this race differs in lighter color, and from *grinnelli* in larger average size of all parts measured except tail, which is actually shorter. Also, *lepida* averages slightly darker colored than *grinnelli*.

The color is slightly lighter to the southward. The actual and relative length of the tail increases to the southward; it is 68 per cent of the length of the head and body in the northeastern corner of the state and increases to 75 per cent in animals from the east side of Grapevine Peak. Because the features differentiating *grinnelli* and *lepida* were unknown to me at the time I examined the specimens in the collection of D. R. Dickey from southern Nevada (Clark County and extreme southern Nye County), the allocation of some specimens in the Dickey Collection to the race *lepida* is tentative. Certain of the specimens may be referable, instead, to the race *grinnelli* which was not named when I examined the specimens. Those from ½ mile south and 1 mile southwest of Pyramid Lake and those from 3 miles east of Reno are intermediate in color between *lepida* and *nevadensis*.

Records of occurrence.—Specimens examined, 455, as follows: *Washoe Co.*: ½ mi. S Pyramid Lake, 3950 ft., 1; 1 mi. SW Pyramid Lake, 3950 ft., 1; 3 mi. E Reno, 1. *Douglas Co.*: Carson River, 5 mi. SE Minden, 4900 ft., 1; Topaz Lake, 1; Desert Creek, Sweetwater Range, 6250 ft., 7. *Storey Co.*: 3 mi. SW Wadsworth, on Truckee Canal, 4100 ft., 1; 6 mi. NE Virginia City, 6000 ft., 2. *Lyon Co.*: 4 mi. W Hazen, 4250 ft., 1; Perretti Ranch, 15 mi. E [by road, and ENE] Dayton, 1 (coll. of U. S. Biol. Surv. Dist. Office, Reno); West Walker River, 12 mi. S Yerington, 4600 ft., 9. *Humboldt Co.*: 18 mi. NE Iron Point, 4600 ft., 1; 2 mi. E Antelope, 4400 ft., 2. *Pershing Co.*: 3½ mi. SE Sulphur, 4950 ft., 2; 8 mi. S Sulphur, 4350 ft., 2; El Dorado Canyon, Humboldt Range, 6000 ft., 1; 30 mi. W and 4 mi. N Lovelock, 4300 ft., 3; S side Granite Peak, East Range, 3; 1 to 3½ mi. W Toulon, 4100–4500 ft., 9; Toulon, 3950 ft., 1. *Churchill Co.*: Mountain Well, 5600 ft., 2; 12 mi. E and 1 mi. S Fallon, 3950 ft., 1; 1 mi. W Hazen, 4020 ft., 1; 3 mi. SW Lahontan Dam, 4100 ft., 1; 8 mi. S and 1 mi. E Eastgate, 1. *Mineral Co.*: 3 mi. S Schurz, 4100 ft., 1; East Walker River, 2 mi. NW Morgans Ranch, 5050–5100 ft., 6; 1 mi. NW Wichman, 5500 ft., 1 (coll. of D. V. Hemphill); ¼ mi. N Wichman, 5500 ft., 1 (coll. of D. V. Hemphill); Stanmoore Mine, 7750 ft., Lapon Canyon, Mt. Grant, 1 (coll. of D. V. Hemphill); Endowment Mine, Excelsior Mts., 6500 ft., 1. *Esmeralda Co.*: 2½ mi. NW Blair Junction, 4950 ft., 1; 3½ mi. SE Coaldale, 4850 ft., 1; 13½ mi. NW Goldfield, 4850 ft., 1; 7 mi. N Arlemont, 5500 ft., 1; Cave Spring, 6200–6248 ft., 13; 1 mi. N Valcalda Spring, 7000 ft., 1; Fish Lake, 4850 ft., 3; 2 mi. S Piper Peak, 7600 ft., 3; Palmetto Wash, 5700 ft., 2 (D. R. Dickey Coll.); 2 mi. E Lida, 1 (D. R. Dickey Coll.); Pigeon Spring, Mt. Magruder, 6400 ft., 3. *Lander Co.*: 1½ mi. NW Cortez, Cortez Mts., 1; Reese River Valley, 7 mi. N Austin, 1; 2½ mi. NE Smiths Creek Ranch, 5800 ft., 2; Smiths Creek, 6000–6800 ft., 2; Campbell Creek, 6900 ft., 1; Peterson Creek, Shoshone Mts., 6500–7300 ft., 4. *Eureka Co.*: Winzell, 1; 4 mi. SE Romano, Diamond Valley, 1; 4 mi. S Romano, 1; 8 mi. W Eureka, 1. *Nye Co.*: Wilson Canyon, 7500 ft., Toquima Range, 1; Wisconsin Creek, 7800 ft., 1; 5 mi. SE Millett P. O., 5300 and 5500 ft., 2; Ophir Creek, 6500 ft., 7; South Twin River, 6500–7000 ft., 1; Greenmonster Canyon, Monitor Range, 7500 ft., 1; Toquima Range, 1 mi. NE Jefferson, 7650 ft., 2; Toquima Range, 1 to 1½ mi. E Jefferson, 7600–8700 ft., 7; Monitor Valley, 9 mi. E Toquima Mtn., 7000 ft., 2; Hot Creek Range, 4 mi. N Hot Creek, 6400 ft., 7; San Antonio, 5400 ft., 2; Hot Creek Range, 7 to 8 mi. W Tybo, 6700–7200 ft.. 4; Burned Corral Canyon, Quinn Canyon Mts., 7000 ft., 2; White River Valley, 14 to 15 mi. SW Sunnyside, 5800 ft., 4; Grant Mts., 19 3/5 mi. WSW Sunnyside, 1; Big Creek, Quinn Canyon Mts., 5700 ft., 1; Garden Valley, 8½ mi. NE Sharp, 4; Old Mill, N end Reveille Valley, 6200 ft., 1; Breen Creek, Kawich Range, 7000 ft., 2; Kawich Mts., 2 4/5 mi. E Silverbow, 7300 ft., 1; Kawich Mts., 2 mi. S Silverbow, 6400 ft., 1; Cactus Spring, Cactus Range, 6500 ft., 1; Cactus Range, 1 mi. SW Cactus Spring, 1; 7 mi. E Cliff Spring, 5900 ft., 2; Belted Range, 3 mi. N Indian Spring, 6700 ft., 1; Belted Range, 2 mi. NW Indian Spring, 6350 ft., 1; Indian Spring, Belted Range, 7450 ft., 1; 2 mi. SE Oak Spring, 5500 ft., 2; 2 mi. S Oak Spring, 5700 ft., 3; 5 mi. E and 1 mi. N Grapevine Peak, 5500 ft., 7; 8 mi. E Grapevine Peak, 5000 ft., 1; 2½ mi. E and 1 mi. S Grapevine Peak, 6700–7000 ft., 12; Amargosa River, 3 to 4 mi. NE Beatty, 3400–3500 ft., 6; 3½ mi. N Pahrump Ranch, 2667 ft., 1 (D. R. Dickey Coll.); Pahrump Ranch, 2667 ft., 1 (D. R. Dickey Coll.). *Elko Co.*: Cedar Creek, 10 mi. NE San Jacinto, 6000 ft., 1; Goose Creek, 2 mi. W Utah boundary, 5000 ft., 3; Tecoma, 4900 ft., 2; Cobre, 6100 ft., 2; 2 mi. SW Cobre, 3; Pilot Peak, ½ mi. W Debbs Creek, 6000 ft., 5; 8 mi. S Wendover, 4700 ft., 9. *White Pine Co.*: Cherry Creek, 6800 ft., 1; 3 mi. W Smith Creek Cave, Mt. Moriah, 6500 ft., 1; 2 mi. W Smith Creek Cave, Mt. Moriah, 6300 ft., 6; Deadman Creek, Mt. Moriah, 6700 ft., 2; near [= within ¼ mile of] Smith

Creek Cave, Mt. Moriah, 5800 ft., 10; 2 mi. E Smith Creek Cave, Mt. Moriah, 1; Halstead Creek, 1 mi. W Illipah, 6200 ft., 1; Hendry Creek, 1½ mi. E Mt. Moriah, 9100 ft., 1; Hendry Creek, 8 mi. SE Mt. Moriah, 6200 ft., 2; Cleve Creek, Shell Creek Range, 6900 ft., 1; 2½ mi. SW Hamilton, 8600 ft., 1; 2 mi. W Baker, 1; Willard Creek, Spring Valley, 7150 ft., 2; Baker Creek, 6600–8500 ft., 22; Water Canyon, 8 mi. N Lund, 5. *Lincoln Co.*: Latitude 38° 17', ¼ mi. W Utah boundary, 7300 ft., 1; Eagle Valley, 3½ mi. N Ursine, 5600 ft., 3; 2 mi. S Pioche, 6000 ft., 1; Panaca, 4700 ft., 1; 11 mi. E Panaca, 6500 ft., 11; E slope Irish Mtn., 6900–7800 ft., 4; 16 mi. W Caliente, 5000 ft., 1; Pahranagat Valley (from Crystal Spring, 9 1/5 mi. NW, 1; 4 mi. NE, 4300 ft., 1; 1½ mi. NE, 4100 ft., 1; 1 2/5 mi. W, 2; Crystal Spring itself, 4000 ft., 1; 2 mi. E, 5000 ft., 1; 4 mi. E, 4300 ft., 1; 1 mi. S, 4000 ft., 1), 9; Meadow Valley Wash, 7 mi. S Caliente, 4500 and 4975 ft., 2; 9 mi. W Groom Baldy, 5500 ft., 1; 16 mi. E Groom Baldy, 4600 ft., 4; SW base Groom Baldy, 7200 ft., 3; Meadow Valley, 24 mi. S Caliente, 3000 ft., 2; 5½ mi. N Summit Spring, 4700 ft., 1; Coyote Spring, 2800 ft., 1. *Clark Co.* (unless otherwise noted, in D. R. Dickey Coll.): Mormon Wells, 6500 ft., 1; Hidden Forest, 8500 ft., 1; Indian Springs, 3120–3500 ft., 7; Muddy River, 1250 ft. (Lost City, 1; ½ mi. E St. Thomas, 1; ½ mi. SE St. Thomas, 1), 3; Corn Creek Station, 2840 ft., 5; ½ mi. W Wheeler Well, 6700 ft., 2; "Charleston Mts.," 3; "Charleston Mts.," 6000 ft., 10; W slope "Charleston Mts.," 9 mi. NE Pahrump, 4000 ft., 1; Kyle Canyon (6500 ft., 18; 4500 ft., 7), 25; 4 mi. NW Las Vegas, 2100 ft., 3; 3½ mi. NW Las Vegas, 2100 ft., 2; Trout Canyon, 6500 ft., 2; 2½ mi. N Hoover (Boulder) Dam Ferry, 2 (Mus. Vert. Zoöl.); Cedar Basin, 3500 ft., 21; N side Potosi Mtn., 7000 ft., 1 (Mus. Vert. Zoöl.).

Additional records: *Washoe Co.* (D. G. Nichols, MS); Hardscrabble Canyon, 4900–5000 ft.; Sutcliffe, 3700–4200 ft.; E shore Pyramid Lake, opposite Anaho Island, 4000 ft. *Storey Co.*: Logamacina (Carl P. Russell, MS). *Mineral Co.* (Goldman, 1910:78): Candelaria. *Lander Co.* (Goldman, 1910:78): Battle Mountain; Silver Creek. *Nye Co.* (Goldman, 1910:78): Peavine; 10 mi. N Ash Meadow. *Clark Co.* (Goldman, 1910:78): Bunkerville.

Neotoma lepida grinnelli Hall
Desert Wood Rat

Neotoma lepida grinnelli Hall, Univ. California Publ. Zoöl., 46:369, July 3, 1942. Type from Colorado River, 20 miles above (by river, but about 12½ miles north by air line) Picacho, Imperial County, California.

Distribution.—Southern Clark County. See figure 370, *a*.

Remarks.—Measurements of ten males and five females from Clark County south of the latitude of Searchlight are: ♂, 299 (278–319), ♀, 276 (255–287); 134 (114–149), 121 (114–130); 31.4 (30–34), 30.4 (29–31); weight, 131.3 (104.7–167.1), 99.0 (67.9–132.2) grams. Tail long, averaging more than 80 per cent of length of head and body; color pale; tympanic bullae well inflated. The animals from the southern part of Clark County have shorter tails than those from farther southward along the western side of the Colorado River in California, but, even so, are referable to *grinnelli* on basis of length of tail and also because of light color. Because the specimens recorded by Burt (1934:417) from farther north in Clark County were not available for study at the time of this writing, it is impossible precisely to determine the northern limit of range of *grinnelli*. The one adult available from 4½ miles west of Boulder City has a long tail and light color as in *grinnelli*.

From *lepida*, this race differs in actually longer tail, smaller average size of most other parts measured, and slightly lighter colored upper parts. From *monstrabilis*, the race to the eastward along the north side of the Colorado River, *grinnelli* differs in longer tail and grayer (less buffy) color. From *devia*, the race to the eastward in Arizona, south of the Colorado River, *grinnelli* differs in longer tail, lighter color, and shorter interparietal. From *felipensis*, the race in northeastern Lower California, Mexico, *grinnelli* differs in shorter hind foot and ear, slightly darker coloration on the average, and narrower rostrum. *N. l. felipensis* averages larger than *grinnelli* in most parts measured and also it has a relatively shorter tail than specimens from the southern part of the range of *grinnelli*.

Records of occurrence.—Specimens examined, 25, as follows: *Clark Co.*: 4½ mi. W Boulder City, 2600 ft., 1; Colorado River, 14 mi. E Searchlight, Jap Ranch, 500 ft., 4; 9 mi. W and 5½ mi. S Searchlight, 4300 ft., 3; 8 mi. S Dead Mtn., 2700 ft., 3; Hiko Spring, 8 mi. SSE Dead Mtn., 1900 ft., 5; 3 mi. SW Hiko Spring, 2400 ft., 4; Colorado River, ½ mi. N Calif.-Nev. Monument, 500 ft., 5.

Neotoma cinerea
Bushy-tailed Wood Rat

Three subspecies of bushy-tailed wood rat occur in Nevada. The marked increase in size to the northward is continued well beyond the northern border of the state.

The total length in adults ranges from 300 to 500 millimeters; length of tail amounts to about three-fourths of length of head and body; foot soles naked as far posteriorly as posterior tubercle; ears thinly haired and projecting prominently beyond fur, and length from notch about a fourth less than length of hind foot; large dermal gland, which secretes distinctive odor, on middle of abdomen; color pattern and general color as described for *Neotoma lepida;* hair on back 20 to 27 mm. long, and 10 to 14 mm. long on underparts; hairs on sides of tail attain a maximum length of 30 mm.; first cheek tooth only slightly wider than last tooth; medial side of first cheek tooth with two re-entrant angles; sphenopalatine vacuities closed in Nevadan animals.

The bushy-tailed wood rat is, in fact, Boreal in habitat preference, and complements in range the Sonoran species, *Neotoma lepida.* A detailed distribution map would show that *cinerea* occupied the Boreal zones and some parts of the Transition Life-zone. To this distribution for *cinerea* there would have to be added the two occurrences at uncommonly low elevations, at Smoke Creek and along the Carson River. At each of these two places in the Upper Sonoran Life-zone, near the edge of the water in the dense shade of deciduous trees, there is a habitat cool enough to permit the rats to live below their normal life-zone. Altitudinally, *cinerea* occurs from as high as timber line (about 11,500 feet) on Wheeler Peak down to 3900 feet at Smoke Creek. At several places, ordinarily where a trap line crossed a canyon, both *N. cinerea* and *N. lepida* were caught within a few yards, or even a few feet, of one another. This was true, for example, on Baker Creek in the Snake Mountains, where a vertical north-facing cliff more than a hundred feet high provided suitable habitat for *cinerea*, whereas on the south-facing, piñon-covered slope a few yards away, *lepida* occurred to the exclusion of *cinerea.*

Pack rat and trade rat, names given to all members of the genus, in Nevada are applied more often to *cinerea* than to *lepida.* *N. cinerea* carries sticks, small rocks, pieces of metal, and almost all objects of a suitable size to its home. It is supposed that when one of these rats carrying an object of its fancy comes to another more attractive object, it drops the first and continues on its way with the second. If the second object be the watch of a camper, who in the morning finds a piece of old bone where the watch lay when the camper went to sleep the evening before, he will think the name trade rat appropriate. The experienced camper will not ordinarily leave his watch or other small object of value thus exposed, but if the watch is lost in such a situation, the camper will do well to search the vicinity carefully for the piles of debris accumulated by pack rats. In one of these there is good chance of finding the watch. Indeed, the watch may be easily found because objects last gathered by the rats most often are placed on the very top of the pile.

Debris often is piled up, to form a "house," at the entrance to a crevice or burrow inhabited by one of these rats. So far as I have observed, in Nevada this species of rat only rarely builds nests in the houses which it constructs. I have seen only one such house. That was in northwestern Nevada in the forks of a large juniper tree. Probably rats in this area, like those in near-by parts of California (see Grinnell, Dixon, and Linsdale, 1930:519), construct houses in trees more commonly than do populations to the southeast. Houses in trees have been found, however, in northeastern Nevada. Relative to the animals in the Ruby Mountains, Borell and Ellis (1934a:31) write essentially as follows: Their houses were found mainly in caves and crevices in rimrock and cliffs. These houses were bulky and were composed mainly of sticks, but occasionally a few weathered bones, bits of bark, green leaves, and other debris were used. A few nests of a different type of construction, in that they were not enclosed in a rat house, were found in mines and deserted buildings. These nests were small, with outside diameters of 8 to 10 inches, and were composed of the bark of sagebrush, cotton, or strips of burlap. One house in the open was 12 feet above the ground in a juniper tree which grew in a mixed stand of juniper and piñon on a dry slope in Overland Pass. Another house at the edge of Willow Creek was built on the horizontal branches of a large willow tree. The tree was entirely surrounded by a dense thicket of willow, aspen, and chokecherry, with an undergrowth of nettle, aconite, bluebell, and wild rose. This house was 10 feet above the ground, and in order to reach it the wood rat had to climb for a distance of 20 feet along sloping branches. The main part of the house, which was 3 feet in diameter at the base and 2 feet high, was composed of short, dry sticks, with pieces of freshly cut chokecherry, bluebell, and nettle scattered over the top. Within the pile was a cavity 12 inches in diameter in which the nest, 6 inches in diameter and entirely composed of dry fibers of willow bark, was situated. Two hundred yards away was another house, 3 feet high, built on the wet ground at the edge of the creek among small willow trees. Another instance of houses in trees in western Nevada was noted (Alcorn, MS) on January 25, 1938. This was 1 mile east of Weeks, along the Carson River, which at that time was overflowing its banks. Large cottonwood trees supported these houses, which were in the crotches of the three or four main trunks forking at 4 to 5 feet above the ground; they were made of sticks and were 2 to 4 feet high. All these houses were above the highest level reached that season by the water, but for several weeks before Alcorn's visit the flood had covered the ground and isolated the trees one from another, except as the limbs touched. Branches of bushes of *Sarcobatus*, which had been used in making the houses, had the bark eaten off, suggesting that the rats were short of food. Wood rats that Alcorn dislodged from the nests in these houses showed real arboreal ability in jumping from one limb to another. One rat that was dislodged from its house escaped into a woodpecker hole 25 feet above the ground.

In Nevada, caves and mine tunnels are favorite places for building nests, and even deserted buildings are used by the rats for this purpose. A nest in one of these places ordinarily is cup-shaped—open at the top—and of a size large enough to accommodate the rat's body. About midday on July 30, 1930, at 8100 feet elevation on Cleve Creek, I pushed open the door of a deserted cabin and saw a female, heavy with embryos, leave her open nest and go to a hole through the wall. Closing the door, I walked around the outside of the cabin and through a window observed the rat for several minutes. She was lying on her side in the nest, but almost immediately got up, went about 5 feet from it, voided body excrements, returned to the nest, and lay down as before. Within a few seconds she got up and reached out of the nest to nibble at some withered *Sambuchus* berries (green), then got out of the nest, went over to a pile of fresh *Sambuchus* berries (all these in panicles), grasped a bunch in her teeth, transferred it to the pile of withered food, and then with the hind part of her body in the nest and the forepart out nibbled at the berries.

This behavior verified a suspicion of mine that the rats keep a supply of green food near enough to these open nests to permit them to eat at all times.

In another cabin we examined the urine that was being expelled by a rat in the roof and found it to be of the consistency of warm molasses and slightly brownish in color. On the sides of some caves in the arid country of Nevada the urine thus expelled at any one of several particular places by rats over a period of many years accumulates to a thickness of several inches, hardens, and becomes semitransparent. Not infrequently this hardened residue is mistaken for a mineral.

Secondary sexual variation is marked in this species and is of greater degree in the northern populations, where the average size is greater than in the southern populations. In every instance females are smaller than males. For example, in populations from the three areas, Ruby Mountains, Snake Mountains, and Charleston Peak, males are larger than females, in total length, to the extent of 15, 6, and 5 per cent, respectively; in length of tail, 14, 4, and 2 per cent; and in basilar length and zygomatic breadth, 10, 5, and 8 per cent.

Of 32 sexually mature females, 5 were pregnant. One female had 3 embryos, each of 2 others had 4, and 2 more had 5. By months, these females were distributed as follows: April, 2 (0 pregnant); June, 15 (4 pregnant); July, 11 (1); August, 4 (0). Two pregnant females from Clark County are recorded by Burt (1934:418) as having 5 and 3 embryos. The average number of embryos would appear to be about 4 and the extremes 3 and 5. In the mountains of Clark County, Burt (*loc. cit.*) took half-grown young as early as May 20 and thought that the breeding season lasts for "most of the summer months." In

Elko County, Borell and Ellis (1934a) similarly found half-grown young as early as May and as late as August.

Neotoma cinerea alticola Hooper
Bushy-tailed Wood Rat

Neotoma cinerea alticola Hooper, Univ. California Publ. Zoöl., 42:409, May 17, 1940. Type from Parker Creek [= Shields Creek, U. S. Forest Service map, edition of 1932], 5500 feet, Warner Mountains, Modoc County, California.
Neotoma cinerea occidentalis, Goldman, N. Amer. Fauna, 31:101, October 19, 1910, part; Taylor, Univ. California Publ. Zoöl., 7:249, June 24, 1911.
Neotoma cinerea cinerea, Goldman, N. Amer. Fauna, 31:95, October 19, 1910, part; Borell and Ellis, Journ. Mamm., 15:31, February 15, 1934.

Distribution.—Northern Nevada south to White Pine County and Lake Tahoe. See figure 370, *b*.

Remarks.—Measurements of a male and four females from Smoke Creek are: ♂, 445, ♀, 390 (384–403); 185, 163 (151–171); 45, 44.0 (40–46); weight, 584.7, 353.0 (323.5–369.8) grams.

Size large; color dark; upper parts dark brownish with considerable black; skull with sphenopalatine vacuities closed.

In his revision of the wood rats, Goldman (1910) referred the specimens here called *alticola* to the races *occidentalis* and *cinerea*. When Hooper (1940:409) named *alticola* he commented upon the specimens from the Ruby Mountains which resembled *alticola* in size and cranial proportions, but referred the animals to *acraia* because of their lighter color. My own review of the specimens leads me to place them in the race *alticola*. This is because the similarity in size and in proportions of the skull has greater weight with me than the slight difference in color.

Records of occurrence.—Specimens examined, 57, as follows: *Washoe Co.:* 2 mi. W Vya, 6200 and 6500 ft., 2; Smoke Creek, 9 mi. E Calif. boundary, 3900 ft., 13; Horse Canyon, Pahrum Peak, 5800 ft., 2. *Humboldt Co.:* Alder Creek, Pine Forest Mts., 5000 ft., 1; 13 to 14 mi. N Paradise Valley, 6400–7000 ft., 3; Leonard Creek, Pine Forest Mts., 6500 ft., 1; Hansen Canyon, Paradise Valley, 1; 18 mi. NE Iron Point, 4600 ft., 2. *Eureka Co.:* Evans, 1. *Elko Co.* (unless otherwise noted, in coll. of Ralph Ellis): 13 mi. SSW Whiterock, 5600 ft., 2 (Mus. Vert. Zoöl.); head of Ackler Creek, 6800 ft., 1; Steels Creek, 7000 ft., 2; South Fork of Long Creek, 7830 ft., 3; Harrison Pass R. S., Green Mtn. Canyon, 6050 ft., 2; W side Ruby Lake, 6 mi. N White Pine Co. line, 6200 ft., 1; W side Ruby Lake, 3 mi. N White Pine Co. line, 6200 ft., 16. *White Pine Co.:* Willow Creek, Ruby Mts., 2 mi. S Elko Co. line, 6500 ft., 4 (3 in coll. of Ralph Ellis).

Additional records: *Washoe Co.* (Carl P. Russell, MS): Truckee Canyon, 15 mi. E Reno; Hunters Creek. *Pershing Co.:* Granite Creek (Goldman, 1910:102). *Elko Co.* (Goldman, 1910:102): Mountain City; Bull Run Mountains.

Neotoma cinerea acraia (Elliot)
Bushy-tailed Wood Rat

Teonoma cinerea acraia Elliot, Field Columb. Mus., zoöl. ser., 3:247, December, 1903. Type from Hot Springs, Long Canyon, Mount Whitney, Inyo County, California.
Neotoma cinerea acraia, Hooper, Univ. California Publ. Zoöl., 42:413, May 17, 1940. Burt, Trans. San Diego Soc. Nat. Hist., 7:418, May 31, 1934, part.
Neotoma cinerea, Linsdale, Amer. Midland Nat., 19:191, January, 1938.
Neotoma cinerea cinerea, Goldman, N. Amer. Fauna, 31:95, October 19, 1910, part.

Distribution.—From Sierra Nevada south of Lake Tahoe eastward across central Nevada; in eastern part of state from northeastern corner south to Sheep Mountains. See figure 370, *b*.

Remarks.—Measurements of twelve males and fifteen females from the Snake Mountains, White Pine County, are: ♂, 380 (350–427), ♀, 359 (336–386); 158 (140–185), 152 (140–163); 42.3 (40–44), 40.5 (38–43); weight, 317.6 (257.2–437.0), 274.0 (218.0–317.7) grams.

Size medium; color grayish; skull with sphenopalatine vacuities closed.

In his revision of the wood rats, Goldman (1910) referred the specimens here called *acraia* to the race *cinerea*. When Hooper (1940:414) studied several races of the species

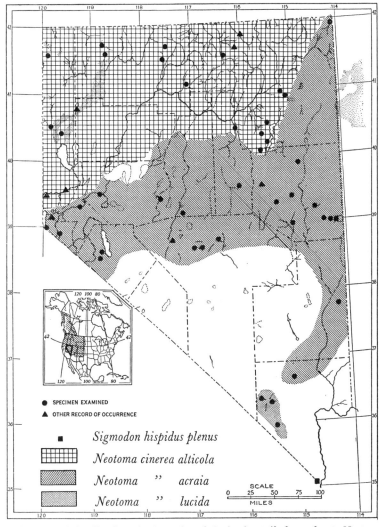

Fig. 370, *b*. Distribution of subspecies of the bushy-tailed wood rat, *Neotoma cinerea*, and cotton rat, *Sigmodon hispidus*, with insert showing range of the bushy-tailed wood rat.

cinerea, he followed Burt in reviving Elliot's name *acraia* and in applying it to the Nevadan animals, which name Goldman earlier had placed under *cinerea*. Burt and Hooper each considered Goldman's name *lucida* (see account of the following treated subspecies) as synonymous with *acraia*.

N. c. acraia is intermediate in size and color, as it is geographically, between *alticola* and *lucida*. The color is about the same as in *N. c. cinerea*, the race to the northeast.

Intergradation with *alticola* is shown by specimens from along the Carson River and by those from the Ruby Mountains, which are referred to *alticola*. Specimens from Hidden Forest in the Sheep Mountains are intermediate toward *lucida*. The size is as in *lucida*, but the color is markedly different, being as in *acraia*. From topotypes of *lucida*, these animals from the Sheep Mountains differ in being grayer (less ochraceous), especially on the sides, but also over all the upper parts. The top of the tail is darker than in *lucida*.

Records of occurrence.—Specimens examined, 81, as follows: *Douglas Co.*: 2 mi. S Zephyr Cove, 1; Carson River, 4900 ft., 5 mi. SE Minden, 1. *Lyon Co.*: Carson River, 5 mi. ENE Weeks, 1; Carson River, 1 mi. E Weeks, 4200 ft., 1. *Churchill Co.*: 5 mi. W Fallon, 1. *Mineral Co.*: Cottonwood Creek, Mt. Grant, 7400 and 7900 ft., 2; Lapon Canyon, Mt. Grant, 8900 ft., 2. *Lander Co.*: Smiths Creek, 6800 and 7700 ft., 2; Kingston R. S., 7500 ft., 3; Kingston Creek, 7000–7100 ft., 4. *Eureka Co.*: 8 mi. W Eureka, 1. *Nye Co.*: Greenmonster Canyon, Monitor Range, 7500 and 8200 ft., 2; Toquima Range, 1 mi. E Jefferson, 7600 ft., 1; Monitor Valley, 9 mi. E Toquima Peak, 7000 ft., 1. *Elko Co.*: Goose Creek, 2 mi. W Utah boundary, 5000 ft., 5. *White Pine Co.*: Cherry Creek, 6800 ft., 4; Gleason Creek, 7300 ft., 4; Halstead Creek, 1 mi. W Illipah, 6200 ft., 1; Cleve Creek, Shell Creek Range, 8100–9900 ft., 5; Snake Mts., ¾ mi. SE Stella Lake, 10,800 ft., 1; Willard Creek, Spring Valley, 7700 ft., 1; mouth of Pole Canyon, south side Baker Creek, Snake Mts., 7300–7500 ft., 8; Baker Creek, 7200–8000 ft., 26; Water Canyon, 8 mi. N Lund, 2. *Lincoln Co.*: 11 mi. E Panaca, 6700 ft., 1. *Clark Co.*: Hidden Forest, 8500 ft., Sheep Mts., 8 (D. R. Dickey Coll.).

Additional records: *Ormsby Co.*: Carson City (Goldman, 1910:98). *Nye Co.*: head of Reese River (Goldman, 1910:102). *White Pine Co.*: Newark Valley, 20 mi. E Eureka (Goldman, 1910:98).

Neotoma cinerea lucida Goldman
Bushy-tailed Wood Rat

Neotoma cinerea lucida Goldman, Proc. Biol. Soc. Washington, 30:107, May 23, 1917. Type from Charleston Peak, Clark County, Nevada.

Neotoma cinerea acraia, Burt, Trans. San Diego Soc. Nat. Hist., 7:418, May 31, 1934, part; Hooper, Univ. California Publ. Zoöl., 42:413, May 17, 1940.

Distribution.—Spring Mountains in Clark County from Charleston Peak south to Potosi Mountain. See figure 370, *b*.

Remarks.—Measurements of eight of each sex from Charleston Peak are: ♂, 356 (310–385), ♀, 339 (320–360); 148 (130–160), 145 (130–155); 41.4 (39–44), 38.3 (36–40); weight not available.

Size small; color pale, upper parts Light Ochraceous Buff finely lined with blackish; skull with sphenopalatine vacuities closed. Comparison with *acraia* is made in the account of that form.

When Goldman (1910) revised the wood rats he had no specimens from within the geographic range of *lucida*. Specimens subsequently acquired were by him (1917:111) named *N. c. lucida*. Burt in 1934 (p. 418) studied more specimens from Charleston Peak than were available to Goldman and concluded that the name *Teonoma cinerea acraia* Elliot, based on specimens from the southern Sierra Nevada, should be used for specimens from Charleston Peak as well as specimens from the southern Sierra Nevada. Hooper, in his study (1940) of more northwestern populations of *Neotoma cinerea*, included a list of more eastern and southern races arranged according to the findings of those who last reported upon them. Therefore, he followed Burt (*loc. cit.*) in placing *lucida* as a synonym of *acraia*. In the autumn of 1940 I was able to examine the specimens from Charleston Peak in the collection of the late Donald R. Dickey. In these the size is less and the color more ochraceous than in more northern populations, which variations lead me to treat *lucida* as a race distinct from *acraia*.

Records of occurrence.—Specimens examined, 49, as follows: *Clark Co.* (unless otherwise noted, in D. R. Dickey Coll.): Clark Canyon, 8000 ft., 3; W side Charleston Peak, 1; Charleston Peak, 11,800 ft., 1; Charleston Peak, 10,000 ft., 9; E slope Charleston Peak, 11,800 ft., 6; Kyle Canyon, Charleston Park, 8000 ft., 21; Kyle Canyon, 6500 ft., 6; N side Potosi Mtn., 7000 ft., 2 (Mus. Vert. Zoöl.).

TABLE 18

CRANIAL MEASUREMENTS (IN MILLIMETERS) OF NEOTOMA

Name and locality	Number of individuals averaged	Sex	Basilar length	Zygomatic breadth	Interorbital breadth	Length of nasals	Length of incisive foramina	Length of palatal bridge	Alveolar length of upper tooth row
Neotoma lepida nevadensis Northern Washoe and Humboldt counties......	9 av.	♂	32.0	20.2	5.0	15.0	8.2	6.8	8.4
	min.		31.2	19.7	4.6	13.8	7.7	6.5	8.2
	max.		33.8	21.3	5.2	16.8	9.1	7.2	8.7
	10 av.	♀	32.7	20.4	5.1	15.0	8.4	6.7	8.2
	min.		29.9	18.9	4.9	13.4	7.5	6.2	8.0
	max.		35.3	21.4	5.6	15.9	9.5	7.2	8.8
Neotoma lepida lepida Great Smoky Valley, Nye Co....................	10 av.	♂	34.3	21.3	5.2	15.8	8.8	7.0	8.1
	min.		33.0	20.2	5.0	14.8	8.1	6.7	7.8
	max.		36.0	22.2	5.4	17.4	9.5	7.5	8.2
	6 av.	♀	33.4	20.8	5.1	15.3	8.5	7.2	8.0
	min.		32.7	20.1	4.7	14.7	8.2	6.8	7.8
	max.		34.3	21.5	5.3	15.7	8.7	7.5	8.2
Neotoma lepida grinnelli Clark Co., S of latitude of Searchlight.............	10 av.	♂	32.7	20.6	5.1	15.1	8.4	6.8	7.9
	min.		30.9	19.2	4.8	14.3	7.8	6.4	7.7
	max.		34.6	21.9	5.3	16.0	8.9	7.6	8.5
	5 av.	♀	31.1	19.8	5.0	14.5	8.0	6.7	8.0
	min.		29.6	17.9	4.9	13.6	7.3	6.4	7.6
	max.		32.8	21.1	5.1	15.2	8.7	7.2	8.2
Neotoma cinerea alticola Smoke Creek.............	1	♂	50.5	30.4	6.8	23.5	13.6	10.3	10.6
	4 av.	♀	44.3	26.7	5.9	20.2	12.7	9.0	10.5
	min.		44.0	26.0	5.6	19.7	12.1	8.3	9.9
	max.		44.8	27.2	6.1	20.2	13.1	9.5	10.7
Neotoma cinerea acraia Snake Mountains..........	12 av.	♂	42.6	26.4	5.9	19.5	11.5	9.1	9.9
	min.		39.5	24.0	5.5	17.6	10.9	8.2	9.4
	max.		48.0	28.9	6.3	22.2	12.6	10.4	10.3
	15 av.	♀	40.6	25.2	5.9	18.6	11.3	9.0	9.6
	min.		39.1	24.3	5.5	17.5	10.7	7.8	9.1
	max.		41.9	26.4	6.3	20.1	11.6	9.1	9.9
Neotoma cinerea lucida Charleston Peak..........	8* av.	♂	42.6	26.0	5.8	19.3	11.3	8.9	9.6
	min.		40.6	25.0	5.4	18.6	10.4	8.5	9.1
	max.		44.6	26.8	6.0	20.4	12.3	9.8	10.4
	8* av.	♀	39.5	24.4	5.8	18.0	10.8	8.2	9.4
	min.		38.1	23.3	5.4	17.5	10.0	7.8	9.1
	max.		42.6	25.0	6.0	18.6	11.9	8.6	10.8

* D. R. Dickey Collection.

Genus **Microtus** Schrank
Meadow Mice

Meadow mice have long, loose pelage, a relatively short tail, short rounded ears nearly concealed by the pelage, smooth (not grooved) anterior faces on the incisor teeth, and hypsodont molar teeth the flat crowns of which are made up of a series of loops and triangles of enamel surrounding areas of dentine. The loops and triangles are separated by re-entrant angles. In Nevadan species m3 has only three closed loops. The dental formula is i. $\frac{1}{1}$, c. $\frac{0}{0}$, p. $\frac{0}{0}$, m. $\frac{3}{3}$.

Meadow mice are characteristically Boreal in distribution. They do not hibernate, but remain active aboveground all year. They frequent places where the vegetation is sufficient to provide protective cover. Runways on top of the ground beneath the cover of vegetation are supplemented by subsurface burrows. The nests are of dry grass and other plant fibers, and are placed below ground, not on the surface. The runways, particularly those on top of the ground, are considerably used by other rodents, especially *Reithrodontomys* and *Peromyscus*. The food in summer is almost entirely green vegetation; in winter, bark, for one thing, is eaten. Relatively large-sized litters, up to eight embryos, have been recorded for each Nevadan species, and the young are born after a gestation period of about 21 days. More than one litter per year is produced, and some females become sexually mature when only 3 weeks old.

Microtus montanus
Montane Meadow Mouse

This species, with six races in Nevada, may be described as: size average for the genus; tail averages 23 to 28 per cent of total length; color dark, resulting from much blackish and reddish in the pelage of most races; skull rugose, heavily ridged in adults, with the incisive foramina constricted posteriorly. Considerable geographic variation exists, and from north to south there is a gradient, or cline. Animals from the northeastern corner of the state have a maximum weight of less than 50 grams, hind foot 19 mm. long, and gray coat, in contrast to a weight of 85 grams, hind foot of 24 mm., and black coat in animals from Ash Meadows, the southernmost population in the state. Between these extremes there are several intermediate stages in *fucosus* and in populations of the race *micropus*.

M. montanus ranges, geographically, as opposed to zonally, over about the same part of the state as does *Microtus longicaudus*, and in addition occurs at two places farther south, namely, in Pahranagat Valley and at Ash Meadows. *M. montanus* occurs mainly in the Upper Sonoran Life-zone, whereas *M. longicaudus* lives mainly in the Boreal life-zones. Nevertheless, *M. montanus* (races *nevadensis* and *fucosus*) occur in the Lower Sonoran Life-zone, and some other populations, for example that at 8000 feet on Baker Creek, are within the Transition Life-zone. The altitudinal extremes recorded for Nevada are 2200 feet in Ash Meadows and 9500 feet on Mount Rose, at the northern end of Lake Tahoe. On Mount Rose, flora of the Upper Sonoran Life-zone extends up to 9500 feet in places, and it is there that *Microtus montanus* lives. The same was true of the top of Mount Grant, at the north end of Walker Lake. There, at 8900 feet, *M. montanus* was taken. Farther down on the slopes of

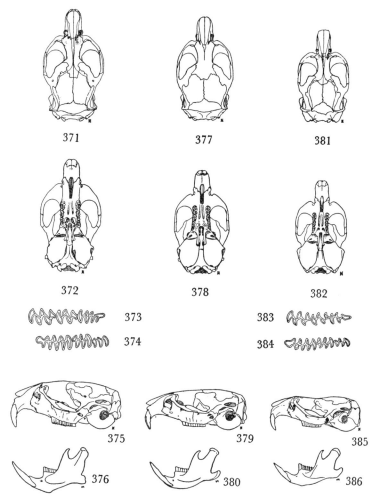

Figs. 371–386. Meadow mice and voles. All, ×1, except occlusal views of teeth (figs. 373, 374, 383, 384) which are ×3⅓.

Figs. 371–376. *Microtus montanus micropus*, Cleveland Ranch, no. 46288, ♂. Occlusal views of teeth (figs. 373, 374) are ×3⅓.
Figs. 377–380. *Microtus longicaudus latus*, Wisconsin Creek, 8500 feet, ♀.
Figs. 381–386. *Lagurus curtatus curtatus*, Chiatovich Creek, 8200 feet, no. 38731, ♂. Occlusal views of teeth (figs. 383, 384) are ×3⅓.

Mount Grant, particularly along the streams, Boreal conditions obtained; the life-zones here were reversed. This explains why, on Mount Grant, *M. montanus* was taken at the higher elevations and *M. longicaudus* at lower elevations. Normally, *montanus* is found in the valleys and *longicaudus* in the mountains.

Microtus montanus ordinarily lives in grass. In this it makes well-defined runways. Since green grass occurs only in moist areas, *montanus* is limited to marshy places, to the vicinities of springs or meadows, or to irrigated fields along the lower courses of streams that flow down from the mountains to the valleys. In the community pasture 7 miles southeast of Fallon, nevertheless, in November, 1939, Alcorn (MS) found that the mice preferred plantings of ladino clover and strawberry clover to meadow fescue as places in which to live. This pasture, not grazed by domestic livestock, had the three forage plants growing in pure stands in strips 30 feet wide and had been given equal amounts of irrigation after being planted at the same time on identical soils. Root stalks of "sour dock," when encountered by *Microtus* in their burrows, about 3 inches underground, had been eaten into at this place.

In the Ruby Mountains, Borell and Ellis (1934a:33) noted that in summer these mice were never captured more than a few feet from water, whereas in winter "their tunnels were found beneath three feet of snow and in some cases these tunnels led over areas which were too dry and open during the summer to be occupied by the species. On December 15, 1927, attention was attracted to an animal that was moving along beneath the snow and raising it to form a ridge or windrow, much as a mole does in soft ground. A quick grab into the moving snow, which was two inches deep, and slightly crusted, produced an adult female *Microtus montanus*. The ability of these mice to make tunnels beneath the snow enables them to forage above ground during the winter. We found that other mammals, such as *Sorex vagrans* and *Peromyscus maniculatus*, made use of *Microtus* tunnels beneath the snow."

Like other mammals of the Upper Sonoran Life-zone, *M. montanus* is subject to fluctuations in numbers, and once, in 1907–1908, in the irrigated area about Lovelock the mice became so abundant as to constitute a serious agricultural pest. Piper's (1909:5) report indicates that there were as many as 8,000 to 12,000 mice per acre. In the autumn of 1934, when I made special search for the mice in this area, no trace of their presence was found. Indication of fluctuation in numbers along the Walker River in the vicinity of Yerington was furnished by Alcorn's taking numerous specimens in the winter of 1939–1940, whereas search there by a party in 1934 yielded only one individual. Increase in numbers to the point where the mice do appreciable damage to crops in Nevada is rare. As already indicated, the areas in Nevada suitable for the mice are of limited extent. Also, in the Sonoran life-zones the huge increases in numbers, such as took place at Lovelock in 1907–1908, occur at wider-spaced and less-regular intervals than in the Boreal life-zones. When an increase does begin, it may be modified by the relatively great checking effect of natural enemies, especially carnivorous mammals and raptorial birds. This is because the population of predaceous vertebrates of a large area

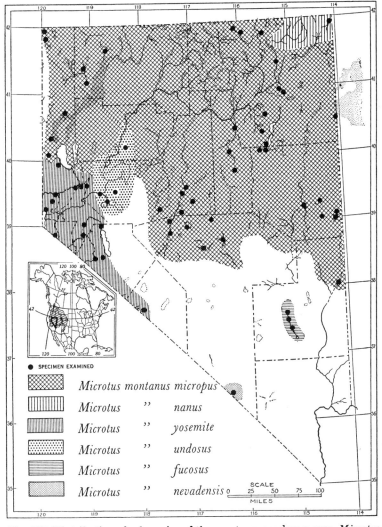

Fig. 387. Distribution of subspecies of the montane meadow mouse, *Microtus montanus*, with insert showing range of the species.

tend to concentrate in their feeding upon the small area occupied by the mice, if mice are abundant enough to make search by the flesh eaters worth while. In areas occupied by *montanus* I have seen coyotes searching for them. In Pahranagat Valley, Bond (1940:165) found that mice of this species comprised more than half (53 per cent) of 394 identified food items in the pellets of the horned owl.

Secondary sexual variation is of slight amount. Males average larger than females by a little more than 1 per cent in external measurements, 5 per cent in weight, and by about 1 per cent in measurements of length of the skull. Measurements of breadth of the skull reveal no difference between the two sexes in the twenty-five individuals of each sex measured, but the width of the auditory bullae appears to be slightly greater in females.

Record of pregnancy was kept for 146 sexually mature females. Of these, 54 contained embryos ranging in number from 2 to 8. The usual number was 5 or 6 and the average was 6.3. By months the females were taken as follows: April, 4 (3 pregnant); May, 48 (18); June, 7 (1); July, 51 (19); August, 23 (8); October, 7 (3); November, 6 (2).

Microtus montanus micropus Hall
Montane Meadow Mouse

Microtus montanus micropus Hall, Univ. California Publ. Zoöl., 40:417, October 25, 1935. Type from Cleveland Ranch, 6000 feet, Spring Valley, White Pine County, Nevada. Hall, Proc. Biol. Soc. Washington, 51:133, August 23, 1938.

Microtus montanus, Linsdale, Amer. Midland Nat., 19:192, January, 1938.

Microtus montanus montanus, Borell and Ellis, Journ. Mamm., 15:32, 73, February 15, 1934.

Distribution.—Northern part of state (the extreme northeastern corner excepted) south to Eagle Valley, Lincoln County; Monitor and Reese River valleys, Nye County; northern end of Virginia Mountains, Washoe County. See figure 387.

Remarks.—Measurements of five topotypes of each sex are: ♂, 172 (158–181), ♀, 162 (159–167); 43.4 (40–50), 41.8 (39–42); 21.4 (20–22), 21.0 (20.0–21.5); weight, 62.6 (60.3–64.5), 49.1 (45.1–55.2) grams.

Size large; tail relatively short, averaging 25 per cent of total length; hind foot small; color relatively blackish, with reduced amount of grayish and reddish; skull of medium size (condylobasal length averaging more than 27 mm.); bullae well inflated; occiput inclined anterodorsally, revealing condyles when skull is viewed from directly above.

From *yosemite*, this race differs in relatively as well as actually shorter tail, less reddish and, except in specimens from Millett, less grayish (therefore, more blackish) coloration, and markedly larger and more inflated tympanic bullae. From topotypes of *M. m. montanus* of north-central California, *micropus* differs in actually and relatively shorter tail and hind foot, less reddish coloration, skull averaging larger in every measurement taken, and more inflated tympanic bullae. From *nevadensis*, *micropus* differs in smaller size throughout, relatively longer tail, less blackish coloration, relatively greater length of nasals and breadth across mastoids, and less depressed rostrum. Comparisons with *fucosus* and *undosus* are made in the accounts of those forms.

Some variation exists between populations here referred to *micropus*. As compared with other specimens of *micropus*, those from 5 to 6 miles southeast of Millett, Great Smoky Valley, are characterized by gray color, a short narrow rostrum, and less heavily ridged skull. In these, the palate is longer, approaching that of *undosus*. Twenty-two specimens from Potts Ranger Station, 6650 feet elevation, Monitor Valley, have big tympanic bullae and short hind feet. Specimens from the Ruby Mountains of Elko and White Pine counties show, on the average, a great disparity between the condylobasal and occipitonasal lengths. Nine specimens from 20 miles south of Owyhee are smaller and grayer than topotypes. Specimens from the two localities last mentioned, along with some other populations mentioned in the account of *nanus*, are intergrades in various degrees between *nanus* and *micropus*.

When I first critically studied and reported (1935b:419) upon the Nevadan material of this species, one immature specimen from the Pine Forest Range and two of similar age from Deep Hole were referred to the race *yosemite*. Since then, two adults have become available from 4 miles southwest of Diessner and one from Round Hole. These show that the animals in northwestern Nevada approach *undosus* in shorter nasals and occipitonasal length (relative to the condylobasal length) and are intermediate in color between the reddish *yosemite*, on the one hand, and the blacker *micropus* and *undosus*, on the other. They agree with *micropus*, to which race they now here are referred, in shorter row of upper cheek teeth, greater mastoidal breadth, and much more inflated auditory bullae. More nearly intermediate still are specimens from the north base of the Virginia Mountains, but these, too, show greater resemblance to *micropus*.

The population from 3½ miles north of Eagle Valley in Lincoln County, although referred to *micropus*, in many features is intermediate between *micropus* and *fucosus*. Agreement with *fucosus* is shown in large hind foot, long nasals, and wide rostrum. Agreement with *micropus* is shown in lesser total length, relatively shorter tail, and lesser zygomatic breadth. The animals are intermediate in coloration, length of skull, palatilar length, and length of upper molars. The occipitonasal length averages more than the condylobasal length, whereas the reverse is true of all other populations of the species *montanus* studied by me.

Records of occurrence.—Specimens examined, 273, as follows: *Washoe Co.:* Barrel Spring, 5700 ft., 9½ mi. E and 3½ mi. N Ft. Bidwell, 4; 4 mi. SW Diessner, 5800 ft., 3; Deep Hole, 4000 ft., 2 (1 in U. S. Nat. Mus., Biol. Surv. Coll.); Round Hole, 3900 ft., 3; Cottonwood Cr., 4400 ft., Virginia Mts., 2; 4¾ mi. S Flanigan, 4200 ft., 1. *Humboldt Co.:* Pine Forest Range, 1 (U. S. Nat. Mus., Biol. Surv. Coll.); Soldier Meadows, 4600 ft., 2; Flowing Spring, 7 mi. E and 3½ mi. N Division Peak, 4200 ft., 1. *Lander Co.:* Reese River Valley, 7 mi. N Austin, 2; Malloy Ranch, 5 mi. W Austin, Reese River, 5500 ft., 8; Birch Creek, 7000 ft., 1; Campbell Creek Ranch, 5500 ft., 3; Kingston R. S., 7500 ft., 3; Kingston Canyon, 7000 ft., 2. *Eureka Co.:* Evans, 12; Winzell, 4; 4 mi. S Romano, Diamond Valley, 3. *Nye Co.:* Potts R. S., 6650 ft., Monitor Valley, 22; Dutch Flat School House, 6715 ft., Reese River, 2; 5 to 6 mi. SE Millett P. O. (Mitchell Field), 5500 ft., 23; Bells Ranch, 6890 ft., Reese River, 1; Fish Spring Valley, 6½ mi. N Fish Lake, 6000 ft., 10; Monitor Valley, 9 to 9¼ mi. E Toquima Peak, 7000 ft., 4. *Elko Co.:* 7 mi. NW Mountain City, Owyhee River, 1; Mountain City, 3 (U. S. Nat. Mus.); summit between heads of Copper and Coon creeks, Jarbidge Mts., 4 (coll. of Ralph Ellis); 20 mi. S Owyhee, 9; Marys River, 5800 ft., 22 mi. N Deeth, 10; head of Ackler Creek, 1 (coll. of Ralph Ellis); Steels Creek, 1 (coll. of Ralph Ellis); Three Lakes, 13 (coll. of Ralph Ellis); Salt Spring, 4200 ft., 1; Harrison Pass R. S., Green Mountain Canyon, 2 (coll. of Ralph Ellis); W side Ruby Lake, 3 mi. N Elko Co. line, 13 (coll. of Ralph Ellis). *White Pine Co.:* Willow Creek, 2 mi. S White Pine Co. line, 3; W side Ruby Lake, 3 mi. S White Pine Co. line, 5; Cleveland Ranch, 6000 ft., Spring Valley, 33; Steptoe Creek, 6400 ft., 5½ mi. SE Ely, 16; 1 mi. N Baker, 3; Baker, 5800 ft., 2; Baker Creek, 6600–8000 ft., 10; 7 mi. SW Osceola, 6100 ft., 2. *Lincoln Co.:* 3½ mi. N Eagle Valley, 5600 ft., 32.

Microtus montanus nanus (Merriam)
Montane Meadow Mouse

Arvicola (Mynomes) nanus Merriam, N. Amer. Fauna, 5:63, July 30, 1891. Type from Pahsimeroi Mountains, head of Pahsimeroi River, 9350 feet, Custer County, Idaho.
Microtus montanus nanus, Hall, Proc. Biol. Soc. Washington, 51:133, August 28, 1938.

Distribution.—Northeastern corner of state. See figure 387.

Remarks.—Measurements of seven males and five females from Goose Creek are: ♂, 162 (145–171), ♀, 160 (155–164); 41.1 (37–46), 38.8 (35–40); 19.6 (19–20), 19.0 (18–20); weight, 38.2 (32.9–48.5), 42.1 (41.1–43.9) grams. These specimens are slightly larger than typical *nanus* and are intergrades toward *micropus*.

Size small; tail short, averaging, in a series of twenty adult animals from near Pocatello, Idaho, 24 per cent of total length; hind foot short, 18.3 (17–20) in same series; color grayish, with relatively little blackish and especially little reddish; skull small; bullae well inflated.

From *micropus*, this race differs in lesser size, grayer (less blackish) color, and relatively larger auditory bullae.

The specimens from Goose Creek are intermediate between *nanus* and *micropus*. Employing topotypes of *micropus* and specimens of *nanus* from the vicinity of Pocatello, Idaho (for precise localities see Whitlow and Hall, 1933:266), it is seen that the animals from Goose Creek closely resemble *nanus* in light color, small size of body, and small size of most of the skull. In longer tail and hind foot, and in wider rostrum, the animals from Goose Creek are intermediate between *nanus* and *micropus*. Even so, when all characters are taken into account, the animals from Goose Creek are nearer *nanus*. Other specimens from northern Nevada, namely, series from Mountain City, 7 miles northwest of Mountain City, and 20 miles south of Owyhee, although almost as small as those from Goose Creek, average darker colored, and the sum total of their characters places them with *micropus*. Continuing southward in Nevada, additional specimens from 22 miles north of Deeth along Marys River and others from several localities farther southward in the Ruby Mountains (see Borell and Ellis, 1934a:32) exhibit a gradual transition from the small, gray-colored *nanus* to the larger, blackish-colored *micropus*.

Record of occurrence.—Specimens examined, 19, as follows: *Elko Co.*: Goose Creek, 5000 ft., 2 mi. W Utah boundary, 19.

Microtus montanus yosemite Grinnell
Montane Meadow Mouse

Microtus montanus yosemite Grinnell, Proc. Biol. Soc. Washington, 27:207, October 31, 1914. Type from Yosemite Valley, 4000 feet, Mariposa County, California. Hall, Univ. California Publ. Zoöl., 40:424, October 25, 1935.

Distribution.—West-central part of the state from Pyramid Lake south to Mount Grant and eastward along Truckee Canal at least to eastern border of Lyon County. See figure 387.

Remarks.—Measurements of four males and six females from 3½ mi. east of Reno are: ♂, 162 (150–190), ♀, 162 (144–175); 40.0 (35–50), 40.1 (37–46); 21.0 (20–22), 20.2 (19–21); weight not recorded. Measurements of five of each sex from the head of Lapon Canyon are: ♂, 175 (163–186), ♀, 171 (152–190); 44.8 (38–51), 43.8 (35–52); 20.6 (20–21), 20.6 (20–22); weight, 47.6 (40.0–58.6), 45.2 (39.2–47.5) grams.

Size medium; tail relatively long, averaging 28 per cent of total length; hind foot small; color relatively reddish, with some grayish, but no blackish; skull of medium size (condylobasal length averaging more than 27 mm.); bullae small and relatively uninflated.

The specimens from Mount Grant and from along the Walker River approach *micropus* rather than *yosemite* in relative shortness of tail, longer nasals, and less reddish coloration. The palate is relatively long, as in *yosemite*, but *undosus* also has a long palate, which feature, as well as the larger tympanic bullae in the animals from along the Walker River, may represent intergradation with *undosus*. The animals from Mount Grant have smaller tympanic bullae essentially of the size found in typical *yosemite*.

The specimens from Fish Lake, Esmeralda County, are geographically intermediate between the three subspecies, *nevadensis* and *yosemite*, and *dutcheri*, the race to the southwest in California. They differ from *dutcheri* in being gray rather than reddish below. Also, the dorsal outline of the skull in longitudinal axis is not evenly convex, the bullae are larger, and the skull is more heavily ridged. The reddish dorsal coloration is nearest to that of *dutcheri*. From *nevadensis*, the animals obtained at Fish Lake differ in that they average smaller in all measurements taken except length of tail, which is greater. The skulls differ in that the nasals are less expanded anteriorly; also, the rostrum is not depressed below the plane of the frontals, although there is a suggestion of this depression, which is lacking in *dutcheri* and in *yosemite*. In color, they average more reddish than *nevadensis*, but resemble *nevadensis* in being blackish rather than grayish above.

The animals from Fish Lake are more reddish above than *yosemite*, have relatively and actually shorter tails, and slightly more heavily ridged skulls, which are a little higher at the junction of the nasals and frontals. They agree with *yosemite* in the gray ventral coloration, in general size, and in degree of inflation of the tympanic bullae. Considering the situation from all angles, the specimens from Fish Lake seem best placed with *yosemite*, although they do approach each of the two geographically adjacent subspecies, *nevadensis* and *dutcheri*.

Records of occurrence.—Specimens examined, 121, as follows: *Washoe Co.:* Pyramid Lake, 2 mi. W Sutcliffe, 8; S side Truckee River, 3 mi. E Reno, 12; 7 mi. S Reno, 10 (7 in coll. of Ralph Ellis); ½ mi. S Mt. Rose, 9500 ft., 4; 3 mi. SSW Mt. Rose, 9000 ft., 2; 3 mi. S Mt. Rose (8600 ft., 3; 8500 ft., 1), 4; Incline Creek, 7100 ft., 1. *Douglas Co.:* Carson River, 4900 ft., 5 mi. SE Minden, 1. *Storey Co.:* Gilpin Spillway, Truckee Canal, 3 mi. WSW Wadsworth, 1. *Lyon Co.:* 2 mi. E Fernley, 3; 2½ mi. W Hazen, Truckee Canal, 1; 2 mi. N Yerington, 4350 ft., 3; West Walker River, 6 mi. S Yerington, 4500 ft., 1. *Mineral Co.:* Schurz Indian dam, Walker River, 4300 ft., 2; Lapon Canyon, 8800–8900 ft., Mt. Grant, 25; N fork of Cat Creek, 8800 ft., Mt. Grant, 5; ¼ mi. E Wichman, 5000 ft., 1 (coll of D. V. Hemphill). *Esmeralda Co.:* Fish Lake, 4800 ft., 37.

Microtus montanus undosus Hall
Montane Meadow Mouse

Microtus montanus undosus Hall, Univ. California Publ. Zoöl., 40:420, October 25, 1935. Type from Lovelock, Pershing County, Nevada.

Distribution.—Humboldt and Carson sinks and lower reaches of Humboldt River. See figure 387.

Remarks.—Measurements of ten males and two females from Lovelock are: ♂, 187 (165–220), ♀, 178, 162; 53 (46–64), 45, 40; 24.8 (24–27), 22, 23; weight of a subadult of each sex from 10 mi. SSE Fallon, ♂, 49.6, ♀, 49.2 grams.

Size large; tail long, averaging, in a series of thirteen adult animals, 28 (23–31) per cent of total length; hind foot long; color relatively blackish, with some reddish; skull large; nasals relatively short; incisors and premaxillae extending appreciably beyond nasals; bullae well inflated; palate long; upper tooth rows long.

From topotypes of *micropus*, this race differs in: maximum and average size greater; tail actually and relatively longer; hind foot longer; coloration slightly more reddish; skull larger and more heavily ridged; brain case relatively longer; tympanic bullae actually, although not relatively, larger; upper incisors projecting farther beyond nasals (occipitonasal length averaging only 95.6 rather than 98 per cent of condylobasal length); upper tooth rows actually and relatively longer; palatilar length averaging 55 rather than 53.2 per cent of the condylobasal length. From *yosemite*, *undosus* differs in greater maximum and average size, longer hind foot, and in being more nearly black. The skull differs in the same features as mentioned in the comparison with *micropus*, except that, relatively, the tympanic bullae are larger in *undosus* and the palatilar lengths are about the same. From *fucosus*, *undosus* differs in: maximum and average size greater; tail and hind foot averaging actually and relatively longer; coloration less blackish; skull averaging larger in all parts measured except nasal length and interorbital constriction; nasals actually and relatively shorter and generally truncate, rather than pointed posteriorly; upper incisors projecting farther beyond nasals; tympanic bullae more inflated and less truncate anteriorly. By actual weight, skulls of an equal degree of maturity differ in the ratio of 9 to 7, *undosus* being the heavier. From practical topotypes of *nevadensis*, *undosus* differs in: greater maximum and average size; actually and relatively longer tail; coloration less blackish; skull less heavily ridged; upper incisors projecting farther beyond nasals; nasals narrower; upper tooth rows, both actually and relatively, slightly longer; mastoidal breadth actually and relatively greater; rostrum less depressed below plane of frontals, resulting in a more nearly straight (rather than highly arched) dorsal outline of skull in longitudinal axis.

Specimens from the Carson Sink (from Stillwater and from 7 to 10 miles to the southeastward of Fallon) differ from those from the Humboldt Sink (topotypes) in having actually and relatively longer nasals and shorter hind feet. The one specimen from 4 miles west of Fallon is not fully adult, and in several features is suggestive of the race *yosemite*, but the larger tympanic bullae, long palate, and some other features, taking into account assumed immaturity of the animal, lead me to refer it to *undosus*. Additional specimens from there would be desirable to ascertain whether the animals are really *undosus*, or, instead, *yosemite*, which may have extended down the Carson River, in times long past, or possibly along the canal which carries water from the Truckee River to the vicinity of Fallon. The one specimen from 4 miles west of Fallon is insufficient to permit the positive identifying of the race there.

Records of occurrence.—Specimens examined, 46, as follows: *Pershing Co.:* Lovelock, 15 (13 in U. S. Nat. Mus., Biol. Surv. Coll.). *Churchill Co.:* 4 mi. W Fallon, 4000 ft., 1; Stillwater, 10 (U. S. Nat. Mus., Biol. Surv. Coll.); community pasture, 7 mi. SE Fallon, 11; 7 mi. S and 3½ mi. E Fallon, 5; 10 mi. SSE Fallon, 4.

Microtus montanus fucosus Hall
Montane Meadow Mouse

Microtus montanus fucosus Hall, Univ. California Publ. Zoöl., 40:421, October 25, 1935. Type from Hiko, 4000 feet, Pahranagat Valley, Lincoln County, Nevada.

Distribution.—Pahranagat Valley in Lincoln County. See figure 387.

Remarks.—Five of each sex measure: ♂, 180 (170–188), ♀, 174 (164–188); 50 (45–60), 44 (39–49); 22.4 (21–24), 21.3 (19.5–20.3); weight, 55.4 (41.8–67.0), 53.7 (46.3–61.5) grams.

Size large; tail relatively long, averaging, in a series of fourteen adult and nearly adult animals, 27 (23–33) per cent of total length; hind foot of medium length; color blackish, with but few overhairs tipped with reddish rather than grayish; skull large; brain case long and narrow; bullae well inflated; nasals long, narrow, and pointed posteriorly; upper tooth rows long.

From *M. m. nevadensis*, this race differs as follows: tail relatively and actually longer; hind foot relatively and actually shorter; skull less heavily ridged and not known to attain a size as large; nasals actually and relatively longer, anteriorly narrower (not expanded at tip), and posteriorly pointed rather than blunt-ended; rostrum on plane with frontals rather than depressed below plane of frontals. Bailey's (1900:34) measurements show a much greater length of tail in *nevadensis* than do our thirteen topotypes. Since most of our specimens of both *nevadensis* and *fucosus* were measured by the same collector, the greater average length of the tail in *fucosus* is regarded as significant. In eight adult and nearly adult *nevadensis* the length of the tail amounts to 23 (19–25) per cent, whereas in ten comparable specimens of *fucosus* the percentage is 27 (23–33). In coloration the two kinds to me are indistinguishable. From *M. m. rivularis*, the race to the eastward, known to me by six topotypes, *fucosus* differs in darker color, larger external measurements, relatively longer tail, and usually broader skull. Every one of the forty-three specimens from Pahranagat Valley is darker than the darkest (least reddish) of the six topotypes of *rivularis* taken only 3 weeks later in the year. Similarly, in relative length of the tail, no overlap has been found between adults and subadults of *fucosus* (average, 27 per cent) and *rivularis*, in which the three older specimens show percentages as follows: 22, 22, 21. Bailey's (1900:30) measurements of the type and one other specimen of *rivularis*, however, show that these two animals have relatively longer tails. From *M. m. arizonensis*, the race to the southeast, known to me by seven topotypes, *fucosus* differs certainly in darker (less reddish) coloration; also, so far as can be judged from the limited material of *arizonensis*, in larger skull, longer tooth rows, and less expansion of the nasals distally. From topotypes and referred specimens of *M. m. micropus*, *fucosus* differs in darker (more blackish) coloration, larger external measurements, relatively longer tail, larger, more heavily ridged skull, anteriorly narrower nasals, and longer tooth rows. Also, the skulls of *fucosus* are larger in almost every measurement taken.

Microtus montanus fucosus is thought to be restricted to Pahranagat Valley. This valley is watered by springs which issue forth at the bases of the surrounding dry mountains. Nowhere else, for a long distance west, north, and east, do habitats suitable for *Microtus montanus* exist. I have not studied the country immediately south of Pahranagat Lake, but according to available information it, also, is too dry to meet the requirements of *Microtus montanus*.

The population nearest to the north, of which there is record, is that from 3½ miles north of Eagle Valley (= Ursine), 5600 feet elevation, in Lincoln County. These animals, although here referred to the subspecies *micropus*, in many features clearly are intermediate between *micropus* and *fucosus*. For example, agreement with *fucosus* is shown in large hind foot, long nasals, and wide rostrum. Nevertheless, they agree with *micropus* in the lesser total length, relatively shorter tail, and lesser zygomatic breadth. They are intermediate in coloration, in length of skull, in palatilar length, and in length of upper molar teeth.

Records of occurrence.—Specimens examined, 67, as follows: *Lincoln Co.*: Pahranagat Valley: Hiko, 4000 ft., 16; 3 mi. N Crystal Spring, 4000 ft., 13; Crystal Spring, 4000 ft., 3; Ash Spring, 3800 ft., 11; 4 mi. S Alamo, 24 (skulls only, from owl pellets).

Microtus montanus nevadensis Bailey
Montane Meadow Mouse

Microtus nevadensis Bailey, Proc. Biol. Soc. Washington, 12:86, April 30, 1898. Type from a big salt marsh below Watkins Ranch, Ash Meadows, Nye County, Nevada. Bailey, N. Amer. Fauna, 17:33, June 6, 1900.
Microtus montanus nevadensis, Hall, Univ. California Publ. Zoöl., 40:423, October 25, 1935.

Distribution.—Ash Meadows in Nye County. See figure 387.

Remarks.—Measurements of four of each sex are: ♂, 175 (162–184), ♀, 167 (140–190); 40.0 (31–44), 39.0 (29–46); 23.8 (22–25), 23.4 (22.5–24.0); weight, 61.3 (57.0–68.6), 61.1 (37.3 and 85.0) grams.

Size large; tail relatively short, averaging, in a series of eight adult and nearly adult animals, 23 (19–25) per cent of total length; hind foot large; color blackish, with but a few overhairs tipped with reddish rather than grayish; skull large; brain case long and narrow; bullae well inflated; nasals short, wide, and posteriorly truncate; rostrum depressed below plane of frontals; upper tooth rows long.

For comparison of *nevadensis* with its structurally most similar relatives, see data for *fucosus* and *undosus*. From both *dutcheri*, the race to the westward in California, and *yosemite*, *nevadensis* differs in: maximum size greater; tail relatively shorter; hind foot longer; coloration more blackish, with less reddish or brownish; skull larger and more heavily ridged; brain case relatively, as well as actually, longer; tympanic bullae larger and more inflated.

Although accorded full specific rank by Bailey (1900), *nevadensis*, in my opinion, is better treated as a subspecies of the species *Microtus montanus*. It differs but little more from *Microtus m. yosemite* than does *fucosus*, and *fucosus* is connected with the *yosemite* stock by a series of intergrading populations found from Pahranagat Valley northward through eastern Nevada and thence westward across the northern part of the state.

In the spring of 1933, when Ward C. Russell and William B. Davis visited Ash Meadows, they could find no sign of *Microtus* in the big salt marsh just below the Watkins Ranch (then occupied by Mr. "Tex" McCall), but they did locate the animals at a place 3½ miles farther north, where, by persistent trapping, a small series was obtained.

Record of occurrence.—Specimens examined: *Nye Co.*: 4 4/5 mi. NW Devils Hole, 2200 ft., 13.

Microtus longicaudus
Long-tailed Meadow Mouse

This species, with three races in Nevada, may be described as: size average for the genus; tail long, averaging 33 to 34 per cent of total length; color grayish; back reddish; sides clearer gray; underparts washed with whitish; tail bicolored, dusky above and whitish below; feet grayish; skull relatively smooth, not heavily ridged, even in adults, and relatively narrow; incisive foramina not abruptly constricted posteriorly, but gradually tapered or as wide posteriorly as anteriorly.

Microtus longicaudus occurs in the Boreal life-zones and down into the Transition Life-zone. Altitudinally, it is recorded from 11,100 feet at the head of Baker Creek down to 4300 feet at Big Creek Ranch of the Pine Forest Mountains. The species does not occur in the high mountains of southern Nevada, for example in the Sheep Range or on Charleston Peak.

Herbaceous vegetation is as much preferred as a place in which to live as is grass, perhaps more so. Ordinarily, mice of this species do not make well-defined runways, and, in this particular, they differ from *Microtus montanus*, which almost always make well-defined runways. *M. longicaudus* is less restricted to marshy situations than is *montanus*. The long-tailed meadow mouse has been taken as far as a half mile from water, and often I have found it several hundred feet from water, particularly in thickets of aspen where scattering green herbaceous vegetation was present. On a north-facing slope south of Wisconsin Creek, Linsdale (1938:193) found *longicaudus* among the sagebrush and *Symphoricarpus*. He says: "Compared with other slopes in the vicinity there was a considerable amount of herbaceous plants, but they were scattered. In this area, which was about ¼ mile square, nearly every bush had runways and holes of *Microtus* beneath it. Also at more than half of these bushes there were piles of bark shredded in small strips and small heaps of recently cut leaves. There were scattered piles of excrement, some fresh but mostly dried. This slope had been covered by snow for most of the winter and, compared with others, late into the spring. A few small drifts remained [late May, 1930] at the upper edge of the area. Above the pure sage there were some scattered mountain mahoganies.

"An explanation which seems probable for the relation of *Microtus* to this sort of habitat is as follows. In winter when the snow is deep here the *Microtus* burrows into it and lives on the bark and leaves of sage and whatever other plants are standing there. After the snow melts and while the ground remains moist, the animals live in burrows beneath the bushes and make [unroofed] paths . . . among the bushes. The young wander to more favorable (more moist) places, downward along the streams and upward along the margin of the retreating snow. Thus the population dwindles until none is left when the ground becomes dry. The . . . following winter starts this . . . cycle over again."

Males appear to average slightly larger than females. Average measurements of thirty-five adult males and thirty-one adult females reveal no difference at all in three cranial measurements, but in length of hind foot and in eight

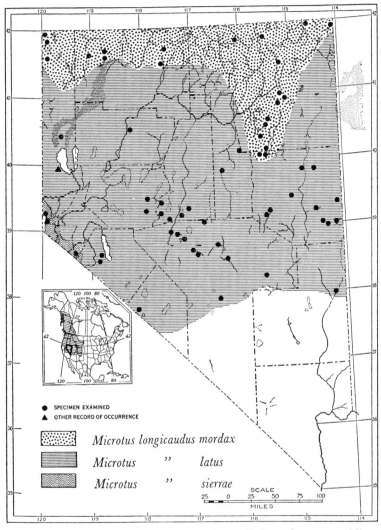

Fig. 388. Distribution of subspecies of the long-tailed meadow mouse, *Microtus longicaudus*, with insert showing range of the species.

cranial measurements males were from 1 to 3 tenths of a millimeter (1 to 2½ per cent) larger. Nevertheless, in total length, length of tail, and weight, the females were a fraction of 1 per cent the larger.

Record of pregnancy was kept in 113 sexually mature females. Of these, 39 contained embryos ranging in number from 2 to 8. The usual number was 5 or 6 and the average was 5.6. By months the females were taken as follows: May, 10 (4 pregnant); June, 26 (10); July, 50 (19); August, 25 (5); October, 2 (1).

Microtus longicaudus mordax (Merriam)
Long-tailed Meadow Mouse

Arvicola (Mynomes) mordax Merriam, N. Amer. Fauna, 5:61, July 30, 1891. Type from Alturas Lake, 7000 feet, Blaine County, Idaho.
Microtus longicaudus mordax, Goldman, Journ. Mamm., 19:491, November 14, 1938.
Microtus mordax, Bailey, N. Amer. Fauna, 17:48, June 6, 1900; Taylor, Univ. California Publ. Zoöl., 7:251, June 24, 1911.
Microtus mordax mordax, Borell and Ellis, Journ. Mamm., 15:33, 73, February 15, 1934.

Distribution.—Northern end of state south into northern White Pine County. See figure 388.

Remarks.—Measurements of ten of each sex from 6 miles southwest of Mountain City are: ♂, 182 (162–193), ♀, 185 (171–194); 62 (51–70), 62 (56–65); 20.5 (20–21), 20.8 (20–22); weight, 46.5 (36.9–56.9), 46.9 (42.0–51.2) grams.

Size large; color dark, with much blackish; skull small and relatively narrow. Nevadan specimens are intermediate between *mordax* and *latus* in color, in size, and in certain cranial proportions. None agrees precisely with topotypes of *mordax*, but, as that race now is understood, specimens from northeastern Nevada more closely resemble it, by a slight degree, than they do *latus*. Specimens from northwestern Washoe County, although referred to *mordax*, appear to be intermediate toward *sierrae*, which view rests on the slightly more reddish color. In specimens from the Ruby Mountains the skulls are narrower than topotypes of *latus*, but the skulls are deep through the interorbital region and at the junction of the frontals and nasals. They are deeper, even, than topotypes of *latus*, but the distal end of the rostrum does not turn down as much as it does in *latus*. These variations and others of a similar nature comprise the basis for regarding the specimens from northern Nevada as intermediates between *mordax* and *latus*. Comparison with *latus* is made in the account of that form. From *sierrae*, *mordax* differs in slightly lesser average size, shorter and especially narrower skull, and less reddish coloration.

Records of occurrence.—Specimens examined, 142, as follows: *Washoe Co.:* Barrel Spring, 9½ mi. E and 3½ mi. N Ft. Bidwell, 5700 ft., 1; 4 mi. SW Diessner, 5800 ft., 8; 2 mi. W Vya, 6500 ft., 1; ½ mi. N Vya, 6000 ft., 3. *Humboldt Co.:* head of Big Creek, Pine Forest Mts., 8000 ft., 6; Big Creek Ranch, Pine Forest Mts., 4350 ft., 1; 5 mi. N Summit Lake, 5900 ft., 1; 13 mi. N Paradise Valley, 6700 ft., 10; Pine Forest Mtn., 8500 ft., 1; Leonard Creek, Pine Forest Mts., 6500 ft., 1; Hansen Canyon, 5 mi. W Paradise Valley, 6200 ft., 1. *Elko Co.:* Cedar Creek, 10 mi. NE San Jacinto, 6000 ft., 5; Goose Creek, 2 mi. W Utah boundary, 5000 ft., 3; summit between heads of Copper and Coon creeks, Jarbidge Mts., 3 (coll. of Ralph Ellis); Cobb Creek, 6 mi. SW Mountain City, 6500–6550 ft., 29; Marys River, 22 mi. N Deeth, 5800 ft., 2; head of Ackler Creek, 6800 ft., 2 (1 in coll. of Ralph Ellis); Steels Creek, 5 (3 in coll. of Ralph Ellis); summit Secret Pass, 6200 ft., 11 (coll. of Ralph Ellis); Three Lakes, 9740 ft., 15 (coll. of Ralph Ellis); south fork of Long Creek, 7343–7830 ft., 7 (coll. of Ralph Ellis); Harrison Pass R. S., Green Mountain Canyon, 6050 ft., 11 (coll. of Ralph Ellis); W side of Ruby Lake, 3 mi. N White Pine Co. line, 6200 ft., 4 (coll. of Ralph Ellis). *White Pine Co.:* Willow Cr., 2 mi. S Elko Co. line, 6500 ft., 8 (6 in coll. of Ralph Ellis); W side Ruby Lake, 3 mi. S Elko Co. line, 6100 ft., 3.

Microtus longicaudus latus Hall
Long-tailed Meadow Mouse

Microtus mordax latus Hall, Univ. California Publ. Zoöl., 37:12, April 10, 1931. Type from Wisconsin Creek, 8500 feet, Toyabe Mountains, Nye County, Nevada.
Microtus longicaudus latus, Goldman, Journ. Mamm., 19:491, November 14, 1938.
Microtus mordax, Bailey, N. Amer. Fauna, 17:48, June 6, 1900; Linsdale, Amer. Midland Nat., 19:192, January, 1938.

Distribution.—Most of Nevada in Boreal zones, excepting Sierra Nevada, Elko County, and northern parts of Humboldt and Washoe counties; not found even in the high mountains south of latitude 37° 30'. See figure 388.

Remarks.—Measurements of ten males and six females from the eastern slope of the Toyabe Mountains are: ♂, 182 (172–190), ♀, 184 (175–190); 59 (56–60), 64 (52–80); 22.4 (20–24), 21.7 (19–25); weight, 47.3 (39.0–56.8), 49.4 (46.0–58.4) grams.

Size medium; coloration pale; brain case broad (see mastoidal breadth); nasals long; tip of rostrum depressed. From *sierrae*, this race differs in: external measurements less; color much paler (less reddish); nasals shorter and interorbital region flat, rather than depressed. From topotypes of *mordax*, *latus* differs in tail slightly shorter; color paler (less blackish); brain case broader; nasals longer; rostrum more depressed at tip. Intergradation with *mordax* is shown by specimens from northern Nevada which are commented on under the account of *mordax*. Specimens from the White Mountains in Esmeralda County show tendencies toward *M. l. sierrae* in both color and cranial characteristics, but are referable to *latus*. Except for the geographic variations noted, these animals are relatively uniform. This uniformity is the more noteworthy because the animals are limited to mountain ranges; populations are separated one from another by territory that is zonally too low to support populations of this species.

Records of occurrence.—Specimens examined, 217, as follows: *Washoe Co.:* Horse Canyon, Pahrum Peak, 5800–6000 ft., 3. *Pershing Co.:* El Dorado Canyon, Humboldt Range, 7800 ft., 5. *Churchill Co.:* Cherry Valley (meadows), 6450 ft., 3; Cherry Creek (spring), 5000 ft., 4; Eastgate, 4400 ft., 1. *Mineral Co.:* Cottonwood Creek, Mt. Grant, 7400–7900 ft., 7; Lapon Canyon, Mt. Grant, 8800 ft., 2. *Esmeralda Co.:* Chiatovich Creek, 8200 ft., 4; ½ mi. W Chiatovich Ranch, 4900 ft., 3. *Lander Co.:* Smiths Creek, 7700 ft., 3; Birch Creek, 7000 ft., 4; Campbell Creek, 6900 ft., 2; Kingston R. S., 7500 ft., 6; Kingston Canyon, 7000 ft., 1; Peterson Creek, Shoshone Mts., 6500–7500 ft., 9. *Eureka Co.:* Union, 2; 4 mi. S Tonkin, Denay Creek, Roberts Mts., 8. *Nye Co.:* Wilson Creek, 7200 ft., Toquima Range, 2; Bells Ranch, Reese River, 6890 ft., 5; Wisconsin Creek, 7800–8500 ft., 17; Ophir Creek, 6500 ft., 1; South Twin River, 6500–7000 ft., 8; Greenmonster Canyon, Monitor Range, 7500 ft., 4; 1 to 1½ mi. E Jefferson, Toquima Range, 7600–7780 ft., 8; 8 to 9 mi. E Toquima Peak, Monitor Valley, 7000–7100 ft., 2; Antone Creek, 2 mi. S Meadow Valley R. S., Toquima Mts., 2; 4 mi. N Hot Creek, Hot Creek Range, 6400 ft., 1; Burned Corral Canyon, Quinn Canyon Mts., 6700 ft., 3; Haws Canyon, 7800 ft., 1; Breen Creek, Kawich Range, 7000 ft., 2. *White Pine Co.:* Cherry Creek, 6800 ft., 2; E side Schellbourne Pass, 6800 ft., 1; Gleason Creek, 7500 ft., 7; Smith Creek (4 mi. W Smith Creek Cave, 6900 ft., 1; Mt. Moriah, 6800 ft., 3; 3 mi. W Smith Creek Cave, 6700 ft., 1; Mt. Moriah, 6500 ft., 1), 6; Hendry Creek, Mt. Moriah, 9800 ft., 3; 1½ mi. E Mt. Moriah, 9100 ft., 26; Cleve Creek, Shell Creek Range, 8100–9580 ft., 30; 3 mi. W Hamilton, 8400 ft., 2; 2½ mi. SW Hamilton, 7300 ft., 1; Willard Creek, Spring Valley, 8200 ft., 2; Baker Creek (8500 ft., 7; 11,100 ft., 4), 11; Stella Lake, Snake Mts., 10,500–10,750 ft., 3. *Lincoln Co.:* 3½ mi. N Ursine, Eagle Valley, 5900 ft., 2.

Additional record: *Washoe Co.:* Hardscrabble Canyon (D. G. Nichols, MS).

Microtus longicaudus sierrae Kellogg
Long-tailed Meadow Mouse

Microtus mordax sierrae Kellogg, Univ. California Publ. Zoöl, 21:288, April 18, 1922. Type from Tuolumne Meadows, Yosemite National Park, Tuolumne County, California.
Microtus longicaudus sierrae, Goldman, Journ. Mamm., 19:481, November 14, 1938.

Distribution.—Sierra Nevada in western Nevada from vicinity of Lake Tahoe south to Desert Creek in Douglas County. See figure 388.

Remarks.—Measurements of two topotypes from California, ♂, no. 23175, and ♀, no. 23174, are: ♂, 204, ♀, 192; 72, 73; 22, 23; weight, 49.3, 45.3 grams.

Size large; color dark, definitely reddish; skull large, often with interorbital region depressed. Comparison with *latus* is made in the account of that form. The one specimen from Desert Creek is a subadult the dark color of which agrees better with that of *sierrae* than with that of *latus*. Of the remaining specimens, the size and the color indicate a relationship as close to *latus* as to *sierrae*. With more abundant material, the resemblance to *sierrae* might be more pronounced. On the basis of specimens now available, it appears

TABLE 19A
CRANIAL MEASUREMENTS (IN MILLIMETERS) OF MICROTUS

Sex	Number of individuals averaged or catalogue no.	Condylobasal length	Occipitonasal length	Nasal length	Zygomatic breadth	Interorbital breadth	Mastoidal breadth	Alveolar length of upper molar series	Width of rostrum	Palatilar length	Width of auditory bullae*
					Microtus montanus micropus, Cleveland Ranch						
♂	5 av.	28.5	28.1	8.3	16.4	3.7	13.1	6.7	5.3	15.1	6.2
	min.	26.7	26.9	7.6	15.1	3.7	12.2	6.5	5.0	13.8	5.9
	max.	29.7	29.3	8.7	16.7	3.8	13.5	6.8	5.6	15.6	6.7
♀	5 av.	28.0	27.7	8.3	16.1	3.7	12.6	6.6	5.1	14.9	6.1
	min.	27.0	26.9	7.8	15.6	3.5	11.7	6.3	4.7	14.1	5.9
	max.	28.2	27.8	8.6	16.0	3.8	12.5	6.9	5.0	15.4	6.3
					Microtus montanus nanus, Goose Creek						
♂	7 av.	26.2	25.6	7.3	15.0	3.6	11.9	6.5	4.7	13.5	5.9
	min.	25.7	25.0	6.6	14.6	3.5	11.4	6.2	4.5	13.0	5.7
	max.	27.6	26.5	7.8	16.2	3.8	12.3	6.7	5.2	14.4	6.1
♀	5 av.	26.6	26.1	7.4	15.4	3.6	12.1	6.5	4.8	14.0	6.0
	min.	26.1	25.6	6.7	14.9	3.3	11.9	6.1	4.6	13.6	5.8
	max.	27.3	26.7	8.1	16.5	3.7	12.2	6.8	5.2	14.8	6.3
					Microtus montanus yosemite, 3½ mi. E Reno						
♂	4 av.	27.3	26.3	7.6	15.5	3.8	12.3	6.7	5.0	14.6	5.8
	min.	26.2	25.5	6.9	14.8	3.7	11.7	6.4	4.7	13.7	5.4
	max.	29.4	28.1	8.8	16.7	3.8	13.3	6.9	5.2	15.7	6.1
♀	6 av.	26.8	26.2	7.7	15.6	3.6	12.1	6.7	4.8	14.4	5.7
	min.	25.0	24.5	6.8	14.0	3.4	11.2	6.5	4.6	13.8	5.6
	max.	27.8	27.4	8.2	16.6	3.8	12.4	6.9	4.9	14.8	5.9
					Microtus montanus undosus, Lovelock						
♂	10 av.	30.0	28.7	8.0	17.3	3.7	13.3	7.5	5.4	16.4	6.4
	min.	28.7	27.6	7.3	16.9	3.4	13.0	7.1	5.1	15.7	6.1
	max.	33.2	30.9	9.2	18.4	4.0	14.1	7.8	5.7	18.0	6.6
♀	156599	30.7	28.6	8.2	17.8	3.6	12.8	7.6	5.6	17.1	6.6
♀	156601	29.0	28.3	8.0	16.8	3.5	12.7	7.4	5.2	16.3	6.4
					Microtus montanus fucosus, Pahranagat Valley						
♂	5 av.	29.1	28.6	8.6	16.7	3.7	12.7	7.3	5.2	15.8	5.8
	min.	27.8	27.5	7.9	16.0	3.6	12.2	7.0	4.9	15.0	5.5
	max.	30.8	30.3	9.2	17.1	3.8	13.0	7.8	5.6	16.5	6.0
♀	5 av.	28.5	27.9	8.3	16.9	3.8	12.6	7.1	5.3	15.5	6.0
	min.	27.3	27.2	8.0	15.7	3.7	12.3	6.8	5.1	14.5	5.8
	max.	29.8	28.7	8.7	17.9	3.8	13.4	7.2	5.6	16.4	6.4

* Measured from anterodorsal face of wall of external auditory meatus to posterior opening of stapedial canal.

TABLE 19A—(Continued)

Sex	Number of individuals averaged or catalogue no.	Condylobasal length	Occipitonasal length	Nasal length	Zygomatic breadth	Interorbital breadth	Mastoidal breadth	Alveolar length of upper molar series	Width of rostrum	Palatilar length	Width of auditory bullae*
					Microtus montanus nevadensis, Ash Meadows						
♂	4 av.	31.3	30.4	8.6	17.7	3.7	13.1	7.4	5.6	16.6	6.4
	min.	29.7	29.1	8.2	16.9	3.5	12.4	6.9	5.2	15.8	6.3
	max.	32.2	31.2	8.9	18.4	3.9	13.6	7.6	5.7	17.3	6.4
♀	4 av.	29.5	28.9	8.2	17.3	3.8	12.5	7.2	5.5	16.0	6.3
	min.	28.1	27.3	7.7	16.1	3.7	11.9	6.9	5.1	15.0	6.0
	max.	31.3	30.3	8.5	18.8	3.8	13.0	7.5	5.8	17.3	6.5
					Microtus longicaudus mordax, 6 mi. SW Mountain City						
♂	10 av.	26.8	26.9	7.8	15.3	3.7	12.3	6.5	5.3	13.2	6.0
	min.	25.6	26.3	7.4	14.5	3.5	11.8	6.2	5.0	12.0	5.7
	max.	27.7	27.7	8.1	16.0	3.9	12.7	6.9	5.5	13.8	6.3
♀	10 av.	26.8	27.0	7.8	15.2	3.6	12.2	6.6	5.1	13.3	6.2
	min.	25.6	26.2	7.1	14.0	3.5	11.5	6.2	4.7	12.5	5.5
	max.	28.4	28.6	8.1	16.0	3.8	13.2	6.9	5.3	13.9	6.5
					Microtus longicaudus latus, Toyabe Mountains						
♂	10 av.	27.3	27.5	8.1	15.5	3.8	12.7	6.7	5.2	13.4	6.2
	min.	25.7	26.3	7.5	14.6	3.5	11.8	6.3	4.8	12.5	5.9
	max.	28.9	29.0	8.8	16.2	3.9	13.3	7.0	5.4	14.3	6.4
♀	6 av.	27.0	26.9	7.7	15.5	3.6	12.4	6.7	5.2	13.4	6.2
	min.	26.0	26.3	7.5	15.0	3.7	12.0	6.3	4.8	12.9	5.8
	max.	27.4	27.5	7.8	15.9	3.5	12.7	6.8	5.4	13.9	6.7
					Microtus longicaudus sierrae, Topotypes						
♂	23175	27.6	27.9	8.2	15.8	3.9	12.8	6.7	5.3	13.8	6.2
♀	23174	27.2	27.7	7.9	14.7	3.5	11.5	7.2	5.2	13.5	6.5

* Measured from anterodorsal face of wall of external auditory meatus to posterior opening of stapedial canal.

that the "Great Basin influence," namely, the characters of *latus*, extends geographically all the way to the eastern shore of Lake Tahoe, although the animals there may be intermediate toward *sierrae*. In fact, with large series of adult specimens available for study from Lake Tahoe, it might turn out that the subspecies *sierrae* is not to be ascribed to Nevada.

Records of occurrence.—Specimens examined, 24, as follows: *Washoe Co.:* ½ mi. S Mt. Rose, 9500 ft., 6; 3 mi. SSW Mt. Rose, 9000 ft., 1; 3 mi. S Mt. Rose, 8500 ft., 12; Incline Creek, 7100 ft., 1. *Ormsby Co.:* Marlette Lake, 8000 ft., 1; ½ mi. S Marlette Lake, 8150 ft., 2. *Douglas Co.:* Desert Creek, Sweetwater Range, 6250 ft., 1.

Lagurus curtatus
Sagebrush Vole

Two races of sagebrush vole occur in Nevada. Distinctive features of the American member of the genus are light gray color and short tail, which amounts to only a fifth or fourth of the length of the head and body. The mammae number the same as in *Microtus*, two pair inguinal and two pair pectoral. Aside from color and length of tail, the external characters are about the same as in *Microtus*, except that there is no well-defined, if any, hip gland in males, and the soles of the feet are more hairy than in some *Microtus*. Cranially, *Lagurus* differs from *Microtus* in that it has complete stapedial canal, more flattened skull than in most species of *Microtus*, and differently formed auditory bullae. The auditory bullae in *Lagurus* are larger, project posteriorly beyond the plane of the occiput, and are cancellous and more foamlike in structure. The dental formula is i. $\frac{1}{1}$, c. $\frac{0}{0}$, p. $\frac{0}{0}$, m. $\frac{3}{3}$.

The American forms have been separated, under the subgeneric name *Lemmiscus* Thomas, from the Old World representatives, subgenus *Lagurus*, on the basis of antitragus present rather than absent, ear more than half the length of hind foot, and cement present in re-entrant angles of molars. These are features in which the American forms agree with *Microtus* and explain why some zoölogists place the sagebrush voles in that genus. Additional differences from the Old World relatives (subgenus *Lagurus*) are longer external auditory canal, four rather than five closed triangles in the third (last) lower molar, and absence of a dark, longitudinal stripe. These features have been held by some to justify elevating the American forms to full generic position under the name *Lemmiscus*.

Zonally, *Lagurus* in Nevada, and elsewhere in North America, is characteristic of the Transition and Upper Sonoran life-zones. Altitudinally, in Nevada, it has been taken from 10,000 feet elevation on Mount Moriah down to 5800 feet on Marys River. At Breen Creek the mice lived in a meadow of sparse dry grass. Some of those along Hendry Creek were in a meadow with widely spaced bushes of *Artemisia*, but at all the other localities of occurrence they were among sagebrush (*Artemisia tridentata*). Their habitat, more exactly defined, is among bushes of sage that are several feet apart and that are of a uniform height of about 2½ feet. These plants of uniform age or stage of growth have the lower branches near the ground. My own experience agrees with that of Borell and Ellis (1934a:35) who said: "All individuals taken at a distance from colonies, or in unusual environments, such as in willow thickets at the water's edge, or among the rocks, proved to be immature." Probably the season's population of young spread out in these ways in order to reach and eventually colonize territory which provides suitable habitat.

At most of the places where these voles were found they lived in colonies. A colony might have as few as eight or as many as thirty entrances to burrows.

The entrance to a burrow usually was situated beneath a sage bush. The runways, which radiated from an entrance, were sometimes discernible for a distance of only about a foot; others were visible all the way from one burrow-opening to an adjacent one. The runways were without cover, and the 2½- to 3-inch width was more than that of the runways made by small- or medium-sized *Microtus*. Blades of green grass or stems of growing plants partly obstructed some runways; in the runway of a *Microtus montanus* these would promptly be cut and eaten, or, at any rate, carried out of the path.

In May of 1927 an area that had been inhabited the preceding winter was located by Miss Annie M. Alexander and Miss Louise Kellogg along Indian Creek, Esmeralda County, "on a north-facing slope at the edge of a snow drift. Indeed only a part of the colony was yet exposed; the remainder, of unknown size, extended beneath the snow drift. The most striking feature of the colony was the *Artemisia* bushes denuded of bark and foliage. Many of the bushes were completely girdled and presumably would die from the effects of the gnawing by the *Lagurus*. Piles of bark, in shreds, and many leaves that the mice had cut off, under cover of the snow, littered the ground. Careful scrutiny indicated that the abundant shreds of bark were removed by the mice so that they could reach the cambium layer which apparently . . . they ate. Many of the masses of shredded bark hung in the tops of sage-bushes and had the appearance of nests but I could find none that, on careful inspection, appeared to have been used as such. However, these shreds of bark and cut leaves had, evidently, functioned as flooring for the runways and large chambers that the mice had made in the snow around and in the tops of the sage-bushes.

"Three burrows that we excavated here were each about twenty-four inches long. Two extended eleven inches underground and the third only six inches. . . . The latter ended in a round chamber three and one-half inches in diameter. Each was unoccupied and contained no nest. No droppings were found in the burrows although they were abundant in the runways." (Hall, 1928:203–204.)

In the colony on Chiatovich Creek, which was more closely studied than any other, the droppings were mostly under bushes, but some were scattered along the paths. The excreta, in shape, resemble those of *Microtus*, and in color they are either green or black.

As shown by the feces, a large proportion of the food is *Artemisia*. One of the animals taken at Chiatovich Creek had sage leaves in its mouth, and at that place there were cut stems of sage, about 3½ inches long, strewn along the runways. Linsdale (1938:194) found freshly cut leaves of sage in two colonies in the Toyabe Mountains in May, and in one of these colonies there were also cut stems and other pieces of herbaceous plants. Fitch (MS), in mid-June, along Hendry Creek, noted that: "Runways, droppings, and cuttings are conspicuous. Most of the cuttings observed were from sage and another shrubby composite and were made several inches above the ground evidently during the winter when the mice were enabled to reach the more tender upper stems of shrubs by making runways to them through the snow. At present, however, they seem to be feeding on succulent leaves of small herbaceous plants, several species of which occur in the area. Partly chewed leaves were found in the mouths of some of the mice caught." On Indian Creek, Esmeralda County, the denuded bushes of *Artemisia* and the rubbish beneath the bushes plainly showed a heavy utilization of this plant in the preceding winter. Here, a lower limb of a foxtail pine (*Pinus balfouriana*), which had been buried under the snow along with the *Artemisia* bushes that had been extensively defoliated by the mice, had not been gnawed, although several runways through the snow passed round and through the clusters of needles. From what has been recorded above about the food, it is clear that although the mice live in an arid habitat distinctly different from the moist habitat of most kinds of voles and that although they have become modified in several features of structure to accord with their habitat, the sagebrush voles have not adapted themselves to the type of food used by most desert rodents, namely, seeds, but still retain the predilection for green foods.

Probably the same kinds of carnivorous mammals and raptorial birds prey on *Lagurus* as prey on other mice. One was found in the stomach of a bobcat 9 miles east of Eastgate.

The mice are not strictly nocturnal. In the colony along Hendry Creek, and in that on Chiatovich Creek, animals were seen moving about in the day, and in the latter colony about as many were taken in the daytime as at night.

By turning over logs along Hendry Creek in mid-June, Fitch (MS) found that many of the animals had runways barely beneath the surface of the ground. Two nests were found under logs. Of one, Fitch says: "I found a litter of young [63 to 71 mm. in total length] in a nest beneath a log. . . . The nest was constructed similarly to that of *Microtus*, but was proportionately smaller. It was composed of a loose mass of dry plant fibers. . . . Five young were captured, but I believe at least one escaped." Concerning the second nest, Fitch says: "[An adult female] *Lagurus* was caught in my trap . . . at one end of a log around which runways were abundant. I overturned the log, but only after considerable effort, probably resulting in disturbance to the animals beneath. Several less-than-half-grown *Lagurus* were running about in exposed runways beneath the log. Four were caught, but possibly others escaped. A loose nest was found in a spherical depression leading into runways on either side. The nest was composed of dried shreds of plant stems. Six newborn [21 to 23 mm. in crown–rump length] young were . . . in the nest. Since only one nest was found beneath the log and only one adult female was trapped in the vicinity, it seemed probable that both newborn and older litters were young of the same female. The female . . . had a much enlarged but empty uterus, indicating that she had recently given birth to young."

Males average 1 to 3 per cent larger than females in most linear measurements taken, and, on the basis of four adult males and three adult females from Chiatovich Creek, are 20 per cent heavier. More complete data probably would show the average difference in weight to be less.

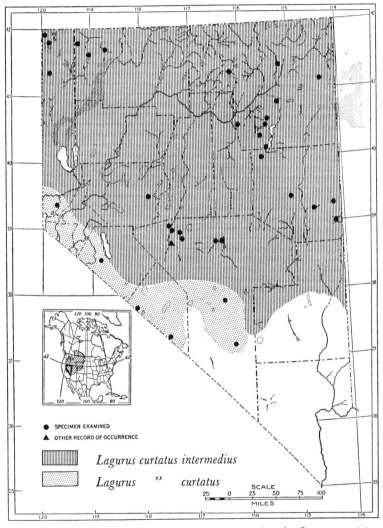

Fig. 389. Distribution of subspecies of the sagebrush vole, *Lagurus curtatus*, with insert showing range of the species.

Record of pregnancy was kept in 35 adult females, 9 of which were pregnant. One female had 3 embryos; 2 had 4 embryos; 3 had 5 embryos; and 3 had 6 embryos, which yields an average of 4.9. By months, these females were taken as follows: April, 2 (0 pregnant); May, 6 (2 pregnant); June, 12 (2); July, 7 (2); August, 7 (3); September, 1 (0).

Lagurus curtatus intermedius (Taylor)
Sagebrush Vole

Microtus (Lagurus) intermedius Taylor, Univ. California Publ. Zoöl., 7:253, June 24, 1911. Type from head of Big Creek, 8000 feet, Pine Forest Mountains, Humboldt County, Nevada.
Lagurus curtatus intermedius, Borell and Ellis, Journ. Mamm., 15:35, February 15, 1934.
Lagurus curtatus, Linsdale, Amer. Midland Nat., 19:194, January, 1938.
Microtus curtatus, Bailey, N. Amer. Fauna, 17:67, June 6, 1900, part.

Distribution.—Over all of state from latitude 38° 30' northward, the southwestern part of state excepted. See figure 389.

Remarks.—Measurements of seven males and ten females from the Ruby Mountains are: ♂, 123 (109–142), ♀, 119 (108–134); 20.4 (15–23), 21.0 (18–26); 17.0 (16–17), 16.5 (15–18). Weight of three females from Hendry Creek, White Pine County, 22.4 (21.8–22.9).

The smaller size and relatively broader skull, by a slight degree, are the only features found that differentiate this race from *curtatus*. Intergradation between them is complete, in that individual specimens provide intermediate stages in size of parts measured. From the race *pauperrimus*, named from southeastern Washington, Taylor (1911:253) indicates that *intermedius* differs in grayer color and slightly smaller size. How the form *L. c. artemisiae* from Ironside, Oregon, differs from *intermedius* is not known at this writing. Of the two names, *intermedius* has priority.

In the animals from Nevada there is an amazing amount of individual variation in size of skull, including size of auditory bullae. The variation is so great that at first it was suspected that two species were involved. Further study showed that both sizes occurred at one locality (Hendry Creek), that animals with skulls and auditory bullae of intermediate size occurred at the same place, and finally that no other features judged to be of systematic worth could be correlated with the mentioned differences in the skull. Only individual, and not specific, variation appears to be involved.

Records of occurrence.—Specimens examined, 97, as follows: *Washoe Co.:* 12 mi. E and 3 mi. N Ft. Bidwell, 5700 ft., 2; 4 mi. S Diessner, 5800 ft., 1; 15 mi. S Vya, 5800 ft., 1. *Humboldt Co.:* longitude 119° 15', 14 mi. S. Oregon boundary, 1 (coll. of Ira La Rivers); head of Big Creek, Pine Forest Mts., 8000 ft., 6; 5 mi. N Summit Lake, 5900 ft., 1. *Churchill Co.:* Cherry Valley (meadows), 6450 ft., 2. *Nye Co.:* Dutch Flat Schoolhouse, Reese River, 6715 ft., 2; Bells Ranch, Reese River, 6890 ft., 1; Wisconsin Creek, 8500 ft., 1; South Twin River, 6500 ft., 2; Greenmonster Canyon, Monitor Range, 7500 ft., 1; 6½ mi. N Fish Lake, Fish Spring Valley, 6700 ft., 1. *Elko Co.:* Marys River, 22 mi. N Deeth, 5800 ft., 2; 1 mi. SE Tuscarora, 5900 ft., 2; Cobre, 6100 ft., 3; summit of Secret Pass, 6200 ft., 1 (coll. of Ralph Ellis); Three Lakes, 9740 ft., 4 (coll. of Ralph Ellis); Long Creek, 7830 ft., 1 (coll. of Ralph Ellis); 5 mi. E Raines, Sulphur Spring Mts., 1; Harrison Pass R. S., Green Mountain Canyon, 6050 ft., 20 (coll. of Ralph Ellis); W side Ruby Lake, 3 mi. N White Pine Co. line, 6200 ft., 1 (coll. of Ralph Ellis). *White Pine Co.:* Willow Creek, 2 mi. S Elko Co. line, 6500 ft., 4 (coll. of Ralph Ellis); Overland Pass, E slope Ruby Mts., 8 mi. S Elko Co. line, 1 (coll. of Ralph Ellis); Gleason Creek, 7300 ft., 6; Hendry Creek, Mt. Moriah, 9800–10,000 ft., 23; Cleve Creek, Shell Creek Range, 8300–8900 ft., 4; Baker Creek, 7200 ft., 2.

Additional records (Bailey, 1900:68): *Nye Co.:* head of Reese River; Indian Creek (near head of Reese River).

Lagurus curtatus curtatus (Cope)
Sagebrush Vole

Arvicola curtata Cope, Proc. Acad. Nat. Sci. Philadelphia, 1868:2. Type from Pigeon Spring, Mount Magruder, Esmeralda County, Nevada.
Lagurus curtatus, Thomas, Ann. and Mag. Nat. Hist. (ser. 8), 9:401. April, 1912.
Lagurus [curtatus], Hall, Journ. Mamm., 9:201, August 9, 1928.
Microtus curtatus, Bailey, N. Amer. Fauna, 17:67, June 6, 1900.

Distribution.—Southwestern Nevada from Pahute Mesa northwest to southern Washoe County. See figure 389.

Remarks.—Measurements of ten of each sex from Chiatovich Creek, Esmeralda County, are: ♂, 128 (119–132), ♀, 127 (121–135); 22.9 (18–28), 21.7 (20–25); 18.0 (17–19), 17.2 (16–18); weight, 29.4 (27.9–30.5), 24.4 (23.0–25.6) grams.

The larger size of individuals of this race in comparison with individuals of races having a more northern distribution is a noteworthy feature and suggests that latitudinally the species behaves to some degree as does *Microtus montanus*, in which there is an increase in size from north to south. However that may be, the range of variation in size from north to south is nowhere near so great as in *montanus*, and *Lagurus*, unlike *Microtus montanus*, appears not to invade the Lower Sonoran Life-zone, or even the lower part of the Upper Sonoran Life-zone; *Microtus montanus*, it will be recalled, lives only in perfectly good Lower Sonoran territory, although the species *montanus* as a whole is mainly boreal in its geographic distribution.

TABLE 19B
CRANIAL MEASUREMENTS (IN MILLIMETERS) OF LAGURUS

Sex	Number of individuals averaged or catalogue no.	Condylobasal length	Occipitonasal length	Nasal length	Zygomatic breadth	Interorbital breadth	Mastoidal breadth	Alveolar length of upper molar series	Width of rostrum	Palatilar length
		Lagurus curtatus intermedius, Ruby Mountains								
♂	7 av.	23.0	22.7	6.2	13.5	3.3	11.8	5.5	4.2	11.6
	min.	21.5	21.4	5.8	13.2	3.1	11.3	5.1	4.0	10.8
	max.	24.0	23.9	6.3	14.2	3.4	12.6	6.0	4.3	12.1
♀	10 av.	22.9	22.9	6.3	13.6	3.2	11.7	5.8	4.2	11.7
	min.	22.0	21.8	5.8	13.2	3.1	11.3	5.5	4.1	11.1
	max.	24.0	23.7	7.1	14.4	3.4	12.1	6.2	4.3	12.3
		Lagurus curtatus curtatus, Chiatovich Creek								
♂	10 av.	24.1	23.6	6.5	14.1	3.4	12.1	5.8	4.3	12.1
	min.	23.1	22.8	6.2	13.6	3.2	11.2	5.4	4.1	11.5
	max.	24.6	24.3	6.8	14.5	3.5	12.6	6.1	4.6	12.8
♀	10 av.	23.6	23.4	6.5	13.9	3.4	11.9	5.8	4.5	11.9
	min.	22.3	22.2	6.0	13.4	3.1	11.5	5.4	4.2	11.3
	max.	24.5	24.0	6.7	14.6	3.6	12.3	6.1	4.7	12.4

In addition to larger size and relatively narrower skull, by a slight degree, no characters have been found that distinguish this race from *intermedius*.

The one specimen from 11 miles southeast of Reno is young, and its reference to the subspecies *curtatus*, rather than to *intermedius*, is made wholly upon the basis of geographic probability.

A revisionary study of the American mice of the genus *Lagurus* is needed to provide an adequate notion of their geographic variation.

Records of occurrence.—Specimens examined, 72, as follows: *Washoe Co.:* 11 mi. SE Reno, on old stage road, 1 (coll. of Ira La Rivers). *Mineral Co.:* Lapon Canyon, Mt. Grant, 8900 ft., 2. *Esmeralda Co.:* Chiatovich Creek, 8200 ft., 36; Indian Spring, Mt. Magruder, 10 (D. R. Dickey Coll.); Log Spring, Mt. Magruder, 17 (D. R. Dickey Coll.). *Nye Co.:* Breen Creek, Kawich Mts., 7000 ft., 5; S end Belted Range, 5½ mi. NW Whiterock Spring, 7200 ft., 1.

Ondatra zibethica
Muskrat

Four races of muskrat are known from Nevada. Characters of the genus are: size large for a microtine rodent (see measurements in table 20); tail nearly as long as body, laterally compressed, with distinct dorsal and ventral keels, and so scantily haired as to reveal scales which are about 2 millimeters in diameter; hind feet relatively large, partly webbed, with fringe of stiff hairs on edge of webs, sides of toes, and metatarsi; mammae eight to ten or even eleven, two pairs inguinal, the rest pectoral; eyes small; ears short, barely projecting beyond the fur, which is dense and "waterproof"; color brown, darkest on back where overhair is thickest; sides more reddish; underparts with silvery tips of underfur showing through the reddish overhairs; overhairs on back attaining a length of 35 millimeters and underfur about half that long; skull rough; squamosals enlarged at expense of parietals; posterior border of palate terminating in median spinous process; incisors with anterior faces smooth; roots of lower incisors on outside of cheek teeth; molars rooted in adults; m3 ordinarily with three or four closed triangles and posterior loop. The dental formula is i. $\frac{1}{1}$, c. $\frac{0}{0}$, p. $\frac{0}{0}$, m. $\frac{3}{3}$.

Muskrats are aquatic mammals which live only in places where there is water deep enough for them to dive into and thus escape enemies.

"At Ruby Lake, muskrats lived in holes in the banks and also in houses which were located among the tules in shallow water, rather than out in the open water" (Borell and Ellis, 1934a:37). Both houses in the water and burrows in cut banks are reported in the marshes north of Stillwater. At Ruby Lake, "One occupied house examined on May 23, 1928, was five feet in diameter at the base and four feet high. It was composed entirely of dead tules and stood in water only six or eight inches deep. When the house was disturbed a muskrat escaped by a hole which entered the mud beneath the house and emerged several feet from it" (Borell and Ellis, loc. cit.).

At most places in Nevada where muskrats occur, they live in burrows, local conditions being such as not to favor the construction of houses. The entrance to a burrow is several inches below water. This permits the animals to enter and leave the burrows without being exposed to land-dwelling enemies.

The muskrat is a vegetarian, although an occasional individual is known to eat some animal matter. In the marshes 5½ miles north of Stillwater, L. R. Emerson, resident there, said that the animals lived almost entirely on the roots and basal 6 inches of the stalks of tules and cattails, the latter being preferred. Borell and Ellis (1934a:37) record that in Ruby Lake, "food of muskrats consisted primarily of the white bases of the stems of tules (Scirpus acutus)." Near Stillwater, Emerson noted that fresh-water mussels were eaten, but apparently only in winter. The food, whether plant or animal, is not eaten immediately upon being brought to the surface, but is carried to an established feeding place. In marshes a mat of tules or cattails ordinarily serves as a feeding place. A sunken log, part of which protrudes above water, or places at the water's edge sheltered by a steep cut bank are common sites for feeding stations along streams.

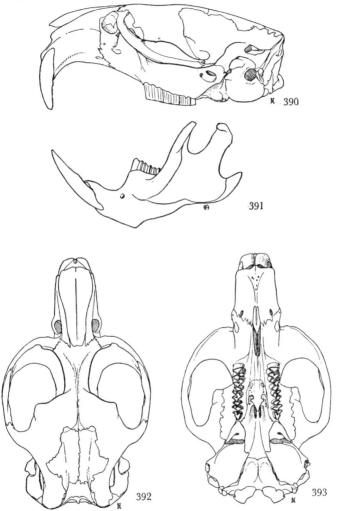

Figs. 390–393. *Ondatra zibethica mergens*, 10 miles southeast Fallon, no. 90544, ♂. ×1.

Although active at night, and perhaps most active then, these animals often are seen swimming in the daytime. In winter, at Ruby Lake, Borell and Ellis (1934*a*:36) often saw muskrats abroad in the afternoon and mention that several were seen walking about on the ice. At one place there, "A muskrat trail led three hundred yards through soft snow from one lagoon to another."

In the vicinity of Fallon muskrats are generally distributed in both the irrigated areas and in the shallow basins where waste water has accumulated. Nevertheless, in most of these places the species is less abundant than in similar situations at places that are higher zonally. Fallon is in the lower part of the Upper Sonoran Life-zone and, like some other areas of similar or lower zonal position, does not produce large numbers of muskrats. One other such place is the well-watered Pahranagat Valley, at the junction of the Upper and Lower Sonoran life-zones. At this place, according to information furnished me by Richard M. Bond, animals from a muskrat farm in Missouri were liberated on the Thiriot Ranch, 6 miles south of Hiko, about 1920, by a Mr. Henry. In the autumn and winter of 1939, three animals, two of them at Hiko, were reported to have been seen in this area. When I visited this valley in May, 1932, no traces of muskrats were seen. Obviously, they do not flourish in this area, even though conditions look to be ideal. Hiko is near the junction of the Upper and Lower Sonoran zones. For muskrats of stocks originating in places of higher zonal position, the lower part of the Upper Sonoran Life-zone and the Lower Sonoran Life-zone appear to be unsuitable. Of course, muskrats live in the Colorado River and in some other streams even farther south in the arid Lower Sonoran Life-zone, but these are muskrats of a notably different sort—subspecies the geographic ranges of which are limited to the Lower Sonoran Life-zone, and they are of a lighter, more reddish color and smaller size than northern races. If muskrats are to be introduced into areas such as Pahranagat Valley, the chances of success would seem to be increased by using stock of the southern races *baileyi* or *goldmani*. An objection to using these races is that the inferior size and light color of the pelts cause them to have less value on the fur market than the larger, darker colored pelts of northern races, say, *mergens* or *osoyoosensis*.

Furs from animals of the two last-mentioned races in many winters command a price of $1 each, whereas those of *bernardi* may bring only about three-fourths as much. In 1942 prices were higher. On March 15, 1942, John W. Keeffe, a fur buyer in Reno paid $586.50 to L. R. Emerson for 401 muskrats trapped by the latter on the Canvas-back Gun Club, about 10 miles east of Fallon. This amounts to $1.46 per rat. Record of several other sales were seen. These were on small lots of nine to thirty skins from the Truckee River. The price ranged from $1.40 to $1.65 per skin.

Muskrats are capable of causing damage to man's property, as, for example, in irrigated areas where their burrows may cause breaks in levees and a consequent loss of water. Decision whether to attempt their introduction into an area where they are lacking, therefore, should be made only after weighing the probable disadvantages against the probable advantages of their presence. In the parts of Nevada where they now occur, the gain from sale of their fur outweighs the inconvenience or damage they cause.

The only place other than Pahranagat Valley of which we have record into which introduction of muskrats was made is Great Smoky Valley. Even as there are doubts concerning where these animals came from—some think it was from Reese River Valley (Linsdale, 1938:194)—so there are doubts whether they have persisted in Great Smoky Valley.

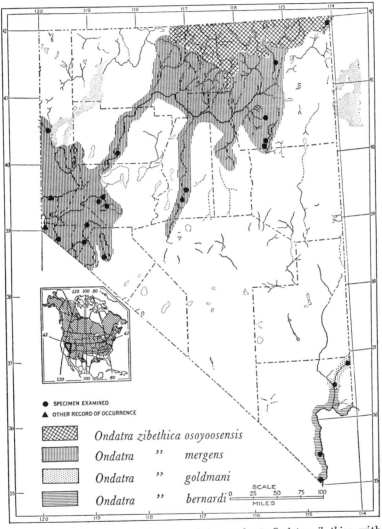

Fig. 394. Distribution of subspecies of the muskrat, *Ondatra zibethica*, with insert showing range of the species.

One of the diseases contracted by muskrats is tularemia. In a letter dated December 27, 1940, to L. T. Turner, Jr., G. H. Hansen writes: "Mr. Dill indicates . . . that the rats in Ruby Lake are carrying tularemia."

The cranial measurements of ten individuals of each sex, all judged to be adults, from Fallon are 2 to 3 per cent larger in males, except that the lengths of the upper molariform tooth rows are the same. External measurements and weights of adults from any one place are either the same in the two sexes or are slightly less in the females.

No records of embryos are available for Nevada-taken specimens. For the race *bernardi* from Imperial Valley, California, Grinnell, Dixon, and Linsdale (1937:746) found the average number of embryos in 23 pregnant females to be 6, with extremes of 3 and 9. In the race *zibethica* (which does not occur in Nevada), the average number of young, in 26 newborn litters, was 6.3, with extremes of 1 and 11. These findings result from Errington's (1937 and 1939) study of a population near Ruthven, Iowa—a study which reveals much about the species that applies probably, but by no means certainly, to other races, including those in Nevada. Selected information is: three litters are produced by some females in one year; no proof was obtained that a female born in the spring bears young the following summer or autumn; the indications are that the period of gestation varies from an atypical minimum of 19 days to a probably more usual minimum of 22 or 23 days, with the ordinary period probably being about 30 days; at birth, young average 21.3 grams in weight or slightly less than 2 per cent of the weight (1,103 grams) of adult females; the eyes open between the twelfth and twentieth day after birth, commonly between the fourteenth and sixteenth day; most young are weaned in the fourth week of their life; the young reach the "kit" stage (about 500 to 650 grams, and, therefore, by weight, are half grown) some time between the seventieth and ninetieth day.

Ondatra zibethica osoyoosensis (Lord)
Muskrat

Fiber Osoyoosensis Lord, Proc. Zoöl. Soc. London, 1863:97. Type from Lake Osoyoos, British Columbia.
Ondatra zibethica osoyoosensis, Miller, Bull. U. S. Nat. Mus., 79:231, December 12, 1931.

Distribution.—Northern Elko County in streams draining into the Snake River. See figure 394.

Remarks.—Measurements for one animal of each sex from Goose Creek are: ♂, 595, ♀, 570; 295, 250; 80, 80; weight, 1,134, 1,000 grams.

Size large; color dark, darker than Prouts Brown above; skull with high interorbital ridge, relatively broad nasals, and small auditory bullae.

From *mergens*, this race differs in darker average color and larger size, including skull and lighter jugals.

Specimens from Goose Creek are in worn summer pelage and their color is therefore of but slight importance in judging of the animal's relationship to *osoyoosensis* or *mergens*. Length of hind foot and length of nasals are more like those in *mergens* than like those in any other named form. Total length and length of tail, and in the skull, basal length, breadth of nasals, and length of tooth row are more like *osoyoosensis*. Considering all features, the animals are intermediate, and, I think, intergrades, between *mergens* and *osoyoosensis*, but show greater resemblance to the latter.

Muskrats probably occur in every one of the several sizable streams which, from

Nevada, drain into the Snake River. Our search was productive on Goose Creek, the only stream where we sought the animals.

Record of occurrence.—Specimens examined: *Elko Co.:* Goose Creek, ½ to 2 mi. W Utah boundary, 5000 ft., 3.

Ondatra zibethica mergens (Hollister)
Muskrat

Fiber zibethicus mergens Hollister, Proc. Biol. Soc. Washington, 23:1, February 2, 1910. Type from Fallon, Churchill County, Nevada. Hollister, N. Amer. Fauna, 32:27, April 29, 1911.
Ondatra zibethica mergens, Miller, Bull. U. S. Nat. Mus., 79:231, December 12, 1931; Borell and Ellis, Journ. Mamm., 15:36, February 15, 1934.
Ondatra zibethica, Linsdale, Amer. Midland Nat., 19:194, January, 1938.

Distribution.—Roughly northern half of Nevada excepting the Snake River drainage; in Smoke Creek and Truckee, Carson, Walker, Humboldt, and Reese rivers. See figure 394.

Remarks.—Measurements of three male and two female topotypes are: ♂, 552 (537–570), ♀, 545, 560; 246 (234–255), 240, 240; 79 (75–82), 80, 76; weights of a male and female from the Walker River are, respectively, 1,132 and 1,000 grams.

Size medium; color dark, darker than Prouts Brown above; skull relatively wide (see fig. 392), but nasals narrow relative to their length.

Comparisons with other races are made in the accounts of those forms. Some geographic variation is discernible when series of skulls from different streams are laid side by side. Skulls from the Humboldt River, including those from near its lower end at Lovelock, are largest and most robust; those from the Walker River are smallest and least robust; and those from Fallon on the Carson River are intermediate. The differences are all slight, and none has been found to be constant.

Tony Petroff told me of having caught muskrats at Glenbrook, in Lake Tahoe.

Records of occurrence.—Specimens examined, 167, as follows: *Washoe Co.:* Smoke Creek (2 mi. E Calif. boundary, 4100 ft., 1; 9 mi. E Calif. boundary, 3900 ft., 1), 2. *Douglas Co.:* Carson River, 5 mi. SE Minden, 4900 ft., 1. *Lyon Co.:* 5 mi. SE Wabuska, 4350 ft., 37 (35 are skulls only); West Walker River, 10½ and 12 mi. S Yerington, 4500 and 4600 ft., 2. *Pershing Co.:* 1 to 4 mi. SE Lovelock, 4000 ft., 37 (35 are skulls only). *Churchill Co.:* Fallon [3970 ft.], 6; 5 mi. SW Fallon, 1; Carson Lake (10 mi. SE, 17; 10 mi. SSE, 21), 38 (all skulls only). *Mineral Co.:* 20 mi. S Schurz, W side Walker Lake, 2. *Lander Co.:* Reese River Valley, 7 mi. N Austin, 1; Gondolpho Ranch, Reese River, 10 mi. SW Austin, 17 (8 are skulls only). *Elko Co.:* Marys River, 22 mi. N Deeth, 5000 ft., 1; Three Lakes, 9700 ft., 2 (coll. of Ralph Ellis); W side Ruby Lake, 6 mi. N White Pine Co. line, 6200 ft., 9 (8 in coll. of Ralph Ellis); W side Ruby Lake, 3 mi. N White Pine Co. line, 6200 ft., 11 (9 in coll. of Ralph Ellis).

Additional records: *Washoe Co.* (Carl P. Russell, MS): Truckee River at Reno; 4 mi. NE Reno; E side Truckee Meadows. *Douglas Co.:* Glenbrook (see text, above).

Ondatra zibethica goldmani Huey
Muskrat

Ondatra zibethica goldmani Huey, Trans. San Diego Soc. Nat. Hist., 8:409, January 18, 1938. Type from St. George, Washington County, Utah.
Ondatra zibethica bernardi, Burt, Trans. San Diego Soc. Nat. Hist., 7:422, May 31, 1934.

Distribution.—Virgin River. See figure 394.

Remarks.—Measurements of an aged male from St. Thomas and of the type specimen, a female, said by Huey (1938:409) to be an adult, are: ♂, 490, ♀, 502; 215, 215; 70, 76. Weights unavailable.

Size medium; color light, Cinnamon Brown or lighter; skull with auditory bullae well inflated, rostrum slender.

From *mergens*, this race differs in lighter color, smaller average size, including measured parts of the skull, and greater average inflation of the auditory bullae. From *bernardi*, *goldmani* differs in larger size, relatively narrower skull, and more inflated auditory bullae; in the specimens available, the color is indistinguishable as between the two races. The one character of *goldmani* which is not intermediate between that of *bernardi*, on the one hand, and that of *mergens* and *osoyoosensis*, on the other hand, is the more inflated auditory bullae.

The aged male from the vicinity of St. Thomas, in every cranial measurement taken, falls within the range shown by skulls of *goldmani*, and in each measurement taken of the skull is larger than the largest *bernardi*. In external measurements it appears to be intermediate between the two kinds, as it is also geographically.

Records of occurrence.—Specimens examined, 10, as follows: *Clark Co.*: Virgin River, 1 mi. SW Mesquite, 10 (4 skins only and 6 skulls only); Muddy Creek, "near St. Thomas," 1 (D.R. Dickey Coll.).

TABLE 20

CRANIAL MEASUREMENTS (IN MILLIMETERS) OF ONDATRA

Name and locality	Number of individuals averaged or catalogue no.	Sex	Basal length	Zygomatic breadth	Length of nasals	Breadth of nasals	Alveolar length of upper molar series
Ondatra zibethica osoyoosensis							
Goose Creek	68606	♂	63.8	40.3	21.8	10.5	16.0
Goose Creek	68605	♀	59.9	37.8	21.7	9.5	15.0
Ondatra zibethica mergens							
Fallon	10 av.	♂	61.8	40.4	21.6	9.1	14.9
	min.		60.5	39.1	20.5	8.7	14.5
	max.		63.3	42.5	23.4	9.5	15.3
Fallon	10 av.	♀	60.6	39.4	21.0	8.9	14.9
	min.		57.2	37.2	20.3	8.3	14.4
	max.		63.3	40.3	21.8	9.6	15.5
Ondatra zibethica goldmani							
1 mi. SW Mesquite	57338	♂?	58.3	39.1	19.6	9.1	15.1
1 mi. SW Mesquite	57339	♀?	55.0	36.3	19.7	9.2	14.8
Ondatra zibethica bernardi		♂					
Colorado River, Nevada	5 av.		54.3	37.2	18.6	8.5	14.2
	min.		53.0	36.6	18.0	8.0	13.8
	max.		55.5	38.0	19.1	8.8	14.6
Colorado River, Nevada	61871	♀	52.8	35.6	18.2	8.1	14.0
Colorado River, Nevada	61876	♀	52.4	35.1	18.0	8.0	14.0

Ondatra zibethica bernardi Goldman
Muskrat

Ondatra zibethica bernardi Goldman, Proc. Biol. Soc. Washington, 45:93, June 21, 1932. Type from 4 mi.
S Gadsden, Yuma County, Arizona.

Distribution.—Colorado River. See figure 394.

Remarks.—Measurements of five males and two females are: ♂, 464 (436–489), ♀, 440, 437; 204 (180–216), 190, 195; 68 (64–70), 65, 65; weight, 697 (609.8–777.0), 601, 541 grams.

Size small; color pale, lighter than Cinnamon Brown; skull with auditory bullae but slightly inflated.

Comparison with *goldmani* is made in the account of that race. The small size and light color are the outstanding characters of *bernardi*. We have no information about the occurrence or nonoccurrence of this animal on the Colorado River above Boulder Dam before its completion and the formation of Lake Mead.

Records of occurrence.—Specimens examined, 8, as follows: *Clark Co.:* Colorado River, Durban Ranch, 14 mi. E Searchlight, 1; Colorado River, 2 mi. N Calif.-Nev. Monument, 500 ft., 7.

Rattus rattus alexandrinus (Geoffroy)
Black Rat

Mus alexandrinus Geoffroy, Catal. Mammif. du Mus. Nat. d'Hist., Paris, p. 192. Type from Alexandria, Egypt.
R[*attus*]. *rattus alexandrinus*, Hinton, Journ. Bombay Nat. Hist. Soc., 26:63, December 20, 1918.

Distribution.—Known only from northeastern outskirts of Reno. See figure 401.

Remarks.—A male and 2 females measure 402, 417, 395; 195 (possibly end missing), 227, 223; 37, 37, 38; height of ear from notch, 23, 22, 25; weight, ——, 172.4, —— grams.

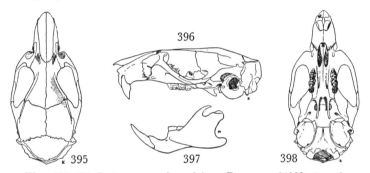

Figs. 395–398. *Rattus rattus alexandrinus*, Reno, no. 94922, ♀. ×1.

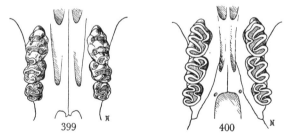

Figs. 399, 400. Enlarged views of the occlusal faces of the upper cheek teeth, of roughly equal degree of wear in the two species. Note the cusps arranged in three longitudinal rows in *Rattus*, and the enclosed lakes and re-entrant angles in *Neotoma*. ×3.

Fig. 399. *Rattus rattus alexandrinus*, Reno, no. 94922, ♀.
Fig. 400. *Neotoma lepida lepida*, Baker Creek, 7300 feet, no. 42031, ♀.

Rats of this genus have scaly, nearly naked tails; nearly naked ears; pelage coarser than native rats of the genus *Neotoma;* temporal ridge developed as a distinct crest which extends from above eye to lambdoidal crest; incisors compressed so that anteroposterior diameter exceeds transverse diameter; three cheek teeth on each side above and below, tuberculate and brachyodont. From the wood rats (*Neotoma*), these rats are distinguished by the tuberculate, as opposed to flat, occlusal faces of the cheek teeth. From the Norway Rat (*Rattus norvegicus*), *Rattus rattus* differs in: size smaller; ears larger; tail longer, rather than shorter, than head and body; females normally with five pairs of mammae (two of which are pectoral) rather than with six pairs (three of which are pectoral); temporal

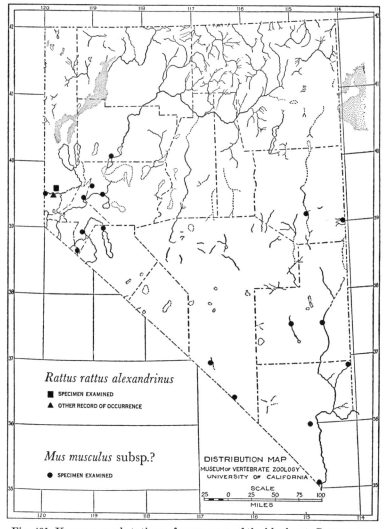

Fig. 401. Known record stations of occurrence of the black rat, *Rattus rattus*, and the house mouse, *Mus musculus*.

ridges bowed outward rather than parallel; length of a parietal measured along a temporal ridge noticeably less than, rather than about equal to, greatest distance between these ridges. The dental formula is i. $\frac{1}{1}$, c. $\frac{0}{0}$, p. $\frac{0}{0}$, m. $\frac{3}{3}$.

This rat is not native to Nevada, but came there following the arrival of white men. The species *Rattus rattus* is a native of the Old World, but now has been conveyed to most all parts of the world and has established itself in the temperate and tropical regions of all continents. By those who prefer to employ common names distinctive for subspecies, *Rattus rattus alexandrinus* is referred to as the Alexandrine rat, and black rat is the name applied to the subspecies *Rattus rattus rattus*. It appears that the subspecific differences between the race *rattus* and *alexandrinus* are matters of color; I know of no cranial differences or differences in size or relative proportions of parts of the body or skull to distinguish the two. Each of our six Nevadan specimens are brownish-gray above and creamy white below, and therefore answer to the description of *alexandrinus*.

In many parts of temperate North America where the species *Rattus rattus* was once fairly abundant it has become rare or has been driven out entirely by the related species *Rattus norvegicus*. In advance of receiving specimens from Reno I supposed that *norvegicus* was the rat found there, but each of the six specimens, all from the area on the northeastern edge of Reno where garbage is unloaded in the desert, are of the species *rattus*. J. R. Alcorn obtained the first one there on August 24, 1939, and T. J. Trelease subsequently took another specimen on February 23, 1940, and four others in early January of 1941, showing that *rattus* and not *norvegicus* is *the* species which lives in that place. Carl P. Russell (MS), a number of years earlier, recorded the same subspecies from 2 miles south of Reno. J. R. Alcorn reports that no trace of introduced rats was found in 1939 when he searched for and inquired about them in Fallon.

Record of occurrence.—Specimens examined: *Washoe Co.:* Reno, 6.
Additional record: *Washoe Co.:* 2 mi. S Reno (Carl P. Russell, MS).

Mus musculus subsp. ?
House Mouse

Mus musculus Linnaeus, Systema Naturae, 10 ed., 1:58, 1758. Type locality probably southern Sweden.
Mus musculus musculus, Burt, Trans. San Diego Soc. Nat. Hist., 7:422, May 31, 1934.

Distribution.—Nonnative, but, nevertheless, now distributed throughout the state. See figure 401.

Remarks.—Measurements of a male and female from Baker are 165, 170; 71, 75; 18, 17.5; ear from notch, 13.5, 13.0; weight, 22.3, —— grams.

Tail thinly haired and scaly; ears large and thinly haired; brownish above and below; underparts often with less blackish than upper parts; tail not sharply bicolored and only slightly lighter below; feet dusky; mammae in five pairs, three pairs pectoral and two pairs abdominal; nasals projecting posteriorly about as far as premaxillae (sometimes farther, but sometimes falling short of premaxillae); incisive foramina large and extending posteriorly almost as far as middle of first upper cheek tooth; rostrum short; incisors smooth on anterior face; occlusal surface of upper incisors notched; three cheek teeth on each side in upper and lower jaw; first upper tooth largest, its length slightly exceeding the combined lengths of the other two; last upper cheek tooth the smallest; crown pattern of cheek tooth essentially as in *Rattus*. The dental formula is i. $\frac{1}{1}$, c. $\frac{0}{0}$, p. $\frac{0}{0}$, m. $\frac{3}{3}$.

Several subspecific names have been proposed for populations of this mouse which is supposed originally to have been restricted to the north temperate part of Europe and southwestern Asia. It is fond of the shelter, warmth, and food provided in man's dwellings, and in his baggage and goods has been distributed over most of the world. Probably it arrived in Nevada with, or shortly after, the first white settlers. Because I suspect that some of the Nevadan animals are the results of crosses between two or more named strains, no attempt here is made to assign subspecific names to the specimens. Most of the specimens have the underparts colored about like the upper parts, but there are some exceptions. The most striking exception is in an animal taken in midwinter, in the wild, along the Colorado River, ½ mile from the California boundary. The underparts of this mouse are white, although the hair is plumbeous basally. Another taken oṅ Desert Creek is lighter below than above, but the underparts are distinctly buffy. The animals most nearly black above are three taken in spring in a house at Baker, White Pine County.

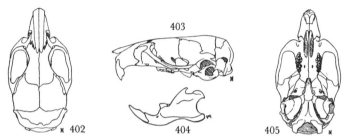

Figs. 402–405. *Mus musculus* subsp. ?, Baker, 5800 feet, no. 41874, ♂. ×1½.

TABLE 21

CRANIAL MEASUREMENTS (IN MILLIMETERS) OF RATTUS AND MUS

Sex	Catalogue no.	Locality	Occipitonasal length	Basilar length	Palatilar length	Length of nasals	Zygomatic breadth	Mastoidal breadth	Width across upper molars	Alveolar length of upper cheek teeth	Alveolar length of lower cheek teeth
			Rattus rattus alexandrinus								
♂	90613	Reno........	45.4	35.9	19.2	16.1	21.6	17.3	8.7	6.6	6.5
♀	94921	Reno........	43.9	33.8	19.1	15.6	20.3	16.2	8.6	6.8	6.6
♀	88129	Reno........	41.9	33.9	18.8	15.0	20.0	17.0	8.5	6.5	6.4
			Mus musculus								
♂	41874	Baker.......	21.9	17.5	9.5	8.5	11.8	9.7	4.6	3.6	2.9
♀	41876	Baker.......	22.2	17.5	9.7	8.0	12.0	9.5	4.7	3.7	3.2

Probably the mice are generally distributed over the state about dwellings occupied by man. In the mild climate of the Lower Sonoran Life-zone and lower part of the Upper Sonoran Life-zone they live all winter out of doors; this is indicated by the taking of specimens in midwinter in the southern tip of the state and in November two and a half miles west of Hazen. In the zonally higher parts of Nevada where the winters are colder the mice in winter probably live almost entirely in or about buildings. In Nevada, house mice often are caught in the same places as harvest mice; grassy areas near water are favored by both species. At times, as indicated by specimens taken on October 1 and 2, 1931, in the vicinity of Mesquite, the house mice live under desert conditions far from water. Judging from the catch in our traps, in this vicinity, on the higher sandy desert as well as in the river bottom, the house mouse was the most common species of mammal.

Under favorable conditions house mice reproduce rapidly; the number of young in a litter seems to average larger than in any rodent of comparable size native to Nevada. The 2 adult females taken in June had 9 and 10 embryos. Six other adult females were without embryos. By months these were taken as follows: January, 1; May, 1; July, 2; August, 1; and September, 1.

Records of occurrence.—Specimens examined, 35, as follows: *Washoe Co.:* W side Truckee River, ½ mi. W Verdi, 4900 ft., 1. *Lyon Co.:* 4 mi. W Hazen, 4250 ft., 1; West Walker River, 6 mi. S Yerington, 4500 ft., 1; Mason Valley, 10 mi. S Yerington, 4500 ft., 1; Desert Creek, Sweetwater Range, 6250 ft., 1. *Pershing Co.:* Toulon, 3930 ft., 1. *Churchill Co.:* 2 mi. W Hazen, Truckee Canal (Lyon County on specimen labels), 8 (skulls only); 1 mi. W Hazen, 4020 ft., 2; 3 mi. W Fallon, 4000 ft., 1. *Mineral Co.:* Schurz Indian dam, Walker River, 4300 ft., 3 (skulls only). *Nye Co.:* Amargosa River, 4 mi. NE Beatty, 3500 ft., 1; Ash Meadows, 4 4/5 mi. NW Devils Hole, 2200 ft., 2. *White Pine Co.:* 5½ mi. SE Ely, 6500 ft., 1; Baker, 5800 ft., 3. *Lincoln Co.:* Crystal Spring, Pahranagat Valley, 4000 ft., 1; 3 mi. S Crystal Spring, 3900 ft., 1; Meadow Valley, 7 mi. S Caliente, 4000 ft., 1. *Clark Co.:* Virgin River, ¾ mi. E Mesquite, 1750 ft., 3; Boulder City, 2400 ft., 1 (Boulder Dam Recreational Area Coll.); Colorado River, ½ mi. N Calif.-Nev. Monument, 500 ft., 1.

Additional record: *Washoe Co.:* 2 mi. S Reno (Carl P. Russell, MS).

Aplodontia rufa californica (Peters)
Mountain Beaver

H[aplodon]. leporinus var. *Californicus* Peters, Monatsber. k. preuss. Akad. Wissensch. Berlin, p. 179, 1864. Type from Sierra Nevada of California (see under remarks).
Aplodontia rufa californica, Trouessart, Catal. Mamm. viv. foss., suppl., p. 348, 1904; Finley, The Murrelet, 22:45, January 20, 1942.

Distribution.—Boreal life-zones of Sierra Nevada. See figure 253, page 354.

Remarks.—Measurements of a male and female from Chinquapin and from near Porcupine Flat, California, respectively, are: ♀, 361, ♂, 347; 40 (sic), 19; 55, 61; weight, ——, 1,014.7 grams. Taylor (1918:440) indicates that males average larger than females, the amount being about 8 per cent in total length.

Tail vestigial, shorter than hind foot; body thick set and legs short; ears small; foot soles naked; five clawed digits on each foot; general body form much as in a pocket gopher (genus *Geomys*), but forelimbs relatively smaller; upper parts ochraceous mixed with black and with some silvery tipped hairs; underparts grayish; hair everywhere plumbeous at base; light spot at base of ear; pelage of young less reddish and grayer; skull remarkably flat, and relatively broad, especially posteriorly; no postorbital processes on frontals; incisive foramina small and not reaching halfway back from incisors to premolars; hard palate behind line connecting last upper molars; angle of mandible greatly expanded transversely; dental formula: i. $\frac{1}{1}$, c. $\frac{0}{0}$, p. $\frac{2}{1}$, m. $\frac{3}{3}$. Cheek teeth hypsodont, of secondarily simple pattern, and, excepting the anterior-most upper premolar, each tooth with a prominent style (labial side of upper teeth and lingual side of lower teeth); fibula not articulating with calcaneum and free from tibia; mammae in three pairs, one pair pectoral and two pair abdominal.

The single living species of the single genus of the family ranges down the coast from southern British Columbia to the Golden Gate, and in the Cascade–Sierra Nevada chain of mountains to Mammoth, Mono County, California. The subspecies *californica* was named in 1864 by Peters who stated that his

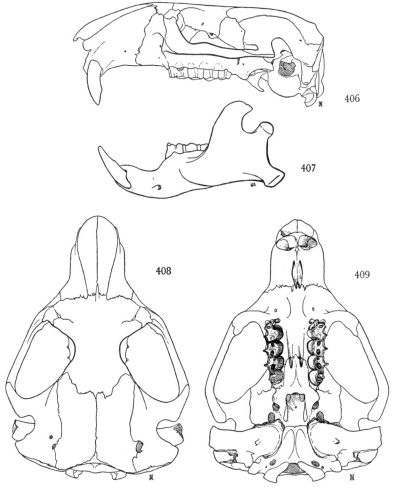

Figs. 406–409. *Aplodontia rufa californica*, ½ mile south Marlette Lake, no. 67066, ♂, young, with worn deciduous premolars still in place. ×1.

specimen came from the mountains of California. Taylor (1918:475) chose to apply the name *californica* to the race in the Sierra Nevada, although some previous American zoölogists regarded the name as untenable. In August, 1937, I examined the type specimen, a young female, in the Berlin Zoölogical Museum. Study of the data on the original label and study of the skin and skull (Hall, 1942:50) made me almost certain that the name was correctly applied by Taylor (*loc. cit.*).

Taylor (1918:450) says that the mountain beaver is "herbivorous, . . . nocturnal, and fossorial. A considerable degree of humidity and an abundant supply of food plants seem to be necessary conditions to its existence. Situations well sheltered by a tangle of vegetation are usually chosen for its burrows. Its nest is made underground, in an enlarged chamber. . . . Sight and hearing are apparently defective; but smell and touch, particularly the latter, appear to make up for any deficiencies in these respects." Detailed notes on the habits of these animals in the Pacific Northwest have been published by

TABLE 22

CRANIAL MEASUREMENTS (IN MILLIMETERS) OF APLODONTIA

Sex and age	Catalogue no.	Locality	Basilar length	Length of nasals	Width of nasals	Zygomatic breadth	Mastoidal breadth	Alveolar length of superior cheek teeth
♂	22620	Chinquapin, California.......	62.3	28.2	11.5	56.0	53.0	20.0
♀	22622	Near Porcupine Flat, Calif....	60.9	26.6	11.7	58.0	54.4	19.9
♂ yg.	67066	½ mi. S Marlette Lake.......	55.9	24.4	10.3	50.4	45.0	17.1

Anthony (1916) and Scheffer (1929), and even fuller observations on Californian animals have been made by Camp (1918).

The specimen from a half mile south of Marlette Lake was trapped in the entrance of a burrow out of which water was running. The burrow was in a dense tangle of willow, honeysuckle, and aspen. This was a place pointed out to me by W. H. Dust, caretaker at Marlette Lake. In years previous to 1934 he had caught several mountain beavers there. The second Nevadan specimen was saved for me by Lester West. Both the Nevadan specimens are young; in each the deciduous fourth upper premolars still are in place. In August, 1934, Jim Howell, fire guard stationed at the north end of Lake Tahoe, described animals seen by him, 2 years before, on the lower part of Incline Creek, that answered to the description of *Aplodontia*. Probably the animals occur in Nevada only in those parts of the Sierra Nevada in the southwestern part of Washoe County, the eastern part of Ormsby County, and the northwestern part of Douglas County.

Records of occurrence.—Specimens examined, 2, as follows: *Washoe Co.:* 2½ mi. W and ⅛ mi. S Lakeview, about 7500 ft., 1. *Ormsby Co.:* ½ mi. S Marlette Lake, 8150 ft., 1.

Additional record: *Washoe Co.:* Incline (see account above).

Zapus princeps
Big Jumping Mouse

There are four subspecies of the big jumping mouse in Nevada. Noteworthy features are the lengthened, five-toed hind foot; tail which averages more than one and a half times the length of the body; four pairs of mammae, one pectoral, two abdominal, and one inguinal; blackish middorsal area sharply set off from, and about same width as, each ochraceous side; underparts pure white all the way to base of hair and sharply set off from sides ordinarily by a narrow lateral line of nearly pure Ochraceous-Buff; skull with broad but tapered rostrum; infraorbital canal proper less than one millimeter in diameter, and at

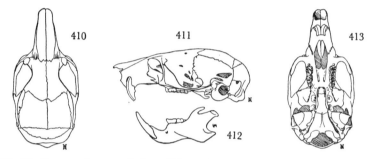

Figs. 410–413. *Zapus princeps palatinus*, Wisconsin Creek, 7800 feet, no. 45871, ♂. ×1½.

the bottom of a false infraorbital foramen, five times greater in diameter, which transmits part of the masseter muscle. The dental formula is i. $\frac{1}{1}$, c. $\frac{0}{0}$, p. $\frac{1}{0}$, m. $\frac{3}{3}$.

Jumping mice are inhabitants of the Boreal life-zones. Altitudinally, they were taken from as low as 6000 to as high as 8500 feet, both of these extreme elevations being in the Pine Forest Mountains. In the sparsely forested area of Nevada, these mice live near streams. Linsdale (1938:195) remarks that "every one [he saved sixteen specimens] was caught within 20 feet of water" in the Toyabe Mountains. This was from May 24 to June 15. Much the same distribution was noted at Cobb Creek from July 22 to 25, and along the creek 13 miles north of Paradise Valley from July 29 to 31, but at each of these places some young individuals were caught in aspen thickets as far as 150 yards from a stream. A typical habitat for *Zapus* was that at the south end of Marlette Lake and along the stream flowing into it from the south where the animals lived amidst a growth of larkspur, monkshood, and aspen. Characteristic signs left by *Zapus* are pieces of stems of herbaceous plants and grass cut in lengths of 1 to 2 inches—pieces longer than those that are cut by *Microtus longicaudus* which lives in the same places.

Jumping mice are nocturnal. They live in globular nests made of dried grass or plant fibers placed on the surface of the ground in tall grass (Borell and Ellis, 1934a:37). In winter they hibernate, usually, it is said, in burrows in the ground. Like other mammals which hibernate, a large supply of fat is accumulated in late summer and autumn. On Cobb Creek from July 22 to 25, 1935, fourteen adult females, three adult males, and 147 young of the year, sex not

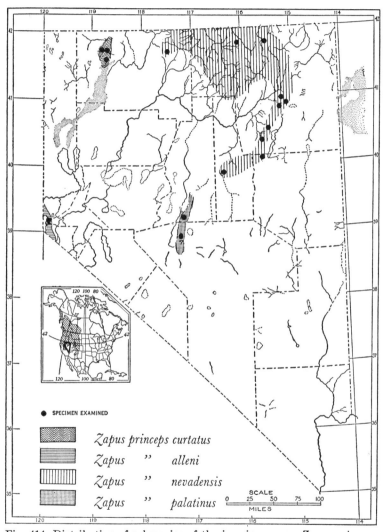

● SPECIMEN EXAMINED

Zapus princeps curtatus

Zapus ” alleni

Zapus ” nevadensis

Zapus ” palatinus

SCALE
0   25   50   75   100
MILES

Fig. 414. Distribution of subspecies of the jumping mouse, *Zapus princeps*, with insert showing range of the species.

recorded, were trapped. Every adult male was "very fat," unlike any of the other specimens. Thirteen miles north of Paradise Valley, in the last 3 days of July of 1935, some of the adult females were definitely fat. These weighed a fourth more (41.3 grams as against 32 grams) than lean adults of the same sex.

Probably the bearing and nursing of young delay the accumulation of fat in females. Judging from our catch, the adult males in the last 3 days of July had already begun hibernation (more properly, estivation) or had at least curtailed their activities more than the adult females had curtailed theirs. At the last-mentioned locality the actual catch of specimens was eight adult females, no adult males, and sixty-six young of the year of both sexes.

Secondary sexual variation apparently is of slight amount. Males appear to average a fraction of 1 per cent larger than females, but too few adult males are available to permit making a positive statement in this regard. By weight, the three adult males taken on July 24 and 25, on Cobb Creek, average 6 per cent heavier than females, but this may be misleading because males seem to accumulate fat in preparation for the long period of dormancy earlier than do females.

Of fifty-seven adult females, nine were pregnant. Three had four embryos each, three had five, two had six, and one had seven, which gives an average of 5.1. By months, the adult females were distributed as follows: May, seven (none pregnant); June, twenty-one (seven pregnant); July, twenty-nine (two).

Zapus princeps curtatus Hall
Big Jumping Mouse

Zapus princeps curtatus Hall, Univ. California Publ. Zoöl., 37:7, April 10, 1931. Type from head of Big Creek, 8000 feet, Pine Forest Mountains, Humboldt County, Nevada.
Zapus princeps oregonus, Taylor, Univ. California Publ. Zoöl., 7:281, June 24, 1911.

Distribution.—Pine Forest Mountains of Humboldt County. See figure 414.

Remarks.—Measurements of a male and four females from the Pine Forest Mountains are: ♂, 213, ♀, 228 (220–235); 130, 132 (125–141); 30, 32 (31–33); weights not recorded.

Size small; coloration pale; lateral line faintly indicated; posterior border of palate convex anteriorly; palatal bridge short; incisive foramina wide posteriorly.

From *Z. p. oregonus*, the race to the northward in Oregon, this form differs in: size less; sides of head and back lighter; lateral stripe less well defined; zygomatic breadth less; palatal bridge shorter; incisive foramina wider, especially posteriorly; brain case narrower; rostrum larger; nasals wider at posterior end. From *Z. p. major*, the race to the westward in the Warner Mountains of northeastern California and southern Oregon, *curtatus* differs in: size less; face lighter; skull more rounded and shorter in posterior part, with brain case more inflated relatively to anterior part of zygomatic structure; zygomatic and mastoidal breadth less; tooth row and palatal bridge shorter; zygomatic arches more bowed out in posterior part. From *Z. p. nevadensis*, *curtatus* differs in: size less; sides more yellowish; skull averaging smaller in all parts measured, except length of upper cheek teeth, which measurement is the same; palatal bridge shorter, averaging 3.2 rather than 3.6 mm. or more. Comparison with *alleni* and *palatinus* are made in the accounts of those forms.

Records of occurrence.—Specimens examined, 19, as follows: *Humboldt Co.:* Pine Forest Mountains; Alder Creek, 6000 ft., 2; head of Big Creek, 8000 ft., 14; Pine Forest Mtn. (= Duffer Peak), 8500 ft., 1; Leonard Creek, 6500 ft., 2.

Zapus princeps alleni Elliot
Big Jumping Mouse

Zapus alleni Elliot, Field Columbian Mus., publ. 27, zoöl. ser., 1:212, March, 1898. Type from Pyramid Peak, Lake Tahoe, Eldorado County, California.

Distribution.—Sierra Nevada in vicinity of Lake Tahoe. See figure 414.

Remarks.—Measurements of ten males and two females from Yosemite National Park are: ♂, 217 (207–232), ♀, 221, 219; 127 (115–138), 135, 128; 31 (30–33), 32, 30; weight of July-taken specimens, 22.1 (17.8–27.5), 19.0, 21.2 grams.

Size small; color bright, sides Ochraceous Buff, causing, in many specimens, the Ochraceous Buff lateral line to be widened to such an extent that it includes all of the side; dorsal dark area sharply set off from sides; skull small; auditory bullae relatively small; incisive foramina narrowed posteriorly; posterior border of palate convex anteriorly.

From each of the other Nevadan races, *alleni* differs in: color much brighter, more ochraceous and less blackish on sides; back with more ochraceous color; auditory bullae relatively as well as actually smaller; incisive foramina narrower posteriorly.

The assignment of *alleni* to the species *princeps* is not done on wholly satisfactory grounds because actual intergrades between *alleni* and any other one of the Nevadan races are lacking. Also, the degree of difference between *alleni* and any other Nevadan race is greater than that between any other two of the races. As between these other races, which also are isolated from one another, the differences are not greater than those which ordinarily exist between subspecies in other groups where actual intergradation takes place. Taking into account all features as best I can, it seems better to treat all four kinds of *Zapus* from Nevada as belonging to the single species *princeps*.

The race *alleni* occurs in Nevada only in the Sierra Nevada of southwestern Washoe County, of eastern Ormsby County, and probably of northwestern Douglas County.

Records of occurrence.—Specimens examined, 8, as follows: *Washoe Co.:* ½ mi. S Mt. Rose, 9500 ft., 2; 3 mi. SSW Mt. Rose, 9000 ft., 1. *Ormsby Co.:* S end Marlette Lake, 8000 ft., 2; ½ mi. S Marlette Lake, 8150 ft., 3.

Zapus princeps nevadensis Preble
Big Jumping Mouse

Zapus nevadensis Preble, N. Amer. Fauna, 15:25, August 8, 1899. Type from Ruby Mountains, Elko County, Nevada.
Zapus princeps nevadensis, Hall, Univ. California Publ. Zoöl., 37:10, April 10, 1931; Borell and Ellis, Journ. Mamm., 15:37, 73, February 15, 1934.

Distribution.—Northeastern Nevada; from Roberts Mountains northward through Ruby Mountains to Jarbidge Mountains and west into Santa Rosa Mountains. See figure 414.

Remarks.—Measurements of five males and seven females from the Ruby Mountains are: ♂, 242 (236–246), ♀, 244 (239–250); 143 (139–147), 144 (139–150); 32.6 (32–34), 32.9 (32–35); weights not recorded, but for three males and eleven females taken in late July from Cobb Creek, weights are: ♂, 32.5 (31.1–34.0) ♀, 31.0 (27.1–37.5) grams.

Size large; coloration pale; lateral line wanting; posterior border of palate convex anteriorly; palatal bridge long; skull broad.

From *Z. p. cinereus*, the race to the northeast, in adjoining parts of Utah and Idaho, *nevadensis* differs in: size greater; tail relatively longer; coloration everywhere darker; side of head between eye and nose Pinkish Buff mixed with black, rather than light gray or whitish. Comparisons with *curtatus* and *palatinus* are made in the accounts of those forms.

The animals from 6 miles southwest of Mountain City agree closely with those from the Ruby Mountains. The animals from 13 miles north of Paradise Valley likewise agree with *nevadensis*, despite their nearness geographically to *curtatus*. From *curtatus*, these specimens from north of Paradise Valley differ in: body longer; tail longer and more distinctly bicolored; hind foot longer; dorsal stripe darker and more definitely outlined; sides with more Ochraceous Buff; occipitonasal length, zygomatic breadth, and length of palate more. In *curtatus*, the posterior margin of the palate is considerably anterior to a line connecting the posterior margins of the last molars, but in *nevadensis* the posterior margin of the palate is only slightly anterior to a line connecting the posterior margins of the last molars. In the animals from north of Paradise Valley, four have the palate as it is in *nevadensis*, three have the palate ending behind the molars, and in two it is even with the

TABLE 23

CRANIAL MEASUREMENTS (IN MILLIMETERS) OF ZAPUS

Sex	Locality	Number of individuals averaged	Occipitonasal length	Zygomatic breadth	Mastoidal breadth	Least interorbital breadth	Length of palatal bridge	Alveolar length of upper tooth row	Height of skull*
					Zapus princeps curtatus				
♂	Pine Forest Mountains.....	1	24.5	12.3	11.0	5.0	3.2	4.3	9.5
♀	Pine Forest Mountains.....	6 av.	24.6	12.5	11.2	4.8	3.2	4.3	9.5
		min.	24.0	12.2	10.8	4.6	2.8	3.9	9.1
		max.	25.3	12.7	11.3	5.0	3.4	4.4	9.7
					Zapus princeps alleni				
♂	Yosemite Nat. Park, Calif..	1	23.4	12.5	10.3	4.4	3.8	3.8	9.3
♀	Yosemite Nat. Park, Calif..	1	23.5	12.5	10.8	4.4	3.2	3.8	9.7
					Zapus princeps nevadensis				
♂	Ruby Mountains...........	5 av.	25.3	12.7	11.4	4.9	3.7	4.4	9.6
		min.	24.9	12.5	11.1	4.8	3.5	4.2	9.5
		max.	25.7	13.0	11.8	5.0	3.8	4.4	9.8
♀	Ruby Mountains...........	7 av.	25.0	12.6	11.4	5.0	3.6	4.3	9.5
		min.	24.0	12.3	11.0	4.8	3.4	4.1	9.4
		max.	25.5	13.7	11.7	5.1	3.8	4.4	9.8
					Zapus princeps palatinus				
♂	Toyabe Mountains.........	12 av.	24.6	12.5	11.4	5.0	3.6	4.3	9.6
		min.	23.8	12.2	11.0	4.8	3.5	4.1	9.3
		max.	25.3	13.0	11.6	5.1	3.8	4.4	9.9
♀	Toyabe Mountains.........	2	25.0	12.7	11.5	5.0	3.6	4.3	9.3
			23.5	12.3	10.8	5.0	3.6	4.2	9.4

* Taken from topmost part of skull to a flat surface on which the skull is supported by the tips of the incisors and tympanic bullae or other ventralmost projection of the basicranial region.

posterior margins of the molars. These detailed comparisons make clear that these westernmost specimens of *nevadensis* show no close approach to *curtatus*.

The adult male from the Roberts Mountains of Eureka County is structurally as well as geographically intermediate between *nevadensis* and *palatinus*. The incisive foramina are narrower, as in *nevadensis*, and the posterior margin of the palate is more anteriorly situated, as in that form, although this margin of the palate is straight or even slightly convex posteriorly, as in typical *palatinus*. Everything considered, the specimen shows greater resemblance to *nevadensis*.

Records of occurrence.—Specimens examined, 147, as follows: *Humboldt Co.:* 13 mi. N Paradise Valley, 6700 ft., 51. *Eureka Co.:* 4 mi. S Tonkin, Denay Creek, Roberts Mts., 1. *Elko Co.* (unless otherwise noted, in coll. of Ralph Ellis): Cobb Creek, 6 mi. SW Mountain City, 6500–6550 ft., 45 (Mus. Vert. Zoöl.); summit between heads of Copper and Coon creeks, Jarbidge Mts., 10 (1 in Mus. Vert. Zoöl.); head of Ackler Creek, 6800 ft., 3 (1 in Mus. Vert. Zoöl.); Steels Creek, 7000 ft., 13 (8 in Mus. Vert. Zoöl.); summit of Secret Pass, 6200 ft., 7; Long Creek, 7830 ft., 4; Harrison Pass R. S., Green Mountain Canyon, 6050 ft., 5. *White Pine Co.:* Willow Creek, 2 mi. S Elko Co. line, 6500 ft., 8 (6 in coll. of Ralph Ellis).

Zapus princeps palatinus Hall
Big Jumping Mouse

Zapus princeps palatinus Hall, Univ. California Publ. Zoöl., 37:8, April 10, 1931. Type from Wisconsin Creek, 7800 feet, Toyabe Mountains, Nye County, Nevada.
Zapus princeps, Linsdale, Amer. Midland Nat., 19:195, January, 1938.

Distribution.—Toyabe Mountains of central Nevada. See figure 414.

Remarks.—Measurements of twelve males and two females are: ♂, 231 (220–240), ♀, 232, 200; 135 (125–147), 131, 113; 32.7 (31–35), 32, 29; weight of adults taken from May 24 to June 6, 26.3 (21.5–28.5), 26.7, —— grams.

Size small; coloration pale; lateral line wanting; tail short; posterior border of palate straight or convex posteriorly; palatal bridge long; incisive foramina wide posteriorly.

From *nevadensis*, this race differs in: body and tail shorter; posterior border of palate straight or convex posteriorly, rather than convex anteriorly; incisive foramina averaging wider posteriorly. From *curtatus*, *palatinus* differs in: sides grayer (less yellowish); posterior border of palate straight or convex posteriorly, rather than convex anteriorly; incisive foramina wider posteriorly, with posterior border more nearly truncate; palatal bridge longer (no overlap in specimens examined); interorbital and mastoidal breadths greater.

The nearest relative of *palatinus* is the race *nevadensis*. To me, the two are indistinguishable in color. In two of the twelve adult specimens of *nevadensis* from the Ruby Mountains the palate is straight, as it is in many individuals of *palatinus*. In one specimen of *palatinus* the palate is convex anteriorly, as it is in *nevadensis*. Nevertheless, even these three specimens are identifiable as to subspecies on the basis of the more anteriorly situated (with respect to the last upper molars) posterior border of the palate in *nevadensis*.

The generally straight or posteriorly convex margin of the palate seems to be unique among named kinds of *Zapus*.

Although looked for in the Desatoya and Shoshone mountain ranges to the west of the Toyabe Range and in the Toquima and Monitor ranges to the eastward, *Zapus* has been taken in central Nevada only in the Toyabe Range.

Records of occurrence.—Specimens examined, 16, as follows: *Lander Co.:* Kingston R. S., 7500 ft., 4. *Nye Co.:* Wisconsin Creek, 7000–8200 ft., 12.

Erethizon epixanthum
Porcupine

Two subspecies of porcupine occur in Nevada. The species may be characterized as: tail less than a third of total length; foot soles naked; four clawed digits on forefeet and five clawed digits on hind feet; mammae in three pairs, one pair pectoral and two pairs abdominal; color of upper parts yellowish or rarely black; nasals extending far behind premaxillae; well-developed sagittal crest in adults; length of diastema more than that of upper cheek teeth; infraorbital canal about twice the area of the foramen magnum; incisors above and below smooth (not grooved) and red on anterior face. The dental formula is i. $\frac{1}{1}$, c. $\frac{0}{0}$, p. $\frac{1}{1}$, m. $\frac{3}{3}$.

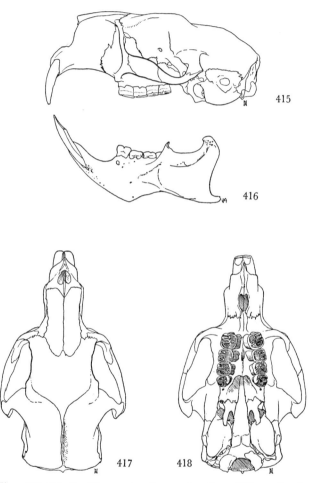

Figs. 415–418. *Erethizon epixanthum epixanthum*, Wilson Creek, 7200 feet, no. 88223, ♂. × ½.

The hair is of three kinds: (1) quills up to 75 mm. long and 2 mm. in diameter, white or light yellowish-white except for about the distal 10 mm., which is black; (2) hair up to 175 mm. long, which is distally yellow, basally white, and black in the middle half (in an occasional specimen the base also is black); (3) fur, in winter-taken specimens up to 100 mm. long, black except for the basal third, which is white. In winter this fur projects beyond and conceals the quills. In summer-taken specimens the fur is absent or so short that it can be found only by parting the spines and looking close to the skin. On the underside of the body, throat, chin, cheeks posteriorly to the level of the eyes, and nose, quills are lacking, the fur is shorter than elsewhere, and the coarser hairs lack the distal yellowish pigment and are black throughout their length.

A young female measuring 483 mm. in total length, taken June 19, 1929, has black fur and black hair which conceals the spines of normal color pattern and gives an all-black appearance except for a few hairs which are white in their distal five-sixths and black in the basal sixth. A subadult female taken June 20, 1929, on Baker Creek, lacks the fur, and the hairs have tips of yellow so short (20 mm.) that the remaining all-black (in this animal) part of the hair and the normally black tips of the quills give the individual a distinctly black appearance. The specimens otherwise appear to be yellow.

The material available at this writing is not adequate to show whether the animal in western North America currently known as *Erethizon epixanthum* is specifically distinct from the earlier named *Erethizon dorsatum* of the more eastern part of the continent.

The quills of porcupines are a defensive armament which effectively protects these large rodents from carnivores. Exception to this probably should be made for inexperienced individuals of the other species of carnivores which occasionally seek to kill a porcupine, and exception probably should also be made for the fisher, which, although unrecorded from Nevada, would be expected to occur only in the limited area about Lake Tahoe. Never have I seen a porcupine attack a tormentor, but almost every porcupine that I have closely approached has reacted by flipping the dangerous tail in my direction. Armed as it is with quills, it is capable of inflicting painful wounds. If quills on the tail happened to be loose, they probably would fall out or conceivably be thrown when the tail is thus flicked. I have never seen this happen, but I suppose that it occasionally does happen and that this is the basis for the belief held by some persons that porcupines throw their quills.

Judging from the vegetation in places where I have found porcupines in Nevada, I think that in spring and in summer they eat more herbaceous plants than they do bark of trees. Kinds of plants which the porcupines are known actually to have eaten in Nevada are: piñon, limber pine, white fir, mountain mahogany, service berry, choke cherry, and willow. The favored habitat is one where piles of large stones, talus, or rocks with crevices afford shelter in or near timber. In my experience the animals are less active in daytime than at dusk and at night.

Taylor (1935) thinks that the gestation period is about 7 months. The quills are said to harden enough within a few hours after birth to afford protection from most enemies. The rule is one young at a birth. None of the four Nevadan specimens (four adult females taken between June 28 and July 24) was pregnant.

Secondary sexual variation in size between our adults amounts to about 7 per cent in external measurements and 9 per cent in cranial measurements, the

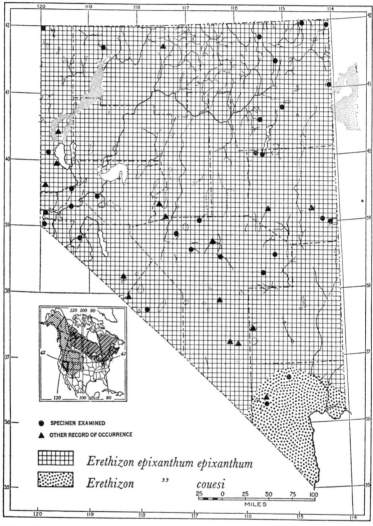

Fig. 419. Distribution of subspecies of the porcupine, *Erethizon epixanthum,* with insert showing range of the genus.

males being the larger. Taylor (1935:38) says males average more than 30 per cent heavier than the females. In the skulls of females, the upper incisors are less prognathous and the sagittal crest is shorter.

Erethizon epixanthum epixanthum Brandt
Porcupine

Erethizon epixanthus Brandt, Mém. Acad. Imp. Sci. St. Petersbourg, ser. 6, vol. 3 (Sci. Nat., vol. 1), p. 390. Type from California.
Erethizon epixanthum, Taylor, Univ. California Publ. Zoöl., 7:287, June 24, 1911; Linsdale, Amer. Midland Nat., 19:195, January, 1938.
Erethizon epixanthum epixanthum, Borell and Ellis, Journ. Mamm., 15:37, 73, February 15, 1934.

Distribution.—Timbered areas above Lower Sonoran Life-zone throughout all the state except Clark County. See figure 419.

Remarks.—Measurements of three males and four females are: ♂, 776 (760–798), ♀, 750 (680–780); 223 (203–238), 205 (175–230); 113 (109–115), 100 (95–111); weight, 26 (24–28), 13¾ (10–17½) lbs.

From *E. e. couesi*, this race is distinguished, so far as can be seen from specimens examined, by larger size (see table 24). Individual variation in color and in relative proportions of the skull is greater than in most kinds of rodents. This variation may have obscured differences in color and shape of parts of the skull that are of subspecific rank. If such exist, they are of an average sort. Individual variation in size also is great, but, nevertheless, there is a subspecific difference in size between the races *epixanthum* and *couesi*.

Records of occurrence.—Specimens examined, 50, as follows: *Washoe Co.:* 12-mile Creek, ½ mi. E Calif. boundary, 5300 ft., 3; Barrel Spring, 9½ mi. E and 3½ mi. N Ft. Bidwell, 5700 ft., 1; Cottonwood Creek, 4400 ft., Virginia Mts., 1; Sandy Point, 5 mi. S Incline, 6300 ft., 1. *Douglas Co.:* 1½ mi. E Edgewood, 1. *Storey Co.:* 8 mi. upriver from Wadsworth, 1. *Lyon Co.:* Carson River, 5 mi. below Weeks, 1; West Walker River, 12 mi. S Yerington, 4600 ft., 1. *Humboldt Co.:* head of Big Creek, Pine Forest Mts., 8000 ft., 1. *Esmeralda Co.:* 2½ mi. S Cave Spring, 7400 ft., 1. *Nye Co.:* Wilson Creek, 7200 ft., 2; ridge south of Wisconsin Creek, 9000 ft., 1; Meadow Creek R. S., Toquima Mts. [= Range], 2; Toquima Range, 1 mi. E Jefferson, 7600 ft., 2; Hot Creek Canyon, 6 mi. W Hot Creek, 6100 ft., 2; Scofield Canyon, Grant Mts., 6400 ft., 1; Burned Corral Canyon, Quinn Canyon Mts., 6700 ft., 1. *Elko Co.:* Cedar Creek, 10 mi. NE San Jacinto, 6000 ft., 1; Goose Creek, 2 mi. W Utah boundary, 5000 ft., 1; summit between heads of Copper and Coon creeks, Jarbidge Mts., 2 (coll. of Ralph Ellis); Marys River, 24 mi. N Deeth, 5800 ft., 1; Pilot Peak, ½ mi. W Debbs Creek, 8800 ft., 1; Jerry Creek (Jerry Crab Springs), 6700 ft., 1 (coll. of Ralph Ellis); Kleckner Creek, 4 mi. E Lee, 7 (coll. of Ralph Ellis). *White Pine Co.:* Willow Creek, 2 mi. S Elko Co. line, 6500 ft., 1 (coll. of Ralph Ellis); W side Ruby Lake, 3 mi. S Elko Co. line, 6100 ft., 1 (coll. of Ralph Ellis); Stella Lake, 10,600 ft., Snake Mts., 1; Treasury Lake, 1; Lehman Creek, 8000 and 8300 ft., 2; Baker Creek, 7300–8500 ft., 7.

Additional records: unmistakable signs, and in some instances the animals themselves, have been seen, unless otherwise noted by myself, at the following places: *Washoe Co.:* Horse Canyon, Pahrum Peak (Johnson, MS); Hardscrabble Canyon, 5500 ft. (D. G. Nichols, MS); N slope Peavine Peak, 6000 ft. (Carl P. Russell). *Humboldt Co.:* 14 mi. N Paradise Valley, 6400 ft. *Mineral Co.:* Excelsior Peak (L. Kellogg, MS). *Esmeralda Co.:* Pinchot Creek, 8200 ft. (Ward C. Russell, MS). *Lander Co.:* Smiths Creek, 5800–7700 ft.; Peterson Creek, 6500 ft., Shoshone Mts. *Nye Co.:* Greenmonster Canyon, 8200 ft.; Breen Creek, 7000 ft.; S end Belted Range, 5½ mi. NW Whiterock Spr., 7200 ft.; Oak Spr., 6000 ft. *White Pine Co.:* Cleve Creek, 8200 ft., Shell Creek Range; 3½ mi. NW Hamilton, 7400–8700 ft. *Lincoln Co.:* S side Groom Baldy.

Erethizon epixanthum couesi Mearns
Porcupine

Erethizon epixanthus couesi Mearns, Proc. U. S. Nat. Mus., 19:723, July 30, 1897. Type from Fort Whipple, Yavapai County, Arizona.
Erethizon epixanthum couesi, Burt, Trans. San Diego Soc. Nat. Hist., 7:422, May 31, 1934.

Distribution.—Upper Sonoran and higher life-zones of Clark County. See figure 419.

Remarks.—Measurements of a male (U. S. Nat. Mus., 205568) from Springerville, Arizona, and a female (U. S. Nat. Mus., 248929) from the Kaibab National Forest, Arizona, are: ♂, 766, ♀, 710; 165, 230; 110, 100; weight, ♂, —, ♀, 15 lbs.

The smaller size of skulls of *couesi* in comparison with those of the subspecies *epixanthum* is the one character of systematic worth found to separate the two.

The skull from Kyle Canyon on Charleston Peak is that of a female which contained one embryo. The fourth premolar above is of full height and is slightly worn. The dimensions of this skull are less than those of any one of the ten adult, subadult, and young porcupines from farther north in Nevada. The female (15885, D. R. Dickey Coll.) from the Sheep Mountains recorded by Burt (1934:423) has not been seen by me, but Donald F. Hoffmeister did examine the skull. From his notes, particularly his statement that the

TABLE 24

CRANIAL MEASUREMENTS (IN MILLIMETERS) OF ERETHIZON

Sex and age	Number of individuals averaged or catalogue no.	Basal length	Basilar length	Occipitonasal length	Palatilar length	Length of nasals	Zygomatic breadth	Mastoidal breadth	Least interorbital breadth	Alveolar length of upper cheek teeth
		Erethizon epixanthum epixanthum, Northern Nevada								
♂	4 av.	106.0	99.5	102.1	54.9	39.5	73.1	46.9	31.4	26.6
	min.	103.3	97.5	97.9	53.7	36.3	68.8	43.5	26.4	24.5
	max.	109.3	102.3	106.5	56.1	44.2	78.3	49.0	37.4	27.5
♀	4 av.	94.7	89.3	94.2	46.4	36.0	70.0	43.3	29.7	25.6
	min.	90.0	85.0	89.0	43.8	34.8	68.1	42.5	26.4	24.6
	max.	101.0	95.4	102.6	51.9	37.5	72.0	44.0	32.2	26.6
		Erethizon epixanthum couesi Sheep Mountains								
♂ ? sad.	15920*	94.3	88.1	93.0	49.3	37.6	67.3	41.4	29.0	23.4
♀ sad.	15885*	87.4	82.0	81.9	44.3	30.8	66.2	41.9	24.2	26.2
		Charleston Peak, Kyle Canyon								
♀ sad.	15821*	74.2	69.1	—	37.1	—	—	36.5	—	22.2

* D. R. Dickey Collection.

fourth upper premolar is but slightly worn, I judge that the age of the specimen was about the same as that of the female from Kyle Canyon. In most measurements this skull is smaller than those of comparable animals from farther north in Nevada. The third skull, also from the Sheep Mountains, is of unknown sex, but judged to be a male. The case for recognizing *couesi* as a race of mammal which occurs in Nevada rests on the small size of the two females. The cranial measurements of these specimens are given in table 24. From all accounts, porcupines are much rarer in these mountains of Clark County than in the mountains farther north in Nevada.

Records of occurrence.—Specimens examined, 2, as follows: *Clark Co.* (D. R. Dickey Coll.): Sheep Mts., 1; Kyle Canyon, 1.

Order LAGOMORPHA
Hares, Rabbits, Pikas

Ochotona princeps
Pika

Four races of pika occur in Nevada. Selected features in which pikas differ from the hares and rabbits of the family Leporidae are as follows: size less; ears shorter and more rounded; hind legs scarcely larger than forelegs; five instead of six upper cheek teeth; no postorbital processes on frontal; rostrum short but slender; nasals widest anteriorly; maxilla not conspicuously fenestrated; palate shorter; jugal long, projecting posteriorly well beyond squamosal; no pubic symphysis. The color of the upper parts ranges from blackish

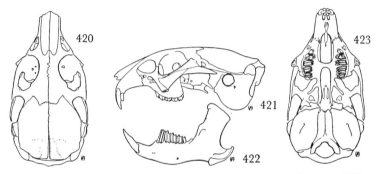

Figs. 420–423. *Ochotona princeps tutelata,* Greenmonster Canyon, 8150 feet, no. 58519, ♂. ×1.

brown in *schisticeps* to near (16′) Ochraceous-Buff in *nevadensis;* sides the same with less overlay of blackish; underparts with hairs tipped with whitish, ochraceous, or both; soles of feet densely haired, only naked parts being pads of toes; hair on soles and tops of forefeet whitish; hair on soles of hind feet blackish; antiplantar faces of hind feet brownish to whitish, depending on subspecies; ears blackish, margined with white. There are four or six mammae, one or two pair pectoral and one pair inguinal. The dental formula is i. $\frac{2}{1}$, c. $\frac{0}{0}$, p. $\frac{2}{2}$, m. $\frac{3}{3}$. Some students regard the cheek teeth as p. $\frac{3}{2}$, m. $\frac{2}{3}$.

The starting point for anyone who wishes to classify pikas with respect to kind is A. H. Howell's "Revision of the American Pikas" (1924). In that paper the kinds now recorded from Nevada were arranged as subspecies of two full species. In the present account these subspecies are arranged as belonging to the one full species, *Ochotona princeps.* Borell (1931:307) made clear that intergradation occurred between the supposedly full species *schisticeps* and *princeps.* The latter name has priority because it was proposed 62 years earlier than *schisticeps.* This accounts for the new combinations of names here used for some of the Nevadan pikas.

Zonally, the pikas are Boreal in distribution; in Nevada they have not been recorded from as low as the piñon belt. They were taken among junipers in northeastern Washoe County where piñons do not occur. Altitudinally, they range from as low as 5700 feet in northern Washoe County up to 11,000 feet in the Toquima Range. Their habitat is talus, the slopes of broken-up rock; we have found them nowhere else. They remain close to their habitat, 20 feet being the farthest I ever saw one from talus. At the near approach of danger, pikas drop into the open spaces between the rocks. Their speed in running is inferior to that of any of the other lagomorphs, and it may be that inferiority in this respect accounts for their remaining near safe retreats.

Pikas are diurnal and, where observed in Nevada, are most active from sunrise until 11 o'clock. They are inactive, or at least relatively little in evidence, between 11 A.M. and 4:30 P.M. From the latter time until sunset they are more active, but less so than in the morning.

Near talus, where pikas live, a person may expect to ascertain their presence by hearing their call, by seeing the animals themselves, by noting their feces, or by finding their hay-piles. In Nevada the characteristic call is a series of "chickch-chickch-chickch" sounds. More often than not, this call will be heard when a person approaches a rock-slide inhabited by pikas. Sometimes they make the sound when they are deep down among the rocks over which a person is walking, but more often they utter the sound while sitting exposed on the top of a boulder. In some places, I have seen the animals running over and among the broken pieces of rocks without making any vocal sound audible to me in the several hours that I spent watching for them. The feces are oblately spherical and are miniatures of those of hares and rabbits. These droppings are scattered about over any area in which the animals spend much time; there seems to be no particular place in which they are deposited.

The hay-piles, sometimes bulking almost as much as a bushel measure, ordinarily are built up under overhanging rocks. On June 19, 1931, in the Toyabe Mountains, Linsdale (1938:196) found the "hay-piles" to consist of "branches of *Artemisia, Chrysothamnus, Symphoricarpus, Ribes,* and a herbaceous plant. The piles were not just accidental leavings, but they were large accumulations of half a bushel or more of material. Most of it was the leafy foliage of bushes. No grass or sedge was available." Borell and Ellis (1934a:38), near the end of the second week in August, in the Ruby Mountains, found one "hay-pile" that "was composed almost entirely of cinquefoil (*Potentilla breweri*). All of the plants used were in blossom. Beneath the new hay was old hay, showing that the place had been used for storage purposes during previous years."

Because food is thus stored, and because, in areas outside Nevada, pikas are found to be active in winter, it is thought that they do not hibernate. Secondary sexual variation is slight, but, as indicated by measurements of twenty-seven adult males and twenty adult females of the subspecies *O. p. tutelata,* males, on the average, are larger than females by about 2 per cent in cranial measurements and by about one-half of 1 per cent in external measurements. Of 23 sexually mature females examined for embryos, 8 were pregnant.

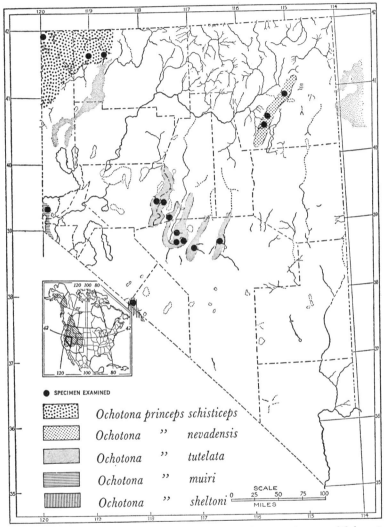

Fig. 424. Distribution of subspecies of the pika, *Ochotona princeps*, with insert showing range of the species.

One had 2 embryos, 5 had 3, and 2 had 4, giving an average of 3.1. Each of the 3 females taken in June was pregnant, as were 5 of the remaining 20, all taken in July.

Ochotona princeps schisticeps (Merriam)
Pika

Lagomys schisticeps Merriam, N. Amer. Fauna, 2:11, October 30, 1889. Type from Donner [= summit], Placer County, California.
Ochotona princeps schisticeps, Miller, A. H., Journ. Mamm., 17:174, May 14, 1936.

Distribution.—Northwestern part of state east to Pine Forest Mountains. See figure 424.

Remarks.—Measurements of two males and two females, the first one of each sex from 5 mi. N Summit Lake and the second from Duffer Peak, are: total length, ♂, 178, 167, ♀, 184, 173; length of hind foot, 30, 28, 27, 27; weight of one male from Duffer Peak, 127.5 grams.

Size medium; in summer pelage upper parts Vinaceous-Cinnamon heavily overlain with blackish; head and nape grayish (with more whitish and less cinnamon); in winter pelage only slightly lighter; skull small, shallow, dorsal outline relatively straight in longitudinal axis; nasals straight-sided; palatal bridge short.

This is the darkest colored race of pika in Nevada. It is smaller than nevadensis and has a relatively shorter palatal bridge. From tutelata, it differs further in having a relatively shallower skull. In advance of study, it was thought that pikas of northwestern Nevada would be referable to the subspecies taylori of northeastern California and adjoining parts of Oregon. More material being available since taylori was named and since Howell (1924) revised the pikas, it is now seen that many of the features thought to distinguish taylori from schisticeps are individual variations. O. p. taylori may be separable from schisticeps on basis of average darker color; but however that may be, our Nevadan specimens are not as dark as the darkest Californian specimens from the range currently assigned to taylori, being about like the average of schisticeps. Probably the animals are much more widely distributed in northwestern Nevada than our three records of occurrence indicate.

Records of occurrence.—Specimens examined, 7, as follows: Washoe Co.: 12 mi. E and 3 mi. N Ft. Bidwell, 5700 ft., 2; Humboldt Co.: Pine Forest Mts., Duffer Peak, 8400–8600 ft., 3; 5 mi. N Summit Lake, 5900 ft., 2.

Ochotona princeps nevadensis Howell
Pika

Ochotona uinta nevadensis Howell, Proc. Biol. Soc. Washington, 32:107, May 20, 1919. Type from Ruby Mountains, southwest of Ruby Valley Post Office, Elko County, Nevada.
Ochotona princeps nevadensis Howell, N. Amer. Fauna, 47:21, August 21, 1924; Borell and Ellis, Journ. Mamm., 15:38, February 15, 1934.

Distribution.—Ruby Mountains. See figure 424.

Remarks.—Measurements of five males and seven females from the Ruby Mountains are: total length, ♂, 189 (171–205), ♀, 193 (174–206); length of hind foot, 30.8 (29–32), 31.1 (30–35); no weights available.

Size large; in summer pelage upper parts near (16') Ochraceous-Buff lightly overlain with blackish except on nape and shoulders where more nearly pure buff; in worn winter pelage upper parts near Light Buff; skull large; nasals straight-sided; palatal bridge wide anteroposteriorly; incisive foramina anteriorly more sharply V-shaped.

From O. p. tutelata, this race differs in larger size and lighter color, because the reddish element is paler and because it is less overlain with blackish. In the skull there is no overlap in occipitonasal length, zygomatic breadth, length of nasals, alveolar length of upper tooth rows, and depth of the skull between a series of twelve nevadensis and nine topotypes of tutelata. Of the five races of pikas in Nevada, nevadensis is lightest colored in the summer pelage.

Records of occurrence.—Specimens examined, 19 (all in the coll. of Ralph Ellis), as follows: Elko Co., Ruby Mts.: Steels Creek, 7000 ft., 1; Three Lakes, 9740 ft., 10; Long Creek, 7830 ft., 8.

Ochotona princeps tutelata Hall
Pika

Ochotona princeps tutelata Hall, Proc. Biol. Soc. Washington, 47:103, June 13, 1934. Type from Greenmonster Canyon, 8150 feet, Monitor Mountains, Nye County, Nevada.
Ochotona schisticeps cinnamomea, Howell, N. Amer. Fauna, 47:47, August 21, 1924.
Ochotona schisticeps, Linsdale, Amer. Midland Nat., 19:196, January, 1938.

Distribution.—Desatoya, Shoshone, Toyabe, Toquima, and Monitor mountain ranges in central Nevada. See figure 424.

Remarks.—Measurements of six male and three female topotypes are: total length, ♂, 174 (155–190), ♀, 164 (155–175); length of hind foot, 28.8 (28–30), 28.3 (28–29); weight, 120.6 (107.7–128.0), for two females, 128.9 and 121.0 grams.

Size medium; in summer pelage upper parts near (14″c) Pinkish Cinnamon lightly overlain with brownish; narrow collar slightly more grayish; in worn winter pelage, lighter cinnamon; skull small, deep, the dorsal outline highly arched in longitudinal axis; nasals straight-sided; palatal bridge short.

The named forms to which *O. p. tutelata* shows greatest resemblance are *O. p. cinnamomea* of Utah and *O. p. muiri*. Compared with topotypes of *cinnamomea*, on the one hand, and *muiri*, from Heather Lake, Eldorado County, California, on the other, *tutelata* is exactly intermediate when in fresh July pelage, but nearer *muiri*, by a slight degree, when in worn winter pelage. From each of these two races, *tutelata* differs in having a skull of greater depth, lesser average length and breadth, and, in specimens of *tutelata* from the Toyabe, Monitor, and Toquima mountains, the palatal bridge shorter. This greater depth of the skull, as measured perpendicularly to a plane touching the tips of the incisors and ventral margins of the tympanic bullae, amounts to 39 per cent or more of the occipitonasal length in each of the five populations of *tutelata* and less than 39 per cent in *muiri* and *cinnamomea*. The greater longitudinal convexity of the dorsal outline of the skull of *tutelata* is a feature constantly separating it from *muiri* and *cinnamomea* when specimens of like age are relied upon.

From *O. p. cinnamomea*, *tutelata* differs also in having the lateral margins of the nasals straight rather than constricted near the middle and in having the foramen magnum smaller and the supraoccipital bone of correspondingly greater depth. Stated in another way, in *cinnamomea* the foramen magnum is larger, relative to the area of the occiput, and the supraoccipital bone is reduced in size.

The pikas in the Toyabe Mountains and those in the Shoshone Mountains probably are not isolated from one another, the two ranges being connected at the south. Otherwise, the pikas in each of the mountain ranges from which *tutelata* is known are isolated from those in each of the other ranges and probably have been so isolated for a long period of time. It is not surprising, therefore, that some geographic variation is shown by the material at hand. Two variations judged to be of a geographic nature are the longer nasals of the animals from the Desatoya Mountains and the greater length (anteroposteriorly) of the palatal bridge in the animals from the Toyabe and Shoshone mountains, which two mountain ranges, it will be remembered, are connected at their southern ends.

Records of occurrence.—Specimens examined, 56, as follows: *Churchill Co.*(?): Desatoya Mts., Toby Canyon, 8100–8400 ft., 5. *Lander Co.*: Desatoya Mts., Smiths Creek, 7500 ft., 3; Shoshone Mts., Peterson Creek, 7300–7800 ft., 8. *Nye Co.*, Toyabe Mts.: Mohawk Canyon [= Mohawk Creek], 2; South Twin River, 4 (U. S. Nat. Mus., Biol. Surv. Coll.); Arc Dome, 5 (U. S. Nat. Mus., Biol. Surv. Coll.); Monitor Range, Greenmonster Canyon, 8600 ft., 10; Toquima Range, SW and W slope Mt. Jefferson, 8700–11,000 ft., 19.

Ochotona princeps muiri Grinnell and Storer
Pika

Ochotona schisticeps muiri Grinnell and Storer, Univ. California Publ. Zoöl., 17:6, August 23, 1916. Type from Ten Lakes, 9300 feet, Yosemite National Park, Tuolumne County, California.
Ochotona princeps muiri, Hall, Proc. Biol. Soc. Washington, 47:103, June 13, 1934.

TABLE 25

CRANIAL MEASUREMENTS (IN MILLIMETERS) OF OCHOTONA

Sex and age	Number of individuals averaged or catalogue no.	Occipitonasal length	Zygomatic breadth	Breadth of brain case	Postorbital breadth	Interorbital breadth	Width (anteroposteriorly) of palatal bridge	Length of nasals	Alveolar length of upper molariform tooth row
				Ochotona princeps schisticeps, 5 mi. N Summit Lake					
♂	74274	41.7	19.9	17.4	13.3	4.3	1.5	14.3	8.1
					Duffer Peak				
♂	66659	41.3	20.2	16.8	13.1	4.7	1.7	13.9	8.0
					5 mi. N Summit Lake				
♀	74273	40.7	20.4	17.9	13.9	4.9	1.6	12.9	8.0
					Duffer Peak				
♀	66660	41.7	20.8	17.9	—	5.0	1.6	13.5	8.2
			Ochotona princeps nevadensis, Ruby Mountains						
♂	5* av.	44.0	21.9	18.6	14.5	5.3	2.3	14.4	8.9
	min.	43.0	21.5	18.4	14.1	5.1	2.1	14.0	8.6
	max.	44.5	22.5	18.9	14.7	5.5	2.4	15.0	9.0
♀	7* av.	43.3	21.4	18.1	14.1	5.2	2.3	14.3	8.6
	min.	42.0	21.0	17.6	13.5	4.5	1.7	14.1	8.2
	max.	44.4	21.7	18.9	14.4	5.5	2.6	14.8	9.0
			Ochotona princeps tutelata, Monitor Range						
♂	6 av.	40.8	20.1	17.2	13.2	5.2	1.4	13.1	7.8
	min.	39.3	19.4	17.0	12.3	4.8	1.3	12.8	7.7
	max.	41.8	20.7	17.6	13.8	5.5	1.7	13.4	8.0
♀	3 av.	39.3	19.5	17.0	13.2	5.0	1.3	12.6	7.9
	min.	38.1	19.3	16.5	13.0	4.8	1.2	12.4	7.8
	max.	41.2	19.9	17.8	13.3	5.3	1.5	13.1	8.0
			Ochotona princeps muiri, Heather Lake, California						
♂	12000	42.3	21.2	18.3	14.0	5.1	1.5	13.7	8.5
♀ sad.	12001	40.7	20.1	17.2	13.9	5.2	1.8	13.2	7.7
			Ochotona princeps sheltoni, ♂ topotype, and ♀ Pinchot Creek						
♂	27553	41.4	20.9	18.2	14.1	4.8	1.5	13.1	8.4
♀	59396	41.7	20.8	18.5	13.9	5.3	1.5	13.2	8.6

* Collection of Ralph Ellis.

Distribution.—Sierra Nevada in vicinity of Lake Tahoe. See figure 424.

Remarks.—Measurements of a male and a subadult female from Heather Lake, California, are: total length, ♂, 187, ♀, 173; length of hind foot, 30, 28; weights not available.

Size medium; in summer pelage upper parts near (14″) Vinaceous Cinnamon overlain with blackish; head and neck grayish; in worn winter pelage slightly lighter; skull of medium size; each nasal rounded posteriorly and not much constricted posteriorly; palatal bridge narrow anteroposteriorly.

From *schisticeps*, this race differs in lighter color and in skull, which averages slightly smaller and relatively narrower. Comparisons with *tutelata* and *sheltoni* are made in the accounts of those forms.

The two specimens available from Nevada are in immature pelage. Although slightly intermediate toward *schisticeps* in color, they far more closely resemble *muiri* in comparable pelage.

Record of occurrence.—Specimens examined: *Washoe Co.:* 3 mi. S Mt. Rose, 8500 ft., 2.

Ochotona princeps sheltoni Grinnell
Pika

Ochotona schisticeps sheltoni Grinnell, Univ. California Publ. Zoöl., 17:429, April 25, 1918. Type from White Mountains, 11,000 feet, near Big Prospector Meadow, Mono County, California.

Distribution.—Northern end of White Mountains in Mineral County. See figure 424.

Remarks.—Measurements of a male from the type locality and a female from 8200 feet on Pinchot Creek are: total length, 175, 192; length of hind foot, 28, 27; weight, for the male, 120.0 grams.

Size large; in summer pelage upper parts near (*a*) Pinkish Cinnamon overlain with blackish and brownish; in worn winter pelage Pinkish Buff without overlay of darker color; head and nape grayish; skull resembling that of *muiri* but averaging shorter and relatively broader.

From *muiri*, the subspecies which *sheltoni* most closely resembles, *sheltoni* differs in darker color in summer pelage and lighter color in winter pelage; and shorter and relatively broader skull.

The two specimens from Nevada were taken on June 3 and 5, 1933, and are in winter pelage. They contrast so strongly with the darker colored summer pelage of all the other California-taken specimens that it was at first difficult to think that the Nevadan and Californian specimens were the same subspecies. Further study shows small, but at first overlooked, patches of winter fur on some of the Californian topotypes, which patches are of the same color as the pelage of the Nevadan animals.

Records of occurrence.—Specimens examined, 2, as follows: *Esmeralda Co.*, White Mts.: Pinchot Creek, 8700 ft., 1; Mustang Mtn., 10,000 ft., 1.

Family LEPORIDAE
Hares and Rabbits

Two genera of Leporidae, *Lepus* and *Sylvilagus*, occur in Nevada. Structural features of family rank, in comparison with the Ochotonidae, are mentioned in the preceding account of the pika. The dental formula is i. $\frac{2}{1}$, c. $\frac{0}{0}$, p. $\frac{3}{2}$, m. $\frac{3}{3}$.

The Nevadan members of this family well illustrate a correlation between structure and function. The functions concerned are those of detecting enemies and escaping from them. The structures most prominently involved are two sense receptors, the eyes and particularly the ears, and the hind legs which

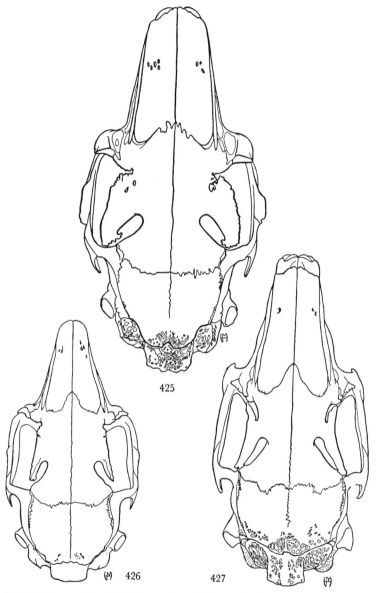

Figs. 425–427. Hares. All, ×1. (Other views of these skulls are shown in figs. 428–430, 431–433, 434–436.)

Fig. 425. *Lepus townsendii townsendii*, north end Ruby Valley, east base Ruby Mountains, no. 4686, coll. of Ralph Ellis, ♀.

Fig. 426. *Lepus americanus tahoensis*, ½ mile south Tahoe Tavern, Lake Tahoe, Placer County, California, no. 37522, ♂.

Fig. 427. *Lepus californicus deserticola*, 4 miles west Fallon, no. 90061, ♂.

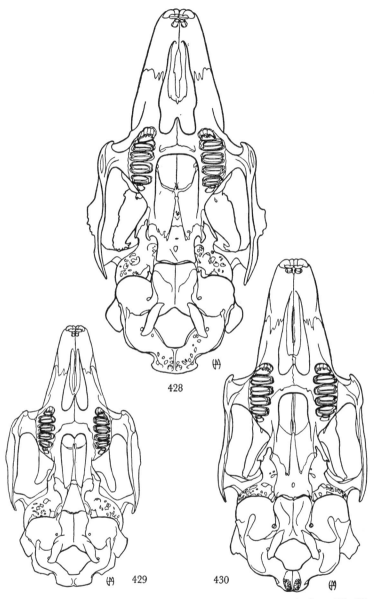

Figs. 428–430. Hares. Different views of these skulls are shown in figs. 425–427. ×1.

Fig. 428. *Lepus townsendii townsendii.*   Fig. 429. *Lepus americanus tahoensis.*

Fig. 430. *Lepus californicus deserticola.*

provide the propulsive power needed in running. At one extreme is *Lepus*. Both kinds of the jack rabbits have long ears and relatively long hind legs and live in the open. The black-tailed jack rabbit, for example, takes alarm when an

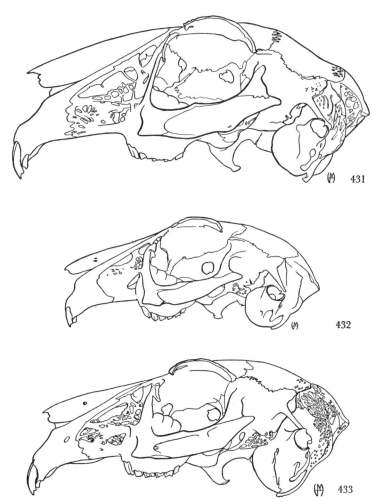

Figs. 431–433. Hares. Different views of these skulls are shown in figs. 425–427. ×1.

Fig. 431. *Lepus townsendii townsendii.*   Fig. 432. *Lepus americanus tahoensis.*
Fig. 433. *Lepus californicus deserticola.*

enemy is relatively a long distance away and seeks safety in outrunning a pursuer. Even when closely followed by an enemy, the jack rabbit relies upon its running ability to escape and does not seek to hide in thick brush or to enter holes in the ground or crevices in rocks. A cottontail has shorter ears and shorter hind legs and lives sometimes in the open but always near dense cover or a safety retreat of some kind. Although ordinarily allowing an enemy to approach more closely than a jack rabbit does and although relying, to some degree, on its running ability for escape, the cottontail flees toward a hole in

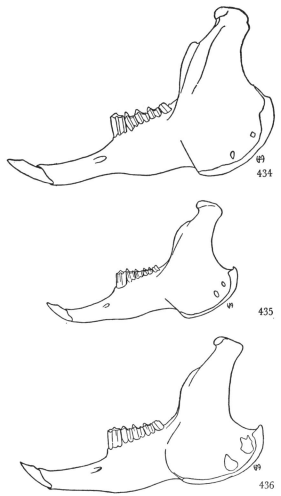

Figs. 434–436. Hares. Lower jaws of skulls shown in figs. 425–427. ×1.
Fig. 434. *Lepus townsendii townsendii.*   Fig. 435. *Lepus americanus tahoensis.*
Fig. 436. *Lepus californicus deserticola.*

the ground, a crevice in the rocks, or dense cover where, without running, it will be safe from its pursuer. The pigmy rabbit, which lives in a hole in the ground, differs still more from the jack rabbit, in that the ears and hind legs are shorter even than in the cottontail. When the pigmy rabbit is out foraging it remains in the brush. At the first sign of danger it doubles and twists a short distance through the brush to the trench leading into its burrow and sits in the trench with just the ears and eyes exposed. At further sign of pursuit the pigmy rabbit scurries on below ground. If the pika, of the family Ochotonidae, be included, it comprises the opposite extreme from the jack rabbit. The pika has short rounded ears and relatively the shortest legs of all. It spends most of its time in and on the rock-slides, where, when danger threatens, it is not required to run at all, but can escape by dropping down into a space between the broken rocks.

The four animals, jack rabbit, cottontail, pigmy rabbit, and pika, all members of the Order Lagomorpha, comprise a gradient series. At one end of the series is the jack rabbit, with large ears, the size of which, together with highly developed hind legs, probably serves mainly the purpose of detecting and evading enemies. At the other end of the series is the pika, with small ears and hind legs but little larger than the forelegs. The observed behavior of the four types agrees closely with what one would expect them to do if he based his expectations on a knowledge of their structure alone.

Genus **Lepus** Linnaeus
Hares

Three species, the white-tailed jack rabbit, the snowshoe rabbit, and the black-tailed jack rabbit, occur in Nevada. Individuals of the species of *Lepus* differ from those of *Sylvilagus* (cottontails and pigmy rabbit) as follows: size larger; relatively longer ears and hind feet; hind legs more highly adapted for running; an interparietal bone that is fused with the parietals rather than distinct throughout life; young born with fur well developed and eyes open, rather than short-haired or naked and blind; the habits of living more in the open and of resting in forms rather than of often resting in holes below ground.

Lepus townsendii townsendii Bachman
White-tailed Jack Rabbit

Lepus townsendii Bachman, Journ. Acad. Nat. Sci. Philadelphia, 8 (pt. 1):90, pl. 2, 1839. Type from Fort Walla Walla, near present town of Wallula, Walla Walla County, Washington.
Lepus campestris townsendii, Nelson, N. Amer. Fauna, 29:78, August 31, 1909.
Lepus townsendii townsendii, Borell and Ellis, Journ. Mamm., 15:39, 73, February 15, 1934.

Distribution.—Northern Nevada and along eastern slope of Sierra Nevada; Upper Sonoran, Transition, and Boreal life-zones. See figure 437.

Remarks.—Seven males and nine females from the Ruby Mountains measure as follows: ♂, 581 (555–618), ♀, 602 (545–655); 82 (72–103), 80 (66–100); 152 (146–165), 154 (145–159); ear from notch on dried skins, 107 (104–109), 104 (98–111); weight, one male, 2,494, five females, 2,976 (2,179–3,440) grams.

Size large; hind foot more than 140 mm.; two annual molts, pelage grayish-brown in summer and white in winter; tail relatively large and white at all seasons, but in some specimens with a dusky middorsal stripe; skull with rostrum broad at base and tapering but little; palatal bridge short; auditory bullae small. The winter pelage is white in all Nevadan animals. If the white guard hairs are parted, the tips of the underfur are seen to vary from Cinnamon to Pinkish-Cinnamon on the rump.

This hare, the largest lagomorph in Nevada, is an inhabitant of the Boreal life-zones and upper part of the Transition Life-zone. In Nevada it has been found in or around the edges of meadows, and occupies a more open habitat than does the black-tailed jack rabbit.

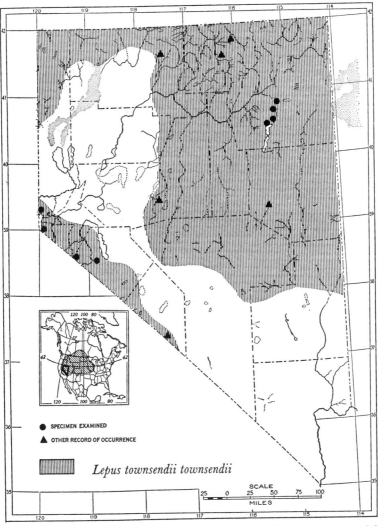

Fig. 437. Distribution of the white-tailed jack rabbit, *Lepus townsendii*, with insert showing range of the species.

The specimens available are from two areas, the Ruby Mountains of northeastern Nevada, and the Sierra Nevada and other mountains to the west of Walker Lake. The animals from the western part of the state would be expected to bear the name *Lepus townsendii sierrae* Merriam. Orr (1940:41, 42) carefully studied specimens from California, Nevada, and Utah and concluded that specimens on which the name *sierrae* was based are inseparable from *townsendii*, as the latter was known to him by the specimens from southern Idaho and northeastern Nevada. I examined the materials used by Orr at the time that he made his study, and, although a few Nevadan specimens have accumulated since then, study of them reveals no basis for a conclusion different from that arrived at by him.

In writing of this species in the Ruby Mountains, Borell and Ellis (1934a:39, 40) noted that "white-tailed jackrabbits were more nocturnal than the black-tailed jackrabbits. During the day no white-tails were seen unless they were jumped from cover. At dusk three or four times as many black-tails as white-tails were observed, but as night advanced this proportion began to change, and after nine o'clock the two species were seen in nearly equal numbers along that part of the road which ran through the territory occupied by the two species." As I interpret the findings of Borell and Ellis, this area was one in which the black-tailed jack rabbits were several times more abundant than the white-tailed jack rabbits.

These same authors noted (*loc. cit.*) also that, "The eyes of this species responded more readily to light reflection than did the eyes of any other species of rabbit inhabiting our territory. When we directed a flashlight or the headlights of the automobile toward one of these rabbits, its eyes returned a fiery red reflection. The shine of its eyes was so much redder and more brilliant than the shine of the eyes of the black-tailed jackrabbit that the two species usually could be distinguished at night by the difference in color of the light reflected by their eyes."

Females from the Ruby Mountains average larger than males by about 1 per cent in external measurements and by 1 to 7 per cent in most cranial measurements.

A female taken on June 1, 1927, at Round Mound was found by James Moffitt to contain three embryos. Borell and Ellis (1934a:40) found that every one of ten adult females taken from June 3 to August 10, in the Ruby Mountains was suckling young.

Evidence was obtained of the presence of these hares in several parts of the state from which no actual specimens are available. On July 29, 1934, Mr. Travis, Forest Ranger, with headquarters at Paradise Valley, said that these hares occurred in the Santa Rosa Mountains. In 1928, Mr. Huey Stewart of Oasis, California, said that rabbits which turned white in winter were known from the top of Mount Magruder. On July 21, 1930, Mr. Zumwalt, then living at the Smith Creek Ranch in Lander County, described "snowshoes" as being of occasional occurrence in the Desatoya Mountains. On July 22, 1934, I saw one 6½ miles southwest of Mountain City and another at Deep Creek in the Bull Run Mountains. On August 20, 1930, Ed Brrch reported white individuals of this species to be common in winter in the vicinity of Hamilton.

Records of occurrence.—Specimens examined, 26, as follows: *Washoe Co.:* 3 mi. S Mt. Rose, 8600 ft., 1. *Douglas Co.:* Round Mound, Lake Tahoe, 1; Edgewood, 1. *Mineral Co.:* Sweetwater Mts., 9000 ft., "5 mi. S and a little E of Desert Creek Point," 1; Lapon Canyon, Mt. Grant, 8900 ft., 1. *Elko Co.* (coll. of Ralph Ellis): summit of Secret Pass, 6200 ft., 5; E base Ruby Mts., N end Ruby Valley, 4; E base Ruby Mts., Arthur P. O., 6400 ft., 2; E base Ruby Mts., 6 mi. S Secret Pass, 1; E base Ruby Mts., 10 mi. S Secret Pass, 6000 ft., 4; 15 mi. S Secret Pass, 2; 20 mi. S Secret Pass, 2; E base Ruby Mts., 20 mi. N Harrison Pass, 1.

Additional records (see text above): *Humboldt Co.:* Santa Rosa Mts. *Esmeralda Co.:* Mt. Magruder. *Lander Co.:* Desatoya Mts. *Elko Co.:* 6½ mi. SW Mountain City; Deep Creek, 13 mi. S and 1 mi. W Whiterock, 1. *White Pine Co.:* Hamilton.

Lepus americanus tahoensis Orr
Snowshoe Rabbit

Lepus washingtoni tahoensis Orr, Journ. Mamm., 14:54, February 14, 1933. Type from ½ mile south of Tahoe Tavern, Placer County, California.

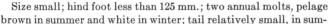

Distribution.—Canadian and possibly upper part of Transition life-zones in Sierra Nevada in vicinity of Lake Tahoe. See figure 253, page 354.

Remarks.—Measurements of a male and female from ½ mile south of Tahoe Tavern, Placer County, California, are: ♂, 367, ♀, 383; 27, 25; 112, 129; ear from notch in dried skin, 70, 71; weight of ♂, 2 lbs.

Size small; hind foot less than 125 mm.; two annual molts, pelage brown in summer and white in winter; tail relatively small, in summer brownish-black above and dusky beneath; skull small, with supraorbital processes slender and only slightly elevated above frontal plane; postorbital projections of supraorbitals slender throughout; anterior palatine foramina usually somewhat constricted posteriorly. If the white guard hairs of the winter coat be parted, the tips of the underfur are seen to vary from Pale Pinkish-Cinnamon almost to Salmon-Buff.

As pointed out by Orr (1940), in the vicinity of Lake Tahoe this hare occupies, in the Boreal life-zones, floral associations which are the counterparts of those in the lower, that is to say, Sonoran, life-zones that are occupied by the brush rabbit (*Sylvilagus bachmani*) on the western slopes of the Sierra Nevada. The snowshoe rabbit lives among the riparian growth, such as alder and willow. It lives also in dense thickets of young conifers, especially firs the branches of which droop to the ground, and in clumps of chaparral made up principally of *Ceanothus* and manzanita.

Like other hares, this species, so far as is known, lives in forms and not in burrows. The young are born with the eyes open and with a good coat of fur.

In 1924, 1 mile west of Spooner, Vernon L. Mills saw a rabbit which his companions identified as a snowshoe rabbit, the short ears, brown color, and build of which made him think of a young Belgian hare. Most residents on the Nevada side of Lake Tahoe testify to having seen snowshoe rabbits, but questioning revealed either that many of the persons were referring to the white-tailed jack rabbit or did not know how to distinguish it from the true snowshoe. On April 3, 1937, about a half mile from the shore of Lake Tahoe, between Incline Creek and the California boundary, I found in the snow, rabbit tracks of two sizes which I tentatively identified as those of cottontails and snowshoes. The larger series of tracks along a willow-lined stream definitely were not those of *Lepus townsendii*. Finally, on June 22, 1941, 350 yards northeast of the junction of the Nevada-California boundary with the north shore of Lake Tahoe, J. R. Alcorn found the remains of a snowshoe (now, no. 95828, Mus. Vert. Zoöl.).

Record of occurrence.—Specimen examined: *Washoe Co.*: "350 yds. NE junction of Nevada state line and [north shore of] Lake Tahoe, 1.

Lepus californicus
Black-tailed Jack Rabbit

Two subspecies of the black-tailed jack rabbit occur in Nevada. Size medium for the genus; hind foot less than 140 mm.; one molt each year; upper parts ashy-gray; tail with black median dorsal stripe and buffy or grayish beneath; skull with rostrum long and tapering; auditory bullae large.

The person who travels across Nevada sees more individuals of this species than of all other kinds of hares and rabbits combined. The black-tailed jack rabbit is abundant throughout the Lower Sonoran and Upper Sonoran life-zones and occurs less commonly in the unforested parts of the Transition Life-zone. It prefers the loose brush, but we have seen it in almost every habitat. I saw a black-tailed jack rabbit more than a mile out on the bare alkali flat about 20 miles southeast of Fallon, and another was seen in Washoe County along the eastern side of Lake Tahoe, 3½ miles south of Incline, among the Jeffrey pines. Altitudinally, it occurs from the lowest parts of the state, in the southern tip, along the Colorado River, up to at least 11,700 feet. At this high elevation, the very top of Mount Jefferson, Frank Gorham shot a young jack rabbit on July 4, 1933. These three occurrences are not typical, but they emphasize the statement made above that this rabbit will be found in almost every kind of habitat.

Borell and Ellis (1934a:40) remark that, "Black-tailed jackrabbits always were more in evidence [in the Ruby Mountains area] at dusk than at any time of the day or than after dark." This agrees with my observations at other places. In Great Smoky Valley, Linsdale (1938:197) noted that animals that were active in the morning had retired to forms by 10 o'clock and that those which began moving about as early as midafternoon sought the shade on the north side of bushes when stopping to rest.

The fluctuation in numbers of this species is so marked that almost every Nevadan resident has noted the phenomenon. Our field experience clearly shows that the rabbits may be near a peak in numbers in one valley, while in some other valley separated from the first by only one range of mountains the jack rabbits may be near the low point in numbers. Ordinarily, the increase to a peak in numbers is accomplished gradually over a period of several years, but the decline in numbers occurs usually in a few months or even weeks. The causes of some of these sudden decreases has been shown to be tularemia, a disease that attacks many kinds of animals. Before this organism (*Bacillus tularense*), which attacks man, was first recognized as distinct from other "mountain fever" organisms, it was credited with a relatively high rate of mortality in man. Now it is known that the rate of mortality is less than was originally thought. In jack rabbits, however, it is highly fatal; at any rate, in some years apparently more than 90 per cent of the jack rabbit population has died from what appears to be tularemia.

Sometimes man's efforts to destroy jack rabbits are given credit for effectiveness when in reality natural disease is responsible. This seemingly had been true in 1931 in Garden Valley, Nye County. In 1932 a rancher told us of how, when he was disturbed by the great abundance of jack rabbits, he distributed finely chopped green alfalfa poisoned with strychnine around the margins of his fields, with the result that the rabbits died in such numbers that they no longer caused him any loss through eating alfalfa. In this same year (1932) jack rabbits were scarce in all parts of this valley that we visited. To us it was inconceivable that the efforts to poison the animals at this one isolated ranch the year before could have decimated the population of rabbits over the entire valley; tularemia or some other disease probably was the factor responsible for reducing this rabbit population.

Observations and reports indicate that disease operated to greatly reduce the jack rabbit population in 1928 at Deep Hole, Washoe County; in 1931, in the country between Tonopah and Caliente and between Beatty and Alamo; and in 1935 or early 1936, many died in northern Washoe County in the vicinity of Hausen.

In Nevada, as in many parts of the western United States where ranches are surrounded by large areas of untilled land, jack rabbits take heavy toll of growing alfalfa in the years when the population of these hares is large. On one 40-acre field of alfalfa at the Chiatovich Ranch in Fish Lake Valley, in June, 1928, I counted more than 200 jack rabbits at dusk one evening. The alfalfa was so heavily browsed by the jack rabbits that it was impossible to get a cutting of hay. Efforts to poison the rabbits, although resulting in the death of some, did not stop the damage to the alfalfa. With thousands of acres of wild land roundabout, it seemed that other rabbits moved in to take the places of those killed. Efforts to eliminate the animals by shooting were made but found far too expensive. The valley is so large and the human population so small that it seemed impractical to attempt rabbit drives. Finally, the 6 miles of fence surrounding a part of the ranch was used for stringing almost 3-foot-high, rabbitproof, woven wire. At that time the cost of the wire was $70 per mile, or $420 in all. The posts already were in place and the labor costs were small. Three years later I visited the ranch and was told that the fence was still effective in excluding jack rabbits. The rancher was of the opinion that the cost of fencing was less than the cost of protecting the alfalfa by any other means, and our observations here and at other similarly isolated ranches led us to agree with him.

The natural enemies of jack rabbits include, certainly, coyotes and golden eagles. Remains of these rabbits have been found in the stomachs of coyotes, and twice I have flushed a pair of golden eagles from the partly eaten carcass of a jack rabbit. Elmer C. Aldrich recovered the foreleg of one from the nest of a prairie falcon, 6 miles east of Carlin.

Several entries in field notebooks mention the jack rabbit's testing of the air and ground with its nose. For example, Orr (MS), in late May of 1932, 5 miles southeast of Millett, observed that jack rabbits going naturally about their business, unmolested by man, used their noses to sniff along the ground. When

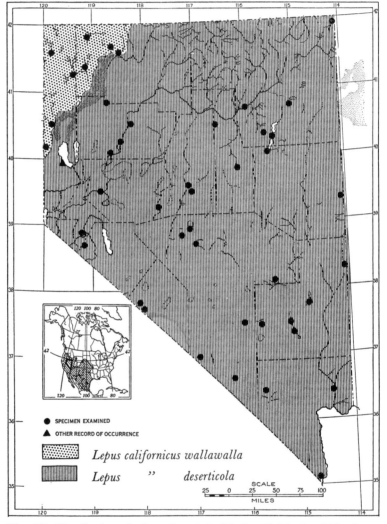

Fig. 438. Distribution of subspecies of the black-tailed jack rabbit, *Lepus californicus*, with insert showing range of the species.

a rabbit was alarmed by a person who remained motionless, the air was tested by the nose while the ears were set erect, indicating that smell as well as hearing and sight were brought to bear in detecting enemies.

Linsdale (1938:197) writes: "An illustration of lack of training of the senses and the little development of fear in the young jack rabbits was noted on May 5, 1930, near South Twin River, 6500 feet. A young individual that I approached started from a form in the center of a sage bush. When I stopped, it froze—up on its toes—and after a minute or so crawled back into the form." Greater caution in older individuals is illustrated by Alcorn's observation, at 7:05 A.M., on August 30, 1940, 13 miles north and 6 miles west of Deep Hole, as he "was resting motionless in the shade of a cut bank of a wash near a small spring. A jack rabbit appeared on the opposite bank not more than 50 feet away and 'zigzagged' down the 10-foot slope of the wash by gentle hops, appearing to be in no hurry. When it approached the edge of the water, it stretched its neck out, apparently as far . . . as possible, and drank for a minute or so. Then it turned and with great speed ran up onto the bank where it stopped and looked about, then leisurely hopped out into the sagebrush." Alcorn thought that the rabbit was not at any time aware of his presence.

Our material is insufficient clearly to show how much if any secondary sexual variation there is in this species, but available data indicate that males average 1 to 2 per cent smaller than females in linear measurements.

In 17 pregnant females from within 12 miles of Fallon the average number of embryos was 3.4, with extremes of 1 and 7. Of 11 females shot on February 14 and 15, 1938, by Alcorn, along the Carson River, 10 to 12 miles west of Fallon, 6 were nursing young and 5 contained embryos. He recorded 4 embryos in each of 2 females killed on May 6. Young of small size seen in all months of the spring, summer, and early autumn show that breeding extends over a correspondingly long time. Our data are not precise enough to show whether a female has more than one litter in the course of a year.

Lepus californicus wallawalla Merriam
Black-tailed Jack Rabbit

Lepus texianus wallawalla Merriam, Proc. Biol. Soc. Washington, 17:137, July 14, 1904. Type from Touchet, Plains of the Columbia, Walla Walla County, Washington.
Lepus californicus wallawalla, Nelson, N. Amer. Fauna, 29:132, August 31, 1909; Taylor, Univ. California Publ. Zoöl., 7:291, June 24, 1911.

Distribution.—Northwestern part of the state from Quinn River Crossing to Flanigan. See figure 438.

Remarks.—Measurements of two males and two females from Virgin Valley and Big Creek Ranch, Humboldt County, are: ♂, 527, 499; ♀, 535, 495; 95, 81; 135, 100; 120, 117; 125, 123; ear from notch on dried skins, 114, 109; 122, 115; weights unavailable.

In addition to the account given of the full species, this race may be characterized as distinctly pinkish on the sides; nasals narrow posteriorly; tympanic bullae small. This race is weakly differentiated from *deserticola*. Topotypes and specimens from eastern Oregon, in comparison with specimens from along the Colorado River in California, have more Pinkish-Buff on the sides and are grayer above. These differences are of only an average sort. In these particulars, most of the specimens from northern Nevada are intermediate. In the skull, the greatest length of the nasals is less and the tympanic bullae appear to be smaller in *wallawalla*. A total of fifteen skulls (eight of *wallawalla* from eastern Oregon and seven of *deserticola* from the vicinity of Fallon, Nevada) was "scrambled" and presented to me for identification upon the understanding that representatives of the two subspecies were included. In my first classification, that based upon size of tympanic bullae, I wrongly identified about half of them. On the basis of width of nasals, posteriorly, I correctly allocated to subspecies all except two, one from Fallon and one from Oregon, which I set aside as intermediates. From this it may be concluded that width of the nasals, posteriorly, provides a better basis for distinguishing skulls from the two areas than does any other feature. Specimens from Elko County are intermediate in width of nasals, but in the sum of their characters seem best referred to the race *deserticola*.

Records of occurrence.—Specimens examined, 16, as follows: *Washoe Co.:* Vya, 6000 ft., 1; mouth of Little High Rock Canyon, 5000 ft., 1; Smoke Creek, 9 mi. E Calif. boundary, 3900 ft., 1; 4½ mi. W Flanigan, 4200 ft., 1. *Humboldt Co.:* Virgin Valley, 5000 ft., 2; Big Creek Ranch, Pine Forest Mts., 4350 ft., 1; Quinn River Crossing, 4100 ft., 4; Soldier Meadows, 4600 ft., 5.

Lepus californicus deserticola Mearns
Black-tailed Jack Rabbit

Lepus texianus deserticola Mearns, Proc. U. S. Nat. Mus., 18:564, June 24, 1896. Type from western edge of Colorado Desert at base of Coast Range, Imperial County, California.

Lepus californicus deserticola, Nelson, N. Amer. Fauna, 29:137, August 31, 1909, Borell and Ellis, Journ. Mamm., 15:40, 73, February 15, 1934; Burt, Trans. San Diego Soc. Nat. Hist., 7:423, May 31, 1934.

Lepus californicus, Linsdale, Amer. Midland Nat., 19:197, January, 1938.

Distribution.—Over entire state except the part northwest of Smoke Creek and Black Rock deserts. See figure 438.

Remarks.—Measurements of four males and three females from 4 miles west of Fallon are: ♂, 544 (539–550), ♀, 528 (515–539); 79 (76–82), 84 (77–90); 124 (120–130), 123 (120–124); ear from notch in dried skins of one male and three females from the west side of Ruby Lake, ♂, 125, ♀, 117 (109–123); weight of twelve males and six nonpregnant females taken February 14 and 15, 1938, 10 to 12 miles west of Fallon, along the Carson River, ♂, 3 2/5 (3–4½), ♀, 4 (3¼–4½) lbs.

In addition to the account given of the full species, this race may be characterized as pale pinkish on the sides, with large auditory bullae and moderately wide rostrum. From *wallawalla, deserticola* differs in less pinkish sides, broader nasals, and, apparently, more inflated tympanic bullae. In the two features first mentioned, the specimens from Elko County show some resemblance to the race *wallawalla*.

Records of occurrence.—Specimens examined, 57, as follows: *Lyon Co.:* West Walker River, 10½ mi. S Yerington, 4500 ft., 1. *Humboldt Co.:* ¾ mi. S Sulphur, 4050 ft., 1. *Pershing Co.:* El Dorado Canyon, Humboldt Range, 5000 ft., 1; 2 mi. N Lovelock, 3; Toulon, 3900 ft., 1. *Churchill Co.:* 1 mi. NW Soda Lake, 4000 ft., 1; 4 mi. W Fallon, 4000 ft., 7. *Mineral Co.:* 2 mi. SW Pine Grove, 7250 ft., 1. *Esmeralda Co.:* Arlemont, 4800–4900 ft., 3; Chiatovich Ranch, 4900 ft., 1; Fish Lake, 4800 ft., 2. *Lander Co.:* Reese River Valley, 7 mi. N Austin, 1; Austin, 1; Campbell Creek, 6900 ft., 1. *Eureka Co.:* 14 mi. NNE Tenabo, 1; 2 mi. S Romano, Diamond Valley, 2. *Nye Co.:* 5 mi. SE Millett P. O., 5500 ft., 2; South Twin River, 6500 ft., 1; top of Mt. Jefferson, Toquima Range, 11,700 ft., 1; Garden Valley, 8½ mi. NE Sharp, 2; Belted Range, 2 mi. N Indian Spring, 6700 ft., 1; 8 mi. E Grapevine Peak, 5000 ft., 1; 23 mi. S and 10 mi. W Wahmonie, 1. *Elko Co.* (unless otherwise noted, in coll. of Ralph Ellis): Goose Creek, ½ mi. W Utah boundary, 5000 ft., 1 (Mus. Vert. Zoöl.); Jerry Creek (Jerry Crab Springs), 6700 ft., 1; 6 mi. E Carlin, 1 (Mus. Vert. Zoöl.); Harrison Pass R. S., Green Mountain Canyon, 6050 ft., 1; W side Ruby Lake, 15 mi. N White Pine Co. line, 1; W side Ruby Lake, 6 mi. N White Pine Co. line, 6200 ft., 1; W side Ruby Lake, 3 mi. N White Pine Co. line, 6200 ft., 3. *White Pine Co.:* W side Ruby Lake, 3 mi. S Elko Co. line, 1 (coll. of Ralph Ellis); 2 mi. E Smith Creek Cave, Mt. Moriah, 5600 ft., 1. *Lincoln Co.:* Latitude 38° 17′, ¼ mi. W Utah boundary, 7300 ft., 1; Desert Valley, 21 mi. W Panaca, 5300 ft., 1; Pahranagat Valley, 1 mi. S Crystal Spring, 4000 ft., 2; SW base Groom Baldy, 7200 ft., 1; Pahranagat Valley, 1 mi. S Alamo, 1. *Clark Co.:* Salt Mine, 6 mi. S St. Thomas, 1; Cold Creek, 6000 ft., 2 (D. R. Dickey Coll.).

Additional records: *Washoe Co.:* Sutcliffe, 3700–4200 ft., 11 (D. G. Nichols, MS). *Clark Co.:* ½ mi. N Calif.-Nev. Monument, Colorado River (Benson, MS).

Genus **Sylvilagus** Gray
Cottontails and Allies

Three species of this genus occur in Nevada. Differential features of generic rank which serve to distinguish cottontails and pigmy rabbits from jack rabbits and snowshoes of the genus *Lepus* are given in the account of the latter. The dental formula is the same. In my experience, the cottontails and pigmy rabbits, in Nevada, are more shy than jack rabbits. Although the two species *nuttallii* and *audubonii* may live in forms in the open, these forms are near dense brush, crevices in rock, or holes in the ground into which the animals can dash for safety if danger threatens. Many individuals of the two species just mentioned and, so far as I have observed, all individuals of the species *idahoensis* stay in holes in the ground in the daytime. The young of all three species are thought to be born in holes in the ground and to be relatively (compared to hares, genus *Lepus*) helpless at birth. All have but one molt per year.

In the vicinity of Fallon, cottontails from the Middle West were liberated between 1910 and 1938. These animals, said to be from Missouri, presumably were of the species *floridanus*. Whether any survived is unknown, but none of the specimens which Vernon L. Mills and J. R. Alcorn saved from this area in 1938 and 1939 are *floridanus;* all are of the species *nuttallii.*

Sylvilagus nuttallii
Nuttall Cottontail

Two subspecies of Nuttall cottontail are recorded from Nevada. The size is intermediate between *audubonii* and *idahoensis,* but nearer the former; hind feet broad and heavily haired on inner surface; grayish-brown above and white beneath; supraorbital processes small, anterior projections abruptly pointed and posterior extensions slender; palatal bridge usually lacking a median spine on posterior border; tympanic bullae small; lateral diameters of posterior halves of second, third, and fourth lower molariform teeth amounting to about one-half of lateral diameters of anterior halves.

Nowhere in Nevada does this species live in the Lower Sonoran Life-zone. It inhabits the territory from the upper part of the Upper Sonoran Life-zone upward through the Transition Life-zone and sometimes above the Transition Zone. One such occurrence was that at 10,400 feet, one mile east of Mount Moriah, where David H. Johnson took a specimen at the upper limit of tree growth. The trees were recorded as a species of spruce, and a five-needled pine. This is the highest altitude among our records of occurrence; the lowest is 3900 feet at the mouth of Big Creek at the base of the Pine Forest Range.

On May 30, 1931, at 9000 feet on the north side of Groom Baldy, I found a nest containing four young which Orr (1940:109) thought were between one and two weeks old. The nest was made of dry grass and rabbit fur. A faint path led

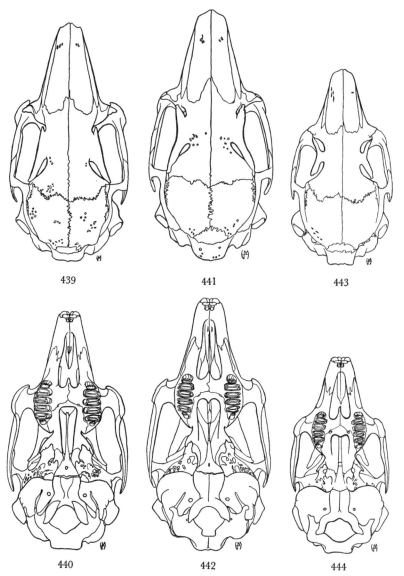

Figs. 439–444. Rabbits. All, × 1. (Other views of these skulls are shown in figs. 445–450.)

Figs. 439, 440. *Sylvilagus nuttallii grangeri*, ½ mile east Jefferson, no. 58527, ♀.
Figs. 441, 442. *Sylvilagus audubonii arizonae*, 3½ miles north Eagle Valley, no. 48960, ♂.
Figs. 443, 444. *Sylvilagus idahoensis*, Millett P. O., no. 37275, ♂.

445

446

447

448

449

450

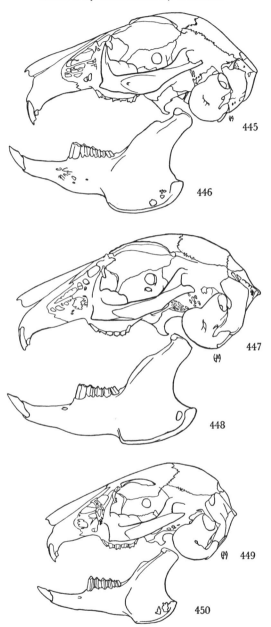

Figs. 445–450. Rabbits. Different views of these skulls are shown in figs. 439–444. ×1.

Figs. 445, 446. *Sylvilagus nuttallii grangeri.*
Figs. 447, 448. *Sylvilagus audubonii arizonae.*
Figs. 449, 450. *Sylvilagus idahoensis.*

away from its opening, which was covered with fur, grass, and a stick ⅜ of an inch in diameter, all placed, I judged, by the female. The nest was on the south side of a piñon trunk one meter through, where the ground was covered with

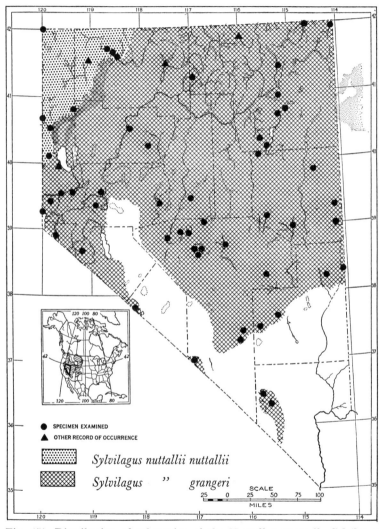

Fig. 451. Distribution of subspecies of the Nuttall cottontail, *Sylvilagus nuttallii*, with insert showing range of the species.

small stones and dry twigs and needles from the piñon. A blind tunnel, which had been built through the 16-inch accumulation of piñon needles on the uphill side of the piñon trunk, led out of the nest and around the same side of the trunk. The small caliber of this tunnel made me think that it had been formed by the young and not by the female. After I reached into the nest, one of the young sought refuge in this tunnel. When taken out of the nest and handled, each of the four young screamed. It was thought that the mother, although looked for, but unfound up to this time, might put in an appearance in response to the cries of her young; but this she did not do. Three of the young, when replaced in the nest, refused to remain there, even though I barricaded the damaged entrance. They were "aroused," and instead of cuddling together, they went pushing here and there, apparently seeking better cover. The rabbits' refusal to remain in the nest was remindful of the behavior of young passerine birds that have been frightened from the nest just prior to the age at which they ordinarily would leave it. These young rabbits were well-furred and had their eyes open. The one taken back to camp weighed 74 grams, had an ear 34 mm. long as measured from the notch, and a hind foot 43 mm. long.

The positive reaction of a cottontail to squeaking sounds made by Linsdale to attract small birds was noted by him in the Toyabe Mountains. In response to these sounds, a cottontail rapidly approached him with apparent concern.

Among the natural enemies of the Nuttall cottontail is to be included the golden eagle; this is indicated by Ward C. Russell's finding of a dead *nuttallii* in a nest occupied by one eaglet on May 20, 1936, 20 miles north of Austin. And these cottontails fall victim to poisoned grain distributed for ground squirrels. Three pregnant females, two of which had six embryos each and the other five, were found by Alcorn to have been killed by poisoned grain in the first half of April, 4 miles west of Fallon.

Of 16 other sexually mature females examined for embryos, 6 were pregnant. The average number of embryos was 5, and the extremes were 4 and 6. By months the females were taken as follows: March, 1 (1 pregnant); April, 1 (1); June, 8 (3); July, 5 (1); September, 1 (0).

As indicated by the cranial and external measurements elsewhere given, males are smaller than females.

Sylvilagus nuttallii nuttallii (Bachman)
Nuttall Cottontail

Lepus nuttallii Bachman, Journ. Acad. Nat. Sci. Philadelphia, 7:345, 1837. Type probably from eastern Oregon, near mouth of Malheur River.

Sylvilagus nuttalli, Lyon, Smiths. Misc. Coll., 45:323, June 15, 1904; Nelson, N. Amer. Fauna, 29:201, August 31, 1909.

Sylvilagus nuttalli grangeri, Taylor, Univ. California Publ. Zoöl., 7:288, June 24, 1911.

Distribution.—Northwestern part of state from Pine Forest Mountains southwest to north end of Virginia Mountains. See figure 451.

Remarks.—Measurements of one male and six females from the Pine Forest Mts. are: ♂, 348, ♀, 354 (350–366); 46, 53 (45–56); 87, 91 (85–95); ear from notch on dried skin, 59, 60 (58–61); weight of a male from Smoke Creek, 658, and of two females from the same place, 783 and 963 grams.

In addition to characters mentioned in the account of the species, this race is further characterized by small size and dark color. These two features are of a comparative nature when contrasted with the race *grangeri*. Nevadan specimens are intergrades between the two races, and those here assigned to the race *nuttallii* are almost as large as *grangeri* and only slightly darker colored on the upper parts.

Records of occurrence.—Specimens examined, 31, as follows: *Washoe Co.:* 12-mile Creek, 5300 ft. (½ mi. E Calif. boundary, 2; 1 mi. E Calif. boundary, 1), 3; Barrel Spring, 5700 ft., 9½ mi. E and 3½ mi. N Ft. Bidwell, 12; ½ mi. S Rock Creek, Granite Mts., 6000 ft., 1; Smoke Creek (from Calif. boundary, ½ mi. E, 5300 ft., 1; 3¼ mi. E, 4000 ft., 1; 9 mi. E, 3900 ft., 1) 3; 4½ mi. S Flanigan, 4100 ft., 1. *Humboldt Co.:* Big Creek, 5000 ft., 1; Big Creek Ranch, 4350 ft., 2; near same, at 5000 ft., 2; mouth of Big Creek, 4300 ft., 1; Quinn River Crossing, 5800 ft., 3.

Additional record (Nelson, 1909:204): Summit Lake.

Sylvilagus nuttallii grangeri (Allen)
Nuttall Cottontail

Lepus sylvaticus grangeri Allen, Bull. Amer. Mus. Nat. Hist., 7:264, 1895. Type from Hill City, Pennington County, South Dakota.
Sylvilagus nuttalli grangeri, Nelson, N. Amer. Fauna, 29:204, August 31, 1909.
Sylvilagus nuttallii grangeri, Borell and Ellis, Journ. Mamm., 15:41, 73, February 15, 1934; Burt, Trans. San Diego Soc. Nat. Hist., 7:423, May 31, 1934.
Sylvilagus nuttallii, Linsdale, Amer. Midland Nat., 19:198, January, 1938.

Distribution.—Upper Sonoran and Transition life-zones of state except part northwest of Black Rock and Smoke Creek deserts. See figure 451.

Remarks.—Measurements of seven males and six females from the Toyabe Mountains area are: ♀, 337 (320–350), ♂, 352 (335–385); 43 (20–57), 52 (30–60); 92 (87–98), 94 (90–96); ear from notch on dried skins, 58 (54–62), 59 (57–63); weight, 641 (600–678), one female, 885 grams.

From the race *nuttallii*, this subspecies differs in being larger and darker colored on the upper parts. In specimens from the southern part of the state, no approach has been noted to the race *pinetis*, which occurs to the southeast of Nevada, but the two animals from Clark County have not been examined with this point in mind.

Records of occurrence.—Specimens examined, 75, as follows: *Washoe Co.:* N side Truckee River, 11¾ mi. E Reno, 4500 ft., 1; 8 mi. S Reno, 1 (coll. of Ralph Ellis); Calvada, N end Lake Tahoe, 6400 ft., 1. *Douglas Co.:* Carson River, 5 mi. SE Minden, 4900 ft., 1. *Storey Co.:* 4 mi. SW Wadsworth, along Truckee Canal, 4100 ft., 1. *Pershing Co.:* El Dorado Canyon, Humboldt Range, 5000 ft., 1; S slope Granite Peak, East Range, 1. *Churchill Co.:* 1 mi. NW Soda Lake, 2; 4 mi. W Fallon, 2; 10 mi. SW Fallon, 2; 15 mi. SW Fallon, 5000 ft., 1. *Mineral Co.:* 2 mi. SW Pine Grove, 7800 ft., 1. *Esmeralda Co.:* Chiatovich Creek, 7000 ft., 2. *Lander Co.:* Austin, 5; Smiths Creek, 7500 ft., 1. *Nye Co.:* White Rock Mtn., 10,170 ft., 1; Wisconsin Creek, 7800 ft., 1; 5 mi. SE Millett P. O., 5500 ft., 7; 2 mi. W Indian Valley, 8300 ft., 1; 1 mi. W Indian Valley, 8000 ft., 1; Fish Spring Valley, ½ mi. N Fish Lake, 6500 ft., 1; Toquima Range, 1½ mi. E Jefferson, 1; Monitor Valley, 8 mi. E Toquima Mtn., 7000 ft., 1; Toquima Range, 2 mi. SE Jefferson, 8800 ft., 1; Antone Creek, 2 mi. S Meadow Valley R. S., Toquima Mts., 1; Burned Corral Canyon, Quinn Canyon Mts., 6500 ft., 1; Belted Range, 2 mi. NW Indian Spring, 6300 ft., 3; S end Belted Range, 5 mi. NW Whiterock Spring, 7200 ft., 1; 2½ mi. E and 1 mi. S Grapevine Peak, 6700 ft., 1. *Elko Co.:* Cedar Creek, 1; 10 mi. NE San Jacinto, 6000 ft., 1; Goose Creek, 2 mi. W Utah boundary, 5000 ft., 1; Marys River, 22 mi. N Deeth, 5800 ft., 1; 10 mi. SW Midas, 5000 ft., 1; Jerry Creek (Jerry Crab Springs), 6700 ft., 1 (coll. of Ralph Ellis); E side Ruby Mts., 10 mi. S Secret Pass, 1 (coll. of Ralph Ellis); W side Ruby Lake, 6 mi. N White Pine Co. line, 6200 ft., 4 (coll. of Ralph Ellis); W side Ruby Lake, 3 mi. N White Pine Co. line, 6200 ft., 3 (coll. of Ralph Ellis). *White Pine Co.:* Willow Creek, 2 mi. S Elko Co. line, 6500 ft., 1 (coll. of Ralph Ellis); E side Schellbourne Pass, 6800 ft., 1; 1 mi. E Mt. Moriah, 10,400 ft., 1; 2½ mi. SW Hamilton, 7600 ft., 1; Lehman Creek (8300 ft., 1; 7200 ft., 1), 2; Baker Creek, 8500 ft., 1; Water Canyon, 8 mi. N Lund, 1. *Lincoln Co.:* Latitude 38° 17′, ¼ mi. W Utah boundary, 7300 ft., 1; Wilson Peak, 7000 ft., Wilson Creek Mts., 1; E slope Irish Mtn., 6900–8250 ft., 5; Groom Baldy, 8400 ft., 1. *Clark Co.:* 1½ mi. N Wheeler Well, 1; Kyle Canyon, Charleston Park, 8000 ft., 1.

Additional records: *Washoe Co.:* Hardscrabble Canyon, 4900–6000 ft. (D. G. Nichols, MS). *Humboldt Co.:* Paradise Valley (Nelson, 1909:207). *Elko Co.:* Mountain City (Nelson, 1909:207).

Sylvilagus audubonii arizonae (Allen)
Audubon Cottontail

(*Lepus sylvaticus*) var. *arizonae* Allen, Monograph of North Amer. Rodentia, p. 332, August, 1877. Type from Beal Springs, 3 miles northwest of Kingman, Mohave County, Arizona.
Sylvilagus auduboni arizonae, Nelson, N. Amer. Fauna, 29:222, August 31, 1909; Burt, Trans. San Diego Soc. Nat. Hist., 8:423, May 31, 1934.

Distribution.—Southern Nevada north to Fish Lake Valley and White River Valley; and in extreme eastern White Pine County. See figure 452.

Remarks.—Measurements of six males and five females from Lincoln and Clark counties are: ♂, 355 (341–372), ♀, 372 (355–382); 42 (35–52), 50 (33–67); 85 (80–88), 87 (83–92); ear

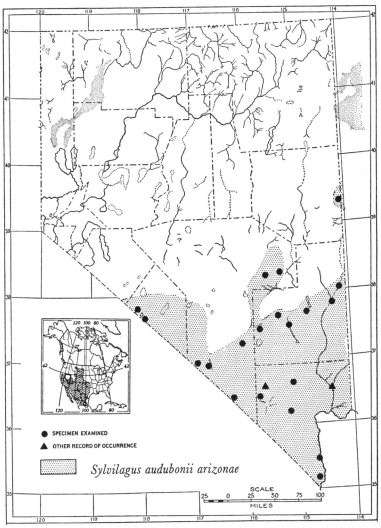

Fig. 452. Distribution of the Audubon cottontail, *Sylvilagus audubonii*.

from notch in dried skins, 74 (69–77), 74 (71–79); weight, 707 (637–771), 792 (679–894) grams.

In size, largest of Nevadan *Sylvilagus;* hind feet slender and lacking the long, dense pelage possessed by *nuttallii;* ears long and sparsely haired on inner surface; supraorbital processes large, anterior projections blunt and posterior extensions broad; palatal bridge usually with median spine on posterior border; tympanic bullae large; lateral diameters of posterior halves of second, third, and fourth lower molariform teeth amounting to about four-fifths of lateral diameter of anterior halves.

The range of *audubonii* is within the Lower Sonoran Life-zone and lower part of the Upper Sonoran Life-zone. Where taken in the same locality with *nuttallii*, *audubonii* almost always lives at a lower elevation in cover of a lower zonal position. Some live in holes in the ground, and some live in forms. Males are smaller than females. In 19 pregnant females from California, Orr found the number of embryos per litter to average 3.6, with extremes of 2 and 6. Of the 3 pregnant specimens from Nevada, all obtained in late May, each of 2 had 4 embryos, and the third had 5. Of the 8 other sexually mature females, 1 was taken in January, 1 in February, 3 in May, and 3 in June. Two of the June-taken animals were suckling young.

Records of occurrence.—Specimens examined, 37, as follows: *Esmeralda Co.:* Arlemont, 4850 ft., 1; Fish Lake, 4800 ft., 4; 3½ mi. E McAfee Ranch, 5450 ft., 1. *Nye Co.:* White River Valley, 15 mi. WSW Sunnyside, 1; Quinn Canyon Mts., 5½ mi. E Nyala, 6300 ft., 1; Oak Spring, 6000 ft., 1; 2 mi. S Oak Spring, 5700 ft., 1; 5 mi. E and 1 mi. N Grapevine Peak, 5500 ft., 1; 3 mi. E Grapevine Peak, 6000 ft., 1; Amargosa River, 3 mi. NE Beatty, 3400 ft., 1; Ash Meadows, 4 4/5 mi. NW Devils Hole, 2200 ft., 2. *White Pine Co.:* 2 mi. E Smith Creek Cave, Mt. Moriah, 5600 ft., 2; 4 mi. E Smith Creek Cave, 1. *Lincoln Co.:* 3½ mi. N Eagle Valley, 5800 ft., 1; 5 mi. E Panaca, 5500 ft., 1; 20 mi. W Caliente, 5000 ft., 1; E slope Irish Mtn., 6900 ft., 1; Pahranagat Valley (4 mi. NE Crystal Spring, 4300 ft., 2; Crystal Spring, 4000 ft., 1; ½ mi. S Crystal Spring, 4000 ft., 1), 4; SW base Groom Baldy, 7200 ft., 1. *Clark Co.:* Hidden Forest, 8500 ft., 1 (D. R. Dickey Coll.); Wheeler Well, 6600 ft., 1 (D. R. Dickey Coll.); 4 mi. NW Las Vegas, 2100 ft., 2 (D. R. Dickey Coll.); Colorado River, 14 mi. E Searchlight, 500 ft., 5; Hiko Spring, 8 mi. SSE Dead Mtn., 1900 ft., 1.

Additional records: *Clark Co.* (Burt, 1934:423): Indian Springs; St. Thomas.

Sylvilagus idahoensis (Merriam)
Pigmy Rabbit

Lepus idahoensis Merriam, N. Amer. Fauna, 5:76, July 30, 1891. Type from head of Pahsimeroi Valley, near Goldburg, Custer County, Idaho.

Sylvilagus idahoensis, Borell and Ellis, Journ. Mamm., 15:41, February 15, 1934; Linsdale, Amer. Midland Nat., 19:198, January, 1938.

Brachylagus idahoensis, Lyon, Smiths. Misc. Coll., 45:323, June 15, 1904; Nelson, N. Amer. Fauna, 29:275, August 31, 1909.

Distribution.—Upper Sonoran Life-zone where *Artemisia tridentata* predominates in the northwestern, northern, and eastern two-thirds of the state south to Sharp in Nye County. See figure 453.

Remarks.—Measurements of fourteen males and five females from Millett are: ♂, 270 (250–290), ♀, 269 (260–288); 25 (20–30), 25 (21–26); 68 (65–72), 68 (62–71); ear from notch in dried skin, 41 (36–48), 41 (37–46); weight of a female taken July 21, 1941, 13 ounces.

Size small (total length less than 300 mm.); ears short and rounded, covered with silky pelage inside and out; upper parts in fresh autumnal pelage with subterminal band varying from Ochraceous-Buff to Pinkish Cinnamon, and terminal band of black varying from conspicuous to inconspicuous with wear and abrasion; pelage of upper parts varies from pinkish to blackish or dark grayish; tail small, dusky above and below; rostrum proportionately short and pointed; antorbital projections of supraorbital processes long compared with those of other *Sylvilagus;* postorbital processes broadest distally where truncate or slightly notched; tympanic bullae large; anterior face of first upper molariform tooth with only one re-entrant angle; lateral diameters of posterior halves of second, third, and fourth lower molariform teeth amounting to about one-half of lateral diameters of anterior halves. Although originally thought to have two annual molts, Nelson (1909:

29), Anthony (1913:20), and Grinnell, Dixon, and Linsdale (1930:557) have maintained that it agrees with other members of the genus *Sylvilagus* in having but one.

The pigmy rabbit has a limited geographic range embracing northeastern California, eastern Oregon, southeastern Washington, and southern Idaho, in

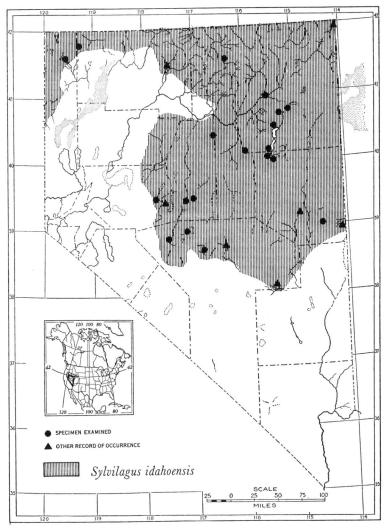

Fig. 453. Distribution of the pigmy rabbit, *Sylvilagus idahoensis*, with insert showing range of the species.

addition to parts of Nevada. Probably it will be found also in Utah. Not only is this rabbit limited in occurrence geographically but also in habitat. I have found it only in relatively dense and tall sagebrush.

TABLE 26

CRANIAL MEASUREMENTS (IN MILLIMETERS) OF LEPUS AND SYLVILAGUS

Sex	Number of individuals averaged or catalogue no.	Basilar length	Zygomatic breadth	Postorbital constriction	Length of nasals	Width of nasals	Length of molar series	Diameter of auditory meatus	Breadth of brain case	Length of palatal bridge
	*Lepus townsendii townsendii*, Ruby Mountains
♂	7* av.	69.7	43.6	14.0	37.2	19.5	16.3	5.8	28.3	5.4
	min.	67.1	43.3	12.3	34.0	18.9	15.6	5.1	26.7	5.2
	max.	73.9	43.8	15.6	40.2	20.2	17.6	6.5	29.2	6.2
♀	9* av.	71.2	45.0	14.1	38.6	20.5	16.9	5.7	29.0	5.7
	min.	66.5	42.9	12.2	37.4	19.0	16.1	5.0	27.3	5.0
	max.	74.2	46.9	15.9	40.1	21.6	17.7	6.5	30.1	7.0
	*Lepus americanus tahoensis*, Placer Co., California
♂	37522	54.0	36.4	11.7	27.0	14.5	12.8	4.8	23.7	6.2
♀	38286	55.7	——	10.7	27.4	15.4	13.2	5.2	23.8	6.9
	*Lepus californicus wallawalla*, Pine Forest Mountains area
♂	8271	67.7	38.8	12.4	32.8	17.9	15.6	6.3	25.6	6.4
♂	8272	66.2	41.2	12.4	33.8	15.8	15.4	5.5	26.5	6.2
♀	8279	71.2	41.9	11.8	35.8	16.2	15.1	6.2	27.1	6.1
♀	12051	69.8	40.7	11.2	34.6	17.1	15.1	5.5	25.5	5.7
	*Lepus californicus deserticola*, 4 mi. W Fallon
♂	4 av.	69.3	41.2	12.2	36.8	18.1	16.0	6.1	26.6	5.4
	min.	66.9	40.6	10.2	34.2	17.5	15.3	5.9	25.9	4.6
	max.	70.8	41.6	14.5	37.9	18.3	16.4	6.3	27.4	6.6
♀	3 av.	68.1	40.3	12.7	34.9	17.8	15.3	6.0	25.2	6.1
	min.	67.0	39.6	11.4	33.9	16.6	14.9	5.7	24.9	5.8
	max.	69.4	41.6	13.7	36.7	18.7	15.7	6.3	25.5	6.4
	*Sylvilagus nuttallii nuttallii*, Pine Forest Mountains area
♂	8263	49.3	32.8	10.8	29.0	13.0	12.1	5.4	21.9	5.0
♀	6 av.	49.2	33.1	10.3	27.9	12.9	12.0	5.0	22.0	5.4
	min.	46.3	32.1	9.3	27.1	12.0	11.1	4.6	21.5	5.2
	max.	50.2	33.7	11.1	29.4	13.7	12.5	5.2	22.9	5.7

* Collection of Ralph Ellis.

TABLE 26—(*Continued*)

Sex	Number of individuals averaged or catalogue no.	Basilar length	Zygomatic breadth	Postorbital constriction	Length of nasals	Width of nasals	Length of molar series	Diameter of auditory meatus	Breadth of brain case	Length of palatal bridge
					Sylvilagus nuttallii grangeri, Toyabe Mountains area					
♂	6 av.	49.3	32.8	10.9	28.6	13.6	12.2	5.0	21.9	5.4
	min.	46.9	32.3	10.4	27.4	12.5	11.3	4.6	21.3	5.3
	max.	51.0	33.3	11.8	30.2	15.1	12.9	5.2	22.3	5.6
♀	6 av.	49.3	32.8	11.3	28.6	13.3	12.2	5.1	22.2	5.4
	min.	48.3	32.3	10.6	27.9	13.0	12.0	4.9	21.5	5.0
	max.	50.1	33.2	12.1	29.3	13.8	12.3	5.5	22.7	5.6
					Sylvilagus audubonii arizonae, Lincoln and Clark counties					
♂	6 av.	50.5	33.2	11.5	28.2	12.3	12.1	5.0	22.2	5.2
	min.	49.2	32.5	10.6	26.8	11.1	11.6	4.5	21.2	4.8
	max.	51.8	34.2	12.9	31.2	13.2	12.5	5.3	23.1	5.5
♀	5 av.	51.0	32.9	11.5	27.7	12.5	12.2	5.1	22.1	5.2
	min.	49.7	31.8	11.0	26.5	11.5	12.1	4.6	21.3	4.8
	max.	53.2	34.0	12.2	29.2	14.0	12.4	5.7	23.6	5.7
					Sylvilagus idahoensis, Millett P. O.					
♂	14 av.	38.6	27.2	9.2	18.8	9.1	9.2	5.0	19.5	3.7
	min.	37.3	26.3	8.3	17.7	8.1	8.8	4.6	18.0	2.9
	max.	40.1	28.1	9.9	19.8	10.3	9.8	5.4	20.2	4.4
♀	5 av.	38.4	27.3	9.2	19.0	9.3	9.2	5.2	19.4	3.9
	min.	38.0	26.9	8.7	18.6	9.1	8.8	5.0	18.7	3.6
	max.	38.8	27.7	10.2	19.5	9.5	10.0	5.3	19.8	4.0

Amid the bushes of sage the rabbits always live, so far as observed in Nevada, in burrows. Nearly all of those burrows examined appeared to have been excavated by the rabbits themselves, and about half of those examined by me had a shallow trench extending out from the mouth of the burrow. When frightened, the rabbit often ran into this trench and stopped just outside the mouth of the burrow, with only the ears and eyes showing above the ground. At further sign of danger, the rabbit disappeared down the burrow. I never found one more than 70 feet from a burrow. A few burrows made originally by badgers were used by the pigmy rabbits.

Bailey (1936:112) reports that the animals eat extensively of sagebrush in winter and that in February of 1908 at Paradise [Valley], Nevada, S. E. Piper learned that the pigmy rabbits seldom were eaten by the people living there because the rabbits tasted so strongly of sage.

The rabbits have been observed outside their burrows in the early morning, at twilight, and at night; their hours of activity appear to be about the same as those of cottontails.

Males and females measured at this writing are of about the same size. It was expected that the females, as in other species of rabbits, would average larger than the males. A larger sample than was available to me might show that the pigmy rabbit is no exception in this respect.

General observations indicate that these rabbits are killed by tularemia. Borell and Ellis (1934a:42) record the remains of one found in the crop of a long-eared owl.

A female taken on June 4, 1925, at Bells Ranch contained six embryos. No embryos are recorded for other females, most of which were taken in winter. From these data and from the meager information on record about the species in California, Oregon, and Idaho, it appears that six young is the rule and that these may be born at any time from late May until early August.

Records of occurrence.—Specimens examined, 56, as follows: *Washoe Co.:* 2 mi. E Massacre Creek, 5800 ft., 1. *Humboldt Co.:* 12 mi. SW Twin Peak, 6000 ft., 1. *Pershing Co.:* 2 mi. NE Alpine, 1 (coll. of J. R. Alcorn). *Lander Co.:* 8 mi. NNE Tenabo, 1; Austin, 2; Gondolpho Ranch, Reese River, 10 mi. W Austin, 11. *Nye Co.:* Millett P. O., 5600 ft., 21; Bells Ranch, Reese River, 6890 ft., 4; Indian Valley, 7500 ft., Shoshone Mts., 1; Monitor Valley, 9 mi. E Mt. Jefferson, 7000 ft., 1; Monitor Valley, 9 mi. E Toquima Peak, 7000 ft., 1. *Elko Co.* (unless otherwise noted, in coll. of Ralph Ellis): 13 mi. SSW Whiterock, 5600 ft., 1 (Mus. Vert. Zoöl.); 3 mi. W Halleck 5200 ft., 1; Jerry Creek (Jerry Crab Springs), 2; Arizona Springs, 6500 ft., 1; W side Ruby Valley, 10 mi. S Secret Pass, 2; east base Ruby Mts., 20 mi. N Harrison Pass, 1; 1½ mi. SE Union, 1 (Mus. Vert. Zoöl.); W side Ruby Lake, 3 mi. N White Pine Co. line, 6200 ft., 1. *White Pine Co.:* W side Ruby Lake, 3 mi. S Elko Co. line, 6100 ft., 1 (coll. of Ralph Ellis); 7 mi. ESE Hobson P. O., 1 (coll. Ralph Ellis); Spring Valley, 7 mi. SW Osceola, 6100 ft., 1.

Additional records (unless otherwise noted, sight records by E. R. Hall): *Humboldt Co.:* Paradise (Nelson, 1909:278). *Lander Co.:* Smiths Creek, 7100 ft. *Nye Co.:* N end Fish Lake, Fish Spring Valley, 8½ mi. NE Sharp. *Elko Co.:* Goose Creek, 1 mi. W Utah boundary. *White Pine Co.:* 10 mi. W Ely; Baker Creek, 6500 ft.

Order ARTIODACTYLA
Even-toed Ungulates

Cervus canadensis nelsoni Bailey
Wapiti

Cervus canadensis nelsoni Bailey, Proc. Biol. Soc. Washington, 48:188, November 15, 1935. Type from Yellowstone National Park [Wyoming ?].

Distribution.—Originally recorded in Shell Creek and Snake Mountains of White Pine County. See figure 458.

Remarks.—Measurements by Joseph S. Dixon of a male, and by Fred M. Packard of a female from Rocky Mountain National Park, Colorado, are: ♂, 2,464, ♀, 2,032; 83, 171; 660, 464; ear from notch, 216, 203; weight of male, 762 lbs.

In size, largest of the true deer; only males possess antlers, which commonly have five to seven points, including well-developed brow tine and bez tine; antlers, measured along the beam, following curves, as much as 66 inches long, and, in exceptional specimens, with a spread of 60 inches; antorbital facial gland present; metatarsal gland oval, about 3 inches long, above middle of metatarsus; nose pad mostly naked, and roughened; neck maned; head and neck dark brown; sides and back grayish-brown; rump and tail lighter, straw-colored; underparts blackish, with white patch between hind legs; legs dark brown;

fawns spotted; canine teeth present in upper jaw, much larger in males. The dental formula is i. $\frac{0}{4}$, c. $\frac{1}{0}$, p. $\frac{3}{3}$, m. $\frac{3}{3}$.

Wapiti must have been of infrequent occurrence in Nevada and were probably present in only a small part of the state, for I have come across only one mention of them by early travelers. This is by Captain J. H. Simpson (1876)

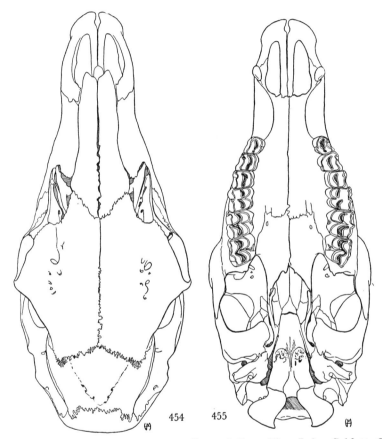

454   455

Figs. 454, 455. *Cervus canadensis nelsoni*, 1 mile north Green River Lakes, Sublette County, Wyoming, 8300 feet, no. 89267, ♀. ×¼.

in his report on explorations for a wagon route from Camp Floyd, Utah, to Genoa, Nevada. On page 121 of his "Report and Journal" he says, under date of July 20, 1859: "An elk was seen for the first time yesterday in Stevenson's Cañon, and one to-day in Red Cañon, also a mountain sheep for the first time." By means of Simpson's map, I place Red Canyon as in the Snake Mountains just north of Wheeler Peak, and Stevensons Canyon as on the west side of the Shell Creek Range, both places in eastern White Pine County.

Sportsmen are said to have introduced wapiti into this general area, on

Mount Moriah or in the territory to the north of this, in White Pine or Elko counties, but whatever original stock was there is thought to have been exterminated before the introductions were made. Wapiti are said to have been introduced also on Charleston Peak, Clark County, between 1930 and 1940. Nothing is known of the fate of these introductions at this writing, 1942.

The name wapiti is used instead of elk bècause in Europe the name elk has for centuries been applied to a different sort of animal, the creature we call a

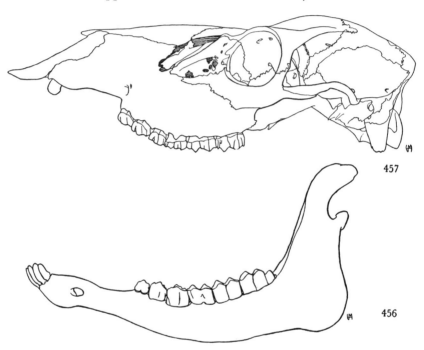

457

456

Figs. 456, 457. Wapiti. ×¼.

Fig. 456. *Cervus canadensis nelsoni*, Estes Park, Colorado, no. 91041, ♀.
Fig. 457. *Cervus canadensis nelsoni*, 1 mile north Green River Lakes, Sublette County, Wyoming, 8300 feet, no. 89267, ♀.

moose. The animal that we call wapiti or elk is known in Europe as the red deer.

Throughout most of its range in the mountainous areas, the wapiti comes down to lower elevations to spend the winter. The antlers are shed in early spring, commonly in March. The calves are born in May or June, after a gestation period of about 8½ months. Except in rare instances, there is but one calf born to a female. In the breeding season, one male gathers several females into a band over which he exercises authority. Except in the breeding season, an older female ordinarily is the leader of a band.

Records of occurrence.—In Shell Creek and Snake ranges of White Pine County, as indicated above.

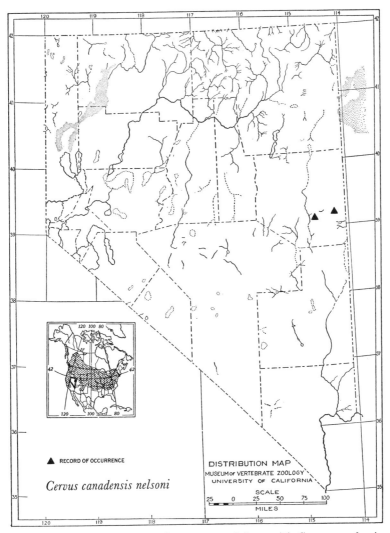

Fig. 458. Two record stations of occurrence of the wapiti, *Cervus canadensis*, with insert showing range of the species.

Odocoileus hemionus hemionus Rafinesque
Black-tailed or Mule Deer

Odocoileus hemionus Rafinesque, Amer. Monthly Mag., 1:436, October, 1817. Type from Sioux River, South Dakota. Taylor, Univ. California Publ. Zoöl., 7:208, June 24, 1911; Linsdale, Amer. Midland Nat., 19:199, January, 1938.

Odocoileus hemionus hemionus, Borell and Ellis, Journ. Mamm., 15:42, 73, February 15, 1934; Burt, Trans. San Diego Soc. Nat. Hist., 7:424, May 31, 1934; Cowan, Calif. Fish and Game, 22:203, July, 1936.

Distribution.—Generally throughout the upper part of the Upper Sonoran Life-zone and higher zones. See figure 463.

Remarks.—Measurements of a male from west side Ruby Lake and three females (no. 74295, 12-mile Cr.; no. 58537, Greenmonster Canyon; no. 58536, N slope Toquima Peak) are: ♂, 1,710, ♀, 1,555, 1,574, 1,540; 134, 180, 170, 145; 585, 480, 465, 455. Weights not available.

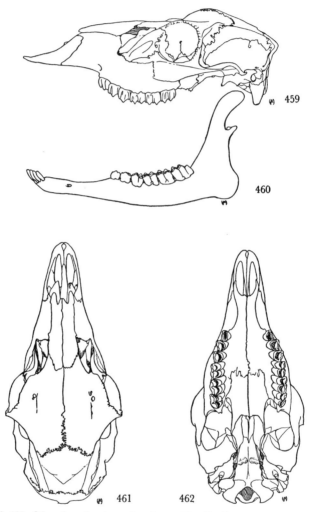

Figs. 459–462. *Odocoileus hemionus hemionus*, 12-mile Creek, no. 74295, ♀. ×¼.

General color of sides and back Cinnamon-Buff to near (c) same; fine black tip to each hair; subterminal band Pinkish Buff; base of each hair Light Drab distally, shading to whitish proximally; dorsal area of animal darker than sides, but without clearly defined middorsal line; brow patch nearly white, bordered anteriorly by V-shaped line of Benzo Brown extending from point on midline of nose, 1½ inches anteriorly to eyes, to point midway along each eyebrow; eyelids black; nose and sides of face whitish, the latter with a wash of Pale Buff extending from angle of mouth to dark color of neck; spots, dorsally and laterally, at base of rhinarium Fuscous Black; chin white; small Fuscous spot on each side of lower lip restricted and generally not meeting on midline; throat white. Outside of ear gray, inside with white spot at base and white extending one-third of way up posterior surface; brisket blackish on midline, shading into dark gray on sides of chest; axilla, inguinal region, belly, inside of foreleg, and inside of hind leg to hock white, with faint wash of fawn varying individually in extent and intensity; genital region, rump, base of tail, and band completely encircling base of tail white; tip of tail black; proximal half of tail naked below. Outside of foreleg, above knee, same color as back; below knee near Clay Color (16″ h); hind leg below hock Pinkish Buff. In summer pelage the color pattern is essentially the same as in winter, but the upper parts are near (c) Cinnamon-Buff, and the animals are "red" as opposed to "blue" in the winter coat. In some specimens there is a well-defined middorsal line; nose and sides of face yellowish-brown; rump patch less extensive than in winter. Metatarsal gland, with two-thirds of its length above midpoint of shank, same color as leg, or slightly lighter and surrounded by narrow area of stiffer, downwardly directed hairs, 30 mm. in length and completely encircling gland; hairs 35 mm. long in a tuft marking location of tarsal gland on median side of tarsus; an interdigital gland on each forefoot as well as on each hind foot; preorbital gland situated just anterior to the internal canthus of the eye and accommodated by a pit in the lacrimal bone; antlers dichotomously branching and present in males only. The dental formula is i. $\frac{0}{4}$, c. $\frac{0}{0}$, p. $\frac{3}{3}$, m. $\frac{3}{3}$.

The above characterization, prepared originally by Cowan (1936) for deer of the race *hemionus* from both California and Nevada, applies to deer in all parts of the state. In other words, even with fairly abundant material, no geographic variation has been found in the Nevadan specimens; so far as we know all Nevadan deer belong to the subspecies *Odocoileus hemionus hemionus*. It is possible that in the vicinity of Lake Tahoe *Odocoileus hemionus columbianus* or *Odocoileus hemionus californicus* will be taken, but none of the specimens seen from Nevada are of these races. Farther south, in the White Mountains of Esmeralda County, deer may be of the subspecies *Odocoileus hemionus inyoensis*, but at this writing no specimens of deer of any kind are available from there.

It may be that indisputable record for Nevada of the entirely distinct species of deer, *Odocoileus virginianus*, probably subspecies *ochrourus*, will yet come to light. Cowan (1936:194, 200) mentions a sight record of a white-tailed deer (*O. virginianus*) for western Washoe County by Donald McLean, and Cowan himself has identified as of this species a shed antler (Mus. Vert. Zoöl., no. 74296) picked up on Granite Peak in the same county. A pair of antlers in a restaurant in Battle Mountain said by several persons to have been Nevada-taken and allegedly pertaining to *Odocoileus virginianus* may be mentioned. Other reported occurrences of *virginianus*, although positively enough made by the persons who reported, have proved to be misidentifications of *O. hemionus* or reports which could not be verified. Although I suppose that white-tailed deer once occurred in Nevada and although some still may be found there, there is no one record known to me which excludes all reasonable doubt of its authenticity.

Deer are truly abundant in many parts of Nevada above the Lower Sonoran Life-zone. Our observations show that areas which are heavily grazed by domestic sheep have far fewer deer than those utilized only by cattle. The Snake Mountains had many deer in 1929 and 1930, but increasingly heavy utilization of the area by sheep was correlated with a reduction in the number of deer, so that 10 years later my impression was that there were not a sixth as many deer as in 1929 and 1930. Numerous other instances were observed where this correlation held, and no exceptions were encountered. I did not learn to my full satisfaction all of the reasons why the presence of sheep in a given area tends to make that area unfavorable for deer, but I think that actual competition for food is involved as one part of the relationship.

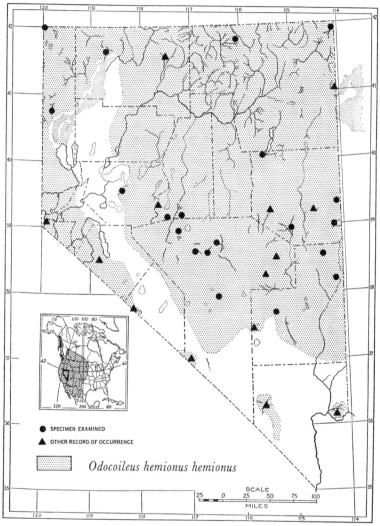

Fig. 463. Distribution of the black-tailed or mule deer, *Odocoileus hemionus*, with insert showing range of the species.

The following notes are ailable avon contents of stomachs of deer: On June 30, 1933, on the north slope of Toquima Peak, at 9300 feet altitude, a yearling buck and an adult doe had fed entirely on leaves of quaking aspen (*Populus tremuloides*). On July 13, 1933, at 8300 feet altitude in Greenmonster Canyon, the stomach of an adult doe contained leaves of aspen mixed with occasional old, yellow leaves of mountain mahogany (*Cercocarpus* sp.). On July 13, 1935, along Goose Creek, two miles west of the Utah boundary, an adult doe had the stomach filled only with leaves of willow (*Salix* sp.). An adult doe shot early on the morning of September 12, 1931, at 7800 feet along Breen Creek, in a burned area among the piñons, contained food items identified by Clarence Cottam as follows: fragments of a number of Agaricaceae (mushrooms), 5%; needle fragments of *Pinus monophylla*, trace; leaves and twigs of *Cowania mexicana*, 72%; leaves and twigs of *Eriogonum* sp., 5%; bud scales and leaf fragments of *Salix* sp., 1%; twelve seeds and plant fiber of *Ranunculus cymbalaria*, 1%; leaf fragments of *Rosa* sp., 1%; plant fiber of *Cercocarpus* sp., 1%; fragments of ten seeds and plant fiber of *Chenopodium* ? *ambrosioides*, 1%; four seeds and plant fiber of *Polygonum* sp., 1%; fragment of seed pod and leaf fragments of legume, 1%; plant fiber of *Artemisia* sp., 1%; undetermined plant fibers, 10%; fragments, mere traces, of several insects which were almost certainly ingested accidentally by the deer while it was eating foliage.

Incomplete as these data are, they serve to illustrate that deer eat a variety of plant foods. Deer are more given to browsing than to grazing. In most places, cattle, which graze more than they browse, compete with deer for food less than do sheep, which graze as well as browse.

The deer are the most hunted of large game mammals in Nevada and are the only large game mammals on which an open season is provided by law. The present (1941) regulations provide that each hunter, in a specified period in the autumn, may legally take one male deer with branched antlers.

Mrs. Lois M. Johnson, Assistant Secretary of the State of Nevada Fish and Game Commission, and J. R. Alcorn have furnished the following record of deer of this kind legally killed and reported for the state:

DEER REPORTED TAKEN IN NEVADA

County	1929	1930	1931	1932	1933	1934	1935	1936	1937	1938	1939	1940
Churchill.....	4	2	7	0	2	3	3	0	1	0	10	5
Clark.........	1	1	0	0	3	1	2	1	0	0	0	4
Douglas.......	2	5	5	2	3	3	5	8	15	10	19	26
Elko..........	48	71	83	64	60	70	76	119	187	189	329	399
Esmeralda....	0	1	0	0	0	0	0	0	0	0	1	2
Eureka........	11	5	15	9	19	8	6	15	9	9	8	30
Humboldt....	55	50	124	62	36	43	67	76	68	71	80	147
Lander........	44	54	58	69	60	63	78	73	95	116	156	186
Lincoln.......	21	30	33	25	12	25	36	38	58	55	59	105
Lyon..........	0	0	0	0	2	1	0	2	0	3	1	0
Mineral.......	1	0	3	1	1	0	0	0	0	1	2	8
Nye..........	56	58	78	78	86	78	67	100	127	130	180	271
Ormsby.......	0	1	2	3	2	4	5	9	5	11	13	12
Pershing......	7	13	8	5	3	2	10	5	11	10	14	10
Storey........	0	0	0	0	0	0	0	0	0	1	2	0
Washoe.......	77	64	122	71	87	76	69	207	201	214	235	291
White Pine....	80	99	144	99	57	74	52	49	89	74	97	221
Total.......	407	454	682	488	433	451	476	702	866	894	1,206	1,717

Many persons think that a much larger number of deer are killed each year than are reported. One reason for this view is that only about one deer is reported for every five deer tags sold. There is reason for thinking that more than 20 per cent of the persons who purchase deer tags do obtain deer. Pertinent data on deer tags issued is as follows:

DEER TAGS REPORTED SOLD IN NEVADA

County	1936	1937	1938	1939	1940
Churchill	216	296	342	364	524
Clark	238	346	326	302	407
Douglas	44	60	49	78	94
Elko	522	817	950	1,297	1,526
Esmeralda	26	40	39	65	114
Eureka	16	38	26	15	28
Humboldt	217	245	292	293	441
Lander	130	165	200	164	210
Lincoln	198	319	357	356	448
Lyon	46	83	112	122	157
Mineral	18	39	38	55	86
Nye	169	217	240	302	408
Ormsby	83	166	177	244	231
Pershing	60	80	76	94	150
Storey	8	19	20	26	37
Washoe	1,037	1,624	1,667	1,848	2,156
White Pine	596	804	916	938	1,269
Deer tags reported distributed free	47	92	120	463	760
Total deer tags issued	3,671	5,450	5,947	7,026	9,046

Comparison of the number of hunting licenses sold with the number of deer tags sold indicates that of every four persons in Nevada who hunt, three hunt deer.

HUNTING LICENSES ISSUED IN NEVADA

	1936	1937	1938	1939	1940
Alien	4	0	7	17	13
Nonresident	193	390	511	559	936
Resident	6,982	7,868	8,556	9,881	11,883
Total licenses issued	7,179	8,258	9,074	10,457	12,832

The name mule deer is firmly established for the subspecies *hemionus*, and the name black-tailed deer (*columbianus*) is applied to the Pacific coastal animal, a different subspecies, which is much smaller, darker colored, and which has a tail that is dark colored all the way down the top side. The differences are as great as those which distinguish several full species of mammals, but in 1936 Cowan showed that there was normal intergradation between the two kinds by way of the intervening "California mule deer" (*Odocoileus hemionus californicus*), which occurs in California. All three of the kinds just mentioned, on the criterion of intergradation, are properly arranged as subspecies of one species. Persons who are inclined to use common names for full species but not for subspecies will therefore have to choose between blacktailed deer and mule deer. In *Odocoileus hemionus hemionus* the large ears suggest those of a mule, and the tail, being constricted at the base may also have suggested to someone the likeness to a mule.

The antlers of deer are a characteristic of the family Cervidae; so many questions occur to so many people about antlers in deer that it is appropriate to set down here some of the known facts concerning them. In the first place, antlers are secondary sexual structures the growth and development of which, it is thought, depends upon the presence of the male sex hormone in the blood. Females, in mule deer, therefore, rarely have antlers; those that do probably are hermaphroditic to a degree that provides the requisite hormone. Careful histological examination of these antlered does would probably reveal that each had substantial amounts of male gonadal tissue.

Further evidence of the close tie-up between antler growth and the sex hormone is furnished by experiments in castrating bucks. If castrated in the first few weeks of life, antlers will not develop at all. If castrated several months after birth, the antlers will develop but will be short and knoblike and will have persistent velvet. If an adult is castrated when the antlers are in the first two-thirds of their annual growth, they will not be shed and will be permanently covered with velvet. If an adult is castrated when the antlers are in the last third of their annual growth, the antlers will be shed within a few weeks and will be replaced with a permanent set which always retain the velvet. Animals with permanent antlers, which always retain the velvet, are commonly designated as stags, although the preferred usage of the word is for the antlered male of the genus *Cervus*, without regard to whether or not he has the male sex glands lost or impaired.

The antler itself, in a mule deer, begins growth from a bud on each frontal bone when the young animal is 3 to 3½ months old. By winter, these protuberances may be 3 inches long and are covered with skin. Growth continues, and in the next year *O. h. hemionus* normally has an antler with one fork. This is shed in winter after the breeding season is past. From the border of the wound left by the shed antler, a thin sheet of skin grows, and in 3 days' time covers the wound. Bony growth occurs underneath, and the new antler is covered by velvet, a modified skin with fine, truly velvetlike hair. Velvet covers the antler until it is full size, after which, by vigorously contacting the antlers with brush and other objects, the velvet is stripped from the antlers. This results in some flow of blood, but apparently the superficial blood vessels by this time have become constricted and the loss of blood is so slight as to be of no serious consequence to the animal. Ossification takes place first on the outside of the antler and gradually progresses inward. The formation of bone within the antler continues after the velvet is shed. Finally, the blood vessels that supply the center of the antler are shut off, and it then becomes a dead structure. Shortly before the antler is mature, the base of the antler and the corona, at the junction with the bony pedicle on which the antler rests, increase in size. Sometime in winter the frontal bone of the skull and the pedicle become highly vascular; the bone between the pedicle and base of the antler breaks down (a peripheral line can then be observed), and from its own weight, or as a result of contact with some other object, the antler breaks off.

The fully formed, polished antler is primarily an offensive weapon, and it is ready for use at the beginning of the breeding season. The size of the antlers is less on a young animal than when the animal has reached full bodily development. Also, the number of points on the antlers are fewer in young deer, and generally fewer in old deer nearing the end of their span of life, than in middle-aged deer which are possessed of full bodily vigor. In old bucks the antlers average shorter than in middle-aged animals. Obviously, the size of the antlers or number of points on them is no sure guide to the age of the animal; sometimes it is impossible to distinguish antlers of senile bucks from those of bucks only 1 or 2 years old. Reference to the teeth does provide a more definite key to age of the individual, but deer hunters probably will derive more pleasure from using the antlers as a basis for such speculation.

In Nevada, deer are migratory in the sense that in autumn they move from areas where snow lies deeply to areas where there is but little or no snow. This results mainly in movement down mountains in autumn and up in spring. In some places the climate is mild enough to allow the deer to occupy the same area the year round.

Mating usually occurs in November, and fawns, one or more, often two, per female, are born in May or June. By September the spots characteristic of the fawns' coats have disappeared. The male seems to take no part in the care of the young.

Records of occurrence.—Specimens examined, 28, as follows: *Washoe Co.:* 12-mile Creek, ½ mi. E Calif. boundary, 5300 ft., 1; 17 mi. W Deep Hole, 4800 ft., 1; Barrel Spring, 1. *Humboldt Co.:* Pine Forest Mts., 1. *Churchill Co.:* 10 mi. E Stillwater, 1. *Lander Co.:* Kingston R. S., 7500 ft., 1; Peterson Creek, Shoshone Mts., 7000 ft., 3. *Nye Co.:* Wisconsin Creek, 8500 ft., 1; Greenmonster Canyon, Monitor Range, 7500 ft., 1; Barley Creek, 7500 and 8500 ft., 2; N slope Toquima Peak, Toquima Range, 9300 and 9400 ft., 2; Breen Creek, Kawich Range, 7000 ft., 1. *Elko Co.:* Goose Creek, 1½ mi. W Utah boundary, 5000 ft., 1; Cobb Creek, 5 mi. SW Mountain City, 6500 ft., 1. *White Pine Co.:* W side Ruby Lake, 3 mi. S White Pine Co. line, 1 (coll. of Ralph Ellis); 1 mi. W Smith Creek Cave, Mt. Moriah, 6200 ft., 1; Lehman Creek, 8800 ft., 1; Baker Creek, 9000 ft., 1; Water Canyon, 8 mi. N Lund, 1. *Lincoln Co.:* Fortification Range, 1; Eagle Valley, 15 mi. N Ursine (= Burnt Canyon, head of Meadow Valley Wash), 3; Monte Spring, near Irish Mtn., 1.

Additional records (unless otherwise noted, based on animals or their sign, as recorded by Hall, MS): *Douglas Co.:* Spooner, 6900 ft. *Humboldt Co.:* 13 mi. N Paradise Valley, 6700 ft. *Mineral Co.:* Lapon Canyon, 8900 ft., Mt. Grant. *Esmeralda Co.:* Indian Creek, 8300 ft., White Mts. *Lander Co.:* Smiths Creek, Desatoya Mts. *Nye Co.:* Scofield Canyon, 5500–7700 ft., Grant Mts.; Burned Corral Canyon, Quinn Canyon Mts.; Grapevine Peak (A. H. Miller, MS). *Elko Co.:* Pilot Peak (Ward C. Russell, MS). *White Pine Co.:* Cleve Creek; vicinity of Hamilton. *Lincoln Co.:* Groom Baldy, 8600 ft. *Clark Co.:* Charleston Peak (Cowan, 1936:210); Bonelli Peak.

Antilocapra americana americana (Ord)
Prong-horned Antelope

Antilope americana Ord, Guthrie's Geography, 2d Amer. ed., 2:292 (described on p. 308), 1815. Type from "Plains and highlands of the Missouri."

Antilocapra americana Ord, Journ. de phys., 87:149, 1818; Taylor, Univ. California Publ. Zoöl., 7:211, June 24, 1911; Nelson, U. S. Dept. Agric., Dept. Bull. no. 1346, 38, August, 1925.

Antilocapra americana americana, Borell and Ellis, Journ. Mamm., 15:43, February 15, 1934; Young, Western Sportsman, 5:78, September, 1940.

Distribution.—Originally probably over all parts of the state in and below the Transition Life-zone; now restricted to several separate areas. See figure 468.

Remarks.—Measurements given by Seton for a male from an unstated locality are 1,320, 89, 432. He gives the weight of an average buck as 100 lbs. An adult female from the Granite Range, Washoe County, measures 1,423, 134, 425, weight 105½ lbs. A female, with M3 only partly erupted, from 5 miles south of Nyala measures 1,270, 80, 440, weight 105 lbs.

Body brown, with strong tinge of cinnamon, darker on mane and paler on legs and ears; muzzle, eyelashes, spots over anterior angle of each eye, edges of ears at tips, and, in many males, a spot at angle of each jaw black or blackish; forehead dark grayish; crown and nape dull brownish; cheeks and lips white; much white on throat, ears, sides, underparts, and rump; white hair on rump long, and capable of being erected by dermal muscles in a way that produces a white "flash" which frequently attracts the attention of a person when he otherwise might not see the animal. Four inguinal mammae; hooves number two on each foot, there rarely being one additional "false hoof," but never two, as in deer; horns present in both sexes, 6 to 10 inches high in average males, 2 inches or less in average females; horn sheaths clearly show their origin from agglutinated hair; sheaths, forked in males, unforked in females, shed annually; bony horn core in each sex persistent (not shed), not forked. The dental formula is i. $\frac{0}{4}$, c. $\frac{0}{0}$, p. $\frac{3}{3}$, m. $\frac{3}{3}$.

The subspecific name *Antilocapra americana oregona* Bailey (1932:45) was based on an animal from Hart Mountain, Oregon, and, in advance of study of specimens, was thought possibly to apply to antelope from northwestern Nevada. Comparison of an adult female topotype of *oregona* in fresh autumn pelage with specimens of similar sex, age, and season from the Granite Range of Washoe County and Railroad Valley of southern Nye County reveals no differences judged to be of systematic worth. The topotype is lighter colored than the Nevadan animals. The latter, from 13 miles north and 6 miles west of Deep Hole, is darker than the animal from Railroad Valley, which is farther from the type locality of *oregona*. Summed up, none of the Nevadan specimens is as light-colored as is the specimen from Oregon, and no reason is seen for applying the subspecific name *oregona* to any of our animals. Lacking comparable specimens from the Great Plains, probably the population on which Ord based his name *Antilope americana*, I cannot be certain, of course, but that all the Nevadan animals, along with those from Oregon, differ enough from the animals from the Great Plains to bear the name *oregona*. Until this uncertainty is cleared away, the better course seems to be to refer the Nevadan animals to the subspecies *americana*.

The animals are said to copulate in September. In Nevada, young are born in May, one or two per female. The young begin to follow the mother when about 3 weeks old and commonly utter a grunting bleat. The females about to have young are solitary. In summer, in northwestern Nevada, I have commonly seen bands of three to twenty animals and also solitary individuals of each sex. In winter, according to reliable report, the pronghorns collect in larger bands. The animals are migratory in the sense that those on the higher part of the summer range move down to lower territory where there is less snow in winter.

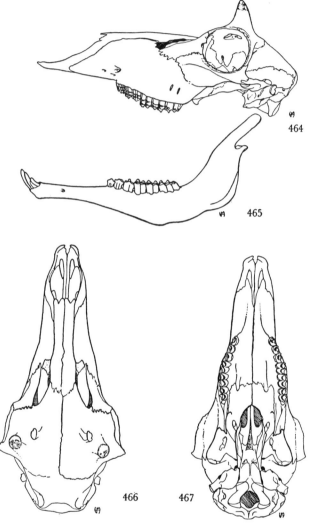

Figs. 464–467. *Antilocapra americana americana,* 13 miles north and 6 miles west Deep Hole, no. 93881, ♀. × ¼.

Although both the area of range and number of animals have been greatly reduced in Nevada, the pronghorn has never become extinct in that state, as it has in several other parts of western North America. Nelson (1925:3, 38, 40) estimated that in 1924 there were 4,253 antelope in Nevada, 3,740 of them in the northwestern part of the state. Young (1940), 16 years later, estimated the number as having increased in the northwestern part of the state (more exactly on the Charles Sheldon Refuge and Range) to 5,000. My own impression is that between 1924 and 1940 the number of antelope except in this northwestern part of the state has remained about the same or is slightly less. The increase recorded in the northwestern part of the state is to be ascribed to the protection given the animals there. In the words of Young (1940:23): "The Charles Sheldon Antelope Refuge, of approximately 34,325 acres, and the Charles Sheldon Antelope Range, of about 547,000 acres, . . . in northwestern Nevada, . . . [are] the result of . . . cooperation with the National Association of Audubon Societies and the Boone and Crockett Club of New York. It was through the generous monetary assistance of these two conservation societies that the private lands held within that part of the public domain were purchased and later donated to the Federal Government. An executive order was then issued on January 26, 1931, setting aside these and adjacent public lands as an antelope refuge, which was named in honor of the late Charles Sheldon. . . . This area is primarily a spring and summer range for antelopes, and it is on these lands that much of the fawning takes place.

". . . adjoining and supplementing the foregoing tract, is the Charles Sheldon Antelope Range. Most of the private lands within that area have been purchased by the Federal Government, and by an executive order on December 21, 1936, it was set aside for the use of antelope in conjunction with the organization of a grazing district under the Taylor Grazing Act of 1934. The area contains lands used by the antelopes for winter range."

Initial efforts to increase the number of the antelope in these areas included great emphasis on destruction of coyotes, which persisted in spite of poison and traps placed for them; but the antelopes seemed to maintain their numbers well irrespective of the number of coyotes, which, in 1941, at least, were abundant in northwestern Nevada. The protection most effective for the antelope seems to be, first, the reduction of illegal shooting and, second, the considerable reduction of domestic livestock, especially in sheep, and to some extent, in cattle and horses.

With the elimination of domestic sheep from the vicinities of many of the springs and other places where antelope drink, conditions were made favorable again for many kinds of animals and plants which had become scarce because of the trampling of plant growth by the sheep near the springs. This trampling not only destroyed the cover of plants, but also the breeding places and food essential to the existence of the several kinds of animals smaller than the antelope.

Nelson (1925:39, 40), in 1924, knew of the existence of antelopes in eleven areas in Nevada. Field notes in the Museum of Vertebrate Zoölogy taken in the years 1928 to 1941, inclusive, mention antelope in ten of these areas.

For area number 1, comprising northern Washoe County, our observations in 1936 and 1941 indicate that the animals are increasing. Nelson estimated 2,000 to 2,500 here.

Area number 2, in central Washoe County, which, according to Nelson, contained about 200 antelope, now (1941) contains more. Five miles south of Flanigan, Ward C. Russell, on April 19, 1941, was told by a local resident that 4 years before, twelve antelope appeared along the north base of the Virginia Mountains, and that by 1941 the band had

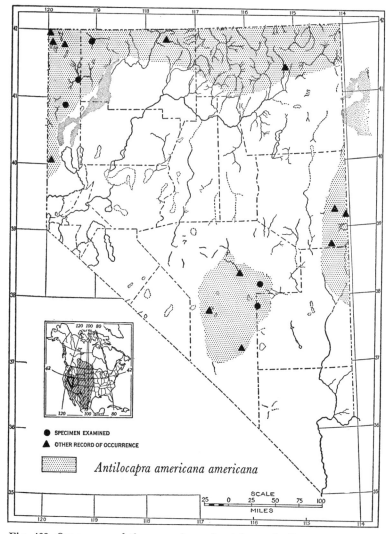

SPECIMEN EXAMINED

OTHER RECORD OF OCCURRENCE

Antilocapra americana americana

SCALE
25   0   25   50   75   100
MILES

Fig. 468. Occurrence of the prong-horned antelope, *Antilocapra americana*, subsequent to 1923, with insert showing range of the species.

increased to twenty-five. Residents thought that the antelope now (1941) never crossed the east to west railroad tracks running through Flanigan. To reach this area the antelope did cross from the north to the south side of the railroad.

In area number 3, the Santa Rosa Game Refuge, where Nelson estimated forty antelope, an undetermined number of antelope were reported in 1935.

In area number 4, comprising much of the Sheldon Antelope Range, Nelson estimated 1,000 antelope. We had reports in 1936 of the animals there, but obtained no estimates of numbers.

In area number 5, northern Elko County, where Nelson estimated 213 animals, I ascertained, in July, 1935, that no less than seven frequented one field along Marys River, 22 miles north of Deeth.

In area number 6, the vicinity of Cobre, Nelson estimated ten animals. I have no knowledge of the status of antelope in this area.

In area number 7, the White Pine Game Refuge, Nelson estimated forty animals. On August 6, 1930, on the western slope of Mount Moriah, I saw tracks of no less than twelve antelope, and on June 2, 1937, David H. Johnson saw one animal at the eastern base of the same mountain.

In area number 8, the territory between Geyser and Pioche, Nelson estimated seventy-five animals. In June, 1929, Doyle C. Robison and W. C. Kirkland said that there were "hundreds" in this area and that they then ranged north of Geyser into the southern end of Spring Valley. Because Robinson and Kirkland were much concerned about the competition for forage between antelope and sheep and were definitely more interested in sheep, their estimate of the number of antelope unconsciously may have been too high. Of this band, Richard M. Bond (MS), in 1940, mentions that there are in Lincoln County fifty to seventy-five animals which range north and east from Pony Springs.

In area number 9, Railroad Valley, Nelson estimated that there were thirty-five to sixty-five antelope. I saw two at a place 5 miles south of Nyala on July 25, 1933, and Alcorn and Longhurst saved a specimen from this place in the autumn of 1940. Our impression is that the animals here are barely holding their own or are decreasing in numbers because of illegal hunting.

In area number 10, near White Blotch [Spring], Lincoln County, and in adjacent parts of Nye County, Nelson estimated 100 antelope, twenty-five more being in the near-by area number 11, Wild Horse Valley, which he indicates lies to the westward of area number 10. On June 3, 1932, I saw one in Penoyer Valley and was told that the animals were decreasing in number there. Richard M. Bond (MS), in 1940, thought that there were about a dozen antelope in Penoyer Valley. On June 3, 1932, Ray Morris told me that at his camp in the meadow at the south end of the Belted Range, 5½ miles northwest of White-rock Spring, at 7200 feet altitude, Nye County, he had seen as many as eighty antelope in summer. He said that these wintered lower down, to the northward, in Kawich Valley and in Gold Flat. Ward C. Russell learned that they occurred in 1932 as far to the northwest as Cactus Spring, Nye County, and, in 1933, three young animals were seen about 6 miles east of Tybo in the same county.

On June 18, 1928, D. H. McNett, resident for more than 50 years in Fish Lake Valley, Esmeralda County, told me that antelope disappeared there in 1901 or 1902, up until which time eight animals came daily to water at the spring at his ranch. Franklin Allen, in March, 1940, said that three antelope had been planted on the slopes of Charleston Peak in the autumn of 1938, but that all of them had died and that no antelope now occurred there.

Records of occurrence.—Specimens examined, 9, as follows: *Washoe Co.:* 8 to 10 mi. SE Swan Lake, 2; High Rock Canyon, 5000 ft., 1; W slope Granite Range, 13 mi. N and 6 mi. W Deep Hole, 1. *Humboldt Co.:* Table Mountain, near Virgin Valley, 1; Virgin Valley, 1; 4 mi. SE Virgin Ranch, 1. *Nye Co.:* 5 mi. S Nyala, 4600 ft., 1. *Lincoln Co.:* Sand Spring Valley (= Penoyer Valley), 1.

Additional records (see text above unless otherwise noted): *Washoe Co.:* 12-mile Creek (Ward C. Russell, MS); 4 mi. S Diessner (Hall, MS); N end Virginia Mts. *Nye Co.:* Hot Creek Valley, east of Tybo (Hall, MS); Cactus Spring; 5½ mi. NW Whiterock Spring, 7200 ft. *Elko Co.:* Marys River, 22 mi. N Deeth. *White Pine Co.:* W side Mt. Moriah; E side Mt. Moriah; S end Spring Valley.

Ovis canadensis
Mountain Sheep

Three subspecies of mountain sheep are thought to have occurred in Nevada. One, and probably two, of these now is extinct within the state. Upper parts brownish (Avellaneous to Wood Brown), becoming darker on sides, neck,

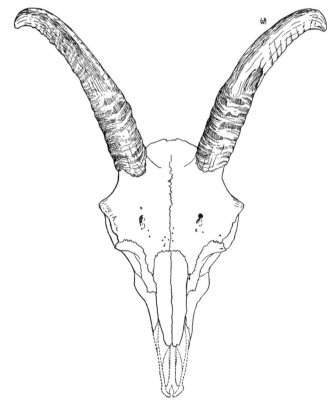

Fig. 469. *Ovis canadensis nelsoni*, 4 miles east Boulder City, no. 71803, ♀. × ¼.

chest, legs, and tail; middorsal line continued onto tail, thus dividing yellowish-white rump patch in two; yellowish patch on brow; face brown; sides of face grayish; nose, inside of ears, and underparts grayish; snout with small naked place between nostrils; glands between toes and under eyes; tail without terminal tuft; feet with four hooves; two mammae; horns, as in all members of the family Bovidae, consist of a horny covering over a bony core; horns in both sexes, those of the ram curling back, around, and up again; horns of ewe smaller and nearly straight. The dental formula is i. $\frac{0}{4}$, c. $\frac{0}{0}$, p. $\frac{3}{3}$, m. $\frac{3}{3}$.

Most of the information about this species in Nevada was provided me by

Joseph C. Allen, Franklin Allen, and Robert E. Towle, employees of the United States Bureau of Biological Survey, in March, 1940, when I visited the Sheep Mountains of Clark County and territory along the Colorado River. As to numbers of sheep in this area, at the time specified, Towle thought that there were about 500 in all, 100 of which were along the Colorado River in Nevada between Searchlight and Bonelli Peak, 100 in the Spring Mountain Range,

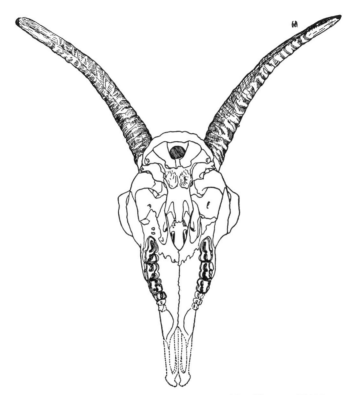

Fig. 470. *Ovis canadensis nelsoni*, 4 miles east Boulder City, no. 71803, ♀. × ¼.

and 300 in the five other mountain ranges designated as Las Vegas, Sheep, Desert, Pintwater, and Spotted.

These animals, in summer at least, are as abundant in the Sheep Mountain Range as in any of the other mountains. J. C. Allen (1939) writes of the animals in this mountain range essentially as follows: For feeding routes, bedding grounds, and all-round living quarters, the bighorn prefers the roughest, most precipitous, and cut-up country, chiefly on or near the mountain tops. Even when forced to travel in lower country, the sheep seek high spots that offer opportunities for them the better to see the surrounding country.

In summer and early autumn there is but little change in the daily routine of the bighorns. Beginning in the early morning they feed for several hours and then bed down, usually in the shade of a tree or the lee of a rock, and sleep until late in the afternoon, when they begin to feed again and continue until sometime in the night. They nibble here and there, taking a bite from a bush or clipping a weed as they go, with no perceptible break in their pace, which is kept up through the feeding period at an approximate rate of 2 to 2½ miles per hour.

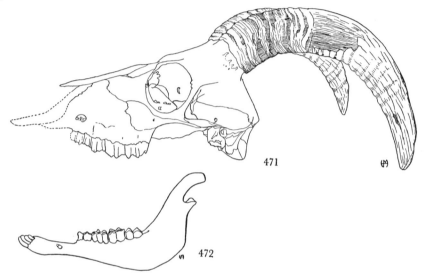

Figs. 471, 472. Mountain Sheep. Both, × ¼.

Fig. 471. *Ovis canadensis nelsoni*, 4 miles east Boulder City, no. 71803, ♀.
Fig. 472. *Ovis canadensis nelsoni*, Deep Canyon, Santa Rosa Mountains, Riverside County, California, no. 2320, ♀.

Each band has a regular feeding route which usually terminates at a bedding ground. Snows and cold in winter cause the sheep to desert these routes and feed along the snow line lower down. In Clark County, temperatures between storms usually rise enough to cause some of the hardier weeds and grasses to sprout where the sun has melted the snow, and it is upon these that the sheep feed in the warmer intervals. When snowstorms are in progress the sheep yard up around growths of mountain mahogany, blackbrush, willow, and other browse. After the storm has passed, the sheep appear at the snow line.

Of foods eaten, probably the fruits of prickly pears (*Opuntia basilaris* and *O. engelmanni*) and those of the ooze apple (*Yucca baccata*) are highest on the list of preferred items. Because these plants bloom late in summer and bear fruit for only a short time in the early autumn, they do not provide a large part of the total food of the sheep. With special reference to the month of July, twenty other plants eaten by mountain sheep, in decreasing order of preference, are: trailing buckwheat, Wright buckwheat brush, wild buckwheat, alfileria, bud sage, shad scale, nine-leaf biscuit root, spider milkweed, Arizona thistle, desert trumpit (*sic*), evening primrose, pink lady fingers, shield leaf, cum vine, little leaf mahogany, desert mallow, beard tongue pentstemon, woolly mule ear, rock vine, and century plant. But, in general, J. C. Allen thought that this order of preference applied fairly well for the year as a whole.

For drinking, where a choice exists, the sheep select springs or waterholes in the most inaccessible, higher parts of the mountains. Two barely perceptible seeps, apparently favorably situated with respect to the requirements of the animals, being below the average snow line, were developed by J. C. Allen into sizable "spring bowls." In speaking further about this, he said: "Response was positive; a small band of eight mountain sheep established its feeding routes and bedding grounds within an area of not more than 250 acres that included these two springs." Franklin Allen thinks that along the Colorado River the mountain sheep may not go to water for long periods when green food is available in cool weather, but he has noticed that the animals in summer drink at the river more regularly.

On March 23, 1940, at about 6000 feet elevation in the canyon leading up to the Hidden Forest in the Sheep Mountains, I saw three ewes each accompanied by one lamb. This is the usual number per female; Towle thought that in Clark County only about one ewe in fifty had two lambs.

Enemies include, first, man, then, probably coyotes and bobcats, and, certainly, golden eagles. J. C. Allen, who witnessed one killing of a lamb by an eagle, says (1939:256): "I have personally observed seventeen such kills of bighorn lambs by eagles." At the time of writing, he favored reducing the number of eagles or at least the killing of some. It probably being true that the mountain sheep were increasing in number on the Sheep Mountain Range, I, personally, could see no reason for making effort to reduce the population of either raptorial birds or carnivorous mammals. Perhaps one important function of this protected area, the Sheep Mountain Range, is to provide sanctuary for both golden eagles and mountain sheep. J. C. Allen (*loc. cit.*) significantly remarks: "Granted favorable solutions of all other problems, success in conserving bighorn sheep in the Nevada ranges depends wholly upon the degree of success attained in stopping poaching." It may be added that, in 1940, no domestic sheep were grazed in the area inhabited by the mountain sheep.

Although the mountain sheep appear to be holding their own or even increasing under protection from poachers in Clark County, they are in most areas of the state formerly inhabited by them either scarce or extinct. Some record of their former status is as follows:

Washoe County: Fremont (1845:216), in early January of 1844, saw many mountain sheep in the mountains between Pyramid and Winnemucca lakes. When these became extinct, I do not know. I saw no trace of mountain sheep in these mountains when I visited them in 1924.

Humboldt County: Paul L. Travis, Forest Ranger, at Paradise Valley, on July 29, 1935, thought that sheep had been extinct for about 30 years in the Santa Rosa Mountains.

Mineral County: In the early spring of 1935, Carl S. Riek reported to Hall McAllister that five animals lived on Pilot Mountain.

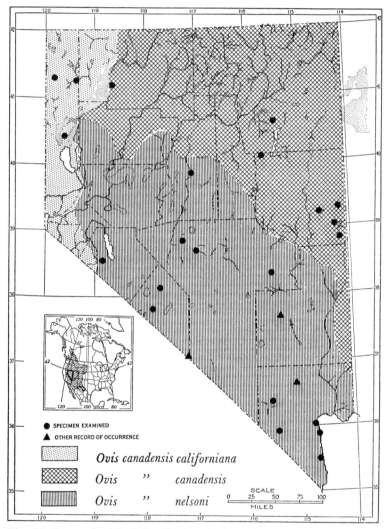

Fig. 473. Assumed original distribution of subspecies of the mountain sheep, *Ovis canadensis*, with insert showing range of the species.

Esmeralda County: In June, 1928, I found fresh droppings and tracks of mountain sheep in the Silver Peak Range between Cave Spring and Piper Peak. Tom Kern, of Fish Lake Valley, reported sheep at this time on White Mountain Peak. D. H. McNett, resident in Fish Lake Valley, had visited Cave Spring and vicinity in the Silver Peak Range regularly for 51 years and believed that the sheep were newcomers because he never saw tracks and sign in the old days as he did in 1928. In February or March of 1935, Carl S. Riek, resident of Coaldale, wrote Hall McAllister that mountain sheep existed in that area, as follows: Coaldale Range, eleven; Stimler Mountain, ninety-seven; Silver Peak, twelve; Lone Mountain, seven.

Nye County: Linsdale (1938:199) had a report of one shot in the Toyabe Mountains in 1931. In July, 1931, I saw sign in the Quinn Canyon Mountains, about 6 miles northeast of Italian Springs, that I felt confident was not more than 4 months old. Alcorn and Longhurst (MS) in the autumn of 1939 saw the mounted head of a ram killed the year before on Troy Creek in the north end of the Quinn Canyon Mountains.

Elko County: So far as I know the last sheep to survive in Elko County were those in the Ruby Mountains. Borell and Ellis (1934a:43) give details of the last records of occurrence. The very last was in October, 1921, when August Rohwer saw three individuals at the head of Smithers Creek (near Verdi Lake).

White Pine County: I saw fresh tracks and droppings of mountain sheep on the northwest shoulder of Wheeler Peak between 10,700 and 11,000 feet on June 30 and July 9, 1929. When I revisited the place in August, 1938, and when William B. Longhurst and J. R. Alcorn visited near-by places in the Snake Range in the autumn of 1939, no trace was found of living mountain sheep. In the Shell Creek Range, the range next to the west, Alec Callcheck, resident for many years on Cleve Creek, reported sheep as present about 15 years ago (therefore in about 1915), when they were hunted by a Mr. Goldman from Washington who saw some but was unable to obtain any.

Lincoln County: On June 11, 1931, Ward C. Russell saw two rams on Irish Mountain.

Summed up, at this May, 1941, writing, my impression is that mountain sheep persist as far north as northern Esmeralda County and in the eastern part of the state as far north as the northern end of the Quinn Canyon Mountains in eastern Nye County, both northern extremities of range being at about the same latitude.

The abundance of domestic sheep and the chance of mistaking one of the old rams, or, as I nearly did once, a billy goat with much curved horns, for mountain sheep, makes it necessary to accept with caution reports of occurrence of bighorns. There is a marked tendency among residents of a given region where mountain sheep have become extinct in the last 10 years to report them as now occurring in the next range of mountains. Mountain sheep, I think, are abundant in Nevada only in places in Clark County, and I would not be surprised if they were entirely extinct north of the 39th parallel.

Ovis canadensis californiana Douglas
Mountain Sheep

Ovis californianus Douglas, Zoöl. Journ., 4:332, January, 1829. Type from near Mount Adams, Yakima County, Washington.

Ovis canadensis californiana, Miller, Bull. U. S. Nat. Mus., 79:396, December 31, 1912; Cowan, Amer. Midland Nat., 24:554, November, 1940.

Distribution.—Western part of state from Oregon boundary south probably to Mineral County. See figure 473.

Remarks.—A male and female from the southern Sierra Nevada of California measure: ♂, 1570, ♀, 1385; 100, 70; 420, 395; weights not available.

Color as described for the species. Differs from race *canadensis*, according to Cowan

(1940:536, 555), in slightly lesser size, more grayish and less reddish color, horns less closely curled; maxillary width of skull and length of upper tooth rows averaging larger. From *O. c. nelsoni, californiana* differs in larger average size of most parts of the skull in females and in smaller horns, on the average, in males.

This race is thought now to be extinct in Nevada, as it is in most of the rest of its former range outside of the state.

Fremont (1845:216), in 1844, in the mountains on the eastern side of Pyramid Lake, and Wistar (1937:109), in 1849, along the Truckee River, saw numbers of sheep, presumably of this subspecies.

Records of occurrence.—Specimens examined, 3, as follows: *Washoe Co.:* Kistler Springs, 15 mi. E Eagleville, Calif., 1 (horns and occipital region of skull); mouth Little High Rock Canyon, 5000 ft., 1 (fragment of skull); Horse Canyon, Pahrum Peak, 6200 ft., 1 (sheath of horn).

Additional records: See above, under remarks and in the account of the full species, *O. canadensis,* under Washoe County.

Ovis canadensis canadensis Shaw
Mountain Sheep

Ovis canadensis Shaw, Naturalists Miscell., vol. 15, text to plate 610. 1804. Type from mountains on Bow River, near Ershaw, Alberta, Canada (see Preble, David Thompson's narrative, p. lxxxi, 1916).
Ovis canadensis (subsp. ?), Borell and Ellis, Journ. Mamm., 15:43, February 15, 1934.

Distribution.—Probably northeastern part of state north and east of a line connecting the Jackson Mountains in Humboldt County with the Snake Mountains in White Pine County. See figure 473.

Remarks.—A male and female from Glacier County, Montana, measure: ♂, 1,726, ♀, 1,433; 95, 121; 482, 406; weights not available.

The description of the full species will apply to this, the darkest colored and largest of the three subspecies found in the state. Comparison with *californiana* is made in the account of that race. *O. c. canadensis* is thought now to be extinct in Nevada. Only two specimens, females, one adult and the other with the last upper molars not yet in place, from King Lea Peak, in the Jackson Mountains of Humboldt County, appear to have been saved. These two specimens, now in the United States National Museum, Biological Surveys Collection, were taken on August 27, 1915, by Theodore Lyman and T. Gardiner. The adult shows some characters of *californiana* and some of *nelsoni.* The relatively short tooth row (33 per cent of basilar length), the relatively narrow rostrum (maxillary width 19 per cent of basilar length), and some other measurements of the skull are about as in the subspecies *canadensis,* to which it is here referred, although the specimen probably is an intergrade between *canadensis,* on the one hand, and, on the other hand, certainly with *californiana,* and, perhaps, with *nelsoni.*

The other occurrences, in Elko and White Pine counties, assigned to this subspecies, are based upon skulls so fragmentary that characters diagnostic of the subspecies are not preserved. The assignment of these occurrences to *canadensis* rather than *nelsoni* is provisional. Identification of the race of sheep which inhabited this area probably will be possible only when skulls preserved as trophies are found. Mountain sheep are thought now to be extinct in this area.

Although Cowan (1940:565) lists under *nelsoni* the specimens here referred to *canadensis,* his map (*op. cit.:* 574) places the locality, King Lea Peak, Jackson Mountains, within the range of *canadensis,* and the other localities fall within an area which he could not certainly assign to either of the two mentioned races.

Records of occurrence.—Specimens examined, 11, as follows: *Humboldt Co.:* King Lea Peak, Jackson Mts., 2 (U. S. Nat. Mus., Biol. Surv. Coll.). *Elko Co.:* above Three Lakes, 10,000 ft., 1 (horns, coll. of Ralph Ellis). *White Pine Co.:* near head of Willow Creek Canyon, 1 (fragment of skull, coll. of Ralph Ellis); Hendry Creek, 1½ mi. E Mt. Moriah, 9100 ft., 1 (cranial fragment); Cleve Creek, Shell Creek Range, 1 (horn core); ¼ mi. SW Stella Lake, 11,800 ft., 1 (part skull); Baker Creek (12,400 ft., 1; 9000 ft., 1; no elevation, 1, U. S. Nat. Mus.. Biol. Surv. Coll.), 3; Granite Mtn., 11,200 ft., 1 (part skull).

TABLE 27
CRANIAL MEASUREMENTS* (IN MILLIMETERS) OF ARTIODACTYLA

Sex	Number of individuals averaged or catalogue no.	Basilar length	Nasal length	Greatest width of nasals	Orbital width	Zygomatic width	Maxillary width	Palatal breadth at M3	Palatal length	Upper molar series
		Cervus canadensis nelsoni, Rocky Mountain National Park, Colorado								
♂	94807	448.0	168.0	70.0	160	173	128	77	207	134
♀	91041	390.0	143.0	61.8	129	163	128	69.5	179	139
		Odocoileus hemionus hemionus, Nevada, north of 37° latitude								
♂	4 av.	272.0	86.4	35.5	85.5	122.2	98.5	58.0	126.0	80.5
	min.	258.0	72.3	31.0	83.0	117.0	93.0	55.6	122.0	76.0
	max.	285.0	101.0	41.0	89.0	128.0	104.0	60.0	130.0	86.7
		Washoe and Nye counties								
♀	3 av.	244.0	72.7	31.9	76.1	107.0	88.7	51.1	121.0	76.1
	min.	241.0	65.5	29.4	74.5	107.0	87.0	49.2	116.0	74.9
	max.	246.0	86.5	36.0	79.0	107.0	90.0	53.0	126.0	78.7
		Antilocapra americana americana, Penoyer Valley								
♂	53277	256.0	106.3	29.0	114.0	109.0	70.0	51.3	142.0	67.0
		Granite Range								
♀	93881	247.0	93.7	27.5	94.0	102.0	71.0	54.1	124.0	72.7
		Ovis canadensis nelsoni, 5 mi. E Coaldale								
♂	211043†	252.8	98.4	45.2	109.0	112.0	85.0	44.0	92.5	85.2
♂	211041†	254.0	104.0	46.5	116.1	119.0	91.4	47.0	95.5	83.5
♀	209704†	228.4	87.2	36.0	101.0	103.5	83.0	42.1	88.7	86.3
♀	209706†	227.0	92.3	32.6	97.3	108.0	82.6	48.2	83.7	80.8
		Ovis canadensis canadensis, Jackson Mountains								
♀	208993†	241.3	95.5	35.0	103.9	117.0	83.0	45.5	94.6	78.5

* Measurements taken according to Cowan (1936:193), except that in *Ovis* the nasal length is the greatest length over all of both nasals and except that the palatal length of *Cervus* and *Ovis* is taken according to Cowan (1940:524).

† United States National Museum, Biological Surveys Collection.

Ovis canadensis nelsoni Merriam
Mountain Sheep

Ovis nelsoni Merriam, Proc. Biol. Soc. Washington, 11:218, July 15, 1897. Type from Grapevine Mountains, on boundary between Inyo County, California, and Esmeralda County, Nevada, just south of latitude 37° N.

Ovis canadensis nelsoni, Lydekker, Wild oxen, sheep and goats of all lands, p. 215, 1898; Burt, Trans. San Diego Soc. Nat. Hist., 7:424, May 31, 1934; Cowan, Amer. Midland Nat., 24:559, November, 1940.

Ovis canadensis, Linsdale, Amer. Midland Nat., 19:199, January, 1938.

Distribution.—Central, southwestern, and southern parts of state. See figure 473.

Remarks.—Average and individual measurements of three males and four females are given below. The first two of each sex are from 5 mi. E Coaldale; the third male is from 4 mi. SE Valcalda Spring; the last two females are from the type locality. ♂, 1,547 (1,530, 1,610, 1,500), ♀, 1,374 (1,410, 1,390, 1,340, 1,355); 104 (97, 116, 99), 95 (70, 90, 110, 110); 401 (398, 390, 416), 356 (365, 360, 350, 350); weights not available.

The description given for the full species will apply to this, the lightest colored of the three subspecies in the state. From the race *canadensis*, *nelsoni* differs in smaller size, lighter color, smaller skull, with relatively longer tooth rows, and relatively broader rostrum. Horns of females are larger than in *canadensis*, and horns of males are more slender, paler, and with the tips more strongly everted than in *canadensis*. Comparison with *californiana* is made in the account of that race.

O. c. nelsoni still is living in Nevada (see account of the full species), and in the southern part of the state is locally abundant.

Records of occurrence.—Specimens examined, 33, as follows: *Mineral Co.:* Middle Fork Cat Creek, 8900 ft., 1. *Esmeralda Co.:* Monte Cristo Mts., 5 mi. E Coaldale, 6 (U. S. Nat. Mus., Biol. Surv. Coll.); Silver Peak Mts., 1 (U. S. Nat. Mus., Biol. Surv. Coll.); near Valcalda Spring, 1 (U. S. Nat. Mus., Biol. Surv. Coll.); ½ mi. NE Cave Spring, 2; 4 mi. S Valcalda Spring, 1 (U. S. Nat. Mus., Biol. Surv. Coll.); Grapevine Mts., on Calif.-Nev. boundary, 10 (U. S. Nat. Mus., Biol. Surv. Coll.). *Lander Co.:* 28 mi. N Austin, 1 (part skull). *Nye Co.:* South Twin River, Toyabe Mts., 2 (U. S. Nat. Mus., Biol. Surv. Coll.); summit of south peak of Mt. Jefferson, Toquima Range, 1 (horn only); a box canyon, 6 mi. NE Italian Spring, Quinn Canyon Mts., 7000 ft., 1 (cranial fragment). *Clark Co.:* east side Charleston Mtn. [= Peak], 2 (U. S. Nat. Mus., Biol. Surv. Coll.); 4 mi. E Boulder City, 800 ft., 1; N side Potosi Mtn., 7500 ft., 1; opposite Willow Beach, 9 mi. S Boulder Dam, Colorado River, 1; Colorado River, 14 mi. E Searchlight, 1 (cranial fragment).

Additional records: *Lincoln Co.:* Irish Mtn. (Ward C. Russell, sight record, 1931). *Clark Co.:* canyon below Hidden Forest, Sheep Mountains (sight record. Hall, 1940).

HYPOTHETICAL LIST

MAMMALS POSSIBLY OCCURRING IN NEVADA OF WHICH

SATISFACTORY RECORD IS LACKING

1. *Myotis lucifugus phasma* Miller and Allen, Big Myotis.—Has been taken in Colorado to the eastward, and to the westward in California in Owens Valley and the Argus Mountains; therefore to be expected in southern Nevada.
2. *Myotis velifer velifer* (J. A. Allen), Broad-toothed Myotis.—Has been taken at Needles, California, and in Arizona, opposite Nevada. Would be expected to occur in summer along the Colorado River in extreme southern Nevada.
3. *Myotis occultus* Hollister, Tawny Myotis.—The type locality is on the west side of the Colorado River, 10 miles above Needles. In summer it would be expected to occur 5 or 6 miles farther up the same side of the river in the southern tip of Nevada.
4. *Tadarida femorosacca* Merriam, Pocketed Free-tailed Bat.—Has been taken in California, to the west of Nevada, and in places to the south of Nevada, and is to be expected in summer in southern Nevada.
5. *Eumops perotis californicus* (Merriam), Mastiff Bat.—Has been taken commonly in southern California and south into Mexico, and may occur in summer in southern Nevada.
6. *Martes pennanti pacifica* (Rhoads), Fisher.—Occurs in the Sierra Nevada of California and may occur in these mountains between Carson City and Reno.
7. *Gulo luscus luteus* Elliot, Wolverine.—Occurs in the Sierra Nevada of California and is to be looked for in these mountains in Nevada between Carson City and Reno, particularly in winter.
8. *Lynx canadensis canadensis* Kerr, Lynx.—Bailey (1936:271), in writing of the mammals of Oregon, says: "There are also a couple of records for Northern Nevada, which seems to be the southern limit of this boreal species in the Great Basin country." In 1940 no specimens from Nevada could be located in the United States National Museum or other collections, and consultation with the late Mr. Bailey indicated that reports of trappers formed the basis for his statement. The large size of bobcats (*Lynx rufus*) in northern Nevada might well mislead one with respect to their specific identity. Until an actual specimen of *Lynx canadensis* is forthcoming from Nevada, it seems best to regard all reports of true lynxes from there as based on large individuals of the bobcat (*Lynx rufus pallescens*).
9. *Citellus beecheyi douglasii* (Richardson), Beechey Ground Squirrel.—Occurs in the Warner Mountains of California, and, particularly, in summer and autumn, when young-of-the-year are seeking new homes, may occur in extreme northwestern Nevada.
10. *Microdipodops megacephalus paululus* Hall and Durrant, Kangaroo Mouse.—Probably occurs in sandy soil in extreme eastern White Pine County, east of Baker. The subspecies has been taken less than 4 miles to the east of the state boundary at points 4 miles south of Gandy and 5 miles south of Garrison.
11. *Castor canadensis shastensis* Taylor, Beaver.—This animal may have once occurred in 12-mile Creek in the extreme northwestern corner of the state. There were no beavers on the part of the creek in Nevada, nor so far as known on any other part of it, in 1936. The only chance of making certain of the occurrence of this subspecies in Nevada would be to find a subfossil skull along 12-mile Creek.
12. *Neotoma lepida monstrabilis* Goldman, Desert Wood Rat.—This subspecies has been recorded from the northwestern corner of Arizona. In the Virgin Mountains, to the south of the town of Mesquite, wood rats of this species almost certainly occur

commonly, but no specimens are available from there and I cannot judge whether they are of the subspecies *monstrabilis*.

13. *Neotoma albigula venusta* True, White-throated Wood Rat.—This species has been recorded from the east bank of the Colorado River opposite Searchlight, Nevada, and from both sides of the Colorado River below Needles, California. Our search for it along the river in extreme southern Nevada was in vain, but it may occur there.

14. *Phenacomys intermedius celsus* A. B. Howell, Gray Phenacomys.—This animal has been taken in the high mountains on the California side of Lake Tahoe and is to be expected on Mount Rose and in other high country above Lake Tahoe in Nevada.

15. *Ochotona princeps muiri* Grinnell and Storer, Pika.—This subspecies of pika occurs in talus of the central Sierra Nevada from Mount Tallac south to Mammoth Pass, and it may occur in Nevada on the higher parts of the Sweetwater Range, near Wichman. If pikas occur there, they almost certainly are of this subspecies.

16. *Odocoileus hemionus inyoensis* Cowan, Black-tailed or Mule Deer.—This subspecies, of the eastern face of the southern Sierra Nevada and head of Owens Valley, may be the race of deer in the White Mountains of Esmeralda County. Although deer are known to occur there, no specimens are available.

17. *Bison bison*, subsp., American Bison.—Statements about the original range of this animal mention "northern Nevada" or "northwestern Nevada," and there are place names in the northwestern part of the state suggesting its former occurrence there, for example, Buffalo Meadows. No sight record by early explorers is known to me, nor do I know of any subfossil remains of the animal recovered from deposits that are unquestionably of Recent age.

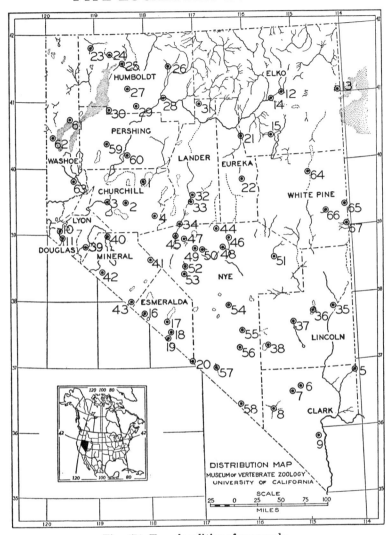

Fig. 474. Type localities of mammals.

Churchill County
1. Dixie Meadows, 3500 feet.
   Thomomys bottae depressus, p. 460.
2. Mountain Well.
   Microdipodops pallidus pallidus, p. 398.
3. Fallon.
   Fiber zibethicus mergens Hollister [*Ondatra zibethica mergens*], p. 567.
4. Eastgate.
   Thomomys bottae lucrificus, p. 461.

[645]

CLARK COUNTY

    5. Virgin River, 7 miles above Bunkerville.
        Perognathus penicillatus sobrinus, p. 376.
    6. Mormon Well, 6500 feet, Sheep Mountains.
        Eutamias dorsalis grinnelli, p. 348.
    7. Hidden Forest, Sheep Mountains.
        Eutamias quadrivittatus nevadensis (8500 ft.), p. 342.
        Thomomys phelleoecus Burt [*Thomomys bottae phelleoecus*], p. 475.
    8. Charleston Peak.
        Callospermophilus lateralis certus Goldman [*Citellus lateralis certus*] (N base of
          Peak), p. 326.
        Eutamias palmeri (8000 ft.), p. 342.
        Eutamias panamintinus juniperus Burt [*Eutamias panamintinus*] (W slope of Peak,
          ½ mi. W Wheeler Well), p. 336.
        Neotoma cinerea lucida, p. 538.
    9. El Dorado Canyon.
        Bassariscus astutus nevadensis, p. 179.

DOUGLAS COUNTY

   10. Carson Valley.
        Citellus mollis washoensis Merriam [*Citellus townsendii mollis*], p. 302.
   11. Gardnerville.
        Peromyscus crinitus scitulus Bangs [*Peromyscus crinitus crinitus*], p. 506.

ELKO COUNTY

   12. Near Deeth, Humboldt River.
        Lutra canadensis nexa, p. 196.
   13. One-half mile west of Debbs Creek, 6000 feet, Pilot Peak.
        Peromyscus truei nevadensis, p. 524.
   14. Halleck.
        Perognathus nevadensis Merriam [*Perognathus longimembris nevadensis*], p. 360.
        Microdipodops [megacephalus] megacephalus, p. 392.
   15. Ruby Mountains.
        Zapus nevadensis Preble [*Zapus princeps nevadensis*], p. 579.
        Ochotona princeps nevadensis (southwest of Ruby Valley P. O.), p. 590.

ESMERALDA COUNTY

   16. Arlemont [= Chiatovich Ranch], 4900 feet.
        Thomomys bottae lacrymalis, p. 463.
   17. Eight miles southeast of Blair, 4500 feet.
        Microdipodops megacephalus lucidus Goldman [*Microdipodops pallidus pallidus*],
          p. 398.
   18. Mount Magruder, 8000 feet.
        Perognathus parvus magruderensis Osgood [*Perognathus parvus olivaceus*], p. 367.
   19. Pigeon Spring, Mount Magruder.
        Arvicola curtata Cope [*Lagurus curtatus curtatus*], p. 560.
   20. Grapevine Mountains, on boundary between Inyo County, California, and Es-
        meralda County, Nevada.
        Ovis nelsoni Merriam [*Ovis canadensis nelsoni*], p. 642.

EUREKA COUNTY

   21. Evans.
        Thomomys townsendii elkoensis, p. 452.
   22. Four miles southeast of Romano, Diamond Valley.
        Dipodomys microps centralis, p. 421.

HUMBOLDT COUNTY
23. Virgin Valley, 4800 feet.
    Neotoma nevadensis Taylor [*Neotoma lepida nevadensis*], p. 530.
24. Head of Big Creek, Pine Forest Mountains, 8000 feet.
    Callospermophilus trepidus Taylor [*Citellus lateralis trepidus*], p. 322.
    Eutamias amoenus celeris, p. 335.
    Microtus intermedius Taylor [*Lagurus curtatus intermedius*], p. 560.
    Zapus princeps curtatus, p. 578.
25. Quinn River Crossing, 4100 feet.
    Thomomys townsendii bachmani, p. 452.
26. Paradise.
    Citellus elegans nevadensis Howell [*Citellus richardsonii nevadensis*], p. 303.
27. Willow Creek Ranch, 20 miles north of Jungo.
    Vulpes macrotis nevadensis, p. 236.
28. Four miles above Winnemucca, Humboldt River.
    Castor canadensis baileyi, p. 488.
29. Eleven miles east and 1 mile north of Jungo, 4200 feet.
    Dipodomys ordii inaquosus, p. 413.
30. One-fourth mile north of Sulphur, 4050 feet.
    Microdipodops megacephalus ambiguus, p. 389.

LANDER COUNTY
31. Three miles south of Izenhood.
    Microdipodops megacephalus nexus, p. 392.
32. Reese River Valley, 7 miles north of Austin.
    Citellus beldingi crebrus, p. 309.
33. Reese River, 5 miles west of Austin.
    Thomomys nevadensis Merriam [*Thomomys townsendii nevadensis*], p. 453.
34. Reese River, at line between Lander and Nye counties.
    Sorex nevadensis Merriam [*Sorex vagrans amoenus*], p. 119.

LINCOLN COUNTY
35. Two miles north of Panaca, 4800 feet.
    Dipodomys ordii fetosus, p. 416.
36. Desert Valley, 5300 feet, 21 miles west of Panaca.
    Microdipodops pallidus albiventer Hall and Durrant [*Microdipodops megacephalus albiventer*], p. 395.
37. Hiko, 4000 feet, Pahranagat Valley.
    Microtus montanus fucosus, p. 548.
38. Fourteen and one-half miles south of Groom Baldy.
    Microdipodops pallidus purus, p. 402.

LYON COUNTY
39. Smiths Valley, West Walker River, 4700 feet.
    Thomomys bottae cinereus, p. 462.

MINERAL COUNTY
40. Three miles south of Schurz, 4100 feet.
    Dipodomys microps occidentalis, p. 422.
41. Fingerrock Wash, 5400 feet.
    Thomomys solitarius Grinnell [*Thomomys bottae solitarius*], p. 464.
42. Fletcher, 6098 feet.
    Microdipodops megacephalus nasutus, p. 389.
43. Queen Station, head of Owens Valley.
    Spermophilus mollis stephensi Merriam [*Citellus townsendii mollis*], p. 301.

NYE COUNTY

44. Potts Ranch, 6900 feet, Monitor Valley.
    Thomomys bottae concisor, p. 468.
45. Bells Ranch, 6890 feet, Reese River Valley.
    Thomomys falcifer Grinnell [*Thomomys talpoides falcifer*], p. 449.
46. Fish Spring Valley, 2 miles southeast of Tulle Peak, 7000 feet.
    Thomomys bottae abstrusus, p. 469.
47. Wisconsin Creek, Toyabe Mountains.
    Microtus mordax latus Hall [*Microtus longicaudus latus*], 8500 feet, p. 552.
    Zapus princeps palatinus, 7800 feet, p. 581.
48. Greenmonster Canyon, 8150 feet, Monitor Mountains.
    Ochotona princeps tutelata, p. 591.
49. Milman Ranch, Moores Creek, 19 miles southeast of Millett P. O.
    Thomomys bottae fumosus, p. 465.
50. Jefferson.
    Marmota flaviventer parvula, p. 289.
    Thomomys bottae vescus (S slope Mt. Jefferson, 9000 ft.), p. 467.
51. Able Spring, 12½ miles south of Lock's Ranch, 5000 feet, Railroad Valley.
    Microdipodops pallidus ammophilus, p. 402.
52. Toyabe Mountains, near Cloverdale.
    Canis lestes Merriam [*Canis latrans lestes*], p. 263.
53. San Antonio, 5400 feet.
    Thomomys bottae curtatus, p. 466.
54. Breen Creek, 7000 feet, Kawich Range.
    Thomomys bottae brevidens, p. 470.
55. Five miles southeast of Kawich P. O., 5400 feet, Kawich Valley.
    Microdipodops megacephalus sabulonis, p. 394.
    Microdipodops pallidus ruficollaris, p. 399.
56. Five and one-half miles northwest of Whiterock Spring, 7200 feet, south end of Belted Range.
    Thomomys bottae nanus, p. 474.
57. Oasis Valley.
    Reithrodontomys megalotis deserti Allen [*Reithrodontomys megalotis megalotis*], p. 497.
58. Ash Meadows, Watkins Ranch.
    Microtus nevadensis Bailey [*Microtus montanus nevadensis*], p. 549.

PERSHING COUNTY

59. Three miles south of Vernon, 4250 feet.
    Microdipodops megacephalus medius, p. 391.
60. Lovelock.
    Microtus montanus undosus, p. 547.

WASHOE COUNTY

61. Deep Hole.
    Thomomys canus Bailey [*Thomomys bottae canus*], p. 459.
62. Latitude 40° 28′, 6 miles east of California boundary, 4000 feet.
    Perognathus formosus melanurus, p. 371.
63. Pyramid Lake.
    Dipodomys merriami nevadensis Merriam [*Dipodomys merriami merriami*], p. 424.

WHITE PINE COUNTY

64. Cherry Creek, 6500 feet.
    Thomomys bottae latus, p. 471.

65. Smith Creek Cave, Mount Moriah.
  Perognathus longimembris gulosus (¼ mi. S Cave, 5800 ft.), p. 364.
  Perognathus formosus incolatus (2 mi. W Cave, 6300 ft.), p. 373.
66. Cleveland Ranch, 6000 feet, Spring Valley.
  Microtus montanus micropus, p. 544.
67. Three miles east of Baker.
  Mustela frenata nevadensis, p. 188.
  Thomomys perpallidus centralis Hall [*Thomomys bottae centralis*] (2½ mi. E Baker, 5700 ft.), p. 471.
COUNTY IN QUESTION
68. Nevada or Utah, along 39th parallel somewhere between Camp Floyd, Utah, and Genoa, Nevada. Not shown on map.
  Neotoma lepida lepida, p. 530.
"Nevada," not shown on map.
  Nyctinomus macrotis nevadensis H. Allen [*Tadarida macrotis*], p. 169.

NAMES CHANGED SINCE BOOK WAS WRITTEN

In the years that have elapsed since the manuscript of this book was written, many advances have been made in our knowledge of North American mammals. As a result, some of the technical names used in this book require modification at the present time, August 30, 1945. These names are as follows:

Page 136. *Myotis evotis chrysonotus* (J. A. Allen) is replaced by *Myotis evotis evotis* (H. Allen). See Dalquest, Proc. Biol. Soc. Washington, 56:1, Feburary 25, 1943.

Page 184. *Mustela cicognanii lepta* (Merriam), Short-tailed Weasel, becomes *Mustela erminea lepta* (Merriam), Ermine. See Hall, Journ. Mammalogy, 26:181, July 13, 1945.

Page 336. *Eutamias panamintinus* (Merriam) becomes *Eutamias panamintinus panamintinus* (Merriam). See Johnson, Univ. California Publ. Zoöl., 48:93, December 24, 1943.

Page 560. *Lagurus curtatus intermedius* (Taylor) as applied to populations from northeastern Nevada should be reconsidered in the light of information provided by Goldman, Proc. Biol. Soc. Washington, 54:69, July 31, 1941, when he named *Lemmiscus curtatus levidensis*.

Page 585. *Erethizon epixanthum epixanthum* Brandt, becomes *Erethizon dorsatum epixanthum* Brandt. See Anderson and Rand, Canadian Journ. Res., 21:293, September 24, 1943.

Page 585. *Erethizon epixanthum couesi* Mearns, in the light of the information provided by Anderson and Rand (*op. cit.*), becomes *Erethizon dorsatum couesi* Mearns.

GAZETTEER

In the gazetteer the aim is to include only, but all of, the place names used in recording the localities of capture and observation of mammals. The entries themselves are not necessarily places of capture or observation. For example, specimens were taken 34 miles east and 1 mile north of Tonopah, but only Tonopah is to be found in the gazetteer.

For brevity and simplicity, abbreviation is resorted to in recording the geographic position of places. This can be illustrated by the first entry in the gazetteer which, if presented in unabbreviated fashion, might read as follows: Able Spring is in Nye County, Nevada, 38 degrees and 27 minutes north of the Equator and 115 degrees and 39 minutes west of Greenwich. The letter c denotes (see end of gazetteer) that the place name was not found on any map but is mentioned in the field notes of a collector, in this instance, E. Raymond Hall. Similarly, full statement of the second entry would be as follows: Ackler Creek: in Elko County, Nevada, with headwaters where the 41st parallel crosses the line of longitude marking 115 degrees and 8 minutes west of Greenwich, flowing northwesterly into Boulder Creek at a point where a line of latitude marking 41 degrees and 2 minutes north of the Equator crosses a line of longitude marking 115 degrees and 16 minutes west of Greenwich. The letter d signifies that the creek is shown and named on the map of Humboldt National Forest, Nevada, U. S. Dept. Agric., Forest Service, 1929. A list of maps is given at the end of the gazetteer. When a topographic feature, as, for example, a creek, has the head shown on one topographic map and the mouth on another, only the map showing the head may be cited for the locality.

The degree of accuracy aimed for is one minute of longitude and latitude. A minute of latitude and, in Nevada, a minute of longitude is about one mile in linear distance. Theoretically, therefore, accuracy to within one-half mile is attainable by this system. If a place is shown on a topographic quadrangle sheet of the United States Geological Survey, this source has been used for ascertaining the longitude and latitude. When not shown on these topographic maps, the position of a place has been ascertained from some other map. The variation between maps with respect to position of the same place introduces a source of error. This and other sources of error should cause the cautious student who needs precise information on the location of a place here listed to consult his own most trusted sources of cartographic information. The gazetteer herewith, then, may be a guide to place names, rather than a source of information for most precisely locating places.

A person who works with place names in Nevada will find helpful the "List of Localities" on pages 14–22 of Linsdale's (1936) "The Birds of Nevada," and the "Index to the Geographical Names of Nevada," by McVaugh and Fosberg (MS, 1941), which latter index aims to locate places from which plants have been collected.

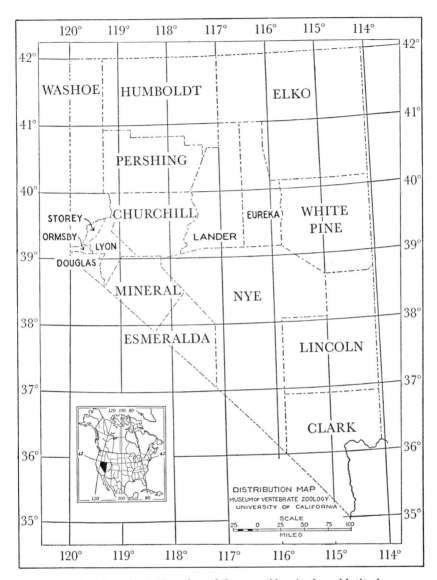

Fig. 475. Counties in Nevada and degrees of longitude and latitude.

One merit which the following list may have is that of giving the "location" of a place name at the time when collections or observations of mammals were labeled as being from that place. For example, Arlemont Post Office, Esmeralda County, at one time is thought to have been almost 20 miles south of the location given here in the gazetteer. The location given refers to the application of this place name in the period 1927–1930, inclusive, when mammals were labeled as captured at Arlemont.

The approximate position of any place named can be learned by examining the name in the gazetteer, noting the county and degrees of longitude and latitude, and then consulting the map, figure 475, which shows the names of the counties and the lines of longitude and latitude. More precise position of a place named will require construction of a guide rule on figure 475, with degrees marked off in 60ths (minutes) or multiples thereof.

Able Spring: Nye Co., 38 27, 115 39. *c* (Hall, July 28, 1933).
Ackler Creek: Elko Co., 41 00, 115 08, NW into Boulder Creek at 41 02, 115 16. *d*.
Adelaide: Humboldt Co., 40 49, 117 32. *a 6*.
Alamo: Lincoln Co., 37 20, 115 09. *b*.
Alder Creek: Humboldt Co., 41 41, 118 43, N to 41 47, 118 45. *a 2*.
Aldridge Grade: Mineral Co., 38 29, 118 54. Oral information from Donald V. Hemphill.
Alpine: Churchill Co., 39 30, 117 48. *b*.
Amargosa Desert: Nye Co., along California boundary from 36 50, SE to 36 25. *a 27*.
Amargosa River: Nye Co., 37 01, 116 44, S to 36 53, 116 45. *a 21*.
Amos: Humboldt Co., 41 24, 117 49. *b*.
Anaho Island: Washoe Co., in Pyramid Lake, 39 57, 119 31. *a 12*.
Anderson: *see* Anderson Ranch, but a place of this name also in Elko Co. at 41 27, 116 05. *b*.
Anderson Ranch: Douglas Co., 38 51, 119 27. George L. Sanford, *in litt.*, Sept. 29, 1941.
Antelope: Humboldt Co., 40 54, 118 31. *a 5*.
Antone Creek: Nye Co., 38 40, 116 58, E to junction with Meadow Creek at 38 40, 116 54. *e*.
Arc Dome: Nye Co., 38 50, 117 21. *a 19*.
Argenta: Lander Co., 40 39, 116 46. *f*.
Arizona Springs: Elko Co., 40 44, 115 05. *d*.
Arlemont (a post office, in 1928 at Chiatovich Ranch): Esmeralda Co., 37 50, 118 05. *a 24*.
Arrowhead: Nye Co., 38 07, 116 10. *f*.
Ash Meadow[s]: Nye Co., 36 25, 116 20. *a 27*.
Ash Spring: Lincoln Co., 37 28, 115 11. *b*.
Askov: Elko Co., 41 42, 116 28. *g*.
Austin: Lander Co., 39 29, 117 05. *b*.

Badger: Humboldt Co., probably refers to Badger Meadows which are at 41 41, 119 18. *a 3*.
Baker: White Pine Co., 39 01, 114 08. *b*.
Baker Creek: White Pine Co., from Baker Peak, 38 58, 114 18, E to town of Baker, 39 01, 114 08. *h*.
Barley Creek: Nye Co., W slope of Monitor Range, 38 44, 116 37, SW to 38 37, thence NW into dry lake, 38 40, 116 45. *e*.
Barrel Spring: Washoe Co., approximately 41 53, 119 58. *c* (Hall, July 11, 1941).
Battle Mountain (a town): Lander Co., 40 39, 116 56. *b*.
Beatty: Nye Co., 36 55, 116 45. *a 27*.
Beaverdam, in state of Arizona: 36 54, 113 59. *g*.
Bells Ranch: Nye Co., on Reese River, 38 56, 117 29. *e*.
Belmont: Nye Co., 38 35, 116 52. *e*.
Belted Peak: Nye Co., 37 34, 116 05. *a 21*.
Belted Range: Nye Co., 37 44, 116 06, S to 37 12, 116 15. *a 21*.
Beowawe: Eureka Co., 40 35, 116 27. *b*.
Big Creek: Humboldt Co., 41 42, 118 40, SE to 41 40, 118 35. *a 2*.

Big Creek: Nye Co., 38 07, 115 43, NW 4 mi. into Railroad Valley. *b.*

Big Creek Ranch: Humboldt Co., 41 40, 118 35. *h.*

Bijou, in state of California: S end Lake Tahoe, 119 58, 38 57. *i.*

Birch Creek: Lander Co., E slope Toyabe Mts., 39 25, 117 05, SE to 39 21, 116 58. *a 9* and *e.*

Birch Creek Ranch: Lander Co., 39 22, 116 58. *a 9.*

Black Canyon: Clark Co., along Colorado River from about 36 02 to 35 52. *b.*

Black Rock Desert: Humboldt Co., 40 57, 119 00, NE to 41 35, 118 30. *b.*

Blair: Esmeralda Co., 37 48, 117 40. *a 23.*

Blair Junction: Esmeralda Co., 38 01, 117 47. *a 19.*

Bliss Ranch: Humboldt Co., said to be in township 40 north, range 43 east, Mount Diablo Base Line and Meridian. Eleanor Bain, *in litt.,* Oct. 3, 1941.

Bonelli Peak: Clark Co., 36 08, 114 15. *f,* but 36 14, 114 13 on *a 29.*

Boulder Canyon: Clark Co., canyon of Colorado River, from about 114 27, W to 114 42. *a 29.*

Boulder City: Clark Co., 35 58, 114 50. *g.*

Boulder Dam (original name was Hoover Dam): Clark Co., 36 01, 114 44. *g.*

Boulder Lake: *see* Lake Mead.

Box Canyon: Nye Co., in Quinn Canyon Mts., about 6 mi. NE Italian Springs, therefore approximately 38 18, 115 38. *j.*

Boynton Pond: Washoe Co., 39 31, 119 45. Frank B. Richardson, *in litt.,* Dec. 6, 1941.

Breen Creek: Nye Co., 37 56, 116 28, SW for 2 mi. *a 21.*

Buena Vista Valley: Pershing Co., 40 38, 117 58, S into Carson Sink at about 40 00, 118 10. *b.*

Bull-head Ranch: Humboldt Co., 41 22, 117 20. Paul L. Travis, *in litt.,* Sept. 23, 1941.

Bull Run: Elko Co., probably refers to Bull Run Basin at 41 39, 116 09, or to Bull Run Creek, which flows through Bull Run Basin. *d.*

Bull Run Mountains: Elko Co., 41 45, 116 05, S to 41 30, 116 08. *b.*

Bullwhack Spring: White Pine Co., 38 50, 114 52. Shown, but unnamed on *k.*

Bunkerville: Clark Co., 36 48, 114 08. *b.*

Burned Corral Canyon (= Burnt Canyon): Nye Co., 38 14, 115 32, W to junction with Spring Creek at 38 14, 115 35. Shown on *h,* but there labeled Burnt Canyon.

Burnt Canyon: Lincoln Co., 38 17, 114 12, S into Meadow Valley Wash of which this is the head. *l.*

Cabin Springs: Clark Co., 36 47, 115 07. *m.*

Cactus Flat: Nye Co., 38 00, 116 45, S to 37 35, 116 35. *a 21.*

Cactus Mountains: *see* Cactus Range.

Cactus Range: Nye Co., 37 50, 116 53, SE to 37 33, 116 42. *a 21.*

Cactus Spring: Nye Co., 37 44, 116 49. *a 21.*

Calico Mountain: Humboldt Co., 41 52, 117 19, S to 41 50, 117 19. Paul L. Travis, *in litt.,* Sept. 18, 1941.

Caliente: Lincoln Co., 37 36, 114 30. *b.*

Callville: Clark Co., 36 05, 114 42. *a 29.*

Calneva: Washoe Co., 39 14, 120 00. *c* (Hall, Aug. 15, 1934).

Calvada: Washoe Co., N end of Lake Tahoe on California boundary, 39 15, 120 00. Used rarely for place designated above as Calneva.

Campbell Creek: Lander Co., 39 15, 117 44, E to 39 13, 117 39. *f.*

Campbell Creek Ranch: Lander Co., 39 13, 117 39. *f.*

Candelaria: Mineral Co., 38 09, 118 05. *a 18.*

Candelaria Junction: Mineral Co., 38 11, 118 11. *a 18.*

Carlin: Elko Co., 40 42, 116 05. *b.*

Carp: Lincoln Co., 37 07, 114 32. *f.*

Carrol Summit: on line between Churchill and Lander counties, 39 16, 117 46. *f.*

Carson City: Ormsby Co., 39 10, 119 46. *a 13.*

Carson Lake: Churchill Co., 39 20, 118 43. *a 10.*

Carson River: from junction of East and West forks at 38 57, 119 48 in Douglas Co., NE through Ormsby and Lyon counties into Churchill Co., originally into Carson Lake and Carson Sink, but now (1939), into Lahontan Reservoir at 39 25, 119 05. *b.*

Carson Sink: Churchill Co., 39 48, 118 34. *a 10.*

Carson Valley: Douglas and Ormsby counties along Carson River where its two forks unite. *a 13* and *b.*

Castle Mountains: Clark Co., from California, barely across state boundary in Nevada at 35 26. *a 31.*

Cat Creek: Mineral Co., 38 32, 118 48, E to 38 33, 118 41. *a 18.*

Cave: Lincoln Co., 38 38, 114 49, *b.*

Cave Spring: Esmeralda Co., 37 48, 117 51. *a 23.*

Cave Valley: 38 50, 114 50 in White Pine Co., S to 38 26, 114 54 in Lincoln Co. Shown, but not named on *b.*

Cedar Basin: Clark Co., about 36 09, 114 13, as plotted by Burt (1934:376).

Cedar Creek: Elko Co., 41 53, 114 29, NW to junction with Shoshone Creek at 41 56, 114 34. *c* (Hall, July 15, 1935). Shown, but not named on *b.*

Charleston Mountains [Spring Mountains]: Clark Co., 36 25, 115 49, S to California boundary at 35 40. *a 28.*

Charleston Park Resort: Clark Co., 36 16, 115 40. *c* (Hall, April 8, 1936; Burt, 1934:385).

Charleston Peak: Clark Co., 36 16, 115 42. *a 28.*

Cherry Creek [Spring]: Churchill Co., on SE slope of Clan Alpine Range, 39 31, 117 52. *b.*

Cherry Creek [P. O.]: White Pine Co., 39 54, 114 53. This place name is used for a railroad station 3 mi. E and ¾ mi. S of the P. O., and a creek of this name extends from the P. O. some 6 mi. farther W. *b* and *k.*

Cherry Valley [Meadows]: Churchill Co., "at head of Cherry Canyon, in Clan Alpine Range . . . ," 39 31, 117 53. *c* (A. M. Alexander and L. Kellogg, p. 14, Nov. 6, 1926).

Chiatovich Creek: Esmeralda Co., from California boundary at 37 48, E to Chiatovich Ranch at 37 50, 118 05. *a 24.*

Chiatovich Ranch (= Arlemont P. O. in 1928): Esmeralda Co., 37 50, 118 05. *a 24.*

Chimney Rock Spring: White Pine Co., 38 50, 114 53. *k.*

Choke Cherry Creek: White Pine Co., 38 48, 114 11, E to 38 47, 114 07. *h.*

Clark Canyon: Clark Co., on lat. 36 20, E to W from 115 42 to 115 49. *a 28.*

Clay City: Nye Co., 36 30, 116 27. *o.*

Cleve Creek: White Pine Co., 39 18, 114 37, SE to 39 13, thence NE to Cleveland Ranch. *h.*

Cleveland Ranch: White Pine Co., 39 15, 114 29. *h.*

Cliff Spring: Nye Co., 37 31, 116 06. *a 21.*

Clover Creek: Humboldt Co., said on label of kit fox to be in vicinity of Jungo.

Cloverdale (a ranch): Nye Co., 38 34, 117 33. *a 19.*

Coaldale: Esmeralda Co., 38 03, 117 54. *a 19.*

Coal Valley: Lincoln Co., 38 03, 115 13, S to 37 44, 115 20. *b.*

Cobb Creek: Elko Co., 41 47, 116 03, SE into Van Duzen Creek at 41 45, 116 02. *c* (Hall, July 22, 1935). Shown, but unnamed on *d.*

Cobre: Elko Co., 41 07, 114 23. *b.*

Cold Creek: Clark Co., 36 25, 115 45, flows northerly for less than a mile (see Burt, 1934: 386). *a 28.*

Cold Creek: Elko Co., 40 43, 115 18, NW to junction with John Day Creek at 40 49, 115 23. *a 7.*

Colorado River: southeastern boundary of state, 36 09, W and S to 35 00. *b.*

Connor Range (= Conner Range, S end of Shell Creek Range): White Pine Co., 39 02, 114 40, S to 38 48, 114 40. *See* Cooper Canyon.

Contact: Elko Co., 41 47, 114 45. *b.*

Coon Creek: Elko Co., 41 47, 115 30, N 4 mi., thence W 5 mi. into Bruneau River. *d.*

Cooper Canyon: White Pine Co., E slope of Connor Range (= S end of Shell Creek Range), 39 08, 114 40, E to 39 06, 114 32 into Spring Valley. *h.*

Copper Creek: Elko Co., 41 46, 115 30, SW 6 mi. into Bruneau River. *d.*

Corn Creek: Clark Co., 36 26, 115 22. *f.*

Corn Creek Station: Clark Co., 36 25, 115 23. *f.*

Cortez: Lander Co., 40 09, 116 36. *b.*

Cortez Mountains: 40 30, 116 10 in Eureka Co., SW to 40 06, 116 35 in Lander Co. *b.*

Cosgrave: Pershing Co., 40 48, 118 01. *a 5.*

Cottonwood Creek: Mineral Co., 38 32, 118 49, N and E into Walker Lake, 38 39, 117 46. *a 18.*

Cottonwood Creek: Nye Co., 39 07, 117 12, W to junction with Reese River at 39 08, 117 22. *e.*

Cottonwood Creek: Washoe Co., N end Virginia Mts., 40 02, 119 48, N to 40 09, 119 49. *a 4.*

Cottonwood Creek: White Pine Co., 39 12, 115 24, N to junction with Illipah Creek at 39 17, 115 24. *h.*

Cottonwood Range (= Santa Rosa Mts.): Humboldt Co., 41 25, 117 45, N to Oregon boundary. *b.*

Cottonwood Springs [Spring]: Clark Co., 36 03, 115 25. *a 28.*

Cottonwood Valley: Clark Co., 35 25, 114 40. *a 30.*

Coyote Spring: Lincoln Co., 37 00, 114 59. *l* (37 03, 114 55. *a*).

Crystal Spring: Lincoln Co., 37 32, 115 14. *l.*

Daniels Ranch: Nye Co., 39 07, 117 01. *e.*

Darroughs Hot Springs: Nye Co., 38 49, 117 11. *a 19.*

Dayton: Lyon Co., 39 14, 119 36. *a 13.*

Deadman Creek: White Pine Co., 39 17, 114 14, NE to junction with Smith Creek at 39 20, 114 09. *h.*

Dead Mountain: Clark Co., 35 17, 114 43. *a 30.*

Dead Mountains: Clark Co., 35 20, 114 44, S to California boundary at 35 02. *a 30.*

Debbs Creek: Elko Co., N side Pilot Peak, approximately 41 01, 114 05, W for 2 mi. *c* (Hall, July 18, 1935).

Deep Creek: Elko Co., 41 34, 116 04, W to junction with South Fork Owyhee River at 41 38, 116 24. *b* and *d.* Deep Creek as a particular place, 41 34, 116 13. Named on *f,* but location ascertained from *d.*

Deep Hole: Washoe Co., 40 43, 119 29. *b.*

Deer Creek: Clark Co., 36 19, 115 38, NE to 36 24, 115 31, SE of Lee Canyon and roughly parallel to same. *h.*

Deeth: Elko Co., 41 04, 115 18. *b.*

Denay Creek: Eureka Co., 39 52, 116 24, N into Horse Creek at 40 08, 116 20. *a 9* and *b.*

Denio, in state of Oregon: 42 00, 118 38. *f.*

Desatoya Mountains: 39 30, 117 36, S to 38 45, 117 52. *b.*

Desert Creek: from California boundary at 38 32, northerly, forming boundary between Douglas and Lyon counties, to 38 40, 119 20, and intermittently, sometimes a mile or so, farther into Smiths Valley. *a 15.*

Desert Creek Point (= Desert Creek Peak ?): Lyon Co., 38 37. 119 19. *a 15.*

Desert Creek Ranch: Lyon Co., 38 39, 119 19. *a 15,* where it is named Simpson.

Desert Ranch: Elko Co., in 1914 said to be 100 mi. NE Golconda. Not found; *see* account of *Sorex m. merriami.*

Desert Valley: Lincoln Co., 37 34, 115 34, S along W base of Silver Canyon Mts. to 37 13, 115 28. A second valley of the same name (Dry Lake Valley on some maps), in the same county, extends from 38 05, 114 50, S to 37 40, 114 50. *b.*

Devil Gate: Eureka Co., 39 34, 116 04. *a 9.*

Devils Hole: Nye Co., 36 25, 116 18. *a 27.*

Diamond Valley: Eureka Co., 39 35, 116 00, N to 40 20, 116 00 in Elko Co. *b.*

Diessner: Washoe Co., 41 54, 119 49. *g.*

Division Peak: Humboldt Co., 41 06, 119 15. *a 3.*

Dixie Meadows: Churchill Co., 39 48, 118 03. *a 10.*

Duck Valley: Lincoln Co., 38 36, 114 35, S to 37 56, 114 22. *b.*

Duckwater: Nye Co., 38 48, 115 40. *b.*

Duffer Peak: Humboldt Co., 41 40, 118 44. *a 2.*

Dugout Camp: Humboldt Co., on Big Creek, 41 40, 118 37. (Taylor, Univ. Calif. Publ. Zoöl., 7:327, 1912.)

Durban Ranch: Clark Co., 35 29, 114 40. *c* (Benson, p. 501, Jan. 8, 1934).

Dutch Flat Schoolhouse: Nye Co., 38 57, 117 28. Clifford W. King, *in litt.*, Oct. 14, 1941.

Dyer: Esmeralda Co., 37 44, 118 06. *a 24.*

Dyer Ranch: Esmeralda Co., 37 46, 118 02. *a 24.*

Eagle Valley: Lincoln Co., 38 03, 114 11, SW 4 or 5 mi. *b.*

Eagleville, in state of California: 41 19, 120 06. Gen. Land Office map, Calif., 1913. Scale 12 miles to the inch.

East Fork Carson River: Douglas Co., from California boundary at 38 47, N to junction with W Fork at 38 57, 119 48. *a 16.*

Eastgate: Churchill Co., 39 21, 117 52. *g.*

East Humboldt Mountains: *see* Ruby Mountains, but name was sometimes applied only to N part of Ruby Mountains.

East Range: Pershing Co., 40 48, 117 52, S to 40 00, 117 52. *b.*

East Walker River: from across California boundary at 38 25, N through Mineral Co. to junction in Lyon Co. with West Walker River at 38 54, 119 11. *a 17, 18, 15.*

Edgewood: Douglas Co., 38 58, 119 56. *i.*

Edwards Creek Ranch: Churchill Co., 39 31, 117 45. *c* (Alexander and Kellogg, Nov. 12, 1928).

Egan Range: White Pine Co., 40 00, 115 00, S to 39 00, 114 54. *b.*

Elburz: Elko Co., 40 56, 115 30. *a 7.*

El Dorado Canyon: Clark Co., 35 45, 114 50, E into Colorado River at 35 44, 114 40. *a 30.*

El Dorado Canyon: Pershing Co., W side Humboldt Range, 40 31, 118 14. *a 5.*

Elgin: Lincoln Co., 37 21, 114 30. *b.*

Elko: Elko Co., 40 50, 115 45. *b.*

Ely: White Pine Co., 39 15, 114 54. *b.*

Emigrant Valley: 37 16, 115 47 in Lincoln Co., SW to 37 04, 116 00 in Nye Co. *b.*

Endowment Mine: Mineral Co., not found on any map, but in field notes of collectors of specimens said to be about 4 mi. N Marietta at head of canyon to E of Excelsior Peak in Excelsior Mountains. *c* (L. Kellogg, June 3, 1928).

Eureka: Eureka Co., 39 32, 115 59. *b.*

Evans: Eureka Co., 40 27, 116 08. *f.*

Excelsior Mountains: Mineral Co., 38 20, 118 10, SW across California boundary at 38 06. *a 18.*

Fairview: Churchill Co., 39 16, 118 12. *a 10.*

Fallon: Churchill Co., 39 28, 118 47. *a 10.*

Fanning: Pershing Co., 40 20, 118 06. *g*.

Favre Lake: Elko Co., 40 34, 115 24. *a 7*.

Fernley: Lyon Co., 39 37, 119 16. *b*.

Fingerrock Wash: Mineral Co., 38 37, 117 57, N to 38 47, 118 05. *a 19, 18*.

Fish Lake: Esmeralda Co., 37 44, 118 03. *a 24*.

Fish Lake: Nye Co., 38 38, 116 29. *b*.

Fish Lake Valley: Esmeralda Co., 37 50, SE along California boundary to 37 30, 117 52. *b*.

Fish Springs: Washoe Co., 40 06, 119 54. Arthur V. Allen, *in litt.*, Oct. 3, 1941.

Fish Spring Valley: Nye Co., 39 00, 116 23, S to 38 36, 116 28. *b*.

Flanigan: Washoe Co., 40 10, 119 53. *g*.

Fletcher: Mineral Co., 38 21, 118 54. *a 18*.

Flowing Spring: Humboldt Co., 41 09, 119 06. Shown, but unnamed on *a 3* (Ward C. Russell, April 23, 1941).

Fort Bidwell, in state of California: 41 51, 120 09. Gen. Land Office, map, Calif., 1913. Scale 12 miles to the inch.

Fort Mohave (Camp Mohave), in state of Arizona: 35 03, 114 37. *b*.

Fortification Range: 38 45, 114 33 in White Pine Co., S to 38 31, 114 28 in Lincoln Co. *b*.

Fox Canyon: Washoe Co., 40 19, 119 35, SW for 3 mi. *c* (D. H. Johnson, May 31, 1937).

Frenchmans Mine: Clark Co., 115 00, 36 10. Burt (1934:393).

Galena Creek: Washoe Co., 39 19, 119 56, E into Pleasant Valley at 39 21, 119 47. *a 13*.

Gambel Ranch: Elko Co., labeled as in vicinity of Montello on skull of coyote.

Garden Valley: 38 10, 115 20 in Nye Co., SW to 37 57, 115 32 in Lincoln Co. *h*.

Gardnerville: Douglas Co., 38 56, 119 45. *a 16*.

Garrison, in state of Utah: 38 55, 114 02. *f*.

Genoa: Douglas Co., 39 00, 119 51. *a 13*.

Gerlach: Washoe Co., 40 39, 119 21. *g*.

Geyser: Lincoln Co., 38 38, 114 37. *f*.

Gilpin Spillway: Storey Co., 39 34, 119 19, on S side Truckee River, nearly on line between Storey and Lyon counties. Oral information from J. R. Alcorn.

Gleason Creek: White Pine Co., 39 26, 115 03, S 3 mi. Elevation of head recorded as 7300 ft. *k*.

Gleason Spring: White Pine Co., 39 26, 115 02. *k*.

Glenbrook: Douglas Co., 39 05, 119 56. *a 13*.

Gold Creek: Elko Co., 41 43, 115 43. *d*.

Golconda: Humboldt Co., 40 57, 117 28. *b*.

Golden: Nye Co., 38 38, 117 34. *b*.

Goldfield: Esmeralda Co., 37 43, 117 14. *a 22*.

Gold Flat: Nye Co., 37 40, 116 27, SW to 37 22, 116 30. *a 21*.

Gold Mountain: Esmeralda Co., 37 15, 117 18. *a 22*.

Gondolpho [Gondolfo] Ranch: Lander Co., 39 26, 117 14. *e*.

Goose Creek: Elko Co., flows NE across Utah border at 41 58. *b*. Drains most of ten townships in NE corner of state.

Granite Creek: Washoe Co., 40 46, 119 23, SE for 5 mi. This creek may have borne this name between 1890 and 1900, but now a creek (heading about 2 mi. E of the head of the Granite Creek of 1900) which flows E instead of SE is locally called Granite Creek, or was in 1936. *c*. *See* account of *Thomomys bottae canus* of present work.

Granite Mountain (= Granite Peak): Washoe Co., 40 48, 119 26. *a 4*.

Granite Mountain (= Granite Peak): White Pine Co., 38 49, 114 13. *h*.

Granite Peak: Pershing Co., 40 17, 117 49. *b*.

Granite Peak: Washoe Co., 40 48, 119 26. *a 4*.

Grant Mountains: *See* Grant Range.

Grant Range: Nye Co., 38 48, 115 15, SW to 38 15, 115 34. *b.*

Grapevine Mountains: across California boundary at 36 55, N in Nye Co. to 37 13, 117 17 in Esmeralda Co. *b.*

Grapevine Peak: Nye Co., 36 58, 117 09. *a 26.*

Greenmonster Canyon: Nye Co., E slope Monitor Range, 38 46, 116 35, SE to 38 43, 116 26. *e.*

Green Mountain Canyon [Creek]: Elko Co., 40 23, 115 32, SW to junction with Toyn Creek at 40 21, 115 38. *d.*

Greens Ranch: White Pine Co., 40 02, 114 46. *f.*

Groom Baldy: Lincoln Co., 37 27, 115 44. *l.*

Halleck: Elko Co., 40 57, 115 25. *a 7.*

Halstead Creek: White Pine Co., 39 20, 115 28, E to 39 21, 115 19. *n.*

Hamilton: White Pine Co., 39 15, 115 30. *b.*

Hancock Summit: Lincoln Co., 37 30, 115 23. *l.*

Hansen Canyon: Humboldt Co., 41 30, 117 40, E to 41 30, 117 36. Paul L. Travis, *in litt.,* Sept. 23, 1941.

Hardscrabble Canyon: Washoe Co., 39 56, 119 39, E into Pyramid Lake at 39 57. *c* (Hall visited place in summer of 1924; shown, but unnamed on *a 12*).

Harrison Pass: Elko Co., 40 19, 115 31. *a 8.*

Harrison Pass Ranger Station: Elko Co., 40 21, 115 36. *a 8.*

Hausen: Washoe Co., 1 mi. E California boundary at 41 10. *g.*

Haws Canyon: Nye Co., 37 58, 116 29, W to 38 00, 116 32. Oral information from E. F. Johnson. Shown, but unnamed on *a 21.*

Hawthorne: Mineral Co., 38 32, 118 38. *a 18.*

Hazen: Churchill Co., 39 34, 119 02. *b.*

Hemenway Wash: Clark Co., 35 59, 114 51, NE into Lake Mead at 36 03, 114 48. Hall visited place on March 18, 1940.

Hendry Creek: White Pine Co., 39 15, 114 11, SW across Utah border at 39 12. *h.*

Hidden Forest: Clark Co., 36 39, 115 13. *m.*

Hiko: Lincoln Co., 37 36, 115 13. *l.*

Hiko Spring: Clark Co., 35 10, 114 41. *c* (Hall, April 11, 1936).

Hiko Spring: Lincoln Co., 37 35, 115 14. *l.*

Hilltop: Lander Co., 40 25, 116 48. *b.*

Hinds Hot Springs: Lyon Co., 38 54, 119 25. *a 15.*

Hobson: Elko Co., 40 04 115 32. *a 8.*

Holbrook: Douglas Co., 38 45, 119 34. *a 16.*

Hoover Dam: *see* Boulder Dam.

Hoover Dam Ferry: Clark Co., *see* Hoover Dam. Ferry was about ½ mi. above site of dam. Oral information from S. B. Benson.

Horse Canyon: Washoe Co., 40 25, 119 38. *c* (D. H. Johnson, May 28, 1937).

Hot Creek (in 1933 a ranch and post office): Nye Co., 38 31, 116 24; creek itself and canyon from 38 36, 116 30, SE to Hot Creek Ranch, and in flood periods farther SE into Hot Creek Valley for about 10 mi. *b.*

Hot Creek Canyon: Nye Co., *see* Hot Creek.

Hot Creek Range: Nye Co., 38 10, 116 25, N across 39 00. *b.*

Hot Creek Valley: Nye Co., 38 37, 116 12, SW to 38 10, 116 20. *b.*

Hot Spring: Humboldt Co., 41 56, 118 42. *a 2.*

Humboldt: Pershing Co., 40 36, 118 15. *a 5.*

Humboldt Range: Pershing Co., 40 35, 118 10, S to 40 00. *b.*

Humboldt River: from junction of East and North forks at 40 56, 115 33, SW into Humboldt Lake and Humboldt Sink, at 40 00, 118 38. *b.*

Hunters Creek: Washoe Co., 39 24, 119 55, N to junction with Truckee River at 39 30, 119 54. *a 13.*

Hunters Lake: Washoe Co., 39 26, 119 55. Shown, but unnamed on *a 13.*

Huntoon Valley: Mineral Co., 38 11, 118 30, SW to 38 06, 118 35. *a 18.*

Illipah: White Pine Co., 39 21, 115 20. *b.*

Incline: Washoe Co., 39 14, 119 57. *a 13.*

Incline Creek: Washoe Co., 39 19, 119 56, S into Lake Tahoe at 39 14, 119 57. *a 13.*

Independence Valley: 41 30, 116 13 in Elko Co., S to 40 50, 116 13 in Eureka Co. *b.*

Indian Creek: Esmeralda Co., from across California boundary at 37 46, NE to 37 48, 118 09. *a 24.*

Indian Creek: Nye Co., 38 46, 117 25, N to junction with Reese River, 38 52, 117 29. *a 19.*

Indian Spring: Esmeralda Co., 37 25, 117 35. *a 22.*

Indian Spring: Nye Co., W slope of Belted Range, 37 26, 116 07. *a 21.*

Indian Springs: Clark Co., 36 34, 115 40. *a 28.*

Indian Springs: Lincoln Co., 38 39, 114 27. W. H. Reppert, *in litt.,* Nov. 28, 1941.

Indian Spring Valley: Clark Co., 36 51, 115 38, SW into Nye Co. to 36 35, 116 04. *a 28.*

Indian Valley: Nye Co., 38 49, 117 30, S to 38 46, 117 30. *a 19.*

Ione Valley: Nye Co., 39 00, 117 40, S to 38 39, 117 43. *a 19.*

Irish Mountain: Lincoln Co., 37 39, 115 23. *b.*

Iron Point: Humboldt Co., 41 00, 117 18. *b.*

Italian Spring (sometimes Italian Springs): Nye Co., 38 15, 115 37. *j.*

Izenhood: Lander Co., 40 56, 116 55. *f* and *g.*

Jack Creek [Jacks Creek]: Elko Co., 41 31, 115 59, NW, then SW to junction with Harrington Creek at 49 30, 116 07. *d.*

Jackson Creek: Humboldt Co., 41 19, 118 28, W to 41 20, 118 34. *a 2.*

Jackson Creek Ranch: Humboldt Co., 41 20, 118 32. *c* (D. H. Johnson, Aug. 3, 1937).

Jackson Mountains: Humboldt Co., 41 30, 118 27, S to 40 54, 118 29. *b.*

Jap Ranch: Clark Co., 35 27, 114 42. *c* (Benson, Jan. 16, 1934).

Jarbidge: Elko Co., 41 53, 115 27. *b.*

Jarbidge Mountains: Elko Co., 41 54, 115 25, S to 41 42, 115 20. *d.*

Jarbidge River: Elko Co., 41 46, 115 23, N across Idaho boundary at 42 00, 115 25. *d.*

Jefferson: Nye Co., 38 43, 117 01. *a 19.*

Jefferson Peak: Nye Co., *see* Mount Jefferson.

Jerry Crab Springs: Elko Co., on Jerry Creek.

Jerry Creek: Elko Co., 40 46, 115 06, E to junction with Warm Creek at 40 45, 115 03. *d.*

Jett (sometimes Jet) Canyon: Nye Co., E side Toyabe Range, 38 46, 117 17, SE to 38 44, 117 13. *a 19.*

John Henry Wash: White Pine Co., 38 58, 114 40, E to about 38 56, 114 34 in Spring Valley. Doyle C. Robison, *in litt.,* Jan. 14, 1940.

Johnnies Water: Nye Co., 37 26, 116 05. *a 21.*

Junction House: Washoe Co., 39 46, 119 41. *a 12.*

Jungo: Humboldt Co., 40 55, 118 23. *a 5.*

Kaolin: Clark Co., 36 32, 114 26. *f.*

Kaolin Reservoir: Clark Co., reservoir of water in Kaolin for domestic use. Oral information from Dwight C. Smiley.

Kawich Mountains: Nye Co., *see* Kawich Range.

Kawich P. O. (= Gold Reed, in 1931 found to be abandoned): Nye Co., 37 33, 116 17. *a 21.*
Kawich Range: Nye Co., 38 08, 116 25, S to 37 15, 116 22. *b.*
Kawich Valley: 37 40, 116 11, S to 37 21, 116 13. *a 21.*
King Lea [King Lear] Peak: Humboldt Co., 41 12, 118 33. *a 2.*
Kingston Canyon: Lander Co., see Kingston Creek.
Kingston Creek: Lander Co., 39 17, 117 08, SW to 117 10, thence SE to 39 12, thence NE to junction with Shoshone Creek at 39 14, 117 02. *i.*
Kingston Ranch: Lander Co., 39 12, 117 05, on Kingston Creek. *e.*
Kingston Ranger Station: Lander Co., 39 15, 117 10. *e.*
Kistler Springs: Washoe Co. On label of mountain sheep said to be 15 mi. E of Eagleville, California.
Kleckner Creek: Elko Co., 40 34, 115 24, W to junction with Rattlesnake Creek at 40 34, 115 36. *a 7* and *d.*
Koalin [Kaolin]: Clark Co., 36 32, 114 26. *f.*
Kyle Canyon: Clark Co., 36 16, 115 40, E to 36 18, 115 27. *a 27.*

Lahontan Dam: Churchill Co., 39 28, 119 04. *f.*
Lake Mead: Clark Co., artificial lake behind Boulder Dam (36 01, 114 45), up Colorado River to Nevada-Arizona boundary at 36 11, 114 03, and with another arm extending up valley of Virgin River. *g.*
Lake Tahoe: 39 00, 120 00, Washoe, Ormsby, and Douglas counties. *b* and *a 13.*
Lake Valley: 38 41, 114 05 in White Pine Co., S to 38 20, 114 03 in Lincoln Co. *b* shows Lake Creek.
Lakeview: Ormsby Co., 39 13, 119 48. *a 13.*
Lapon Canyon: Mineral Co., 38 32, 118 50, W to 38 33, 118 52. *a 18.*
Lamoille: Elko Co., 40 44, 115 29. *a 7.*
Las Vegas: Clark Co., 36 10, 115 09. *a 28.*
Las Vegas Wash [Vegas Wash]: Clark Co., 36 30, 115 39, SE to junction with Colorado River at 36 05, 114 46. *b.*
Leadville: Washoe Co., 41 02, 119 22. *f.*
Lee: Elko Co., 40 35, 115 37. *b.*
Lee Canyon: Clark Co., 36 19, 115 41, NE to 36 22, 115 37. *a 28.*
Lehman Cave: White Pine Co., 39 00, 114 13. *h.*
Lehman Creek: White Pine Co., 39 00, 114 18, E to junction with Baker Creek at 39 01, 114 07. *h.*
Leonard Creek: Humboldt Co., 41 40, 118 43, S to 41 30, 118 44. *a 2.*
Lida: Esmeralda Co., 37 28, 117 30. *a 22.*
Little Falls: Clark Co., 36 16, 115 39. Burt (1934:385). *h.*
Little High Rock Canyon: Washoe Co., 41 15, 119 24, E to 41 16, 119 18. *a 3.*
Little Humboldt Ranch: Humboldt Co., 41 30, 117 02. Paul L. Travis, *in litt.*, Sept. 23, 1941.
Little Log Spring: Esmeralda Co., 37 23, 117 39. *a 22.*
Little Owyhee River: 41 48, 117 18 in Humboldt Co., NE across Elko Co. line, then N across Idaho boundary at 116 56. *b.*
Little Rye Patch: Nye Co., 38 09, 116 39. *b.*
Lock's Ranch: Nye Co., 38 39, 115 38. *c* (Hall, July 29, 1933).
Logamacina (now Lockwood Ranch): Storey Co., 39 30, 119 39. Carl P. Russell, *in litt.*, Oct. 14, 1941.
Logandale: Clark Co., 36 36, 114 27. *f.*
Log Spring: Esmeralda Co., 37 23, 117 39. *a 22.*
Lone Mountain: Esmeralda Co., 38 02, 117 30. *a 19.*

Long Creek [Long Canyon on *a 7* and South Furlong Creek on *d*]: Elko Co., 40 30, 115 26, NW to junction with Mahogany Creek, *a*, or North Furlong Creek, *d*, at 40 33, 115 30. *a 7.*

Long Valley Ranch: Washoe Co., 41 33, 119 51. *c* (Ward C. Russell, July 22, 1936).

Lost City: Clark Co , 36 32, 114 25. *f.*

Lovelock (or Lovelocks): Pershing Co., 40 11, 118 28. *a 5.*

Lund: White Pine Co., 38 51, 115 00. *b.*

Mahogany [Creek]: Humboldt Co., 41 59, 117 21, E to junction with another stream at 41 59, 117 06. Paul L. Travis, *in litt.*, Sept. 23, 1941.

Mahogany Canyon: Lander Co., 39 15, 117 08, W to junction with Kingston Creek at 39 15, 117 10. Shown, but unnamed on *e*. Oral information from J. M. Linsdale.

Malloy Ranch: Lander Co., 39 32, 117 09. *e.*

Manhattan: Nye Co., 38 32, 117 04. *a 19.*

Marble: Nye Co., 39 00, 118 04. *b* (39 00, 117 53 on *a 18*).

Marietta: Mineral Co., 38 15, 118 20. *a 18.*

Marlette Lake: Washoe Co., 39 10, 119 54. *a 13.*

Martin Creek Ranger Station: Humboldt Co., 41 41, 117 32. *d.*

Marys River: Elko Co., 41 40, 115 14, S into Humboldt River at 41 04, 115 16. *b.*

Mason Valley: Lyon Co., 39 10, 119 12, S to 38 40, 119 02. *a 14, 15.*

Massacre Creek: Washoe Co., 41 32, 119 35, N into Massacre Lake at 41 38, 119 36. *a 3.*

McAfee Ranch: Esmeralda Co., 37 39, 118 03. *a 24.*

McDermitt: Humboldt Co., 42 00, 117 44, *d.*

McNett Ranch: Esmeralda Co. at 37 49, 118 10, elevation of 5600 ft., is ranch called Upper McNett Ranch, and at 37 51, 118 01, elevation of 4800 ft., is Lower McNett Ranch. *a 24.*

Meadow Creek: Nye Co., E slope Toquima Range, 38 44, 116 56, SE to 38 38, thence NE into dry lake at 38 40, 116 45. *e.*

Meadow Valley [Wash]: *see* Meadow Valley Wash. *b.*

Meadow Valley Ranger Station: Nye Co., 38 41, 116 55. *e.*

Meadow Valley Wash: 37 52, 114 18 in Lincoln Co., S to 36 41, 114 36 in Clark Co. *b.*

Mesquite: Clark Co., 36 49, 114 05. *b.*

Metropolis: Elko Co., 41 14, 115 03. *b.*

Midas: Elko Co., 41 15, 116 47. *b.*

Middle Creek: Esmeralda Co., 37 50, 118 18, E to junction with Chiatovich Creek at 37 50, 118 12. *a 24.*

Middle Stormy Spring: Nye Co., 38 29, 115 39. *c* (Hall, July 28, 1933).

Millers [Millers Wells]: Esmeralda Co., 38 08, 117 27. *a 19.*

Millett P. O.: Nye Co., 39 01, 117 11. *b.*

Milman Ranch: Nye Co. On labels of pocket gophers said to be on Moores Creek, hence near 38 52, 117 00.

Minden: Douglas Co., 38 57, 119 46. *a 16*, where named Millerville.

Mitchell Field (5 mi. SE Millett P. O.): Nye Co., 38 58, 117 07. *c* (Alexander and Kellogg, Dec. 29, 1927).

Mohawk Canyon [Mohawk Creek]: Nye Co., 38 58, 117 19, NW to junction with Reese River at 39 02, 117 25. *e.*

Monitor Range: 39 20, 116 30 in Eureka Co., S to 38 15, 116 50 in Nye Co. *b.*

Monitor Valley: Nye Co., 39 15, 116 40, S to 38 30, 116 57. *b.*

Monte Cristo Mountains: Esmeralda Co., 38 18, 117 50, S to 38 02, 117 49. *a 19.*

Montello: Elko Co., 41 16, 114 11. *b.*

Monte Spring: Lincoln Co., 37 41, 115 32. Albert F. Sander, *in litt.*, Oct. 17, 1941.

Monument Peak: Douglas Co., 38 55, 119 54. *a 16.*

Moores Creek: Nye Co., 38 49, 116 55, N and W to 38 53, 117 04. *e.*
Morgans Ranch: Mineral Co., on East Walker River, 38 33, 118 57. *a 18.*
Mormon Well: Clark Co., 36 39, 115 06. *a 28.*
Mount Grant: Mineral Co., 38 34, 118 47. *a 18.*
Mount Jefferson: Nye Co., 38 45, 116 56. *e.*
Mount Magruder: Esmeralda Co., 37 25, 117 32. *a 22.*
Mount Moriah: White Pine Co., 39 16, 114 12. *h.*
Mount Patterson: *see* Patterson Mountain.
Mount Rose: Washoe Co., 39 21, 119 55. *a 13.*
Mount Siegel: Douglas Co., 38 53, 119 30. *a 16* [Galena Peak].
Mount Sugar (= Sugar Loaf): Douglas Co., 38 51, 119 33. *a 16.*
Mountain City: Elko Co., 41 51, 115 58. *b.*
Mountain View: Elko Co., 41 02, 115 15. Borell and Ellis (1934*a*:14, 16).
Mountain Well: Churchill Co., 39 27, 118 22. *a 10.*
Muddy Creek [Muddy River]: Clark Co., 36 41, 114 36, S to junction with Virgin River at 36 28, 114 19. *g.* Shown, but unnamed on *a 29.*
Muddy River: *see* Muddy Creek.
Mud Lake: Nye Co., 37 54, 117 06. *b.*
Muriel Bee Mine: Mineral Co., 38 34, 119 01. Oral information from Donald V. Hemphill.
Mustang Mountain: Esmeralda Co., 37 53, 118 18. *a 24.*

Nay Ranch: Nye Co., 38 37, 116 42. *e.*
Needles: *see* The Needles.
New Reveille: Nye Co., 38 00, 116 12. *a 21.*
Newark Valley: White Pine Co., 39 33, 115 37, S to 39 18, 115 40. *b.*
New York Mountains: Clark Co., barely cross California boundary into Nevada at 35 25. *a 31.*
Nixon: Washoe Co., Piute Indian trading post near mouth of Truckee River, 39 50, 119 22. *g* (same as Piute Indian Agency on *a 11*).
North Fork [Humboldt River]: Elko Co., 41 35, 115 59, S to junction with East Fork of Humboldt River at 40 56, 115 32. *b.*
Nyala: Nye Co., 38 15, 115 44. *f* and *h.*

Oak Spring: Nye Co., 37 14, 116 05. *a 21.*
Oasis, in state of California: 37 29, 117 55. *a 22.*
Oasis Valley: Nye Co., 37 04, 116 41, S to 36 54, 116 46. *a 21, 27.*
Ocala: Churchill Co., 39 55, 118 44. *a 10.*
Old Fort Churchill: Lyon Co., N side Carson River, 39 18, 119 17. *g.*
Old Mill: Nye Co., 38 03, 116 19. *f.*
Old River: Churchill Co., 39 29, 118 49, E to 39 29, 118 35. *a 10.*
Omco: Mineral Co., "in the Bell Mining District . . . in the northerly end of the Cedar Mountain Range," G. L. Sanford, *in litt.*, Sept. 29, 1941.
Ophir Creek: Nye Co., 38 56, 117 19, E to about 38 56, 117 13. *a 19.*
Oreana: Pershing Co., 40 20, 118 19. *a 5.*
Osceola: White Pine Co., 39 06, 114 23. *b.*
Osobb Valley: Churchill Co., 39 35, 118 05, S to 39 10, 118 20; named Dixie Valley on recent maps. *b.*
Overland Pass (Hastings Pass): White Pine Co., 40 01, 115 35. *a 8.*
Overton: Clark Co., 36 33, 114 26. *a 29.*
Owyhee: Elko Co., 41 57, 116 04. *b.*
Owyhee River: Elko Co., 41 30, 115 47, N across Idaho boundary at 42 00, 116 10. *b.*

Pablo: Nye Co., 38 42, 117 13. *a 19.*

Pahranagat Valley: Lincoln Co., 37 35, 115 15, S to 37 12, 115 05. *b.*

Pahroc Spring: Lincoln Co., 37 40, 114 59. *b.*

Pahrum Peak: Washoe Co., 40 24, 119 35. *a 4.*

Pahrump Ranch: Nye Co., 36 12, 115 59. *a 28.*

Pahrump Valley: along California boundary in southern Nye Co., S into western Clark Co. *b.*

Painted Point: Washoe Co., 41 36, 119 41. *à 3.*

Palisade: Eureka Co., 40 37, 116 12. *b.*

Palmetto: Esmeralda Co., 37 27, 117 42. *a 22.*

Palmetto Wash: Esmeralda Co., 37 25, 117 39, NW to 37 27, 117 49. *a 22.*

Panaca: Lincoln Co., 37 48, 114 24. *a 20.*

Paradise Valley (a town): Humboldt Co., 41 30, 117 32. *b.*

Patterson Mountain (Mount Patterson): White Pine Co., 38 41, 114 42. *n.*

Peavine Ranch: Nye Co., 38 34, 117 16. *a 19.*

Penelas Mine: Nye Co., 39 05, 117 47. Oral information from Kay Beech.

Penoyer Valley (Sand Spring Valley): 37 57, 115 45 in Lincoln Co., SW to 37 35, 116 00 in Nye Co. *b.*

Peretti Ranch: Lyon Co.; said on label of a desert wood rat to be 15 mi. by road ENE of Dayton.

Peterson Creek: Lander Co., W side Shoshone Mts., 39 10, 117 29, N and W about 6 mi. into an alkali flat. *e.*

Pigeon Spring: Esmeralda Co., 37 25, 117 40. *a 22.*

Pigeon Stamp Mill: Esmeralda Co., 37 25, 117 40. *a 22.*

Pilot Peak: Elko Co., 41 01, 114 05. *f.*

Pinchot Creek: Esmeralda Co., 37 56, 118 17, NE intermittently for 5 mi. *a 24.*

Pine Creek: Eureka Co., 40 16, 116 10, N at least to 40 32, 116 09. *b.*

Pine Creek: Nye Co., on E side Toquima Range, 38 47, 116 56, E at least to Pine Creek Ranch at 38 47, 116 49. *e.*

Pine Creek Ranch: Nye Co., 38 47, 116 49. *e.*

Pine Forest Mountains: Humboldt Co., 41 55, 118 40, S to 41 30, 118 44. *b.*

Pine Grove: Mineral Co., 38 41, 119 07. *a 15.*

Pinnacles: *see* The Pinnacles.

Pioche: Lincoln Co., 37 56, 114 26. *a 20.*

Piper Peak: Esmeralda Co., 37 42, 117 55. *a 23.*

Pole Canyon: White Pine Co., on E slope Snake Range, 38 58, 114 16, NE to junction with canyon of Baker Creek at 38 59, 114 14. Another canyon of same name on W slope of same mountain range, 38 54, 114 20, W 3 mi. into Spring Valley. Pole Canyon is the name used for canyon on E slope, and Pole Canyon, W slope Snake Mts., is used to designate the canyon on the W slope. *h.*

Poney (Pony) Springs: Lincoln Co., 38 19, 114 34. *b* (at 114 37 on *l*).

Potosi Mountain: Clark Co., 35 58, 115 30. *a 31.*

Potts: Nye Co., 39 05, 116 38. *a 9.*

Potts Ranch: Nye Co., 39 05, 116 38. *a 9.*

Potts Ranger Station: Nye Co., *see* Potts.

Pyramid: Washoe Co., 39 52, 119 37. *a 12.*

Pyramid Lake: Washoe Co., 40 00, 119 35. *b.*

Queen (Station): Mineral Co., 37 56, 118 25. *a 24.*

Quinn Canyon Mountains: 38 12, 115 35 in Nye Co., S to 38 00, 115 45 in Lincoln Co. *b.*

Quinn River Crossing (Masons Crossing): Humboldt Co., 41 35, 118 26. *a 2.*

Rabbit Hole Mountains (Antelope Range on some maps, and Kamma Mts. on others): 40 52, 118 39 in Humboldt Co., S to 40 42, 118 45 in Pershing Co. Name once may have been applied to peaks called Seven Troughs Range which extends S to 40 27, 118 50. The locality name applies to specimens collected by Vernon Bailey on one of his early trips when he camped at Rabbit Hole Springs. *a 5.*

Rabbit Hole Springs: Pershing Co., 40 45, 118 45. *a 5.*

Railroad Pass: Lander Co., 39 22, 117 23. *e.*

Railroad Valley: Nye Co., 38 45, 115 33, S and W to 38 00, 116 00. *b.*

Rainbow Canyon: Lincoln Co., the part of Meadow Valley Wash from Elgin to a point 4 mi. S thereof, but name sometimes applied also to part of canyon from Elgin N for several miles. Oral information from R. M. Bond.

Rainbow Falls: Clark Co., 36 14, 115 39, about 1 mi. S of and at about the same elevation as Little Falls. Oral information from A. M. Alexander.

Raines: Eureka Co., 40 29, 116 08. *f* and *g.*

Ralston Valley: Nye Co., from the angle in the E line of Esmeralda Co. at 38 00 one arm of valley extends N to 38 25, 117 06, and another arm E and N to 38 28, 116 35. *b.*

Raspberry Creek: Pershing Co., 40 47, 117 56, W to 40 47, 118 00. *a 6.*

Rawhide, Esmeralda Co., 39 01, 118 24. *a 10.*

Red Butte: Humboldt Co., 41 11, 118 36. *f* and *g.*

Reese River: 38 46, 117 30 in Nye Co., N in interrupted fashion to Humboldt Valley at town of Battle Mountain in Lander Co. *b.*

Reglis Ranch: Eureka Co.; on label of coyote skull said to be in vicinity of Eureka.

Reno: Washoe Co., 39 32, 119 49. *a 13.*

Reveille Valley: Nye Co., 38 04, 116 20, S to 37 40, 116 15. *b.*

Rhyolite: Nye Co., 36 54, 116 50. *a 27.*

Roberts Creek Ranch: Lander Co., 39 45, 116 17. *a 9.*

Roberts Mountains: Eureka Co., 39 59, 116 12, SW to 39 45, 116 23. *a 9.*

Rock Creek: Washoe Co., E slope Granite Mtn., 40 48, 119 23, SE for 2 mi. *c* (Hall, July 10, 1936).

Rockhill: Esmeralda Co., 38 08, 117 56. *f.*

Romano (= Romano Ranch, in 1936 found to be abandoned): Eureka Co., 39 52, 116 04. *a 9.*

Roop: Washoe Co., 40 35, 119 59. *b.*

Rose Creek: Mineral Co., 38 34, 118 47, NE into Walker Lake at 38 37, 118 44. *a 18.*

Round Hole: Washoe Co., 40 19, 119 48. *g.*

Round Mound: Douglas Co., 38 59, 119 57. *a 16.*

Round Mountain: Nye Co., 38 43, 117 04. *a 19.*

Rox [Station]: Lincoln Co., 36 54, 114 40. *f.*

Royal Blue Mine: Esmeralda Co., 38 19, 117 32. Oral information from Emery F. Johnson.

Royston: Esmeralda Co., 38 19, 117 32. Oral information from Emery F. Johnson.

Ruby Lake: 40 18, 115 25 in Elko Co., S to 40 04, 115 29 in White Pine Co. *b.*

Ruby Mountains: 40 46, 115 15 in Elko Co., S to 40 01, 115 35 in White Pine Co. *b.*

Ruby Valley: 40 27, 115 18 in Elko Co., S to 40 03, 115 30 in White Pine Co. *b.*

Rye Grass Canyon: White Pine Co., 39 21, 114 17, SE to 39 20, 114 11. *h.*

Salt Spring (sometimes Salt Springs): Elko Co., 40 29, 114 03. *b.*

San Antonio: Nye Co., 38 28, 117 17. *a 19.*

Sand Harbor: Washoe Co., 39 12, 119 56. *i.*

Sand Pass: Washoe Co., 40 16, 119 48. *g.*

Sand Spring Valley [Penoyer Valley]: 37 57, 115 45 in Lincoln Co., SW to 37 35, 116 00 in Nye Co. *b.*

Sandy Point: Washoe Co., W side Lake Tahoe, 39 12, 119 56. *i*.

San Jacinto: Elko Co., 41 53, 114 40. *b*.

San Juan Creek: Nye Co., 39 05, 117 16, N to junction with Cottonwood Creek at 39 09, 117 17. *e*.

Schellbourne: White Pine Co., 39 48, 114 41. *b*.

Schellbourne Pass: White Pine Co., 38 48, 114 40. *c* (Hall, Aug. 10, 1930).

Schurz: Mineral Co., 38 57, 117 48. *a 18*.

Schurz Indian Dam [Weber Dam]: Mineral Co., 39 01, 118 52. On Walker River, 6 mi. above Schurz. Dale H. Reed, *in litt.*, Sept. 22, 1941.

Schwartz Ranch: Humboldt Co.; recorded as 1 mi. W Paradise Valley on label of a pocket gopher, *Thomomys t. bachmani*.

Scofield Canyon: Nye Co., on E slope of Quinn Canyon Range, 38 19, 115 30, E to 38 16, 115 24 in Garden Valley. *h*.

Searchlight: Clark Co., 35 28, 114 57. *b*.

Searchlight Ferry: Clark Co., in the year 1934, at 35 30, 114 40. *c* (Benson, map following p. 549, 1934).

Secret Pass: Elko Co., 40 49, 115 12. *a 7*.

Seeman Pass: Lincoln Co., 37 42, 115 15, pass leading from Coal Valley into Pahranagat Valley. *c* (Hall, May 22, 1932).

Shady Run: Churchill Co., 39 48, 118 14. *a 10*.

Sharp: Nye Co., 38 07, 115 36 (in 1933). *c* (Hall, June 4, 1932).

Sheep Mountains [Sheep Range]: 37 00, 115 05 in Lincoln Co., S to 36 27, 115 16 in Clark Co. *b*.

Shell Creek Range: White Pine Co., 39 50, 114 38, S to or beyond Lincoln Co. line. *b*.

Shingle Mountains: Lincoln Co., 38 40, 114 57, S to 38 31, 114 52. *c* (Hall, Aug. 13, 1930, visited same).

Shingle Pass: Lincoln Co., 38 33, 114 54. *l*.

Shoshone Mountains: 38 33, 117 33, N to beyond 39 20. *b*.

Shoshone P. O.: White Pine Co., 38 51, 114 24. *b*.

Silverbow: Nye Co., 37 53, 116 30. *a 21*.

Silver Creek: Lander Co., 39 38, 116 58, W to junction with Italian Creek at 39 36, 117 05. *e*.

Silver Creek: White Pine Co., 38 49, 114 53. *k*.

Silver Peak (a mining camp): Esmeralda Co., 37 45, 117 38. *a 23*.

Silver Peak Range: Esmeralda Co., 38 00, 117 55, SE to Mt. Magruder at 37 25, 117 33. *a 22*.

Silver Range (Stillwater Range): Churchill Co., 40 00, 118 05, S to 39 16, 118 22. *b*.

Skelton: Elko Co., 40 25, 115 40. *b*.

Skull Mountain: Nye Co., 36 46, 116 11. *a 27*.

Slys Ranch: Nye Co., 38 49, 117 30. *a 19*.

Smith Creek: White Pine Co., 39 21, 114 17, E across Utah boundary at 39 20. *h*.

Smith Creek Cave: White Pine Co., 39 20, 114 06, on N side of Smith Creek. *c* (D. H. Johnson, June 4, 1937, and oral information from him).

Smith Ranch: Esmeralda Co., on W side of Fish Lake at 37 45, 118 03. *c* (Hall, May 27, 1928). Shown, but unnamed on *a 24*.

Smiths Creek: Lander Co., 39 22, 117 42, E into dry lake at 39 19, 117 32. *b*.

Smiths Creek Ranch: Lander Co., on Smiths Creek at E base of Desatoya Mts., approximately 39 22, 117 36. *c* (Hall, July 23, 1934).

Smiths Creek Valley: Lander Co., 39 35, 117 28, S to 39 08, 117 40. *b*.

Smiths Valley: Lyon Co., 39 00, 119 20, S to 38 40, 119 20. *b*.

Smoke Creek: Washoe Co., from across California boundary at 40 37, SE to 40 30, 119 52. *a 4*.

Smoke Creek Desert: Washoe Co., 40 43, 119 34, S to 40 16, 119 45. *b.*

Snake Creek: White Pine Co., 38 57, 114 17, E to Utah boundary at 38 56. *h.*

Snake Mountains (Snake Range): 39 35, 114 15 in White Pine Co., S to about 38 30, 114 15 in Lincoln Co. *b.*

Snake Range: *see* Snake Mountains. *b.*

Soda Lake: Churchill Co., 39 32, 118 52. *a 10.*

Sodaville: Mineral Co., 38 21, 118 06. *a 18.*

Soldier Meadows: Humboldt Co., 41 22, 119 11. *a 3.*

Sonoma: Mineral Co., 38 26, 119 06. *a 17.*

South Furlong Creek: *see* Long Creek.

South Twin River: Nye Co. 38 48, 117 17, NE to 38 54, 117 11. *a 19.*

Spanish Springs: Washoe Co., 39 37, 119 41. *a 12.*

Spooner: Douglas Co., 39 06, 119 55. *a 13.*

Springdale: Nye Co., 37 01, 116 43. *a 21.*

Springdale Canyon: Esmeralda Co., on E slope of Lone Mountain, 38 02, 117 29, E for 2 mi. *a 19.*

Spring Mountain (Charleston Mountains): Clark Co., 36 29, 115 50, S across California boundary at 35 42, 115 33. *b.*

Spring Valley: White Pine Co., 39 38, 114 26, S to 38 50, 114 26. *b.*

Stanmoore (sometimes Stanmore) Mine: Mineral Co., 38 32, 118 50. J. J. Connelly, *in litt.*, Jan 11, 1941.

State-line Peak: Washoe Co., 40 02, 119 59. *a 4.*

Steels Creek: Elko Co., 40 55, 115 07, E for 7 mi. into dry flat. *a 7.*

Stella Lake: White Pine Co., 39 00, 114 18. *h* (Teresa Lake on map, but Stella Lake on labels of specimens).

Steptoe Creek: White Pine Co., 38 53, 114 39, W, thence N, down Steptoe Valley to 39 16, 114 51. *b.*

Steptoe Valley: White Pine Co., 40 07, 114 40, S to 38 45, 114 47. *b.*

Stewart Valley: Mineral Co., 38 33, 117 55, NW to 38 40, 118 02. *a 19, 18.*

Stillwater: Churchill Co., 39 31, 118 33. *a 10.*

Stocade Spring [s]: Esmeralda Co., 37 22, 117 37. *a 22.*

Stones Ferry [Stone Ferry]: Clark Co., 36 07, 114 24. *a 29.*

Stonewall Flat: Nye Co., center of flat near 37 35, 117 05. *a 22.*

Stonewall Mountain: Nye Co., 37 30, 117 02. *a 22.*

Stormy Spring: Nye Co., a few miles (memory [of Hall] indicates 1 and certainly not more than 10) N of Middle Stormy Spring, which see. *c* (Hall, July 28, 1933).

St. Thomas: Clark Co., 36 28, 114 21. *a 29.*

Sugar Loaf: Douglas Co., 38 51, 119 33. *a 16.*

Sulphur: Humboldt Co., 40 52, 118 44. *a 5.*

Sulphur Cow Creek: Humboldt Co., possibly is Cow Creek, now in Pershing Co., 40 35, 118 46, N to junction with Rabbit Hole Creek at 40 41, 118 42; about 15 mi. S of Sulphur. *a 5.*

Sulphur Spring Mountains: 40 35, 116 00 in Elko Co., S to 39 47, 116 07 in Eureka Co. *a 7* and *b.*

Summit Lake: Humboldt Co., 41 31, 119 04. *a 3.*

Summit Spring (sometimes Summit Springs): Lincoln Co., 37 12, 115 34. *f.*

Sunnyside: Nye Co., 38 25, 115 01. *b.*

Sutcliffe: Washoe Co., 39 57, 119 36. *g.*

Swan Lake: Washoe Co., 41 49, 119 30. *b.*

Sweetwater Range: from California boundary at 38 30, N in Mineral and Lyon counties to 39 33, 119 18. *a 15.*

Table Mountain: Humboldt Co., each of three flat-topped areas near Virgin Creek is referred to in field notes as Table Mountain. These three areas are situated at 41 55, 119 05; 41 50, 119 10; and 41 45, 119 05. Antelope mentioned from Table Mountain were taken in the second or third of these areas. *a 3.*

Taylors Canyon: Elko Co., 41 13, 116 00, NW to 41 18, 116 08. *d.*

Tecoma: Elko Co., 41 20, 114 05. *b.*

Teels Marsh: Mineral Co., 38 12, 118 22. *a 18.*

Tenabo: Lander Co., 40 18, 116 40. *b.*

Tennille Ranch: Lincoln Co., in Meadow Valley Wash, about 3 mi., by road, S Caliente, and extending, along road, for 4 or more mi. S. Field observation, Hall, June 18, 1931.

Teresa Lake: White Pine Co., 39 00, 114 18. *h.*

The Crossing: Esmeralda Co., 37 52, 117 58. *a 23.*

The Needles [The Pinnacles]: Washoe Co., 40 08, 119 41. *a 4.*

The Pinnacles: *see* The Needles.

The Pyramid: Washoe Co., a rock formation in Pyramid Lake near E shore, 39 59, 119 30. *a 11, 12.*

30-mile Spring: White Pine Co., 39 33, 115 06. *n.*

Thorp (or Thorps) Mill: Nye Co., 37 13, 117 06. *a 22.*

Thousand Creek: Humboldt Co., 41 53, 119 01, E to 41 52, 118 45. *a 3, 2.*

Three Lakes: Elko Co., 40 35, 115 25. *a 7* (Borell and Ellis, 1934*a*:14).

Timber Lake: Churchill Co., in Carson Sink. Osgood (1909:93) gives "Carson Sink, near Timber Lake."

Timber Mountain: Nye Co., 37 05, 116 28. *a 21.*

Timpahute Mountains [Timpahute Range]: Lincoln Co., 37 42, 115 30, SW to 37 20, 115 56. *b.*

Toby Canyon: Churchill Co., estimated at 2 mi. NW of temporary camp at 7100 ft. on Smiths Creek. *c.* "Second canyon to the north of Smith Creek" (Ward C. Russell, p. 726, July 23, 1934). If estimate is correct, position is 39 24, 117 41.

Tonkin: Eureka Co., 39 56, 116 25. *a 9.*

Tonopah: Nye Co., 38 04, 117 14. *a 19.*

Topaz Lake: Douglas Co., 38 40, 119 31. *f* and *g.*

Toquima Peak: Nye Co., 38 40, 116 58. *e.*

Toquima Range: 39 15, 116 48 in Lander Co., S to 38 35, 117 04 in Nye Co. *b.*

Toulon: Pershing Co., 40 04, 118 38. *a 5.*

Toyabe Mountains: *see* Toyabe Range.

Toyabe Range: 40 00, 116 42 in Lander Co., S to 38 32, 117 20 in Nye Co. *b.*

Toyn Creek: Elko Co., 40 20, 115 31, NW to junction with Corral Creek at 40 21, 115 37. *a 8.*

Treasury Lake: White Pine Co., 38 57, 114 17. *h.*

Tregaskis Well: Humboldt Co., 41 26, 118 17. *c* (Taylor, 1909, sketch map in notebook).

Trout Canyon: Clark Co., 36 13, 115 41, S and W into Pahrump Valley at about 36 08, 115 46. *a 28.*

Trout Creek Ranch: Humboldt Co., on the creek which extends from 41 17, 118 29, SE to 41 10, 118 23. *a 2.*

Troy Creek: Nye Co., 38 20, 115 30, NW to 38 23, 115 38. *h.*

Truckee Canal: 39 34, 119 28 in Storey Co., SE into Lahontan Reservoir at 39 28, 119 04. *a 11* and *f.*

Truckee Canyon: 39 31, 119 41, E to 39 36, 119 22. *a 12, 11.*

Truckee Meadows: Washoe Co., 39 33, 119 44, S to 39 23, 119 44. *a 12, 13.*

Truckee River: from across California boundary at 39 28, E and N through Washoe Co. into Pyramid Lake. *a 12, 11.*

Tulle Peak: Nye Co., 38 50, 116 30. *e* [Tulle Mtn.].

Tuscarora: Elko Co., 41 19, 116 14. *b.*

12-mile Creek: Washoe Co., from Oregon boundary at 119 59, E 1½ mi., thence into Oregon near 119 57. *a 3.*

21-mile Ranch: Elko Co.; on label of badger skull said to be in vicinity of Montello.

Twin Peak: Humboldt Co., 41 59, 119 00. *b.*

Twin Spring: Nye Co., 38 13, 116 11. *b.*

Twin Springs: Nye Co., 38 34, 115 43. *f.*

Tybo: Nye Co., 38 23, 116 23. *b.*

Union: Eureka Co., 40 10, 116 02. *f.*

Unionville: Pershing Co., 40 27, 118 08. *a 5.*

Ursine: Lincoln Co., 37 58, 114 14. *b.*

Valcalda Spring: Esmeralda Co., 37 46, 117 47. *a 23.*

Valley of Fire: Clark Co., 36 26, 114 30. *f.*

Vegas Valley: Clark Co., 36 28, 115 25, SE to 36 03, 114 58. *b.*

Vegas Wash: *see* Las Vegas Wash.

Verdi: Washoe Co., 39 31, 119 59. *a 12.*

Vernon: Pershing Co., 40 26, 118 47. *a 5.*

Virginia City: Storey Co., 39 19, 119 39. *a 13.*

Virginia Mountains: Washoe Co., 40 08, 119 49, S to 39 40, 119 36. *b.*

Virgin Ranch: Humboldt Co.; an antelope labeled as having been obtained 4 mi. SE Virgin Ranch, Virgin Valley, gives basis for locating the ranch as at about 41 51, 119 02.

Virgin River: Clark Co., from across Arizona boundary at 36 50, SW to junction with Colorado River at 36 09, 114 22. *a 29.*

Virgin Valley: Humboldt Co., a small valley about 8 mi. wide, centering near 41 51, 119 03. *a 3.*

Vya: Washoe Co., 41 35, 119 51. *g.*

Wabuska: Lyon Co., 39 09, 119 13. *b.*

Wadsworth: Lyon Co., 39 38, 119 17. *a 11.*

Wahmonie: Nye Co., 36 49, 116 09. *g.*

Walker Lake: Mineral Co., 38 54, 118 47, S to 38 34, 118 40. *a 18.*

Walker River: from junction of West Walker River and East Walker River at 38 54, 119 11 in Lyon Co., N and then S into N end Walker Lake at 38 54, 118 47 in Mineral Co. *a 15, 14, 10, 18.*

Washington Creek: Lander Co., 39 10, 117 11, SW into Nye Co., thence back into Lander Co. to junction with Reese River at 39 12, 117 20. *e.*

Washoe: Washoe Co., 39 20, 119 48. *a 13.*

Washoe City: Washoe Co., 39 20, 119 48. *a 13*, where designated as Washoe.

Washoe Lake: Washoe Co., 39 15, 119 47. *a 13.*

Water Canyon: White Pine Co., 39 00, 114 53, SW into valley near Lund at 38 52, 115 01. *h.*

Weeks: Lyon Co., 39 17, 119 17. J. R. Alcorn, *in litt.*, March 3, 1941.

Wellington: Lyon Co., 38 44, 119 23. *b.*

Wells: Elko Co., 41 08, 114 59. *b.*

Wendover: Elko Co., 40 44, 114 03. *f.*

West Walker River: from across California boundary at 38 39, NE through Douglas Co., to junction in Lyon Co. with East Walker River at 38 54, 119 11. *a 15.*

Wheelbarrow Peak: Nye Co., in Belted Range, 37 27, 116 05. *a 21.*

Wheeler Creek: Humboldt Co., 41 52, 118 27, S to Quinn River Crossing. *a 2.*

Wheeler Peak: White Pine Co., 38 59, 114 19. *b.*

Wheeler Well: Clark Co., 36 23, 115 50. *a 28*.

White Mountains: from across California boundary, N in Esmeralda Co. to near 37 50. *b*.

White River: 38 58, 115 25 in White Pine Co., E and S interruptedly to 38 10, 115 05 in Nye Co. *b*.

White River Valley: 38 58, 115 25 in White Pine Co., E and S to 38 15, 115 15 in Nye Co. *b*.

Whiterock: Elko Co., 41 45, 116 11. *b*.

White Rock Mountain: Nye Co., 39 04, 116 48. *a 9*.

Whiterock Spring: Nye Co., 37 12, 116 08. *a 21*.

White Sage Valley: White Pine Co., 39 29, 115 14, S to 39 04, 115 15. *b*.

Wichman: Mineral Co., 38 34, 118 57. *b*. In recent years a change in county boundary places Wichman in Lyon County (see page 11).

Wildhorse Valley: Nye Co., name applied by Nelson (1925:40) to the part of Ralston Valley adjoining Wildhorse Spring, which spring is at 37 44, 117 05. *a 22*.

Willard Creek: White Pine Co., W slope Snake Range, 39 01, 114 20, W 3 or 4 mi. into Spring Valley. *h*.

Williams Ranch: White Pine Co., 38 58, 115 11. *h*.

Willow Beach, in state of Arizona: 35 52, 114 40. *g*.

Willow Creek: Clark Co., 36 25, 115 48. *a 28*.

Willow Creek: White Pine Co., 40 06, 115 37, W to junction with Sestonovich Creek at 40 06, 115 44. *d*.

Willow Creek Ranch: Humboldt Co., ranch on Willow Creek, which creek extends from 41 16, 118 24, SE to 41 12, 118 21. *a 2*.

Willow Point: Humboldt Co., 41 15, 117 35. *b*.

Wilson Canyon: Lyon Co., on West Walker River, 38 50, 119 16, E to 39 50, 119 11. Unnamed on *a 15*.

Wilson Canyon: Nye Co., 39 03, 116 48, W, N, then NE to 39 08, 116 41. *a 9*.

Wilson Creek: Lincoln Co., 38 16, 114 22, NW to 38 23, 114 29. *l*.

Wilson Creek: Nye Co., 39 03, 116 48, W, N, then NE to 39 08, 117 41. *a 9*.

Wilson Creek Mountains: Lincoln Co., 38 28, 114 20, SE to 38 01, 114 15. *l*. Cedar Range on some maps.

Wilson Peak (Mount Wilson): Lincoln Co., 38 15, 114 24. *l*.

Wilson Ranch: Lyon Co., 38 50, 119 11. *f*.

Winnemucca: Humboldt Co., 40 59, 117 45. *b*.

Winters Mine: Douglas Co., 38 52, 119 28. George L. Sanford, *in litt.*, Sept. 23, 1941.

Winzell: Eureka Co., 40 06, 116 19. *g*.

Wiregrass [Wire] Spring: Clark Co., 36 37, 115 15. *m*.

Wisconsin Creek: Nye Co., 38 58, 117 17, ESE to 38 57, 117 15. *a 19*.

Yerington: Lyon Co., on Walker River, 38 59, 119 10. *a 15*.

Zephyr Cove: Douglas Co., E side Lake Tahoe, 39 00, 119 57. *a 13*.

MAPS AND OTHER SOURCES OF INFORMATION USED IN DEFINING THE POSITIONS OF PLACES NAMED IN THE GAZETTEER

a Topographic maps (quadrangles here used are either one degree or one-half degree in linear dimensions), U. S. Dept. Interior, U. S. Geol. Survey, Washington, D. C. (listed below from N to S in same order as sections are numbered in a township). For each quadrangle (sheet, on the older maps) the longitude and latitude of the right lower corner is given. If the map is one which gives only ½ of a degree in linear dimensions, the fraction ¼ is added to distinguish it from a map which covers all four quarters of a quadrangle.

1. Paradise sheet, edition of Nov. 1893, reprinted March 1903. 41 00, 117 00.
2. Disaster sheet, ed. Nov. 1893, reprinted Jan. 1909. 41 00, 118 00.
3. Long Valley sheet, ed. Feb. 1894, reprinted 1920. 41 00, 119 00.
4. Granite Range sheet, ed. Jan. 1894, reprinted Sept. 1908. 40 00, 119 00.
5. Lovelock quadrangle, ed. 1935. 40 00, 118 00.
6. Sonoma Range quadrangle, advanced sheet subject to correction, surveyed in 1931 and 1932. 40 00, 117 00.
7. Halleck quadrangle, ed. 1935. 40 30, 115 00. ¼.
8. Jiggs quadrangle, ed. 1937. 40 00, 115 30. ¼.
9. Roberts Mountains quadrangle, ed. 1929. 39 00, 116 00.
10. Carson Sink quadrangle, ed. May 1910. 39 00, 118 00.
11. Wadsworth sheet, ed. Sept. 1894, reprinted 1906. 39 30, 119 00. ¼.
12. Reno sheet, ed. Dec. 1893, reprinted Oct. 1912. 39 30, 119 30. ¼.
13. Carson sheet, ed. Nov. 1893, reprinted Aug. 1904. 39 00, 119 30. ¼.
14. Wabuska sheet, ed. Sept. 1894, reprinted Nov. 1906. 39 00, 119 00. ¼.
15. Wellington sheet, ed. Nov. 1893, reprinted Jan. 1899. 38 30, 119 00. ¼.
16. Markleville sheet, ed. Nov. 1893, reprinted 1916. 38 30, 119 30. ¼.
17. Bridgeport quadrangle, ed. Dec. 1911. 38 00, 119 00. ¼.
18. Hawthorne quadrangle, May 1911. 38 00, 118 00.
19. Tonopah quadrangle, ed. June 1908, reprinted 1922. 38 00, 117 00.
20. Pioche sheet, ed. Dec. 1885, reprinted Dec. 1914. 37 00, 114 00.
21. Kawich quadrangle, ed. June 1908, 37 00, 116 00.
22. Lida quadrangle, ed. Oct. 1913. 37 00, 117 00.
23. Silverpeak (included in Lida sheet) ed. June 1900, reprinted Dec. 1906. 37 30, 117 30. ¼.
24. White Mountain quadrangle, ed. 1917, reprinted 1926. 37 30, 118 00. ¼.
25. Mt. Morrison quadrangle, ed. June 1914. 37 30, 118 30. ¼.
26. Ballarat quadrangle, ed. March 1908. 36 00, 117 00.
27. Furnace Creek quadrangle, ed. April 1910, reprinted 1920. 36 00, 116 00.
28. Las Vegas quadrangle, ed. March 1908. 36 00, 115 00.
29. St. Thomas sheet, ed. April 1886, reprinted March 1908. 36 00, 114 00.
30. Camp Mohave sheet, ed. March 1892, reprinted Aug. 1905. 35 00, 114 00.
31. Ivanpah quadrangle, ed. June 1912. 35 00, 115 00.

b State of Nevada. Gen. Land Office, U. S. Dept. Interior, Washington, D. C., 1914. Scale 12 miles to the inch.

c "Field notes, Museum of Vertebrate Zoölogy" are kept by all regular staff members engaged in field work and are filed alphabetically by author and under author chronologically.

d Humboldt National Forest, Nevada. Mt. Diablo Meridian. 1929. Scale 4 miles to the inch. Compiled at Washington Office, 1928, by H. S. Meekham. Traced by F. E. Sizer. U. S. Dept. Agriculture, Forest Service. Includes Ruby, Humboldt, and Santa Rosa divisions of the Humboldt National Forest.

e Toyabe National Forest, Nevada. Mt. Diablo Meridian. 1928. Scale 4 miles to the inch. Compiled at District Office by C. J. Truscott. Traced by G. L. Nichols. U. S. Dept. Agriculture, Forest Service.

f Automobile road map of the State of Nevada. Map service of the Automobile Club of Southern California, 2601 South Figueroa Street, Los Angeles. Scale 16 miles to the inch. Received in 1936.

g Shell official road map, Nevada and Utah. Scale 30 miles to inch. Distributed by Shell Oil Company at its gasoline filling stations. Undated, but includes "radio log . . . in effect as of July 1, 1937."

h Nevada National Forest, Nevada. Mt. Diablo Meridian. 1937. Scale 4 miles to the inch. Includes Snake Range, Shell Creek Range, Egan Range, White Pine Range, with intervening valleys, and Quinn Canyon Range, and Charleston Peak, each with adjoining territory.

i Tahoe National Forest, California and Nevada. Mt. Diablo Meridian. 1930. Scale 4 miles to the inch. Compiled at District Office, San Francisco, 1929, by H. A. Sedelmeyer. Traced by A. [L. ?] Bell. U. S. Dept. Agriculture, Forest Service.

j Nevada National Forest. Mt. Diablo Meridian. 1919. Scale 4 miles to the inch. Compiled at District Office, Ogden, 1918, by O. C. Lockhart. Traced by C. B. Noyes. U. S. Dept. Agriculture, Forest Service.

k White Pine County, Nevada, 1930, revised. Scale 4 miles to the inch. Compiled from personal surveys, records, and other reliable sources by Ed. Millard & Son, Ely, Nevada.

l Lincoln County, Nevada [received Dec. 27, 1939, freshly printed]. Scale 4 miles to the inch. Supervision, although not so stated, of preparation by Dr. Richard M. Bond. U. S. Dept. Agriculture, Soil Conservation Service.

m Desert Game Range, Clark and Lincoln counties, Nevada. Jan. 6, 1940. Scale 4 miles to the inch. Prepared at Desert Game Range by Joseph C. Allen, of the Fish and Wildlife Service, U. S. Dept. Interior.

n White Pine Division of Nevada National Forest. March 1924. Scale 1 mile to the inch. Compiled by [Mud] Townsend. Traced by Corn.

o Nevada precipitation map. Scale 50 miles to the inch. From map prepared by Nevada Agric. Exp. Station. 1936.

GLOSSARY

abdominal, *adj.*—Of or pertaining to that part of the body (excepting the back) between the thorax and the pelvis.

alisphenoid, *adj. & n.*—Pertaining to or designating the right or left bone in front of the squamosal bone and behind the orbitosphenoid bone. See figure 479.

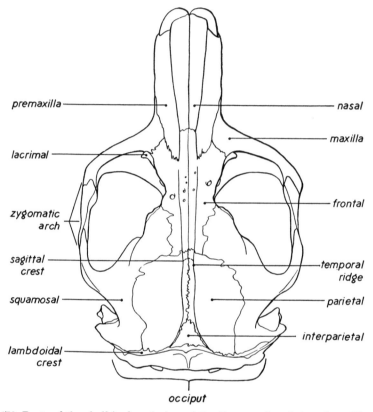

premaxilla — nasal

maxilla

lacrimal

frontal

zygomatic arch

sagittal crest — temporal ridge

squamosal — parietal

interparietal

lambdoidal crest

occiput

Fig. 476. Parts of the skull in dorsal view of the Townsend pocket gopher, *Thomomys townsendii nevadensis*, from Malloy Ranch, 5 miles west Austin, no. 37073, ♂. ×2.

alveolus (plural, alveoli), *n.*—A small cavity or pit, as a socket for a tooth.

angular process, *n.*—In lower jaw, posteroventral process below the articular process. See figure 481.

ankylose (anchylose), *v.t.*—To unite, consolidate, and become immovable; said of bones that grow together.

anterior, *adj.*—Before, or toward the front, in place—opposed to posterior.

anterior nares (singular, naris), *n.*—Opening out of the skull, of the nasal cavities. See figure 482.

anterior palatine foramina (singular, foramen), *n.*—The incisive foramina, openings through the bony roof of the mouth at the juncture of the premaxillary and maxillary bones. See figure 477.

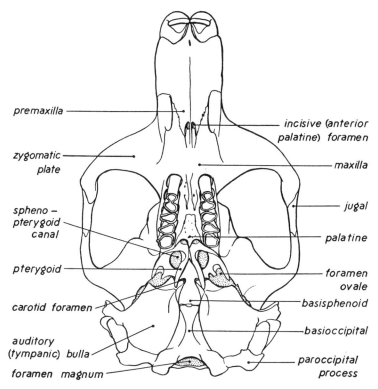

Fig. 477. Parts of the skull in ventral view of the Townsend pocket gopher. ×2. (Same specimen shown in fig. 476.)

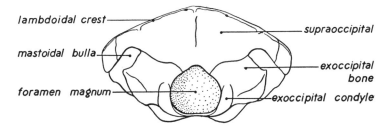

Fig. 478. Posterior view of occiput of the Townsend pocket gopher. × 2. (Same specimen shown in fig. 476.)

antorbital (process) projection.—Forward extended arm of the supraorbital process of the frontal bone in rabbits. See figure 484.

arboreal, *adj.*—Inhabiting or frequenting trees—contrasted with fossorial, aquatic, and cursorial.

auditory bulla (plural, bullae), *n.*—A hollow, bony prominence of rounded form (usually formed of the tympanic bone) partly enclosing structures of the middle and inner ear. See figure 477.

audital bullae.—See auditory bulla.

auditory meatus.—As here used, refers to the external auditory meatus which is the opening leading from the external ear to the eardrum (tympanic membrane). See figure 479.

baculum (plural, bacula), *n.*—The os penis or bone in the penis (male copulatory organ) of mammals of the orders Carnivora, Pinnipedia, and many kinds of Rodentia.

basal length.—Distance on skull from the anteriormost inferior border of the foramen magnum to a line connecting the anteriormost parts of the premaxillary bones. See figure 483.

basilar length.—Distance on skull from the anteriormost inferior border of the foramen magnum to a line connecting the posteriormost margins of the alveoli of the first upper incisors. See figure 483.

basioccipital, *adj. & n.*—Pertaining to or designating the bone (unpaired) immediately in front of the foramen magnum. See figure 477.

basisphenoid, *adj. & n.*—Pertaining to or designating the bone (unpaired) immediately in front of the basioccipital bone. See figures 477, 480.

bicolor, *adj.*—Of two colors.

brachyodont, *adj.*—Having teeth with low, shallow crowns and well-developed roots—opposed to hypsodont.

brain case, *n.*—The part of the skull enclosing the brain.

buccal, *adj.*—Of or pertaining to the cheeks. When applied to the cusps of the teeth, the opposite is lingual.

bulla (plural, bullae), *n.*—A hollow prominence of rounded form, as the auditory bulla of the skull.

calcar, *n.*—In bats, a process connected with the calcaneum, helping to support the uropatagium between the leg and tail.

canal, *n.*—A passage, often tubular, through some part of the body, which provides passage for something which ordinarily is not a part of the structure, organ, or part pierced by the canal.

canine, *adj. & n.*—Of, pertaining to, or designating the tooth next to the incisors in mammals. See figure 483. Of or pertaining to dogs or to the family Canidae.

carnassial, *adj. & n.*—Pertaining to or designating certain teeth in mammals of the order Carnivora, usually adapted for cutting. In these mammals the last premolar in each upper jaw and first true molar in each lower jaw is a carnassial tooth. See figure 483.

carnivorous, *adj.*—Eating flesh; preying or feeding on animals—opposed to herbivorous.

carotid foramen.—The foramen transmitting the internal carotid artery; in many rodents the artery lies in merely a groove on the medial wall of the tympanic bulla; the medial wall of the groove is formed by the basioccipital and basisphenoid bones. See figure 477.

carpal, *adj. & n.*—Of or pertaining to the carpus or wrist; carpal bone.

caudal, *adj.*—Of, pertaining to, or like a tail, situated in or near or directed toward the tail or hind end of the animal.

cheek teeth.—Teeth behind the canines.

cingulum, *n.*—A band or girdle, or structure likened to a girdle, as a ridge on the base of a tooth about the crown. See figure 485.

conch (plural, concha), *n.*—Any of various anatomical structures shaped like a shell, as the entire external ear.

condyle, *n.*—An articular prominence on a bone.

condylobasal length.—Least distance on skull from a line connecting the posteriormost projections of the exoccipital condyles to a line connecting the anteriormost projections of the premaxillary bones. See figure 483.

coronoid process.—The upward projecting process of the posterior part of the lower mandible, giving attachment on its outward side to the masseter muscle and on its inner side to the temporal muscle. See figure 481.

Cowpers gland.—A gland (paired) discharging into the male urethra.

cranial, *adj.*—Of or pertaining to the skull.

cranium, *n.*—The skull without the lower jaws, in a more restricted sense the part of the skull which encloses the brain, and in a more general sense the skull with lower jaws.

crepuscular, *adj.*—Of, pertaining to, or like twilight; active in the twilight, as certain bats.

cusp, *n.*—A point, especially on the crown of a tooth.

cusplet, *n.*—A diminutive cusp at the side, front, or back of a cusp, especially of the crown of a tooth.

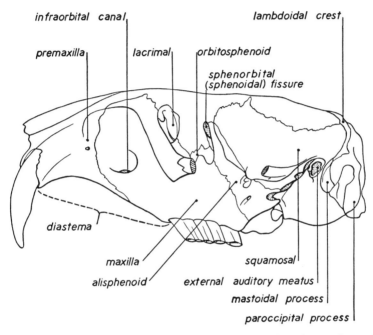

Fig. 479. Lateral view of left side of skull of the Townsend pocket gopher. × 2. (Same specimen shown in fig. 476.)

deciduous, *adj.*—Falling off, or shed, or falling out at maturity, at certain seasons, or at certain ages, as antlers of deer, hair of mammals, or first (milk) set of teeth of most kinds of mammals.

dental formula (plural, formulae).—A brief method for expressing the number and kind of teeth of mammals. The abbreviations i. (incisor), c. (canine), p. or pm. (premolar), and m. (molar) indicate the kinds in the permanent dentition, and the number in each jaw is written like a fraction, the figures above the horizontal line showing the number in the upper jaw, and those below, the number in the lower jaw. The dental formula of an adult weasel from Nevada is i. $\frac{3}{3}$, c. $\frac{1}{1}$, p. $\frac{3}{3}$, m. $\frac{1}{2}$.

dentine, *n.*—A calcareous material harder and denser than bone which composes the principal mass of a tooth.

dentition, *n.*—The teeth of an animal considered collectively.

deuterocone, *n.*—One of the cusps of a premolar tooth of a mammal corresponding in position to the protocone of a true molar. See figure 485.

diastema, *n.*—A vacant space or gap between teeth in a jaw. See figure 479.

diurnal, *adj.*—Active by day—opposed to nocturnal.

dorsal, *adj.*—Pertaining to or situated near or on the back or dorsum of a mammal—opposed to ventral.

enamel, *n.*—Of teeth, the hardest substance of the mammalian body, which forms a thin layer that caps or partly covers the teeth.

entepicondylar foramen.—A foramen near the distal end of the humerus (upper arm bone) above the median epicondyle; present in some kinds of mammals.

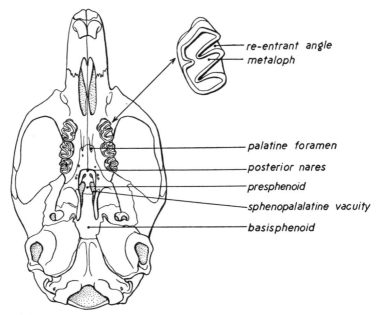

Fig. 480. Parts of the skull in ventral view of the desert wood rat, *Neotoma lepida lepida.* Different view of skull shown in figs. 363–365. ×2.

entoconid, *n.*—The principal posterointernal cusp of the talonid (heel) of a lower molar tooth. See figure 485.

exoccipital, *adj. & n.*—Pertaining to or designating the right or left bone on the side of the foramen magnum at the back of the cranium. See figure 478.

fanglomerate, *n.*—Relatively unworn material in an alluvial fan, extensive amounts of which occur in alluvial fans in deserts. The term is sometimes applied exclusively to desert situations.

feces (singular and plural), *n.*—Intestinal excrement.

femur (plural, femora), *n.*—The proximal bone of the leg of the hind limb.

fibula, *n.*—The outer and usually the smaller of the two bones of the hind limb (or leg) below the knee.

fimbriated, *adj.*—Having a fringed border, as the sides of the hind foot of a water shrew which have a growth of stiff hairs that enlarges the propulsive surface of the hind foot.

foramen (plural, foramina), *n.*—A small orifice, opening, or perforation.

foramen magnum.—The large opening in the back of the skull through which the spinal cord passes to become the medulla oblongata of the brain. See figures 477, 478, 483.

foramen ovale.—An opening in the alisphenoid bone transmitting the third or mandibular branch of the fifth cranial or trigeminal nerve. See figure 477.

fossa (plural, fossae).—A pit, cavity, or depression, as the glenoid fossa into which the articular condyle of the lower jaw fits.

fossorial, *adj.*—Fitted for digging.

frontal, *adj. & n.*—Pertaining to or designating the bone (paired) immediately in front of the parietal bone and behind the nasal. See figure 476.

frontal sinus.—The air space between the tables of the frontal bone above the orbit on each side of the cranium.

genitalia, *n.*—The external sexual organs.

glenoid fossa.—The fossa (depression) which accommodates the articular condyle of the lower jaw. See figure 483.

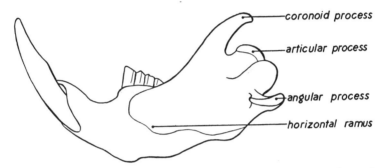

coronoid process
articular process
angular process
horizontal ramus

Fig. 481. Parts of the left lower jaw in lateral view of the Townsend pocket gopher. ×2. (Same specimen shown in fig. 476.)

guard hairs.—The stiffer, longer hairs which grow up through the limber, shorter hairs (fur) of a mammal's pelage.

hamular process.—A hooklike process, as the hamular process of the lacrimal bone.

heterodont, *adj.*—Having the teeth differentiated into incisors, canines, premolars, and molars.

hyoid, *adj. & n.*—Designating or pertaining to a bone or several connected bones situated at the base of the tongue.

hypoconid, *n.*—The principal posteroexternal cusp of the talonid (heel) of a lower molar tooth. See figure 485.

hypsodont, *adj.*—Having teeth with high or deep crowns and short roots, as in the molar teeth of meadow mice—opposed to brachydont.

incisive foramen.—The anterior palatine foramina, of which there are two in the bony roof of the anterior part of the cavity of the mouth at the juncture of the premaxillary and maxillary bones, transmit the nasal branches of the palatine arteries and the naso-palatine ducts of Jacobson. See figure 477.

incisor, *adj. & n.*—Pertaining to or designating one of the teeth in front of the canine tooth; those in the upper jaw invariably are in the premaxillary bone. See figure 483.

infraorbital, *adj.*—Designating a canal through the maxillary bone from the orbit to the face, the foramen by which the canal opens on the face of the bone, or the structures which the canal conducts.

infraorbital foramen.—The opening, on the facial side of the maxillary bone, of the infraorbital canal. The canal pierces the maxillary bone and opens on the face of the skull and into the anterior wall of the orbit, transmitting the infraorbital nerve and blood vessels. See figure 479 for infraorbital canal.

inguinal, *adj.*—Pertaining to or in the region of the groin.

insectivorous, *adj.*—Eating insects; preying or feeding on insects.

interfemoral membrane.—The fold of skin in a bat stretching from hind legs to tail.

interorbital constriction.—The least distance across the top of the skull between the orbits (eye sockets). See figure 482.

interparietal, *adj. & n.*—Pertaining to or designating the bone (rarely paired) immediately in front of the supraoccipital bone and between the two parietal or temporal bones. See figure 476.

jugal, *adj. & n.*—Pertaining to or designating the bone in the zygomatic arch which lies between the maxillary and squamosal. See figure 477.

labial, *adj.*—Of or pertaining to the lips. When applied to cusps of the teeth, the opposite of lingual.

lacrimal bone.—The bone pierced by the lacrimal duct (tear duct) between the frontal bone and maxillary bone at the anterior end of the orbit. See figures 476, 479.

lambdoidal, *adj.*—Of or pertaining to the suture and sometimes crest where the occipital bones join the parietal and squamosal bones. See figures 476, 478, 479 for lambdoidal crest.

length of tooth rows.—Measurement parallel to long axis of cranium of over-all length of rows of upper teeth. See figure 483.

lingual, *adj.*—Of or pertaining to the tongue. When applied to cusps of teeth, the opposite of buccal.

loph, *n.*—A combining form used as the terminal part of certain words and denoting the ridges (or areas) composed of several cusps and styles on the occlusal face of a tooth, as protoloph. See metaloph in figure 480.

lyrate, *adj.*—Shaped like a lyre.

M1.—Designation of the front true molar of the permanent dentition in the upper jaw of a mammal. See figure 485.

m1.—Designation of the front true molar of the permanent dentition in the lower jaw of a mammal. See figure 485.

mammae (singular, mamma), *n.*—The glandular organs for secreting milk, characteristic of all mammals.

mandible, *n.*—In mammals, the dentary bone comprising either the right or left half of the lower jaw.

mastoid, *adj. & n.*—Designating or pertaining to the mastoid bone (paired) or its process. This bone is bounded by the squamosal bone, exoccipital bone, and tympanic bone. See figures 478, 479.

mastoidal breadth.—Greatest distance across mastoid bones perpendicular to long axis of skull. See figure 482.

maxilla (plural, maxillae), *n.*—The bone (paired) which bears the molars and premolar teeth. See figures 476, 477, 479.

maxillary breadth.—Width of skull from some designated place on the lateral face of the right maxilla to the corresponding point on the left maxilla. In shrews, across the ends of the zygomatic processes of the maxillae.

meatus, *n.*—A natural passage or canal or the opening of such a passage, as the external auditory meatus. See figure 479.

metacarpal, *adj. & n.*—Of or pertaining to the metacarpus. The five bones between the wrist and the fingers of five-fingered animals are metacarpal bones.

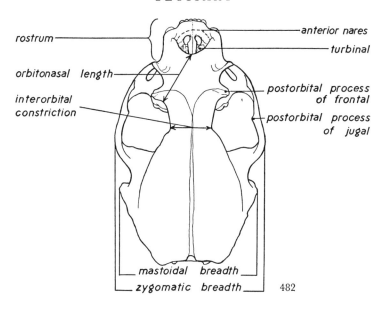

rostrum

anterior nares

turbinal

orbitonasal length

postorbital process of frontal

interorbital constriction

postorbital process of jugal

mastoidal breadth

zygomatic breadth

482

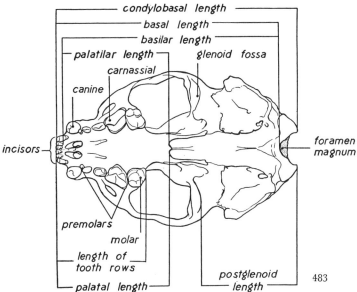

condylobasal length

basal length

basilar length

palatilar length

glenoid fossa

carnassial

canine

incisors

foramen magnum

premolars

molar

length of tooth rows

palatal length

postglenoid length

483

Figs. 482, 483. Parts of the skull of the river otter, *Lutra canadensis*, and points, or parallels, as the measurement may require, between which cranial measurements were taken. × ½. (Same specimen shown in figs. 130–133.)

Fig. 482. Dorsal view.　　　　　　Fig. 483. Ventral view.

metaconid, *n*.—The posterointernal cusp of a mammalian lower molar. See figure 485.

metaconule, *n*.—The posterior intermediate cusp of a mammalian upper molar between the hypocone and the metacone.

middorsal, *adj*.—Of or pertaining to something along the middle of the top of the back, as a middorsal stripe extending from the head to the tail.

molar, *adj. & n*.—One of the posterior teeth (three on each side in upper jaw and in lower jaw in coyote, making twelve in all) not preceded by deciduous teeth. See figure 483.

molariform, *adj*.—Of or pertaining to teeth the form of which is like that of a molar, as the molars and premolars when the latter are like molars in form.

nares, *n*.—The openings of the nose. See posterior nares, figure 480, and anterior nares, figure 482.

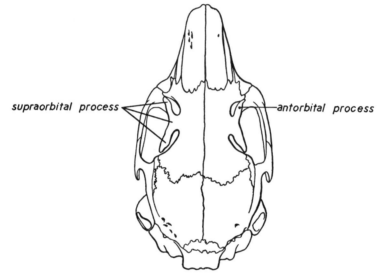

supraorbital process   antorbital process

Fig. 484. Parts of the skull of the pigmy rabbit. × 1½. (Same specimen shown in figs. 443, 444.)

nasal, *adj. & n*.—Of or pertaining to the nose, as a nasal bone (paired) on the dorsal surface of the skull at its anterior end. See figure 476.

nocturnal, *adj*.—Active by night—opposed to diurnal.

nomen nudem.—Literally, a "nude name," applied to scientific zoölogical names of kinds of animals when at the time the name was coined or first proposed there was no recognizable description accompanying the name.

oblately, *adv*.—Flattened or depressed at the poles, as an oblate spheroid.

occiput, *n*.—The back part of the head or skull. In the skull, made up of the posterior aspect of the four occipital bones which surround the foramen magnum. See figure 476.

occlusal, *adj*.—Of or pertaining to the grinding or biting (occluding) surface of a tooth.

omnivorous, *adj*.—Eating both animal and vegetable food.

operculum, *n*.—A lid or covering flap in animals and plants.

orbit, *n*.—The eye socket of the skull.

orbitonasal length.—Distance on anterior part of skull from posterior margin of base of postorbital process of frontal bone to posteriormost part of anterior border of nasal bone on same side of skull. See figure 482.

os penis.—The bone in the penis (male copulatory organ) of mammals of the orders Carnivora, Pinnipedia, and many kinds of the order Rodentia.

P4.—Designation of the last premolar in the upper jaw of a mammal; lies next to the first molar. See figure 485.

p4.—Designation of the last premolar in the lower jaw of a mammal; lies next to the first molar. See figure 485.

palatal length.—Distance on the skull from the anteriormost point on the posterior border of the palate (palatine bones) to a line connecting the anteriormost parts of the premaxillary bones. See figure 483.

palate, n.—Designates, in the present work, the bony roof of the mouth comprised of the two palatine bones, two maxillary bones, and two premaxillary bones.

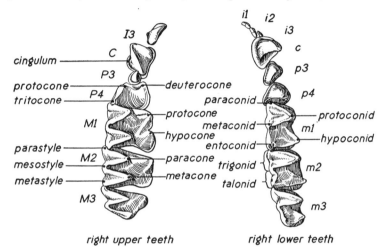

right upper teeth   right lower teeth

Fig. 485. Occlusal views of teeth of Mexican free-tailed bat, *Tadarida mexicana*, showing names applied to parts. × 7½. (Same specimen shown in fig. 69.)

palatilar length.—Distance on skull from the anteriormost point on the posterior border of the palate (palatine bones) to a line connecting the posteriormost margins of the alveoli of the first upper incisors. See figure 483.

parastyle, n.—The small cusp, on the anterolateral crown of an upper molar, in front of the paracone, as in a ground squirrel. See figure 485.

parietal, adj. & n.—Pertaining to or designating the parietal bone (paired) roofing the brain case. This bone is behind the frontal bone and in front of the occipital bones. See figure 476.

paroccipital, adj.—Pertaining to the ventrally projecting process on each exoccipital bone. See figures 477, 479.

pectoral, adj.—Of, pertaining to, situated, or occurring in or on the chest.

pelage, n.—The covering or coat of a mammal, as of hair, fur, or wool.

penicillate, adj.—Ending in a tuft of fine hairs, as the tail of a kangaroo rat.

phalanges (singular, phalanx), n.—The bones of the fingers and toes distal to the metacarpals and metatarsals.

phlanax (plural, phalanges), n.—A bone in a finger distal to the metacarpus or a bone in a toe distal to the metatarsus.

plantar, adj.—Of or pertaining to the sole of the foot.

plantigrade, *adj.*—Walking on the sole with the heel touching the ground, as man and sometimes bears.

pollex (plural, pollices), *n.*—The first (preaxial) digit of the forelimb, the thumb.

postauricular, *adj.*—Situated behind the ear.

posterior, *adj.*—At or toward the hinder end of the body.

postglenoid length.—Length on a mammalian skull from a line connecting the posterior walls of the glenoid fossae to a line connecting the posteriormost tips of the exoccipital condyles. See figure 483.

postorbital, *adj.*—Situated behind the eye, as postorbital process of the frontal bone or postorbital process of the jugal bone. See figure 482.

premaxilla (plural, premaxillae), *n.*—The bone (paired) in the mammalian skull bearing the incisor teeth of the upper jaw, situated in front of the maxilla. See figures 476, 477, 479.

premolar, *adj.* & *n.*—Designating or pertaining to one of the teeth (four on each side in upper jaw and in lower jaw in coyote, making sixteen in all) in front of the true molars. When canine teeth are present, premolars are behind these teeth; premolars are preceded by deciduous teeth, and in the upper jaw are confined to the maxillary bone. See figure 483.

preorbital, *adj.*—In front of the eyes, as preorbital part of skull.

presphenoid, *adj.* & *n.*—Designating or pertaining to a bone (single) in the base of the brain case in front of the basisphenoid bone and between the two alisphenoid bones. See figure 480.

prognathous, *adj.*—Having the jaws projecting beyond the upper part of the face.

protocone, *n.*—The central of the three cusps of a primitive upper molar; in higher forms, the principal anterointernal cusp. See figure 485.

protoconid, *n.*—The principal anteroexternal cusp of a molar in the lower jaw. See figure 485.

protoconule, *n.*—The anterior intermediate cusp between protocone and paracone of an upper molar.

pseudostyloid process.—A projection on the ulnar side of the distal end of the radius, as in a pocket gopher.

pterygoid, *adj.*—Designating, pertaining to, or in the region of a bone (paired) behind the palatine bone, as pterygoid bone and pterygoid muscle. See figure 477.

pubic symphysis.—The immovable or more or less movable articulation of the two pubic bones on the ventral side of the pelvis.

radius, *n.*—The shorter of the two bones of the forearm; at its distal end it articulates with the anterointernal part of the wrist.

ramus (plural, rami), *n.*—In an animal, a branch, a projecting part or elongated process, a ramification, as the horizontal ramus (part) of the dentary bone bearing the lower teeth of a mammal. See figure 481 for horizontal ramus of lower mandible.

rectum, *n.*—The terminal part of the intestine.

re-entrant angle.—An infold of the enamel layer on the side, front, or back of a cheek tooth, as in a molar of a muskrat or a wood rat. See figure 480.

rostral breadth.—Width, transverse to long axis of the skull, of the rostrum.

rostrum, *n.*—The anteriorly projecting part of a mammalian skull in front of the orbits. See figure 482.

sagittal crest.—The raised ridge of bone at the juncture of the two parietal bones resulting from the coalescence of the temporal ridges; in old individuals of many species of mammals the crest extends from the middle of the lambdoidal crest anteriorly onto the frontal bones, where it divides into two temporal ridges each of which ends anterolaterally on the posterior edge of the postorbital process of the frontal bone. See figure 476.

scapula (plural, scapulae), *n.*—The shoulder blade, a bone of the pectoral arch.

secondary sexual variation.—A difference, apart from the primary sexual organs, distinguishing individuals of one sex from the other, as the heavy facial beard of man or the antlers of male deer (genus *Odocoileus*).

sectorial, *adj.*—Adapted for cutting, as a sectorial tooth.

sinus (plural, sinuses), *n.*—A cavity in the substance of a bone of the skull which communicates with the nasal cavity and contains air, as the frontal sinus.

skull, *n.*—The skeleton of the head; in mammals, of a bony nature.

sphenoidal fissure.—See sphenorbital fissure.

sphenopalatine vacuity.—A fissure (a right or a left) at the side of the basisphenoid and presphenoid, as in *Neotoma lepida*. See figure 480.

sphenopterygoid canal.—A canal or foramen (paired) with its posterior opening near the pterygoid fossa; when present, usually transmits the internal maxillary vein. See figure 477.

sphenorbital (or sphenoidal) fissure.—An opening (paired) in the alisphenoid bone, as in a pocket gopher (*Thomomys*), transmitting nerves and blood vessels. See figure 479.

squamosal, *adj.* & *n.*—Designating or pertaining to the bone (paired) ventral to the parietal; the posterior root of the zygomatic arch is a process of the squamosal bone. See figures 476, 479.

stapedial canal.—A bony, tubular passage transmitting the stapedial artery in the cavity of the tympanic bulla.

style (plural, styles), *n.*—Any of several small cusps or elevations of the cingulum of a molar tooth, as the metastyle just posterior to the metacone. See figure 485.

submalar stripe.—A stripe on the lower part of the region of the upper jaw, as in a chipmunk.

submedian dark dorsal stripe.—The first dark stripe either to the right or left of the median longitudinal dark stripe, as in a chipmunk.

supraoccipital bone.—The bone (unpaired) immediately above the foramen magnum. See figure 478.

supraorbital process.—The process of the frontal bone on the top rim of the orbit, as in a rabbit. See figure 484.

suture, *n.*—The line of union in an immovable articulation, like one of the articulations between two bones of the skull.

symphysis (plural, symphyses), *n.*—Immovable or more or less movable articulation of certain bones in the median plane of the body, as the pubic symphysis.

synonym, *n.*—In the zoölogical sense, a systematic name, as of a subspecies, species, or genus, regarded as incorrectly applied or as incorrect in the form of spelling. It may have been the accepted name which was afterwards rejected in favor of another either because of evidence of priority of that other or evidence establishing a more natural, assumedly genetic classification.

tactile, *adj.*—Of, pertaining to, or relating to the sense of touch, as a tactile organ.

talonid, *n.*—The crushing region, the heel, of a lower molar tooth. See figure 485.

tarsal, *adj.*—Of or pertaining to the tarsus.

tarsus (plural, tarsi), *n.*—The ankle; the part of a vertebrate between the metatarsus and the leg.

temporal ridges.—Two curved, raised lines on each side of the brain case marking the upper limit of attachment of the fascia of the temporal muscle. The temporal ridges are prominent on the parietal bones, frequently extend anteriorly onto the frontal bones, and in some mammals extend posteriorly onto the interparietal bone. When present, the sagittal crest is formed by the coalescence of the temporal ridges. See figure 476.

terrestrial, *adj.*—Inhabiting the land, rather than water, trees, or the air.

thoracic, *adj.*—Of, pertaining to, located with, or in the region of the thorax, which is the part of the body of a mammal situated between the neck anteriorly and the abdomen posteriorly.

tibia (plural, tibiae), *n.*—The inner and usually the larger of the two bones of the hind limb (or leg) between the knee and the ankle.

topotype, *n.*—A specimen of a species or subspecies of animal obtained at the locality at which the original type specimen (holotype) was obtained.

total length.—Distance from the tip of the nose to the end of the fleshy part of the tail (hairs projecting beyond fleshy part are excluded) when the mammal is laid out straight but not stretched beyond its normal length in this position.

tragus (plural, tragi), *n.*—The prominence or process in front of the external opening of the ear.

trenchant, *adj.*—Adapted for cutting or shearing, sharp-edged, as the carnassial tooth of a bobcat.

trigonid, *n.*—The cutting region in front of the talonid of a lower molar tooth. See figure 485.

trochanter, *n.*—A prominence or process; in mammals it is on the proximal end of the bone of the thigh.

trochin, *n.*—The lesser tuberosity (*tuberculum minimus*) on the end nearest the body of the bone (humerus) of the upper arm.

trochiter, *n.*—The greater tuberosity (*tuberculum magnus*) on the end nearest the body of the bone (humerus) of the upper arm.

truncate, *adj.*—Having the end square or even, as if cut off.

tuberculate, *adj.*—Provided with tubercules. Tubercules are prominences, as on the crown of a tooth.

tympanic bulla.—The hollow, rounded prominence of bone enclosing the three auditory ossicles and related structures of the middle and inner ear. Referred to often as auditory bulla and sometimes audital bulla. See figure 477.

type locality.—The place where a type specimen was obtained.

type specimen.—The specimen or individual on which the scientific name and accompanying diagnosis of a species or subspecies is based.

ulna, *n.*—The longer of the two bones of the forearm; at its distal end it articulates with the posteroexternal part of the wrist.

unicuspid, *adj. & n.*—Pertaining to or designating any one of the teeth in a shrew behind the anteriormost tooth (it is an incisor), in front of the fourth premolar in the upper jaw, and in front of the first true molar in the lower jaw.

unicuspidate, *adj.*—Having one principal cusp, used in reference to anterior teeth of shrews.

urethra (plural, urethrae), *n.*—The canal which in most mammals carries off the urine from the bladder, and in the male serves also as a genital duct.

uroptagium, *n.*—The interfemoral membrane of a bat, that is to say, the fold of skin which stretches from the hind legs to the tail.

ventrad, *adv.*—Toward the ventral side.

ventral, *adj.*—Designating, pertaining to, or situated on the lower side—opposed to dorsal.

vertebra (plural, vertebrae), *n.*—One of the segments of the spinal column or backbone; the first vertebra is immediately behind and in contact with the skull and the last is the segment in the tip of the tail.

vibrissa (plural, vibrissae), *n.*—One of the stiff tactile hairs on the wrist or face of a mammal, as the so-called whiskers of a cat.

zygoma (plural, zygomata), *n.*—The whole zygomatic arch.

zygomatic arch.—The arch of bone which extends along the side of the skull beneath the orbit; formed in most mammals by the union of the jugal bone with the maxillary bone in front and the zygomatic arm of the squamosal bone behind. See figure 476.

zygomatic breadth.—Greatest distance across zygomatic arches of cranium perpendicular to long axis of skull. See figure 482.

zygomatic plate.—The plate of bone comprised in the zygomatic arm of the maxilla. See figure 477.

LITERATURE CITED

ALCORN, J. R.
  1940a. Life history notes on the Piute ground squirrel. Journ. Mamm., 21:160–170, 1 fig. in text, May 14, 1940.
  1940b. Color variation in the Piute ground squirrel. Journ. Mamm., 21:218, May 14, 1940.
  1941. Counts of embryos in Nevadan kangaroo rats (genus Dipodomys). Journ. Mamm., 22:88–89, 1 fig. in text, February 14, 1941.
ALLEN, G. M.
  1916. Bats of the genus Corynorhinus. Bull. Mus. Comp. Zoöl., Harvard College, 60:333–356, 1 pl., April, 1916.
ALLEN, J. A.
  1890. A review of some of the North American ground squirrels of the genus Tamias. Bull. Amer. Mus. Nat. Hist., 3:45–116, December, 1890.
  1894. Descriptions of ten new North American mammals, and remarks on others. Bull. Amer. Mus. Nat. Hist., 6:317–332, November 7, 1894.
ALLEN, J[OSEPH]. C.
  1939. Ecology and management of Nelson's bighorn on the Nevada mountain ranges. Trans. Fourth N. Amer. Wildlife Conference, pp. 253–256, 1939.
ANTEVS, ERNST
  1925. On the Pleistocene history of the Great Basin. Carnegie Institution of Washington Publ. 352, pp. 51–114, July, 1925.
ANTHONY, H. E.
  1913. Mammals of northern Malheur County, Oregon. Bull. Amer. Mus. Nat. Hist., 32:1–27, 2 pls., March 7, 1913.
  1916. Habits of Aplodontia. Bull. Amer. Mus. Nat. Hist., 35:53–63, April 1, 1916.
BAILEY, V.
  1900. Revision of American voles of the genus Microtus. U. S. Dept. Agric., Bur. Biol. Surv., N. Amer. Fauna, 17:1–88, 5 pls., 17 figs. in text, June 6, 1900.
  1915. Revision of the pocket gophers of the genus Thomomys. U. S. Dept. Agric., N. Amer. Fauna, 39:1–136, 8 pls., 10 figs., November 15, 1915.
  1929. Life history and habits of grasshopper mice, genus Onychomys. U. S. Dept. Agric., Tech. Bull., 145 (pt. 1):1–15, November, 1929.
  1932. The Oregon antelope. Proc. Biol. Soc. Washington, 45:45–46, April 2, 1932.
  1936. The mammals and life zones of Oregon. U. S. Dept. Agric., Bur. Biol. Surv., N. Amer. Fauna, 55:1–416, 51 pls. (nos. 2–52), 102 figs. in text, 1 map, August 29, 1936.
BANGS, O.
  1897. Notes on the lynxes of eastern North America, with descriptions of two new species. Proc. Biol. Soc. Washington, 11:47–51, 1 pl., March 16, 1897.
BENSON, S. B.
  1934. Description of a race of Dipodomys merriami from Arizona. Proc. Biol. Soc. Washington, 47:181–184, October 2, 1934.
  1938. Notes on kit foxes (Vulpes macrotis) from Mexico. Proc. Biol. Soc. Washington, 51:17–24, February 18, 1938.
BENSON, S. B. and BOND, R. M.
  1939. Notes on Sorex merriami Dobson. Journ. Mamm., 20:348–351, 2 figs., August 14, 1939.
BOND, R. M.
  1940. Food habits of horned owls in the Pahranagat Valley, Nevada. Condor, 42:164–165, May 15, 1940.

BORELL, A. E.
1931. A new pika from Idaho. Journ. Mamm., 12:306–308, August 24, 1931.

BORELL, A. E., and ELLIS, R.
1934a. Mammals of the Ruby Mountains region of northeastern Nevada. Journ. Mamm., 15:12–44, 6 pls., 1 fig., February 15, 1934.
1934b. Mammals found near Jarbidge, Elko County, Nevada. Journ. Mamm., 15:72–73, February 15, 1934.

BURT, W. H.
1934. The mammals of southern Nevada. Trans. San Diego Soc. Nat. Hist., 7:375–427, 1 map, May, 1934.

BUXTON, P. A.
1923. Animal life in deserts. Edward Arnold & Co., London, xv + 176 pp., 43 figs. in text.

CAMP, C. L.
1918. Excavations of burrows of the rodent Aplodontia, with observations on the habits of the animal. Univ. California Publ. Zoöl., 17:517–536, 6 figs. in text, June 22, 1918.

COLLINS, H. H.
1918. Studies of normal moult and of artificially induced regeneration of pelage in Peromyscus. Journ. Exp. Zoöl., 27:73–98, 2 pls., 3 figs. in text, October, 1918.
1923. Studies of the pelage phases and of the nature and color variations in mice of the genus Peromyscus. Journ. Exp. Zoöl., 38:45–107, 7 pls., 15 figs. in text, August, 1923.

COWAN, I. Mc.
1936. Distribution and variation in deer (Genus Odocoileus) of the Pacific coastal region of North America. California Fish and Game, 22:155–246, 13 figs. in text, July, 1936.
1940. Distribution and variation in the native sheep of North America. Amer. Midland Nat., 24:505–580, 4 pls., 1 map, November, 1940.

COY, O. C.
1923. The genesis of California counties. Publ. California Hist. Surv. Comm., Berkeley, California, xi + 92 pp., illustrated.

DAVIS, W. B.
1934. Notes on the Utah chipmunk. Murrelet, 15:20–22, January, 1934.
1937. Variations in Townsend pocket gophers. Journ. Mamm., 18:145–158, May 14, 1937.
1939. The Recent mammals of Idaho. The Caxton Printers, Caldwell, Idaho, 400 pp., 2 full page half-tones, 33 figs. in text, April 5, 1939.

DICE, L. R.
1935. A study of racial hybrids in the deer-mouse, Peromyscus maniculatus. Occas. Papers, Mus. Zoöl., Univ. Michigan, 312:1–22, May 3, 1935.

DURRANT, S. D., and HALL, E. R.
1939. Deux sous-espèces nouvelles du rongeur «Dipodomys ordii» de l'ouest des Etats-Unis d'Amerique. Mammalia, 3:10–16, 1 pl., Mars, 1939.

ELLIOTT, T. C.
1910. The Peter Skene Ogden Journals. Editorial notes. Oregon Hist. Quarterly, 11:201–222, 355–396, June–December, 1910.

ENGELS, W. L.
1936. Distribution of races of the brown bat (Eptesicus) in western North America. Amer. Midland Nat., 17:653–660, May, 1936.

ERRINGTON, P. L.
  1937.   The breeding season of the muskrat in northwest Iowa. Journ. Mamm., 18: 333–337, August 14, 1937.
  1939.   Observation on young muskrats in Iowa. Journ. Mamm., 20:465–478, November 14, 1939.
FINLEY, ROBERT B., JR.
  1942.   Geographic variation in the rodent Aplodontia rufa. Murrelet, 22:45–49, January 20, 1942.
FREMONT, J. C.
  1845.   Report of the exploring expeditions to the Rocky Mountains in the year 1842, and to Oregon and North California in the years 1843–'44. Washington, D. C., 693 pp., illustrated.
GIDLEY, J. W.
  1913.   Preliminary report on a recently discovered Pleistocene cave deposit near Cumberland, Maryland. Proc. U. S. Nat. Mus., 46:93–102, August 23, 1913.
GOLDMAN, E. A.
  1910.   Revision of the wood rats of the genus Neotoma. U. S. Dept. Agric., Bur. Biol. Surv., N. Amer. Fauna, 31:1–124, 8 pls., 14 figs. in text, October 19, 1910.
  1917.   New mammals from North and Middle America. Proc. Biol. Soc. Washington, 30:107–116, May 23, 1917.
  1931.   Two new desert foxes. Journ. Washington Acad. Sci., 21:249–251, June 4, 1931.
  1935.   New American mustelids of the genera Martes, Gulo, and Lutra. Proc. Biol. Soc. Washington, 48:175–186, November, 1935.
  1937a. The wolves of North America. Journ. Mamm., 18:37–45, February 14, 1937.
  1937b. The Colorado river as a barrier in mammalian distribution. Journ. Mamm., 18:427–435, November 14, 1937.
  1939a. A new pocket mouse of the genus Perognathus from Nevada. Proc. Biol. Soc. Washington, 52:33–36, March 11, 1939.
  1939b. Nine new mammals from islands in Great Salt Lake, Utah. Journ. Mamm., 20:351–357, August 14, 1939.
  1941.   Three new wolves from North America. Proc. Biol. Soc. Washington, 54:109–114, September 30, 1941.
GRATER, R. K.
  1939.   The desert kit fox moves his family. Nature Notes (J. H. Sedgwick, ed. and publ., Peoria, Ill.), 6:77–81, 3 photographs, April, 1939.
GRIFFIN, D. R.
  1936.   Bat banding. Journ. Mamm., 17:235–239, August 14, 1936.
GRINNELL, J.
  1914.   An account of the mammals and birds of the lower Colorado Valley with especial reference to the distributional problems presented. Univ. California Publ. Zoöl., 12:51–294, 11 pls., 9 figs. in text, March 20, 1914.
  1922.   A geographical study of the kangaroo rats of California. Univ. California Publ. Zoöl., 24:1–124, 7 pls., 24 figs. in text, June 17, 1922.
  1923.   The burrowing rodents of California as agents in soil formation. Journ. Mammalogy, 4:137–149, 3 pls., August 10, 1923.
  1933.   Review of the Recent mammal fauna of California. Univ. California Publ. Zoöl., 40:71–234, September 26, 1933.
GRINNELL, J., and DIXON, J.
  1919.   Natural history of the ground squirrels of California. Monthly Bull. State Comm. Horticulture [Sacramento, California], 7:597–708, 5 pls., 30 figs., January 27, 1919.

1923. The systematic status of the mountain lion of California. Univ. California Publ. Zoöl., 21:325–332, 2 pls., April 27, 1923.

1924. Revision of the genus Lynx in California. Univ. California Publ. Zoöl., 21:339–354, 1 pl., 1 fig. in text, January 24, 1924.

GRINNELL, J., DIXON, J., and LINSDALE, J. M.

1930. Vertebrate natural history of a section of northern California through the Lassen Peak region. Univ. California Publ. Zoöl., 35:1–594, 181 figs. in text, October, 1930.

1937. Fur-bearing mammals of California: their natural history, systematic status, and relations to man. Univ. California Press, Berkeley, California, 2 vols., xii + 375 and xiii + 377–777 pp., 13 colored pls., 345 figs., July 22, 1937.

GRINNELL, J., and STORER, T. I.

1924. Animal life in the Yosemite. Univ. California Press, Berkeley, California, xviii + 752 pp., 62 pls., 65 figs., 1924.

HALL, E. R.

1926. Systematic notes on the subspecies of Bassariscus astutus with description of one new form from California. Univ. California Publ. Zoöl., 30:39–50, 2 pls., September 8, 1926.

1927. Species of the mammalian subfamily Bassariscinae. Univ. California Publ. Bull. Dept. Geol. Sci., 16:435–448, 1 pl., 2 figs., March 17, 1927.

1928. Notes on the life history of the sage-brush meadow mouse (Lagurus). Journ. Mamm., 9:201–204, August 9, 1928.

1930a. Three new pocket gophers from Utah and Nevada. Univ. California Publ. Zoöl., 32:443–447, July 8, 1930.

1930b. Predatory mammal destruction. Journ. Mamm., 11:362–372, August 9, 1930.

1931a. Critical comments on mammals from Utah, with descriptions of new forms from Utah, Nevada and Washington. Univ. California Publ. Zoöl., 37:1–13, April 10, 1931.

1931b. Tree-climbing Callospermophilus. Murrelet, 12:54–55, May, 1931.

1931c. The coyote and his control. California Fish and Game, 17:283–290, 2 figs., July, 1931.

1932. New pocket gophers from Nevada. Univ. California Publ. Zoöl., 38:325–333, February 27, 1932.

1933. Sorex leucogenys in Arizona. Journ. Mamm., 14:153–154, May 15, 1933.

1934. A new pika (mammalian genus Ochotona) from central Nevada. Proc. Biol. Soc. Washington, 47:103–106, June 13, 1934.

1935a. Occurrence of the spotted bat at Reno, Nevada. Journ. Mamm., 16:148, May 15, 1935.

1935b. Nevadan races of the Microtus montanus group of meadow mice. Univ. California Publ. Zoöl., 40:417–427, October 25, 1935.

1936. Mustelid mammals from the Pleistocene of North America, with systematic notes on some Recent members of the genera Mustela, Taxidea and Mephitis. Carnegie Institution of Washington Publ. 473:41–119, 5 pls., 6 figs., November 20, 1936.

1938a. Gestation period in the long-tailed weasel. Journ. Mamm., 19:249–250, May 14, 1938.

1938b. Notes on the meadow mice Microtus montanus and M. nanus with description of a new subspecies from Colorado. Proc. Biol. Soc. Washington, 51:131–134, August 23, 1938.

1939. The grizzly bear of California. California Fish and Game, 25:237–244, 2 pls., 1 fig. in text.

1940. A new race of Belding ground squirrel from Nevada. Murrelet, 21:59–61, 1 fig., December 20, 1940.

1941a. New heteromyid rodents from Nevada. Proc. Biol. Soc. Washington, 54:55–62, May 20, 1941.

1941b. Revision of the rodent genus Microdipodops. Zoöl. Series, Field Mus. Nat. Hist., 27:233–277, 8 figs. in text, December 8, 1941.

1942. The type specimen of Aplodontia rufa californica (Peters). Murrelet, 22:50–51, January 20, 1942.

HALL, E. R., and BOWLUS, H. LORRAINE

1938. A new pika (mammalian genus Ochotona) from southeastern Idaho with notes on near-by subspecies. Univ. California Publ. Zoöl., 42:335–340, 1 fig., October 12, 1938.

HALL, E. R., and DALE, F. H.

1939. Geographic races of the kangaroo rat, Dipodomys microps. Occas. Papers Mus. Zoöl., Louisiana State Univ., no. 4:47–63, 3 figs., November 10, 1939.

HALL, E. R., and DAVIS, W. B.

1935. Geographic distribution of pocket gophers (genus Thomomys) in Nevada. Univ. California Publ. Zoöl., 40:387–402, 1 fig., March 13, 1935.

HALL, E. R., and DURHAM, F. E.

1938. A new pocket gopher from Nevada. Proc. Biol. Soc. Washington, 51:15–16, February 18, 1938.

HALL, E. R., and DURRANT, S. D.

1937. A new kangaroo mouse (Microdipodops) of Utah and Nevada. Journ. Mamm., 18:357–359, August 14, 1937.

1941. Two new kangaroo-mice from Utah. Murrelet, 22:5–7, April 30, 1941.

HALL, E. R., and GILMORE, R. M.

1932. New mammals from St. Lawrence Island, Bering Sea, Alaska. Univ. California Publ. Zoöl., 38:391–404, 1 fig., 2 pls., September 17, 1932.

HALL, E. R., and HATFIELD, D. M.

1934. A new race of chipmunk from the Great Basin of western United States. Univ. California Publ. Zoöl., 40:321–326, 1 fig., February 12, 1934.

HALL, E. R., and HOFFMEISTER, D. F.

1940. The pinyon mouse (Peromyscus truei) in Nevada, with description of a new subspecies. Univ. California Publ. Zoöl., 42:401–406, 1 fig., April 30, 1940.

1942. Geographic variation in the canyon mouse, Peromyscus crinitus. Journ. Mamm., 23:51–65, 1 fig. in text, February 14, 1942.

HALL, E. R., and JOHNSON, D. H.

1940. A new chipmunk of the Eutamias amoenus group from Nevada. Proc. Biol. Soc. Washington, 53:155–156, December 19, 1940.

HALL, E. R., and LINSDALE, J. M.

1929. Notes on the life history of the kangaroo mouse (Microdipodops). Journ. Mamm., 10:298–305, 1 pl., November 11, 1929.

HAMILTON, W. J., JR.

1933. The weasels of New York. Amer. Midland Nat., 14:289–344, 4 pls., 3 figs., 2 maps, July, 1933.

HARDMAN, G., and VENSTROM, C.

1941. A 100-year record of Truckee River runoff estimated from changes in levels and volumes of Pyramid and Winnemucca lakes. Trans. Amer. Geophysical Union, pt. 1 for 1941, pp. 71–90, 5 figs., MS [processed literature].

HATFIELD, D. M.

1936. Revision of the Pipistrellus hesperus group of bats. Journ. Mamm., 17:257–262, August, 1936.

1937. Notes on the behavior of the California leaf-nosed bat. Journ. Mamm., 18: 96–97, February 14, 1937.

HATT, R. T.
1932. The vertebral columns of ricochetal rodents. Bull. Amer. Mus. Nat. Hist., 63:599–738, 10 pls., 27 figs. in text, November 26, 1932.

HILL, J. E.
1937. Morphology of the pocket gopher mammalian genus Thomomys, Univ. California Publ. Zoöl., 42:81–171, 26 figs. in text, August 25, 1937.

HOLLISTER, N.
1914. A systematic account of the grasshopper mice. Proc. U. S. Nat. Mus., 47:427–489, 1 pl., October 29, 1914.

HOOPER, E. T.
1940. Geographic variation in bushy-tailed wood rats. Univ. California Publ. Zoöl., 42:407–424, 2 figs. in text, May 17, 1940.

HOWELL, A. B.
1932. The saltatorial rodent Dipodomys: the functional and comparative anatomy of its muscular and osseous systems. Proc. Amer. Acad. Arts and Sciences, 67:375–536, frontispiece, 28 figs. in text, December, 1932.

HOWELL, A. B., and GERSH, I.
1935. Conservation of water by the rodent Dipodomys. Journ. Mamm., 16:1–9, February 14, 1935.

HOWELL, A. H.
1901. Revision of the skunks of the genus Chincha. U. S. Dept. Agric., Bur. Biol. Surv., N. Amer. Fauna, 20:1–62, 8 pls., August 31, 1901.

1906. Revision of the skunks of the genus Spilogale. U. S. Dept. Agric., Bur. Biol. Surv., N. Amer. Fauna, 26:1–55, 10 pls., November 24, 1906.

1914. Revision of the American harvest mice (Genus Reithrodontomys). U. S. Dept. Agric., Bur. Biol. Surv., N. Amer. Fauna, 36:1–97, 7 pls., 6 figs. in text, June 5, 1914.

1915. Revision of the American marmots. U. S. Dept. Agric., Bur. Biol. Surv., N. Amer. Fauna, 37:1–80, 15 pls., 3 figs. in text, April 7, 1915.

1918. Revision of the American flying squirrels. U. S. Dept. Agric., Bur. Biol. Surv., N. Amer. Fauna, 44:1–64, 7 pls., 4 figs. in text, June 13, 1918.

1924. Revision of the American pikas (genus Ochotona). U. S. Dept. Agric., Bur. Biol. Surv., N. Amer. Fauna, 47:1–57, 6 pls., 4 figs. in text, August 21, 1924.

1929. Revision of the American chipmunks (genera Tamias and Eutamias). U. S. Dept. Agric., Bur. Biol. Surv., N. Amer. Fauna, 52:1–157, 10 pls., 9 figs. in text, November 30, 1929.

1938. Revision of the North American ground squirrels with a classification of North American Sciuridae. U. S. Dept. Agric., Bur. Biol. Surv., N. Amer. Fauna, 56:1–256, 32 pls. (some colored), 20 figs. in text, May 18, 1938.

1939. [Review of] Davis, William B. The Recent Mammals of Idaho. . . . Journ. Mamm., 20:389–390, August 14, 1939.

HUEY, L. M.
1938. A new muskrat from Utah. Trans. San Diego Soc. Nat. Hist., 8:409–410, January 18, 1938.

HUXLEY, J. S.
1939a. Ecology and taxonomic differentiation. Journ. Ecology (Cambridge, England), 27:408–420, August, 1939.

1939b. Clines: an auxiliary method in Taxonomy. Bijdr. Dierk. (Holland) (vol. for 1939):491–520.

JACKSON, H. H. T.
1915. A review of the American moles. U. S. Dept. Agric., Bur. Biol. Surv., N. Amer. Fauna, 38:1–100, 6 pls., 27 figs., September 30, 1915.
1928. A taxonomic review of the American long-tailed shrews. U. S. Dept. Agric., Bur. Biol. Surv., N. Amer. Fauna, 51:vi + 238, 13 pls., 24 figs., July, 1928.

JOHNSON, D. H.
1943. Systematic review of the chipmunks (genus Eutamias) of California. Univ. California Publ. Zoöl., 48:63–148, 1 pl., 12 figs. in text, December 24, 1943.

LAWSON, A. C., GILBERT, G. K., et al.
1908. Atlas of maps and seismographs accompanying the report of the State Earthquake Investigation Commission upon the California earthquake of April 18, 1906. Carnegie Institution of Washington, Washington, D. C., 1908.

LA RIVERS, IRA
1941. The Mormon cricket as food for birds. Condor, 43:65–69, January 15, 1941.

LINSDALE, J. M.
1936. The birds of Nevada. Pacific Coast Avifauna, Cooper Ornith. Club, 23:1–145, February 7, 1936.
1938. Environmental responses of vertebrates in the Great Basin. Amer. Midland Nat., 19:1–206, 12 figs., January, 1938.
1940. Amphibians and reptiles in Nevada. Proc. Amer. Acad. Arts and Sciences, 73:197–257, 29 figs. in text, May, 1940.

McVAUGH, R., and FOSBERG, F. R.
1941. Index to the geographical names of Nevada. U. S. Dept. Agric., Div. Plant Expl. and Introduction, Bur. Plant Indust. Works Progress Admst. Nev. Collaborator, Univ. Nevada. Contributions toward a flora of Nevada, No. 29: 1–216 [processed literature, not printed].

MERRIAM, C. H.
1890. Results of a biological survey of the San Francisco Mountain region and desert of the Little Colorado in Arizona. U. S. Dept. Agric., Div. Ornith. and Mamm., N. Amer. Fauna, 3:1–101, frontispiece, 2 figs. in text, September 11, 1890.
1891. Description of a new genus and species of dwarf kangaroo rat from Nevada (Microdipodops megacephalus). U. S. Dept. Agric., Div. Ornith. and Mamm., N. Amer. Fauna, 5:115–117, July 30, 1891.
1897. Revision of the coyotes or prairie wolves, with descriptions of new forms. Proc. Biol. Soc. Washington, 11:19–33, 1897.
1900. Preliminary revision of the North American red foxes. Proc. Washington Acad. Sci., 2:661–676, 2 pls., December 28, 1900.

MILLER, G. S., JR.
1897. Revision of the North American bats of the family Vespertilionidae. U. S. Dept. Agric., Div. Biol. Surv., N. Amer. Fauna, 13:1–140, 3 pls., 40 figs. in text, October, 1897.
1907. The families and genera of bats. U. S. Nat. Mus. Bull., 57:xvii + 282, 14 pls., 49 figs. in text, June, 1907.
1913. A new cacomistle from Nevada. Proc. Biol. Soc. Washington, 26:159–160, June 30, 1913.

MILLER, G. S., JR., and ALLEN, G. M.
1928. The American bats of the genera Myotis and Pizonyx. U. S. Nat. Mus. Bull., 144:viii + 218, 1 pl., 1 fig., 13 maps, May, 1928.

NELSON, E. W.
1909. The rabbits of North America. U. S. Dept. Agric., Bur. Biol. Surv., N. Amer. Fauna, 29:1–314, 13 pls., 19 figs. in text, August 31, 1909.

1925.   Status of the pronghorned antelope, 1922–1924. U. S. Dept. Agric., Dept. Bull., 1346:1–64, 6 pls., 21 figs. in text, August, 1925.

1927.   Description of a new subspecies of beaver. Proc. Biol. Soc. Washington, 40: 125–126, September 26, 1927.

NELSON, E. W., and GOLDMAN, E. A.
1929.   List of the pumas, with three described as new. Journ. Mamm., 10:345–350, November 11, 1929.

1931.   Three new pumas. Journ. Washington Acad. Sci., 21:209–212, May 19, 1931.

ORR, R. T.
1939.   Longevity in Perognathus longimembris. Journ. Mamm., 20:505, November 14, 1941.

1940.   The rabbits of California. Occas. Papers California Acad. Sci., 19:1–207, 10 pls., 30 figs., May 25, 1940.

OSGOOD, W. H.
1900.   Revision of the pocket mice of the genus Perognathus. U. S. Dept. Agric., Div. Biol. Surv., N. Amer. Fauna, 18:1–72, 4 pls., 15 figs. in text, September 20, 1900.

1909.   Revision of the mice of the American genus Peromyscus. U. S. Dept. Agric., Bur. Biol. Surv., N. Amer. Fauna, 28:1–285, 8 pls., 12 figs., April 17, 1909.

PALMER, F. G.
1937.   Geographic variation in the mole Scapanus latimanus. Journ. Mamm., 18: 280–314, 2 pls., 1 fig., 2 tables, August 14, 1937.

PERKINS, I. J.
1928.   A visit to a bat cave—Pyramid Lake, Nevada. Year Book, Public Mus. City Milwaukee, for 1927, 7:1–195, 178 figs., June 1, 1928.

PIPER, S. E.
1909.   The Nevada mouse plague of 1907–8. U. S. Dept. Agric., Farmers' Bull., 352:1–23, 9 figs., 1909.

RECORDS, E[DWARD].
1919 to 1934. Biennial report of the State Rabies Commission for 1917–1918, pp. 1–10, 1919; for 1919–1920, pp. 1–8, 1921; for 1921–1922, pp. 1–11, 1923; for 1923–1924, pp. 1–10, 1925; for 1925–1926, pp. 1–9, 1927; for 1927–1928, pp. 1–10, 1929; for 1929–1930, pp. 1–9, 1931; for Jan. 1, 1931 to June 30, 1932, pp. 1–8, 1932; for July 1, 1932 to June 30, 1934, pp. 1–8, State Printing Office, Carson City, Nevada, included in appendices to journals of Senate and Assembly of the Legislature of the State of Nevada.

RIDGWAY, R.
1912.   Color standards and color nomenclature. Washington, D. C. Privately printed, iv + 44 pp., 53 pls.

RUSSELL, I. C.
1885.   Geological history of Lake Lahontan. Monogr. U. S. Geol. Surv., 11:xiv + 288 45 pls., 36 figs. in text.

SCHEFFER, T. H.
1929.   Mountain beavers in the Pacific Northwest: their habits, economic status, and control. U. S. Dept. Agric., Farmers' Bull., 1598:1–18, 13 figs., August, 1929.

SETON, E. T.
1929.   Lives of game animals. Doubleday, Doran & Co., Inc., New York City, 4 vols.: 1, xxxix + 640; 2, xvii + 746; 3, xix + 780; 4, xxii + 949, profusely illustrated.

SHAMEL, H.
1931.   Notes on the American bats of the genus Tadarida. Proc. U. S. Nat. Mus., 78:1–27, May 6, 1931.

SHAW, W. T.
1928.   The spring and summer activities of the dusky skunk in captivity. New York State Museum handbook, 4:1–103, 40 figs., 1928.

SIMPSON, J. H.
1876.   Report of explorations across the Great Basin of the territory of Utah for a direct wagon-route from Camp Floyd to Genoa, in Carson Valley, in 1859. U. S. Engineer Dept., Washington Govt. Printing Office, pp. 1–518, with maps.

SPERRY, C. C.
1929.   Laboratory studies of the food of Onychomys. U. S. Dept. Agric., Tech. Bull., 145 (pt. 2):15–20, November, 1929.

STONE, W.
1904.   Notes on a collection of Californian mammals. Proc. Acad. Nat. Sci. Philadelphia, 1904:586–591, October 17, 1904.

SUMNER, F. B.
1932.   Genetic, distributional, and evolutionary studies of the subspecies of deer mice (Peromyscus). Bibliographia Genetica, 9:1–106, 1932.

SVIHLA, A.
1932.   A comparative life history study of the mice of the genus *Peromyscus*. Univ. Michigan Mus. Zoöl., Miscell. Publ., 24:1–39, July 8, 1932.

SVIHLA, R. D.
1936.   Breeding and young of the grasshopper mouse (Onychomys leucogaster fuscogriseus). Journ. Mamm., 17:172–173, May 14, 1936.

TAYLOR, W. P.
1911.   Mammals of the Alexander Nevada Expedition of 1909. Univ. California Publ. Zoöl., 7:205–307, 2 figs. in text, June 24, 1911.
1912.   Field notes on amphibians, reptiles and birds of northern Humboldt County, Nevada with a discussion of some of the faunal features of the region. Univ. California Publ. Zoöl., 7:319–436, 6 pls., February 14, 1912.
1918.   Revision of the rodent genus Aplodontia. Univ. California Publ. Zoöl., 17:435–504, 5 pls., 16 figs. in text, May 29, 1918.
1935.   Ecology and life history of the porcupine (*Erethizon epixanthum*) as related to the forests of Arizona and the southwestern United States. Univ. Arizona Bull. (Biol. Sci. Bull., no. 3), 6 (no. 5):1–177, 8 pls., 18 figs. in text, July 1, 1935.

TIMOFEEFF-RESSOVSKY, N. W.
1940.   Mutations and geographical variation, pp. 73–136, 38 figs. in text, *in* The New Systematics, edited by Julian S. Huxley, Oxford, England, Clarendon Press, 1940.

WHITLOW, W. B., and HALL, E. R.
1933.   Mammals of the Pocatello region of southeastern Idaho. Univ. California Publ. Zoöl., 40:235–275, 3 figs. in text, September 30, 1933.

WISTAR, I. J.
1937.   Autobiography of Isaac Jones Wistar . . . , vii + 528 pp., Wistar Institute of Anatomy and Biology, Philadelphia, 1937.

WOOD, A. E.
1935.   Evolution and relationship of the heteromyid rodents with new forms from the Tertiary of western North America. Ann. Carnegie Mus., 24:73–262, 157 figs. in text, May 13, 1935.

YOUNG, S. P.
1940.   The comeback of the antelope. Western Sportsman, 5 (no. 4):7, 8, 23, 31, 7 figs., September, 1940.

Transmitted June 29, 1942.

INDEX